WITNESSES
TO A VANISHING
AMERICA

1. James Mooney, "Hopi Kachinas of the Powamu or 'Bean-planting Ceremony,'" Walpi Pueblo, Arizona, 1893. Photograph. The National Anthropological Archives, Smithsonian Institution.

WITNESSES
TO A VANISHING
AMERICA

THE NINETEENTH-CENTURY
RESPONSE

LEE CLARK MITCHELL

PRINCETON UNIVERSITY PRESS

Published by Princeton University Press, Princeton, New Jersey
In the United Kingdom: Princeton University Press, Guildford, Surrey

Library of Congress Cataloging in Publication Data will be
found on the last printed page of this book

Publication of this book has been aided by a grant from
the Paul Mellon Fund of Princeton University Press

This book has been composed in linotype Baskerville

Clothbound editions of Princeton University Press books
are printed on acid-free paper, and binding materials are
chosen for strength and durability

Printed in the United States of America by Princeton
University Press, Princeton, New Jersey

Designed by Laury A. Egan

For my mother and father

YONNONDIO*

Walt Whitman, 1883

A song, a poem of itself—the word itself a dirge,
Amid the winds, the rocks, the storm and wintry night,
To me such misty, strange tableaux the syllables
    calling up;
Yonnondio—I see, far in the west or north, a limitless
    ravine, with plains and mountains dark,
I see swarms of stalwart chieftains, medicine-men, and
    warriors,
As flitting by like clouds of ghosts, they pass and are
    gone in the twilight,
(Race of the woods, the landscapes free, and the falls!
No picture, poem, statement, passing them to the future:)
Yonnondio! Yonnondio!—unlimn'd they disappear;
To-day gives place, and fades—the cities, farms,
    factories fade;
A muffled sonorous sound, a wailing word is borne
    through the air for a moment,
Then blank and gone and still, and utterly lost.

* The sense of the word is *lament for the aborigines.* It is an
Iroquois term; and has been used for a personal name.
[Whitman's note]

CONTENTS

LIST OF ILLUSTRATIONS

PREFACE

[Travelers] never describe things as they
really are, but bend them and mask them
according to the point of view from which
they see things.
  —*Montaigne, Essays*

Everything is extraordinary in America.
  —*Alexis de Tocqueville*
  Democracy in America

Propelled across the continent by notions of "rugged individualism,"
"course of empire," "inexhaustible resources," and "manifest destiny,"
pioneer Americans soon discovered that such slogans masked the other
side of progress: empire building required the destruction of a wilderness. In the nineteenth century, that devastation proceeded at a
rate alarming enough to arouse growing apprehensions about America's westward mission itself. Optimistic catch-phrases could hardly
calm the suspicion that much, perhaps too much, was being sacrificed
to the future. Was the promise of empire worth the price? Concern
for the vanishing wilderness would ultimately lead Americans to
question their culture itself. The following pages explore this critical
attitude as it emerged, paradoxically, from the continental conquest
meant to redeem that culture.

A wide variety of documents reveals, in ways never before made
clear, that the prospect of a vanishing "wilderness" provoked nineteenth-century Americans to commitments of astonishing diversity,
energy, and consequence. Diaries, novels, and reminiscences; letters
and all-too-conventional poems; newspaper essays, artists' journals,
and scientific notes and reports—all hint at a deep sense of foreboding. This feeling in turn inspired projects aimed at forestalling the
effects of westward "progress." Grasping as they did at America's
promised future, countless Americans nonetheless attempted to preserve its landscape in words, oils, and photographs. Quickly tamed
pioneer life elicited a similar response, as citizens strove to capture
their own evanescent histories. Others focused on Indian Tribes, recording alien images and cultures before the inevitable changes that

white encroachment would bring. This undercurrent of apprehension touched even those who did not go west. Local drives for historical societies, city parks, and woodland conservation spurred broad support among citizens all across the nation into awareness of the toll exacted by America's supposedly manifest destiny. Similar concerns sparked national movements in literature, painting, and photography, as well as in archaeology and anthropology.

These interrelated developments call for a revision in our notions of American history by revealing the ambivalence felt among even those who participated in the nation's triumphant conquest of the wilderness. The reassessment required by this view, however, also compels a reassessment of ourselves. Issues that we assume are modern—conservation, protection of endangered species, native rights, and questioning of the price of progress—actually originated early in the nineteenth century. As such, they form a uniquely American legacy.

To provide a context for understanding the emergence of these alternative attitudes, the opening chapter reviews common American assumptions about nature and culture. Chapter Two then assesses the growing number of laments over the passing of America's wilderness. Manifested most simply as nostalgic regret, the impulse to fix a record spread with astonishing rapidity—as rapidly as landscape seemed to alter and wild game to disappear. Explorers, frontiersmen, and scientists, settlers and tourists all came to feel that the "West" they preserved on paper was being diminished in more profound and troubling ways than it was being developed. Some even came to view the land as valuable in itself and worth holding intact. Federal park and conservation movements of the late nineteenth century expressed an active national commitment to issues once endorsed only by isolated individuals.

Americans' desire to capture the quickly passing moment of untamed wilderness focused first upon the plains, forests, mountains, and wildlife of the West. But a vanishing wilderness included more than topography, flora, and fauna, however exotic. Chapter Three examines those who came to prize human activity not merely as a picturesque embellishment on the natural landscape, but for its own sake. Seemingly overnight, settlements grew into towns and cities, as pioneer histories and frontier folkways passed into memory. Before too much was thus lost to recollection, many felt impelled to preserve their firsthand experiences, the lore quickly acquired of necessity and as soon outmoded by "progress."

The most compelling actor in the wilderness—indeed, the human symbol of that evanescent experience—was the Indian. Americans committed to rendering accounts of native life for the sake of future generations clearly realized that they were in a race against the destruction of their subjects—if not by outright extinction, then by more insidious white influences. Chapter Four traces the career of George Catlin, the first person to devote a full career to preserving in paint and words an exhaustive record of the Indians. The strength of his lifelong dedication, the trenchancy of his insights, and the quality of his completed record make him a major representative of the themes we are examining. Chapters Five and Six consider the historical context for Catlin's singular energies, surveying the painters and photographers of threatened Indian life and reviewing the work of nineteenth-century ethnographers. First attracted to the West by notions of the exotic and colorful, all of these chroniclers completed their records out of serious apprehensions about the impact of white expansion on native tribes.

Curiosity about Indian cultures often led beyond respect, and those willing to shake off preconceptions sometimes felt a wistful envy. Herman Melville's experiences in Polynesia during the 1840s helped him to anticipate a melancholy question toward which others would struggle in the next half century: Could native cultures, nonwhite and heathen, provide a richer life for their members than that which was replacing them? Chapter Seven, on Melville's sophisticated reading of Polynesian life, enters directly into the suggestive possibilities of that question.

Chapter Eight traces the series of increasingly complex responses to indigenous tribes that Melville had anticipated. Painters, scientists, and others began by merely hoping to record one moment in history; yet contact with alien peoples often educated them to the mysterious intricacies and emotional satisfactions of cultures they knew were doomed. For the more sensitive, study of native tribes finally meant probing, sometimes radically, the idea of culture itself. Absolutist notions of the superiority of Western civilization eroded before evidence demanding more sympathetic and relativisitic interpretations. Once again, "wilderness" connoted far more than mere landscape, and nineteenth-century Americans gradually became aware of ever more complex experiences associated with that word—experiences imperiled by the westward expansion of white Americans.

The Conclusion describes the self-conscious assessments of Western civilization that resulted from admiration for tribal life. In addition, it pursues well into the twentieth century the themes raised in earlier chapters. Without consciously doing so, Americans fostered a dialogue challenging to the very premises of their own way of life. The dialogue continues today, though of course its terms have shifted and the voices have grown more strident. Yet we too often comfort ourselves with the rather threadbare blanket of modernity; Americans have ventured neither as far nor as willingly as most assume concerning issues of conservation, endangered wildlife, and native American rights. Nor have the more humane attitudes suddenly emerged from nowhere. Our nineteenth-century predecessors swaggered with less thoughtless confidence than the accepted historical record suggests, and we need to view them as aware of, even puzzled by issues that now trouble us—to recognize that they could be nearly as troubled as we are. Accepting such a heritage should help us to discern a more complex American character than that suggested by slogans blazoned across consciousness and continents.

A WORD of caution: anyone familiar with the criticism will realize that my readings of Cooper, Melville, and Mark Twain are hardly new. They are not meant to be. The newness here lies in depicting the world from which they emerged. As a graduate student, I was fascinated by these writers' criticism of their westering culture, the collective "No, in thunder" with which they repudiated popular clichés. Increasingly, however, I came to see them as less isolated in their resistance than they, their critics, or I had assumed. The place of these writers here, then, is not as uniquely perceptive figures but as spokesmen for a broad intellectual movement shared with their many less articulate contemporaries. Instead of illuminating independent texts from a new vantage, I want to place familiar works in a surprisingly more sympathetic historical context.

To the extent that scholarly books represent joint projects, this one is more so than most and has incurred for me a long and fortunate series of debts. At the University of Washington, Martha Banta helped to shape its first dissertation stages, and I continue to be grateful for her generous advice. At that same time, Ann Meyrich shared my enthusiasm for ideas still disturbingly vague. That she may not immediately recognize them in this, their final form cannot diminish the fact that they would not first have seemed worth engaging without her calm encouragement.

Others have since read intermediate drafts, interrupting harried schedules to help me map a tangled intellectual landscape. Carlos Baker, Frank Bergon, Alfred L. Bush, Emory Elliott, Douglas Gordon, William L. Howarth, Bruce Johnson, A. Walton Litz, Jr., Richard M. Ludwig, Jarold Ramsey, and Harold Simonson—all have variously altered my ideas, in the process steering me from hidden pitfalls and toward untested possibilities. Even while dissenting, I rarely failed to learn from them. Or from Susan McCloskey, who was at first unfamiliar with the wilderness I was struggling to order. She nonetheless turned a keen eye and exacting ear to the project, affirming throughout her undiminished confidence in the writer and the work. I hope this book fulfills some part of the promise she saw.

More than to anyone else, however, this book owes its existence to Howard C. Horsford. He first suggested the idea, and from early dissertation drafts to final page proof has read nearly every word. That I have subbornly refused his advice means that I must alone claim responsibility for its flaws. But the debt goes deeper than this book. A dozen years ago, he taught me to see in the academic profession more than a worthy vocation. The very example of his unregenerate curiosity, rigorous standards, and wry patience has been for me, as for many other students and colleagues, the fincst model of how to engage life.

Fellowships awarded by the American Council of Learned Societies and the Surdna Foundation freed me to write, and I am grateful for their generosity. I would also like to thank the Princeton University Committee on Research in the Humanities and Social Sciences for extending funds to cover costs of travel and typing. The staffs at various libraries, including those at the University of Washington, Princeton University, the American Antiquarian Society, and the Huntington (and there, in particular, Virginia Renner), made my research far more of a pleasure than I could have hoped. Miriam Brokaw and Gail Filion first took an editorial interest in this book, and it has clearly benefited from their attention. I have been especially fortunate in both my copyeditor, Gretchen Oberfranc, whose blue pencil rarely errs, and in my research assistant, Kathryn G. Humphreys, who skillfully helped to prepare the index. Under the pressure of assorted deadlines, Helen Wright silently corrected flawed grammar and erratic footnotes, producing fair copy out of drafts barely readable to their author. I can only add my heartfelt appreciation to that of many others associated with her through the American Studies Program at Princeton.

Finally, the dedication confirms my fullest, least redeemable debt. This is a study of the offering presented by preceding generations to their successors—"a gift to posterity," as it was for a time entitled. To register here my father's reverence for American landscape and my mother's Quaker faith in unstated truths is to identify only part of what I cherish in them. Yet by attending to these considerations in the following pages, I want to offer my own small gift in return for all they have given me.

CHAPTER ONE

FROM LANDSCAPE TO CULTURE, PRESERVATION TO CRITIQUE

Let us conquer space.
—*John C. Calhoun*, 1817

The wonders of inanimate nature leave [Americans] cold, and, one may almost say, they do not see the marvelous forests surrounding them until they begin to fall beneath the ax. What they see is something different. The American people see themselves marching through wildernesses, drying up marshes, diverting rivers, peopling the wilds, and subduing nature. It is not just occasionally that their imagination catches a glimpse of this magnificent vision. . . . it is always flitting before [their] mind.
—*Alexis de Tocqueville*
Democracy in America (1835)

THE NEW WORLD has long fascinated the Old by seeming to promise regeneration to a civilization tired of itself. That America was as old as Europe geologically; that its native population was as large and, in places, as concentrated; that its civilizations claimed illustrious pedigrees—these facts mattered little against such a powerfully attractive conception.[1] The land could hardly resist. Its assumed physical newness meant that for as long as territory lay open, a setting might be found for every sort of utopian second chance. Popular belief went so far as to ascribe rejuvenating powers to the very soil itself.[2] If Europe seemed religiously, politically, or economically stale, its institutions unresponsive to individual needs, the New World represented an opportunity to create a more nearly perfect society amid fresh surroundings.

John Winthrop's projected "city on a hill," J. Hector St. John de Crèvecoeur's celebrated American farmer, Thomas Jefferson's yeoman, Benjamin Franklin's autodidact, Ralph Waldo Emerson's self-reliant Yankee, and Frederick Jackson Turner's frontier democrat—the model holds a stalwart pose under dramatically varied trappings. In each instance, the pose proclaims: We have abandoned tradition-clogged societies to embrace a new, a free, a far richer life. America's wilderness seemed to provide a physically limitless and ahistorical setting in which men and women could imagine their finest self-conceptions fulfilled. The powerful fascination of that hope entwines more than three centuries of colonial and national experience.[3]

[1] Wilbur R. Jacobs, in calling for more attention to "what might be called the Indian point of view," has confirmed these historical actualities. See especially his "The Indian and the Frontier in American History—A Need for Revision," *Western Historical Quarterly*, 4 (January 1973), 43-56, and "The Tip of an Iceberg: Pre-Columbian Indian Demography and Some Implications for Revisionism," *William and Mary Quarterly*, 3d ser., 31 (January 1974), 123-32.

[2] Gilbert Chinard, "The American Dream," chap. 15 of Robert E. Spiller *et al.*, eds., *Literary History of the United States: History*, 3d ed. rev. (New York: Macmillan Co., 1963), pp. 195ff.

[3] The cultural context within which these assumptions emerged as effective symbols has been amply documented, most notably by: Perry Miller, "The Romantic Dilemma in American Nationalism and the Concept of Nature," *Harvard Theological Review*, 48 (October 1955), 239-53; Henry Nash Smith, *Virgin Land: The American West as Symbol and Myth* (New York: Random House, 1950); R.W.B. Lewis, *The American Adam: Innocence, Tragedy, and Tradition in the Nineteenth Century* (Chicago: University of Chicago Press, 1955); Howard Mumford Jones, *O Strange New World—American Culture: The Formative Years* (New York: Viking, 1964). See also John Conron, *The American Landscape: A Critical Anthology of Prose and Poetry* (New York: Oxford University Press, 1974), p. xviii; Loren Baritz, "The Idea of the West," *American Historical Review*, 66 (April 1961), 618-40.

What might be termed the "idea of America" integrated a set of apparently untroubled assumptions about nature, progress, and the past. However inconsistent, these assumptions nonetheless induced belief through the constant lure of a fresh start. America would foster the new citizen in a new society without materially diminishing the new-found world. Far from fearing the effects on the land, most commentators stressed its promised transformation. Even by the end of the nineteenth century, few Americans understood Thoreau's eccentric plea for wildness as the preservation of the world.[4] The continent's natural plentitude seemed inexhaustible, yet its true value could not be realized while the land remained uncultivated. The "virgin land" would find fulfillment in marriage to the plow, not in unproductive spinsterhood. So European tools conquered the continent, and the land came to serve a technological progress based increasingly on American notions of advancement. How could a democratic republic fail to thrive in the economic soil of freehold agrarianism or, later, of laissez-faire capitalist industrialism?[5]

Assumptions about natural plentitude and cultural progress combined to encourage a fierce rejection of older values. At the same time, the westward trek to a better American future signaled escape from a desultory history of economic trial and social error that most observers wanted to associate peculiarly with Europe. America offered "a new field of opportunity," in Frederick Jackson Turner's conception, and presented "a gate of escape from the bondage of the past."[6] American frontiersmen exuberantly rejected tradition, if for no other reason than that it was traditional. Customs, laws, manners, and governments all were suspect. It was necessary to adopt a new life. In the most celebrated definition of what it meant to be an American, Crèvecoeur evoked qualities that seem appropriately baptismal: *"He is an American who, leaving behind him all his ancient prejudices and manners, receives new ones from the new mode of life he has embraced, the new government he obeys, and the new rank he holds."*[7]

Yet such proud exuberance is deceptive. From this early passage, Crèvecoeur's narrative moves steadily, letter by letter, toward despair-

---

[4] Henry David Thoreau, "Walking," in *Excursions* (1863; rpt. New York: Corinth Books, 1962), p. 185.

[5] See Smith, *Virgin Land*, p. 138.

[6] Frederick Jackson Turner, "The Significance of the Frontier in American History" (1893), in Turner, *The Frontier in American History* (New York: Henry Holt, 1921), p. 38.

[7] Michel-Guillaume St. Jean de Crèvecoeur [J. Hector St. Jean de Crèvecoeur], *Letters from an American Farmer . . .* (1782; rpt. New York: E. P. Dutton, 1957), p. 39.

ing disillusionment with the new world. However much Americans think they can abandon mistakes, however completely one's past seems mere encumbrance, that past has at least the virtue of familiarity. Marcus Cunliffe sharply qualifies Crèvecoeur's embrace of his new life, detecting "an almost inherent American tendency to believe that one has been cut off decisively from the past as if by a physical barrier . . . [that] has, understandably, revealed itself in regrets and neuroses as well as in pride and exuberance."[8] Juxtaposed against America's cheering connotations as a land of hope and progress, freedom and opportunity, this statement may seem overly pessimistic. Nonetheless, it helps to clarify Americans' paradoxical melancholy, anxiety, and restlessness "in the midst of their prosperity,"[9] which Alexis de Tocqueville so presciently observed. Cut off from the past, even by an act of free will, one is compelled to view the present as equally imperiled by a deracinating future. Of course, if the breach is not self-willed, it may prove yet more unsettling.

Expounded by such orators as Daniel Webster, Henry Clay, and Thomas Hart Benton, the official faith of nineteenth-century America remained floridly optimistic, in tune with the formal symbol America represented. Yet spread-eagle rhetoric does not altogether mask a strain of misgiving, and many historians have identified what one calls an "apprehension of doom" characterizing nineteenth-century statements.[10] Such foreboding was widespread, provoked at least in part by the westering process itself. For example, the prospect loomed vague but insistent that American expansion might destroy those aspects of

[8] Cunliffe, "American Watersheds," *American Quarterly*, 13 (Winter 1961), 489.

[9] De Tocqueville, *Democracy in America* (1835), trans. George Lawrence, ed. J. P. Mayer (New York: Doubleday, Anchor Books, 1969), p. 535. See also Jones, *Strange New World*, pp. 379, 383-86; David Lowenthal, "The Place of the Past in the American Landscape," in David Lowenthal and Martyn J. Bowden, eds., *Geographies of the Mind: Essays in Historical Geosophy* (New York: Oxford University Press, 1976), pp. 89-117.

[10] Miller, "Romantic Dilemma," p. 251. See also Curtis Dahl, "The American School of Catastrophe," *American Quarterly*, 11 (Fall 1959), 380-90; Leo Marx, *The Machine in the Garden: Technology and the Pastoral Ideal in America* (New York: Oxford University Press, 1964); William R. Taylor, *Cavalier and Yankee: The Old South and American National Character* (New York: Braziller, 1961), esp. p. 98; Marvin Meyers, *The Jacksonian Persuasion: Politics and Belief* (Stanford: Stanford University Press, 1957); Fred Somkin, *Unquiet Eagle: Memory and Desire in the Idea of American Freedom, 1815-1860* (Ithaca: Cornell University Press, 1967); Roderick Nash, *Wilderness and the American Mind*, rev. ed. (New Haven: Yale Univeristy Press, 1973); Neil Harris, *The Artist in American Society: The Formative Years, 1790-1860* (New York: Simon and Schuster, 1966), pp. 158-59, 166-67; Jay Martin, *Harvests of Change: American Literature, 1865-1914* (Englewood Cliffs, N.J.: Prentice-Hall, 1967), pp. 85-86; Klaus J. Hansen, "The Millennium, the West, and Race in the Antebellum American Mind," *Western Historical Quarterly*, 3 (October 1972), 376.

frontier life that had first attracted pioneers; that material progress would introduce serious new social and psychological pressures; that America was developing according to a cyclic pattern of rise and fall characteristic of other celebrated empires; or even that a culture could be advanced without being white, Christian, or industrial. Few in the nineteenth century could comprehend these as intellectual propositions; fewer still could ignore them. By mid-century a young whaler's fictive nightmare epitomized the vague anxiety that a considerable segment of American society was beginning to feel about its flight from the past into the future. "Uppermost was the impression," Melville's Ishmael reflects, "that whatever swift, rushing thing I stood on was not so much bound to any haven ahead as rushing from all havens astern. A stark, bewildered feeling, as of death, came over me."[11] Those unenthusiastic about America's "progress" usually expressed themselves less severely. Nonetheless, as slight, isolated, unimaginative, or inconsistent as their expressions so often prove to be, they occur with remarkable frequency in nineteenth-century writings.

Among the unwelcome prospects mentioned above, the first excited greatest distress: that national expansion might diminish as well as develop the landscape. America had been imagined from the beginning in terms of timeless space, as a vacant land awaiting the starter's gun of history. Once the historical race began, the continent lent itself readily to the uses of progress and civilization. The first systematic mappers early in the nineteenth century preceded the immigration of millions committed to removing native tribes, hunting vast quantities of game, clearing forests for farms, erecting cities on open plains, and finally, crossing the continent with rails. The land would pass from Indian to trapper and prospector, from frontier trader to urban businessman, from homesteader to corporate farmer. All of these actors in the national drama clearly anticipated the landscape's transformation. Given the formulistic text of the "official faith," however, most never questioned the process, much less resisted it.

LANDSCAPE, PRESERVATION, AND DOUBTS

In the 1820s and 1830s, Americans felt vaguely uncertain about, and sometimes cringed mentally at, their altering of the land. They had begun to recognize that the continent was not merely a vacant landscape awaiting axes and plows but possessed intrinsic delights, values,

[11] Herman Meville, *Moby-Dick; or, The Whale*, ed. Harrison Hayford and Hershel Parker (New York: W. W. Norton, 1967), p. 354.

and order.[12] Of course, they were not conservationists, certainly not as we know the term. Those few who suggested preserving as they were the Indian or the buffalo or the forests were considered mere fools. Yet many ruefully anticipated the passing of the wilderness, and thousands hastened westward to see it while it lasted. "We are prone to speak of ourselves as the inhabitants of a *new* world," wrote Orsanus Turner near mid-century, "and yet we are confronted with such evidences of antiquity! We clear away the forests and speak familiarly of subduing a 'virgin soil';—and yet the plough up-turns the skulls of those whose history is lost! We say that Columbus discovered a *new* world. Why not that he helped to make two *old* ones acquainted with each other?"[13]

One reason "why not" concerned prevailing public opinion. Ready-to-hand clichés, including "virgin soil," "new world," and "course of empire," substituted for incisive assessments of specific local relationships between man and nature. "The westward-making Americans had no instructed image of the land they were bent on possessing," Bernard DeVoto has concluded. "Manifest Destiny was blindfolded."[14] The first to raise their blindfolds expressed only tentative doubts, if any, about what they saw, and public constraints drove even these expressions into various forms of private writings. Like nuggets of placer gold, they turn up not in the mainstream of books and speeches but in the side currents of prefaces and conclusions, in the eddies of allusions, dropped comments, and sometimes merely suggestive phrasings. Frontier journals, diaries, travel books, editorials, exploration accounts, and letters home by people of all classes and occupations reveal increasing apprehension.

Of course, far from a majority of those who crossed the continent had second thoughts. Nor could many anticipate the effects of their westering society. Lewis Mumford has nicely characterized the settlement of America as "a large-scale mushroom hunt: in the pursuit of a single object, urban sites, coal mines, gold, or oil, every other attribute of the landscape was neglected."[15] Even for those not quite so single-minded, the "mushroom hunt" seemed both inevitable and right.

[12] See Barbara Novak, "On Divers Themes from Nature: A Selection of Texts," in Kynaston McShine, ed., *The Natural Paradise: Painting in America, 1800-1950* (Boston: New York Graphic Society, 1976), p. 60.

[13] Turner, *Pioneer History of the Holland Purchase of Western New York* (Buffalo: Jewett, Thomas and Co., 1849), pp. 18-19.

[14] DeVoto, *Across the Wide Missouri* (Boston: Houghton Mifflin Co., 1947), p. 397.

[15] Mumford, *The Brown Decades. A Study of the Arts in America, 1865-1895* (1931; rpt. New York: Dover Publications, 1955), pp. 67-68.

Yet if they rarely questioned the transition, a considerable number felt impelled to document the "West" before it vanished.

That impulse may at first seem little more than an antiquarian quirk. However, Marcus Cunliffe's description of the American as one who believes himself "cut off decisively from the past as if by a physical barrier" challenges such a dismissive view by placing recorders of the passing frontier within a larger context. They accomplished the very objective to which most nineteenth-century American artists aspired: to arrest in realistic terms an accurate view of nature.[16] In literature, painting, and photography, work after work during this period concentrates on accurate observation and detailed rendering of the physical world. As the youthful Thoreau declared, "Nature will bear the closest inspection."[17] Landscape and genre paintings, novels and even poems declare themselves to be honest transcriptions not merely of nature but of specific locales. Perhaps it is true that "people robbed of their past seem to make the most fervent picture takers."[18] American enthusiasm for realism, whether in photography or in other art forms, certainly seems to derive from an all-encompassing historical concern. From transcendentalist essays to luminist canvases, in the Leatherstocking tales and *Moby-Dick* as in the landscape photographs of Carleton Watkins and William Henry Jackson, the finest American art maintains what has been elsewhere characterized as "a vested interest in the preservation of the fact."[19]

Throughout America and western Europe, change seemed far too rapid in the nineteenth century. Americans, however, had forsaken traditional institutions that might have insulated against the shock of change. Pioneers traveled west to escape their pasts, moving spatially, as it were, to escape time. But one truly escapes time only by arresting it, as art fixes an image. Thus, the later chroniclers who hurried west to document a vanishing world were propelled by the same impulses that had moved earlier immigrants, who, buffeted by change, had begun to regret their lost pasts. All wanted at least to ease uncertainty by holding on to the landscape of an ephemeral present.

Whatever its causes, this impulse toward preservation ramified within a definite historical frame, commencing in the 1820s. Perhaps

16 See John Ewers, *Artists of the Old West* (Garden City, N.Y.: Doubleday and Co., 1965), p. 7; Donald A. Ringe, *The Pictorial Mode: Space and Time in the Art of Bryant, Irving, and Cooper* (Lexington: University Press of Kentucky, 1971), p. 1.

17 Thoreau, "A Natural History of Massachusetts" (1842), in *Excursions*, p. 42.

18 Susan Sontag, *On Photography* (New York: Farrar, Straus and Giroux, 1977), p. 10; see also pp. 9, 62-63, 76.

19 Barbara Novak, *American Painting of the Nineteenth Century: Realism, Idealism, and the American Experience* (New York: Praeger, 1969), p. 59.

the new technology's awesome capacity to destroy the landscape first spurred those anxious about its disappearance.[20] Or perhaps such anxiety grew from other causes: from the sense of nationhood that first emerged after the War of 1812; from resistance to the swelling emigration to the trans-Appalachian west; or from dismay at an ideology affirming inexhaustibility even as land was visibly impoverished and wildlife decimated. Perhaps such concern grew, ironically, in response to proliferating documents themselves, which finally fixed landscapes, wildlife, and Indian tribes on record. As Susan Sontag asserts, "our oppressive sense of the transience of everything is more acute since cameras gave us the means to 'fix' the fleeting moment."[21] For whatever reasons, people did not begin to express their apprehensions until after 1820. Tentatively stated at first, by the end of the century the issues were headlined in popular magazines, and government officials were formulating responses in terms of national policies.

The shift in public attitudes occurred less uniformly than this review may suggest. In the 1870s, worried observers of an altering landscape unknowingly repeated the caveats spoken and implied half a century earlier. On the other hand, those who in the seventies began vaguely to question white civilization's alleged superiority to indigenous cultures had few precursors. Tacking into strange seas of cultural thought, they deserve consideration less for their numerical strength than for their intellectual daring. The most important insights they provided struck at the heart of assumptions about civilization itself. Whites for the first time looked closely at native cultures and came to appreciate their extraordinary diversity, intricacy, and autonomy —even their values. Though treated as one for centuries, Indian tribes shared far fewer characteristics than European nations; at last, the diversity of their histories and cultures began to be recognized.[22]

Whites returning from more objective studies began to reassess assumptions about progress. Evidence suggested that so-called primitive tribes, far from lacking institutional controls, were structured by social codes sometimes more complex and frequently more fulfilling

[20] For general background see Richard Lillard, *The Great Forest* (New York: Alfred A. Knopf, 1947), esp. pp. 138-208; Stewart L. Udall, *The Quiet Crisis* (New York: Avon, 1963), pp. 67-68. John William Ward, in *Andrew Jackson: Symbol for an Age* (New York: Oxford University Press, 1955), p. 45, has observed the effects of this increasing conflict during the 1820s between the claims of technology and those of the wilderness.

[21] Sontag, *On Photography*, p. 179.

[22] See Wilcomb E. Washburn, *The Indian in America* (New York: Harper and Row, 1975), p. xvi. See also William Brandon, *The Last Americans: The Indian in American Culture* (New York: McGraw-Hill, 1974), p. 20.

than those of white society. Was progress an absolute conception? Were cultures only relative conditions? More and more persistently, the study of native tribes sparked questions to trouble Americans' complacency about themselves and their mission westward.

LITERARY BOOKENDS

At the same time that ethnographers began to develop greater respect for the intrinsic value of native cultures, paintings of Indians changed more in perspective and content than ever before. Nevertheless, two literary works offer the most vivid illustration of these changing attitudes toward native Americans. St. John de Crèvecoeur's *Letters from an American Farmer* (1782) and Willa Cather's *The Professor's House* (1925) explore problems of contemporary society and the possibilities posed by native life in nicely contrasting terms. Standing outside the historical limits of this study, they conveniently summarize the cultural expectations that dominated the respective ends of the century.

Crèvecoeur's letters hymn the virtues of America's freehold, agrarian society. The yeoman working his own land is an enviable social model: both temporally and spatially, he is the perfect median between the extremes of barbaric frontier freedom and decadent European tradition. The system affords him maximum economic incentive with minimal social constraints. "This formerly rude soil has been converted by my father into a pleasant farm," Crèvecoeur's Farmer James declares, "and in return it has established all our rights; on it is founded our rank, our freedom, our power as citizens, our importance as inhabitants of such a district."[23] This "devout agrarianism"[24] depends on two dovetailed assumptions: that the land exists to be cleared, plowed, and planted, and that it belongs to those best capable of making such a transformation. Few eighteenth-century Americans would have disagreed.

Crèvecoeur revealed his essentially conventional perspective more tellingly in the claims that Farmer James makes for the northeastern Indian tribes. Despite the Frenchman's firsthand knowledge of native life, his descriptions merely depict the noble savage of Enlightenment discourse—indistinguishable tribe from tribe, person from person. Native societies apparently lack all social forms and restrictions. Viewing the increased dangers of life on the frontier that the forthcoming war with Britain would bring, Farmer James philosophically contemplates the prospect of life among the Indians:

23 Crèvecoeur, *Letters from an American Farmer*, pp. 20-21.
24 Henry Nash Smith, *Virgin Land*, p. 16, uses this phrase to refer to Jefferson's similar economic philosophy.

As soon as possible after my arrival, I design to build myself a wigwam, after the same manner and size with the rest, in order to avoid being thought singular, or giving occasion for any railleries. . . . I shall erect it hard by the lands which they propose to allot me, and will endeavour that my wife, my children, and myself may be adopted soon after our arrival. Thus becoming truly inhabitants of their village, we shall immediately occupy that rank within the pale of their society, which will afford us all the amends we can possibly expect for the loss we have met with by the convulsions of our own.[25]

Crèvecoeur sounds as if he thought Farmer James were moving cross-town instead of cross-culturally. Far from being genuinely interested in a specific Indian tribe, he invokes the subject solely as an excuse for reflection about his own society: "Thus shall we metamorphose ourselves, from neat, decent, opulent planters, surrounded with every convenience . . . into a still simpler people divested of everything beside hope, food, and the raiment of the woods." As did Rousseau before and Thoreau after, Crèvecoeur finds that primitive society offers him an opportunity intelligently to simplify his life: "Rest and peace of mind will make us the most ample amends for what we shall leave behind."[26] For Crèvecoeur, as for most of his contemporaries, European values represented an absolute cultural standard, and tribal life constituted merely the negation of supposedly "civilized" ways. The idea that "primitive" societies might perfect virtues to which Europeans and Americans gave only lip service or which their civilization actually subverted was beyond contemplation.[27]

A century and a half later, these unsettling ideas had become commonplace, even as the transformation from an agrarian economy to an urban and industrial one had given them a more complex edge. The dazzling array of comforts offered by nineteenth-century technology could not ease that technology's disproportionate costs, and the sober recognition of this contributed to the *fin de siècle* malaise of Henry and Brooks Adams, Mark Twain, and William Dean Howells. Even for those less thoughtful, the game did not seem worth the candle. The enthusiasm with which late-nineteenth-century

[25] Crèvecoeur, *Letters from an American Farmer*, p. 215.

[26] Ibid., p. 218. See Roy Harvey Pearce, *Savagism and Civilization: A Study of the Indian and the American Mind*, rev. ed. (Baltimore: Johns Hopkins University Press, 1965), pp. 139-41.

[27] For one possible exception in Crèvecoeur's prose to this state of mind, see his *Journey into Northern Pennsylvania and the State of New York* (1801), trans. Clarissa Spencer Bostelmann, 3 vols. in 1 (Ann Arbor: University of Michigan Press, 1964), p. 11.

Americans devoted their energies to progressive social and political movements was generated in part by a feeling that technological advancements had undermined traditional values.[28] As Felix Frankfurter later noted about the leader of the Progressive party: "Behind the diverse and discordant movements for reform to which [Theodore] Roosevelt gave voice lay the assumption that the traditional hopes of American democracy had been defeated by social and economic forces not contemplated by the founders of our nation."[29]

In Willa Cather's *The Professor's House*, young Tom Outland keenly inveighs against these changes. Visiting Washington, D.C., with grand enthusiasm early in the twentieth century, he leaves the city without regret:

> How it did use to depress me to see all the hundreds of clerks come pouring out of that big building at sunset! Their lives seemed to me so petty, so slavish. The couple I lived with gave me a prejudice against that kind of life. . . . They asked me not to mention the fact that I paid rent, as they had told their friends I was making them a visit. It was like that in everything; they spent their lives trying to keep up appearances, and to make his salary do more than it could. When they weren't discussing where she should go in the summer, they talked about the promotions in his department; how much the other clerks got and how they spent it, how many new dresses their wives had. And there was always a struggle going on for an invitation to a dinner or a reception, or even a tea-party. When once they got the invitation they had been scheming for, then came the terrible question of what Mrs. Bixby should wear.[30]

Obviously, in this bleak urban landscape the promise of Crèvecoeur's fresh green world has disappeared as even an imaginative desire. Themes of corruption, crass commercialism, and unintended betrayal interweave throughout Cather's novel, reinforcing an image of American society beyond possible redemption. Technology has prostituted America's integrity. Underscoring the theme, Cather's central character, Professor Godfrey St. Peter, concludes a class with the sardonic request: "You might tell me next week, Miller, what you

[28] See, for example, Herbert Croly, *The Promise of American Life* (1909; rpt. New York: Bobbs-Merrill, 1965).

[29] Cited by John William Ward in his introduction to Croly, *Promise of American Life*, p. viii. This quotation is from an article written by Frankfurter for *New Republic*, July 16, 1930, p. 247.

[30] Willa Cather, *The Professor's House* (New York: Alfred A. Knopf, 1925), p. 232. All subsequent references will be to this edition.

think science has done for us, besides making us very comfortable" (69).

Against this despair over modern technology's joyless comforts, Cather contrasts the imagined cultural richness of an ancient race of cliff dwellers. Outland, Professor St. Peter's former student, discovers while patiently excavating an abandoned mesa village that only an advanced culture could have erected such a stunning, yet functional, complex. Father Duchene, a friend more experienced in archaeology, concludes, " 'your tribe were a superior people. Perhaps they were not so when they first came upon this mesa, but in an orderly and secure life they developed considerably the arts of peace. There is evidence on every hand that they lived for something more than food and shelter' " (219). Examining this evidence with care, Father Duchene imagines how Tom's tribe "humanized" the mesa:

> "I see them here, isolated, cut off from other tribes, working out their destiny, making their mesa more and more worthy to be a home for man, purifying life by religious ceremonies and observances, caring respectfully for their dead, protecting the children, doubtless entertaining some feelings of affection and sentiment for this stronghold where they were at once so safe and so comfortable, where they had practically overcome the worst hardships that primitive man had to fear. They were, perhaps, too far advanced for their time and environment." (220-221)

Crèvecoeur might have found little to disagree with in this description. The measure of how far attitudes had altered lies rather in the contrast between his bland conception of native life as a mere escape from contemporary political convulsions and Cather's portrayal of a tribal culture as a rich improvement upon modern life. Thoreau followed Crèvecoeur in ironically juxtaposing the frame house of Concord against the Indian wigwam to illustrate the issue of economy.[31] Far more than money and man-hours of labor were at issue for Cather.

In almost every respect, Crèvecoeur and Cather brought quite different associations to essentially similar symbols. Farmer James escapes to the frontier to avoid temporary social distress, not to embark upon permanent cultural change. He neither embraces a particular Indian tribe nor considers abandoning his fixed agrarian values. So easy an escape was not possible for Cather; social philoso

[31] Thoreau, *Walden*, ed. J. Lyndon Shanley (Princeton: Princeton University Press, 1971), pp. 27ff.

phers and anthropologists had radically altered the terms. Supposedly absolute cultural norms had been reduced to a conditional status, ranked according to their cumulative humanizing effect. A culture might be evaluated according to the sense of participation shared by its members in conceiving and achieving their destiny. The extinct southwestern culture uncovered by Tom Outland provides—in sharp contrast to Crèvecoeur's unnamed northeastern tribes—a telling critique of American and European civilization. The passage cited above goes on to suggest the symbolic link between Washington bureaucrats who allow the mesa ruins to be ravaged and a supposed Navaho horde that may have slaughtered the cliff dwellers. Progress forecloses as well as fulfills possibilities; material comforts may diminish as well as enrich individual lives.

SUBDUING THE LAND

Before Americans came to question progress in terms of Indian cultures, they found themselves first questioning their assumptions about nature. Those assumptions concerned not only particular aspects of the natural landscape but also man's relationship to the earth, to the North American continent, and to the technology he applied to it. At an elementary level, most believed that the earth was created for man's use. Textbooks repeatedly invoked Genesis 1:26-28, describing God's gift of "dominion" and his command to Adam and Eve to "subdue" the earth.[32] Such a perspective tacitly acknowledges an impersonal relationship to nature by conceiving of man as disconnected from the physical world and of God as independent of both. Of course, technological advance itself demanded these "scientific" premises. Only a civilization imbued with such thinking could have achieved the expertise Americans enjoyed in the nineteenth century. On the other hand, only such a civilization could have devastated the landscape as Americans did or exterminated so many indigenous peoples. It is one irony among many that Indians never quite comprehended those who, precisely because they conceived of God, nature, and man as independent, could acquire the power to destroy them.

[32] See Ruth Miller Elson, *Guardians of Tradition: American Schoolbooks of the Nineteenth Century* (Lincoln: University of Nebraska Press, 1964), pp. 16-40; Wilbur R. Jacobs, *Dispossessing the American Indian: Indians and Whites on the Colonial Frontier* (New York: Charles Scribner's Sons, 1972), pp. 19-25; Roderick Nash, *Wilderness and the American Mind*, esp. pp. 19, 31, 59, 104-5, 193; Nash, *The American Environment: Readings in the History of Conservation*, 2d ed. (Reading, Mass.: Addison-Wesley, 1968), pp. 3-4.

Notwithstanding the special symbolic status of the New World as a new beginning, America had seemed a physical, and thereby cultural, extension of Europe ever since its discovery. In one respect, however, this was not true: the Europeans' hard-won respect for the land never took root in American soil. Enclaves of German farmers practiced Old World conservation in their new Pennsylvania communities, but they were exceptional in a country where land had always been cheaper than labor. Whether one interprets Americans' careless use of the land in social, religious, psychological, or even sexual terms—as, say, a compensation for lapsed faith, or a ravishing of the feminine earth—the fact remains that an astonishing portion of the American forest was destroyed. In the seventeenth century it covered half the continent; by the end of the nineteenth it had been burned over, logged, and cleared to only one-fifth the original acreage. Abundance may at first have encouraged myths of inexhaustibility. Eroded lands, flooded fields, stump-spotted forests, and ruined prairies too soon stood in silent judgment of those who had acted so irresponsibly.[33]

In part, this exuberant irresponsibility testified to Americans' characteristically progressive rather than conservative perspective. Wild nature represented promise, not fulfillment, and the continent presented a vividly physical challenge to white energies. At the same time that Americans eagerly accepted that challenge, new patterns undermined their confidence in their westward mission. Tourism and pleasure traveling, for example, were activities restricted to the rich in 1800. By 1900, when they had become popular pastimes,[34] people could see for themselves the magnificence, and the devastation, of their continent.

Belief in the unhealthiness of urban life also contributed to a heightened appreciation for landscape. This romantic bias against

[33] For background information on these developments, see: Paul W. Gates, *The Economic History of the United States*, vol. 3, *The Farmer's Age: Agriculture, 1815-1860* (New York: Holt, Rinehart and Winston, 1960); Clarence J. Glacken, "Changing Ideas of the Habitable World," in William L. Thomas, ed., *Man's Role in Changing the Face of the Earth* (Chicago: University of Chicago Press, 1956), pp. 70-92; Russel B. Nye, *This Almost Chosen People: Essays in the History of American Ideas* (East Lansing: Michigan State University Press, 1966), pp. 256-304; Udall, *Quiet Crisis*, esp. pp. 31-81. See as well, for revisionist assessments of some of these judgments: Gordon M. Day, "The Indian as an Ecological Factor in the Northeastern Forest," *Ecology*, 34 (April 1953), 329-45; Daniel Q. Thompson and Ralph H. Smith, "The Forest Primeval in the Northeast—A Great Myth?" in *Annual Proceedings: Tall Timbers Fire Ecology Conference, No. 10* (Fredericton, New Brunswick: Tall Timbers Research Station, 1970), pp. 255-65.

[34] See Earl Pomeroy, *In Search of the Golden West: The Tourist in Western America* (New York: Alfred A. Knopf, 1957).

cities—found even in grammar school texts as early as 1813—acquired powerful reinforcement as reformers publicized the obvious human costs of industrialism. The various epidemics that periodically plagued the antebellum East further confirmed the impulse.[35] As well, Americans began to take pride in what was now their land. Emerson touched a resonant chord in his "American Scholar" address (1837) when he called for an art that glorified indigenous themes. Reviewers encouraged American writers and painters to take pristine nature as their subject; those who resisted did so at peril of losing public favor. Against the dominant commitment to conquer the continent, then, a vigorous celebration of its untransformed virtues thrived.

However inconsistent this conjunction of ideas, virtually everyone conceded a corollary: the continent, whether put to the axe or not, belonged to those who knew how best to use it. Crèvecoeur voiced this assumption, and nineteenth-century school texts reflect its general acceptance.[36] Though Americans may have occasionally confessed injustices toward Indians, they fell back on the right of usage, which abrogated all other rights of even the most peaceable tribes when challenged by white farmers. By whatever terms the issue may have been defined—communal versus private ownership, red skin versus white, hunting versus agrarian exploitation—the native claim seemed inferior. It could hardly have proved otherwise.

During the last third of the century, this cast of thought acquired even more extreme coloration. Social Darwinism offered "scientific" confirmation to those who believed that the less fit ought to suffer extinction, and Americans generated greater support for the theory than any other nationality. Against Europeans who responded sympathetically to the Indians' plight, Americans countered that the Old World could hardly afford to do so, having only just shaken off centuries of mistreating Africans, Asians, and Latin American Indians. Moreover, Europeans, according to Americans, retained only faulty appreciation for the requirements of turning native soil into national homeland.[37]

Europeans and Americans together were blind to the virtues of tribal cultures, largely because of irreconcilable epistemologies. In

[35] Elson, *Guardians of Tradition*, pp. 25-35. For an exemplary study of the costs of and attitudes toward disease in nineteenth-century America, see Charles E. Rosenberg, *The Cholera Years* (Chicago: University of Chicago Press, 1962).

[36] Elson, *Guardians of Tradition*, pp. 65ff.

[37] See Hugh Honour, *The New Golden Land: European Images of America from the Discoveries to the Present Time* (New York: Pantheon, 1975), pp. 219ff.; Richard Hofstadter, *Social Darwinism in American Thought*, rev. ed. (Boston: Beacon Press, 1955), pp. 82ff.

nontechnological societies, natural cycles connect man with the phenomenal world. His culture serves at every point to ensure an integrating harmony; goodness and God exist in the complete immersion within natural cycles, whether ethical, aesthetic, or economic. The tribal individual cannot conceive of himself *as* an individual, somehow isolated from a world resonating with religious significance. By contrast, technological societies render the world in physical, not moral, terms. Nature is to be dominated first for man's welfare, perhaps later for the glory of God. Instead of "family" or "tribal" individuals, technological societies assume the existence of "universal man," the "reasonable" individual who acknowledges social and political codes as absolute as those that govern his science.[38]

Native tribes could do little to halt the crusade of white America westward. The fine, pragmatic turn of mind that had produced their technological marvels, and in the process made them awesomely destructive, also blinded whites to the merits of native societies. All their standards confirmed the Indians' inadequacy.[39] Nor could the Indians understand what strange compulsions drove on their invaders. Washington Irving reported the wry response of one Sioux to a missionary imploring "the necessity of industry, etc., to happiness": " 'Father, I don't understand this kind of happiness you talk of. You tell me to cut down tree—to lop it—to make fence—to plough—this you call being happy—I no like such happiness.' "[40] In terms far more profound than this rejection of the work ethic, natives came sadly to recognize the indifferent universe that whites inhabited. Committed willy-nilly to the intellectual imagination, its technological tools and purely abstract codes, whites seemed starved in every other important

[38] For more precise discussion, see Gary B. Nash, "The Image of the Indian in the Southern Colonial Mind," *William and Mary Quarterly*, 3d ser., 29 (April 1972), 197-230; F.S.C. Northrop, "Man's Relation to the Earth in Its Bearing on His Aesthetic, Ethical, and Legal Values," in Thomas, ed., *Man's Role in Changing the Face of the Earth*, pp. 1052-67; Robert Redfield, *The Primitive World and Its Transformations* (Ithaca: Cornell University Press, 1953).

[39] See Gary B. Nash, "Image of the Indian," pp. 197-211; Nash, "Red, White and Black: The Origins of Racism in Colonial America," in Gary B. Nash and Richard Weiss, eds., *The Great Fear: Race in the Mind of America* (New York: Holt, Rinehart and Winston, 1970), pp. 1-9; Philip Borden, "Found Cumbering the Soil: Manifest Destiny and the Indian in the Nineteenth Century," in ibid., pp. 72-88; Louise K. Barnett, *The Ignoble Savage: American Literary Racism, 1790-1890*, Contributions in American Studies, no. 18 (Westport, Conn.: Greenwood Press, 1975), pp. 100ff.

[40] *The Western Journals of Washington Irving*, ed. John Francis McDermott (Norman: University of Oklahoma Press, 1944), pp. 103-4. For an excellent objective analysis of the historical effects of such a conflict of cultures, see Anthony F. C. Wallace, *The Death and Rebirth of the Seneca* (New York: Alfred A. Knopf, 1970), esp. pp. 184ff.

respect—emotionally, aesthetically, and spiritually. Some intellectuals had already begun to consider issues from this perspective. Experiencing the contrast of Indian life itself, however, helped others to reconsider the toll their civilization was taking. As well, it opened them to novel assessments of the very concept of culture.

THE MEANINGS OF CULTURE

Few words have enjoyed so striking a transition in meaning as *culture*. Prior to the nineteenth century, western Europeans rarely doubted that their civilization embodied the preeminent social qualities. Noble savages existed in a precivilized state, with both its virtues and puerile vices. Like children, they lacked social graces. Human nature being everywhere the same, however, they could appreciate the force of reason whether or not they lived by its dictates. Even Caliban might learn table manners.[41]

Increasing contact after 1800 proved that tribes did not warrant this easy dismissal. At the same time, European society was in upheaval, violently challenged by forces unanticipated only a few decades earlier. Civilization itself appeared to be under attack, perhaps even breaking down. The response to this turmoil was a more exacting assessment of the social contract that most had until then taken for granted. Thomas Carlyle, John Stuart Mill, John Ruskin, and Matthew Arnold studied the web of their society in ways that suggested its conditional status, while later cultural evolutionists, drawing on Darwin's work, posited developmental stages in social history. Implicit in all these normative analyses, however, was the familiar notion of absolute progress with European civilization epitomizing its direction. In contrast to Enlightenment assumptions about the noble savage, however,

[41] For a general history and discussion of the meaning of the word *culture* and of the noble savage see: A. L. Kroeber, *Anthropology: Race, Language, Culture, Psychology, Prehistory*, rev. ed. (New York: Harcourt, Brace and Co., 1948), pp. 265-66; Julian H. Steward, "Evolution and Process," and David Bidney, "The Concept of Value in Modern Anthropology," in A. L. Kroeber, ed., *Anthropology Today: An Encyclopedic Inventory* (Chicago: University of Chicago Press, 1953), pp. 313-26 and 686-99; David Bidney, "The Idea of the Savage in North American Ethnohistory," *Journal of the History of Ideas*, 15 (April 1954), 322-27; Henri Baudet, *Paradise on Earth: Some Thoughts on European Images of Non-European Man* (1959), trans. Elizabeth Wentholt (New Haven: Yale University Press, 1965), esp. pp. 5-29; George W. Stocking Jr., *Race, Culture, and Evolution: Essays in the History of Anthropology* (New York: Free Press, 1968), pp. 36-40, 69-132; Karl J. Weintraub, *Visions of Culture* (Chicago: University of Chicago Press, 1966); David M. Schneider, "Notes toward a Theory of Culture," in Keith H. Basso and Henry A. Selby, eds., *Meaning in Anthropology* (Albuquerque: University of New Mexico Press, 1976), pp. 197-220.

nineteenth-century evolutionists recognized that the moral values of so-called primitive cultures functioned like those that framed their own society. This was a radical turn of thought. Indeed, by conceding that every society, no matter how alien or seemingly savage, possesses an institutional structure with its own integrity, evolutionists made modern anthropological study possible.[42]

The hard-won recognition that there exists no such universal as "human nature" gained acceptance only slowly. Sympathetic anthropologists, much less the general public, had to struggle to accept the fact that cultures, all cultures, form necessary contexts for becoming very different kinds of human beings. Even today, the acknowledgement of other cultures as intrinsically worth respect does not draw wide support. On the other hand, this relativism implies a supposed detachment from one's deepest cultural assumptions, a detachment as delusive as any belief in Enlightenment absolutism. For better or worse, all individuals are bound by their societies; they can never be neutral. To claim to be free from arbitrary mores, perhaps out of respectful tolerance for other modes of behavior, is self-deceptively to ignore that tolerance itself is an arbitrary cultural more.[43] Properly employed, relativism leads not to a blithe stepping aside from one's culturally defined cast of thought but to a growing recognition that it is neither biologically nor racially determined. "So-called primitive societies," according to Claude Lévi-Strauss, ". . . have specialized in ways different from those which we have chosen. Perhaps they have, in certain respects, remained closer to the very ancient conditions of life, but this does not preclude the possibility that in other respects they are farther from those conditions than we are."[44]

The possibility that different societies provide appropriate satisfaction of their members' needs or that the histories of various cultures might complement rather than duplicate one another derives from recent studies, many of which focus on native American tribes. Only at the turn of the century did the American anthropologist Franz Boas define these premises as basic axioms of professional anthro-

[42] Raymond Williams has best defined the emergence of the distinct idea of culture in western European intellectual history; see his *Culture and Society: 1780-1950* (New York: Harper and Row, 1958). According to Williams, the concept of culture did not begin to emerge until the end of the eighteenth century; see pp. 59-60.

[43] The most cogent discussion of issues raised by culture and cultural relativism is contained in Clifford Geertz's *The Interpretation of Cultures: Selected Essays* (New York: Basic Books, 1973), to which much of this discussion is indebted.

[44] Lévi-Strauss, Inaugural Lecture, Collège de France, January 5, 1960, published as *The Scope of Anthropology*, trans. Sherry Ortner Paul and Robert A. Paul (London: Jonathan Cape, 1967), p. 46.

pology.[45] But even earlier, those who helped to create a context for Boas's breakthroughs, who roughly anticipated some of his conclusions, were Americans with firsthand experience of native tribes. They had come to appreciate the vital autonomy of those tribes and found unacceptable the normative ideals of evolutionists, especially since Western civilization served so inadequately as a measure by which to judge Indian tribes.

Conventional strains of thought could not help but distort even firsthand observation, however. Roy Harvey Pearce notes these incongruities in discussing Henry Rowe Schoolcraft's work on Indian tribes:

> The complexity of Indian customs and traits, the richness of Indian legend and belief, the stubborn self-sufficiency of Indian cultures, are embodied in his six volumes, as they are, if one looks hard enough for them, in most earlier works on the Indian. In the *Historical and Statistical Information* [1851-1857], we can see how data deny conclusions—how, for example, Schoolcraft's Indians do find in their religious meanings and rewards, motives for living and dying, which he cannot be satisfied with and so cannot see for what they are.[46]

The failure of these early studies lay in the ethnologists' condescending perspective. Yet native materials collectively belied such interpretations and sometimes converted those less single-minded than Schoolcraft to a broader view of cultural possibilities. Even those far more casual than he began during the middle part of the nineteenth century to see native cultures for what they in fact so often were— rich, vital, autonomous, and severely threatened.[47]

To trace the exact development of such patterns of thought is impossible, like trying to fix on a color spectrum the point at which yellow turns to green. Still, amid the diverse influences shaping popular thought there emerges an intellectual sequence uniquely American: widespread concern for recording a threatened wilderness landscape created a context for anxious ethnographic efforts. To some extent, of course, anthropology always springs from the impulse to preserve human cultures from the ravages of time, to fix them descriptively in order to understand them.[48] But this admission hardly places the ideas traced here in a less distinctly national perspective. Instead,

---

[45] For a discussion of Boas's transformation of the concepts of culture, see Stocking, *Race, Culture, and Evolution*, pp. 133-307.

[46] Pearce, *Savagism and Civilization*, p. 127.

[47] Ibid., p. 129.

[48] See Lévi-Strauss, *Scope of Anthropology*, p. 51.

it clarifies a pattern linking the concern for a vanishing wilderness with that for cultural pluralism, a pattern that uniquely characterizes an era in American history.

No other country or historical period has experienced the complex undercurrents examined here. In Africa, South America, and Australia, landscapes and native peoples suffered at the hands of invaders in ways strikingly similar to those in America. For a number of reasons connected with settlement patterns, however, the invaders' perceptions of their own impact were never as conflicted. In South America, the Spanish and Portuguese clung to the coast; Africa saw only transient exploiters, except in the south, where natives nevertheless far outnumbered colonists; in Australia, conversely, the aborigines were few, and settlements remained coastal. What follows in these pages, then, is not a comparative study but a more precise examination of the conflicting impulses that Crèvecoeur, De Tocqueville, and many since have found so fascinating and bewildering in the American character.

CHAPTER TWO

THE VANISHING
WILDERNESS

And change with hurried hand has swept these scenes:
The woods have fallen, across the meadow-lot
The hunter's trail and trap-path is forgot,
And fire has drunk the swamps of evergreens;
Yet for a moment let my fancy plant
These autumn hills again . . .
>   —*Frederick Goddard Tuckerman*
>   Sonnet XVIII (ca. 1854-60)

The notes of a single observer, even in a limited district, describing accurately its features, civil, natural and social, are of more interest, and often of more value, than the grander view and broader generalizations of history.
>   —*Anonymous epigraph to Bela Hubbard*
>   *Memorials of a Half-Century* (1887)

AFTER LIVING happily abroad for seventeen years, Washington Irving (1783-1859) sailed home in the spring of 1832. During those years, he had garnered an illustrious reputation as America's first internationally acclaimed writer. Sophisticated, cosmopolitan, fully at ease in the best European court circles, Irving was returning at the height of his powers. For months beforehand, the New York City press heralded the arrival of the man who to most Americans personified success. Yet he also represented a silent, possibly reproving, judgment of his countrymen's sometimes rude Jacksonian virtues. Others crossing the Atlantic to view the young "democratic experiment" had frequently damned it with faint praise, when they praised it at all. Only a few years later, James Fenimore Cooper would return from a much shorter sojourn abroad to flay his countrymen and their institutions. If Americans felt uncertain about Irving's long-delayed return, however, they praised generously and held their questions.[1]

Irving's motives were in fact quite mixed. Nearly fifty years old, without a position, and having just lost his publisher, he shrewdly hoped to capitalize on an American reputation grown larger than his European prospects. He had a ready-made audience in America, one eager to offer approval. As well, he felt genuinely curious about his country. Reports abroad challenged memory and quickened his long-standing resolve to write on native themes. Irving worked best when he traveled, and he knew that his writing depended upon an accurate evocation of place. Perhaps the change of scene would rekindle a literary imagination temporarily gone cold.

On shipboard, Irving befriended two men who helped him to decide his itinerary: a Swiss count named Albert-Alexandre de Pourtalès and his older English companion, Charles J. Latrobe. Latrobe had been hired by the Pourtalès family to counsel the young libertine in sowing his wild oats abroad, and their joint enthusiasm for seeing the frontier soon inspired their new American friend. After

---

[1] This material on Irving and that to follow relies on the three standard modern biographies: Stanley T. Williams, *The Life of Washington Irving*, 2 vols. (New York: Oxford University Press, 1935), esp. 2:1-90; Edward Wagenknecht, *Washington Irving: Moderation Displayed* (New York: Oxford University Press, 1962); and Johanna Johnston, *The Heart That Would Not Hold: A Biography of Washington Irving* (New York: M. Evans and Co., 1971), esp. pp. 323ff. See also William Charvat, *The Profession of Authorship in America, 1800-1870: The Papers of William Charvat*, ed. Matthew J. Bruccoli (Columbus: Ohio State University Press, 1968), pp. 9-46.

arriving in New York, the trio made several short summer excursions up the Hudson River into the Green Mountains. In late August they struck out for the West. The measure of how powerfully the American wilderness gripped the imagination may be inferred from the eagerness with which these sophisticated gentlemen put aside more conventional pleasures to see it.

As they were traveling across Lake Erie toward Detroit, the friends met one of the new government commissioners for western tribes, Henry Leavitt Ellsworth. Once again, Irving caught another's enthusiasm for travel. Ellsworth persuaded the friends to accompany him to Arkansas, and in a letter to his brother later that year, Irving explained his own motive for risking the formidable hazards of such a venture: "The offer was too tempting to be resisted: I should have an opportunity of seeing the remnants of those great Indian tribes which are now about to disappear as independent nations, or to be amalgamated under some new form of government. I should see those fine countries of the 'far west,' while still in a state of pristine wilderness, and behold herds of buffaloes scouring their native prairies, before they are driven beyond the reach of a civilized tourist."[2]

Professional habit invariably compelled Irving to record his experiences. On this trip, however, his recognition of the transiency of wilderness reinforced habit to ensure an accurate account of what was already quickly receding. Although the resulting book, *A Tour of the Prairies* (1832), represents little other than a polished journal of a trip remarkable more for initial motive than for either itinerary or informed commentary, the trip profoundly influenced Irving's career. Stimulated by what he had seen, he spent the next five years in documenting aspects of his own and others' western experiences.

The separate accounts written by Irving's fellow travelers offer similar rationales for having accepted Ellsworth's invitation. Ellsworth himself showed no awareness of a threat to the wilderness. Latrobe's motives, on the other hand, matched Irving's. He too hoped to see Indian tribes and buffalo herds while they still freely roamed the plains, but like Irving, he ventured little beyond conventional predictions and laments in his completed book.[3] Only Latrobe's young charge exhibited a sophisticated understanding of their experiences, though he did so in a rather unorthodox fashion. Pourtalès's eagerness to learn the Osage language, for instance, fails to withstand close

---

[2] *The Western Journals of Washington Irving*, ed. John Francis McDermott (Norman: University of Oklahoma Press, 1944), p. 10.

[3] Charles Joseph Latrobe, *The Rambler in North America: 1832-1833*, 2 vols. (London: R. B. Seeley and W. Burnside, 1835), esp. 1:6, 166-67, 203, 2:172.

scrutiny, particularly in light of his successful seductions of native girls. Yet intimacy may curiously have shaped an exemplary insight. The vigorous count achieved a respect for the Osage as individuals and a sympathetic concern for their threatened way of life far deeper than that of his more primly buttoned companions.[4] Searching as the comments in his journal and correspondence appear, however, they fail to form the basis for an extended examination of the Osage or of the passing West. Only Irving found himself reverting again and again to the topic.

In *Astoria* (1836), Irving compiled what he hoped was the definitive history of western riverboatmen and fur traders. As in *A Tour of the Prairies*, he wrote with one eye to the expectations of a reading public addicted to frontier subjects and sentimentalized themes. John Jacob Astor had entreated him to use the voluminous manuscripts in his private collection to complete a popular, authoritative history, and the book is an important document because it includes paraphrases of manuscripts that have since disappeared. More important, asides throughout the narrative indicate Irving's awareness that his subject itself was vanishing. "It is the object of our task," he initially claims, "to present scenes of the rough life of the wilderness, and we are tempted to fix these few memorials of a transient state of things fast passing into oblivion."[5] Irving never questions the effects of the fur trade on indigenous populations. Though he openly sympathizes with their decline, his object was to document not the Indians but a distinct mode of white frontier life that was passing unrecorded.[6]

The Adventures of Captain Bonneville, U.S.A. (1837), the last work in Irving's western series, suffers from many of the weaknesses that flaw *Astoria*, including a too scrupulous attention to details copied from journals and interviews and an inability to report without sentimentality or cliché. Irving's special affection for a book that is little more than a miscellany of information on the West has never been shared by readers. Yet his intentions for the book, best revealed in its conclusion, bear close examination:

> We here close our picturings of the Rocky Mountains and their wild inhabitants, and of the wild life that prevails there; which we have been anxious to fix on record, because we are aware that

[4] Pourtalès, *On the Western Tour with Washington Irving: The Journal and Letters of Count de Pourtalès*, ed. George F. Spaulding (Norman: University of Oklahoma Press, 1968), esp. pp. 19, 21-22.

[5] *Astoria, or Anecdotes of an Enterprise Beyond the Rocky Mountains*, ed. Edgeley W. Todd (Norman: University of Oklahoma Press, 1964), p. 14.

[6] Ibid., esp. p. 517.

this singular state of things is full of mutation, and must soon undergo great changes, if not entirely pass away. The fur trade, itself, which has given life to all this portraiture, is essentially evanescent. . . . The mad carouse in the midst of danger, the night attack, the stampado, the scamper, the fierce skirmish among rocks and cliffs—all this romance of savage life, which yet exists among the mountains, will then exist but in frontier story, and seem like the fiction of chivalry or fairy tale.[7]

This passage suggests better than almost any other single quotation the kind of concerned commitment, at various levels of intensity, manifested in countless works on the West during this period.

FIXING A RECORD

People "anxious to fix on record" their "picturings" of the West almost literally elbowed each other aside. John James Audubon, for instance, returning from one of his painting expeditions, traveled aboard the same Mississippi steamboat that carried the Irving entourage.[8] Also during the summer of 1832, George Catlin visited the same dwindling Osage tribe whose language Count Pourtalès so closely studied. These men differed little from their countrymen in anticipating the dramatic changes soon to occur and in expressing the need to record an image of the original. The question then arises: Why should such feelings have appeared so early? The continent was still largely unmapped and unstudied, its resources still largely undiminished.

The answer may be found in part in a vague, but widespread, anxiety that scholars have only recently detected both in America and abroad. Granted, the psychological condition of any nation resists diagnosis; a constellation of variables keeps social complacency and unrest in constant flux. Nevertheless, nineteenth-century Americans appear to have had more cause than most nationalities for strains of uncertainty. The insidious psychological pressures predictable in a society claiming no impediments to success, the social upheavals brought about by new urban and industrial patterns of life, and the growing regional dissension over racial and economic issues form only a partial listing of causes to account for the recurrent images of apocalypse and catastrophe, the camouflaged themes of decline and doom that characterized Jacksonian American rhetoric. Anxiety about

---

[7] *The Adventures of Captain Bonneville, U.S.A., in the Rocky Mountains and the Far West*, ed. Edgeley W. Todd (Norman: University of Oklahoma Press, 1961), p. 372.

[8] Williams, *Washington Irving*, p. 43.

the wilderness gusted fitfully in this turbulent national atmosphere. By the time Americans considered their republic more than an experiment, around 1820, they had already long been abandoning worn-out farmland and unproductive plantations along the east coast. The very prevalence of this pattern was portentous. How could one assuage the suspicion that Indian extermination and then land exhaustion would transform the West as they had the East? Would not the cycle be successively repeated across the continent?

That Americans experienced such doubts should cause less surprise than that they felt them so early. Unlike Europeans in Africa or Australia, Americans felt more than a proprietary interest in the continent. True, they too had been colonials, with primary allegiance to the mother country. Following the Revolution, however, the continent connoted far more than, say, India would to the British or Mexico and Peru to the Spanish. Once entirely their own, the land formed a kind of collective self-extension, defining Americans even as it continued to be defined by them. In a country that had changed so rapidly, the salvaged record offered sole evidence of the earlier definitions. It alone could testify to the natural delights that had first attracted the pioneer. Few challenged the tenets of their progressive faith, caught up as they were in building new lives. Yet more than a few attempted to capture a permanent view that would form the sole content of another generation's knowledge of its heritage.

Among the myriad reasons given by those who would record their experiences, many reflect no specific urge to preserve a wilderness vision. On the other hand, certain people clearly felt so impelled, and yet failed to articulate that feeling. The impulse is sometimes evidenced in the very paintings and photographs they produced, in the ethnological or archaeological work they pursued, or in the commitment they made to collecting for museums and to establishing local and national preserves. Toward the end of the century especially, people apparently took for granted an understanding of their sometimes frenetic exertions. This chapter, however, concentrates on people who explicitly and self-consciously voiced apprehensions about the continent. In prefaces, allusions, asides, and occasional direct avowals, they committed themselves to detailing an accurate portrait of the wilderness, its forests, wildlife, scenic wonders, and Indians.

In their simpler forms, these expressions hardly cut very deep. An inescapable sense of loss is at times registered in tones of vague regret, more frequently as mild bewilderment. Some express a kind of anticipatory nostalgia for that which, however threatened, had not yet passed. They lamented what still stood in front of them. Voices were raised energetically in hymns of progress; but the more thoughtful found in the refrain "how the times have swept us by" sufficient cause to sing in a minor key.[9]

This lamentation for something departing also helps to account for the plethora of travel journals and diaries, what one scholar has termed "the characteristic literature of the period."[10] Permanent frontier settlers and travelers who, like Irving, Latrobe, and Pourtalès, hurried west to see it still undiminished wrote accounts intentionally to preserve their firsthand impressions. They appreciated their timely good fortune. Already by the 1830s and early 1840s, these varied observers included: the trapper Osborne Russell, one of the early visitors to the Yellowstone region; western judge and popular novelist James Hall; Indian captive Oliver M. Spencer; rifleman and later regimental General Thomas James; and the famous chronicler of the Santa Fe Trail, Josiah Gregg.[11] All these men shared an attitude composed of contradictory impulses, best described by a fellow spirit nearly half a century later: "In ten or fifteen years more, perhaps, this cannot be said, but as yet we may still feel a delight, keen as a woman's in the possession of a rare jewel, in the scene which surrounds us and which so few others have enjoyed."[12] Hesitation, a sense of imminent foreclosure, coupled with the immediate pleasure evoked by the wilderness—these elements characterize many of the explanations given for recording firsthand impressions.

[9] Jeremiah Church, *Journal of Travels, Adventures, and Remarks, of Jerry Church* (Harrisburg, Pa.: n.p., 1845), p. 72.

[10] William Goetzmann, *Army Exploration in the American West, 1803-1863* (New Haven: Yale University Press, 1959), p. 471.

[11] Osborne Russell, *Journal of a Trapper* . . . , ed. Aubrey L. Haines (Portland: Oregon Historical Society, 1955), esp. pp. 4, 112, 123, 138, 143-45, 154; James Hall, *Legends of the West: Sketches Illustrative of the Habits, Occupations, Privations, Adventures and Sports of the Pioneers of the West* (1832; rpt. Cincinnati: Applegate and Co., 1857), pp. v, xii-xiv; Oliver M. Spencer, *Indian Captivity* (1835; rpt. Ann Arbor: University Microfilms, 1966), pp. 11-12; Gen. Thomas James, *Three Years among the Indians and Mexicans* (1846; rpt. Chicago: R. R. Donnelley and Sons, 1953), pp. xx, 17, 93-94; Josiah Gregg, *Commerce of the Prairies* (1844), ed. Max L. Moorhead (Norman: University of Oklahoma Press, 1954), pp. 369-70, 396; William Cullen Bryant, *Letters of a Traveller; or, Notes of Things Seen in Europe and America* (1850), 4th ed. (New York: G. P. Putnam and Co., 1855), pp. 79, 302; Peter Skene Ogden, *Traits of American-Indian Life and Character by a Fur Trader* (London: Smith, Elder and Co., 1853), p. xi; John Treat Irving Jr., *Indian Sketches Taken During an Expedition to the Pawnee Tribes [1833]* (1835), ed. John Francis McDermott (Norman: University of Oklahoma Press, 1955), p. 22; George Frederick Ruxton, *Life in the Far West* (1848), ed. LeRoy R. Hafen (Norman: University of Oklahoma Press, 1951), pp. 100, 106, 112.

[12] S. C. Robertson, "An Army Hunter's Notes on Our North-Western Game," *Outing*, 11 (January 1888), 305.

People otherwise confident about the westward progress of white settlement often betrayed deep resistance to the devastation thereby entailed. They felt alternately proud of their settlements and disoriented by the rapidity with which these were axed out of the wilderness. Praising America in the abstract, they shrank from the actual wounds inflicted on the land. Descriptions belie their complacency: "magnificent forests which the axe has not yet despoiled"; "innumerable spots where nature is invulnerable"; "while the wilderness still glowed in its pristine luxuriance."[13] The *yets* and *stills*, the hesitations and exceptions, the rhetorical graspings for a land slipping away proliferate in western accounts. Bayard Taylor, that American Marco Polo who enthralled his countrymen with descriptions of faraway lands, never jeopardized his popularity or royalties by challenging popular assumptions. Yet even he felt dismay at how far below his American dream fell the vulgar reality. Returning to California ten years after his first visit in 1849, he sadly observed in an account that otherwise continually soothes American ambitions: "Nature here reminds one of a princess fallen into the hands of robbers, who cut off her fingers for the sake of the jewels she wears."[14]

Ambivalence about this American experience characterizes much travel writing of the century, until elegy gives way to concern and then consternation in ever clearer tones.[15] From private diarists to

[13] The quotations, respectively, are from: Timothy Flint, *Recollections of the Last Ten Years Passed in Occasional Residences and Journeyings in the Valley of the Mississippi . . .* (Boston: Cummings, Hilliard, and Co., 1826), pp. 27-28; John A. Butler, "Some Western Resorts," *Harper's New Monthly Magazine*, 65 (August 1882), 326; and Benjamin Drake, *The Life and Adventures of Black Hawk* (1838), 7th ed. rev. (Cincinnati: E. Morgan and Co., 1850), p. 256. See also Rev. James Wallis Eastburn, *Yamoyden, A Tale of the Wars of King Philip: In Six Cantos* (New York: n.p., 1820), pp. 3-4, 27-29; Henry Marie Brackenridge, *Recollections of Persons and Places in the West* (Philadelphia: James Kay, Jun. and Brother, 1834), pp. 71-72; Robert Montgomery Bird, *Calavar; or, The Knight of the Conquest: A Romance of Mexico* (1834), 2d ed., 2 vols. (Philadelphia: Carey, Lea, and Blanchard, 1835), 1:v; James H. Lawrence, "Discovery of the Nevada Fall," *Overland Monthly*, 2d ser., 4 (October 1884), 371.

[14] Taylor, *At Home and Abroad: A Sketch-Book of Life, Scenery, and Men*, 2d ser. (New York: G. P. Putnam, 1862), p. 155. See Kevin Starr, *Americans and the California Dream, 1850-1915* (New York: Oxford University Press, 1973), pp. 174-75, for discussion of widespread sympathy with Taylor's attitude among California tourists.

[15] For an apt illustration of this transition, see: Timothy Dwight, *Travels in New-England and New York*, 4 vols. (London: William Baynes and Son, 1823), 1:vi; Sarah Kemble Knight, *The Journal of Madam Knight* (Boston: Small, Maynard and Co., 1920), p. xii; William C. Spengemann, *The Adventurous Muse: The Poetics of American Fiction, 1789-1900* (New Haven: Yale University Press, 1977), p. 45. See also Gabriel Franchère, *Narrative of a Voyage to the Northwest Coast of America in the Years 1811, 1812, 1813, and 1814; or The First American Settlement*

famous writers, housewives to professional journalists, the intent altered little: "to picture a fleeting phase of our national life"; "[to hand] down to posterity a faithful record"; "to delineate the character, customs and habits of the Indian tribes, who have passed, and are passing, so fast away, that little more will soon be left of them to sight or memory." Decidedly, "he who would write of the 'wilds of the West, beyond the bounds of civilization' must write quickly."[16] Some surely hoped to chart the national progress by defining initial conditions—intent, as it were, on taking a "before" picture in what they expected would make a dramatic "before-and-after" sequence. Yet the attention of later nineteenth-century picture takers seems less calmly focused in proud expectation. Their prose acquires a shrill tone and a more agitated rhythm, punctuated by expressions of mild regret.[17]

Perhaps the clearest insight into this rough transition in public attitudes can be gained by assembling a series of statements made during the course of the century. Far from reflecting a uniform shift

---

on the Pacific (1820), trans. and ed. J. V. Huntington (1854), reprinted in vol. 6 of Reubon Gold Thwaites, ed. Early Western Travels: 1748-1846, 32 vols. (Cleveland: Arthur H. Clark Co., 1904-07), p. 175; John Burroughs's introduction to Robert Buchanan, Life and Adventures of Audubon the Naturalist (1868; rpt. New York: E. P. Dutton, 1913),·p. vii.

[16] The quotations are from: Albert D. Richardson, Beyond the Mississippi: From the Great River to the Great Ocean . . . (Hartford, Conn.: American Publishing Co., 1867), p. i; Caroline Matilda Kirkland, A New Home—Who'll Follow? or, Glimpses of Western Life (1839), 3d ed. (New York: Charles S. Francis, 1841), p. 7; George H. Colton, Tecumseh; or, The West Thirty Years Since. A Poem (New York: Wiley and Putnam, 1842), preface; I. Winslow Ayer, Life in the Wilds of America, and Wonders of the West in and beyond the Bounds of Civilization (Grand Rapids, Mich.: Central Publishing Co., 1880), p. 15.

[17] Those intent on a "before" shot while still possible include: Charles Loring Brace, The New West: or, California in 1867-1868 (New York: G. P. Putnam and Son, 1869), p. iv; Fortescue Cuming, Sketches of a Tour to the Western Country, Through the States of Ohio and Kentucky . . . 1807-1809 (1810), reprinted in vol. 4 of Thwaites, ed., Early Western Travels, p. 23; Joseph Henry Taylor, Sketches of Frontier and Indian Life (Pottstown, Pa.: n.p., 1889), pp. 6-7. Those intent merely on salvaging some accurate record include: Frances Chamberlain Holley, Once Their Home; or, Our Legacy From the Dahkotahs (Chicago: Donohue and Henneberry, 1890), p. 18; Emerson Hough, The Way to the West (Indianapolis: Bobbs-Merrill, 1903), p. 423; Bela Hubbard, "Ancient Garden Beds of Michigan," American Antiquarian, 1 (April 1878), 1; Humphrey Marshall, The History of Kentucky (Frankfort: n.p., 1824), introduction; Charles Alston Messiter, Sport and Adventures among the North-American Indians (London: R. H. Porter, 1890), pp. v-vi; John Lewis Peyton, Over the Alleghanies and Across the Prairies: Personal Recollections of the Far West (London: Simpkin, Marshall and Co., 1869), p. xi; Gilbert Malcolm Sproat, Scenes and Studies of Savage Life (London: Smith, Elder and Co., 1868), p. 10. See also Annette Kolodny's reference to William Gilmore Simms in The Lay of the Land: Metaphor as Experience and History in American Life and Letters (Chapel Hill: University of North Carolina Press, 1975), p. 104.

in public opinion, these statements serve rather as a paradigm for the history of an idea. The first statement was delivered in 1834 by the leading citizen of a burgeoning Cincinnati. Lecturing the city's finest on their "history, character, and prospects," he observed: "Thus the teeming and beautiful landscape of nature fades away like a dream of poetry. . . . Before this transformation is finished, a portrait should be taken, that our children may contemplate the primitive physiognomy of their native land, and feast their eyes on its virgin charms."[18] As if to reinforce this suggestion, he called attention to the recent disappearance of local game and encouraged the collecting of fossil remains and Indian artifacts before they were plowed under.

Near mid-century a less well-known resident of western New York State wrote a number of volumes on pioneer life and Iroquois traditions. Introducing one of them, he reflected wryly, "strange as it may appear, the history of this important country . . . will only attract the attention it demands, in the remote periods of future ages. The records of memory are fast fading away. The remnant of a once mighty nation is rapidly disappearing. Indian tradition, with all its vivacity and interest, is fearfully becoming extinct. A few short years and nothing new can possibly be gleaned."[19]

More than twenty years later, an antiquarian prefaced his collection of pioneer accounts by way of both apology and exhortation. "It is a great pity that the simple and unlettered actors in the rude and eventful old Border days recorded so little. . . . It is now, alas! almost too late. What can yet be done, however, should speedily be done to rescue from oblivion the evanescent memories of days that are past; to supply existing deficiencies; to correct the many errors which prevail; and to restore some degree of order to the great confusion existing among Border Chronicles and Traditions."[20]

The three statements share a similar concern, but they also suggest distinct differences in the quality of that concern as it developed over a forty-year period. Their common subject elicits a successively more intense emotional engagement. The conditional future perspective of the 1830s ("a portrait should be taken"), glowingly elaborated and calmly confident in its linked clauses, gives way in the second quotation to a reflection phrased in more agitated syntactic units. Parti-

[18] Daniel Drake, M.D., *Discourse on the History, Character, and Prospects of the West* (1834; rpt. Gainesville, Fla.: Scholars' Facsimiles and Reprints, 1955), p. 17; see also pp. 16-21.

[19] Joshua V. H. Clark, *Onondaga; or Reminiscenses of Earlier and Later Times . . .* , 2 vols. (Syracuse: Stoddard and Babcock, 1849), 1:xiv; see also 1:xiii, 77.

[20] Charles McKnight, *Our Western Border . . . One Hundred Years Ago* (Philadelphia: J. C. McCurdy and Co., 1875), p. x, also p. xi.

ciples seem to teeter on the fulcrum of tense, present and past; the sentences shrink, increasingly isolated, as each becomes more simply declarative, less structurally related to its predecessor. The style, that is, reflects an underlying sense of loss. Although the final statement may not seem to move as dramatically along the spectrum of attitudes, its combination of resignation and determination, its almost business-like assessment of missed opportunities and remaining possibilities nevertheless defines the kind of response many finally made in recording the vanishing appearance of the frontier. Of course, the rhetorical differences detailed here may illustrate stylistic idiosyncrasies as well as historical changes in response. Still, quotations similar to these can easily be replicated, alternating between assurances that there is "still time" and regrets that it is "too late."

For the most part, those concerned about the threatened landscape lacked the training in art, the professional experience as writers, or the unsparing commitment that might have shaped full careers in documenting the West. Though sharing a common historiographic bond, they usually acknowledged it only once, in diaries, essays, or illustrations that stand as unique efforts, not as part of lifelong missions. Most exceptions to this pattern, predictably, were trained artists or scientists, often members of government-sponsored surveys of the Far West. They devoted years, even decades, to preserving records of a wilderness threatened by the very opportunities revealed in their reports, whether for potential railroad routings or possible settlement locations.

As early as 1802, President Thomas Jefferson encouraged Meriwether Lewis to gather notes and materials along his continental trek, apparently with some sense of the need for a record. Jefferson long maintained not only a wide curiosity about the wilderness but also an incipient appreciation for its passing. For thirty years he collected ethnographic materials precisely because he recognized that tribes were dying off without leaving their histories behind.[21] Such awareness and accompanying commitment, rare in the eighteenth century, became characteristic, especially of particular groups of professionals, in the nineteenth. The letters and diaries of survey artists, for example, confirm this development. Even more convincing, the

---

[21] See Paul Russell Cutright, *Lewis and Clark: Pioneering Naturalists* (Urbana: University of Illinois Press, 1969), esp. p. 7, where he quotes from Jefferson's *Notes on the State of Virginia*: " 'It is to be lamented, then, very much to be lamented, that we have suffered so many of the Indian tribes already to extinguish, without our having previously collected and deposited in the records of literature, the general rudiment at least of the languages they spoke.' "

injunctions of art critics toward the end of the century suggest a broad public endorsement of such work.[22]

PAINTERS AS HISTORIANS OF THE WILDERNESS

The work of three major artists whose careers collectively spanned the middle two quarters of the nineteenth century suggests the extent of this concern for wilderness and the extraordinary efforts it produced. John James Audubon, Thomas Cole, and Albert Bierstadt were all immigrants who came or were brought to America for a new and better life; the paintings of each memorialize scenes they had initially wanted to celebrate. Audubon (1785-1851) was the first whose considerable ambitions were strengthened by a sense of imminent threat to the landscape. In 1820, seventeen years after leaving Santo Domingo, he began the vast project of illustrating all of America's birds, and for the next eighteen years he traveled through the North American wilderness, collecting specimens, dashing off sketches, taking voluminous notes, and finishing color plates for his masterwork, *Birds of America* (1827-1838).

The journals Audubon kept of his travels powerfully evoke his growing uneasiness over the incursions settlers were making. The Tennessee warbler and belted kingfisher, the passenger pigeon and yellow-throated vireo represented only a small part of what was threatened. "Nature herself seems perishing," he mourned in the early 1830s,[23] then going on to detail the ravaged landscape, the dwindled herds of buffalo and deer, the disease-ridden Indian tribes. In 1843 he described the Ohio River as it had seemed to him only twenty years earlier, and he concluded:

22 Thomas Nuttall, for example, explained his motives for publishing: "As it may contain some physical remarks connected with the history of the country, and with that of the unfortunate aborigines, who are so rapidly dwindling into oblivion, and whose fate may, in succeeding generations, excite a curiosity and compassion denied them by the present, I have considered myself partly excused in offering a small edition to the scientific part of the community". (Nuttall, *A Journal of Travels into the Arkansas Territory, During the year 1819* . . . [1821], reprinted as vol. 13 of Thwaites, ed., *Early Western Travels*, p. 27). See also Joseph Kastner, *A Species of Eternity* (New York: Alfred A. Knopf, 1977), pp. 254-83; Jessie Poesch, *Titian Ramsey Peale and His Journals of the Wilkes Expedition, 1799-1885* (Philadelphia: American Philosophical Society, 1961), pp. 22-26; S.G.W. Benjamin, *Art in America: A Critical and Historical Sketch* (New York: Harper and Brothers, 1880), p. 88; and Franz Stenzel, *James Madison Alden: Yankee Artist of the Pacific Coast, 1854-1860* (Fort Worth: Amon Carter Museum, 1975), pp. 9-18.

23 Maria R. Audubon, *Audubon and His Journals*, 2 vols. (New York: Charles Scribner's Sons, 1897), 1:407; See also 1:10-11, 406. For good background materials, see Kastner, *A Species of Eternity*, pp. 207-39.

I feel with regret that there are on record no satisfactory accounts of the state of that portion of the country from the time when our people first settled on it. . . . However, it is not too late yet; and I sincerely hope that either or both [Washington Irving and James Fenimore Cooper] will ere long furnish the generations to come with those delightful descriptions which they are so well qualified to give, of the original state of a country that has been so rapidly forced to change her form and attire under the influence of increasing population.[24]

Audubon's cherished hope for an "immortal" picture of "the country as it once existed" found at least some fulfillment in the works of both writers.[25]

Audubon himself set about fixing elements of the landscape in his own immortal picture, and his call to others to join in the task only confirms a personal sense of mission. Professionally ambitious, he nonetheless also felt a less selfish urge to use his skills in capturing pictures of American nature before its transformation. "Audubon attempted to stop time altogether," one scholar has pointed out, "and preserve the static continuity of a soaring bird and a landscape 'before population had greatly advanced.' "[26] That he spent the last decade of his strenuous career preparing *Viviparous Quadrupeds of North America* (1845-1854) testifies to the strength and widening scope of that motivation to stop time. Had he lived longer, Audubon might well have attempted other subjects whose despoliation he had long openly regretted.

Audubon's contemporary fame depended on Americans' new clamoring for paintings with indigenous subjects, a demand most fully satisfied by the Englishman Thomas Cole (1801-1848). Between 1825, when his oils were discovered in a Greenwich Village shop window, and 1848, the year of his death, Cole reigned as America's most popular painter. Buyers of his landscapes demanded accurate transcriptions of specific locales, and, as had Audubon, he learned to take voluminous notes in preparation for his highly detailed compositions. Indeed, Cole would come to feel that his paintings achieved a documentary status. Claiming special privileges for American artists be-

[24] Audubon, *Delineations of American Scenery and Character* (New York: G. A. Baker and Co., 1926), pp. 4-5. See also Robert V. Hine and Edwin R. Bingham, eds., *The American Frontier: Readings and Documents* (Boston: Little, Brown and Co., 1972), pp. 302-4; Alice Ford, *John James Audubon* (Norman: University of Oklahoma Press, 1964), p. 401.

[25] Maria R. Audubon, *Audubon and His Journals*, 1:182-83.

[26] Kolodny, *Lay of the Land*, p. 88.

cause "all nature here is new to art,"[27] he also recognized their collective responsibility to the landscape that was so rapidly passing away. The "meagre utilitarianism" of contemporaries who seemed willing to sacrifice the landscape to the "ravages of the axe" enraged Cole. In an 1835 public address he implored Americans to remember that "we are still in Eden; the wall that shuts us out of the garden is our own ignorance and folly."[28]

As forceful as were his speeches on behalf of preservation, Cole proved far more persuasive as a painter. In some cases, to be sure, his canvases are merely didactic. One, for instance, presents a woodsman senselessly attacking a tree in the midst of a clearing he has already hacked out of the forest.[29] A more profound vision emerges in Cole's celebrated five-panel series, *The Course of Empire* (1836), in which the final two scenes illustrate time's ravaging force as "The Destruction of Empire" and "Desolation."[30] Cole knew from visits to Europe the dangers that Western civilization offered to unprotected landscape. Against his strong sense of historical cycles ever turning to ruinous waste, his native scenes often work as Audubon's color plates had: to hold an image of the fleeting wilderness forever fixed in time. They do not incidentally illustrate the American landscape before mid-century; they were created for that very purpose.[31]

By the mid-1840s, Cole had abandoned efforts to synthesize ideal conceptions with graphic detail. In his last painting, *View of the Falls of Munda* (1847), he completely abandoned a priori formulas to embrace an almost photographic accuracy. "The real and the ideal," one critic has observed, "which had so often conflicted in his art, seem to have separated out like oil and water."[32] A partial reason for this

27 Cited in Louis L. Noble, *The Course of Empire, Voyage of Life, and Other Pictures of Thomas Cole, N.A.* (New York: Lamport, Blakeman and Law, 1853), p. 202.

28 Cole, "Lecture on American Scenery, Delivered before the Catskill Lyceum, April 1st, 1841," *Northern Light*, 1 (May 1841), 25-26. See also Cole's poem, "The Lament of the Forest," *Knickerbocker*, 17 (June 1841), 516-19.

29 See Richard Rudisill, *Mirror Image: The Influence of the Daguerreotype on American Society* (Albuquerque: University of New Mexico Press, 1971), p. 8.

30 See Louis Legrand Noble, *The Life and Works of Thomas Cole* (1853), ed. Elliot S. Vesell (Cambridge, Mass.: Harvard University Press, 1964), pp. xxi, 129.

31 See Howard S. Merritt, *Thomas Cole* (Rochester: University of Rochester Memorial Art Gallery, 1969), p. 24. On Cole's "Kaaterskill Falls" (1827) Merritt remarks: "As recorded in the drawing there were, even at this early date, an observation pavilion and guard rails at the head of the falls. Typically, Cole carefully omits these in the painting, thereby emphasizing, or one should say restoring, the unspoiled wilderness of the scene—further underscored by the inclusion of an Indian."

32 Barbara Novak, *American Painting of the Nineteenth Century: Realism, Idealism, and the American Experience* (New York: Praeger, 1969), p. 79. See also James

2. Thomas Cole, *Landscape: The Wilderness Axeman*, 1825. Oil on canvas. The Minneapolis Institute of Arts.

clarification is suggested in the notes Cole made just prior to his death for an art book taking wilderness as its main theme: "Love of nature more intense and diffused among the moderns than the ancients. One cause of it—the wilderness passing away, and the necessity of saving and perpetuating its features."[33] Whether he would have completed that book had he lived, Cole would certainly have moved landscape painting toward more exacting documentation.

Of course, more detailed landscapes offer in themselves no particular evidence of swelling concern for the wilderness. Cole's successor as America's premier painter, Asher Durand, practiced a far more literal landscape style without ever expressing disquietude over

Thomas Flexner, *That Wilder Image: The Painting of America's Native School from Thomas Cole to Winslow Homer* (1962; rpt. New York: Dover Publications, 1970), pp. 34ff.; Roderick Nash, *Wilderness and the American Mind*, rev. ed. (New Haven: Yale University Press, 1973), p. 97; Arthur A. Ekirch Jr., *Man and Nature in America* (New York: Columbia University Press, 1963), p. 27.

[33] Cited in Noble, *Course of Empire*, p. 398.

the passing of America's forests. Nevertheless, Durand, other Hudson River School practitioners, and American painters generally could not remain unaffected when even art critics elaborated on Cole's pleas. An anonymous reviewer of two Jasper Cropsey landscapes in 1847, for example, ranked the painter with both Cole and Durand because he illustrated the high mission of the American painter. "The axe of civilization is busy with our old forests," the reviewer declared. "Yankee enterprise has little sympathy with the picturesque, and it behooves our artists to rescue from its grasp the little that is left, before it is for ever too late."[34] Artists heeded the plea. Indeed, one art historian has verified this impulse in pre-Civil War America, declaring that "no object is so frequently found in its landscape art as the tree stump."[35] Of course, then as now, artists primarily responded to special aesthetic considerations or more general ones of public remuneration. But some satisfied personal standards and popular taste even as they fulfilled a "high mission."

Albert Bierstadt (1830-1902) does not exemplify this fusion. Capitulating to easy popularity in his grandiloquent landscapes, he and his reputation have suffered the consequences in modern appreciation. During the 1870s and 1880s, however, he epitomized a major strain in national taste and pride by giving form to Americans' vague image of the Far West. Melodramatic in his composition and lighting, unimaginative in his application of colors, Bierstadt can hardly be said to follow either Audubon or the later Cole. Nonetheless, in his finest painting, *The Rocky Mountains* (1863), he offers a paradigm for the intertwined commitments to both landscape and indigenous peoples. The huge canvas presents a grandiose mountain scene that all but compels closer inspection, inspection that reveals a group of Bannock Indians camped on the valley floor. The eye moves, in other words, from an overwhelming alpine vista to the natives below. Without overburdening the analogy, one might note that the initial desire to preserve images of the unaltered land similarly encouraged initial inquiries about the tribes living there.[36]

However seldom Bierstadt's paintings reflect the theses of Audubon or Cole, he identified with their principles on one occasion at least. In 1859, on his first trip to the Rockies, he sent a public letter back

[34] Review of Exhibition of National Academy of Design, *Literary World*, May 15, 1847, p. 348.
[35] Nicolai Cikovsky Jr., " 'The Ravages of the Axe': The Meaning of the Tree Stump in Nineteenth-Century American Art," *Art Bulletin*, 61 (December 1979), 626.
[36] See John C. Ewers, *Artists of the Old West* (Garden City, N.Y.: Doubleday and Co., 1965), p. 183. See also Ellwood Parry, *The Image of the Indian and the Black Man in American Art, 1590-1900* (New York: George Braziller, 1974), pp. 114-16.

3. Albert Bierstadt, *The Rocky Mountains,* 1863. Chromolithograph. Collection of Alfred L. Bush, Princeton, New Jersey.

east, reiterating what others had long proclaimed: "For a figure-painter, there is an abundance of fine subjects. The manners and customs of the Indians are still as they were hundreds of years ago, and now is the time to paint them, for they are rapidly passing away, and soon will be known only in history. I think that the artist ought to tell his portion of their history."[37] Bierstadt later ignored his own injunction, but he could hardly ignore an aspect of the trip that will demand later attention: the presence of a professional photographer. The camera's extraordinary capacity for documentary realism, however little it shaped his own art, provided for countless others a tool to preserve images imminently threatened in the West.[38]

[37] Bierstadt, "Letter from the Rocky Mountains, July 10, 1859," *Crayon,* (September 1859), 287.

[38] Josiah Gregg supposedly made daguerreotype plates on the Santa Fe Trail in 1846. John Mix Stanley had made some three years before on his first trip west, as documented by Russell E. Belous and Robert A. Weinstein in *Will Soule: Indian Photographer at Fort Sill, Oklahoma, 1869-74* (Los Angeles: Ward Ritchie Press, 1969), p. 13. The railroad surveys of the fifties invariably included a photographer, who often focused on Indians and Indian life in the areas visited. Richard and Edward Kern, for example, accompanied John C. Frémont's fourth Southwest expedition; among their plates "are illustrations of designs on fragments of Indian pottery, Indian hieroglyphics, and ground plans of several pueblos, invaluable for the archaeolog[ist]" today, according to Robert Taft in *Artists and Illustrators of*

WRITERS AS HISTORIANS OF THE WILDERNESS

Photography powerfully influenced those ignorant of the craft itself. Not until the last quarter of the century did major innovations in the photographic process make the camera a convenient tool for those interested in documentation. Its language had already crept into general usage, however, and its new perspectives had long since fostered new attitudes among those anxious about the threatened landscape. Hardly three decades after Louis Daguerre and William Henry Fox Talbot perfected the process, Francis Parkman completed a volume of his North American history in which he claimed "to secure the greatest possible accuracy of statement, and to reproduce an image of the past with photographic clearness and truth."[39] For Parkman, as for other historians, the camera provided more than a convenient metaphor. It clarified the very premises of his profession, especially as that profession faced the complex phenomenon of the American West.

---

the Old West 1850-1900 (New York: Charles Scribner's Sons, 1953), p. 258. S. N. Carvalho's work for Frémont's fifth expedition in 1853 and John Mix Stanley's prints for Isaac Stevens's survey that same year both included a number of studies of Indians and Indian culture, although both men's work has since been lost or destroyed. See also Edward Vischer, *Vischer's Pictorial of California: Landscape, Trees and Forest Scenes; Grand Features of California Scenery, Life, Traffic and Customs,* 5 series of 12 numbers each (San Francisco: n.p., April 1870), pp. 1-2; Vischer, *Sketches of the Washoe Mining Region: Photographs Reduced from Originals* (San Francisco: Valentine and Co., 1862), pp. 6-7; John Warner Barber and Henry Howe, *All the Western States and Territories . . .* (Cincinnati: Howe's Subscription Book Concern, 1868), p. 4; Freeman Tilden, *Following the Frontier with F. Jay Haynes: Pioneer Photographer of the Old West* (New York: Alfred A. Knopf, 1964), esp. pp. 26, 197, 223, 359ff.; F. Jay Haynes, *Indian Types of the North-West* (New York: Adolph Wittemann, ca. 1885), p. 3; Mark H. Brown and W. R. Felton, *Before Barbed Wire: L. A. Huffman, Photographer on Horseback* (1956; rpt. New York: Bramhall House, 1961), pp. 10-12, 19-21; Mark H. Brown and W. R. Felton, *The Frontier Years: L. A. Huffman, Photographer of the Plains* (New York: Bramhall House, 1955); John S. Hittell, *Yosemite: Its Wonders and Its Beauties* (San Francisco: H. H. Bancroft and Co., 1868); William Henry Jackson, *Descriptive Catalogue of Photographs of North American Indians,* U.S. Geological and Geographical Survey of the Territories, Miscellaneous Publication no. 9 (Washington: G.P.O., 1877), pp. iii-v; *The Diaries of William Henry Jackson: Frontier Photographer,* ed. LeRoy R. Hafen and Ann W. Hafen (Glendale, Calif.: Arthur H. Clark Co., 1959), pp. 275-76, 314; and Victoria Thomas Olson, "Pioneer Conservationist A. P. Hill: 'He Saved the Redwoods,'" *American West,* 14 (September-October 1977), 32-40.

[39] Francis Parkman, *The Jesuits of North America in the Seventeenth Century* (1867), vols. 3-4 of the Champlain Edition (Boston: Little, Brown and Co., 1897), 3:vii. Thirteen years later a reviewer of Francis Parkman's collected works invoked the same metaphor: "As we peruse them now, remembering the mighty changes which have been wrought in yesterday's wilderness, we realize that they have a peculiar value of their own. For they are a photographic record of a state of things which has passed away never to return" (Edward G. Mason, "Francis Parkman" *Dial,* 1 [December 1880], 149).

Parkman (1823-1893) resembles Washington Irving both in his career as historian and in his fascination with America's wilderness. With greater deliberation than Irving and for a longer period, however, he attempted both to explore those wild regions and to document them. In 1841, for example, he hiked into the White Mountains "to see the wilderness where it was as yet uninvaded by the hand of man."[40] Five years later, weak health and a strong desire to observe at firsthand the life of the Plains Sioux led Parkman to make a summer's trek to the West, a trip that confirmed him in his career. Returning to write a personal narrative, *The Oregon Trail* (1849), he followed it with what became a nine-volume study, *France and England in North America* (1892). The first volume in this series, *The Conspiracy of Pontiac* (1851), documents the Anglo-French struggle in colonial America and openly declares both its purpose and Parkman's continuing motive: "The history of that epoch . . . has been, as yet, unwritten, buried in the archives of governments, or among the obscurer records of private adventure. To rescue it from oblivion is the object of the following work. It aims to portray the American forest and the American Indian at the period when both received their final doom."[41] Parkman felt almost compelled to rescue American history from fading memories and crumbling manuscripts, and he even came to view his earlier endeavors in this light. Though he wrote *The Oregon Trail* with no explicitly preservationist purpose, his prefaces to subsequent editions increasingly invest the work with special value. In each he laments the passing of the wilderness, and by 1892 he could conclude: "The Wild West is tamed, and its savage charms have withered. If this book can help to keep their memory alive, it will have done its part."[42]

This concern to preserve America's frontier history may seem incongruous in a sophisticated Boston Brahmin. Insulated by birth, education, and predisposition from the wilderness dramas he described, Parkman nonetheless kept returning to America's past in

[40] *The Journals of Francis Parkman*, ed. Mason Wade, 2 vols. (New York: Harper and Brothers, 1947), 1:31.

[41] *The Conspiracy of Pontiac and the Indian War after the Conquest of Canada* (1851), vols. 16-18 of the Champlain Edition (Boston: Little, Brown and Co., 1898), 16:ix.

[42] *The Oregon Trail: Sketches of Prairie and Rocky-Mountain Life* (1849), ed. E. N. Feltskog (Madison: University of Wisconsin Press, 1969), p. ix. For discussion of Parkman's earlier dismay at the losses incurred through "civilizing" the West (as reflected in *The Oregon Trail*), see esp. Howard Doughty, *Francis Parkman* (New York: Macmillan Co., 1962), pp. 116-17, 151-58. For a more contemporary response admiring Parkman's preservationist achievement, see Mason, "Francis Parkman," p. 150.

order to document the continent as it once had been. Against his rather romantic vision of the American West pressed a strong intimation of loss. Yet, unlike Thomas Cole, who explored this very conjunction in his art, Parkman failed to pursue its darker implications in his historical series. Indeed, his unquestioning belief in material progress prevented him from ever specifically formulating the issue.

A contemporary who failed in a similar fashion was James Fenimore Cooper (1789-1851), though he at least attempted to deal with the implications of progress. Toiling in fictional rather than historical fields, Cooper suffered similar uneasiness about what was being eroded, what plowed under in America's wilderness history. In fact, Parkman's preface to *The Conspiracy of Pontiac* (1851), proclaiming accuracy in his rescued record, may itself have been prompted by Cooper's efforts to reclaim native soil. Following the novelist's death later that year, Parkman wrote a eulogy suggesting such an influence. Though he missed the moral ambiguities at the heart of Cooper's mythic vision, the historian analyzed tellingly in one section:

> Civilization has a destroying as well as a creating power. It is exterminating the buffalo and the Indian, over whose fate too many lamentations, real or affected, have been sounded for us to renew them here. It must, moreover, eventually sweep from before it a class of men, its own precursors and pioneers, so remarkable both in their virtues and their faults, that few will see their extinction without regret. Of these men, Leatherstocking is the representative . . . [and] worthy of permanent remembrance. His life conveys in some sort an epitome of American history, during one of its more busy and decisive periods.[43]

Parkman failed only to grant Cooper the self-conscious intent he argued for his own labors.

Prefaces to the Leatherstocking tales repeatedly proclaim Cooper's fidelity to the wilderness experience. His declaration, for example, that "though the scenes of this book are believed to have once been as nearly accurate as required by the laws which govern fiction, they are so no longer,"[44] is reiterated in three of the four other tales in the series. While New York's eastern woodlands had altered dra-

[43] Parkman, "The Works of James Fenimore Cooper," *North American Review*, 74 (January 1852), 151-52.

[44] Cooper, *The Pathfinder, or The Inland Sea* (New York: W. A. Townsend and Co., 1859), p. viii. All future references will be to this edition of Cooper's works, known as the Author's Revised Edition, illustrated by F.O.C. Darley. See other volumes from this edition, including *The Pioneers*, p. ix; *The Last of the Mohicans*, p. ix; and *The Deerslayer*, p. xiii.

matically between his childhood there and the beginning of his writing career in the 1820s, Cooper hoped to preserve a memory of them through his art, providing historical footnotes that verify otherwise improbable scenes and, in subsequent editions, refuting challenges to portrayed events.[45]

His narrative technique itself manifests a documentary concern that readers from the beginning have identified with the visual arts. His scenes, in the words of one, are "sharp visual images conceived as if they were paintings lacking the dimension of time."[46] Cooper intended that static quality in his novels; those that mythicize the young Leatherstocking, especially, give the impression of stopping time altogether. And this impression holds even in *The Pioneers* (1823) and *The Prairie* (1828), which portray an old and garrulous Natty Bumppo posed against the new pioneer order. Both novels present dislocation in such a way as to make it seem permanent. More profoundly than any of his contemporaries, Cooper felt impelled to flesh out a way of life already relegated to the past.[47]

The commitment to preserving a record of the wilderness that he had known as a child may be seen as an extension of his father's concern for eastern forests. Judge William Cooper settled his family on his vast landholdings in Cooperstown, New York, with the declared intention "to cause the Wilderness to bloom and fructify."[48] But against that promise intruded the fear that America's continental woodlands were inadequate to Americans' usage. In a careful analysis, Judge Cooper defined the specific conditions inevitably leading to a shortage of forested lands. Primary among these was man's thought-

[45] See, for example, *The Pioneers*, pp. 255, 257, 468; *The Prairie*, pp. 10, 11, 23, 27, 67, 124; *The Deerslayer*, p. 263.

[46] Henry Nash Smith, introduction to Cooper, *The Prairie: A Tale* (New York: Holt, Rinehart and Winston, 1950), p. ix. See also Honoré de Balzac, "Lettres sur la littérature," *Revue Parisienne*, July 23, 1840, trans. Warren S. Walker, in Walker, ed., *Leatherstocking and the Critics* (Chicago: Scott, Foresman and Co., 1965), p. 2; Blake Nevius, *Cooper's Landscapes: An Essay on the Picturesque Vision* (Berkeley: University of California Press, 1976); H. Daniel Peck, *A World by Itself: The Pastoral Moment in Cooper's Fiction* (New Haven: Yale University Press, 1977), esp. pp. 3-17.

[47] According to William Goetzmann, Cooper makes "time *and* progress stand still." "His great achievement was to render the historical process of change during a period of cultural genesis somehow timeless and permanent while at the same time capturing all of the ambiguities, dislocations, and anomalies of a culture in the throes of a process of acceleration more rapid than any ever seen before" (Goetzmann, "James Fenimore Cooper: *The Prairie*," in Hennig Cohen, ed. *Landmarks of American Writing* [New York: Basic Books, 1969], p. 71).

[48] William Cooper, *A Guide in the Wilderness: or the History of the First Settlements in the Western Counties of New-York with Useful Instructions to Future Settlers* (1810; rpt. New York: George P. Humphrey, 1897), p. 6. Cited in Roderick Nash, *Wilderness and the American Mind*, p. 32.

less waste. Cautioning against such prodigality, he offered informed suggestions for preventing this projected dearth.[49]

Once he began to write professionally, then, young James Fenimore could rely on more than a well-stocked memory of childhood experiences in frontier Cooperstown. The combination of parental opinion, personal temperament, and extensive research led Cooper into a paradox far more extreme than that troubling his father: deeply cherishing undomesticated wilderness, he nonetheless felt deeply pulled by America's westering development. Clearly, the novelist approved the spread of what he thought was the best of western European civilization across the continent. At the same time, he responded powerfully to the claims of an unsettled continent.[50] Cooper's lack of self-awareness about that conflict—hence, his inability to resolve it—prevents his fiction from finally transcending his own profound ambivalences.

Fitfully divided about the issue of civilization versus nature, Cooper nonetheless wanted to do more than preserve an accurate picture of the latter. Even as he celebrated white America's prospects in his essays and letters, in his fiction he gives the impression of wanting to preserve actual wilderness itself—land, Indians, and lone frontiersmen. As did his friend Thomas Cole, he sensed that Americans were selling their patrimony to destruction in the name of progress. Cooper best explores this issue of agrarian progress westward versus undomesticated nature in his Leatherstocking saga, most tellingly in *The Pioneers* and in *The Prairie*. *The Pioneers*, especially, highlights Cooper's imaginative "conflict of allegiances,"[51] perhaps because it is so closely autobiographical, more likely because it inaugurates the series. Artistically less self-conscious than he would be even in his next book, Cooper more readily incorporated contradictory elements into the narrative, defining at its most resonant levels his ambivalence toward America's westering society.[52] The stumps of felled trees sur-

[49] Roderick Nash, *Wilderness and the American Mind*, p. 23. Other public examples of this anticipatory concern include Samuel Akerly, "On the Cultivation of Forest Trees; In a Letter Addressed to Jonathan Thompson," broadside, 1823, American Antiquarian Society, Worcester, Mass.; and D. C. Banks, "To the Citizens of Kentucky," broadside, February 15, 1840, American Antiquarian Society.

[50] For further proof of the strength of Cooper's later feelings in this regard, see John J. McAleer, "Biblical Analogy in the Leatherstocking Tales," *Nineteenth-Century Fiction*, 17 (December 1962), 221-22.

[51] Smith, *Virgin Land*, p. 66.

[52] See D. H. Lawrence, *Studies in Classic American Literature* (1923; rpt. New York: Viking, 1966), pp. 50-51; Edwin Fussell, *Frontier: American Literature and the American West* (Princeton: Princeton University Press, 1965), pp. 56-64; Donald Ringe, *James Fenimore Cooper* (New York: Twayne, 1962), pp. 80ff.; Howard Mumford Jones, "Prose and Pictures: James Fenimore Cooper" (1951),

rounding the village of Templeton (to use a deliberately minor example) reappear with surprising frequency, and the very imagery associated with their appearances reflects Cooper's dismay at the necessary process of clearing. In our first view of Templeton, the narrator describes the way stumps "abounded in the open fields, adjacent to the village, and were accompanied occasionally, by the ruin of a pine or a hemlock that had been stripped of its bark, and which waved in melancholy grandeur its naked limbs to the blast, a skeleton of its former glory."[53] A quiet leitmotiv, these stumps reinforce a larger view of advancement as loss, of gain felt more compellingly as sacrifice.

Cooper equates progress with despoliation in each of the novel's major set pieces. Spurred on by civic leaders, the villagers cheerfully exhaust the natural environment, depleting the forests of sugar maples, the lakes of bass, the skies of passenger pigeons. Yet Cooper's distress is not at what Thomas Cole later decried as "meagre utilitarianism." Rather, he indicts the pioneers for their complacent extravagance in turning nature to profit, their thriftless waste in hacking out a community. The outspoken sheriff, Richard Jones, epitomizes this attitude in explaining urban planning to Elizabeth: " 'We must run our streets by the compass, coz, and disregard trees, hills, ponds, stumps, or, in fact, anything but posterity.' "[54]

Cooper best subverts the advocates of such progress through Natty Bumppo, who in *The Pioneers* lives on the outskirts of Templeton. He wins few admirers for his querulous ranting, whether against the villagers' extravagances or the village itself, but the narrative effectively supports his claims. "Civilization" and "progress" appear to Natty to be little more than rubrics justifying wholesale destruction of nature, and though his narrow view does not necessarily bound Cooper's own, the novel nonetheless offers little to counteract the hunter's suspicious conservatism.

A decade after fleeing westward from the sound of Templeton axes, Natty still cannot escape the crash of falling timber. In the first major action of *The Prairie*, he encounters the ironically named Bush family in the act of brutishly axing down the only grove of trees in sight. The image sets the tone for the novel, since, as Natty later observes,

in Jones, *History and the Contemporary: Essays in Nineteenth-Century Literature* (Madison: University of Wisconsin Press, 1964), p. 76. See also Charvat, *Profession of Authorship in America*, ed. Bruccoli, pp. 68-83; Peck, *A World by Itself*, pp. 61-62, 102-7.

[53] *The Pioneers*, p. 46. See Donald Ringe, *The Pictorial Mode: Space and Time in the Art of Bryant, Irving, and Cooper*. (Lexington: University Press of Kentucky, 1971), pp. 85, 124; Cikovsky, " 'Ravages of the Axe,' " pp. 611-26.

[54] *The Pioneers*, p. 199.

the demise of those trees prefigures his own.[55] Cooper depicts the white "rape of the wilderness" far less equivocally here than elsewhere in the series.[56] For instance, in his initial entrance, Abiram White confirms his defective moral standing when he declares: "The 'arth was made for our comfort; and, for that matter, so ar' its creatur's."[57] Through imagery and characterization, the novel confutes just this assertion. The very immensity of the landscape, the limitless horizon of the prairie, dramatically emphasizes a natural order that all should acknowledge. Cooper's proud Americans fail to do this. Dr. Obed Bat's imposition of a sterile taxonomy on nature is only the humorous obverse of Ishmael Bush's wasteful selfishness; both evince a contemptible arrogance toward the environment.[58]

But against the powerful scene of the axed grove of trees, Cooper places an equally forceful image. In the midst of the vast immensity glimmers the small, lighted circle of family relation as the Bush family camps for the night atop a great rock outcropping. Cooper could not reconcile this conflict between the separate claims of undefiled nature and westward progress. At the heart of his mythic interpretation of America, regret intensifies to tragic loss.[59] For all the value in that small circle of the family on the rock, these Americans represent changes that do not themselves seem inherently desirable. This incipient challenge to Western civilization's premises derives from more complex issues than that of America's vanishing wilderness and will be further examined in Chapter Eight.

For the moment, it is enough to observe that Cooper's disquietude about man's ravaging of nature gave him sufficient reason to document the landscape. Similar distress compelled others to radically different, more concerted forms of preservation that Cooper may never have considered, including the possibility of setting aside actual reserves. His and his father's efforts, however, coincided with the advent of public recommendations for city parks, state preserves, and national forests.

[55] See Joel Porte, *The Romance in America: Studies in Cooper, Poe, Hawthorne, Melville, and James* (Middletown, Conn.: Wesleyan University Press, 1967), pp. 45-46.

[56] See Ringe, *James Fenimore Cooper*, p. 45.

[57] *The Prairie*, p. 25.

[58] See Donald Ringe, "Man and Nature in Cooper's *The Prairie*," *Nineteenth-Century Fiction*, 15 (March 1961), 316-18.

[59] Henry Nash Smith first noted this in his Introduction to *The Prairie*, p. xvi. For other discussions, see Porte, *Romance in America*, p. 52, and Roy Harvey Pearce *Savagism and Civilization. A Study of the Indian and the American Mind*, rev. ed. (Baltimore: Johns Hopkins University Press, 1965), p. 202.

PRESERVATIONISTS AS HISTORIANS

The commitment to preservation of the land itself grew out of state efforts to set aside scenic wonders and cities' recognition of the benefits of public parks. Supporters of these causes became increasingly involved through the nineteenth century in deciding the future of America's larger wilderness landscape. Frederick Law Olmsted, John Muir, and Henry George, each in his own fashion, aroused Americans to the special claims of their continent. In their separate strategies for preservation, they nicely represent the spectrum of conservationism in the nineteenth century.

The first proposals for public parks, small "blocks of green," came on both sides of the Atlantic during the 1830s. This post-Renaissance idea had initially been conceived for royal, sometimes noble, purposes. Not until the nineteenth century, however, would it be adopted for the common welfare, and nowhere as in America would the pressure grow for city parks as "nature museums." Worldwide romanticism had contributed to an efflorescence of activities associated with the out-of-doors, as well as a growing resistance to the encroachments of the new urban industrialism. The rapid transformation of wilderness to settlement and settlement to crowded city encouraged Americans in particular to feel that urban enclaves should be preserved against the inroads of progress. Similar American patterns would energize indigenous movements for physical culture, landscape architecture, and rural cemeteries. By the 1840s and 1850s, advocates as little known as Thoreau and as popular as landscape architect Andrew Jackson Downing were repeatedly encouraging Americans to set aside generous tracts of city land.[60]

Such proposals united even political rivals. Among the few beliefs shared by William Cullen Bryant, the fiercely Democratic editor of the *New York Evening Post,* and Horace Greeley, editor of the Whiggish *New-York Tribune,* one was that Americans should be proscribed from destroying certain woodlands. More specifically, both men desired a park for New York City. Bryant phrased the need well in an editorial dated July 3, 1844: "As we are now going on, we are making

[60] Thoreau, *The Maine Woods* (1864), ed. Joseph J. Moldenhauer (Princeton: Princeton University Press, 1972), p. 205. See as well *The Journal of Henry David Thoreau,* ed. Bradford Torrey and Francis H. Allen (Boston: Houghton Mifflin Co., 1906), pp. 341, 1529, 1740-41; Andrew Jackson Downing, ed., *The Horticulturist, and Journal of Rural Art and Rural Taste,* 3 (October 1848), 153-57, 4 (July 1849), 9-12, 5 (October 1850), 153-56; and, for a useful survey, Albert Matthews, "The Word Park in the United States," *Publication of the Colonial Society of Massachusetts: Transactions,* 8 (1906), 373-97.

a belt of muddy docks all around the island. We should be glad to see one small part of the shore without them, one place at least where the tides may be allowed to flow pure, and the ancient brim of rocks which border the waters left in its original picturesqueness and beauty."[61] Seven years later, Central Park was conceived, though planned for the center of the city rather than the island's shores. Construction began in 1856, largely at Bryant's initiative.

Frederick Law Olmsted (1822-1903) made his name with the prize-winning design for Central Park. The flattering imitations for which he was commissioned following its 1861 completion—Fairmount Park in Philadelphia, Prospect Park in Brooklyn, South Park in Chicago, Mount Royal Park in Montreal, and park systems in Buffalo and Boston, to name but the largest—attest to the eight-hundred-acre park's resounding success. Olmsted's deft reliance on natural features, as well as his anticipation of future demands, became standards for later park planners. "He had without doubt," according to Lewis Mumford, "one of the best minds that the Brown Decades produced."[62] Driven by an ambition as great as his abilities, Olmsted pursued numerous careers: gentleman farmer, travel writer, editor of *Putnam's Magazine*, co-founder of the *Nation*, and executive secretary of the United States Sanitary Commission. His fame, however, rests on his landscape architecture and his efforts to ensure the preservation of "open spaces."

Olmsted's vision extended well beyond city limits; he recognized that more than urban development needed to be controlled. Government, he believed, had a responsibility to protect all the land for citizens living and unborn. Settlement must be regulated, even proscribed in certain spectacular locations, such as Niagara Falls. The falls, of course, had long attracted visitors, but completion of the Erie Canal in 1825 eased access and attracted a swarm of speculators. The earliest proposals for the site's preservation had been made at the time

[61] William Cullen Bryant, "A New Public Park," *New York Evening Post*, July 3, 1844, p. 2; Horace Greeley, *Glances at Europe* (New York: Dewitt and Davenport, 1851), pp. 38-39. See also James Russell Lowell, who made a similar statement in *Crayon*, 55 (1857). Bryant expressed a larger concern with the threat to America's landscape in his poetry, usually stated (as in Cooper) through Indian personas. See his *Poems* (Philadelphia: Carey and Hart), esp. pp. 70-72, 88-91, 94-97, 175-76.

[62] Mumford, *The Brown Decades: A Study of the Arts in America, 1865-1895* (1931; rpt. New York: Dover Publications, 1955), p. 93. The discussion of Olmsted relies on three studies: Elizabeth Barlow, *Frederick Law Olmsted's New York* (New York: Praeger, 1972), esp. pp. 5-32; Albert Fein, *Frederick Law Olmsted and the American Environmental Tradition* (New York: George Braziller, 1972); and Laura Wood Roper, *FLO: A Biography of Frederick Law Olmsted* (Baltimore: Johns Hopkins University Press, 1973), esp. pp. 232-87.

Olmsted first visited the falls as an adolescent. The legislation that finally withdrew it from the public domain thirty-odd years later resulted largely from his efforts. It is not merely Olmsted's responsiveness to untransformed landscape, then, that distinguishes him from his contemporaries, but rather his ability to move beyond vague concern to successful political action.

Olmsted helped to shape the most important decade in the history of park preservation. Moving to California in 1863 for reasons of health and career, the landscape architect was soon caught up in the fight for Yosemite Valley and the Mariposa Big Tree Grove. Congress had withdrawn these lands from public sale and granted them to the state of California. Not knowing what to do with them, California established the Yosemite Commission and appointed Olmsted chairman. His 1865 report, according to his biographer, provided "the first systematic exposition of the right and duty of a democracy to take the action that Congress had taken in reserving the Yosemite Valley and the Mariposa Big Tree Grove from private preemption for the enjoyment of all the people."[63] In defending the park premise, Olmsted moved far beyond the commonplace rationale that the out-of-doors ensured "health and vigor." According to him, whole species of indigenous flora had been destroyed back east and supplanted by foreign "weeds"[64]—a calamity he hoped to prevent at Yosemite by creating a "museum of natural science." Despite, or perhaps because of, his conclusion that the state had a "duty of preservation," the report was quietly suppressed. Another quarter of a century would pass before preservationists such as John Muir convinced Congress to adopt Olmsted's recommendations for Yosemite.

Nevertheless, the publicity that he generated inspired others, especially painters, to preservationist efforts. Frederick Edwin Church, one of Thomas Cole's last students, completed numerous drawings of Niagara Falls, and in 1869 he conveyed to Olmsted his hope that the area would be preserved. Fighting together for years against commercial developers, they finally helped to establish an international park in 1885. Thomas Moran's spectacular landscapes of the Yellowstone Canyon likewise energized public support for the first national park in 1872 and garnered him the sobriquet of "the father of the

63 Roper, *FLO*, p. 283. See also Starr, *Americans and the California Dream*, pp. 182-83.

64 Frederick Law Olmsted, "The Yosemite Valley and the Mariposa Big Trees: A Preliminary Report" (1865), with an introductory note by Laura Wood Roper, *Landscape Architecture*, 43 (October 1952), 22. For a more general, but valuable, discussion of the background to popular conceptions of the idea of a "wild park," see Roderick Nash, "The American Invention of National Parks," *American Quarterly*, 22 (Fall 1970), 726-35.

4. Thomas Moran, *Giant Geyser*, 1872. Watercolor. Private collection, New York City.

park system."[65] Similarly, in the 1890s, photographer A. P. Hill used his art to popularize the California redwoods and thereby prevent their destruction. In each case, however, actual preservation depended on those who shared Olmsted's administrative skills.

This protective attitude toward spectacular sites emerged slowly but steadily through the century, forming a major strand in the development of the land conservation movement in America. The movement's vigorous growth can be attributed in part to America's unique possession of a public domain; all land not privately owned remained the common property of the American people. As early as 1815, Thomas Jefferson had refused to sell Virginia's Natural Bridge because he viewed it as a "public trust." Later efforts on behalf of national parklands grew out of similar concern, though almost always for "natural wonders," never for undistinguished virgin forests or wildlife breeding areas. After all, America seemed to have limitless wilderness regions at its disposal. Although more than two million acres were set aside in 1872 to establish Yellowstone National Park, few who supported this bill felt concerned about the wilderness as such. As one historian of the public domain observed in 1880: "Natural wonders and venerable or interesting relics of architectural value or domestic use on the public domain should be preserved. The Shoshone Falls, on Snake River, Idaho . . . [and] many of the old Indian and Mexican ruins . . . should be reserved, along with other remains of former civilizations. The big trees of California . . . should also be reserved."[66] Only afterwards did people realize that they had saved unspoiled forests and waterways along with historical curiosities, threatened species of wild game along with natural wonders.[67]

[65] See Ronald L. Way, *Ontario's Niagara Parks: A History* (Niagara: Niagara Parks Commission, 1946), pp. 15-18. Albert Fein, in *Frederick Law Olmsted*, pp. 42ff., further describes this history, while Kermit Vanderbilt has documented the substantial efforts of Charles Eliot Norton in preserving a park at Niagara Falls in *Charles Eliot Norton: Apostle of Culture in a Democracy* (Cambridge, Mass.: Harvard University Press, 1959), pp. 188-90. Norton was, moreover, close friends with his cousin, Francis Parkman, as confirmed by Howard Doughty in *Francis Parkman*, pp. 145-46. See also Thurman Wilkins, *Thomas Moran: Artist of the Mountains* (Norman: University of Oklahoma Press, 1966), pp. 4-6, 33, 70.

[66] Thomas Donaldson, *The Public Domain: Its History, with Statistics*, 3d ed. (Washington: G.O.P., 1884), p. 1294. Jefferson expressed his views to William Caruthers, March 15, 1815; cited in Roper, *FLO*, p. 285. For a contrasting view of the history of forest preservation, see Ralph H. Brown, *Historical Geography of the United States* (New York: Harcourt, Brace and World, 1948), esp. pp. 107-8.

[67] See Ferdinand Vandeveer Hayden, *The Great West: Its Attractions and Resources* (Philadelphia: Franklin Publishing Co., 1880), p. 36; Hiram Martin Chittenden, *The Yellowstone National Park* (1895), ed. Richard A. Bartlett (Norman: University of Oklahoma Press, 1964), esp. pp. 86ff.; Richard A. Bartlett, *Nature's Yellowstone* (Albuquerque: University of New Mexico Press, 1974), esp. pp. 194-97.

The movement to preserve intact less spectacular acreage did not develop until after the Civil War. DeWitt Clinton in the 1820s and Washington Irving in the 1830s had separately proposed that large tracts of otherwise unexceptional wilderness be maintained in their pristine state, but these early suggestions lacked popular support.[68] Not until Americans anticipated the closing of the frontier—not until the devastation of the land had altered from threatening portent to confirmed pattern—did they sympathize not merely with preservation but with conservation.[69]

The single individual most instrumental in altering public attitudes was John Muir (1838-1914), who arrived in Yosemite three years after Olmsted's ill-fated 1865 report on California lands. During the next forty years, he became America's premier naturalist, the first to popularize the western wilds, including Alaska, and to celebrate their undomesticated virtues in widely read essays. He also ensured that legislation on behalf of conservation never suffered from public ignorance, and he deserves special credit for the Yosemite Act, passed by Congress in 1890. Olmsted's earlier pressure to withdraw state lands made possible Muir's successful efforts to establish fifteen hundred square miles of national parkland.[70] More than in particular

[68] John F. Reiger, *American Sportsmen and the Origins of Conservation* (New York: Winchester Press, 1975), p. 86; Irving, *Captain Bonneville*, ed. Todd, p. 372. See also Akerly, "Cultivation of Forest Trees"; Lt. Francis Hall, *Travels in Canada, and the United-States in 1816 and 1817*, 2d ed. (London: Longman, Hurst, Rees, Orme and Brown, 1819), pp. 35-36; Andrew S. Fuller, *The Forest Tree Culturist: A Treatise on the Cultivation of American Forest Trees* (New York: George E. and F. W. Woodward, 1866), pp. iv, 5-6; Roderick Nash, *Wilderness and the American Mind*, esp. p. 98.

[69] See Charles William Eliot, *Charles Eliot: Landscape Architect* (Boston: Houghton Mifflin and Co., 1902), esp. 304-49; John Gifford, ed., *The New Jersey Forester: A Bi-Monthly Pamphlet Devoted to the Development of Our Forests*, 1 (January 1895), 1; "Forests," *Hours at Home*, 3 (September 1866), 398-402; Isabella James, "American Forests," *Lippincott's Magazine*, 1 (June 1868), 598-602; Franklin B. Hough, "On the Duty of Governments in the Preservation of Forests," *Proceedings of the American Association for the Advancement of Science*, 22, pt. 2 (1873), 1-10; Felix L. Oswald, "The Preservation of Forests," *North American Review*, 128 (1879), 46; Charles Howard Shinn, *Mining Camps: A Study in American Frontier Government* (1885; rpt. New York: Alfred A. Knopf, 1948), p. xvi; Henry George, *Our Land and Land Policy* (1871; rpt. New York: Doubleday Page and Co., 1904); Starr, *Americans and the California Dream*, p. 175; Stewart L. Udall, *The Quiet Crisis* (New York: Avon, 1963), pp. 69-74; Roderick Nash, *Wilderness and the American Mind*; Hans Huth, "Yosemite: The Story of an Idea," *Sierra Club Bulletin*, 33 (March 1948), 47ff. See also Huth, *Nature and the American: Three Centuries of Changing Attitudes* (Berkeley: University of California Press, 1957); H. Duane Hampton, *How the U.S. Cavalry Saved Our National Parks* (Bloomington: Indiana University Press, 1971), esp. pp. 5-19; Ekirch, *Man and Nature in America*, esp. pp. 29-30; Alfred Runte, *National Parks: The American Experience* (Lincoln: University of Nebraska Press, 1979), esp. pp. 1-9, 38-81.

[70] Roderick Nash, *Wilderness and the American Mind*, pp. 131-32.

legislative coups, Muir's achievement lies in having educated Americans to the intrinsic value of wild places. He applied transcendentalist principles to the public domain so successfully that an aging Emerson came to see at first hand the region that Muir celebrated.

Whereas Emerson's insights had given inspiration to Muir's preservation goals, Henry George's ideas helped to direct his conservation ethos. The federal government's prodigal history of land cession had troubled George (1839-1897). Three years after Muir arrived at Yosemite, the San Francisco-based journalist concluded his preliminary study of *Our Land and Land Policy* (1871). "A generation hence," he declared, "our children will look with astonishment at the recklessness with which the public domain has been squandered. It will seem to them that we must have been mad."[71] Although George failed to offer specific remedies for this squandering, the expanded version of his study, *Progress and Poverty* (1879), awakened Americans to the unequal disposition of their continent as no one might have predicted. The rather simple economic solution he offered was never adopted; nonetheless, George became nineteenth-century America's most popular nonfiction author by engaging Americans' emotions. His damning history of land waste inspired thousands—John Muir most importantly[72]—who then were able to formulate and carry through practical legislation. The question George asked in 1871 crackled with too much rhetorical charge to be ignored: "Why should we seek so diligently to get rid of this public domain as if for the mere pleasure of getting rid of it? What have the buffaloes done to us that we should sacrifice the heritage of our children to see the last of them extirpated before we die?"[73] In the next three decades, Americans would find themselves similarly troubled by the disappearance not only of wild lands but of wildlife as well.

GAME PROTECTION AND THE LAND

The conservation movement brought together trappers and transcendentalists, animal lovers and hunters. Indeed, as important as were "pure" conservationists such as Muir and Olmsted, their projects

[71] George, *Our Land and Land Policy*, p. 11, also p. 91.

[72] Linnie Marsh Wolfe, *Son of the Wilderness: The Life of John Muir* (New York: Alfred A. Knopf, 1945), p. 182; see pp. 184, 227-28, 245-46, 251 for supporting documentation of this passage. See also John Muir, *Our National Parks* (New York: Houghton Mifflin Co., 1901), pp. 337, 364; Douglas H. Strong, "The Sierra Club—A History. Part 1: Origins and Outings," *Sierra*, October 1977, pp. 10-14; Starr, *Americans and the California Dream*, pp. 183-91.

[73] George, *Our Land and Land Policy*, p. 91.

might well have failed in Congress without the support of the thousands of sports hunters who shared their goals, though they were often seen as adversaries.[74] Irving and Cooper again offer apt examples. Irving's tour of the prairies had made him aware of the threatened extinction of buffalo and beaver, perhaps all fur-bearing animals, and in his subsequent western books he prayed that "the avidity of the hunter [might] be restrained within proper limitations."[75] Indeed, he even proposed the establishment of a permanent wilderness preserve.[76] Similarly, Cooper put into the mouth of his expert hunter, Natty Bumppo, his own fears about the slaughter of passenger pigeons and made a narrative case for restrictive hunting laws.[77]

By the end of the century, sportsmen and animal lovers alike would be concerned for many species, above all, for the buffalo. Long before Henry George deplored their disappearance, John James Audubon, himself a skilled marksman, had noted their precipitous decline. "What a terrible destruction of life as it were for nothing," he sadly mused in 1843. "Daily we see so many that we hardly notice them more than the cattle in our pastures about our homes. But this cannot last; even now there is a perceptible difference in the size of the herds, and before many years the Buffalo, like the Great Auk, will have disappeared."[78] From the early 1820s, when buffalo roamed in enormous herds even east of the Mississippi, until the mid-1880s, when they were reduced to a scraggly few, hunters and travelers concurred on their steady demise.[79] The *even nows* and *before longs* abound

74 This is John Reiger's main thesis in *American Sportsmen and the Origins of Conservation.* See also Starr, *Americans and the California Dream,* p. 176. For two convincing examples of conservationist hunters, see William Elliott, *Carolina Sports by Land and Water* (1867?; rpt. Columbia, S.C.: State Co., 1918), pp. 252-60, and Samual H. Hammond, *Wild Northern Scenes; or Sporting Adventures with the Rifle and the Rod* (New York: Derby and Jackson, 1857), p. 83.

75 Irving, *Captain Bonneville,* ed. Todd, p. 372; Irving, *Astoria,* pp. 516-17.

76 Irving, *Captain Bonneville,* ed. Todd, p. 372.

77 Cooper, *The Pioneers,* pp. 270-74.

78 Cited in Francis Hobart Herrick, *Audubon the Naturalist: A History of His Life and Time,* 2d ed., 2 vols. (New York: D. Appleton-Century Co., 1938), 2:255-56.

79 See Edwin James, *Account of an Expedition from Pittsburgh to the Rocky Mountains,* 2 vols. (1822-23; rpt. Ann Arbor: University Microfilms, 1966), p. 472; William A. Bell, *New Tracks in North America: A Journal of Travel and Adventure Whilst Engaged in the Survey for a Southern Railroad to the Pacific Ocean During 1867-8* (Albuquerque: Horn and Wallace, 1965), p. xx; Col. Richard Irving Dodge, *The Plains of the Great West and Their Inhabitants* (New York: G. P. Putnam's Sons, 1877), pp. 131-32; George Bird Grinnell, *The Passing of the Great West: Selected Papers of George Bird Grinnell,* ed. John F. Reiger (New York: Winchester Press, 1972), pp. 62, 65, 118-19; Pierre Jean de Smet S J, *Western Missions and Missionaries: A Series of Letters* (1859) (2d ed. 1863; rpt. Shannon: Irish University Press, 1972), pp. 5, 55; Messiter, *Sport and Adventures,* p. v; Col.

in their narratives, as if many observers realized that the scenes they were describing rarely equaled those seen by the earlier travelers whose accounts had inspired their own westward journeys. "Taming" the land seemed to require exterminating the species.

By the 1880s, the federal government finally grew alarmed at the dire prospects for the buffalo. Along with the bald eagle and the wild turkey, the buffalo had always seemed to symbolize the spirit of America itself. Yet hunting proceeded ruthlessly, and even the attempt to supplement stuffed models in the national collection seemed an eleventh-hour effort. Spencer F. Baird, secretary of the Smithsonian Institution (who had been nominated for the job, appropriately, by Audubon), decided in the mid-1880s to inaugurate a search for a representative bison before the species' extinction:

> The work of exterminating the American bison had made most alarming progress, and also . . . the representatives of this species then in the National Museum were far from being what they should be. . . . Realizing the imperative need of securing at once and at all hazards a complete and unexceptional series of fresh skins for mounting, before it should become too late, the Secretary directed the chief taxidermist, Mr. Hornaday, to take immediate steps toward the accomplishment of that end.[80]

William Hornaday's subsequent report severely criticized the national attitudes that had led to the crisis. He hoped a lesson had been learned that would benefit other large indigenous game. In phrasing similar to Henry George's, he declared, "A continuation of the record we have lately made as wholesale butchers will justify posterity in dating us back with the mound-builders and cave-dwellers, when man's only function was to slay and eat."[81] Hornaday at last won protection for the few buffalo herds that remained.

The shaggy buffalo head came to represent the issue of game preservation at about the time that other wildlife species acquired

---

Randolph Barnes Marcy, *Thirty Years of Army Life on the Border* (New York: Harper and Brothers, 1866), pp. 334ff.; George Frederick Ruxton, *Ruxton of the Rockies*, ed. LeRoy R. Hafen (Norman: University of Oklahoma Press, 1950), pp. 249, 252; Theodore B. Comstock, cited in Reiger, *American Sportsmen*, p. 99. See also Frank Luther Mott, *A History of American Magazines, 1865-1885*, 3 (Cambridge, Mass.: Harvard University Press, 1938), pp. 60-61; Robertson, "An Army Hunter's Notes," p. 305.

80 Spencer F. Baird, "Letter from the Secretary of the Smithsonian Institution," in *Annual Report of the Board of Regents of the Smithsonian Institution for the Year Ending June 30, 1887* (Washington: G.P.O., 1889), pp. 5-6.

81 Hornaday, *The Extermination of the American Bison* (Washington: G.P.O., 1889), p. 464.

constituencies working on their behalf. After the Civil War, books and essays increasingly helped to inform national discussion on the subject, detailing threats to wild cattle, elk, deer, antelope, mountain sheep, and even wolves.[82] An article from 1870 is representative in its concluding hope: "May you and I, my reader, live to see the day when the game-laws of our land, now inefficient and worthless, shall be redeemed; when the wholesale, cruel, indiscriminate, and unmanly slaughter which is now carried on shall be abolished."[83] The 1860s had already witnessed the first organized concern for declining wildlife in the formation of the Audubon Society and the American Ornithological Union, meant to protect bird species threatened by millinery fashion's insatiable demand for feathers.[84] Sportsmen's associations such as the Boone and Crockett Club and the Rocky Mountain Sportsmen's Association would soon organize outdoorsmen to call for further protective government legislation and for more energetic enforcement of existing laws.[85] By the end of a century often characterized as driven by brute manifest destiny, one popular author found it possible seriously to claim: "Animals are creatures with wants and feelings differing in degree only from our own."[86]

The patrician George Bird Grinnell (1849-1938) may seem an unlikely choice as the figure most representative of these and other aspects of wilderness conservation. Nevertheless, in addition to helping to found nearly all of the organizations mentioned above, he publicly, tirelessly, and self-effacingly encouraged far-sighted national

[82] See Robertson, "An Army Hunter's Notes," p. 308; Frederick Schwatka, "An Elk-Hunt on the Plains," *Century Magazine*, 35 (January 1888), 447; Frederick Gerstaecker, *Wild Sports in the Far West* (Boston: Crosby, Nichols and Co., 1859), p. v; De Smet, *Western Missions*, p. 5; *Ruxton of the Rockies*, ed. Hafen, pp. 255-57; George P. Belden, *Belden, The White Chief; or Twelve Years Among the Wild Indians of the Plains*, ed. Gen. James S. Brisbin (1870; rpt. Cincinnati: E. W. Starr and Co., 1875), p. 90; *The Journals of Captain Nathaniel J. Wyeth* (Fairfield, Wash.: Ye Galleon Press, 1969), p. 131.

[83] W. Waddle Jr., "The Game Water-Fowl of America," *Harper's New Monthly Magazine*, 40 (February 1870), 437.

[84] See Frank M. Chapman, *Autobiography of a Bird-Lover* (New York: D. Appleton-Century Co., 1933), esp. pp. 37-38, 180-82; Reiger, *American Sportsmen*, esp. pp. 65ff. See also *The Letters of Theodore Roosevelt*, ed. Elting E. Morison, 8 vols. (Cambridge, Mass.: Harvard University Press, 1951), 1:948, 1292, 1421-22.

[85] See Reiger, *American Sportsmen*. See also *American Big-Game Hunting: The Book of the Boone and Crockett Club*, ed. Theodore Roosevelt and George Bird Grinnell (New York: Forest and Stream Publishing Co., 1893), pp. 9-10, 240-70, 326-33; *American Big Game Hunting in Its Haunts*, ed. George Bird Grinnell (New York: Forest and Stream Publishing Co., 1904), p. 7; Earl Pomeroy, *In Search of the Golden West: The Tourist in Western America* (New York: Alfred A. Knopf, 1957), pp. 03-04.

[86] Ernest Seton-Thompson, *Wild Animals I Have Known* (New York: Charles Scribner's Sons, 1898), p. 12.

policies toward birds, buffalo, and large game, as well as toward forests and wilderness areas. Grinnell could lay claim to a number of conservation firsts, including the very use of the word *conservation* in its modern ecological sense.[87] As a young scientist accompanying the famous Ludlow expedition to Yellowstone in 1875, he wrote a letter included in the official report, a plea for federal restrictions on hide hunters.[88] The initial issue of *Forest and Stream* (1873), the publication he had helped to found and would edit through the last quarter of the century, proclaimed battle on all those willing to see American forests diminished. The magazine provided a continuing forum for writers who favored restricting development of natural resources. In the early 1880s, Grinnell vigorously endorsed the "Save the Adirondacks" campaign, which resulted in 715,000 acres being set aside as state forests. His editorials on game extinction in Yellowstone during the same period, and his later defense of the national park system, aroused sportsmen against the depredations of industry, fashion, land speculation, and a thoughtlessly westering mentality. Grinnell became the leader of America's conservation movement just when it was gaining an identifiable constituency.[89]

Of course, concern for the threatened landscape was not a matter for sportsmen alone. Increasing leisure time and disposable income in the post-Civil War period offered greater numbers of men and women the opportunity to hunt and fish, which in turn swelled the constituency supporting conservation at a national level. In addition, these economic forces spawned the middle-class western tourist.[90] Earlier in the century, travel had at best meant discomfort and delay; at worst, it involved genuine danger. Besides, it required substantial means, and only the adventurous and restless felt the effort worth the expense. With the completion of the transcontinental railway in 1869, cross-country travel became steadily safer, more reliable and comfortable, and increasingly attractive to Americans of moderate means. Among those who embarked on western excursions, some returned in alarm at what they had witnessed. The buffalo they had come to marvel at had been thoughtlessly sacrificed to the very railroad crews that made their trips possible. Wonder gave way to regret as they glimpsed uniquely American scenes that their children would never know.

[87] Reiger, *American Sportsmen*, p. 84. Reiger's is the finest treatment of Grinnell's efforts on behalf of conservation.

[88] Grinnell, *Passing of the Great West*, ed. Reiger, pp. 118-19.

[89] See Pomeroy, *In Search of the Golden West*, pp. 93-94.

[90] See ibid. for background to this section.

CONSERVATION

Roderick Nash has sharply observed those factors unique to America that contributed to national conservationist activity in the nineteenth century: a public domain; tracts of wilderness still untenanted; settlement patterns; and the national affluence that made preservation of natural resources conceivable at all. In Nash's wry phrasing: "Ironically, our success in exploiting the environment increased the likelihood of its protection."[91] Out of the nineteenth century's particular pairing of opportunities and apprehensions, Americans "invented" a national park and forest reserve system. Conservation, at least by the last two decades of the nineteenth century, gained headlines in newspapers, supporters in legislatures, and students in new university schools of forestry. The examples of German forestry measures and royal hunting preserves in England fundamentally influenced American thinking, to be sure.[92] But even the conservation ideas propounded in Europe had been reciprocally shaped by the thinking of Americans, in particular by George Perkins Marsh (1801-1882).

Marsh's varied career as lawyer, businessman, linguist, politician, and diplomat offers little clue to the seminal importance of his ideas on conservation. In the 1840s, as a one-term congressman from Vermont, he had lobbied vigorously for a national museum to preserve artifacts of natural and human history. Joining forces with John Quincy Adams, he persuaded his colleagues to use the bequest of the English scientist James Smithson to establish such an institution.[93] Through this and like efforts, Marsh gained a reputation as the defender of a variety of endangered objects, from human artifacts to state forests and woodlands. In an 1847 speech to a Vermont agricultural society, he condemned devastation of the landscape and called for a prohibition on agricultural clearing in order that future generations might enjoy American wilderness.[94] Seventeen years later, Marsh extended these ideas in a profound study of conservation that ranks among the seminal works of the nineteenth century. Appearing long before the word *ecology* even existed, *Man and Nature* (1864) assiduously defines that science, much as Grinnell had first helped

[91] Roderick Nash, "American Invention of National Parks," pp. 726-34.

[92] See Clarence J. Glacken, "Changing Ideas of the Habitable World," in William L. Thomas, ed., *Man's Role in Changing the Face of the Earth* (Chicago: University of Chicago Press, 1956), p. 74.

[93] David Lowenthal, *George Perkins Marsh: Versatile Vermonter* (New York: Columbia University Press, 1958), pp. 82ff.

[94] Marsh *Address Delivered Before the Agricultural Society of Rutland County, Sept. 30, 1847* (Rutland, Vt.: n.p., 1848), esp. pp. 17-19.

to develop conservation into firm legislative policies. The book became, in Lewis Mumford's words, "the fountain-head of the conservation movement."[95]

Marsh opens with an indictment of characteristic western European thoughtlessness about the natural environment: "Man has too long forgotten that the earth was given to him for usufruct alone, not for consumption, still less for profligate waste."[96] Quickly moving beyond moral outrage, he demonstrates in chapter-by-chapter analysis the tremendous economic waste exacted by the carnage of buffalo, beaver, cattle, walrus, and whales. That whole species neared extinction seemed condemnation enough. Even worse, in his judgment, was the threatened imbalance of entire ecological systems. Deforestation, for instance, results first in blighted landscapes, then in drought, flooding, mud slides, and general soil exhaustion. Its effects were already apparent: "The earth is fast becoming an unfit home for its noblest inhabitant, and another era of equal human crime and human improvidence . . . would reduce it to such a condition of impoverished productiveness, of shattered surface, of climatic excess, as to threaten the deprivation, barbarism, and perhaps even extinction of the species."[97] Wantonly to kill animals or destroy trees meant simply to threaten one's own welfare.

To Marsh, the solution seemed obvious, at least politically: each state should preserve the woodland it presently possessed. True material progress, as contrasted with hasty national expansion, could be achieved only through social foresight. "Careful control and intelligent planning" might help to heal the wounds already inflicted.[98] Marsh's conclusion recalls Thomas Cole's earlier plea: "It is . . . a question of vast importance, how far it is practicable to restore the garden we have wasted."[99]

Man and Nature drew a highly favorable response both in war-torn America and abroad, selling out its first edition within months. Subsequent editions and translations brought Marsh firm disciples, including Muir and Olmsted, who developed his proposals into practical legislation. According to Marsh's biographer:

> Together with the enthusiasm for tree-planting, which swept the country in the Arbor Day movement, *Man and Nature* inaugu-

[95] Mumford, *Brown Decades*, p. 78.

[96] Marsh, *Man and Nature* (1864), ed. David Lowenthal (Cambridge, Mass.: Harvard University Press, 1965), p. 36.

[97] Ibid., p. 43.　　　　　　　　　　[98] Ibid., p. 272.

[99] Ibid., p. 353. See as well Marsh, "The Study of Nature," *Christian Examiner*, 5th ser., 68 (January 1860), esp. p. 33.

rated a revolutionary reversal of American attitudes toward resources. It stimulated the American Association for the Advancement of Science to submit a memorial on forests to Congress in 1873; the outcome was a national forestry commission, the establishment of forest reserves and the national forest system in 1891, then watershed protection, eventually a governmental program for the conservation of all natural resources. A quarter of a century after Marsh's death, *Man and Nature* was still the only work in its field.[100]

However, with the exception of Carl Schurz, Secretary of the Interior Department under President Hayes, federal policy remained indifferent to conservation in the decades following the Civil War. Lower-ranking government officials, including John Wesley Powell and W. J. McGee, read Marsh, but it was not until the late 1880s that they would finally effect new federal policies on land usage and development.[101] Counseled by his good friend Gifford Pinchot, President

[100] Lowenthal, *George Perkins Marsh*, p. 268. The methods of Marsh's disciples are discussed by Lowenthal on pp. 246ff. For only two examples, see N. H. Egleston, "What We Owe to the Trees," *Harper's New Monthly Magazine*, 64 (April 1882), 675-82; G. W. Powell, "American Forests," ibid., 59 (August 1879), 371-74.

[101] See Claude Moore Fuess, *Carl Schurz: Reformer (1829-1906)* (New York: Dodd, Mead and Co., 1932), pp. 267-68; Wallace Stegner, *Beyond the Hundredth Meridian: John Wesley Powell and the Second Opening of the West* (Boston: Houghton Mifflin Co., 1954), pp. 6, 210ff.; John Upton Terrell, *The Man Who Rediscovered America: A Biography of John Wesley Powell* (New York: Weybright and Talley, 1969), pp. 1-8; Henry Nash Smith, "Clarence King, John Wesley Powell, and the Establishment of the United States Geological Survey," *Mississippi Valley Historical Review*, 34 (June 1947), 37-58; William Goetzmann, *Exploration and Empire: The Explorer and the Scientist in the Winning of the American West* (New York: Alfred A. Knopf, 1966), esp. pp. 530-31; W. J. McGee, "The Conservation of Natural Resources," *Proceedings of the Mississippi Valley Historical Association*, 3 (1909-10), 361-79; Bernhard Eduard Fernow, *Economics of Forestry: A Reference Book for Students of Political Economy and Professional and Lay Students of Forestry* (New York: Thomas Y. Crowell, 1902), esp. pp. 1-10, 369ff.; Fernow, *Report upon the Forestry Investigations of the United States Department of Agriculture, 1877-1898* (Washington: G.P.O., 1899), pp. 3-6. For good general surveys of the development of conservationist sentiments toward the end of the nineteenth century, see: Ekirch, *Man and Nature in America*, esp. pp. 70-120; Hampton, *How the U.S. Cavalry Saved Our National Parks*, esp. pp. 18ff.; Russell Lord, *The Care of the Earth: A History of Husbandry* (New York: Thomas Nelson and Sons, 1962), pp. 225-47; Maxine E. McCloskey and James P. Gilligan, eds., *Wilderness and the Quality of Life* (New York: Sierra Club, 1969), pp. vii, 66-73; Roderick Nash, *Wilderness and the American Mind*, pp. 96-160; Nash, ed., *The American Environment: Readings in the History of Conservation* (Reading, Mass.: Addison-Wesley, 1968), pp. 24-71; Russel B. Nye, *This Almost Chosen People: Essays in the History of American Ideas* (East Lansing: Michigan State University Press, 1966), pp. 256-304; Robert Shankland, *Steve Mather of the National Parks* (New York: Alfred A. Knopf, 1951), pp. 4, 48ff.; Donald C. Swain, *Wilderness Defender: Horace M. Albright and Conservation* (Chicago: University of Chicago

Theodore Roosevelt, looking back on a long history of developing apprehensions as well as more recent efforts responsibly to ease them, succeeded in making conservation a major component of his domestic policy. Together, the President and his chief of the forestry division of the Department of Agriculture withdrew tens and hundreds of thousands of acres from the public domain; encouraged game legislation, as well as stricter enforcement of existing laws; and they provided government grants for universities to establish forestry departments.[102] In a variety of fashions, the public encouraged its legislators, and was encouraged by them, to save what remained of the once unspoiled continent.

CONCLUSION

The widespread public commitment to conservation reflects only one aspect of concern for the wilderness—important historically, to be sure, but less a development in the concept of "wilderness" than in that of preservation. By the time Americans appreciated the natural landscape enough to want to save actual forests and wildlife, the need for mere records had subsided. Only a few diehards any longer rushed west with pencils in hand to transcribe the landscape. That "wilderness," Americans had come to recognize, deserved preservation in fact, not on paper.

Apprehension about the landscape radiated out along the fissures of Americans' awareness, and—whatever the hopes for America's prospects—this feeling encouraged efforts both to record it and to save it. Wilderness, after all, remains a vaguely idyllic sanctuary only so long as one remains in the East. Come west, and immediately its soft outlines firm. The rubrics of "wilderness" and "frontier" break down not only into slaughtered flocks of passenger pigeons and herds of buffalo, devastated forests, and mine-ravaged mountain valleys, but they also bring to mind other images and activities, including fur trapping, prospecting, pioneer farming, and cow-punching. Material

Press, 1970), esp. pp. 46ff.; Runte, *National Parks*; Andrew Denny Rodgers III, *Bernhard Eduard Fernow: The Story of North American Forestry* (Princeton: Princeton University Press, 1951). For a corrective to some of the overstatements of these books, see Sherry H. Olson, *The Depletion Myth: A History of Railroad Use of Timber* (Cambridge, Mass.: Harvard University Press, 1971), esp. pp. 31-40, 75ff., 178-92. Also see Udall, *Quiet Crisis*, pp. 81-170.

[102] William H. Harbaugh, *The Life and Times of Theodore Roosevelt*, rev. ed. (New York: Oxford University Press, 1963), pp. 304ff.; Harold T. Pinkett, *Gifford Pinchot: Private and Public Forester* (Urbana: University of Illinois Press, 1970), esp. pp. 44-81; M. Nelson McGeary, *Gifford Pinchot: Forester-Politician* (Princeton: Princeton University Press, 1960).

progress threatened these vocations just as predictably as it did the land, and with an intrinsic irony: human success at these activities posed a threat to the land and thereby, finally, to the very way of life that had made success possible. Far-sighted individuals realized this danger and set about to ensure that frontier life would not pass unrecorded, that successive generations would know it as something more than embellished myth. If their histories took an affectionate, sometimes uncritical perspective, it was because they recognized how imperiled the white frontier was.

CHAPTER THREE

PRESERVING
FRONTIER HISTORY

[T]o record the events connected with the
early history of the country, to note characteristics of its early inhabitants, to delineate the privations and hardships experienced by its pioneers . . . is a useful and
laudable undertaking. . . . [It] will soon
be the only record left of a class of people
fast fading from the view of those who
now occupy the stage of public life.
      —*Henry S. Baird*
   "Recollections of the Early History
   of Northern Wisconsin" (1859)

All these subjects of my description—
men, conditions of life, races of aboriginal
inhabitants, and adventurous hunters and
pioneers—are passing away. . . . It can not
be entirely in vain that any one contributes that which he knows from personal
experience, however little, to aid in preserving the memory of the people and the
customs of the West in the middle of the
nineteenth century.
      Col. Randolph Barns Marcy
   Thirty Years of Army Life on the Border
      (1866)

J̶o Hector St. John de Crèvecoeur fully shared his contemporaries' belief in westward progress. His *Journey in Northern Pennsylvania and the State of New York* (1801)—that lively journal-dialogue of frontier peregrinations made more than thirty years earlier—rarely strays from well-beaten paths through the intellectual wilderness. At one point, however, Crèvecoeur remarks on the whirlwind transformation of pioneer communities and unexpectedly suggests preserving their scattered ruins, the "traces of the passing of generations that preceded us." He adds: "instead of hastening the ruin of this debris, one should consider its destruction a sacrilege; its conservation a religious act."[1]

At the turn of the century, Crèvecoeur's adjuration stands alone, unsupported by him and ignored by others. His contemporaries no more considered preserving log cabins than woodlands; nor did they deem worthwhile a record of those who had built the cabins and developed the land. Yet during the nineteenth century, as many came to value a threatened wilderness, concern also grew for the pioneers who were being similarly displaced. By mid-century, Francis Parkman could assume that public consensus had shifted. In his eulogy of James Fenimore Cooper he claimed that Cooper's fame would endure for more than artistic reasons. The novelist had ensured the "permanent remembrance" of a "class of men" suddenly swept from history.[2]

Although Parkman referred to only one frontier type, the hunter-trapper represented by Leatherstocking, material progress had also swept aside a distressing number of other characteristically American classes of men and women. The shift from early frontier settlements to burgeoning agricultural and industrial centers transformed Americans even as they transformed the landscape.[3] Nor were the evolving characteristics of American life the result merely of accumulating assumptions; also critical was a casting off of old ways. Americans became their most distinctive selves through the activities and vocations that sprang up, blossomed, and died off like rare prairie wildflowers,

[1] Crèvecoeur, *Journey into Northern Pennsylvania and the State of New York* (1801), trans. Clarissa Spencer Bostelmann, 3 vols. in 1 (Ann Arbor: University of Michigan Press, 1964), p. 102.

[2] Francis Parkman, "The Works of James Fenimore Cooper," *North American Review*, 74 (January 1852), 151. Parkman himself had performed a similar service in his portrait of the mountain man and guide Henri Chatillon (1816-1875), in *The Oregon Trail* (1849).

[3] Frederick Jackson Turner first formulated this, his frontier theory, in his essay, "The Significance of the Frontier in American History" (1893).

never to bloom again. Trappers, keelboatmen, and placer miners; pony express riders and cowboys; army scouts, stagecoach hands, and booster newspapermen—among a myriad of other types, these burst onto the western scene as quickly as buffalo disappeared from it, and then vanished themselves before the next, scarcely more stable arrivals. Frequently, apocryphal anecdotes of their exploits alone survived. Or, as one self-styled "gold miner, trader, merchant, rancher and politician" mused at the turn of the century, "It would be impossible to make persons not present on the Montana cattle ranges realize the rapid change that took place on those ranges in two years. In 1880 the country was practically uninhabited. One could travel for miles without seeing so much as a trapper's bivouac. Thousands of buffalo darkened the rolling plains. . . . In the fall of 1883 there was not one buffalo remaining. . . . In 1880 no one had heard tell of a cowboy . . . but in the fall of 1883 there were six hundred thousand head of cattle on the range."[4]

The land had always demanded as much in energy and adaptability, imagination and sheer brute force as it promised in opportunity. But by the 1880s, Americans' power to alter the land, and thereby to be altered themselves, had risen exponentially. They rarely argued against that power or its promise, of course, however buffeted they felt by gusts of progress. Jobs went out of date like fashions, almost annually, and boom and ghost towns only underscored the difficulty of prophesying what or where development would occur. The enthusiastic pioneer quoted above marveled at the transformation of an entire region, the miraculous advent of a whole way of life. Others, though equally impressed by the pace of change, could only regret the lost ways. Out West in 1894 to collect material for stories that would eventually mythicize the cowboy, Owen Wister wrote to his patrician Philadelphian mother, "The frontier has yielded to a merely commonplace society. . . . The survivors of Tombstone sit there and dwell on how things used to be. In 1882 there were from six to eight thousand people; there are now six hundred, and all over the adjacent hills stand silent silver mines—the machinery rusty, falling to pieces, and a good deal of it burned."[5]

Such matter-of-fact observations on the rapidity of change and its human toll were commonplace long before the end of the century.

[4] *Forty Years on the Frontier as seen in the Journals and Reminiscences of Granville Stuart, Gold-Miner, Trader, Merchant, Rancher and Politician*, ed. Paul C. Phillips, 2 vols. (1925; rpt. Glendale, Calif.: Arthur H. Clark Co., 1957), 2:187-88.

[5] *Owen Wister Out West: His Journals and Letters*, ed. Fanny Kemble Wister (Chicago: University of Chicago Press, 1958), p. 210.

To be sure, frontier conditions had been altering ever since the settlement of Jamestown and the Massachusetts Bay Colony. Yet reflections on those altering conditions only begin to appear around 1820, as already noted. The land needed to be stamped "American" by wars in 1776 and 1812 before its citizens came to recognize that their national heritage was the vanishing landscape.

Individuals felt impelled to preserve records of passing white history only as that history also began to seem uniquely and nationally American. As the society grew self-conscious about its claim to a special identity, a more demanding audience, its nationalist appetite whetted, consumed all kinds of histories, biographies, and genre paintings and illustrations. In the words of one energetic publisher of American works, "the tendency of the present age has been justly and philosophically designated historick."[6] Americans wanted to find out all about themselves. They also wanted to ensure that the contemporary selves they did know would be preserved—written about, painted, or photographed—before passing from the western scene. This is hardly surprising. Indeed, it is less remarkable that the trapper's rapid advent and decline should have prompted anxious attempts at documentation than that the buffalo's far slower demise, as we have seen, encouraged similar endeavors.

The reasons for these attempts are as diverse as their subjects. Even more than those who first documented the landscape, recorders of frontier life strove to present exotic instances of the American experience to jaded easterners. Rocky Mountain fur trader Hugh Glass, for example, inspired countless writers with his incredible story of survival in the 1820s. Left for dead by his companions after having been horribly mauled by a grizzly bear, Glass crawled more than a hundred miles, feeding on berries and buffalo carcasses, before reaching aid. Setting out after his former companions, he joined a party that was soon attacked by Indians. Glass alone escaped with his life. After further trials and failures, he finally caught up with his companions, confronted them, and recovered his rifle. Glass's exploits are the stuff of legend. Yet, however unreliable such accounts, whatever the impulse to record them, Americans recognized a transience to these and less extraordinary frontier experiences.

Mountain men and frontiersmen themselves sometimes wrote with

[6] Cited in Eric F. Goldman, "The Historians," in Robert E. Spiller et al., eds., *Literary History of the United States: History*, 3d ed. rev. (New York: Macmillan Co., 1963), pp. 526-27. See for a good general survey, George H. Callcott, *History in the United States, 1800-1860: Its Practice and Purpose* (Baltimore: Johns Hopkins University Press, 1970), esp. pp. 25-53, 83-173.

the clear intention of setting the record straight. They wanted to humanize the mythical pose into which writers like Cooper had cast them and to correct Americans' distorted view of their history and perhaps of their illiteracy.[7] Those lacking firsthand experience sought out old hunters and trappers or collected extensive records in order to depict what the popular novelist Timothy Flint characterized in 1831 as "a race passing unrecorded from history."[8]

Whether buckskin-fringed scout or gregarious flatboatman, hunter or trapper, the frontiersman represents only one colorful aspect of American life in the West. Likewise, those who labored to preserve records of him represent only part of a more considerable movement. Long-suffering "black-robes" and frontier camp revivalists; battles between "blue coats" and recalcitrant tribes; county wars between ranchers and farmers—all were recognizably passing from experience and were salvaged for history by anxious observers.[9] Old frontier ways acquired a retrospective allure they may only rarely have held for those who learned them of necessity. The allure was especially strong in a nation progressively more self-conscious about what it was sacrificing to the charms of progress. More important, these fleeting

[7] For instance, see Howard Louis Conrad, *"Uncle Dick" Wootton, the Pioneer Frontiersman of the Rocky Mountain Region* (Chicago: W. E. Dribble and Co., 1890), preface (unpaginated); William Thomas Hamilton, *My Sixty Years on the Plains: Trapping, Trading, and Indian Fighting* (1905; rpt. Norman: University of Oklahoma Press, 1960), p. 3; George Frederick Ruxton, *Life in the Far West*, ed. Le-Roy R. Hafen (Norman: University of Oklahoma Press, 1951), esp. pp. xiii, 112.

[8] Timothy Flint, ed., *The Personal Narrative of James O. Pattie of Kentucky* (1831), reprinted in vol. 18 of Reuben Gold Thwaites, ed., *Early Western Travels: 1748-1846*, 32 vols. (Cleveland: Arthur H. Clarke Co., 1904-07), p. 27. See also Col. Randolph Barnes Marcy, *Thirty Years of Army Life on the Border* (New York: Harper and Brothers, 1866), pp. 356, 397; David H. Coyner, *The Lost Trappers: A Collection of Interesting Scenes and Events in the Rocky Mountains* (Cincinnati: J. A. and U. P. James, 1847), p. 240; Samual Asahel Clarke, *Pioneer Days of Oregon History*, 2 vols. (Portland, J. K. Gill Co., 1905), 1:84; Mrs. Anna Brownell Jameson, *Winter Studies and Summer Rambles in Canada*, 2 vols. (New York: Wiley and Putnam, 1839), 2:205; Mrs. Frances Fuller Victor, *The River of the West: Life and Adventure in the Rocky Mountains and Oregon* (Hartford, Conn.: R. W. Bliss and Co., 1869), pp. iv-vi; John Crittenden Duval, *Early Times in Texas* (Austin: H.P.N. Gammel and Co., 1892), preface (unpaginated).

[9] Rev. Asa Mahan, *Autobiography: Intellectual, Moral and Spiritual* (London: T. Woolmer, 1882), p. 215; Rev. Stephen R. Beggs, *Pages from the Early History of the West and North-West* (Cincinnati: Methodist Book Concern, 1868), introduction by T. M. Eddy (unpaginated); Mrs. Margaret I. Carrington, *Absaraka, Home of the Crows* (1868), ed. Milo Milton Quaife (Chicago: R. R. Donnelley and Sons, 1950), pp. 63-64; Gen. Randolph B. Marcy, *Border Reminiscences* (New York: Harper and Brothers, 1872), pp. v-vi, 358; James W. Steele, *Frontier Army Sketches* (Chicago: Jansen, McClurg and Co., 1883), pp. 3-4; John Bauman, "On a Western Ranche," *Fortnightly Review*, new ser., 41 (1887), 516, 535; Emerson Hough, *The Story of the Cowboy* (New York: D. Appleton and Co., 1897), pp. v-vi.

forms of life were not to be abandoned in this the most forward-looking of countries and ages without energetic efforts to preserve their images.

GENRE PAINTING AND PHOTOGRAPHY

The impulse to preserve the western experience took its clearest form in the commitment to pictorial representation, a commitment partly registered in the sizable number of painters and illustrators attracted to the frontier. Motives once again resist easy recovery. Moreover, eastern enthusiasm for frontier scenes made most pictorial efforts at best a compound of commercial and historical hopes. Currier and Ives, for instance, identified a strong public desire for sentimental prints of American life and scenery and from mid-century on tapped it with unprecedented success. They produced numerous images of threatened rural and pioneer life as well, though neither publisher ever intimated historical preservation as his motive.[10] Perhaps they did not need to do so. National pride mixed with curiosity to keep genre art popular enough for publishers to look only to profits. On a deeper, psychological level, paintings of passing ways helped to calm forebodings by giving a face to the process of change itself. Pictures of "Home, Sweet Frontier Home" warmed pioneer parlors not just by defining the distance that proud owners had come; they also recalled conditions too easily fading in memory.

Thomas Cole had clarified the aims of the Hudson River School when he pleaded with his countrymen to revere their native scenes. Similarly, America's leading genre artist, George Caleb Bingham (1811-1879)—the only major painter raised on the frontier—identified widely held aspirations in one of his rare comments about art. Referring to the claim that his and his colleagues' paintings would have on future attention, Bingham observed, "The humorous productions of [William Sydney] Mount and others as seen in the 'Bargaining for a horse,' 'The Jolly Flatboatmen' and 'County Election,' assure us that our social and political characteristics as daily and annually exhibited will not be lost in the lapse of time for want of an Art record rendering them full justice."[11] Indeed, one must today consult the work of these painters in order to see what the West looked like in its early settle-

10 Yet see A. K. Baragwanath's introduction to *Currier and Ives: Chronicles of America*, ed. John Lowell Pratt (Maplewood, N.J.: Hammond Inc., 1968), p. 13.

11 Letter written June 19, 1871, cited in Albert Christ-Janer, *George Caleb Bingham of Missouri: The Story of an Artist* (New York: Dodd, Mead and Co., 1940), pp. 109-10.

ment period.¹² The paintings that Bingham completed in the decade after 1845 form an authentic chronicle of the life that Mark Twain would later nostalgically recall. Bingham's canvases of trappers and riverboatmen, of squatters and county politicians self-consciously preserve a way of life never to be restored.¹³

In the late 1830s, at the very time that Bingham first devoted himself to "historic painting," the invention of the daguerreotype encouraged those less patient or well trained to render scenes more simply and objectively.¹⁴ Improvements in the photographic process throughout the century induced practitioners to risk westward travel in order to capture images of what they had hitherto only heard and read about. Celebrated for his stunning photographic record of the Civil War, Alexander Gardner traveled to Kansas in 1867 to preserve images of frontier life.¹⁵ Indeed, the Civil War released dozens of trained battlefield photographers who turned west after Appomattox. Others soon followed. Solomon D. Butcher spent the last quarter of the century compiling a superb chronicle of midwestern homesteading. Starting early in the eighties, George Edward Anderson spent the next forty-odd years shooting thousands of photographs of rural industry, civic activities, and community celebrations in Mormon Utah. Erwin E. Smith devoted himself in the early 1900s to photographing cowboy life on the Texas range. These and others, amateur and professional alike, received little pay for their countless uncommissioned photographs of local life in the West. Few confessed their motives

12 Henry Worrall, for only one example, pursued a career like Bingham's as a pictorial recorder of western community life, though in the post-Civil War period. See Robert Taft, *Artists and Illustrators of the Old West, 1850-1900* (New York: Charles Scribner's Sons, 1953), pp. 117-28.

13 For background on Bingham, see Christ-Janer, *George Caleb Bingham*; E. Maurice Bloch, *George Caleb Bingham: The Evolution of an Artist* (Berkeley: University of California Press, 1967); Larry Curry, *The American West: Painters from Catlin to Russell* (New York: Viking, 1972), pp. 21-22. Contemporaries appreciated Bingham's efforts for similar reasons; see, for example, a statement from an 1847 issue of the *Missouri Republican*: "Mr. Bingham has struck out for himself an entire new field of historic painting, if we may so term it. He has taken our Western rivers, our boats and boatmen, and the banks of the streams for his subjects" (cited in Barbara Novak, *American Painting of the Nineteenth Century: Realism, Idealism, and the American Experience* [New York: Praeger, 1969], pp. 152-53).

14 The advent of the camera accompanied a renewed concern for detailed accuracy, as described in the preceding chapter. Nor was this a particularly American phenomenon, as many have noted. Susan Sontag, in *On Photography* (New York: Farrar, Straus and Giroux, 1977), has provided a provocative examination of many of the issues to be discussed here and later; see especially pp. 56-62, 65-70.

15 See Russell E. Belous and Robert A Weinstein, *Will Soule: Indian Photographer at Fort Sill, Oklahoma, 1869-74* (Los Angeles: Ward Ritchie Press, 1969), p. 15.

5. George Caleb Bingham, *The County Election (2)*, 1852. Oil on canvas. Collection of The Boatmen's National Bank of St. Louis.

6. Solomon D. Butcher, "Log Cabin of E. S. Finch in Early Days. Built in 1875." From the photograph reproduced in S. D. Butcher's *Pioneer History of Custer County* (Broken Bow, Nebr., 1901).

in writing, whatever their accomplishments.[16] Yet their work, bankruptcies, and broken homes tacitly attest to costly, arduous commitments.

FRONTIER AND PIONEER HISTORIES

An exhaustive record of frontier life could not be compiled through pictures alone. Nor were frontier activities the only subjects of those concerned with rescuing documents. Far less dramatic aspects of western life also cried out to be preserved, and most Americans who responded did so in writing, either from firsthand experience or from others' collected histories. As one amateur historian before mid-century observed about his efforts:

> There having been no historical account published of the first settlement of the Ohio Company at Marietta . . . and the materials on which it was to be founded becoming annually more and more scarce, from the death of the early inhabitants, the author, in the year 1841, was led to commence this difficult, but, to him, pleasant labor. . . . One mode of collecting materials for the history, was to employ some of the few that remained of the first settlers to write down their recollections . . . and by collating these several sketches, the truth could be very nearly ascertained. The larger portion of these men are now dead, and many of the events would have perished with them, had they not been preserved in this manner.[17]

Extraordinary as this man's devotion to the task may seem, such statements of intention might be multiplied almost indefinitely. Even the dull prose is representative, intimating the slogging, unimaginative presentation of so many of these accounts. Too often they merely recite events unique in name and date alone. And in so doing, they defeat their stated purpose by reducing uncommon past experiences to commonplaces.

16 *Frontier America: The Far West* (Boston: Museum of Fine Arts, 1975), introduction by Jonathan L. Fairbanks, p. 130; J. Evetts Haley, *Life on the Texas Range*, with photographs by Erwin E. Smith (Austin: University of Texas Press, 1952), esp. pp. 15, 18, 23, 29; Rell G. Francis, "Views of Mormon Country: The Life and Photographs of George Edward Anderson," *American West*, 15 (November-December 1978), 14-29. For exceptions to the rule of implicit commitment, see Ferdinand Vandeveer Hayden, *Sun Pictures of Rocky Mountain Scenery* (New York: Julius Bien, 1870), p. 33; *Centenniel State, 1776-1882: A Memorial Offering of the Business Men and Pioneers of Denver, Colorado* (Denver: Rebanks, Wilson and Co., 1882).

17 S. P. Hildreth, *Pioneer History: Being an Account of the First Examinations of the Ohio Valley and the Early Settlement of the Northwest Territory* (Cincinnati: H. W. Derby and Co., 1848), pp. v-vi.

Yet intention should not be faulted for poor execution. However cliché-ridden and repetitive, these works claim our attention because of their expressed hopes: "Facts and circumstances, which may now be attested to by the living, in a few years, could only be reported upon the faith of tradition."[18] Like the refrain of a backwoods ballad, the plea for old-timers to recollect their experiences recurs. A quick review of such accounts illustrates the limited variety of these pleas, all sung in the same key: "almost too late"; "soon be the only record"; "now was the time"; "might have been lost"; "must now be very quickly done, if done at all"; "an almost-dead past"; "to rescue and preserve some of the doings of the common people."[19] Life in the West was changing as quickly as the landscape, and similar phrasings echo across the continent and the nineteenth century. Kentucky in the 1820s, Ohio and the old Northwest Territory in the 1840s, California in the 1860s—each locale felt similar concern at the time when pioneers settling there began progressively to abandon frontier modes and manners.[20]

Of course, more than a touch of nostalgia fed this impulse, distorting accounts that were in many cases hastily prepared. But the impulse could also encourage accuracy,[21] to the extent that some felt un-

[18] Humphrey Marshall, *The History of Kentucky* (Frankfort: n.p., 1824), introduction (unpaginated).

[19] Respectively, the quotations are from: Charles McKnight, *Our Western Border . . . One Hundred Years Ago* (Philadelphia: J. C. McCurdy and Co., 1875), p. x; Henry S. Baird, "Recollections of the Early History of Northern Wisconsin," *Collections of the State Historical Society of Wisconsin*, 4 (1859), 197; Alice Polk Hill, *Tales of the Colorado Pioneers* (Denver: Pierson and Gardiner, 1884), preface (unpaginated); Clarke, *Pioneer Days of Oregon History*, 1:iii; Arthur A. Denny, *Pioneer Days on Puget Sound* (1888; rpt. Seattle: Alice Harriman Co., 1908), p. 22; Frances Chamberlain Holley, *Once Their Homes; or, Our Legacy from the Dahkotahs* (Chicago: Donohue and Henneberry, 1890), p. v, also p. 18; John Carr, *Pioneer Days in California* (Eureka, Calif.: Times Publishing Co., 1891), p. 24. See also Charles Loring Brace, *The New West: or, California in 1867-1868* (New York: G. P. Putnam and Son, 1869), pp. iii-iv, 371-73; J.D.B. Stillman, *Seeking the Golden Fleece; A Record of Pioneer Life in California* (San Francisco: A. Roman and Co., 1877), p. 5.

[20] Kevin Starr, in *Americans and the California Dream, 1850-1915* (New York: Oxford University Press, 1973), pp. 110ff., claims that "From the start, Californians cherished their history." The rest of his chap. 4 documents both individual and institutional efforts in this state at mid-century and after. See also Thomas D. Clark, *Frontier America: The Story of the Westward Movement*, 2d ed. (New York: Charles Scribner's Sons, 1969), pp. 22-23; Callcott, *History in the United States*, pp. 67-82.

[21] See, for example, *The American Pioneer: A Monthly Periodical, Devoted to the Objects of the Logan Historical Society; or, To Collecting and Publishing Sketches to the Early Settlement and Successive Improvement of the Country* (Cincinnati), ed. John S. Williams, 1 (January 1842), 3; Ferdinand F. Crèvecoeur, *Old Settlers' Tales . . ,* (Onaga, Kan.: n.p., 1909), pp. 9-41 Bela Hubbard, *Memorials of a Half-Century* (New York: G. P. Putnam's Sons, 1887), p. iii; Henry H. Hurlbut, *Chicago Antiquities* (Chicago: n.p., 1881), p. 4; Albert D. Richardson, *Beyond the Mississippi: From the*

equal to the task, ruefully self-conscious about their lack of talent or knowledge.[22] Others awoke to the value of old diaries and letters that preserved what they only much later realized was ephemeral. Still others began to rummage through collections for the public's sake— in the words of one, "simply to rescue from the hopeless oblivion to which they would soon be consigned, a few facts, concerning the people and their doings of those early times, that ought to be preserved, if ever a full and correct history is written."[23] Family pride only partly explains the willingness of relatives of pioneers to meet the expense of printing old reminiscences and family histories, pedestrian accounts and banal correspondence.[24] The larger purpose threading together all of these publishing ventures was a strong preservationist motive.[25]

Great River to the Great Ocean . . . 1857-1867 (Hartford: American Publishing Co., 1867), p. i; J. Fletcher Williams, "A History of the City of St. Paul and of the County of Ramsey, Minnesota," *Collections of the Minnesota Historical Society*, 4 (1876), 3; I. Winslow Ayer, *Life in the Wilds of America, and Wonders of the West in and beyond the Bounds of Civilization* (Grand Rapids, Mich.: Central Publishing Co., 1880), pp. 7-8, 15.

[22] See Mrs. John H. [Juliette Augusta] Kinzie, *Wau-Bun, The "Early Day" in the North-West* (New York: Derby and Jackson, 1856), pp. vi-vii; Peter H. Burnett, *Recollections and Opinions of an Old Pioneer* (New York: D. Appleton and Co., 1880), pp. vi-vii; Annie D. Tallent, *The Black Hills; or, The Last Hunting Ground of the Dakotahs* (St. Louis: Nixon-Jones, 1899), pp. v-vii; Francis Parkman, *The Oregon Trail: Sketches of Prairie and Rocky-Mountain Life* (1849), ed. E. N. Feltskog (Madison: University of Wisconsin Press, 1969), pp. viii-ix.

[23] Rev. George R. Carroll, *Pioneer Life In and Around Cedar Rapids, Iowa from 1839 to 1849* (Cedar Rapids: n.p., 1895), preface (unpaginated). See also Horatio Hale, *An International Idiom: A Manual of the Oregon Trade Language or "Chinook Jargon"* (London: Whittaker and Co., 1890), pp. 19-20; Alexander Ross, *Adventures of the First Settlers on the Oregon or Columbia River . . .* (1849), reprinted as vol. 7 of Thwaites, ed., *Early Western Travels*, p. 22.

[24] Preface to J. W. Spencer, *Reminiscences of Pioneer Life in the Mississippi Valley* (1872), reprinted in Milo Milton Quaife, ed., *The Early Days of Rock Island and Davenport* (Chicago: R. R. Donnelley and Sons, 1942), p. iii. See also Daniel Drake, *Pioneer Life in Kentucky: A Series of Reminiscential Letters from Daniel Drake, M.D., of Cincinnati, to His Children*, ed. Charles Drake (Cincinnati: Robert Clarke and Co., 1870), pp. v-vi; Gabriel Franchère, *Narrative of a Voyage to the Northwest Coast of America in the Years 1811, 1812, 1813, and 1814; or, The First American Settlement on the Pacific* (1820), trans. and ed. J. V. Huntington (1854), reprinted in vol. 6 of Thwaites, ed., *Early Western Travels*, p. 175; Edmund De Schweinitz, *The Life and Times of David Zeisberger: The Western Pioneer and Apostle of the Indians* (Philadelphia: J. B. Lippincott and Co., 1870), pp. 161-62.

[25] See, for example, Hermann E. Ludewig, *The Literature of American Local History: A Bibliographical Essay* (New York: R. Craighead, 1846). For a general background to travel literature as well as to local histories during this period, see John Francis McDermott, ed., *Research Opportunities in American Cultural History* (Lexington: University Press of Kentucky, 1961), esp. Thomas Clark, "Travel Literature," pp. 46-65, and Richard M. Dorson, "Folklore and Cultural History," pp. 102-23.

Antiquarians, Historians, and Societies

Preservationist sentiment did not grow uniformly throughout the century, though it is possible to see offhand comments giving way to determined efforts, isolated gestures to committed careers. In some cases, determination and commitment emerged already fully formed. For example, Jared Sparks, later Harvard's and America's first professor of history, undertook the first archival tour of the country in 1826. Examining as many colonial and Revolutionary materials as he could uncover along the eastern seaboard, he returned to his Cambridge study to establish "an editorial assembly-line" where those and other original accounts, purchased and borrowed, could be duplicated.[26]

Though most recorders had neither the time nor the funds for such selfless dedication, some at least shared Sparks's initiative. John Leeds Bozman in Maryland in the 1830s, Reverend William B. Sprague in New York in the 1840s, and Hubert Howe Bancroft in California in the 1850s assiduously sought out pioneers, tracked down books, pamphlets and manuscripts, and ferreted out a wide assortment of other half forgotten and disintegrating materials.[27]

Among these remarkable individuals, Lyman Draper (1815-1891) towers over his contemporaries in his devotion to the task of historical preservation. As a student in Ohio in the mid-1830s, Draper had found himself absorbed by the lives and deeds of local pioneers, and he began to write to them. It occurred to him that "very much precious historical incident must still be treasured up in the memory of aged Western Pioneers, which would perish with them if not quickly rescued."[28] His mission in life soon took form: to search out those individuals, their relatives and descendants; to pry into memories already hazy; to ransack attics and packing barrels for letters and documents; to buy what he could and transcribe what he could not.

Blessed with a charm that made his enthusiasm contagious, Draper convinced Mobile businessman Peter Remsen to become his patron.

[26] Lyman H. Butterfield, "Draper's Predecessors and Contemporaries," in Donald R. McNeil, ed., *The American Collector* (Madison: State Historical Society of Wisconsin, 1955), p. 16; see also p. 7.

[27] See John Leeds Bozman, *The History of Maryland*, 2 vols. (Baltimore: James Lucas and E. K. Deaver, 1837); Hubert Howe Bancroft, *The Early American Chroniclers* (San Francisco: A. L. Bancroft and Co., 1883); "California Historical Society, 1852-1922," *California Historical Society Quarterly*, 1 (July 1922), 10; Butterfield, "Draper's Predecessors and Contemporaries," pp. 11-15.

[28] Draper to Mrs. Lucy S. Green, October 28, 1849. Cited in William B. Hesseltine, *Pioneer's Mission: The Story of Lyman Copeland Draper* (Madison: State Historical Society of Wisconsin, 1954), p. 27. This paragraph relies on Hesseltine's account.

This arrangement freed him to roam the Allegheny region in the 1840s, "delving and rummaging,"[29] interviewing and corresponding, and always collecting. Local antiquarians willingly helped. Following Remsen's death in late 1851, historical societies eagerly offered to house Draper's well-known collection, but the historian needed a new source of funding in order to continue his mission. Moving to Madison, Wisconsin, a year later, he won the appointment of secretary to the State Historical Society in 1854, a post he held for the next thirty years.

Draper's career embodies the strain of apprehension felt by so many of his contemporaries at less committed, less professional levels. As were Reubon T. Durret, William M. Darlington, and Philip Ashton Rollins later in the century, he was an impressive collector of invaluable materials "against accident and the mouldering of time."[30] But he moved beyond even them in encouraging the establishment of antiquarian and historical societies in order to ensure that second-generation settlers, given to discarding reminders of old frontier ways, did not thereby altogether frustrate the possibility of a record.

European countries had long provided models for similar organizations in the form of research libraries and private archives. London's Society of Antiquarians, for instance, had been established in 1572. The evidence suggests, however, that America's historical societies emerged largely uninfluenced by foreign models.[31] First seriously supported in the years following national independence, they proliferated during the antebellum period. During that three-quarters of a century, moreover, the tone with which these sober societies asserted themselves underwent a significant change, reflecting the increasing urgency with which Americans established them. In 1791 Bostonians founded the first such American group, the Massachusetts Historical Society, with calmly measured words: "the professed design of [the society] is, to collect, preserve and communicate materials for a complete history of this country, and accounts of all valuable efforts of human ingenuity and industry, from the beginning of its settle-

29 The phrase is Hesseltine's, in ibid., p. 47. See also *Dr. J.G.M. Ramsey: Autobiography and Letters,* ed. William B. Hesseltine (Nashville: Tennessee Historical Commission, 1954).

30 The phrase is John Leeds Bozman's, in *The History of Maryland,* 1:v; see also pp. viii-ix.

31 Leslie W. Dunlap, *American Historical Societies, 1790-1860* (Madison: privately printed, 1944), pp. 7-19; Henry Nash Smith, "The Widening of Horizons," in Spiller et al., eds., *Literary History of the United States,* pp. 644-46; Arthur Palmer Hudson, "Folklore," in ibid., pp. 717ff.; Jay Martin, *Harvests of Change: American Literature, 1865-1914* (Englewood Cliffs, N.J.: Prentice-Hall, 1967), p. 83n. For a comparative view, see Richard M. Dorson, "Folklore and Cultural History," esp. pp. 104-8.

ment."[32] The resolution inaugurating the Indiana Historical Society in 1830 struck a more forceful, more anxious note: "This meeting is fully impressed with the importance and necessity of collecting and preserving the materials for a comprehensive and accurate history of our country, natural, civil and political, [which] in the absence of well directed efforts to preserve them are rapidly passing into oblivion. . . ."[33] In the 1860s and 1870s, newly admitted western states formed similar organizations in an ever more self-conscious race against time and progress.[34]

The professionalization of antiquarian efforts, combined with the establishment of sixty-five major state and private historical societies by 1860, attests to unusual enthusiasm in a young society. These and similar efforts reached a fever pitch in the immediate post-Civil War years, and the founding of the American Folklore Society in 1888 consolidated hitherto fragmented efforts into a national organization. Ancestral societies such as the Sons of the American Revolution (1889) and the Colonial Dames of America (1890) gave form to this same spirit, which also prompted those further west to establish the Society of California Pioneers (1850) and the Daughters of the Republic of Texas (1891). Perhaps this historical interest was intensified psychologically by a war that destroyed a beloved southern subculture. Or perhaps less precise reasons contributed: a new ease of transcontinental travel, which stepped up the process of change, or an accelerating industrialization and urbanization, which fostered increasing social discontent. More important, after a half century of dizzying national growth, coupled with a new self-consciousness about what "modernization" had displaced, efforts to preserve records of earlier patterns no longer appeared quixotic. On the contrary, respected postbellum figures acquired additional prestige through their efforts to preserve features of pioneer life.

FIVE REPRESENTATIVE FIGURES

Four men who powerfully shaped post-Civil War popular opinion— George Bird Grinnell, Theodore Roosevelt, Frederick Remington,

[32] "Circular Letter of the Historical Society," *Proceedings of the Massachusetts Historical Society*, 1 (1791-1835), 1. See also Roy Harvey Pearce, *Savagism and Civilization: A Study of the Indian and the American Mind*, rev. ed. (Baltimore: Johns Hopkins University Press, 1965), 112-14; "Petition to the Massachusetts Legislature" (October 1812), *American Antiquarian Society Collections*, 1 (1820), 17-18.

[33] "Minutes of the Indiana Historical Society for December 11, 1830," *Indiana Historical Society Publications: Proceedings of the Indiana Historical Society, 1830-1886,* 1 (1897), 9.

[34] For one example among many, see the "General Circular Issued by the State Librarian," *Pioneer Collections: Report of the Pioneer Society of the State of Michigan*, 1 (1877), 3-4.

and Owen Wister—all grew up in eastern, patrician families. As young men, they attended either Harvard or Yale; in their early twenties, each traveled to Montana or the Dakotas. Enamored of western life, Remington and Roosevelt even bought sizable ranches. Common backgrounds, interests, and experiences encouraged friendships and influences among them and make them an unusually representative group. Once again, their individual popularity hinged upon a growing public interest in efforts on behalf of wilderness preservation and frontier history; but that interest took shape in turn from their own accomplishments.

Easily the most popular of the four, Roosevelt (1858-1919) is usually remembered for his bold conservation policy while president. Nearly two decades before being elected president, he wrote a series of essays from his North Dakota ranch in which his enthusiasm for western ranch life was tempered by a wry regret for its imminent demise. It is, he observed, "a phase of American life as fascinating as it is evanescent, and one well deserving an historian."[35] After he returned east to politics and Sagamore Hill, Roosevelt continued to turn out essays lamenting the rude transformation of western landscape and life. Published in popular periodicals such as *Century Magazine*, his accounts of "Frontier Types" and "Ranch Life in the Far West in the Cattle Country" celebrated the occupations still to be found on the frontier: trapper, cowpuncher, horse thief, buckskin maker, highwayman, hunter.[36] He read widely in the literature, corresponded frequently with fellow western artists and historians, and continued throughout his career to press for the West's accurate documentation. Whether or not his direct experiences made him a conservationist later, Roosevelt certainly lent a presidential "seal of approval" to writing about western life.

One of Roosevelt's correspondents was Frederic Remington (1861-1909), who was commissioned by *Century Magazine* to illustrate some of the politician's early genre essays. The young artist grew to admire the writer whose prose so brightly complemented his own style. According to his later recollection, Remington conceived his artistic purpose at nineteen while sitting around a Montana campfire. An old wagon freighter concluded a reminiscence by bemoaning that "now

35 Roosevelt, *Hunting Trips of A Ranchman / Hunting Trips on the Prairie and in the Mountains* (1885; rpt. New York: G. P. Putnam's Sons, 1905), p. 35; see also pp. 24-25, 55, 261, 269-70.

36 Roosevelt, "Frontier Types," *Century Magazine*, 36 (October 1888), 832-43; "Ranch Life in the Far West," ibid., 35 (February 1888), 495-510. See also "The Ranchman's Rifle on Crag and Prairie," ibid., 36 (June 1888), 200-212; "Sheriff's Work on A Ranch," ibid., 36 (May 1888), 39-51.

7. Frederic Remington, *A Fur Train from the Far North*, 1888. Wood engraving from *Harper's Weekly*, August 25, 1888.

there is no more West." "The old man had closed my very entrancing book almost at the first chapter. I knew the railroad was coming. . . . I knew the wild riders and the vacant land were about to vanish forever—and the more I considered the subject, the bigger the *forever* loomed. Without knowing exactly how to do it, I began to try to record some facts around me, and the more I looked the more the panorama unfolded."[37] This passage, written through nearly a quarter century of affectionate hindsight, helps to explain Remington's stylistic precision, from his first published pictures half a year later, in 1882, through much of the career to follow. By the end of the eighties, both subject matter and treatment allowed him to command hefty commissions from America's best-selling periodicals, including *Harper's Weekly*, *Century Magazine*, and *Outing Magazine*.

[37] Cited in Harold McCracken, *Frederic Remington: Artist of the Old West* (Philadelphia: J. B. Lippincott Co., 1947), pp. 34, 36. See also G. Edward White, *The Eastern Establishment and the Western Experience· The West of Frederic Remington, Theodore Roosevelt, and Owen Wister* (New Haven: Yale University Press, 1968), p. 121.

As did Grinnell and Roosevelt, Remington spent much of the 1880s wandering through the West. Success allowed him to travel extensively, but it also constrained him to popular forms. His illustrations, paintings, and sculptures too often border on the sentimental, barely redeemed by their accurate detail, the result of his concern to document what was already past or passing. Even his rather maudlin essays on aspects of western life rarely fail to point to their subject's evanescence. His popular western stories, collected in *Pony Tracks* (1895) and *Crooked Trails* (1898), incorporate this strain of ephemerality in their very structures. In one, for example, two boys meet an "old-time Texas Ranger" and begin "the approaches by which we hoped to loosen the history of a wild past from one of the very few tongues which can still wag on the days when the Texans, the Comanches, and the Mexicans chased one another over the plains of Texas."[38] Other examples imitate this narrative premise of rescuing valuable western lore in the nick of time.

Owen Wister (1860-1938) also looked back from the peak of his success to recall his reasons for writing about the West:

> And so one Autumn evening of 1891, fresh from Wyoming and its wild glories, I sat in the club dining with a man as enamored of the West as I was. . . . From oysters to coffee we compared experiences. Why wasn't some Kipling saving the sage-brush for American literature, before the sage-brush and all that it signified went the way of the California forty-niner, went the way of the Mississippi steamboat, went the way of everything? Roosevelt had seen the sage-brush, true, had felt its poetry; and also Remington, who illustrated his articles so well. But what was fiction doing, fiction, the only thing that has always outlived facts?[39]

Wister had asked himself that question some time earlier and attempted to fill the need. In fact, his trip during that summer of 1891 had been planned in order to study the people of Wyoming, their activities and habits. Wister strove tirelessly to ensure fictional authenticity in a conscious race against time.[40] He too lamented the rapidly changing character of western life, growing at once bitter about civilized progress and mythic in his characterization of the men

---

[38] Remington, "How the Law Got into Chaparral," in *Crooked Trails* (1898; rpt. Freeport, N.Y.: Books for Libraries Press, 1969), pp. 1-2, also p. 63.

[39] *Owen Wister Out West*, ed. F. K. Wister, pp. 11-12. See also p. 35 for a journal entry dated July 16, 1885, which partly verifies this later recollection.

[40] Ben Merchant Vorpahl, ed., *My Dear Wister: The Frederic Remington-Owen Wister Letters* (Palo Alto, Calif.: American West Publishing Co., 1972), p. 28. On Wister's commitment, one should look particularly at *Owen Wister Out West*, ed. F. K. Wister, pp. 123-24, 209-10, for appropriate references in his letters to his mother during the nineties.

and order it replaced. His short stories in the 1890s led finally to *The Virginian* (1902), which not only established the general outlines for subsequent western fiction but also recovered an encyclopedic array of colloquial expressions. By this time, as his preface notes, the Far West had been "tamed."[41]

As we have already seen, George Bird Grinnell, the fourth and eldest member of this group, educated his friends and his generation to the need for forest and wildlife legislation. His career began as a graduate student of the Yale paleontologist O. C. Marsh, on one of whose collecting expeditions he had already traveled west in 1870. That early experience sparked his interest in the West, and during the next forty-odd years, he devoted himself to all forms of preservation—records and objects, wilderness and wild game—as well as to ethnology and frontier history.[42] Late in his life, in a preface to a series of sketches entitled *Beyond the Old Frontier* (1913), Grinnell expressed encouragement about the growing efforts to preserve what remained of western materials:

> Not many years ago a change began to take place in the viewpoint of many Americans. Far-sighted men and women came to feel that the history made by their fathers and mothers was worth preserving, and they began to write and talk about this. What they said fell on sympathetic ears, and interest was easily aroused, so that before long, in many of the Western States historical societies were established, and earnest men gave time and effort to the work of inducing the early settlers to set down their recollections—to describe the events in which they had taken part. Later came the marking of historic spots and trails by monuments.[43]

Roosevelt, Remington, and Wister had won considerable acclaim by the closing decade of the nineteenth century. Contemporary reviewers fully recognized the historical and sociological value of their western records.[44] Yet, even as these critics wrote, the Wild West was

41 Wister, *The Virginian: A Horseman of the Plains* (1902; rpt. New York: Macmillan Co., 1903), p. viii.

42 John Reiger suggests that Grinnell's very background encouraged this commitment: "He possessed the aristocrat's dislike for change, a characteristic that compelled him to record his experiences in an effort to preserve—at least on paper—the life they represented" (in Grinnell, *The Passing of the Great West: Selected Papers of George Bird Grinnell*, ed. Reiger [New York: Winchester Press, 1972], p. 2, also pp. 100-104).

43 Grinnell, *Beyond the Old Frontier: Adventures of Indian-Fighters, Hunters, and Fur Traders* (New York: Charles Scribner's Sons, 1913), p. vii.

44 See the review of Roosevelt, *The Wilderness Hunter*, in *Atlantic Monthly*, 75 (June 1895), 829-30. For a similar statement, see "Roosevelt's Ranch Life," review of Roosevelt, *Ranch Life and the Hunting Trail*, in *Overland Monthly*, 2d ser., 28 (November 1896), 604.

no longer there for artists to see, much less to preserve through the "sharp realism" admired by their contemporaries.[45] By the close of the century, that landscape could be mapped only in memory or imagination. Artists like Remington and Wister, for all their preservationist intentions, found themselves drawn rather to outsized, mythic renderings. Their willing acceptance of such a style, and the public's enthusiasm for it, suggests a larger issue worth examining later: the growing aversion to eastern, industrial society.

Here, attention should shift for a moment away from these gifted easterners inclined toward nostalgic wistfulness. Perhaps favored backgrounds or national influence and popularity encouraged them to express historiographic motives rarely voiced, though felt, by others. Remington's foremost rival, Charles Marion Russell (1864-1926), for instance, lacked the Yale education and small income that eased Remington's excursions. In 1880, at the age of sixteen, Russell ran away from his St. Louis home to live among the cowboys and Indians of Montana, where he longed to teach himself the skills required to sketch their life. If Russell suffered from the common tendency to sentimentalize the Old West, despite his long apprenticeship in hardship, he nevertheless broke important stereotypes, unlike Remington and artists inferior to them both. For example, he rarely depicted white frontiersmen in conflict with one another or with native tribes. Instead, his vignettes attempt to isolate frontier modes of life, illustrating codes, patterns, and activities from a neutral perspective. The one theme common to his paintings, one spiritually binding all Indians to all frontiersmen, is the threat of mechanical progress. His very titles indicate Russell's resistance: *When Guns Were Their Passports; When Meat Was Plentiful; Before the White Man Came.* Like Wister and Remington, he rued the loss of a frontier world by confirming it in the past tense and then elevating it to the stature of myth. Whether or not he ever articulated the impulse, his paintings express a lifelong commitment to documenting not only those pioneer experiences that were so obviously passing but also those that loomed heroic in memory against the banal exigencies of the present.[46]

[45] "Mr. Remington as Artist and Author," review of Remington, *Crooked Trails,* in *Dial,* 25 (October 16, 1898), 265. See also Julian Ralph, "Frederic Remington," *Harper's Weekly,* 39 (July 20, 1895), 688.

[46] For background on Russell, see: Charles M. Russell, *Good Medicine: Memories of the Real West* (New York: Garden City Publishing Co., 1929); Harold McCracken, *The Charles M. Russell Book: The Life and Work of the Cowboy Artist* (Garden City, N.Y.: Doubleday and Co., 1957); Ramon F. Adams and Homer E. Britzman, *Charles M. Russell: The Cowboy Artist* (Pasadena: Trail's End Publishing Co., 1948); J. Frank

FICTIONAL PRESERVES

The urge to preserve records of life on the frontier was expressed in two characteristic voices, which are easily identifiable late in the century, but can also be discerned in earlier statements. The louder one spoke out for historical documents, and everyone from genre painters and local antiquarians to professional historians and their societies joined in. The second voice, somewhat fainter, expressed a more diffuse commitment to preservation in fictional forms. As Owen Wister demanded after a summer of collecting "local colour," "what was fiction doing, fiction, the only thing that has always outlived facts?"[47] Of course, Americans had always wanted to forge a literature of their own from indigenous materials. That desire bears little relationship to the self-conscious documenting of characteristic, threatened modes of life, however. Cooper, for instance, created one of America's most powerful myths in the figure of Leatherstocking. But his acceptance of the formal conventions of the English novel of manners and the historical romance suggests that he was less concerned at first with establishing a uniquely American fictional world than with recording his experiences.

Other novelists in the 1820s and 1830s shared this commitment, though they only declared it openly in their essays and nonfiction studies. Timothy Flint's *Recollections of the Last Ten Years* (1826), Robert Montgomery Bird's *Peter Pilgrim; or, A Rambler's Recollections* (1838), and Mrs. Caroline Kirkland's *A New Home—Who'll Follow?* (1839) represent, as do the later paintings of Bingham, Remington, and Russell, a considerable investment in documenting frontier experience for its own value. Mrs. Kirkland, for instance, had found life in an early Michigan settlement altogether unlike what she had expected from reading Châteaubriand's sentimental *Atala*. Her trials as a frontier housewife provoked her to a brisk account of pretentious rustic belles and old-maid gossips, crass woodsmen and flamboyant embezzlers, unfailingly generous neighbors and crude frontier holidays. Like Bird and Flint, she aspired to a degree of accuracy about which she seems unduly defensive when she forthrightly offers her book as a "veritable history; an unimpeachable transcript of reality."[48]

Dobie, *The Conservatism of Charles M. Russell* (El Paso: C. R. Smith, 1950); Frank Bird Linderman, *Recollections of Charley Russell*, ed. H. G. Merriam (Norman: University of Oklahoma Press, 1963), esp. pp. 52ff.

[47] *Owen Wister Out West*, ed. F. K. Wister, pp. 11-12.

[48] Caroline Matilda Kirkland, *A New Home—Who'll Follow? or, Glimpses of Western Life* (1839) ed William S. Osborne (New Haven: College and University Press,

Each of the three popular authors vigorously proclaimed their documentarian intentions, which suggests that in later fictionalizing these settings and subjects, their motives changed little.[49]

Likewise, the attempt accurately to portray frontier life through fiction made a well-worn device, that of a narrator discovering a pioneer's long-forgotten manuscript, a frequently used framework during this period. The first American novel about whaling provides a curious instance. Joseph Hart's *Miriam Coffin* (1834) is now justly ignored by all but literary scholars, whose interest derives solely from Melville's having incorporated sections of it into *Moby-Dick*. Yet its contrived rationale reflects another aspect of the growing concern for frontier histories.[50] In an extended introduction, Hart denies having written the ensuing narrative of eighteenth-century Nantucket. Instead, he claims to have sailed to the island in order to prepare a study of whaling. There he searched out an old pioneer "possessing a remarkably retentive memory,—particularly in what related to the early history of the island." Garrulously answering Hart's queries, the man at last ends the interview by offering his visitor a bulky manuscript, which, he assures Hart, will explain all. It satisfies as well Hart's reiterated desire to preserve such moldering accounts by publishing them.[51]

Such artifices and motifs were by no means restricted to a special brand of pioneer fiction. Following the Civil War, regionalism and the local-color movement rose to prominence, taking over the task of preservation hitherto shouldered by professional and amateur historians. Writers turned to the delineation of local folkways and dialects in order to perpetuate in literature the patterns rapidly being abandoned or disrupted. Their efforts, like those of the artists discussed above, often ease into nostalgia or sacrifice accuracy for an ideal. Yet they were motivated by the same concern we have seen elsewhere, as Carlos Baker notes: "At a crucial period in American history, when

---

1965), p. iii. See also William S. Osborne, *Caroline M. Kirkland* (New York: Twayne Publishers, 1972), esp. pp. 7-10, 36-37.

[49] Timothy Flint, *Recollections of the Last Ten Years Passed in Occasional Residences and Journeyings in the Valley of the Mississippi* . . . (Boston: Cummings, Hilliard, and Co., 1826), pp. 188-89, also pp. 27-28, 53, 203, 389-90; Robert Montgomery Bird, *Peter Pilgrim; or, A Rambler's Recollections* 2 vols. (Philadelphia: Lea and Blanchard, 1838), 1:23; Kirkland, *A New Home*, p. 7.

[50] See Benjamin Keen, *The Aztec Image in Western Thought* (New Brunswick: Rutgers University Press, 1971), pp. 373-74; Louise K. Barnett, *The Ignoble Savage: American Literary Racism, 1790-1890*, Contributions in American Studies, no. 18 (Westport, Conn.: Greenwood Press, 1975), pp. 39-40.

[51] Col. Joseph C. Hart, *Miriam Coffin, or The Whale Fishermen: A Tale* (1834), new ed., 2 vols. in one (San Francisco: H. R. Coleman, 1872), p. xvii; see the whole introduction, pp. ix-xxviii.

old faces, manners, customs, recipes, styles, attitudes, and prejudices were undergoing rapid change or total extirpation, they seized and perpetuated, through the medium of fictional character, the cultural landscape: the native idiom, the still unravished rural peace, the feel and flavor of things as they were, and would never be again."[52]

The local-color and regionalist movements were fueled by paradoxically opposed impulses: on the one hand, writers attempted to idealize the quickly passing; on the other, they wanted to correct idealistically accurate depictions. The efforts of authors who glorified the agrarian past, such as Thomas Nelson Page of Virginia and Sarah Orne Jewett of Maine, and those of western regionalists such as Edgar Watson Howe and Hamlin Garland, whose grim portraits of pioneer life challenge such conceptions, reflect motives essentially aesthetic or sociological rather than historiographic.[53] In any case, local color and regionalism grew more readily in the Northeast and the South than in the West, partly because the West changed almost too rapidly to accommodate serious fiction.[54] There were exceptions, of course. Edward Eggleston wrote *A Hoosier Schoolmaster* (1871), as he said, to subvert James Fenimore Cooper's "unreal world" and to capture in realistic fiction the "manners, customs, thoughts and feelings" of "life in the back-country districts of the Western States."[55] For the most part, however, writers were inadequate to the region—understandably so, given the frenetic rate at which the unstoried frontier gave way to full-scale agrarian and industrial development. The pace of change helps to explain why those who began their careers by writing realistic western fiction often found that they could do justice to the region only by writing histories.[56]

[52] Carlos Baker, "Delineation of Life and Character," in Spiller et al., eds., *Literary History of the United States*, p. 861, also pp. 847-48, 856.

[53] See Warner Berthoff, *The Ferment of Realism: American Literature, 1884-1919* (New York: Free Press, 1965), pp. 90-100; Martin, *Harvests of Change*, pp. 86-88, 111-59. For a contrasting instance, see Hamlin Garland, *Crumbling Idols: Twelve Essays on Art Dealing Chiefly with Literature Painting and the Drama* (1894), ed. Jane Johnson (Cambridge, Mass.: Harvard University Press, 1960), pp. 59-60, 62, 65.

[54] See Baker, "Delineation of Life and Character," pp. 844, 848; Berthoff, *Ferment of Realism*, pp. 90-91.

[55] Edward Eggleston, *The Hoosier Schoolmaster* (1871; rpt. New York: Orange Judd Co., 1890), pp. 5-6. See also Ernest E. Leisy, *The American Historical Novel* (Norman: University of Oklahoma Press, 1950), pp. 125ff.; [Augustus Baldwin Longstreet], *Georgia Scenes, Characters, Incidents, &c. in the First Half Century of the Republic*, 2d ed. (New York: Harper and Brothers, 1860), p. iii.

[56] Joseph Kirkland, for example, a generation after his mother, Caroline, documented the building of *A New Home*, turned for just this reason from writing novels about small town life in the Middle West to compiling chronicles and local histories.

PHYSICAL PRESERVATION

The popularity of the local-color movement reflects a national disposition to hold on to ways of life obviously in decline. True, that mood did not confine itself to national borders or continental limits. Thomas Hardy proved a more thorough and better "chronicler of decay" than Edward Eggleston; European artists also seized on their own threatened local lore. In America, however, partly because so much more in addition to historical lore was vanishing, the regionalist movement drew more widespread support. Perhaps it contributed in turn to more literal kinds of preservation than envisioned by those who wrote fiction or those who collected histories. The preceding chapter suggested that no clear connection can be made between those who recorded wilderness landscapes and those who struggled in political arenas for their preservation. To link recorders of pioneer history, local-color artists, and the relatively few who worked to preserve actual artifacts would prove even more difficult.

Most nineteenth-century Americans remained unaware of any need for physical preservation. George Washington's neglected home began to be rescued by the newly formed Mount Vernon Ladies' Association only in 1858 and was not secured until the 1870s.[57] The homes of other political notables, much less anonymous log cabins or adobe houses, hardly seemed worth the trouble or expense of preservation.

Toward the end of the century, the Spanish missions of southern California almost alone escaped decay due to apathy. Monuments to a distinctly non-Anglo Saxon past, they had been allowed to suffer years of crumbling disrepair, until two concerned Los Angeles civic leaders, George Wharton James and Charles F. Lummis, encouraged their restoration in the 1880s. Their friend, the photographer Adam Clark Vroman, felt anxious enough about the missions' dilapidated state to spend the decade after 1895 photographing an exhaustive record of them. Delivering lectures throughout the state, these three men gathered support for the Association for the Preservation of the Missions, organized in 1888. The language James used, curiously, bears comparison with that of contemporary conservationists speaking about forests and wild game: "Buildings that come down to us out of the past, if ever worth anything, are worth preserving,—keeping, just as they are, as a valuable heirloom *that is not ours* except to look at, use, and pass on to our posterity. Our science is daily broadening. . . . Therefore we have awakened senses as to our duty to

[57] Gerald W. Johnson, *Mount Vernon: The Story of a Shrine* (New York: Random House, 1953), pp. 21-24, 42-43.

8. Adam Clark Vroman, "San Luis Rey Mission, Entrance to the Inner Court," 1897. Photograph. The Natural History Museum of Los Angeles County.

the historic remains of the past and the rights and claims of those who will come after us to them."[58] By 1900, shrewdly opportunistic Randolph Hearst sensed the popular enthusiasm for saving the missions and threw the influence of his *San Francisco Examiner* behind the movement.[59]

In the same way that conservationists came to defend all wilderness, not merely spectacular enclaves, all worthy historic buildings, not just

[58] George Wharton James, *In and Out of the Old Missions of California: An Historical and Pictorial Account of the Franciscan Missions* (Boston: Little, Brown and Co., 1905), p. 383. See also James, *Old Missions and Mission Indians of California* (Los Angeles: B. R. Baumgardt and Co., 1895), esp. pp. 29, 52, 121; Ruth I. Mahood, *Photographer of the Southwest: Adam Clark Vroman, 1856-1916* (New York: Bonanza Books, 1961), pp. 23-24; Dudley C. Gordon, *Charles F. Lummis: Crusader in Corduroy* (Los Angeles: Cultural Assets Press, 1972), esp. pp. 90-91; Charles Howard Shinn, "San Fernando Mission by Moonlight," *Land of Sunshine*, 2 (April 1895), 80.

For a contrasting example, see the antiquarian photography of Philadelphia's older buildings completed by Frederick Richards, ca. 1859, in *Philadelphia: Three Centuries of American Art*, Catalogue of Bicentennial Exhibit (Philadelphia Museum of Art, 1976), p. 31.

[59] James, *In and Out of the Old Missions*, pp. 387-88.

the Spanish missions, came to be seen as deserving preservation. The Landmarks Club, incorporated in 1896 to safeguard and reclaim any "historic monuments, relics, or landmarks" in southern California,[60] drew support from members of the Sierra Club and other wilderness conservation groups. Elsewhere across the nation similar concern had led to the organization of the Association for the Preservation of Virginia Antiquities (1889) and the American Scenic and Historic Preservation Society (1895). These would be followed by numerous preservation organizations at the turn of the century. Unlike the conservation movement, however, the relatively few citizens committed to landmark preservation maintained a primarily local solidarity.

CONCLUSION

Frederick Jackson Turner first formulated how the risks and rewards of an ever-retreating western frontier had uniquely shaped America's national character. To understand that character requires an understanding of the pioneer experiences that molded it. In large part, as Turner also noted, the passing of the frontier confirmed the passing of America's most challenging guarantee of political, social, and moral growth. Perhaps substituting "settler" for Emerson's "savage" best identifies the irony here: "In history the great moment is when the [settler] is just ceasing to be a [settler]. . . . Everything good in nature and the world is in that moment."[61] The ideal American society, in other words, needs continuous regeneration through contact with nature, but nature everywhere recedes before that society. That this ideal could only be approached in the process of passing, that is, in the pioneer experience, clarifies an irresolvable contradiction at the heart of America's self-conception. Few of those touched by this social paradox in the nineteenth century could appreciate it. We can better understand their attachment to frontier life, cherished less in the present than in the past tense, sometimes in the form of sentimental tales, sometimes in attempted histories, but increasingly as irrecoverable experience.

In the broadest sense, nineteenth-century Americans wanted to freeze all aspects of the wilderness experience. Vanishing forests, polluted streams, and eroded prairies; decimated flocks, dwindling herds, and disappearing evidence of pioneer exploits—each reminder elicited sympathetic attempts to preserve what was left for posterity, either

60 Ibid., p. 384.
61 Ralph Waldo Emerson, "Power," in *The Complete Writings of Ralph Waldo Emerson*, 2 vols. (New York: William H. Wise, 1929), 1:541.

through accurate records or by physical conservation. Missing from that list, however, is a far more striking embodiment of North America's wilderness: the Indian, human representative of all that the continent had symbolized prior to white settlement. Assuredly, he was not absent from the nineteenth-century consciousness of passing wilderness. But white understanding of native ways—much less white concern for their passing—remained complex and contradictory. Before examining the varied responses to the Indian and his place in the wilderness, we might first turn to a man who committed his life to preserving both images and records of vanishing native tribes. In so doing, we shall find in the paradigm of George Catlin's career all the issues traced so far.

CHAPTER FOUR

GEORGE CATLIN'S
MISSION

Those tribes, sir, that have preceded
us, to whose lands we have succeeded, and
who have no written memorials of their
laws, their habits, and their manners, are
all passing away to the world of forgetfulness. Their likeness, manners, and
customs are portrayed with more accuracy
and truth in this collection by Catlin than
in all the other drawings and representations on the face of the earth. Somebody
in this country ought to possess this collection. . . .

. . . I go for this as an American subject—as a thing belonging to us—to our
history—to the history of a race whose
lands we till, whose obscure graves and
bones we tread every day. I look upon it
as a thing more appropriate for us than
the ascertaining of the South Pole, or anything that can be discovered in the Dead
Sea, or the River Jordan.

Daniel Webster
Senate speech (1849)

F EW NINETEENTH-CENTURY AMERICANS committed themselves as completely to America's vanishing wilderness as did George Catlin (1796-1872). Others, witness to troubling changes, went to extraordinary pains to compile accurate records. But they did so only as the western experience touched some part of their careers, and even then only as isolated gestures against the inevitable. The conventional demands of work and family prevented greater sacrifice. Indeed, Catlin's devotion to such a professional life led some to regard him as merely eccentric, a judgment he himself encouraged. In *Shut Your Mouth and Save Your Life* (1860), for instance, he attempted to prove that whites are less healthy than Indians because they snore.[1] Happily, such aberrant theories had little effect on the popularity Catlin won for his lifelong efforts. That broad popularity, moreover, helps to define the age's aspirations.

Most recent historians have not appreciated this context, coupling praise for Catlin's paintings with strained arguments for his supposedly unique vision.[2] Yet Catlin differed from his fellow Americans less in the substance of his beliefs than in the quality of his devotion. His commitments to preservation—whether of forests or game, Indian ethnography or painting—remain unusual only in having characterized one man's life. The uniqueness of his career resulted from his having recognized the vital interrelation between the destruction of indigenous cultures and a vanishing landscape. He rarely viewed tribes in isolation from their surroundings or apart from the effects of white Americans on the land and its wildlife. As early as the summer of 1832, while on his first painting expedition to the West, he lamented the decline of wild game in the upper Missouri country.[3] Using sketchbooks and canvases to preserve an accurate image of the remaining buffalo herds, he at the same time created the very conventions of buffalo painting that other painters would adopt.[4]

[1] Catlin, *Shut Your Mouth and Save Your Life* (1860; rpt. London: Trübner and Co., 1876).

[2] See, for instance, James Thomas Flexner, *That Wilder Image: The Painting of America's Native School from Thomas Cole to Winslow Homer* (1962; rpt. New York: Dover Publications, 1970), esp. pp. 69-71; Bernard DeVoto, *Across the Wide Missouri* (Boston: Houghton Mifflin Co., 1947), pp. 394-95; Harold McCracken, *George Catlin and the Old Frontier* (New York: Bonanza Books 1959), p. 16. For a more tempered assessment, see Larry Curry, *The American West: Painters from Catlin to Russell* (New York: Viking, 1972), p. 19.

[3] George Catlin, *Letters and Notes on the Manners, Customs, and Conditions of the North American Indians* (1844), reprinted with an introduction by Marjorie Halpin, 2 vols. (New York: Dover Publications, 1973), 1:256.

[4] See DeVoto, *Across the Wide Missouri*, p. 395; Flexner, *That Wilder Image*, p. 74.

9. George Catlin, *Buffalo Bulls Fighting in Running Season, Upper Missouri,* 1830-1839. Oil on canvas. The National Collection of Fine Arts, Smithsonian Institution; gift of Mrs. Sarah Harrison.

But Catlin did more than rescue the buffalo's image for posterity. He formulated a reasonable alternative to its extinction, which he viewed as connected with the decline of native cultures and, more broadly, with the transformation of the land itself. In 1833 he publicly suggested a stunningly original undertaking: a national park system.

And what a splendid contemplation too, when one (who has travelled these realms, and can duly appreciate them) imagines them as they *might* in future be seen (by some great protecting policy of government) preserved in their pristine beauty and wildness, in a *magnificent park*, where the world could see for ages to come, the native Indian in his classic attire. . . . A *nation's Park*, containing man and beast, in all the wild and freshness of their nature's beauty!

I would ask no other monument to my memory, nor any other

enrollment of my name amongst the famous dead, than the reputation of having been the founder of such an institution.[5]

Olmsted's, Bryant's and Greeley's plans for city parks each were radical anticipations of public concern for preservation. Catlin's earlier conception attests to a greater awareness of the problems of western expansion and a more incisive perception of the necessary solution. He urged the government to withdraw most of the high plains country; a preserve any smaller, he knew, would have the same effect on native life as none at all.

The very originality of his suggestion meant that few took it seriously. Those sympathetic to proposals for a national park system would not gain power for nearly forty years. Yet Catlin's accomplishments in the 1830s and his widespread self-publicizing in the 1840s shaped a change in public attitudes toward the West. Of course, he achieved his greatest fame as a painter of Indians, a preeminence confirmed not only by his general popularity and the interest he stimulated among ethnologists but also by his dominant effect on almost every other artist similarly engaged.[6] At a minimum, his paintings provided credible source material for the less adventurous. But he also inspired others to follow him to Indian country.

BORN IN 1796, George Catlin grew up in the wilderness area separating Pennsylvania and New York that was so affectionately described by Crèvecoeur some two decades earlier. Like other frontier children, he spent much of his youth fantasizing about "wild Indians," listening to tales of older settlers, and searching out abandoned campsites. Catlin may have found these occasions particularly vivid: his own mother and grandmother had been briefly captured by Miami Indians in the celebrated Wyoming Valley massacre of 1778, and his mother's playmate had been permanently adopted by the tribe. Interest in such history spurred an adolescent delight in sketching his frontier environs that was sustained through a short stint as a lawyer. In 1823 Catlin finally abandoned the law to take his growing portfolio of portrait miniatures to Philadelphia, where within months he attracted professional attention and lucrative commissions. By 1826, he enjoyed a reputation that extended throughout the East.[7]

---

5 Catlin, *Letters and Notes*, 1:261-62.

6 See Flexner, *That Wilder Image*, p. 79; John C. Ewers, *Artists of the Old West* (Garden City, N.Y.: Doubleday and Co., 1965), p. 94.

7 Marjorie Catlin Roehm, ed., *The Letters of George Catlin and His Family: A Chronicle of the American West* (Berkeley: University of California Press, 1966), p. 29; Royal Hassrick, *George Catlin Book of American Indians* (New York: Watson-

Catlin discovered his life's mission during his first year in Philadelphia. As he later recalled, he had been "continually reaching for some branch or enterprise of the art, on which to devote a whole life-time of enthusiasm,"[8] when in 1824 a native delegation from the "Far West" passed through Philadelphia. The young painter was indelibly impressed. "The history and customs of such a people, preserved by pictorial illustrations," he later declared, "are themes worthy the life-time of one man, and nothing short of the loss of my life, shall prevent me from visiting their country, and of becoming their historian."[9]

During the rest of the 1820s, Catlin drew more portraits, broached his idea to possible patrons, and in general set about acquiring financial support for his proposed expeditions. A sympathetic New York City publisher, Colonel William F. Stone, finally made it possible for the painter to turn west.[10] In the spring of 1832, as the ice was breaking on the river, he boarded the steamboat *Yellowstone* for its historic first journey up the Missouri. Catlin knew what he wanted, as he made clear in a letter to Colonel Stone. One long passage is worth quoting in full:

> I have, for many years past, contemplated the noble races of red men who are now spread over these trackless forests and boundless prairies, melting away at the approach of civilization. Their rights invaded, their morals corrupted, their lands wrested from them, their customs changed, and therefore lost to the world; and they at last sunk into the earth, and the ploughshare turning the sod over their graves, and I have flown to their rescue—not of their lives or of their race (for they are *"doomed"* and must perish), but to the rescue of their looks and their modes, at which the acquisitive world may hurl their poison and every besom of destruction, and trample them down and crush them to death; yet, phoenix-like, they may rise from the "stain on a painter's palette," and live again upon canvass, and stand forth for centuries yet to come, the living monuments of a noble race. For this purpose, I have designed to visit every tribe of Indians on the Continent, if my life should be ·spared; for the purpose of procuring portraits of distinguished Indians, of both sexes in each tribe, painted in their

Guptill, 1977), p. 20; Catlin, *Letters and Notes*, 1:vii-viii; William Goetzmann, *Exploration and Empire: The Explorer and the Scientist in the Winning of the American West* (New York: Alfred A. Knopf, 1966), pp. 184-91.

[8] Catlin, *Letters and Notes*, 1:2.

[9] Ibid.

[10] Hassrick, *Catlin Book*, pp. 20, 25; George Catlin, *Letters and Notes on the North American Indians*, ed. and abr. Michael MacDonald Mooney (New York: Clarkson N. Potter, 1975), pp. 14-19; Roehm, ed., *Catlin Family Letters*, pp. 47-49.

native costume; accompanied with pictures of their villages, domestic habits, games, mysteries, religious ceremonies, etc. with anecdotes, traditions, and history of their respective nations.[11]

Catlin's theme is clear; the need to race against time, to paint as many tribes as possible before they alter forever, recurs in his writings often enough to form a personal manifesto.

The *Yellowstone*'s three-month, two-thousand-mile voyage upriver inaugurated Catlin's true western career and also modified his notions of what that career would entail. To refresh his memory for later studies, for instance, he scribbled notes on the tribes he observed, reminders that soon grew into an extensive encyclopedia finally published as his *Letters and Notes*. Moreover, the focus of his painting shifted from an initial concentration on portraits to a fascination with exuberant scenes of tribal life, including dances, ceremonies, architecture, buffalo hunts, artwork, and domestic activities. Even his style evolved. Catlin's furious pace, dictated by his desire to record as much as possible, often meant a sacrifice of conventional artistic standards of composition, perspective, and even color in the numerous sketches he completed. Yet he converted liabilities into assets, moving beyond a forgivable crudeness to achieve masterful studies. Entranced by the Assiniboin, Blackfoot, Crow, and Cree Indians at Fort Union, Montana, he spent a full month sketching scenes that he would later only rarely excel.[12]

During his return trip by canoe that summer, Catlin visited the two remaining Mandan villages located north of present-day Bismarck, North Dakota. At once he sensed the importance of this beleaguered tribe, which remained one of the most complex of Plains Indian cultures: "so forcibly have I been struck with the peculiar ease and elegance of these people, together with . . . their peculiar and unaccountable customs, that I am fully convinced that they have sprung from some other origin than that of the other North American tribes, or that they are an amalgam of natives with some civilized race."[13] Catlin soaked up information, "trusting that by further intimacy and familiarity with these people I may yet arrive at more satisfactory and important results."[14] In only a fortnight he gained an extraordinary intimacy. Permitted to attend rituals rarely witnessed by

11 Catlin, *Letters and Notes*, intro. by Halpin, 1:16.
12 Roehm, ed., *Catlin Family Letters*, pp. 57, 64-65; Thomas Donaldson, *The George Catlin Indian Gallery in the United States National Museum*, author's ed. (Washington: G.P.O., 1887), pp. 369, 438; Hassrick, *Catlin Book*, pp. 21-25.
13 Catlin, *Letters and Notes*, 1:93.
14 Ibid., 1:177.

whites, Catlin completed a series of invaluable canvases, the most celebrated of which illustrate the Mandans' renowned four-day torture
ceremony. His description of the O-kee-pa ceremony, in which initiates
were suspended by splints in their flesh, challenges credulity even
today, especially since his was one of the few records made. When
Audubon visited the Mandans in 1843—six years after a smallpox
epidemic decimated the tribe—he could only lament: "Ah! Mr. Catlin, I am now sorry to see and to read your accounts of the Indians
you saw—how very different they must have been from any that I have
seen!"[15] Audubon's description of thieving Mandans scavenging
among putrid, drowned buffaloes and crowding into hovels during
winter storms forms a cruel juxtaposition to Catlin's account.

Catlin devoted the year 1833 to completing his rough sketches and
painting large oil canvases. He returned to Indian territory the following year, this time to the southern plains of the little-known
Comanches and Kiowas, which had also become the home of the
displaced Osage, Choctaws, and Cherokees. Continuing to make sometimes dangerous, always exhausting, tours in search of other tribes,
by late 1836 he had nearly completed his "Indian Gallery": 422 paintings and thousands of sketches made among at least forty-eight tribes.

Starting with his first trip to St. Louis in 1830, the financial costs
of his seven-year venture were substantial. In turning to the public,
Catlin hoped at once to recoup his losses and to gain a permanent
museum for his collection. It was time to inspire others. Catlin opened
the first major exhibit of his Indian Gallery in New York City in 1837,
successfully moving it later to Washington, Philadelphia, and Boston.[16] Hundreds came to see the enormous collection of costumes and
artifacts, as well as paintings, and to purchase Catlin's thirty-six-page
catalogue. For the first time, easterners were treated to a large western
exhibit—a precursor of the shows that Buffalo Bill Cody would make
commercially popular half a century later. If Catlin's innate show-
manship helped to draw enthusiastic crowds, however, his poor business sense ensured that costs soon exceeded admission fees. Financial
pressures finally became · intolerable after the federal government
narrowly refused to purchase his collection in 1839.

15 Cited in Maria R. Audubon, *Audubon and His Journals*, 2 vols. (New York:
Charles Scribner's Sons, 1897), 1:497, 2:10-11. See also Alice Ford, *John James Audubon* (Norman: University of Oklahoma Press, 1964), p. 398; Robert Buchanan, *Life
and Adventures of Audubon the Naturalist* (1868; rpt. New York: E. P. Dutton and
Co., 1913). p. 321.
16 See DeVoto, *Across the Wide Missouri*, p. 391; Roehm, ed., *Catlin Family Letters*, pp. 119-22.

10. George Catlin, *The Cutting Scene, Mandan O-kee-pa Ceremony*, 1832. Oil on canvas. The Harmsen Collection, Denver.

Hoping to win a reputation abroad that would convince a future Congress to reverse this decision, Catlin sailed for Liverpool that fall with eight tons of freight, including paintings, Indian artifacts, and two live grizzly bears.[17] As Bernard DeVoto describes Catlin's European tour: "There were more than six hundred paintings and Catlin went on adding to them through the years. (He also made many copies, some of which hang in English town and country houses today.) A visitor who remained unsatiated after looking at six hundred canvases could go on to two dozen dummies dressed in genuine Indian costumes and a sizable museum of medicine bundles, shields, amulets, baskets, robes, travois, moccasins, weapons, pipes, and other artifacts. There were learned, dramatic lectures by the proprietor and *tableaux vivants* posed by local supernumeraries in Indian dress."[18] His reception in London and Paris augured well. Royalty feted him; artists as

[17] DeVoto, *Across the Wide Missouri*, pp. 391-92.
[18] Ibid.

diverse as Charles Dickens, Charles Baudelaire, Eugène Delacroix, and George Sand showered accolades upon him.

At this peak of interest, Catlin decided to bring out his *Letters and Notes*, hoping thereby to encourage a solid financial commitment from his countrymen. Many, it might go without saying, were simply impressed by Catlin's exotic subjects; they thronged to his shows or purchased his book because it was the fashionable thing to do.[19] But others genuinely appreciated Catlin's achievement in terms he himself might have formulated. "Had he been like other mortals," one anonymous American reviewer observed, "he would probably have lived a quiet and decent citizen of his native State; and the tribes of the more remote western territories might perhaps for ever have remained unvisited by any one capable of thus portraying to the world their habits and features. It is a well known fact that the interesting tribe of Mandans . . . exist now only on his canvass and in his pages. Since the visit of Mr. Catlin they have been swept by disease from the face of the earth, and little else than a few ruined huts now remains to tell that a people once existed there. So may it perhaps be with many others of the nations among whom he dwelt. . . ."[20] Americans and Europeans alike realized that Catlin's work justified his fame. American artists living in Paris, in the late 1840s, including John Vanderlyn, William Morris Hunt, John Frederick Kensett, and William B. Chambers, supported his efforts and urgently petitioned Congress to purchase the collection "as a nucleus for a national museum, where American artists may freely study that bold race who once held possession of our country, and who are so fast disappearing before the tide of civilization."[21] Senators Henry Clay and William Henry Seward attempted to rally fellow legislators to Catlin's cause. Daniel Webster's Senate plea that "this race is going into forgetfulness" and that America "ought to possess this collection"[22] nearly clinched the vote, despite Catlin's steep offering price. By a narrow margin of four votes, however, Congress again decided against the purchase. Three years later, in 1852, that decision was confirmed when a similar bill was tabled, this time by a single vote.

19 Hugh Honour, *The New Golden Land: European Images of America from the Discoveries to the Present Time* (New York: Pantheon Books, 1975), pp. 236-37; Roehm, ed., *Catlin Family Letters*, pp. 170, 176, 305-7, 309-12.

20 Review of "Catlin's North American Indians," *United States Magazine, and Democratic Review*, new ser., 11 (July 1842), 45.

21 Donaldson, *Catlin Indian Gallery*, p. 747.

22 Ibid., p. 770. See also Lloyd Haberly, *Pursuit of the Horizon: A Life of George Catlin, Painter and Recorder of the American Indian* (New York: Macmillan Co., 1948), pp. 110, 114; Catlin, *Letters and Notes*, ed. Mooney, pp. 66-67; Flexner, *That Wilder Image*, p. 80.

Catlin, now heavily overextended, suffered a short incarceration in Britain's debtors' prison before a sympathetic creditor, a rich American boilermaker, bought the collection and shipped it to his Philadelphia warehouse. (Little could the disappointed Catlin guess that his paintings would thereby be saved from the devastating Smithsonian Institution fire of 1865.) At fifty-six he felt beaten: his family had been destroyed through disease and debt; his life's work lay bundled in a warehouse; his health was ruined.[23]

Nevertheless, Catlin abandoned neither his conception of a public gallery nor his commitment to record threatened tribes. In 1852 he left Europe for South America, once again to paint Indians in their native habitats. At the same time, he patiently recreated from sketches and memory much of his original collection. His style further evolved, as did the mood he expressed through his art. In uncolored pencil sketches he presented South American Indians as accurately as ever. Yet they "stare with level-fronting eyes at some tragic vision that is to each his own but which they all share," one art historian has noted. "These exotic-faced dreams composed separately together personify a stoic nobility that transcends the world's troubles. But Catlin's renditions of ceremonies and hunts, where the world has interposed, where people are conscious of each other and acting in concert, express a bitterness, a revulsion, and all-embracing cruelty he had never felt when in actuality among the tribes."[24] Reflecting in part his own feelings, these later studies also evince the diminished prospects available to American tribes in the second half of the nineteenth century.

Though embittered, Catlin never lost his sense of mission. Only a few years before he died in 1872, he wrote a long manuscript to accompany his new collection, prefaced by a statement of purpose that differs hardly at all from the one he had written on the *Yellowstone* more than thirty-five years earlier:

> Nations of people yet unborn, and even many of those of the present generation, will look through the pages of this work with feelings of surprise and profound regret that a numerous Race of human beings, with the looks and customs herein described, existing over most parts of the American Continent in the middle of the nineteenth century, should have passed away before the destructive wave of civilization, leaving few, if any, monuments behind them. . . .
>
> Deeply impressed with the irresistible fate awaiting these poor people . . . I conceived the plan of visiting their various countries

<hr/>

[23] Catlin, *Letters and Notes*, 1:xii.   [24] Flexner, *That Wilder Image*, p. 81.

with my canvass and brushes, and note book, gathering and rescuing from oblivion everything I could of their looks and customs,
for the instruction of future ages. . . . I resolved, if my life should
be spared, to make a pictorial history of those vanishing Races.[25]

Catlin cherished an unassailable belief in the value of his labors.
Never reconciled to America's failure to purchase his original Indian
Gallery, he wondered even on his deathbed about its fate.[26] Seven
years later, in 1879, the owner made a gift of it to the nation.

To Americans then as now, Catlin's career epitomized intelligent
concern for the vanishing wilderness and particularly for the Indian.
Numerous countrymen shared his anxiety; others supported his efforts. Yet, if his intentions were rarely questioned, his actual skills
provoked doubts. Just as Herman Melville's descriptions of Polynesian
cannibals met with disbelief, so did Catlin's Mandans and their
"strange and peculiar" rituals.[27] Particularly damaging was the bitter
war of letters in which Henry Rowe Schoolcraft engaged him. The respected ethnologist arrogantly questioned every aspect of Catlin's
Mandan report well after the few other reliable witnesses to the
O-kee-pa ceremony had substantiated Catlin.

Bernard DeVoto well sums up Catlin's faults and achievements: "It
is true that he was an enthusiast and even a monomaniac, that he
misunderstood much of what he saw, as anyone in his place must have
done, that he held some wildly untenable theories, that he never lost
his Rousseauian prepossessions about savages in a state of nature,
that he made many mistakes, and even that he falsified or invented
some details. Nevertheless, he is in the main reliable and both his
books and paintings have been immensely important to American
ethnology ever since 1837."[28] Insofar as one may claim, as DeVoto
does, that American ethnology began with Catlin, it is because Catlin
for the most part succeeded in painting what he saw, rather than what

[25] Preface to Catlin, "The North Americans in the Middle of the Nineteenth Century: A Numerous and Noble Race of Human Beings fast passing to oblivion and
leaving no monuments of their own behind them," bound ms., Huntington Library,
San Marino.

[26] Roehm, ed., Catlin Family Letters, p. 411.

[27] Catlin, Letters and Notes, 1:55. See Donaldson, Catlin Indian Gallery, pp. 376-
83; Roehm, ed., Catlin Family Letters, pp. 344-45. John C. Ewers has best described
the reception and continuing importance of Catlin's descriptions in his introduction
to George Catlin, O-kee-pa: A Religious Ceremony and Other Customs of the Mandans, ed. John C. Ewers (New Haven: Yale University Press, 1967), pp. 1-33.

[28] DeVoto, Across the Wide Missouri, p. 392. See, for only one example of con-
temporary disbelief by knowledgeable observers among tribes Catlin had visited,
Edwin Thompson Denig, Five Indian Tribes of the Upper Missouri, ed. John C.
Ewers (Norman: University of Oklahoma Press, 1961), pp. xxx-xxxi.

11. George Catlin, *Bull Dance, Part of Mandan Okipa Ceremony,* ca. 1838. Oil on canvas. The National Collection of Fine Arts, Smithsonian Institution; gift of Mrs. Sarah Harrison.

he said he saw. For in his writings he sentimentalized Indians as noble savages, a conception differing little from the alleged childlike quality that Schoolcraft condemned. Catlin too believed that "the Indian's mind is a beautiful blank, on which anything might be written, if the right mode were taken to do it."[29] Neither man could appreciate the cultural integrity their very descriptions revealed.

In important ways, Catlin fell victim to his sense of mission. The same considerations impelling him to document individuals and tribal activities also define flaws in his work. He was obsessed by the fact that Indians were, as he noted, "on the wane," which explains his repeated urging "that the traveller who would see these people in their native simplicity and beauty, must needs be hastily on his way to the prairies and Rocky Mountains, or he will see them only as they

[29] Catlin, *Letters and Notes,* 2:245. See also Catlin, *Life Among the Indians* (London: Gall and Inglis, [187?]), pp. 18-20.

are now seen on the frontiers, as a basket of *dead game*,—harassed, chased, bleeding and dead."[30] In one sense, however, such adjurations exacted the consequence against which they warned. Inspired imitators would demoralize western tribes by their very enthusiasm, their eagerness to confirm and picture sacred rites. In another sense, Catlin's imperative haste suggests why ethnologists have sometimes found his portraits and genre scenes inadequately detailed. They compare poorly, for example, with those painted by his Swiss contemporary, Karl Bodmer. As established critics of the time observed, Catlin seemed an "intrepid traveler" but a "mediocre painter."[31]

Catlin cherished little affection for conventional artistic standards, having realized that the older methods were inadequate to the mammoth task he had set himself and to the unforgiving demands of time. The challenges posed by frontier conditions led him to employ shortcuts in field sketches—using pigments in their unmixed form, or painting in thin, quick-drying layers—that could be compensated for later in his studio. Probably his most trying problem resulted from Indians' common reluctance to having their portraits painted. Well into the twentieth century they warily resisted those who came to "steal" their likenesses, fearing the consequences of this unknown ritual: that they would never again sleep, since their painted eyes remained open; that profile portraits might destroy the unrendered side of their faces; or, even worse, that their souls would escape into the paintings. Though Catlin learned to persuade his models otherwise, assurances rarely stood warrant for long, and finishing a portrait expeditiously offered the sole guarantee of finishing one at all. Luckily, as one wag put it, Catlin had the fastest brush in the West.[32] He sometimes sketched half a dozen portraits in a single day, and during his 1832 canoe trip down the Missouri River, he completed one hundred oils. Of course, this meant that he sometimes sacrificed or simplified detail, compounding his problems of landscape perspective and figural proportions. Yet, with few exceptions, Catlin painted "with passionate accuracy."[33] The certificates of authenticity that he obtained from reliable officials are still attached to some paintings. More important, he gained a fresh realism that even the trained

30 Catlin, *Letters and Notes*, 1:10.

31 Honour, *The New Golden Land*, p. 237; Hassrick, *Catlin Book*, p. 29; Catlin, *Letters and Notes*, ed. Mooney, p. 81; Catlin, *Letters and Notes*, intro. by Halpin, 1:xiv; DeVoto, *Across the Wide Missouri*, p. 405; Flexner, *That Wilder Image*, pp. 75-76. For information on Bodmer, see Chapter Five, p. 127.

32 Cited by Hassrick, *Catlin Book*, p. 29.

33 Flexner, *That Wilder Image*, p. 72. See also pp. 73-74; Catlin, *Letters and Notes*, ed. Mooney, editor's introduction; DeVoto, *Across the Wide Missouri*, p. 394.

draftsman Bodmer failed to achieve. To say, as did one admirer, that "Bodmer was painting real paintings, Catlin real Indians,"[34] defines the special strength of Catlin's vision. Another critic has more revealingly characterized his Indians "as neither the bloodthirsty enemies nor the pathetic victims of the march of progress."[35] Catlin portrayed his subjects as individual human beings.

At the age of seventy-five, reflecting on his career, Catlin hoped that future generations would "find enough of historical interest excited by faithful resemblance to the physiognomy and customs of these people to compensate for what may be deficient in them as works of art."[36] Before the camera made a different kind of exact documentation possible, he completed paintings that can be trusted to present scenes as he saw them. Before westward expansion in the 1840s forever altered Plains Indian life, he captured nearly the final impression of those cultures as they had continued for generations. In words he repeated frequently, "I was luckily born in time to see these people in their native dignity, and beauty, and independence."[37]

Catlin was the first to teach his countrymen to observe their western landscape and to examine the people who lived there. The viewing public, which had contented itself with the sentimental "Lo, The Poor Indian" or the savage "Death of Jane McCrea," began to appreciate the inadequacies of such uninformed fantasies and to demand more from its artists.[38] Catlin covered more territory in the 1840s and depicted more different tribes in greater detail than did any other painter who followed.[39] But he was certainly not alone. Many of those who took their lead from him and went on to surpass him in the quality of their records will be discussed in Chapter Five. The achievements of those spurred to more exacting ethnographic efforts by his written descriptions of native behavior will be examined in Chapter Six. Yet few shared commitments to the range of interests that both these forms of preserved record exemplify.

For all Catlin's extraordinary popularity, his long moment in the sun ended rather abruptly. Nor was he ever to emerge from under the cloud of debt that ruined him in 1852. His concern for dwindling

[34] Quoted in Catlin, *Letters and Notes*, ed. Mooney, p. 81. See also DeVoto, *Across the Wide Missouri*, p. 395.

[35] Honour, *The New Golden Land*, p. 236.

[36] Catlin, *Letters and Notes*, ed. Mooney, p. 82. See also Flexner, *That Wilder Image*, pp. 74-75, 81-82.

[37] Cited in Donaldson, *Catlin Indian Gallery*, p. 745.

[38] Ellwood Parry, *The Image of the Indian and the Black Man in American Art, 1590-1900* (New York: George Braziller, 1974), p. 83.

[39] DeVoto, *Across the Wide Missouri*, p. 393.

tribes, despite the many individuals thus spurred to similar efforts, seemed excessive, even perverse, to others who thought him a "flaming enthusiast."[40] His strong claims and speculations, sometimes bordering on the ridiculous—for example, that the Mandans were related to migrating Welsh tribes and that all Indians displayed uniformly temperate, generous spirits[41]—seemed proof of a lack of perspective, placing even his firsthand reports under suspicion. By the time he published his theory of Indian health in 1860, he had long since fallen into obscurity.

A fierce irony to Catlin's career is that his hopes for his collection approached fulfillment shortly after he died. In 1879 the secretary of the Smithsonian Institution and a few others finally persuaded the boilermaker's generous widow to give the Indian Gallery—by then badly water damaged—to the nation.[42] Less than a decade later, a dedicated government employee, Thomas Donaldson, ferreted out as much information about Catlin as possible in compiling a thick government publication, *The George Catlin Indian Gallery in the United States Museum* (1887). The work is uncritical and sometimes inaccurate. Nonetheless, Donaldson felt that the sixty-odd years since Catlin saw his first Indian delegation had wrought changes that only confirmed his lifelong mission: "The plains are silent; neither structure nor monument tells their past glory. . . . The painter's art, the museum, and the art preservative alone tell the story."[43] Catlin himself stated the issue more exactly, and for once less rhetorically, when in 1868 he recalled the efforts that had shaped his unique career: "I have said that I was lucky enough to have been born at the right time to have seen these people (Indians) in their nature, dignity, and elegance; and thanks to Him in whose hands the destinies of all men are, that my life has been spared to visit most of the tribes in every latitude of the American continent, and my hands enabled to delineate their personal looks and their modes, to be seen and to be criticized after this people and myself shall have passed away."[44]

40 Ibid., p. 404.

41 Catlin, *Letters and Notes*, 1:8-10, 23, 61, 205-7, 2:277; Catlin, *Life Among the Indians*, pp. 18-19. Also see Donaldson, *Catlin Indian Gallery*, pp. 463-66.

42 Catlin, *Letters and Notes*, ed. Mooney, p. 79; Hassrick, *Catlin Book*, p. 33; McCracken, *Catlin and the Old Frontier*, pp. 207-8.

43 Donaldson, *Catlin Indian Gallery*, p. 742. See DeVoto, *Across the Wide Missouri*, p. 393, for a critique of this effort.

44 Cited by Donaldson, *Catlin Indian Gallery*, p. 745. Yet even at this time, Catlin worked to see his record permanently installed, as suggested by his 1872 proposal for a monument to the Indian to be erected in Central Park: a sheet-iron replica of

Catlin's fears for the vanishing Indian were hardly unique. But he attempted sooner, more completely, and more publicly than most to rescue an invaluable history. And with no predecessors of any influence, he produced a comprehensive image that continues to inform our understanding of the West.

---

a Crow wigwam, seventy-five feet high, inside of which was to be contained his paintings and artifacts. See *Frank Leslie's Illustrated Newspaper* (New York), March 2, 1872, pp. 385, 391, cited by Richard A. Bartlett, *The New Country: A Social History of the American Frontier, 1776-1890* (New York: Oxford University Press, 1974), p. 19.

CHAPTER FIVE

INDIANS AND
IMAGE CATCHERS

I began my work among them twenty-two years ago, and have seen many changes. Entire tribes have been destroyed by disease, and others have been scattered by encroaching civilization. The Indian, as an Indian, is rapidly disappearing. He is adopting the white man's ways and losing his tribal characteristics. He is gradually giving up his deeply significant nature-lore, his religions and his ceremonies, and it will not be long before his tribal communities, ancestral manners and customs will have passed from his life.

Realizing these conditions, I have devoted many years to the making of an ethnographic record of the Indians, photographing their life, manners and habitat, and thus preserving for future generations a picture-history which will show what these most interesting early Americans were like, before they were disturbed by the influences of the white man.

—*Frederick Monsen*
"Picturing Indians with the Camera"
(1910)

F EW MAJOR AMERICAN WRITERS in the first half of the nineteenth century seemed less interested in Indian tribes than Nathaniel Hawthorne. His literary career traces a series of moral and symbolic fictions; efforts at authentication led him more often to the seventeenth century than to the nineteenth, to New England than to the West. At the age of thirty-one, however, with his career still before him, Hawthorne recognized with some sadness a direction that his writing would not take: "It has often been a matter of regret to me, that I was shut out from the most peculiar field of American fiction, by an inability to see any romance, or poetry, or grandeur, or beauty in the Indian character, at least, till such traits were pointed out by others. I do abhor an Indian story. Yet no writer can be more secure of a permanent place in our literature, than the biographer of the Indian chiefs. His subject, as referring to tribes which have mostly vanished from the earth, gives him a right to be placed on a classic shelf, apart from the merits which will sustain him there."[1] This curious mix of sentiments reveals the pervasive grip that the idea of the Indian had on nineteenth-century American thought. Catlin, traveling among Plains Indians even as Hawthorne penned these words in his Salem study, was neither alone nor first in wanting to document tribes that would soon, according to Hawthorne, "have mostly vanished from the earth."

Portraits and biographies of various tribal dignitaries had spiced America's artistic and literary diet for centuries. Even Catlin's patron, Colonel William L. Stone, contributed to that tradition in the 1830s by writing commendable biographies of Joseph Brant and Red-Jacket.[2] Following prescribed convention, Stone presented his Indian chiefs as models of the unacculturated, not as exemplary products of alternative cultures. Their claim on white attention depended on the white virtues they displayed in red-face, traits that supposedly explained their tribal preeminence. Up to 1800, most white Americans conceived of Indians in Crèvecoeur's terms, as merely uncivilized, having neither cultural constraints nor intellectual capacities. Oblivious to sometimes radical tribal differences, they authored biographies and painted portraits that reveal far more of themselves than of their

[1] Nathaniel Hawthorne, "Our Evening Party Among the Mountains," in *Mosses from an Old Manse* (1835; rpt. Ohio State University Press, 1974), p. 428.

[2] William L. Stone, *Life of Joseph Brant—Thayendanegea, Including the Indian Wars of the American Revolution*, 2 vols. (New York: George Dearborn and Co., 1838), and *The Life and Times of Red-Jacket, or Sa-Go-Ye-Wat-Ha; Being the Sequel to the History of the Six Nations* (New York: Wiley and Putnam, 1841).

subjects. Predictably, early portraits of the savage seem bland and interchangeable;[3] biographies reflect distinctly European assumptions about individual motivation and historical causality. Colorful exaggerations and inaccuracies abound in descriptions of tribal life and accounts of historical events. Conventional assumptions about Indian "savagery" so thoroughly shaped artists' responses that objective representation was almost impossible.[4]

"In America," Perry Miller once claimed, "the artist has a calling above and beyond an accurate reporting of scenery: he must work fast . . . to strive to fix the fleeting moment of primitive grandeur."[5] Yet, although white men and red had lived together for nearly three centuries, the need to preserve an accurate record of the Indians' "primitive grandeur" was not widely felt until the early nineteenth century. Of course, Europeans and Americans from Columbus on had been intensely curious about native life. But the westward advance of settlement brought to the raw new federal city on the Potomac Indian delegations hoping to influence national policy toward their tribes. Now these compellingly real reminders of the exotic West jostled elbows with the men and women trying to establish an "American" culture.[6]

Coincidentally, older conventions of idealization in American painting gave way to a singular devotion to pictorial accuracy. As Barbara Novak has observed, art increasingly concentrated on "the stopped moment, the frozen continuum, the fixation of becoming to being."[7] The transcendentalists' delight in the ultimate significance of the immediate and particular constituted one aspect of this development. The Hudson River School paintings reflect another, as do those of local genre artists. This increasing attentiveness to painterly detail, requiring "greater accuracy, or objectivity, or truth to nature by allowing each subject to begin to speak for itself, instead of imposing

[3] For remarkable exceptions to this general rule, however, see William J. Buck, "Lappawinzo and Tishcohan, Chiefs of the Lenni Lenape," *Pennsylvania Magazine of History and Biography*, 7 (1883), 215-318; Luke Vincent Lockwood, "The St. Memin Indian Portraits," *New-York Historical Society Quarterly Bulletin*, 12 (April 1928), 3-26; Ellwood Parry, *The Image of the Indian and the Black Man in American Art, 1590-1900* (New York: George Braziller, 1974), pp. 24, 64-65.

[4] Parry, *Image of the Indian*, pp. 53-64; Roy Harvey Pearce, *Savagism and Civilization: A Study of the Indian and the American Mind*, rev. ed. (Baltimore: Johns Hopkins University Press, 1965).

[5] Perry Miller, "The Romantic Dilemma in American Nationalism and the Concept of Nationalism," *Harvard Theological Review*, 48 (October 1955), p. 240.

[6] Parry, *Image of the Indian*, pp. 68ff.

[7] Barbara Novak, *American Painting of the Nineteenth Century: Realism, Idealism, and the American Experience* (New York: Praeger, 1969), p. 121. See also Parry, *Image of the Indian*, p. 82.

artificial or extrinsic interpretations,"[8] grew from a variety of causes. At least one of the reasons, however, as we have already seen in the discussions of Thomas Cole and George Caleb Bingham, was a sense of their subjects' ephemerality, a recognition that Indian delegations were traveling east precisely to negotiate terms by which their present lives might be preserved.

Thus, both style and interest converged when artists for the first time recognized Indian cultures as at once fragile and irrevocably disappearing. In addition, the romantic movement swept much of western Europe into an excessive regard for the effects of time's passing. "The nostalgia and pity aroused by the dying race," one historian notes, "produced the best romantic sentiments and gave that sense of fleeting time beloved of romantic sensibilities."[9] Another has claimed that with "economic mastery of nature and the physical world" arises the urge to render it with artistic exactness.[10] Whatever its origins, a widely shared impulse developed among American painters and, later, photographers to fix the various images of the Indian. By the 1890s, when the extinction or acculturation of nearly every North American tribe had been effected, pictorial artists had recorded much of what had been. Self-consciously, they completed an ex-

[8] Parry, *Image of the Indians*, p. 82. See also Warner Berthoff, *The Example of Melville* (1962; rpt. New York: W. W. Norton, 1972), pp. 81-82.

[9] Robert F. Berkhofer Jr., *The White Man's Indian: Images of the American Indian from Columbus to the Present* (New York: Alfred A. Knopf, 1978), p. 88. See also A. Irving Hallowell, "The Backwash of the Frontier: The Impact of the Indian on American Culture," in Walker D. Wyman and Clifton B. Kroeber, eds., *The Frontier in Perspective* (Madison: University of Wisconsin Press, 1957), pp. 232-33. Brian William Dippie, in "The Vanishing American: Popular Attitudes and American Indian Policy in the Nineteenth Century" (Ph.D. diss., University of Texas, Austin, 1970), claims that "the Vanishing Indian" was mere tradition and did not reflect actual conditions. Yet he also admits, "In one way or another it colored all thought on the Indian throughout the nineteenth century" (v). See also ibid., pp. 1, 7, 27.

[10] Berthoff, *Example of Melville*, p. 64. See also Hallowell, "Backwash of the Frontier," p. 248; Richard Rudisill, *Mirror Image: The Influence of the Daguerreotype on American Society* (Albuquerque: University of New Mexico Press, 1971), pp. 9-28; Dorothy Harmsen, *Harmsen's Western Americana: A Collection of One Hundred Western Paintings with Biographical Profiles of the Artists* (Flagstaff: Northland Press, 1971), p. 2; Frank Weitenkampf, "Early Pictures of North American Indians: A Question of Ethnology," *Bulletin of the New York Public Library*, 53 (December 1949), 596-598; John C. Ewers, *Artists of the Old West* (Garden City, N.Y.: Doubleday and Co., 1965), pp. 7-8; Ewers, "Fact and Fiction in the Documentary Art of the American West," in John Francis McDermott, ed., *The Frontier Reexamined* (Urbana: University of Illinois Press, 1967), pp. 79ff.; Jonathan L. Fairbanks, introduction to *Frontier America: The Far West* (Boston: Museum of Fine Arts, 1975), pp. 15-16; James Thomas Flexner, *That Wilder Image: The Painting of America's Native School from Thomas Cole to Winslow Homer* (1962; rpt. New York: Dover Publications, 1970), p. 66.

tensive gallery of pencil sketches, watercolors, and oil paintings, daguerreotypes and photographs documenting the lives of native Americans in their cultural richness.

Even among people as committed as these, however, few found it possible to abandon stereotypes. From Catlin across the century to Edward Curtis, artists allowed earnest sympathy to blind them to the complexities of Indian cultures. Yet, as Catlin's work demonstrates, their reasonably objective illustrations mostly escape the distorting influence of their otherwise facile ideas. In aspiring to exact documentation, moreover, the very fact of close observation brought some to a more profound understanding of native life. Later in the century, this greater understanding encouraged a shift away from simple notions of cultural absolutism. Heroic portraits of characteristic types or of celebrated chieftains in the 1820s gradually gave way to more precise illustrations of otherwise unremarkable figures and of everyday domestic life.

By the late 1830s, as Hawthorne's regretful claim and the popularity of Catlin's exhibit suggest, many Americans accepted the value of preserving accounts and illustrations of ephemeral tribal life.[11] Even within the elite literary circle defined by Hawthorne and his friends, the scholarly, cosmopolitan Margaret Fuller came to appreciate these issues. Before making a trip to Chicago in the early 1840s, she "read all the books I could find about the new region," including Catlin's and Irving's, and in turn wrote perceptively of life in northern Illinois and Wisconsin.[12] Repeatedly, deploring the depredations whites had made on the wilderness, she empathized with the original occupants of the land: "I have no hope of liberalizing the missionary, of humanizing the sharks of trade, of infusing the conscientious drop into the flinty bosom of policy, of saving the Indian from immediate degradation and speedy death. . . . Yet ere they depart I wish there might be some masterly attempt to reproduce in art or literature what is proper to them. . . . We hope some other mind may be bent upon it, ere too late."[13] Her high regard for Catlin led her to hope that others would complete the record he had begun.

Fuller looked to more than individual effort, however. That the federal government should support such endeavors was an idea possibly suggested to her by Catlin's book. "We hope there will be a na-

[11] See, for example, Jessie Poesch, *Titian Ramsey Peale and His Journals of the Wilkes Expedition, 1799-1885* (Philadelphia: American Philosophical Society, 1961), p. 24.

[12] Margaret Fuller, *Summer on the Lakes* (1843), in *The Writings of Margaret Fuller*, ed. Mason Wade (New York: Viking, 1941), pp. 24-25.

[13] Ibid., p. 88.

tional institute containing all the remains of the Indians, all that has been preserved by official intercourse at Washington, Catlin's collection, and a picture-gallery as complete as can be made, with a collection of skulls from all parts of the country. To this should be joined the scanty library that exists on the subject."[14] Three years later, responding to a campaign begun long before Fuller's advocacy, Congress established this "national institute," the Smithsonian. Somewhat ironically, given the federal government's expansionist policies, Fuller's predecessors included government bureaucrats using federal funds first to achieve, then to popularize, a full record of American Indian life.

THOMAS McKENNEY'S INDIAN ARCHIVES

During the first third of the nineteenth century, the single most influential official concerned with the destinies of America's Indian tribes was Colonel Thomas L. McKenney (1785-1859). Serving under four presidents, from James Madison to Andrew Jackson, he persuaded the government to invite delegates from Indian tribes to Washington for treaty negotiations, and he acquired a reputation as a fierce champion of their human rights, first as Superintendent of the Indian Trade Bureau and then as chief of the Bureau of Indian Affairs. His sympathy for the native plight hardly altered immediate government policy, however. Jackson's administration, bent on permanently removing the Indian population out of the white man's way, had no place for McKenney and finally forced him from office.[15]

To be sure, McKenney like many other well-intentioned officials up to the present, wanted to save the native population by assimilating it into white American culture. But although he deliberately encouraged the dismantling of tribal cultures for what he took to be their own good, he valued their manifold accomplishments nonetheless. Of greater consequence than his pleas to the federal government on behalf of Indian rights was what he liked to call his "Archives," a

14 Ibid., p. 91.

15 For background material on McKenney, see Herman J. Viola, *Thomas L. McKenney, Architect of America's Early Indian Policy: 1816-1830* (Chicago: Swallow Press, 1974), esp. pp. 143-44, 185ff.; Thomas L. McKenney, *Memoirs, Official and Personal; With Sketches of Travels among the Northern and Southern Indians,* 2d ed., 2 vols. (New York: Paine and Burgess, 1846); Michael Rogin "Indian Extinction, American Regeneration," *Journal of Ethnic Studies,* 2 (Spring 1974), 96-97; James D. Horan, *The McKenney-Hall Portrait Gallery of American Indians* (New York: Crown, 1972), pp. 21-111; Bernard W. Sheehan, *Seeds of Extinction: Jeffersonian Philanthropy and the American Indian* (New York: W. W. Norton, 1973), pp. 121ff.

collection of items "relating to our aborigines preserved there for the inspection of the curious and for the information of future generations and long after the Indians will have been no more."[16] While on far-ranging travels along the western and southern frontiers, he gathered countless artifacts, as well as a series of anecdotes, narratives, and myths. At an early stage, McKenney realized the unique power of his position as Superintendent of the Indian Trade Bureau, and by 1817 he was sending general requests to anyone who might be of help. Missionaries, Indian agents, frontiersmen, factors, and government representatives soon forwarded journals, tribal vocabularies, descriptions of Indian medicinal lore, and much other information. "Apparently it became known on the frontier," one scholar has observed, "that McKenney was collecting anything to do with Indian culture; there was always a letter from an old frontiersman offering a 'manuscript' or a 'journal' of Indian captivity or a missionary with 'a scholarly work on the tribes.' "[17] In McKenney's words, he set this project in motion "with the view of preserving in the archives of the Government whatever of the aboriginal man can be rescued from the destruction which awaits his race."[18]

McKenney was already dreaming of an Indian archive when he took office in 1816. The idea of a portrait gallery occurred to him in the winter of 1821-1822, when a large delegation of midwestern natives arrived in Washington. Caught up in the town's enthusiasm, he commissioned from the reputable portraitist Charles Bird King twenty-five paintings of chiefs and warriors in that delegation. King, though he continued to paint Indian visitors in his Washington studio for twenty more years, never shared the younger Catlin's extraordinary excitement for this work. McKenney, however, came much closer to that feeling and worked indefatigably to persuade his immediate superiors of the value of such records. John C. Calhoun, Secretary of War at the time, was already convinced that native tribes

16 Cited in Horan, *McKenney-Hall Portrait Gallery*, p. 23; see also p. 51.
17 Ibid., p. 62.
18 Cited in ibid., p. 61. Herman J. Viola, in *Thomas L. McKenney*, p. 244, quotes from the circular that McKenney sent to all superintendents, agents, and missionaries on August 22, 1825: " 'It is for us of the present generation, if possible, to put it in the power of history to say something more of these wonderful people, than that "they once lived." ' Although all Indian languages were important to the study, McKenney asked that particular attention be given to 'any such isolated being known to you as the "last man" of his Tribe—to get from him the words called for. Such a man may be looked upon as the connecting link between time and eternity, as to all that regards his people; and which, if it be lost, all that relates to his Tribe is gone forever! When a preservation of it might lead to the most enlightening and gratifying results.' "

were "about to become extinct,"[19] and in 1824 he formalized and extended King's commission. The unflagging McKenney then encouraged Calhoun to employ another painter as well. From that point on, King made portraits of chiefs visiting the nation's capital, while the self-taught artist James Otto Lewis worked out of St. Louis, painting treaty negotiations on the spot.[20]

Calhoun's successor as Secretary of War, James Barbour, shared his predecessor's regretful conviction and gladly extended the official arrangements.[21] However, a belt-tightening Congress compelled McKenney to account for nearly every penny expended by his office. In an 1828 letter to the public, the bureau chief defended his policy in familiar terms: he and his colleagues were preserving a record of an aspect of American life that was too rapidly disappearing.[22] His motives failed to move Indian-despising congressmen, who charged the beleaguered chief with having wasted $3,190, as one sneered, "for the pictures of those wretches."[23] Following McKenney's dismissal in 1830, such expenditures ceased.

By the spring of 1832, as George Catlin set out on his seven-year research mission, McKenney had already pressed well ahead on an elephant folio of color lithographs of Indian portraits. Judge James Hall, a popular western novelist and man of letters, had agreed to write an accompanying text for McKenney's materials. Though a financially ruinous project, the three-volume *History of the Indian Tribes of North America* (1836-1844) proved far more fortunate than Hall could have guessed or McKenney would ever know: the devastating 1865 fire in the Smithsonian Institution destroyed McKenney's entire archives, with the exception of only thirty of the hundreds of original portraits by King and Lewis.[24]

Of the four men involved in this project, Judge Hall seems the least likely to have concerned himself with Indians. Nevertheless, his narrow race prejudice did not prevent him from coming to recognize

---

[19] Cited in Flexner, *That Wilder Image*, p. 78.

[20] See Herman J. Viola, *The Indian Legacy of Charles Bird King* (Washington: Smithsonian Institution Press, 1976), for discussion of King's career.

[21] See Thomas L. McKenney and James Hall, *The Indian Tribes of North America, with Biographical Sketches and Anecdotes of the Principal Chiefs* (1836-44), new ed. Frederick Webb Hodge, 3 vols. (Edinburgh: John Grant, 1933-34), 1:xxxiii.

[22] Ibid., 1:xxxiv. See also Flexner, *That Wilder Image*, p. 78.

[23] Horan, *McKenney-Hall Portrait Gallery*, p. 91; Viola, *Thomas L. McKenney*, pp. 248-50.

[24] See Bernard DeVoto, *Across the Wide Missouri* (Boston: Houghton Mifflin Co., 1947), p. 399.

12. Charles Bird King, *No-Way-Ke-Sug-Ga, Oto Tribe*, 1837. Lithograph colored with watercolor. Author's collection.

the need for a comprehensive record.[25] Similar motives seem to have compelled the two painters. Certainly Lewis felt this way, as he made clear in the introduction to his *North American Aboriginal Port-Folio* (1835-1836).[26] Although King left no written record of his reasons for undertaking the 143 portraits he completed in the course of twenty years, a great deal is suggested by his willingness to paint nearly thirty portraits of native dignitaries—some without remuneration—during the years following McKenney's dismissal.[27]

Aside from its quality and exhaustiveness, McKenney's project continues to deserve praise, along with Catlin's, as one of the few private attempts to publish western scenes. Lewis and King completed the first paintings we have of the Plains Indians, and the *History of the Indian Tribes* remains "a monument of American culture, solely because of the portraits."[28] More to the point, the four men wanted to ensure a pictorial record of vanishing native life. McKenney in particular committed himself no less energetically than Catlin and over a similarly long career, and like Catlin too, he saw that extraordinary commitment completely drain his funds. An 1830 guide to Washington best describes the monument to his pennilessness. Directing visitors to the "Indian Archives" on the second floor of the War Department building, it concludes: "But for this gallery, our posterity would ask in vain—'what sort of a looking being was the red man of this country?' In vain would the inquirers be told to *read* descriptions of him—these never could satisfy. He must be *seen* to be known. Here then is a gift to posterity."[29]

SURVEY PAINTERS AND THE EASTMANS IN THE 1840S

Prior to the 1850s, the prohibitive expense of lithographed or steel-engraved prints meant that publishers only rarely considered the venture; crude wood-block sketches served well enough. The federal government alone could consistently afford to send artists west and to illustrate subsequent reports with fine-lined prints.[30] The character-

[25] James Hall, *Sketches of History, Life, and Manners in the West*, 2 vols. (Philadelphia: Harrison Hall, 1835), p. 27.

[26] James Otto Lewis, *The North American Aboriginal Port-Folio* (1835-36; rpt. New York: J. P. Callender, 1838), p. 2. See also DeVoto, *Across the Wide Missouri*, pp. 399-400, for background information.

[27] Viola, *Charles Bird King*, p. 88.

[28] DeVoto, *Across the Wide Missouri*, p. 399.

[29] Cited in Viola, *Thomas L. McKenney*, p. 231. For another tribute, see Minnie Myrtle, *The Iroquois; or, The Bright Side of Indian Character* (New York: D. Appleton and Co., 1855), pp. 14-15.

[30] DeVoto, *Across the Wide Missouri*, p. 398.

istic art of the West before mid-century, then, resulted not from costly individual efforts but from railroad surveys and army exploratory expeditions.

Men like Samuel Seymour, Titian Ramsey Peale, and Samuel Carvalho, Gustavus Sohon, George Gibbs, and Edward and Richard Kern accompanied the various government expeditions of the second quarter of the century, giving Americans their earliest accurate images of the newly explored West and its inhabitants.[31] Characteristically, they left few written accounts; many surely sought their positions in hopes of excitement and exotic scenes and the promise of security offered by regular salary and relatively comfortable travel. Yet how can one account for the frequent attempts by these artists and draftsmen to achieve a far more exhaustive illustration of tribal life than required? The accounts left by a handful of survey artists from the 1840s and 1850s, including those of Balduin Möllhausen, Carl Wimar, Albert Bierstadt, and especially John Mix Stanley, reveal their self-conscious urge to complete such illustrations before whites had irrevocably altered native life.[32] Far from applying their skills indiscriminately,

[31] John Francis McDermott, "Samuel Seymour: Pioneer Artist of the Plains and the Rockies," in *Annual Report of the Board of Regents of the Smithsonian Institution, 1950* (Washington: G.P.O., 1951), pp. 498-501; Poesch, *Titan Ramsey Peale*, esp. pp. 22-24; Joan Sturhahn, *Carvalho: Artist—Photographer—Adventurer —Patriot: Portrait of a Forgotten American* (Merrick, N.Y.: Richwood Publishing Co., 1976), esp. pp. 70, 85-88, 105-6, 115; John C. Ewers, "Gustavus Sohon's Portraits of Flathead and Pend D'Oreille Indians, 1854," *Smithsonian Miscellaneous Collections*, 110 (Washington: G.P.O., 1948), 5-6; George Gibbs, *Indian Tribes of Washington Territory: Pacific Northwest Letters of George Gibbs* (1854; rpt. Fairfield, Wash.: Ye Galleon Press, 1967); David I. Bushnell Jr., "Drawings by George Gibbs in the Far Northwest, 1849-1851," *Smithsonian Miscellaneous Collections*, 97 (Washington: G.P.O., 1938), 1-28; Lt. James H. Simpson, *Journal of a Military Reconnaissance from Santa Fé, New Mexico to the Navajo Country* (Philadelphia: Lippincott, Grambo and Co., 1852); Robert V. Hine, *Edward Kern and American Expansion* (New Haven: Yale University Press, 1962); *The Published Pictures, Portraits and Maps Collectively Depicting the Indians, Scenery and Topography of the Far West, Drawn by Edward Kern and Richard Kern, 1846-1851*, Fort Sutter Papers, vol. 39, Huntington Library, San Marino; Ewers, "Fact and Fiction," pp. 79-89; H. Chadwick Hunter, "The American Indian in Painting," *Art and Archaeology*, 8 (April 1919), 80-96; Fairbanks, introduction to *Frontier America*, pp. 15-23; William H. Truettner, "Natural History and the Natural Man: Art and Science in the West," in *Frontier America*, pp. 40-42.

[32] Balduin Möllhausen, *Diary of a Journey from the Mississippi to the Coasts of the Pacific*, trans. Mrs. Percy Sinnett, 2 vols. (London: Longman, Brown, Green, Longmans, and Roberts, 1858), esp. 1:xii-xiii; Preston Albert Barba, *Balduin Möllhausen: The German Cooper* (Philadelphia: University of Pennsylvania Press, 1914), pp. 46-52, 135-36; Perry T. Rathbone, *Charles Wimar, 1828-1862: Painter of the Indian Frontier* (St. Louis: City Art Museum, 1946), pp. 5, 15-17; William Romaine Hodges, *Carl Wimar: A Biography* (Galveston: Charles Reymershoffer, 1908), esp. epigraph; Gordon Hendricks, *Albert Bierstadt: Painter of the American West* (New York:

these men pursued positions with western surveys expressly to paint Indian tribes as they still remained.[33]

From the 1820s on, the army's developing system of forts in Indian country provided military personnel a unique opportunity to fill sketchbooks with illustrations of Indian life. Lieutenant Seth Eastman (1809-1875), a West Point graduate trained in art, was first assigned to Fort Snelling, Minnesota, in the spring of 1830. Almost immediately, he conceived the idea of producing an Indian gallery, and on his own time he started drawing nearby tribes.[34] His project was interrupted early in 1833 for tours of duty at West Point and in Florida. Only in 1841 was he able to rejoin the regiment at Fort Snelling. During the next seven years he learned a number of Dakota languages fluently and devoted his free hours to unobtrusively sketching Chippewa and Sioux domestic scenes and ceremonies. So careful a student could hardly fail to notice the new patterns altering tribal life. For this reason, perhaps, his sketching was "not a mere occupation"; according to his wife, "it became a passion with him."[35]

By 1846 Eastman had completed more than four hundred oils and watercolors. A visitor to the fort that summer who wandered into Eastman's crowded little studio, described his amazement at the stunning canvases "comprising every variety of scenes, from the grand Medicine Dance to the singular and affecting Indian Grave. When

Harry N. Abrams, 1974), pp. 63, 69-70, 94; Hendricks, "The First Three Western Journeys of Albert Bierstadt," *Art Bulletin*, 46 (September 1964), 337-39; John Mix Stanley, "Portraits of North American Indians with Sketches of Scenery, Etc.," *Smithsonian Miscellaneous Collections*, 2 (1862), 1-76; Nellie B. Pipes, "John Mix Stanley, Indian Painter," *Oregon Historical Quarterly*, 33 (September 1932), 253, 256; W. Vernon Kinietz, *John Mix Stanley and His Indian Paintings* (Ann Arbor: University of Michigan Press, 1942); Robert Taft, *Artists and Illustrators of the Old West 1850-1900* (New York: Charles Scribner's Sons, 1953), pp. 27, 35, 258-59, 8, 18.

33 John Mix Stanley, whose career included the most extensive experiences of any major western artist, joined a number of expeditions in the 1840s for just this reason. In 1852 he loaned his marvelous collection to the Smithsonian Institution, declaring in his preface to the catalogue of 152 paintings: "Even these brief sketches, it is hoped, will not fail to interest those who look at their portraits, and excite some desire that the memory, at least, of these tribes may not become extinct" ("Portraits of North American Indians," preface). Unfortunately, his paintings were lost in the great Smithsonian fire, and he left no other testament to his motives. See also DeVoto, *Across the Wide Missouri*, pp. 398-99, 450-51; Harold McCracken, *Portrait of the Old West, With a Biographical Check List of Western Artists* (New York: McGraw-Hill, 1952), pp. 97-98; Larry Curry, *The American West: Painters from Catlin to Russell* (New York: Viking, 1972), p. 23.

34 John Francis McDermott, *Seth Eastman: Pictorial Historian of the Indian* (Norman: University of Oklahoma Press, 1961), p. 3.

35 Mary Eastman to Benjamin Pringle, March 14, 1856, cited in McDermott, *Seth Eastman*, p. 30. See also ibid., pp. 4-5, 56-57, 92, 91-92, 102-110; David I. Bushnell Jr., "Seth Eastman: The Master Painter of the North American Indian," *Smithsonian Miscellaneous Collections*, 87 (April 11, 1932).

13. Seth Eastman, *Indians Playing Draught*, 1848. Oil on canvas. Private collection. Photograph courtesy of M. Knoedler & Co., Inc., New York.

the extent and character of this Indian Gallery are considered, it must be acknowledged the most valuable in the country, not even excepting that of George Catlin."[36] Eastman had steadily refused to part with any paintings, even rejecting handsome professional offers

[36] Charles Lanman, *A Summer in the Wilderness*, p. 59, cited in John Francis McDermott, *Seth Eastman's Mississippi: A Lost Portfolio Recovered* (Urbana: University of Illinois Press, 1973), p. 6.

in order to continue among the tribes he knew so well.[37] In the three years after 1848, however, he sold twenty-odd paintings to the Western Art Union in Cincinnati and the American Art Union in New York, where they were immediately exhibited—striking evidence of his almost instant popularity.

During this same period, Congress authorized the Office of Indian Affairs to publish an exhaustive volume on American Indian tribes. Legislative sympathies had altered dramatically in the dozen years since McKenney's project had been terminated. Henry Rowe Schoolcraft, considered the most distinguished ethnologist in America, agreed to collect material and write the text. George Catlin, the most celebrated among contemporary painters of the Indian, haughtily refused to supply illustrations to a government that had refused to purchase his collection. On the other hand, Schoolcraft's second choice actively solicited the position. In 1849 Eastman was transferred to Washington, where for the next six years he prepared three hundred plates for Schoolcraft's celebrated *Indian Tribes of the United States* (1851-1857).[38]

Eastman's achievement warrants consideration for a number of reasons. As a trained watercolorist, he anticipated by more than a quarter century the effects that other American artists would achieve in landscape technique. As a documentarian, his careful studies of Indian artifacts, paintings, and costumes attest to an extraordinary ethnological knowledge. A journalist once remarked of him that he knew the Sioux so well he could "read the private history of a chief or brave by the ornaments which decorate his person."[39] Although this kind of knowledge may have differed only in degree from that of many another sensitive army officer in the West, Eastman's ability to preserve this knowledge in paint and in the descriptive notes he attached to each finished canvas sets him and his achievement apart from all others.

No less committed to preserving a record of Plains Indian life, and more explicit in her reasons for doing so, was Eastman's wife, the author Mary Eastman (1818-1880). The pattern of their joint careers suggests that she spoke for him as well. Although she achieved her greatest commercial success in 1852 with *Aunt Phillis' Cabin*, a rejoinder to Harriet Beecher Stowe,[40] she had earlier devoted years of

[37] Ibid., pp. 6ff.   [38] McDermott, *Seth Eastman*, pp. 63-78.

[39] Cited in David Lavender, *The American Heritage History of the Great West*, ed. Alvin M. Josephy Jr. (New York: American Heritage, 1965), p. 150. See also McDermott, *Seth Eastman*, pp. 90-91; Rudisill, *Mirror Image*, p. 96.

[40] McDermott, *Seth Eastman*, p. 93. See also Herbert Ross Brown, *The Sentimental Novel in America, 1789-1860* (Chapel Hill: Duke University Press, 1940), pp. 260-67.

energy to recording northern Sioux culture. Already aware by the 1840s of the parlous condition of tribes near Fort Snelling, she acquired a working knowledge of their languages as an entrance into their lives. The texts she wrote to accompany her husband's plates in *The Romance of Indian Life* (1853) and *The American Aboriginal Portfolio* (1853) stress both the red man's imminent disappearance and the value of the "faithfully depicted" record that she and her husband had compiled.[41] In their first collaboration, *Dahcotah; or, Life and Legends of the Sioux Around Fort Snelling* (1849), she specified more explicitly the reasons for their commitments:

> It will still be my endeavor to depict all the customs, feasts and ceremonies of the Sioux, before it be too late. The account of them may be interesting, when the people who so long believed in them will be no more. . . . They are receding rapidly, and with feeble resistance, before the giant strides of civilization. The hunting grounds of a few savages will soon become the haunts of densely peopled, civilized settlements. We should be better reconciled to this manifest destiny of the aborigines, if the inroads of civilization were worthy of it.[42]

This short preface intimates the pattern of the study, to be developed in the course of the following chapters: the transition from early, rushed attempts to depict and understand a disappearing native culture to somber questioning of the supplanting white culture. Of course, for all their manifest concern to record native life, the Eastmans never seriously doubted the superiority of white culture or even shed their conventional, sentimental assumptions about the Sioux they so sympathetically fixed in colors and words. Mary Eastman's final clause above barely suggests a troubling possibility.

INDEPENDENT PAINTERS IN THE 1850S

Although the federal government was one of the few reliable employers of artists in the West before the Civil War, hiring men like Eastman for its own purposes and then allowing them to fulfill personal missions, financial considerations did not altogether prevent private individuals from pursuing similar projects. Among these, a number of Europeans, with perhaps a greater sense of the exotic or

[41] Mary H. Eastman, *The American Aboriginal Portfolio* (Philadelphia: Lippincott, Grambo and Co., [1853]), p. v, and *The Romance of Indian Life* (Philadelphia: Lippincott, Grambo and Co., 1853), p. xi.

[42] Mary H. Eastman, *Dahcotah; or, Life and Legends of the Sioux Around Fort Snelling* (Minneapolis: Ross and Haines, 1962), p. xvi.

a more wistful yearning, came to the North American continent expressly to document a threatened wilderness and its inhabitants.

In the case of the Prussian Prince Maximilian zu Wied, who brought the talented young Swiss artist Karl Bodmer to accompany his 1833 ethnological tour of the upper Missouri territory, financial considerations were even more obviously irrelevant. Maximilian's wealth bought a priceless record. Painting far fewer tribes than had Catlin the summer before, Bodmer achieved far more detailed portraits. Where those paintings duplicate Catlin's subjects, the advantages of Bodmer's training as a draftsman and, more important, his leisurely pace are obvious. Anthropologists and art critics consider his eighty-one paintings among the finest completed in the antebellum period. Bodmer himself left nothing in words to indicate his intentions or responses, and he apparently never looked back on that part of his career from his subsequent success in France. On the other hand, scholars have long acknowledged the surpassing historical significance of Maximilian's *Travels in the Interior of North America* (1839), in which the prince claims motives similar to those of Catlin, McKenney, and the Eastmans.[43]

Another adventurous aristocrat, Sir William Drummond Stewart, visited the Rockies half a dozen times beginning in 1833, and he commissioned the young American artist Alfred Jacob Miller to accompany his 1837 tour of the West. In *Altowan* (1846), Stewart's later fictionalized record, he too expressed appreciation for the threat to landscape and native inhabitants.[44]

Important as their records are, these European aristocrats represent only a small proportion of the committed individuals who sought out the experiences of the West. Impecunious artists drawn to wilderness scenes by imagined commissions, tourists with sketch pads in hand, missionaries with a bent for illustration as well as writing—all attempted "artistic delineations," as one observed, that might "preserve from obliteration the likenesses, habits and customs of some at least, of the unfortunate race of red men."[45] If the names Felix O. C.

[43] Maximilian zu Wied, *Travels in the Interior of North America* (1843), reprinted as vols. 22-24 of Reubon Gold Thwaites, ed., *Early Western Travels 1748-1846* (Cleveland: Arthur H. Clark Co., 1906), pp. 26-28, 70-71. See also Maximilian zu Wied, *People of the First Man: Life among the Plains Indians in Their Final Days of Glory*, ed. Davis Thomas and Karin Ronnefeldt (New York: E. P. Dutton, 1976), pp. 6-13, 50, 120; DeVoto, *Across the Wide Missouri*, p. 402.

[44] Stewart, *Altowan; or, Incidents of Life and Adventure in the Rocky Mountains by an Amateur Traveler*, ed. J. Watson Webb, 2 vols. (New York: Harper and Brothers, 1846), pp. iii, vi.

[45] Winter, *The Journals and Indian Paintings of George Winter, 1837-1839* (Indianapolis: Indian Historical Society, 1948), p. 152.

Darley, George Winter, Rudolph Friedrich Kurz, Nicolas Point, and Peter Rindisbacher elicit no recognition today, it is not because these men felt less apprehensive or committed themselves less wholeheartedly than Catlin or McKenney.[46] Rather, their anonymity reflects their lesser accomplishment. That these individuals also undertook severe privations without government aid or private financing only confirms the extent of the mid-nineteenth-century movement to paint a record of Indian life.

Evidence further suggests that Catlin's self-publicizing in the 1840s encouraged similar careers on the part of other painters, including Charles Deas, Frank Blackwell Mayer, and John Mix Stanley.[47] Among them, the Canadian Paul Kane (1810-1871) most self-consciously patterned his own ambitions on Catlin's. As an art student in Europe, he was befriended by the older painter, who had just left New York City to exhibit his collection abroad. Catlin's influence, plus Kane's reading of books that called attention to the passing wilderness, confirmed the student in his new-found mission.[48] In 1845 he returned to Toronto, impelled by the need to "see the aborigines of this country in their original state."[49] Luckily, Kane found a sympathetic patron who commissioned from him one hundred Indian

[46] Felix O. C. Darley, *Scenes in Indian Life*, 4 nos. (Philadelphia: J. R. Colon, April-July 1843); Parry, *Image of the Indian*, pp. 77-79; Winter, *Journals and Indian Paintings*, pp. 96, 98, 105-8, 111, 119-20; *Journal of Rudolph Friedrich Kurz: An Account of His Experiences among Fur Traders and American Indians on the Mississippi and the Upper Missouri Rivers During the Years 1846 to 1852*, trans. Myrtis Jarrell, ed. J.N.B. Hewitt, Smithsonian Institution, Bureau of American Ethnology, Bulletin 115 (Washington: G.P.O., 1937), pp. 2, 129; *Wilderness Kingdom—Indian Life in the Rocky Mountains: 1840-1847. The Journals and Paintings of Nicolas Point, S.J.*, trans. Joseph P. Donnelly, S.J. (New York: Holt, Rinehart and Winston, 1967); Pierre Jean de Smet, S.J., *Oregon Missions and Travels Over the Rocky Mountains, in 1845-46* (1847), illus. by Nicholas Point, S.J., reprinted as vol. 29 of Thwaites, ed., *Early Western Travels* p. 111; Alvin M. Josephy Jr., *The Artist Was a Young Man: The Life Story of Peter Rindisbacher* (Fort Worth: Amon Carter Museum, 1970); DeVoto, *Across the Wide Missouri*, pp. 393-94; McCracken, *Portrait of the Old West*; Hugh Honour, *The New Golden Land: European Images of America from the Discoveries to the Present Time* (New York: Pantheon Books, 1975), p. 238; Ewers, *Artists of the Old West*. See also Gibbs, *Indian Tribes of Washington Territory*; Bushnell, "Drawings by George Gibbs."

[47] Parry, *Image of the Indian*, pp. 77-79; McCracken, *Portrait of the Old West*, pp. 97-98; Frank Blackwell Mayer, *With Pen and Pencil on the Frontier in 1851: The Diary and Sketches of Frank Blackwell Mayer*, ed. Bertha L. Heilbron (St. Paul: Minnesota Historical Society, 1932), pp. 2-6, 14-15.

[48] For details of Kane's career, see *Paul Kane's Frontier*, ed. J. Russell Harper (Austin: University of Texas Press, 1971), pt. 1; Albert H. Robson, *Paul Kane* (Toronto: Ryerson Press, 1938), pp. 4-14.

[49] Kane, *Wanderings of an Artist among the Indians of North America from Canada to Vancouver's Island and Oregon through the Hudson's Bay Company's Territory* (1859; rpt. Toronto: Radisson Society of Canada, 1925), pp. lii-liii.

paintings. During the next two and a half years he traversed Canada, completing more than five hundred sketches, detailed portraits, and genre scenes in order to produce a finished cycle of paintings that would memorialize all phases of native life.

The careful travel journal Kane published with his sketches, *Wanderings of an Artist among the Indians of North America* (1859), sold out within a few months; three foreign-language editions followed within four years. Perhaps most strikingly, foreign reviews reveal the pervasiveness of the popular anxieties that Kane touched. The London *Athenaeum* thought he "had devoted himself to an American purpose, sketching and recording the deeds and outward forms of an unhappily vanishing race."[50] A French reviewer took twenty-three pages in the prestigious *Revue des deux mondes* to make the same point, and he particularly praised Kane's documentary presentation.[51]

The popular reception for Kane, Seth Eastman, John Mix Stanley, Karl Bodmer, and George Catlin indicates the tenor of national and international concern developing for native American life. Most whites felt indifferent to the Indian and his fate. Even the more intelligently aware welcomed western artists because they, like their less perceptive contemporaries, were simply intrigued by the configuration of the country and its inhabitants. Yet if we do no more than speculate from the kind of critical reception accorded Kane and others, their enthusiasm also issued from a more profound realization of the need to make records before opportunities passed.

Many looked to the federal government to support such efforts. Though, as we have seen, McKenney did not win enough congressional support to continue his collecting and was indeed cut off, he did for a time receive government financing. Two decades later, despite a crippling economic depression, Congress came within a hair's breadth of purchasing Catlin's large collection. By 1853, McKenney's successor in the Bureau of Indian Affairs sensed "an increasing regret that the Government has not taken more timely and efficient measures for preserving memorials of the race. A National Portrait Gallery of distinguished Indians permanently located at the seat of Government, would certainly be an object of general interest and that interest would continue to increase with the lapse of time."[52]

Private owners of paintings of Indians began near mid-century to

---

50 Cited in J. Russell Harper's introduction to *Paul Kane's Frontier*, p. 40.

51 Cited by Harper in ibid., p. 41.

52 Commissioner of Indian Affairs Luke Lea to W. Sebastian, cited in Viola, *Indian Legacy of Charles Bird King*, p. 115.

14. Paul Kane, *Sault Ste. Marie (Ojibwa Village)*, 1845-1848. Oil on canvas. The Royal Ontario Museum, Toronto.

give them to state and local historical societies for safe-keeping as well as for public enjoyment.[53] Joseph Henry, who by 1858 had served as secretary of the Smithsonian Institution for more than a decade, warned in his annual report for that year that the paintings and artifacts already gathered from native tribes were irreplaceable. Additionally, he "hoped that Congress will in due time purchase the portraits belonging to Mr. [John Mix] Stanley which will become more and more valuable in the progress of the gradual extinction of the race of which they are such faithful representations."[54] During the next twenty years, Henry labored assiduously to convince the owner of Catlin's collection to bequeath it to the nation.

POST-CIVIL WAR PAINTERS

Following the Civil War, spiritual descendants of Catlin, Bodmer, and Kane proliferated, encouraged by public enthusiasm for their

[53] Buck, "Lappawinzo and Tishcohan," pp. 215-18; Lockwood, "St. Memin Indian Portraits," p. 3.

[54] Joseph Henry, "Report of the Secretary for 1858," in *Annual Report of the Board of Regents of the Smithsonian Institution* (Washington: G.P.O., 1859), p. 42.

work. Perhaps that popularity itself made it unnecessary for them to express their seemingly self-evident commitment. Men like William dc la Montagne Cary, Henry Farny, Edwin W. Deming, Elbridge Ayer Burbank, Ralph A. Blakelock, and Charles Schreyvogel traveled west to acquire realistic documents of tribal life.[55] Although the popular magazines that bought their illustrations demanded only colorful sketches, these artists sought both accuracy and sympathetic insight. Some, like George de Forest Brush, Charles M. Russell, DeCost Smith, and Charles Craig, spent months and years learning Indian languages or living among tribes.[56] Admiring native skills and tradition, they deplored the forces threatening them. Ironically, their finished work often appears to idealize and sentimentalize, since so often they found the Indian's already reduced circumstances less interesting, and more appalling, than his life prior to white influence. These artists hoped to preserve a record of what had already distinctly passed.

In a very few areas, traditional Indian culture managed to survive intact through the 1890s. The pueblos of the Southwest, for example, had secured themselves against European invaders and external attractions for centuries. Traditional, mysterious, peaceable even to the point of apparent passivity—these tribes treasured a land that seemed harshly unappealing, indeed, actively hostile, to immigrants bent on finding a place for permanent settlement. The Hopi, Zuni, and Rio Grande Pueblos, as well as the Navaho, Pima, and Papago, enjoyed isolation at a time when aggressive pioneers forced their brethren elsewhere to conform to white dictates. Largely ignored, they were thereby able to retain their distinctive cultures. During the late 1880s, when artists and anthropologists finally realized the extent of rich tribal experience waiting to be documented, time had not already run out.

[55] Harmsen, *Harmsen's Western Americana*, pp. 26-27, 38, 42; Curry, *American West*, p. 30; Peter Hassrick *The Way West: Art of Frontier America* (New York: Harry N. Abrams, 1977), pp. 192ff.; Taft, *Artists and Illustrators of the Old West*, pp. 214, 217-25, 227-30; McCracken, *Portrait of the Old West*; Norman A. Geske, "Ralph Albert Blakelock in the West," *American Art Review*, 3 (January-February 1976), 123-35; James D. Horan, *The Life and Art of Charles Schreyvogel: Painter-Historian of the Indian-Fighting Army of the American West* (New York: Crown, 1969), pp. 17, 27-28.

[56] George de Forest Brush, "An Artist Among the Indians," *Century Magazine*, 30 (May 1885), 54-57; Harold McCracken, *The Charles M. Russell Book: The Life and Work of the Cowboy Artist* (Garden City N.Y.: Doubleday and Co., 1957); Ewers, *Artists of the Old West*, p. 232; Harmsen, *Harmsen's Western Americana*, pp. 54, 182. See also Howard Doughty, *Francis Parkman* (New York: Macmillan Co., 1962), p. 392n; Searles R. Boynton, "The Pomo Indian Portraits of Grace Carpenter Hudson," *American West*, 14 (September-October 1977), 25.

The schools of painters that established themselves around Taos and Santa Fe shared little more than an attraction to the Southwest and a self-conscious commitment to record "what was thought of as a dying race and the grandeur of an austere landscape."[57] Joseph Sharp (1859-1953), around whom the Taos art colony later grew, first visited the pueblo in 1893. Realizing that the tribe had created a complex culture, he attempted to reproduce with ethnographic accuracy their distinctive facial structure and costumes, ceremonials and customs. Over a long career, he came to be known as "the anthropologist" by fellow artists, many of whom he had already persuaded in the early 1890s to leave eastern and European studios behind in order to settle in the region.

Like Catlin and Stanley more than half a century before, Sharp traveled throughout the Far West in order to document tribes already in their last phases as autonomous cultures. Describing an 1899 painting trip to the heart of the old Sioux country in southeastern Montana, he explained, "I went north because I realized Taos would last longer."[58] Sharp spent two years in Montana—the second year in a cabin built under President Theodore Roosevelt's authorization next to the old Custer battlefield—painting hundreds of Plains Indian studies. He returned to New Mexico in 1902 to contir ie the work for which he and his colleagues subsequently became famous. "In the past years I have seen so many things and made studies that probably no other living artist ever saw," Sharp once claimed, "that if I do not paint none ever will."[59] Today, Sharp's scrupulously detailed studies of tribal life are considered accurate enough to justify their inclusion in university anthropology collections and in the Smithsonian's Bureau of Ethnology.

Despite the genuine accomplishments of Sharp and others, the pictorial record of Indian life undertaken after the Civil War suffers in comparison with that completed earlier. Artists of the late 1850s and 1860s in general turned away from the individually distinctive toward the characteristic gesture or type. George Catlin and Seth Eastman had strived to paint precisely what they saw; Henry Farny and Joseph Sharp attempted in larger part to *recreate* a recent past.

[57] Van Deren Coke, *Taos and Santa Fe: The Artist's Environment, 1882-1942* (Albuquerque: University of New Mexico Press, 1963), p. 9, also pp. 11-16. See also Laura M. Bickerstaff, *Pioneer Artists of Taos* (Denver: Sage Books, 1955), esp. pp. 85-87; Patricia Trenton, "Picturesque Images of Taos and Santa Fe," *American Art Review*, 1 (March-April 1974), 97-98; Harmsen, *Harmsen's Western Americana*, p. 178.

[58] Cited in Bickerstaff, *Pioneer Artists of Taos*, p. 86.

[59] Cited in Coke, *Taos and Santa Fe*, p. 16.

15. Joseph Sharp, *Taos Indian Portrait*, 1914. Oil on canvas. Museum of New Mexico, Santa Fe.

Canvases completed after the Civil War, however detailed, fully register the impact of white civilization, whether through the melancholy tone of portraits or the projected idealization of domestic and genre scenes. Attempting to do more than transcribe, these latter-day artists too often succumbed to their sympathies. By contrast, Catlin conceived of his mission as a more narrowly documentary project and rarely revealed his own feelings in his paintings.

THE FRONTIER PHOTOGRAPHER

Perhaps one reason for this shift from representational accuracy was the invention of the daguerreotype in 1839. Throughout the next half century, as rapid improvements in the photographic process encouraged hundreds to haul equipment west, the camera gradually replaced the paintbrush as the documentarian's tool of choice. The very nature of painting—demanding lengthy sessions for each canvas, the artist's conscious or unconscious conformity to conventions and innovations—prevented a complete or unbiased ethnographic record. Painters like Sharp still voiced a commitment to accuracy, but similar expressions occur far more frequently among those known to their subjects as the "shadow catchers."

Despite the bulky equipment, time-consuming processing, and unpredictable results of daguerreotype and wet-plate photography, as well as the skill and inordinate patience they required, American archaeologists and ethnologists quickly comprehended the camera's inestimable value for on-site work. The early photographic successes of Seth Eastman, Frederick Catherwood, and Henry Rowe Schoolcraft encouraged the first tentative use of photographic equipment on western expeditions. Secretary of the Smithsonian, Joseph Henry, in his 1858 annual report, added his enjoinder that photography be used particularly to document tribes yet unchanged.[60] For those sensitive to such developments, the replacement of the survey artist by the staff photographer seemed only a matter of a few technological improvements to aid portability. Even prior to such improvements, individuals like A. Zeno Shindler, C. M. Bell, and Alexander Gardner took off in the late fifties to work on their own as professional photographers among the western tribes.[61]

The corps of photographic teams equipped by Matthew Brady during the Civil War provided a training ground for many western

[60] Henry, "Report of the Secretary for 1858," pp. 41-42. See also Henry, "Circular Relating to Collections in Archaeology and Ethnology," *Smithsonian Miscellaneous Collections*, 8 (1868), pp. 1-2; Viola, *Indian Legacy of Charles Bird King*, p. 114.

[61] For background, see Chapters Two and Three above; Robert Taft, *Photography and the American Scene: A Social History, 1839-1889* (New York: Macmillan Co., 1938), pp. 282-283; Joanna Cohan Scherer, *Indians: The Great Photographs that Reveal North American Indian Life, 1847-1929* . . . (New York: Crown, 1973), esp. pp. 12-21; Gen. William J. Palmer, *Report of Surveys Across the Continent in 1867-'68 on the 35th and 32nd Parallels for a Route extending the Kansas Pacific Railway* (Philadelphia, 1869), esp. plates 16, 17.

practitioners. As well, wartime improvements transformed the camera into an efficient, reliable, and extremely accurate instrument. By the 1870s, an established group of well-trained, well-equipped photographers was available to act on the deepening concern for documenting vanishing tribes. Ironically, however, improvements in photography at the same time added pounds of equipment and demanded proportionately greater skill. Moreover, the kind of account that the camera might have provided of folk and subcultures in Europe and America was no longer possible by the time it was invented. Scholars have regretted that "as the technical means for providing a brilliant and vivid record of Indian life finally became available to the photographer, conditions of Indian life had so deteriorated that what remains is, for the most part, a visual record of a harassed, defeated, and degraded people."[62] Indeed, the very technology that could enable the most accurate depiction of native American cultures had already, in pernicious manifestations of gun, barbed wire, and windmill, hastened the decline of those cultures.

The peace at Appomattox that released dozens of accomplished photographers also released dozens of well-trained army battalions for western service. Making the West safe for settlement meant at best dislocation, at worst extermination of relatively defenseless tribes. Thus, despite the unquestionably superior objectivity of photography, most post-Civil War practitioners lacked the opportunity to surpass or even equal the insights into Indian culture gained by the pre-Civil War painters. Catlin's depiction of the vital coherence of the complex Mandan culture alone makes his series of paintings more valuable than most photographic records made only a half century later.

Of course, many photographers themselves, especially those aware of the diminished possibilities, felt the same documentarian motives as painters before them. In 1866 one Ridgeway Glover reportedly planned a photographic excursion specifically "to illustrate the life and character of the wild men of the prairie."[63] He hardly traveled alone. In the next fifteen years, more Indian photographs of historical and ethnological value were produced than ever before or since.[64]

[62] Robert A. Weinstein and William Webb, *Dwellers at the Source: Southwestern Indian Photographs of A. C. Vroman, 1895-1904* (New York: Grossman, 1973), p. 10, also p. 14. See also Susan Sontag, *On Photography* (New York: Farrar, Straus and Giroux, 1977), pp. 15-16, 65, 76.

[63] Cited in Russell E. Belous and Robert A Weinstein, *Will Soule: Indian Photographer at Fort Sill, Oklahoma, 1869-74* (Los Angeles: Ward Ritchie Press, 1969), p. 14.

[64] Ibid., p. 15, also pp. 13-14. See also Taft, *Photography and the American Scene*, pp. 282-83.

Government survey photographers were joined by independents who packed their gear west to open studios and galleries. The works of E. A. Bonine in Arizona, Major G. W. Ingalls and Will Soule in Oklahoma, Major Horatio Nelson Rust in southern California, Laton Huffman and Frank Haynes in the Dakotas confirm their commitments to documentation, though, again, not one verified that commitment in writing.[65] Their reasons for photographing Indians, however mixed, would not have been financial, since studio work offered little profit and excursions to tribal grounds even less.

After the Civil War, as before, and for similar reasons, federally sponsored expeditions made possible the most extensive records of the West. Even in the 1850s, expedition artists—John Mix Stanley on Governor Isaac Stevens's Northwest survey and Samuel Carvalho on General John C. Frémont's Southwest expeditions—packed daguerreotyping equipment to record native tribes.[66] Three of the finest postwar photographers, John K. Hillers, Timothy H. O'Sullivan, and William Henry Jackson, were hired by western surveys that produced major published reports. Although O'Sullivan and Hillers never wrote of their responses to the native Americans at whom they so frequently pointed cameras, Major John Wesley Powell did. Leader of the 1872 Colorado River Survey and other important expeditions throughout the decade, he had hired Hillers in the explicit belief that the threatened western tribes cried out for immediate documentation.[67]

[65] E. A. Bonine collection of photographs, Huntington Library, San Marino, California; Gary F. Kurutz, "Pictorial Resources: The Henry E. Huntington Library's California and American West Collections," *California Historical Quarterly*, 54 (Summer 1975), esp. 178; Belous and Weinstein, *Will Soule*, esp. pp. 11-20; Horatio Nelson Rust Collection, Huntington Library, San Marino; Mark H. Brown and W. R. Felton, *The Frontier Years: L. A. Huffman, Photographer of the Plains* (New York: Bramhall House, 1955), esp. p. 238; Brown and Felton, *Before Barbed Wire: L. A. Huffman, Photographer on Horseback* (1956; rpt. New York: Bramhall House, 1961), pp. 12, 19-21; Freeman Tilden, *Following the Frontier with F. Jay Haynes: Pioneer Photographer of the Old West* (New York: Alfred A. Knopf, 1964), pp. 197ff.; F. Jay Haynes, *Indian Types of the North West* (New York: Adolph Wittemann, ca. 1885), esp. p. 3. See also "Photographic Portraits of North American Indians in the Gallery of the Smithsonian Institution," *Smithsonian Miscellaneous Collections*, 14 (1867), 1-42.

[66] Pipes, "John Mix Stanley," p. 255; Sturhahn, *Carvalho* pp. 68-70. Susan Sontag, in *On Photography*, p. 76, has claimed: "From the start, photographers not only set themselves the task of recording a disappearing world but were so employed by those hastening its disappearance." See also ibid., pp. 64-65.

[67] Wallace Stegner, *Beyond the Hundredth Meridian: John Wesley Powell and the Second Opening of the West* (Boston: Houghton Mifflin Co., 1954), p. 130. Powell's own energetic efforts will be examined in the following chapter; see here *"Photographed All the Best Scenery": Jack Hillers' Diary of the Powell Expeditions, 1871-1875*, ed. Don D. Fowler (Salt Lake City: University of Utah Press, 1972); Julian H.

16. Timothy H. O'Sullivan, "Aboriginal Life among the Navajoe Indians near Old Fort Defiance, New Mexico," 1873. Stereoptican photograph. Collection of Alfred L. Bush.

The frontier photographer who traveled farthest throughout the continent, achieved the greatest popularity and respect, and left the most comprehensive written record of his intentions and responses was William Henry Jackson (1843-1942). After a short stint in Nebraska as a free-lance photographer following the war, he accepted Ferdinand Vandeveer Hayden's offer to join his 1870 survey of the western territories. Perhaps Hayden first persuaded the young cameraman of the historical value of photographing native tribes. The commander already felt convinced of the logic of preserving vast tracts of wilderness as they were, and he vigorously encouraged documentation of wilderness scenes and frontier life as well as ethnographic studies of the waning Indian tribes.[68] His dramatic example, in fact, probably influenced Jackson's 1870 studies of the famous Shoshone chief Washakie and the tepee village at South Pass, Wyoming, which are among the earliest photographs of indigenous tribes prior to reservation conditions.[69]

Jackson's 1868 photographs of Indians near Omaha, as well as his later career, suggest that he needed little urging. Openly regretting missed opportunities on his first expedition, he nevertheless felt relieved at having obtained illustrations of native peoples and archaeological sites before they succumbed to white devastation. Jackson continued to travel throughout the West, and by 1877 he had compiled an extensive catalogue of available photographs—his own as well as those of others—of twenty-five tribes made over as many years. The short preface that his old mentor wrote enthusiastically described the collection as "undoubtedly the largest and most valu-

Steward, "Notes on Hillers' Photographs of the Paiute and Ute Indians Taken on the Powell Expedition of 1873," *Smithsonian Miscellaneous Collections*, 98 (1939), esp. p. 2. See also James D. Horan, *Timothy O'Sullivan, America's Forgotten Photographer* (Garden City, N.Y.: Doubleday and Co., 1966), pp. 153, 239; Beaumont and Nancy Newhall, *T. H. O'Sullivan: Photographer* (Rochester: George Eastman House, 1966); Taft, *Photography and the American Scene*, pp. 284-92.

[68] Ferdinand Vandever Hayden, *Sun Pictures of Rocky Mountain Scenery* (New York: Julius Bien, 1878), pp. 32-33; Hayden, *The Great West: Its Attractions and Resources* (Philadelphia: Franklin Publishing Co., 1880) p. 36; Hayden, prefatory note to Washington Matthews, *Ethnography nd Philology of the Hidatsa Indians*, U.S. Geological and Geographical Survey, Miscellaneous Publications, no. 7 (Washington: G.P.O., 1877), pp. iii-iv.

[69] Taft, *Photography and the American Scene*, pp. 293-94. For details of Jackson's career, see Clarence S. Jackson, *Picture Maker of the Old West: William H. Jackson* (New York: Bonanza Books, 1947); William Henry Jackson, *Time Exposure: The Autobiography of William Henry Jackson* (New York: G. P. Putnam's Sons, 1940); *The Diaries of William Henry Jackson: Frontier Photographer*, ed. LeRoy R. and Ann W. Hafen (Glendale, Calif.: Arthur H. Clark Co., 1959). Useful but untrustworthy is Beaumont Newhall and Diana E. Edkins, *William H. Jackson* (Fort Worth: Amon Carter Museum, 1974).

17. William Henry Jackson, "Crow Eyes. Pawnee," 1869. Albumen photograph. Amon Carter Museum, Fort Worth, Texas.

able one extant."[70] Notably, Hayden valued the collection not only for the usual general reasons but also because it preserved evidence of specific artifacts, a consideration that was gaining importance among ethnographers. In his own prefatory note, Jackson tersely concurred.[71]

THE PASADENA EIGHT

Nowhere in the last two decades of the century were artifacts so well preserved or, as mentioned earlier, tribal cultures so richly intact as in the Southwest. Serious photographers wandered through the region in an active, explicit commitment to compiling ethnographic records. Unlike the similarly motivated paintings of Joseph Sharp and the Taos and Santa Fe schools, their work attracted only moderate attention from the general public. Though the scientific community embraced such efforts, it lacked the means to support them. Their tepid public reception almost ensured that these craftsmen would be loners, existing on limited funds, searching out remote tribes and scenes, and transporting heavy chemical supplies and fragile view camera equipment on their own by wagon.

A singular anomaly in this general pattern of loner photographers was a small group of far-sighted southern Californians who became so closely associated that students still confuse their work. Chapter Three described Charles Lummis's and George Wharton James's spearheading of a movement in the 1890s to preserve California's Spanish missions. Outside the state, they directed another project: the preservation of a record of the tribes of the Southwest. Others from Pasadena shared their commitment, including a former book-dealer, Adam Clark Vroman, the studio and expedition photographers C. J. Crandall, Frederick I. Monsen, and Carl Moon, and two dealers in Indian artifacts, Horatio Rust and Grace Nicholson. Each of these eight people appears to have known all the others, and some were close friends. From the 1870s, each made photographic trips to the pueblos of Arizona and New Mexico, sometimes annually and sometimes in the company of other members of the group. They produced tens of thousands of photographs over a span of forty years out of the recognized need to preserve "for future generations

[70] F. W. Hayden, prefatory note to William Henry Jackson, *Descriptive Catalogue of Photographs of North American Indians*, United States Geological and Geographical Survey of the Territories, Miscellaneous Publications, no. 9 (Washington: G.P.O., 1877), p. iii.

[71] Ibid., p. v. See also Terry William Mangan, *Colorado on Glass: Colorado's First Half-Century as Seen by the Camera* (Denver: Sundance Ltd., 1975), p. 112.

18. Carl Moon, "Navaho Weaver, Canyon de Chelly," ca. 1907-1914. Photograph. The Henry E. Huntington Library and Art Gallery, San Marino, California.

a picture-history which will show what these most interesting early Americans were like."[72]

In their acknowledged motives, an additional reason appears frequently: the need to understand these mysterious cultures on their own terms. Surely this is also implied in the excited note Adam Clark Vroman scrawled on the back of a photograph taken at his first Hopi Snake Dance in 1895:

> . . . the Dance is Over.
>
> Words cannot picture it at all. The location, the surroundings, the costumes which are beautiful, the bodies of Dancers died a rich brown with the entire chin *white*, making [the] face look almost hideous.
>
> My first thought was after it was all over was to see it again and know more about it, why it was and how it is planned. I felt I could spend a year right there, be one of them, and learn their ways and beliefs. It is a sacred rite with them and carried out to the letter and they believe it.[73]

Vroman expresses a common feeling among those entranced by the southwestern cultures. Yet like Catlin's paintings, his photographs— "unexpressive, uncondescending, unsentimental"[74]—resist the easy conversion of subject matter into sentimental plea.

[72] Frederick I. Monsen, "Picturing Indians with the Camera," *Photo-Era*, 25 (October 1910), 165. For additional such statements, plus background information on these people, see: Ruth I. Mahood, ed., *Photographer of the Southwest: Adam Clark Vroman, 1856-1916* (n.p.: Ward Ritchie Press, 1961), esp. pp. 9-10, 17-19, 222-24; Webb and Weinstein, *Dwellers at the Source*; A. C. Vroman's Diary, Hopi Indians, Huntington Library, San Marino; Frederick Monsen's Ethnographic Indian Photographs, 13 vol., Huntington Library; Frederick Monsen, *With A Kodak in the Land of the Navajo* (Rochester: Eastman Kodak, 1907?), esp. pp. 16-26; Kristina Wilkinson, "Frederick Monsen, F.R.G.S.: Explorer and Ethnographer," *Noticias*, Summer 1969, pp. 16-23; Frederick Monsen, "The Destruction of our Indians: What Civilization Is Doing to Extinguish an Ancient and Highly Intelligent Race by Taking Away its Arts, Industries, and Religion," *Craftsman*, 11 (March 1907), 683-91; Carl Moon, "A Brief Account of the Making of This Collection of Indian Pictures," typescript, 1924, Huntington Library; Carl Moon, "Photographing the Vanishing Red Man," *Leslie's Illustrated*, March 10, 1914; Carl Moon, "American Indians of the Southwest," *Century Magazine*, 74 (October 1907), 923-27; W. Jerome, "Karl Moon's Indian Photographs," *Craftsman*, 20 (April 1911), 24-32; Horatio Nelson Rust Collection, Huntington Library, esp. boxes 4, 6, 12, 13, 16; Grace Nicholson Collection, Huntington Library; Jane Apostol, "The Indian Summers of Miss Grace Nicholson," typescript, Huntington Library; Winifred Starr Dobyns, "A Treasure House," *Woman Citizen*, 56, old ser. (December 1927), 12-14; Kurutz, "Pictorial Resources," pp. 175-82. See also Gar and Maggy Packard, *Southwest 1880: With Ben Wittick, Pioneer Photographer of Indians and Frontier Life* (Santa Fe: Packard Publications, 1970), esp. pp. 3, 46.

[73] A. C. Vroman's Diary, no. 14

[74] Sontag, *On Photography*, p. 62. Sontag further observes about them: "They are not moving, they are not idiomatic, they do not invite sympathy; they make no propaganda for the Indians."

19. Adam Clark Vroman, "Gathering Snakes at the End of the Ceremony, Walpi," 1897. Photograph. The Natural History Museum of Los Angeles County.

20. Frederick I. Monsen, "Snake Dance, Oraibi, Hopi," ca. 1889-1894. Photograph. The Henry E. Huntington Library and Art Gallery, San Marino, California.

The careers of Vroman and his Pasadena housemate, Frederick I. Monsen (1865-1929), best represent the commitment made by countless other western photographers. Monsen, a young immigrant Norwegian, already had Geological Survey field experience under his belt when he discovered pueblo life in the late 1880s. Intrigued, he studied the Hopi and then the Navaho in an earnest attempt to adapt himself to their alien worlds, "so far as was possible for a white man,"[75] and began photographing the first of more than ten thousand scenes. From the turn of the century, Monsen gained a reputation as an authority on Pueblo life and was acclaimed as photographer, anthropologist, and lecturer. An unusual insight into his career can be found in his account of early enthusiasm for that work:

> It seemed to me that any truthful record of the lives and customs of the people of the Pueblos, made while they were yet unspoiled, would have an ethnological and historical value even greater than the quality of picturesqueness that is now coming to to be of such keen interest to artists. The only way to gain the true impression that alone would be of value, instead of merely gathering a collection of unusual and attractive pictures, was to become intimate with the people, to understand them and be understood by them, to gain their friendship and so coax them by imperceptible degrees to forget to be watchful and conscious in the presence of a stranger, and to live and pursue their daily occupations as if no camera or sketch-block had ever been brought within the borders of the Great Desert.[76]

In 1879, the same year that Monsen took his first photographs of the Hopi, George Eastman perfected the portable roll-film camera. Half a dozen years later, Adam Clark Vroman came west, hiring on as a Kodak dealer along with Monsen; they worked closely together, supplemented each other's ideas, and contributed to each other's collections.[77] The new Kodaks kept the pair solvent even as the cameras offered them invaluable photographic possibilities, allowing Monsen in particular to take more candid pictures than before and to complete them with far less trouble. Unfortunately, the San Francisco earthquake and fire of 1906 destroyed most of his vast collection of negatives. The few hundred that survive attest to the extraordinary range of his interests in native life, his excellent handling of the

[75] Monsen, "Destruction of Our Indians," p. 684.

[76] Ibid., pp. 683-84.

[77] See letter from Monsen's son, Courtenay, to Gary F. Kurutz, June 17, 1973, Huntington Library.

camera, and his honest, unsentimental view. Of course, Monsen lost a distinct edge in the quality of his prints to those who persisted with the more precise view cameras. On the other hand, he gained immeasurably in the range of cultural experiences available for photographic preservation; that is, he could achieve pictures that, because unposed, revealed less of the photographer's necessary preconceptions than of the native's characteristic habits and modes. In Monsen's own words, "the unconscious expression of daily life and character was what I had set my heart on obtaining."[78]

EDWARD CURTIS AND THE END OF AN ERA

As has already been noted, camera technology developed to the point where a close transcription of native life could be considered at just the time when native life was being seriously eroded. The camera itself confirmed that decline in what has been characterized as "the colonization through photography."[79] Eastman had succeeded by the turn of the century in making snapshot photography generally available; at the same time, Thomas Edison had created a popular demand for motion picture films of exotic activities. Discreet amateurs like Monsen and Vroman, respectful of their subjects, signaled the advent of a horde of tourists rudely eager for a "good shot." Poking their noses into holy places and their unwelcome cameras at native ceremonials, unflappable whites crassly paid for poses, and in some cases forever altered ceremonials whose strength inhered in their secrecy. Technological progress in the form of the camera brought a rapid end to the very experiences it was employed to preserve.

Neither Monsen nor his colleagues possessed the resources, and perhaps not the energy or inclination, to transform extensive photographic collections into published documents. At their deaths, what remained of their collections fell into disarray, remembered only by friends. In some cases, it was decades before they were rediscovered, reassembled, and published—to reveal a commitment focused intensively on only a few southwestern tribes. The usefulness of these unexcelled collections is diminished, however, by their creators' failure to leave a written record explaining the scenes they had photographed.

Only one man in the post-Civil War era surpassed the Pasadena group in his ambitions, though Edward S. Curtis (1868-1952) accomplished little in his first thirty years that might have presaged his later

[78] Monsen, "Destruction of Our Indians," p. 686.
[79] Sontag, *On Photography*, p. 64; see also p. 65.

career. As a young photographer in the vigorous Seattle of the 1890s, he specialized in portraits of the socially elite, a lucrative profession that gave him the freedom to explore the surrounding mountains during the summers. In 1898, on an excursion up Mount Rainier, Curtis stumbled upon a party of lost climbers and guided them down safely. That party happened to include George Bird Grinnell and Gifford Pinchot, both of whom took an immediate liking to the resourceful guide. Young Pinchot had yet to establish his formidable reputation as dean of American foresters. Grinnell, on the other hand, was already the recognized leader of the new movement concerned with conservation, wildlife management, and Indian ethnography. Two years later Grinnell invited Curtis on a trip to the Blackfoot reservation in Montana, which Curtis's daughter long after described as the "pivotal experience" of his life. The older admirer of Blackfoot culture and collector of Indian tales imparted his enthusiasm to the young photographer. "He often spoke of it afterward. To most people it would have been just a bunch of Indians. To him it was something that soon would never be seen again."[80] During this trip, Curtis finally committed himself to an idea he had been quietly mulling over for two years: photographing and studying all the Indian tribes still remaining west of the Mississippi River. Grinnell warmly encouraged him to turn his skills to the mammoth task and within ten days after returning to Seattle from Montana, Curtis was in southern Arizona photographing the Hopi.

Seven years later, in the introduction to the first volume of what would become a twenty-volume photographic record, Curtis asserted that he had been working arduously since the first trip "in accumulating the data necessary to form a comprehensive and permanent record of all the important tribes of the United States and Alaska that still retain to a considerable degree their primitive customs and traditions."[81] He further acknowledged that "it represents the result of personal study of a people who are rapidly losing the traces of their aboriginal character and who are destined ultimately to become assimilated with the 'superior race.' "[82] Curtis readily appreciated how late his commitment had come, late enough to throw into question the very completion of his project. In terms that reiterate the apprehensions of many before him, he emphasized this theme:

[80] Florence Curtis Graybill and Victor Boesen, *Edward Sheriff Curtis: Visions of a Vanishing Race* (New York: Thomas Y. Crowell, 1976), p. 12.

[81] Curtis, *The North American Indian: Being a Series of Volumes Picturing and Describing the Indians of the United States, and Alaska*, ed. Frederick Webb Hodge, 20 vols. (Cambridge, Mass.: Harvard University Press, 1907-30), 1:xiii.

[82] Ibid.

The great changes in practically every phase of the Indian's life that have taken place . . . have been such that had the time for collecting much of the material . . . been delayed, it would have been lost forever. The passing of every old man or woman means the passing of some tradition, some knowledge of sacred rites possessed by no other; consequently the information that is to be gathered, for the benefit of future generations . . . must be collected at once or the opportunity will be lost for all time. It is this need that has inspired the present task.[83]

Within a year after he committed himself to his life's task, in 1900, Curtis received widespread public encouragement. Early exhibits of his work in San Francisco drew reviews attesting to its "immense ethnological value,"[84] and Grinnell persuaded his old friend President Roosevelt to support the photographer. By Roosevelt's second term Curtis had won substantial encouragement from America's art and financial communities. As one important New York reviewer wrote in 1905, "the undertaking is the most remarkable artistic and historical work thus far attempted by photography in America."[85] In that same year, partly through Roosevelt's special efforts, J. P. Morgan agreed to subsidize the costly publication of Curtis's complete works. This extraordinary alliance of political and financial support secured his reputation as the most acclaimed of Indian photographers.

The weaknesses of Curtis's studies are more clearly apparent today, analogous to those of the Indian paintings of Charles Russell or of the Taos school. Instead of attempting realistic photographs of the contemporary lives of the tribes he visited, Curtis invariably portrayed a Hopi or a Crow or a Tlingit "as he moved about before he ever saw a paleface."[86] Predictably, many of these photographic studies suffer from sentimentality and stylization. They reflect what Monsen warned against as the "photographer's idea" rather than portraying the native experience. To compound the well-meant distortions, Curtis frequently carried costumes for his intended models and posed them in stereotypical groupings or sentimental actions.

Nonetheless, Curtis's fundamental motives were admirable. No one since Catlin had conceived so comprehensive a plan for preserving

[83] Ibid., 1:xvi-xvii.

[84] Arnold Genthe, review essay in *Camera Craft*, 11 (February 1901), 310, cited in Mahood, ed., *Photographer of the Southweast*, p. 18.

[85] John Tennent, review essay in *Photo-Miniaturem* 6 (September 1905), 663, cited in Mahood, ed. *Photographer of the Southwest*, p. 19. See also Theodore Roosevelt's foreword to Curtis, *North American Indian*, vol. 1.

[86] Curtis, cited in Graybill and Boesen, *Edward Sheriff Curtis*, p. 13.

21. Edward S. Curtis, "Kotsuis and Hohhuq—Nakoaktok," Kwakiutl, 1914. Photogravure from Curtis, *The North American Indian*, portfolio X.

the image of a vanishing race or had visited so many tribes.[87] In the inclusiveness of his intentions, indeed, Curtis far exceeded even Catlin.[88] More systematically than any painter or photographer before or since, he collected a massive fund of ethnological information, which he published in volumes accompanying his photographic portfolio. Yet he sadly recognized, like other serious students to be discussed in the following chapter, that "the years of a single life are insufficient for the task of treating in minute detail all the intricacies of the social structure and the arts and beliefs of many tribes."[89] Curtis's particular achievement, setting him worlds apart from those who may have shared this knowledge, lay in making the Indian's worlds more generally available through the medium of photography.

Within four years after Curtis first published his exhaustive studies, Ishi, the last "wild Indian" uninfluenced by white civilization, wan-

[87] See, however, Frederick Starr, *Indians of Southern Mexico: An Ethnographic Album* (Chicago: privately published, 1899); Starr, *Notes upon the Ethnography of Southern Mexico*, 2 vols. (Davenport, Ia.: Putnam Memorial Publication Fund, 1900-1902), esp. pp. 2-3.

[88] Curtis, *North American Indian*, 1:xvi-xvii.

[89] Ibid., 1:xvi.

dered fearfully into tiny Oroville, California, only to be forced into trousers and handcuffs by an equally bewildered sheriff.[90] In less than a century, nearly two hundred indigenous tribes had disappeared entirely or had been harried, deceived, and beaten into acceptance of white rule. Their various ways of life manifested fewer and fewer distinctive characteristics as they now imitated the clothes, hair styles, work habits, and manners of the culture that had displaced them.

CLEARLY, Catlin does not stand alone in his commitment to compiling a permanent pictorial record of the western tribes. Yet most of the painters who preceded him and many of the painters and photographers who followed never fully appreciated the work completed by their contemporaries. Catlin inspired others to the task, but for the most part artists worked in isolation and learned little from one another. A tradition of artists committed to preserving such records never existed, any more than a consistent, self-conscious pattern came to define those committed to recording the passing wilderness landscape or the disappearance of wildlife. Through a century of displacement, acculturation, and extinction, however, an increasing number came with increasing urgency to realize that much of value was being consigned to oblivion. This "mournful vision of loss,"[91] according to one historian, defines a fundamental strain of American photography. The West specifically, and the Indian in particular, emblematized all that was changing. In the many documentary photographs made through the course of the century, a "vision of loss" confronts the viewer.[92]

Before the end of the nineteenth century, pictorial records drew the serious attention of ethnologists and historians. The drawings, sketches, oils, and photographs of tribes completed years earlier and in many cases long since forgotten acquired significance for the very reasons that the original artists had claimed.[93] For tribes that had disappeared, the earlier pictorial evidence proved as helpful as it was accurate. Yet, despite the information that such records contained, they could by their very nature provide accounts of no more than physical design, the visible form, the dramatic gesture. Questions of

[90] Theodora Kroeber, *Ishi in Two Worlds: A Biography of the Last Wild Indian in North America* (1961; rpt. Berkeley: University of California Press, 1971).

[91] Sontag, *On Photography*, p. 67; see also pp. 56, 76.

[92] Hallowell, "Backwash of the Frontier," pp. 248, 250.

[93] Ewers, "Fact and Fiction," esp. pp. 79-82; Herman J. Viola, "How *Did* an Indian Chief Really Look?" *Smithsonian*, 8 (June 1977), 100-104; Weitenkampf, "Early Pictures of North American Indians," pp. 591-614; Herman Ten Kate, "On Paintings of North American Indians and Their Ethnographical Value," *Anthropos*, 7 (1911), 521-45.

meaning, of belief, of value required the efforts of individuals committed to more than vanishing appearances. So just as artists had been drawn westward by the idea of saving an image of native life, those more scientifically inclined endured similar privations in order to secure records of Indian cultural experiences.

Despite their similar missions, artists and scientists rarely worked together. Whether or not the artist would have helped the scientist to see his subject more clearly, it seems likely that the scientist might well have helped the artist. For it was first the Indian biographer, then the ethnologist, and finally the anthropologist who came to appreciate the complexity of all cultural structures. Those who rescued tribal vocabularies and ceremonial descriptions early in the century often found more than they had suspected. Nathaniel Hawthorne may have regretted never finding an "Indian story" interesting, but others turned their ears attentively and in the process not merely salvaged remnants from the ruins but came to recognize a previously rich autonomy to tribes now sadly dependent.

CHAPTER SIX

THEIR TRIBAL LORE
PRESERVED

As a race they have withered from the
land. Their arrows are broken, their
springs are dried up, their cabins are in
the dust. . . . Ages hence, the inquisitive
white man, as he stands by some growing
city, will ponder on the structure of their
disturbed remains, and wonder to what
manner of persons they belonged. They
will live only in the songs and chronicles
of their exterminators. Let these be faithful to their rude virtues as men, and pay
due tribute to their unhappy fate as a
people.
　　—McGuffey's *Newly Revised*
　　　Rhetorical Guide (1853)

Give not, give not the yawning graves their plunder;
　　Save, save the lore, for future ages' joy;
The stories full of beauty and of wonder
　　The songs more pristine than the songs of Troy,
The ancient speech forever to be vanished—
　　Lore that tomorrow to the grave goes down!
All other thought from our horizon vanished,
　　Let any sacrifice our labor crown.
　　　—*John Peabody Harrington*
　　　　(1884-1961)

O<small>N</small> D<small>ECEMBER</small> 20, 1819, an Episcopal minister stepped before the New-York Historical Society to present a "Discourse on the Religion of the Indian Tribes of North America." The Reverend Samuel Farmar Jarvis could claim firsthand knowledge neither of the Indians he chose to speak of that day nor of their religion. Yet his speech, culled mostly from published sources and printed by the society the following year, reveals an unusually sensitive mind and presages some of the major issues that would trouble Americans throughout the rest of the century. Declaring that woodland Indians had long since ceased to inspire fear among settled white communities, Jarvis added: "In the room of fear, should now arise a sentiment of pity. The red men are melting, to borrow the expressive metaphor of one of their most celebrated warriors—'like snow before the sun'; and we should be anxious, before it is too late, to copy the evanescent features of their character, and to perpetuate them on the page of history."[1] Of course, Jarvis acknowledged, those eastern tribes in closest contact with expansion-minded whites had long since abandoned the beliefs and manners most worth preserving and studying: "When a race of men are mingled with others, who consider them as inferiors, they inevitably become so."[2] Instead of the specimen that Cooper would soon portray as Mohegan John—reduced by rum to basket weaving—Jarvis demanded that historians search out the still "uncivilized" and undegraded Chingachgook: "if we wish to see him in his original character, we must follow him to his native forests.— There, surely, he is worthy of our attention."[3] Once there, however, white researchers should not recklessly leap to facile conclusions or mistake reticence for ignorance.

> The Indians themselves are not communicative in relation to their religion; and it requires a good deal of familiar, attentive, and I may add, unsuspected observation, to obtain any knowledge respecting it. Hence, many who have been transiently resident among them, have very confidently pronounced, that they have no religion; an assertion, which subsequent and more accurate travellers have shown to be entirely unfounded.

[1] Jarvis, *A Discourse on the Religion of the Indian Tribes of North America* . . . (New York: C. Wiley and Co., 1820), p. 6. See also Elémire Zolla, *The Writer and the Shaman: A Morphology of the American Indian* (1969), trans. Raymond Rosenthal (New York: Harcourt Brace Jovanovich, 1973), p. 173.

[2] Jarvis, *Discourse*, p. 6.

[3] Ibid., p. 7.

Those, also, on whom we rely for information, have either been too little informed to know what to observe, or they have been influenced by peculiar modes of thinking, which have given a tinge to all they have said on the subject.[4]

Jarvis developed these ideas in some detail before concluding with the conventional exhortation that Americans had a duty to "civilize" and "Christianize" the "scanty remnants" of Indian tribes.[5]

Jarvis's encouragements and caveats to some of New York City's most respected citizens express insights far removed from the notions generally current in 1819. He proposed that indigenous populations were rapidly declining, that their religions, "character," and cultures remained unrecorded, and that only a willing suspension of disbelief plus patient study might reveal these complex subjects. No more than a few other Americans—notably Thomas L. McKenny—had actively responded to these issues in the first decades of the nineteenth century. McKenney's and King's documentation in paint, however, differed radically from the kind of effort Jarvis demanded of the student of culture. The artist ought to transcribe appearances; the student needed to press beneath them. Only then could he comprehend native assumptions at their most resonant levels.

That Charles Bird King and Karl Bodmer, Adam Clark Vroman and Frederick I. Monsen knew little about native values, sometimes after years of familiarity with tribes, hardly detracts from their records. As were many others, they were motivated by the prospect of physical rather than ideational loss. Jarvis's supposition that cultural values were imperiled found less immediate endorsement than the call for preservation of exotic scenes and artifacts that seemed to be disappearing. Exceptional figures such as George Catlin and Seth and Mary Eastman worked to preserve both physical image and cultural experience in paint and words. But before mid-century most considered these separate, sometimes even mutually exclusive activities.

Individual painters who hurried in the 1830s and 1840s to document indigenous tribes were largely unaffected by earlier sentimental representations of the Indian. Abstract painterly norms and contemporary aesthetic theory influenced them far more than reductive assumptions about native cultures. Clearly, however, those who recognized a more compelling value in disappearing vocabularies and myths, traditions and customs were too often influenced by such assumptions. To understand why whites, almost without exception, fell victim to simplistic interpretations of native cultures requires a

[4] Ibid., pp. 7-8.   [5] Ibid., pp. 63-64.

quick review of intellectual history. Only against the backdrop of received ideas about race and culture can one appreciate the actual achievement of those in the nineteenth century who attempted to preserve a record of disappearing tribal cultures.

The tribes peopling the Western Hemisphere descended from successive bands of Asiatic nomads that migrated via a land bridge across the Bering Strait at least ten thousand years before Christ. Subsequent isolation ensured genetic uniformity, while tribal exchanges over the millenniums assured similar social, economic, even religious characteristics. Despite these similarities, however, the groups of "Indians" observed by Columbus and subsequent explorers proved to be far more various than whites imagined.[6] They differed radically in cultural assumptions and, in 1492, spoke between one and two thousand separate languages. The diversity suggested by this figure was compounded by European conquerors and colonials, who altered native life in obvious ways and in others more subtle, including trading and settlement patterns.[7]

This broad spectrum of cultural variation had little effect upon successive waves of European explorers and settlers, who continued generation after generation to project assumptions onto "the Indian."[8] In the earliest years, colonists admired the natives' communal ownership, simple fashions in dress, and apparently lax sexual morality.[9]

[6] On this point, see William Brandon, *The Last American: The Indian in American Culture* (New York: McGraw-Hill, 1974); Alfred W. Crosby Jr., *The Columbian Exchange: Biological and Cultural Consequences of 1492*, Contributions in American Studies, no. 2 (Westport, Conn.: Greenwood Publishing Co., 1972), esp. pp. 21ff.; John C. Ewers, "When Red and White Men Meet," *Western Historical Quarterly*, 2 (April 1971), 133-35; Edward H. Spicer, *Cycles of Conquest: The Impact of Spain, Mexico, and the United States on the Indians of the Southwest, 1533-1960* (Tucson: University of Arizona Press, 1962); Robert F. Berkhofer Jr., *The White Man's Indian: Images of the American Indian from Columbus to the Present* (New York: Alfred A. Knopf, 1978), esp. pp. 5-29; Wilbur R. Jacobs, "The Tip of an Iceberg: Pre-Columbian Indian Demography and Some Implications for Revisionism," *William and Mary Quarterly*, 3d ser., 31 (January 1974), 123-32; Wilcomb E. Washburn, *The Indian in America* (New York: Harper and Row, 1975), esp. pp. xv-xvii; Philip Borden, "Found Cumbering the Soil: Manifest Destiny and the Indian in the Nineteenth Century," in Gary B. Nash and Richard Weiss, eds., *The Great Fear: Race in the Mind of America* (New York: Holt, Rinehart and Winston, 1970), pp. 78-79; Stuart Levine, "*Sacred Circles*: Native American Art and American Culture," *American Quarterly*, 30 (Spring 1978), 108-23.

[7] See Oscar Lewis, *The Effects of White Contact upon Blackfoot Culture, with Special Reference to the Role of the Fur Trade*, monograph of the American Ethnological Society, vol. 6 (New York: J. J. Augustin, 1942); Spicer, *Cycles of Conquest*, pp. 1-5.

[8] Roy Harvey Pearce, *Savagism and Civilization: A Study of the Indian and the American Mind*, rev. ed. (Baltimore: Johns Hopkins University Press, 1965), Berkhofer, *White Man's Indian*.

[9] Brandon, *The Last Americans*, pp. 4-6.

Disaffected European intellectuals may have idealized this "natural" state through the eighteenth century, but American colonials abandoned the convention far earlier.[10] Indeed, the 1622 Jamestown massacre confirmed a racism in the southern colonies equal to that of the Massachusetts religious settlements. The need to justify displacement or extermination, to vindicate a sense of westward mission, steeled contemptuous colonists to dismiss "savage" ways. Of course, this kind of uninformed racism only mirrors the earlier idealization: both responses essentially ignored tribal cultures by reducing them to a single, limited group of values.

Exceptional figures resisted such stereotypes. John Smith and Roger Williams, for two early examples, studied local tribes with critical admiration and recorded their religious practices.[11] Others traveling among eastern tribes in the next two centuries also awoke to their unexpectedly rich cultural life. Missionaries in particular—John Eliot, Joseph Lafitau, and Gabriel Sagard, for example—attempted to understand those whom they intended to convert. They lived with woodland tribes and made extensive ethnographic studies of "their dances, songs, and other silly ceremonies," as Father Sagard entitled a chapter of his subsequent account.[12] Yet for all of their tolerant interest in native life, that description dramatically betrays the condescending air that most whites shared toward Indians.

Though some eighteenth-century European intellectuals were considering issues of culture and civilization, relatively few travel accounts of the period evince appreciation for indigenous tribes on their own cultural terms. The variously bedaubed and bedecked subjects

[10] Gary B. Nash, "The Image of the Indian in the Southern Colonial Mind," *William and Mary Quarterly*, 3d ser., 29 (April 1972), 217; Nash, "Red, White and Black: The Origins of Racism in Colonial America," in Nash and Weiss, eds., *The Great Fear*, pp. 4-9; Berkhofer, *White Man's Indian*, pp. 23-25; Bordon, "Found Cumbering the Soil," pp. 72ff.; Wilbur R. Jacobs, *Dispossessing the American Indian: Indians and Whites on the Colonial Frontier* (New York: Charles Scribner's Sons, 1972), esp. pp. 2-5; Winthrop D. Jordan, *White Over Black: American Attitudes toward the Negro, 1550-1812* (Chapel Hill: University of North Carolina Press, 1968), pp. ix, 26-27; Frank Shuffelton, "Indian Devils and Pilgrim Fathers: Squanto, Hobomok, and the English Conception of Indian Religion," *New England Quarterly*, 49 (March 1976), 108-16; Benjamin Keen, *The Aztec Image in Western Thought* (New Brunswick: Rutgers University Press, 1971), esp. pp. 55, 307-9, 352-56.

[11] Nash, "Image of the Indian," pp. 215, 223; Thomas F. Gossett, *Race: The History of an Idea in America* (Dallas: Southern Methodist University Press, 1963), p. 19.

[12] Sagard, *The Long Journey to the Country of the Hurons* (1639), trans. H. H. Langton, ed. George M. Wrong (Toronto: Champlain Society, 1939), p. 115. See also Zolla, *The Writer and the Shaman*, pp. 41ff.; Brandon, *The Last Americans*, p. 5; John Hopkins Kennedy, *Jesuit and Savage in New France* (New Haven: Yale University Press, 1950), esp. pp. 103-9.

sometimes peer through an imposed mask of primitiveness to claim their humanity; but these examples were too few to effect even subtle change in the European conception of the Indian as deficient. He required conversion, sacred and secular. Individuals such as the Virginia planter Robert Beverley or John Heckewelder, the Moravian missionary in Pennsylvania, may have admired elements of tribal life, just so long as these did not counter their own Christian assumptions.[13]

This inability to see native Americans without prejudice persisted well into the nineteenth century. Again, the intentions of those hoping to educate and Christianize childlike primitives differed little in effect, if not motive, from the determination of those bent on destroying brute savages.[14] Kindness, as Indians soon discovered, could kill as effectively as bullets. Nineteenth-century activists attracted far more support in efforts to reform native tribes than had their few philanthropical predecessors a century earlier. Yet even they held little more informed estimations of the tribes they proposed to help.[15] Archaeologists claimed that indigenous peoples were incapable of constructing the earthwork mounds that dotted the landscape east of the Mississippi River; the structures seemed too complex, their treasures too wonderful. Instead, they devised theories of glorious mound builders destroyed in some distant past by ravaging hordes, the ancestors of present Indian tribes.[16] Ethnologists created elaborate proofs for Indian inferiority based on skull size and house structure.[17]

[13] Nash, "Image of the Indian," pp. 222, 226; Nash, "Red, White and Black," p. 9; Zolla, *The Writer and the Shaman,* pp. 63-77. For Heckewelder's nonetheless incisive descriptions, see *30,000 Miles with John Heckewelder,* ed. Paul A. W. Wallace (Pittsburgh: University of Pittsburgh Press, 1958), esp. pp. v-vii, 44-45, 331-33.

[14] Bernard W. Sheehan, *Seeds of Extinction: Jeffersonian Philanthropy and the American Indian* (New York: W. W. Norton, 1973). See also Michael Rogin, review of Sheehan, *Seeds of Extinction,* and Slotkin, *Regeneration through Violence,* in *Journal of Ethnic Studies,* 2 (Spring 1974), 93-104.

[15] Francis Paul Prucha, S.J., ed., *Americanizing the American Indians: Writings by the "Friends of the Indian," 1880-1900* (Cambridge, Mass.: Harvard University Press, 1973), esp. pp. 1-8, 45; Prucha, "Indian Policy Reform and American Protestantism, 1880-1900," in Ray Allen Billington, ed., *People of the Plains and Mountains,* Contributions in American History, no. 25 (Westport, Conn.: Greenwood Press, 1973), pp. 120-45; Robert A. Trennert Jr., *Alternative to Extinction: Federal Indian Policy and the Beginnings of the Reservation System, 1846-51* (Philadelphia: Temple University Press, 1975); Robert Winston Mardock, *The Reformers and the American Indian* (Columbia: University of Missouri Press, 1971), esp. pp. 1-3, 87; Henry E. Fritz, *The Movement for Indian Assimilation, 1860-1890* (Philadelphia: University of Pennsylvania Press, 1963).

[16] Robert Silverberg, *Mound Builders of Ancient America: The Archaeology of a Myth* (Greenwich, Conn.: New York Graphic Society, 1968), pp. 6ff., 97-103, 170.

[17] William Stanton, *The Leopard's Spots: Scientific Attitudes toward Race in America, 1815-59* (Chicago: University of Chicago Press, 1960), esp. pp. 25-45, 85-86; Gossett, *Race,* esp. pp. 54ff., 228ff.

McGuffey readers and other popular grade-school texts rationalized extermination of tribes on religious and philosophical grounds.[18] Professional historians rarely quarreled with this view. As Thoreau observed in his journal, "though he professes more humanity than the trapper, mountain man, or gold digger, who shoots one as a wild beast, [the historian] really exhibits and practices a similar inhumanity to [the Indian], wielding a pen instead of a rifle."[19]

Nevertheless, against this essentially static background of cultural thought, one can discern a swelling undercurrent of concern to record native life, an undercurrent that finally surfaced in the 1820s.[20] Earlier chapters have noted the anxiety that impelled the documenting of landscapes and wildlife. A similar feeling spurred similar attempts on behalf of native tribes. As well, eastern white communities felt relatively secure from tribal retaliation at just the time when the romantic movement encouraged the sentimentalization of the primitive. Whatever the constellation of causes, interest in recording threatened vocabularies, myths, and traditions followed a pattern similar to that of the earlier concern for documenting the native American's physical world. That urge to preserve visual representations of the Indian as the prime human constituent of a vanishing wilderness led first to vague sketches and random portraits and then grew into efforts at systematic, comprehensive pictorials. Similarly, concern to fix on record not only the painted or photographed "exterior" but also the more complex "interior" forms evolved from upsophisticated adjurations among a smattering of enthusiasts into a chorus of serious ethnographic efforts.[21]

[18] Richard D. Mosier, *Making the American Mind: Social and Moral Ideas in the McGuffey Readers* (New York: Columbia University Press, 1947), pp. 148-51; Ruth Miller Elson, *Guardians of Tradition: American Schoolbooks of the Nineteenth Century* (Lincoln: University of Nebraska Press, 1964), pp. 71-79.

[19] Thoreau, *Journal*, cited in Jacobs, *Dispossessing the American Indian*, p. 19. See also Louise K. Barnett, *The Ignoble Savage: American Literary Racism, 1790-1890*, Contributions in American Studies, no. 18 (Westport, Conn.: Greenwood Press, 1975), p. 190; David Levin, *History as Romantic Art: Bancroft, Prescott, Motley, and Parkman* (Stanford: Stanford University Press, 1959), esp. pp. 136-38.

[20] Cf. Guillaume T. F. Raynal, *Histoire philosophique des Indes* (1773), cited in Kennedy, *Jesuit and Savage in ·New France*, p. 191. See also Nash, "Image of the Indian," p. 222. For a contrary opinion, see Berkhofer, *White Man's Indian*, pp. 88-89.

[21] In part, this effort may have reflected a general response to the widespread assumption of Indian extinction. See Robert F. Sayre, *Thoreau and the American Indians* (Princeton: Princeton University Press, 1977), p. 27; Berkhofer, *White Man's Indian*, pp. 88-89; Brian William Dippie, "The Vanishing American: Popular Attitudes and American Indian Policy in the Nineteenth Century" (Ph.D. diss., University of Texas, Austin, 1970), p. v; Richard Slotkin, *Regeneration through Violence: The Mythology of the American Frontier, 1600-1860* (Middletown, Conn.: Wesleyan University Press, 1973), p. 357.

Once again, little coherent thinking on the issue, much less a consolidated movement, ever developed. Few knew of like-minded enthusiasts in archaeology and archival collecting, linguistic ethnology and cultural anthropology. Yet taken together, the concerns of these men and women define a growing unrest with the state of knowledge of native tribes. Most important, that unrest forms more than an interesting strand in American intellectual history, for it fostered extensive, systematic study of numerous nonwhite cultures.

FRONTIER JOURNALS AND INDIAN BIOGRAPHIES

At its most elementary level, apprehension for vanishing tribes revealed itself in diaries, memoirs, and informal travel accounts. Such expressions, which continued nearly to the present day, consist of no more than vague laments. Joshua Clark, for example, noted in 1849 that "Indian tradition, with all its vivacity and interest, is fearfully becoming extinct. A few short years and nothing new can possibly be gleaned."[22] Reiterating this motive, frontiersmen kept journals that bracket useful accounts of native habits with predictions of their decline. Others fed a popular appetite for such material by bringing together anecdotes collected either directly from natives or from manuscripts and books.[23] Indians themselves sometimes used acquired

[22] Joshua V. H. Clark, *Onondaga; or, Reminiscences of Earlier and Later Times . . .* , 2 vols. (Syracuse: Stoddard and Babcock, 1849), 1:xiv. See also *Biblical Reportory and Princeton Review*, 10 (October 1838), 513; Abbé Emmanuel Domenech, *Seven Years' Residence in the Great Deserts of North America*, 2 vols. (London: Longman, Green, Longman, and Roberts, 1860), 1:vii-xi, 439, 461; James Buchanan, *Sketches of the History, Manners and Customs of the North American Indians* (London: Black, Young, and Young, 1824), pp. vii-ix, 1, 9, 13; Peter Skene Ogden, *Traits of American-Indian Life and Character by a Fur Trader* (London: Smith, Elder and Co., 1853), p. xi; *Peter Skene Ogden's Snake Country Journal, 1826-27*, ed. K. G. Davies, intro. by Dorothy O. Johansen, Publications of the Hudson's Bay Record Society, 23 (London: Hudson's Bay Record Society, 1961), pp. lxxi, 35, 68; John Dunn, *History of the Oregon Territory* (London: Edwards and Hughes, 1844), pp. 54-57; George Frederick Ruxton, *Life in the Far West* (1848), ed. LeRoy R. Hafen (Norman: University of Oklahoma Press, 1951), pp. 90-91, 99-100, 105-6; *Ruxton of the Rockies*, ed. LeRoy R. Hafen (Norman: University of Oklahoma Press, 1950), p. 46; John C. Cremony, *Life Among the Apaches* (San Francisco: A. Roman and Co., 1868), pp. 11-12, 310-13.

[23] See Alfred Benjamin Meacham, *Wigwam and War-Path; or, The Royal Chief in Chains*, rev. ed. (Boston: John P. Dale and Co., 1875), intro. by Wendell Phillips, p. iv; Fannie Reed Giffen, *Oo-Mah-Ha Ta-Wa-Tha (Omaha City)* (Lincoln, Nebr.: n.p., 1898), p. 7; Walter McClintock, *Old Indian Trails* (Boston: Houghton Mifflin Co., 1923), p. viii; George Wharton James, *Indian Basketry* (Pasadena: n.p., 1901), pp. 9-10, 16; review of John Dunn Hunter, *Memoirs of a Captivity among the Indians of North America*, and James Buchanan, *Sketches of the History, Manners and Customs of the North American Indians*, in *Quarterly Review*, 31 (1825), 76-77.

skills to preserve an accurate memory of their experiences. As one Pawnee chief regretfully noted in the 1880s, "Already the old things are being lost, and those who knew the secrets are many of them dead. If we had known how to write, we would have put all these things down, and they would not have been forgotten. . . . It may be that they have changed as they passed from father to son, and it is well that they should be put down, so that our children, when they are like the white people, can know what were their fathers' ways."[24] George Copway, the great Ojibwa chief and later Wesleyan missionary, prefaced his *Traditional History and Characteristic Sketches of the Ojibway Nation* (1850) with a rationale at once similar and yet more profound: "I feel incompetent for my work, but am impelled forward by the thought that the nation whose history I here feebly sketch seems passing away, and that unless a work like this is sent forth, much, very much, that is interesting and instructive in that nation's actions, will with it pass away."[25] He added that the remaining Indians "hold a key which will unlock a library of information, the like of which is not. It is for the present generation to say, whether the last remnants of a powerful people shall perish through neglect, and as they depart bear with them that key."[26] The notion that whites held an obligation to themselves as well as to posterity—that Indian experience could be valuable in and of itself, learned from as well as documented—appears increasingly throughout the nineteenth century and forms a recurrent theme in this and following chapters.

White and native self-consciousness about the need for records lends an ironic continuity to the efforts of the Eastman family. In the 1840s, Mary Eastman asked her friend Caroline Kirkland to compose a preface for her collection of Dakota Sioux myths. Attempting to explain Mrs. Eastman's project, the popular novelist declared that the Indian is "our own, and passing away—while we take no pains to arrest their fleeting traits or to record their picturesque traditions. . . . We are continually reproached by British writers for the obtuse carelessness with which we are allowing these people . . . to go into the annihilation which seems their inevitable fate as civilization advances, without

[24] Cited in George Bird Grinnell, *Pawnee Hero Stories and Folk-Tales with Notes on the Origin, Customs and Character of the Pawnee People* (New York: Charles Scribner's Sons, 1890), p. vi, also pp. vi-xvii, 406-8.

[25] George Copway, *The Traditional History and Characteristic Sketches of the Ojibway Nation* (London: Charles Gilpin, 1850), p. vii. See also Copway, *The Life, History, and Travels of Kah-Ge-Ga-Gah-Bowh* (Albany: n.p., 1847), pp. 7, 55.

[26] Copway, *Traditional History*, p. viii.

an effort to secure and record all that they are able to communicate respecting themselves."[27] Little could she have guessed at the double edge to her words. One of painter Seth Eastman's intimate contacts with the Dakota Sioux prior to his marriage would result in a grandson, Charles Eastman, who would write prolifically of his Sioux childhood before receiving a Dartmouth and medical education.[28] Dr. Eastman's various reminiscences did not pretend to scientific exactitude any more than had Copway's. Yet, as his white grandfather had been motivated to paint, he intended his autobiographies to preserve a history that few others could hope to know and record.[29]

Earlier in the nineteenth century, Indian biography, not autobiography, enjoyed wide popularity, analogous in many ways to the public enthusiasm for studio portraits of tribal chieftains. Consisting of European literary conventions stalely imposed upon native materials, these works rather crudely combine extensive passages of tribal history with narratives of exemplary figures. Nevertheless, impelling their authors was a desire "not merely to introduce to the reading public the Leading Men of the Indian Territory their laws and customs, etc.," as one practitioner stumblingly announced, "but to perpetuate for all time the memories of the most illustrious among the great American aborigines."[30]

Catlin's patron, publisher William Stone, had planned a comprehensive six-volume history of the famous Iroquois Confederacy long before he met the obsessed young painter. So strong was the biographical convention, however, that the two volumes he completed

[27] C. M. Kirkland, preface to Mary Eastman, *Dahcotah; or, Life and Legends of the Sioux Around Fort Snelling* (1849; rpt. Minneapolis: Ross and Haines, 1962), pp. vi, viii.

[28] John Francis McDermott, *Seth Eastman: Pictorial Historian of the Indian* (Norman: University of Oklahoma Press, 1961), p. 18.

[29] Charles Alexander Eastman, *Indian Boyhood*, illus. by E. L. Blumenschein (1902; rpt. Boston: Little, Brown and Co., 1918), esp. pp. 1, 181; Eastman, *The Soul of the Indian: An Interpretation* (Boston: Houghton Mifflin Co., 1911), foreword; Eastman, *From the Deep Woods to Civilization: Chapters in the Autobiography of an Indian* (1916; rpt. Boston: Little, Brown and Co., 1917), esp. pp. 166-67.

[30] Harry F. O'Beirne, *Leaders and Leading Men of the Indian Territory*, vol. 1, *Choctows and Chickasaws* (Chicago: American Publishers' Association, 1891), p. i. See also Minnie Myrtle, *The Iroquois; or, The Bright Side of Indian Character* (New York: D. Appleton and Co., 1855), pp. 12, 14-15, 24-25, 298; Zolla, *The Writer and the Shaman*, pp. 183-84. Roy Harvey Pearce discusses this subject in *Savagism and Civilization*, esp. p. 118, concentrating on the two best-known antiquarian scholars, Benjamin Thatcher and Samuel Gardner Drake. In contrast to Pearce's conclusions, see an anonymous review of Thatcher's *Indian Biography* (1833) in *Knickerbocker*, 2 (August 1833), 139, and Benjamin Drake, *The Life and Adventures of Black Hawk* (1838), 7th ed. rev. (Cincinnati: E. Morgan and Co., 1850).

before his death in 1844 each focused on a famous Indian leader.[31] Inspiring him was the explicit fear that the events, traditions, and myths that he had learned as a boy, and that still lived in the memories of local natives, were disappearing with old-timers into the grave.[32] For his efforts in searching out yellowing manuscripts and graying survivors, Stone won plaudits from whites and an honorary chieftainship from the Seneca tribe.

VOCABULARIES AND GRAMMARS

Although praiseworthy in intent, Stone's and others' ventures achieved little of value. More sharply focused, deliberate, and even scientific attempts to preserve the facts of Indian cultural life had been undertaken since before the turn of the century. For the most part, these efforts were directed at recording vocabularies and grammars. Thomas Jefferson, for example, lamented in his *Notes* the loss to history even by 1782 of linguistic accounts of "so many of the Indian tribes."[33] But he did more than lament. As he observed in 1809 to a like-minded friend, "I have now been thirty years availing myself of every possible opportunity of procuring Indian vocabularies to the same set of words; my opportunities were probably better than will ever occur again to any person having the same desire."[34] One of those opportunities had been the expedition on which he sent Meriwether Lewis and William Clark half a dozen years earlier. Subsequent surveys were also encouraged to collect ethnological information and were joined in these efforts by private historical and antiquarian societies.[35]

[31] William L. Stone, *Life of Joseph Brant—Thayendanegea, Including the Indian Wars of the American Revolution*, 2 vols. (New York: George Dearborn and Co., 1838); Stone, *The Life and Times of Red-Jacket, or Sa-Go-Ye-Wat-Ha; Being the Sequel to the History of the Six Nations* (New York: Wiley and Putnam, 1841).

[32] See William L. Stone Jr., "Memoir," in the 1866 edition of *The Life and Times of Red-Jacket*, p. 74.

[33] Cited in Paul Russell Cutright, *Lewis and Clark: Pioneering Naturalists* (Urbana: University of Illinois Press, 1969), p. 7. Henry R. Schoolcraft liked this statement also, invoking it in his *Archives of Aboriginal Knowledge*, 6 vols. (Philadelphia: J. B. Lippincott and Co., 1860), 5:viii. See also Pearce, *Savagism and Civilization*, pp. 78ff.

[34] Cited by Cutright, *Lewis and Clark*, p. 7.

[35] See Rev. Jedidiah Morse, *A Report to the Secretary of War of the United States on Indian Affairs . . .* (New Haven: S. Converse, 1822), esp. pp. 31-32, 66-67; Lt. Amiel Weeks Whipple, *Reports on Explorations and Surveys . . .* , Senate Executive Documents, 33d Cong., 2d sess., 185?, vol. 3, no. 78, esp. pt. 3, pp. 43ff.; Gibbs, *Indian Tribes of Washington Territory: Pacific Northwest Letters of George Gibbs* (1854; rpt. Fairfield, Wash.: Ye Galleon Press, 1976). See as well Constantin F. C. Volney, *A View of the Soil and Climate of the United States of America* (London: J. Johnson, 1804), pp. 488-89. For a curiously opposite contemporary

Amateur linguistic ethnologists began to appear in significant numbers only in the 1820s. There were exceptions, of course, including most singularly Jefferson. Two centuries earlier, Christian missionaries had collected word lists as aids to conversion and in rare cases had made extensive notes explicitly to preserve languages imperiled by their missionary efforts.[36] By the mid-1840s, the indefatigable Reverend Stephen R. Riggs was self-consciously following the example of early ethnographers in his admirable series of grammars and vocabularies of northern Plains tribes.[37] Enthusiastic and sometimes talented, these self-styled linguists—army personnel, boundary commissioners, frontiersmen, doctors, even a Canadian magistrate—worked diligently against time with little hope of reward.[38] Near mid-century, one of them regretted how little of Indian life remained in characteristic tones. "What was once an easy attainment, was then neglected," he observed, deploring the inadequate word lists made earlier by those with greater opportunity. "Such as it is, however, we feel very grateful for it; though small, still it is precious. . . ."[39] This alternation between regret at the loss and relief at what had been

response, see the anonymous review of Morse's *Report* in *North American Review*, 16 (January 1823), esp. 30-33, 39-40. See also Pearce, *Savagism and Civilization*, pp. 112ff.

[36] Edmund De Schweinitz, *The Life and Times of David Zeisberger: The Western Pioneer and Apostle of the Indians* (Philadelphia: J. B. Lippincott and Co., 1870), pp. 161-62, 189, 253, 686; Kennedy, *Jesuit and Savage in New France*, esp. pp. 97ff., 191.

[37] See Leslie A. White's introduction to Lewis Henry Morgan, *The Indian Journals, 1859-62*, ed. White (Ann Arbor: University of Michigan Press, 1959), pp. 7-8; William Goetzmann, *Exploration and Empire: The Explorer and the Scientist in the Winning of the American West* (New York: Alfred A. Knopf, 1966), p. 232; Stephen R. Riggs, *Dakota-English Dictionary* (1852), Contributions to North American Ethnology, no. 7 (Washington: G.P.O., 1897), p. 1. See also Rev. Marie Charles Pandosy, *Grammar and Dictionary of the Yakima Language*, trans. and ed. George Gibbs and J. G. Shea (New York: Cramoisy Press, 1862), p. 1.

[38] John Russell Bartlett, *Personal Narrative of Explorations and Incidents in Texas, New Mexico, California, Sonora, and Chihuahua, Connected with the United States and Mexican Boundary Commission, During the Years 1850, '51, '52, and '53*, 2 vols. (New York: D. Appleton and Co., 1854), esp. 1:vi; Robert V. Hine, *Bartlett's West: Drawing the Mexican Boundary* (New Haven: Yale University Press, 1968), esp. pp. 54, 63-65; Joshua V. H. Clark, *Lights and Lines of Indian Character and Scenes of Pioneer Life* (Syracuse: E. H. Babcock and Co., 1854), pp. iii-iv; Myrtle, *The Iroquois*, pp. 13-14; Joseph Barrett, *The Indian of New-England and the North-Eastern Provinces* (Middletown, Conn.: Charles H. Pelton, 1851), esp. p. 2; Gilbert Malcolm Sproat, *Scenes and Studies of Savage Life* (London: Smith, Elder and Co., 1868), p. 10; *The Journals of Captain Nathaniel J. Wyeth* (Fairfield, Wash.: Ye Galleon Press, 1969), pp. 106-9, 118-20, 129-31. On Wyeth, see Joseph Kastner, *A Species of Eternity* (New York: Alfred A. Knopf, 1977), pp. 277-80.

[39] Barrett, *Indian of New-England*, p. 2.

salvaged forms a basic rhythm to statements by collectors throughout the century.

To repeat, then, the urgent need for a comprehensive linguistic study of Indian tribes was apparent by the 1820s. Albert Gallatin, Jefferson's illustrious secretary of the Treasury and Monroe's minister to France, began in 1823 to collect word lists. Retiring from public life eight years later, he turned fully to the project. By 1843, he had published the most exhaustive contemporary study of native vocabularies, helped to found and become the first president of the American Ethnological Society of New York, and achieved the reputation of "father of American ethnology."[40] Others similarly anxious and similarly interested in comparative philology set out near mid-century to rescue vocabularies collected earlier but forgotten.[41] At the end of the century, however, sophisticated studies in linguistic anthropology were still operating under the premises of early, amateur efforts. Franz Boas's linguistic analyses and Gallatin's tribal word lists, separated by more than seventy years, share a common belief that language, like a master key, would open a series of locked cultural doors.

Though linguistic interpretation advanced relatively little in the nineteenth century, the number of those collecting tribal vocabularies grew dramatically. Confirming the heightened consciousness of a need for haste is the incidence of such phrases as "yet attainable," "while we may," "none too soon," and "will be too late."[42] Moreover, collectors recognized that the task required greater ingenuity. Horatio Hale, America's most distinguished nineteenth-century linguist after Gallatin, effected a dramatic coup in 1870 by seeking out "the lone centurion surviving fullblood" of the Tutelo tribe and patiently transcribing the Tutelo language.[43] Other vocabularies would be snatched

[40] Henry Adams, *The Life of Albert Gallatin* (Philadelphia: J. B. Lippincott, 1880), p. 644. See also *Selected Writings of Albert Gallatin*, ed. E. James Ferguson (New York: Bobbs-Merrill, 1967); Albert Gallatin, "A Synopsis of the Indian Tribes of North America," *Archaeologica Americana: Transactions and Collections of the American Antiquarian Society*, 2 (1836), 1-422; Gallatin, "Notes on the Semi-Civilized Nations of Mexico, Yucatan, and Central America," *Transactions of the American Ethnological Society*, 1 (1845), 1-352; Pearce, *Savagism and Civilization*, p. 114n.

[41] See Hermann E. Ludewig, *The Literature of American Aboriginal Languages*, ed. Nicolas Trübner (London: Trübner and Co., 1858), pp. vi, xi.

[42] See John Wesley Powell, *Introduction to the Study of Indian Languages with Words Phrases and Sentences to be Collected* (1877), 2d ed. (Washington: G.P.O., 1880), p. v.

[43] William N. Fenton, introduction to Horatio Hale, ed., *The Iroquois Book of Rites* (1883), ed. Fenton (Toronto: University of Toronto Press, 1963), p. xii.

from the grave by other ethnologists struggling alone, motivated by a similar sense of personal mission.[44]

The federal government, led by Secretary of the Smithsonian Institution Joseph Henry, increasingly recognized its responsibility for preserving and studying information on the western tribes. The institution's first thirty years chronicle a pattern of continual official pleading for ethnological collecting.[45] Under pressure from the forceful, far-sighted John Wesley Powell (1834-1902), Congress finally established the Bureau of American Ethnology as a branch of the Smithsonian in 1879.[46] Powell, who pursued careers enough for three men, all aimed at intelligent settlement of western lands, directed the newly formed bureau into two decades of large-scale, well-funded, expert compiling of vocabularies "of those languages which can still be successfully studied."[47] During his very first year in office, he publicly pleaded for American scholars to devote themselves to such work.[48] Accomplished scientists, including Washington Matthews, James C. Pilling, and George A. Dorsey, heeded his call, often out of explicit agreement with Powell's forebodings.[49] Even though much

[44] See, for instance, Albert Gatschet, "The Karankawa Indians, the Coast People of Texas," *Archaeological and Ethnological Papers of the Peabody Museum*, 1, no. 2 (1891), 69-70.

[45] Henry, "Circular Relating to Collections in Archaeology and Ethnology," *Smithsonian Miscellaneous Collections*, 8 (1868), 1-2; Henry, "Circular in Reference to American Archaeology," ibid., 15 (1878), 1. See also Pearce, *Savagism and Civilization*, pp. 129-30; William Henry Holmes, *Archaeological Studies among the Ancient Cities of Mexico*, Field Columbian Museum Publication, 8, 16 (Chicago, 1895), p. 15; Edgar L. Hewitt, "The Groundwork of American Archaeology," *Papers of the School of American Archaeology*, 1 (1908), reprinted in *American Anthropologist*, 10 (October-December 1908), 595.

[46] Neil M. Judd, *The Bureau of American Ethnology: A Partial History* (Norman: University of Oklahoma Press, 1967), pp. 2-4.

[47] John Wesley Powell, "Preface," *Bureau of Ethnology: Annual Reports*, 2 (1880-81), xx. See also William Culp Darrah, *Powell of the Colorado* (Princeton: Princeton University Press, 1951), esp. pp. 194, 255-56, 259, 262; Wallace Stegner, *Beyond the Hundredth Meridian: John Wesley Powell and the Second Opening of the West* (Boston: Houghton Mifflin Co., 1954), esp. pp. 256-60; John Upton Terrell, *The Man Who Rediscovered America: A Biography of John Wesley Powell* (New York: Weybright and Talley, 1969), pp. 162ff. See also Judd, *Bureau of American Ethnology*, p. 19; Brian M. Fagan, *Elusive Treasure: The Story of Early Archaeologists in the Americas* (New York: Charles Scribner's Sons, 1977), 285-95; Goetzmann, *Exploration and Empire*, pp. 530-76.

[48] Powell, *Study of Indian Languages*, p. viii.

[49] Washington Matthews, *Ethnology and Philology of the Hidatsa Indians*, U.S. Geological and Geographical Survey, Miscellaneous Publications, no. 7 (Washington: G.P.O., 1877), pp. 30-31; George A. Dorsey, *The Arapaho Sun Dance: The Ceremony of the Offerings Lodge*, Field Columbian Museum Publication 75 (Chicago, 1903), p. 2; Dorsey, *Traditions of the Osage*, Field Museum Publication 88 (Chicago, 1904), p. v; Dorsey, *The Cheyenne*, vol. 1, *Ceremonial Organization*, Field Columbian Museum

of the best anthropology at the century's end narrowed its focus to linguistic considerations, it did not ignore the contexts newly provided by cultural and physical anthropologists. "A language is best understood," Powell admonished, "when the habits, customs, institutions, philosophy,—the subject-matter of thought imbodied in the language are best known. The student of language should be a student of the people who speak the language."[50]

CUSTOMS AND LORE

Half a century before Powell espoused his ethnographic principle, others with little sense for the possibilities of linguistic anthropology dismissed the supposedly narrow assumptions of word-list gatherers. Such simplistic efforts, they thought, misrepresented the complexity of native languages; even worse, these enthusiasts ignored other, more valuable materials equally imperiled.[51] Crèvecoeur in 1800 was certainly not the first layman, nor Edmund Wilson in 1947 the last, enthralled enough by native myths and rituals to want to transcribe them.[52] In the nineteenth century, however, the sheer number of amateurs who set down native folklore and traditions represents a striking testament to white apprehension. Their efforts—those of Mary Eastman with Dakota tribes in the 1840s and of George Bird Grinnell among the Montana Pawnee and Blackfoot in the 1870s— derived almost entirely from a consciousness of imminent loss.[53] Simi-

---

Publication 99 (Chicago, 1905), p. v; Dorsey, *The Ponca Sun Dance*, Field Columbian Museum Publication 102 (Chicago, 1905), p. 67; James Constantine Pilling, *Bibliography of the Siouan Languages*, Bureau of American Ethnology, Bulletin no. 5 (Washington: G.P.O., 1887); Pilling, *Bibliography of the Chinookan Languages* (Washington: G.P.O., 1893), p. vi.

[50] Powell, *Study of Indian Languages*, p. vi.

[51] See, for instance, Caleb Atwater's animadversions on missionary vocabularies as fundamentally simplistic, in *Remarks Made on a Tour to Prairie Du Chien; Thence to Washington City, in 1829* (Columbus: Isaac N. Whiting, 1831), pp. 78-81.

[52] Michel-Guillaume St. Jean de Crèvecoeur, *Journey into Northern Pennsylvania and the State of New York* (1801), trans. Clarissa Spencer Bostelmann, 3 vols. in 1 (Ann Arbor: University of Michigan Press, 1964), pp. 221-35; Edmund Wilson, *Red, Black, Blond and Olive—Studies in Four Civilizations: Zuni, Haiti, Soviet Russia, Israel* (New York: Oxford University Press, 1956), pp. 23ff.

[53] Grinnell, *Pawnee Hero Stories*, p. x; Eastman, *Dahcotah*, p. xvi; Eastman, *The American Aboriginal Portfolio* (Philadelphia: Lippincott, Grambo and Co., [1853]), pp. v, xi, xii, 80. See also George Bird Grinnell, *Blackfoot Lodge Tales: The Story of a Prairie People* (1903?; rpt. Lincoln: University of Nebraska Press, 1962), pp. ix, xi-xv; *The Passing of the Great West: Selected Papers of George Bird Grinnell*, ed. John T. Rieger (New York: Winchester Press, 1972), esp. pp. 2, 65, 69. Missionaries also transcribed native myths out of similar apprehensions. See, for example: Pierre Jean De Smet, S.J., *Oregon Missions and Travels Over the Rocky Mountains, in 1845-46* (1847), rpt. in vol. 29 of Reubon Gold Thwaites, ed., *Early Western Travels: 1748-*

larly, the popular essayist Charles Godfrey Leland attempted to transcribe all he could of the surprisingly rich oral tradition still extant in the 1880s among the Algonquin Passamaquoddy. In resisting interpretive comment, he nicely expressed what many responsible ethnographers also felt: "when the Indian shall have passed away there will come far better ethnologists than I am, who will be much more obliged to me for collecting raw material than for cooking it."[54] Leland was right not only in maintaining this cautious critical stance but also in recognizing the cumulative value of his and others' work. Whether or not his pleas for broad public participation in such efforts converted his contemporaries, many were already attempting to track down "every scrap of information" before "the Indians shall have departed."[55]

Leland's appreciation of native life preceded his initiation into the Kaw tribe of Kansas. Other whites awoke to the value of recording the knowledge they had gained of native tribes only after they had spent many years in close contact with them. Initiation itself spurred their sense of responsibility for preserving otherwise forgotten lore.[56]

1846 (Cleveland: Arthur H. Clark Co., 1904), p. 111; Nicolas Point, S.J., *Wilderness Kingdom—Indian Life in the Rocky Mountains: 1840-1847. The Journals and Paintings of Nicolas Point, S.J.*, trans. Joseph P. Donnelly, S.J. (New York: Holt, Rinehart and Winston, 1967), pp. 120-21; Rev. Gideon H. Pond, "Dakota Superstitions," *Collections of the Minnesota Historical Society*, 2 (1860-67), 215; Gregory Mengarini, S.J., *Recollections of the Flathead Mission*, trans. and ed. Gloria Ricci Lothrop (Glendale, Calif.: Arthur H. Clark Co., 1977); Slotkin, *Regeneration through Violence*, p. 211.

[54] Leland, *The Algonquin Legends of New England, or Myths and Folk Lore of the Micmac, Passamaquoddy, and Penobscot Tribes* (Boston: Houghton, Mifflin and Co., 1884), p. iv, also pp. iii, 5, 8, 13. See also Zolla, *The Writer and the Shaman*, pp. 148, 175-77, for a useful discussion of Leland.

[55] Ernest Whitney, *Legends of the Pike's Peak Region: The Sacred Myths of the Manitou* (Denver: Chain and Hardy Co., 1892), pp. 12, 52; Harriet Maxwell Converse, "Myths and Legends of the New York State Iroquois," *New York State Museum Bulletin* (Albany: University of the State of New York, 1908), pp. 14, 27, 31ff. See also Zolla, *The Writer and the Shaman*, p. 179.

[56] James Athearn Jones, *Traditions of the North American Indians*, 3 vols. (1830; rpt. Upper Saddle River, N.J.: Literature House, 1970), 1:ix-xi, xv; *The Journal of Major John Norton, 1816*, ed. Carl F. Klinck and James J. Talman (Toronto: Champlain Society, 1970), pp. xvii-xxiv; Sarah Winnemucca Hopkins, *Life Among the Piutes: Their Wrongs and Claims*, ed. Mrs. Horace [Mary] Mann (Boston: n.p., 1883), p. 3; George P. Belden, *Belden, The White Chief; or Twelve Years Among the Wild Indians of the Plains*, ed. Gen. James S. Brisbin (1870; rpt. Cincinnati: E. W. Starr and Co., 1875); Mary Ellicott Arnold and Mabel Reed, *In the Land of the Grasshopper Song: A Story of Two Girls in Indian Country in 1908-09* (New York: Vantage Press, 1957), pp. 3-5; C. D. Willard, "The New Editor [Charles F. Lummis]," *Land of Sunshine*, (December 1894), 12; Edwin Thompson Denig, *Five Indian Tribes of the Upper Missouri* ed John C. Ewers (Norman. University of Oklahoma Press, 1961), p. xxix; Jean Louis Berlandier, *The Indians of Texas in 1830*, trans. Patricia Reading Leclercq, ed. John C. Ewers (Washington: Smithsonian Institution, 1969), pp. 22-24, 153ff.

Before the Civil War, those expressing such concern tended to be frontiersmen on close terms with individual tribes. After the late 1860s, the ones to volunteer records were often military personnel who had come to feel sympathy for the very peoples they had been ordered to force onto reservations.[57]

The recognition that tribal lore needed to be preserved did not itself encourage the development of cultural tolerance, much less pluralism. Henry Rowe Schoolcraft (1793-1864), for example, the single most important ethnographer before the Civil War, empathized with Indian tribes enough to have learned a number of native dialects, spent a lifetime studying tribal lore, and married the granddaughter of an Ojibwa chief. But, to repeat, his ethnocentrism colored his views so thoroughly that the very data his monumental studies provide frequently refute his conclusions.

At the age of twenty-seven, Schoolcraft accompanied an 1820 government expedition to the Lake Superior copper region as geologist and geographer. Soon less interested in topography than in local tribes, he developed that interest during the next four decades into a career as the first ethnologist of American Indian life. Rocks, Schoolcraft felt, might wait another century or two; native cultures would not.[58] He returned to the Lake Superior region the following year as a federal Indian agent, a role that perfectly clarifies the conflict informing Schoolcraft's attitude toward indigenous tribes: the post facilitated his gathering of native materials even as it required him to negotiate against native tribes. Schoolcraft himself never appreciated the contradiction, applying the same pedantic meticulousness of his scholarship to shrewd treaties for white expansion.[59] In that regard, he exemplifies the thesis of this chapter, laboring anxiously against the loss of materials that were threatened by his own official actions.

[57] Ewers, "When Red and White Men Meet," pp. 144-45. Ewers first suggested this revisionist reading, one developed well by Thomas Leonard in *Above the Battle: War-Making in America from Appomattox to Versailles* (New York: Oxford University Press, 1978), chap. 3. See, for two instances, John G. Bourke, *On the Border with Crook* (New York: Charles Scribner's Sons, 1891), pp. 112-14; Bourke, "The Medicine-Men of the Apaches," in Bureau of American Ethnology, *Ninth Annual Report, 1887-88* (Washington: G.P.O., 1892), p. 451; Frederic Webb Hodge, "In Memoriam—John Gregory Bourke," *Journal of American Folk-Lore,* 9 (1896), esp. p. 141; Col. Randolph Barnes Marcy, *Thirty Years of Army Life on the Border* (New York: Harper and Brothers, 1866), pp. 97ff. See also Garrick Mallery, *Picture Writing of the American Indians,* 2 vols. (1893; rpt. New York: Dover Publications, 1972).

[58] Henry Rowe Schoolcraft, *Narrative Journal of Travels Through the Northwestern Regions of the United States . . .* (1821), ed. Mentor Williams (East Lansing: Michigan State College Press, 1953), p. 203.

[59] See Zolla, *The Writer and the Shaman,* pp. 148-62; Pearce, *Savagism and Civilization,* pp. 120-28.

In studies over thirty years, resulting in a series of encyclopedic published collections, Schoolcraft kept returning to the legends of his wife's Algonquin-speaking tribe, always for the same reasons. *Algic Researches* (1839), his first collection of mythological tales and, in a later version, Longfellow's source for *Hiawatha* (1855), offers "General Considerations" for the undertaking.

> Every year is diminishing [the Indians'] numbers and adding to the obscurity of their traditions. Many of the tribes and languages are already extinct, and we can allude to at least one of the still existing smaller tribes who have lost the use of their vernacular tongue and adopted the English. Distinct from every benevolent consideration, weighty as these are, it is exceedingly desirable that the record of facts, from which they are to be judged, should be completed, as early as possible. It is conceived that, in rescuing their oral tales and fictitious legends, an important link in the chain has been supplied. But it is believed that still higher testimony remains.[60]

Throughout his distinguished career, Schoolcraft circled back to this theme, rededicating himself to ensuring a record of Indian life and tradition.

Not surprisingly, his Ojibwa wife, Jane, shared this concern and may even have helped him to define it more clearly. A visitor once described this European-educated woman as having "a melancholy and pity in her voice, when speaking of [her people], as if she did indeed consider them a doomed race."[61] She joined her husband in recording and translating tribal myths, but she failed to help him break through a narrow assessment of Indian cultures. Schoolcraft's lifelong study of what he referred to as the "mental character" and "interior man" of native life gave him no more than a bare inkling of the complexity of his subjects.[62] Never moving beyond the stereotypical Indian-agent cast of thought, he deplored the failure of natives to adopt white habits of industry, thrift, and cleanliness, and his occasional translations of Indian poetry confirm European, not native,

[60] *Schoolcraft's Indian Legends*, ed. Mentor Williams (East Lansing: Michigan State University Press, 1956), pp. 10-11, also p. 302. See also Hodges, *Carl Wimar*, p. 10.

[61] Mrs. Anna Brownell Jameson, *Winter Studies and Summer Rambles in Canada*, 2 vols. (New York: Wiley and Putnam, 1839), 2:148. See also Charles S. and Stellanora Osborn, *Schoolcraft—Longfellow—Hiawatha* (Lancaster, Pa.: Jacques Cattell Press, 1942), pp. 520-39.

[62] Henry Rowe Schoolcraft, *The Myth of Hiawatha and Other Oral Legends* (Philadelphia: J. B. Lippincott and Co., 1856), pp. viii, x; Schoolcraft, *Archives of Aboriginal Knowledge*, 1:vi.

conventions.[63] Nevertheless, Schoolcraft's exhaustive research remains invaluable. Completed at the very moment tribes were disappearing, his collection of myths, legends, and narratives attests to a richness and diversity of native experience that he himself could not appreciate.

By mid-century, a national reputation helped Schoolcraft to persuade others of the need for last-minute collecting of cultural documents. Amateurs and professionals alike felt a new urgency to compile such materials and came almost to resent the seemingly constitutional reserve of their informants. "This reticence on the part of the Indian may finally disappear," one prominent anthropologist wrote in 1892, reiterating a judgment made for decades; "still, it is quite time that their myths and traditions were collected, lest with the breaking up of customs on which that reticence is founded the memory of the past will be lost."[64] Of course, reticence itself betokened cultural strength, testifying to the continuing vitality of norms and taboos. The paradox here—that traditions could be transcribed only when dead, when their function and full meaning had become obsolete—was hardly lost upon recorders. Like the photographers who discovered this same truth, they nonetheless continued to work toward a cultural image as accurate as possible. By the 1890s, even popular magazines touted such efforts in patriotic terms. An article in *Harper's Monthly* announced:

> Old traditions, old customs, old aspirations, are fading swiftly and surely in the presence of the white man. It is humiliating not only for an American, but for any educated human being, to realize that in this great, rich, powerful United States, boasting ever of its general enlightenment, there is neither the intelligent public spirit nor the sustained private devotion to the wider aspects of science to secure the myths and traditions and lore of those wonderful people before this page now open upon the Story of Man shall be closed forever. For nowhere else upon this planet does this particular illumining phase of human life exist, nor will it come again. There are many fields of science in which it does not make very much difference if the work which is waiting

---

[63] In this context, see also Lewis Cass, *Inquiries, Respecting the History, Traditions, Languages, Manners, Customs, Religion, &c. of the Indians, Living within the United States* (Detroit: Sheldon and Reed, 1823), pp. 2ff.; Cass, "Indians of North America," *North American Review*, 22 (1826), 54-58.

[64] Adolph F. Bandelier, "Final Report of Investigations among the Indians of the Southwestern United States, Carried on Mainly in the Years from 1880 to 1885," pt. 2, *Papers of the Archaeological Institute of America, American Series*, 4 (1892), 6.

to be done shall wait a little longer. A decade more or less is of little importance in the end. But here delay is fatal.[65]

Perhaps as clearly as anywhere, this declaration evinces how an exuberant nationalism may thinly veil the uncertainties about vanishing native cultures that troubled increasing numbers of Americans toward the end of the century.

RECOVERING EARLY RECORDS

The most dramatic instances of rescued traditions involved the discovery of unique manuscripts by happenstance. It was as if a Mayan codex had been seized from the flames of Bishop Landa's sixteenth-century bonfire. Horatio Hale, an eminent ethnologist, accomplished such a feat by transcribing the sole copy of *The Iroquois Book of Rites* and publishing it in 1883. In the process, he reclaimed the cultural heritage of that great woodland confederacy, thoroughly transformed by long contact with European culture. As Hale recognized, the book's value lay in just this point, in having been "framed long before [the Iroquois] were affected by any influences from abroad."[66]

In 1884 Daniel Brinton, who achieved a correspondingly eminent reputation in linguistics, similarly resurrected "one of the most curious records of ancient American history," the *Walam Olum*.[67] Supposedly lost to history, this chronicle of the Delaware tribe now stands as a great epic poem and an invaluable anthropological document. A year later, Brinton prefaced his *Annals of the Cakchiquels* (1885) with a statement strikingly similar to Hale's evaluation of the *Book of Rites*.[68]

Such dramatic coups were rare, however—the result less of diligence than of serendipity. From the 1840s, individuals more commonly devoted themselves to collecting a literature transcribed long before, sometimes even published, but abandoned in attics or forgotten in library alcoves. They were motivated by the same concerns that prompted others to search dusty shelves for word lists and grammars, but they ranged more widely and organized more extensive ma-

[65] T. Mitchell Prudden, "An Elder Brother to the Cliff-Dwellers," *Harper's Monthly Magazine*, 95 (June 1897), 57.

[66] Hale, ed., *Iroquois Book of Rites*, ed. Fenton, p. 82.

[67] Brinton, *The Lenâpé and Their Legends* (1885; rpt. New York: Ams Press, 1969), p. v.

[68] Brinton, *The Annals of the Cakchiquels* (1885; rpt. New York: Ams Press, 1969), p. v. See also Franz Boas, *Chinook Texts*, Bureau of American Ethnology (Washington: G.P.O., 1894), pp. 5-6; Pilling, *Bibliography of the Chinookan Languages*, pp. v-vi.

terials in order to reconstruct a history. Hiram Beckwith, for example, described his own antiquarian efforts as a synthesis of "gleanings over a wide field of antiquated books of travel and maps long since out of print, or copies of manuscript-correspondence of a private or official character, little of which is accessible to the general reader."[69] He deplored the current state of knowledge of eastern woodland tribes. "The little information that has been preserved concerning them is so scattered through the volumes of authors who wrote from other motives, or at different dates, or of different nations, without taking thought to discriminate, that no satisfactory account of any particular tribe is now attainable. The best that may be done is to select such of these disjointed scraps as bear evidence of being the most reliable, and arrange them in something like chronological order."[70]

Statements of regret, compilations of "gleanings," and rueful observations on the appalling lack of documentary evidence might be multiplied almost indefinitely.[71] Thoreau himself—who, according to one scholar, "had Indians on the brain" as early as the 1840s[72]— spent the decade before his death in 1862 working almost exclusively on eleven manuscript notebooks that comprise more than a thousand pages of materials on North American Indians. Thoreau wanted merely to preserve, and to educate himself, in materials fast fading away.

This impulse reverberated across the continent. Hubert Howe Bancroft, the eccentric San Francisco book dealer, had become an energetic collector of Americana in 1859. He stated one of the reasons that persuaded him to become a professional historian in *The Native Races of the Pacific States*: "To gather and arrange in systematic com-

---

69 Hiram W. Beckwith, *The Illinois and Indiana Indians* (Chicago: Fergus Printing Co., 1884), p. v.

70 Ibid.

71 For a sampling, see: *Graphic Sketches from Old and Authentic Works, Illustrating the Costume, Habits, and Character of the Aborigines of America* (New York: J. and H. G. Langley, 1841), p. 3; John W. De Forest, *History of the Indians of Connecticut from the Earliest Known Period to 1850* (Hartford: William James Hamersley, 1853), pp. 1-2; William T. Corbusier, *Verde to San Carlos: Recollections of a Famous Army Surgeon and His Observant Family on the Western Frontier, 1869-1886* (Tucson: Dale Stuart King, 1969); Samuel Asahel Clarke, *Pioneer Days of Oregon History*, 2 vols. (Portland: J. K. Gill Co., 1905), 1:iii, 84ff.; James Buchanan, *Sketches of the History, Manners, and Customs of the North American Indians with a Plan for Their Melioration*, 2 vols. (New York: W. Borradaile, 1824), 1:ix, 13; John Halkett, *Historical Notes Respecting the Indians of North America* . . . (London: Archibald Constable and Co., 1825).

72 Sayre, *Thoreau and the American Indians*, p. 97. See also Albert Keiser, "Thoreau's Manuscripts on the Indians," *Journal of English and Germanic Philology*, 27 (April 1928), esp. 198-99.

pact form all that is known of these people; to rescue some facts, perhaps, from oblivion, to bring others from inaccessible nooks, to render all available to science and to the general reader. . . ."[73] More traditional, thorough, and accomplished historians, including Francis Parkman and William Hickling Prescott, also attempted to weave together forgotten native materials into solid but readable works. Among nineteenth-century historians of America, those devoted to the Indian experience seem to have felt the burden and urgency of documentation most heavily.[74]

A thin line divided the writing of history from that of belles-lettres in the mid-nineteenth century. The height of romanticism in America encouraged an outpouring of sentimental poems, novels, plays, and even operas with Indian themes, Longfellow's *Hiawatha* being only the best-known example. "Writers of frontier romances," one student of the genre has observed, "believed that Indians would soon exist only in their pages."[75] More serious artists, including James Fenimore Cooper, responded to the hopes expressed by Hawthorne and Margaret Fuller, that "there might be some masterly attempt to reproduce in art or literature what is proper to them."[76] Surprising as it may appear to readers of, say, *The Deerslayer*, Cooper was among the first devoted to faithful fictional portraits of native tribes. Never troubling to travel among the tribes he described, he nonetheless read extensively in missionary reports, histories, and government surveys in order to authenticate narrative depictions of tribes declining or extinct by the time he wrote.[77]

Some authors self-consciously resisted the trend toward adapting

[73] Bancroft, *The Native Races of the Pacific States of North America*, 5 vols. (New York: D. Appleton and Co., 1875-1876), 1:x-xi.

[74] See, for example, the discussion of Francis Parkman in Chapter Two above. See also Howard Doughty, *Francis Parkman* (New York: Macmillan, 1962), pp. 390-91. Parkman, *The Jesuits in North America in the Seventeenth Century* (1867), vols. 3-4 of the Champlain ed. of *The Works of Francis Parkman* (Boston: Little, Brown and Co., 1897), 3:vi-vii; Edward G. Mason, "Francis Parkman," *Dial*, 1 (December 1880), 150. For useful discussions of Parkman, see Pearce, *Savagism and Civilization*, pp. 162-68; Zolla, *The Writer and the Shaman*, pp. 139-43.

[75] Barnett, *Ignoble Savage*, p. 39. See also Keen, *Aztec Image*, p. 363. For one explicit example of this, see Mrs. Mary H. Eastman, *The Romance of Indian Life* (Philadelphia: Lippincott, Grambo and Co., 1853), p. xi.

[76] *The Writings of Margaret Fuller*, ed. Mason Wade (New York: Viking, 1941), p. 88.

[77] See Gregory Lansing Paine, "The Indians of the Leather-Stocking Tales," *Studies in Philology*, 23 (1926), 20-21, 30, 39; John T. Frederick, "Cooper's Eloquent Indians," *Publications of the Modern Language Association*, 71 (1956), 1006; Paul A. W. Wallace, "Cooper's Indians," *New York History*, 35 (October 1954), 404 ff.; Henry Nash Smith, introduction to Cooper, *The Prairie* (New York: Holt, Rinehart and Winston, 1950), pp. vi-viii.

fiction to documentary ends.[78] Too many others followed Cooper's romantic lead without bothering to imitate even his second hand scholarship.[79] Not surprisingly, many frontier romancers were, in one scholar's words, "men on whom a great deal was lost."[80] But even had they been more sensitive, more intelligent, better informed, they would likely have failed in their portrayals, since no treatment that satisfies western European literary conventions could have adequately encompassed the native experience. In a vain attempt to compensate for the perceived deficiency, authors in the last decade of the century completed works that barely sustain a fictional life. Adolph Bandelier's *The Delight Makers* (1890), for instance, and Edna Dean Procter's poem *The Song of the Ancient People* (1893) are riddled with anthropological data.[81] Such efforts frequently demonstrated little more sensitivity, and often less cultural tolerance, than might have been gained from straightforward scientific accounts. They can only be praised for attempting to break from the powerful sentimentalizing influence of Longfellow and his imitators. Longfellow himself had wanted merely to romanticize Schoolcraft's Ojibwa legends in his *Song of Hiawatha* and never shared Bandelier's or Procter's concern for preservation or authenticity. Nonetheless, the poem's spectacular popularity sparked numerous attempts to collect native legends and oral traditions before time ran out.[82] Perhaps this, for all the expressed hopes of other writers, remains the single notable legacy of nineteenth-century imagings of the Indian.[83]

[78] Cf. Charles Dickens, *American Notes and Pictures from Italy* (1842; rpt. New York: E. P. Dutton, 1908), pp. 163-64.

[79] See, for example, George H. Colton, *Tecumseh; or, The West Thirty Years Since. A Poem* (New York: Wiley and Putnam, 1842), preface (unpaginated).

[80] Barnett, *Ignoble Savage*, pp. 189-90.

[81] Zolla, *The Writer and the Shaman*, pp. 166-72; Barnett, *Ignoble Savage*, pp. 191-95.

[82] Ellwood Parry, *The Image of the Indian and the Black Man in American Art, 1590-1900* (New York: George Braziller, 1974), p. 125.

[83] Unlike Longfellow, many frontier romancers did want to preserve an accurate image of native history and lore. See, among others: Rev. James Wallis Eastburn, *Yamoyden, A Tale of the Wars of King Philip: In Six Cantos* (New York: n.p., 1820), esp. pp. 3-4, 27ff.; Sir William George Drummond Stewart, *Altowan; or, Incidents of Life and Adventure in the Rocky Mountains by an Amateur Traveler*, ed. J. Watson Webb, 2 vols. (New York: Harper and Brothers, 1846), 1:iv-v; Rev. J. J. Methvin, *Andele, or The Mexican-Kiowa Captive: A Story of Real Life Among the Indians* (Louisville: Pentecostal Herald Press, 1899), p. 3; Homer F. Barnes, *Charles Fenno Hoffman* (New York: Columbia University Press, 1930), pp. 216, 315; Lewis Leary, *That Rascal Freneau: A Study in Literary Failure* (New Brunswick: Rutgers University Press, 1941), pp. 260-61. See also William H. Gardiner, review of Cooper, *The Spy*, in *North American Review*, 15 (1822), 257-58. See also Keen, *Aztec Image*, pp. 373ff.

ARCHAEOLOGY

Just as renewed collecting of myths and legends inspired fictional treatments and was inspired by them, fascination with archaeology was spurred by popular romances about the extinct mound builders.[84] Increasing numbers of enthusiasts in the 1850s, impelled by romances or scientific rationales, posed a considerable threat to sites not already destroyed by farmers' plows and the spades of artifact hunters. The innumerable earthwork mounds dotting the eastern and southern landscape of America had always attracted the curiosity of men like Henry Brackenridge and Thomas Jefferson (who made the first study of one).[85] In the nineteenth century, however, as people came to view the mounds less as mere obstacles to be demolished, interest increased markedly. As one expert has remarked, "In 1800, an Ohioan with a mound on his property was likely to level it so he could plant his crops; in 1840 it was probable that he would conduct a careful excavation and fill his house with an array of ancient artifacts."[86] Obviously, this new attitude posed almost as many problems to the emerging professional as did the old one.

In September 1820, an anonymous letter to the editor of the newly established *Detroit Gazette* asserted: "The origin and history of our Aborigines can only be discovered by a minute investigation of their numerous works of art. This investigation is rendered the more necessary as the rapidly increasing population and cultivation of our country have already occasioned the destruction of many monuments of Indian labor, and it is greatly to be feared, that other of our antiquarian relics will soon suffer the same fate. We ought to urge the more enlightened part of our comunity to draw correct plans and describe the various circumvallatory ramparts which still exist. . . ."[87] Whether or not this particular letter touched other than local sympathies, a wide variety of people—showmen, lawyers, artifact hunters, missionaries, naturalists and scientists, Governor DeWitt Clinton of New York, and Lewis Cass, governor of the Michigan Territory—

[84] Silverberg, *Mound Builders*, esp. pp. 6ff.

[85] Ibid., pp. 97ff.; Cutright, *Lewis and Clark*, p. 6; C. W. Ceram [Kurt W. Marek], *The First American: A Story of North American Archaeology* (New York: Harcourt Brace Jovanovich, 1971), pp. 4-9; Gordon R. Willey and Jeremy A. Sabloff, *A History of American Archaeology* (London: Thames and Hudson, 1974), pp. 33, 36-38; Fagan, *Elusive Treasure*, pp. 94-99.

[86] Silverberg, *Mound Builders*, p. 97.

[87] "Letters to the Editor, on Indian Antiquities. Letter I," *Detroit Gazette*, September 1, 1820, p. 1.

expressed equal concern.[88] Few committed their lives to the tasks they so energetically proclaimed. Nor did many assume that the mound builders were the direct ancestors of present tribes. A handful of devoted archaeologists, however, usually concluded just such a relationship.

Caleb Atwater, Ephraim Squier, and Cyrus Thomas—professionals whose careers neatly span the nineteenth century—attempted to compile accurate records of mounds everywhere being looted and ravaged. Early in his career, in 1820, Atwater had predicted that the mounds at Circleville, Ohio, "will entirely disappear in a few years." He "used the only means within my power, to perpetuate their memory," a drawing and a brief description.[89] For the next two decades, Atwater, and then Squier for twenty years after him, prepared accurate maps and reports of the thousands of mounds still visible. Over and over, these two rued their inadequate means and the enormity of their task.[90]

In the 1880s, Cyrus Thomas, with the funds of the Archaeological Institute of America at his disposal, was faced with the problem of how best to make a comprehensive survey of the earth structures. He rejected the idea of mapping first and investigating later. Private collectors and impatient farmers might have left nothing by the time he could return to a particular site. But if he thoroughly investigated a select few, as Robert Silverberg has noted, "the constant destruction

[88] Constantine Samuel Rafinesque, *The Ancient Monuments of North and South America*, 2d ed. (Philadelphia: n.p., 1838), p. 12; Rafinesque, *A Life of Travels and Researches in North America and South Europe* (Philadelphia: n.p., 1836), p. 62; Kastner, *A Species of Eternity*, pp. 240-53; Alexander W. Bradford, *American Antiquities and Researches into the Origin and History of the Red Race* (New York: Dayton and Saxton, 1841), pp. 1, 12-13; Chauncey Wales Riggs, *How We Find Relics: A Series of Letters* (Chicago: W. B. Conkey Co., 1893), pp. 20-21, also pp. 78-79; *Bishop [Henry Benjamin] Whipple's Southern Diary, 1843-1844*, ed. Lester B. Shippee (Minneapolis: University of Minnesota Press, 1937), pp. 147-48; Bela Hubbard, "Ancient Garden Beds of Michigan," *American Antiquarian*, 1 (April 1878), 1, 8-9; "[Thomas] Nuttall's Travels into the Old Northwest: An Unpublished 1810 Diary," ed. Jeannette E. Graustein, *Chronica Botanica*, 14 (Autumn 1951), 66-67; DeWitt Clinton, *A Memoir on the Antiquities of the Western Parts of the State of New York* (Albany: I. W. Clark, 1818), pp. 3-4; [Lewis Cass], *Ontwa, the Son of the Forest. A Poem* (New York: Wiley and Halsted, 1822), pp. 116-20. See also Curtis Dahl, "Mound-Builders, Mormons, and William Cullen Bryant," *New England Quarterly*, 34 (June 1961), 180ff.; Willey and Sabloff, *History of American Archaeology*, pp. 31-63; Silverberg, *Mound Builders*.

[89] Quoted in Silverberg, *Mound Builders*, p. 64.

[90] Caleb Atwater, *The Writings of Caleb Atwater* (Columbus: n.p., 1833), p. 6; Silverberg, *Mound Builders*, p. 61; Willey and Sabloff, *History of American Archaeology*, pp. 38-39, 43-49; Ephraim G. Squier, *The Serpent Symbol*, American Archaeological Researches, no. 1 (New York: George P. Putnam, 1851), preface (unpaginated), pp. 13-14; Squier, *Antiquities of the State of New York* (Buffalo: George H. Derby and Co., 1851), pp. 7-8, 11, 14. See also Fagan, *Elusive Treasure*, pp. 109-14, 118, 214-24; Ceram, *The First American*, pp. 201-2.

of mounds by natural erosion, private excavation, and public ignorance would remove from study many of the most interesting monuments, no matter which zone was chosen first for intensive exploration."[91] Thomas finally decided on the narrower, but more definitive,
choice and in the process set a model for other workers in the field.

Most of the century's swelling group of archaeologists realized the
concomitant needs for accuracy and haste, whether they studied
eastern mounds or southwestern pueblos, and the inaugural report
of the Archaeological Institute of America expressed this collective
purpose in 1879.[92] More than thirty years earlier, however, a popular
travel writer had garnered enduring fame by practicing and popular-
izing these principles in his studies of Central American archaeology.
John Lloyd Stephens's "great eyes" had long excited the young Herman Melville with the wonders they had seen in Europe and the
Levant.[93] But not until he was sent as a minister to Guatemala in
1839 did Stephens find his true mission. Accompanied by the English
draftsman Frederick Catherwood, Stephens soon became fascinated
with the ruins near Belize and with the native peoples themselves.
The arduous trek he made with Catherwood to Copan and Tikal,
followed by explorations and further study of all other known sites,
led to his reputation as "the father of Mayan archaeology."

The two books that Stephens published from his careful notes and
from the drawings of his companion remain standard texts on their
subject. His motives, explained in 1843, sound remarkably similar to
those of other observers, amateur and professional: "In a few generations, great edifices, their facades covered with sculptured ornaments,
already cracked and yawning, must fall, and become mere shapeless
mounds. It has been the fortune of the author to step between them
and the entire destruction to which they are destined; and it is his
hope to snatch from oblivion these perishing but still gigantic memorials of a mysterious people."[94] Indeed, Stephens and Catherwood
did "snatch from oblivion" the first, in some cases the only, accurate

91 Silverberg, *Mound Builders*, p. 203. See also Wiley and Sabloff, *History of
American Archaeology*, pp. 49-50; Fagan, *Elusive Treasure*, pp. 293-300.

92 See Charles Eliot Norton, Francis Parkman, and Alexander Agassiz, "First
Annual Report of the Executive Committee, with Accompanying Papers. 1879-80,"
in *Archaeological Institute of America* (Cambridge, Mass.: John Wilson and Co.,
1880), p. 20. See also Wiley and Sabloff, *History of American Archaeology*, pp.
48-49.

93 Melville, *Redburn: His First Voyage* (1849; rpt. New York: Doubleday and
Co., 1957), p. 4.

94 Stephens, *Incidents of Travel in Yucatan*, 2 vols. (1843; rpt. New York: Dover
Publications, 1963), 1:v. For biographical information, consult Victor Von Hagan,
Maya Explorer: John Lloyd Stephens (Norman: University of Oklahoma Press,
1947).

record of numerous Mayan ruins. Moreover, Stephens's earnestness and his fine literary talents combined to awaken his countrymen, including eminent scientists and historians, to the eroding possibilities of archaeological and anthropological study.[95]

ETHNOLOGICAL SOCIETIES

The voices of Stephens, Atwater, Squier, and Thomas were only four among hundreds clamoring for the immediate collecting of indigenous materials.[96] As mentioned earlier, state governments had been organizing historical societies as repositories for all kinds of artifacts and records since the 1790s. The "Circular Letter" establishing the first of these, in Boston, dispassionately expressed the special importance of native materials among items to be collected: "Monuments and relicks of the ancient Indians; number and present state of any remaining Indians among you."[97] In 1831, in less fragmentary syntax, a tone of disquietude entered the Maine Historical Society's adjuration. Americans must transcribe Indian histories, since they "will be likely to excite higher interest as they recede more and more from future ages."[98] Little more than forty years later, excited urgency had displaced uneasy premonitions, as the "General Circular" stating the principles of the Michigan Pioneer Society reveals: "The interesting traces of the prehistoric races . . . are fast disappearing. The aboriginal tribes, our more immediate ancestors, are fast passing away, and with them the traces of their ancestors, and all traditions of the more recent events in their own unwritten history. . . . these should not be lost, but should be recorded, and that history be carefully preserved."[99]

Also in the period 1830-1880, numerous anthropological societies and museums, public and private, were founded with the purpose of collecting and preserving native materials. The federal government

[95] Richard L. Predmore, introduction to Stephens's *Incidents of Travel in Central America, Chiapas, and Yucatan* (1841), ed. Predmore, 2 vols. (New Brunswick: Rutgers University Press, 1949), 1:xviii; Willey and Sabloff, *History of American Archaeology*, pp. 64-65; Fagan, *Elusive Treasure*, pp. 138-204.

[96] Silverberg, *Mound Builders*, p. 97.

[97] "Circular Letter of the Historical Society," *Proceedings of the Massachusetts Historical Society*, 8 (1791-1835), 1. Henry Nash Smith provides a sharper historical focus to this phenomenon: "Thirty-five local and state historical societies were established between 1820 and 1850 (only three, Massachusetts, New York, Pennsylvania, had been established before 1820). In the same period collectors like John Carter Brown of Providence and James Lennox of New York began to form libraries of Americana" (Smith, "The Widening of Horizons," in Robert E. Spiller et al., eds., *Literary History of the United States: History*, 3d ed. rev. [New York: Macmillan Co., 1963], pp. 644-45).

[98] Cited in Pearce, *Savagism and Civilization*, p. 113.

[99] "General Circular Issued by the State Librarian," *Pioneer Collections: Report of the Pioneer Society of the State of Michigan*, 1 (1877), 3.

demonstrated its own increasing commitment in the programs authorized first by the Smithsonian and later by the Bureau of American Ethnology. More than any other individual, John Wesley Powell was responsible for the coordination of many scattered efforts. His dramatic initial exploration of the Colorado River in 1869 had brought him into contact with remote tribes unaware of the existence of whites. Returning to Zuni Pueblo ten years later with a larger team plus a staff photographer, he felt almost consumed by the need for active, extensive anthropological efforts. "The field of research is speedily narrowing because of the rapid change in the Indian population now in progress," he announced. "All habits, customs, and opinions are fading away; even languages are disappearing; and in a very few years it will be impossible to study our North American Indians in their primitive condition, except for recorded history. For this reason ethnologic studies in America should be pushed with the utmost vigor."[100] Acting on these principles, Powell turned the Bureau of American Ethnology away from its authorized study of historical sites and toward more encompassing ethnological efforts among living tribes.[101] An extraordinary administrator able to attract and hold together a variety of talented scholars, Powell organized the first systematic research in American Indian ethnology.

By the 1880s and 1890s, the federal government had clearly assumed responsibility for concerted, large-scale collecting of indigenous materials. Individuals convinced of the need for such work joined government-funded expeditions or submitted their work for publication in government periodicals. Again, as was true half a century earlier, only a few prominent individuals could afford not to consider government sponsorship, among them some who financed institutions and brought together collections on their own. The expatriate investment banker George Peabody, one of the richest Americans at the time, provides a spectacular example. He gave $150,000 to Harvard University in 1866 to establish the Peabody Museum of Archaeology and Ethnology, "to be devoted wholly to the acquirement and preservation of the fast disappearing material relating to primitive man."[102]

---

[100] Cited in Darrah, *Powell of the Colorado*, p. 255, also pp. 262, 278, 359. For expressions by Powell of similar sentiments, see his *Study of Indian Languages*, pp. v, vi, viii, and "Preface," p. xx. See also Stegner, *Beyond the Hundredth Meridian*, p. 130, and Carl Resek, *Lewis Henry Morgan: American Scholar* (Chicago: University of Chicago Press, 1960), pp. 142, 150.

[101] Judd, *Bureau of American Ethnology*, esp. pp. 4, 19-20; Darrah, *Powell of the Colorado*, pp. 258ff.; Terrell, *The Man Who Rediscovered America*, pp. 209-10, 226ff.

[102] Charles C. Willoughby, "The Peabody Museum of Archaeology and Ethnology, Harvard University," *Harvard Graduates' Magazine*, 31 (June 1923), 495. See also "Letter of Gift, October 8, 1866," *Reports of the Peabody Museum of*

Twenty years later, the Reverend Sheldon Jackson established a small museum in Sitka, Alaska, for similar reasons.[103] Just after the turn of the century, a young engineer, George Heye, the son of a successful Standard Oil executive, set out on his own to acquire artifacts and information from tribes of the Southwest. The endeavor resulted in the Heye Museum of the American Indian in New York City, which organized one of the largest collections of American tribal materials in the world.[104]

These enterprises were the direct descendents of McKenney's "Archives" and Catlin's "Gallery," though undertaken with scientific standards that neither of those men considered necessary. Following the Civil War, the growing appreciation of the link between artifact and ritual, art and world view dictated caution even among commercial collectors. Although relics, tools, and art pieces had excited popular interest well before the Civil War, only toward the end of the century did white observers realize the complex role such artifacts played in Indian cultural life. Recognition of the need for care and accuracy more and more tempered the urgency with which individuals approached collecting.

The single most important artifact in educating white collectors to native culture was the woven basket.[105] Shapes, styles, colors, and intricate reed patterns represented an integration of the sacred, social, ceremonial, and aesthetic values of the culture that produced them. In the process of cultural dissolution, however, weavers abandoned old methods of construction for more profitable ones. Metal proved cheaper than reed and was more durable. White collectors, sensitive to such inexorable developments, compiled voluminous notes and

American Archaeology and Ethnology with Harvard University, 1 (1868-76), 25-26; Charles Schuchert and Clara Mae LeVene, *O. C. Marsh: Pioneer in Paleontology* (New Haven: Yale University Press, 1940), pp. 76-93; Franklin Parker, *George Peabody: A Biography* (Nashville: Vanderbilt University Press, 1971), pp. 139-56.

103 Sheldon Jackson Museum pamphlet and leaflet, Sheldon Jackson Museum (est. 1888), Sitka, Alaska. See also Rev. Sheldon Jackson, *Alaska, and Missions on the North Pacific Coast* (New York: Dodd, Mead and Co., 1880), esp. pp. 86ff.

104 J. Alden Mason, *George J. Heye, 1874-1957* (New York: American Indian Heye Foundation, 1958), esp. pp. 10-12. Another notable instance is the Massachusetts philanthropist Mary Hemenway, who in 1886 financed the Hemenway Southwestern Archaeological Expedition, which brought together Adolph Bandelier, Frank H. Cushing, and others. See Fagan, *Elusive Treasure*, p. 248.

105 C. H. Green, "Brief History of Cliff Dwellers, Their Relics and Ruins," in *Catalogue of a Unique Collection of Cliff Dweller Relics* (Chicago: Art Institute, 1891), p. 19; Horatio Nelson Rust Collection, Huntington Library, San Marino; Charles F. Lummis, "The Palmer Collection," *Land of Sunshine*, 2 (February 1895), 69; J.B.B., "The Yates Collections," *Land of Sunshine*, 2 (May 1895), 98.

made extensive photographic records of both artisans and artifacts.[106] In certain cases they encouraged natives to resurrect old methods and patterns or sought out practitioners who still recalled the significance of the rich basket symbolism.[107] Commercial collectors, in other words, sometimes became good amateur ethnologists, helping professionals and museums to preserve the best still available.

THE RISE OF THE PROFESSIONAL ANTHROPOLOGIST

This chapter has so far sketched the transition from simple concern for native words to a progressively more varied, more anxious, more complex valuation of native modes of thought. Such a well-defined, linear transition never actually occurred, yet the outline characterizes the general tenor of altering assumptions. From memoirs, journal entries, and Indian biographies to more studied attempts at word lists and vocabularies, to active collection of tribal legends and lore, to rediscovery of materials already transcribed or preservation of Indian experiences through fictional means—the thematic sequence suggests an increasing concern for, if not greater understanding of, the felt experience of native cultures. As the outer form of Indian cultures came to be appreciated, many realized that the inner life also demanded attention. Even the act of collecting, preserving, and displaying physical artifacts took on a greater respect for the total cultural life. More and more, amateur and professional collectors learned to view native experience as a complexly integrated whole, larger than the sum of its variously preservable parts.[108]

[106] Livingston Farrand, "Basketry Designs of the Salish Indians," in Franz Boas, ed., *Memoirs of the American Museum of Natural History: Jesup North Pacific Expedition,* 1 (1898-1900), 391-92; James, *Indian Basketry,* pp. 9-10, 16; Otis Tufton Mason, "Aboriginal American Basketry: Studies in a Textile Art Without Machinery," in *Smithsonian Institution Annual Report, 1902* (Washington: G.P.O., 1904), esp. pp. 312-13, 315, 538-40; Frank G. Speck, *Decorative Art of Indian Tribes of Connecticut,* no. 10 Anthropological Series, Canada Department of Mines (Ottawa: G.P. Bureau, 1915), p. 6.

[107] J. Torrey Connor, "Confessions of a Basket Collector," *Land of Sunshine,* 5 (June 1896), 3, 10. See the Grace Nicholson Collection, Huntington Library, San Marino. See esp. Box 1, letter from Mary M. Bradford, November 18, 1906; Box 4; Box 5, letter from Otis T. Mason, July 1, 1902; Box 16, Nicholson's 1906 diary; Nicholson Photograph Album "B," pp. 60-90. See also Apostol, The Indian Summers of Miss Grace Nicholson, pp. 1-3; Winifred Starr Dobyns, "A Treasure House," *Woman Citizen,* 56, old ser. (December 1927), 13-14.

[108] For just two examples, see Myrtle, The Iroquois, p. 30; and Joseph K. Dixon, *The Vanishing Race: The Last Great Indian Council* (Garden City N.Y.: Doubleday, Page and Co., 1913), pp. xv, 5, 9-10. See as well Brandon, *The Last Americans,* p. 20.

As early as 1826, one prominent westerner declared: "Of the external habits of the Indians, if we may so speak, we have the most ample details. But of the moral character and feelings of the Indians, of their mental discipline, of their peculiar opinions, mythological and religious, and of all that is most valuable to man in the history of man, we are about as ignorant, as when Jacques Cartier first ascended the St. Lawrence."[109] Of course, a culturally prescribed ethnocentrism too often prevented those similarly committed from seeing what was in front of them. Nonetheless, some diligently tried not merely to collect materials but also to make interpretive sense of them. In part, again, they wanted to verify what complementary materials needed to be preserved before time ran out.

The greatest of these nineteenth-century ethnographers, Lewis Henry Morgan (1818-1881), established American anthropology on true professional grounds. In the 1840s, the young lawyer from Rochester, New York, began to study the social organization of the nearby Iroquois. In fact, the Seneca so fascinated him that his legal career faltered until he found a way to combine avocation and profession. The federal government had been threatening this westernmost tribe of the Iroquois confederates with removal from their attractive reserves, and in the mid-1840s Morgan joined the legal fight to allow them to stay. Success appeared far from imminent, and in the following years Morgan worked ever more urgently to preserve a record of imperiled Iroquois customs, enjoining others to similar efforts.[110]

Morgan's failing law practice finally convinced him to publish the voluminous notes he had collected and to abandon further study. His careful elucidation of social organization, written up in six hectic months as *The League of the Iroquois* (1851), achieved what John Wesley Powell praised as "the first scientific account of an Indian tribe ever given to the world."[111] Morgan's plans to salvage his legal career ended rather than began with the book's completion. That delightfully lively work confirmed him in his continuing avocation, and in the next thirty years, his intensive researches and radical theories established him as the "father of American anthropology."[112]

109 Cass, "Indians of North America," pp. 54-55.

110 Resek, *Lewis Henry Morgan*, p. 18. See also, for background information on Morgan, Leslie A. White's introduction to Morgan, *Indians Journals*, ed. White, pp. 3-12.

111 Powell, "Sketch of Lewis Henry Morgan," *Popular Science Monthly*, November 1880, p. 115.

112 For useful discussions of Morgan, see: Pearce, *Savagism and Civilization*, pp. 130-34; Berkhofer, *White Man's Indian*, pp. 52-54; Zolla, *The Writer and the Shaman*, pp. 162-68; Dwight W. Hoover, *The Red and the Black* (Chicago: Rand

More important even than Morgan's own efforts were his adjurations to contemporaries to record and systematize information on the American Indian everywhere. In a famous review of Hubert Howe Bancroft's *Native Races of the Pacific States*, he claimed:

> The question is still before us, as a nation, whether we will undertake the work of furnishing to the world a scientific exposition of Indian society, or leave it as it now appears, crude, unmeaning, unintelligible, a chaos of contradictions and puerile absurdities. With a field of unequalled richness and of vast extent . . . more persons ought to be found willing to work upon this material for the credit of American scholarship. It will be necessary for them to do as Herodotus did in Asia and Africa, to visit the native tribes at their villages and encampments, and study their institutions as living organisms, their condition, and their plan of life.[113]

A year later, Morgan lamented that time was too short to complete the necessary work, that Indian institutions and traditions were disappearing ever more rapidly, and that the efforts of American ethnologists were inadequate.[114] The very ease with which he was gaining information manifested the degree of demoralization among the Iroquois; ceremonies once carefully guarded had become performances.

Morgan's particular genius lay in his recognition of the need for more than careful description. He wanted to turn ethnology into a comparative science in which institutions might be classified and societies evaluated. Like many of his notable colleagues, including Powell and Daniel Brinton, Morgan never conceded to native cultural institutions a value comparable to that of white ones. Yet, his patronizing assumptions notwithstanding, he exactingly defined structural links between tribes, using information gathered from western field trips and from a seven-page questionnaire sent in 1859 to thirty western informants. Morgan's subsequent work, his monumental *Systems of Consanguinity* (1871), transformed responsible thinking about native peoples. He not only collated a mass of invaluable data but

---

McNally, 1976), pp. 97-100, 157-60; Idus L. Murphree, "The Evolutionary Anthropologists: The Progress of Mankind. The Concepts of Progress and Culture in the Thought of John Lubbock, Edward B. Tylor, and Lewis H. Morgan," *Proceedings of the American Philosophical Society*, 105 (June 1961), 272, 291-97; Keen, *Aztec Image*, pp. 380-410.

113 Morgan, "Montezuma's Dinner," *North American Review*, 122 (1876), 268-69.

114 Morgan, *Ancient Society, or Researches in the Lines of Human Progress from Savagery through Barbarism to Civilization* (New York: Henry Holt and Co., 1877), pp. vii-viii.

also created the science of kinship in what has been termed "perhaps the most original and brilliant single achievement in the history of anthropology."[115] What most considered curious facts or exotic traditions could no longer be accepted as less than the warp and woof of an entire cultural fabric. Morgan helped fellow intellectuals to understand how native societies functioned. Before him, for example, Indian tribes had been described in specious terms of kingship and feudalism. Morgan, on the other hand, authenticated their fundamentally socialist character. Though he never freed himself from a rigid cultural absolutism, he nonetheless created the possibility that others could do so and through rigorously objective standards helped to reveal native societies for what they were.

Morgan was by far the most influential person to appreciate the complex integrity of native cultures and their institutions. Beginning in the 1870s, his work achieved international recognition, inspiring Frederick Engels, for instance, to radically new socioeconomic speculations.[116] In America, he gained ardent disciples impressed by the caliber of his theorizing and converted by his urgings of haste. His classic study of *Ancient Society* (1877), which applied questionable evolutionary theory to primitive cultures, eloquently pleaded the case of native studies. Morgan directly challenged his contemporaries, whom he described as "workmen [who] have been unequal to the work. Moreover, while fossil remains buried in the earth will keep for the future student, the remains of Indian arts, languages and institutions will not. They are perishing daily, and have been perishing for upwards of three centuries. . . . After a few more years, facts that may now be gathered with ease will become impossible of discovery. These circumstances appeal strongly to Americans to enter this great field and gather its abundant harvest."[117]

Among those stimulated by Morgan was his most outstanding student, Adolph Bandelier (1840-1914). Nearly commanded by his paternal mentor to study the pueblo cultures of the Southwest, Bandelier traveled to Santa Fe in 1882, where he commenced more than a decade of painstaking study that would establish anthropology in the Southwest. In his voluminous journals and thorough manuscripts, he coordinated archaeological, ethnological, and historical evidence into

115 George P. Murdock, *Social Structure* (New York: Macmillan Co., 1949), pp. 4-5, cited in Leslie A. White, introduction to Morgan, *Indian Journals*, ed. White, p. 10. See also Brandon, *The Last Americans*, pp. 6-7.

116 Friedrich Engels, *The Origin of the Family, Private Property and the State in the Light of the Researches of Lewis H. Morgan* (1884), trans. Ernest Untermann (New York: International Publishers, 1942), pp. 5-6, 25-27.

117 Morgan, *Ancient Society*, p. viii.

an integrated picture of culture. Ever Morgan's student, his work is informed throughout by the sense that much was soon to be lost.[118]

During the next twenty years, numerous serious ethnographers labored in the field explicitly to preserve what was clearly threatened. John Dunbar among the Pawnees; James Owen Dorsey among the Ponca, Osage, and Omaha tribes; George Dorsey among the Cheyenne, Arapaho, and Hopi; Frederick Starr in Mexico; J. A. Costello, James G. Swan, and Franz Boas in the Pacific Northwest; Edward Nelson among the Eskimos; Alexander Stephen with the Hopi; Washington Matthews among the Navaho; Matilda Coxe Stevenson and J. Walter Fewkes among the Zuni[119]—these are only a few of the dedicated professionals who feared that even strenuous ethnological efforts could not save enough of what was threatened. By the century's end, precipitate changes were engulfing the little that was left of Indian life. The elegiac sentiments of the early years of the century had by the 1880s evolved into large-scale, systematic, and imaginative interdisciplinary research.[120]

[118] See Leslie A. White, ed., *Pioneers in American Anthropology: The Bandelier-Morgan Letters, 1873-1883*, 2 vols. (Albuquerque: University of New Mexico Press, 1940). More particularly, see Bandelier, "Historical Introduction to Studies among the Sedentary Tribes of New Mexico," *Papers of the Archaeological Institute of America, American Series*, 1, pt. 1 (1883), 28-29; Bandelier "Final Report," pp. 3, 6.

[119] John B. Dunbar, "The Pawnee Indians: Their Habits and Customs," *Magazine of American History*, 8 (November 1882), 751; J. A. Costello, *The Siwash, Their Life, Legends and Tales* (Seattle: Calvert Co., 1895), preface (unpaginated); James G. Swan, *The Northwest Coast; or, Three Years' Residence in Washington Territory* (1857; rpt. Seattle: University of Washington Press, 1969), pp. ix, xvii, 110; Edward William Nelson, "The Eskimo About Bering Strait," in *Bureau of American Ethnology Annual Report 1896-97* (Washington: G.P.O., 1899), pp. 20-21; *Hopi Journal of Alexander M. Stephen*, ed. Elsie Clews Parson, 2 vols. (New York: Columbia University Press, 1936), 1:xlviii; Matthews, *Ethnography and Philology of the Hidatsa Indians*, pp. 30-31; *A Journal of American Ethnology and Archaeology*, ed. J. Walter Fewkes, 5 vols. (Boston: Houghton, Mifflin and Co., 1891-1908), 1:1; Matilda Coxe Stevenson, *The Zuñi Indians: Their Mythology, Esoteric Fraternities, and Ceremonies* (1905; rpt. New York: Johnson Reprint Corp., 1970), p. 608, also p. 18; Capt. John G. Bourke, *The Snake-Dance of the Moquis of Arizona* . . . (New York: Charles Scribner's Sons, 1884), pp. 14ff.; Sylvester Baxter, "The Father of the Pueblos," *Harper's New Monthly Magazine*, 65 (June 1882), 72-73; James Mooney, *The Ghost-Dance Religion and the Sioux Outbreak of 1890* (1896), ed. Anthony F. C. Wallace (New York: Dover Publications, 1972), pp. 1-2.

[120] It was with this enterprise in view that the *Journal of American Folk-Lore* announced in its inaugural issue a claim many had come to learn by heart: the need for concerted eleventh-hour anthropological efforts ("Preface," *Journal of American Folk-Lore*, ed. W. W. Newell et al., 1 [1888], 5-6). See also Justin Winson, ed., *Narrative and Critical History of America*, 8 vols. (New York: Houghton, Mifflin and Co., 1889), 1:438; Leslie W. Dunlap, *American Historical Societies, 1790-1860* (Madison, Wis.: privately printed, 1944), p. 19.

Public respect for deliberate scientific examinations grew, as it had for the work of similarly motivated painters, photographers, and writers. Popular magazines catered to this new enthusiasm, and universities followed the trend by establishing departments of anthropology in the late 1880s and 1890s. Museums flourished, especially after inaugurating changes modeled on Franz Boas's daring curatorial success at Chicago's Columbian Exposition in 1893. By the beginning of the twentieth century, a tremendous salvage operation was underway. Individuals would sacrifice careers and families, in some cases risk their lives, in order to preserve information. "All other thought from our horizon banished, / Let any sacrifice our labor crown."[121] And yet, much of the enormous amount of information preserved by these professionals has in turn "vanished" in unread manuscripts and academic monographs. Having once saved them, researchers too often failed either to study or to enjoy native traditions and lore.

By 1900, the wilderness seemed to have vanished. The Wild West of the cowboy and rancher, the army scout, miner, and trapper, the frontier and Indian communities existed only as shades of their former selves, when extant at all. What many had long prophesied had come to pass. Scientists still hastened west, but they found themselves forced to deal with information collected earlier. Artists became either elegiac or mythic in their treatments of western history. Yet the passing of the wilderness helped to effect fundamental changes in attitudes and assumptions. With surprising frequency, especially toward the end of the century, Americans found their national complacency challenged. The heavy costs that a technologically progressive civilization entailed, especially vivid in the western landscape, tested cultural allegiances.

Among those who traveled west, the initial urge to document what was passing often developed into a strong inclination to question what would replace it. At its most sentimental, the question turned on the issue of progress. Did factories, cities, and farms improve upon plains and forests or impoverish them? And what of those who lived or worked in them? Few at mid-century gave more than cursory attention to Thoreau's challenging contrast of the Indian shelter and the village house. Far more listened in patriotic agreement to Senator Thomas Hart Benton in his enthusiasm for unrestrained national expansion. Yet, later in the century, cooler and more sensible heads began to view skeptically the claim that America's manifest destiny

---

121 John Peabody Harrington, quoted in Carobeth Laird, *Encounter with an Angry God: Recollections of My Life with John Peabody Harrington* (New York: Ballantine, 1975), p. v.

was desirable, however fated. Those who hastened to preserve tribal experiences were especially beset with doubts about the arbitrary premises of their own western European heritage. Was white civilization measurably more satisfying, more intelligent, more humane, than Indian cultures? Did it offer a greater, more significant sense of participation in social and religious endeavors? The Reverend Samuel Farmar Jarvis would have been jolted to the tips of his Episcopal whiskers at the very notion. How could he guess that those who answered his call in 1819 "to copy the evanescent features of [the Indian] character" would in time believe these questions possible. Chapter Eight will demonstrate that many did come to share this belief—or, at least, this suspension of disbelief. Perhaps the best introduction to their uncertainties is the work of an artist still in the cradle when Jarvis spoke that winter day. By the time he was thirty, though, he would have explored the issues suggested above as well as anyone and, in the process, helped to define the terms by which cultural relativism might be considered.

CHAPTER SEVEN

MELVILLE'S CANNIBALS
AND CHRISTIANS

We are all of us—Anglo-Saxons, Dyaks,
and Indians—sprung from one head, and
made in one image. And if we regret this
brotherhood now, we shall be forced to
join hands hereafter. A misfortune is not
a fault; and good luck is not meritorious.
The savage is born a savage; and the
civilized being inherits his civilization,
nothing more.
　　—*Melville* review of Parkman,
　　The California and Oregon Trail
　　　　　(March 1849)

"It's a mutual, joint-stock world, in all
meridians. We cannibals must help these
Christians."
　　　　　—*Moby-Dick* (1851)

Herman Melville's *Moby-Dick* (1851) either stimulates or stymies its reader with its plethoric display of knowledge about whales. From its opening "Etymology" and "Extracts" of whaling quotations, through its long disquisitions on cetology and its taxonomy of species and hunting tools, to its catalogue of whaling paintings, the book aspires to exhaust the possibilities of its material. Critics have rightly interpreted this exhaustiveness in thematic terms: in spite of all one can learn about whaling, the whale itself forever evades the harpoon of definition.[1]

The impressive array of facts marshaled in this metaphysical quest also presents another aspect: a genre picture of an imperiled way of life. Melville could not have predicted Daniel Drake's success in drilling for petroleum in August 1859 at Titusville, Pennsylvania, or guessed at its consequences for the whaling industry. Yet by the time he had completed *Moby-Dick* the sperm whale industry was already sinking into its long decline, while extinction itself threatened right and gray whales. Confident Ishmael answers the question titling one chapter, "—Will He Perish?" by invoking a contrast with the extermination of buffalo in Illinois: "the far different nature of the whale-hunt peremptorily forbids so inglorious an end to the Leviathan" (383). Perhaps thematic necessity dictated so sanguine a conclusion. Without full consciousness of the need for such a record, Melville nonetheless labored to document the business of whaling as thoroughly as possible. Few others possessed such knowledge. Though Melville was hardly the harpooner of two and a half years' experience he sometimes whimsically claimed to be, still, as for Ishmael, a whaleship was his Yale College and his Harvard. It provided him with experiences other authors might envy and made him one of the few capable of documenting the whaling industry in its heyday of the 1840s. His efforts compare strikingly with, say, those of George Caleb Bingham on the Missouri frontier.

Four of the five novels Melville wrote prior to *Moby-Dick* document contemporary cultures. *Typee* (1846) and *Omoo* (1847) proclaim themselves accurate records of Polynesian life at the very

---

[1] Or, as Ishmael remarks, in trying merely to comprehend the whale's tail: "The more I consider this mighty tail, the more do I deplore my inability to express it. . . . Dissect him how I may, then, I but go skin deep; I know him not, and never will. But if I know not even the tail of this whale, how understand his head? much more, how comprehend his face, when face he has none?" Melville, *Moby-Dick; or, The Whale*, ed. Harrison Hayford and Hershel Parker (New York: W. W. Norton, 1967), pp. 317-18. All subsequent references are to this edition.

moment that Christian missionaries and white sailors threatened it. Melville hurriedly finished *Redburn* (1849) for needed advance, roughly sketching out his initial experiences at sea of a decade earlier and incidentally documenting merchant-marine life in the North Atlantic. *White-Jacket* (1850), also more or less autobiographical, claims scholarly accuracy in illustrating shipboard life on an American man-of-war. Midway through his narrative Melville reflects that he feels himself "actuated by the same motive which has prompted many worthy old chroniclers, to set down the merest trifles concerning things that are destined to pass away entirely from the earth, and which, if not preserved in the nick of time, must infallibly perish from the memories of man. Who knows that this humble narrative may not hereafter prove the history of any obsolete barbarism? Who knows that, when men-of-war shall be no more, *White Jacket* may not be quoted to show to the people in the Millennium what a man-of-war was?"[2] This sentiment informs much of the energy of *Moby-Dick* as well.

Melville possessed, as critics like to remind us, the most thoroughly symbolic as well as the most "appropriative" imagination ever nurtured by American soil and salt water. His densely textured world is firmly rooted in mid-century social life, boldly anchored in contemporary factual currents.[3] Yet as keen an observer as he was, he serves representatively here for other reasons. Factualism was, after all, not unique; others, especially James Fenimore Cooper, had already devoted themselves to recording ways of life evanescently American. Melville's experiences propelled him farther, in part because, unlike Cooper, he had encountered at firsthand supposedly primitive life. He anticipated ways of thinking about vanishing tribes, as well as questions of progress and culture, that others adopted only much later. George Catlin's preservationist crusade made him a representative figure for issues examined earlier; his career combined so many allied commitments. A far greater artist, Melville was at the same time far less programmatically narrow in his manipulation of a fictional wilderness. In this regard, he provides a profound entrance into issues others would explore only later.

At twenty, lacking other employment, Herman Melville (1819-1891) shipped as a cabin boy from the economically depressed Amer-

---

[2] Melville, *White-Jacket, or The World in a Man-of-War*, ed. Harrison Hayford, Hershel Parker, and G. Thomas Tanselle (Evanston: Northwestern University Press and The Newberry Library, 1970), p. 282. All subsequent references are to this edition.

[3] See Warner Berthoff, *The Example of Melville* (1962; rpt. New York: W. W. Norton, 1972), pp. 21-22.

ica of the late 1830s. By the time he was discharged at Boston five years later, he had served in the merchant marine, the American navy, and aboard Pacific whalers; he had seen the Atlantic and the North and South Pacific; he had jumped ship, been held captive by a tribe of Polynesian cannibals, and spent time as a vagabond in both Tahiti and Hawaii. These five most active years of his life provided him with an admiral's knot of experiences to unravel. Like Henry Rowe Schoolcraft after his first frontier expedition, converted from geology to ethnology; like George Catlin and Lewis Henry Morgan, who abandoned portrait painting and a legal career, respectively, for anthropology—Melville returned from the South Seas with a fund of adventures that would dictate the course of his life. He had little inclination to pursue the staid professions his family might have hoped for him. Instead, he began a narrative about Polynesian natives, one that branded him with the vexing reputation of a "man who lived among the cannibals."[4]

Melville had certainly not hurried to the "West" intending to document its passing, however much his early fiction may suggest such a purpose.[5] Yet he had quickly realized the importance of his experiences as an early visitor to a still unaltered native environment. By combining observations made during four years in the Pacific with exhaustive reading of contemporary accounts, he created an invaluable ethnographic record. Moreover, he explored an intellectual pattern that many others would trace more firmly later in the century among American Indians. Polynesian and Indian cultures were threatened with extinction by white encroachment, and both sets evoked similar responses from concerned white Americans.

Of course, Melville later achieved far more in his career than relates to our purposes. His maturing as an artist in the ten years from the publication of *Typee* and *Omoo* through *Moby-Dick* to the completion of *The Confidence-Man* in 1856 entailed a progressive disengagement from purely cultural questions and an increasing devotion to issues metaphysical and moral. Naturally, with his memories of them receding, the distinctive elements of his South Seas adventures seem less and less fresh where they appear in later work. But this de-

---

[4] Melville to Nathaniel Hawthorne, June 1?, 1851, in *The Letters of Herman Melville*, ed. Merrill R. Davis and William H. Gilman (New Haven: Yale University Press, 1960), p. 130.

[5] See Melville, *Typee: A Peep at Polynesian Life*, ed. Harrison Hayford, Hershel Parker, and G. Thomas Tanselle (Evanston: Northwestern University Press, 1968), p. xiii; *Omoo: A Narrative in the South Seas*, ed. Harrison Hayford, Hershel Parker, and G. Thomas Tanselle (Evanston: Northwestern University Press, 1968), pp. xiv, 184. All subsequent references are to these editions.

velopment also resulted from Melville's more deliberately symbolic characterizations. Although *Typee*, "Benito Cereno" (1855), and *The Confidence-Man*, for example, share relevant themes, the last two handle the subject of racial variations in highly charged, highly allusive modes. Much of the present chapter concentrates on *Typee* and *Omoo* in order to define more straightforwardly the effect that native peoples had on Melville. Later works will warrant attention precisely to the extent that they form incisive, if highly symbolic, examinations of truths that Melville discovered in first reflecting upon his stay among the Marquesans and Tahitians.

One of Melville's most persistent fictional themes concerns man's imposing of belief upon experience, a theme that first appears in *Typee*, predictably in cultural garb. It is best typified in an early passage describing the island reception awaiting the narrator and his mates:

> How often is the term "savages" incorrectly applied! None really deserving of it were ever yet discovered by voyagers or by travellers. They have discovered heathens and barbarians, whom by horrible cruelties they have exasperated into savages. It may be asserted without fear of contradiction, that in all the cases of outrages committed by Polynesians, Europeans have at some time or other been the aggressors, and that the cruel and blood-thirsty disposition of some of the islanders is mainly to be ascribed to the influence of such examples. (27)

Melville tracks this theme through the rest of *Typee* and *Omoo* and tightens it to its fullest resonances in *Moby-Dick*. Following his frightening encounter with the kindly cannibal Queequeg, Ishmael might agree with Tommo: "Thus it is that they whom we denominate 'savages' are made to deserve the title" (26).[6]

The notion that primitive peoples often become what they were labeled finds its best formulation in *The Confidence-Man*, in those chapters devoted to "The Metaphysics of Indian-Hating." But by now, Melville treats the Indian so symbolically as to render the fiction an

---

[6] One of the valuable sources Melville researched prior to composing this passage claimed a similar provenance for native antagonism toward whites. According to Charles S. Stewart, "It has principally been in resentment for some real or supposed outrage on the part of civilized man" (Stewart, *A Visit to the South Seas in the U.S. Ship Vincennes, During the Years 1829 and 1830*, 2 vols. [1831; rpt. New York: Praeger Publishers, 1970], 1:317). Earlier, Stewart had angrily charged that "it is in such aggression and barbarity on the part of civilized and nominally Christian men, that more than half the reputed savageness of the heathen world has its origin" (ibid., p. 298).

allegorical satire on the evil that Christians do in the name of good.[7] Indian-hating, epitomized by John Moredock, reduces the white to the very evils he has vowed to eradicate. The creed that Christ preached, taken too narrowly to heart, degenerates to its most wretched inversion in the hands of its most vigorous proponents.

One must approach these chapters with caution, however, for it is easy to gloss over their inner complexities, ignoring the clues that suggest the story be read as one more instance in the book's catalogue of self-deception and misplaced confidence. Though Melville's Indians loom as mere symbolic grotesques, the fearful embodiment of irrational, ineluctable evil, the Moredock story may also be read in the light of Tommo's statement that "they whom we denominate 'savages' are made to deserve the title." The Indian fills for the Indian-hater a projected role as Devil, in other words, just as Moby Dick does for Captain Ahab; both apparently become what their adversaries expect of them.

Chapter Twenty-six on "The Metaphysics of Indian-Hating" provides a description of "backwoods education," an education obsessively devoted to "histories of Indian lying, Indian theft, Indian double-dealing, Indian fraud and perfidy, Indian want of conscience, Indian blood-thirstiness, Indian diabolism" (126). The narrator reveals the perspective from which to interpret the chapter in his caveat: "Still, all this is less advanced as truths of the Indians than as examples of the backwoodsman's impression of them" (127). Obsession blinds the backwoodsman to any interpretation but his own. Some Indians may stoop to treachery, but the Indian-hater cannot distinguish the many who do not. Pointedly, the narrator implies that native treachery represents a predictable response to evils perpetrated by whites. Mocmohoc, for instance, the alleged epitome of savage vengeance, is chief of "a dwindled tribe" (128). We are left to infer that the tribe has dwindled for the usual melancholy reasons connected with white settlement of adjacent lands. The question that more broadly demands our consideration, though, is put by the narrator: "But are all Indians like Mocmohoc?" (129). According to the backwoodsman, whether or not all act alike, they should be treated alike.

The original Moredock party was massacred by "a band of twenty renegades from various tribes, outlaws even among Indians" (133). The action sets off John Moredock on an obsessed career, namely, the destruction of this small band, followed by vengeance on the entire

[7] See Hershel Parker, "The Metaphysics of Indian-Hating," *Nineteenth-Century Fiction*, 18 (September 1963), reprinted in Herman Melville, *The Confidence-Man: His Masquerade*, ed. Hershel Parker (New York: W. W. Norton, 1971), p. 330.

race. He vows to exterminate the very tribes that had originally banished the twenty renegades. Ignoring his own inconsistencies, the
Indian-hater acts constantly so as to provoke a predictable native
response. Stressing Moredock's self-dehumanization, the satire exposes him as an armed paranoiac, compelling from others precisely
the actions he most fears. More to the point, he resembles the South
Seas sailors whose unprovoked aggressions Melville had vividly
described.

Of course, the notion that primitives respond as they are treated
illuminates little about relative cultural development. Yet the issue
of cultural imposition necessarily involved for Melville a contrast in
values between the supposedly civilized and the primitive. His narrator in *Typee* asks, in respect of a resplendently attired admiral and
a naked savage, "may not the savage be the happier man of the two?"
(29). If he lacks the comforts bestowed by material progress, the
Typee native is also free of its concomitant problems. As facile as this
Rousseauistic comparison may seem, Melville pressed through its conventional sentiment to a troubling series of judgments. Informed
sympathy for Polynesian societies allowed him to see what others
would only later begin to approach, that every culture represents just
one of many expressions of a common humanity. Western European
institutions could maintain no claim to inherent superiority.

Melville's development of these issues hardly followed a logical
progression and must be assessed in the terms used in earlier chapters
to define whole eras: moving from apprehensive concern for a preserved record, to tolerant understanding of what was recorded, to
incipient cultural relativism. In beginning with Melville's rationale
for his first two novels, one finds that it duplicates in part the motivation of artists discussed earlier. Though he never confessed an intention to record Marquesan culture before it changed irrevocably, he
called strongly and persistently for an accurate record of it while deploring its imminent loss. That desire for accuracy led Melville to
confirm firsthand experience with research.[8] He had spent a mere four
weeks among the Typees, not the four months claimed by Tommo—

---

[8] For corroboration of Melville's accounts, see H. Bruce Franklin, *The Wake of the
Gods: Melville's Mythology* (Stanford: Stanford University Press, 1963), pp. 106-7;
Charles Roberts Anderson, *Melville in the South Seas* (1939; rpt. New York: Dover
Publications, 1966), pp. 190, 270; James Baird, *Ishmael: A Study of the Symbolic
Mode in Primitivism* (New York: Harper and Brothers, 1956), pp. 9, 109; *Typee*, pp.
291-93; *Omoo*, pp. 322-25. When Melville occasionally strays from faithful renderings
to embellish his account—as, for instance, in his "Characteristic Anecdote of the
Queen of Nukuheva" or his description of boating excursions with the beautiful
Fayaway—he does so to epitomize conditions, not to distort them.

hardly time to learn so difficult a language or to understand so complex a tribe. To refresh his memory, then, and to supplement his partial knowledge, he read "almost every available account of the Marquesas."⁹ Indeed, Melville borrowed freely from the works of Charles S. Stewart, Captain David Porter, William Ellis, and Georg H. von Langsdorff, though he maintained a shrewd distrust of any single account, even his own. He knew too well how Western observers grossly misinterpreted "primitive" behavior out of familiar preconceptions, unconfirmed assumptions, or religious or cultural narrowness. *Typee*, in fact, deftly satirizes the complacent ethnologist and the agreeably imaginative native respondent, whose "powers of invention increase with the credulity of his auditors. He knows just the sort of information wanted, and furnishes it to any extent" (170).

Melville conscientiously refused to extrapolate from cultural data, as he states explicitly in *Typee* and *Omoo* and acknowledges tacitly in the premises informing episodes in his later fiction.¹⁰ The humor of Ishmael's "unwarrantable prejudices" on first seeing the cannibal Queequeg; the near-tragedy of Captain Amasa Delano's blithe presumptions about Babo and the black slaves in "Benito Cereno"; and the dark satire of Moredock's obsessive hatred of Indians in *The Confidence-Man*—each of these perspectives on cultural interpretation stresses its dangers, suggesting that even at best it is always in part projection. Each perspective derives by contrast from Melville's own tolerant, even open-ended, reading of cultural behavior.

This concern for pure description hinged upon Melville's sense that the Typee culture would soon pass beyond the possibility of accurate recording. The cause of its degeneration appeared to him in part internal, more largely external. Native religion had seemed to be declining even prior to the advent of whites, as Tommo notes: "In truth, I regard the Typees as a back-slidden generation. They are sunk in religious sloth, and require a spiritual revival. A long prosperity of bread-fruit and cocoa nuts has rendered them remiss in the performance of their higher obligations" (179). True, Melville is enjoying his sly ironies at the expense of a god-haunted and insistently pious American society.¹¹ Nevertheless, he did intuit a cultural

⁹ Franklin, *Wake of the Gods*, p. 9. Melville commented on the difficulty of the Typee language in *Typee*, pp. 24-25. See also Anderson, *Melville in the South Seas*, p. 146.

¹⁰ *Typee*, p. xiii; *Omoo*, p. xiv. Charles Anderson, in *Melville in the South Seas*, pp. 108, 137, 167-68, discusses the author's intelligent caution in such matters.

¹¹ See *Typee*, p. 174. See also Baird, *Ishmael*, pp. 103-4; Anderson, *Melville in the South Seas*, p. 175; Stewart, *Visit to the South Seas*, 1:292.

decline confirmed by later, more scientific studies. Cultural dissolution from within allowed whites more quickly to undermine social values, but even this process was less appalling than the threat to the very existence of the native population. In both *Typee* and *Omoo* Melville deplored the sharp drop in island numbers, attributing it to irreversible causes that made extinction no longer inconceivable.[12] *Omoo*, in fact, deliberately exaggerates the decline in population in order to dramatize Melville's apprehensions. This decline resulted entirely from the enforced adoption of Western modes, which proved meaningless to a native population. Only their own culture could sustain the Marquesans: "Nay, as a race, they can not otherwise long exist" (190). Even as late as an 1858-1859 lecture on "The South Seas," Melville reiterates this concern: "So the result of civilization, at the Sandwich Islands and elsewhere, is found productive to the civilizers, destructive to the civilizees. It is said to be compensation—a very philosophical word; but it appears to be very much on the principle of the old game, 'You lose, I win': good philosophy for the winner."[13] A dozen years earlier, he had written more bluntly: "Their prospects are hopeless."[14]

As imminent as the destruction of Polynesian cultures and peoples seemed, especially in Tahiti and Hawaii, much of the vigorous life on remoter islands continued in the 1840s. Melville cherished his opportunity as perhaps the last white, certainly the last to write an account, with direct knowledge of Marquesan culture prior to the encroachment of Western civilization.[15] The islands were still "tenanted by beings as strange and barbarous as ever."[16] This remark appears in *Omoo* as well, and even the later lecture refers to island enclaves "yet uncontaminated by the contact of civilization."[17] Melville seized upon just such threatened occasions, as early reviewers knew, congratulating him for having plucked from the Pacific Ocean accurate records of an uncorrupted, but sinking, native culture.[18]

[12] *Typee*, pp. 154-56, 188-89, 191-93, 195; *Omoo*, p. 125. See also, Louise K. Barnett, *The Ignoble Savage: American Literary Racism, 1790-1890*, Contributions in American Studies, no. 18 (Westport, Conn.: Greenwood Press, 1975), p. 173.

[13] Merton M. Sealts Jr., *Melville as Lecturer* (Cambridge, Mass.: Harvard University Press, 1957), p. 179. Although Melville never published this or other public lectures, Sealts has reconstructed as much as can be known of them from contemporary newspaper accounts.

[14] *Omoo*, p. 192.

[15] Compare William Ellis's similar response a quarter century before Melville, in *Polynesian Researches: Polynesia*, 2d ed. (1831; rpt. Rutland, Vt.: Charles E. Tuttle, Co., 1969), p. xiv.

[16] *Typee*, p. 5, also p. 11. See also Stewart, *Visit to the South Seas*, 1:212.

[17] *Omoo*, p. 265; Sealts, *Melville as Lecturer*, p. 180. See also *Typee*, pp. 5, 11.

[18] Hugh W. Hetherington, *Melville's Reviewers: British and American, 1846-1891* (Chapel Hill: University of North Carolina Press, 1961), pp. 34ff.

Yet the abandonment of indigenous ways troubled Melville far less because it deprived history of an account than because natives were losing a vital, autonomous culture. In diametrical opposition to many contemporaries who "sighed for the beginning of missionary instruction among them,"[19] the novelist felt, in James Baird's words, "that no affront to primitive man exceeds the missionary's intent to strip him of his native symbolism and leave him naked in the world, save for the ill-fitting habiliments of a misunderstood Christianity."[20] Melville admired the healthy integrity of Marquesan institutions, which had already resulted in an apparently ideal society in which government remained at a minimum and economic and social equality extended to all.[21] Of course, his enthusiasm echoed what had been considered "enlightened" sentiment since the eighteenth century. Yet his was an informed enthusiasm; personal experience allowed him to substantiate a realistic account of coherent native culture.

In *Typee* Melville presents an entire society living together peacefully and productively. "These islanders were heathens! savages! ay, cannibals! and how came they, without the aid of established law, to exhibit, in so eminent a degree, that social order which is the greatest blessing and highest pride of the social state?" (200). Taboo, the immediate answer, hardly satisfies the broader implications of the question. That Typee culture seemed incomprehensible to Western whites was no reason to assume that it functioned less adequately for its members than did western European culture.

Another, related point deserves mention here. Melville never forgot the extent to which he remained an outsider in Polynesia. It was notably astute of him to recognize the implications of that fact so early, and the insight explains one major motif in *Typee*, that of the alien confused by a culture whose rules and values are inaccessible to him. Repeatedly, Tommo observes native behavior without being able to comprehend its meaning. Though he vows to record "their practical every-day operation" (173), religion and its rites prove "a complete mystery" to him. Typee culture retains a vitality, despite signs of decay, that is best evident in its impenetrability. "I was utterly at a loss how to account for their singular conduct," Tommo confesses in one form or another throughout the narrative.[22] In part, his hesitation merely confirms Melville's initial refusal to venture unverifiable in-

[19] Stewart, *Visit to the South Seas*, 1:295.

[20] Baird, *Ishmael*, p. 99. For a larger view of Melville's attitude toward culture and society, see Harry B. Henderson III, *Versions of the Past: The Historical Imagination in American Fiction* (New York: Oxford University Press, 1974), p. 129.

[21] Anderson, *Melville in the South Seas*, pp. 132, 140, 169-70.

[22] *Typee*, pp. 120, 166, 169, 173, 177, 186-87, 189, 200, 221, 224, 232, 236.

ferences. In larger part, Tommo's bewilderment attests to the extraordinary complexity of Polynesian cultures. Even so astute an observer as he cannot penetrate their workings, as his lengthy, but self-consciously inadequate, appraisals of taboo demonstrate.[23]

That quality of mystery thwarting the alien observer of cultural behavior converts "Benito Cereno" from a mere grotesquerie to a subtle examination of guilt, evil, and epistemology. Melville, as he freely concedes, took the basic plot from the first-person narrative of Amasa Delano, an American sea captain who spent a bewildered and anxious day on board a Spanish slave ship. As Melville transforms the story, its vaguely threatening power emerges through Delano's misunderstanding of the enigmatic poses taken by the blacks: picking oakum, polishing rusty hatchets, scraping a wooden platter, dipping rope strands into pitch. More vividly developed is Delano's confrontation with enigmas that hint at a life wholly unknown to him. The nursing black mothers, for example, or the royally unyielding bearing of the slave king Atufal suggest a mysterious social ethic at work.

This story exaggerates the tendency evident in Melville's later prose toward the syntactically ambiguous and ambivalent. Locutions like "seems," "as if," and "he thought . . . but" further create the ambience achieved at times in *Typee*. Babo, Atufal, and the other blacks—like Kory-Kory, Mehevi, and other Polynesians in *Typee*—act in ways incomprehensible to the white observer. But whereas Tommo consciously refuses to interpret the Typees' taboo behavior, Delano indulges in facile, myopic assumptions. Melville transformed the actual Delano into a naive racist, one who poses a telling contrast to the more restrained, perceptive example provided by Tommo.[24] That Tommo tolerantly allows the alien phenomena of native culture to remain mysterious in their irreducible complexity finally redeems his efforts; that Delano interprets them reductively according to his own narrow lights almost proves his undoing.

From the beginning, Melville cast a skeptical eye on the progressive values his white contemporaries unquestioningly assumed. Tolerant admiration of Polynesian cultures prompted him to condemn the supposedly civilizing influence of such values, whether introduced by whalers, merchantmen, or French missionary expeditions. *Omoo* illustrates the devastation of Tahitian and Hawaiian cultures over half a century by religious and commercial solicitation, illustrations that pulse even more damningly in juxtaposition with the record of

---

[23] *Typee*, pp. 91, 221-23. See also Anderson, *Melville in the South Seas*, pp. 166-68.
[24] Henderson, *Versions of the Past*, p. 150.

unspoiled Marquesan life provided only a year before in *Typee*.[25] The "semi-civilization" of Tahiti, as Melville reveals it in the later book, exemplifies the worst of both worlds. At its least harmful, this transitional state elicits merely ridiculous behavior. A half-understood code pressures native churchgoers, for example, into wearing outlandish costumes, so that at one service there appear "half-a-dozen strapping fellows, in white shirts and no pantaloons" (171). Those who strutted awkwardly in European suits, hats, and petticoats had abandoned native costumes "graceful in the extreme, modest to all but the prudish, and peculiarly adapted to the climate" (182).

More insidiously, Christian civilization renders the natives defenseless against the corruption, diseases, and brutal exploitation introduced by the whites. They had coerced natives into abandoning old customs without offering a viable cultural system in return. The subsequent "amazing decrease" (191) in population seems less cruel, ironically, than the "physical degeneracy" (128) of the survivors. Stable native societies based on polyandrous family units gave way to an anarchy of self-destructive licentiousness. "In view of these things, who can remain blind to the fact, that, so far as mere temporal felicity is concerned, the Tahitians are far worse off now, than formerly" (192).

Responsibility for much of this destruction, of course, lies with the least respectable elements of white civilization. In the very beginning of *Typee*, Tommo describes the greeting given his ship by native girls upon its arrival at Nukuheva. The natives' kindness, openness, and generous welcome are met by the crew's licentiousness and "most shameful inebriety." He continues bitterly, "Alas for the poor savages when exposed to the influence of these polluting examples! Unsophisticated and confiding, they are easily led into every vice, and humanity weeps over the ruin thus remorselessly inflicted upon them by their European civilizers. Thrice happy are they who, inhabiting some yet undiscovered island in the midst of the ocean, have never been brought into contaminating contact with the white man" (15). This description would have surprised few readers, as it differs little from the accounts of Captain Cook or, more contemporaneously, J. Ross Browne, Captain David Porter, and Charles S. Stewart.[26] But Melville alone pursued the theme. Moving well beyond an exposition of out-

---

[25] Melville thought the Marquesans destined to the exploitative pattern of their island counterparts. See *Typee*, pp. 6, 188-89, 195. See also, for confirmation, Anderson, *Melville in the South Seas*, p, 175; Baird, *Ishmael*, p, 103; *Omoo*, pp. 184-89.

[26] Anderson, *Melville in the South Seas*, pp. 37-38, 96; Stewart, *Visit to the South Seas*, 1:298.

rages committed by rough sailors and unscrupulous traders, he came to see such incidents as symptomatic of, not marginal exceptions to, western European civilization.[27]

The true representatives of a tolerant Christian civilization in Polynesia should have been the missionaries, both French and English. Yet neither nationality tolerates the other, each pursuing its own narrow notions of native policy. These "saviors of the heathen" dismiss Polynesian customs and beliefs out-of-hand, complacently assuming the benefits to be gained from their cultural imperialism. Deeply racist, they segregate schooling for their children and introduce rickshaw taxi service, with natives "civilized into draught horses, and evangelized into beasts of burden" (196). A line of these vehicles stands at the same mission churches where they preach the democratizing love of Christ.[28] Hypocrisy aside, this scene best symbolizes native enslavement to a class-structured, work-driven culture. More than a decade after writing *Omoo*, Melville still felt his old animus, revealed in the conclusion to his lecture on "The South Seas." "I hope that these Edens of the South Seas . . . will long remain unspoiled in their simplicity, beauty, and purity. And as for annexation, I beg to offer up an earnest prayer—and I entreat all present and all Christians to join me in it—that the banns of that union should be forbidden until *we* have found for ourselves a civilization morally, mentally, and physically higher than one which has culminated in almshouses, prisons, and hospitals."[29]

Exercised as he continued to be by this issue, Melville must have appreciated what an easy target it offered for criticism. All human societies bear flaws, surely; neither vice nor corruption is a sufficient argument against fundamental institutions. Yet, for Melville, civilized vices, however destructive, proved less insidiously damaging than the enforced virtues. Appropriate as Western ways may have been for whites, they only incapacitated Polynesians. As the narrator of *Omoo* states after hearing a missionary's sermon, "In fact, there is, perhaps, no race upon earth, less disposed, by nature, to the monitions of Christianity, than the people of the South Sea" (174). Even when "the missionaries were prompted by a sincere desire for good . . . the effect has been lamentable." Forced to think abstractly, to work diligently, to forgo games and celebrations in favor of more "serious" employment, to worship with studied restraint rather than with emotional abandon, the natives found the very bases of an individualistic,

[27] See especially *Typee*, pp. 188-89, and *Omoo*, p. 127.
[28] Franklin, *Wake of the Gods*, p. 15.
[29] Sealts, *Melville as Lecturer*, p. 180.

success-oriented, materialistic Western culture dissatisfying. These cultural values need not prove ultimately inadequate; but they are not simply transportable truths, to be rudely imposed on any or all societies.

By the same token, Tommo feels no more comfortable with the equally rigorous, arbitrary, and mystifying beliefs of the natives. Despite certain manifest advantages to their way of life, the Typees display as blind an intolerance and as unyielding a disposition as the missionaries. They listen to their wooden idol, Moa Artua, and interpret his godly message as "generally of a complimentary nature" (176). Standing outside such belief, Tommo can only wonder at the degree of communal projection laid bare here, the self-deception characterizing not only primitive religion but also, by extension, all such rituals. He treats this religious myopia rather lightheartedly at first; the natives, at least, unlike the missionaries, do not seem to proselytize. Yet when every one of the Typees vigorously supports Karky in his demand to tattoo Tommo, the captive sailor perceives that the basis of their desire is to make a conversion as complete as that which the missionaries plan in their turn. None of the Typees comprehends Tommo's refusal, his evident rejection of their values. Like the white sailors and missionaries against whom they are thematically posed, the natives cannot move beyond a cultural absolutism.

To be sure, two natives—the beautiful Fayaway and the gentle old man Marheyo—seem able to transcend their culture's values, at least a little. "Of all the natives," Tommo remarks of his island consort, "she alone seemed to appreciate the effect which the peculiarity of the circumstances in which we were placed had produced upon the minds of [Toby] and myself. In addressing me, . . . there was a tenderness in her manner which it was impossible to misunderstand or resist" (108). Similarly, Marheyo, in the midst of Tommo's dramatic escape from his kindly captors, comes to his side. "He placed his arm upon my shoulder, and emphatically pronounced the only two English words I had taught him—'Home' and 'Mother.' I at once understood what he meant" (248). Marheyo then commands his son to carry Tommo to the beach and to freedom. These two instances, however, seem so thoroughly colored by romantic sentimentality that they only reinforce the original contention respecting any culture's narrow angle of vision.

Nevertheless, the possibility that cultural limits can give way to a shared humanity, that absolutism and intolerance of whatever stripe might moderate, persistently attracted Melville. Tommo's desperate escape at the end of the novel represents resistance to all cultural absolutes. He must if need be put a boathook into the throat of his erstwhile friend, the one-eyed chief Mow-Mow. In doing so, of course, he defends his threatened life and his Western identity. But he also puts a boathook into all one-eyed, one-sided interpretations of experience, all cultural absolutes. He gains freedom to return to a sea world where at least the possibility of contingent relationships and cultural relativity still exists.

Clearly, Melville rejected the notion that a particular culture or race can hold a warrant on truth. "What plays the mischief with the truth," he wrote in a famous letter to Hawthorne as he was finishing *Moby-Dick* in 1851, "is that men will insist upon the universal application of a temporary feeling or opinion."[30] One could easily extend this thought, without misconstruing Melville's meaning, to include "or the universal application of particular cultural patterns or goals." Melville denied that certain races were inherently depraved or, conversely, that others were superior. Captain Delano's blindness to circumstances aboard the *San Dominique,* for instance, largely results from his bland racism, his willingness truly to believe that "Most negroes are natural valets and hairdressers . . . [with] a certain easy cheerfulness, harmonious in every glance and gesture" (306, 314). In *Typee* Melville most clearly states the need for an open attitude toward cross-cultural variations:

> Civilization does not engross all the virtues of humanity: she has not even her full share of them. They flourish in greater abundance and attain greater strength among many barbarous people. The hospitality of the wild Arab, the courage of the North American Indian, and the faithful friendships of some of the Polynesian nations, far surpass any thing of a similar kind among the polished communities of Europe. If truth and justice, and the better principles of our nature, cannot exist unless enforced by the statute-book, how are we to account for the social condition of the Typees? (202-3)

His belief that genuinely complex systems structured non-Western cultures distinguishes Melville from most of his contemporaries. He seems to have understood that cultures form indigenous patterns both expressive of and responsive to communal needs. This approximation of cultural relativism, derived almost by definition from Melville's informed tolerance, is revealed nicely in the description of Wooloo

---

30 *Letters of Herman Melville*, ed. Davis and Gilman, p. 131. See also Louise Barnett's discussion of this theme in *Ignoble Savage*, pp. 173-80.

the Polynesian in *White-Jacket*. "In our man-of-war, this semi-savage, wandering about the gun-deck in his barbaric robe, seemed a being from some other sphere. His tastes were our abominations: ours his. Our creed he rejected: his we. We thought him a loon: he fancied us fools. Had the case been reversed; had we been Polynesians and he an American, our mutual opinion of each other would still have remained the same. A fact proving that neither was wrong, but both right" (118). Among Melville's contemporaries, Hawthorne most closely characterized the man he had yet to meet in his review of *Typee*. He particularly praised the author's "freedom of view—it would be too harsh to call it levity of principle—which renders him tolerant of codes of morals that may be little in accordance with our own."[31]

More than just "freedom of view," which can be cultivated in Salem as readily as in the South Seas, Melville stressed the need for intimate exposure to native life. Only then can true cultural tolerance be tested. The most striking development of this idea occurs in *Typee* when Tommo confronts cannibalism. From the beginning, Tommo invokes the natives' reputed love of human flesh as a source of awful suspense. This theme alters during his stay, however, from a melodramatic one to one more profound. Despite his fears, Tommo finds the Typees enchanting, and when, after a week among them, his companion remarks on their anthropophagic tastes, he replies, "Granted, . . . but a more humane, gentlemanly, and amiable set of epicures do not probably exist in the Pacific" (97). He later compares their "epicurism" favorably with countless "examples of civilized barbarity" even as he deprecates the charge of cannibalism by dismissing exaggerated accounts. Only toward the end of his stay is he again plagued by fears. This alternation in narrative perspective hardly demonstrates Tommo's reversion to the usual contemporary response, however.[32] It is one thing to contemplate cannibalism with equanimity; it is quite another to face being eaten oneself! Intimate exposure had allowed Tommo to judge this communion ceremony more tolerantly; but his "freedom of view" did not extend to partaking himself, or being partaken of.

Typee's development of the subject of cannibalism reveals the depth of Melville's tolerance for alien cultures. Although *Moby-Dick* propounds issues at once more symbolically ambitious, more metaphysical, and correspondingly less cultural, it also focuses on a cannibal in elaborating its major themes. That elaboration best reveals

---

[31] Cited in Hetherington, *Melville's Reviewers*, p. 51.
[32] See, for another reading, Anderson, *Melville in the South Seas*, p. 110.

discoveries Melville had made in *Typee* and best anticipates those that others would make more than a generation later. On a rather simple level, as already suggested, the entire novel is committed to documenting a major mid-century enterprise. Yet understated symbols throughout the narrative enforce the sense of irrecoverability, of experiences beyond the possibility of recording. The *Pequod* itself is named for "a celebrated tribe of Massachusetts Indians, now extinct as the ancient Medes" (67). That the ship emblematizes the questing, cannibalistic spirit of industrial society also links white predatory success with native decline. Similarly, quiet Tashtego, the second harpooner, represents the only Indian among the "Anacharsis Clootz deputation from all the isles of the sea" (108) that constitutes the *Pequod*'s crew. He comes from "Gay Head . . . where there exists the last remnant of a village of red men" (107). These descriptions serve as quiet reminders of the human costs dictated by white America's western progress.[33]

Structurally, *Moby-Dick* splits into two sections usually identified according to the dominant characters: Ishmael in the opening third; Ahab thereafter. The split might be more fruitfully identified, however, as one between Queequeg and Ahab, each of whom educates Ishmael in alternative responses to experience. When Ahab appears, the limits to his dramatic vision have already been identified by contrast to Queequeg's tolerance, generosity, and responsiveness. Ahab's gesture against the white whale is Promethean, but Queequeg has made it possible for Ishmael to realize the self-projecting nature of Ahab's torment, "that vulture the very creature he creates" (175). The captain heaps on the "dead wall" of Moby Dick's brow his own angry burden of hate, as the backwoodsman did to the Indian and as Tommo, in a less defiant, more fearful way, initially did to the Typees. Melville masterfully develops the dramatic possibilities of Ahab's moral absolutism, his fierce conversion of belief into truth. Yet the severest challenge to that absolutism comes not from those who openly resist his monomaniacal hunt for Moby Dick but from Queequeg's example.

Thrown into the strange bed of a tattooed Polynesian near the opening of the novel, Ishmael finds his fears instantly aroused by "unwarrantable prejudices." He watches Queequeg carefully, first in his preparations for bed and the next morning during his ablutions, and describes every action with an almost ethnological care. His initial response to Queequeg's "strange antics" and "queer proceed-

[33] See Barnett, *Ignoble Savage*, pp. 170, 176, 180, for a similar discussion of these issues.

ings" (30) resembles Captain Delano's reductive interpretation of mysteries aboard the *San Dominique*. Unlike Delano, he grows wide-eyed with fear in anticipation of some cannibal violence. In the very midst of his paralysis, nonetheless, he counsels himself to tolerance. "What's all this fuss I have been making about, thought I to myself—the man's a human being just as I am: he has just as much reason to fear me, as I have to be afraid of him" (31). Queequeg, in fact, soon bears out this confidence.

As he becomes a "bosom friend" of Queequeg, Ishmael learns to respect more fully those mysterious, unacculturated aspects of behavior beyond his ken. Queequeg's oblations to his idol, Yojo; his curious notions about sickness, death, and friendship; his daylong Ramadan—all define a system of beliefs completely outside Ishmael's cultural inheritance. Of course, they pique his curiosity and encourage his "rational" adjurations. But Melville thoroughly rejects any moral absolutism, even Ishmael's kindly sort.

> After all, I do not think that my remarks about religion made much impression upon Queequeg. Because, in the first place, he somehow seemed dull of hearing on that important subject, unless considered from his own point of view; and, in the second place, he did not more than one third understand me, couch my ideas simply as I would; and, finally, he no doubt thought he knew a good deal more about the true religion than I did. He looked at me with a sort of condescending concern and compassion, as though he thought it a great pity that such a sensible young man should be so hopelessly lost to evangelical pagan piety. (82)

The ironies here compound one another. Ishmael's arch tone, meant to puncture Queequeg's complacency, ends in self-deflation as well. Assessing the shortcomings of an intolerant Polynesian religion, he reveals his own mild intolerance. Ishmael's saving grace is his appreciation of the irony of their mutually condescending proselytizings.

Religion in particular divides within and between cultures by enforcing formal barriers to a common humanity. Recognizing this, Ishmael offers a mock-humorous rationalization for joining Queequeg in his worship:

> I was a good Christian; born and bred in the bosom of the infallible Presbyterian Church. How then could I unite with this wild idolator in worshipping his piece of wood? But what is worship? thought I. Do you suppose now, Ishmael, that the magnani-

mous God of heaven and earth—pagans and all included—can possibly be jealous of an insignificant bit of black wood? Impossible! But what is worship?—to do the will of God—*that* is worship. And what is the will of God?—to do to my fellow man what I would have my fellow man to do to me—*that* is the will of God. Now, Queequeg is my fellow man. And what do I wish that this Queequeg would do to me? Why, unite with me in my particular Presbyterian form of worship. Consequently, I must then unite with him in his; ergo, I must turn idolator. So I kindled the shavings. . . . (54)

Later, Queequeg's outraged exclamation on nearly losing his hand to the still-snapping jaws of a dead shark illustrates the ultimate insignificance of all cultural labels: "Queequeg no care what god made him shark, . . . wedder Fejee god or Nantucket god; but de god wat made shark must be one dam Ingin" (257).

The "sharkish world" sometimes breaks down cultural patterns to reveal a shared humanity. More often, cultural patterns alone articulate complex human impulses. When Queequeg "pressed his forehead against mine, clasped me round the waist, and said that henceforth we were married" (53), he expresses affection in the only way he knows how—wonderfully strange to Ishmael, yet unmistakable. Remarkably, Melville could stand slightly aside from his own culture as well and see it *as* a culture with its own distinct prescriptions. This "negative capability" meant that Melville could see Western behavior from a Polynesian perspective as both strangely arbitrary and understandable. Tommo and his companion, Toby, for instance, first enter the Typee Valley at once afraid and stalwart. Their demeanor—fully understandable from a Western perspective—ironically evokes nearly identical fears from the first Typees they see, who are scared off because the two act like "white cannibals" (69). Later, the sailors are invited to try a dish of poee-poee. Melville inverts the convention of the natives unable to cope with the civilization of fork and spoon by having the pair's unpracticed attempts to eat with their fingers "convulse the bystanders with uncontrollable laughter" (73). Once again, *Moby-Dick* best explores the theme of culturally fixed patterns when Queequeg recounts his first ignorant handling of a wheelbarrow. Carrying it on his back, he found, attracted condescending attention. But his ignorance differed little from that of a merchant captain who, visiting Queequeg's native island, had mistaken a punch bowl for a finger dish. " 'Now,' said Queequeg, 'what you tink now?—Didn't our people laugh?' " (59).

Melville never developed his thinking about cultural forms beyond this anecdotal and rather mechanical level. But perhaps that level was best suited to revealing their fundamental arbitrariness. Queequeg looks ridiculous as an "undergraduate" in western civilization, as did the Tahitians and Hawaiians in *Omoo*. He crawls under the bed in only his top hat to put on the boots that New Bedford society demands. "He was just enough civilized to show off his outlandishness in the strangest possible manner" (34). Yet his example, here as elsewhere, exposes the strict dogmatism of Western fashion, of dress codes, as well as of considerations of modesty. Moreover, Queequeg's attempt to conform to Western codes debilitates rather than enhances him morally. In providing the biography of this Polynesian prince, Ishmael describes his reason for emigrating: "at bottom—so he told me—he was actuated by a profound desire to learn among the Christians, the arts whereby to make his people still happier than they were; and more than that, still better than they were" (57). He soon learned "that even Christians could be both miserable and wicked; infinitely more so, than all his father's heathens" (57). In an ironic twist to the stereotypical tale of lapsed Christian morality, Queequeg can no longer return to inherit his kingship: "he was fearful Christianity, or rather Christians, had unfitted him for ascending the pure and undefiled throne of thirty pagan Kings before him" (57).

In earlier novels Melville attacked Western practices by juxtaposing them with native practices commonly condemned by whites, especially cannibalism. In *Moby-Dick* he remonstrated against cruel and wasteful consumption in a similar fashion:

> Go to the meat-market of a Saturday night and see the crowds of live bipeds staring up at the long rows of dead quadrupeds. Does not that sight take a tooth out of the cannibal's jaw? Cannibals? who is not a cannibal? I tell you it will be more tolerable for the Fejee that salted down a lean missionary in his cellar against a coming famine; it will be more tolerable for that provident Fejee, I say, in the day of judgment, than for thee, civilized and enlightened gourmand, who nailest geese to the ground and feastest on their bloated livers in thy paté-de-foie-gras. (255-56)

This question of true and false cannibalism informs the entire novel. The *Pequod*, on a predatory mission, is itself described in cannibalistic terms. Queequeg alone can educate Ishmael to considerations of tolerance, generosity, and selflessness. Later, Ahab will educate him to the contrasted terms of Western society, terms that Melville had hinted at in his earlier fiction. The whaling ship *Dolly*, for example, rejected by Tommo in the opening chapter of *Typee*, symbolizes Western civilization at its most blindly exploitative. Like the *Pequod*, its contempt for more elementary levels of natural and animal life, its scorn for native societies, finally becomes grotesquely cannibalistic. The story of the ship *Perseverance*, whose skipper simply touched port for replenishments and then headed back to whaling grounds, suggests an entire civilization ever questing and taking, eternally unsatisfied. The *Dolly* will also continue to sail until the last reminder of land and animal life, Pedro the rooster, is devoured. Only then will the ship return to land, taking more provisions for life it never replenishes. This coldly rational, power-impelled civilization is epitomized in Ahab's quest, his brutal social domination for private ends. He heroically perfects his society's assumptions. In *Israel Potter* (1855) Melville developed this indictment of Western "cannibalism" into a searching question, one at once less sententious and less easily dismissed than the "meat-market" passage quoted above: "What separates the enlightened man from the savage? Is civilization a thing distinct, or is it an advanced stage of barbarism?"[34]

Melville's later reflections on his experiences among Polynesian cultures convinced him of more than their autonomous vitality. Compared with his society, they seemed in surprising respects genuinely superior. Their democratic, fraternal nature delighted him, as did such socially reinforced characteristics as a "sense of delicacy," politeness, and the serene self-sufficiency that Queequeg representatively manifests. Indeed, if "the contemporary view of Christian civilization toward Oceania and Asia" was, in James Baird's words, "as *the regions of darkness*," then for Melville, by a radical inversion, those areas were "to become the only regions of light." For him, Baird goes on to claim, "the achievement of persuading an agreeable people (those of Tahiti, for example), to give up a traditional symbolism in answer to vague mumblings of peace, where peace and good will were already known, was an act of sacrilege, suspect in itself of 'civilized' evil. This feat of persuasion was a virtual token of the symbolic impoverishment in which the zeal of the missions originated."[35]

Beyond such improvishment, however, Melville saw nineteenth-century Western civilization in actively, humanly destructive terms. London, its symbol, appeared to him "the City of Dis," with emissaries convincingly more barbaric than those whom they deemed "barbarians."[36] In *White-Jacket*, his young narrator queries rhetorically:

[34] Melville, *His Fifty Years of Exile (Israel Potter)*, ed. Lewis Leary (New York: Sagamore Press, 1957), p. 186, also p. 170.
[35] Baird, *Ishmael*, p. 99, also p. 16. See also Barnett, *Ignoble Savage*, pp. 168ff.
[36] *Israel Potter*, p. 225.

"Are there no Moravians in the Moon, that not a missionary has yet visited this poor pagan planet of ours, to civilize civilization and Christianize Christendom?" (267). Earlier, in *Typee*, Tommo had not even phrased it as a question: "The term 'Savage' is, I conceive, often misapplied, and indeed when I consider the vices, cruelties, and enormities of every kind that spring up in the tainted atmosphere of a feverish civilization, I am inclined to think that so far as the relative wickedness of the parties is concerned, four or five Marquesan Islanders sent to the United States as Missionaries might be quite as useful as an equal number of Americans despatched to the Islands in a similar capacity" (125-26).

A more compellingly bitter articulation of this attitude occurs in Melville's later lecture, where he describes the efforts of actual missionaries:

> I am sorry to say we whites have a sad reputation among many of the Polynesians. The natives of these islands are naturally of a kindly and hospitable temper, but there has been planted among them an almost instinctive hate of the white man. They esteem us, with rare exceptions, such as *some* of the missionaries, the most barbarous, treacherous, irreligious, and devilish creatures on the earth. This may of course be a mere prejudice of these unlettered savages, for have not our traders always treated them with brotherly affection? Who has ever heard of a vessel sustaining the honor of a Christian flag and the spirit of the Christian Gospel by opening its batteries in indiscriminate massacre upon some poor little village on the seaside—splattering the torn bamboo huts with blood and brains of women and children, defenseless and innocent.[37]

Little of Cooper's ambivalence regarding the spread of "civilization" along the frontier is evident here. Already, the disillusionment savors of the sort that later spiced Mark Twain's writings. A decided shift has taken place along the spectrum of attitudes outlined earlier in the discussion of Crèvecoeur and Cather.

Melville enjoyed resounding popularity with his first two books— more than he ever again received. Some pious critics found his strictures on missionaries blasphemous; most enjoyed the lively view he presented of Polynesia. Yet, with regard to other exotic captivity and travel narratives popular at the time, none matched Melville's easy

[37] Sealts, *Melville as Lecturer*, pp. 168-69. See also Anderson, *Melville in the South Seas*, p. 447; Richard Slotkin, *Regeneration through Violence: The Mythology of the American Frontier, 1600-1860* (Middletown, Conn.: Wesleyan University Press, 1973), p. 550.

sophistication with other cultures or his correspondingly severe cross-cultural critiques and reverse comparisons. He anticipated a constellation of attitudes toward primitive cultures that became commonplaces only near the end of the century: the need for broad tolerance, for a recognition of a culture's autonomy as well as of its mysterious inner complexity. The question remains whether his contemporaries tacitly endorsed the controversial views expressed in *Typee, Omoo,* and, had they read it, *Moby-Dick*.

To judge only by some of the quotations offered in preceding chapters, many shared at least some of these attitudes. They too had learned to appreciate complex values in tribal life, though they were unable to integrate them as Melville had. To what extent was Melville at mid-century only one among the avant-garde? The answer to that question will require a full examination of those who, whether or not they began by commiting themselves to records of imperiled indigenous cultures, discovered nonetheless an authentic and autonomous value to them. The intellectual history of their explorations matches, in striking ways, the template offered by Melville's fictions. Moreover, they would subscribe to profound new assumptions about cultural life at which he had only hinted.

CHAPTER EIGHT

TOWARD CULTURAL RELATIVISM

It is related by Æsop, that a forester once meeting with a lion, they travelled together for a time, and conversed amicably without much differing in opinion. At length a dispute happening to arise upon the question of superiority between their respective races, the former, in the absence of a better argument, pointed to a monument, on which was sculptured, in marble, the statue of a man striding over the body of a vanquished lion. "If this," said the lion, "is all you have to say, let us be the sculptors, and you will see the lion striding over the vanquished man."

The moral of this fable should ever be borne in mind when contemplating the character of that brave and ill-used race of men, now melting away before the Anglo-Saxons like the snow beneath a vertical sun—the aboriginals of America. The Indians are no sculptors.
> —*Col William L. Stone*
> *Life of Joseph Brant* (1838)

The data of ethnology prove that not only our knowledge, but also our emotions are the result of the form of our social life and of the history of the people to whom we belong. If we desire to understand the development of human culture we must try to free ourselves of these shackles. This is possible only to those who are willing to adapt themselves to the strange ways of thinking and feeling of primitive people.
> —*Franz Boas*
> "The Aims of Ethnology" (1888)

An EMINENT MODERN ANTHROPOLOGIST has provided a simple touchstone for studies by his fellow practitioners. "Know what he thinks a savage is," Clifford Geertz claims, with a gleam in his eye, "and you have the key to his work."[1] Despite his assurances, such a simple key aids more surely in theory than in practice. In part, this is because the concept of the "savage"—the "primitive" or the "wild man"—masks such a welter of attitudes as to render the label inadequate to those it purports to define. Melville, for a prime instance, explored the concept in ways unmatched in the mid-nineteenth century, the result of unique personal adventures, exhaustive reading, and a searching artistry. He therefore exposes most convincingly the limits to Geertz's attractive dictum. Although Melville's idea of the savage might well be found in *Typee*, it can hardly be reduced to less than the narrative whole. No simple key to his work exists. Geertz realizes this, of course, as his elaboration confirms: "You know what he thinks he himself is and, knowing what he thinks he himself is, you know in general what sort of thing he is going to say about whatever tribes he happens to be studying. All ethnography is part philosophy, and a good deal of the rest is confession."[2] Whatever one believes of the savage invokes the fullest conceptions of oneself and one's culture.

Impelled by greater self-consciousness about their own value systems, twentieth-century anthropologists have abandoned their predecessors' absolutist perspectives. Yet that rejection itself represents only one more step in a history of increasingly sophisticated perspectives, all rejected in their own turn. Most people in the eighteenth century lacked the experience that might have encouraged them to move beyond contemporary stereotypes to relative judgments of other societies. Nevertheless, significant numbers began in the nineteenth century to treat exotic cultures more circumspectly. Some of the writers, artists, and photographers introduced in Chapters Five and Six, for example, discerned in the records they had preserved a challenge to their assumptions about tribal life. The realization that Indians might well be valued for more than pictorial or antiquarian reasons in turn brought into question received opinion on the issue of culture itself—a development so controversial that it continues to shake conventional assumptions.[3]

[1] Clifford Geertz, *The Interpretation of Cultures: Selected Essays* (New York: Basic Books, 1973), p. 346.

[2] Ibid.

[3] For background, see: David Bidney, "The Concept of Value in Modern Anthropology," in A. L. Kroeber, ed., *Anthropology Today: An Encyclopedic Inventory*

This chapter elaborates a sequence intimated in the preceding discussion of Melville, tracing four progressively more complex understandings of Indian tribes. Those who recognized an autonomous value to native cultures frequently stopped at that, incapable of pressing insight further. A more perceptive group appreciated as well their mystery and warned against easy hypotheses about these "closed" social worlds. Others went on to stress the need for intimate and protracted association. To comprehend the native, they realized, required learning to live and to think like one. Finally, one group won its way to an acceptance of primitive societies as comparable, and in many ways superior, to their own—a cultural relativism that in turn fueled inquiries into the concepts of advanced civilizations and material progress. These four lines of thought hardly developed as a distinct historical progression, nor are they necessarily linked. It is difficult nonetheless to conceive of the emergence of later, more complex forms of appreciation without the insights brought about by increasingly respectful tolerance.

The word *culture* itself underwent a remarkable transformation through the nineteenth century, acquiring new meanings at the same time that it crept into common parlance. Fuller understanding of this change may be gained here from a review of attitudes that Europeans initially held toward Indians, a review that risks sounding reductive only because European attitudes generally were so. From the sixteenth century on, most whites could not help but distort information about native life. One example is the imposed notion of kingship, as in the case of the misnamed King Philip's War. In fact, virtually no tribe lived under anything resembling a monarchy. In other respects, the long-developed European concept of wildness—defined by Hayden White as part of a "set of culturally self-authenticating devices which includes, among many others, the ideas of 'madness' and 'heresy' "[4]—

(Chicago: University of Chicago Press, 1953), pp. 682-99; Bidney, "The Idea of the Savage in North American Ethnohistory," *Journal of the History of Ideas*, 15 (April 1954), 322-27; F. R. Cowell, *Culture in Private and Public Life* (London: Thames and Hudson, 1954), esp. pp. 235ff.; Marvin Harris, *Culture, People, Nature: An Introduction to General Anthropology*, 2d ed. (New York: Thomas Y. Crowell, 1975), esp. pp. 146-47; George W. Stocking Jr., *Race, Culture, and Evolution: Essays in the History of Anthropology* (New York: Free Press, 1968); Raymond Williams, *Culture and Society: 1780-1950* (Harper and Row, 1958), pp. xiv, 58-65; Geertz, " 'From the Native's Point of View': On the Nature of Anthropological Understanding," in Keith H. Basso and Henry A. Selby, eds., *Meaning in Anthropology* (Albuquerque: University of New Mexico Press, 1976), pp. 221-37; David M. Schneider, "Notes toward a Theory of Culture," in ibid., pp. 197-220.

[4] Hayden White, "The Forms of Wildness: Archaeology of an Idea," in Edward Dudley and Maximillian E. Novak, eds., *The Wild Man Within: An Image in Western Thought from the Renaissance to Romanticism* (Pittsburgh: University

provided ready-made categories for defining the denizens of this paradigmatic wilderness.

Historians have offered compelling reasons for the persistence of this narrow, negative view of indigenous tribes. The strength of certain Christian mores predisposed Europeans to see Indians as a kind of negative definition of themselves, as deficient whites. Settling the land according to European economic practice in any case meant dispossessing native tribes, which further encouraged dehumanizing assumptions as a way of absolving guilt. Through the eighteenth century, then, ethnocentrism fostered an image of the Indian composed of largely Western patterns of intention and desire.

Even those intellectuals who professed a kind of moral tolerance rarely considered making inductive observations. They merely conceived of the Indian as the "other." The "noble savage" fathered by Diderot, Rousseau, Freneau, and Franklin was little more than a twin to wretched Caliban, both of whom had been delivered without aid of the midwife culture. Only the values ascribed to their births differed. Instead of damning him, Enlightenment intellectuals comforted the primitive child as a way of reflexively criticizing their own civilization. This reaction, itself an impressive development, allowed them to recognize some of their own society's arbitrary modes. As early as 1582, Montaigne shrewdly observed "that everyone gives the title of barbarism to everything that is not according to his usage; as, indeed, we have no other criterion of truth and reason than the example and pattern of the opinions and customs of the country where-

of Pittsburgh Press, 1972), p. 4, also pp. 3-38. See also Peter S. Thorslev Jr., "The Wild Man's Revenge," in ibid., pp. 281-307; Gary B. Nash, "Red, White and Black: The Origins of Racism in Colonial America," in Nash and Richard Weiss, eds., *The Great Fear: Race in the Mind of America* (New York: Holt, Rinehart and Winston, 1970), pp. 1-26; Nash "The Image of the Indian in the Southern Colonial Mind," *William and Mary Quarterly*, 3d ser., 29 (April 1972), 197-230; Roy Harvey Pearce, *Savagism and Civilization: A Study of the American Mind*, rev. ed. (Baltimore: Johns Hopkins University Press, 1965); Henri Baudet, *Paradise on Earth: Some Thoughts on European Images of Non-European Man* (1959), trans. Elizabeth Werthoff (New Haven: Yale University Press, 1965), esp. pp. vii, 5-25; Richard Slotkin, *Regeneration through Violence: The Mythology of the American Frontier, 1600-1860* (Middletown, Conn.: Wesleyan University Press, 1973), esp. pp. 116ff.; Robert F. Berkhofer Jr., *The White Man's Indian: Images of the American Indian from Columbus to the Present* (New York: Alfred A. Knopf, 1978), esp. pp. 5-7, 10-11, 25-27; Elémire Zolla, *The Writer and the Shaman: A Morphology of the American Indian* (1969), trans. Raymond Rosenthal (New York: Harcourt Brace Jovanovich, 1973), esp. pp. 5-27; Benjamin Keen, *The Aztec Image in Western Thought* (New Brunswick: Rutgers University Press, 1971), pp. 217-309; Michael Paul Rogin, "Liberal Society and the Indian Question," *Politics and Society*, 1 (May 1971), 269-312; Hoxie Neale Fairchild, *The Noble Savage: A Study in Romantic Naturalism* (New York: Columbia University Press, 1928).

in we live."⁵ Two centuries later, Benjamin Franklin could add little, despite firsthand knowledge the French philosopher could not claim: "Savages we call them, because their Manners differ from ours, which we think the Perfection of Civility. They think the same of theirs."⁶

The tolerance that grew in America as threats of Indian attack on eastern colonies diminished probably reflected little more than that abeyance. Certainly, the old ethnocentric ideas died hard even among those few closely acquainted with tribal life. Though missionaries and traders, explorers and Indian captives had always been capable of sympathetic assessments of specific native societies, they did not abandon a secure confidence in white superiority. Appreciation of a complex tribal diversity rarely developed into more profound attempts to understand native cultures on their own terms, much less into more penetrating assessments of the issue of culture itself.⁷ More to the point, such appreciation, even when it existed, seldom extended beyond a select group.

Well into the nineteenth century, Americans continued to subscribe to fixed cultural assumptions. Polygenesis, the dominant scientific concept in this era, offered a rational defense for longstanding racism. Government policy, though occasionally deflected or softened, rarely abandoned the reductive premise that Indians were children unable to appreciate their beleaguered past or their circumscribed future. This hoary notion found spokesmen among people as tolerant as Carl Schurz, President Hayes's secretary of the Interior Department. "We must not expect them, therefore, to evolve out of their own consciousness what is best for their salvation," Schurz counseled.

⁵ *Montaigne: Selected Essays*, ed. Blanchard Bates (New York: Random House, Modern Library, 1949), p. 77.

⁶ Benjamin Franklin, "Remarks Concerning the Savages of North America," Papers of Benjamin Franklin, Library of Congress microcopy (1941), 2d ser., vol. 10, no. 2334-2344, p. 1. See as well, for outstanding instances of this form of Enlightenment relativism: [Joseph Addison], *The Spectator*, April 27, 1711, pp. 1-2; *Captain Cook's Journal . . . 1768-71*, ed. Captain W.J.L. Wharton (London: Elliott Stock, 1893), p. 232; Alan Moorehead, *The Fatal Impact: An Account of the Invasion of the South Pacific, 1767-1840* (New York: Harper and Row, 1966), p. 70; *The Prose of Philip Freneau*, ed. Philip M. Marsh (New Brunswick: Scarecrow Press, 1955), pp. 332-42; *The Western Journals of Washington Irving*, ed. John Francis McDermott (Norman: University of Oklahoma Press, 1944), pp. 103-4; John Francis McDermott, "Up the Wide Missouri: Travelers and Their Diaries, 1794-1861," in McDermott, ed., *Travelers on the Western Frontier* (Urbana: University of Illinois Press, 1970), pp. 21-23; Pearce, *Savagism and Civilization*, pp. 138-41; Stocking, *Race, Culture, and Evolution*, p. 37; Robert F. Sayre, *Thoreau and the American Indians* (Princeton: Princeton University Press, 1977), Leslie Fiedler, *The Return of the Vanishing American* (New York: Stein and Day, 1968), pp. 41ff.

⁷ Gary B. Nash, "Red, White and Black," p. 9; Nash, "Image of the Indian," pp. 222, 225, 229; Berkhofer, *White Man's Indian*, p. 49; Pearce, *Savagism and Civilization*, p. 91.

"We must in a great measure do the necessary thinking for them, and then in the most humane way possible induce them to accept our conclusions."[8] Apart from his sheer patronization, Schurz reveals the inability of most otherwise sympathetic individuals to recognize the extraordinary variety of Indian cultures.[9]

Yet if this overview illustrates in large brushstrokes the attitudes generally shared by whites, it also paints over the emergence of significant resistance to and revision of those attitudes. In the nineteenth century, many of those who ventured west not only experienced revelations about Indian tribes shared by relatively few others for centuries, but they also stumbled into radically new ways of thinking about them. This development coincided in the 1860s with the emergence of anthropology as a central intellectual issue in an age rocked by geological, biological, and religious controversies.[10] To be sure, the ensuing mood of unsettled questioning was an international phenomenon, in large part the result of theoretical breakthroughs unconnected with the North American continent. Nonetheless, countless travelers on the western frontier contributed to this reassessment of notions of culture. Tourists, explorers, and amateur and professional ethnologists began during the second quarter of the nineteenth century to see native cultures as rich, vital, and autonomous, the evidence of their experiences among western tribes having patently contradicted longstanding theory and pressed them to more adequate interpretations. Ironically, acknowledgment of the viability of indigenous cultures—and with it, attitudes of respect, tolerance, even cultural relativism—gained acceptance just as Americans finally undermined most of those cultures.

The broad transition outlined in the following pages, then, is from cultural absolutism and ethnocentrism to cultural relativism. These terms, briefly discussed in Chapter One, reflect a progressively less complacent, more self-conscious appraisal of cultural thought and

[8] Carl Schurz, "Present Aspects of the Indian Problem," *North American Review*, 133 (July 1881), 19. For background to this paragraph, see: Stocking, *Race, Culture, and Evolution*, p. 39; Philip Borden, "Found Cumbering the Soil: Manifest Destiny and the Indian in the Nineteenth Century," in Nash and Weiss, eds., *The Great Fear*, p. 96.

[9] Borden, "Found Cumbering the Soil," p. 78; Wilcomb E. Washburn, *Red Man's Land/White Man's Law: A Study of the Past and Present Status of the American Indian* (New York: Charles Scribner's Sons, 1971), pp. 60-75; Alan Heimert, "Puritanism, the Wilderness, and the Frontier," *New England Quarterly*, 26 (September 1953), 371ff.; Richard Drinnon, *White Savage: The Case of John Dunn Hunter* (New York: Schocken Books, 1972), p. 241.

[10] Stocking, *Race, Culture, and Evolution*, p. 74, H. Bruce Franklin, *The Wake of the Gods: Melville's Mythology* (Stanford: Stanford University Press, 1963), pp. 3-4; Borden, "Found Cumbering the Soil," p. 92.

behavior. Historically, the shift has been from an initial belief in the exclusive worth of one's institutions to a hierarchical theory. Known as cultural evolutionism, this view grudgingly concedes value to other societies insofar as they share supposedly earlier or incipient forms of one's own institutions. This social-stages-of-history theory, given fictional garb by James Fenimore Cooper, in turn bowed to a pluralistic one: that cultures can not be evaluated against absolute norms, because each one intrinsically may warrant as much respect as another. Whether this sort of pure tolerance can ever be achieved, it forms an admirable goal, and the development of that recognition forms a fascinating history.

AWARENESS OF CULTURAL AUTONOMY

To reiterate, the majority of white Americans in the nineteenth century accepted a legacy of racial stereotypes: the good and bad Indian, the noble savage and unconscionable devil. In the nineteenth century, however, for reasons already discussed, the number of those who rejected that legacy grew significantly for the first time. They began to regard natives as complex human beings, as diverse as whites and equally admirable though differing radically in thought and behavior. Offering greatest impetus for this more widespread altering of attitudes were those who had actually lived among tribes, including Indian captive John Dunn Hunter, fur trapper Osborne Russell, and painter-ethnologist George Catlin.[11] Many others adopted their tolerance—but without following their example—through the next half century. In the 1870s, individuals as different as General George Crook and anthropologist James Mooney would feel the need to reiterate to an ever more receptive public what Commissioner of Indian Affairs Jedidiah Morse had perceptively remarked in the 1820s: "There is as visible a difference of character among the different tribes, as there is in our own population; few general observations, therefore, will apply to them as a body."[12] Perhaps the best articulation of this view ap-

[11] John Dunn Hunter, *Memoirs of a Captivity Among the Indians of North America* (1824), ed. Richard Drinnon (New York: Schocken Books, 1973), pp. xiv-xv, xxii-xxiii, 207, 210-12; Osborne Russell, *Journal of a Trapper* (1914), ed. Aubrey L. Haines (Portland: Oregon Historical Society, 1955), pp. 113, 121; George Catlin, *Letters and Notes on the Manners, Customs, and Conditions of the North American Indians*, 2 vols. (1844; rpt. New York: Dover Publications, 1973), 1:23; Oliver M. Spencer, *Indian Captivity* (1835; rpt. Ann Arbor: University Microfilms, 1966), esp. pp. 72-93, 102-7, 120-23.

[12] Cited in *A Collection of Indian Ancedotes* (Concord, N.H.: William White, 1838), p. xi; Gen. George Crook, *General George Crook: His Autobiography*, 2d ed., ed. Martin F. Schmitt (Norman: University of Oklahoma Press, 1960), p, 271;

peared in a letter written to *Century Magazine* in July 1889, criticizing
Frederic Remington's painted Indians:

> There are Indians and Indians, and he who should form his
> general impression of the Indian from a glimpse of the savagery
> of individual Apaches would find it necessary to discard his work
> and begin anew in the presence of the peaceful and skillful Zuni.
> . . . Those who have studied the question on the ground are
> agreed that while the Army view, the view of the frontiersman,
> and the view of the philanthropist are each true in individual
> cases, none of them contains the whole truth. The Indian char-
> acter is as varied as the character of the white man who sits in
> judgment upon him.[13]

Yet the concepts of human variety and even tribal diversity proved
less difficult to grasp than that of cultural complexity. Observers
were repeatedly astonished at the degree to which Iroquois, Kwakiutl,
Sioux, Algonquin, Papago, and Cherokee tribal life constituted whole
and extensive cultures, with idiosyncratic institutions shaping nearly
every facet of human behavior. Far from simple collectives, these and
other native cultures comprised intricate structures. Each aspect of
tribal life—religious, linguistic, political, artistic, economic, and social
—meshed into a mutually reinforcing whole, altogether unlike the
divisive strains of white society.[14]

Confirming this profound social integrity, redeemed white captives
sometimes described their experiences in terms very much like those
Melville invoked in *Typee*.[15] Others provided an even more sympa-

---

James Mooney, *The Ghost-Dance Religion and the Sioux Outbreak of 1890* (1896),
ed. Anthony F. C. Wallace (New York: Dover Publications, 1972), p. ix. See also Rev.
Jedidiah Morse, *A Report to the Secretary of War of the United States on Indian
Affairs . . .* (New Haven: S. Converse, 1822), pp. 66-67, 82; Col. Richard Irving Dodge,
*Our Wild Indians: Thirty-Three Years' Personal Experience Among the Red Men
of the Great West . . .* (Hartford, Conn.: A. D. Worthington and Co., 1883), pp. 53-54;
Ewers, "When Red and White Men Meet," *Western Historical Quarterly*, 2 (April
1971), 134. For a more general, and contradictory, reading of the period, see Pearce,
Savagism and Civilization, pp. 108-9; Berkhofer, *White Man's Indian*, pp. 19-11, 26,
71ff.

13 Hamilton Wright Mabie, "Indians, and Indians," *Century Magazine*, 38 (July
1889), 471.

14 For suggestions of this novel insight, see: Robert V. Hine, *Bartlett's West:
Drawing the Mexican Boundary* (New Haven: Yale University Press, 1968), pp. 63-
65; Charles Granville Johnson, *History of the Territory of Arizona*, 3 vols. (San
Francisco: Vincent Ryan and Co., 1868), 1:11; Charles G. Leland, *The Algonquin
Legends of New England, or Myths and Folk Lore of the Micmac, Passamaquoddy,
and Penobscot Tribes* (Boston: Houghton, Mifflin and Co., 1884), pp. 3-5, 13. See
also Stocking, *Race, Culture, and Evolution*, esp. p. 87

15 The earliest such description is "The Narrative of Alvar Nunez Cabeza de Vaca,"
trans. (Thomas) Buckingham Smith, ed. Frederick W. Hodge, in *Spanish Explorers*

thetic gloss on their experience by freely returning to native life without published comment. Their actions stood as judgment on their "captivities."[16] Former compatriots dismissed these eccentrics out-of-hand, of course, for voluntarily sacrificing "civilized" restraints for "savage freedom." Others, however, recognized the attraction of the highly socialized, if alien, character of tribal life. John Dunn Hunter's case is the most celebrated. In the early 1820s he caused a minor national uproar with the publication of his *Manners and Customs of the Indian Tribes Located West of the Mississippi* (1823), the record of his captivity, adoption, and training since childhood among woodland tribes. His eloquent ambivalence about white society, his generous validation of native life, his sympathy for people whom he characterized in fully human terms—all divided readers sharply into those supporting him and those charging fraud.[17]

Being held captive, of course, was no prerequisite for appreciating native cultures. Near mid-century, James Swan voluntarily chose to live among the Chehalis and Chinook Indians of the Pacific Northwest in order to study their complex societies. This somewhat eccentric frontiersman, who served as translator for Isaac Stevens's exploring expeditions, argued forcibly against the territorial governor's efforts toward "civilizing and Christianizing the Indians."[18] Speaking of the tribes' willingness to trade with the whites, he countered:

> They neither wish to adopt the white man's style of living, or his language, or religion.
>
> They feel as we would if a foreign people came among us, and attempted to force their customs on us whether we liked them or

---

in the Southern United States, 1528-1543, Original Narratives of Early American History Series (New York: Charles Scribner's Sons, 1907), pp. 1-126. See also John R. Jewitt, *A Narrative of the Adventures and Sufferings of John R. Jewitt During a Captivity of Nearly Three Years Among the Savages of Nootka Sound* (1815), 3d ed. (New York, 1816), esp. pp. 34-35, 197; Edwin James, ed., *A Narrative of the Captivity and Adventures of John Tanner . . .* (1830; rpt. Minneapolis: Ross and Haines, 1956); Pearce, *Savagism and Civilization*, pp. 116-18; Slotkin, *Regeneration through Violence*; Michael J. Colacurcio, review of Slotkin, *Regeneration*, in *Early American Literature*, 9 (Winter 1975), 336.

[16] J. Norman Heard, *White into Red: A Study of the Assimilation of White Persons Captured by Indians* (Metuchen, N.J.: Scarecrow Press, 1973), esp. pp. 1-6, 11-13, 138, 156; Slotkin, *Regeneration through Violence*, pp. 100-102.

[17] Hunter, *Memoirs of a Captivity*. See also Drinnon, *White Savage*, esp. pp. xvi-xvii, 12, 30, 37-39; [John P. Foote?], review of John D. Hunter, *Manners and Customs of the Indian Tribes Located West of the Mississippi*, in *Cincinnati Literary Gazette*, 1 (January 1, 10, 1824), 1-2, 9-10; review of Hunter, *Memoirs*, in *Quarterly Review*, 31 (1825), 76-80.

[18] James G. Swan, *The Northwest Coast, or, Three Years' Residence in Washington Territory* (1857; rpt. Seattle: University of Washington Press, 1969), p. 367.

not. We are willing the foreigners should come, and settle, and live with us; but if they attempted to force upon us their language and religion, and make us leave our old homes and take up new ones, we would certainly rebel; and it would only be by a long intercourse of years that our manners could be made to approximate.[19]

This recognition of cultural autonomy in native life constitutes perhaps the greatest strength of Swan's account. Moreover, the kind of argument he made had numerous advocates by mid-century.[20] John Wesley Powell spoke for a large segment of the educated population of 1878 when he asserted "Savagery is not inchoate civilization; it is a distinct status of society with its own institutions, customs, philosophies, and religion."[21] Like other cultural evolutionists who believed in a historical progression through increasingly more advanced social organizations, Powell could not accept an equation between "savagery" and "civilization." But he demonstrated the kind of respect for native tribes that formed a prerequisite to such acceptance.

Only recently have anthropologists exposed the fallacy common to all of the above statements, that culture supposedly reduces to man-

[19] Ibid., p. 368, also pp. ix, xi.
[20] See, for instance, John Beeson, *A Plea for the Indians* . . . (New York: J. Beeson, 1857), preface (unpaginated), pp. 112-14; William Watts H. Davis, *El Gringo; or, New Mexico and Her People* (New York: Harper and Brothers, 1857), esp. pp. 133-34; "Mrs. J. E. De Camp Sweet's Narrative of Her Captivity in the Sioux Outbreak of 1862," *Collections of the Minnesota Historical Society*, 6 (1894), 382-84: *Captivity and Adventures of John Tanner*, ed. James, pp. xvii-xviii, xxviii-xxix, xxxi. See also, Edward P. Dozier, "Resistance to Acculturation and Assimilation in an Indian Pueblo," *American Anthropologist*, 53 (January-March 1951), 56-66.
[21] Cited by William Culp Darrah, *Powell of the Colorado* (Princeton: Princeton University Press, 1951), p. 256. For similar statements, see Henry A. Boller, *Among the Indians. Eight Years in the Far West: 1858-1866* (Philadelphia: T. Ellwood Zell, 1868), p. 54; Daniel G. Brinton, *Essays of an Americanist* (Philadelphia: David McKay, 1890), p. 103; Brinton, *The Myths of the New World: A Treatise on the Symbolism and Mythology of the Red Race of America* (1868), 3d ed. (Philadelphia: David McKay, 1896), p. 15; Capt. John G. Bourke, *The Snake-Dance of the Moquis of Arizona* . . . (New York: Charles Scribner's Sons, 1884), p. 14; Catlin, *Letters and Notes*, 1:11, 26; Edward S. Curtis, *The North American Indian; Being a Series of Volumes Picturing and Describing the Indians of the United States, and Alaska*, ed. Frederick Webb Hodge, 20 vols. (Cambridge, Mass.: Harvard University Press, 1907-30), 1:xv-xvi; George Bird Grinnell, *Pawnee Hero Stories and Folk-Tales with Notes on the Origin, Customs and Character of the Pawnee People* (New York: Charles Scribner's Sons, 1890), pp. xii-xv; George Frederick Ruxton, *Ruxton of the Rockies*, ed. LeRoy R. Hafen (Norman: University of Oklahoma Press, 1950), p. 46; Matilda Coxe Stevenson, *The Zuñi Indians: Their Mythology, Esoteric Fraternities, and Ceremonies* (1905; rpt. New York: Johnson Reprint Corp., 1970), pp. 20, 607-8; Charles F. Lummis, *Bullying the Moqui*, ed. Robert Easton and Mackenzie Brown (Flagstaff: Prescott College Press, 1968), esp. pp. 3-4, 30ff.

ners and that human nature remains the same independent of time and place. Similar desires do not, like common physiques, appear under different cultural garbs. In fact, "cultural universal" suggests a contradiction, since human nature emerges only in particular contexts. "Culture," Clifford Geertz observes, "is not just an ornament of human existence but . . . an essential condition for it. . . . To be human here is thus not to be Everyman; it is to be a particular kind of man, and of course men differ."[22] Ironically, Geertz here defines the very terms of an older understanding of culture against which the best-intentioned ethnologists in the nineteenth century so stridently fought. Experiences with western tribes had led these more sensitive observers to honor various cultures as manifestations of identical human capacities; different conditioning seemed merely to give expression to a common human nature. The sole premise Geertz shares with their formulations—a significant one—is a fundamental respect for all cultural forms.

Those few times that writers ventured it in fiction, cultural relativism offered a clumsy perspective. Cooper's Leatherstocking tales represent a partial exception, defining whites and Indians in a roughly cultural fashion according to the repeated distinction between "gifts" and "natur'." In *The Deerslayer* (1841), Natty Bumppo provides the best definitions of these terms for Judith Hutter:

> "You find different colors on 'arth, as anyone may see, but you don't find different natur's. Different gifts, but only one natur'."
>
> "In what is a gift different from a nature? Is not nature itself a gift from God?"
>
> "Sartain; that's quick-thoughted and creditable, Judith, though the main idee is wrong. A natur' is the creatur' itself; its wishes, wants, idees, and feelin's, as all are born in him. This natur' never can be changed in the main, though it may undergo some increase or lessening. Now, gifts come of sarcunstances. Thus, if you put a man in a town, he gets town gifts; in a settlement, settlement gifts. . . . All these increase and strengthen until they get to fortify natur', as it might be, and excuse a thousand acts and idees. Still, the creatur' is the same at the bottom. . . ."[23]

---

[22] Geertz, *Interpretation of Cultures*, pp. 46, 53.

[23] Cooper, *The Deerslayer; or, The First War-Path* (New York: W. A. Townsend and Co., 1859), p. 477. (All further references to Cooper's works will be to this collected edition known as the Author's Revised Edition, illustrated by F.O.C. Darley and printed between 1859 and 1861.) Cooper has Bumppo provide this, his most thorough explanation, largely in order to elucidate a distinction that had been mired in vague contradiction since its initial presentation fifteen years earlier in *The Last of the Mohicans* (1826). Nevertheless, the hunter-philosopher has

Despite glaring inconsistencies in Bumppo's "gifts" thesis, Cooper achieved a remarkable assessment of cultural values. For the first time in American fiction, Iroquois and Sioux, Delaware and Pawnee move in relatively authentic native contexts, not just in worlds defined negatively by white standards. Within the limitations of his art and his conservative theories of evolutionary social history, Cooper represented Indians as complex beings in authentic cultures. He could never detail those cultures, nor could he believe them equal to European civilization. Yet his Indian was no longer a stock primitive, either mere savage negation or noble epitome, though both types do appear in his pages.

Cooper established a rough system of native values counter to those that whites wanted to impose. The novels declare that every person must be measured against the standards of behavior inculcated by his own society; behavior thereby deemed appropriate for one person may not be so for another. According to Natty, Indians differ as radically from whites in their conception of an afterlife as in that of battlefield courage; both concepts, however, pose acceptable alternatives to European notions of redemption and chivalry. Throughout the novels, the native is expected to be grudgingly implacable, his white counterparts forgiving. The former's culture values the laconic and reserved; the latter's, a genial openness and sociability. The Indian's alertness and shrewd deceptiveness contrast with the white's mean, complaining manner. Within what he posits as the framework of a common humanity, Cooper allows for workable variations in behavior. Or, as Natty remarks at one point, "In my judgment, every man is to be esteemed or condemned according to his gifts."[24]

Culture ever takes precedence, determining the ethical context within which to judge personal behavior. Natty Bumppo tells Chingachgook that "no christianizing will ever make even a Delaware a white man, nor any whooping and yelling convart a paleface into a redskin."[25] Underlying the implicit racism of these contrasted ex-

invoked the terms throughout the tales with reference to such a medley of idiosyncrasies, prejudices, habits, and culturally sanctioned customs, and mixed them so frequently (in the final two tales, an average of once every ten pages), as to render this concluding explanation nearly meaningless.

[24] *The Pathfinder*, p. 100. See also ibid., pp. 37, 41, 53, 67, 72, 81-82, 133, 338, 435, 476, 479; *The Last of the Mohicans*, pp. 174, 243, 259, 263; *The Deerslayer*, pp. 48, 91, 162, 226. Edwin Fussell, in *Frontier: American Literature and the American West* (Princeton: Princeton University Press, 1965), pp. 63-67, comments intelligently on such supposed racial differentiation.

[25] *The Pathfinder*, p. 130. See also ibid., pp. 242, 338; *The Deerslayer*, p. 87. For an interpretation of this line that is at odds with my own, see Joel Porte, *The Romance in America: Studies in Cooper, Poe, Hawthorne, Melville, and James* (Middletown, Conn.: Wesleyan University Press, 1969), p. 16.

amples—Christianity versus "whooping and yelling"—is an elementary recognition of cultural integrity. Despite his lack of firsthand experience, despite the thoroughgoing romanticism of his plots, with however little intellectual sophistication and in however contradictory a fashion, Cooper produced a fictional testament to his conditional respect for other cultures on their own terms.

Cooper stood with a distinct minority in the 1830s and 1840s. Contemporaries had as much difficulty in conceding the cultural terms of his fictions as they did, say, in accepting that the great ancient American cultures were indigenous, not introduced. Only in the 1880s would John Wesley Powell and Cyrus Thomas finally dispel the myth of a supposedly white-skinned race—the mound builders—exterminated by Indian savages. Yet George Catlin and Albert Gallatin had authoritatively declared half a century earlier that the very ancestors of nineteenth-century Indians had built the impressive ruins.[26] Similarly, their perceptive contemporaries, Alexander Bradford and Theodore Parker, had been quick to recognize the sophistication of the great civilizations of Central and South America, the Toltecs, Aztecs, and Incas. Parker, in fact, quarreled at length with William Hickling Prescott's monumental *History of the Conquest of Mexico* (1843) for its bland defense of Cortez's vile depredations and its patronizing attitude toward an Aztec civilization Parker considered the equal of Spain's.[27]

As mentioned in Chapter Six, the most successful popularizer of these radical concepts, John Lloyd Stephens, discovered and described many ancient Mayan ruins in the early 1840s. But he did far more. His boldly documented and marvelously illustrated claim for the autonomy of a native Indian civilization, its superb complexity and high sophistication, refuted the notion of Indians as simple, primitive, or barbarically savage. In the first of his two Mayan books, *Incidents of Travel in Central American, Chiapas, and Yucatan* (1841), he described his response to the massive temple at Copan, the first site he uncovered:

[26] Catlin, *Life Among the Indians* (London: Gall and Inglis, 187?), p. 21; Albert Gallatin, "A Synopsis of the Indian Tribes in North America," *Archaeologica Americana: Transactions and Collections of the American Antiquarian Society*, 2 (1836), 6, 147. See above, Chapter Six, p. 157, for a discussion of nineteenth-century interest in the mound builders.

[27] Alexander W. Bradford, *American Antiquities and Researches into the Origin and History of the Red Race* (New York: Dayton and Saxton, 1841), p. 72; Theodore Parker, "Prescott's Conquest of Mexico" (1849), reprinted in Theodore Parker, *The American Scholar*, ed. George Willis Cooke (Boston: American Unitarian Association, 1907), pp. 248-49, 265.

America, say historians, was peopled by savages; but savages never reared these structures, savages never carved these stones. When we asked the Indians who had made them, their dull answer was "Quién sabe? (Who knows?)" There were no associations connected with the place. . . . But architecture, sculpture, and painting, all the arts which embellish life, had flourished in this overgrown forest; orators, warriors, and statesmen, beauty, ambition, and glory had lived and passed away, and none knew that such things had been, or could tell of their past existence. Books, the records of knowledge, are silent on this theme.[28]

Stephens went on to offer persuasive reasons why this culture had to have been indigenous and to show its approximation to the glory of ancient Greece and Egypt. Indeed, his sensitivity to the ruins was as important, finally, as his documentation of them.

Yet the idea that *contemporary* Indian tribes also had intricate cultures gained popular acceptance far less readily, despite increasing numbers of individual proponents. Before mid-century, most ridiculed native cultures as at best a fiction of romantic sensibilities, at worst, an impediment to quick acculturation.[29] Institutions like the Carlisle School for Indians (and its counterpart, Hampton Institute for blacks) persisted in turning their charges into motivated bourgeois. At the same time, however, whites were increasingly recognizing Indian cultures for what they actually were and not merely for what they initially appeared to be. Their mysteriously complex structures began at last to demand fuller respect.

THE NEED FOR INTELLIGENT CAUTION

By the time Melville sardonically inveighed against the complacent ethnologist to a broad popular readership, others were also refusing to slip into the trap of unverifiable hypotheses. This cautious response became commonplace only late in the nineteenth century; even today, the full extent of necessary caution continues to trouble anthropologists. Yet Stephens, Melville, and other careful students of alien cultures established for ethnologists a pattern of continuous, self-conscious uncertainty that Clifford Geertz regards as basic to the science:

[28] Stephens, *Incidents of Travel in Central America, Chiapas, and Yucatan* (1841), ed. Richard L. Predmore, 2 vols. (New Brunswick: Rutgers University Press, 1949), 1:80-81. See also Victor Von Hagan, *Maya Explorer: John Lloyd Stephens* (Norman: University of Oklahoma Press, 1947), pp. 195-96.

[29] See, for a good description of these attitudes, Pearce, *Savagism and Civilization*, pp. 96-97; see also pp. 105ff.

"Cultural analysis is intrinsically incomplete. And, worse than that, the more deeply it goes the less complete it is. It is a strange science whose most telling assertions are its most tremulously based, in which to get somewhere with the matter at hand is to intensify the suspicion, both your own and that of others, that you are not quite getting it right. But that, along with plaguing subtle people with obtuse questions, is what being an ethnographer is like."[30] The very fact of recognizing one's informants as "subtle people" "plagued" by one's questions suggests a perspective too sensitive by half for ethnographers to appreciate until late in the nineteenth century.

Yet long before Geertz, many observers suffered honest, intelligent confusion about the peoples they studied, recognizing a more startling complexity to native life than any proposed in the fictions of alleged authorities. Captain James Cook, that most intrepid of eighteenth-century explorers, repeatedly acknowledged the inadequacy of his observations made in the Pacific. As James Boswell noted after breakfasting with the celebrated voyager, "He candidly confessed to me that he and his companions who visited the South Sea Islands could not be certain of any information they got, or supposed they got, except as to objects falling under the observation of the senses; their knowledge of the language was so imperfect they required the aid of their senses, and anything which they learnt about religion, government, or traditions might be quite erroneous."[31] As in so many other respects, Cook stood nearly alone, his exemplary caution imitated by few contemporaries.

By 1819, Reverend Jarvis, in his speech before the New-York Historical Society, could set forth certain ethnographic principles for those pursuing field research:

> If we wish to see him in his original character, we must follow him to his native forests. —There, surely, he is worthy of our attention.
>
> The Indians themselves are not communicative in relation to their religion; and it requires a good deal of familiar, attentive, and I may add, unsuspected observation, to obtain any knowledge respecting it. Hence, many who have been transiently resident among them, have very confidently pronounced, that they have no religion, an assertion, which subsequent and more accurate travellers have shown to be entirely unfounded.

[30] Geertz, *Interpretation of Cultures*, p. 29.
[31] James Boswell, *Boswell: The Ominous Years, 1774-1776*, ed. Charles Ryskamp and Frederick Pottle (New York: McGraw-Hill, 1963), p. 341.

Those, also, on whom we rely for information, have either been too little informed to know what to observe, or they have been influenced by peculiar modes of thinking, which have given a tinge to all they have said on the subject.[32]

Jarvis, more deliberately than Cook and long before Geertz, encouraged intelligent respect for tribal cultures. Only the dull and insensitive would assume easy access to them.

By the mid-1830s, even someone as inexperienced as Washington Irving espoused these principles. Rewriting the notes of fur magnate John Jacob Astor into *Astoria* (1836), he at one point remarked, "The religious belief of these people was extremely limited and confined," but quickly added, "or rather, in all probability, their explanations were but little understood by their visitors."[33] Having never seen the tribes, Irving nonetheless assumed their integrity and therefore the inaccuracy of the traders' reports. In spite of such isolated statements on the one hand, however, or the widely popular example of John Lloyd Stephens on the other, this attitude took hold only in the period following the Civil War, when it received the encouragement of professionals such as Powell, Grinnell, Hale, and Bandelier.[34]

One major pitfall of ethnographic research, then, was to assume too little, reducing native behavior to barely more than irrational impulse. Another danger, more problematic because less readily discernible, was to assume too much. As the painter Frederic Remington counseled about tribes of the Southwest, "The searching of the ethnologist must not penetrate his thoughts too rapidly, or he will find that he is reasoning for the Indian, and not with him."[35] Lewis Henry Morgan, the father of American anthropology, best articulated this resistance to facile ethnological interpretation in 1876. He flailed earlier recorders for succumbing to imaginative sentimentality: "Ig-

[32] Samuel Farmar Jarvis, *A Discourse on the Religion of the Indian Tribes of North America. Delivered Before the New-York Historical Society, Dec. 20, 1819* (New York: C. Wiley and Co., 1820), pp. 7-8.

[33] Irving, *Astoria, or Anecdotes of an Enterprise Beyond the Rocky Mountains*, ed. Edgeley W. Todd (Norman: University of Oklahoma Press, 1964), p. 334.

[34] Darrah, *Powell of the Colorado*, p. 255; Grinnell, *Pawnee Hero Stories*, pp. xi-xii; Horatio Hale, ed., *The Iroquois Book of Rites* (1883), ed. William N. Fenton (Toronto: University of Toronto Press, 1963), p. 37; Adolph F. Bandelier, "Final Report of Investigations among the Indians of the Southwestern United States," pt. 1, *Papers of the Archaeological Institute of America, American Series*, 3, (1890), 316. See also Gilbert Malcolm Sproat, *Scenes and Studies of Savage Life* (London: Smith, Elder and Co., 1868), p. 203; Stevenson, *Zuñi Indians*, pp. 607-8.

[35] Frederic Remington, "On the Indian Reservations," *Century Magazine*, 38 (July 1889), 400. See also the entry for October 30 in C. F. Saunders, Pocket Diary for 1909 Tour, Box 9, Saunders Collection, Huntington Library.

norant of its [Indian culture's] structure and principles, and unable to comprehend its peculiarities, they invoked the imagination to supply whatever was necessary to fill out the picture. When the reason, from want of facts, is unable to understand and therefore to explain the structure of a given society, imagination walks bravely in and fearlessly rears its glittering fabric to the sky."[36]

Morgan's caveat made eminent sense to increasing numbers of Americans in the next thirty years, who learned for themselves what Thoreau, Catlin, and Melville had discovered at least thirty years before.[37] One absolutely had to maintain cautious respect, to withhold judgment, neither assuming little nor imagining much, in order to come to understand the far more profound imaginative reaches of the people under study. Increasing familiarity with certain tribes led whites to remark with increasing frequency an indefinable, even recondite quality. A whole array of curiously implicit laws dictated social behavior. Particular occasions could not be isolated; they were enmeshed in a web of cultural assumptions that vibrated at every point when touched at one. As an army colonel later admitted about his fascination with Plains Indian religions in the 1870s, "One peculiarity of a people grows out of or is involved in, other peculiarities, and I soon found that I could give no explanation of the Indian religion which would be satisfactory even to myself, without a thorough knowledge of all his other characteristics and peculiarities. From the study of his religion I began to study the man."[38] Though frustration in this case led to renewed efforts, in many others it produced only a deepened sense of inadequacy.

By the early 1890s, the finest early anthropologist to work among the Hopi had lost nearly all confidence in his ability to understand

---

[36] Morgan, "Montezuma's Dinner," *North American Review*, 122 (1876), 268.

[37] Thoreau, *The Maine Woods* (1864), ed. Joseph J. Moldenhauer (Princeton: Princeton University Press, 1972), pp. 178-79; Catlin, *Life Among the Indians*, p. 9. See also Brinton, *Essays of an Americanist*, pp. iii-iv, 103; John C. Ewers, "Jean Louis Berlandier: A French Scientist among the Wild Comanches of Texas in 1828," in McDermott, ed., *Travelers on the Western Frontier*, esp. pp. 296-99; *Selected Prose of John Wesley Powell*, ed. George Crossette (Boston: David R. Godine, 1970), p. 115; Curtis, *North American Indian*, 1:xv-xvi.

[38] Dodge, *Our Wild Indians*, p. 40. See also John T. Flanagan, introduction to William Joseph Snelling, *Tales of the Northwest* (1830; rpt. Minneapolis: University of Minnesota Press, 1936), pp. xviii-xix; William Philo Clark, *The Indian Sign Language, with Brief Explanatory Notes* . . . (Philadelphia: L. R. Hamersly and Co., 1884), pp. 13-17; Col. Randolph B. Marcy, *Thirty Years of Army Life on the Border* (New York: Harper and Brothers, 1866), pp. 101 ff.; Francis Parkman, *The Conspiracy of Pontiac and the Indian War after the Conquest of Canada* (1851), vols. 16-18 of the Champlain Edition of *The Works of Francis Parkman* (Boston: Little, Brown and Co., 1898), 16:43; Alfred Robinson, *Life in California* (New York: Wiley and Putnam, 1846), pp. 235-36.

them. "The *Journal* is primarily a record of the ceremonial life," observes the editor of Alexander Stephen's *Hopi Journal*, "which is so full and so elaborated that it causes the Journalist to exclaim in despair that it is beyond the compass of a man's lifetime to understand and that it argues the possession of a sixth sense in the townspeople whom he finds at times very dull, i.e. unresponsive to his own terms of thought. It is the integration of the ceremonial life with the general life which is his despair, and ours."[39] Naturally, part of this mysteriousness in Indian behavior was due to the native's fear that by explaining activities he would expose to the white outsider not just himself, in the sense of personal privacy, but his source of being, his access to divine power. Among others, James Swan and Lieutenant Amiel Weeks Whipple had inferred this motive behind what the photographer Edward Curtis termed "the deep-rooted superstition, conservatism, and secretiveness so characteristic of primitive people, who are ever loath to afford a glimpse of their inner life to those who are not of their own."[40] Furthermore, only privileged figures—the sachems, society priests, and chiefs—fully understood sacred rituals or had access to the most cherished of cultural secrets.

Captain John G. Bourke, stationed in the Southwest for fifteen years, also discovered fierce native resistance to the inquiries he pursued in his spare time among local tribes. The research that proved unusually difficult for him, later published as *The Snake-Dance of the Moquis of Arizona* (1884), describes one of the most famous of all tribal ceremonies, during the most compelling moments of which dancers hold rattlesnakes in their mouths. Explaining the Moqui (or Hopi) tribe's animus toward him, Bourke vividly recalls the explanation offered by an "unusually bright Indian" named Nanahe:

> "You must not ask me to give you any information about that order. I am a member of it. It is a secret order, and under no circumstances can any of its secrets be made known. Very few

[39] Elsie Clews Parsons, introduction to *Hopi Journal of Alexander M. Stephen*, ed. Parsons, 2 vols. (New York: Columbia University Press, 1936), 1:xlviii. See also *David Thompson's Narrative of His Explorations in Western America, 1784-1812*, ed. Joseph Burr Tyrrell (Toronto: Champlain Society, 1916), pp. 81-82; Charles Alexander Eastman, *Indian Boyhood* (1902; rpt. Boston: Little, Brown and Co., 1918), p. 181.

[40] Curtis, *North American Indian*, 1:xiv. See also Swan, *The Northwest Coast*, pp. 151-52; Lt. Amiel Weeks Whipple, *Reports on Explorations and Surveys . . .*, *Senate Executive Documents*, 33d Cong., 2d sess., 185?, vol. 3, no. 78, p. 104; Bourke, *Snake-Dance of the Moquis*, p. 14; Catlin, *Letters and Notes*, 1:8-9; Charles G. Leland, "Legends of the Passamaquoddy," *Century Magazine*, 28 (September 1884), 676; J. Walter Fewkes, "Summer Ceremonials at Zuni Pueblo," *Journal of American Ethnology and Archaeology*, 1 (1891), 1n; Bandelier, "Final Report," pt. 1, p. 6.

people, even among the Moquis, know anything about it, and its members would be more careful to keep its affairs from the knowledge of the Moquis, not members, than they would from you. . . . We tell all sorts of stories to outsiders, even in Moqui.

"Of course that is lying, but if we adopted any other course our secrets wouldn't be kept very long. You must not get angry at me for speaking thus to you, but I cannot tell you what you want to know, and I don't want to deceive you."[41]

Momentarily, Nanahe's apologetic explanation shifts in tone as he severely rebukes Bourke's apparent lack of consideration for Hopi values and beliefs:

"We saw you writing down everything as you sat in the Estufa, and we knew that you had all that man could learn from his eyes. We didn't like to have you down there. No other man has ever shown so little regard for what we thought, but we knew that you had come there under orders, and that you were only doing what you thought you ought to do to learn all about our ceremonies. So we concluded to let you stay.

"No man—no man"—(with much emphasis) "has ever seen what you have seen—what you have seen—and I don't think that any stranger will ever see it again. One of our strictest rules is never to shake hands with a stranger while this business is going on, but you shook hands with nearly all of us, and you shook them very hard too. There never was a man who took notes of the dance while it was going on until you did; any one who says he did tells a lie."[42]

As any reader will discover, Bourke conveys extreme sensitivity, especially for Hopi efforts to defend the integrity of their sacred institutions. His very recounting of this reproach bears out that impression.

Wordsworth's phrase, "We murder to dissect," might have seemed an apt characterization of Bourke's and others' efforts. The information they acquired could never evoke the ineffable sense of the living social organism. Yet without their attempts, which themselves threatened cultural integrity, native traditions would have fallen into the grave of unrecorded history. If tribal resistance spurred them to haste,

---

[41] Bourke, *Snake-Dance of the Moquis*, pp. 180-81.

[42] Ibid., pp. 181-82. See also Bourke, "The Medicine-Men of the Apaches," in Bureau of American Ethnology, *Ninth Annual Report, 1887-88* (Washington: G.P.O., 1892), p. 451; Frederick Webb Hodge, "In Memoriam—John Gregory Bourke," *Journal of American Folk-Lore*, 9 (1896), 141. For a similar exclamation from a native, see Margaret Mead, *Ruth Benedict* (New York: Columbia University Press, 1974), pp. 31-32.

however, it also encouraged a more intelligent spirit of inquiry, tempered by renewed respect. Early in the twentieth century, Dr. Charles Eastman listed his reasons for describing his religious life prior to his conversion to Christianity. He felt as George Copway had half a century earlier: haste alone would not help whites to acquire a record of sacred lore.

> The religion of the Indian is the last thing about him that the man of another race will ever understand.
>
> First, the Indian does not speak of these deep matters so long as he believes in them, and when he has ceased to believe he speaks inaccurately and slightingly.
>
> Second, even if he can be induced to speak, the racial and religious prejudice of the other stands in the way of his sympathetic comprehension.
>
> Third, practically all existing studies on this subject have been made during the transition period, when the original beliefs and philosophy of the native American were already undergoing rapid disintegration.[43]

Deeper significances than met the eye required, paradoxically, both haste and caution from white observers desiring to understand tribal cultures as they truly persisted.

THE NEED FOR INTIMATE ASSOCIATION

That tribal life would ever elude simple, straightforward attempts at understanding led to the corollary recognition of the need to suspend cultural bias. Only by adopting a native perspective, or coming as close to it as possible, could one comprehend the strength of tribal culture. By 1884, the observation by a student of native sign languages that "one must train the mind to *think* like the Indians" before drawing conclusions may well have seemed commonplace.[44] More than half a century earlier, in 1830, a redeemed Indian captive had noted even more pointedly, "It is quite impossible that any one, who has not been among and 'of' the North American Indians, should be able to form even a tolerable idea of the extent to which they are acted upon by their superstitions."[45] During the years spanned by these

[43] Eastman, *The Soul of the Indian: An Interpretation* (Boston: Houghton Mifflin Co., 1911), foreword (unpaginated); George Copway, *The Life, History, and Travels of Kah-Ge-Ga-Gah-Bowh* (Albany: n.p., 1847), p. 55.

[44] Clark, *Indian Sign Language*, p. 17, also pp. 18-19.

[45] James Athearn Jones, *Traditions of the North American Indians*, 3 vols. (1830; rpt. Upper Saddle River, N.J.: Literature House, 1970), 1:x-xi. See also Jean Louis

two statements, scores of ethnographers and historians sought to unravel the mysteries of tribal life.

Of course, many refused to consider the native perspective, among
them William Hickling Prescott: as his *Conquest of Mexico* suggests,
their work suffered for that refusal.[46] On the other hand, some put
aside an initial skepticism to find themselves deeply moved by native
customs and modes. Dr. Washington Matthews, one of America's
finest field ethnographers, came to cherish a particular admiration
for the Southwest Pueblo tribes, and he revealed their complexity
in a series of careful studies to a scientific community still beset with
monographs dismissing native art and religion as puerile. For more
than eight years in the 1880s and 1890s, Matthews devoted all his
spare time to studying native life near Fort Wingate in the heart of
Navaho country. Initially delighted with weaving and silverwork, his
interest in physical anthropology gave way to a fascination with the impressive Navaho chants that his best later work examines. Matthews discovered that his sensibilities grew more refined as he attended more
carefully and that what he first took for a "succession of grunts" revealed themselves to an educated ear as an extraordinarily sophisticated body of lore: "thousands of significant songs—or poems as they
might be called—which have been composed with care and handed
down, for centuries perhaps, from teacher to pupil, from father to son,
as a precious heritage."[47]

Understandably, chants presented an almost impenetrable experience for white listeners, however fully they wanted to cross cultural
boundaries. Musical conventions are far more arbitrary than representational artistic modes, far less satisfying to any but initiates, and
even Matthews could cultivate little more than an intellectual appreciation. The account Alice C. Fletcher offered of the Omaha is all
the more surprising, then, in its encompassingly emotional quality.
A brilliant anthropologist devoted to the study of Indian music, Miss
Fletcher long afterwards recalled her initial work in the early 1880s:

> My first studies were crude and full of difficulties, difficulties
> that I afterward learned were bred of preconceived ideas, the

---

Berlandier *The Indians of Texas in 1830*, trans. Patricia Reading Leclercq, ed. John
C. Ewers (Washington: Smithsonian Institution, 1969), pp. 11, 22; Edwin Thompson
Denig, *Five Indian Tribes of the Upper Missouri*, ed. John C. Ewers (Norman: Uni-
versity of Oklahoma Press, 1961), pp. xxxi-xxxii.

46 See Keen, *Aztec Image*, p. 363. Harry B. Henderson III, in *Versions of the Past:
The Historical Imagination in American Fiction* (New York: Oxford University
Press, 1974), p. 32, offers an alternative interpretation.

47 Actually, these are the words of a Dr. Jona Letherman in an 1856 report, revised
and published by Dr. Washington Matthews as "Songs of the Navajos" in *Land of
Sunshine*, 5 (October 1896), 197; see also p. 201.

influence of generally accepted theories concerning "savage" music. . . . For a considerable time I was more inclined to distrust my ears than my theories, but when I strove to find facts that would agree with these theories I met only failure. . . . During these investigations I was stricken with a severe illness and lay for months ministered to in part by Indian friends. While I was thus shut in from the rest of the world . . . they would often at my request sing for me. They sang softly because I was weak, and there was no drum, and then it was that the distraction of noise and confusion of theory were dispelled, and the sweetness, the beauty and meaning of these songs were revealed to me.[48]

Matthews's and Fletcher's famous contemporary in American anthropology, Daniel G. Brinton, spoke more generally along these lines in 1890: "Savage symbolism is rich and is expressed both in object and word; and what appears cruelty, puerility or obscenity assumes a very different aspect when regarded from the correct, the native, point of view, with a full knowledge of the surroundings and the intentions of the myth-makers themselves."[49] At the same time, the only way to learn "the correct, the native, point of view" was to move in their closed world for extended periods. Or, in the words of one amateur ethnologist as early as 1830, "a man must live, emphatically, *live*, with Indians; share with them their lodges, their food, and their blankets, for years, before he can comprehend their ideas, or enter into their feelings."[50] The implicit corollary to this injunction is that only by living with them can the white alien be trusted enough for natives to open up to him. George Belden among the Plains tribes, Henry Boller with the Minnetarees, James G. Swan among the Pacific Northwest Chinooks, George Bird Grinnell among the Pawnee, and Adolph Bandelier, Captain John G. Bourke, Alexander M. Stephen, and in particular, Frank Hamilton Cushing with the Southwest Pueblo tribes—these are only some of the more notable among a wide variety of people who forsook white ways, if only temporarily, in order to gain more complete access to native modes.[51]

[48] Alice C. Fletcher, "A Study of Omaha Indian Music," *Archaeological and Ethnological Papers of the Peabody Museum*, 1, no. 5 (June 1893), 8.

[49] Brinton, *Essays of an Americanist*, p. 103. See also Dwight W. Hoover, *The Red and the Black* (Chicago: Rand McNally, 1976), p. 162; Thoreau, *The Maine Woods*, ed. Moldenhauer, p. 237.

[50] Snelling, *Tales of the Northwest*, p. 3.

[51] George P. Belden, *Belden, The White Chief; or Twelve Years Among the Wild Indians of the Plains*, ed. Gen. James S. Brisbin (1870; rpt. Cincinnati: E. W. Starr and Co., 1875), pp. 90ff.; Boller, *Among the Indians*, p. 48; Swan, *The Northwest Coast*, p. 148; Grinnell, *Pawnee Hero Stories*. See as well Thomas P. Wentworth, *Early*

In his flamboyant yet mysterious fashion, Cushing best embodies the different strains of this chapter. More brilliantly than any person before and most since, he comprehended the inner life of a native American culture, experiencing it as few others had from within. Curiously, the career he forged for himself precisely fits the famous definition Crèvecoeur offered for an American: *"He* is an American, who, leaving behind him all his ancient prejudices and manners, receives new ones from the new mode of life he has embraced."[52] Cushing's new "prejudices and manners" made him, in a way the eighteenth-century farmer-philosopher could never have imagined, the most extraordinary figure in the history of American anthropology.

Born in western New York State in 1857, Cushing suffered frail health all his life and died prematurely in 1900. By the time he was fourteen, he owned an impressive collection of pre-Columbian arrowheads; at seventeen, he published his first article on Indian folklore. Though largely self-taught, he was appointed a year later to the Smithsonian as an assistant in ethnology. By the age of twenty, Cushing had already gained an enviable reputation among anthropologists. Joining the Bureau of American Ethnology in 1879, he accompanied an expedition that fall to the Southwest, where he became fascinated with the secretive Zuni tribe. A decade after John Wesley Powell had seen them, the Zuni remained of all tribes the least influenced by white settlers. Others in the expedition collected artifacts and took photographs and notes. (A *Harper's* journalist reported their efforts in the long familiar terms of loss, necessity of haste, and danger of naiveté.)[53] But Cushing quickly chafed against the tribe's close-lipped resistance in matters of apparent internal importance. "Much dis-

---

Life Among the Indians: Reminiscences from the Life of Benjamin G. Armstrong (Ashland, Wis.: A. W. Bowron, 1891), esp. p. 147; James Willard Schultz, *My Life as an Indian: The Story of a Red Woman and a White Man in the Lodge of the Blackfeet* (1906-07; rpt. Boston: Houghton Mifflin Co., 1914), pp. iii, 6, 45; Daniel W. Jones, *Forty Years Among the Indians* (Salt Lake City: Juvenile Instructor Office, 1890), pp. 363-64; Walter Hough, *The Moki Snake Dance* (Chicago: Passenger Department, Santa Fe Route, 1898), pp. 50-51.

[52] Crèvecoeur, *Letters from an American Farmer* (1782; rpt. New York: E. P. Dutton, 1957), p. 39.

[53] Sylvester Baxter, "The Father of the Pueblos," *Harper's New Monthly Magazine*, 65 (June 1882), 75. Baxter's two articles on Cushing—this one and "An Aboriginal Pilgrimage," *Century Magazine* 24 (August 1882), 526-36—are the best contemporary accounts. For the most judicious biography of Cushing, see Jessie Green's introduction to *Zuni: Selected Writings of Frank Hamilton Cushing*, ed. Green (Lincoln: University of Nebraska Press, 1979), pp. 3-34. The following account was written prior to my reading of Green but has been partially revised according to his findings. See also Fagan, *Elusive Treasure*, pp. 248-55.

couraged," he later wrote of his first months there, "at last I determined to try living with the Indians."[54]

Surprising both his white colleagues and the Zuni, Cushing decided to move into the pueblo, remaining as anthropology's first "participant observer" after the expedition completed its two-month investigation. "Until I could overcome the suspicion and secure the full confidence of the Indians," he noted, "it would be impossible to gain any knowledge of importance regarding their inner life."[55] Despite his fears of being reduced to a "doomed exile," Cushing took an increasing part in tribal activities and doggedly learned to speak the difficult language. The Zuni accepted him, but only on their own terms, expecting to make him one of them. They were dismayed by Cushing's ever present sketchbook—just as Bourke's notebook had alienated the Hopi—and finally decided to use physical means to oppose this crude invasion of their cultural life. The sacred dance called the Kea-k'ok-shi was about to begin when Cushing found himself cornered in his room:

> "Leave your books and pencils behind, then," said they.
> "No, I must carry them wherever I go."
> "If you put the shadows of the great dance down on the leaves of your books to-day, we shall cut them to pieces," they threatened.
> Suddenly wrenching away from them, I pulled a knife out from the bottom of my pouch, and, bracing up against the wall, brandished it, and said that whatever hand grabbed my arm again would be cut off, that whoever cut my books to pieces would only cut himself to pieces with my knife. It was a doubtful game of bluff, but the chiefs fell back a little, and I darted through the door. Although they followed me throughout the whole day, they did not again offer to molest me, but the people gathered so closely around me that I could scarcely find opportunity for sketching.[56]

After the Zuni's initial wariness passed, Cushing acquired close friends, assumed full Zuni costume, and accepted foster parents. Similarly, when he set aside his own notions of taboo and allowed his ears to be pierced, he was adopted into the Macaw clan and given the name Ténatsali, or Medicine Flower, a name that "only one man in a

[54] Cushing, "My Adventures in Zuni," *Century Magazine*, 25 (December 1882), 199.
[55] Ibid., p. 204.
[56] Ibid., p. 205.

generation could bear."[57] For four and a half years Cushing lived in full acceptance among the tribe, participating in sacred ceremonies, serving on the tribal council, and even gaining admittance to a secret medicine fraternity. His most notable distinction came in 1881, with his initiation into the Priesthood of the Bow, one of the most esoteric orders and the most powerful. According to his biographer, "As he improved his knowledge of the language and assimilated the complexities of the Zuni social order, he assumed an influential role in the government of the tribe. And, a gifted raconteur, he became not only a recognized authority in matters of Zuni history, myth, and ceremony but a favorite among the tribal storytellers, making contributions of his own to the collective story."[58] Perceptive, intelligent, and sensitive, Cushing achieved far greater participation than any other white, even more than most Zuni, advancing in the priesthood to assistant chief. Ultimately, after taking the requisite enemy scalp—probably the only scientist to do so in the line of duty—he was made head war chief.

Suddenly, in early 1894, Cushing left Zuni without public explanation, never to return. White Americans were both fascinated and confused by this long-haired, earringed man, the only person in history to justifiably identify himself, as he once officially did, with the double title "1st War Chief of Zuni, U.S. Asst. Ethnologist."[59] In fact, Cushing had been officially recalled for having successfully defended Zuni land rights against powerful federal interests, thereby jeopardizing the Bureau of American Ethnology itself. But these circumstances were unknown to readers of *Century* and *Atlantic*, whose interest had been excited by Cushing's descriptions of his exotic experiences. Nor was the public aware of his recurrent illnesses, which only confirmed his chronic inability to complete written reports. All they knew was that he seemed voluntarily to refrain from publishing everything but a score or so of pieces from his vast collection of materials. He never organized that collection, never catalogued his many masks and dolls, and never completed his fine study of Zuni mythology. The volumes he did publish, along with his manuscripts, suggest Cushing's profound insight into Zuni culture. They also underscore the painful loss to anthropology of a wealth of unrecorded knowledge and experiences. It was as if a door had been shut firmly on the finest five years of nineteenth-century ethnology.

[57] Cushing, "My Adventures in Zuni. II.," *Century Magazine*, 26 (February 1883), 511.

[58] Green, introduction to Cushing, *Zuni*, ed. Green, p. 10.

[59] Ibid., pp. 5-6.

During the next two years, Cushing pursued archaeological investigation along the Gila and Salt Rivers in Arizona, before ill health in the winter of 1888-1889 forced him to leave the region forever.[60] He never again achieved the acceptance he had won among the Zuni in the early 1880s. Thomas Eakins's famous 1895 portrait of the thirty-eight-year-old ethnologist reveals a lanky, melancholy figure apparently locked in memories evoked by the Zuni fetishes that surround him. Eakins's biographer has written that the painting "celebrates a disappearing culture and the dying man who devoted his life to studying it. Tragic possibility is written in Cushing's face, in an understanding that is beyond solace and in the emaciated figure of the man. . . . The man exists alone and in the broader experience of the age, expressing his reverence for a civilization being engulfed and destroyed in nineteenth-century America."[61]

This interpretation somewhat sentimentalizes Cushing's actual response to the Zuni, whom he did not think were declining, either numerically or culturally. (He even subscribed to a mild form of cultural evolutionism, and thought a more advanced white culture should eventually assimilate the Zuni.) Yet like other ethnologists, he found much in native culture superior to his own, including ethical, spiritual, and even agricultural knowledge. He wanted to make available to his white contemporaries the system of Zuni philosophy within its cultural context, but his inability to reveal so much of what his intelligent, persistent efforts had unveiled may have been owing to more than merely constitutional reasons.[62] Informed speculation leads to the conclusion that he may consciously have refused to publicize important materials. Like the priests who attempted to prevent him from taking notes during his first months in Zuni, he certainly came to appreciate the intricate, fragile balance of belief with mystery, significant gesture with sacred knowledge. True cultural relativism may never be attainable, as modern anthropologists affirm. To the extent that Cushing chose between the alternatives of white openness and native secrecy, he embraced the latter.

For other ethnologists, if apparently not for Cushing, tribal life hardly could support theories of progressive social stages in an evolutionary spectrum of cultures. Increasingly, it appeared structured by

---

[60] For a description of Cushing's contributions to archaeology in these years, see Gordon R. Willey and Jeremy A. Sabloff, *A History of American Archaeology* (London: Thames and Hudson, 1974), pp. 59-60, 114.

[61] Sylven Schendler, *Eakins* (Boston: Little, Brown and Co., 1967), p. 137; see also p. 136.

[62] See, for evidence supporting the claims of this paragraph, Cushing, *Zuni*, ed. Green, pp. 145, 166, 184, 218, 252-54, 427-28.

22. Thomas Eakins, *Frank Hamilton Cushing*, 1894-1895. Oil on canvas. The Thomas Gilcrease Institute of American History and Art, Tulsa, Oklahoma.

institutions whose complexity rivaled and surpassed that of institutions in supposedly more advanced societies. Though less flexible, perhaps less "intelligent" or "rational" than that of western Europe, native American cultures could also manifest an integrity, a significance, a value for their members in ways more satisfying. As Melville had discovered, those whites who allowed themselves to accept that possibility and to share that perspective found that the tables might be turned. "Indian tribes look upon the whites as an inferior race," observed one midwesterner in 1868 after having lived with the Minnetaree tribe, "pretty much in the same light that we formerly regarded plantation negroes."[63]

THE PROSPECT OF CULTURAL RELATIVISM

The notions that native Americans could make serious judgments on white institutions and patterns and that, by extension, white Americans might assess western European civilization from the perspective of native ones set the terms for a fourth way of looking at culture. Before the nineteenth century, expressions such as Benjamin Franklin's on the "Savage" perspective reflect a certain abstract admiration for native life.[64] Yet this incipient relativism had negligible influence, in part because real tolerance for particular native institutions was too wholly constrained by Western assumptions. Circumspect questions about cultural variations would rarely be posed until well into the nineteenth century, much less answered. Even then, recognition of the complex autonomy of native cultures developed slowly and uncertainly among the most perceptive and willing of whites. Since the perspective that true cultural relativism allows depends upon a prior acknowledgment of cultural autonomy, insights more informed than Franklin's had to wait half a century.

An assortment of important discoveries encouraged this new attitude, especially those in the fields of comparative religion and mythology. Such investigations, along with those in biology and geography, "turned much of Western Scripture from historical fact into metaphorical or psychological fact—or, perhaps, mere fancy."[65] That the psychological bases for Western civilization differed little from those for any other culture was one of the most radical ideas to emerge in the late nineteenth century. Again, the implication is not what many liberal thinkers have often believed, that beneath outer

63 Bollor, *Among the Indians*, p. 54.
64 See above, p. 218.
65 Franklin, *Wake of the Gods*, p. 3.

cultural forms all humans share a common psychological nature. "No two languages are ever sufficiently similar to be considered as representing the same social reality," Edward Sapir noted in a different context half a century ago. "The worlds in which different societies live are distinct worlds, not merely the same world with different labels attached."[66] On the other hand, differences between societies reveal nothing about differences in supposed racial capacities or predispositions.

More than a few came to suspect that savagery and civilization were not absolute conditions but relative states, or, as one man described them in 1843, matters of "taste."[67] Partly, this suspicion grew as people recognized "the weakness of arbitrary technological criteria of cultural progress."[68] The San Francisco bibliophile and amateur historian Hubert Howe Bancroft attacked Lewis Henry Morgan's deprecatory assessment of the Aztecs on these very terms. What, he asked in 1883, was meant by "half-civilization, or quarter-civilization, or wholly civilized? A half-civilized nation is a nation half as civilized as ours. But is our civilization fully civilized?"[69] Others also recognized, some more pointedly and in detail, that whites could by no means claim sole possession of superior knowledge and that native tribes had often served as instructors. "It is the common cry among us," declared one historian in 1825, "that the savage must now at length be taught to till the ground, to sow, and to reap; we all the while forgetting that it was the same savage who actually taught the European emigrant how to cultivate the American soil, to clear the stubborn forest by degrees, and to grow that valuable grain, the maize, or Indian corn; and that the farmers even of the present day . . . do little more than follow the agricultural lessons taught to their progenitors by the Indians."[70]

Alfred W. Crosby and Virgil J. Vogel have detailed the enormous debt incurred by European settlers to native Americans, especially in

[66] Sapir, "Linguistics," *Language*, 5 (1929), epigraph, cited in Drinnon, *White Savage*, p. 125.

[67] Felix O. C. Darley, *Scenes in Indian Life*, 4 nos. (Philadelphia: J. R. Colon, April-July 1843), no. 2, May 1843.

[68] Keen, *Aztec Image*, p. 391.

[69] Hubert Howe Bancroft, *The Early American Chroniclers* (San Francisco: A. L. Bancroft and Co., 1883), p. 10. See also Kevin Starr, *Americans and the California Dream, 1850-1915* (New York: Oxford University Press, 1973), p. 125; Keen, *Aztec Image*, pp. 403ff.; John Walton Caughey, *Hubert Howe Bancroft, Historian of the West* (Berkeley: University of California Press, 1946), pp. 122ff.

[70] John Halkett, *Historical Notes Respecting the Indians of North America . . .* (London: Archibald Constable and Co., 1825), p. 325, also pp. 2, 26, 338.

medicine and agriculture.[71] Cooper dramatized this debt from a more sardonic perspective in his first Leatherstocking novel. *The Pioneers* early presents the Mohican healer Chingachgook and Dr. Elnathon Todd jointly attending the wounded young hero. Not only are Todd's ministrations revealed as patently ineffective, but he unashamedly steals the Indian's medicinal ointments. As the narrator observes, "It was fortunate for Dr. Todd that his principles were so liberal, as, coupled with his practice, they were the means by which he acquired all his knowledge, and by which he was gradually qualifying himself for the duties of his profession."[72] Less wryly, but no less aware of equivalent cultural differences, Thoreau remarked in the late 1850s, "One revelation has been made to the Indian, another to the white man. I have much to learn of the Indian, nothing of the missionary. I am not sure but all that would tempt me to teach the Indian my religion would be his promise to teach me *his*."[73]

This recognition paralleled, perhaps even contributed to, an increasing circumspection about the national policy of "civilizing" the Indian. "The Choctaws and Chickasaws will not long retain such a knowledge of *astronomy* and *surveying*," charged the scientist Edwin James in 1830, "as would be useful to guide their wanderings, or make out their possessions in those scorched and sterile wastes to which it is our fixed intention to drive them. The giving to a few individuals of a tribe an education which, as far as it has any influence, tends directly to unfit them for the course of life they are destined to lead, with whatever intention it may be undertaken, is certainly far from being an act of kindness."[74]

A quarter century later, James Swan expressed similar sympathy for the Chinooks, who were resisting white cultural patterns. A half century after Swan, the Pasadena Eight grew to cherish a profound respect for the Hopi and Navaho. "Only to be among these Indians," Frederick Monsen once declared of the Hopi, "to hear them talk, and to observe their treatment of one another and of the casual stranger that is within their gates, is to have forced upon one the realization that here is the unspoiled remnant of a great race, a race of men who have, from time immemorial, lived quiet, sane, whole-

[71] Alfred W. Crosby Jr., *The Columbian Exchange: Biological and Cultural Consequences of 1492*, Contributions in American Studies, no. 2 (Westport, Conn.: Greenwood Publishing Co., 1972); Virgil J. Vogel, *American Indian Medicine* (Norman: University of Oklahoma Press, 1970).

[72] Cooper, *The Pioneers*, p. 95.

[73] Thoreau, *The Maine Woods*, ed. Moldenhauer, p. 239.

[74] James, ed., *Captivity and Adventures of John Tanner*, p. xxviii, also p. xxxi.

some lives very close to Nature."[75] Appreciating the integrity of Hopi life and its religious strength, Monsen deplored its destruction by a "too-benevolent white race."[76] Sadly, he conceded that "the world is losing something of pure beauty because it knows no better than to thrust aside these things. . . . Some day when it is too late, we may realize what we have lost by 'educating' the Indian, and forcing him to accept our more complex but far inferior standards of life, work and art."[77]

Now perhaps we are in a better position to recognize a strain that has been present intermittently, incompletely throughout these chapters. Crèvecoeur half entertained it; in Melville it is mockingly explicit. From Washington Irving and George Catlin near the beginning of the century, to translator William Philo Clark and painter Charles M. Russell near the end, commentators on the effects of white attempts to civilize Indian tribes took an increasingly critical view of the value system offered in place of native modes, and they later scrutinized it ever more carefully from the native perspective itself.[78] Far from assisting natives, material progress seemed actually to unfit both Polynesians and Indians for life either in their own communities or in the white one. As one amateur ethnologist observed in 1909, "true philanthropy is to make way for them the path of development along the lines which they themselves have started and wonderfully continued till Washington discovered them."[79]

From this critical outlook, it was only a slight step to the suggestion that the intrinsic value of native cultures might even excel that of Western civilization. So radical a notion, naturally, persuaded few but the most disaffected or the most perceptive. Still, the very fact that it was considered at all reflects the extent of appreciation for native

[75] Frederick I. Monsen, "Picturing Indians with the Camera," *Photo-Era,* 25 (October 1910), 170.

[76] Frederick Monsen, "The Destruction of Our Indians: What Civilization Is Doing to Extinguish an Ancient and Highly Intelligent Race by Taking Away Its Arts, Industries, and Religion," *Craftsman,* 11 (March 1907), 688.

[77] Ibid., p. 691.

[78] Irving, *Western Journals,* ed. McDermott, pp. 103-4; Catlin, *Letters and Notes,* 1:245, 272; Catlin, *Life Among the Indians,* p. 19; Clark, *Indian Sign Language,* pp. 18-20; Harold McCracken, *The Charles M. Russell Book: The Life and Work of the Cowboy Artist* (Garden City, N.Y.: Doubleday and Co., 1957), pp. 130-31. See also Parker, "Prescott's Conquest," p. 263; Mrs. Anna Brownell Jameson, *Winter Studies and Summer Rambles in Canada,* 2 vols. (New York: Wiley and Putnam, 1839), 2:335, also 2:231-33.

[79] Charles Francis Saunders, Pocket Diary for 1909 Tour of the Pueblos, Box 9, November 26. With less restraint, he had earlier quipped, "Let 'em go to hell their own way—I think anyhow they have as good a chance of keeping out of hell as I have" (ibid., entry for August 1).

societies.[80] Fur traders of the 1830s, for example, recognized some truth in native assertions that their community life put that of whites to shame.[81] More tellingly, assorted individuals began in the 1820s to trouble over the alarming rate of recidivism among redeemed white captives.[82] Whether more former captives returned to their captors than remained in civilized society is an issue still debated. Of greater importance is the question "why individuals of both races who experienced both civilizations so frequently preferred the Indian life style. It would appear that Indian family life offered much to the fulfillment of the individual that was lacking in the more advanced civilization."[83] Another historian has hypothesized that these "white Indians" discovered "a kind of unity of thought and action and a kind of social cohesion which deeply appealed to them, and which they did not find with the whites, especially not with the pioneers."[84] Some of those who chose to remain with their "own kind" expressed just such comparative judgments, casting serious doubts on the premises of Western society even as they praised the possibilities defined in native ones.

In this light, we can understand nineteenth-century scientists' energetic theorizing about these questions. Britain's John Lubbock and Edward Tylor and America's Lewis Henry Morgan, for instance, independently grappled with issues that others had been content merely to brush up against, and they defined thereby fuller possibilities for the science of anthropology. Matthew Arnold's celebrated *Culture and*

[80] See Father Gabriel Sagard, *The Long Journey to the Country of the Hurons* (1639), trans. H. H. Langton, ed. George M. Wrong (Toronto: Champlain Society, 1939), pp. 58, 138, 213; Mrs. John H. Kinzie, *Wau-Bun, The "Early Day" in the North-West* (New York: Derby and Jackson, 1856), pp. vii, 340-42, 363; Charles Alexander Eastman, *From the Deep Woods to Civilization: Chapters in the Autobiography of an Indian* (1916; rpt. Boston: Little, Brown, and Co., 1917), pp. 143, 194; Robert F. Berkhofer Jr., *Salvation and the Savage: An Analysis of Protestant Missions and American Indian Response, 1787-1862* (Louisville: University of Kentucky, 1965), pp. 107-11.

[81] Lewis O. Saum, *The Fur Trader and the Indian* (Seattle: University of Washington Press, 1965), pp. 244-45, also pp. 110, 113, 197, 223.

[82] See, among others, *Letters and Other Writings of James Madison*, 4 vols. (Philadelphia: J. B. Lippincott and Co., 1865), 3:64-65; Halkett, *Historical Notes Respecting the Indians*, p. 316; John F. Meginess, *Biography of Frances Slocum, the Lost Sister of Wyoming* (1891; rpt. New York: Arno Press, 1974), pp. 68ff.; Kinzie, *Wau-Bun*, p. 287; Drinnon, *White Savage*, pp. 11-12, 37.

[83] Heard, *White into Red*, p. 13. See also Slotkin, *Regeneration through Violence*, pp. 100-101, 265.

[84] Erwin H. Ackerknecht, " 'White Indians': Psychological and Physiological Peculiarities of White Children Abducted and Reared by North American Indians," *Bulletin of the History of Medicine*, 15 (January 1944), 34, also pp. 19-21, 28-31. See also John R. Swanton, "Notes on the Mental Assimilation of Races," *Journal of the Washington Academy of Sciences*, 16 (November 1926), 493-502.

Anarchy (1869) educated his age to a humanist meaning of culture that was quickly adopted by anthropologists. Yet Arnold "could never have called a work *Primitive Culture*," as George Stocking has shrewdly noted about Tylor's masterwork, which appeared two years later; "the very idea would have been to him a contradiction in terms. To argue that culture actually existed among all men, in however 'crude' or 'primitive' a form, may be viewed as a major step toward the anthropological concept."[85] Despite the breakthrough they pioneered in notions of primitive culture, neither Tylor nor Morgan could move beyond the dominant paradigm of their time—an ethnocentric cultural evolutionism.[86]

The truly radical assessments of the concept of culture occurred among those working in the field. Firsthand experience led the more tolerant to challenge the finely phrased assumptions of even so brilliant a theorist as Tylor, sometimes only implicitly, sometimes in a rather rough-and-ready fashion. More than any other single person, Franz Boas (1858-1942) made this challenge explicit, far-ranging, and convincing. His experiences among native American tribes in the 1880s led him to theoretical interpretations of a kind that Melville could only guess at. His long subsequent career forced him back repeatedly to field work for confirmation of these extraordinary speculations. Moreover, his life's work defines a decisive curve in the idea of culture as it has come to be accepted. Like Frank Hamilton Cushing, the other figure representative of this chapter, Boas was shocked into respect for the intense cultural life of supposedly "primitive" societies. Unlike Cushing, he transformed that realization into a brilliant set of ideas and went on to train some of the finest anthropologists America has produced.[87]

Again in contrast to Cushing, young Boas had not started out with any particular interest in anthropology. German-born and raised, having studied physics and geography for a doctorate, he had every intention of spending his life in the German academic world of "hard

---

[85] Stocking, *Race, Culture, and Evolution*, p. 87. See also Idus L. Murphree, "The Evolutionary Anthropologists: The Progress of Mankind. The Concepts of Progress and Culture in the Thought of John Lubbuck, Edward B. Tylor, and Lewis H. Morgan," *Proceeding of the American Philosophical Society*, 105 (June 1961), 265-300.

[86] See Stocking, *Race, Culture, and Evolution*, pp. 81-82; Bidney, "Concept of Value," pp. 687ff.; Saum, *Fur Trader and the Indian*, pp. 198-223.

[87] For background, see: Stocking, *Race, Culture, and Evolution*, pp. 148, 156-59, 200-209, 228-30; Berkhofer, *White Man's Indian*, pp. 62-65; Keen, *Aztec Image*, pp. 404-5; Hoover, *The Red and the Black*, pp. 211-17; Willey and Sabloff, *History of American Archaeology*, pp. 86-87, 89, 91; Margaret Mead and Ruth L. Bunzel, eds., *The Golden Age of American Anthropology* (New York: Braziller, 1960), pp. 306, 400, 461, 577ff.

science." Like Melville, Schoolcraft, Catlin, and Morgan, however, he discovered in his early twenties the absolute irrelevance of the first career on which he had set his life. On a scientific expedition to Baffin Island in the mid-1880s, he lived for some weeks with local Eskimos. Intrigued by their culture, he turned to the larger idea of culture itself. Boas never turned back, and, more remarkably, over the decades in which he then gave himself to that idea, his thought shows astonishing consistency. There is little of the changing, progressive sweep of ideas building out of or contradicting early discoveries that so often characterizes great innovative thinkers. His finest, most incisive ideas were there at the beginning, only waiting to be fully developed. In that first winter of 1883-1884, for instance, Boas complimented his Eskimo hosts with certain seminal observations in his notebook:

> I often ask myself what advantages our "good society" possesses over that of the "savages." The more I see of their customs, the more I realize that we have no right to look down on them. Where amongst our people would you find such true hospitality? . . . We have no right to blame them for their forms and superstitions which may seem ridiculous to us. We "highly educated people" are much worse, relatively speaking. . . . As a thinking person, for me the most important result of this trip lies in the strengthening of my point of view that the idea of a "cultured" individual is merely relative and that a person's worth should be judged by his *Herzenbildung*.[88]

This observation cut through the thick flesh of evolutionary bias to the bones of a radical theory that Boas would spend his entire career articulating. The special value of this observation for anthropology was that, unlike others who made similar comments, Boas had a rigorous scientific background, which forced him to more than mere tolerant conjecture.

By 1888, Boas had emigrated to America and become an accomplished anthropologist. However narrowly focused his essays on those Pacific Northwest tribes he considered his special province, his writings implicitly espouse the view of culture he first glimpsed on Baffin Island. "At least by implication," one noted historian has observed about an early essay, "On Alternating Sounds" (1888), "it sees cultural phenomena in terms of the imposition of conventional meaning on the flux of experience. It sees them as historically conditioned and transmitted by the learning process. It sees them as determinants of our very perceptions of the external world. And it sees them in

88 Cited in Stocking, *Race, Culture, and Evolution*, p. 148.

relative rather than in absolute terms. Much of Boas' later work, and that of his students after him, can be viewed simply as the working out of implications present in this article."[89] Instead of moving from conventional premises to specific interpretations, Boas worked inductively; he wanted not to define culture in the singular and abstract but rather to understand in their particularity a variety of autonomous tribal cultures.

The consistency of Boas's career may best be illustrated through his celebrated accomplishments in the special field of museum arrangements. In 1887 he wrote an astonishing series of letters to John Wesley Powell and Otis Mason, the Smithsonian Institution's curator of ethnology. Boas clarified his resistance to Mason's arrangement of specimens according to commonly accepted practice, that is, by alleged cultural stages operating regardless of time or place. Boas thought materials should be arranged by ethnological, not typological, connections—by tribe, not function. Rather than placing, say, all baskets together, he thought it far more important to show how baskets from a particular tribe fitted in with its other cultural artifacts. Only then could the tribe's integrity, to say nothing of its uniqueness, be appreciated. Boas was given a chance to put his theory into practice half a dozen years later, when he was appointed chief assistant in anthropology at Chicago's World Columbian Exposition of 1893. Supervising the ethnology arrangement that was later converted into the Field Museum of Natural History, he established a model that transformed museum collections the world over. Boas deeply believed in a concept of total culture, one that placed human activities within a specific cultural context and stressed as well the need for "study of the thoughts, emotional life, and ethical standards of the common people"[90] more than those of the select classes of priests and chiefs.

The prerequisite to such knowledge, manifestly, was study carried out according to strict scientific rules of observation and evidence. In such work lay Boas's true genius. Prolific as a scholar, indefatigable as a field researcher, innovative as a curator, he could have secured fame in any one of these fields alone. His most substantial contribution, however, was to attract and train an entire generation of talented scholars. With his appointment to Columbia University in the mid-1890s, he began to establish the world's finest graduate program in anthropology. As one of his students later wrote, "He brought to anthropology rigorous standards of proof, a critical skepticism toward all generalization, and the physicist's unwillingness to accept any gen-

[89] Ibid., p. 159.
[90] Franz Boas, "The Ethnological Significance of Esoteric Doctrines," in Boas, *Race, Language and Culture* (New York: Macmillan Co., 1940), p. 315.

eralization or explanation as anything more than a useful hypothesis until it has been clearly demonstrated that no other explanation is possible."[91] Boas demanded much from his students—like Morgan, sometimes dictating professional, even private, decisions—but he also inculcated by stern example the possibilities of his considered view of culture.

Boas's own work in the 1890s among the Pacific Northwest Coast tribes only confirmed his early dismissal of cultural absolutism. His contributions to linguistic anthropology, including the countless native texts he collected, demonstrated that "primitive" languages equaled, even surpassed Indo-European varieties in their formal complexity. His rejection of simple anthropological evolution opened the possibility of a diverse body of cultures, none to be shunted under specious eveluative rubrics. To turn away from the dominant comparative method, Boas asserted, was to turn away from belief in any fixed standard of judgment. The strength of anthropology was in its ability "to impress us with the relative value of all forms of culture," as he claimed in 1904, "and thus serve as a check to an exaggerated valuation of the standpoint of our own period, which we are only too liable to consider the ultimate goal of human evolution."[92] Precisely because other cultures differed so radically from one's own, the very notion of objective scientific valuation of them was invalidated. In Boas's simple assertion. "There is no absolute progress."[93] The western European prejudice for rationality, for instance, was no better than the modes of thought peculiar to other cultures, nor was it any less determined by cultural tradition.

> It is somewhat difficult for us to recognize that the value which we attribute to our own civilization is due to the fact that we participate in this civilization, and that it has been controlling all our actions since the time of our birth; but it is certainly conceivable that there may be other civilizations, based perhaps on different traditions and on a different equilibrium of emotion and reason which are of no less value than ours, although it may be impossible for us to appreciate their values without having grown up under their influence.[94]

[91] Ruth L. Bunzel, in Mead and Bunzel, eds., *Golden Age of Anthropology*, p. 403.
[92] Boas, "The History of Anthropology," in *The Shaping of American Anthropology, 1883-1911: A Franz Boas Reader*, ed. George W. Stocking Jr. (New York: Basic Books, 1974), p. 36.
[93] Boas, *The Mind of Primitive Man* (1911), rev. ed. (New York: Macmillan Co., 1930), p. 208.
[94] Ibid., p. 225. For a discussion of this passage, see Stocking, *Race, Culture, and Evolution*, pp. 103-4. See also Bidney, "Concept of Value," pp. 687-88.

Boas thrust through to an entirely new way of thinking about issues long discussed and consequences long conceded. Moreover, the orientation he provided remains standard in principle among anthropologists. Most Americans did not share his assessments of native tribes at the time; perhaps few more do so today. Yet others had come to a roughly similar point of view. That is to say, by the last third of the nineteenth century, a broad spectrum of Americans sympathized with Indian tribes in ways altogether different from earlier attitudes.[95]

It should be noted that modern anthropologists consider cultural relativism a suspect concept.[96] Acculturated beings ourselves, they argue, we cannot help rendering value judgments. Boas himself assumed certain tenets as absolutely good, including freedom, tolerance, rationality, and mutual respect. By theoretical definition, however, true cultural relativism would be completely neutral. The important point historically is not that true cultural relativism is inherently unattainable. Rather, it is how that belief affected people at the time —that so many white Americans, from the most humane of motives, dismissed ethnocentrism to embrace a larger view. They could hardly realize the psychological depths of the assumptions they made in their attempt to be open-minded toward aliens. But they had nevertheless taken the first steps toward such a realization.

Once again in the nineteenth century, a vanishing wilderness altered Americans' sense of themselves. In each of the preceding cases—landscape and wild game, white frontiersmen, native tribes seen first as merely exotic, then as intrinsically worthy of respect—Americans had

[95] See, for instance, Parker Gillmore, *A Hunter's Adventures in the Great West* (London: Hurst and Blackett, 1871), pp. 4-5; Beeson, *Plea for the Indians*; Helen Hunt Jackson, *Glimpses of California and the Missions* (1883; rpt. Boston: Little, Brown and Co., 1903), esp. pp. 32, 97, 101, 173; Jackson, *A Century of Dishonor: The Early Crusade for Indian Reform* (1881) ed. Andrew F. Rolle (New York: Harper and Row, 1965), pp. 9-11, 27, 64, 102, 118, 185; Henry Benjamin Whipple, *Lights and Shadows of a Long Episcopate: Being Reminiscences and Recollections of The Right Reverend Henry Benjamin Whipple, Bishop of Minnesota* (New York: Macmillan Co., 1899), esp. pp. 34ff. See, in a slightly different context, William Graham Sumner, *Folkways: A Study of the Sociological Importance of Usages, Manners, Customs, Mores, and Morals* (1906; rpt. New York: New American Library, 1940), esp. pp. 27-28, 30-31. See also Robert Winston Mardock, *The Reformers and the American Indian* (Columbia: University of Missouri Press, 1971); Willey and Sabloff, *History of American Archaeology*, pp. 86-87; George W. Stocking Jr., "Introduction: The Basic Assumptions of Boasian Anthropology," in Boas, *Shaping of American Anthropology*, ed. Stocking, pp. 18-20.

[96] Geertz, *Interpretation of Cultures*, pp. 37, 40, 43-44, 53; Stocking, *Race, Culture, and Evolution*, pp. 88, 231; Bidney, "Idea of the Savage," p. 326; Bidney, "Concept of Value," pp. 687-94; Fiedler, *Return of the Vanishing American*, p. 170; Mead and Bunzel, eds., *Golden Age of American Anthropology*, p. 403; Hoover, *The Red and the Black*, pp. 214, 297-98, 366.

felt the tremendous costs entailed by their conquest of the wilderness. Before the century's end, few counted the cost too high. But a significant number gradually, grudgingly wondered how their own allegedly more advanced civilization so often failed at what native tribes so eminently succeeded in doing. Melville's condemnation in *Typee* of the smug complacency of French missionaries and American sailors found many unconscious analogues during the rest of the century. The sole difference would be in the degree of their progressively more damning criticisms of American civilization.

CHAPTER NINE

WEIGHED, MEASURED, AND FOUND WANTING

"Ye see, Hinnissy, th' Indyun is bound f'r to give way to th' onward march iv white civilization. You 'an me, Hinnissy, is th' white civilization. . . . Th' on'y hope f'r th' Indyun is to put his house on rollers, an' keep a team hitched to it, an', whin he sees a white man, to start f'r th' settin' sun. . . . Th' onward march iv th' white civilization, with morgedges an' other modhern improvements, is slowly but surely, as Hogan says, chasin' him out. . . ."
—*Finley Peter Dunne*
"On the Indian War" (1898)

October 12, the Discovery. It was wonderful to find America, but it would have been more wonderful to miss it.
—*Mark Twain*
"Pudd'nhead Wilson's Calendar" (1894)

IN 1845 a popular southern author explained the reasons for "our blinding prejudices against the [Indian] race—prejudices which seem to have been fostered as necessary to justify the reckless and unsparing hand with which we have smitten them in their habitations, and expelled them from their country. We must prove them unreasoning beings, to sustain our pretensions as human ones—show them to have been irreclaimable, to maintain our own claims to the regards and respect of civilization."[1] Or, as Melville allowed Tommo to consider a year later, "they whom we denominate 'savages' are made to deserve the title." Sardonic puncturings of white complacency were hardly new to the nineteenth century. Directed not against their society itself but at its dramatic depredations and self-justifying logic, such reformist protests had a long history, if to little effect. Increasingly respectful admiration for native tribes, however, prompted many in the nineteenth century to a more profoundly disturbing outrage at the very terms of their culture itself. As Clifford Geertz reminds us, one's notion of the savage necessarily invokes one's self-conception. To see others as no longer savage negations is not necessarily to deny the contrast with one's own culture but to raise the prospect that that contrast might be reversed, that one's society might itself be fundamentally "savage." Cultural relativism, then, more than inspiring envious admiration of native tribes, encouraged a devastating indictment of American society from the very perspective offered by tribal life.

At its least telling, reflexive critiques of this sort merely challenged the effect of sacred and secular efforts to "redeem" native souls and to "advance" their societies. Such efforts had achieved little more than the corruption of both. Deploring the natives' wretched treatment, some travelers shrewdly noted that behind the policy of removing Indian tribes westward lay the paradoxical premise that contact with whites would only drive them to further depths of supposed savagery. Others, more outraged if less sophisticated, scathingly indicted a history of broken treaties, fraud, and corruption in the federal government's displacement of the Indian.[2] George Catlin, the most vocal

[1] William Gilmore Simms, *Views and Reviews in American Literature, History and Fiction, First Series* (1845), ed. C. Hugh Holman (Cambridge, Mass.: Harvard University Press, 1962), p. 142.

[2] See Count de Pourtalès, *On the Western Tour with Washington Irving: The Journal and Letters of Count de Pourtalès*, ed. George F. Spaulding (Norman: University of Oklahoma Press, 1968), p. 62; George Frederick Ruxton, *Life in the Far West* (1848), ed. LeRoy R. Hafen (Norman: University of Oklahoma Press, 1951), pp. 99-100; Bishop [Henry B.] *Whipple's Southern Diary, 1843-1844*, ed. Lester B. Shippee (Minneapolis: University of Minnesota Press, 1937), p. 63; Frederic Remington,

protestor before the Civil War, formulated the issue well but never more succinctly or more forcefully than did Lewis Henry Morgan in his conclusion to *League of the Iroquois*: "It cannot be forgotten, that in after years our Republic must render an account, to the civilized world, for the disposal which it makes of the Indian. It is not sufficient, before this tribunal, to plead inevitable destiny."[3]

By the mid-1860s, even someone who shared as fully in his society's prejudices as did the youthful Mark Twain could satirize missionary efforts among the Hawaiians: "The contrast is so strong—the wonderful benefit conferred upon this people by the missionaries is so prominent, so palpable, and so unquestionable, that the frankest compliment I can pay them, and the best, is simply to point to the condition of the Sandwich Islanders of Captain Cook's time, and their condition today. Their work speaks for itself."[4] Twain later exposes the deadly effectiveness of missionaries' work in alluding to the statistical condition of the Hawaiian race: "Doubtless this purifying is not far off, when we reflect that contact with civilization and the whites has reduced the native population from *four hundred thousand* (Captain Cook's estimate) to *fifty-five thousand* in something over eighty years!"[5]

Within the next third of a century, such cuts and thrusts at white civilization slashed through a large body of public expression, though the notion that manifest destiny merely meant genocide was never welcome. True, Americans had long satirized the deplorable treatment of Indian tribes; but in the past these excesses had seemed necessary evils, the predictable exceptions to a humane rule. More and more widely through the nineteenth century, however, the rule of Western civilization itself seemed suspect, and respect for indigenous cultures spurred further doubts about continental platitudes. Even in the instances of less facile white assumptions, those invoking the scales

---

"Artist Wanderings Among the Cheyennes," *Century Magazine*, 38 (August 1889), 541; Capt. D. C. Poole, *Among the Sioux of Dakota: Eighteen Months' Experience as an Indian Agent* (New York: D. Van Nostrand, 1881), pp. 225-28; Benjamin Drake, *The Life and Adventures of Black Hawk* (1838), 7th ed. rev. (E. Morgan and Co., 1850), p. 5. For a calmer statement directed at this same issue, see Young Joseph, "An Indian's Views of Indian Affairs," *North American Review*, 128 (1879), esp. 432-33.

[3] Morgan, *League of the Ho-De-No Sau-Nee or Iroquois* (1851), rpt. 2 vols. in 1 (New Haven: Human Relations Area Files, 1954), 2:123.

[4] *Mark Twain's Letters from Hawaii*, ed. A. Grove Day (New York: Appleton-Century, 1966), pp. 54-55; see also pp. 52-53, 129-30.

[5] Samuel Clemens [Mark Twain], *Roughing It*, ed. Franklin R. Togers (Berkeley: University of California Press, 1972), pp. 423-24; see also pp. 411-13, 423ff. For background, see Justin Kaplan, *Mr. Clemens and Mark Twain: A Biography* (New York: Simon and Schuster, 1966), p. 30; Walter Francis Frear, *Mark Twain and Hawaii* (Chicago: Lakeside Press, 1947), pp. 33-34, 128-32, 490-500.

of cultural contrast weighed, measured, and found them also wanting.[6] When Theodore Parker and Alexander Bradford suggested as early as the 1840s that Cortez's destruction of the Aztec empire was the act of a barbarian, they sounded a note that would echo down the century. Montezuma's civilization, however militaristic, turned on less inherently destructive modes than those the Spanish conquistadors introduced; in other ways, it seemed superior. As Parker and Bradford sharply observed, contemporary America's self-complacent faith in its institutions was similarly unwarranted, similarly deplorable.[7]

Albert Gallatin opposed President Polk's expansionist administration during the 1840s by likewise arguing vigorously, in his editor's words, against the "white-man's burden argument that justified annexation as conferring the benefits of higher civilization upon the backward Mexicans."[8] A decade later, Mary Eastman would conclude her elegiac lament for the vanishing Sioux with the weighted profession: "We should be better reconciled to this manifest destiny of the aborigines, if the inroads of civilization were worthy of it."[9] In each of these and other cases, doubts about the tenets and practices of western European culture had evolved out of admiration for those of native American ones. By the end of the century, Boas could even reverse the intellectual sequence, warning in dire terms against cultural absolutism precisely because it fed a nationalistic arrogance.[10]

Of course, other domestic and foreign issues aroused Americans, certainly by the time Boas spoke. Resistance to militant missionizing

[6] See Mrs. Anna Brownell Jameson, *Winter Studies and Summer Rambles in Canada*, 2 vols. (New York: Wiley and Putnam, 1839), 2:231-33; James F. Rusling, *Across America: Or, The Great West and the Pacific Coast* (New York: Sheldon and Co., 1874), p. 138.

[7] Theodore Parker, "Prescott's Conquest of Mexico" (1849), reprinted in Parker, *The American Scholar*, ed. George Willis Cooke (Boston: American Unitarian Association, 1907), pp. 246-51, 261-67; Alexander W. Bradford, *American Antiquities and Researches into the Origin and History of the Red Race* (New York: Dayton and Saxton, 1841), pp. 72, 82-83, 160-61.

[8] *Selected Writings of Albert Gallatin*, ed. E. James Ferguson (New York: Bobbs-Merrill, 1967), p. 456; see also p. v.

[9] Mrs. Mary H. Eastman, *Dahcotah; or, Life and Legends of the Sioux Around Fort Snelling* (1849; rpt. Minneapolis: Ross and Haines, 1962), p. xvi. For similar statements, see Francis Parkman, "Preface to the Illustrated Edition" (September 16, 1892), and "Preface to the Fourth Edition" (March 30, 1872), both in *The Oregon Trail: Sketches of Prairie and Rocky-Mountain Life*, ed. E. N. Feltskog (Madison: University of Wisconsin Press, 1969), pp. vii, ix, xi-xii; Ben Merchant Vorpahl, ed., *My Dear Wister: The Frederic Remington–Owen Wister Letters*, ed. Ben Merchant Vorpahl (Palo Alto, Calif.: American West Co., 1972), pp. 95-96; and Daniel G. Brinton, *Races and Peoples: Lectures on the Science of Ethnography* (Philadelphia: David McKay, 1901), pp. 289-300.

[10] See David Bidney, "The Concept of Value in Modern Anthropology," in A. L. Kroeber, ed., *Anthropology Today: An Encyclopedic Inventory* (Chicago: University of Chicago Press, 1953), pp. 687-88.

had swollen into a flood tide of public opinion, and alienation from contemporary society expressed itself most outspokenly against America's ruthless imperialism in the Philippines, in China, in Central America, and, not least, in the American West, where the frontier was closing. A collective sense of powerlessness, of victimization by forces that might otherwise have been converted to beneficent ends, led to a reexamination of American society's basic tenets. Although the larger terms of this revaluation do not figure here, they offer a context of revulsion from arrogant Western assumptions that was shared most readily by individuals willing to adopt a native perspective.[11]

COMPELLED by an uneasiness, then a disillusionment with white American institutions, Cooper explored the terms of this perspective more profoundly than any other author besides Melville in the first half of the nineteenth century. He certainly failed in his Leatherstocking tales to do justice to native societies or psychology. Dissatisfied with what he saw America becoming, however, he adopted the native point of view in later novels of the series as a means of censuring white society. Both Dew of June, the kindly Tuscarora in *The Pathfinder*, and Rivenoak, the wise Huron in *The Deerslayer*, deliver scathing, irrefutable indictments of whites. In response to the Huron chief's criticisms, simple-minded Hetty Hutter pleads to her friend Wah-ta!-Wah, "there can't be two sides to truth." Wah-ta!-Wah ruefully responds, "Well, to poor Injin girl it seem everything *can* be to palefaces. . . . One time 'ey say white, and one time 'ey say black. Why *never can be*?"[12] Melville's description of Shakespeare here applies to Cooper: in the mouths of his characters he puts terrific truths that would be madness to utter in his own person.

[11] For nineteenth-century assumptions about progress, see: Arthur Alphonse Ekirch Jr., *The Idea of Progress in America, 1815-1860*, Studies in History, Economics and Public Law, no. 511 (New York: Columbia University Press, 1944); David Levin, *History as Romantic Art: Bancroft, Prescott, Motley, and Parkman* (Stanford: Stanford University Press, 1959), pp. 27ff.; Fred Somkin, *Unquiet Eagle: Memory and Desire in the Idea of American Freedom, 1815-1860* (Ithaca: Cornell University Press, 1967); David W. Noble, *The Paradox of Progressive Thought* (Minneapolis: University of Minnesota Press, 1958); Henry F. May, *The End of American Innocence: A Study of the First Years of Our Own Time, 1912-1917* (New York: Alfred A. Knopf, 1959).

[12] Cooper, *The Deerslayer; or, The First War-Path* (New York: W. A. Townsend and Co., 1859), p. 208. (All further references to Cooper's works will be to this collected edition, known as the Author's Revised Edition, illustrated by F.O.C. Darley and printed between 1859 and 1861. See also Donald A. Ringe, *James Fenimore Cooper* (New York: Twayne Publishers, 1962), pp. 8off.; Howard Mumford Jones, "Prose and Pictures: James Fenimore Cooper" (1951), reprinted in Jones, *History and the Contemporary: Essays in Nineteenth-Century Literature* (Madison: University of Wisconsin Press, 1964), p. 76; Marius Bewley, *The Eccentric Design: Form in the Classic American Novel* (New York: Columbia University Press, 1957), p. 96.

Once sensitized to this strain, one can recognize it even in the speech of an otherwise unlikely character, Magua, from *The Last of the Mohicans*. Though, as Magua notes, all peoples are created by a godly spirit, the races display profound differences:

> "Some He made with faces paler than the ermine of the forests: and these He ordered to be traders; dogs to their women, and wolves to their slaves. He gave this people . . . appetites to devour the earth. He gave them tongues like the false call of the wild-cat; hearts like rabbits; the cunning of the hog (but none of the fox). . . . With his tongue [the white man] sops the ears of the Indians . . . and his arms inclose the land from the shores of the salt-water to the islands of the great lake. His gluttony makes him sick. God gave him enough, and yet he wants all. Such are the pale-faces!"[13]

Self-serving as it is, Magua's speech nevertheless seems corroborated by his following eulogy to his race, voiced with what one reader has characterized as "all the accents of poetic truth that Cooper can muster."[14] Ratifying this judgment is the acknowledgment offered by Tamenund, the far less vindictive Mohican chief, sometimes called a "spokesman for the novelist."[15] Indeed, the novel supports these assessments. Nearly all the respectable white characters are incompetent or tedious, while Uncas emerges as the series' hero. If his death augurs that of native experience itself, the entire novel confirms a bleaker vision that juxtaposes the loss of wilderness against the dubious gain of white civilization.

Although Cooper elsewhere vouched support for America's westward mission, his novels as a whole register a telling skepticism about its fulfillment.[16] The contradiction in his conception—social good deriving from careless greed and irresponsible anarchy—repeatedly converts a mythic rendition of pioneering into a dark prognosis for America. The Leatherstocking tales in particular express something

13 Cooper, *Last of the Mohicans*, pp. 380-81.

14 Joel Porte, *The Romance in America: Studies in Cooper, Poe, Hawthorne, Melville, and James* (Middletown, Conn.: Wesleyan University Press, 1967), p. 19.

15 Edwin Fussell, *Frontier: American Literature and the American West* (Princeton: Princeton University Press, 1965), p. 43.

16 See Henry Nash Smith, introduction to Cooper, *The Prairie: A Tale* (New York: Holt, Rinehart and Winston, 1950), pp. ix, xvi; Porte, *Romance in America*, p. 52; Jones, "Prose and Pictures," p. 74; Robert H. Zoellner, "Conceptual Ambivalence in Cooper's Leatherstocking," *American Literature*, 31 (January 1960), 397-420; Donald Ringe, "Man and Nature in Cooper's *The Prairie*," *Nineteenth-Century Fiction*, 15 (March 1961), 313-23; Charles A. Brady, "James Fenimore Cooper, 1789-1851: Mythmaker and Christian Romancer," in Harold C. Gardiner, S.J., ed., *American Classics Reconsidered: A Christian Appraisal* (New York: Charles Scribner's Sons, 1958), p. 61.

more than dramatic regret that the wilderness is fated to pass, since the drama they unfold converts that regret into tragic loss. The imagined future rarely glimmers more desirably than the lost past.[17]

Readers no more grasped this strain in the popular series than did Cooper, certainly not before mid-century. Moreover, the issues raised by a nation pulling apart tended to close off debate on such topics until after the Civil War, when despoliation of the wilderness and of wild game, abandonment of frontier patterns, and subduing of native tribes all revived at a madcap pace. "The last gun fired at Appomattox," Stewart Udall has felicitously observed, "was, in effect, the starter's gun in an intensified race for resources."[18] The nation could turn renewed energies and a sophisticated technology on the West, which is merely to say that "the peace at Appomattox meant war for the Indian."[19]

At the same time, broad-based resistance to the government's treatment of Indians rapidly began to develop. Indeed, the very men sent to impose a sentence of death often sympathized with their enemy's tragic circumstances. Even General Philip Sheridan, the renowned Indian fighter who coined the popular "good Indian, dead Indian" tag, confessed, "We took away their country and their means of support, broke up their mode of living, their habits of life, introduced disease and decay among them and it was for this and against this they made war. Could anyone expect less?"[20] The upshot of this question for those who asked was disillusionment with one's government and, finally, one's culture. "In the West," according to one army historian, "the Indian often seemed more than a worthy opponent: he cast doubt on the value of war for civilization itself. Empathizing with the red man while fighting him was an unsettling experience. . . ."[21]

[17] John Lynen, in *The Design of the Present: Essays on Time and Form in American Literature* (New Haven: Yale University Press, 1969), p. 174, has stated similarly: "In essence the action of *The Pioneers* is the process of discovering the basis of community. Cooper's regret for the passing of the wilderness is more than sentimental nostalgia; it arises from the agonizing doubt whether civilization is worth the terrible price men pay for it." See also ibid., pp. 168-200; Richard Slotkin, *Regeneration through Violence: The Mythology of the American Frontier, 1600-1860* (Middletown, Conn.: Wesleyan University Press, 1973), pp. 509-15.

[18] Stewart L. Udall, *The Quiet Crisis* (New York: Avon, 1963), p. 96.

[19] Thomas C. Leonard, *Above the Battle: War-Making in America from Appomattox to Versailles* (New York: Oxford University Press, 1978), p. 43.

[20] Cited in ibid., p. 46.

[21] Ibid. See as well Perkins, *Three Years in California: William Perkins' Journal of Life at Sonoma, 1849-1852*, ed. Dale L. Morgan and James R. Scobie (Berkeley: University of California Press, 1964), pp. 123-25; Lewis Henry Morgan, "Letter to the Editor: The Hue-&-Cry Against the Indians," *Nation*, July 20, 1876, pp. 40-41; *General George Crook: His Autobiography*, 2d ed., ed. Martin F. Schmitt (Norman: University of Oklahoma Press, 1960), pp. 15-16, 228-29, 269-71; Nelson Miles, *Personal*

Among the minority who were so unsettled, of course, none resigned his commission or otherwise resisted. Nor did those appalled by the Indian solution abandon their conviction that the price of civilization was not too high. But soldiers during the post-Civil War period, with some major exceptions, viewed themselves less and less as conquerors, more and more in the frustrating role of policemen of treaties broken by the federal government.[22] Inadequate as their divided feelings were to the devastation wrought, such disquietude was expressed with increasing, and increasingly public, stridency.

Apart from questions of the reasonableness of Indian policy, corruption permeated the Indian service in the late 1860s to a degree that outraged Americans more directly at their society's excesses. As early as 1857, one self-styled reformer attributed the Indians' squalid condition entirely to the effects of a decadent white civilization. Slavery and an impending civil war, he intimated, exposed the moral inadequacy of a society no better than the ones it was wantonly destroying.[23] Others, sharing in this self-revulsion, worked to reform the Indian service. Perhaps surprisingly, these reformers drew their greatest strength not from eastern sentimentalists but from western settlers who saw at first hand the frequently fraudulent, otherwise indifferent federal management of native affairs. Their efforts culminated in the Dawes Act of 1887, which broke up the reservations and assimilated individual Indians into white society. However dubious the achievement, especially in its devastating social effects upon the natives, the act institutionalized racial egalitarianism for the first time as federal policy.[24]

Recollections and Observations of General Nelson A. Miles . . . (New York: Werner Co., 1897), p. 88; Miles, *Serving the Republic: Memoirs of the Civil and Military Life of Nelson A. Miles . . .* (New York: Harper and Brothers, 1911), pp. 113-15, 116-17; Mrs. Margaret I. Carrington, *Absaraka, Home of the Crows* (1868), ed. Milo Milton Quaife (Chicago: R. R. Donnelley and Sons, 1950), p. 211; Edward S. Ellis, *The Indian Wars of the United States* (New York: Cassell Publishing Co., 1892), introduction (unpaginated).

22 Leonard, *Above the Battle*, pp. 43-44. See as well, John C. Ewers, "When Red and White Men Meet," *Western Historical Quarterly*, 2 (April 1971), 141-45; Robert M. Utley, *Frontiersmen in Blue: The United States Army and the Indian, 1848-1865* (New York: Macmillan Co., 1967), pp. 110, 341, 346.

23 John Beeson, *A Plea for the Indians; With Facts and Features of the Late War in Oregon* (New York: J. Beeson, 1857), p. 131.

24 Henry E. Fritz, *The Movement for Indian Assimilation, 1860-1890* (Philadelphia: University of Pennsylvania Press, 1963), p. 34. See also Francis Paul Prucha, S.J., ed. *Americanizing the American Indians: Writings by the "Friends of the Indian," 1880-1900* (Cambridge, Mass.: Harvard University Press, 1973), and Prucha, "Indian Policy Reform and American Protestantism, 1880-1900," in Ray Allen Billington, ed., *People of the Plains and Mountains*, Contributions in American History, no. 25 (Westport, Conn.: Greenwood Press, 1973), pp. 120-45.

The person most successful in arousing public opinion, Helen Hunt Jackson, published *A Century of Dishonor* (1881) precisely to document the history of governmental injustice. Offering a particularly bitter indictment of treaties broken with the Delaware tribe, she concluded "Such uprooting, such perplexity, such loss, such confusion and uncertainty, inflicted once on any community of white people anywhere in our land, would be considered quite enough to destroy its energies and blight its prospects for years."[25] Her more damning statement appeared three years later. *Ramona* (1884), intended to accomplish for Indians what *Uncle Tom's Cabin* (1852) had for blacks, enjoyed resounding success and in fact garnered considerable support for reform. Unfortunately, the book encouraged the kind of improved treatment that American bureaucracy has historically provided in crises—too little and too late.[26] Despite the novel's sentimentality, Mrs. Jackson developed a telling critique of American values from what she assumed was an indigenous point of view. Against the fragile love of the Indian Alessandro and the half-Indian Ramona, the novelist depicts the rapine of land-hungry settlers. Alessandro's father is brutally murdered and his southern Californian village destroyed; nowhere can he and Ramona escape the white hordes. Finally driven insane, Alessandro is killed by a representative of the society whose winning of the land only confirms its inhumanity.

By the end of the century, the tide of factors eroding American idealism and simple-minded faith in progress—the dehumanization of industrial labor, for one notable example, and the gross inequalities between poverty and ostentatious wealth for another—had risen dangerously. Among these, the recognition of superior values in cultures not obsessed with progress and self-serving Darwinian analogies may seem less significant, but it unquestionably forms a basis for sterner judgments and bleaker disillusions.

Moreover, the ever present complement of this revulsion against traditional attitudes toward the Indian—criticism of land policy and mindless exploitation—was gaining urgency. Long before the Civil War, Thoreau, Catlin, and Cole had deplored mere utilitarian valuation of the land, as Chapter Two illustrated. Adopting a far more analytical approach in *Our Land and Land Policy* (1871), Henry George attacked his countrymen's assumptions by illustrating their

25 Jackson, *A Century of Dishonor: The Early Crusade for Indian Reform* (1881), ed. Andrew F. Rolle (New York: Harper and Row, 1965), p. 64. For similar observations see her *Glimpses of California and the Missions* (1883; rpt. Boston: Little, Brown and Co., 1903).

26 Wallace Stegner, "Western Record and Romance," in Robert E. Spiller et al., eds. *Literary History of the United States: History*, 3d ed. rev. (New York: Macmillan Co., 1963), p. 869.

mismanagement of the wilderness. "Evidently," he stated, referring to the federal government's own General Land Office figures, "if we get rid of our remaining public land at the rate which we have been . . . it will be all gone some time before the year 1890."[27] Dismayed at the bureaucratic resistance his popular ideas met, George turned more radical, finally questioning material progress itself. Civilization's advance across the continent, as he came to understand it, actually encouraged greater economic dislocation. Speaking on "The Crime of Poverty" in 1885, he asked, "What is the most astonishing thing in our civilization? Why, the most astonishing thing to those Sioux chiefs who were recently brought from the Far West and taken through our manufacturing cities in the East, was not the marvelous inventions that enabled machinery to act almost as if it had intellect . . . but the fact that amid this marvelous development of productive power, they found little children at work."[28] Despite the "marvelous inventions" industry had fostered, conditions in America were too quickly replicating European ones. According to George, "the general condition of the working classes is becoming worse instead of better."[29] Formulating a difficult but necessary question, he continued, "A very Sodom's apple seems this 'progress' of ours to the classes that have the most need to progress. We have been 'developing the country' fast enough. We have been building railroads, and peopling the wilderness, and extending our cities. But what is the gain? . . . are the masses of the people any better off?"[30]

Admirers of native cultures had come to see that white depredations were less exceptions to than expressions of their culture's basic tenets. So too those who, like George, treasured the landscape—not more than they desired the good of society, but precisely for society's good —realized that the enemy was themselves. A connection would seem to follow. At every point—wilderness conservation on the one hand and tribal preservation on the other, appreciation for the land and respect for indigenous cultures, destruction of the environment and extinction of Indian tribes—the issues seem to fall into logical, even obvious associations.[31] As if only further to conjoin the two sets of

[27] George, *Our Land and Land Policy* (1871; rpt. New York: Doubleday Page and Co., 1904), pp. 9, 11. See also Edward T. Peters, "Evils of Our Public Land Policy," *Century Magazine*, 25 (February 1883), 599-601.

[28] George, *Moses/The Crime of Poverty* (New York: International Joseph Fels Commission, 1918), p. 39, also p. 34; George, *Progress and Poverty* (1879; rpt. New York: Robert Schalkenbach Foundation, 1954), pp. 7-8.

[29] George, *Our Land and Land Policy*, p. 119.

[30] Ibid.

[31] Wilbur R. Jacobs, in *Dispossessing the American Indian: Indians and Whites on the Colonial Frontier* (New York: Charles Scribner's Sons, 1972), pp. 19-20, 25, is one of the few recent scholars to have noted this interrelationship.

issues, most tribes shared a sacred respect for their regions' ecological balance and were revolted by the arrogant indifference to the natural environment that characterized successive waves of pioneers. It is a little surprising, then, that obvious thematic associations in fact do not correspond to actual historical patterns. Few whites who valued wilderness conservation were also committed to Indian rights. Still, both groups contributed to revaluating a fundamental cultural assumption, and under pressure from some of America's best minds, the postulate of inevitable human progress began to erode.

MARK TWAIN, the quintessential exponent of intricate technology and bonanza schemes for quick wealth, can hardly be expected to serve as a compelling example of these thematic strains. Perhaps for that reason, however, he illustrates a more common state of unrest in late nineteenth-century America, and in so doing, he nicely complements Cooper's uneasiness. *A Connecticut Yankee in King Arthur's Court* (1889), Twain's longest essay into cultural comparison, was meant to confute sentimental nostalgias by comparing a primitive with an industrial society, to the latter's advantage, of course. Yet in Twain's hands, the two cultures share more than salient features. The perspective of a backward society, defined by nineteenth-century standards, finally exposes the bankruptcy of those very standards. What begins as a contemptuous account of the squalor and filth of Arthurian life becomes a paean to a pastoral beauty that industrialism renders irrecoverable.

Hank Morgan, suddenly transported back hundreds of years to Arthurian Britain, sets about freeing a feudal society enslaved by monarchism, caste, ignorance, and superstition. Like Christian missionaries among native American tribes, he hopes to subvert the religious and social institutions of the rude Celts in order to convert them to his brand of industrial progress. Twain had intended along the way to excoriate the fashionable admiration for medieval life and English institutions, but, interestingly, he shifted ground in the process of writing. His opening depiction of the population as alternately "childlike" and "savage" is challenged by the later view that nobility, courage, and compassion are encouraged by feudal training. The novel switches disconcertingly between Hank's claims for progressive industrial democracy and Twain's incipient doubts about it. Nowhere else in his works does he voice such fervid hopes for the economic, political, and social progress of the American system, and yet nowhere else are his confusions as vivid. Developing the comic premise of a mechanical wizard in a backward land only exposed his deep reservations about material progress and dictated in the process a perversely uncomical novel. As he later recognized, rewriting it would require "a pen warmed-up in hell."[32]

Part of the problem is that Hank does not live up to his advance billing as the engineer of a social revolution that will truly improve Arthurian society. During his seven-year tenure as "The Boss," his technological know-how provides little more than telephones, bicycles, and explosives. More than half a century earlier, Cooper had also intended his Leatherstocking tales to demonstrate the superiority of European civilization over life on the American frontier. Just as he failed to create credible patricians illustrative of his socially progressive theory, Twain later could not endow his own allegedly superior conceptions with fictional authenticity.[33]

More distressing than the ends Hank achieves are his suspect means of instituting a capitalist, industrial American way of life. Introducing consumer goods through crass commercialism and vulgar advertising ploys only confirms his willingness to reduce everything to cost-accounting. He abruptly dismisses the Grail quest as unprofitable; instead, he orders stove-pipe hats for King Arthur's knights, better to equip them to peddle shoe polish, sewing machines, and barbed wire. The population's illiteracy hardly curbs Hank's distribution of a "Court Circular," a daily newspaper, and a prohibition journal. All these publications, of course, are meant either for comic deflation or as occasions of parody. More often than not, however, a wary reader sees the possibility of such instances cutting sharply the other way. Instead of conceiving sensitive solutions to social problems, Hank imposes useless products and services with Procrustean willfulness. He replaces jousting with "armored" baseball and converts a hermit's religious abasement into the power source for a shirt factory. Aspiring to recognition as the modern man *par excellence*—like Napoleon III in *Innocents Abroad*, "representative of the highest modern civilization, progress, and refinement"[34]—he achieves successes as trivial as Merlin's.

[32] Frederick Anderson, William M. Gibson, and Henry Nash Smith, eds., *Selected Mark Twain-Howells Letters, 1872-1910* (1960; rpt. New York: Atheneum, 1968), p. 287.

[33] See Roger B. Saloman, *Twain and the Image of History* (New Haven: Yale University Press, 1961), pp. 113, 118-19; James M. Cox, *Mark Twain: The Fate of Humor* (Princeton: Princeton University Press, 1966), pp. 216-17; Henry Nash Smith, *Mark Twain's Fable of Progress: Political and Economic Ideas in "A Connecticut Yankee"* (New Brunswick: Rutgers University Press, 1964), pp. 80-87.

[34] Samuel Clemens [Mark Twain], *The Innocents Abroad, or, The New Pilgrim's Progress* (1869; rpt. Hartford, Conn.: American Publishing Co., 1890), p. 126.

Where Hank himself fails to do so, those he attempts to civilize call his perspective into question. At first, he can join in their humor at his expense, appreciating that his actions reflect a social training as restrictive as theirs. "Inherited ideas are a curious thing, and interesting to observe and examine. I had mine, the king and his people had theirs. In both cases they flowed in ruts worn deep by time and habit, and the man who should have proposed to divert them by reason and argument would have had a long contract on his hands."[35] Hank acknowledges his dogmatism only infrequently thereafter; he even denies having been shaped by cultural patterns as constrictingly inhumane as the Arthurians'. Nonetheless, the novel displays a representative Hank with moral deficiencies more troubling than those apparent in the people he wants to raise. The novel's grim conclusion ironically exposes him as the true barbarian Arthurians first suspected. Long before the end, Twain points to the ambivalent nature of Hank's talents. The opening reference to his nineteenth-century employer, the Colt arms factory, for example, reminds us of technology's capacity for destruction as well as for material progress. And however little the novel substantiates genuine progress, it amply illustrates the machine's destructive efficiency. Early in his career as "The Boss," Hank revealingly speaks of his secret factories operating like "a serene volcano, standing innocent with its smokeless summit in the blue sky and giving no sign of the rising hell in its bowels."[36] The conclusion, perhaps the most grotesque in American literature, figures forth the appalling implications of this image in what is also the most elaborate manifestation of Hank's technology. He and his small band of boys electrocute, drown, and gun down twenty-five thousand men, only to succumb themselves to a miasma of rotting flesh. The whole gruesomely acknowledges the moral exhaustion of Hank's scientific philosophy and, by extension, of Twain's economic and political beliefs.[37]

This seemingly unintended repudiation of industrial technology was not informed by any genuine understanding of the possibilities offered by another culture. Twain's youthful excursion to the Sandwich Islands and encounters with native Hawaiians may have lent certain qualities to his basic conception in *A Connecticut Yankee*. But if so, he practiced a device differing in degree, not kind, from Enlightenment instancings of primitive peoples to measure their cul-

35 Clemens, *A Connecticut Yankee in King Arthur's Court* (New York: Charles L. Webster and Co., 1889), p. 98.

36 Ibid., p. 120.

37 See Henry Nash Smith, *Fable of Progress*, pp. 6-7, and Smith, *Mark Twain: The Development of a Writer* (1962; rpt. New York: Atheneum, 1967), p. 12.

ture's inadequacies. That degree, however, was considerable, and had as much to do with the passing of the nineteenth century as with the talents of any particular writer.

More to present purposes, Twain combined in his fictional assessment three strains we have already seen emerging in the nineteenth century. Starting with a basic revaluation of primitive culture, he soon evinced deeply ambivalent feelings about his own society. Indeed, his work goes on to reveal the fundamental incompatibility of pastoral simplicity, as expressed in Sandy, with the surging volcano of technological industry. Finally, he could do nothing more than expose the moral bankruptcy of his technology, its all-embracing destructiveness. Perhaps the very fact that Twain did not intend this sequence or even fully realize its implications suggests how compelling these strains were for him and his contemporaries. He had arrived at a fictional view that many individuals by the last third of the century perceived more directly and factually: that western European civilization, particularly its American variant, might have little to redeem it from a charge of fundamental inhumanity.

Just as Rebecca Harding Davis's story "Life in the Iron Mills" (1861) presaged the muckrakers' efforts of the early 1900s, so a feature article in the popular *Harper's New Monthly Magazine* of May 1870 discreetly raised the question, "What is a Barbarian? What is a Civilized Man?" It concluded with the uncertain query: "Is civilization a good or an evil?"[38] Doubtless, neither the writer nor his readers hesitated more than a comfortable few minutes over the question. As should be all too clear by now, however, this predictable response hardly concedes what one recent historian has claimed, that "altogether what infuriated the white man was the Indians' indifference to that which was so obvious: the superiority of the white man's civilization."[39]

Increasingly toward the century's turn, those familiar with native cultures found themselves forced to challenge their civilization. By 1896 the famous anthropologist of the Ghost-Dance religion, James Mooney, could adopt the native perspective to a similar end: "The wise men tell us that the world is growing happier—that we live longer than did our fathers, have more comfort and less of toil, fewer wars and discords, and higher hopes and aspirations. So say the wise men; but deep in our own hearts we know they are wrong. . . . We

[38] Benson J. Lossing, "Our Barbarian Brethren," *Harper's New Monthly Magazine*, 40 (May 1870), 793, 811.
[39] Howard H. Peckham, "Indian Relations in the United States," in John Francis McDermott, ed., *Research Opportunities in American Cultural History* (Lexington: University Press of Kentucky, 1961), p. 31.

found the glory that had lured us onward was only the sunset glow that fades into darkness while we look, and leaves us at the very goal to sink down, tired in body and sick at heart. . . . As with men, so it is with nations."[40] Manifestly, though speaking for Indians, Mooney was also expressing a judgment on white America. Boas remarked more directly and pointedly that "greater lack of cultural values than that found in the inner life of some strata of our modern population is hardly found anywhere."[41] By the time he said this, America could seem well into the later scenes of Thomas Cole's *Course of Empire*.

[40] James Mooney, *The Ghost-Dance Religion and the Sioux Outbreak of 1890* (1896), ed. Anthony F. C. Wallace (New York: Dover Publications, 1972), p. 1.

[41] Cited by William Brandon, *The Last Americans: The Indian in American Culture* (New York: McGraw-Hill, 1974), p. 3. See also Bidney, "Concept of Value," pp. 687-88.

CHAPTER TEN

EPILOGUE

Conservation is getting nowhere because it is incompatible with our Abrahamic concept of land. We abuse land because we regard it as a commodity belonging to us. When we see land as a community to which we belong, we may begin to use it with love and respect. There is no other way for land to survive the impact of mechanized man.

—Aldo Leopold
A Sand County Almanac (1949)

So-called primitive societies, of course, exist in history; their past is as old as ours, since it goes back to the origin of the species. . . . But they have specialized in ways different from those which we have chosen. Perhaps they have, in certain respects, remained closer to the very ancient conditions of life, but this does not preclude the possibility that in other respects they are farther from those conditions than we are.

—Claude Lévi-Strauss
Inaugural Lecture, Collège de France
(January 1960)

IT IS CUSTOMARY in literary and cultural history to see the catastrophe of World War I as closing a century of faith in rationality and progress. Perhaps so, but the state of mind associated with the young American men and women thereafter had more distant antecedents. From the vantage of 1900, glancing over figures dotting this book's landscape, we can see these latter-day doubts evolving long before 1918. Whether they were prompted by aesthetic, historical, or cultural considerations, or some mix of the three; whether they expressed their concerns through federal and institutional efforts or those characteristically private (not to say eccentric); whether they used their experiences to make knowledgeable, sometimes brilliant assessments or merely to reiterate conventional wisdom—Americans in the nineteenth century felt growing uncertainties about the possibilities foreclosed by a westering, progressive ideology. Of course, this uneasy ferment was hardly unique to America. The terrifying rapidity of industrial transformation going on throughout Western civilization also generated European equivalents—the preservation of country villages, the encouragement of nearly lost handicrafts, and so on.[1] But what invests American history with a peculiar, indeed a tragic intensity is the once compelling Edenic myth of hope, regeneration, and perfection. Nowhere else did there exist just that conjunction of magnificent wilderness, a once unparalleled plentitude of animal life, a wide variety of intrinsically self-contained alien cultures, and an energetic, pioneering intruder. Only in America, that is, were conditions quite so ready for the emergence of the strains outlined here at so many levels of awareness and intensity.

The point nonetheless bears repeating that far less than a majority ever felt the apprehensions, much less entertained the ideas, suggested above. Those who have leafed through western Americana collections can testify that every expression of concern for the physical continent, native tribes, or American society is discovered only after turning over countless volumes mindlessly effusing over the promise of westward expansion. Public opinion may have constrained some of these to write what they did not quite believe, but most remained deaf to the troubling observations of their contemporaries. Only a mildly intractable minority gave voice to the underlying uncertainties that the larger group perhaps felt but could not articulate because so at odds with the acceptable commonplaces of American life. Whether

[1] See, for example, John Ward, *Pyramids and Progress: Sketches From Egypt* (London: Eyre and Spottiswoode, 1900), p. xvii.

or not America actually experienced its most rapid transformation during the mid-nineteenth century, it is true that never before did Americans feel so intensely deracinated. "We have the St. Vitus' dance," declared Thoreau, appalled at his countrymen's frenetic westering.[2] But few thought to slow the dance that would alter the landscape seemingly overnight. Still fewer guessed to what it would lead.

By 1900, white Americans had effectively settled and "civilized" the continent. They had reduced native tribes to their weakest state, in part by reducing them to a number fewer than ever before or since.[3] The Eleventh United States Census of 1890 offered figures on which Frederick Jackson Turner three years later based his thesis of the closing of the frontier. That same document was also, ironically, "one of the most exhaustive sources of information on the American Indian ever published."[4] In other words, the census signaled both that wilderness no longer existed and that its human symbol was no longer an alien. A ward of the government, the Indian was at best a museum piece, at worst a scorned anachronism. The process that had shaped America even as it exterminated many of its indigenous populations was supposedly at an end, having confirmed what Americans both desired and feared.

The advent of the twentieth century, far from calming eight or so decades of apprehensions, meant instead their intensification. To develop an account of the further shifts in attitude during these last eight decades would require another book as long as this one. Indeed, the survey would be lengthier, since the conflicts have grown that much more complex, public and private endeavors that much more various. How shall we today reconcile these violently contradictory actions and consequences? On the one hand, there is the Alaska Native Claims Settlement Act of 1971, which deeded extraordinarily generous grants of land to native populations, set aside vast tracts for conservation, and otherwise protects against exploitation. For the first time, Congress refused to impose paternalistic terms of use on tribal recipients, abandoning solutions based on removal, reservations, and wardship. As well, it legislated respect for a fragile ecology, to be protected at all costs against the consequences of thoughtless developers and careless oil companies intent only on completing a pipe-

2 Thoreau, *Walden* (1854), ed. J. Lyndon Shanley (Princeton: Princeton University Press, 1971), p. 93.

3 Wilbur R. Jacobs, "The Indian and the Frontier in American History—A Need for Revision," *Western Historical Quarterly*, 4 (January 1973), 47.

4 Robert Taft, in *Artists and Illustrators of the Old West 1850-1900* (New York: Charles Scribner's Sons, 1953), p. 215, speaking of the *Report on Indians Taxed and Indians Not Taxed in the United States (Except Alaska) at the Eleventh Census: 1890* (1894).

line across the state.[5] On the other hand, consider the more recent legislation authorizing what is by the Department of the Interior's own evaluation the useless damming of the Little Tennessee River. It means the dispossession of a sturdy yeomanry, the inundation of a uniquely beautiful and fertile valley, and the ruthless disregard for the archaeological sites of the Cherokees' ancestral religious center— all, so far as can be determined, for the real benefit only of certain land developers and the political fortunes of a senator.[6] The debate continues, as present jobs vie with future generations, native rights and conservation contend with a powerfully exploitative ethos.

Yet there are signs—most of them hopeful, though still tentative— and perhaps it is worth the risk of superficiality to name at least some of them. To write a history of conservation for our time would be to start with Theodore Roosevelt's friendship with Gifford Pinchot, which led to the most sustained public movement ever on behalf of conservation.[7] Special-interest and private groups, in some cases modeled after California's Sierra Club, also helped to convince Americans of the need to husband natural resources.[8] Government officials such as Steve Mather and Horace M. Albright successfully encouraged fellow countrymen to "See America First" and at the same time aggrandized power to the National Park Service.[9] According to one scholar, "It is no exaggeration to say that by 1921 the conservation of natural resources had become a well-established government function.[10]

During this period, the setting aside of large tracts of unspoiled land became a mark of good citizenship for the well-to-do, especially following the example of John D. Rockefeller.[11] An innovative land-

5 See Robert D. Arnold, *Alaska Native Land Claims* (Anchorage: Alaska Native Foundation, 1976); Wilcomb E. Washburn, *Red Man's Land, White Man's Law: A Study of the Past and Present Status of the American Indian* (New York: Charles Scribner's Sons, 1971), pp. 124ff.; John McPhee, *Coming into the Country* (New York: Farrar, Straus and Giroux, 1977), pp. 18-21, 34-36, 152, 391-93.

6 See Peter Matthiessen, "How to Kill a Valley," *New York Review of Books*, February 7, 1980, pp. 31-36.

7 William H. Harbaugh, *The Life and Times of Theodore Roosevelt*, rev. ed. (New York: Oxford University Press, 1963), pp. 304ff.

8 Douglas H. Strong, "The Sierra Club—A History. Part I: Origins and Outings," *Sierra*, October 1977, pp. 10-14; Strong, "The Sierra Club—A History. Part II: Conservation," *Sierra*, November-December 1977, pp. 16-20.

9 Donald C. Swain, *Wilderness Defender: Horace M. Albright and Conservation* (Chicago: University of Chicago Press, 1970), esp. pp. 46ff.; Robert Shankland, *Steve Mather of the National Parks* (New York: Alfred A. Knopf, 1951), pp. 4, 12-13.

10 Donald C. Swain, *Federal Conservation Policy, 1921-1933*, University of California Publications in History, 76 (Los Angeles: University of California Press, 1963), p. 5.

11 Stewart L. Udall, *The Quiet Crisis* (New York: Avon, 1963), pp. 161-64.

scape architect, Clarence Stein, popularized Olmsted's ideas in conceiving entire greenbelt towns designed in accordance with, rather than as impositions on, the natural environment.[12] In a rather crude and anarchic fashion, modern suburban sprawl has seemed to adopt this principle. Perhaps we may feel less ambiguity about the continuing popularity of *A Sand County Almanac* (1949), in which retired forester Aldo Leopold formulated an ethos of respect for the land as a community in which man is only one participant. Leopold declared that man had no more, perhaps less, inherent right to alter that environment to his ends and that we need to evolve "an ethical relation to the land" based on "love, respect, and admiration.[13] To be sure, Leopold's vision borders on the sentimental. But the degree of serious consideration given to like-minded philosophies by the 1930s and 1940s suggests a radical change in Americans' regard for the continent.

Similarly, Americans revised their opinion of Indians in the first half of this century, though the process differed in two substantial ways: fewer whites shared in this revaluation, and Indians themselves considerably shaped those altered assumptions. The Dawes Severalty Act of 1887 finally completed the process of destruction where wars, diseases, and removal had not quite succeeded. Aside from indirectly effecting the loss of more than two-thirds of the remaining reservation lands, it struck a catastrophic psychological blow at Indians. By 1928, when the Secretary of the Interior was presented with the well-researched Lewis Merriam report, the documented record of the bankruptcy of government policy came as little surprise. At least one of the report's conclusions, however, pointed to a genuine rethinking of possibilities: "He who wants to remain an Indian and live according to his old culture should be aided in doing so."[14] This idea formed the basis of the next phase of federal policy, pressed into law by perhaps the most remarkable white man to serve the federal government in the cause of Indian affairs.

Nearly a decade before the Merriam report, John Collier felt completely diseffected with post-World War I America, "its externalism

---

[12] Ada Louise Huxtable, "Clarence Stein—The Champion of the Neighborhood," *New York Times*, January 16, 1977, pp. 23, 28.

[13] Leopold, *A Sand County Almanac* (1949; rpt. New York: Ballantine, 1970), p. 261. See also Roderick Nash, ed., *The American Environment: Readings in the History of Conservation* (Reading, Mass.: Addison-Wesley, 1968), pp. 105ff.

[14] Cited in Washburn, *Red Man's Land*, p. 77. See as well Harold E. Driver, *Indians of North America*, 2d ed. rev. (Chicago: University of Chicago Press, 1969), pp. 493-95. Note the reception during this period given Ruth Benedict's *Patterns of Culture* (Boston: Houghton Mifflin Co., 1934), the most popular anthropology text ever sold.

and receptive sensualism, its hostility to human diversity, its fanatical devotion to downgrading standardization, its exploitative myopia, and that world fascism and home fascism which the boundless, all-haunting insecurity and the consequent lust for personal advantage were bringing to fatal power."[15] Moving to the Southwest in 1920, he became fascinated with the kind of life still maintained by local tribes. The election of Franklin Delano Roosevelt in 1932 brought the unexpected appointment of Collier, long a caustic critic of America's Indian policies, as Commissioner of Indian Affairs. Immediately, he set about preparing legislation that would result in the Indian Reorganization Act of 1934. Instead of attempting to assimilate natives into a supposed American melting pot, the act encouraged communal ownership of lands, separate tribal constitutions, and the revival of native arts, crafts, and education. Though the bill was Collier's inspiration, he realized that its passage into law reflected a more general change in attitudes. The 1934 act did not redress the long history of wrongs perpetrated against native tribes. It did not even mark a final stage in progressively more enlightened attitudes among white Americans, for within twenty years Congress gutted the Indian New Deal. Yet those programs for the first time registered the American government's respectful acceptance of native tribes on their own terms.

By the time Franklin Roosevelt took office, in other words, selfless efforts on behalf of the land and of native peoples had at last won a measure of nationwide respect. Curiously, the two large issues still attracted different sets of proponents, but with one notable exception: Harold L. Ickes, Roosevelt's Secretary of the Interior. A charter member of the American Indian Defense Association, Ickes deserves primary credit for the appointment of Collier as Commissioner of Indian Affairs. At the same time, his commitment to land conservation urged him to try to remake the Department of the Interior into a Department of Conservation.

Likewise, twentieth-century artists have fictionally explored the interlinked issues of the rights of indigenous natives and those of the land itself. Willa Cather, for example, whose *The Professor's House* was

[15] John Collier, *The Indians of the Americas* (New York: W. W. Norton, 1947), p. 18, also pp. 244ff. See also Driver, *Indians of North America*, p. 494; Robert F. Berkhofer Jr., *The White Man's Indian: Images of the American Indian from Columbus to the Present* (New York: Alfred A. Knopf, 1978), pp. 178-88; Washburn, *Red Man's Land*, pp. 78ff.; Washburn, *The Indian in America* (New York: Harper and Row, 1975), pp. 253-54; Kenneth R. Philip, "John Collier and the Controversy over the Wheeler-Howard Bill," in Jane F. Smith and Robert M. Krasnicka, eds., *Indian-White Relations: A Persistent Paradox* (Washington: Howard University Press, 1976), pp. 171-200; Lawrence C. Kelly, "John Collier and the Indian New Deal: An Assessment," in ibid., pp. 227-41.

discussed earlier, attempted such a synthesis in her celebrated novel
Death Comes for the Archbishop (1927). Father Jean Latour, bishop
to the mid-nineteenth-century diocese of New Mexico, grows to respect the peacable Hopi and Navaho in their relation to the land. At
first, however, neither appeals to him; the people seem as formidably
inaccessible as the landscape: "he was quite willing to believe that
behind Jacinto," the narrator notes about the bishop's response to his
Hopi guide, "there was a long tradition, a story of experience, which
no language could translate to him. A chill came with the darkness."[16]

Latour first fears, then comes to respect this "kind of life out of
reach." As he learns, native religion values all nature as sacred; it is
not to be altered by proud man but merely "passed through."[17] Devotion to his project of a great cathedral is thematically balanced against
this deepening appreciation. Near the close of his life, however, Latour
recognizes the defects of his own white influence. "Men travel faster
now," a Navaho comments to the dying archbishop, reflecting on the
recent railroad as Thoreau had; "but I do not know if they go to
better things."[18] Santa Fe's tawdry new buildings come to represent for
Latour the loss of something "in the air," and he regrets not having
recorded the old native legends and myths, now forever lost.[19] Most important, Cather intimates his distress at the civilized consciousness
that arbitrarily isolates individual acts from spatial context, man
from nature, a culture from the landscape. One scholar has probed
this idea to even more troubling depths in reflecting on "the last
Americans":

> The important point is that the Indian world may really have
> been a genuine, influential civilization worth taking seriously in
> American history. It may really have been a civilization so firmly
> committed to its strange attitudes that it nourished its own con-
> querors and abetted its own conquest. It may really have been a
> civilization so incomprehensibly foreign to Europeans that Euro-
> peans could not recognize its existence even while in mortal em-
> brace with it, somewhat as in the case of the dark planets imag-
> ined by Alfred North Whitehead that move on a scale of space
> and time so radically different from our own as to be undetectable
> to our sense and instruments. And finally it may have been a

[16] Cather, *Death Comes for the Archbishop* (1927; rpt. New York: Random House,
1971), p. 92.
[17] Ibid., pp. 103, 233-35.
[18] Ibid., p. 291.
[19] Ibid., pp. 275, 277.

civilization affecting not only our past but still to affect our future.[20]

More than responsible scholarship is clearly involved here. As always, questions of gain and loss obtrude, of what material progress genuinely accomplishes against what it rudely sacrifices. Or, rather, during the century and a half since Americans first voiced them, these considerations have become as complex as the changing conditions of American life.

Technological progress and constant economic growth, far from shimmering in attractive prospect, have tarnished badly in the event. "The more science, technology, and the gross national product grow," one respected economist has written, "the more nasty, brutish, vile and precarious becomes human existence."[21] While extending prosperity, modern industrial economies have also compelled ever larger numbers to labor at ever less satisfying and meaningful tasks. Some observers further argue that trying to correct these unforeseen consequences of progress will only contribute to greater social enslavement.

It is no surprise that a much less vocal minority in the nineteenth century sensed this distinction between a technical and a moral ordering of experience, between their own epistemology, which was relatively indifferent to humankind, and a supposedly primitive one that encouraged individuals in responsible action.[22] Perhaps less obvious, however, are the ways in which contemporary unease with Western culture ironically mirrors that first expressed by native Americans and acknowledged by some whites. To credit what popular literature, cinema, and television inadvertently reveal, we feel about modern technology much as Indians felt about the pioneers who introduced them to its earlier forms. Sophisticated machines, computers in particular, challenge our humane values even as they offer material benefits. Their extraordinary capacity for quantitative analysis inspires awe, to be sure. But it also instills a sense of dread, since such knowledge and consequent power seem ever greater threats to human auton-

[20] William Brandon, *The Last Americans: The Indian in American Culture* (New York: McGraw-Hill, 1974), p. 22. See also, for a tangential comment, Jarold Ramsey, *Coyote Was Going There: Indian Literature of the Oregon Country* (Seattle: Washington University Press, 1977), p. xxxi.

[21] Leonard Silk, "Bigger Badder," review of E. J. Mishan, *The Economic Growth Debate*, in *New York Times Book Review*, February 5, 1978, p. 12.

[22] Walter J. Ong, S.J., "World as View and World as Event," *American Anthropologist*, 71 (August 1969), 634-47; Robert Redfield, *The Primitive World and Its Transformations* (Ithaca: Cornell University Press, 1953), esp. pp. 22-24, 81-83, 102-10.

omy. Native tribes received pioneers no differently, regarding them with both envy and disgust. Even as they wonderingly accepted a technology of guns, traps, and textiles, Indians abhorred the day-to-day patterns that whites demanded they adopt. How could they embrace ways of life so contrary to all they cherished in life itself? How could they accept modes and mores that violated sacred knowledge? The mixed reception they gave to whites and, in turn, white Americans' growing appreciation of the reasons offer means for understanding our present circumstances.

Clearly, the issues traced here still shape attitudes and actions; in large ways and small, in public legislation as in private fears, they mold our responses. This study has not assumed an easy progression from misgivings early in the nineteenth century to our tentative resolutions of them. Nor should we make any larger claim for recent efforts than they warrant. Yet it is true that a whole array of private and government programs have lately focused public energies on endangered species and land conservation. Grants supporting preservation and revival of native lore proliferate, as do newsweekly essays encouraging them. A national constituency subscribes to such groups as the Sierra Club, the Society for Endangered Species, and the American Indian Movement, each of which is devoted to a holding action in the erosion of landscape and cultures. Predictably, scholars still claim that too little is being done too slowly and too late. Indian tribes have turned, so some allege, into what whites always imagined them: a single entity, bound together by economic necessity and social ostracism.[23] While this charge partially describes native affairs, characteristically from a white perspective, people nonetheless have tried as never before to understand, even to learn from native points of view.[24] Anthropologists now find themselves joined by historians and government officials.[25] All of these efforts only barely indicate how variously the impulse to leave a record for future generations continues to affect Americans.

Perhaps fiction, once again, offers the best touchstone, since it more concisely reveals the multiple extensions of contemporary response. By that standard, Barry Lopez's short story "The Photographer" (1977) is exemplary, summing up in all of two pages the issues we have been exploring throughout. A young man decides to make a gallery of "endangered and possibly extinct animals. He

[23] Berkhofer, *White Man's Indian*, p. 195; Frederick Turner, " 'Tribe' Is a White Man's Concept," *New York Times*, January 8, 1978, Week in Review section, p. 2.

[24] Wilbur R. Jacobs, *Dispossessing the American Indian: Indians and Whites on the Colonial Frontier* (New York: Charles Scribner's Sons, 1972), p. 25.

[25] For a good review of current trends, see Francis Paul Prucha, "Doing Indian History," in Smith and Krasnicka, eds., *Indian-White Relations*, pp. 3-10.

would go to the places where the last of a species had been reported and he would systematically set about capturing the animals on film."[26] After spending "some years" among Plains Indians learning wilderness lore, the unnamed photographer sets out on his mission. Over nearly a decade, he patiently completes thirty-one portraits of birds, rodents, and mammals listed as extinct or endangered. In each one he achieves "exactly what he wanted. A portrait of an endangered species that would terrify."

Exhibited in New York City, the photographs garner instant acclaim. But their "unsettling" quality soon converts enthusiasm to "a sort of fear." Conservationists and art scholars decide to reproduce the invaluable portraits, since the negatives have been destroyed. Yet as they begin, the photographs start to fade and within a few hours become unrecognizable blurs. The photographer himself had refused payment, publicity, or further commission: "he thought privately that he had done what he set out to do and that in an odd way he was now free to go." Unconcerned with his photographs' fate, he abandons his camera equipment and travels to Alaska "to study the behavior of humpback whales."

The story is hardly representative of actual history, perhaps least so in the photographer's final abjuration of responsibility—so different from the fierce perseverance of contemporaries committed to so many holding actions against industrial progress. Still, the story nicely integrates the kinds of careers and many of the themes we have been studying: the concern for vanishing wildlife; the impulse to document it; the artistic preparation for the self-imposed task; the appreciation of native American lore in best comprehending the wilderness; the discovery, in compiling that record, of aspects more compelling than had been anticipated; and finally, the photographer's conclusion, despite excursions elsewhere, that "there was nothing outside North America that held his interest."

The story grips the imagination for reasons that, as with all literature, ultimately elude analysis. In part it does so, for the American reader at least, by concisely imaging a constellation of ideas and attitudes that our history has rehearsed. The constellation is a lesser one, certainly, within the galaxy of America's social, economic, and intellectual history. Yet a vanishing continental wilderness elicited apprehensions and commitments that in telling ways continue to define us as a people. Which is simply to say that whatever we may mean to evoke by the phrase "American character" must not ignore that mixed strain of regret about the process of westering that ramified so variously, so vigorously through the nineteenth century.

26 Lopez, "The Photographer," *North American Review*, 262 (Fall 1977), 66-67.

SELECTED BIBLIOGRAPHY

MANUSCRIPT COLLECTIONS

Akerly, Samuel. "On the Cultivation of Forest Trees; In a Letter Addressed to Jonathan Thompson, Esq. Collector of the Customs of the Port of New York." Broadside. 1823. American Antiquarian Society. Worcester, Massachusetts.

Banks, D. C. "To the Citizens of Kentucky." Broadside. February 15, 1840. American Antiquarian Society.

Bonine, E. A. Collection of Photographs. Henry E. Huntington Library, San Marino, California.

Catlin, George. "The North Americans in the Middle of the Nineteenth Century: A Numerous and Noble Race of Human Beings fast passing to oblivion and leaving no monuments of their own behind them." Bound folio. George Catlin Collection. Huntington Library.

Hillers, Jack. Photographic Views of Ancient Ruins of Hopi Villages. 9 original photographs mounted and bound. 1880s? Huntington Library.

James, George Wharton. Photographs; stereophotos. Box 5. Huntington Library.

Kern, Edward, and Kern, Richard. *The Published Pictures, Portraits and Maps Collectively Depicting the Indians, Scenery and Topography of the Far West, Drawn by Edward Kern and Richard Kern, 1846-1851.* Fort Sutter Papers. Vol. 39. Huntington Library.

Monsen, Frederick. *Frederick Monsen's Ethnographic Indian Photographs.* 13 vols. Huntington Library.

Moon, Carl, "A Brief Account of the Making of this Collection of Indian Pictures." Typescript. Dated: Pasadena, Calif., 1924. Huntington Library.

————. Letter to Grace Nicholson. January 14, 1931. Box 6, Nicholson Collection. Huntington Library.

Nicholson, Grace. Grace Nicholson Photograph Albums "A"–"E." Huntington Library.

————. Nicholson Collection. Boxes I-XVI. Huntington Library.

————. *Nicholson (Grace) Collection: Summary Report.* Huntington Library.

Rollins, Philip. Philip Rollins Western Americana Collection. Firestone Library. Princeton University. Princeton, New Jersey.

Rust, Horatio Nelson. Horatio Nelson Rust Collection. Huntington Library.

Saunders, Charles Francis. Pocket Diary for 1909, July 31–September 5, tour of the pueblos. Box 9, Saunders (Charles Francis) Collection. Huntington Library.

———. Pocket Diary for 1909 Tour, September 25–November 18. Box 9, Saunders Collection. Huntington Library.

Vroman, A. C. A. C. Vroman's Diary, Hopi Indians. Ca. 1895. Huntington Library.

PUBLISHED SOURCES

Primary

Atwater, Caleb. *Remarks Made on a Tour to Prairie Du Chien; Thence to Washington City, in 1829.* Columbus: Isaac N. Whiting, 1831.

———. *The Writings of Caleb Atwater.* Columbus: n.p., 1833.

Audubon, John James. *Delineations of American Scenery and Character.* New York: G. A. Baker and Co., 1926.

Audubon, Maria R. *Audubon and His Journals.* 2 vols. New York: Charles Scribner's Sons, 1897.

Ayer, I. Winslow. *Life in the Wilds of America, and Wonders of the West in and beyond the Bounds of Civilization.* Grand Rapids, Mich.: Central Publishing Co., 1880.

J.B.B. "The Yates Collections." *Land of Sunshine*, 2 (May 1895), 98.

Baird, Henry S. "Recollections of the Early History of Northern Wisconsin." *Collections of the State Historical Society of Wisconsin*, 4 (1859), 197-221.

Baird, Spencer F. "Letter from the Secretary of the Smithsonian Institution." In *Annual Report of the Board of Regents of the Smithsonian Institution for the Year Ending June 30, 1887*, pp. 1-27. Washington: G.P.O., 1889.

Bancroft, Hubert Howe. *The Early American Chroniclers.* San Francisco: A. L. Bancroft and Co., 1883.

———. *The Narrative Races of the Pacific States of North America.* 5 vols. New York: D. Appleton and Co., 1875-76.

Bandelier, Adolph F. *Papers of the Archaeological Institute of America, American Series.* 5 vols. Boston: Cupples, Upham, and Co., 1883-92.

Barrett, Joseph, M.D. *The Indian of New-England and the North-Eastern Provinces.* Middletown, Conn.: Charles H. Pelton, 1851.

Bartlett, John Russell. *Personal Narrative of Explorations and Incidents in Texas, New Mexico, California, Sonora, and Chihuahua, Connected with the United States and Mexican Boundary Commission, During the Years 1850, '51, '52, and '53.* 2 vols. New York: D. Appleton and Co., 1854.

Baxter, Sylvester. "An Aboriginal Pilgrimage." *Century Magazine,* 24 (August 1882), 526-36.

———. "The Father of the Pueblos." *Harper's New Monthly Magazine,* 65 (June 1882), 72-91.

Beckwith, Hiram W. *The Illinois and Indiana Indians.* Chicago: Fergus Printing Co., 1884.

Beeson, John. *A Plea for the Indians; With Facts and Features of the Late War in Oregon.* New York: J. Beeson, 1857.

Beggs, Rev. Stephen R. *Pages from the Early History of the West and Northwest.* . . . Cincinnati: Methodist Book Concern, 1868.

Benjamin, S.G.W. *Art in America: A Critical and Historical Sketch.* New York: Harper and Brothers, 1880.

Berlandier, Jean Louis. *The Indians of Texas in 1830.* Translated by Patricia Reading Leclercq. Edited by John C. Ewers. Washington: Smithsonian Institution, 1969.

Bierstadt, Albert. "Letter from the Rocky Mountains, July 10, 1859." *Crayon,* 6 (September 1859), 287.

Bird, Robert Montgomery. *Peter Pilgrim; or, A Rambler's Recollections.* 2 vols. Philadelphia: Lea and Blanchard, 1838.

Boas, Franz. *Chinook Texts.* Bureau of American Ethnology. Washington: G.P.O., 1894.

———. *Race, Language and Culture.* New York: Macmillan Co., 1940.

———. *The Shaping of American Anthropology, 1883-1911: A Franz Boas Reader.* Edited with an introduction by George W. Stocking Jr. New York: Basic Books, 1974.

Boller, Henry A. *Among the Indians. Eight Years in the Far West: 1858-1866.* Philadelphia: T. Ellwood Zell, 1868.

Bourke, Capt. John G. *On the Border with Crook.* New York: Charles Scribner's Sons, 1891.

———. *The Snake-Dance of the Moquis of Arizona.* . . . New York: Charles Scribner's Sons, 1884.

Brace, Charles Loring. *The New West; or, California in 1867-1868.* New York: G. P. Putnam and Son, 1869.

Brackenridge, Henry Marie. *Recollections of Persons and Places in the West*. Philadelphia: James Kay, Jun. and Brother, 1834.

Bradford, Alexander W. *American Antiquities and Researches into the Origin and History of the Red Race*. New York: Dayton and Saxton, 1841.

Brinton, Daniel G. *The Annals of the Cakchiquels*. 1885. Reprint. New York: Ams Press, 1969.

————. *Essays of an Americanist*. Philadelphia: David McKay, 1890.

————. *The Lenâpé and Their Legends*. 1885. Reprint. New York: Ams Press, 1969.

————. *Races and Peoples: Lectures on the Science of Ethnography*. Philadelphia: David McKay, 1901.

Brush, George de Forest. "An Artist Among the Indians." *Century Magazine*, 30 (May 1885), 54-57.

Bryant, William Cullen. *Letters of a Traveller; or, Notes of Things Seen in Europe and America*. 1850. 4th ed. New York: G. P. Putnam and Co., 1855.

————. "A New Public Park." *New York Evening Post*, July 3, 1844, p. 2.

————. *Poems*. Philadelphia: Carey and Hart, 1848.

Buchanan, James. *Sketches of the History, Manners, and Customs of the North American Indians with a Plan for Their Melioration*. 2 vols. New York: W. Borradaile, 1824.

Buck, William J. "Lappawinzo and Tishcohan, Chiefs of the Lenni Lenape." *Pennsylvania Magazine of History and Biography*, 7 (1883) 215-18.

Carr, John. *Pioneer Days in California*. Eureka, Calif.: Times Publishing Co., 1891.

Carrington, Mrs. Margaret I. *Absaraka, Home of the Crows*. 1868. Edited by Milo Milton Quaife. Chicago: R. R. Donnelley and Sons, 1950.

Carroll, Rev. George R. *Pioneer Life in and Around Cedar Rapids, Iowa from 1839 to 1849*. Cedar Rapids: n.p., 1895.

Cass, Lewis. "Indians of North America." *North American Review*, 22 (1826), 53-119.

————. *Inquiries, Respecting the History, Traditions, Languages, Manners, Customs, Religion, &c. of the Indians, Living within the United States*. Detroit: Sheldon and Reed, 1823.

[————]. *Ontwa, the Son of the Forest. A Poem*. New York: Wiley and Halsted, 1822.

Catlin, George. *Letters and Notes on the Manners, Customs, and Conditions of the North American Indians*. 2 vols. 1844. Reprinted with an introduction by Marjorie Halpin. New York: Dover Publications, 1973.

————. *Life Among the Indians*. London: Gall and Inglis, [187?].

————. *O-kee-pa: A Religious Ceremony and Other Customs of the Mandans*. Edited by John C. Ewers. New Haven: Yale University Press, 1967.

————. *Shut Your Mouth and Save Your Life*. 1860. Reprint. London: Trübner and Co., 1875.

Chapman, Frank M. *Autobiography of a Bird-Lover*. New York: D. Appleton-Century Co., 1933.

Clark, Joshua V. H. *Lights and Lines of Indian Character and Scenes of Pioneer Life*. Syracuse: E. H. Babcock and Co., 1854.

————. *Onondaga; or Reminiscences of Earlier and Later Times*. . . . 2 vols. Syracuse: Stoddard and Babcock, 1849.

Clark, William Philo. *The Indian Sign Language, with Brief Explanatory Notes*. . . . Philadelphia: L. R. Hamersly and Co., 1884.

Clarke, Samuel Asahel. *Pioneer Days of Oregon History*. 2 vols. Portland: J. K. Gill Co., 1905.

Clinton, DeWitt. *A Memoir on the Antiquities of the Western Parts of the State of New York*. Albany: I. W. Clark, 1818.

Cole, Thomas. "The Lament of the Forest." *Knickerbocker*, 17 (June 1841), 516-19.

————. "Lecture on American Scenery, Delivered before the Catskill Lyceum, April 1st, 1841." *Northern Light*, 1 (May 1841), 25-26.

Collection of Indian Anecdotes, A. Concord, N.H.: William White, 1838.

Colton, George H. *Tecumseh; or, The West Thirty Years Since. A Poem*. New York: Wiley and Putnam, 1842.

Connor, J. Torrey. "Confessions of a Basket Collector." *Land of Sunshine*, 5 (June 1896), 3-10.

Conrad, Howard Louis. *"Uncle Dick" Wootton, the Pioneer Frontiersman of the Rocky Mountain Region*. Chicago: W. E. Dribble and Co., 1890.

Converse, Harriet Maxwell. "Myths and Legends of the New York State Iroquois." *New York State Museum Bulletin* 125. Albany: University of the State of New York, 1908.

Cook, James. *Captain Cook's Journal . . . 1768-71*. Edited by Capt. W.J.L. Wharton. London: Elliott Stock, 1893.

Cooper, Judge William. *A Guide in the Wilderness: or the History of the First Settlements in the Western Counties of New-York with Useful Instructions to Future Settlers*. 1810. Reprinted with an introduction by James Fenimore Cooper. Rochester, N.Y.: George P. Humphrey, 1897.

Copway, George. *The Life, History, and Travels of Kah-Ge-Ga-Gah-Bowh*. Albany: n.p., 1847.

———. *The Traditional History and Characteristic Sketches of the Ojibway Nation*. London: Charles Gilpin, 1850.

Costello, J. A. *The Siwash, Their Life, Legends and Tales*. Seattle: Calvert Co., 1895.

Cremony, John C. *Life Among the Apaches*. San Francisco: A. Roman and Co., 1868.

Crèvecoeur, Ferdinand F. *Old Settlers' Tales.* . . . Onaga, Kan.: n.p., 1902.

Crèvecoeur, Michel-Guillaume St. Jean de [J. Hector Saint John de Crèvecoeur]. *Journey into Northern Pennsylvania and the State of New York*. 1801. Translated by Clarissa Spencer Bostelmann. 3 vols. in one. Ann Arbor: University of Michigan Press, 1964.

Crook, George. *General George Crook: His Autobiography*. 2d ed. Edited by Martin F. Schmitt. Norman: University of Oklahoma Press, 1960.

Curtis, Edward S. *The North American Indian; Being a Series of Volumes Picturing and Describing the Indians of the United States, and Alaska*. Edited by Frederick Webb Hodge. Foreword by Theodore Roosevelt. 20 vols. Cambridge, Mass.: Harvard University Press, 1907-30.

Cushing, Frank Hamilton. "My Adventures in Zuni." *Century Magazine*, 25 (December 1882), 191-207.

———. "My Adventures in Zuni. II." *Century Magazine*, 26 (February 1883), 500-11.

———. *Zuni: Selected Writings of Frank Hamilton Cushing*. Edited and with an introduction by Jesse Green. Lincoln: University of Nebraska Press, 1979.

Darley, Felix O. C. *Scenes in Indian Life*. 4 numbers. Philadelphia: J. R. Colon, April-July 1843.

De Forest, John W. *History of the Indians of Connecticut from the Earliest Known Period to 1850*. Hartford: William James Hamersley, 1853.

Denig, Edwin Thompson, *Five Indian Tribes of the Upper Missouri*. Edited by John C. Ewers. Norman: University of Oklahoma Press, 1961.

Denny, Arthur A. *Pioneer Days on Puget Sound*. 1888. Reprint. Seattle: Alice Harriman Co., 1908.

De Schweinitz, Edmund. *The Life and Times of David Zeisberger: The Western Pioneer and Apostle of the Indians.* Philadelphia: J. B. Lippincott and Co., 1870.

De Smet, Pierre Jean, S.J. *Oregon Missions and Travels Over the Rocky Mountains, in 1845-46.* Illustrated by Nicolas Point. 1847. Reprinted in vol. 29 of Thwaites, ed., *Early Western Travels,* pp. 103-424.

Dixon, Joseph K. *The Vanishing Race: The Last Great Indian Council.* Garden City, N.Y.: Doubleday, Page and Co., 1913.

Dodge, Col. Richard Irving. *Our Wild Indians: Thirty-Three Years' Personal Experience Among the Red Men of the Great West. . . .* Hartford, Conn.: A. D. Worthington and Co., 1883.

Domenech, Abbé Emmanuel. *Seven Years' Residence in the Great Deserts of North America.* 2 vols. London: Longman, Green, Longman, and Roberts, 1860.

Donaldson, Thomas. *The George Catlin Indian Gallery in the U.S. National Museum.* Author's edition. Washington: G.P.O., 1887.

―――. *The Public Domain: Its History, with Statistics.* 1880. 3d ed. Washington: G.P.O., 1884.

Dorsey, George A. *The Arapaho Sun Dance: The Ceremony of the Offerings Lodge.* Field Columbian Museum Publication 75. Chicago, 1903.

―――. *The Cheyenne.* Vol. 1: *Ceremonial Organization.* Field Columbian Museum Publication 99. Anthropological Series, vol. 9, no. 1. Chicago, 1905.

―――. *The Ponca Sun Dance.* Field Columbian Museum Publication 102. Anthropological Series, vol. 7, no. 2. Chicago, 1905.

Downing, Andrew Jackson, ed. *The Horticulturist and Journal of Rural Art and Rural Taste.* 1 (1846-47), 6 (1851-52).

Drake, Benjamin. *The Life and Adventures of Black Hawk.* 1838. 7th ed. rev. Cincinnati: E. Morgan and Co., 1850.

Drake, Daniel, M.D. *Discourse on the History, Character, and Prospects of the West.* 1834. Reprint. Gainesville, Fla.: Scholars' Facsimiles and Reprints, 1955.

―――. *Pioneer Life in Kentucky: A Series of Reminiscential Letters from Daniel Drake, M.D., of Cincinnati, to His Children.* Edited by Charles D. Drake. Cincinnati: Robert Clarke and Co., 1870.

Dunbar, John B. "The Pawnee Indians: Their Habits and Customs." *Magazine of American History,* 8 (November 1882), 734-54.

Duval, John Crittenden. *Early Times in Texas.* Austin: H.P.N. Gammel and Co., 1892.

Dwight, Timothy. *Travels in New-England and New-York*. 4 vols. London: William Baynes and Son, 1823.

Eastman, Charles Alexander [Ohiyesa]. *From the Deep Woods to Civilization: Chapters in the Autobiography of an Indian*. 1916. Reprint. Boston: Little, Brown and Co., 1917.

————. *Indian Boyhood*. Illustrated by E. L. Blumenschein. 1902. Reprint. Boston: Little, Brown and Co., 1918.

————. *The Soul of the Indian: An Interpretation*, Boston: Houghton Mifflin Co., 1911.

Eastman, Mrs. Mary H. *The American Aboriginal Portfolio*. Illustrated by Seth Eastman. Philadelphia: Lippincott, Grambo and Co., [1853].

————. *Dahcotah; or, Life and Legends of the Sioux Around Fort Snelling*. Illustrated by Seth Eastman. 1849. Reprint. Minneapolis: Ross and Haines, 1962.

————. *The Romance of Indian Life*. Philadelphia: Lippincott, Grambo and Co., 1853.

Eggleston, Edward. *The Hoosier Schoolmaster*. 1871. Reprint. New York: Orange Judd Co., 1890.

Egleston, N. H. "What We Owe to the Trees." *Harper's New Monthly Magazine*, 64 (April 1882), 675-87.

Eliot, Charles William. *Charles Eliot: Landscape Architect*. Boston: Houghton Mifflin and Co., 1902.

Elliott, William. *Carolina Sports by Land and Water*. 1867? Reprint. Columbia, S.C.: State Co., 1918.

Farrand, Livingston. "Basketry Designs of the Salish Indians." In Franz Boas, ed., *Memoirs of the American Museum of Natural History: Jesup North Pacific Expedition*, 1 (1898-1900), 391-412.

Fernow, Bernhard Eduard. *Economics of Forestry: A Reference Book for Students of Political Economy and Professional and Lay Students of Forestry*. New York: Thomas Y. Crowell, 1902.

————. *Report upon the Forestry Investigations of the United States Department of Agriculture, 1877-1898*. Washington: G.P.O., 1899.

Fewkes, J. Walter, ed. *A Journal of American Ethnology and Archaeology*. 5 vols. Boston: Houghton Mifflin and Co., 1891-1908.

Fletcher, Alice C. "A Study of Omaha Indian Music." *Archaeological and Ethnological Papers of the Peabody Museum*, 1, No. 5 (June 1893), 231-382.

Flint, Timothy. *The Personal Narrative of James O. Pattie of Kentucky*. 1831. Reprinted in vol. 18 of Thwaites, ed., *Early Western Travels*.

————. *Recollections of the Last Ten Years Passed in Occasional Residences and Journeyings in the Valley of the Mississippi . . . In a Series of Letters. . . .* Boston: Cummings, Hilliard, and Co., 1826.

[Foote, John P.]. Review of John D. Hunter, *Manners and Customs of the Indian tribes located west of the Mississippi. Cincinnati Literary Gazette,* 1 (January 1, 10, 1824), 1-2, 9-10.

"Forests." *Hours at Home,* 3 (September 1866), 398-402.

Franchère, Gabriel. *Narrative of a Voyage to the Northwest Coast of America in the Years 1811, 1812, 1813, and 1814; or The First American Settlement on the Pacific.* 1820. Translated and edited by J. V. Huntington, 1854. Reprinted in vol. 6 of Thwaites, ed., *Early Western Travels.*

Franklin, Benjamin. "Remarks Concerning the Savages of North America." Papers of Benjamin Franklin. Library of Congress microcopy. 1941. 2d Ser., vol. 10, no. 2334-2344.

Freneau, Philip. *The Prose of Philip Freneau.* Edited by Philip M. Marsh. New Brunswick: Scarecrow Press, 1955.

Fuller, Margaret. *The Writings of Margaret Fuller.* Edited by Mason Wade. New York: Viking, 1941.

Gallatin, Albert. *Selected Writings of Albert Gallatin.* Edited by E. James Ferguson. New York: Bobbs-Merrill, 1967.

Garland, Hamlin. *Crumbling Idols: Twelve Essays on Art Dealing Chiefly with Literature Painting and the Drama.* 1894. Edited by Jane Johnson. Cambridge, Mass.: Harvard University Press, 1960.

Gatschet, Albert. "The Karankawa Indians, the Coast People of Texas." *Archaeological and Ethnological Papers of the Peabody Museum,* 1, No. 2 (1891), 65-103.

George, Henry. *Moses/The Crime of Poverty.* New York: International Joseph Fels Commission, 1918.

————. *Our Land and Land Policy.* 1871. Reprint. New York: Doubleday Page and Co., 1904. Expanded in 1878 to *Progress and Poverty.*

————. *Progress and Poverty.* 1879. Reprint. New York: Robert Schalkenbach Foundation, 1954.

Gibbs, George. *Indian Tribes of Washington Territory. Pacific Northwest Letters of George Gibbs.* 1854. Reprint. Fairfield, Wash.: Ye Galleon Press, 1967.

Giffen, Fannie Reed. *Oo-Mah-Ha Ta-Wa-Tha (Omaha City).* Lincoln, Nebr.: n.p., 1898.

Gifford, John, ed. *The New Jersey Forester: A Bi-Monthly Pamphlet Devoted to the Development of Our Forests.* 1-2 (1895-1896).

Gillmore, Parker. *A Hunter's Adventures in the Great West.* London: Hurst and Blackett, 1871.

Greeley, Horace. *Glances at Europe.* New York: Dewitt and Davenport, 1851.

Green, C. H. "Brief History of Cliff Dwellers, Their Relics and Ruins." In *Catalogue of a Unique Collection of Cliff Dweller Relics.* Chicago: Art Institute, 1891.

Grinnell, George Bird. *Beyond the Old Frontier: Adventures of Indian-Fighters, Hunters, and Fur-Traders.* New York: Charles Scribner's Sons, 1913.

————. *Blackfoot Lodge Tales: The Story of a Prairie People.* 1903? Reprint. Lincoln: University of Nebraska Press, 1962.

————. *The Passing of the Great West: Selected Papers of George Bird Grinnell.* Edited by John T. Reiger. New York: Winchester Press, 1972.

————. *Pawnee Hero Stories and Folk-Tales with Notes on the Origin, Customs and Character of the Pawnee People.* New York: Charles Scribner's Sons, 1890.

————, ed. *American Big Game Hunting in Its Haunts.* New York: Forest and Stream Publishing Co., 1904.

Hale, Horatio. *An International Idiom: A Manual of the Oregon Trade Language or "Chinook Jargon."* London: Whittaker and Co., 1890.

————, ed. *The Iroquois Book of Rites.* 1883. Edited by William N. Fenton. Toronto: University of Toronto Press, 1963. Originally no. 2 of D. G. "Brinton's Library of Aboriginal Literature" (Philadelphia).

Halkett, John. *Historical Notes Respecting the Indians of North America: With Remarks on the Attempts Made to Convert and Civilize Them.* London: Archibald Constable and Co., 1825.

Hall, James. *Legends of the West: Sketches Illustrative of the Habits, Occupations, Privations, Adventures and Sports of the Pioneers of the West.* 1832. Reprint. Cincinnati: Applegate and Co., 1857.

————. *Sketches of History, Life, and Manners in the West.* 2 vols. Philadelphia: Harrison Hall, 1835.

Hamilton, William Thomas. *My Sixty Years on the Plains: Trapping, Trading, and Indian Fighting.* 1905. Reprint. Norman: University of Oklahoma Press, 1960.

Hammond, Samuel H. *Wild Northern Scenes; or Sporting Adventures with the Rifle and the Rod.* New York: Derby and Jackson, 1857.

Hart, Col. Joseph C. *Miriam Coffin, or The Whale Fishermen: A Tale*. 1834. New ed. 2 vols. in 1. San Francisco: H. R. Coleman, 1872.

Hawthorne, Nathaniel. *The American Notebooks*. Edited by Claude M. Simpson. Columbus: Ohio State University Press, 1972.

———. "Sketches from Memory." 1835. Reprinted in *Mosses from an Old Manse*, pp. 422-38. Vol. 10 of Centenary Ed. Columbus: Ohio State University Press, 1974.

Henry, Joseph. "Circular Relating to Collections in Archaeology and Ethnology." *Smithsonian Miscellaneous Collections*, 8 (1868), 1-2.

———. "Report of the Secretary for 1858." In *Annual Report of the Board of Regents of the Smithsonian Institution*, pp. 13-43. Washington: G.P.O., 1859.

Hildreth, S. P. *Pioneer History: Being an Account of the First Examinations of the Ohio Valley and the Early Settlement of the Northwest Territory*. Cincinnati: H. W. Derby and Co., 1848.

Hill, Alice Polk. *Tales of the Colorado Pioneers*. Denver: Pierson and Gardiner, 1884.

Hillers, Jack. *"Photographed All the Best Scenery": Jack Hillers' Diary of the Powell Expeditions, 1871-1875*. Edited by Don D. Fowler. Salt Lake City: University of Utah Press, 1972.

Holley, Frances Chamberlain. *Once Their Home; or, Our Legacy from the Dahkotahs*. Chicago: Donohue and Henneberry, 1890.

Holmes, William Henry. *Archaeological Studies among the Ancient Cities of Mexico*. Field Columbian Museum Publication 8, 16. Anthropological Series, vol. 1, no. 1. Chicago, 1895.

Hopkins, Sarah Winnemucca. *Life Among the Piutes: Their Wrongs and Claims*. Edited by Mrs. Horace [Mary] Mann. Boston: n.p., 1883.

Hornaday, William T. *The Extermination of the American Bison*. Washington: G.P.O., 1889.

Hough, Emerson. *The Story of the Cowboy*. New York: D. Appleton and Co., 1897.

Hough, Franklin B. "On the Duty of Governments in the Preservation of Forests." *Proceedings of the American Association for the Advancement of Science*, 22, pt. 2 (1873), 1-10.

Hubbard, Belà. "Ancient Garden Beds of Michigan." *American Antiquarian*, 1 (April 1878), 1-9.

———. *Memorials of a Half-Century*. New York: G. P. Putnam's Sons, 1887.

Hunter, John Dunn. *Memoirs of a Captivity Among the Indians of*

North America. 1824. Edited by Richard Drinnon. New York: Schocken Books, 1973.

Hurlbut, Henry H. *Chicago Antiquities.* Chicago: n.p., 1881.

Irving, John Treat, Jr. *Indian Sketches Taken During an Expedition to the Pawnee Tribes [1833].* 1835. Edited by John Francis Mc-Dermott. Norman: University of Oklahoma Press, 1955.

Irving, Washington. *The Adventures of Captain Bonneville, U.S.A., in the Rocky Mountains and the Far West.* 1837. Edited by Edgeley W. Todd. Norman: University of Oklahoma Press, 1961.

————. *Astoria, or Anecdotes of an Enterprise Beyond the Rocky Mountains.* Edited by Edgeley W. Todd. Norman: University of Oklahoma Press, 1964.

————. *The Western Journals of Washington Irving.* Edited by John Francis McDermott. Norman: University of Oklahoma Press, 1944.

Jackson, Helen Hunt. *A Century of Dishonor: The Early Crusade for Indian Reform.* 1881. Edited by Andrew F. Rolle. New York: Harper and Row, 1965.

————. *Glimpses of California and the Missions.* 1883. Reprint. Boston: Little, Brown and Co., 1903.

Jackson, Rev. Sheldon. *Alaska, and Missions on the North Pacific Coast.* New York: Dodd, Mead and Co., 1880.

Jackson, William Henry. *Descriptive Catalogue of Photographs of North American Indians.* With a prefatory note by F. W. Hayden. United States Geological and Geographical Survey of the Territories. Miscellaneous Publications, no. 9. Washington: G.P.O., 1877.

James, Edwin, ed. *A Narrative of the Captivity and Adventures of John Tanner During Thirty Years Residence Among the Indians in the Interior of North America.* 1830. Reprint. Minneapolis: Ross and Haines, 1956.

James, George Wharton. *In and Out of the Old Missions of California: An Historical and Pictorial Account of the Franciscan Missions.* Boston: Little, Brown and Co., 1905.

————. *Indian Basketry.* Pasadena: n.p., 1901.

————. *Old Missions and Mission Indians of California.* Los Angeles: B. R. Baumgardt and Co., 1895.

James, Isabella. "American Forests." *Lippincott's Magazine,* 1 (June 1868), 596-602.

James, Gen. Thomas. *Three Years among the Indians and Mexicans.* 1846. Reprint. Chicago: R. R. Donnelley and Sons, 1953.

Jameson, Mrs. Anna Brownell. *Winter Studies and Summer Rambles in Canada.* 2 vols. New York: Wiley and Putnam, 1839.

Jarvis, Samuel Farmar. *A Discourse on the Religion of the Indian Tribes of North America. Delivered Before the New-York Historical Society, Dec. 20, 1819.* New York: C. Wiley and Co., 1820.

Jerome, W. "Karl Moon's Indian Photographs." *Craftsman,* 20 (April 1911), 24-32.

Jones, James Athearn. *Traditions of the North American Indians.* 1830. 3 vols. Reprint. Upper Saddle River, N.J.: Literature House, 1970.

Journal of American Folk-Lore, The. Edited by W. W. Newell, Franz Boas, T. Frederick Crane, J. Owen Dorsey. Vol. 1. Boston: Houghton Mifflin and Co., 1888.

Kane, Paul. *Wanderings of an Artist among the Indians of North America from Canada to Vancouver's Island and Oregon through the Hudson's Bay Company's Territory.* 1859. Reprint. Toronto: Radisson Society of Canada, 1925.

Kinzie, Mrs. John H. [Juliette Augusta]. *Wau-Bun, The "Early Day" in the North-West.* New York: Derby and Jackson, 1856.

Knight, Sarah Kemble. *The Journal of Madam Knight.* Boston: Small, Maynard and Co., 1920.

Latrobe, Charles Joseph. *The Rambler in North America: 1832-1833.* 2 vols. London: R. B. Seeley and W. Burnside, 1835.

Lawrence, James H. "Discovery of the Nevada Fall." *Overland Monthly.* 2d ser., 4 (October 1884), 360-71.

Leland, Charles G. *The Algonquin Legends of New England, or Myths and Folk Lore of the Micmac, Passamaquoddy, and Penobscot Tribes.* Boston: Houghton Mifflin and Co., 1884.

———. "Legends of the Passamaquoddy." *Century Magazine,* 28 (September 1884), 668-77.

"Letters to the Editor, on Indian Antiquities. Letter I." *Detroit Gazette,* September 1, 1820, p. 1.

Lewis, James Otto. *The North American Aboriginal Port-Folio.* 1835-36. New York: J. P. Callender, 1838.

[Longstreet, Augustus Baldwin]. *Georgia Scenes, Characters, Incidents &c. in the First Half Century of the Republic.* 2d ed. New York: Harper and Brothers, 1860.

Lossing, Benson J. "Our Barbarian Brethren." *Harper's New Monthly Magazine,* 40 (May 1870), 793-811.

Ludewig, Hermann E. *The Literature of American Aboriginal Languages. Edited by Nicholas Trübner.* London. Trübner and Co., 1858.

Lummis, Charles F. "The Palmer Collection." *Land of Sunshine*, 2 (February 1895), 68-69.

Mabie, Hamilton Wright. "Indians, and Indians." *Century Magazine*, 38 (July 1889), 471-72.

McClintock, Walter. *Old Indian Trails*. Boston: Houghton Mifflin Co., 1923.

McGee, W. J. "The Conservation of Natural Resources." *Proceedings of the Mississippi Valley Historical Association*, 3 (1909-10), 361-79.

McKenney, Thomas L., and Hall, James. *The Indian Tribes of North America, with Biographical Sketches and Anecdotes of the Principal Chiefs*. 1836-44. New ed. Edited by Frederick Webb Hodge. 3 vols. Edinburgh: John Grant, 1933-34.

McKnight, Charles. *Our Western Border . . . One Hundred Years Ago*. Philadelphia: J. C. McCurdy and Co., 1875.

Mahan, Rev. Asa. *Autobiography: Intellectual, Moral and Spiritual*. London: T. Woolmer, 1882.

Marcy, Randolph Barnes. *Border Reminiscences*. New York: Harper and Brothers, 1872.

―――. *Thirty Years of Army Life on the Border*. New York: Harper and Brothers, 1866.

Marsh, George Perkins. *Address Delivered Before the Agricultural Society of Rutland County, Sept. 30, 1847*. Rutland, Vt.: n.p., 1848.

―――. *Man and Nature*. 1864. Edited by David Lowenthal. Cambridge, Mass.: Harvard University Press, 1965.

―――. "The Study of Nature." Review of Alexander von Humboldt, *Views of Nature* (1850), and W. R. Alger, *Lessons for Mankind from the Life and Death of Humboldt* (1859). *Christian Examiner*, 5th ser., 68 (January 1860), 33-62.

Marshall, Humphrey. *The History of Kentucky*. Frankfort: n.p., 1824.

Mason, Edward G. "Francis Parkman." *Dial*, 1 (December 1880), 149-51.

Mason, Otis Tufton. "Aboriginal American Basketry: Studies in a Textile Art without Machinery." In *Smithsonian Institution Annual Report, 1902*, pp. 171-548. Washington: G.P.O., 1904.

Matthews, Washington. *Ethnography and Philology of the Hidatsa Indians*. With a preface by F. V. Hayden. United States Geological and Geographical Survey, Miscellaneous Publications, no. 7. Washington: G.P.O., 1877.

———. "Songs of the Navajos." *Land of Sunshine,* 5 (October 1896), 197-201.

Maximilian zu Wied. *People of the First Man: Life among the Plains Indians in Their Final Days of Glory.* Edited by Davis Thomas and Karin Ronnefeldt. New York: E. P. Dutton, 1976.

———. *Travels in the Interior of North America.* Translated by H. Evans Lloyd. 1843. Reprinted as vols. 22-24 of Thwaites, ed., *Early Western Travels.*

Mayer, Frank Blackwell. *With Pen and Pencil on the Frontier in 1851: The Diary and Sketches of Frank Blackwell Mayer.* Edited by Bertha L. Heilbron. Saint Paul: Minnesota Historical Society, 1932.

Meacham, Alfred Benjamin. *Wigwam and War-Path; or The Royal Chief in Chains.* Rev. ed. Boston: John P. Dale and Co., 1875.

Messiter, Charles Alston. *Sport and Adventures among the North American Indians.* London: R. H. Porter, 1890.

Methvin, Rev. J. J. *Andele, or The Mexican-Kiowa Captive: A Story of Real Life Among the Indians.* Louisville: Pentecostal Herald Press, 1899.

Miles, Nelson. *Personal Recollections and Observations of General Nelson A. Miles. . . .* New York: Werner Co., 1897.

"Mr. Remington as Artist and Author." Review of Remington, *Crooked Trails. Dial,* 25 (October 1898), 265.

Monsen, Frederick I. "The Destruction of Our Indians: What Civilization Is Doing to Extinguish an Ancient and Highly Intelligent Race by Taking Away Its Arts, Industries, and Religion." *Craftsman,* 11 (March 1907), 683-91.

———. "Picturing Indians with the Camera." *Photo-Era,* 25 (October 1910), 165-78.

Moon, Carl. "Photographing the Vanishing Red Man." *Leslie's* Illustrated, March 10, 1914.

Mooney, James. *The Ghost-Dance Religion and the Sioux Outbreak of 1890.* 1896. Edited by Anthony F. C. Wallace. New York: Dover Publications, 1972.

Morgan, Lewis H. *Ancient Society, or Researches in the Lines of Human Progress from Savagery through Barbarism to Civilization.* New York: Henry Holt and Co., 1877.

———. *The Indian Journals, 1859-62.* Edited by Leslie A. White. Ann Arbor: University of Michigan Press, 1959.

———. *League of the Ho-De-No Sau-Nee or Iroquois.* 1851. Reprint 2 vols. in 1. New Haven: Human Relations Area Files, 1954.

Morgan, Lewis H. "Letter to the Editor: The Hue-&-Cry Against the Indians." Dated Rochester, July 10, 1876. *Nation*, July 20, 1876, pp. 40-41.

———. "Montezuma's Dinner." Review of H. H. Bancroft, *Native Races of the Pacific States. North American Review*, 122 (1876), 265-308.

Morse, Rev. Jedidiah. *A Report to the Secretary of War of the United States on Indian Affairs Comprising a Narrative of a Tour Performed in the Summer of 1820*. New Haven: S. Converse, 1822.

Muir, John. *Our National Parks*. New York: Houghton Mifflin Co., 1901.

Myrtle, Minnie. *The Iroquois; or, The Bright Side of Indian Character*. New York: D. Appleton and Co., 1855.

Nelson, Edward William. "The Eskimo About Bering Strait." In *Bureau of American Ethnology Annual Report, 1896-97*. Washington: G.P.O., 1899.

Noble, Louis L. *The Course of Empire, Voyage of Life, and Other Pictures of Thomas Cole, N.A.* New York: Lamport, Blakeman and Law, 1853.

Norton, Charles Eliot; Parkman, Francis; and Agassiz, Alexander. "First Annual Report of the Executive Committee, with Accompanying Papers, 1879-80." In *Archaeological Institute of America*. Cambridge, Mass.: John Wilson and Co., 1880.

Norton, John. *The Journal of Major John Norton, 1816*. Edited by Carl F. Klinck and James J. Talman. Toronto: Champlain Society, 1970.

Nuttall, Thomas. *A Journal of Travels into the Arkansas Territory, During the Year 1819. . . .* 1821. Reprint as vol. 13 of Thwaites, ed., *Early Western Travels*.

O'Beirne, Harry F. *Leaders and Leading Men of the Indian Territory*. Vol. 1: *Choctaws and Chickasaws*. Chicago: American Publishers' Association, 1891.

Ogden, Peter Skene. *Peter Skene Ogden's Snake Country Journal, 1826-27*. Edited by K. G. Davies. With an introduction by Dorothy O. Johansen. Publications of The Hudson's Bay Record Society, 23. London: Hudson's Bay Record Society, 1961.

———. *Traits of American-Indian Life and Character by a Fur Trader*. London: Smith, Elder and Co., 1853.

Olmsted, Frederick Law. *The Papers of Frederick Law Olmsted*. Vol. 1: *The Formative Years, 1822 to 1852*. Edited by Charles Capen McLaughlin. Baltimore: Johns Hopkins University Press, 1977.

———. "The Yosemite Valley and the Mariposa Big Trees: A Preliminary Report (1865)." With introductory note by Laura Wood Roper. *Landscape Architecture*, 43 (October 1952), 12-25.

Pandosy, Rev. Marie Charles. *Grammar and Dictionary of the Yakama Language*. Translated and edited by George Gibbs and J. G. Shea. New York: Cramoisy Press, 1862.

Parkman, Francis. *The Conspiracy of Pontiac and the Indian War after the Conquest of Canada*. 1851. Vols. 16-18 of the Champlain Edition of *The Works of Francis Parkman*. Boston: Little, Brown and Co., 1898.

———. *The Jesuits in North America in the Seventeenth Century*. 1867. Vols. 3-4 of the Champlain Edition of *The Works of Francis Parkman*. Boston: Little, Brown and Co., 1897.

———. *The Oregon Trail: Sketches of Prairie and Rocky-Mountain Life*. 1849. Edited by E. N. Feltskog. Madison: University of Wisconsin Press, 1969.

———. "The Works of James Fenimore Cooper." *North American Review*, 74 (January 1852), 147-61.

Peters, Edward T. "Evils of Our Public Land Policy." *Century Magazine*, 25 (February 1883), 599-601.

"Petition to the Massachusetts Legislature," October, 1812. In *American Antiquarian Society Collections*, 1:17-18. Worcester, Mass., 1820.

Peyton, John Lewis. *Over the Alleghanies and Across the Prairies: Personal Recollections of the Far West*. London: Simpkin, Marshall and Co., 1869.

"Photographic Portraits of North American Indians in the Gallery of the Smithsonian Institution." *Smithsonian Miscellaneous Collections*, 14 (1867), 1-42.

Pilling, James Constantine. *Bibliography of the Chinookan Languages*. Washington: G.P.O., 1893.

———. *Bibliography of the Siouan Languages*. Bureau of American Ethnology, Bulletin 5. Washington: G.P.O., 1887.

Pourtalès, Count de. *On the Western Tour with Washington Irving: The Journal and Letters of Count de Pourtalès*. Edited by George F. Spaulding. Norman: University of Oklahoma Press, 1968.

Powell, G. W. "American Forests." *Harper's New Monthly Magazine*, 59 (August 1879), 371-74.

Powell, John Wesley. *Introduction to the Study of Indian Languages with Words Phrases and Sentences to be Collected*. 1877. 2d ed. Washington: G.P.O., 1880.

Powell, John Wesley. "Preface." *Bureau of Ethnology: Annual Reports*, 2 (1880-81).

———. *Selected Prose of John Wesley Powell*. Edited by George Crossette. Boston: David R. Godine, 1970.

———. "Sketch of Lewis Henry Morgan." *Popular Science Monthly*, November 1880, pp. 114-21.

Pratt, John Lowell, ed. *Currier and Ives: Chronicles of America*. Introduction by A. K. Baragwanath. Maplewood, N.J.: Hammond Inc., 1968.

Prudden, T. Mitchell. "An Elder Brother to the Cliff-Dwellers." *Harper's Monthly Magazine*, 95 (June 1897), 56-62.

Rafinesque, Constantine Samuel. *The Ancient Monuments of North and South America*. 2d ed. Philadelphia: n.p., 1838.

———. *A Life of Travels and Researches in North America and South Europe*. Philadelphia: n.p., 1836.

Ralph, Julian. "Frederic Remington." *Harper's Weekly*, 39 (July 20, 1895), 688.

Remington, Frederic. *Crooked Trails*. 1898. Reprint. Freeport, N.Y.: Books for Libraries Press, 1969.

———. "On the Indian Reservations." *Century Magazine*, 38 (July 1889), 394-405.

Review of "Catlin's North American Indians." *United States Magazine, and Democratic Review*, new ser., 11 (July 1892), 44-52.

Review of Exhibition of National Academy of Design. *Literary World*, May 15, 1847, pp. 347-48.

Review of Roosevelt, *Ranch Life and the Hunting Trail*. *Overland Monthly*, 2d ser., 28 (November 1896), 604.

Richardson, Albert D. *Beyond the Mississippi: From the Great River to the Great Ocean, Life and Adventure on the Prairies, Mountains, and Pacific Coast . . . 1857-1867*. Hartford, Conn.: American Publishing Co., 1867.

Riggs, Stephen R. *Dakota-English Dictionary*. 1852. Contributions to North American Ethnology, no. 7. Washington: G.P.O., 1897.

Robertson, S. C. "An Army Hunter's Notes on Our North-Western Game." *Outing*, 11 (January 1888), 302-09.

Robinson, Alfred. *Life in California*. New York: Wiley and Putnam, 1846.

Roehm, Marjorie Catlin, ed. *The Letters of George Catlin and His Family: A Chronicle of the American West*. Berkeley: University of California Press, 1966).

Roosevelt, Theodore. "Frontier Types." *Century Magazine*, 36 (October 1888), 832-43.

————. *Hunting Trips of a Ranchman/Hunting Trips on the Prairie and in the Mountains.* 1885. Reprint. New York: G. P. Putnam's Sons, 1905.

————. *The Letters of Theodore Roosevelt.* Edited by Elting E. Morison. 8 vols. Cambridge, Mass.: Harvard University Press, 1951.

————. "Ranch Life in the Far West." *Century Magazine,* 35 (February 1888), 495-510.

————. "The Ranchman's Rifle on Crag and Prairie." *Century Magazine,* 36 (June 1888), 200-212.

————. "Sheriff's Work on a Ranch." *Century Magazine,* 36 (May 1888), 39-51.

————, and Grinnell, George Bird, eds. *American Big-Game Hunting: The Book of the Boone and Crockett Club.* New York: Forest and Stream Publishing Co., 1893.

Ross, Alexander. *Adventures of the First Settlers on the Oregon or Columbia River* . . . 1849. Reprinted as vol. 7 of Thwaites, ed., *Early Western Travels.*

Rusling, James F. *Across America: Or, The Great West and the Pacific Coast.* New York: Sheldon and Co., 1874.

Russell, Osborne. *Journal of a Trapper.* . . . Edited by Aubrey L. Haines. Portland: Oregon Historical Society, 1955.

Ruxton, George Frederick. *Life in the Far West.* 1848. Edited by LeRoy R. Hafen. Norman: University of Oklahoma Press, 1951.

Sagard, Gabriel. *The Long Journey to the Country of the Hurons.* 1639. Translated by H. H. Langton. Edited by George M. Wrong. Toronto: Champlain Society, 1939.

Schoolcraft, Henry R. *Archives of Aboriginal Knowledge.* 6 vols. Philadelphia: J. B. Lippincott and Co., 1860.

————. *Narrative Journal of Travels Through the Northwestern Regions of the United States Extending from Detroit through the Great Chain of American Lakes to the Sources of the Mississippi River in the Year 1820.* 1821. Edited by Mentor Williams. East Lansing: Michigan State College Press, 1953.

————. *Schoolcraft's Indian Legends.* Edited by Mentor Williams. East Lansing: Michigan State University Press, 1956.

Schultz, James Willard [Apikuni]. *My Life as an Indian: The Story of a Red Woman and a White Man in the Lodge of the Blackfeet.* Boston: Houghton Mifflin Co., 1914. Serialized 1906-1907 in *Forest & Stream* as "In the Lodges of the Blackfeet."

Schurz, Carl. "Present Aspects of the Indian Problem." *North American Review,* 133 (July 1881), 1-24.

Schwatka, Frederick. "An Elk-Hunt on the Plains." *Century Magazine*, 35 (January 1888), 447-56.

Seton-Thompson, Ernest. *Wild Animals I Have Known*. New York: Charles Scribner's Sons, 1898.

Shinn, Charles Howard. "San Fernando Mission by Moonlight." *Land of Sunshine*, 2 (April 1895), 79-80.

Simms, William Gilmore. *Views and Reviews in American Literature, History and Fiction, First Series*. 1845. Edited by C. Hugh Holman. Cambridge, Mass.: Harvard University Press, 1962.

Simpson, Lt. James H. *Journal of a Military Reconnaissance from Santa Fé, New Mexico to the Navajo Country*. Philadelphia: Lippincott, Grambo and Co., 1852.

Snelling, William Joseph. *Tales of the Northwest*. 1830. Reprint. Minneapolis: University of Minnesota Press, 1936.

Speck, Frank G. *Decorative Art of Indian Tribes of Connecticut*. No. 10 Anthropological Series, Canada Department of Mines. Ottawa: G. P. Bureau, 1915.

Spencer, J. W. *Reminiscences of Pioneer Life in the Mississippi Valley*. 1872. Reprinted in Milo Milton Quaife, ed., *The Early Days of Rock Island and Davenport*, pp. 1-85. Chicago: R. R. Donnelley and Sons, 1942.

Spencer, Oliver M. *Indian Captivity*. 1835. Reprint. Ann Arbor: University Microfilms, 1966.

Sproat, Gilbert Malcolm. *Scenes and Studies of Savage Life*. London: Smith, Elder and Co., 1868.

Squier, Ephraim G. *Antiquities of the State of New York*. Buffalo: George H. Derby and Co., 1851.

————. *The Serpent Symbol*. American Archaeological Researches, no. 1. New York: George P. Putnam, 1851.

Stanley, John Mix. "Portraits of North American Indians with Sketches of Scenery, Etc." *Smithsonian Miscellaneous Collections*, 2 (1862), 1-76.

Starr, Frederick. *Notes upon the Ethnography of Southern Mexico*. 2 vols. Davenport, Ia.: Putnam Memorial Publication Fund, 1900-1902.

Stephen, Alexander M. *Hopi Journal of Alexander M. Stephen*. Edited by Elsie Clews Parsons. 2 vols. New York: Columbia University Press, 1936.

Stephens, John Lloyd. *Incidents of Travel in Central America, Chiapas, and Yucatan*. 1841. Edited by Richard L. Predmore. 2 vols. New Brunswick: Rutgers University Press, 1949.

————. *Incidents of Travel in Yucatan.* 2 vols. 1843. Reprint. New York: Dover Publications, 1963.

Stevenson, Matilda Coxe. *The Zuñi Indians: Their Mythology, Esoteric Fraternities, and Ceremonies.* 1905. Reprint. New York: Johnson Reprint Corp., 1970.

Stewart, Sir William Drummond. *Altowan; or Incidents of Life and Adventure in the Rocky Mountains by an Amateur Traveler.* Edited by J. Watson Webb. 2 vols. New York: Harper and Brothers, 1846.

Stillman, J.D.B. *Seeking the Golden Fleece; A Record of Pioneer Life in California.* San Francisco: A. Roman ad Co., 1877.

Stone, William L. *The Life and Times of Red-Jacket, or Sa-Go-Ye-Wat-Ha; Being the Sequel to the History of the Six Nations.* New York: Wiley and Putnam, 1841.

————. *Life of Joseph Brant—Thayendanegea, Including the Indian Wars of the American Revolution.* 2 vols. New York: George Dearborn and Co., 1838.

Stuart, Granville. *Forty Years on the Frontier as seen in the Journals and Reminiscences of Granville Stuart, Gold-Miner, Trader, Merchant, Rancher and Politician.* Edited by Paul C. Phillips. 2 vols. 1925. Reprint. Glendale, Calif.: Arthur H. Clark Co., 1957.

Swan, James G. *The Northwest Coast; or, Three Years' Residence in Washington Territory.* 1857. Reprint. With an introduction by Norman H. Clark. Seattle: University of Washington Press, 1969.

Sweet, Mrs. J. E. De Camp. "Mrs. J. E. De Camp Sweet's Narrative of Her Captivity in the Sioux Outbreak of 1862." *Collections of the Minnesota Historical Society,* 6 (1894), 354-80.

Tallent, Annie D. *The Black Hills; or, The Last Hunting Ground of Dakotahs.* St. Louis: Nixon-Jones, 1899.

Taylor, Bayard. *At Home and Abroad: A Sketch-Book of Life, Scenery, and Men.* 2d ser. New York: G. P. Putnam, 1862.

Taylor, Joseph Henry. *Sketches of Frontier and Indian Life.* Pottstown, Pa.: n.p., 1889.

Thwaites, Reuben Gold, ed. *Early Western Travels: 1748-1846.* 32 vols. Cleveland, Ohio: Arthur H. Clark Co., 1904-07.

Turner, O. *Pioneer History of the Holland Purchase of Western New York.* Buffalo: Jewett, Thomas and Co., 1849.

Victor, Mrs. Francis Fuller. *The River of the West: Life and Adventure in the Rocky Mountains and Oregon* Hartford, Conn.: R. W. Bliss and Co., 1869.

Vischer, Edward. *Sketches of the Washoe Mining Region: Photographs Reduced from Originals.* San Francisco: Valentine and Co., 1862.

Vischer's Pictorial of California: Landscape, Trees and Forest Scenes; Grand Features of California Scenery, Life, Traffic and Customs. 5 series of 12 numbers each. San Francisco: n.p., April 1870.

Volney, Constantin François Chasseboeuf. *A View of the Soil and Climate of the United States of America.* London: J. Johnson, 1804.

Vorphal, Ben Merchant, ed. *My Dear Wister: The Frederic Remington–Owen Wister Letters.* Palo Alto, Calif.: American West Publishing Co., 1972.

Waddle, W., Jr. "The Game Water-Fowl of America." *Harper's New Monthly Magazine,* 40 (February 1870), 433-37.

Wallace, Paul A. W., ed. *30,000 Miles with John Heckewelder.* Pittsburgh: University of Pittsburgh Press, 1958.

Whipple, Lt. Amiel Weeks. *Reports on Explorations and Surveys, To Ascertain the Most Practicable and Economical Route for a Railroad from the Mississippi River to the Pacific Ocean, 1853-4.* Senate Executive Documents, 33d Cong., 2d sess., 185?, vol. 3, no. 78, pt. 3, pp. 1-127.

White, Leslie A., ed. *Pioneers in American Anthropology: The Bandelier–Morgan Letters, 1873-1883.* 2 vols. Albuquerque: University of New Mexico Press, 1940.

Whitney, Ernest. *Legends of the Pike's Peak Region: The Sacred Myths of the Manitou.* Denver: Chain and Hardy Co., 1892.

"The Wilderness Hunter." *Atlantic Monthly,* 75 (June 1895), 826-30.

Willard, C. D. "The New Editor [Charles F. Lummis]. *Land of Sunshine,* 1 (December 1894), 12-13.

Williams, J. Fletcher. "A History of the City of Saint Paul and of the County of Ramsey, Minnesota." *Collections of the Minnesota Historical Society,* 4 (1876).

Williams, John S., ed. *The American Pioneer: A Monthly Periodical, Devoted to the Objects of the Logan Historical Society; or, To Collecting and Publishing Sketches Relative to the Early Settlement and Successive Improvement of the Country.* Cincinnati, Ohio. 1 (1842); 2 (January-October 1843).

Winter, George. *The Journals and Indian Paintings of George Winter, 1837-1839.* Indianapolis: Indiana Historical Society, 1948.

Wister, Owen. *Owen Wister Out West: His Journals and Letters.* Edited by Fanny Kemble Wister. Chicago: University of Chicago Press, 1958.

Wyeth, Nathaniel J. *The Journals of Captain Nathaniel J. Wyeth.* Fairfield, Wash.: Ye Galleon Press, 1969.

Secondary

Ackerknecht, Erwin H. " 'White Indians': Psychological and Physiological Peculiarities of White Children Abducted and Reared by North American Indians." *Bulletin of the History of Medicine,* 15 (January 1944), 15-36.

Apostol, Jane. "Francis of the Flowers: An Appreciation of Charles Francis Saunders." *California History,* 58 (Spring 1979), 38-47.

———. "Saving Grace." *Westways,* 68 (October 1976), 22-24, 71-72.

Arnold, Robert D. *Alaska Native Land Claims.* Anchorage: Alaska Native Foundation, 1976.

Baird, James. *Ishmael: A Study of the Symbolic Mode in Primitivism.* New York: Harper and Brothers, 1956.

Barlow, Elizabeth. *Frederic Law Olmsted's New York.* New York: Praeger, 1972.

Barnett, Louise K. *The Ignoble Savage: American Literary Racism, 1790-1890.* Contributions in American Studies, no. 18. Westport, Conn.: Greenwood Press, 1975.

Bartlett, Richard A. *Nature's Yellowstone.* Albuquerque: University of New Mexico Press, 1974.

Berkhofer, Robert F., Jr. *Salvation and the Savage: An Analysis of Protestant Missions and American Indian Response, 1787-1862.* Lexington: University Press of Kentucky, 1965.

———. *The White Man's Indian: Images of the American Indian from Columbus to the Present.* New York: Alfred A. Knopf, 1978.

Bickerstaff, Laura M. *Pioneer Artists of Taos.* Denver: Sage Books, 1955.

Bidney, David. "The Concept of Value in Modern Anthropology." In A. L. Kroeber, ed., *Anthropology Today: An Encyclopedic Inventory,* pp. 682-94. Chicago: University of Chicago Press, 1953.

———. "The Idea of the Savage in North American Ethnohistory." *Journal of the History of Ideas,* 15 (April 1954), 322-27.

Borden, Philip. "Found Cumbering the Soil: Manifest Destiny and the Indian in the Nineteenth Century." In Nash and Weiss, eds., *The Great Fear.*

Brandon, William. *The Last Americans: The Indian in American Culture.* New York: McGraw-Hill, 1974.

Brown, Mark H., and Felton, W. R. *Before Barbed Wire: L. A. Huffman, Photographer on Horseback.* 1956. Reprint. New York: Bramhall House, 1961.

Brown, Mark H., and Felton, W. R. *The Frontier Years: L. A. Huffman, Photographer of the Plains.* New York: Bramhall House, 1955.

Butterfield, Lyman H. "Draper's Predecessors and Contemporaries." In Donald R. McNeil, ed., *The American Collector*, p. 16. Madison: State Historical Society of Wisconsin, 1955.

Callcott, George H. *History in the United States, 1800-1860, Its Practice and Purpose.* Baltimore: Johns Hopkins University Press, 1970.

Carter, Everett. *The American Idea: The Literary Response to American Optimism.* Chapel Hill: University of North Carolina Press, 1977.

Caughey, John Walton. *Hubert Howe Bancroft, Historian of the West.* Berkeley: University of California Press, 1946.

Ceram, C. W. [Kurt W. Marek]. *The First American: A Study of North American Archaeology.* New York: Harcourt Brace Jovanovich, 1971.

Cikovsky, Nicolai, Jr. " 'The Ravages of the Axe': The Meaning of the Tree Stump in Nineteenth Century American Art." *Art Bulletin*, 61 (December 1979), 611-26.

Coke, Van Deren. *Taos and Santa Fe: The Artist's Environment, 1882-1942.* Albuquerque: University of New Mexico Press, 1963.

Cunliffe, Marcus. "American Watersheds." *American Quarterly*, 13 (Winter 1961), 480-94.

Curry, Larry. *The American West: Painters from Catlin to Russell.* New York: Viking, 1972.

Cutright, Paul Russell. *Lewis and Clark: Pioneering Naturalists.* Urbana: University of Illinois Press, 1969.

Dahl, Curtis. "The American School of Catastrophe." *American Quarterly*, 11 (Fall 1959), 380-90.

———. "Mound-Builders, Mormons, and William Cullen Bryant." *New England Quarterly*, 34 (June 1961), 178-90.

Darrah, William Culp. *Powell of the Colorado.* Princeton: Princeton University Press, 1951.

DeVoto, Bernard. *Across the Wide Missouri.* Boston: Houghton Mifflin Co., 1947.

Dippie, Brian William. "The Vanishing American: Popular Attitudes and American Indian Policy in the Nineteenth Century." Ph.D. diss., University of Texas, Austin, 1970.

Dobyns, Winifred Starr. "A Treasure House." *Woman Citizen*, 56, old ser. (December 1927), 12-14.

Doughty, Howard. *Francis Parkman.* New York: Macmillan Co., 1962.

Dozier, Edward P. "Resistance to Acculturation and Assimilation in an Indian Pueblo." *American Anthropologist,* 53 (January-March 1951), 56-66.

Drinnon, Richard. *White Savage: The Case of John Dunn Hunter.* New York: Schocken Books, 1972.

Dudley, Edward, and Novak, Maximillian E., eds. *The Wild Man Within: An Image in Western Thought from the Renaissance to Romanticism.* Pittsburgh: University of Pittsburgh Press, 1972.

Elson, Ruth Miller. *Guardians of Tradition: American Schoolbooks of the Nineteenth Century.* Lincoln: University of Nebraska Press, 1964.

Ewers, John C. *Artists of the Old West.* Garden City, N.Y.: Double-day and Co., 1965.

———. "Fact and Fiction in the Documentary Art of the American West." In John Francis McDermott, ed., *The Frontier Re-examined,* pp. 79-95. Urbana: University of Illinois Press, 1967.

———. "Jean Louis Berlandier: A French Scientist among the Wild Comanches of Texas in 1828." In McDermott, ed., *Travelers on the Western Frontier,* pp. 290-300.

———. "When Red and White Men Meet." *Western Historical Quarterly,* 2 (April 1971), 133-50.

Fagan, Brian M. *Elusive Treasure: The Story of Early Archaeologists in the Americas.* New York: Charles Scribner's Sons, 1977.

Fairbanks, Jonathan L. Introduction to *Frontier America: The Far West,* pp. 13-23. Boston: Museum of Fine Arts, 1975.

Fein, Albert. *Frederick Law Olmsted and the American Environmental Tradition.* New York: George Braziller, 1972.

Francis, Rell G. "Views of Mormon Country: The Life and Photographs of George Edward Anderson." *American West,* 15 (November-December 1978), 14-29.

Fritz, Henry E. *The Movement for Indian Assimilation, 1860-1890.* Philadelphia: University of Pennsylvania Press, 1963.

Fuess, Claude Moore. *Carl Schurz: Reformer (1829-1906).* New York: Dodd, Mead and Co., 1932.

Geertz, Clifford. " 'From the Native's Point of View': On the Nature of Anthropological Understanding." In Keith H. Basso and Henry A. Selby, eds., *Meaning in Anthropology,* pp. 221-37. Albuquerque: University of New Mexico Press, 1976.

———. *The Interpretation of Cultures: Selected Essays.* New York: Basic Books, 1973.

Geske, Norman A. "Ralph Albert Blakelock in the West." *American Art Review,* 3 (January-February 1976), 123-35.

Glacken, Clarence J. "Changing Ideas of the Habitable World." In William L. Thomas, ed., *Man's Role in Changing the Face of the Earth*, pp. 70-92. Chicago: University of Chicago Press, 1956.

Goetzmann, William. *Exploration and Empire: The Explorer and the Scientist in the Winning of the American West*. New York: Alfred A. Knopf, 1966.

Gordon, Dudley C. *Charles F. Lummis: Crusader in Corduroy*. Los Angeles: Cultural Assets Press, 1972.

Graybill, Florence Curtis, and Boesen, Victor. *Edward Sheriff Curtis: Visions of a Vanishing Race*. New York: Thomas Y. Crowell, 1976.

Haley, J. Evetts. *Life on the Texas Range*. With photographs by Erwin E. Smith. Austin: University of Texas Press, 1952.

Hampton, H. Duane. *How the U.S. Cavalry Saved Our National Parks*. Bloomington: Indiana University Press, 1971.

Harmsen, Dorothy. *Harmsen's Western Americana: A Collection of One Hundred Western Paintings with Biographical Profiles of the Artists*. Flagstaff: Northland Press, 1971.

Harper, J. Russell, ed. *Paul Kane's Frontier*. Austin: University of Texas Press, 1971.

Hassrick, Peter. *The Way West: Art of Frontier America*. New York: Harry N. Abrams, 1977.

Hassrick, Royal. *George Catlin Book of American Indians*. New York: Watson-Guptill, 1977.

Heard, J. Norman. *White into Red: A Study of the Assimilation of White Persons Captured by Indians*. Metuchen, N.J.: Scarecrow Press, 1973.

Hesseltine, William B. *Pioneer's Mission: The Story of Lyman Copeland Draper*. Madison: State Historical Society of Wisconsin, 1954.

Hine, Robert V. *Bartlett's West: Drawing the Mexican Boundary*. New Haven: Yale University Press, 1968.

———. *Edward Kern and American Expansion*. New Haven: Yale University Press, 1962.

Hoover, Dwight W. *The Red and the Black*. Chicago: Rand McNally, 1976.

Horan, James D. *The McKenney-Hall Portrait Gallery of American Indians*. New York: Crown, 1972.

Huth, Hans. *Nature and the American: Three Centuries of Changing Attitudes*. Berkeley: University of California Press, 1957.

———. "Yosemite: The Story of an Idea." *Sierra Club Bulletin*, 33 (March 1948), 47-78.

Jackson, Clarence S. *Picture Maker of the Old West: William H. Jackson.* New York: Bonanza Books, 1947.

Jacobs, Wilbur R. "The Indian and the Frontier in American History—A Need for Revision." *Western Historical Quarterly,* 4 (January 1973), 43-56.

———. "The Tip of an Iceberg: Pre-Columbian Indian Demography and Some Implications for Revisionism." *William and Mary Quarterly,* 3d ser., 31 (January 1974), 123-32.

Johnson, Gerald W. *Mount Vernon: The Story of a Shrine.* New York: Random House, 1953.

Judd, Neil M. *The Bureau of American Ethnology: A Partial History.* Norman: University of Oklahoma Press, 1967.

Keen, Benjamin. *The Aztec Image in Western Thought.* New Brunswick: Rutgers University Press, 1971.

Kennedy, John Hopkins. *Jesuit and Savage in New France.* New Haven: Yale University Press, 1950.

Kroeber, A. L. *Anthropology: Race, Language, Culture, Psychology, Prehistory.* Rev. ed. New York: Harcourt, Brace and Co., 1948.

Kroeber, Theodora. *Ishi in Two Worlds: A Biography of the Last Wild Indian in North America.* 1961. Reprint. Berkeley: University of California Press, 1971.

Kurutz, Gary F. "Pictorial Resources: The Henry E. Huntington Library's California and American West Collections." *California Historical Quarterly,* 54 (Summer 1975), 175-82.

Leonard, Thomas. *Above the Battle: War-Making in America from Appomattox to Versailles.* New York: Oxford University Press, 1978.

Lévi-Strauss, Claude. *The Scope of Anthropology.* Translated by Sherry Ortner Paul and Robert A. Paul. London: Jonathan Cape, 1967.

Lillard, Richard. *The Great Forest.* New York: Alfred A. Knopf, 1947.

Lopez, Barry. "The Photographer." *North American Review,* 262 (Fall 1977), 66-67.

Lowenthal, David. *George Perkins Marsh: Versatile Vermonter.* New York: Columbia University Press, 1958.

McCloskey, Maxine E., and Gilligan, James P., eds. *Wilderness and the Quality of Life.* New York: Sierra Club, 1969.

McCracken, Harold. *The Charles M. Russell Book: The Life and Work of the Cowboy Artist.* Garden City, N.Y.: Doubleday and Co., 1957.

McCracken, Harold. *Frederic Remington: Artist of the Old West.* Philadelphia: J. B. Lippincott Co., 1947.

———. *George Catlin and the Old Frontier.* New York: Bonanza Books, 1959.

McDermott, John Francis. *Seth Eastman: Pictorial Historian of the Indian.* Norman: University of Oklahoma Press, 1961.

———. *Seth Eastman's Mississippi: A Lost Portfolio Recovered.* Urbana: University of Illinois Press, 1973.

———, ed. *Travelers on the Western Frontier.* Urbana: University of Illinois Press, 1970.

Mahood, Ruth I., ed. *Photographer of the Southwest: Adam Clark Vroman, 1856-1919.* N.p.: Ward Ritchie Press, 1961.

Mardock, Robert Winston. *The Reformers and the American Indian.* Columbia: University of Missouri Press, 1971.

Mason, J. Alden. *George J. Heye, 1874-1957.* Leaflets of the American Indian Heye Foundation, no. 6. New York, 1958.

Matthiessen, Peter. "How to Kill a Valley." *New York Review of Books,* February 7, 1980, pp. 31-36.

Miller, Perry. "The Romantic Dilemma in American Nationalism and the Concept of Nature." *Harvard Theological Review,* 48 (October 1955), 239-53.

Mosier, Richard D. *Making the American Mind: Social and Moral Ideas in the McGuffey Readers.* New York: Columbia University Press, 1947.

Murphree, Idus L. "The Evolutionary Anthropologists: The Progress of Mankind. The Concepts of Progress and Culture in the Thought of John Lubbuck, Edward B. Tylor, and Lewis H. Morgan." *Proceedings of the American Philosophical Society,* 105 (June 1961), 265-300.

Nash, Gary B. "The Image of the Indian in the Southern Colonial Mind." *William and Mary Quarterly,* 3d ser., 29 (April 1972), 197-230.

———, and Weiss, Richard, eds. *The Great Fear: Race in the Mind of America.* New York: Holt, Rinehart and Winston, 1970.

Nash, Roderick. "The American Invention of National Parks." *American Quarterly,* 22 (Fall 1970), 726-35.

———. *Wilderness and the American Mind.* Rev. ed. New Haven: Yale University Press, 1973.

———, ed. *The American Environment: Readings in the History of Conservation.* 2d ed. Reading, Mass.: Addison-Wesley, 1976.

Northrop, F.S.C. "Man's Relation to the Earth in Its Bearing on His Aesthetic, Ethical, and Legal Values." In William L. Thomas, ed., *Man's Role in Changing the Face of the Earth*, pp. 1052-67. Chicago: University of Chicago Press, 1956.

Novak, Barbara. *American Painting of the Nineteenth Century: Realism, Idealism, and the American Experience.* New York: Praeger, 1969.

Olson, Victoria Thomas. "Pioneer Conservationist A. P. Hill: 'He Saved the Redwoods.'" *American West*, 14 (September-October 1977), 32-40.

Ong, Walter J., S.J. "World as View and World as Event." *American Anthropologist*, 71 (August 1969), 634-47.

Packard, Gar, and Packard, Maggy. *Southwest 1880: With Ben Wittick, Pioneer Photographer of Indian and Frontier Life.* With photographs from the Museum of New Mexico. Santa Fe: Packard Publications, 1970.

Parker, Franklin. *George Peabody: A Biography.* Nashville: Vanderbilt University Press, 1971.

Parry, Ellwood. *The Image of the Indian and the Black Man in American Art, 1590-1900.* New York: George Braziller, 1974.

Pearce, Roy Harvey. *Savagism and Civilization: A Study of the American Mind.* Baltimore: Johns Hopkins University Press, 1965.

Pinkett, Harold T. *Gifford Pinchot: Private and Public Forester.* Urbana: University of Illinois Press, 1970.

Pipes, Nellie B. "John Mix Stanley, Indian Painter." *Oregon Historical Quarterly*, 33 (September 1932), 250-58.

Poesch, Jessie. *Titian Ramsey Peale and His Journals of the Wilkes Expedition, 1799-1885.* Philadelphia: American Philosophical Society, 1961.

Pomeroy, Earl. *In Search of the Golden West: The Tourist in Western America.* New York: Alfred A. Knopf, 1957.

Prucha, Francis Paul, S.J., ed. *Americanizing the American Indians: Writings by the "Friends of the Indian" 1880-1900.* Cambridge, Mass.: Harvard University Press, 1973.

Rathbone, Perry T. *Charles Wimar, 1828-1862: Painter of the Indian Frontier.* St. Louis: City Art Museum, 1946.

Reiger, John F. *American Sportsmen and the Origins of Conservation.* New York: Winchester Press, 1975.

Resek, Carl. *Lewis Henry Morgan: American Scholar.* Chicago: University of Chicago Press, 1960.

Ringe, Donald A. *The Pictorial Mode: Space and Time in the Art of Bryant, Irving, and Cooper.* Lexington: University Press of Kentucky, 1971.

Rodgers, Andrew Denny, III. *Bernhard Eduard Fernow: The Story of North American Forestry.* Princeton: Princeton University Press, 1951.

Roper, Laura Wood. *FLO: A Biography of Frederick Law Olmsted.* Baltimore: Johns Hopkins University Press, 1973.

Rudisill, Richard. *Mirror Image: The Influence of the Daguerreotype on American Society.* Albuquerque: University of New Mexico Press, 1971.

Runte, Alfred. *National Parks: The American Experience.* Lincoln: University of Nebraska Press, 1979.

Saum, Lewis O. *The Fur Trader and the Indian.* Seattle: University of Washington Press, 1965.

Scherer, Joanna Cohan. *Indians: The Great Photographs that Reveal North American Indian Life, 1847-1929, from the Unique Collection of the Smithsonian Institution.* New York: Crown, 1973.

Shankland, Robert. *Steve Mather of the National Parks.* New York: Alfred A. Knopf, 1951.

Sheehan, Bernard W. *Seeds of Extinction: Jeffersonian Philanthropy and the American Indian.* New York: W. W. Norton, 1973.

Silverberg, Robert. *Mound Builders of Ancient America: The Archaeology of a Myth.* Greenwich, Conn.: New York Graphic Society, 1968.

Smith, Jane F., and Krasnicka, Robert M., eds. *Indian-White Relations: A Persistent Paradox.* Washington: Howard University Press, 1976.

Somkin, Fred. *Unquiet Eagle: Memory and Desire in the Idea of American Freedom, 1815-1860.* Ithaca: Cornell University Press, 1967.

Spengemann, William C. *The Adventurous Muse: The Poetics of American Fiction, 1789-1900.* New Haven: Yale University Press, 1977.

Spicer, Edward H. *Cycles of Conquest: The Impact of Spain, Mexico, and the United States on the Indians of the Southwest, 1533-1960.* Tucson: University of Arizona Press, 1962.

Stanton, William. *The Leopard's Spots: Scientific Attitudes toward Race in America, 1815-59.* Chicago: University of Chicago Press, 1960.

Starr, Kevin. *Americans and the California Dream, 1850-1915.* New York: Oxford University Press, 1973.

Steward, Julian. "Evolution and Process." In A. L. Kroeber, ed., *Anthropology Today: An Encyclopedic Inventory,* pp. 313-26. Chicago: University of Chicago Press, 1953.

Stocking, George W., Jr. *Race, Culture, and Evolution: Essays in the History of Anthropology.* New York: Free Press, 1968.

Strong, Douglas H. "The Sierra Club—A History. Part I: Origins and Outings." *Sierra,* October 1977, pp. 10-14.

———. "The Sierra Club—A History. Part II: Conservation." *Sierra,* November-December 1977, pp. 16-20.

Sturhahn, Joan. *Carvalho: Artist—Photographer—Adventurer—Patriot: Portrait of a Forgotten American.* Merrick, N.Y.: Richwood Publishing Co., 1976.

Swain, Donald C. *Federal Conservation Policy, 1921-1933.* University of California Publications in History, 76. Los Angeles: University of California Press, 1963.

———. *Wilderness Defender: Horace M. Albright and Conservation.* Chicago: University of Chicago Press, 1970.

Swanton, John R. "Notes on the Menal Assimilation of Races." *Journal of the Washington Academy of Sciences,* 16 (November 1926), 493-502.

Taft, Robert. *Artists and Illustrators of the Old West 1850-1900.* New York: Charles Scribner's Sons, 1953.

———. *Photography and the American Scene: A Social History, 1839-1889.* New York: Macmillan Co., 1938.

Ten Kate, Herman. "On Paintings of North American Indians and Their Ethnological Value." *Anthropos,* 7 (1911), 521-45.

Tilden, Freeman. *Following the Frontier with F. Jay Haynes: Pioneer Photographer of the Old West.* New York: Alfred A. Knopf, 1964.

Trennert, Robert A., Jr. *Alternative to Extinction: Federal Indian Policy and the Beginnings of the Reservation System, 1846-51.* Philadelphia: Temple University Press, 1975.

Trenton, Patricia. "Picturesque Images of Taos and Santa Fe." *American Art Review,* 1 (March-April 1974), 96-111.

Udall, Stewart L. *The Quiet Crisis.* New York: Avon, 1963.

Utley, Robert M. *Frontiersmen in Blue: The United States Army and the Indian, 1848-1865.* New York: Macmillan Co., 1967.

Viola, Herman J. "How *Did* an Indian Chief Really Look?" *Smithsonian,* 8 (June 1977), 100-104.

———. *The Indian Legacy of Charles Bird King.* Smithsonian Institution Press, 1976.

Von Hagan, Victor. *Maya Explorer: John Lloyd Stephens.* Norman: University of Oklahoma Press, 1947

Washburn, Wilcomb E. *Red Man's Land/White Man's Law: A Study of the Past and Present Status of the American Indian.* New York: Charles Scribner's Sons, 1971.

Way, Ronald L. *Ontario's Niagara Parks: A History.* Niagara: Niagara Parks Commission, 1946.

Webb, William, and Weinstein, Robert A. *Dwellers at the Source: Southwestern Indian Photographs of A. C. Vroman, 1895-1904.* New York: Grossman, 1973.

White, G. Edward. *The Eastern Establishment and the Western Experience: The West of Frederic Remington, Theodore Roosevelt, and Owen Wister.* New Haven: Yale University Press, 1968.

Wilkinson, Kristina. "Frederick Monsen, F.R.G.S.: Explorer and Ethnographer." *Noticias,* Summer 1969, pp. 16-23.

Williams, Stanley T. *The Life of Washington Irving.* 2 vols. New York: Oxford University Press, 1935.

Willoughby, Charles C. "The Peabody Museum of Archaeology and Ethnology, Harvard University." *Harvard Graduates' Magazine,* 31 (June 1923), 495-503.

Zolla, Elémire. *The Writer and the Shaman: A Morphology of the American Indian.* 1969. Translated by Raymond Rosenthal. New York: Harcourt Brace Jovanovich, 1973.

INDEX

Library of Congress Cataloging in Publication Data

Mitchell, Lee Clark, 1957-
    Witnesses to a vanishing America.

    Bibliography: p.
    Includes index.
    1. Nature conservation—United States—History.   2. Conservation of
natural resources—United States—History.   3. Frontier and pioneer life—
United States—History.   I. Title.
QH76.M54   333.95'0973   80-8567
ISBN 0-691-06461-X

Black Africa

Black Africa
A Comparative Handbook

Donald George Morrison
Robert Cameron Mitchell
John Naber Paden
Hugh Michael Stevenson

with

Lynn F. Fisher

Joseph Kaufert

Kenneth E. Larimore

C. William Schweers, Jr.

The Free Press, New York

Collier-Macmillan Ltd., London

Copyright © 1972 by The Free Press
A Division of The Macmillan Company

Printed in the United States of America

The Free Press
A Division of The Macmillan Company
866 Third Avenue, New York, New York 10022

Collier–Macmillan Canada Ltd., Toronto, Ontario

Library of Congress Catalog Card Number: 72–143505

printing number

1 2 3 4 5 6 7 8 9 10

Abbreviated Table of Contents

Detailed Table of Contents

PART III Cross-National Research on Africa: Issues and Context   383

Types of political integration; the organization of the data; data omissions; the colonial legacy: a problem in comparing African nations; theory and research

2 Comparative Analysis of African Nations: On the Uses and Limitations of Cross-National Data
Nations as units of analysis in comparative research; the problem of unit equivalence; the equivalence of nations; the development of African nations; Africa and cross-national comparisons; five approaches to cross-national analysis; methodological issues in cross-national generalization

The nature of reliability; source reliability; reliability assessment; conclusion

List of Abbreviations

Africa   Jeune Afrique. *Africa* New York: Africana, annual.

Africa Contemporary Record   Colin Legum and John Drysdale, eds. *Africa Contemporary Record: Annual Survey and Documents.* Exeter, England: Africa Research Limited, annual.

AID Economic Data Book   United States Agency for International Development. Office of Program and Policy Division. *AID Economic Data Book: Africa.* AID 3/00/0309. Washington, D.C.: Clearinghouse, December 1967. Subsequent editions issued irregularly and noted by date.

Démographie Comparée   Francis Gendreau. *Centres Urbains.* Afrique Noire, Madagascar, Comores, démographie comparée, vol. 2. Paris: Délégation Générale Recherche Scientifique et Technique, 1966.

ECA Statistical Bulletin   United Nations, Economic Commission for Africa. *Statistical Bulletin for Africa.* No. 2. Three parts. Addis Ababa: Economic Commission for Africa, March 1967.

Étude Monographique   *Étude Monographique de trente et un pays africains.* 4 vols. Paris: Union Africaine et Malgache de Coopération Économique, 1964.

Europa Yearbook   *The Europa Yearbook.* Vol. 2, Africa, London: Europa Publications, annual.

Overseas Business Reports 1966   *Overseas Business Reports.* Washington, D.C.: Bureau of Commerce, 1966. Issued separately by country.

Statesman's Yearbook   S. H. Steinberg, ed. *Statesman's Year-Book.* New York: St. Martin's Press, annual.

UA   *Urban Agglomeration.*

UN Demographic Yearbook   United Nations. *Demographic Yearbook.* New York: United Nations, annual.

UN Statistical Yearbook   United Nations. *Statistical Yearbook.* New York: United Nations, annual.

UNESCO Statistical Yearbook   United Nations Educational, Scientific and Cultural Organization. *Statistical Yearbook.* Paris: UNESCO, annual.

World Bank Atlas   International Bank for Reconstruction and Finance. *World Bank Atlas: Population, Per Capita Product and Growth Rates.* Washington, D.C.: International Bank for Reconstruction and Finance, annual.

List of Tables and Figures

Preface

This Handbook presents in a clear and readily accessible form the latest comparable information available (up to publication time) for 32 independent black African nations. We have culled from a wide variety of sources the most reliable data describing the political, economic, and social dimensions of these new nations. We have made every effort to give the data sources so that the student preparing a paper, the scholar undertaking a cross-national study, or the civil servant or businessman writing a report can utilize the data or pursue the topic further. As a further help we include a map and a selected bibliography for each of the 32 countries.

The idea for this Handbook occurred a few years ago when one of the co-authors took a course in African urbanization. The instructor asked several students to undertake a report on a cross-national analysis of the relationship of urbanization in African countries to such factors as area, population size, former colonial rule, and national income per capita. The students quickly found that they were unable to do a satisfactory job on the assignment because the existing general comparative data handbooks such as those authored by Russett,[1] Banks and Textor,[2] and Ginsberg[3] did not have enough data on Africa, or their data on Africa was ill-suited to regional comparison. Only a few African countries were covered in publications available at that time since only a few nations on the continent had been independent for any length of time; most were only recently independent; and data for Africa was given in a scaled form based upon a distribution for the world so that, on measures of urbanization, for example, black African countries fell uniformly into the same category: "low." Surely studies of world social and political patterns needed to include the African states if they were to be truly comprehensive, and surely the data was available if only researchers had the time and access to a good library to compile it. Since the Northwestern University Africana Library is one of the foremost collections of material on Black Africa, the situation seemed remediable.

It was in this conviction that we began in 1967 a study of national integration and political stability in Black Africa, for which we hoped to utilize the hospitable combination of inter-disciplinary, inter-societal, and African studies offered by the Council for Intersocietal Studies and the Program of African Studies at Northwestern University. The senior authors of this book have been trained in diverse intellectual traditions: economics and applied mathematics (Morrison), sociology (Mitchell), and political science (Paden and Stevenson), and each of us has lived and worked in Africa, as have all the junior authors of the book. It was from this generalized commitment to social science and comparative studies, and involvement and concern with political development in Africa, that this Handbook took shape.

The integration of nation-states and their political stability is important to us not because we see intrinsic value in either nation-states or established governments, but because we believe that the quality of life and the degree of freedom available to the individual are critically restricted by violent political conflicts and coercive national governments. To what extent such restrictions follow from or precede particular kinds of political instability, and to what extent they are contingent on the wider social, economic, and political structure of the nation-state itself are questions that we hope can begin to be answered with the help of data such as those presented in this Handbook. In this regard, we have been encouraged by African statesmen and social scientists to view national integration as one of the two major research priorities in Africa (the other is economic development). The cost of this project has been met by Ford Foundation grants to the Council for Intersocietal Studies and the Program of African Studies at Northwestern University—partly in response to the requests from African universities for more "relevant" research by American social scientists.

The importance of social science in the consideration of problems of political development is not that it avoids the questions of value or ideology in the definition of problems in social life, but that it makes public its criteria for problem selection and its criteria for problem solving. One of the purposes of this Handbook is to suggest that "facts" are inevitably based on social perception, theoretical screening, and construction of statistical indices, and we have tried to indicate clearly our theoretical and methodological interpretation of the observations we report here.

In their *original* form, the data summarized in this book are public information to be found in diverse scholarly journals, books, government publications, United Nations' documents, and reference works. There is nothing in this volume that is not already known to governments, corporations, and individuals who have interests other than our own, but our intention has been to make this information easily available to, and easily usable by, individuals who do not have the resources or interests of governments.

Prefaces are most efficiently constructed when the important business of thanking those who have assisted in the preparation of a book is dismissed with rapid, but loyal, mention of employers, friends, and family, and with riders to the effect that the names of those to whom debts are owed are "too numerous to mention," and that "responsibility falls to the author alone." In the case of this book, the names of the authors are probably too numerous to mention, but since we have mentioned so many names on the title page alone, we shall attempt to be as informative as possible about the many contributions made to this handbook.

For any project which has been as intimate as this in terms of personal relationships, intellectual stimulation, and the paucity of physical space, the allocation of authorship is an invidious task. Time spent on the job seems as useful a guide to selection as the more appropriate, but impossible, evaluation of the quality of intellectual contributions. Following this principle, the senior authors have broken with the honorable practice of alphabetizing their nomination in order to indicate the especially burdensome administrative work load assumed by Donald Morrison. Further, the junior authors are junior only in the sense that their work on the project was more limited in historical time. One who

should probably rank as the single senior author of the book if we stuck more resolutely to our rule, and, perhaps if women's liberation were more advanced at this time, is our secretary Janice Caplan, whose contribution has been inestimable both in terms of time and quality.

Very important contributions have been made to the collection of data reported here by others whose work, following our rule, cannot be individually credited, but to whom much of any credit given the authors belongs: Vaughn Bishop, Virginia Chene, Richard Klimala, George Martens, Marcia Muldrow, Elone Nwabuzor, Harry Ododa, Oscar Rosenblum, Norman Rothman, Frank Stark, and Mary Welfling.

In addition, there has been a legion of capable people, whose more active extra-project life kept us from exploiting them more, but whose skills greatly improved this book: Mary Aitkin, Judy Ashton, Cathie Boccio, Jan Carstin, Rick Cunningham, Mike Ford, Richard Greenfield, Laura Helrung, Nancy Johnson, Kim Nuzzo, Debbie Pellow, Debbie Phillips, Anne Potter, Nicholas Reynolds, Amos Sawyer, Gus Stevens, Mary Weber, and Barbara Yagerman.

A number of our colleagues at other colleges and universities have read portions of the manuscript and offered us their critical comments: an indispensable service for a Handbook of this kind. We are indebted to Lucy C. Behrman (University of Pennsylvania), A. A. Castagno (Boston University), William Foltz (Yale University), David Gardinier (Marquette University), Svend Holsoe (University of Delaware), Ronald J. Horvath (University of California, Santa Barbara), George Jenkins, Michael W. Kuhn (University of California, Santa Barbara), Faye Leary (Temple University), René Lemarchand (University of Florida), Raoul Naroll (State University of New York, Buffalo), Barry Riddell (Queens University, Ontario), Marc Ross (Bryn Mawr College), Robert I. Rotberg (Massachusetts Institute of Technology), Richard L. Sklar (University of California, Los Angeles), Jan Vansina (University of Wisconsin), and M. Crawford Young (University of Wisconsin).

Our colleagues at Northwestern and Swarthmore have been exceptionally patient and helpful in meeting our numerous requests for help, and we are grateful to Clement Cottingham, Remi Clignet, Maurice Goodman, Raymond F. Hopkins, Asmaron Legesse (now at Boston University), Raymond Moses, Edward Soja, Richard Spears, Howard Williams, and Hans Panovsky and his colleagues in the Africana Library at Northwestern University. Donald G. Campbell provided financial support for Donald Morrison, in addition to his useful methodological advice. Finally, this Handbook could not have come to be were it not for the help of Richard D. Schwartz and Gwendolen M. Carter. Professor Schwartz, former Director of Northwestern's Council for Intersocietal Studies (now Dean of the Law School, State University of New York at Buffalo), enthusiastically encouraged the project at its inception and throughout its subsequent development, and his Council has borne the major financial burden of our activities. The Program of African Studies at Northwestern provided an essential scholarly environment at all stages of our work, and Professor Carter, the program's director, was most generous in providing the financial support which has made the preparation of this manuscript possible.

DGM
RCM
JNP
HMS

Notes

1 Bruce M. Russett, et al., *World Handbook of Political and Social Indicators* (New Haven, Conn.: Yale University Press, 1964).

2 Arthur S. Banks and Robert Textor, *A Cross-Polity Survey* (Cambridge, Mass.: Massachusetts Institute of Technology Press, 1963).

3 Norton Ginsburg, ed., *Atlas of Economic Development* (Chicago: University of Chicago Press, 1961).

Introduction

Background on Black Africa

Since January 1, 1956, when Sudan became an independent nation, thirty-one other black African nations have celebrated the end of colonial rule. Together with the ancient Kingdom of Ethiopia and the century-old Republic of Liberia these new nations have brought Black Africa dramatically into the world's consciousness.

TABLE 1 Date of Independence of the Thirty-Four Independent Black African States

Country	Date of Independence
Ethiopia	Ancient Kingdom
Liberia	July 26, 1847
Sudan	Jan. 1, 1956
Ghana	Mar. 6, 1957
Guinea	Oct. 2, 1958
Cameroon	Jan. 1, 1960
Togo	Apr. 27, 1960
Zaire (Congo-Kinshasa)	June 30, 1960
Somalia	July 1, 1960
Dahomey	Aug. 1, 1960
Niger	Aug. 3, 1960
Upper Volta	Aug. 5, 1960
Ivory Coast	Aug. 7, 1960
Chad	Aug. 11, 1960
Central African Republic	Aug. 13. 1960
Congo (Brazzaville)	Aug. 15, 1960
Gabon	Aug. 17, 1960
Senegal	Aug. 20, 1960
Mali	Sept. 22, 1960
Nigeria	Oct. 1, 1960
Mauritania	Nov. 28, 1960
Sierra Leone	Apr. 27, 1961
Tanzania	Dec. 9, 1961
Burundi	July 1, 1962
Rwanda	July 1, 1962
Uganda	Oct. 9, 1962
Kenya	Dec. 12, 1963
Malawi	July 6, 1964
Zambia	Oct. 24, 1964
Gambia	Feb. 18, 1965
Botswana	Sept. 30, 1966
Lesotho	Oct. 4, 1966
Swaziland	Sept. 6, 1968
Equatorial Guinea	Oct. 12, 1968

The independent black African nations fill the middle two-thirds of the African continent. This is an extremely compact continent whose smooth coastline lacks many natural harbors. Its interior is a vast plateau broken by the great river systems of the Nile, Niger, and Zaire rivers and the great Rift valley in Eastern Africa. Transversed by the equator, its climate varies widely. Only a relatively small portion of the continent, the Zaire basin and parts of West Africa, have rain forests with jungle foliage. Vast savannah grasslands characterize much of the continent's interior. It was under conditions like this that earliest man is thought to have evolved in Africa some two million years ago.

To the north, across the vast Sahara desert, lie the nations of North Africa. Although relatively distinct in culture and religion from Black Africa, caravans have traversed the far from impenetrable Sahara for countless centuries, facilitating both trade and culture contact. To the south lie a number of countries culturally similar to the independent black nations but still under the control of whites: Angola, Rhodesia, Mozambique, South and South West Africa

In order to understand Black Africa's dynamic response to modernization it is important to realize that the traditional culture of its peoples was tribal rather than peasant. This means that the basis of social organization lies in kinship units larger than the immediate family rather than in villages and the immediate family; that land rights are held by groups such as clans, lineages (people tracing their relationship to a common ancestor), or extended families (kin groups larger than the parent-children unit) rather than by individuals; that political authority often involves checks and balances ensuring to some degree the consent of the governed rather than being vested in a relatively absolute ruler; that traditional African religion involves local cults and ceremonies rather than a universal religion; that villages or homesteads rather than cities are the characteristic places of residence; and that culture is transmitted by oral rather than written tradition.

These generalizations admit to some exceptions, of course. To name a few, the rural Amhara people in central Ethiopia have a way of life that is more peasant than tribal. Those areas where Islam has become the dominant religion, such as parts of northern Nigeria, northern Sudan, and Somalia, have a universal religion at the heart of their culture. Finally, before the Western impact, the Yoruba in Nigeria had cities of up to 100,000 population although the vast majority of these city dwellers were farmers.

Within the tribal framework, the diversity of the traditional culture of the 800 or more African peoples is very large. Some peoples are nations of ten million like the Yoruba, while others are just a few thousand strong. Some have complex state political systems, while at the other extreme there are peoples with minimal political institutions above the authority of the family. Although inheritance in most African peoples passes through the father's line (patrilineal), a significant number of peoples are matrilineal. A herding way of life centered around cattle characterizes some peoples such as the Fulani of West Africa and the Masai of Eastern Africa, but most peoples are settled on the land and follow an agricultural way of life. A small number of peoples such as the pygmies of the Zaire forests and the Bushmen of the Kalahari desert in Botswana and South West Africa follow the ancient hunting and gathering way of life.

African culture has never been static. For millennia the continent has known migrations, wars, cultural innovation, and cultural diffusion. With the Western colonial impact of the nineteenth century the tempo of change quickened. The major colonial powers were the British, French, Belgians, Portugese and, until the end of World War I, the Germans. They arbitrarily divided the continent into large political units and imposed Western culture. Following initial resistance and a period of hesitancy, most African peoples responded in a dramatic fashion—crowding the primary and secondary schools, migrating to the cities in search of jobs, and sacrificing to send the most brilliant students to universities overseas and, later, at home. It is in this context of traditional tribal cultures responding to modernization that the new nations of Africa have come into being.

Scope of the Handbook

George H. T. Kimble has written, "The darkest thing about Africa has always been our ignorance of it." True as this statement is, the Western desire to learn about Africa has a long history. Although the ancients were not able to explore the interior of Africa, Ptolemy's geography (A.D. 125–155) summarized the results of numerous voyages along its perimeter.[1] In the nineteenth century, the Victorians were fascinated by the puzzle of the origins of the Nile and the Niger rivers and acclaimed the explorers who finally "discovered" these origins. Now that black African countries are members of the United Nations and an important part of the world community of nations, both Africans and non-Africans are seeking more knowledge about contemporary Africa.

This Handbook is designed to assist the study of independent black African nations by making available in readily accessible form comparable data on a wide range of topics. Although the reader interested in a specific country will find much that is of interest to him in this book, we have prepared the volume especially to encourage the comparative study of these nations.

We identify as "Black Africa" the thirty-two sub-Saharan nations that were sovereign states when this project was initiated in 1967, and which were governed by black people. This is not to argue that there is a "White Africa," but only to indicate that non-liberated territories governed by white minorities, and the North African states are not considered comparable for the purposes of this Handbook. Since 1967 two more small black African nations have achieved independence: Swaziland (pop. 385,000) on September 6, 1968, and Equatorial Guinea (pop. 281,000) on October 12, 1968. As of this book's time of publication, active liberation movements were fighting in the Portugese territories of Angola, Portugese Guinea, and Mozambique, in Rhodesia, in South Africa, and in the South African-controlled territory of South West Africa. We hope that future editions of this Handbook will include additional independent nations.

This Handbook is not intended to be a distillation

of *all* available data dealing with Black Africa. Rather, it is designed to provide the most reliable information available to facilitate the enterprise of comparative political, economic and social analysis and inquiry, and therefore, the development of theory and empirically verified generalization. This information was collected not because "it was there," but because it seemed important to the study of problems in the development of nations.

The African National Integration Project at Northwestern University, out of which this Handbook has developed, was designed to investigate problems of national integration and political stability. Nations, we argued, are political systems that are functionally equivalent units of analysis in that they have in common properties of territoriality, citizenship, and sovereignty. Changes in the boundaries of national territory, in the opportunities and obligations of citizens, and in the coerciveness and justice of the exercise of sovereignty seemed to be critical problems in the lives of men and women throughout Africa, and it seemed desirable to attempt to discover empirical regularities or generalizations about the development of nations. We were especially interested in two related processes of nation-building: the degree to which national political systems are radically altered by violent breakdowns in the authority relationships between different segments of the national population, and the degree to which elements of national populations become politically unified in increasing contact, cooperation, and consensus. In the organization and substance of this book, therefore, we give special attention to the requirements for a theoretical analysis of African political development. For a further discussion of the theoretical context of the data collection, see Part III, Chapter 1.

Organization of the Handbook

Part I, Comparative Profiles, presents 172 tables of quantitative data which are not only of intrinsic interest but also necessary to the measurement of concepts and the testing of theory. In general, the data are based on existing, quantitative information, which we have checked for consistency between different sources; in some cases we have constructed indices for concepts we believe to be theoretically important, but for which there is no available quantitative measurement.

Part II, Country Profiles, gives information about each country's ethnic, linguistic, urban, and political situation. Where the index construction in Part I has required extensive aggregation from smaller units for each country, the country profiles give the original data for each unit. For example, as an index for urbanization in Part I, we include the percentage of population in cities of 20,000 people or more (Table 15.2). In the country profiles, each of these cities is listed with its population. This same pattern is followed for pluralism and political development. Part II also includes a map and selected bibliography for each country.

In Part III, Cross National Research on Africa: Issues and Context, we discuss some of the important methodological issues in the comparative analysis of black African nations. These include an elaboration of the theoretical focus on integration and instability, the relevance and peculiar problems of generalizations based on cross-national research, the treatment of ethnicity in comparative research on Africa, and the reliability of aggregate data such as those we present in this book. The chapter on ethnic units (Chapter 4) provides a detailed discussion of the system of ethnic classification used in Part II.

The present Handbook is a selection of material from a larger data bank[2]—a selection which represents the most reliable and significant data we have presently available. We have made only a beginning; there are undoubtedly gaps in the information already stored and omissions and errors which are no doubt reflected in this publication. Our hope is that any errors and omissions will be isolated in critical readings of this book, and that the work in its present form will stimulate greater international cooperation in the collection and sharing of information about Africa.[3] This hope is based not only on the assumption that the systematic collection, evaluation, and open publication of information is the essence of scholarship, but also on the feeling that this kind of enterprise is ultimately rewarding to Africans themselves. From the vantage point of

African nations and their citizens, the development of national autonomy depends on being able to get information, as power depends on having information and being able to use it.

> A society or community that is to steer itself must continue to receive a full flow of three kinds of information: first, information about the world outside; second, information from the past, with a wide range of recall and recombination; and third, information about itself and its own parts. Let any one of these three streams be long interrupted, such as by oppression or secrecy, and the society becomes an automaton, a walking corpse. It loses control over its own behavior, not only for some of its parts, but also eventually at its very top.[4]

This Handbook, then, represents an attempt to provide comparative information—i.e., information about a country, which, in its very presentation, is information about a "world" of countries outside.

As it is analyzed, modified, and added to, this information may make some contribution to the potential autonomy of African nations. That, at least, is the intention of the authors.

Notes

1 Robert I. Rotberg, *A Political History of Africa* (New York: Harcourt Brace, 1965), pp. 3–33.
2 The data bank developed by the African National Integration Project contains approximately 1200 variables coded for each of 32 black African nations, as well as data on the background of elites, the cultural characteristics of ethnic groups, and information on urban centers. See Appendices 1 and 2 for information about the availability of these data on computer tape.
3 The authors would be most grateful if readers finding any errors would bring them to our attention. Communications should be addressed to R. C. Mitchell, Department of Sociology, Swarthmore College, Swarthmore, Pa. 19081.
4 Karl W. Deutsch, *The Nerves of Government* (New York: The Free Press, 1963), p. 129.

Part I
Comparative Profiles

AFRICA

Independent
Black Africa

MADEIRA
ISLANDS
(Port.)

CANARY
ISLANDS
(Spain)

El Aaiún

SPANISH
SAHARA

MAURITANIA

• Nouakchott

SENEGAL
Dakar
Bathurst
GAMBIA
PORT.
GUINEA
Bissau
GUINEA
Conakry
Freetown
SIERRA LEONE
Monrovia
LIBERIA

MALI

Bamako
• Ouagadougou
UPPER VOLTA
IVORY
COAST
GHANA
Abidjan
Accra

Tunis
Algiers
TUNISIA
Tripoli

Rabat
MOROCCO

ALGERIA

LIBYA

Benghazi

Cairo

UNITED
ARAB
REPUBLIC

Eritrea

NIGER

Niamey

CHAD

Khartoum

SUDAN

Fort-Lamy

DAHOMEY
TOGO
Porto-Novo
Lomé
Lagos

NIGERIA

CAMEROON

Santa
Isabel
FERNANDO PO

CENTRAL
AFRICAN
REPUBLIC

Bangui

Southern
SUDAN

Addis
Ababa

Djibouti

ETHIOPIA

SOMALIA

Mogadiscio

EQUATORIAL
GUINEA
PRÍNCIPE
(Port)
SÃO TOMÉ
(Port)
ANNOBÓN

Yaoundé
Libreville
GABON

REP. OF THE CONGO

Brazzaville
Kinshasa

ZAIRE

Kampala
UGANDA
RWANDA
Kigali
Bujumbura
BURUNDI

KENYA
Nairobi

PEMBA
ZANZIBAR
Dar es Salaam

Luanda

TANZANIA

COMORO
ISLANDS (Fr.)

ANGOLA
(Port.)

MALAWI

ZAMBIA

Lusaka

Zomba

Salisbury

Tananarive

SOUTH-WEST
AFRICA
(Int. Terr.)
(NAMIBIA)

WALVIS BAY
(Rep. of S.Af.)

Windhoek

RHODESIA
(ZIMBABWE)

BOTSWANA

Gaberone
Pretoria
Mbabane
Maseru LESOTHO

MOZAMBIQUE
(Port.)

MALAGASY
REPUBLIC

MAURITIUS

Port Louis

RÉUNION (Fr.)

Lourenco Marques
SWAZILAND

SOUTH
AFRICA

Miles
0   500   1000

0   500   1000
Kilometers

Introduction

Part I presents data on 172 variables for the 32 black African nations. By "variable" is meant a measurable aspect of these countries which varies over a range of possibilities such as telephones per 10,000 population (Table 6.5) which varied in 1967 from 4 to 114. The variables are grouped by topic into sixteen chapters. Each chapter includes: (a) a brief discussion of the topic and its importance for an understanding of Black Africa, (b) references to some of the latest and most important articles and books on the topic, (c) an explanation of the selection of variables* we made for the topic, and (d) an evaluation of the data sources for these variables plus, if possible, our assessment of the accuracy of the data. Chapters in this section are not intended to interpret the meaning of the data patterns themselves.

Each of the 172 tables presents the data for one variable. These data consist of the values for each country on that variable plus a variety of statistics. Many readers will consult the table simply for the values. Consulting Table 6.5, for instance, they will learn that Zambia has the highest number of telephones per 10,000 population (114). The statistics, however, provide additional useful information about the distribution of the values for that variable showing, for instance, that Zambia's value of 114 is far above the mean of 32 telephones per 10,000 population.

In Figure I.1, Table 9.9 is reprinted as a sample table. Each element of the table is explained in detail so that the reader may use all the information in the tables, if he wishes, to aid his interpretation of the data.

Guide to Reading the Tables in Part I

Table 9.9 is reprinted here as a sample table.

(A) = *Title*: The table title describes the variable

* A total of 172 variables are presented in the sixteen chapters. These are a selection from a much larger data bank on Black Africa. In selecting the data for inclusion in this Handbook we have been guided by the principle that data readily available elsewhere should not be included in that form in this book. Instead we try to provide sufficient references to the literature so that the user might locate

those data and we go on to present either other data, or these data in another form such as percent increase or per capita. The appendices contain a code book and listing of these 172 variables plus a further selection of data from the African data bank in a form suitable for punching on data cards if desired.

Figure I.1

Ⓐ

TABLE 9.9 Direct Taxes as a Percent of Total Government Revenue, 1966

Ⓑ *Definition*: Direct taxes include income and profit taxes and all other taxes paid directly to the government without passing through an intermediary.

Ⓖ RANGE =	41.00					
Ⓘ MEAN =	23.25					
Ⓙ STANDARD DEVIATION =		11.07				

POPULATION PERCENT Ⓛ Ⓚ CUM. COUNTRY	Ⓕ RANK	COUNTRY NAME	Ⓔ VALUE	Ⓗ RANGE DECILE
3.8	3.8	1.0	GHANA	43	1
12.9	9.1	2.5	ZAIRE	40	
14.7	1.8	2.5	ZAMBIA	40	
19.5	4.8	4.0	KENYA	37	2
30.4	10.9	5.5	ETHIOPIA	34	3
36.1	5.7	5.5	TANZANIA	34	
36.6	0.5	7.0	LIBERIA	33	
38.1	1.5	8.5	BURUNDI	31	
40.0	1.9	8.5	MALAWI	31	
41.7	1.7	10.0	NIGER	29	4
42.0	0.3	11.0	BOTSWANA	27	
67.0	25.0	12.5	NIGERIA	25	5
69.3	2.3	12.5	UPPER VOLTA	25	
70.0	0.7	14.0	CAR	24	
72.2	2.2	15.0	MALI	23	
73.3	1.1	16.5	SIERRA LEONE	22	6
77.5	4.2	16.5	UGANDA	22	
80.0	2.5	18.5	CAMEROON	20	
81.6	1.6	18.5	CHAD	20	
82.0	0.4	20.5	CONGO (BRA)	18	7
82.2	0.2	20.5	GABON	18	
83.7	1.5	22.0	RWANDA	11	8
85.6	1.9	23.0	IVORY COAST	10	9
86.4	0.8	24.0	TOGO	9	
87.6	1.2	25.5	DAHOMEY	8	
94.3	6.7	25.5	SUDAN	8	
95.5	1.2	27.0	SOMALIA	7	
97.2	1.7	28.0	GUINEA	2	10

Ⓓ DATA NOT AVAILABLE FOR THE FOLLOWING COUNTRIES

GAMBIA   LESOTHO   MAURITANIA   SENEGAL

Ⓒ SOURCES: *AID Economic Data Book*. Cameroon, CAR, Chad, Congo (*Brazzaville*), Gabon: International Monetary Fund, *Surveys of African Economies*, Vol. 1; *Kenya, Somalia, Tanzania, Uganda: ibid.*, Vol. 2.

and the year. In this case the variable is direct taxes as a percent of total government revenue and the year is 1966.

(B) = *Definition*: When it is necessary to define the variable more precisely and less ambiguously, additional information is given here.

(C) = *Sources*: The principal source is listed first. When subsidiary sources are used or additional information is given about particular countries, the countries involved are listed. The general source for Table 9.9 is the *AID Economic Data Book* (whose full reference is given in the List of Abbreviations on page xv). The data for nine of the countries in the table come from another source, however. *Surveys of African Economies*, Vol. 1, was used for Cameroon, CAR, Chad, Congo (Brazzaville) and Gabon, while Vol. 2 was used for Kenya, Somalia, Tanzania and Uganda.

(D) = *Data Not Available*: Whenever data is unavailable on a variable for any of the 32 countries covered in this Handbook, the names of the missing countries are listed here.

(E) = *Value*: The data in this column are the values for the variable for each country. The 43 opposite Ghana indicates that 43 percent of Ghana's total government revenue in 1966 came from direct taxes. The unit (percent or millions of U.S. dollars, etc.) is always specified in the table title.

(F) = *Rank*: The countries are listed in the table in rank order from those which have the highest value of the variable to those which have the lowest value. This column gives the rank of every country on the variable. It shows that Ghana is first, Botswana eleventh and Guinea twenty-eighth out of 28 countries in direct taxes as a percent of government revenue, 1966. Countries which are *tied* at the same value, such as Cameroon and Chad which both have a value of 20, are given the same rank. This is calculated as the average of the ranks which they cover.

In the case of Cameroon and Chad these ranks are 18 and 19. The average is 18.5 which is the rank given to each.

The next four statistics provide a simple summary of some aspects of the distribution of the values for the 28 countries in the table. They are all expressed in the original measurement units, in this case percentages.

(G) = *Range*: This is the distance between the highest and the lowest value of the variable and shows the limits within which all measurements fall. In this case the distance between Ghana's 43 percent and Guinea's 3 percent gives a range of 41.

(H) = *Range Decile*: The numbers in this column show which countries fall into which decile (or tenth) of the range. In this case the range is 41 so each decile is 4.1. Each country in Table 9.9 whose value is between 43 (highest value) and 38.1 (lowest value within one decile of the highest value) is in the first decile of the range, etc. Thus Ghana (value 43), Zaire (Congo K.) [value 40], and Zambia (value 40) are all in the first decile. Kenya is the only country in the second decile while five countries are in the third decile, etc. A glance at the range decile column will show how evenly or unevenly the countries are distributed across the range. For instance, when the country having the highest value is in decile 1 and the country with the next highest value is in decile 8, the distribution across the range is highly uneven. In the case of Table 9.9 the distribution across the range is fairly even except in the lower deciles (8, 9, and 10).

(I) = *Mean*: The mean may be thought of as the central tendency of the distribution. It is that score about which deviations in one direction equal deviations in the other. It is calculated by taking the sum of all the values (in column E) and dividing them by the total number of values (in this case by 28). The mean for Table 9.9 is 23.25. In cases where the distribution is skewed, the countries with values closest to the mean will be closer to the top or the bottom of the rank ordered countries.

(J) = *Standard Deviation*: This is an index of variability or how the values depart from the central tendency or the mean of a distribution. It is the square root of the variance for a distribution. For Table 9.9 the standard deviation is 11.07. The higher the standard deviation, the greater the countries' dissimilarity as a whole.

As as aid in interpreting the data, the remaining two sets of figures give information about the size of each country relative to the other countries covered by this Handbook.

(K) = *Country Population Percent*: The figures in this column give the percent each country's population is of the total population for all 32 countries. Adding the 1969 population figures for all the countries we get 236,000,000 as the total population. The figures in this column show that Congo (Brazzaville)'s population of 880,000 comprises less than one half of one percent of the total (.4) while Nigeria's 56,700,000 people comprises 25 percent of the total (25.0). A glance at this column will show such things as whether the smaller countries are grouped at the top or the bottom of a distribution. In the case of Table 9.9 the distribution by size of country is fairly even, although the lower values tend to be held by small countries. The country population percent is also a useful reminder of absolute values. In a table presented in Chapter 6, "Telephones per 10,000 Population, 1967," Congo (Brazzaville) has a higher value than Nigeria. Of course the more populous Nigeria has a much larger number of telephones (702,000) than tiny Congo (Brazzaville) (5,600), but Congo has the greater percentage.

(L) = *Cumulative Population Percent*: The figures in this column give the country population percent (K) in a cumulative fashion beginning with the country population percent of the country with the highest value. At every point in the distribution of the value it shows the percentage of the total 32-country population accounted for by those countries which hold that value or a higher one. For example, the 13 countries in Table 9.9 that have a value of 25 or higher account for 69.3 percent of the total population of all 32 countries. The figure of 97.2 opposite Guinea in this column shows that the 28 countries for which data were available on this variable account for 97.2 percent of the total population.

1. Ecology and Demography

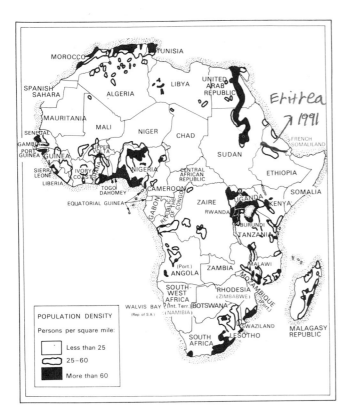

POPULATION DENSITY

Persons per square mile:

Less than 25

25–60

More than 60

The characteristics of the physical environment and of the human populations, and their interaction for each nation, are fundamental to comparative analysis. These characteristics are among the more difficult categories to measure with reasonable accuracy, however, particularly for the developing nations.

This chapter gives the latest available data on those aspects of ecology and demography that are readily amenable to cross-national depiction with reasonable accuracy. These variables can only show the basic parameters of the African situation, however. Readers are referred to the several recent geographies on Africa as a whole[1] and the increasing number of individual country geographies for detailed data on the ecology of Black Africa. Two important works on demography, published in 1968, provide a sophisticated review of the present state of African population studies.[2]

Agriculture and herding remain the principal economic pursuits of the vast majority of Africans. About three-fifths of the total cultivated area of tropical Africa is devoted to subsistence farming. William Hance[3] has described tropical Africa (including the Portuguese colonies and Rhodesia but excluding the Union of South Africa) as topographically a plateau continent, possessing few good natural harbors, with narrow coastal plains, two-fifths of which is steppe or desert and one-third savanna. The soils in the rainforest and savanna areas are poorly structured and leached latosols which require careful cultivation. Neither land nor solar radiation are lacking, however. Only inadequacies in technique and deficiencies in rainfall stand in the way of abundant agricultural productivity.[4] The forests (Africa has 17 percent of the world's forest areas) represent an important and valuable resource which has been only modestly exploited to date. Cattle and the well-known African wildlife form very large faunal resources, and fisheries are rapidly expanding.

The mineral exploitation potential and the availability of energy resources for export and for supplying power to manufacturing industries vary widely from country to country. Iron ore is mined in Mauritania, Guinea, Sierra Leone, and Liberia, and coal deposits are either exploited or known to exist in five of the countries discussed in this Handbook. There are important copper mines in Zambia and Zaire (Congo K.), tin mines in Nigeria and Zaire (Congo K.), bauxite reserves in Guinea, Sierra Leone, and Ghana, manganese mines in Gabon, and commercial production of diamonds in Sierra Leone, Liberia, and Central African Republic. As of 1970 most of these mines and most of the presently known potential mineral resources were in West and Equatorial Africa. Since few areas of Black Africa have had thorough geological surveys, new discoveries may be expected.

According to Hance, Africa has the greatest water power potential in the world. Add to this the possession of some of the world's greatest known

6

reserves of uranium ore (which could fuel nuclear power stations), large petroleum discoveries in Nigeria and potential commercial oil fields in Gabon, Congo (Brazzaville), and elsewhere in West Africa, plus the natural gas fields in Nigeria, and a promising energy picture emerges. The major drawback is the shortage of coking coal, necessary for the production of iron and steel, and the unequal distribution of fuel resources in the various countries.

Ecology

We have limited our presentation of data on the ecology of Africa to three variables: (1) Area of Country in Square Kilometers, (2) Acres of Agricultural Land per Capita and (3) Non-Agricultural Development Potential Index (Tables 1.1–1.3). Further variables could have been included on other aspects of land use, but even the relatively simple variables we have chosen present serious reliability problems. For instance, the area size of African countries is seemingly a straightforward variable which is highly amenable to measurement. Nevertheless, the United Nations and its agency, the Economic Commission for Africa, give slightly different figures for Mali, Botswana, and Mauritania, and other sources offer even more divergent estimates. We resolve this dilemma without solving it by presenting in Table 1.1 a UN figure in square kilometers as a size variable.[5] Then, in the country section, Part II, we give the size of each country in square miles along with the names of those U.S. states which in combination approximate the same land area.

With the second ecological variable, agricultural land per capita, the reliability problems become quite serious. Norton Ginsburg in his *Atlas of Economic Development* labeled this variable "highly suspect for many of the poorer countries"[6] because reliable information is difficult to obtain and the definitions of "cultivated" and "potentially cultivatable" land are open to different interpretations. In our data-gathering operations we located three other measures of this variable (or variables very similar to it, such as "cultivated land in hectares per capita"). In a factor analysis of all our ecological and demo-graphic data, the four variables fell on three different factors instead of the same factor, indicating a definite multidimensionality instead of the hoped-for unidimensionality. Since, with few exceptions, we did not have access to special information that would allow us to resolve these difficulties or to improve upon existing data, we took our data from a single recent source. Of course, this variable does not take into account the quality and character of the land involved, but it provides (hopefully) a rough comparative indicator of agricultural potential.

The third variable in this set is qualitative, based upon a series of assessments by William A. Hance of certain aspects of the non-agricultural potential of the thirty-two countries included in this Handbook. Hance, in his book *African Economic Development*, surveys the development of all of Black Africa, country by country. He summarizes this discussion in a table which rates each country on a number of factors which inhibit development (overpopulation, aridity, remoteness, etc.) and also on various short- and medium-run opportunities for development. We present a variable which is the sum of the scores for each country on the short- and medium-run opportunities for non-agricultural development in the following areas: forestry, fishing, mining, hydro-power, and manufacturing. The rankings on this variable give a rough ranking of the development potential of the thirty-two countries. Qualitative and judgmental as this variable is, it has the advantage of coming from a readily accessible source which contains a detailed justification for these judgments.

Demography

The populations of these countries constitute a human resource of utmost importance. Development planning requires accurate data regarding population size and its characteristics in order to allocate national resources in a manner consistent with national goals. These data are no less vital in theoretical research which must account for variations in systemic scale. It will be noted that many variables contained in this Handbook have been standardized by population size for greater unit comparability. Although population counts of one kind or another have been undertaken in Black Africa for several decades, it is only since about 1960 that enumerations using modern census techniques have been used.[7] Even today relatively few countries have undertaken full censuses, although most have used the technique of the sampling survey which was first introduced to Africa in 1948 and was subsequently adopted by most of the former French colonies, Zaire (Congo K.), and Sudan.

The building of an accurate demographic data base in Africa has just begun. For this reason the reliability of the various important demographic measures such as birth rate, death rate, infant mortality rate, size of the working force, etc., are generally low and extremely variable across the countries. In this Handbook we have restricted ourselves to the inclusion of an estimate for population size, a growth rate or rate of natural increase estimate, a population density figure, and two variables on European population as percent of population.

As with area size, population size is difficult to measure with accuracy. A successful census is an enormous bureaucratic undertaking that requires the availability of highly specialized technicians and statisticians, and a considerable expenditure of funds. It also requires the cooperation of the population. In the colonial era census undercounts commonly resulted because people feared taxation or otherwise misunderstood the purpose of the census; in the contemporary post-independence era the opposite may hold as the rewards of parliamentary representation and resource allocation threaten to bias the results towards overcounts. In general the pre-modern censuses have been undercounts, although the governments of Sierra Leone and Liberia unexpectedly found that their populations had been considerably overestimated.

Nigeria is a dramatic example of the contemporary threat of overcounting. The first census to be taken in the 1960s (1962) was branded fraudulent and scrapped. The regional officials had allegedly conspired to preserve or change the political balance in their favor by inflating their returns. A second census, taken the next year with similar returns, was accepted by the politicians but not by the demographers

because it indicated an exceedingly high and irregular growth rate. Thus, although the United Nations dutifully reports the official figure of sixty-one million for 1967, a non-governmental study of Nigerian human resource development based its analysis on an estimate of fifty million.[8]

Migratory movements, mostly of a seasonal variety, have a significant influence on the populations of several African countries which is difficult to take into account. The inland countries of West Africa—Mali, Upper Volta, and Niger—supply male immigrants to coastal countries, especially to Ghana, Nigeria, and Ivory Coast. In the 1960 Ghana census, 12 percent of the population were immigrant aliens. If the census had been taken earlier in the year the figure would have been even higher since many of the immigrants had returned to their home countries after the harvest (before the March–April date of the census).[9] Hance estimates that Ivory Coast annually receives about 200,000 semi-permanent immigrants from both Mali and Guinea, and 500,000 from Upper Volta—equivalent to about one-fourth of her total population. Mining and industrial locations in Rhodesia and South Africa attract migrants from Zambia and especially Malawi in Central Africa, and one-sixth of the working force in Zambia itself are immigrants.[10]

Another category of immigrants are political refugees. According to the *Statesman's Yearbook 1967* the following countries had received refugees, some of them in very substantial numbers: Zaire (Congo K.) 350,000 (300,000 from Angola, others from Rwanda and Sudan), Tanzania 33,000 (12,000 from Mozambique, 13,500 from Rwanda, the rest from Zaire [Congo K.]), Uganda 155,000 (55,000 from Sudan, 67,000 from Rwanda, and 33,000 from Zaire [Congo K.]), and Zambia 6,500 (from Angola and Mozambique).

The population size data we present are taken directly from the *United Nations Demographic Yearbook 1969*, as are the census dates. The reliability estimates presented in Table 1.4 are a summary index derived from information presented in the *Statistical Yearbook* on the nature of the base data, its recency, and the method and quality of time adjustment. Our index represents the following error ranges:[11]

1	Good	2–8%
2	Fair	9–12%
3	Poor	13–19%
4	Very poor	20–30%

The variable on population density (Table 1.5) shows the comparatively low density which characterizes the African continent. Australia is the only continent that has lower density. To understand the meaning of population density in terms of over- or under-population we must take into account the relatively low carrying capacity of much of African land including the "arable" portions. William Hance has reviewed the arguments pro and con regarding Africa's "underpopulation" and seems to feel that the danger lies in the direction of over-population in the habitable zones if the expected high growth rates are experienced.[12]

A population growth rate consists of the balance of in- and out-migration and the rate of natural increase (births minus deaths). Although we present a natural increase variable (Table 1.6), it should be noted that its reliability is not very high.[13] The method of estimating this variable is presented in Appendix 5. Having compared the two independent attempts to estimate mortality and fertility by demographers at Princeton University and at the Economic Commission for Africa, J. C. Caldwell[14] concludes that fertility in tropical Africa is "very high, but not quite uniformly so." Mortality rates are falling, "perhaps rapidly." With the mortality transition and without a fertility transition as yet, Africa is in the early phase of rapidly accelerating population growth.[15] As one consequence of this situation, more than two-fifths of the population in most African countries are under fifteen years of age.

White population is an important variable reflecting the differential colonial impact. Table 1.7 presents data for the 1920's. The latest data presented on white population is for 1960 (Table 1.8); this date is too early to indicate the post-colonial situation exactly, but it probably approximates the immediate post-colonial years except for Zaire (Congo K.) where there was a considerable out-migration of Belgians following independence. That even a relatively small percentage of whites can exert a dominant neo-colonial influence is illustrated by the case of Gabon in the early 1960s, which has been described by the former American ambassador to that country.[16]

Since the white populations in the thirty-two countries were relatively small and under the direct control of the colonial regimes, the data on them is likely to be relatively reliable, even for earlier periods. The definition of "European" complicates the reliability of the variable: Indian or Levantine immigrants may be counted separately from "whites" in one country, such as Kenya, and together with them in another, such as Nigeria.

Notes

[1] R. J. Harrison Church, et al., *Africa and the Islands* (New York: John Wiley, 1965); William A. Hance, *The Geography of Modern Africa* (New York: Columbia University Press, 1964); George H. T. Kimble, *Tropical Africa*, 2 vols. (New York: The Twentieth Century Fund, 1960); P. Ady, ed., *Oxford Regional Economic Atlas—Africa* (Oxford: Clarendon Press, 1965).

[2] J. C. Caldwell and C. Okonjo, *The Population of Tropical Africa*, (London: Longmans, 1968); and William Brass, et al., *The Demography of Tropical Africa* (Princeton, N.J.: Princeton University Press, 1968).

[3] William A. Hance, *African Economic Development*, 2nd ed. (New York: Praeger, 1967).

[4] Pierre Gourou, "Agriculture in the African Tropics: The Observations of a Geographer," in *Africa*, ed. P. J. McEwan (London: Oxford University Press, 1968), pp. 128–138. Among other discussions of African agriculture are: William Allan, *The African Husbandman* (Edinburgh: Oliver and Boyd, 1965); René Dumont, *False Start in Africa* (New York: Praeger, 1966); David Hapgood and Max F. Millikan, *No Easy Harvest: The Dilemma of Agriculture in Underdeveloped Countries* (Boston: Little, Brown, 1967).

[5] *UN Demographic Yearbook 1967*.

[6] Norton Ginsburg, *Atlas of Economic Development* (Chicago: University of Chicago Press, 1961), p. 46.

[7] Complete house-to-house censuses had been carried out, however, as early as 1948. Frank Lorimer, "Introduction," in *The Demography of Tropical Africa*, eds. William Brass, et al., p. 5.

[8] Education and World Affairs, *Nigerian Human Resource Development and Utilization* (New York: Education and World Affairs, 1967), p. 18.

[9] B. Gil, "Immigration into Ghana and Its Contribution in Skill," in Department of Economic and Social Affairs, *Proceedings of the World Population Conference* (New York: United Nations, 1967), p. 202. In late 1969 the Ghanaian government expelled many of the estimated two million aliens then resident in the country.

[10] C. A. L. Myburgh, "Migration in Relationship to the Economic Development of Rhodesia, Zambia and Malawi," in *ibid.*, p. 216 and William A. Hance, *Population, Migration, and Urbanization in Africa* (New York: Columbia University Press, 1970), pp. 128–208.

[11] For a useful discussion of the United Nations' population data reliability see Bruce M. Russett, *World Handbook of Social and Political Indicators* (New Haven, Conn.: Yale University Press, 1964), pp. 15–17.

[12] William A. Hance, "The Race Between Population and Resources," *Africa Report*, 13 (January 1968): 6–12 and Hance, *Population, Migration and Urbanization in Africa*, pp. 43–127.

[13] Of the two different estimates of natural increase mentioned, the estimate given in this Handbook conforms more to the Economic Commission for Africa estimates, which are generally higher than the Princeton estimates.

[14] J. C. Caldwell, "The Demographic Situation," in Caldwell and Okonjo, *The Population of Tropical Africa*, pp. 8–15.

[15] In about two decades, Africa may have the highest population growth rate of the world regions. R. K. Som, "Some Demographic Indicators for Africa," in Caldwell and Okonjo, *op. cit.*, p. 197.

[16] Charles and Alice Darlington, *African Betrayal* (New York: David McKay Co., 1967).

TABLE 1.1 Area of Country

Definition: Total area enclosed within the natural boundaries, including that covered by water. Value is in 1,000 square kilometers.

```
RANGE      =    2495.00
MEAN       =     597.47
STANDARD DEVIATION =            621.44
```

POPULATION PERCENT CUM.	COUNTRY	RANK	COUNTRY NAME	VALUE	RANGE DECILE
6.7	6.7	1.0	SUDAN	2506	1
15.8	9.1	2.0	ZAIRE	2345	
17.4	1.6	3.0	CHAD	1284	5
19.1	1.7	4.0	NIGER	1267	
21.3	2.2	5.0	MALI	1240	6
32.2	10.9	6.0	ETHIOPIA	1222	
32.7	0.5	7.0	MAURITANIA	1031	
38.4	5.7	8.0	TANZANIA	940	7
63.4	25.0	9.0	NIGERIA	924	
65.2	1.8	10.0	ZAMBIA	753	8
66.4	1.2	11.0	SOMALIA	638	
67.1	0.7	12.0	CAR	623	
67.4	0.3	13.0	BOTSWANA	600	
72.2	4.8	14.0	KENYA	583	
74.7	2.5	15.0	CAMEROON	475	9
75.1	0.4	16.0	CONGO (BRA)	342	
77.0	1.9	17.0	IVORY COAST	322	
79.3	2.3	18.0	UPPER VOLTA	274	
79.5	0.2	19.0	GABON	268	
81.2	1.7	20.0	GUINEA	246	10
85.0	3.8	21.0	GHANA	239	
89.2	4.2	22.0	UGANDA	236	
90.9	1.7	23.0	SENEGAL	196	
92.8	1.9	24.0	MALAWI	118	
94.0	1.2	25.0	DAHOMEY	113	
94.5	0.5	26.0	LIBERIA	111	
95.6	1.1	27.0	SIERRA LEONE	72	
96.4	0.8	28.0	TOGO	56	
96.8	0.4	29.0	LESOTHO	30	
98.3	1.5	30.0	BURUNDI	28	
99.8	1.5	31.0	RWANDA	26	
100.0	0.2	32.0	GAMBIA	11	

source: *UN Statistical Yearbook, 1969*. See Part II, Country Profiles, for country area in square miles.

TABLE 1.2 Acres of Agricultural Land per Capita, 1968

Comment: These figures are only rough estimates and are based on varying definitions of agricultural land. For the sake of consistency a single source was used.

```
RANGE      =     166.00
MEAN       =      14.69
STANDARD DEVIATION =             31.77
```

POPULATION PERCENT CUM.	COUNTRY	RANK	COUNTRY NAME	VALUE	RANGE DECILE
0.3	0.3	1.0	BOTSWANA	167	1
0.8	0.5	2.0	MAURITANIA	88	5
2.4	1.6	3.0	CHAD	37	8
4.2	1.8	4.0	ZAMBIA	22	9
5.4	1.2	5.0	SOMALIA	20	
7.6	2.2	6.0	MALI	19	
13.3	5.7	7.0	TANZANIA	16	10
15.0	1.7	8.0	NIGER	12	
15.7	0.7	9.0	CAR	10	
16.2	0.5	10.0	LIBERIA	9	
25.3	9.1	12.0	ZAIRE	8	
36.2	10.9	12.0	ETHIOPIA	8	
36.6	0.4	12.0	LESOTHO	8	
39.1	2.5	14.0	CAMEROON	7	
40.2	1.1	15.0	SIERRA LEONE	6	
46.9	6.7	16.0	SUDAN	5	
47.1	0.2	17.5	GAMBIA	4	
48.8	1.7	17.5	SENEGAL	4	
49.6	0.8	19.0	TOGO	3	
50.0	0.4	21.5	CONGO (BRA)	2	
51.2	1.2	21.5	DAHOMEY	2	
52.9	1.7	21.5	GUINEA	2	
55.2	2.3	21.5	UPPER VOLTA	2	
56.7	1.5	28.0	BURUNDI	1	
56.9	0.2	28.0	GABON	1	
60.7	3.8	28.0	GHANA	1	
62.6	1.9	28.0	IVORY COAST	1	
67.4	4.8	28.0	KENYA	1	
69.3	1.9	28.0	MALAWI	1	
94.3	25.0	28.0	NIGERIA	1	
95.8	1.5	28.0	RWANDA	1	
100.0	4.2	28.0	UGANDA	1	

source: U.S. Department of State, *Africa: . . . this new dialogue . . .* (Washington, D.C.: Government Printing Office, 1970), pp. 38–39. *Ivory Coast, Uganda, Rwanda, Mali*: arable land only. *Botswana, Somalia, Sudan, Cameroon, Chad, Sierra Leone, Ethiopia, Kenya*: large percentage of the land is pasture. *Tanzania*: more than half rough grazing land.

TABLE 1.3 Non-Agricultural Development Potential Index

Definition: Summation of ranking on "short- and medium-run opportunities for development" in (a) forestry, (b) fishing, (c) mining, (d) hydropower, and (e) manufacturing. Scores can be interpreted as follows:

4–7 Poor
8–11 Fair
12–14 Good
15–19 Excellent

```
RANGE =        12.00
MEAN =          8.59
STANDARD DEVIATION =          3.99
```

POPULATION PERCENT					
CUM.	COUNTRY	RANK	COUNTRY NAME	VALUE	RANGE DECILE
0.2	0.2	1.5	GABON	16	1
25.2	25.0	1.5	NIGERIA	16	
34.3	9.1	3.0	ZAIRE	15	
36.0	1.7	5.0	GUINEA	14	2
37.9	1.9	5.0	IVORY COAST	14	
39.7	1.8	5.0	ZAMBIA	14	
42.2	2.5	7.5	CAMEROON	13	3
42.7	0.5	7.5	LIBERIA	13	
43.1	0.4	9.5	CONGO (BRA)	12	4
46.9	3.8	9.5	GHANA	12	
51.7	4.8	11.0	KENYA	10	6
52.2	0.5	12.5	MAURITANIA	9	
57.9	5.7	12.5	TANZANIA	9	
68.8	10.9	15.5	ETHIOPIA	8	7
70.7	1.9	15.5	MALAWI	8	
72.4	1.7	15.5	SENEGAL	8	
73.5	1.1	15.5	SIERRA LEONE	8	
74.7	1.2	19.0	DAHOMEY	7	8
81.4	6.7	19.0	SUDAN	7	
85.6	4.2	19.0	UGANDA	7	
86.4	0.8	21.0	TOGO	6	9
86.7	0.3	24.0	BOTSWANA	5	10
87.4	0.7	24.0	CAR	5	
87.6	0.2	24.0	GAMBIA	5	
89.8	2.2	24.0	MALI	5	
91.3	1.5	24.0	RWANDA	5	
92.8	1.5	29.5	BURUNDI	4	
94.4	1.6	29.5	CHAD	4	
94.8	0.4	29.5	LESOTHO	4	
96.5	1.7	29.5	NIGER	4	
97.7	1.2	29.5	SOMALIA	4	
100.0	2.3	29.5	UPPER VOLTA	4	

SOURCE: William A. Hance, *African Economic Development*, pp. 290–291.

TABLE 1.4 Estimated Population 1969, Year of Latest Census, and Reliability Estimate

Definition: Year of latest census also includes year of sample survey if no census has been taken. Reliability estimate is coded:
1. Basically complete census in the five years prior to 1969.
2. Complete census within eight years or sample survey within four years prior to 1969.
3. Complete census or sample survey within twelve years prior to 1969 or a partial registration within two years prior to 1969.
4. Older censuses or sample surveys.
5. No census or sample survey taken by 1969.

```
RANGE =      56343.00
MEAN =        7076.34
STANDARD DEVIATION =      10575.55
```

POPULATION PERCENT							
CUM.	COUNTRY	RANK	COUNTRY NAME	VALUE	RANGE DECILE	TOTAL	
25.0	25.0	1.0	NIGERIA	56700	1	63	3
35.9	10.9	2.0	ETHIOPIA	24769	6	0	5
45.0	9.1	3.0	ZAIRE	20564	7	69	2
51.7	6.7	4.0	SUDAN	15186	8	56	4
57.4	5.7	5.0	TANZANIA	12926		67	1
62.2	4.8	6.0	KENYA	10890	9	69	1
66.4	4.2	7.0	UGANDA	9526		69	1
70.2	3.8	8.0	GHANA	8546		70	1
72.7	2.5	9.0	CAMEROON	5680	10	69	2
75.0	2.3	10.0	UPPER VOLTA	5278		61	3
77.2	2.2	11.0	MALI	4881		61	3
79.1	1.9	12.0	MALAWI	4398		66	1
81.0	1.9	13.0	IVORY COAST	4195		58	3
82.8	1.8	14.0	ZAMBIA	4056		69	1
84.5	1.7	15.0	NIGER	3909		60	3
86.2	1.7	16.0	GUINEA	3890		55	4
87.9	1.7	17.0	SENEGAL	3780		61	3
89.5	1.6	18.0	CHAD	3510		62	3
91.0	1.5	19.0	RWANDA	3500		52	4
92.5	1.5	20.0	BURUNDI	3475		65	3
93.7	1.2	21.0	SOMALIA	2730		0	5
94.9	1.2	22.0	DAHOMEY	2640		61	3
96.0	1.1	23.0	SIERRA LEONE	2510		63	2
96.8	0.8	24.0	TOGO	1815		59	3
97.5	0.7	25.0	CAR	1518		65	3
98.0	0.5	26.0	LIBERIA	1150		62	2
98.5	0.5	27.0	MAURITANIA	1140		65	2
98.9	0.4	28.0	LESOTHO	930		66	1
99.3	0.4	29.0	CONGO (BRA)	880		61	3
99.6	0.3	30.0	BOTSWANA	629		64	1
99.8	0.2	31.0	GABON	485		61	3
100.0	0.2	32.0	GAMBIA	357		63	2

SOURCES: *UN Demographic Yearbook 1969*, Table 4. *Nigeria*: See Appendix 5 of this Handbook; *Zaire (Congo K.)*: results of a provisional census taken in 1969–1970 as reported in *African Contemporary Record 1969–70*, p. B417; *Kenya, Uganda*: results of censuses in August 1969 as reported in *African Contemporary Record 1969–70*, pp. B138, B225.

TABLE 1.5 Population Density, 1969

Definition: Value is persons per square kilometer. Area estimates include inland waters.

```
RANGE =        124.00
MEAN =          20.94
STANDARD DEVIATION =        23.70
```

POPULATION PERCENT CUM.	COUNTRY	RANK	COUNTRY NAME	VALUE	RANGE DECILE
1.5	1.5	1.0	BURUNDI	125	1
26.5	25.0	2.0	NIGERIA	61	6
30.7	4.2	3.0	UGANDA	40	7
32.6	1.9	4.0	MALAWI	37	8
36.4	3.8	5.0	GHANA	36	
37.5	1.1	6.0	SIERRA LEONE	35	
39.0	1.5	7.0	RWANDA	33	
39.2	0.2	8.5	GAMBIA	32	
40.0	0.8	8.5	TOGO	32	
40.4	0.4	10.0	LESOTHO	31	
41.6	1.2	11.0	DAHOMEY	23	9
52.5	10.9	12.0	ETHIOPIA	20	
57.3	4.8	14.0	KENYA	19	
59.0	1.7	14.0	SENEGAL	19	
61.3	2.3	14.0	UPPER VOLTA	19	
63.0	1.7	16.0	GUINEA	16	
64.9	1.9	17.5	IVORY COAST	13	10
70.6	5.7	17.5	TANZANIA	13	
73.1	2.5	19.0	CAMEROON	12	
73.6	0.5	20.0	LIBERIA	10	
82.7	9.1	21.0	ZAIRE	9	
89.4	6.7	22.5	SUDAN	6	
91.2	1.8	22.5	ZAMBIA	6	
93.4	2.2	24.5	MALI	4	
94.6	1.2	24.5	SOMALIA	4	
96.2	1.6	27.0	CHAD	3	
96.6	0.4	27.0	CONGO (BRA)	3	
98.3	1.7	27.0	NIGER	3	
99.0	0.7	29.5	CAR	2	
99.2	0.2	29.5	GABON	2	
99.5	0.3	31.5	BOTSWANA	1	
100.0	0.5	31.5	MAURITANIA	1	

SOURCE: Population data from Table 1.4; area data from *UN Statistical Yearbook 1969*, Table 16.

TABLE 1.6 Estimated Percent Rate of Natural Population Increase, 1969

Definition: Population increase is obtained by subtracting the death rate from the birth rate.

```
RANGE =        2.80
MEAN =         2.62
STANDARD DEVIATION =        0.65
```

POPULATION PERCENT CUM.	COUNTRY	RANK	COUNTRY NAME	VALUE	RANGE DECILE
1.2	1.2	1.0	SOMALIA	3.7	1
2.9	1.7	3.0	NIGER	3.5	
4.4	1.5	3.0	RWANDA	3.5	
6.2	1.8	3.0	ZAMBIA	3.5	
11.0	4.8	5.0	KENYA	3.4	2
11.4	0.4	6.0	LESOTHO	3.3	
18.1	6.7	7.5	SUDAN	3.2	
23.8	5.7	7.5	TANZANIA	3.2	
25.0	1.2	9.0	DAHOMEY	3.1	3
25.8	0.8	10.0	TOGO	3.0	
29.6	3.8	11.0	GHANA	2.9	
30.3	0.7	13.0	CAR	2.8	4
32.0	1.7	13.0	GUINEA	2.8	
36.2	4.2	13.0	UGANDA	2.8	
38.1	1.9	15.5	IVORY COAST	2.7	
39.8	1.7	15.5	SENEGAL	2.7	
40.1	0.3	18.0	BOTSWANA	2.6	
42.0	1.9	18.0	MALAWI	2.6	
67.0	25.0	18.0	NIGERIA	2.6	
76.1	9.1	20.5	ZAIRE	2.5	5
78.4	2.3	20.5	UPPER VOLTA	2.5	
79.9	1.5	22.0	BURUNDI	2.4	
82.4	2.5	23.5	CAMEROON	2.3	
84.6	2.2	23.5	MALI	2.3	
84.8	0.2	25.5	GAMBIA	2.1	6
85.3	0.5	25.5	MAURITANIA	2.1	
85.8	0.5	27.0	LIBERIA	2.0	7
96.7	10.9	28.0	ETHIOPIA	1.9	
98.3	1.6	29.5	CHAD	1.7	8
98.7	0.4	29.5	CONGO (BRA)	1.7	
99.8	1.1	31.0	SIERRA LEONE	1.5	
100.0	0.2	32.0	GABON	0.9	10

SOURCE: See Appendix 5 for the method of calculation and sources.

TABLE 1.7 Percent European Population in 1920s

Definition: "European" includes all whites. Cameroon includes the European population of Douala only, Ghana includes British Togoland.

```
RANGE =            0.68
MEAN =             0.14
STANDARD DEVIATION =          0.16
```

POPULATION PERCENT CUM.	COUNTRY	RANK	COUNTRY NAME	VALUE	RANGE DECILE
0.3	0.3	1.0	BOTSWANA	0.69	1
2.1	1.8	2.0	ZAMBIA	0.54	3
3.8	1.7	3.0	SENEGAL	0.36	5
8.6	4.8	4.5	KENYA	0.34	6
9.0	0.4	4.5	LESOTHO	0.34	
18.1	9.1	6.0	ZAIRE	0.26	7
18.3	0.2	7.0	GABON	0.17	8
18.7	0.4	9.0	CONGO (BRA)	0.13	9
19.9	1.2	9.0	SOMALIA	0.13	
25.6	5.7	9.0	TANZANIA	0.13	
26.3	0.7	12.0	CAR	0.10	
26.5	0.2	12.0	GAMBIA	0.10	
28.2	1.7	12.0	GUINEA	0.10	
30.1	1.9	14.5	MALAWI	0.08	
30.9	0.8	14.5	TOGO	0.08	
33.4	2.5	17.5	CAMEROON	0.07	10
37.2	3.8	17.5	GHANA	0.07	
39.1	1.9	17.5	IVORY COAST	0.07	
40.2	1.1	17.5	SIERRA LEONE	0.07	
41.4	1.2	20.5	DAHOMEY	0.06	
43.6	2.2	20.5	MALI	0.06	
47.8	4.2	22.0	UGANDA	0.05	
48.3	0.5	23.0	MAURITANIA	0.04	
49.9	1.6	24.5	CHAD	0.03	
60.8	10.9	24.5	ETHIOPIA	0.03	
62.5	1.7	27.0	NIGER	0.02	
87.5	25.0	27.0	NIGERIA	0.02	
89.8	2.3	27.0	UPPER VOLTA	0.02	
90.3	0.5	29.0	LIBERIA	0.01	

DATA NOT AVAILABLE FOR THE FOLLOWING COUNTRIES

BURUNDI   RWANDA   SUDAN

SOURCES: O. Martens and O. Karstedt, *The African Handbook*, 2nd ed. (London: Allen and Unwin, 1938). Population data for the years indicated is from Appendix 5. *Central African Republic, Congo (Brazzaville), Gabon*: J. Brummelkamp, *Social Geografie van Afrika*, Vol. 2 (Groningen: J. B. Wolters, 1930); *Liberia*: R. P. Strong, ed., *The African Republic of Liberia and the Belgian Congo* (Cambridge: Harvard University Press, 1930), pp. 42–44.

YEARS: Data is for 1926 except for: *Botswana, Gambia, Sierra Leone*: 1921; *Ethiopia*: 1927; *Liberia, Nigeria, Tanzania, Zambia*: 1928; *Cameroon, Dahomey, Kenya, Lesotho, Malawi, Somalia, Togo, Uganda, Upper Volta*: 1929; *Zaire (Congo K.)*: 1930; *Ghana*: 1931; *Central African Republic, Guinea, Mali*: 1926 estimates were made by extrapolating between 1920 and 1930 data.

TABLE 1.8 Percent European Population, ca. 1960

Definition: "European" includes all whites.

```
RANGE =          2.25
MEAN =           0.45
STANDARD DEVIATION =          0.56
```

POPULATION PERCENT CUM.	COUNTRY	RANK	COUNTRY NAME	VALUE	RANGE DECILE
1.8	1.8	1.0	ZAMBIA	2.31	1
3.5	1.7	2.0	SENEGAL	2.00	2
3.9	0.4	3.0	CONGO (BRA)	1.56	4
4.1	0.2	4.0	GABON	1.12	6
13.2	9.1	5.0	ZAIRE	0.84	7
13.5	0.3	6.0	BOTSWANA	0.80	
18.3	4.8	7.0	KENYA	0.73	8
20.2	1.9	8.0	IVORY COAST	0.56	
22.7	2.5	9.0	CAMEROON	0.42	9
23.4	0.7	10.0	CAR	0.40	
23.6	0.2	11.0	GAMBIA	0.33	
24.0	0.4	12.0	LESOTHO	0.28	10
25.2	1.2	13.0	SOMALIA	0.24	
30.9	5.7	14.0	TANZANIA	0.22	
31.4	0.5	15.0	MAURITANIA	0.21	
31.9	0.5	16.0	LIBERIA	0.20	
35.7	3.8	17.5	GHANA	0.19	
37.9	2.2	17.5	MALI	0.19	
39.8	1.9	19.5	MALAWI	0.17	
44.0	4.2	19.5	UGANDA	0.17	
45.2	1.2	21.5	DAHOMEY	0.15	
46.7	1.5	21.5	RWANDA	0.15	
47.5	0.8	23.0	TOGO	0.14	
49.2	1.7	24.0	NIGER	0.11	
50.8	1.6	25.0	CHAD	0.10	
51.9	1.1	26.5	SIERRA LEONE	0.09	
54.2	2.3	26.5	UPPER VOLTA	0.09	
55.7	1.5	28.5	BURUNDI	0.07	
80.7	25.0	28.5	NIGERIA	0.07	
82.4	1.7	30.0	GUINEA	0.06	
89.1	6.7	31.5	SUDAN	0.06	

DATA NOT AVAILABLE FOR THE FOLLOWING COUNTRIES

ETHIOPIA

SOURCES: Unless otherwise indicated, data source is an official government census report. *Cameroon, CAR, Gabon, Liberia, Mali, Mauritania, Niger: Outre-mer 1958* (Paris: Republique Française, Ministère d'Outre-mer, Service des Statistics, 1960); *Nigeria, Somalia*: Francisco H. Blasco, *Africa Tercer Mundo* (Barcelona: Corona, 1966); *Sierra Leone, Tanzania: UN Statistical Yearbook 1961–62; Burundi, Rwanda*: Office de l'Information et des Relations Publique du Congo Belge et du Ruanda-Urundi, *Ruanda-Urundi Geography and History* (Brussels: 1960), p. 52; *Ghana*: Walter Birmingham, et al., eds., *A Study of Contemporary Ghana*, Vol. 2 (London: Allen and Unwin, 1967); *Dahomey*: Includes all non-indigenous population; *Burundi, Guinea, Rwanda*: For the main urban centers only; *Ivory Coast*: 1965 figure; *Chad: Guide Afrique Equatoriale 1962–63; Zaire (Congo K.)*: Howard M. Epstein, ed., *Revolt in Congo 1960–1964* (New York: Facts on File, 1965), p. 173; *Zambia*: George Kay, *A Social Geography of Zambia* (London: University of London Press, 1967); *Botswana, Burundi, Cameroon, Chad, Congo (Brazzaville), Dahomey, Gambia, Guinea, Ivory Coast, Kenya, Lesotho, Malawi, Mali, Mauritania, Nigeria, Rwanda, Senegal, Sierra Leone, Somalia, Sudan, Tanzania, Upper Volta*: extrapolations on a straight line basis were made for these countries.

2. Cultural Pluralism

Three major types of cultural pluralism in Black Africa are based on differences in language, religion, and ethnicity. The first two are treated in this chapter, and ethnic pluralism will be discussed in Chapter 16. Pluralism refers to the existence of two or more social sub-systems within a large context, such as the national state. Even in cases where such sub-systems are structurally interrelated in the political and/or economic spheres, there is usually some degree of autonomy in the social sphere. It is recognized that both language and religion may, in certain circumstances, be affiliational or voluntaristic types of grouping. In broad demographic terms, however, religion and language tend to represent a potential for more basic social boundaries. At the same time both language and religion represent some of the most powerful linkages between ethnic groups, especially in terms of communications capacity.

a. Language Pluralism

Language Distribution and Classification

According to Knappert,[1] there are 993 indigenous languages in the thirty-two countries in this Handbook. Many linguists estimate the actual number to be considerably higher. Language distribution is difficult to assess in Africa because scholars disagree on whether a particular designation refers to the dialect of a language, a single language, or a group of closely related languages. A number of classification schemes have been proposed. Most tend to follow one or the other of two major organizing principles: (1) etiological or historical relatedness between languages (exemplified in the work of Westermann and Bryan,[2] and Guthrie[3]); (2) typologies based on similarities between languages (exemplified in the work of Greenberg[4] and the Voegelins[5]). A good deal of controversy has surrounded the issue of classification, but such literature[6] will not be reviewed in this Handbook. For our purpose, to illustrate the idea of language families, we selected the Greenberg classification. This classification, which first appeared in 1955, and then in revised form (with fewer over-all categories) in 1963, has come to be widely accepted.

The Greenberg classification identifies four major language families (or "macro-phyla," according to the Voegelins), which may be regarded as roughly comparable in degree of comprehensiveness to the "Indo-European" language family (which includes such widely different languages as Russian, Persian, English, and Hindi). The four language families are: (I) *Congo-Kordofanian*, which includes both the Bantu of East and Central Africa, as well as most of the languages of West Africa; (II) *Nilo-Saharan*, which groups such languages of the Sudanic belt as Songhai and Kanuri together with the several Nilotic northeastern languages; (III) *Afro-Asiatic*, including Arabic, the Semitic languages of Ethiopia, the Berber languages of North Africa, ancient Egyptian (now extinct), and Hausa; (IV) *Khoisan*, which is limited to a few pockets in southern Africa, including the Bushmen and Hottentots, who are characterized by "click" sounds in their languages.

The basis of the Greenberg classification is typological: i.e. a comparison of basic vocabulary and grammatical elements between the various African languages for similarity of sound (phonology) and meaning or function (semantics and morphology). The major sections within each of the four language families are summarized in Figure 2.1. Notice that Bantu languages form only a sub-category in the Benue-Congo section of Congo-Kordofanian. Although Guthrie suggests major families within the Bantu languages,[7] we have not made such distinctions at this time in our own coding of language families. In Part II of this Handbook, every language group of 5 percent or more within each African country is coded according to the language family and major sections listed in Figure 2.1.

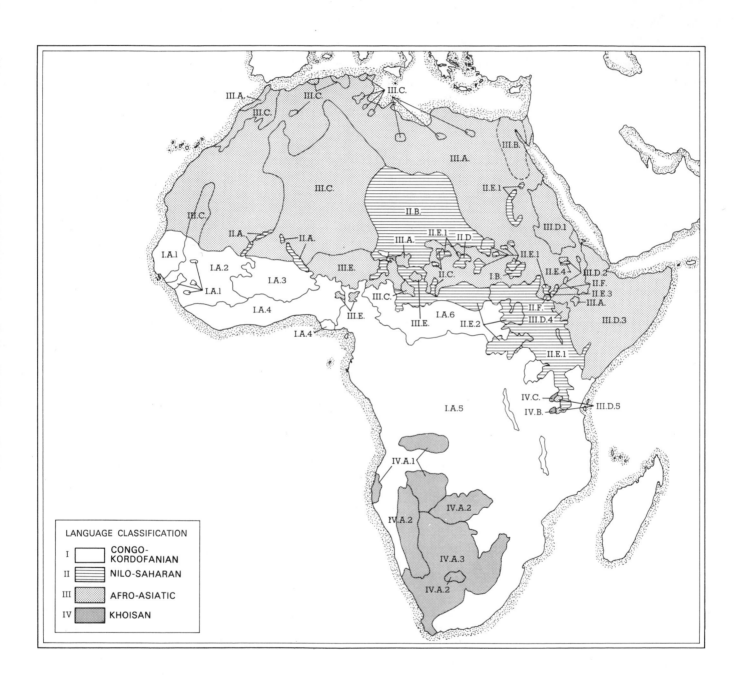

LANGUAGE CLASSIFICATION

I ☐ CONGO-KORDOFANIAN

II ☰ NILO-SAHARAN

III ▦ AFRO-ASIATIC

IV ▦ KHOISAN

Figure 2.1 Language Families of Africa: Greenberg's 1963 Classification

Language Family (*macro-phylum*)	*Major Sections* (*phyla/families*)	*Examples of individual languages or groups*
I. Congo-Kordofanian	A. Niger-Congo	
	A–1. West Atlantic	Fulani, Wolof, Serer, Temne, Limba
	A–2. Mande	Soninke, Malinké, Bambara, Kpellé
	A–3. Voltaic (Gur)	Senufo, Mossi, Grusi, Kabre, Bargu
	A–4. Kwa ("others")	Kru, Bété, Bassa, Ewé, Akan, Yoruba
	A–5. Benue-Congo	Bantu family, Tiv, Ibibio, Basa, Mbum
	A–6. Adamawa	Gbaya, Banda, Mbaka, Sango
	B. Kordofanian	
	B–1. Koalib	Kanderma
	B–2. Tegali	Rashad
	B–3. Talodi	Lafofa
	B–4. Tumtum	Tuleshi
	B–5. Katla	Tima
II. Nilo-Saharan	A. Songhai	
	B. Saharan	Kanuri (Kanembu)
	C. Maban	Maba
	D. Fur	
	E. Chari-Nile	
	E–1. Eastern Sudanic	Nubian group, Nilotic family, (Acholi, Lango, Nuer)
	E–2. Central Sudanic	
	E–3. Berta	
	E–4. Kunama	
	F. Koman	Koma
III. Afro-Asiatic	A. Semitic	Arabic
	B. Egyptian	
	C. Berber	
	D. Cushitic	
	D–1. Northern Cushitic	Beja
	D–2. Central Cushitic	Bogo
	D–3. Eastern Cushitic	Saho-Afar, Somali, Galla
	D–4. Western Cushitic	Janjero
	D–5. Southern Cushitic	Burungi
	E. Chad	Hausa, Bana, Banana (Masa)
IV. Khoisan	A. South African Khoisan	(Not significant in countries contained in this Handbook)
	A–1. Northern South African Khoisan	
	A–2. Central South African Khoisan	
	A–3. Southern South African Khoisan	
	B. Sandawe	
	C. Hatsa	

Language and National Integration

The relationship between language patterns and national integration has been explored by a number of scholars.[8] The distinction between a nation-state and a multinational state largely revolves around the issue of language. Many scholars have used language pluralism as a measure of cultural diversity within a country. Banks and Textor[9] suggest two such variables: (a) "linguistic homogeneity" (countries with 85 percent of the adult populations speaking a common language are coded as homogeneous); (b) speakers of dominant language as percentage of population. Adelman and Morris[10] use language diversity as the major indicator of national integration. Anderson, von der Mehden, and Young[11] use an ordinal scale to show the degree of linguistic pluralism within a country. When language distribution is viewed from a national context in Africa, there is a tremendous range between those countries which have only one or two languages, and those which have up to two hundred. In this Handbook we present three variables on language homogeneity (Tables 2.1–2.3).

Yet quite apart from the actual number of languages within a state is the issue of the number of language families, which is probably some measure of the "degree of language corpus distance"[12] within a country (Table 2.4). According to Kloss:

> It would seem that close linguistic kinship facilitates collaboration and mutual understanding between the leading ethnic nationalities, whereas fundamental linguistic distance tends to make for mutual distrust and to be an obstacle (though not an unsurmountable one) to a national feeling of belonging together.[13]

This hypothesis may be tested within the African context. At the first view, some countries which appear to have a large number of languages, such as CAR, Congo (Brazzaville), or Tanzania, actually contain languages which are all of a single sub-category (IA6, IA5, and IA5 respectively), while countries such as Mauritania (which had severe language riots in 1966) have a more limited number of languages which nevertheless represent different macro-phyla (IIIA and IA1). On the other hand, countries such as Nigeria which have a large number of languages can own compound language prob-lems since virtually all major language families and sub-categories are represented.

Within the African context, statesmen are clearly aware of the significance of language to national integration. Some have even suggested that all internal administrative districts within the state follow linguistic lines.[14]

At this point the question of *lingua francas*, or "languages of wider communication,"[15] becomes extremely important (Table 2.5). A leading Tanzanian newspaper writes: "A common indigenous language in the modern nation states is a powerful factor for unity. Cutting across tribal and ethnic lines, it promotes a feeling of single community. . . . In Tanzania we have been blessed with such a language —Swahili."[16] In most African states there exist languages of wider communication, although to date very little research has been done on *lingua francas* or multilingualism.[17]

For purposes of this volume, we have defined a *lingua franca* as a second language spoken by 5 percent or more of the population. In terms of potential for wider communication, we would suggest that the degree of standardization of a language or *lingua franca* is of prime importance (Table 2.6). If language standardization has reached a stage where wide-spread publishing is possible, the communications potential is greater than in cases where orthographies have not been devised. Most of the major languages of Africa are becoming standardized, particularly those languages which exist in more than one country (e.g. Hausa and Swahili). It is clear that govern-mental policy regarding language patterns is important to national integration (Table 2.7). Policy regarding use of official languages, languages of mass media, and of education, is central to the processes of national communication and cooperation.[18]

The Formulation of Language Variables

Many social scientists have suggested the importance of language classification variables. Barrett[19] has coded ethnic groups per African country on a dichotomous language-family variable (Bantu/non-Bantu). In Part II of this Handbook, we have included data on language pluralism within the capital cities of the thirty-two African states. (The capital city context may be more relevant to certain types of social science analysis than the national context.)

In formulating variables dealing with language pluralism in Africa it is important to recognize the limitations of source materials. Both Adelman and Morris, and Banks and Textor draw almost exclusively for their African language data on Mac-Dougald.[20] This study was done in the '40s—besides being incomplete for several African countries, its reliability is questionable (see below). In all cases, it is important to recognize when scholars are using ethnic distribution data as a surrogate for language distribution data and vice versa.

The variables we have chosen to formulate and include in this Handbook may be divided into two categories: (1) language distribution, and (2) national communications potential. Language distribution refers to the total number of distinct languages within a country (Table 2.3), the degree to which a single language predominates—including both percent of total population (Table 2.1) and relationship to second largest language (Table 2.3), and the degree to which languages within a country are part of the same, or different language families (Table 2.4).

National communications potential in vernacular languages refers to the types, if any, of *lingua franca* within a country (Table 2.5), the extent of standardization of the major languages (Table 2.6), and governmental policy with regard to use of vernaculars in communications, education, and government (Table 2.7). It should be noted that we have not included exoglossic (i.e., non-indigenous) language variables (such as degree of literacy in French or English) since such data is contained in the education section.

With regard to the future formulation of national language policy variables, it is clear that time-series data will be of special importance. The language policies of most countries in Africa have changed over time, and the timing of these changes may well be correlated with other important events within the countries. In Nigeria, for example, the *number* of vernacular languages used in education and broadcasting changed in 1960, 1966, 1967, and —according to official statements—will change again now that the civil war is over.

Data Sources and Reliability

On the question of language distribution within a country, there is a wide difference of opinion among scholars. The three major comprehensive attempts to code dominant language as percent of total population have been MacDougald (1944),[21] Knappert (1965),[22] and Rustow (1968).[23] Not only is there considerable variation in the percentages attributed (see Figure 2.2), but in eight countries (Cameroon,

Figure 2.2 Estimated Reliability of Major Language (Inter-coder Estimates of Major Language as Percent of Total Population)*

Country	Language	MacDougald Estimate	Knappert Estimate	Rustow Estimate	Range of Estimate†
1. Botswana	Tswana	—	100%	69%	31%
2. Burundi	Rundi	84%	100	28	72
3. Chad	Arabic	—	40	33	7
4. Congo (Bra)	Kongo	—	40	50	10
5. Dahomey	Fon	51	50	58	8
6. Ethiopia	Amharic	61	71	49	22
7. Gambia	Mandingo	—	100	46**	54
8. Ghana	Akan	62	57	44	18
9. Guinea	Fulani	62	33	39	29

* Includes all countries in first alphabetical half of thirty-two country sample, excluding those where there was no agreement on choice of primary language.

† Average range of estimate is 28 percent.

** Includes Malinke-Bambara-Dyula.

CAR, Zaire [Congo K.], Gabon, Ivory Coast, Kenya, Sierra Leone, Tanzania) there is a lack of agreement as to which is the dominant language.

Part of this lack of coding congruence is probably definitional, since Rustow is apparently referring to languages as the equivalent of ethnic groups, while Knappert is apparently referring to speakers of a given language (including second-language speakers). We have adopted the latter procedure. Thus, in twenty-three out of thirty-two countries, the dominant language is—at least to some extent—a *lingua franca* within the country, and hence is invariably larger than the "ethnic group" who may speak it as a mother tongue. Our estimates of whether a dominant language acts as a *lingua franca* are based on individual country studies of language distribution (cited in Part II) and on our own estimates. These estimates should be regarded as very rough approximations.

Our estimates of the degree of standardization of dominant languages (first or second language) is also based on country-specific literature. In his discussion of a standardization criteria, Kloss[24] provides some paradigms from the African context. He regards French as a "mature standard language," Luganda as a "young standard language," Somali as an "unstandardized alphabetized language," and Galla as a "pre-literate language." We have coded only four African languages as "mature standard languages": Arabic, Amharic, Swalili, Hausa. As the UNESCO studies of language distribution and characteristics in Africa become available, it may be possible to refine the distinctions between African languages on such matters as standardization of orthography, extent of vernacular literature, and range/number of vocabulary words. The world-wide language survey[25] directed by Kloss should also yield valuable data on the African countries.

Our judgments as to official language policy within the African countries are also rough approximations, especially since such policies may change over time or may be "unofficial." In general, the French-speaking areas have not used vernacular languages in education, but in the post-independence period they have used vernaculars in broadcasting. English-speaking areas have been receptive to using the vernacular in government, education, and mass media. The regional and/or national official languages of each country are cited in Part II by country.

b. Religion

The three major religious traditions in contemporary Africa are African traditional religion, Islam, and Christianity. Traditional religion, which consists of a wide variety of localized religious practices and beliefs, is presently declining in institutional vigor and importance, giving way to Islam and Christianity. The underlying philosophy or world view[26] common to African traditional religions has by no means shared in this decline, however. It persists in important ways such as the African adaptations of Islam and Christianity, the continued demand for the divinatory powers, witchcraft protection, and healing skills of traditional practitioners, and in aspects of the new African culture.

Islam[27] has been an important religious influence in Africa south of the Sahara, especially since the days of Ibn Yasin, an eleventh-century Muslim missionary who established himself among the Berbers in present-day Mauritania. Christianity[28] has an even longer history of contact back to the fourth-century introduction of Coptic Christianity to the Kingdom of Axum (present-day Ethiopia). The Ethiopian Orthodox Church remains today the most important Christian Church in Ethiopia. However, the centuries-long contact between Roman Catholic Portugal and Central and West Africa which began in the fifteenth century was ultimately unsuccessful in establishing a lasting mission. A sustained Christian missionary effort on the part of Protestants and Roman Catholics ultimately occurred in the nineteenth century. Today the northern part of Black Africa is heavily Muslim, while certain countries to the south, such as Gabon, have Christian majorities. Present indications suggest an accelerated movement towards these two major world religions so that by 1980 avowed adherents of traditional African religion will be a very small minority in Black Africa.

Islam and Christianity have been important forces for change in Africa. Each embodies a distinctive universalistic culture which it transmits to its

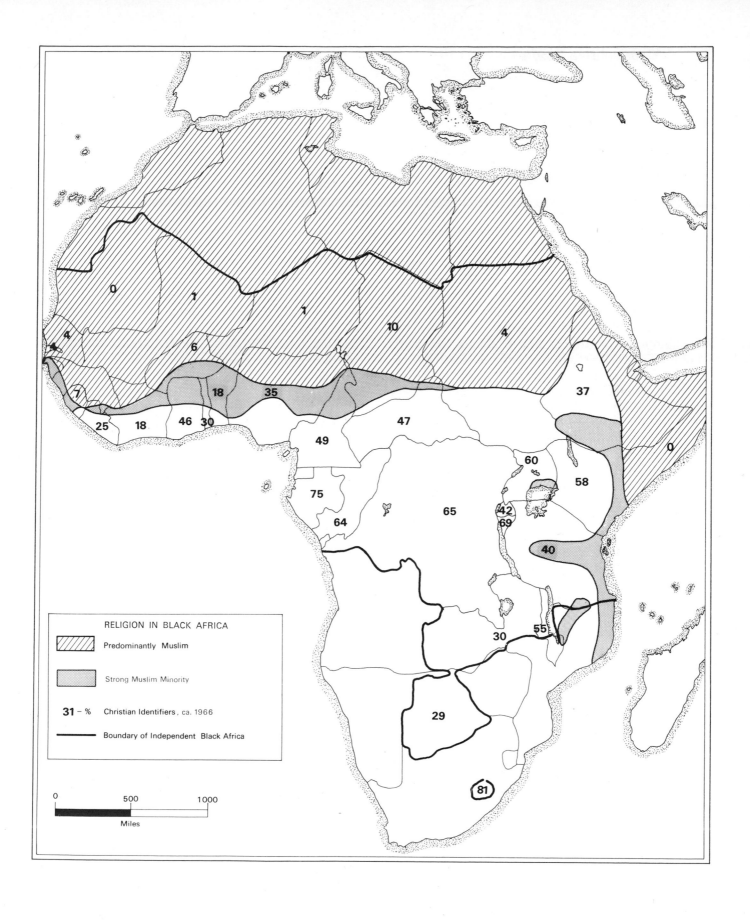

RELIGION IN BLACK AFRICA

Predominantly Muslim

Strong Muslim Minority

31 – % Christian Identifiers, ca. 1966

Boundary of Independent Black Africa

0   500   1000

Miles

converts through the teachings of its religious leaders, its religious ceremonies, and special experiences such as the Muslim pilgrimage to Mecca. Christianity, as the religion of the colonial powers, came to enjoy high prestige with those Africans who aspired to elite positions in the modern social structure. One of the special attractions of Christianity was the widespread network of mission schools. Developed from the beginning of missionary work in each area so as to instruct the new believers in the Bible, these schools quickly broadened to serve a wider clientele, providing a fuller curriculum and attracting financial support from the colonial governments. As a consequence the colonial governments, especially the British, opened relatively few secular government schools. Today it is not uncommon to find that 60–75 percent of the schools in a country are still owned by the churches.[29] Islam, of course, offers Koranic instruction through local Koranic schools.

One of the few quantitative cross-national studies of a sample of African nations examined the effect of Christianity in ten mainly English-speaking countries and concluded that Christian missionaries have been an important cause of social mobilization.[30] Although the conclusions of this study have been called into question on methodological grounds,[31] the relationship of religion to social change in Africa remains one of considerable interest.

The pattern of the relationship between religion and politics in contemporary Africa is far from clear at this point in the development of African nations. In most African countries thus far Christianity and Islam have avoided direct confrontations with the State, but the cases of Guinea, Senegal, and Ghana suggest a certain potential for contributing to political opposition on the part of religious groups and leaders. On the other hand, the Islamic character of Mauritania and Somalia and the established Ethiopian Orthodox Church in Ethiopia probably contributes to the political integration of these countries. In countries where there is no one dominant faith, religion has the potential for acting as a cross-cutting cleavage between ethnic groups.

Concepts and Definitions

In order to satisfactorily employ religion as a variable in the analysis of African societies it is necessary to understand how Muslims and Christians differentiate themselves. Islam, to the non-Muslim, often appears to be a monolithic, homogeneous entity. Actually it contains important divisions between the various legal schools, the Sufi brotherhoods, the believers and the nonbelievers in a Mahdi, and the reformed and conservative groups. Only two of the legal schools are important in Africa: the Maliki in the North and West, and the Shafi'i on the eastern coast. Among the many Sufi brotherhoods in Africa, the Tidjaniyya and the Qadiriyya are especially important in West Africa. Claimants to the Mahdiship have occasionally appeared in Islamic Africa, most notably in the Sudan. The Pakistani Ahmadiyya Muslim group, which considers the late Ghulam Ahmad to have been the Mahdi, also undertakes active missionary work in Africa.[32] Although much of African Islam is very conservative, reform groups exist, particularly in urban settings where they show a concern for modernizing Islamic education and the role of women. Unfortunately, data are unavailable on a cross-national basis for Muslim sub-groupings and we are unable to include them in the variables for this section.

The three major traditions of Christianity are Orthodoxy, Roman Catholicism, and Protestantism. The Ethiopian Orthodox Church is the major expression of Orthodoxy in Africa, while Roman Catholicism is represented by various missionary orders such as the White Fathers. With the exception of part of Eritrea in Ethiopia, the Catholic areas in our sample of countries are under the authority of *Propaganda Fide* in Rome. Protestantism is divided into a large number of denominations. These denominations may be further grouped into the "main line" mission denominations such as the Methodists and Anglicans, the "third force" or sect-type mission groups such as the Seventh Day Adventists and Church of God, and the African independent churches.[33] The latter are Christian groups which either broke away from the mission churches or spontaneously emerged as a response to the work of African Christian diviner-healers or prophets. Data are available for most of the Christian sub-groupings, a small selection of which is presented in Tables 2.12–2.18.

"Membership" in a religious group has various meanings depending upon the context. Typically the official membership figures of the various Christian religious groups in Africa are far below the aggregate claims of individuals who are individually polled in a national survey or census. The individual tells the census taker that he is a "Protestant" or "Catholic" in the sense of stating a preference. He may rarely or never occupy a pew—perhaps he has never even been baptized. The Christian groups themselves, on the other hand, generally count as full members only those who have fulfilled certain requirements (such as confirmation). Even when they label a broader category of people as "catechumens" or as the "Christian community," they still reserve these labels for people who have demonstrated their religious preference through their actions in en-rolling as catechumens and/or their attendance at church services. It is important to note that Muslims and traditionalists do not make this distinction: in these religions the individual's self-definition is the sole criterion for "membership."

In this Handbook we will make a basic distinction for the Christian groups, between these two types of involvement or identification with religion in terms of: (a) *Identifiers*, or those who claim a traditional, Muslim, or Christian identity (as in a census), and (b) *Affiliators*, a category applicable *only to Christianity*, which denotes those claimed by the Christian groups themselves as members, catechumens, or adherents. Our "affiliators" category is comparable to the "total Christian community" claimed by each Protestant denomination in the *World Christian Handbook*,[34] a major source for data. The most comparable Roman Catholic category for affiliators is the sum of their "Catholics" (baptized, including children) and their "catechumens" (under instructions for baptism) categories.[35] Although we will not do so here, it is possible to break the Protestant data into categories of affiliators such as communicants or "full members," and catechumens or inquirers. In Africa the catechumen category is typically swollen out of proportion to other parts of the world because the Roman Catholic Church and many Protestant churches do not baptize polygynists.

All too often the presentation of data on Christian-ity in Africa fails to make this important distinction between identifiers and affiliators and the reader is left uncertain as to how the author defines membership. Figure 2.3 illustrates this problem and shows

Figure 2.3 Estimates of Christians in Ghana and Nigeria, 1960s

	Beetham's Data on "Percent Christian"[1]	Christian Affiliators[2]	Christian Identifiers[3]
Ghana	36% (c. 1964)	17% (1962)	43% (1960)
Nigeria	8 (c. 1964)	6 (1962)	35 (1963)

[1] T. A. Beetham, *Christianity in Africa* (London: Pall Mall, 1965).
[2] *World Christian Handbook 1962* (London: World Dominion Press, 1963). This source presents official Protestant and Roman Catholic reports on membership (full members plus catechumens).
[3] Ghana Census, 1960, and Nigerian Census, 1963.

the marked differences between national data on affiliators and identifiers. T. A. Beetham's book reports data identified as "percent Christian" and footnoted as being based on "official Roman Catholic and Protestant statistics." In fact, only the Nigerian figure resembles the official Christian data. His Ghanaian figure is much closer to the figure reported in the Ghanaian 1960 census. The difference in years between the figures cannot account for this great a difference.

Data Sources and Reliability

The best source for data on religious *identifiers* are official censuses or sample surveys. Unfortunately religion is not always included in African censuses (nor in the U.S. census for that matter), so for the most part other authorities have to be relied upon in making estimates of identifiers. These authorities' reliability is impossible to estimate, but an error margin of 10 percent or more may be assumed at the present time.

The *affiliation* category for the Christian data presents a more hopeful situation with regard to data reliability. The annual church membership reports compiled by the national church authorities represent one of the most extensive statistical operations in Africa, and provide a relatively thorough and consistent data base. There are many chances for misreporting and non-reporting in this operation, however, as anyone knows who has tried to collect religious data on the local level in Africa.

The Roman Catholic membership figures are published annually, diocese by diocese (but not by nation), for the whole world in *Annuario Pontificio* (Vatican City). Compilations on the national level for Africa are made by the International Fides Service and have been published in *Ready Information about Africa*,[36] *Bilan du Monde*,[37] and the Protestant *World Christian Handbook*.[38] The sources of bias in the Roman Catholic reporting process are unknown.

Protestant data are published periodically in the *World Christian Handbook*. The *Handbook* obtains its data by sending questionnaires to all Protestant denominations requesting data on a number of categories. It publishes these data in country tables which list each denomination and their reported data. Until recently the reliability of the *Handbook's* data left much to be desired.[39] Errors of considerable magnitude, such as its 1957 report that the Free Presbyterian Church of Scotland had one thousand ordained pastors in the Union of South Africa whereas in fact they had only one, found publication with alarming frequency. Churches were sometimes counted more than once when multiple reports were received under variations of the church's name.[40] Finally, no attempt was made to include the African independent churches, thus ignoring several million African Christians. Gross errors of this sort were eliminated from the 1968 *Handbook*, by its new African editor, David B. Barrett. Future editions of the *Handbook* are to be combined with the Roman Catholic *Bilan du Monde*, and Barrett and his co-editors are making serious efforts to improve the comprehensiveness and reliability of the African data.

The Data

The first five tables, 2.8–2.12, give estimates of the percentage of the population who identify (as defined above) with Islam, Christianity, Protestantism, Roman Catholicism and traditional religion. These estimates correspond to the statements in other reference books that 50 percent of the population in country X is Muslim, 32 percent is Christian, etc. The figures given here vary from the available estimates in standard international reference works, some-

times considerably. Since they are based on the latest available data as detailed in the source notes to the tables, overall they should provide a more satisfactory estimate, but the reader should keep the suggested error margin of at least 10 percent in mind.

Although there are sources for Christian affiliators which present data over time,[41] nothing comparable is available for Christian, Muslim and traditional identifiers. The Christian affiliator data sources for the years prior to World War II suffer from two weaknesses, however. Their reliability is very hard to assess since they give totals for each country but do not break these totals down to the component denominations. Secondly, their coverage is poor—they only present data for about 21 of our 32 countries.

In an attempt to overcome these weaknesses we present data on mission stations per million population in 1925 (Tables 2.13–2.15). The data source is a map which clearly locates these stations.[42] The decision to use mission stations instead of members or missionaries per million population reduces the validity of the variables somewhat, but it can be argued that the mission stations were important indicators of the Christian presence in Africa at that time. Hildegard Johnson has described the role of the mission station in this regard:

> . . . With their chapels, residences, dormitories, schools, dispensaries, gardens, utility buildings, water-supply systems, and good access roads they stand in great contrast with their immediate surroundings. In the confrontation of Europeans with African ways of life these stations have been for the missionaries a refuge, a symbol of achievement, and a home; for the Africans they have been strongholds of alien ways from religion to agriculture. . . .[43]

Variables which indicate change are highly desirable and we present a change variable for Roman Catholic membership growth 1963–1967 (Table 2.18). After careful consideration it was concluded that a reliable Protestant growth estimate for a comparable time period could not be made at this time.[44]

Only two recent variables on the level of Christian adherence are included here because many of these variables are available in the *World Christian Handbook* and will also be published in the forthcoming second edition of the *World Handbook of Social and*

Political Indicators.[45] Because the data for an estimate of total Christian affiliators ca. 1967 is not available in the above handbooks,[46] however, we present that variable (Table 2.16) and also David Barrett's estimates of the adherents of the African Independent Churches (Table 2.17).

Notes

[1] Jan Knappert, "Language Problems of the New Nations of Africa," *Africa Quarterly*, 5 (1965): 95–105.

[2] See Diedrich Westermann and Margaret Bryan, *Languages of West Africa, Handbook of African Languages* (London: Oxford University Press, 1952).

[3] Malcolm Guthrie, *The Classification of the Bantu Languages* (London: Oxford University Press, 1948); also, "Bantu Origins: A Tentative New Hypothesis," *Journal of African Languages*, 1 (1962): 9–21.

[4] Joseph H. Greenberg, *The Languages of Africa* (Bloomington: Indiana University Press, 1966); also, *Studies in African Linguistic Classification* (New Haven, Conn.: Compass Publishing Company, 1955).

[5] C. F. and F. M. Voegelin, "Languages of the World: African Fascicle One," *Anthropological Linguistics*, 6 (May 1964): 1–339.

[6] See, F. D. D. Winston, "Greenberg's Classification of African Languages," *African Language Studies*, 7 (1966): 160–170; David Dalby, "Levels of Relationship in the Comparative Study of African Languages," *African Language Studies*, 7 (1966): 171–179; Diedrich Westermann, "African Linguistic Classifications," *Africa*, 22 (1952): 250–256; Istvan Fodor, "La classification des langues negro-africaines et la theorie de J. H. Greenberg," *Cahiers d'études Africaine*, 7 (1968): 617–631; Istvan Fodor, *The Problems in the Classification of the African Languages: Methodological and Theoretical Conclusions Concerning the Classification System of Joseph H. Greenberg* (Budapest: Center for Afro-Asian Research of the Hungarian Academy of Sciences, 1966); J. H. Kwabena Nketia, "The Language Problem and the African Personality," *Présence Africaine*, no. 67 (1968): 157–171; Jean Mfoulou, "Science et pseudo-science des langues Africaines," *Présence Africaine*, no. 70 (1969): 147–161: Pierre Alexandre, *Langues et Langage en Afrique Noire* (Paris: Payot, 1967); "Table ronde sur les langues Africaines," *Présence Africaine*, no. 67 (1968): 53–156; Jack Berry, "Language Systems and Literature" in *The African Experience*, Vol. 1, eds. John Paden and Edward Soja (Evanston, Ill.: Northwestern University Press, 1970).

[7] Guthrie, *Classification of the Bantu Languages.*

[8] See Joshua A. Fishman, Charles A. Ferguson, and Jyotirindra Das Gupta, eds., *Language Problems of Developing Nations* (New York: John Wiley, 1968). Within this anthology, see in particular, Jyotirindra Das Gupta, "Language Diversity and National Development," pp. 17–26; Joshua A. Fishman, "Nationality-Nationalism and Nation-Nationism," pp. 39–52; Joshua A. Fishman, "Some Contrasts between Linguistically Homogenous and Linguistically Heterogenous Politics," pp. 53–68; Heinz Kloss, "Notes Concerning a Language-Nation Typology," pp. 69–86; Dankwart Rustow, "Language, Modernization and Nationhood—An attempt at Typology," pp. 87—106; Pierre Alexandre, "Some Linguistic Problems of Nation Building in Negro Africa," pp. 119–120, John N. Paden, "Language Problems of National Integration in Nigeria: The Special Position of Hausa," pp. 199–214; Joshua Fishman,

"Language Problems and Types of Political and Sociocultural Integration," pp. 491–498.

[9] Arthur S. Banks and Robert B. Textor, *A Cross-Polity Survey* (Cambridge: Massachusetts Institute of Technology Press, 1963).

[10] Irma Adelman and Cynthia Taft Morris, *Society, Politics, and Economic Development: A Quantitative Approach* (Baltimore, Md.: Johns Hopkins Press, 1967), p. 54–56.

[11] Charles Anderson, Fred von der Mehden and Crawford Young, *Issues of Political Development* (Englewood Cliffs, N.J.: Prentice-Hall, 1967).

[12] Kloss, "Notes Concerning a Language-Nation Typology," p. 75.

[13] *Ibid.*

[14] See, for example, Obafemi Awolowo, *The People's Republic* (Ibadan: Oxford University Press, 1968); also *Thoughts on Nigerian Constitution* (Ibadan: Oxford University Press, 1966).

[15] See Joshua A. Fishman, "National Languages and Languages of Wider Communication in the Developing Nations," *Anthropological Linguistics*, 11 (April 1969): 11–135.

[16] *The Nationalist*, December 20, 1968 (quoted in *ibid.*, p. 118).

[17] For a discussion of multilingualism, see Scientific Council for Africa, *Symposium on Multilingualism: Brazzaville, 1962*, Publication no. 87. (London: 1962). For a summary of a pilot research project on multilingualism, see Jack Berry, "The Madina Project; Sociolinguistic Research in Ghana" in *Expanding Horizons in African Studies*, eds. Gwendolen M. Carter and Ann Paden (Evanson, Ill.: Northwestern University Press, 1969), pp. 303–314. The most recent work is W. H. Whiteley, ed., *Language Use and Social Change: Problems of Multilingualism with Special Reference to Eastern Africa* (London: Oxford University Press, 1971).

[18] See John Spencer, ed., *Language in Africa* (Cambridge, England: Cambridge University Press, 1963); also, Istvan Fodor, "Linguistic Problems and 'Language Planning' in Africa," *Linguistics*, 25 (September 1966): 18–33.

[19] David Barrett, *Schism and Renewal in Africa: An Analysis of Six Thousand Contemporary Religious Movements* (Nairobi: Oxford University Press, 1968).

[20] Duncan MacDougald, Jr., *The Languages and Press of Africa*, University of Pennsylvania Press (Philadelphia: 1944).

[21] *Ibid.*

[22] Knappert, "Language Problems of the New Nations of Africa."

[23] Dankwart Rustow, "Language, Modernization and Nationhood—An Attempt at Typology" in *Language Problems of Developing Nations*, eds. Fishman et al., pp. 87–106. Rustow codes "Mother Tongue of Largest Group" as "Per Cent of Population." Although he codes all the countries in the world, most of his coding for the African states is based on "Source C," which is S. I. Bruk, ed. *Chislennost' i Rasselenie Naradov Mira* (Moscow: Izdatel'stvo Akademii Nauk S.S.S.R., Institut Etnografii, 1962).

[24] Kloss, "Notes Concerning a Language-Nation Typology," p. 81.

[25] The survey is being conducted at the International Center for Research on Bilingualism, Cité Universitaire, Québec, Canada. It is administering mail questionnaires to assess linguistic aspects of "language corpus," demographic distribution of languages, and literary uses of language.

[26] Daryll Forde, ed., *African Worlds: Studies in the Cosmological Ideas and Social Values of African Peoples* (London: Oxford University Press, 1954); John S. Mbiti, *African Religions and Philosophy* (New York: Praeger, 1969); John V. Taylor, *The Primal Vision: Christian Presence amid African Religion* (London: SCM Press, 1963); Fr. Placide Tempels, *La Philosophie Bantoue* (Elizabethville: Editions Louvania, 1945).

[27] Jean C. Froelich, *Les Musulmans d'Afrique Noire* (Paris: Editions de l'Orante, 1962): I. M. Lewis, ed., *Islam in Tropical Africa* (London: Oxford University Press, 1966); Vincent Monteil, *L'Islam Noire* (Paris: Editions de Seuil, 1964); J. Spencer Trimingham, *The Influence of Islam upon Africa* (London: Longmans, 1968); J. Kritzeck and W. I. Lewis, eds., *Islam in Africa* (Cincinnati, Ohio: Van Nostrand/Reinhold, 1969). See also the forthcoming *Islam en Afrique* (Brussels: Pro Mundi Vita, 1969 or 1970). The latter source gives estimates of Muslim identification for the African nations.

[28] C. G. Baeta, ed., *Christianity in Tropical Africa* (London: Oxford University Press, 1968); T. A. Beetham, *Christianity and the New Africa* (London: Pall Mall, 1967). See also the new journal, *Journal of Religion in Africa* (Leiden, the Netherlands: E. J. Brill) and C. P. Groves, *The Planting of Christianity in Africa*, 4 vols. (London: Lutterworth Press, 1948–1958).

[29] R. P. Beaver, ed., *Christianity and African Education* (Grand Rapids, Mich.: Eerdmans, 1966).

[30] Raymond F. Hopkins, "Christianity and Sociopolitical Change in Sub-Saharan Africa," *Social Forces*, 44 (1966): 555–562.

[31] Robert Cameron Mitchell and Donald George Morrison, "On Christianity and Sociopolitical Change," *Social Forces*, 48 (1970): 397–408.

[32] H. J. Fisher, *Ahmadiyyah: A Study in Contemporary Islam on the West African Coast* (London: Oxford University Press, 1963).

[33] David B. Barrett, *Schism and Renewal in Africa: An Analysis of Six Thousand Contemporary Religious Movements* (Nairobi: Oxford University Press, 1968); Robert Cameron Mitchell and Harold W. Turner, eds., *A Comprehensive Bibliography of Modern African Religious Movements* (Evanston, Ill.: Northwestern University Press, 1967).

[34] The latest edition of this handbook is H. Wakelin Coxill and Kenneth Grubb, eds., *World Christian Handbook 1968* (London: Lutterworth Press, 1968). Previous editions of this work appeared in 1949, 1952, 1957 and 1962. This source does not date its data, but it is presumed that they generally are for the year preceding each edition, so in using the 1968 *Handbook* we refer to 1967 data. The *Handbook* is probably the most commonly referred to source for Protestant data in Africa, and is used widely as authoritative despite its various faults.

[35] These two groupings are not exactly comparable as the Protestant "Christian community" category is somewhat broader. The official definition for the Christian community category given in the *World Christian Handbook* says that the category includes all communicants and full members and in addition "all participants in the life of your church, such as regular worshippers, children of Christian parents, catechumens, and members of functional groups etc." Of course the Roman Catholic data always includes baptized children as members, but even the Catholic catechumen category would not necessarily include "regular worshippers."

[36] The latest edition available to us is Mission Information Centre, *Ready Information about Africa* (London: Mission Information Centre, 1965). Previous editions appeared in 1956 and 1962. It presents the *Propaganda Fide* data for 1963.

[37] Eglise Vivant, *Bilan du Monde* (Paris: Casterman, 1964). A previous edition appeared in 1958–1959.

[38] Regrettably, the 1968 *Handbook* presented the Catholic data only for "Roman Catholics," omitting the "catechumen" category which it had included in the 1962 *Handbook*. The *Handbook* gets its data from official Roman Catholic sources.

[39] It should be noted that each edition of the *Handbook* points out the problems of unreliability and urges caution in the use of the data, especially over time. The editors mention missing information, the varying quality of the information supplied, the duplication of churches, and the respondents' differing interpretations of the categories they are asked to use, as the major sources of error in the *Handbook*.

[40] Rycroft and Clemmer, in a useful compilation of religious and non-religious data on Africa, present a table giving Protestant totals for nations which edits the 1962 *Handbook* data to eliminate these duplications. W. Stanley Rycroft and Myrtle M. Clemmer, *A Factual Study of Sub-Saharan Africa* (New York: Commission on Ecumenical Mission and Relations, The United Presbyterian Church in the U.S.A., 1962), p. 110.

[41] Two of the most important of these sources are: Harlan P. Beach and Charles H. Fahs, eds., *World Missionary Atlas* (New York: Institute of Social and Religious Research, 1925); and Joseph I. Parker, *Interpretative Statistical Survey of the World Mission of the Christian Church* (New York: International Missionary Council, 1938).

[42] Hildegard Binder Johnson, "Christian Mission Stations in Africa 1920's," *The Geographical Review*, 57, no. 2 (1961), Plate 1.

[43] Hildegard Binder Johnson, "The Location of Christian Missions in Africa," *The Geographical Review*, 57, no. 2 (1961), p. 168.

[44] It would seem that the data in the *Handbook*, when given, are relatively reliable. A fairly precise change measure could be developed for a limited number of Protestant denominations by calculating the growth of only those denominations whose data could be traced through the different editions of the *World Christian Handbook*. This would eliminate missing data. It would of course be biased towards the bigger, more main-line denominations, and also towards those with the more reliable data-gathering procedures. It should be noted that data cited in a later *Handbook* as coming from the previous *Handbook* are sometimes from an even earlier *Handbook*, thereby vastly complicating the calculation of Protestant growth rates.

[45] The Christian religion data in the first edition of this work were drawn from the *World Christian Handbook* and therefore represent indicators of adherence. The data for the sixth edition, forthcoming, will be supplied by David Barrett and will include the African Independent Churches in the Christian category—again the Christian variables will be of adherence. Bruce M. Russett, ed., *World Handbook of Political and Social Indicators* (New Haven, Conn.: Yale University Press, 1964).

[46] The new edition of the Russett volume will present a "total Christian" variable, but the Roman Catholic data used in this variable only includes "Roman Catholics" (baptized only), thus leaving out Roman Catholic catechumens, while the corresponding Protestant data includes catechumens. This results in an underestimate of adherence, particularly in the heavily Roman Catholic countries. We attempt to compensate here for the lack of catechumen data for 1966 by calculating for each nation a ratio of catechumens to Roman Catholics for 1963, the latest year for which both variables are available. We then multiply the ratio by the 1966 Roman Catholic data. The result is an estimate of the 1966 catechumens for each country. We add this estimate to the 1966 Roman Catholic figure and then add the result, estimated Roman Catholic adherents 1966, to the Protestant, African Independent Churches, and Ethiopian Orthodox data to obtain "total Christian affiliators."

TABLE 2.1 Percent Speaking Dominant Vernacular Language, ca. 1967

Definition: Percent of the total population who speak the dominant vernacular language as a first or second language.

RANGE = 84.00
MEAN = 57.28
STANDARD DEVIATION = 22.23

POPULATION PERCENT CUM. COUNTRY		RANK	COUNTRY NAME	VALUE	RANGE DECILE
0.3	0.3	1.5	BOTSWANA	99	1
0.7	0.4	1.5	LESOTHO	99	
1.9	1.2	3.0	SOMALIA	97	
3.4	1.5	4.5	BURUNDI	90	2
4.9	1.5	4.5	RWANDA	90	
10.6	5.7	6.0	TANZANIA	88	
11.1	0.5	7.0	MAURITANIA	87	
12.8	1.7	8.0	NIGER	70	4
17.6	4.8	9.0	KENYA	65	5
18.8	1.2	11.5	DAHOMEY	60	
19.0	0.2	11.5	GAMBIA	60	
20.7	1.7	11.5	SENEGAL	60	
27.4	6.7	11.5	SUDAN	60	
29.0	1.6	14.5	CHAD	55	6
31.3	2.3	14.5	UPPER VOLTA	55	
31.7	0.4	16.0	CONGO (BRA)	52	
33.6	1.9	17.0	MALAWI	51	
44.5	10.9	20.0	ETHIOPIA	50	
44.7	0.2	20.0	GABON	50	
46.9	2.2	20.0	MALI	50	
71.9	25.0	20.0	NIGERIA	50	
72.7	0.8	20.0	TOGO	50	
74.4	1.7	23.0	GUINEA	48	7
75.5	1.1	24.0	SIERRA LEONE	45	
79.3	3.8	25.5	GHANA	44	
79.8	0.5	25.5	LIBERIA	44	
84.0	4.2	27.0	UGANDA	33	8
84.7	0.7	28.0	CAR	31	9
87.2	2.5	29.5	CAMEROON	30	
96.3	9.1	29.5	ZAIRE	30	
98.2	1.9	31.0	IVORY COAST	25	
100.0	1.8	32.0	ZAMBIA	15	10

SOURCES: Estimates based on data by Jan Knappert, "Language Problems of the New Nations of Africa," *Africa Quarterly*, 5 (1965): 95–105; Dankwart Rustow, "Language, Modernization and Nationhood—An Attempt at Typology," in *Language Problems of Developing Nations*, eds. Joshua A. Fishman et al. (New York: John Wiley, 1968); Duncan MacDougald, *The Languages and Press of Africa* (Philadelphia: University of Pennsylvania Press, 1944). For discussions of estimations and languages for each country see Part II of this Handbook.

TABLE 2.2 Primacy of First Language, ca. 1967

Definition: Primacy ratio based on percent speakers of the first (most widely spoken) language divided by the percent speakers of the second language. The higher the ratio, the greater the primacy.

RANGE = 98.00
MEAN = 9.94
STANDARD DEVIATION = 23.65

POPULATION PERCENT CUM. COUNTRY		RANK	COUNTRY NAME	VALUE	RANGE DECILE
0.3	0.3	1.5	BOTSWANA	99	1
0.7	0.4	1.5	LESOTHO	99	
1.9	1.2	3.0	SOMALIA	32	7
3.4	1.5	4.5	BURUNDI	9	10
4.9	1.5	4.5	RWANDA	9	
10.6	5.7	6.0	TANZANIA	7	
11.1	0.5	7.0	MAURITANIA	6	
17.8	6.7	8.0	SUDAN	5	
18.0	0.2	9.0	GAMBIA	3	
19.7	1.7	10.0	NIGER	3	
22.0	2.3	11.0	UPPER VOLTA	3	
25.8	3.8	12.0	GHANA	2	
30.6	4.8	13.5	KENYA	2	
32.5	1.9	13.5	MALAWI	2	
33.7	1.2	16.5	DAHOMEY	2	
33.9	0.2	16.5	GABON	2	
58.9	25.0	16.5	NIGERIA	2	
60.6	1.7	16.5	SENEGAL	2	
62.8	2.2	19.0	MALI	2	
63.2	0.4	20.0	CONGO (BRA)	2	
64.0	0.8	21.0	TOGO	2	
65.6	1.6	22.0	CHAD	2	
69.8	4.2	23.0	UGANDA	1	
71.5	1.7	24.0	GUINEA	1	
73.4	1.9	25.0	IVORY COAST	1	
75.9	2.5	27.5	CAMEROON	1	
85.0	9.1	27.5	ZAIRE	1	
86.1	1.1	27.5	SIERRA LEONE	1	
87.9	1.8	27.5	ZAMBIA	1	
88.4	0.5	30.0	LIBERIA	1	
89.1	0.7	31.5	CAR	1	
100.0	10.9	31.5	ETHIOPIA	1	

SOURCES: Estimates for percent speakers of second and first languages are detailed by country in Part II.

TABLE 2.3 Estimated Number of Languages per Million Population and Total Languages, ca. 1967

Definition and Comments: This is the number of individual indigenous languages. The source gives a figure of 993 such languages for the thirty-two countries, but many experts regard this as an under-estimate. The major problem is in deciding whether a language is a dialect of another language or a language in its own right.

```
RANGE =         31.10
MEAN =           7.24
STANDARD DEVIATION =        7.91
```

POPULATION PERCENT						
		RANK	COUNTRY NAME	VALUE	RANGE DECILE	TOTAL
CUM.	COUNTRY					
0.2	0.2	1.0	GABON	31.7	1	15
0.9	0.7	2.0	CAR	28.1	2	41
1.4	0.5	3.0	LIBERIA	26.1		29
3.2	1.8	4.0	ZAMBIA	17.5	5	69
5.1	1.9	5.0	IVORY COAST	14.2	6	57
11.8	6.7	6.0	SUDAN	11.9	7	171
12.6	0.8	7.0	TOGO	9.3	8	56
15.1	2.5	8.0	CAMEROON	9.1		50
15.5	0.4	9.0	CONGO (BRA)	8.1		7
17.1	1.6	10.0	CHAD	6.5	9	22
18.3	1.2	11.0	DAHOMEY	6.0		15
20.0	1.7	12.0	GUINEA	5.9		22
20.2	0.2	13.0	GAMBIA	5.8		2
22.5	2.3	14.0	UPPER VOLTA	5.3		27
26.3	3.8	15.5	GHANA	4.5		37
32.0	5.7	15.5	TANZANIA	4.5		56
33.7	1.7	17.0	NIGER	3.9		14
42.8	9.1	18.0	ZAIRE	3.7	10	61
43.1	0.3	19.0	BOTSWANA	3.4		2
44.2	1.1	20.0	SIERRA LEONE	3.3		8
46.4	2.2	21.0	MALI	3.2		15
50.6	4.2	22.0	UGANDA	3.0		24
61.5	10.9	23.0	ETHIOPIA	2.7		63
61.9	0.4	24.5	LESOTHO	2.3		2
86.9	25.0	24.5	NIGERIA	2.3		125
91.7	4.8	26.5	KENYA	2.2		22
93.4	1.7	26.5	SENEGAL	2.2		8
93.9	0.5	28.0	MAURITANIA	1.8		2
95.8	1.9	29.0	MALAWI	1.2		5
97.0	1.2	30.0	SOMALIA	0.8		2
98.5	1.5	31.5	BURUNDI	0.6		2
100.0	1.5	31.5	RWANDA	0.6		2

SOURCE: Based on data in Knappert, "Language Problems of the New Nations of Africa."

TABLE 2.4 Language Classification: Corpus Distance Index

Definition: The following categories are an ordinal scale on the degree of linguistic similarity between the vernacular languages of a country's ethnic units.

1. One category, no internal sub-categories (all indigenous languages are in the same linguistic classification category).
2. One category, two or three internal sub-categories.
3. One category, more than three sub-categories.
4. Two major categories, no internal sub-categories.
5. Two major categories, two or three internal sub-categories.
6. Two major categories, more than three internal sub-categories.
7. Three major categories, no internal sub-categories.
8. Three major categories, two or three internal sub-categories.

The higher the number on the scale, the more linguistically heterogeneous are the country's ethnic units.

```
RANGE =         7.00
MEAN =          3.03
STANDARD DEVIATION =        2.30
```

POPULATION PERCENT					
		RANK	COUNTRY NAME	VALUE	RANGE DECILE
CUM.	COUNTRY				
2.2	2.2	2.5	MALI	8	1
3.9	1.7	2.5	NIGER	8	
28.9	25.0	2.5	NIGERIA	8	
35.6	6.7	2.5	SUDAN	8	
38.1	2.5	5.0	CAMEROON	6	3
39.7	1.6	6.5	CHAD	5	5
43.9	4.2	6.5	UGANDA	5	
45.4	1.5	9.5	BURUNDI	4	6
50.2	4.8	9.5	KENYA	4	
50.7	0.5	9.5	MAURITANIA	4	
52.2	1.5	9.5	RWANDA	4	
61.3	9.1	17.5	ZAIRE	2	9
62.5	1.2	17.5	DAHOMEY	2	
73.4	10.9	17.5	ETHIOPIA	2	
73.6	0.2	17.5	GAMBIA	2	
77.4	3.8	17.5	GHANA	2	
79.1	1.7	17.5	GUINEA	2	
81.0	1.9	17.5	IVORY COAST	2	
81.5	0.5	17.5	LIBERIA	2	
83.2	1.7	17.5	SENEGAL	2	
84.3	1.1	17.5	SIERRA LEONE	2	
85.1	0.8	17.5	TOGO	2	
87.4	2.3	17.5	UPPER VOLTA	2	
87.7	0.3	28.0	BOTSWANA	1	
88.4	0.7	28.0	CAR	1	
88.8	0.4	28.0	CONGO (BRA)	1	
89.0	0.2	28.0	GABON	1	
89.4	0.4	28.0	LESOTHO	1	
91.3	1.9	28.0	MALAWI	1	
92.5	1.2	28.0	SOMALIA	1	
98.2	5.7	28.0	TANZANIA	1	
100.0	1.8	28.0	ZAMBIA	1	

SOURCE: Calculated on the basis of the classifications in J. Greenberg, *The Languages of Africa* (Bloomington: Indiana University, 1966). See Part II, Country Profiles, for the individual ethnic unit language classifications.

TABLE 2.5 Vernacular Lingua Franca

Definition: *Lingua franca* refers to a language which is spoken by 5 percent or more of the total population as a "second" language. This ordinally scaled variable is coded as follows.

1. No vernacular *lingua franca* in the country.
2. Existence of a *lingua franca* in the country which is neither the largest nor the second largest language.
3. Second largest language serves as a *lingua franca*.
4. Largest language serves as a *lingua franca*.
5. Largest and second largest languages both serve as *lingua francas*.

```
RANGE     =        4.00
MEAN      =        3.78
STANDARD DEVIATION =            1.05
```

POPULATION PERCENT CUM.	COUNTRY	RANK	COUNTRY NAME	VALUE	RANGE DECILE
1.5	1.5	4.0	BURUNDI	5	1
10.6	9.1	4.0	ZAIRE	5	
21.5	10.9	4.0	ETHIOPIA	5	
23.2	1.7	4.0	GUINEA	5	
24.7	1.5	4.0	RWANDA	5	
28.9	4.2	4.0	UGANDA	5	
31.2	2.3	4.0	UPPER VOLTA	5	
31.5	0.3	16.5	BOTSWANA	4	3
33.1	1.6	16.5	CHAD	4	
33.5	0.4	16.5	CONGO (BRA)	4	
34.7	1.2	16.5	DAHOMEY	4	
34.9	0.2	16.5	GABON	4	
35.1	0.2	16.5	GAMBIA	4	
39.9	4.8	16.5	KENYA	4	
40.3	0.4	16.5	LESOTHO	4	
42.2	1.9	16.5	MALAWI	4	
42.7	0.5	16.5	MAURITANIA	4	
44.9	2.2	16.5	MALI	4	
46.6	1.7	16.5	NIGER	4	
71.6	25.0	16.5	NIGERIA	4	
73.3	1.7	16.5	SENEGAL	4	
74.5	1.2	16.5	SOMALIA	4	
81.2	6.7	16.5	SUDAN	4	
86.9	5.7	16.5	TANZANIA	4	
87.7	0.8	16.5	TOGO	4	
88.8	1.1	26.0	SIERRA LEONE	3	5
91.3	2.5	29.0	CAMEROON	2	8
92.0	0.7	29.0	CAR	2	
95.8	3.8	29.0	GHANA	2	
97.7	1.9	29.0	IVORY COAST	2	
98.2	0.5	29.0	LIBERIA	2	
100.0	1.8	32.0	ZAMBIA	1	10

SOURCE: See Part II for a discussion of this coding for each country

TABLE 2.6 Primary Language Standardization

Definition: The first or second largest vernacular language (depending on which is most standardized) is judged on its degree of standardization (i.e., orthography and literary tradition). The four-fold ordinal scale is coded as follows:

1. Pre-literate language.
2. Unstandardized alphabetized language.
3. Young standardized language.
4. Mature standardized language.

```
RANGE     =        3.00
MEAN      =        2.84
STANDARD DEVIATION =            0.97
```

POPULATION PERCENT CUM.	COUNTRY	RANK	COUNTRY NAME	VALUE	RANGE DECILE
1.5	1.5	6.5	BURUNDI	4	1
3.1	1.6	6.5	CHAD	4	
12.2	9.1	6.5	ZAIRE	4	
23.1	10.9	6.5	ETHIOPIA	4	
27.9	4.8	6.5	KENYA	4	
28.4	0.5	6.5	MAURITANIA	4	
30.1	1.7	6.5	NIGER	4	
55.1	25.0	6.5	NIGERIA	4	
56.6	1.5	6.5	RWANDA	4	
63.3	6.7	6.5	SUDAN	4	
69.0	5.7	6.5	TANZANIA	4	
73.2	4.2	6.5	UGANDA	4	
73.4	0.2	14.5	GAMBIA	3	4
75.1	1.7	14.5	GUINEA	3	
77.3	2.2	14.5	MALI	3	
79.0	1.7	14.5	SENEGAL	3	
79.3	0.3	24.0	BOTSWANA	2	7
81.8	2.5	24.0	CAMEROON	2	
82.5	0.7	24.0	CAR	2	
82.9	0.4	24.0	CONGO (BRA)	2	
84.1	1.2	24.0	DAHOMEY	2	
84.3	0.2	24.0	GABON	2	
88.1	3.8	24.0	GHANA	2	
90.0	1.9	24.0	IVORY COAST	2	
90.4	0.4	24.0	LESOTHO	2	
90.9	0.5	24.0	LIBERIA	2	
92.8	1.9	24.0	MALAWI	2	
93.9	1.1	24.0	SIERRA LEONE	2	
94.7	0.8	24.0	TOGO	2	
97.0	2.3	24.0	UPPER VOLTA	2	
98.8	1.8	24.0	ZAMBIA	2	
100.0	1.2	32.0	SOMALIA	1	10

SOURCE: Scale adapted from Heinz Kloss, "Notes Concerning a Language-Nation Typology," in *Language Problems of Developing Nations*, eds. Fishman et al., pp. 77–83. *Burundi, Zaire (Congo K.), Gambia, Guinea, Mali, Senegal, Uganda*: Standardization calculated on second largest language rather than first.

TABLE 2.7 Vernacular Language Policy, ca. 1969

Definition: An ordinal scale based on the degree of official government encouragement of the use of vernacular language, ranging from the complete lack of utilization to complete utilization.

1. Non-indigenous (exoglossic) language primacy as government policy (e.g. French or English).
2. Use of the vernacular in public communications *media* (e.g. radio).
3. Use of vernacular in *educational* institutions (any level, but excluding adult literacy campaigns).
4. Existence of one or more official *regional* vernacular languages.
5. Existence of an official national vernacular language, which is *symbolic* but not used in government operations.
6. Existence of an *official* national vernacular language (usually co-equal with an exoglossic language in which the government conducts a significant number of operations).
7. Existence of an official national vernacular language (which is clearly dominant over any exoglossic language) which constitutes the major *working* language of the government.

```
RANGE              =      5.00
MEAN               =      3.84
STANDARD DEVIATION =              1.95
```

POPULATION PERCENT CUM.	COUNTRY	RANK	COUNTRY NAME	VALUE	RANGE DECILE
10.9	10.9	2.0	ETHIOPIA	7	1
17.6	6.7	2.0	SUDAN	7	
23.3	5.7	2.0	TANZANIA	7	
23.6	0.3	7.5	BOTSWANA	6	2
25.1	1.5	7.5	BURUNDI	6	3
34.2	9.1	7.5	ZAIRE	6	
39.0	4.8	7.5	KENYA	6	
39.4	0.4	7.5	LESOTHO	6	
39.9	0.5	7.5	MAURITANIA	6	
41.4	1.5	7.5	RWANDA	6	
42.6	1.2	7.5	SOMALIA	6	
43.3	0.7	12.5	CAR	5	4
44.1	0.8	12.5	TOGO	5	5
69.1	25.0	14.5	NIGERIA	4	6
73.3	4.2	14.5	UGANDA	4	7
73.5	0.2	16.5	GAMBIA	3	8
74.6	1.1	16.5	SIERRA LEONE	3	9
77.1	2.5	25.0	CAMEROON	2	10
78.7	1.6	25.0	CHAD	2	
79.1	0.4	25.0	CONGO (BRA)	2	
80.3	1.2	25.0	DAHOMEY	2	
80.5	0.2	25.0	GABON	2	
84.3	3.8	25.0	GHANA	2	
86.0	1.7	25.0	GUINEA	2	
87.9	1.9	25.0	IVORY COAST	2	
88.4	0.5	25.0	LIBERIA	2	
90.3	1.9	25.0	MALAWI	2	
92.5	2.2	25.0	MALI	2	
94.2	1.7	25.0	NIGER	2	
95.9	1.7	25.0	SENEGAL	2	
98.2	2.3	25.0	UPPER VOLTA	2	
100.0	1.8	25.0	ZAMBIA	2	

SOURCE: Scale developed by Kloss, "Notes Concerning a Language-Nation Typology" pp. 79–81. See Part II for discussion of each nation's language policy.

TABLE 2.8 Estimated Percent Identifiers with Islam, ca. 1966

Definition: Identifiers refers to those who would identify with a particular religion when asked their religion by someone such as a census taker.

```
RANGE              =      99.00
MEAN               =      30.56
STANDARD DEVIATION =              32.50
```

POPULATION PERCENT CUM.	COUNTRY	RANK	COUNTRY NAME	VALUE	RANGE DECILE
1.2	1.2	1.0	SOMALIA	99	1
1.7	0.5	2.0	MAURITANIA	96	
1.9	0.2	3.0	GAMBIA	90	
3.6	1.7	4.0	NIGER	85	2
5.3	1.7	5.0	SENEGAL	82	
12.0	6.7	6.0	SUDAN	71	3
13.7	1.7	7.5	GUINEA	60	4
15.9	2.2	7.5	MALI	60	
40.9	25.0	9.0	NIGERIA	52	5
42.5	1.6	10.0	CHAD	50	
53.4	10.9	11.0	ETHIOPIA	40	6
54.5	1.1	12.0	SIERRA LEONE	30	7
56.4	1.9	13.5	IVORY COAST	23	8
62.1	5.7	13.5	TANZANIA	23	
64.4	2.3	15.0	UPPER VOLTA	22	
68.2	3.8	16.0	GHANA	19	9
70.7	2.5	17.5	CAMEROON	15	
71.2	0.5	17.5	LIBERIA	15	
73.1	1.9	19.0	MALAWI	12	
73.9	0.8	20.0	TOGO	8	10
78.1	4.2	21.0	UGANDA	6	
78.8	0.7	22.5	CAR	5	
80.0	1.2	22.5	DAHOMEY	15	
84.8	4.8	24.0	KENYA	4	
86.3	1.5	27.5	BURUNDI	1	
86.7	0.4	27.5	CONGO (BRA)	1	
95.8	9.1	27.5	ZAIRE	1	
96.0	0.2	27.5	GABON	1	
97.5	1.5	27.5	RWANDA	1	
99.3	1.8	27.5	ZAMBIA	1	
99.6	0.3	31.5	BOTSWANA	0	
100.0	0.4	31.5	LESOTHO	0	

SOURCES: Unless otherwise noted, the estimates are based on J. S. Trimingham, *The Influence of Islam upon Africa* (London: Longmans, 1968), pp. 113–114 and the *Statesman's Yearbook 1967–68*. Official government census or sample survey data were available on religion and used to make the estimates for: *Ghana, Dahomey, Kenya, Lesotho, Mali, Nigeria* and *Senegal*. Cameroon: *Islam en Afrique* (Brussels: Pro Mundi Vita, forthcoming); *Tanzania*: L. W. Swantz, "Church, Mission and State Relations in Pre- and Post-Independence Tanzania (1955–1964)," Occasional Paper No. 19 (Syracuse: Program of East African Studies, 1966).

TABLE 2.9 Estimated Percent Identifiers with Christianity, ca. 1966

Definition: Identifiers refers to those who would identify with a particular religion when asked their religion by someone such as a census taker. Includes the African Independent Churches, the Orthodox Churches as well as the Protestant and Roman Catholic Churches.

```
RANGE =           81.00
MEAN =            31.59
STANDARD DEVIATION =            25.09
```

POPULATION PERCENT CUM.	COUNTRY	RANK	COUNTRY NAME	VALUE	RANGE DECILE
0.4	0.4	1.0	LESOTHO	81	1
0.6	0.2	2.0	GABON	75	
2.1	1.5	3.0	BURUNDI	69	2
11.2	9.1	4.0	ZAIRE	65	
11.6	0.4	5.0	CONGO (BRA)	64	3
15.8	4.2	6.0	UGANDA	60	
20.6	4.8	7.0	KENYA	58	
22.5	1.9	8.0	MALAWI	55	4
25.0	2.5	9.0	CAMEROON	49	
25.7	0.7	10.0	CAR	47	5
29.5	3.8	11.0	GHANA	46	
31.0	1.5	12.0	RWANDA	42	
36.7	5.7	13.0	TANZANIA	40	6
47.6	10.9	14.0	ETHIOPIA	37	
72.6	25.0	15.0	NIGERIA	35	
73.4	0.8	16.5	TOGO	30	7
75.2	1.8	16.5	ZAMBIA	30	
75.5	0.3	18.0	BOTSWANA	29	
76.0	0.5	19.0	LIBERIA	25	
77.2	1.2	20.5	DAHOMEY	18	8
79.1	1.9	20.5	IVORY COAST	18	
80.7	1.6	22.0	CHAD	10	9
81.8	1.1	23.0	SIERRA LEONE	7	10
84.1	2.3	24.0	UPPER VOLTA	6	
84.3	0.2	26.0	GAMBIA	4	
86.0	1.7	26.0	SENEGAL	4	
92.7	6.7	26.0	SUDAN	4	
94.4	1.7	29.0	GUINEA	1	
96.6	2.2	29.0	MALI	1	
98.3	1.7	29.0	NIGER	1	
98.8	0.5	31.5	MAURITANIA	0	
100.0	1.2	31.5	SOMALIA	0	

SOURCES: These estimates were made by Robert Cameron Mitchell. They are based on the following assumptions: (1) Islam and Christianity are growing rapidly in Black Africa today, (2) Christianity is growing most rapidly where it is already the religion of a strong minority, (3) national census data or sample survey data for 1966 represent the most satisfactory estimate possible, (4) the reported data for affiliators (members and adherents) given by Protestant churches in the *World Christian Handbook* considerably underestimate the Protestant identifiers, especially where Protestants constitute a strong minority (see Figure 2.3), and (5) official Roman Catholic affiliator data also underestimates Roman Catholic identifiers, but to a lesser extent than the Protestant data. The following notes attempt to specify the process of estimation as fully as possible. The principal source upon which the estimate is based is given along with any change in the data. Five or six different estimates of identifiers were consulted in the process of making these estimates.

Botswana: Beetham, *Christianity and the New Africa,* plus 2 percent; *Burundi:* Handbook plus 2 percent; *Cameroon:* Handbook plus 18 percent.

CAR: AID Economic Data Book; Chad: Handbook plus 4 percent; *Congo (Brazzaville): Handbook* plus 10 percent; *Zaire (Congo K.): Handbook* plus 10 percent; *Dahomey:* 1961 sample survey plus slight extrapolation; *Ethiopia:* George Lipsky, *Ethiopia* (New Haven, Conn.: HRAF Press, 1962) (a conservative estimate of 7,600,000 Ethiopian Orthodox identifiers was used); *Gabon: Handbook* plus 8 percent; *Gambia: Handbook; Ghana:* census plus 3 percent; *Guinea: Handbook; Ivory Coast: Handbook* plus 8 percent; *Kenya:* census 1964; *Lesotho:* census 1956 plus 10 percent; *Liberia: Handbook* plus 13 percent; *Malawi: Handbook* plus 16 percent or lower end of *Statesman's Yearbook 1968–69* estimate; *Mali:* sample survey 1964–1965; *Mauritania, Niger: Handbook; Nigeria:* census 1963; *Rwanda: Handbook* plus 12 percent; *Senegal:* census 1960–1961; *Sierra Leone: Handbook* plus 3 percent; *Somalia: Handbook; Sudan: Europa Yearbook 1967; Tanzania:* Swantz, "Church, Mission and State Relations"; *Togo: Statesman's Yearbook 1967–68* plus 3 percent; *Uganda: Area Handbook for Uganda,* pp. 161–162; *Upper Volta: Handbook* plus 1 percent; *Zambia: Area Handbook for Zambia,* p. 185.

TABLE 2.10   Estimated Percent Identifiers with Protestantism, ca. 1966

Definition: Identifiers refers to those who would identify with a particular religion when asked their religion by someone such as a census taker. Protestantism includes the African Independent Churches but not the Orthodox Churches.

```
RANGE    =        39.00
MEAN     =        12.34
STANDARD DEVIATION =         11.79
```

POPULATION PERCENT CUM.	COUNTRY	RANK	COUNTRY NAME	VALUE	RANGE DECILE
0.4	0.4	1.0	LESOTHO	39	1
5.2	4.8	2.0	KENYA	36	
7.1	1.9	3.0	MALAWI	35	2
7.4	0.3	4.0	BOTSWANA	26	4
11.6	4.2	5.0	UGANDA	25	
12.1	0.5	6.0	LIBERIA	24	
15.9	3.8	7.0	GHANA	23	5
16.3	0.4	8.0	CONGO (BRA)	22	
18.8	2.5	9.5	CAMEROON	20	
27.9	9.1	9.5	ZAIRE	20	
28.6	0.7	11.5	CAR	19	6
28.8	0.2	11.5	GABON	19	
53.8	25.0	13.0	NIGERIA	18	
59.5	5.7	14.0	TANZANIA	14	7
61.0	1.5	15.5	BURUNDI	9	8
62.8	1.8	15.5	ZAMBIA	9	
64.3	1.5	17.5	RWANDA	7	9
65.1	0.8	17.5	TOGO	7	
66.7	1.6	20.0	CHAD	5	
68.6	1.9	20.0	IVORY COAST	5	
69.7	1.1	20.0	SIERRA LEONE	5	
70.9	1.2	22.0	DAHOMEY	3	10
71.1	0.2	23.0	GAMBIA	2	
82.0	10.9	25.0	ETHIOPIA	1	
88.7	6.7	25.0	SUDAN	1	
91.0	2.3	25.0	UPPER VOLTA	1	
92.7	1.7	29.5	GUINEA	0	
93.2	0.5	29.5	MAURITANIA	0	
95.4	2.2	29.5	MALI	0	
97.1	1.7	29.5	NIGER	0	
98.8	1.7	29.5	SENEGAL	0	
100.0	1.2	29.5	SOMALIA	0	

SOURCES: See sources for Table 2.9.

TABLE 2.11   Estimated Percent Identifiers with Roman Catholicism, ca. 1966

Definition: Identifiers refers to those who would identify with a particular religion when asked their religion by someone such as a census taker.

```
RANGE    =        60.00
MEAN     =        18.16
STANDARD DEVIATION =          17.37
```

POPULATION PERCENT CUM.	COUNTRY	RANK	COUNTRY NAME	VALUE	RANGE DECILE
1.5	1.5	1.0	BURUNDI	60	1
1.7	0.2	2.0	GABON	56	
10.8	9.1	3.0	ZAIRE	45	3
11.2	0.4	4.5	CONGO (BRA)	42	4
11.6	0.4	4.5	LESOTHO	42	
13.1	1.5	6.5	RWANDA	35	5
17.3	4.2	6.5	UGANDA	35	
19.8	2.5	8.0	CAMEROON	29	6
20.5	0.7	9.0	CAR	28	
26.2	5.7	10.0	TANZANIA	26	
30.0	3.8	11.5	GHANA	23	7
30.8	0.8	11.5	TOGO	23	
35.6	4.8	13.0	KENYA	22	
37.4	1.8	14.0	ZAMBIA	21	
39.3	1.9	15.0	MALAWI	20	
64.3	25.0	16.0	NIGERIA	17	8
65.5	1.2	17.0	DAHOMEY	15	
67.4	1.9	18.0	IVORY COAST	13	
69.0	1.6	19.5	CHAD	5	10
71.3	2.3	19.5	UPPER VOLTA	5	
73.0	1.7	21.0	SENEGAL	4	
73.3	0.3	22.5	BOTSWANA	3	
80.0	6.7	22.5	SUDAN	3	
80.2	0.2	24.5	GAMBIA	2	
81.3	1.1	24.5	SIERRA LEONE	2	
92.2	10.9	28.0	ETHIOPIA	1	
93.9	1.7	28.0	GUINEA	1	
94.4	0.5	28.0	LIBERIA	1	
96.6	2.2	28.0	MALI	1	
98.3	1.7	28.0	NIGER	1	
98.8	0.5	31.5	MAURITANIA	0	
100.0	1.2	31.5	SOMALIA	0	

SOURCES: See sources for Table 2.9.

TABLE 2.12 Estimated Percent Identifiers with Traditional African Religions, ca. 1966

Definition: Identifiers refers to those who would identify with a particular religion when asked their religion by someone such as a census taker.

```
RANGE    =        71.00
MEAN     =        37.47
STANDARD DEVIATION =          20.20
```

POPULATION PERCENT CUM.	COUNTRY	RANK	COUNTRY NAME	VALUE	RANGE DECILE
2.3	2.3	1.0	UPPER VOLTA	72	1
2.6	0.3	2.0	BOTSWANA	71	
4.4	1.8	3.0	ZAMBIA	69	
5.6	1.2	4.0	DAHOMEY	67	
6.7	1.1	5.0	SIERRA LEONE	63	2
7.5	0.8	6.0	TOGO	62	
8.0	0.5	7.0	LIBERIA	60	
9.9	1.9	8.0	IVORY COAST	59	
11.4	1.5	9.0	RWANDA	57	3
12.1	0.7	10.0	CAR	48	4
13.7	1.6	11.0	CHAD	40	5
15.4	1.7	12.5	GUINEA	39	
17.6	2.2	12.5	MALI	39	
23.3	5.7	14.0	TANZANIA	37	
25.8	2.5	15.5	CAMEROON	36	6
30.6	4.8	15.5	KENYA	36	
31.0	0.4	17.5	CONGO (BRA)	35	
34.8	3.8	17.5	GHANA	35	
43.9	9.1	19.5	ZAIRE	34	
48.1	4.2	19.5	UGANDA	34	
50.0	1.9	21.0	MALAWI	33	
51.5	1.5	22.0	BURUNDI	30	
58.2	6.7	23.0	SUDAN	25	7
58.4	0.2	24.0	GABON	24	
69.3	10.9	25.0	ETHIOPIA	23	
69.7	0.4	26.0	LESOTHO	19	8
71.4	1.7	27.5	NIGER	14	9
73.1	1.7	27.5	SENEGAL	14	
98.1	25.0	29.0	NIGERIA	13	
98.3	0.2	30.0	GAMBIA	6	10
98.8	0.5	31.0	MAURITANIA	4	
100.0	1.2	32.0	SOMALIA	1	

SOURCES: See sources for Table 2.9. In the cases where official census or sample survey data were not available, the traditionalists represent the residual after percentages of Muslims and Christians had been estimated. *Kenya*: The 2 percent classified as having "no religion" in the census are not included in any of these tables, hence Christians, Muslims and Traditionalists do not add up to 100 percent in this case.

TABLE 2.13 Protestant Mission Stations per Million Population, ca. 1925

```
RANGE    =        431.00
MEAN     =         97.28
STANDARD DEVIATION =        116.62
```

POPULATION PERCENT CUM.	COUNTRY	RANK	COUNTRY NAME	VALUE	RANGE DECILE
0.4	0.4	1.0	LESOTHO	431	1
2.2	1.8	2.0	ZAMBIA	406	
2.7	0.5	3.0	LIBERIA	363	2
11.8	9.1	4.0	ZAIRE	223	5
12.1	0.3	5.0	BOTSWANA	214	6
13.2	1.1	6.0	SIERRA LEONE	178	
18.9	5.7	7.0	TANZANIA	159	7
19.3	0.4	8.0	CONGO (BRA)	141	
21.2	1.9	9.0	MALAWI	139	
26.0	4.8	10.0	KENYA	132	
26.2	0.2	11.0	GABON	126	8
28.7	2.5	12.0	CAMEROON	109	
30.2	1.5	13.0	RWANDA	57	9
34.0	3.8	14.0	GHANA	54	
38.2	4.2	15.0	UGANDA	45	
38.4	0.2	16.0	GAMBIA	44	
40.1	1.7	17.0	GUINEA	39	10
40.8	0.7	18.0	CAR	35	
42.3	1.5	19.5	BURUNDI	34	
43.1	0.8	19.5	TOGO	34	
68.1	25.0	21.0	NIGERIA	33	
69.3	1.2	22.0	SOMALIA	32	
76.0	6.7	23.0	SUDAN	30	
76.5	0.5	24.0	MAURITANIA	17	
78.7	2.2	25.0	MALI	11	
89.6	10.9	26.0	ETHIOPIA	10	
90.8	1.2	27.0	DAHOMEY	7	
93.1	2.3	28.0	UPPER VOLTA	6	
94.7	1.6	29.0	CHAD	4	
96.6	1.9	31.0	IVORY COAST	0	
98.3	1.7	31.0	NIGER	0	
100.0	1.7	31.0	SENEGAL	0	

SOURCES: Foldout map with Hildegard B. Johnson, "The Location of Christian Missions in Africa," *The Geographical Review*, 57 (April 1967): 168–202. Population data for 1925 from Appendix 5 in this Handbook.

TABLE 2.14 **Roman Catholic Mission Stations per Million Population, ca. 1925**

```
RANGE =         503.00
MEAN =           78.16
STANDARD DEVIATION =            93.42
```

POPULATION PERCENT CUM.	COUNTRY	RANK	COUNTRY NAME	VALUE	RANGE DECILE
0.2	0.2	1.0	GABON	503	1
0.6	0.4	2.0	CONGO (BRA)	228	6
1.0	0.4	3.0	LESOTHO	204	
10.1	9.1	4.0	ZAIRE	155	7
15.8	5.7	5.0	TANZANIA	132	8
16.9	1.1	6.0	SIERRA LEONE	111	
17.7	0.8	7.0	TOGO	102	
19.4	1.7	8.0	SENEGAL	96	9
21.2	1.8	9.0	ZAMBIA	92	
21.4	0.2	10.0	GAMBIA	87	
22.9	1.5	11.5	RWANDA	80	
27.1	4.2	11.5	UGANDA	80	
29.0	1.9	13.0	IVORY COAST	67	
29.7	0.7	14.0	CAR	58	
30.9	1.2	15.0	DAHOMEY	50	10
32.6	1.7	16.0	GUINEA	49	
34.5	1.9	17.0	MALAWI	46	
35.0	0.5	18.0	LIBERIA	44	
38.8	3.8	19.0	GHANA	36	
39.3	0.5	20.0	MAURITANIA	34	
39.6	0.3	21.5	BOTSWANA	33	
41.8	2.2	21.5	MALI	33	
43.0	1.2	23.0	SOMALIA	32	
45.5	2.5	24.0	CAMEROON	29	
47.0	1.5	25.5	BURUNDI	27	
51.8	4.8	25.5	KENYA	27	
58.5	6.7	27.0	SUDAN	21	
60.8	2.3	28.0	UPPER VOLTA	18	
71.7	10.9	29.0	ETHIOPIA	17	
96.7	25.0	30.0	NIGERIA	10	
98.3	1.6	31.5	CHAD	0	
100.0	1.7	31.5	NIGER	0	

SOURCE: Foldout map with Johnson, "The Location of Christian Missions in Africa."

TABLE 2.15 **Total Christian Mission Stations per Million Population, ca. 1925**

Definition: Sum of Protestant and Roman Catholic Stations.

```
RANGE =         635.00
MEAN =          174.63
STANDARD DEVIATION =           171.16
```

POPULATION PERCENT CUM.	COUNTRY	RANK	COUNTRY NAME	VALUE	RANGE DECILE
0.4	0.4	1.0	LESOTHO	635	1
0.6	0.2	2.0	GABON	629	
2.4	1.8	3.0	ZAMBIA	498	3
2.9	0.5	4.0	LIBERIA	407	4
12.0	9.1	5.0	ZAIRE	378	5
12.4	0.4	6.0	CONGO (BRA)	349	
18.1	5.7	7.0	TANZANIA	291	6
19.2	1.1	8.0	SIERRA LEONE	289	
19.5	0.3	9.0	BOTSWANA	245	7
21.4	1.9	10.0	MALAWI	185	8
26.2	4.8	11.0	KENYA	159	
28.7	2.5	12.0	CAMEROON	138	
30.2	1.5	13.0	RWANDA	137	
31.0	0.8	14.0	TOGO	136	
31.2	0.2	15.0	GAMBIA	131	
35.4	4.2	16.0	UGANDA	125	9
37.1	1.7	17.0	SENEGAL	96	
37.8	0.7	18.0	CAR	93	
41.6	3.8	19.0	GHANA	90	
43.3	1.7	20.0	GUINEA	88	
45.2	1.9	21.0	IVORY COAST	67	
46.4	1.2	22.0	SOMALIA	64	
47.9	1.5	23.0	BURUNDI	60	10
49.1	1.2	24.0	DAHOMEY	57	
49.6	0.5	25.5	MAURITANIA	51	
56.3	6.7	25.5	SUDAN	51	
58.5	2.2	27.0	MALI	44	
83.5	25.0	28.0	NIGERIA	40	
94.4	10.9	29.0	ETHIOPIA	27	
96.7	2.3	30.0	UPPER VOLTA	24	
98.3	1.6	31.0	CHAD	4	
100.0	1.7	32.0	NIGER	0	

SOURCE: Foldout map with Johnson, "The Location of Christian Missions in Africa."

TABLE 2.16 Percent Christian Affiliators, ca. 1967

Definition: Adherents and full members claimed by the Churches themselves. Total of "Roman Catholics" and Roman Catholic catechumens, Protestant "Christian community," estimated African independent church membership, and Ethiopian Orthodox members. Includes children.

```
RANGE  =           76.00
MEAN   =           25.00
STANDARD DEVIATION =        22.15
```

POPULATION PERCENT					
CUM.	COUNTRY	RANK	COUNTRY NAME	VALUE	RANGE DECILE
0.2	0.2	1.0	GABON	76	1
0.6	0.4	2.0	LESOTHO	74	
1.0	0.4	3.0	CONGO (BRA)	62	2
2.5	1.5	4.0	BURUNDI	60	3
11.6	9.1	5.0	ZAIRE	59	
15.8	4.2	6.0	UGANDA	51	4
17.3	1.5	7.0	RWANDA	40	5
28.2	10.9	8.0	ETHIOPIA	35	6
30.7	2.5	9.5	CAMEROON	34	
32.6	1.9	9.5	MALAWI	34	
38.3	5.7	11.0	TANZANIA	32	
39.0	0.7	12.5	CAR	27	7
43.8	4.8	12.5	KENYA	27	
45.6	1.8	14.0	ZAMBIA	25	
45.9	0.3	15.0	BOTSWANA	24	
46.7	0.8	16.0	TOGO	23	
50.5	3.8	17.0	GHANA	22	8
52.4	1.9	18.0	IVORY COAST	17	
53.6	1.2	19.0	DAHOMEY	16	
54.1	0.5	20.0	LIBERIA	15	9
79.1	25.0	21.0	NIGERIA	12	
80.7	1.6	22.0	CHAD	7	10
81.8	1.1	23.5	SIERRA LEONE	6	
84.1	2.3	23.5	UPPER VOLTA	6	
85.8	1.7	25.0	SENEGAL	5	
86.0	0.2	26.5	GAMBIA	4	
92.7	6.7	26.5	SUDAN	4	
94.4	1.7	29.0	GUINEA	1	
96.6	2.2	29.0	MALI	1	
98.3	1.7	29.0	NIGER	1	
98.8	0.5	31.5	MAURITANIA	0	
100.0	1.2	31.5	SOMALIA	0	

sources: *Ready Information about Africa* and *World Christian Handbook 1968*; for Roman Catholic data, the proportion of catechumens to "Roman Catholics" in 1962 being used to calculate the 1967 catechumens from the "Roman Catholics" figure; *World Christian Handbook 1968* for Protestants; David Barrett, *Schism and Renewal* (Nairobi: Oxford University Press, 1968) for independents; and an Ethiopian Orthodox estimate of 7,800,000. Population data for 1967 from Appendix 5 in this Handbook.

TABLE 2.17 Thousands of Estimated Affiliators of African Independent Churches per Million Population, ca. 1965

Definition: Barrett defines independency as "the formation and existence within a tribe or tribal unit, temporarily or permanently, of any organized religious movement with a distinct name and membership, even as small as a single organized congregation, which claims the title Christian in that it acknowledges Jesus Christ as Lord, and which has either separated by secession from a mission church or an existing African independent church, or has been founded outside the mission churches as a new kind of religious entity under African initiative and leadership." (p. 50). His data include both members and adherents claimed by the churches. Children are presumably included in these figures.

```
RANGE  =           61.00
MEAN   =           12.88
STANDARD DEVIATION =        18.80
```

POPULATION PERCENT					
CUM.	COUNTRY	RANK	COUNTRY NAME	VALUE	RANGE DECILE
9.1	9.1	1.0	ZAIRE	61	1
13.9	4.8	2.0	KENYA	60	
14.3	0.4	3.0	LESOTHO	57	
16.2	1.9	4.0	IVORY COAST	50	2
16.7	0.5	5.0	LIBERIA	27	6
20.5	3.8	6.5	GHANA	25	
22.3	1.8	6.5	ZAMBIA	25	
22.7	0.4	8.0	CONGO (BRA)	23	7
22.9	0.2	9.0	GABON	21	
23.2	0.3	10.0	BOTSWANA	17	8
25.7	2.5	11.0	CAMEROON	11	9
50.7	25.0	12.0	NIGERIA	8	
52.6	1.9	13.0	MALAWI	7	
54.1	1.5	14.0	BURUNDI	6	10
54.8	0.7	15.0	CAR	5	
56.0	1.2	16.5	DAHOMEY	2	
61.7	5.7	16.5	TANZANIA	2	
63.3	1.6	20.0	CHAD	1	
74.2	10.9	20.0	ETHIOPIA	1	
75.3	1.1	20.0	SIERRA LEONE	1	
76.1	0.8	20.0	TOGO	1	
80.3	4.2	20.0	UGANDA	1	
80.5	0.2	27.5	GAMBIA	0	
82.2	1.7	27.5	GUINEA	0	
82.7	0.5	27.5	MAURITANIA	0	
84.9	2.2	27.5	MALI	0	
86.6	1.7	27.5	NIGER	0	
88.1	1.5	27.5	RWANDA	0	
89.8	1.7	27.5	SENEGAL	0	
91.0	1.2	27.5	SOMALIA	0	
97.7	6.7	27.5	SUDAN	0	
100.0	2.3	27.5	UPPER VOLTA	0	

sources: Barrett, *Schism and Renewal*, pp. 77–80. *Liberia*: An estimate of 5,000 affiliators was substituted for Barrett's 30,000 estimate. The lower estimate was made by Professor Harold W. Turner and is based on his field experience in Liberia studying the independent churches (personal communication, 1970); *Nigeria*: A 300,000 estimate was substituted for 500,000 by Robert Cameron Mitchell.

TABLE 2.18   Percent Growth of Roman Catholic Affiliators, 1963–1967

Definition: Change in number of "Roman Catholics" from 1963 to 1967 divided by data on "Roman Catholics" for 1963 times 100. Includes children but excludes catechumens.

```
RANGE  =        180.00
MEAN  =          16.35
STANDARD DEVIATION =            34.86
```

POPULATION PERCENT CUM.	COUNTRY	RANK	COUNTRY NAME	VALUE	RANGE DECILE
1.2	1.2	1.0	SOMALIA	167	1
2.9	1.7	2.0	NIGER	113	4
4.1	1.2	3.0	DAHOMEY	40	8
9.8	5.7	4.0	TANZANIA	35	
10.9	1.1	5.0	SIERRA LEONE	23	9
11.1	0.2	6.0	GAMBIA	20	
12.8	1.7	7.0	GUINEA	17	
13.1	0.3	8.0	BOTSWANA	14	
15.3	2.2	9.0	MALI	11	
24.4	9.1	10.0	ZAIRE	10	
24.6	0.2	11.5	GABON	9	
49.6	25.0	11.5	NIGERIA	9	
51.1	1.5	14.0	BURUNDI	8	
51.8	0.7	14.0	CAR	8	
52.3	0.5	14.0	LIBERIA	8	
54.8	2.5	16.5	CAMEROON	7	
57.1	2.3	16.5	UPPER VOLTA	7	
60.9	3.8	19.0	GHANA	5	10
61.3	0.4	19.0	LESOTHO	5	
65.5	4.2	19.0	UGANDA	5	
67.4	1.9	21.0	MALAWI	4	
69.2	1.8	22.0	ZAMBIA	3	
74.0	4.8	23.0	KENYA	2	
74.4	0.4	25.0	CONGO (BRA)	1	
76.1	1.7	25.0	SENEGAL	1	
76.9	0.8	25.0	TOGO	1	
87.8	10.9	27.0	ETHIOPIA	0	
89.3	1.5	28.5	RWANDA	-1	
96.0	6.7	28.5	SUDAN	-1	
97.9	1.9	30.0	IVORY COAST	-11	
99.5	1.6	31.0	CHAD	-13	

```
DATA NOT AVAILABLE FOR THE FOLLOWING COUNTRIES

MAURITANIA
```

SOURCES: *Ready Information about Africa* and the *World Christian Handbook 1968*.

3. Labor, Energy, and Investment

Economic systems can be described in terms of the interaction, development, and institutional organization of the labor force, mineral and energy resources, physical capital, and financial and distribution systems. Economic development is the process by which economic systems grow in the direction of preferred rates and distributions of output, which are conventionally measured as increases in aggregate income. The major sources of such growth are related to increased skills and education, economies of large-scale production, capital accumulation, and technological development.[1]

In this chapter, we discuss the major factors of production—human capital or labor, energy resources, and investment and physical capital. In Chapter 4, we discuss the productivity of African economies as measured by their aggregate output and welfare. In Chapter 5, we deal with the special questions of human resource development by relating formal education to economic and political development, and, in Chapter 6, we discuss communication and transportation facilities as social overhead capital. Finally, in Chapter 9, there is a discussion of the role of government in the national economy.

Economic Development

Increase in agricultural production and industrialization are primary objectives in virtually all countries, rich and poor alike. The theory and planning of economic development emphasize the creation and augmentation of productive capabilities—an emphasis which is hardly questioned. However, while there may be unanimity as to the goal of economic development, the means of such growth and the appropriate response to economic gain are questions that are not amenable to purely "technical" answers; they may create more conflict than unanimity. Economic development is a problem of the selection of both ends and means,[2] in which the range of alternatives is already apparent in the approaches of various African leaders. Economic policy ranges

from the emphasis on foreign investment as the "engine of growth" in countries like Liberia, Gabon, and Ivory Coast, to the emphasis on indigenous public development and ownership in countries like Guinea, Tanzania, and recently, perhaps, Sudan. The very complex issues involved in decisions about appropriate investment, savings, and distribution patterns cannot be adequately discussed with the aggregate data we present here.[3] It is important, however, that we emphasize the political nature of decisions on these questions, and not overlook their importance in considering the potential for economic development in African economic systems.

While sub-Saharan Africa is one of the wealthier areas of the world in terms of energy resources, mineral resources, and cultivable land, these are only necessary, not sufficient, conditions for economic development. Human and physical capital must be mobilized to handle increasingly complex and specialized tasks.[4] The development of capacities for the manipulation and adaptation of the environment can be analyzed from data on the characteristics of the labor force, the development of energy resources, the extent of industrialization, and rates of investment. These measures are relevant not only to theories of economic development, but also to sociological concepts of social differentiation and modernization.

Labor

Important characteristics of the labor force are the number of persons in the wage economy, the percent of the population in subsistence agriculture, and the dependence on the government for wage earning employment. Data on these variables is given in Tables 3.1, 3.2, 3.3, and in Table 7.3. Part of the process of development involves the transfer of labor resources from low productivity, subsistence farming[5] to higher productivity jobs, including urban employment and cash cropping, in the modern sector. The lower the percentage of subsistence farmers, the greater the labor pool potentially available for use in the development of a modern sector. This process produces a dualistic economy in which modern and traditional sectors exist side by side, and in which productivity in both agricultural and industrial sectors is likely to increase as workers in modern-sector employment are socialized into the values associated with regular income and participation in a money economy. This last point is important in the consideration of the development of economic productivity, which is a function not only of the nature of "modern" jobs, but also of the commitment of the worker to the values associated with modern employment.[6] The simple consideration of aggregate levels of labor mobility as indicators of economic development is further qualified by important research indicating that the internalization of "modern values" is not consistently related to levels of exposure to modern occupations and skills.[7]

Energy Resources

An essential indicator of economic development is the growth in the energy-output-per-man, and, by implication, his productivity. Aggregate data on the consumption of energy resources can be used as indicators of productive capability. However, energy resources may be so concentrated in single, capital intensive industries, that they do not adequately reflect the development of the productivity of the total labor force. In Ghana and Zambia, for example, large percentages of power go to producing, for export, alumina and copper, and it may not be true to say that the productivity per worker in Ghana and Zambia is proportionately higher than that in countries where such industries do not exist on the same scale. These qualifications should be considered in using the data on energy consumption in Tables 3.4 and 3.5. The data on the number of possible industrial types that can be developed by 1980, given in Table 3.6, should also be used in conjunction with the energy data as an indication of the possible diversification of energy deployment.

Investment and Capital

Investment is the mechanism by which a society accumulates the capital resources necessary to increase productivity by industrialization and to transfer the work burden from man to machine. Levels of investment are reflected in the data in Table 3.7 on gross domestic capital formation. This measure represents the total investment in fixed capital—buildings, equipment, communications facilities, inventories—in a given year, without accounting for depreciation in the value of the initial capital stock. Gross domestic capital is developed by private and public investment, and data on public investment are given in Tables 3.8 and 3.9. An additional source of domestic capital formation is foreign investment; in Table 3.10 we give an ordinal ranking of the size of United States' investment by 1965. Finally, a summary measure of the difficulty of achieving economic growth as a result of inadequate economic resources is given in Table 3.11.

Reliability

The measurement of factors of production in the industrial or modern sector of the economy requires methodological sophistication and considerable expenditures on manpower and facilities. There is generally more accurate and comprehensive data available for the wealthier, more industrialized countries than for poorer countries. Furthermore, important methodological problems center around the time of measurement, the classification of observations, and the reliability and generalizability of the information gathered.[8]

The data on the labor force are particularly subject to these methodological problems. The actual number of wage and salary earners is usually well defined since the total number is relatively small in most African countries, and concentrated within a few major sectors of employment.[9] Nevertheless, even if the data are accurate for a particular point in time, seasonal variations are not accounted for in presenting the data. In general, data are presented in a form consistent with UN procedures, but no consistent estimates of reliablity for these measures exists.

Data on energy consumption are required by energy-producing facilities, and as a result should be reliable. However, the data on capital accumulation and investment are difficult to evaluate. Inconsistencies in definition of gross domestic capital formation and of public investment may limit the comparability of such data.

Dimensionality

A factor analysis of over two hundred economic variables indicates a solution in which seven factors account for 87 percent of the variance of the intercorrelation matrix. The analysis included measures of the factors of production as well as measures of welfare discussed in the next chapter. Four of the factors reflect independent dimensions of: (1) labor use and stock, (2) investment levels, (3) energy production, and (4) per capita energy production. The tables in this section give what we judge to be the most reliable measures of each of these dimensions. The factor structure itself gives some assurance of the reliability of the data by indicating the close intercorrelation and similar loading pattern of indicators that are conceptually related but collected by different agencies at different times.

Notes

1 For a discussion of these and other terms that is intelligible to the non-economist, see Robert L. Heilbroner, *Understanding Macro-Economics* (Englewood Cliffs, N.J.: Prentice-Hall, 1965). The literature on economic development is enormous; the following represent important introductions to the questions considered in this brief outline. (1) Human Resource Development: H. Correa, *The Economics of Human Resources* (Amsterdam: North Holland, 1962); Samuel Bowles, "The Efficient Allocation of Resources in Education," *Quarterly Journal of Economics*, 81 (May 1967): 189–219; T. Schultz, "Capital Formation by Education," *Journal of Political Economy*, 68 (1960): 571–583; and Gary Becker, *Human Capital* (New York: National Bureau, 1965). (2) Production and Investment: Robert

Solow, "Technical Change and the Aggregate Production Function," *Review of Economics and Statistics*, 39 (August 1957): 312–332; Solow, "Technical Progress, Capital Formation, and Economic Growth," *American Economic Review*, 52 (May 1962): 76–86; H. Chenery and A. Stout, "Foreign Assistance and Economic Development," *American Economic Review*, 56 (September 1966): 679–733; Albert Waterson, *Development Planning* (Baltimore: Johns Hopkins Press, 1967); and Hla Myint, "Economic Theory and the Underdeveloped Countries," *Journal of Political Economy*, 73 (October 1965): 475–491.

2 "The desire for or commitment to economic development as an end does not necessarily include desire for or commitment to economic development as a means. The fact that these two aspects of development can vary somewhat independently means that even though the desire for development as a goal may exist and be physically achievable, commitment to development as a process of change may not exist." Wilbert E. Moore and Arnold S. Feldman, eds., *Labor Commitment and Social Change in Developing Areas* (New York: Social Science Research Council, 1960), p. 6.

3 For a consideration of the problems associated with extensive foreign investment as a means of achieving economic development, and for a consideration of the possibilities and alternatives in the redistribution of economic gain, see Harry G. Shaffer and Jon Prybla, eds., *From Underdevelopment to Affluence* (New York; Appleton, 1968); Robert Clower et al., *Growth without Development* (Evanston, Ill.: Northwestern University Press, 1967); and S. Enke, *Economics for Development* (London: Dennis Dobson, 1964). For a discussion of the nature of African socialism and the problems of the conversion of ideology into economic policy, see Elliot J. Berg, "Socialism and Economic Development in Tropical Africa," *Quarterly Journal of Economics*, 78 (November 1964): 549–573.

4 ". . . The wealth of a nation and its potential for social, economic and political growth stem from the power to develop and effectively utilize the innate capacities of people." Frederick Harbison and Charles A. Meyers, *Education, Manpower, and Economic Growth* (New York: McGraw-Hill, 1964), p. 14.

5 The marginal productivity of farm labor *may* even be negative where production increases when workers leave the farm.

6 See Moore and Feldman, eds., *Labor Commitment and Social Change.*

7 See Arnold S. Feldman and Christopher Hurn, "The Experience of Modernization," *Sociometry*, 29 (December 1966): 378–395; and George R. Horner, "Selected Cultural Barriers to the Modernization of Labor," in *French-Speaking Africa*, ed. William H. Lewis (New York: Walker and Company, 1965), pp. 166–175.

8 See Oskar Morgenstern, *On the Accuracy of Economic Observations* (Princeton: Princeton University Press, 1963).

9 In Cameroon a sample survey representing a universe of about 80 percent of the labor force in the modern economy has been completed, and should provide accurate data on labor-force characteristics. The high quality of this survey is unusual for Africa. See Jean Chaumont, Remi Clignet, and Phillip Foster, "Economic Development and the Labor Force in Cameroon," forthcoming.

TABLE 3.1   Percent Labor Force in Agriculture, ca. 1968

```
RANGE     =       40.00
MEAN      =       84.09
STANDARD DEVIATION =                 8.94
```

POPULATION PERCENT		RANK	COUNTRY NAME	VALUE	RANGE DECILE
CUM.	COUNTRY				
1.7	1.7	1.0	NIGER	96	1
3.2	1.5	3.0	BURUNDI	95	
4.7	1.5	3.0	RWANDA	95	
10.4	5.7	3.0	TANZANIA	95	
12.0	1.6	5.0	CHAD	92	2
12.3	0.3	6.0	BOTSWANA	91	
13.0	0.7	8.0	CAR	90	
13.4	0.4	8.0	LESOTHO	90	
15.6	2.2	8.0	MALI	90	
16.1	0.5	11.0	MAURITANIA	89	
17.3	1.2	11.0	SOMALIA	89	
21.5	4.2	11.0	UGANDA	89	
32.4	10.9	13.5	ETHIOPIA	88	3
37.2	4.8	13.5	KENYA	88	
37.4	0.2	15.5	GAMBIA	87	
39.7	2.3	15.5	UPPER VOLTA	87	
41.6	1.9	17.0	IVORY COAST	86	
43.3	1.7	18.0	GUINEA	85	
45.8	2.5	20.0	CAMEROON	84	4
47.0	1.2	20.0	DAHOMEY	84	
47.2	0.2	20.0	GABON	84	
49.1	1.9	22.5	MALAWI	81	
50.9	1.8	22.5	ZAMBIA	81	
51.4	0.5	24.5	LIBERIA	80	5
76.4	25.0	24.5	NIGERIA	80	
77.2	0.8	26.0	TOGO	79	
83.9	6.7	27.0	SUDAN	78	
85.0	1.1	28.0	SIERRA LEONE	75	6
86.7	1.7	29.0	SENEGAL	74	
95.8	9.1	30.0	ZAIRE	69	7
96.2	0.4	31.0	CONGO (BRA)	64	8
100.0	3.8	32.0	GHANA	56	10

SOURCES: *AID Economic Data Book* (1970). *Lesotho*: *Europa Yearbook 1967*.

TABLE 3.2   Number of Wage Earners, 1963

```
RANGE     =      119700.00
MEAN      =       16254.69
STANDARD DEVIATION =             23239.49
```

POPULATION PERCENT		RANK	COUNTRY NAME	VALUE	RANGE DECILE
CUM.	COUNTRY				
9.1	9.1	1.0	ZAIRE	120000	1
13.9	4.8	2.0	KENYA	53500	6
38.9	25.0	3.0	NIGERIA	42300	7
44.6	5.7	4.0	TANZANIA	40000	
48.4	3.8	5.5	GHANA	35000	8
55.1	6.7	5.5	SUDAN	35000	
56.9	1.8	7.0	ZAMBIA	26640	
61.1	4.2	8.0	UGANDA	22100	9
63.0	1.9	9.0	IVORY COAST	17100	
65.5	2.5	10.0	CAMEROON	16000	
67.4	1.9	11.0	MALAWI	13500	
69.1	1.7	12.0	SENEGAL	12000	10
69.6	0.5	13.5	LIBERIA	10000	
71.1	1.5	13.5	RWANDA	10000	
72.6	1.5	15.0	BURUNDI	9000	
73.7	1.1	16.0	SIERRA LEONE	8000	
74.1	0.4	17.0	CONGO (BRA)	7000	
75.8	1.7	18.0	GUINEA	6500	
86.7	10.9	19.0	ETHIOPIA	5520	
87.4	0.7	20.0	CAR	5500	
87.6	0.2	21.5	GABON	3500	
88.8	1.2	21.5	SOMALIA	3500	
90.4	1.6	23.0	CHAD	3200	
92.7	2.3	24.0	UPPER VOLTA	2750	
93.0	0.3	25.5	BOTSWANA	2500	
94.2	1.2	25.5	DAHOMEY	2500	
96.4	2.2	27.0	MALI	1880	
96.9	0.5	28.0	MAURITANIA	1850	
98.6	1.7	29.0	NIGER	1350	
99.4	0.8	30.0	TOGO	1160	
99.6	0.2	31.0	GAMBIA	1000	
100.0	0.4	32.0	LESOTHO	300	

SOURCES: *Étude Monographique*, p. 15. *Botswana*: Gross estimate based on low-wage employment in the country according to *Europa Yearbook 1967*, p. 104; *Ethiopia, Sudan*: *AID Economic Data Book*; *Malawi, Somalia, Zambia*: *Overseas Business Reports 1966*.

TABLE 3.3 Number of Wage Earners as Percent of Active Population, 1963

Definition: Number of wage earners divided by the total adult working-age population.

```
RANGE           =        16.00
MEAN            =         7.39
STANDARD DEVIATION =              4.51
```

POPULATION PERCENT CUM.	COUNTRY	RANK	COUNTRY NAME	VALUE	RANGE DECILE
0.2	0.2	1.0	GABON	18	1
0.6	0.4	2.5	CONGO (BRA)	17	
9.7	9.1	2.5	ZAIRE	17	
14.5	4.8	5.0	KENYA	12	4
15.0	0.5	5.0	LIBERIA	12	
16.8	1.8	5.0	ZAMBIA	12	
17.5	0.7	7.0	CAR	11	5
21.3	3.8	9.0	GHANA	10	
23.2	1.9	9.0	IVORY COAST	10	
29.9	6.7	9.0	SUDAN	10	
31.4	1.5	12.0	BURUNDI	8	7
33.1	1.7	12.0	SENEGAL	8	
38.8	5.7	12.0	TANZANIA	8	
41.3	2.5	15.0	CAMEROON	7	
42.8	1.5	15.0	RWANDA	7	
43.9	1.1	15.0	SIERRA LEONE	7	
44.1	0.2	18.0	GAMBIA	6	8
46.0	1.9	18.0	MALAWI	6	
50.2	4.2	18.0	UGANDA	6	
50.7	0.5	20.0	MAURITANIA	5	9
52.4	1.7	21.0	GUINEA	4	
54.0	1.6	25.5	CHAD	3	10
55.2	1.2	25.5	DAHOMEY	3	
66.1	10.9	25.5	ETHIOPIA	3	
68.3	2.2	25.5	MALI	3	
70.0	1.7	25.5	NIGER	3	
71.2	1.2	25.5	SOMALIA	3	
72.0	0.8	25.5	TOGO	3	
74.3	2.3	25.5	UPPER VOLTA	3	
74.6	0.3	30.0	BOTSWANA	2	
99.6	25.0	31.5	NIGERIA	2	

DATA NOT AVAILABLE FOR THE FOLLOWING COUNTRIES

LESOTHO

SOURCES: *Étude Monographique*, p. 15. *Zaire (Congo K.)*: *Directory of Labor Organizations, Africa*, Vol. I (Washington, D.C.: Dept. of Labor, 1966); *Botswana, Malawi, Somalia, Zambia*: Active population: *Europa Yearbook 1967*, number of wage earners, 1963: see Table 3.2; *Sudan*: Percentage of wage earners engaged in manufacturing, services and administration; *Ethiopia*: *AID Economic Data Book*.

TABLE 3.4 Per Capita Energy Consumption in Kilograms of Coal Equivalent, 1966

```
RANGE           =       422.00
MEAN            =        87.50
STANDARD DEVIATION =              96.47
```

POPULATION PERCENT CUM.	COUNTRY	RANK	COUNTRY NAME	VALUE	RANGE DECILE
1.8	1.8	1.0	ZAMBIA	434	1
2.3	0.5	2.0	LIBERIA	294	4
2.5	0.2	3.0	GABON	280	
2.9	0.4	4.0	CONGO (BRA)	180	7
4.8	1.9	5.0	IVORY COAST	159	
6.5	1.7	6.0	SENEGAL	145	
11.3	4.8	7.0	KENYA	124	8
13.0	1.7	8.0	GUINEA	99	
16.8	3.8	9.0	GHANA	95	9
25.9	9.1	10.0	ZAIRE	90	
32.6	6.7	11.0	SUDAN	78	
35.1	2.5	12.0	CAMEROON	73	
40.8	5.7	13.0	TANZANIA	62	
41.6	0.8	14.0	TOGO	54	10
42.1	0.5	15.0	MAURITANIA	53	
67.1	25.0	16.0	NIGERIA	52	
71.3	4.2	17.0	UGANDA	50	
71.5	0.2	18.0	GAMBIA	42	
72.6	1.1	19.0	SIERRA LEONE	38	
74.5	1.9	20.0	MALAWI	37	
75.2	0.7	21.0	CAR	33	
76.4	1.2	22.0	SOMALIA	26	
77.6	1.2	23.0	DAHOMEY	24	
79.8	2.2	24.0	MALI	21	
90.7	10.9	25.5	ETHIOPIA	16	
92.2	1.5	25.5	RWANDA	16	
93.9	1.7	27.0	NIGER	14	
95.4	1.5	28.0	BURUNDI	12	
97.0	1.6	29.0	CHAD	12	
99.3	2.3	31.0	UPPER VOLTA	12	

DATA NOT AVAILABLE FOR THE FOLLOWING COUNTRIES

BOTSWANA   LESOTHO

SOURCE: *UN Statistical Yearbook 1967*, p. 343, Table 142.

TABLE 3.5　Growth of Electricity Production, 1963–1968

Definition: Ratio of electricity production in 1968 to electricity production in 1963 times 100.

```
RANGE  =      461.00
MEAN   =      192.53
STANDARD DEVIATION =        82.94
```

| POPULATION PERCENT | | | COUNTRY | | RANGE |
CUM.	COUNTRY	RANK	NAME	VALUE	DECILE
3.8	3.8	1.0	GHANA	551	1
5.3	1.5	2.5	RWANDA	273	7
6.1	0.8	2.5	TOGO	273	
6.6	0.5	4.0	LIBERIA	264	
8.5	1.9	5.0	MALAWI	251	
10.1	1.6	6.0	CHAD	238	
16.8	6.7	7.0	SUDAN	236	
18.7	1.9	8.0	IVORY COAST	234	
18.9	0.2	9.0	GAMBIA	217	8
19.6	0.7	10.5	CAR	206	
30.5	10.9	10.5	ETHIOPIA	206	
31.6	1.1	12.0	SIERRA LEONE	200	
31.8	0.2	13.0	GABON	188	
33.5	1.7	14.0	NIGER	179	9
34.7	1.2	15.0	SOMALIA	178	
40.4	5.7	16.0	TANZANIA	172	
40.9	0.5	17.5	MAURITANIA	167	
43.1	2.2	17.5	MALI	167	
47.3	4.2	19.0	UGANDA	147	
56.4	9.1	20.0	ZAIRE	145	
58.7	2.3	21.0	UPPER VOLTA	144	
60.4	1.7	22.0	SENEGAL	141	
61.6	1.2	23.0	DAHOMEY	139	
66.4	4.8	24.0	KENYA	134	10
68.2	1.8	25.0	ZAMBIA	133	
68.6	0.4	26.5	CONGO (BRA)	129	
70.3	1.7	26.5	GUINEA	129	
95.3	25.0	28.0	NIGERIA	124	
96.8	1.5	29.0	BURUNDI	121	
99.3	2.5	30.0	CAMEROON	90	

```
DATA NOT AVAILABLE FOR THE FOLLOWING COUNTRIES

BOTSWANA    LESOTHO
```

SOURCES: *AID Economic Data Book* (1970). *Mauritania*: 1964 to 1962 ratio, *UN Statistical Yearbook 1965*, Table 142.

TABLE 3.6　Number of Industrial Types Possible by 1980

Definition: Ewing estimated the number of different types of industries which normally require a market of two or three countries that could be established in each country by 1980. The totals are presented here.

```
RANGE  =       28.00
MEAN   =        9.50
STANDARD DEVIATION =         7.29
```

| POPULATION PERCENT | | | COUNTRY | | RANGE |
CUM.	COUNTRY	RANK	NAME	VALUE	DECILE
25.0	25.0	1.0	NIGERIA	29	1
29.8	4.8	2.0	KENYA	27	
33.6	3.8	3.0	GHANA	19	4
35.4	1.8	4.0	ZAMBIA	18	
37.1	1.7	5.0	SENEGAL	17	5
46.2	9.1	6.0	ZAIRE	16	
48.7	2.5	7.5	CAMEROON	15	
49.1	0.4	7.5	CONGO (BRA)	15	
51.0	1.9	9.0	IVORY COAST	13	6
56.7	5.7	10.5	TANZANIA	12	7
60.9	4.2	10.5	UGANDA	12	
63.1	2.2	12.0	MALI	11	
64.8	1.7	13.0	GUINEA	9	8
71.5	6.7	14.0	SUDAN	8	
82.4	10.9	16.0	ETHIOPIA	7	
82.6	0.2	16.0	GABON	7	
83.7	1.1	16.0	SIERRA LEONE	7	
85.3	1.6	18.0	CHAD	6	9
86.5	1.2	20.5	DAHOMEY	5	
87.0	0.5	20.5	LIBERIA	5	
87.5	0.5	20.5	MAURITANIA	5	
89.8	2.3	20.5	UPPER VOLTA	5	
91.5	1.7	23.0	NIGER	4	
92.2	0.7	24.5	CAR	3	10
93.0	0.8	24.5	TOGO	3	
94.5	1.5	26.5	RWANDA	2	
95.7	1.2	26.5	SOMALIA	2	
97.2	1.5	28.0	BURUNDI	1	
97.4	0.2	29.0	GAMBIA	1	
99.3	1.9	31.0	MALAWI	1	

```
DATA NOT AVAILABLE FOR THE FOLLOWING COUNTRIES

BOTSWANA    LESOTHO
```

SOURCE: A. F. Ewing, *Industry in Africa* (London: Oxford University Press, 1968).

TABLE 3.7 Gross Domestic Capital Formation as a Percent of GDP and Gross Domestic Capital Formation in Millions of U.S. Dollars, 1963

Definition: Gross domestic capital formation is the value at the official exchange rate of all buildings, equipment, inventories, and all other increments to the economies' physical capital.

```
RANGE  =          33.10
MEAN   =          12.99
STANDARD DEVIATION =          6.96
```

POPULATION PERCENT					
CUM.	COUNTRY	RANK	COUNTRY NAME	VALUE	RANGE DECILE
0.5	0.5	1.0	MAURITANIA	36.9	1
1.0	0.5	2.0	LIBERIA	27.1	3
1.2	0.2	3.0	GABON	25.7	4
5.0	3.8	4.0	GHANA	18.5	6
6.7	1.7	5.0	GUINEA	16.0	7
8.5	1.8	6.0	ZAMBIA	15.3	
10.4	1.9	7.0	IVORY COAST	15.2	
12.3	1.9	8.0	MALAWI	14.5	
18.0	5.7	9.0	TANZANIA	13.1	8
27.1	9.1	10.0	ZAIRE	12.7	
28.2	1.1	11.0	SIERRA LEONE	11.4	
39.1	10.9	12.0	ETHIOPIA	11.3	
64.1	25.0	13.0	NIGERIA	10.8	
65.7	1.6	14.5	CHAD	10.5	
67.9	2.2	14.5	MALI	10.5	
72.7	4.8	16.0	KENYA	10.4	9
74.4	1.7	17.0	SENEGAL	10.2	
78.6	4.2	18.0	UGANDA	10.0	
80.3	1.7	19.0	NIGER	9.9	
81.8	1.5	20.5	BURUNDI	9.3	
84.1	2.3	20.5	UPPER VOLTA	9.3	
85.6	1.5	22.0	RWANDA	9.2	
86.4	0.8	23.0	TOGO	9.0	
88.9	2.5	24.0	CAMEROON	8.9	
90.1	1.2	25.0	SOMALIA	6.8	10
90.3	0.2	26.0	GAMBIA	4.5	
91.5	1.2	27.0	DAHOMEY	3.8	

DATA NOT AVAILABLE FOR THE FOLLOWING COUNTRIES

BOTSWANA   CAR   CONGO (BRA)   LESOTHO
SUDAN

SOURCE: *Economic Bulletin for Africa*, Vol. 7, pp. 8–9. *Gabon*: 1960 data; *Cameroon, Zaire (Congo K.)*: 1964 data.

TABLE 3.8 Public Investment per Capita in Hundreds of CFA Francs, 1960*

* Conversion rate is 247 CFA francs = 1 U.S. dollar.

```
RANGE  =        137.00
MEAN   =         20.68
STANDARD DEVIATION =          24.85
```

POPULATION PERCENT					
CUM.	COUNTRY	RANK	COUNTRY NAME	VALUE	RANGE DECILE
0.2	0.2	1.0	GABON	139	1
2.0	1.8	2.0	ZAMBIA	40	8
2.5	0.5	3.0	MAURITANIA	33	
4.2	1.7	4.0	GUINEA	30	
4.7	0.5	5.0	LIBERIA	28	9
8.5	3.8	7.0	GHANA	26	
10.4	1.9	7.0	IVORY COAST	26	
11.5	1.1	7.0	SIERRA LEONE	26	
11.9	0.4	9.5	CONGO (BRA)	25	
13.8	1.9	9.5	MALAWI	25	
15.5	1.7	11.0	SENEGAL	24	
15.7	0.2	12.5	GAMBIA	16	
22.4	6.7	12.5	SUDAN	16	
24.9	2.5	14.0	CAMEROON	14	10
35.8	10.9	15.5	ETHIOPIA	12	
40.0	4.2	15.5	UGANDA	12	
41.2	1.2	17.5	DAHOMEY	11	
46.0	4.8	17.5	KENYA	11	
47.2	1.2	19.0	SOMALIA	10	
47.9	0.7	20.0	CAR	9	
50.1	2.2	21.0	MALI	8	
51.7	1.6	22.5	CHAD	7	
53.4	1.7	22.5	NIGER	7	
78.4	25.0	25.0	NIGERIA	6	
84.1	5.7	25.0	TANZANIA	6	
84.9	0.8	25.0	TOGO	6	
87.2	2.3	27.0	UPPER VOLTA	4	
96.3	9.1	28.0	ZAIRE	2	

DATA NOT AVAILABLE FOR THE FOLLOWING COUNTRIES

BOTSWANA   BURUNDI   LESOTHO   RWANDA

SOURCES: *Étude Monographique. Sierra Leone*: Estimated from Liberian figure; *Ethiopia, Malawi, Sudan*: *ECA Statistical Bulletin*, Table 15; *Somalia*: Estimated from Kenyan figure.

TABLE 3.9 Public Investment as Percent of Gross Domestic Product, 1960

```
RANGE =          18.50
MEAN =            7.36
STANDARD DEVIATION =        4.38
```

POPULATION PERCENT		RANK	COUNTRY NAME	VALUE	RANGE DECILE
CUM.	COUNTRY				
0.2	0.2	1.5	GABON	19.5	1
0.7	0.5	1.5	MAURITANIA	19.5	
2.4	1.7	3.0	GUINEA	13.4	4
4.3	1.9	4.0	MALAWI	12.9	
5.5	1.2	5.5	SOMALIA	10.0	6
12.2	6.7	5.5	SUDAN	10.0	
12.4	0.2	7.0	GAMBIA	9.3	
14.2	1.8	8.0	ZAMBIA	8.5	
18.4	4.2	9.0	UGANDA	8.2	7
18.8	0.4	10.0	CONGO (BRA)	7.5	
29.7	10.9	11.5	ETHIOPIA	7.0	
34.5	4.8	11.5	KENYA	7.0	
35.7	1.2	13.0	DAHOMEY	6.6	
36.2	0.5	14.5	LIBERIA	6.5	8
37.3	1.1	14.5	SIERRA LEONE	6.5	
39.2	1.9	16.0	IVORY COAST	6.2	
43.0	3.8	17.0	GHANA	5.3	
44.7	1.7	18.0	SENEGAL	5.0	
46.9	2.2	19.0	MALI	4.8	
49.4	2.5	20.0	CAMEROON	4.7	9
51.0	1.6	22.0	CHAD	4.3	
52.7	1.7	22.0	NIGER	4.3	
58.4	5.7	22.0	TANZANIA	4.3	
60.7	2.3	24.0	UPPER VOLTA	4.2	
61.4	0.7	25.0	CAR	3.3	
86.4	25.0	26.5	NIGERIA	3.2	
87.2	0.8	26.5	TOGO	3.2	
96.3	9.1	28.0	ZAIRE	1.0	

```
DATA NOT AVAILABLE FOR THE FOLLOWING COUNTRIES

BOTSWANA     BURUNDI     LESOTHO     RWANDA
```

SOURCES: *Étude Monographique*, p. 30. *Malawi*: Estimate from *ECA Statistical Bulletin*, not yet converted to percent; *Somalia*: Estimate from Kenyan and Ugandan figures; *Sudan*, *Zambia*: Estimate from Uganda and *ECA Statistical Bulletin*; *Ethiopia*: Estimate based on Kenyan figures and *ECA Statistical Bulletin*.

TABLE 3.10 Rating of Size of U.S. Investment by 1965

Definition:
1. Low—no significant U.S. investment
2. Medium—some limited U.S. investment
3. High—significant U.S. investment

```
RANGE =           2.00
MEAN =            1.72
STANDARD DEVIATION =        0.87
```

POPULATION PERCENT		RANK	COUNTRY NAME	VALUE	RANGE DECILE
CUM.	COUNTRY				
9.1	9.1	5.0	ZAIRE	3	1
20.0	10.9	5.0	ETHIOPIA	3	
20.2	0.2	5.0	GABON	3	
24.0	3.8	5.0	GHANA	3	
25.7	1.7	5.0	GUINEA	3	
30.5	4.8	5.0	KENYA	3	
31.0	0.5	5.0	LIBERIA	3	
56.0	25.0	5.0	NIGERIA	3	
57.8	1.8	5.0	ZAMBIA	3	
58.5	0.7	12.0	CAR	2	5
60.4	1.9	12.0	IVORY COAST	2	
61.5	1.1	12.0	SIERRA LEONE	2	
68.2	6.7	12.0	SUDAN	2	
69.0	0.8	12.0	TOGO	2	
69.3	0.3	23.5	BOTSWANA	1	10
70.8	1.5	23.5	BURUNDI	1	
73.3	2.5	23.5	CAMEROON	1	
74.9	1.6	23.5	CHAD	1	
75.3	0.4	23.5	CONGO (BRA)	1	
76.5	1.2	23.5	DAHOMEY	1	
76.7	0.2	23.5	GAMBIA	1	
77.1	0.4	23.5	LESOTHO	1	
79.0	1.9	23.5	MALAWI	1	
79.5	0.5	23.5	MAURITANIA	1	
81.7	2.2	23.5	MALI	1	
83.4	1.7	23.5	NIGER	1	
84.9	1.5	23.5	RWANDA	1	
86.6	1.7	23.5	SENEGAL	1	
87.8	1.2	23.5	SOMALIA	1	
93.5	5.7	23.5	TANZANIA	1	
97.7	4.2	23.5	UGANDA	1	
100.0	2.3	23.5	UPPER VOLTA	1	

SOURCE: *Overseas Business Reports 1966*.

**TABLE 3.11   Difficulty in Achieving Long-Run Economic
Growth, ca. 1967**

Definition:
1. Growth not difficult
2. Growth not very difficult
3. Growth difficult
4. Growth very difficult

```
RANGE  =           3.00
MEAN   =           2.77
STANDARD DEVIATION =           1.09
```

POPULATION PERCENT		RANK	COUNTRY NAME	VALUE	RANGE DECILE
CUM.	COUNTRY				
1.5	1.5	6.0	BURUNDI	4	1
2.2	0.7	6.0	CAR	4	
3.8	1.6	6.0	CHAD	4	
5.0	1.2	6.0	DAHOMEY	4	
5.2	0.2	6.0	GAMBIA	4	
7.4	2.2	6.0	MALI	4	
9.1	1.7	6.0	NIGER	4	
10.6	1.5	6.0	RWANDA	4	
11.8	1.2	6.0	SOMALIA	4	
12.6	0.8	6.0	TOGO	4	
14.9	2.3	6.0	UPPER VOLTA	4	
15.3	0.4	14.0	CONGO (BRA)	3	4
17.2	1.9	14.0	MALAWI	3	
17.7	0.5	14.0	MAURITANIA	3	
18.8	1.1	14.0	SIERRA LEONE	3	
24.5	5.7	14.0	TANZANIA	3	
27.0	2.5	21.5	CAMEROON	2	7
36.1	9.1	21.5	ZAIRE	2	
47.0	10.9	21.5	ETHIOPIA	2	
50.8	3.8	21.5	GHANA	2	
55.6	4.8	21.5	KENYA	2	
56.1	0.5	21.5	LIBERIA	2	
81.1	25.0	21.5	NIGERIA	2	
82.8	1.7	21.5	SENEGAL	2	
89.5	6.7	21.5	SUDAN	2	
91.3	1.8	21.5	ZAMBIA	2	
91.5	0.2	27.0	GABON	1	10
93.2	1.7	28.0	GUINEA	1	
95.1	1.9	30.5	IVORY COAST	1	
99.3	4.2	30.5	UGANDA	1	

```
DATA NOT AVAILABLE FOR THE FOLLOWING COUNTRIES

BOTSWANA       LESOTHO
```

SOURCE: William Hance, *African Economic Development*, 2nd ed.
(New York: Praeger, 1967), Table 13, pp. 290–291.

4. Social and Economic Welfare

Welfare is the degree to which individuals and groups achieve those things they value. All values, therefore, are important in the consideration of welfare but, characteristically, the focus of the term is restricted to considerations of wealth and health, and, in particular, to an analysis of the distribution of income, consumption, and facilities for the maintenance of physical well-being. The universality of positive responses to these values is commonly assumed in social scientific analysis,[1] but it is clear that great variation in values exists in any human grouping, and the study of welfare is therefore complicated by questions of the measurement and comparison of individual welfare (utility functions) and social welfare.[2]

Welfare

Some of the most intensive and sophisticated theory in the economic literature is to be found in the study of welfare, but the conceptual complexity and mathematical level of this work has limited the degree to which it has been understood and utilized in other areas of social inquiry. Furthermore, the difficulties involved in the operational treatment of concepts like individual and social utility have meant that development economists themselves often pay little attention to the major theoretical questions of welfare economics. Nevertheless, all social scientists are interested in welfare as that branch of inquiry which relates to the maximization, optimization, or satisficing of human values.[3]

The measurement of welfare is further related to the theoretical analysis of change and stability in social and political organization. Welfare data are used by social scientists to analyze the process of social mobilization, in which individuals are rewarded and reinforced for changing values and patterns of behavior.[4] Welfare data are also used in the analysis of the growth and stability of democratic institutions,[5] the analysis of social stratification and inequality,[6] and the intensity of social conflict and instability.[7]

In this chapter we present data on national income, price structure, agricultural productivity, and health facilities. The use of such data in the evaluation of the welfare outputs of economic and political systems, and in the operationalization of such concepts as frustration, deprivation, or power[8] is subject to several limitations. First, definitions of welfare—what is to be valued, and in what order—are not simply technical or rational economic decisions.[9] They are political decisions which may vary from country to country in important aspects, and low scores on the measures given here may not be valid indications of relative levels of welfare, as it is defined in different countries and by different groups within them. Second, the critical questions of within-nation differences in the distribution of aggregate income are not answered by reference to these data, since sufficient data are not available for the construction of indices of inequality such as the Gini index.[10]

Data Validity and Reliability

A further set of problems relates to the methods of constructing measures of aggregate income, and the difficulties in assessing the reliability of such measures. Gross National Product (GNP) is the value to the final consumer of all goods and services consumed in a country (Tables 4.3–4.5). Gross Domestic Product (GDP) is GNP minus the difference between the value of goods imported and exported by the country (Tables 4.1, 4.2). The analysis of the value of goods and services consumed in a sample of nations is made difficult by problems of comparability in the accounting of the types of goods and services considered, and in the values assigned to the items that are included.[11]

The countries in our sample have large subsistence sectors where exchanges of goods and services are not recorded in the market, but must be imputed in income calculations. As economies grow, many services enter the marketplace which have previously been performed at home or communally, and were therefore not included in measures of income.[12] Because of the confines of the operational definition of GNP and GDP, "it is only exceptionally thought appropriate to impute economic values to activities that do not enter the market, as for instance the rental value of owner-occupied housing or the unsold part of the product of one's 'own trade,' as the UN system puts it. (But) in underdeveloped countries where the market plays a smaller part, imputation becomes necessary on a very large scale if income and product are to have any meaning at all."[13]

The validity and reliability of aggregate income measurement is also impaired by the standards of value applied to goods and services consumed. The usual practice is to calculate income estimates in the national currency and convert to U.S. dollars, or some other unit of international exchange, at the official exchange rate. Such a method probably *understates* the value of goods in domestic markets, and accentuates the differences between rich and poor nations, since the price of foreign exchange is primarily related to those goods and services which do or might enter foreign trade. Products and services which by their nature are consumed locally are at best indirectly affected by prices of foreign goods. Furthermore, the exchange rate used is often a non-equilibrium rate which is periodically devalued and hence an inaccurate measure of value even for internationally traded goods and services. For cross-national, comparative purposes, figures should compare purchasing prices for the range of items used in income calculation. The effects of such a procedure are illustrated in a study cited by the *World Bank Atlas*, in which the per capita product in the U.S. compared to that in India was in ratio 30 to 1, whereas calculations based on purchasing power parities yielded a ratio of only 12 to 1.[14] A related difficulty in the valuation of domestic income is the problem of currency inflation. The data in this chapter are given at factor cost whenever possible, which corrects for taxation differences, but these are probably minimal. The correction of prices for inflation can only be done for a small subset of African nations since appropriate GDP deflators do not exist. Care must therefore be taken, particularly

with the data on GDP growth, since different growth rates reflect both real changes and those which result from currency inflation.

When income measures are standardized for population differences, additional sources of error emerge. Added to the problems of accounting already discussed are the errors attributable to the estimates of population used in ratio measures. Until recently, population figures for Africa were very unreliable; as a result, the error range in these ratios can be considerable. If, however, the errors in the annual ratios are correlated, the accuracy of dynamic indicators may be greater than that for individual static measures.[15]

Prices are clearly related to welfare inasmuch as they limit the purchasing power of income, and reflect the imbalance between the supply of, and demand for, consumption goods. Although we do not have full information for the deflation of income measures to a constant base year, we do have a partial measure of deflation in the consumer price index given in Table 4.6. Price levels are indicators of the money necessary to buy a given "basket of goods." When prices go up for the same quantity and mix of goods, the index in this table goes up as a ratio to the price of such goods in 1959.

It is important to note that the inflation measured by the consumer price index may be the result of different economic processes. The ability to increase productive capacity in some nations is very limited in the face of increased expectations and demands for welfare. On the other hand, nations with greater productive capacity may invest resources in unproductive economic enterprises so that they bring about inflation more than have it thrust upon them. This difference is relevant to the interpretation of the respective positions of Somalia and Ghana, for example, in Table 4.6.

The output of the economy in terms of consumption goods is critical to the analysis of welfare. Ideally, one would want to know the range and quantity of different goods produced, as well as the growth in different sectors of production. Particularly relevant to theories of economic development is the relative importance, or primacy, of increasing productivity in the agricultural and industrial sectors. Underdeveloped countries in Africa are often dependent for growth on the generation of agricultural surpluses, which not only release agrarian labor for industrial employment, but also provide for growth in the commercial marketing of agricultural produce, and thereby create profits for domestic saving and investment. The data in Table 4.7 is an index of the change in total agricultural output from 1954 to about 1960–61. The base year is defined as 100, and the value of 201 for Ivory Coast, for example, represents a 101 percent *increase* over the 1954 production, while the value of 91 for Zaire (Congo K.) represents a *decrease* of 9 percent in that time period. The relevance of these data to the analysis of standards of living and the potential for economic growth is limited by the fact that large proportions of the agricultural produce in some countries is traded in international markets, and not available for domestic consumption. Furthermore, the reliability of indices such as these is affected by the difficulty of accurately estimating that production which is smuggled out of the country.

Aggregate measures of physical well-being in African nations can be developed from data on disease levels, infant mortality, hospital facilities, caloric intake, and number of medical practitioners. In our data, the measures of these factors that we have are highly intercorrelated with the measure of physicians per capita given in Table 4.8, a growth measure for which is given in Table 4.9. A disadvantage of this measure is the lack of comparability in the qualifications required in different countries for medical practice. Furthermore, the actual practice of medicine is not necessarily equated with the qualifications for such practice; figures for Cameroon, for example, show that 20 percent of the qualified doctors living there were not actually practicing medicine in 1968.[16]

The reliability of the measures reported in this chapter or, at a minimum, their stability is subject to the numerous sources of confusion and error that we have discussed. We are unable to give any quantitative estimate of the reliability of these figures, and they should be used with caution. The dimensionality of income, price structure, agricultural productivity, and health facilities is, however, clearly illustrated in a factor analysis of 172 variables in which six factors account for 81 percent of the variance. Factor analysis, furthermore, indicates that measures of similar concepts, taken at different times by different agencies, are closely associated, which may be taken as some basis for confidence in their reliability.

Notes

[1] It should be emphasized that the restrictive emphasis on wealth and health obscures the range of values that might be analyzed. Values on power and security, for example, held both by researchers and by those who allocate welfare may be of greater weight in the determination of the allocation of welfare than those widely distributed values on wealth and health.

[2] James S. Coleman, "The Possibility of a Social Welfare Function," *American Economic Review*, 56 (December 1966): 1105–1122.

[3] Useful introductions to the scope of welfare economics are J. R. Hicks, "The Foundation of Welfare Economics," *Econometrica*, 7 (1939): 215–228; I. M. D. Little, *A Critique of Welfare Economics* (London: Oxford University Press, 1950); Kenneth Arrow, *Social Choice and Individual Values* (New York: John Wiley, 1963); T. C. Koopmans, *Three Essays on the State of Economic Science* (New York: McGraw-Hill, 1957); E. J. Mishan, "A Survey of Welfare Economics, 1939–1959," *Economic Journal*, 70 (1960): 197–265; Paul Samuelson, *Foundations of Economic Analysis* (Cambridge: Harvard University Press, 1947); and Tibor Scitovsky, "A Note on Welfare Propositions in Economics," *Review of Economic Studies*, 9 (November 1941): 77–88; K. Arrow and T. Scitovsky, eds., *A.E.A. Readings in Welfare Economics* (Homewood, Ill.: Irwin, 1970). Examples of the use of the theory of welfare economics outside of economics are Herbert A. Simon, *Administrative Behavior* (New York: Macmillan, 1947); Robert A. Dahl and Charles E. Lindblom, *Politics, Economics, and Welfare* (New York: Harper and Row, 1953); and Anthony Downs, *An Economic Theory of Democracy* (New York: Harper and Row, 1957).

[4] This approach is most directly related to the work of Karl W. Deutsch and, in particular, to his stimulating article, "Social Mobilization and Political Development," *American Political Science Review*, 55 (September 1961): 493–514.

[5] See Seymour M. Lipset, *Political Man* (Garden City, N.Y.: Doubleday Anchor Books, 1960).

[6] See, for example, Bruce M. Russett, "Inequality and Instability: The Relation of Land Tenure to Politics," *World Politics*, 16 (April 1964): 442–54.

[7] See the footnotes in Chapter 11.

[8] The use of income measures as operationalizations of national power in the study of international relations is discussed in Karl W. Deutsch, *The Analysis of International Relations* (Englewood Cliffs, N.J.: Prentice-Hall, 1968).

[9] See Kenneth E. Boulding, "Economics as a Moral Science," *American Economic Review*, 59 (March 1969): 1–12.

[10] For discussions and data on the Gini index, see Bruce M. Russett, ed., *The World Handbook of Political and Social Indicators* (New Haven: Yale University Press, 1964), and Hayward R. Alker, Jr., and B. Russett, "Indices for Comparing Inequality," in *Comparing Nations*, eds. R. Merritt and S. Rokkan (New Haven, Conn.: Yale University Press, 1966), pp. 337–348.

[11] For information on the details of national income calculation in Africa, see Peter Ady and Michel Courcier, *Systems of National Accounts in Africa* (Paris: Organization for European Economic

Cooperation, 1960); and D. A. Lury, "National Accounts in Africa," *Journal of Modern African Studies*, 2 (1964): 94–110.

[12] For discussions of traditional markets and occupational structures, see Paul Bohannan and George Dalton, *Primitive Economies* (New York: Doubleday, 1964).

[13] Goran Ohlin, "Aggregate Comparisons: Problems and Prospects of Quantitative Analysis Based on National Accounts," in *Comparative Research across Cultures and Nations*, ed. S. Rokkan (Paris: Mouton, 1968).

[14] *World Bank Atlas* (Washington, D.C.: International Bank for Reconstruction and Development, 1969).

[15] See Gustav Ranis and John C. H. Fei, "A Theory of Economic Development," *American Economic Review*, 51 (1961): 533–565; and S. Hymer and S. Resnick, "A Model of an Agrarian Economy with Non-agricultural Activities," *American Economic Review*, 59 (September 1969): 493–506.

[16] Personal communication from Kenneth E. Larimore based upon field research in Cameroon, 1968–1969.

TABLE 4.1　GDP in Tens of Millions of U.S. Dollars, ca. 1961

```
RANGE    =      326.00
MEAN     =       44.78
STANDARD DEVIATION =          61.99
```

POPULATION PERCENT			COUNTRY		RANGE
CUM.	COUNTRY	RANK	NAME	VALUE	DECILE
25.0	25.0	1.0	NIGERIA	328	1
28.8	3.8	2.0	GHANA	132	7
37.9	9.1	3.0	ZAIRE	122	
44.6	6.7	4.0	SUDAN	113	
55.5	10.9	5.0	ETHIOPIA	90	8
60.3	4.8	6.0	KENYA	80	
66.0	5.7	7.0	TANZANIA	56	9
68.5	2.5	8.0	CAMEROON	54	
70.2	1.7	9.0	SENEGAL	53	
72.0	1.8	10.0	ZAMBIA	52	
73.9	1.9	11.5	IVORY COAST	47	
78.1	4.2	11.5	UGANDA	47	
80.3	2.2	13.0	MALI	25	10
82.0	1.7	14.0	GUINEA	19	
83.1	1.1	15.5	SIERRA LEONE	18	
85.4	2.3	15.5	UPPER VOLTA	18	
87.1	1.7	17.0	NIGER	17	
88.7	1.6	19.0	CHAD	16	
89.9	1.2	19.0	DAHOMEY	16	
90.4	0.5	19.0	LIBERIA	16	
90.6	0.2	21.0	GABON	15	
91.3	0.7	22.0	CAR	14	
92.5	1.2	23.0	SOMALIA	13	
94.4	1.9	24.0	MALAWI	12	
95.9	1.5	26.0	BURUNDI	11	
97.4	1.5	26.0	RWANDA	11	
98.2	0.8	26.0	TOGO	11	
98.6	0.4	28.5	CONGO (BRA)	9	
99.1	0.5	28.5	MAURITANIA	9	
99.5	0.4	30.0	LESOTHO	4	
99.7	0.2	31.0	GAMBIA	3	
100.0	0.3	32.0	BOTSWANA	2	

SOURCES: "Comparative Survey of per Capita Income in Africa," *Africa Report*, 8 (August, 1963): 32. *Burundi, Chad, Congo (Brazzaville), Zaire (Congo K.), Dahomey, Ghana, Guinea, Ivory Coast, Malawi, Niger, Tanzania, Togo*: UN, *Housing in Africa*, 1965, pp. 182–183.

TABLE 4.2　GDP at Current Market Prices, 1965, in Millions of U.S. Dollars

```
RANGE    =     4824.00
MEAN     =      615.97
STANDARD DEVIATION =          904.25
```

POPULATION PERCENT			COUNTRY		RANGE
CUM.	COUNTRY	RANK	NAME	VALUE	DECILE
25.0	25.0	1.0	NIGERIA	4852	1
28.8	3.8	2.0	GHANA	2207	6
35.5	6.7	3.0	SUDAN	1387	8
44.6	9.1	4.0	ZAIRE	1273	
55.5	10.9	5.0	ETHIOPIA	1171	
57.4	1.9	6.0	IVORY COAST	963	9
62.2	4.8	7.0	KENYA	846	
64.0	1.8	8.0	ZAMBIA	842	
69.7	5.7	9.0	TANZANIA	751	
71.4	1.7	10.0	SENEGAL	680	
73.9	2.5	11.0	CAMEROON	670	
78.1	4.2	12.0	UGANDA	658	
79.2	1.1	13.0	SIERRA LEONE	344	10
81.4	2.2	14.0	MALI	297	
83.1	1.7	15.5	GUINEA	257	
85.4	2.3	15.5	UPPER VOLTA	257	
87.1	1.7	17.0	NIGER	250	
88.7	1.6	18.0	CHAD	237	
89.2	0.5	19.0	LIBERIA	213	
90.4	1.2	20.0	DAHOMEY	165	
92.3	1.9	21.0	MALAWI	163	
93.1	0.8	22.0	TOGO	156	
94.6	1.5	23.0	RWANDA	155	
95.8	1.2	24.0	SOMALIA	150	
97.3	1.5	25.0	BURUNDI	140	
97.7	0.4	26.0	CONGO (BRA)	138	
97.9	0.2	27.0	GABON	130	
98.4	0.5	28.0	MAURITANIA	127	
99.1	0.7	29.0	CAR	122	
99.5	0.4	30.0	LESOTHO	48	
99.8	0.3	31.0	BOTSWANA	34	
100.0	0.2	32.0	GAMBIA	28	

SOURCES: *Africa 1968*, p. 108. *Botswana:* Estimate based on $60.00 per capita GNP from *AID Economic Data Book*; *Lesotho:* Estimate based on $58.00 per capita GNP.

TABLE 4.3 Per Capita GNP in U.S. Dollars, 1963

```
RANGE     =     287.00
MEAN  =         105.91
STANDARD DEVIATION =          63.74
```

POPULATION PERCENT CUM.	COUNTRY	RANK	COUNTRY NAME	VALUE	RANGE DECILE
0.2	0.2	1.0	GABON	325	1
0.7	0.5	2.0	LIBERIA	238	4
4.5	3.8	3.0	GHANA	207	5
6.4	1.9	4.0	IVORY COAST	188	
8.1	1.7	5.0	SENEGAL	183	
8.5	0.4	6.0	CONGO (BRA)	172	6
10.3	1.8	7.0	ZAMBIA	158	
11.4	1.1	8.0	SIERRA LEONE	123	8
20.5	9.1	9.0	ZAIRE	116	
23.0	2.5	10.0	CAMEROON	109	
23.7	0.7	11.0	CAR	106	
24.2	0.5	12.0	MAURITANIA	102	
29.0	4.8	13.0	KENYA	97	
30.7	1.7	14.0	GUINEA	96	
37.4	6.7	15.0	SUDAN	94	9
38.9	1.5	16.5	BURUNDI	81	
40.4	1.5	16.5	RWANDA	81	
41.2	0.8	18.0	TOGO	79	
42.9	1.7	19.0	NIGER	77	
44.1	1.2	20.5	DAHOMEY	70	
44.3	0.2	20.5	GAMBIA	70	
48.5	4.2	22.0	UGANDA	69	
50.7	2.2	23.0	MALI	66	10
51.9	1.2	24.5	SOMALIA	65	
57.6	5.7	24.5	TANZANIA	65	
59.2	1.6	26.0	CHAD	64	
84.2	25.0	27.0	NIGERIA	61	
84.5	0.3	28.0	BOTSWANA	51	
84.9	0.4	29.0	LESOTHO	48	
95.8	10.9	30.5	ETHIOPIA	45	
98.1	2.3	30.5	UPPER VOLTA	45	
100.0	1.9	32.0	MALAWI	38	

SOURCE: *UN Statistical Yearbook, 1967*, Table 185, p. 576. *Botswana, Lesotho*: Estimates based on extrapolation around 1963.

TABLE 4.4 Per Capita GNP in U.S. Dollars, 1968

Comment: World Bank figures are mostly computed for 1968 as extrapolations of U.S. dollar estimates previously determined for 1964. These 1964 estimates were derived in most cases from the respective national currency figures on the basis of the then prevailing official or par value exchange rates. This procedure, which is described in more detail in the source, is intended to minimize the distorting effects of inflation and the impact of non-internationally traded goods on the total national product of developing nations.

```
RANGE     =     260.00
MEAN  =         120.63
STANDARD DEVIATION =          65.43
```

POPULATION PERCENT CUM.	COUNTRY	RANK	COUNTRY NAME	VALUE	RANGE DECILE
0.2	0.2	1.0	GABON	310	1
2.1	1.9	2.0	IVORY COAST	260	2
2.5	0.4	3.0	CONGO (BRA)	230	4
4.3	1.8	4.0	ZAMBIA	220	
4.8	0.5	5.0	LIBERIA	210	
5.3	0.5	6.0	MAURITANIA	180	6
9.1	3.8	7.5	GHANA	170	
10.8	1.7	7.5	SENEGAL	170	
11.9	1.1	9.0	SIERRA LEONE	150	7
14.4	2.5	10.0	CAMEROON	140	
19.2	4.8	11.0	KENYA	130	
19.9	0.7	12.0	CAR	120	8
24.1	4.2	13.0	UGANDA	110	
24.4	0.3	15.5	BOTSWANA	100	9
24.6	0.2	15.5	GAMBIA	100	
31.3	6.7	15.5	SUDAN	100	
32.1	0.8	15.5	TOGO	100	
41.2	9.1	19.0	ZAIRE	90	
42.9	1.7	19.0	GUINEA	90	
45.1	2.2	19.0	MALI	90	
46.3	1.2	22.0	DAHOMEY	80	
46.7	0.4	22.0	LESOTHO	80	
52.4	5.7	22.0	TANZANIA	80	
63.3	10.9	25.5	ETHIOPIA	70	10
65.0	1.7	25.5	NIGER	70	
90.0	25.0	25.5	NIGERIA	70	
91.5	1.5	25.5	RWANDA	70	
93.1	1.6	28.5	CHAD	60	
94.3	1.2	28.5	SOMALIA	60	
95.8	1.5	31.0	BURUNDI	50	
97.7	1.9	31.0	MALAWI	50	
100.0	2.3	31.0	UPPER VOLTA	50	

SOURCE: *World Bank Atlas 1970. Botswana, Gambia, Lesotho, Rwanda, Somalia*: Estimates are tentative.

TABLE 4.5 Average Annual Growth Rate of GNP Per Capita, 1961–1968

Definition and Comment: The average annual growth rates given are the compounded rates of growth between 1961 and 1968. Over an extended period, and except where marked cyclical or irregular factors are present, this method may generally be taken to yield a fair approximation of the trend according to the World Bank.

```
RANGE     =        12.90
MEAN      =         1.15
STANDARD DEVIATION =           2.30
```

POPULATION PERCENT CUM.	POPULATION PERCENT COUNTRY	RANK	COUNTRY NAME	VALUE	RANGE DECILE
0.5	0.5	1.0	MAURITANIA	11.3	1
2.4	1.9	2.0	IVORY COAST	4.8	6
4.2	1.8	3.0	ZAMBIA	3.6	
5.9	1.7	4.0	GUINEA	2.7	7
16.8	10.9	5.0	ETHIOPIA	2.6	
17.2	0.4	6.5	CONGO (BRA)	2.2	8
19.1	1.9	6.5	MALAWI	2.2	
20.6	1.5	8.5	RWANDA	1.5	
21.7	1.1	8.5	SIERRA LEONE	1.5	
26.5	4.8	10.0	KENYA	1.4	
28.7	2.2	11.0	MALI	1.3	
29.1	0.4	12.5	LESOTHO	1.2	
34.8	5.7	12.5	TANZANIA	1.2	
37.3	2.5	15.0	CAMEROON	1.1	
38.5	1.2	15.0	DAHOMEY	1.1	
42.7	4.2	15.0	UGANDA	1.1	
43.0	0.3	17.0	BOTSWANA	0.8	9
43.2	0.2	18.5	GABON	0.7	
43.7	0.5	18.5	LIBERIA	0.7	
44.5	0.8	20.0	TOGO	0.5	
45.7	1.2	21.0	SOMALIA	0.2	
48.0	2.3	22.0	UPPER VOLTA	0.1	
49.5	1.5	23.0	BURUNDI	0.0	
49.7	0.2	24.0	GAMBIA	-0.1	
58.8	9.1	25.5	ZAIRE	-0.3	
83.8	25.0	25.5	NIGERIA	-0.3	
90.5	6.7	27.0	SUDAN	-0.4	10
91.2	0.7	28.0	CAR	-0.6	
95.0	3.8	29.0	GHANA	-0.7	
96.7	1.7	30.0	SENEGAL	-1.4	
98.3	1.6	31.0	CHAD	-1.5	
100.0	1.7	32.0	NIGER	-1.6	

SOURCE: *World Bank Atlas 1970. Botswana, Gambia, Lesotho, Rwanda, Somalia:* Estimates are tentative.

TABLE 4.6 Consumer Price Index, 1965

Definition: Ratio of prices in 1965 to prices in 1958 times 100. Increase of index indicates rising prices.

```
RANGE     =        80.00
MEAN      =       126.08
STANDARD DEVIATION =           19.67
```

POPULATION PERCENT CUM.	POPULATION PERCENT COUNTRY	RANK	COUNTRY NAME	VALUE	RANGE DECILE
3.8	3.8	1.0	GHANA	181	1
5.0	1.2	2.0	SOMALIA	160	3
6.6	1.6	3.0	CHAD	151	4
8.1	1.5	4.5	BURUNDI	150	
10.4	2.3	4.5	UPPER VOLTA	150	
10.8	0.6	6.0	CONGO (BRA)	145	5
11.5	0.7	7.0	CAR	134	6
13.0	1.5	8.0	RWANDA	130	7
23.9	10.9	9.0	ETHIOPIA	128	
25.6	1.7	10.0	SENEGAL	126	
26.7	1.1	11.0	SIERRA LEONE	124	8
30.9	4.2	12.0	UGANDA	123	
31.4	0.5	13.0	MAURITANIA	121	
33.9	2.5	14.0	CAMEROON	119	
58.9	25.0	15.5	NIGERIA	117	9
65.6	6.7	15.5	SUDAN	117	
67.4	1.8	17.0	ZAMBIA	116	
67.6	0.2	18.5	GABON	114	
69.5	1.9	18.5	IVORY COAST	114	
74.3	4.8	20.0	KENYA	112	
76.2	1.9	21.0	MALAWI	106	10
81.9	5.7	22.0	TANZANIA	105	
91.0	9.1	23.5	ZAIRE	104	
92.7	1.7	23.5	NIGER	104	
93.2	0.5	25.0	LIBERIA	101	

DATA NOT AVAILABLE FOR THE FOLLOWING COUNTRIES

BOTSWANA	DAHOMEY	GAMBIA	GUINEA
LESOTHO	MALI	TOGO	

SOURCES: *ECA Statistical Bulletin II*, Table 63A, pp. 314–316. *Burundi, Rwanda: Overseas Business Reports 1966.*

TABLE 4.7 Index of Agricultural Production, 1960–1961

Definition: Ratio ca. 1960–1961 to 1954 production times 100.

```
RANGE     =      110.00
MEAN      =      128.63
STANDARD DEVIATION =          21.32
```

POPULATION PERCENT CUM.	COUNTRY	RANK	COUNTRY NAME	VALUE	RANGE DECILE
1.9	1.9	1.0	IVORY COAST	201	1
3.1	1.2	2.0	SOMALIA	179.	2
6.9	3.8	3.5	GHANA	148	5
8.6	1.7	3.5	NIGER	148	
13.4	4.8	5.0	KENYA	145	6
19.1	5.7	6.0	TANZANIA	141	
21.0	1.9	8.0	MALAWI	140	
22.7	1.7	8.0	SENEGAL	140	
24.5	1.8	8.0	ZAMBIA	140	
27.0	2.5	10.0	CAMEROON	136	
52.0	25.0	11.0	NIGERIA	131	7
58.7	6.7	12.0	SUDAN	127	
60.2	1.5	14.0	BURUNDI	125	
61.7	1.5	14.0	RWANDA	125	
62.5	0.8	14.0	TOGO	125	
64.2	1.7	16.5	GUINEA	122	8
68.4	4.2	16.5	UGANDA	122	
68.9	0.5	18.0	MAURITANIA	120	
69.6	0.7	20.5	CAR	119	
71.2	1.6	20.5	CHAD	119	
71.6	0.4	20.5	CONGO (BRA)	119	
71.8	0.2	20.5	GABON	119	
74.0	2.2	23.0	MALI	116	
84.9	10.9	24.0	ETHIOPIA	114	
87.2	2.3	25.0	UPPER VOLTA	113	9
88.4	1.2	26.0	DAHOMEY	111	
88.6	0.2	27.0	GAMBIA	110	
89.1	0.5	28.0	LIBERIA	107	
90.2	1.1	29.0	SIERRA LEONE	106	
99.3	9.1	30.0	ZAIRE	91	10

```
DATA NOT AVAILABLE FOR THE FOLLOWING COUNTRIES

BOTSWANA    LESOTHO
```

SOURCES: *International Commercial Supplement* (Washington, D.C.: U.S. Department of Commerce, 1963), p. 97. *Malawi, Zambia*: Report Index for Federation of Rhodesia and Nyasaland; *Burundi*: Estimate based on export figures of coffee, 1958–1960, *Étude Monographique*, Vol. 3, p. 218; *Rwanda*: Estimate based on production levels of subsistence agriculture and tea, *ibid.*; *Mauritania*: Estimate based on mean index of Mali and Senegal which have comparable agricultural characteristics.

TABLE 4.8 Inhabitants per Physician, in Hundreds, ca. 1967–1968

```
RANGE     =      695.00
MEAN      =      306.81
STANDARD DEVIATION =          202.69
```

POPULATION PERCENT CUM.	COUNTRY	RANK	COUNTRY NAME	VALUE	RANGE DECILE
2.3	2.3	1.0	UPPER VOLTA	762	1
3.9	1.6	2.0	CHAD	724	
6.1	2.2	3.0	MALI	652	2
17.0	10.9	4.0	ETHIOPIA	627	
18.5	1.5	5.0	RWANDA	624	
20.2	1.7	6.0	NIGER	588	3
21.7	1.5	7.0	BURUNDI	563	
23.6	1.9	8.0	MALAWI	469	5
48.6	25.0	9.0	NIGERIA	365	6
49.3	0.7	10.0	CAR	360	
50.5	1.2	11.0	DAHOMEY	315	7
51.0	0.5	12.0	MAURITANIA	300	
52.2	1.2	13.0	SOMALIA	283	
54.7	2.5	14.0	CAMEROON	267	8
55.1	0.4	15.0	LESOTHO	261	
61.8	6.7	16.0	SUDAN	246	
62.6	0.8	17.0	TOGO	221	
71.7	9.1	18.0	ZAIRE	211	
73.4	1.7	19.0	GUINEA	205	9
73.7	0.3	20.0	BOTSWANA	197	
73.9	0.2	21.0	GAMBIA	187	
75.8	1.9	22.0	IVORY COAST	173	
81.5	5.7	23.0	TANZANIA	168	
83.2	1.7	24.0	SENEGAL	167	
84.3	1.1	25.0	SIERRA LEONE	164	
88.1	3.8	26.0	GHANA	141	
88.5	0.4	27.5	CONGO (BRA)	116	10
90.3	1.8	27.5	ZAMBIA	116	
90.8	0.5	29.0	LIBERIA	106	
95.6	4.8	30.0	KENYA	95	
99.8	4.2	31.0	UGANDA	78	
100.0	0.2	32.0	GABON	67	

SOURCE: *AID Economic Data Book 1970.*

TABLE 4.9 Average Annual Percent Change in Number of Physicians, ca. 1960–1963

```
RANGE  =        125.00
MEAN   =         11.94
STANDARD DEVIATION =         21.59
```

POPULATION PERCENT		RANK	COUNTRY NAME	VALUE	RANGE DECILE
CUM.	COUNTRY				
9.1	9.1	1.0	ZAIRE	117	1
12.9	3.8	2.0	GHANA	44	6
14.7	1.8	3.0	ZAMBIA	32	7
15.9	1.2	4.0	DAHOMEY	28	8
17.8	1.9	5.0	IVORY COAST	22	
18.6	0.8	6.0	TOGO	20	
29.5	10.9	7.0	ETHIOPIA	15	9
29.9	0.4	8.5	CONGO (BRA)	11	
30.1	0.2	8.5	GABON	11	
34.9	4.8	10.0	KENYA	10	
37.2	2.3	11.0	UPPER VOLTA	9	
39.7	2.5	13.0	CAMEROON	8	
41.3	1.6	13.0	CHAD	8	
41.8	0.5	13.0	MAURITANIA	8	
42.0	0.2	15.5	GAMBIA	7	
43.7	1.7	15.5	SENEGAL	7	
45.9	2.2	18.0	MALI	5	
52.6	6.7	18.0	SUDAN	5	
58.3	5.7	18.0	TANZANIA	5	
59.8	1.5	21.5	BURUNDI	4	10
60.3	0.5	21.5	LIBERIA	4	
62.2	1.9	21.5	MALAWI	4	
63.3	1.1	21.5	SIERRA LEONE	4	
65.0	1.7	24.0	NIGER	3	
90.0	25.0	25.0	NIGERIA	1	
90.7	0.7	28.0	CAR	0	
92.4	1.7	28.0	GUINEA	0	
93.9	1.5	28.0	RWANDA	0	
95.1	1.2	28.0	SOMALIA	0	
99.3	4.2	28.0	UGANDA	0	
99.7	0.4	31.0	LESOTHO	-2	
100.0	0.3	32.0	BOTSWANA	-8	

SOURCE: *ECA Statistical Bulletin II*, Table 73, p. 382.

5. Education

Education may be identified as the more or less consciously pursued or programmatic phase of acculturation in all societies from traditional to modern. It involves the cognition and internalization of social norms, values, ideas, and substantive information necessary for the full participation and survival of the individual in his social and ecological setting. From the perspective of structural-functional theory,[1] educational institutions are often viewed as essentially conservative forces insuring the perpetuation of existing cultural patterns, value orientations, and behavioral norms. This perspective is, however, not applicable to the Western-based educational systems in Africa, which have been key instruments of transition and potential conflict in the colonial period and after.[2]

Four Approaches

Social scientists have examined the impact of education in Africa and other developing areas of the world from varying points of view. One approach adopted by economic planners has been to view educational systems as the developers and mobilizers of human capital for the modern sector of the economy.[3] Those who take this approach view human capital formation as one of several factors determining increased national production and consumption.

A second approach emphasizes the "mass mobilizing" aspect of education. Political scientists and sociologists who take this point of view treat education as an important transformer of traditional social values and norms and a stimulant to participation in modern institutions. In this sense, education is one of six major categories of indicators in the "auditing of modernization,"[4] suggested by Daniel Lerner. He compares elementary, vocational, teacher training, and university enrollment per capita for several Middle Eastern countries and observes that an important requisite for non-erratic social change and political stability is balanced growth among major categories of indicators and among indicators within

one category (e.g., teacher training must keep pace with elementary enrollment).[5] S. N. Eisenstadt expresses similar views by describing development in the educational field as a basic characteristic of modernization.[6] A more direct, empirical study of the influence of early educational experience on the political system in terms of adult political participation was conducted by Gabriel Almond and Sidney Verba.[7] They found a positive relationship between participation in decision-making in the home and classroom and later political participation in adulthood.[8]

In contrast to this, the third approach is the "elite formation" emphasis of scholars such as C. Arnold Anderson, Remi Clignet, and Philip Foster. They examine the impact of education on the social structure of African countries and argue that while education has in fact accelerated individual social mobility along new paths, certain groups or categories of people in the population have greater opportunity for education than others. Most particularly, the educated elite's children enjoy an advantage in pursuing educational qualifications. These scholars question whether schooling has had much effect on the intensity of ethnic identification and inequalities based on the same.[9] The importance of modern education in Africa is seen by this approach in terms of its "elite" effects rather than as a mass mobilizing process in which general psychological commitments are reformed.[10]

A fourth approach takes a particular aspect of modernization, the developing of a sense of national identification which transcends ethnic loyalties,[11] and assesses the contribution made to this process by the modern educational system. While positive attitudes toward the national political system may be internalized in the early stages of the formal educational process,[12] the effective transmission of such attitudes increases as education itself becomes accepted as a social value.[13] This process is not, however, without difficulties. Although education at the mass level continues to inculcate the national loyalties and participatory values necessary for the perpetuation of modern political systems, the danger remains that the somewhat less than universal access to modern education in new nations will accentuate a growing rift between traditional and modern sectors of the population.[14] And, as Coleman argues, inequalities in the distribution of education "may intensify divisions among different ethnic, regional, and parochial groups out of which nation-builders, partly through education, must forge a larger sense of national identity."[15]

As this highly eclectic review of theoretical relationships between education and national development suggests, there are numerous hypotheses worth testing, but only if adequate data can be brought to bear on them. Although quantitative information pertaining to education in Africa has been produced in abundance first by colonial administrators and, since the First World War, by governmental and international organizations, literature on this subject, until recently, has been largely descriptive and unit specific rather than quantitative or broadly comparative.[16]

Data Sources

A precursor to comparative research in African education was the publication of the widely acclaimed Phelps-Stokes reports in 1922 and 1925 under the editorship of T. J. Jones. These reports included a comprehensive evaluation of the various colonial educational systems together with enrollment estimates and recommendations for reform.[17] In recent years several works, including those by Donald G. Burns on education in Commonwealth nations and Abdou Moumouni on the former French African territories,[18] have been produced which are broadly comparative in their approach and offer a liberal selection of cross-national data.

The availability of what might be classed as original data sources—official government publications, colonial reports on education, and statistical periodicals emanating from official sources—is somewhat limited, at least in the United States, to several larger institutions.[19] British colonial governments characteristically issued yearly reports often with detailed data on enrollment and expenditures in all

administrative subdivisions. During the Second World War, however, statistical reporting was negligible due to the lack of funds and personnel. Comprehensive data on the French areas, published in Paris, are available for approximately the final eight years of colonial domination.[20]

By far the largest and most useful single body of statistical information on enrollment and expenditure for education at various levels is available in *A World Survey of Education*, published by UNESCO in four volumes between the years 1955 and 1966.[21] The above publications, together with material from the *UN Statistical Yearbook* for the most recent years, represent the major sources of data on enrollment and expenditures for the tables which follow in this chapter. Represented here are four broad categories of indicators of the state of educational development:

(1) student enrollment
(2) literacy
(3) expenditures
(4) staffing or teaching personnel

(1) Data on student enrollment are given in Tables 5.1–5.15. These data are reported in terms of the numbers of persons enrolled in different levels of education—primary, secondary, and higher education. Furthermore we provide, in addition to aggregate size, enrollment data standardized by population, rates of change over periods extending from 1930 onwards, and indicators relating to female enrollment.[22] One of the problems confronting educational planners has been to determine the appropriate "mix" of primary and secondary school places. Tables 5.13 and 5.14 present data on the ratio of secondary to primary pupils.

It should be noted here that student enrollment *per se* is not as sensitive a measure of education as it might appear. Census reports for certain nations often contain information on the percentages of the population which have attained various levels of education, but complete information on this subject is still needed.[23] For many contexts, it is more useful to learn the ratio of enrollment for a population of a given age, but data which pertain to age cohort groups are not systematically available for these countries.[24] For use in some research, enrollment figures may require adjustment according to attendance rates, which vary across countries and also radically within territorial units, and according to season of the year.[25] Systematic data on attendance rates were unavailable to us. Finally, these figures do not include secondary students who are studying abroad.

(2) Tables 5.16 and 5.17 relate to current literacy estimates and increased literacy rates from 1950 to 1967. Data in this category are admittedly less reliable than enrollment figures and countries may use different definitions of literacy. However, individual values should not be in error more than plus or minus 10 percent. Figure 5.2, below, shows that for all units the correlation between literacy and per capita primary enrollment is quite high.

(3) A number of economic indicators which relate to educational expenditure have been employed in quantitative analyses. Three types are included in this chapter: expenditure on primary education as a percent of total educational expenditure (Table 5.18); total educational expenditure as a percent of national income (Table 5.19); and as a percent of total government expenditures (Table 5.20). Thus we present a measure of level emphasis, a control for economic development, and lastly a measure of relative emphasis on educational development as opposed to other national priorities. Other variables not included here which are of interest include: educational expenditure per capita[26] and expenditure per pupil enrolled (possibly an indicator of instructional quality).[27]

(4) Measures of teaching or staffing capability in the educational system are presented in Tables 5.22 and 5.23. Additional data on the number of teachers at different levels of the educational system and the number of students enrolled in teacher training are available in Appendix 1.

Dimensionality and Reliability

A factor analysis of 74 indicators of educational development confirmed the utility of focusing on enrollment, expenditures, and staffing as independent dimensions. In addition, the factor solution shows well defined and independent dimensions of size

(absolute enrollment figures), and change in enrollment. Furthermore, primary and secondary enrollment figures fall on separate dimensions, showing the importance of concentrating on differences in educational development at different levels.

The relatively low level of abstraction involved in the measures discussed here should not produce a false sense of security in regard to their reliability. Unfortunately, educational figures on Africa, especially for the earlier colonial period, are sometimes merely estimates, and poor ones at that. In the collection of the present data and in our continuing attempt to discover additional sources to fill in missing data, a number of problems have come to the surface which are the result of both random and systematic errors in existing published, quantitative information on African education.

Errors which specifically relate to educational variables are often the result of definitional ambiguity relating to and stemming from structural differences in school systems. These differences include: varying lengths in the duration of primary and secondary programs, the categorizing of pre-primary grades or middle-level grades (where they exist) as primary-level education, and defining vocational and teacher-training enrollment as secondary-level or parallel-level education.[28] The variety of school systems within one national unit is itself a continual source of error. For example, separate systems within British territories during the colonial era have included: official government schools (usually only a small percentage of the total), native authority schools, assisted (usually mission) schools and unassisted institutions, and inspected and uninspected schools. The accuracy of reporting, the chance of inclusion in official published figures, and consistency in standards maintained can be presumed to decrease with the distance from control by the central administration.[29]

Techniques to Assess Reliability

Other than careful discrimination among reporting agencies in the actual choice of data using the criteria of reputation and professional accountability, the number of available strategies open to the researcher for insuring against unreliable aggregate data are

Figure 5.1   Trends in Public and Private Enrollment in French Togo, 1921–1937.

few. Certain reliability checks, of course, can be applied. These are based on several simple assumptions about the variation of the data across time and in relation to other indicators. These assumptions are:

(1) That indicators such as enrollment are relatively stable and, with few exceptions, increase with geometric regularity (as with population). Unusual fluctuations from one time period to another thus signal possible significant changes in accounting procedures, a redefinition of categories by reporters, or generally unreliable reporting methods. The fact that indicators of enrollment across different time periods fall unambiguously on the same factors in the factor analysis of the data facilitates reasonably accurate interpolation for unreported years, and helps establish the reliability of the individual measures.

(2) That variation is affected by external factors and temporal conditions. For example, the trend on

all indices from the introduction of Western education to the present has been generally upward; however, events such as the world wars and, in particular, the great depression have had a generally negative effect on enrollment in colonies which relied on mission support for a large part of the education program. The trend of public and private enrollment for the French mandate territory of Togo demonstrates this effect (see Figure 5.1).[30] Questionable data must therefore be assessed in terms of over-all trends within the total time continuum and in consideration of the unique systemic characteristics of the territorial units studied.

(3) That certain testable propositions as to the relationship among variables across time can be hypothesized. While the finding of no relationship is by no means prima-facie evidence of unreliability, those in support of the hypothesized relationship offer a degree of credibility. This sort of test was applied to the two available sets of literacy estimates included

Figure 5.2 Correlations between Literacy and Primary Enrollment per Capita for 32 African Countries.

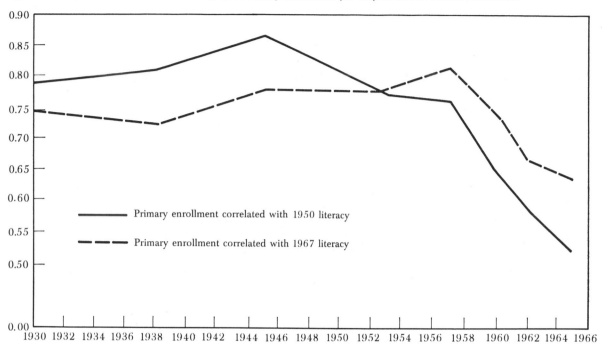

in the tables for which we had a much lesser degree of confidence than for the various indices of enrollment. Literacy is presumably a strong correlate of primary education.[31] Using factor analysis, we found that these literacy measures loaded highly on the same factor as the per capita measures of primary enrollment. This suggests co-variation but does not permit us to make a very strong conclusion as to the reliability of the literacy data. We can further hypothesize that there will be an increasingly stronger relationship between literacy (as a percentage of the population above 15 years of age) at specific points of time with aggregate indicators of educational experience which precede the literacy estimates in time. As the impact of changing early primary enrollment patterns will not be felt in terms of adult literacy for several years, evidence of a time-lag should be apparent in the correlational measures. It can be argued that correlations between literacy and subsequent enrollment patterns in the 1960s *following* the date of the literacy estimate should fall sharply, not only due to the absence of direct causality but as a result of the implementation of comprehensive policy

changes brought about by independence. These bivariate correlations were inspected and appear in Figure 5.2.

The expectations in this case are essentially realized. Comparing literacy estimates for 1950 and 1967 with nine measures of per capita primary enrollment from 1930 to 1965, literacy in 1950 correlates highest with enrollment in 1945 (.88) and literacy in 1967 with enrollment in 1957 (.82).

Notes

[1] Structural–functionalism involves the basic proposition that social systems can be compared in terms of functions which are performed by structures which vary. This is described for political systems in developing nations by Gabriel A. Almond and G. B. Powell, *Comparative Politics, A Developmental Approach* (Boston: Little, Brown and Co., 1966) Chapter 2, pp. 16–41.

[2] Clignet and Foster in a recent work on secondary education in the Ivory Coast, state: "The school in Africa is inevitably an agent of change. . . . Schools in Africa can never become agencies of simple culture transmission facilitating consensus and stability whether the content of instruction is African or European." Remi Clignet and Philip Foster, *The Fortunate Few, A Study of Secondary Schools and Students in the Ivory Coast* (Evanston, Ill.: Northwestern University Press, 1966), p. 201.

³ A composite index of human resource development is employed in Frederick Harbison and Charles A. Myers, *Education, Manpower and Economic Growth* (New York: McGraw-Hill, 1964). This is calculated as the sum of second level and five times the third level enrollment ratios. In another report of quantitative analysis, Irma Adelman and C. T. Morris, *Society, Politics and Economic Development* (Baltimore, Md.: Johns Hopkins Press, 1967), the Harbison and Myers Index is used in addition to a number of other social and political measures.

Also see Gary S. Becker, *Human Capital, A Theoretical and Empirical Analysis with Special Reference to Education* (New York: National Bureau of Economic Research, 1964); H. Correa, *The Economics of Human Resources* (Amsterdam: North Holland Publishing Co., 1963); Stephen Enke, *Economics for Development* (Englewood Cliffs, N.J.: Prentice-Hall, 1963), especially Chapter 2, "Productivity and Education," pp. 385–397; Ladislav Gerych, *Problems of Aid to Education in Developing Countries* (New York: Praeger, 1965); and Frederick H. Harbison and Charles A. Meyers, eds., *Manpower and Education* (New York: McGraw-Hill, 1965). It is not surprising that while economists such as Gerych, Becker, and Harbison stress secondary and higher education as important factors in development, theorists concerned with development in other spheres focus more often on primary education, the source of literacy skills, and modern political value orientations.

⁴ Others include literacy, voting, media consumption, and media production. Daniel Lerner, *The Passing of Traditional Society, Modernizing the Middle East* (Glencoe, Ill.: The Free Press, 1958) p. 86.

⁵ *Ibid.*, pp. 87–89. The mass media, as well as presumably educational systems, work to create what Lerner terms "mobile personalities," who have "high capacity for identification with new aspects of (their) environment," p. 49.

⁶ S. N. Eisenstadt, *Modernization: Protest and Change* (Englewood Cliffs, N.J.: Prentice-Hall, 1966), pp. 16–18.

⁷ Gabriel A. Almond and Sidney Verba, *The Civic Culture* (Boston: Little, Brown and Co., 1963), Chapter 9, "Political Socialization and Civic Competence," pp. 208–243.

⁸ Also see Lucian W. Pye, *Politics, Personality, and Nation Building; Burma's Search for Identity* (New Haven, Conn.: Yale University Press, 1962) and Robert E. Scott, "Mexico, The Established Revolution," in *Political Culture and Political Development*, eds. L. W. Pye and Sidney Verba (Princeton, N.J.: Princeton University Press, 1965), pp. 330–395. In Mexico, according to Scott, the educational system's relationship to change is ambivalent; many institutions tend to reinforce traditional attitudes.

⁹ C. Arnold Anderson, "Patterns and Variability in the Distribution and Diffusion of Schooling," in *Education and Economic Development*, eds. C. Arnold Anderson and Mary Jean Bowman (Chicago: Aldine Co., 1965); Remi Clignet, "Ethnicity, Social Differentiation and Secondary Schooling in West Africa," *Cahiers D'Etudes Africaines*, 7 (1967): 360–378; Philip Foster, "Secondary Schooling and Social Mobility in a West African Nation," *Sociology of Education*, 37 (1963): 159; Philip Foster, *Education and Social Change in Ghana* (Chicago: University of Chicago Press, 1965).

¹⁰ Clignet goes on to state that his findings suggest "ethnic differentials in attitude do not seem to be deeply eroded by education," thus challenging the assertion that educational systems operate as powerful agents for re-socialization to modern commitments. Clignet, "Ethnicity, Social Differentiation and Secondary Schooling . . ." p. 378.

¹¹ For works on political socialization relating to the early acquisition of national identification, the first resulting from case studies, the second from the quantitative analysis of data from a large sample, see Erik H. Erikson, *Childhood and Society*, 2nd printing rev. (New York: W. W. Norton & Co., 1963) and Robert D. Hess and Judith V. Torney, *The Development of Political Attitudes in Children* (New York: Doubleday & Co., 1968).

¹² Robert A. LeVine, "Political Socialization and Culture Change," in *Old Societies and New States*, ed. Clifford Geertz (New York: The Free Press of Glencoe, 1963), pp. 280–303.

¹³ Penelope Roach, *Political Socialization in the New Nations of Africa* (New York: Teachers College Press, Columbia University, 1967).

¹⁴ Primary enrollment ratios as late as 1957 did not exceed 40 percent in most African territories and were somewhat smaller in many.

¹⁵ James S. Coleman, ed., *Education and Political Development* (Princeton, N.J.: Princeton University Press, 1965), p. 30. In his introduction (pp. 3–32) Coleman offers a discussion of education and political socialization, recruitment, and integration. He points out that on the whole both political scientists and educators have failed to recognize the importance of the "education-polity nexus"; the efforts of educators themselves in cross-national research has been largely limited to intra-system analysis as if education were an autonomous sector of activity.

Jerry B. Bolibaugh describes how in former French Africa the educated elite was developed as a controlling link between the metropole and the masses: Jerry B. Bolibaugh and Paul R. Hanna, *Education as an Instrument of National Policy in Selected Newly Developing Nations* (Stanford, Calif.: Comparative Education Center, School of Education, Stanford University, 1964), p. 96.

¹⁶ However, much of the descriptive material is especially useful for general familiarization with the variety of educational systems and their unique problems. Important works of this type, recently published, are: Gray L. Cowan, James O'Connell, and David G. Scanlon, eds., *Education and Nation Building in Africa* (New York: Praeger, 1965); John W. Hanson and Cole S. Brembeck, eds., *Education and the Development of Nations* (New York: Holt, Rinehart and Winston, 1966); David G. Scanlon, ed., *Church, State and Education in Africa* (New York: Teachers College Press, Columbia University, 1966); David G. Scanlon, ed., *Traditions of African Education* (New York: Teachers College Press, Columbia University, 1964); John Wilson, *Education and Changing West African Culture* (New York: Teachers College Press, Columbia University, 1963).

¹⁷ Thomas Jesse Jones, *Education in Africa* (New York: The Phelps-Stokes Fund, 1922); and Thomas Jesse Jones, ed., *Education in East Africa* (London: Edinburgh House Press, 1925). Also see L. J. Lewis, ed., *Phelps-Stokes Reports on Education in Africa* (London: Oxford University Press, 1962).

¹⁸ Donald G. Burns, *African Education, An Introductory Survey of Education in Commonwealth Countries* (London: Oxford University Press, 1965). For former French territories, Abdou Moumouni, *Education in Africa*, trans. by Phyllis N. Ott (New York: Praeger, 1968), originally published under the title *L'Education en Afrique*, (Paris: François Maspero, 1964). While this volume has been unfavourably reviewed by both Clignet and Foster, it offers broad cross-national comparisons with a strong quantitative orientation. Also, Elliot Berg, "French Educational Policy in Senegal, Guinea, and the Ivory Coast," in Harbison and Myers, *Manpower and Education*, pp. 232–267. For an excellent overview of the continent, see Guy Hunter, "Education in Africa," *African Affairs*, 66 (April 1967): 127–139.

¹⁹ Extensive holdings of education reports, primarily for British territories exist at the following locations: The Library of Congress, Washington, D.C.; Teachers College Library (Columbia University); The Cubberley Library (Stanford University); and the Library of the Department of Health, Education, and Welfare, Washington, D.C.

[20] *Enseignement Outre-mer: Bulletin de l'inspection general de l'enseignement et de la jeuness du ministère de la France d'outre-mer* (Paris: Ministère de la France d'Outre-mer, issued yearly from approximately 1950 through 1958). These issues are available for reference at the Teachers College Library, Columbia University.

[21] UNESCO, *World Survey of Education* (Paris: UNESCO); Vol. 1 (General), 1955; Vol. 2 (Primary Education), 1958; Vol. 3 (Secondary Education), 1961; Vol. 4 (Higher Education), 1966.

[22] There are ways, other than those we use, of calculating changes in enrollment. The following formula is provided for calculating rates of increase from given enrollment ratios for the beginning and end date of a span of years:

$p_n = p_o (1 \pm r)^t$

p_o = ratio at the beginning of period

p_n = ratio at the end of period

r = rate of increase or decrease per year

t = number of years $(n - o)$

[23] For a discussion of this need see Harbison and Myers, *Education, Manpower and Economic Growth*, pp. 24–25.

[24] Enrollment by class, age, or number of years of education completed is available in certain of the more detailed reports from Commonwealth nations and territories. A general discussion of measuring enrollment is found (in addition to the *World Survey* volumes), in *Manual of Education Statistics* (Paris: UNESCO, 1961), and W. L. Kendall, *Statistics of Education in Developing Countries, an Introduction to their Collection and Presentation* (Paris: UNESCO, 1968).

[25] For example, comparing attendance rates for seven districts in Tanzania in 1964 and 1965, Jane King reports a range of variation between 11 percent and 79 percent. Jane King, *Planning Non-formal Education in Tanzania*, African Research Monograph 16 (Paris: UNESCO International Institute for Educational Planning, 1967), p. 23. These research monographs are useful data sources for educational planning in Africa; each deals with a particular national unit.

[26] Daniel Blot and Michel Debeauvais, "Educational Expenditure in Developing Areas: Some Statistical Aspects," in *Financing of Education for Economic Growth*, ed. Lucille Reifman (Paris: Organization for Economic Co-operation and Development, 1964).

[27] For a use of this measure see UNESCO *World Survey of Education*, *Vol. 3, Secondary Education* (individual country reports).

[28] A detailed outline and comparison of all contemporary African educational structures is found in Martena Sasnett and Inez Sepmeyer, *Educational Systems of Africa* (Berkeley: University of California Press, 1966). This information corresponds to earlier descriptions found in individual national unit sections of the UNESCO, *World Survey of Education* series.

[29] For a discussion of the problems of cross-national comparisons see Kendall, *Statistics of Education in Developing Countries*, pp. 74–78.

[30] Data used to construct this figure were taken from L. Pechoux, *Le Mandat Français sur le Togo* (Paris: A. Pedone, 1939), pp. 344, 347.

[31] Statistical relationships between expenditures and other educational measures in order to test reliability are also plausible. Blot and Debeauvais, for example, investigate the predictive relationship between educational expenditure and GDP which correlates at .94, Blot and Debeauvais, "Educational Expenditure in Developing Areas."

TABLE 5.1   Primary School Enrollment per 1000 Population and Total Primary Enrollment, 1930

Definition: Total enrollment in primary or first-level education (typically including the first six to eight years of education) in all schools public and private, divided by the national population estimate for this year.

```
RANGE =           146.00
MEAN =             15.00
STANDARD DEVIATION =              27.21
```

POPULATION PERCENT CUM.	COUNTRY	RANK	COUNTRY NAME	VALUE	RANGE DECILE	TOTAL
0.4	0.4	1.0	LESOTHO	147	1	70000
4.6	4.2	2.0	UGANDA	54	7	229078
6.5	1.9	3.0	MALAWI	46		112721
8.3	1.8	4.0	ZAMBIA	42	8	78732
8.6	0.3	5.0	BOTSWANA	27	9	8000
14.3	5.7	6.0	TANZANIA	21		133773
19.1	4.8	7.0	KENYA	17		85815
28.2	9.1	8.0	ZAIRE	15	10	145106
28.7	0.5	9.0	LIBERIA	14		10250
32.5	3.8	10.0	GHANA	11		51241
32.7	0.2	11.0	GABON	9		3243
34.2	1.5	13.5	BURUNDI	7		17009
35.7	1.5	13.5	RWANDA	7		11524
36.8	1.1	13.5	SIERRA LEONE	7		12418
37.6	0.8	13.5	TOGO	7		6630
38.0	0.4	17.0	CONGO (BRA)	6		3753
39.2	1.2	17.0	DAHOMEY	6		8989
39.4	0.2	17.0	GAMBIA	6		1500
64.4	25.0	19.5	NIGERIA	5		193473
71.1	6.7	19.5	SUDAN	5		38900
72.8	1.7	21.0	SENEGAL	4		10000
75.0	2.2	22.0	MALI	3		10000
77.5	2.5	24.5	CAMEROON	2		6959
78.2	0.7	24.5	CAR	2		1748
79.9	1.7	24.5	GUINEA	2		6000
81.8	1.9	24.5	IVORY COAST	2		6174
83.4	1.6	29.5	CHAD	1		425
94.3	10.9	29.5	ETHIOPIA	1		4036
94.8	0.5	29.5	MAURITANIA	1		400
96.5	1.7	29.5	NIGER	1		2500
97.7	1.2	29.5	SOMALIA	1		1390
100.0	2.3	29.5	UPPER VOLTA	1		3446

SOURCES: Population estimates for this and the following tables are from Appendix 5. Otto Martens and O. Karstedt, *The African Handbook and Travelers Guide* (London: Allen and Unwin, 1932). *Botswana, Gambia, Guinea, Lesotho, Mali, Mauritania, Niger, Senegal, Upper Volta*: Estimates for 1930 based on reported figures for 1934 or 1935: *Ghana, Kenya, Malawi, Nigeria, Sierra Leone, Tanzania, Uganda, Zambia*: Reports from individual colonial departments of education for 1930; *Tanzania*: Total for Tanzania is the officially reported enrollment for Tanganyika and Zanzibar combined; *Zaire (Congo K.), Ethiopia, Sudan*: UNESCO *World Survey of Education*, Vol. 2, "Primary Education" (Paris: 1958), see separate country reports; *CAR, Chad, Congo (Brazzaville), Gabon: Historique et Organization General de l'Enseignement en A.E.F.* (Brazzaville: Gouvernement Generale de l'Afrique Equatoriale Française, 1931); *Burundi, Rwanda*: Enrollment for Burundi and Rwanda calculated by applying the estimated total population ratio for these units in 1930 to the total enrollment given by UNESCO for Ruanda-Urundi; *Togo*: L. Pechoux, *Le Mandat*

Français sur le Togo (Paris: A. Pedone, 1939); *Dahomey*: "Rapports et Compte-Rendu du Congres intercolonial de l'Enseignement dans les Colonies et les Pays d'Outre-mer," *L'Adaptation de l'Enseignement dans les Colonies* (Paris: Henri Didier, 1932); *Cameroon*: This figure is for British Cameroons only; enrollment in the French mandate is probably somewhat larger; *Ivory Coast*: The enrollment given by Martens and Karstedt for the Ivory Coast is assumed to include Upper Volta which was part of the Ivory Coast from 1932 to 1947. The ratio of total enrollment between the two units in 1948 was applied to obtain an estimate for each in 1930; *Ethiopia*: For Eritrea only, and may include children of Italian personnel. Enrollment in Ethiopia proper (except for traditional Coptic schools) at this time was negligible; *Somalia*: I. M. Lewis, *The Modern History of Somaliland*, (New York: Praeger, 1965), p. 97. Lewis states that non-traditional schools were not begun in British Somaliland until after World War II; therefore, this figure represents enrollment in the Italian mandate only.

TABLE 5.2 Primary School Enrollment per 1000 Population and Total Primary Enrollment, 1953

Definition: Total enrollment in primary or first-level education (typically including the first six to eight years of education) in all schools public and private, divided by the national population estimated for this year.

```
RANGE      =      148.00
MEAN       =       36.63
STANDARD DEVIATION =          31.73
```

POPULATION PERCENT CUM.	COUNTRY	RANK	COUNTRY NAME	VALUE	RANGE DECILE	TOTAL
0.4	0.4	1.0	LESOTHO	151	1	93000
0.8	0.4	2.5	CONGO (BRA)	80	5	56683
4.6	3.8	2.5	GHANA	80		468118
13.7	9.1	4.0	ZAIRE	79		974287
15.6	1.9	5.0	MALAWI	71	6	218488
15.8	0.2	6.0	GABON	68		28754
17.6	1.8	7.0	ZAMBIA	63		166210
20.1	2.5	8.5	CAMEROON	50	7	209145
24.3	4.2	8.5	UGANDA	50		288799
29.1	4.8	10.0	KENYA	48		330190
29.6	0.5	11.0	LIBERIA	45	8	39976
29.9	0.3	12.0	BOTSWANA	44		19000
30.7	0.8	13.0	TOGO	43		52697
31.9	1.2	14.0	DAHOMEY	35		53822
37.6	5.7	15.0	TANZANIA	30	9	257553
38.3	0.7	16.0	CAR	28		30001
39.8	1.5	17.5	BURUNDI	25		64186
41.3	1.5	17.5	RWANDA	25		54853
66.3	25.0	19.0	NIGERIA	24		1094200
67.4	1.1	20.0	SIERRA LEONE	21		43203
69.1	1.7	21.0	SENEGAL	18		50339
71.0	1.9	22.5	IVORY COAST	16	10	46567
77.7	6.7	22.5	SUDAN	16		161090
77.9	0.2	24.0	GAMBIA	15		4253
79.6	1.7	25.5	GUINEA	9		23541
81.8	2.2	25.5	MALI	9		32397
83.0	1.2	27.5	SOMALIA	6		10342
85.3	2.3	27.5	UPPER VOLTA	6		21064
86.9	1.6	29.5	CHAD	5		13740
87.4	0.5	29.5	MAURITANIA	5		4135
98.3	10.9	31.0	ETHIOPIA	4		68691
100.0	1.7	32.0	NIGER	3		7982

SOURCES: *Enseignement Outre-mer*: Bulletin de l'inspection général de l'enseignement et de la jeunesse du ministère de France d'outre-mer. (Paris: Ministère de la France d'Outre-mer, December 1954). *Botswana, Burundi, Zaire (Congo K.), Ethiopia, Ghana, Kenya, Lesotho, Liberia, Malawi, Nigeria, Rwanda, Sierra Leone, Somalia, Tanzania, Uganda, Zambia*: Reports from individual colonial departments of education, 1953; *Cameroon, Gambia, Sudan*: UN Statistical Yearbook, 1955–1960; *Cameroon*: Combined figures for French and British areas; *Tanzania*: Calculated as for 1930; *Nigeria*: Includes the British Cameroons; *Somalia*: Combined figures for British and Italian areas.

TABLE 5.3 Primary School Enrollment per 1000 Population and Total Primary Enrollment, 1960

Definition: Total enrollment in primary or first-level education (typically including the first six to eight years of education) in all schools public and private, divided by the national population estimated for this year.

```
RANGE      =      181.00
MEAN       =       58.44
STANDARD DEVIATION =          41.81
```

POPULATION PERCENT CUM.	COUNTRY	RANK	COUNTRY NAME	VALUE	RANGE DECILE	TOTAL
0.4	0.4	1.0	LESOTHO	189	1	136143
0.8	0.4	2.0	CONGO (BRA)	150	3	115331
1.0	0.2	3.0	GABON	123	4	55000
10.1	9.1	4.0	ZAIRE	105	5	1460753
14.9	4.8	5.0	KENYA	97	6	781293
17.4	2.5	6.0	CAMEROON	92		435497
19.2	1.8	7.0	ZAMBIA	88		280000
21.1	1.9	8.0	MALAWI	82		285163
25.3	4.2	9.0	UGANDA	80	7	532918
29.1	3.8	10.0	GHANA	72		490000
29.4	0.3	11.0	BOTSWANA	70		35225
31.3	1.9	12.0	IVORY COAST	65		220000
32.1	0.8	13.0	TOGO	63		90000
32.6	0.5	14.0	LIBERIA	56	8	54500
33.3	0.7	15.0	CAR	55		67510
58.3	25.0	16.0	NIGERIA	54		2805896
59.8	1.5	18.0	BURUNDI	47		137092
61.3	1.5	18.0	RWANDA	47		126547
67.0	5.7	18.0	TANZANIA	47		470000
68.2	1.2	20.0	DAHOMEY	44	9	90000
69.9	1.7	21.0	SENEGAL	37		115000
71.0	1.1	22.0	SIERRA LEONE	36		80000
72.7	1.7	23.0	GUINEA	31		95000
79.4	6.7	24.0	SUDAN	26	10	300000
81.0	1.6	25.5	CHAD	23		70000
81.2	0.2	25.5	GAMBIA	23		7047
83.4	2.2	27.0	MALI	16		64902
85.7	2.3	28.0	UPPER VOLTA	13		56598
86.2	0.5	29.0	MAURITANIA	12		12000
87.4	1.2	30.0	SOMALIA	11		22341
98.3	10.9	31.5	ETHIOPIA	8		176522
100.0	1.7	31.5	NIGER	8		22000

SOURCES: *UN Statistical Yearbooks 1962–1964. Burundi, Chad, Dahomey, Gabon, Ghana, Guinea, Ivory Coast, Mauritania, Niger, Rwanda, Senegal, Sierra Leone, Tanzania, Togo, Zambia*: Estimates of 1960 enrollment based on 1959, 1961, and 1962 data given in the same source; *Burundi, Rwanda*: Enrollment for Burundi and Rwanda calculated by applying the estimated total population ratio for these units in 1960 to the total enrollment given for Ruanda-Urundi.

TABLE 5.4   Percent Change in Primary School Enrollment per Capita, 1953–1960

```
RANGE =          370.00
MEAN =            94.13
STANDARD DEVIATION =        78.07
```

POPULATION PERCENT CUM. COUNTRY		RANK	COUNTRY NAME	VALUE	RANGE DECILE
1.6	1.6	1.0	CHAD	360	1
3.5	1.9	2.0	IVORY COAST	306	2
5.2	1.7	3.0	GUINEA	244	4
6.9	1.7	4.0	NIGER	166	6
7.4	0.5	5.0	MAURITANIA	140	
32.4	25.0	6.0	NIGERIA	125	7
34.7	2.3	7.0	UPPER VOLTA	116	
36.4	1.7	8.0	SENEGAL	105	
41.2	4.8	9.0	KENYA	102	
52.1	10.9	10.0	ETHIOPIA	100	8
52.8	0.7	11.0	CAR	96	
54.3	1.5	12.5	BURUNDI	88	
55.8	1.5	12.5	RWANDA	88	
56.2	0.4	14.0	CONGO (BRA)	87	
58.7	2.5	15.0	CAMEROON	84	
59.9	1.2	16.0	SOMALIA	83	
60.1	0.2	17.0	GABON	81	
62.3	2.2	18.0	MALI	78	
63.4	1.1	19.0	SIERRA LEONE	71	
70.1	6.7	20.0	SUDAN	62	9
74.3	4.2	21.0	UGANDA	60	
74.6	0.3	22.5	BOTSWANA	59	
80.3	5.7	22.5	TANZANIA	59	
80.5	0.2	24.0	GAMBIA	53	
81.3	0.8	25.0	TOGO	46	
83.1	1.8	26.0	ZAMBIA	40	
92.2	9.1	27.0	ZAIRE	33	
93.4	1.2	28.0	DAHOMEY	26	10
93.8	0.4	29.0	LESOTHO	25	
94.3	0.5	30.0	LIBERIA	24	
96.2	1.9	31.0	MALAWI	15	
100.0	3.8	32.0	GHANA	-10	

SOURCE: See Tables 5.2, 5.3.

TABLE 5.5   Primary School Enrollment per 1000 Population and Total Primary Enrollment, 1966

Definition: Total enrollment in primary or first-level education (typically including the first six to eight years of education) in all schools public and private, divided by the national population estimated for this year.

```
RANGE =          210.00
MEAN =            81.25
STANDARD DEVIATION =        53.11
```

POPULATION PERCENT CUM. COUNTRY		RANK	COUNTRY NAME	VALUE	RANGE DECILE	TOTAL
0.4	0.4	1.0	CONGO (BRA)	221	1	186544
0.8	0.4	2.0	LESOTHO	195	2	167169
1.0	0.2	3.0	GABON	169	3	79162
4.8	3.8	4.0	GHANA	163		1292213
7.3	2.5	5.0	CAMEROON	133	5	713557
16.4	9.1	6.0	ZAIRE	130		1995000
16.7	0.3	7.5	BOTSWANA	124		71557
18.5	1.8	7.5	ZAMBIA	124		473432
19.2	0.7	9.5	CAR	105	6	148845
24.0	4.8	9.5	KENYA	105		1010889
24.5	0.5	11.0	LIBERIA	101		110251
26.4	1.9	12.0	IVORY COAST	98		381452
27.2	0.8	13.0	TOGO	94	7	157548
31.4	4.2	14.0	UGANDA	73	8	564190
33.3	1.9	15.0	MALAWI	71		286753
39.0	5.7	16.0	TANZANIA	63		740991
40.7	1.7	17.0	SENEGAL	61		218795
42.2	1.5	18.5	BURUNDI	57		183366
43.7	1.5	18.5	RWANDA	57		176176
44.9	1.2	20.0	DAHOMEY	55		132690
46.0	1.1	21.0	SIERRA LEONE	52	9	125943
47.6	1.6	22.5	CHAD	51		172485
72.6	25.0	22.5	NIGERIA	51		3025981
74.3	1.7	24.0	GUINEA	46		164119
74.5	0.2	25.0	GAMBIA	42		14218
76.7	2.2	26.5	MALI	35		161605
83.4	6.7	26.5	SUDAN	35		492085
85.7	2.3	28.0	UPPER VOLTA	22	10	107588
87.4	1.7	29.0	NIGER	21		70656
87.9	0.5	30.0	MAURITANIA	19		20000
98.8	10.9	31.0	ETHIOPIA	16		378750
100.0	1.2	32.0	SOMALIA	11		28890

SOURCE: *UNESCO Statistical Yearbook 1968*, Table 2.7. *Rwanda*: 1963 data; *Gambia, Guinea, Mauritania, Senegal, Sudan, Upper Volta*: 1965; *Botswana, Malawi*: 1967.

TABLE 5.6 Average Annual Percent Change in Primary School Enrollment per Capita, 1960–1966

Definition: Values are shown in whole percentiles in the table below.

```
RANGE =            176.00
MEAN =              51.78
STANDARD DEVIATION =          42.05
```

POPULATION PERCENT CUM.	COUNTRY	RANK	COUNTRY NAME	VALUE	RANGE DECILE
1.7	1.7	1.0	NIGER	163	1
5.5	3.8	2.0	GHANA	126	3
7.1	1.6	3.0	CHAD	122	
9.3	2.2	4.0	MALI	119	
20.2	10.9	5.0	ETHIOPIA	100	4
20.9	0.7	6.0	CAR	91	5
21.1	0.2	7.0	GAMBIA	83	
21.6	0.5	8.0	LIBERIA	80	
21.9	0.3	9.0	BOTSWANA	77	
24.2	2.3	10.0	UPPER VOLTA	69	6
25.9	1.7	11.0	SENEGAL	65	
26.4	0.5	12.0	MAURITANIA	58	
28.3	1.9	13.0	IVORY COAST	51	7
29.1	0.8	14.0	TOGO	49	
30.8	1.7	15.0	GUINEA	48	
31.2	0.4	16.0	CONGO (BRA)	47	
33.7	2.5	17.0	CAMEROON	45	
34.8	1.1	18.0	SIERRA LEONE	44	
35.0	0.2	19.0	GABON	37	8
36.8	1.8	20.0	ZAMBIA	36	
43.5	6.7	21.0	SUDAN	35	
49.2	5.7	22.0	TANZANIA	34	
50.4	1.2	23.0	DAHOMEY	25	
59.5	9.1	24.0	ZAIRE	24	
61.0	1.5	25.5	BURUNDI	21	9
62.5	1.5	25.5	RWANDA	21	
67.3	4.8	27.0	KENYA	12	
67.7	0.4	28.0	LESOTHO	3	10
68.9	1.2	29.0	SOMALIA	0	
93.9	25.0	30.0	NIGERIA	−6	
98.1	4.2	31.0	UGANDA	−9	
100.0	1.9	32.0	MALAWI	−13	

SOURCES: See Tables 5.3 and 5.5.

TABLE 5.7 Percent Change in Primary School Enrollment per Capita from Two Years before to Two Years after Independence

Definition: For many cases in which independence was achieved in 1960, the relevant years are 1958 and 1962. See Part II for each country's date of independence. In order to include Ethiopia and Liberia in the comparison, an artificial "date of independence" of 1960 was used.

```
RANGE =            197.00
MEAN =              43.03
STANDARD DEVIATION =          44.75
```

POPULATION PERCENT CUM.	COUNTRY	RANK	COUNTRY NAME	VALUE	RANGE DECILE
1.6	1.6	1.0	CHAD	177	1
2.1	0.5	2.0	MAURITANIA	157	2
3.8	1.7	3.0	NIGER	133	3
6.0	2.2	4.0	MALI	83	5
7.7	1.7	5.0	SENEGAL	76	6
8.1	0.4	6.0	CONGO (BRA)	73	
19.0	10.9	7.0	ETHIOPIA	63	
19.7	0.7	8.0	CAR	62	
22.2	2.5	9.0	CAMEROON	57	7
24.1	1.9	10.0	IVORY COAST	52	
30.8	6.7	11.5	SUDAN	50	
33.1	2.3	11.5	UPPER VOLTA	50	
34.2	1.1	13.5	SIERRA LEONE	44	
35.0	0.8	13.5	TOGO	44	
35.2	0.2	15.0	GAMBIA	38	8
35.4	0.2	16.0	GABON	35	
39.2	3.8	17.0	GHANA	34	
40.7	1.5	18.5	BURUNDI	33	
42.2	1.5	18.5	RWANDA	33	
42.7	0.5	20.0	LIBERIA	31	
44.5	1.8	21.0	ZAMBIA	28	
50.2	5.7	22.0	TANZANIA	16	9
59.3	9.1	23.0	ZAIRE	15	
60.5	1.2	24.0	SOMALIA	13	
61.7	1.2	25.0	DAHOMEY	7	
62.0	0.3	26.0	BOTSWANA	5	
66.8	4.8	27.0	KENYA	4	
68.5	1.7	28.5	GUINEA	0	
93.9	25.0	28.5	NIGERIA	0	
93.9	0.4	30.0	LESOTHO	−6	10
98.1	4.2	31.0	UGANDA	−10	
100.0	1.9	32.0	MALAWI	−20	

SOURCES: See previous tables.

TABLE 5.8 Females Enrolled in Primary Education per 100 Primary School Students, 1960

```
RANGE           =       58.00
MEAN            =       43.25
STANDARD DEVIATION =          12.25
```

POPULATION PERCENT CUM.	COUNTRY	RANK	COUNTRY NAME	VALUE	RANGE DECILE
1.6	1.6	1.0	CHAD	86	1
3.3	1.7	2.0	GUINEA	61	5
3.7	0.4	3.5	CONGO (BRA)	60	
4.5	0.8	3.5	TOGO	60	
5.2	0.7	5.0	CAR	58	
5.6	0.4	6.0	LESOTHO	54	6
8.1	2.5	7.0	CAMEROON	51	7
9.9	1.8	8.0	ZAMBIA	50	
12.1	2.2	9.0	MALI	49	
14.4	2.3	10.0	UPPER VOLTA	47	
14.6	0.2	11.0	GABON	46	
20.3	5.7	12.0	TANZANIA	45	8
22.0	1.7	13.0	NIGER	43	
23.9	1.9	15.0	IVORY COAST	42	
28.7	4.8	15.0	KENYA	42	
35.4	6.7	15.0	SUDAN	42	
36.6	1.2	17.5	DAHOMEY	41	
38.5	1.9	17.5	MALAWI	41	
47.6	9.1	19.0	ZAIRE	40	
49.1	1.5	20.5	BURUNDI	39	9
50.6	1.5	20.5	RWANDA	39	
51.7	1.1	22.0	SIERRA LEONE	36	
53.4	1.7	23.0	SENEGAL	35	
64.3	10.9	24.0	ETHIOPIA	33	10
64.6	0.3	25.5	BOTSWANA	32	
65.1	0.5	25.5	MAURITANIA	32	
65.3	0.2	28.0	GAMBIA	31	
69.1	3.8	28.0	GHANA	31	
69.6	0.5	28.0	LIBERIA	31	
94.6	25.0	30.0	NIGERIA	30	
98.8	4.2	31.0	UGANDA	29	
100.0	1.2	32.0	SOMALIA	28	

SOURCES: *UNESCO Statistical Yearbook 1968*, Table 2.7. *Burundi*: Data for 1961; *Zaire (Congo K.)* and *Senegal*: *UN Compendium of Social Statistics* (New York: UN, 1963).

TABLE 5.9 Secondary School Enrollment per 10,000 Population and Total Secondary Enrollment, 1950

Definition: Enrollment in general secondary education, excluding teacher training and vocational enrollment, in all schools public and private, divided by national population estimated for this year.

```
RANGE           =       280.00
MEAN            =       40.72
STANDARD DEVIATION =          49.13
```

POPULATION PERCENT CUM.	COUNTRY	RANK	COUNTRY NAME	VALUE	RANGE DECILE	TOTAL
3.8	3.8	1.0	GHANA	281	1	6162
4.0	0.2	2.0	GAMBIA	89	7	545
4.2	0.2	3.0	GABON	84	8	485
4.7	0.5	4.0	LIBERIA	61		924
7.2	2.5	5.5	CAMEROON	60		1634
8.9	1.7	5.5	SENEGAL	60		2288
10.8	1.9	7.0	IVORY COAST	57	9	1268
17.5	6.7	8.5	SUDAN	56		3682
21.7	4.2	8.5	UGANDA	56		6306
22.5	0.8	10.0	TOGO	53		671
31.6	9.1	11.5	ZAIRE	51		6953
32.7	1.1	11.5	SIERRA LEONE	51		2792
57.7	25.0	13.0	NIGERIA	43		21437
62.5	4.8	14.0	KENYA	35		8000
63.7	1.2	15.0	DAHOMEY	29	10	803
64.4	0.7	16.5	CAR	24		237
65.6	1.2	16.5	SOMALIA	24		295
67.4	1.8	18.0	ZAMBIA	23		337
67.8	0.4	19.0	CONGO (BRA)	21		933
73.5	5.7	20.0	TANZANIA	19		9679
73.8	0.3	21.0	BOTSWANA	17		132
74.2	0.4	22.0	LESOTHO	15		726
75.7	1.5	23.0	BURUNDI	13		350
77.4	1.7	25.5	GUINEA	12		430
79.3	1.9	25.5	MALAWI	12		142
81.5	2.2	25.5	MALI	12		942
83.0	1.5	25.5	RWANDA	12		247
84.6	1.6	28.0	CHAD	10		106
86.3	1.7	29.0	NIGER	8		202
97.2	10.9	30.5	ETHIOPIA	7		1079
99.5	2.3	30.5	UPPER VOLTA	7		356
100.0	0.5	32.0	MAURITANIA	1		146

SOURCES: *UNESCO Statistical Yearbook 1968*, Table 2.8. *Gambia*: Data for 1961; *Ethiopia*: UNESCO, *World Survey of Education*, Vol. I (Paris: UNESCO, 1955); *Burundi*: The only data available include general secondary, vocational and teacher-training enrollment in one figure. An estimate of the secondary component was made on the basis of the 1961 distribution of the three types of education; *Kenya*: The African educational system was reorganized in 1951, lengthening the primary school course from 6 to 8 years and shortening the secondary school course from 6 to 4 years. Our figure is an estimate of the enrollment for the 4 year secondary equivalent in 1950; *Chad*: Value is less than one per 10,000 population; *Somalia*: Data refer to the former Territory of Somaliland (Italian administration).

TABLE 5.10 Secondary School Enrollment per 10,000 Population and Total Secondary Enrollment, 1966

Definition: Enrollment in general secondary education, excluding teacher training and vocational enrollment, in all schools public and private, divided by national population estimated for this year.

RANGE =   211.00
MEAN =   54.50
STANDARD DEVIATION =   46.02

POPULATION PERCENT CUM.	POPULATION PERCENT COUNTRY	RANK	COUNTRY NAME	VALUE	RANGE DECILE	TOTAL
3.8	3.8	1.0	GHANA	213	1	168729
4.2	0.4	2.0	CONGO (BRA)	151	3	12778
8.4	4.2	3.0	UGANDA	118	5	90904
8.6	0.2	4.0	GAMBIA	110		3689
9.1	0.5	5.0	LIBERIA	104	6	11324
9.3	0.2	6.0	GABON	101		4750
11.2	1.9	7.0	IVORY COAST	83	7	32590
12.0	0.8	8.0	TOGO	75		12589
13.7	1.7	9.0	SENEGAL	72		25574
20.4	6.7	10.0	SUDAN	66		92407
22.2	1.8	11.0	ZAMBIA	63	8	24005
23.3	1.1	12.0	SIERRA LEONE	57		13589
25.8	2.5	13.0	CAMEROON	53		28529
30.6	4.8	14.0	KENYA	51		49223
32.3	1.7	15.0	GUINEA	46		16698
33.5	1.2	16.0	DAHOMEY	43	9	10425
58.5	25.0	17.0	NIGERIA	39		202683
59.2	0.7	19.0	CAR	33		4668
68.3	9.1	19.0	ZAIRE	33		52309
68.7	0.4	19.0	LESOTHO	33		2825
69.0	0.3	21.0	BOTSWANA	32		1854
70.2	1.2	22.0	SOMALIA	28		7104
71.8	1.6	23.0	CHAD	24		7993
82.7	10.9	24.0	ETHIOPIA	22	10	50438
88.4	5.7	25.0	TANZANIA	20		23836
90.3	1.9	26.0	MALAWI	17		6718
90.8	0.5	27.0	MAURITANIA	14		1500
92.3	1.5	28.0	BURUNDI	12		2932
94.6	2.3	29.0	UPPER VOLTA	11		5468
96.3	1.7	30.5	NIGER	9		3068
97.8	1.5	30.5	RWANDA	9		2900
100.0	2.2	32.0	MALI	2		1011

SOURCE: *UN Statistical Yearbook 1968.*

TABLE 5.11 Percent Change in Secondary School Enrollment per Capita 1962–1966

RANGE =   1383.00
MEAN =   105.84
STANDARD DEVIATION =   247.27

POPULATION PERCENT CUM.	POPULATION PERCENT COUNTRY	RANK	COUNTRY NAME	VALUE	RANGE DECILE
0.5	0.5	1.0	MAURITANIA	1300	1
0.9	0.4	2.0	CONGO (BRA)	619	5
2.6	1.7	3.0	GUINEA	283	8
13.5	10.9	4.0	ETHIOPIA	214	
15.3	1.8	5.0	ZAMBIA	174	9
16.9	1.6	6.0	CHAD	140	
17.3	0.4	7.0	LESOTHO	120	
21.5	4.2	8.0	UGANDA	111	
21.8	0.3	9.0	BOTSWANA	88	
22.3	0.5	10.0	LIBERIA	70	
24.6	2.3	11.0	UPPER VOLTA	57	
25.8	1.2	12.0	DAHOMEY	48	10
27.7	1.9	13.5	IVORY COAST	46	
32.5	4.8	13.5	KENYA	46	
34.4	1.9	15.5	MALAWI	42	
35.2	0.8	15.5	TOGO	42	
35.9	0.7	17.0	CAR	38	
36.1	0.2	18.0	GAMBIA	24	
36.3	0.2	19.5	GABON	20	
38.0	1.7	19.5	SENEGAL	20	
44.7	6.7	21.0	SUDAN	18	
45.9	1.2	22.0	SOMALIA	17	
47.6	1.7	23.0	NIGER	13	
48.7	1.1	24.0	SIERRA LEONE	12	
73.7	25.0	25.0	NIGERIA	9	
79.4	5.7	26.0	TANZANIA	5	
80.9	1.5	27.0	BURUNDI	-8	
83.4	2.5	28.0	CAMEROON	-12	
84.9	1.5	29.0	RWANDA	-25	
88.7	3.8	30.0	GHANA	-26	
97.8	9.1	31.0	ZAIRE	-35	
100.0	2.2	32.0	MALI	-83	

SOURCE: The 1962 enrollment data appear in Appendix 1, and the 1966 figures are from Table 5.10.

TABLE 5.12 Females Enrolled in Secondary Schools per 100 Secondary Students, 1960

Definition: Enrollment in general secondary education, excluding teacher training and vocational enrollment, in all schools public and private.

```
RANGE              =      40.00
MEAN               =      20.69
STANDARD DEVIATION =              9.39
```

POPULATION PERCENT CUM.	COUNTRY	RANK	COUNTRY NAME	VALUE	RANGE DECILE
0.3	0.3	1.0	BOTSWANA	45	1
0.7	0.4	2.0	LESOTHO	43	
5.5	4.8	3.0	KENYA	36	3
11.2	5.7	4.0	TANZANIA	32	4
11.6	0.4	5.0	CONGO (BRA)	29	5
12.8	1.2	7.0	DAHOMEY	28	
14.5	1.7	7.0	SENEGAL	28	
15.6	1.1	7.0	SIERRA LEONE	28	
15.8	0.2	9.0	GAMBIA	26	
19.6	3.8	10.0	GHANA	24	6
19.8	0.2	12.5	GABON	21	7
44.8	25.0	12.5	NIGERIA	21	
45.6	0.8	12.5	TOGO	21	
49.8	4.2	12.5	UGANDA	21	
50.3	0.5	15.5	LIBERIA	20	
52.5	2.2	15.5	MALI	20	
54.0	1.5	18.0	BURUNDI	19	
55.5	1.5	18.0	RWANDA	19	
57.8	2.3	18.0	UPPER VOLTA	19	
60.3	2.5	20.0	CAMEROON	18	
62.2	1.9	21.5	MALAWI	17	8
68.9	6.7	21.5	SUDAN	17	
70.6	1.7	23.0	NIGER	16	
72.4	1.8	24.0	ZAMBIA	15	
73.1	0.7	25.0	CAR	14	
74.8	1.7	26.0	GUINEA	13	9
76.7	1.9	27.0	IVORY COAST	12	
85.8	9.1	28.5	ZAIRE	10	
96.7	10.9	28.5	ETHIOPIA	10	
97.9	1.2	30.0	SOMALIA	8	10
99.5	1.6	31.0	CHAD	7	
100.0	0.5	32.0	MAURITANIA	5	

SOURCE: *UNESCO Statistical Yearbook 1968*, Table 2.8. *Burundi, Rwanda*: Data refer to the former Trust Territory of Ruanda-Urundi.

TABLE 5.13 Secondary Students per 1000 Primary Students, 1952

```
RANGE              =     253.00
MEAN               =      79.03
STANDARD DEVIATION =              62.70
```

POPULATION PERCENT CUM.	COUNTRY	RANK	COUNTRY NAME	VALUE	RANGE DECILE
0.2	0.2	1.0	GAMBIA	259	1
1.4	1.2	2.0	SOMALIA	245	
8.1	6.7	3.0	SUDAN	188	3
12.3	4.2	4.0	UGANDA	161	4
23.2	10.9	5.0	ETHIOPIA	133	5
27.0	3.8	6.0	GHANA	131	6
28.7	1.7	7.0	SENEGAL	117	
29.8	1.1	8.0	SIERRA LEONE	108	
31.5	1.7	9.5	GUINEA	103	7
32.0	0.5	9.5	LIBERIA	103	
33.9	1.9	11.0	IVORY COAST	85	
34.7	0.8	12.0	TOGO	80	8
35.9	1.2	13.0	DAHOMEY	79	
36.4	0.5	14.0	MAURITANIA	75	
36.8	0.4	15.0	CONGO (BRA)	68	
61.8	25.0	16.0	NIGERIA	67	
62.0	0.2	17.0	GABON	60	
64.3	2.3	18.5	UPPER VOLTA	51	9
66.1	1.8	18.5	ZAMBIA	51	
70.9	4.8	20.0	KENYA	48	
72.5	1.6	21.0	CHAD	46	
74.2	1.7	22.0	NIGER	43	
76.7	2.5	23.0	CAMEROON	40	
82.4	5.7	24.0	TANZANIA	32	
83.1	0.7	25.0	CAR	31	10
83.4	0.3	26.5	BOTSWANA	26	
92.5	9.1	26.5	ZAIRE	26	
94.4	1.9	28.0	MALAWI	23	
95.9	1.5	29.0	BURUNDI	19	
96.3	0.4	30.0	LESOTHO	17	
97.8	1.5	31.0	RWANDA	8	
100.0	2.2	32.0	MALI	6	

SOURCES: For 1952 primary and secondary enrollment: UNESCO, *World Survey of Education*, Vols. 2, 3 and 4; *UN Statistical Yearbook 1955–1960*; *Enseignement Outre-mer* (December 1953); *Education in the United Kingdom Dependencies.*

TABLE 5.14 Percent Change in Secondary to Primary Ratio, 1952–ca. 1966

Definition: The percent change in secondary students per 1000 primary students. The higher the number, the greater the increase in the proportion of secondary students.

```
RANGE              =     1141.00
MEAN               =      183.72
STANDARD DEVIATION =              244.74
```

POPULATION PERCENT		RANK	COUNTRY NAME	VALUE	RANGE DECILE
CUM.	COUNTRY				
1.9	1.9	1.0	MALAWI	1050	1
3.7	1.8	2.0	ZAMBIA	750	3
7.5	3.8	3.0	GHANA	524	5
14.2	6.7	4.0	SUDAN	487	
15.4	1.2	5.0	SOMALIA	457	6
19.6	4.2	6.0	UGANDA	373	
20.1	0.5	7.0	LIBERIA	348	7
20.9	0.8	8.0	TOGO	300	
31.8	10.9	9.0	ETHIOPIA	291	
32.0	0.2	10.0	GABON	186	8
57.0	25.0	11.0	NIGERIA	158	
58.7	1.7	12.0	GUINEA	139	
59.0	0.3	13.0	BOTSWANA	136	9
59.7	0.7	14.0	CAR	121	
64.5	4.8	15.0	KENYA	100	
65.7	1.2	16.0	DAHOMEY	88	
67.3	1.6	17.0	CHAD	84	
69.8	2.5	18.0	CAMEROON	82	
70.0	0.2	19.0	GAMBIA	73	
71.9	1.9	20.5	IVORY COAST	70	
72.3	0.4	20.5	LESOTHO	70	
74.6	2.3	22.0	UPPER VOLTA	55	
76.3	1.7	23.0	NIGER	43	
76.7	0.4	24.0	CONGO (BRA)	23	10
85.8	9.1	25.0	ZAIRE	18	
86.3	0.5	26.0	MAURITANIA	14	
88.0	1.7	27.0	SENEGAL	10	
89.1	1.1	28.0	SIERRA LEONE	5	
90.6	1.5	29.0	BURUNDI	-5	
92.1	1.5	30.0	RWANDA	-33	
97.8	5.7	31.0	TANZANIA	-47	
100.0	2.2	32.0	MALI	-91	

sources: See Table 5.13 for 1952 ratio. For the 1965–66 ratio, see the *UN Statistical Yearbook 1968*. The values for the 1965–66 ratio are listed in Appendix 1.

TABLE 5.15 Students in Higher Education as a Percent of the 20–24 Year Old Age Group and Total Students in Higher Education, 1961

Definition: Figures on which these calculations were made include students at home and abroad.

```
RANGE              =        7.90
MEAN               =        2.13
STANDARD DEVIATION =              1.77
```

POPULATION PERCENT		RANK	COUNTRY NAME	VALUE	RANGE DECILE	TOTAL
CUM.	COUNTRY					
0.5	0.5	1.0	LIBERIA	8.0	1	701
0.9	0.4	2.5	CONGO (BRA)	5.0	4	280
2.6	1.7	2.5	SENEGAL	5.0		951
5.1	2.5	6.0	CAMEROON	4.0	6	1111
5.3	0.2	6.0	GABON	4.0		131
9.1	3.8	6.0	GHANA	4.0		2061
11.0	1.9	6.0	IVORY COAST	4.0		1002
17.7	6.7	6.0	SUDAN	4.0		3737
18.9	1.2	9.0	DAHOMEY	3.0	7	395
19.1	0.2	13.5	GAMBIA	2.0	8	48
20.8	1.7	13.5	GUINEA	2.0		448
25.6	4.8	13.5	KENYA	2.0		972
26.0	0.4	13.5	LESOTHO	2.0		100
51.0	25.0	13.5	NIGERIA	2.0		5430
52.1	1.1	13.5	SIERRA LEONE	2.0		399
53.3	1.2	13.5	SOMALIA	2.0		262
54.1	0.8	13.5	TOGO	2.0		255
59.8	5.7	18.0	TANZANIA	1.6	9	1038
68.9	9.1	20.0	ZAIRE	1.0		1147
79.8	10.9	20.0	ETHIOPIA	1.0		1808
84.0	4.2	20.0	UGANDA	1.0		660
84.7	0.7	23.0	CAR	0.9		76
85.2	0.5	23.0	MAURITANIA	0.9		48
87.4	2.2	23.0	MALI	0.9		271
88.9	1.5	25.5	BURUNDI	0.8	10	137
90.4	1.5	25.5	RWANDA	0.8		133
90.7	0.3	27.0	BOTSWANA	0.7		17
92.3	1.6	28.5	CHAD	0.5		93
94.6	2.3	28.5	UPPER VOLTA	0.5		125
96.3	1.7	30.0	NIGER	0.3		62
98.2	1.9	31.5	MALAWI	0.1		225
100.0	1.8	31.5	ZAMBIA	0.1		200

source: UNESCO, *Development of Higher Education in Africa*, Report of the Conference on the Development of Higher Education in Africa (Paris: UNESCO, 1962), p. 226. *Burundi, Rwanda*: Separate estimates were made from the 270 total for Ruanda-Urundi; *Malawi, Zambia*: Estimates were made from the combined figure given for the Federation of Rhodesia and Nyasaland.

TABLE 5.16   Estimated Percent of Population Literate, 1965

Definitions and Comments: The United Nations recommended definition of literacy is the ability both to read and write. A literate person must be able to read with understanding, and to write a short statement on everyday life, in any one language. We assume that the AID's definition of literacy is similar to that of the UN.

```
RANGE     =        57.00
MEAN      =        16.44
STANDARD DEVIATION =          13.12
```

POPULATION PERCENT		RANK	COUNTRY NAME	VALUE	RANGE DECILE
CUM.	COUNTRY				
0.4	0.4	1.0	LESOTHO	60	1
9.5	9.1	2.5	ZAIRE	40	4
11.3	1.8	2.5	ZAMBIA	40	
36.3	25.0	4.0	NIGERIA	33	5
36.6	0.3	6.0	BOTSWANA	30	6
40.4	3.8	6.0	GHANA	30	
44.6	4.2	6.0	UGANDA	30	
49.4	4.8	8.0	KENYA	25	7
49.8	0.4	9.0	CONGO (BRA)	23	
51.7	1.9	10.0	IVORY COAST	20	8
57.4	5.7	11.0	TANZANIA	17	
58.1	0.7	12.0	CAR	15	
58.3	0.2	13.5	GABON	13	9
65.0	6.7	13.5	SUDAN	13	
66.5	1.5	19.0	BURUNDI	10	
69.0	2.5	19.0	CAMEROON	10	
69.2	0.2	19.0	GAMBIA	10	
70.9	1.7	19.0	GUINEA	10	
71.4	0.5	19.0	LIBERIA	10	
73.3	1.9	19.0	MALAWI	10	
74.8	1.5	19.0	RWANDA	10	
75.9	1.1	19.0	SIERRA LEONE	10	
76.7	0.8	19.0	TOGO	10	
78.4	1.7	24.5	SENEGAL	7	10
80.7	2.3	24.5	UPPER VOLTA	7	
82.3	1.6	28.5	CHAD	5	
83.5	1.2	28.5	DAHOMEY	5	
94.4	10.9	28.5	ETHIOPIA	5	
94.9	0.5	28.5	MAURITANIA	5	
97.1	2.2	28.5	MALI	5	
98.3	1.2	28.5	SOMALIA	5	
100.0	1.7	32.0	NIGER	3	

SOURCES: *AID Economic Data Book 1967*, p. 5. Data are assumed to represent percent of total population literate. *Botswana, Ghana, Lesotho, Uganda*: AID estimate considered unreliable in these instances; an estimate has been made on the basis of earlier census reports included in: *UN Report on the World Social Situation* (New York: 1957), *UN Compendium of Social Statistics, 1967*, and UNESCO, *Basic Facts and Figures* (Paris: 1952); *Burundi, Zaire (Congo K.), Kenya, Malawi, Mauritania, Rwanda, Togo*: Cases for which a range is given and, due to consideration of earlier data, the highest value of the range has been taken; *Congo (Brazzaville), Gabon, Mali, Nigeria, Senegal, Sudan, Tanzania, Upper Volta*: Cases for which a range is given and the mid-point has been taken.

TABLE 5.17   Percent Change in Literacy Rate, ca. 1955–1965

Definition and Comments: Data for 1955 are given by the source as "percent literate in the 1950s". Where the sources provide a range (e.g. 35–40 percent), a midpoint value has been chosen, often with the aid of additional sources. It should be noted that all the former French West and French Equatorial African countries were estimated at between 5 and 10 percent literate for 1955.

```
RANGE     =       659.00
MEAN      =       133.03
STANDARD DEVIATION =          165.06
```

POPULATION PERCENT		RANK	COUNTRY NAME	VALUE	RANGE DECILE
CUM.	COUNTRY				
0.4	0.4	1.0	CONGO (BRA)	667	1
2.3	1.9	2.0	IVORY COAST	567	2
3.0	0.7	3.5	CAR	400	5
4.2	1.2	3.5	SOMALIA	400	
4.4	0.2	5.0	GABON	333	6
6.1	1.7	6.0	GUINEA	233	7
31.1	25.0	7.0	NIGERIA	230	
32.8	1.7	8.0	NIGER	200	8
34.5	1.7	9.5	SENEGAL	133	9
36.8	2.3	9.5	UPPER VOLTA	133	
42.5	5.7	11.0	TANZANIA	113	
49.2	6.7	12.0	SUDAN	86	
51.0	1.8	13.0	ZAMBIA	74	
52.6	1.6	16.0	CHAD	67	10
53.8	1.2	16.0	DAHOMEY	67	
64.7	10.9	16.0	ETHIOPIA	67	
65.2	0.5	16.0	MAURITANIA	67	
67.4	2.2	16.0	MALI	67	
69.9	2.5	19.5	CAMEROON	43	
70.1	0.2	19.5	GAMBIA	43	
70.4	0.3	21.5	BOTSWANA	30	
74.2	3.8	21.5	GHANA	30	
75.7	1.5	25.5	BURUNDI	25	
76.2	0.5	25.5	LIBERIA	25	
78.1	1.9	25.5	MALAWI	25	
79.6	1.5	25.5	RWANDA	25	
80.7	1.1	25.5	SIERRA LEONE	25	
81.5	0.8	25.5	TOGO	25	
81.9	0.4	29.5	LESOTHO	20	
86.1	4.2	29.5	UGANDA	20	
90.9	4.8	31.0	KENYA	9	
100.0	9.1	32.0	ZAIRE	8	

SOURCES: See previous table for 1965. For ca. 1955: *UN Report on the World Social Situation. Cameroon, Zaire (Congo K.), Nigeria, Somalia*: UNESCO, *Basic Facts and Figures*; *Botswana, Gabon, Lesotho, Niger, Senegal, Sudan, Uganda, Zambia*: Census reports from *UN Compendium of Social Statistics, 1967*.

TABLE 5.18 Expenditure on Primary Education as a Percent of Total Educational Budget, ca. 1965

```
RANGE =          60.20
MEAN =           52.57
STANDARD DEVIATION =         15.26
```

POPULATION PERCENT CUM.	COUNTRY	RANK	COUNTRY NAME	VALUE	RANGE DECILE
1.5	1.5	1.0	RWANDA	85.1	1
2.3	0.8	2.0	TOGO	83.2	
4.1	1.8	3.0	ZAMBIA	81.8	
4.5	0.4	4.0	LESOTHO	73.6	2
6.0	1.5	5.0	BURUNDI	72.8	3
6.5	0.5	6.0	MAURITANIA	66.8	4
7.2	0.7	7.0	CAR	59.7	5
9.4	2.2	8.0	MALI	58.9	
15.1	5.7	9.0	TANZANIA	58.1	
17.0	1.9	10.5	MALAWI	57.8	
18.7	1.7	10.5	NIGER	57.8	
20.4	1.7	12.0	SENEGAL	57.4	
20.8	0.4	13.0	CONGO (BRA)	56.7	
22.0	1.2	14.0	DAHOMEY	54.5	6
26.8	4.8	15.0	KENYA	54.4	
29.3	2.5	16.0	CAMEROON	53.6	
29.6	0.3	17.0	BOTSWANA	49.7	
33.8	4.2	18.0	UGANDA	49.6	
42.9	9.1	19.0	ZAIRE	49.5	
44.1	1.2	20.0	SOMALIA	48.7	7
69.1	25.0	21.0	NIGERIA	47.9	
69.6	0.5	22.0	LIBERIA	46.3	
71.3	1.7	23.0	GUINEA	46.2	
73.6	2.3	24.0	UPPER VOLTA	44.7	
84.5	10.9	25.0	ETHIOPIA	41.7	8
86.1	1.6	26.0	CHAD	37.6	
86.3	0.2	27.0	GAMBIA	36.6	9
87.4	1.1	28.0	SIERRA LEONE	34.9	
91.2	3.8	29.0	GHANA	31.0	
97.9	6.7	30.0	SUDAN	30.9	10
99.8	1.9	31.0	IVORY COAST	30.0	
100.0	0.2	32.0	GABON	24.9	

SOURCES: *UN Statistical Yearbooks 1967–1968*. Percentages computed from absolute figures given in local currencies for all levels. *Rwanda*: Data for 1963; *Lesotho, Nigeria, Togo*: Data for 1966; *Ivory Coast, Mauritania*: Data for 1964; *Uganda*: Data for 1960; *Ivory Coast*: Jacques Hallak and Raymond Poignant, *Les aspects financiers d'education en Cote-d'Ivoire* (Paris: UNESCO, Institut international de planification de l'education, 1966), p. 33.

TABLE 5.19 Educational Expenditure as a Percent of Gross Domestic Product, 1965

```
RANGE =           4.00
MEAN =            2.88
STANDARD DEVIATION =          1.07
```

POPULATION PERCENT CUM.	COUNTRY	RANK	COUNTRY NAME	VALUE	RANGE DECILE
1.5	1.5	1.0	BURUNDI	5.0	1
5.3	3.8	2.0	GHANA	4.8	
14.4	9.1	3.0	ZAIRE	4.6	2
14.8	0.4	4.0	CONGO (BRA)	4.3	
15.1	0.3	5.5	BOTSWANA	4.0	3
19.9	4.8	5.5	KENYA	4.0	
21.6	1.7	7.0	GUINEA	3.9	
22.8	1.2	8.5	DAHOMEY	3.8	
24.7	1.9	8.5	MALAWI	3.8	
30.4	5.7	12.0	TANZANIA	3.7	4
30.6	0.2	12.0	GAMBIA	3.2	5
32.5	1.9	12.0	IVORY COAST	3.2	
32.9	0.4	12.0	LESOTHO	3.2	
33.1	0.2	12.0	GABON	3.1	
34.7	1.6	15.0	CHAD	2.9	6
35.4	0.7	17.0	CAR	2.8	
42.1	6.7	17.0	SUDAN	2.8	
43.9	1.8	17.0	GAMBIA	2.8	
45.0	1.1	19.5	SIERRA LEONE	2.6	
47.3	2.3	19.5	UPPER VOLTA	2.6	
49.8	2.5	22.5	CAMEROON	2.1	8
50.3	0.5	22.5	MAURITANIA	2.1	
51.8	1.5	22.5	RWANDA	2.1	
53.5	1.7	22.5	SENEGAL	2.1	
54.0	0.5	25.0	LIBERIA	2.0	
54.8	0.8	26.0	TOGO	1.9	
57.0	2.2	27.0	MALI	1.7	9
58.7	1.7	28.5	NIGER	1.6	
83.7	25.0	28.5	NIGERIA	1.6	
87.9	4.2	30.0	UGANDA	1.5	
98.8	10.9	31.0	ETHIOPIA	1.3	10
100.0	1.2	32.0	SOMALIA	1.0	

SOURCES: Sources for Table 5.18 apply here also. For cases in which data pertain to years other than 1965, computation of percent of GDP has been made using GDP figures for the corresponding year, thus providing an estimate of the 1965 value. Gross Domestic Product data from *UN Statistical Yearbook 1968*, pp. 184 and 190. *Ivory Coast*: Hallak and Poignant, *Les aspects financiers d'education en Cote-d'Ivoire*, p. 13.

TABLE 5.20   Educational Expenditure as a Percent of Total Government Expenditure, 1965

Definition: For cases in which educational expenditure data pertain to a year other than 1965, computation of percent of total government expenditure has been made using budget figures for the corresponding year, thus providing an estimate of the 1965 allocation.

RANGE   =   23.10
MEAN   =   16.28
STANDARD DEVIATION =   5.09

POPULATION PERCENT		RANK	COUNTRY NAME	VALUE	RANGE DECILE
CUM.	COUNTRY				
1.7	1.7	1.0	GUINEA	30.1	1
2.1	0.4	2.0	LESOTHO	27.9	
3.6	1.5	3.0	BURUNDI	23.0	4
12.7	9.1	4.0	ZAIRE	21.4	
16.5	3.8	5.0	GHANA	20.9	
18.0	1.5	6.0	RWANDA	20.5	5
18.4	0.4	7.0	CONGO (BRA)	20.3	
25.1	6.7	8.0	SUDAN	20.1	
26.2	1.1	9.0	SIERRA LEONE	19.4	
27.8	1.6	10.0	CHAD	18.5	6
28.6	0.8	11.0	TOGO	17.9	
34.3	5.7	12.0	TANZANIA	17.8	
36.2	1.9	13.0	IVORY COAST	16.7	
37.4	1.2	14.0	DAHOMEY	16.5	
39.9	2.5	15.0	CAMEROON	16.4	
40.2	0.3	16.0	BOTSWANA	16.2	7
42.5	2.3	17.0	UPPER VOLTA	16.1	
67.5	25.0	18.0	NIGERIA	16.0	
69.4	1.9	19.0	MALAWI	15.0	
69.9	0.5	20.0	MAURITANIA	14.3	
70.6	0.7	21.0	CAR	13.6	8
71.1	0.5	22.0	LIBERIA	13.5	
73.3	2.2	23.0	MALI	12.9	
73.5	0.2	24.0	GAMBIA	12.6	
75.2	1.7	25.0	NIGER	12.2	
75.4	0.2	26.0	GABON	12.1	
80.2	4.8	27.0	KENYA	11.9	
84.4	4.2	28.0	UGANDA	10.8	9
86.2	1.8	29.0	ZAMBIA	10.6	
97.1	10.9	30.0	ETHIOPIA	10.2	
98.8	1.7	31.0	SENEGAL	8.7	10
100.0	1.2	32.0	SOMALIA	7.0	

sources: See Table 5.18. Total government expenditure based on *Europa Yearbook 1967* and *UN Statistical Yearbook 1967*. *Ivory Coast*: Hallak and Poignant, *Les aspects financiers d'education en Cote-d'Ivoire*, p. 13.

TABLE 5.21   Percent Change in Educational Expenditure as a Proportion of Total Government Budget, 1958–1965

Comment: The higher the number the greater the increase in the percent of the total government budget which is devoted to education.

RANGE   =   373.00
MEAN   =   -22.90
STANDARD DEVIATION =   76.36

POPULATION PERCENT		RANK	COUNTRY NAME	VALUE	RANGE DECILE
CUM.	COUNTRY				
1.7	1.7	1.0	GUINEA	145	1
8.4	6.7	2.0	SUDAN	104	2
8.8	0.4	3.0	LESOTHO	91	
10.4	1.6	4.0	CHAD	70	3
19.5	9.1	5.0	ZAIRE	41	
22.0	2.5	6.0	CAMEROON	24	4
22.2	0.2	7.0	GAMBIA	20	
23.7	1.5	8.5	BURUNDI	13	
24.5	0.8	8.5	TOGO	13	
24.8	0.3	10.0	BOTSWANA	11	
26.5	1.7	11.0	NIGER	-1	
28.8	2.3	12.0	UPPER VOLTA	-3	
29.3	0.5	13.0	MAURITANIA	-7	5
33.1	3.8	14.0	GHANA	-10	
44.0	10.9	15.0	ETHIOPIA	-11	
45.9	1.9	16.5	IVORY COAST	-12	
47.4	1.5	16.5	RWANDA	-12	
49.2	1.8	18.0	ZAMBIA	-25	
50.9	1.7	19.0	SENEGAL	-38	
52.0	1.1	20.0	SIERRA LEONE	-48	6
53.9	1.9	21.0	MALAWI	-54	
54.6	0.7	22.0	CAR	-57	
55.0	0.4	23.0	CONGO (BRA)	-59	
55.2	0.2	24.0	GABON	-75	
56.4	1.2	25.0	DAHOMEY	-81	7
60.6	4.2	26.0	UGANDA	-106	
65.4	4.8	27.0	KENYA	-115	
67.6	2.2	28.0	MALI	-117	8
73.3	5.7	29.0	TANZANIA	-160	9
98.3	25.0	30.0	NIGERIA	-228	

DATA NOT AVAILABLE FOR THE FOLLOWING COUNTRIES

LIBERIA   SOMALIA

sources: Data for educational and total government expenditure for 1958 are from: *Enseignement Outre-mer* (December 1958) (individual unit reports give percent of total government expenditure allocated for education); *Europa Yearbook 1961*, Vol. 2; *UN Statistical Yearbook 1968*, Table 185; UNESCO, *World Survey of Education*, Vol. 3; *United Nations Trusteeship Report on Ruanda-Urundi* (New York: 1960), p. 68. For 1965 refer to Table 5.20.

TABLE 5.22 Primary Pupils per Teacher and Total Number of Primary Teachers, 1966

Definition: Teachers include both full-time and part-time teachers, excluding other instructional personnel without teaching functions (e.g. certain principals, librarians, etc.).

```
RANGE     =    132.00
MEAN      =     47.09
STANDARD DEVIATION =        23.02
```

POPULATION PERCENT CUM.	COUNTRY	RANK	COUNTRY NAME	VALUE	RANGE DECILE	TOTAL
0.8	0.8	1.0	TOGO	152	1	1044
2.4	1.6	2.0	CHAD	81	6	1315
3.9	1.5	3.0	RWANDA	74		4892
6.2	2.3	4.0	UPPER VOLTA	63	7	1488
6.6	0.4	5.5	CONGO (BRA)	60		2201
7.0	0.4	5.5	LESOTHO	60		2536
7.7	0.7	7.0	CAR	59	8	1161
9.5	1.8	8.0	ZAMBIA	51		6453
15.2	5.7	9.0	TANZANIA	50		10566
21.9	6.7	10.0	SUDAN	48		8879
24.4	2.5	11.0	CAMEROON	47		6334
26.3	1.9	12.0	IVORY COAST	46	9	7209
28.0	1.7	13.0	NIGER	44		1097
38.9	10.9	14.5	ETHIOPIA	43		7660
40.6	1.7	14.5	SENEGAL	43		3997
40.9	0.3	16.0	BOTSWANA	42		1236
41.1	0.2	17.5	GABON	41		1490
42.8	1.7	17.5	GUINEA	41		2436
44.0	1.2	19.0	DAHOMEY	40		2552
45.5	1.5	20.5	BURUNDI	39		2848
54.6	9.1	20.5	ZAIRE	39		48220
56.8	2.2	22.0	MALI	38		1530
58.7	1.9	23.0	MALAWI	37		7271
59.2	0.5	24.0	LIBERIA	35		2158
84.2	25.0	25.0	NIGERIA	33	10	99335
88.4	4.2	26.0	UGANDA	32		17331
88.6	0.2	28.0	GAMBIA	31		318
93.4	4.8	28.0	KENYA	31		22655
94.5	1.1	28.0	SIERRA LEONE	31		3189
95.7	1.2	30.0	SOMALIA	30		920
99.5	3.8	31.0	GHANA	26		30517
100.0	0.5	32.0	MAURITANIA	20		937

SOURCE: *UNESCO Statistical Yearbook 1968*, Table 2.7. *Rwanda*: 1963 data; *Gambia, Guinea, Mauritania, Senegal, Sudan, Upper Volta*: 1965; *Botswana, Malawi*: 1967.

TABLE 5.23 Average Annual Percent Change in Primary Pupils per Teacher, 1960–1966

Definition and Comment: See Table 5.22. The average annual figure is used here because some of the data in the source are for years other than 1960–1966.

```
RANGE     =    162.00
MEAN      =      4.19
STANDARD DEVIATION =        30.75
```

POPULATION PERCENT CUM.	COUNTRY	RANK	COUNTRY NAME	VALUE	RANGE DECILE
1.5	1.5	1.0	RWANDA	87	1
3.8	2.3	2.0	UPPER VOLTA	65	2
4.1	0.3	3.0	BOTSWANA	47	3
15.0	10.9	4.0	ETHIOPIA	29	4
21.7	6.7	5.0	SUDAN	26	
22.1	0.4	6.5	CONGO (BRA)	22	5
24.0	1.9	6.5	IVORY COAST	22	
25.5	1.5	9.0	BURUNDI	18	
27.1	1.6	9.0	CHAD	18	
27.5	0.4	9.0	LESOTHO	18	
52.5	25.0	11.5	NIGERIA	17	
58.2	5.7	11.5	TANZANIA	17	
58.7	0.5	13.0	LIBERIA	14	
60.4	1.7	14.0	NIGER	9	
61.6	1.2	15.0	SOMALIA	8	
65.8	4.2	16.0	UGANDA	5	6
66.5	0.7	17.0	CAR	4	
69.0	2.5	18.0	CAMEROON	2	
69.2	0.2	19.5	GAMBIA	1	
71.0	1.8	19.5	ZAMBIA	1	
72.2	1.2	21.0	DAHOMEY	-2	
81.3	9.1	22.5	ZAIRE	-5	
81.8	0.5	22.5	MAURITANIA	-5	
85.6	3.8	24.0	GHANA	-12	7
87.5	1.9	25.5	MALAWI	-15	
89.2	1.7	25.5	SENEGAL	-15	
90.0	0.8	27.0	TOGO	-24	
91.1	1.1	28.0	SIERRA LEONE	-25	
93.3	2.2	29.0	MALI	-26	
98.1	4.8	30.0	KENYA	-43	9
98.3	0.2	31.0	GABON	-49	
100.0	1.7	32.0	GUINEA	-75	

SOURCE: *UNESCO Statistical Yearbook 1968*, Table 2.7. See source information for Table 5.22 for information regarding the 1966 data. All the data for "1960" are for that year with the exception of Burundi whose data is for 1961.

6. Mass Communications and Transportation Systems

The circulation and flow of information (communications) and the movement of physical goods and populations (transportation) have been emphasized in theories of both economic and political development.[1] In this chapter we present data on mass communication and transportation systems—i.e. the facilities available for communication and transport —but it is useful to introduce these data in the context of theories which concern the effects of actual flows of information, goods and people on economic and political development.

Theoretical Importance of Communication

In terms of *economic development*, communications play a critical role in (1) the creation of demands for the goods and benefits of an industrial society and the associated "revolution of rising expectations," and (2) the transmission of values and norms compatible with an integrated and industrialized economic system.[2] The growth of communications and transport systems have additional economic ramifications since they represent a major aspect of the development of social overhead capital.[3] Once constructed, facilities for mass communication and transportation frequently effect considerable economies of scale in the movement of goods and information, providing increasingly large pay-offs as usage increases without concomitant increases in the investment in infrastructure. Extensions of communication and transportation systems, therefore, can enlarge existing markets, diminish the size and isolation of subsistence sectors, and satisfy some minimum conditions for the establishment of manufacturing industries.

One should, nevertheless, be wary of any simplistic equation of the growth of communication and transportation infrastructure with growth in national income. Relatively easy though it is to persuade foreign aid agencies of the utility of infrastructure development, and satisfying though it may be for government officials to have themselves associated with the visible facilities of progress, "the role of infrastructure facilities in development is coordinate with that of many other pieces of capital equipment and changes in management practices and in institutions. Increasingly large infrastructure facilities have their place in the course of development, but they deserve no special niche as absolute or near-absolute prerequisites to growth."[4]

In theories of *political development*, the growth of communication and transportation systems is linked to the shift from traditional to modern society, the development of democratic decision-making structures, and the integration of national political communities. A unifying explanatory concept related to these hypothesized developments is Daniel Lerner's notion of empathy, or the capacity of the individual to place himself in the role of others. Lerner sees modernization as a progressive diffusion of empathy which is characteristic of people who display relatively higher levels of physical, social and psychic mobility, and he argues that empathy is a consequence of the sequential effects of urbanization and literacy and is "multiplied" by exposure to mass media.

Lerner's emphasis on the role of communications in changing the traditional habits and world-view of individuals and thus effecting a transition to modern society, is clearly reflected in the work of political scientists who see the growth of modern society as the result of a multidimensional process of social mobilization. Karl Deutsch has described social mobilization as the overall process of change involving large segments of the population, "in which major clusters of social, economic and psychological commitments are eroded or broken and people become available for new patterns of socialization and behavior."[5] Deutsch emphasizes the role of radio and newsprint in mobilizing populations into an awareness of new styles of life,[6] and Gabriel Almond and G. B. Powell argue that social mobilization is "in large part a communications phenomenon" that must occur before the development of political and economic capabilities.[7]

The consequences of social mobilization in terms

of the political systems that result from the growth of communication and transportation are not yet well understood, although there is a considerable body of social research that emphasizes the linkage between increasing communications and increasingly democratic political organization. Both Lerner and Deutsch remark on the association between mass political participation and increasing social mobilization. In this connection, a notable empirical analysis by Philips Cutwright describes a strong association between political development, operationalized as the presence and persistence of aspects of democratic institutionalization, and the extent of mass communication. Comparing seventy-one countries on these two variables Cutwright reported a correlation of .80.[8]

In addition to the development of empathy, rationality,[9] and democratic behavior as hypothesized consequences of an increasing experience of mass communication and transportation, theories of political development emphasize the disruptive political consequences implied in the conceptualization of social mobilization as a breakdown of traditional patterns of thought and behavior, and a mechanism for the development of new and potentially unsatisfiable demands. Depending, therefore, on the ratio of demand arousal to demand satisfaction, communication development may result in political instability in new nations.[10] But as social mobilization dislocates people from their habitual environment and provides for the intensification of formerly unexpressed demands and inter-group conflicts, so the development of communications and transportation may facilitate the integration of political communities. Integration is the increasing linkage, interdependence, cohesion, unification and consensus characteristic of social groupings (see Part III, Chapter One), and the use of communication facilities for increasing transactions between spatially and socially disparate political actors is a crucial aspect of political integration.[11]

The measurement of integration with data on communication and transportation facilities of the kind presented in this chapter is, it must be emphasized, subject to some reservation. Communication potential as measured by the number and type of mass media and transportation facilities in each national unit is neither indicative of the intensity of communications and transactions nor is it specific as to the geographical and social location of the source and receivers of goods and messages.[12] Empirical analysis of national integration must eventually incorporate measures of within-nation transaction flows, since the theoretical linkage between communication development and national integration is based on the argument that, aside from official boundaries, the composition of functional political communities can be determined by the identification of discontinuities in the flow of mutually rewarding transactions between members of a given nation. The model of this kind of analysis is to be found in studies of international or regional integration, an example of which is a study by Edward Soja, in which the salience of telephonic communications between urban centers in Kenya, Uganda, and Tanzania between 1961 and 1965 was reduced and a pattern of intra-national clustering became more clearly evident.[13]

Measuring Communication

The data presented in the tables which follow have been chosen to cover a broad range of communications and transport phenomena within the limits of aggregate measurement. Information concerning radios (Tables 6.1 and 6.2), newspapers (Tables 6.3 and 6.4), telephones (Tables 6.5 and 6.6), cinemas (Table 6.7), roads (Table 6.8), passenger cars (Table 6.11), commercial vehicles (Tables 6.9 and 6.10), and miles of railroad track (Table 6.12) are included. Per capita figures are usually presented for two years in the last decade, and the road mileage measure has been standardized on the basis of area of the country. Further, percentage changes are given to show relative rates of growth.

These data are directly applicable to the operationalization of social mobilization and social overhead capital as conceptual explanations of political and economic development. There are serious difficulties, however, in justifying these aggregate measures as indicators of national integration, as the explanation of the mechanisms linking communications development to the growth of democracy, political instability, or economic development is by no means obvious. Summary indicators of the scale of communication and transportation facilities in a given country obscure the details of who uses such facilities, how often people use them and how mutually rewarding the transactions are, who controls them, and what consequences are entailed by patterns of usage and control for the content and effectiveness of communications.

In interpreting the data in this chapter, therefore, one must have in mind the unidentified variation between African nations in the concentration of communications in particular sectors of the population. Deutsch has specified several levels of social communication which are differentiated both by the actors involved and the media employed.[14] If one distinguishes broadly between the elite, opinion leaders, and the mass public in any nation, it is necessary, from the point of view of satisfying explanations of political and economic development, to know (1) how great is the concentration of ownership,[15] control,[16] and usage[17] of communications by the elite; (2) how clearly communications from the elite to the mass public are transmitted in the two-step flow[18] of messages from opinion leaders to the average citizen; and (3) to what extent reactive media like telephones, transportation, and face-to-face communications differ in their effects on individual perception and feeling from nonreactive media like radios, television, newspapers, and cinemas.

Reliability

Most communications data are generated in accordance with the maintenance and accounting requirements of the various operating systems, and can be expected to have high reliability. Accurate measures of communications volume within nations are often readily available to the researcher, although not in disaggregated form. Nevertheless, each of the variables included in this chapter has certain specific reliability problems.

The most serious reliability problems are two which are associated with the measurement of radios. The first is occasioned by the procedure in some countries in which radios must be licensed, while the number of radios is only estimated in those countries without licensing requirements. Furthermore, since the licensing process is usually a taxing device, understatement is to be expected in those countries where radio licenses are the basis of measurement. Whenever available, the numbers reported in Tables 6.1 and 6.2 are estimates of the total number of receivers in a given country. A second measurement problem occurs when estimates of radio receivers obtained from available sources show considerable variance for the same or adjacent years.[19]

Daily newspapers (Tables 6.3 and 6.4) are a major source of information for the literate population, and are capable of presenting a variety of positions that government owned or regulated radio stations may not present—this, of course, provided that newspapers are not owned or censored by government. The difficulty with measures of newspaper circulation, however, is that the definition of daily newspapers is not always consistently adhered to by the reporting countries. The figures given in this chapter are intended to include the circulation of all indigenous newspapers issued regularly, either daily or at least three to four times a week.

We expect telephones (Tables 6.5 and 6.6), passenger cars (Table 6.11), and commercial vehicles (Tables 6.9 and 6.10) to be reported with reasonable accuracy in original sources, since telephonic technology requires accurate measures of usage, and, unlike radios, the licensing of vehicles is generally enforceable. Conversely, the measures of improved roads (Table 6.8) are plagued by a lack of clear-cut definition of "improved."[20] Nevertheless, this latter figure should provide a rudimentary ranking of the countries with respect to road density. Railroad mileage is, in principle, a well-defined measure, but secondary track and side spurs are sometimes included with figures for primary track mileage.[21] The variable reported in Table 6.13 is intended to represent primary track mileage only.

In addition to lending general support to the reliability of the data in this chapter by showing high intercorrelations between different measures of the same variable, a factor analysis of seventy-four communications and transport variables showed an interesting pattern of dimensionality. Four factors, accounting for 85 percent of the total variance, may be characterized as follows:

1. Radios, newspapers, cinemas (mass or non-reactive communications)
2. Telephones, passenger cars, railroad mileage (personal or reactive communications)
3. Commercial transport
4. Air transport

The data in this chapter have been selected to provide coverage of these dimensions and to indicate temporal aspects of communications development based on figures for the time of independence and the latest year for which adequate coverage is available.[22]

Notes

[1] See, for example: Lucian Pye, ed., *Communications and Political Development* (Princeton: Princeton University Press, 1962); Karl W. Deutsch, *Nationalism and Social Communications: An Inquiry into the Foundations of Nationalism* (New York: The Technology Press of M.I.T. and John Wiley, 1953); Philip Jacob and James V. Toscano, eds., *The Integration of Political Communities* (New York: J. B. Lippincott Co., 1964); Daniel Lerner, *The Passing of Traditional Society* (Glencoe, Ill.: The Free Press, 1958); Everett Rogers, *Modernization Among Peasants: The Impact of Communication* (New York: Holt, Rinehart and Winston, 1969).

[2] For a discussion of the importance of communication in the development of labor commitment in developing nations see Peter B. Hammond, "Management in Economic Transition," in Wilbert E. Moore and Arnold S. Feldman, eds., *Labor Commitment and Social Change in Developing Areas* (New York: Social Science Research Council, 1960), pp. 109–122; and for an analysis of the positive effects of mass media exposure on individual innovation, see Rogers, *Modernization Among Peasants*, Chapter 5.

[3] For a discussion of social overhead capital, see Stephen Enke, *Economics For Development* (London: Dennis Dobson, 1963).

[4] Everett E. Hagen, *The Economics of Development* (Homewood, Illinois: Richard D. Irwin Inc., 1968), p. 129.

[5] Daniel Lerner, *The Passing of Traditional Society*, pp. 47–65.

[6] Karl W. Deutsch, "Social Mobilization and Political Development," *American Political Science Review*, 55 (September 1961): 494.

[7] Gabriel A. Almond and G. B. Powell, Jr., *Comparative Politics: A Developmental Approach* (Boston: Little, Brown and Co., 1966), p. 177.

[8] Philips Cutwright, "National Political Development: Measurement and Analysis," *American Sociological Review*, 28 (1963): 253–264. For related discussions of these concepts, see Deane N. Neubauer, "Some Conditions of Democracy," *American Political Science Review*, 61 (1967): 1002–1009; Marvin E. Olsen, "Multivariate Analysis of National Political Development," *American Sociological Review*, 33 (1968): 699–712; and Arthur K. Smith, Jr., "Socio-Economic Development and Political Democracy: A Causal Analysis," *Midwest Journal of Political Science* (1969): 96–125.

[9] For the importance of communications in the development of political rationality, see, for example, Lucien Pye, *Aspects of Political Development* (Boston: Little, Brown and Co., 1966), Chapter 8.

[10] See the clear-cut formulation of this problem in Deutsch, "Social Mobilization and Political Development."

[11] See Karl W. Deutsch, "Communication Theory and Political Integration," and "Transaction Flows as Indicators of Political Cohesion," in *The Integration of Political Communities*, Jacob and Toscano, eds., pp. 46–74 and 75–97.

[12] See the discussion and analysis in Donald G. Morrison and Hugh Michael Stevenson, *Conflict and Change in African Political Development* (New York: Free Press, forthcoming in 1972).

[13] See Edward W. Soja, "Communication and Territorial Integration in East Africa: An Introduction to Transaction Flow Analysis," in *The Structure of Political Geography*, ed. Roger E. Kasperson and Julian V. Menghi (Chicago: Aldine Publishing Company, 1969), pp. 231–242. The salience of communications is determined by the value of the relative acceptance index, first introduced by I. R. Savage and Karl W. Deutsch, "A Statistical Model of the Gross Analysis of Transaction Flows," *Econometrica*, 28 (1960) 551–572. This index is a measure of the significance of the actual or observed flow of communications as a proportion of the flow expected by a chance or "null" model.

[14] See Karl W. Deutsch, *The Analysis of International Relations* (Englewood Cliffs, N.J.: Prentice-Hall, 1968), pp. 101–110.

[15] Annual compendia such as *Europa Yearbook* and the *Statesman's Yearbook* contain detailed information on radio and the press in African countries. See also *The Commercial Radio in Africa* (German African Society, October 1969) and Fritz Feuereisen and Ernst Schmacke, eds, *Africa: A Guide to Newspapers and Magazines* (New York: Africana, 1970).

[16] Reports on press censorship covering some of the black African countries are available from the University of Missouri and Indiana University.

[17] The concentration of facilities and usage in government offices and capital cities may be illustrated by the fact that of the 25,513 telephones in Senegal in 1967, 20,373 were in Dakar. *Statesman's Yearbook, 1968–1969.*

[18] For the "two-step flow" hypothesis that "ideas often flow from radio and print to opinion leaders and from them to the less active sections of the population" see Paul F. Lazarsfeld, et al., *The People's Choice* (New York: Meredith Press, 1944) and Elihu Katz, "The Two-Step Flow of Communication: An Up-To-Date Report on an Hypothesis," *Public Opinion Quarterly*, 21 (1957): 61–78.

[19] For example, the *UN Statistical Yearbook 1967* reports 58,000 radio receivers in Ivory Coast in 1964. Another report for the same year, in *Africa Report*, 9 (February 1964): 32, gives a figure of 100,000 receivers. A third source *Africa 1968*, reports 300,000 radio receivers in Ivory Coast in 1965.

[20] This can be observed by comparing the figures on improved roads in *AID Economic Data Book: Africa 1970* with more detailed descriptions of road surface in *Statesman's Yearbook 1968–69.*

[21] It should be noted that Sierra Leone's uneconomical railway is to be phased out by 1972 and replaced with improved roads.

[22] Air transport data were not included because data were lacking for a third of the countries.

TABLE 6.1 Radios per 1,000 Population and Total Radios, 1966

```
RANGE       =     147.00
MEAN        =      35.16
STANDARD DEVIATION =          35.80
```

POPULATION PERCENT		RANK	COUNTRY NAME	VALUE	RANGE DECILE	TOTAL
CUM.	COUNTRY					
0.2	0.2	1.0	GAMBIA	150	1	60
0.7	0.5	2.0	LIBERIA	139		152
0.9	0.2	3.0	GABON	85	5	40
1.3	0.4	4.0	CONGO (BRA)	74	6	60
3.0	1.7	5.0	SENEGAL	73		260
6.8	3.8	6.0	GHANA	70		555
11.0	4.2	7.0	UGANDA	61	7	473
12.1	1.1	8.0	SIERRA LEONE	44	8	105
14.6	2.5	9.5	CAMEROON	39		200
19.4	4.8	9.5	KENYA	39		375
20.1	0.7	11.0	CAR	33		48
20.5	0.4	12.0	LESOTHO	31	9	25
22.4	1.9	13.5	MALAWI	29		85
22.9	0.5	13.5	MAURITANIA	29		31
24.6	1.7	15.0	GUINEA	21		75
26.3	1.7	16.0	NIGER	20		70
27.5	1.2	17.0	DAHOMEY	19		45
28.3	0.8	18.0	TOGO	18		31
39.2	10.9	19.5	ETHIOPIA	16	10	358
45.9	6.7	19.5	SUDAN	16		225
47.8	1.9	21.0	IVORY COAST	15		60
49.0	1.2	22.5	SOMALIA	14		36
50.8	1.8	22.5	ZAMBIA	14		55
59.9	9.1	24.0	ZAIRE	13		200
84.9	25.0	25.0	NIGERIA	12		660
90.6	5.7	26.5	TANZANIA	10		120
92.9	2.3	26.5	UPPER VOLTA	10		50
94.5	1.6	28.0	CHAD	9		30
94.8	0.3	29.0	BOTSWANA	7		4
96.3	1.5	30.5	BURUNDI	6		20
98.5	2.2	30.5	MALI	6		30
100.0	1.5	32.0	RWANDA	3		10

SOURCES: *UN Statistical Yearbook 1969. Cameroon, Congo (Brazzaville), Lesotho: UNESCO Statistical Yearbook 1968; Burundi, Rwanda:* "Press and Radio in Africa," *Africa Report,* 9 (1964): 32; *Zaire (Congo K.), Ethiopia, Mauritania, Nigeria, Sierra Leone, Sudan: UN Statistical Yearbook 1967* (1964 data).

TABLE 6.2 Percent Increase in Radios per 1,000 Population, 1960 to 1966

```
RANGE       =    1011.00
MEAN        =     274.34
STANDARD DEVIATION =         306.42
```

POPULATION PERCENT		RANK	COUNTRY NAME	VALUE	RANGE DECILE
CUM.	COUNTRY				
2.5	2.5	2.5	CAMEROON	999	1
4.2	1.7	2.5	NIGER	999	
5.3	1.1	2.5	SIERRA LEONE	999	
6.5	1.2	2.5	SOMALIA	999	
7.7	1.2	5.0	DAHOMEY	533	5
8.1	0.4	6.0	CONGO (BRA)	428	6
8.5	0.4	7.0	LESOTHO	416	
9.2	0.7	8.0	CAR	371	7
18.3	9.1	9.5	ZAIRE	333	
23.1	4.8	9.5	KENYA	333	
27.3	4.2	11.0	UGANDA	307	
38.2	10.9	12.0	ETHIOPIA	220	8
42.0	3.8	13.0	GHANA	218	
43.6	1.6	14.5	CHAD	200	
45.8	2.2	14.5	MALI	200	
47.6	1.8	16.0	ZAMBIA	180	9
47.8	0.2	17.0	GAMBIA	179	
49.7	1.9	18.0	MALAWI	162	
55.4	5.7	19.0	TANZANIA	150	
55.9	0.5	20.0	MAURITANIA	81	10
56.4	0.5	21.0	LIBERIA	78	
56.6	0.2	22.0	GABON	77	
56.9	0.3	23.0	BOTSWANA	75	
57.7	0.8	24.0	TOGO	64	
59.4	1.7	25.0	GUINEA	62	
61.1	1.7	26.0	SENEGAL	52	
63.4	2.3	27.0	UPPER VOLTA	43	
70.1	6.7	28.0	SUDAN	33	
71.6	1.5	30.0	BURUNDI	0	
96.6	25.0	30.0	NIGERIA	0	
98.1	1.5	30.0	RWANDA	0	
100.0	1.9	32.0	IVORY COAST	-12	

SOURCE: 1966 data from Table 6.1.

TABLE 6.3 Daily Newspaper Circulation per 1,000 Population and Total Daily Circulation, 1968

Definition: Total daily circulation is given in hundreds.

```
RANGE    =     350.00
MEAN =          41.09
STANDARD DEVIATION =          63.89
```

POPULATION PERCENT CUM.	COUNTRY	RANK	NAME	VALUE	RANGE DECILE	TOTAL
3.8	3.8	1.0	GHANA	350	1	2950
8.6	4.8	3.5	KENYA	90	8	850
9.1	0.5	3.5	LIBERIA	90		70
34.1	25.0	3.5	NIGERIA	90		4040
35.2	1.1	3.5	SIERRA LEONE	90		220
39.4	4.2	6.0	UGANDA	80		630
41.2	1.8	7.0	ZAMBIA	70	9	280
42.9	1.7	8.5	SENEGAL	60		200
43.7	0.8	8.5	TOGO	60		100
43.9	0.2	10.5	GAMBIA	50		15
50.6	6.7	10.5	SUDAN	50		650
53.1	2.5	12.5	CAMEROON	40		180
58.8	5.7	12.5	TANZANIA	40		340
67.9	9.1	14.5	ZAIRE	30	10	550
69.8	1.9	14.5	IVORY COAST	30		100
80.7	10.9	16.5	ETHIOPIA	20		340
81.9	1.2	16.5	SOMALIA	20		55
82.3	0.4	18.0	CONGO (BRA)	12		11
83.5	1.2	19.5	DAHOMEY	10		20
83.7	0.2	19.5	GABON	10		5
85.9	2.2	21.0	MALI	6		30
86.6	0.7	22.0	CAR	5		6
88.2	1.6	23.5	CHAD	4		15
89.9	1.7	23.5	NIGER	4		13
91.6	1.7	25.5	GUINEA	2		25
93.9	2.3	25.5	UPPER VOLTA	2		15
94.2	0.3	29.5	BOTSWANA	0		0
95.7	1.5	29.5	BURUNDI	0		0
96.1	0.4	29.5	LESOTHO	0		0
98.0	1.9	29.5	MALAWI	0		0
98.5	0.5	29.5	MAURITANIA	0		0
100.0	1.5	29.5	RWANDA	0		0

SOURCE: *UN Statistical Yearbook 1968.*

TABLE 6.4 Percent Increase in Newspaper Circulation, 1960 to 1968

```
RANGE  =       250.00
MEAN =          19.44
STANDARD DEVIATION =          44.12
```

POPULATION PERCENT CUM.	COUNTRY	RANK	NAME	VALUE	RANGE DECILE
0.5	0.5	1.0	LIBERIA	200	1
1.7	1.2	2.5	SOMALIA	100	5
4.0	2.3	2.5	UPPER VOLTA	100	
13.1	9.1	4.5	ZAIRE	50	7
13.9	0.8	4.5	TOGO	50	
15.7	1.8	6.0	ZAMBIA	40	
18.2	2.5	7.5	CAMEROON	33	
19.8	1.6	7.5	CHAD	33	
20.5	0.7	9.5	CAR	25	8
27.2	6.7	9.5	SUDAN	25	
27.6	0.4	11.0	CONGO (BRA)	20	
52.6	25.0	12.5	NIGERIA	13	
53.7	1.1	12.5	SIERRA LEONE	13	
57.5	3.8	14.0	GHANA	9	
57.8	0.3	22.0	BOTSWANA	0	9
59.3	1.5	22.0	BURUNDI	0	
70.2	10.9	22.0	ETHIOPIA	0	
70.4	0.2	22.0	GABON	0	
70.6	0.2	22.0	GAMBIA	0	
72.3	1.7	22.0	GUINEA	0	
74.2	1.9	22.0	IVORY COAST	0	
74.6	0.4	22.0	LESOTHO	0	
76.5	1.9	22.0	MALAWI	0	
77.0	0.5	22.0	MAURITANIA	0	
78.7	1.7	22.0	NIGER	0	
80.2	1.5	22.0	RWANDA	0	
81.9	1.7	22.0	SENEGAL	0	
87.6	5.7	22.0	TANZANIA	0	
91.8	4.2	22.0	UGANDA	0	
94.0	2.2	30.0	MALI	-8	
98.8	4.8	31.0	KENYA	-31	10
100.0	1.2	32.0	DAHOMEY	-50	

SOURCE: *UN Statistical Yearbook 1968.*

TABLE 6.5   Telephones per 10,000 Population, 1967

```
RANGE =            110.00
MEAN =              32.00
STANDARD DEVIATION =            27.44
```

POPULATION PERCENT CUM.	COUNTRY	RANK	COUNTRY NAME	VALUE	RANGE DECILE
1.8	1.8	1.0	ZAMBIA	114	1
2.2	0.4	2.0	CONGO (BRA)	103	2
2.4	0.2	3.0	GABON	86	3
4.1	1.7	4.0	SENEGAL	67	5
8.9	4.8	5.0	KENYA	61	
10.8	1.9	6.0	IVORY COAST	59	6
11.1	0.3	7.0	BOTSWANA	50	
14.9	3.8	8.0	GHANA	42	7
15.1	0.2	9.0	GAMBIA	38	
19.3	4.2	10.0	UGANDA	31	8
19.8	0.5	11.5	LIBERIA	30	
26.5	6.7	11.5	SUDAN	30	
27.6	1.1	13.0	SIERRA LEONE	28	
28.1	0.5	14.0	MAURITANIA	25	9
30.0	1.9	15.5	MALAWI	23	
35.7	5.7	15.5	TANZANIA	23	
36.1	0.4	17.0	LESOTHO	20	
36.8	0.7	18.5	CAR	19	
38.0	1.2	18.5	DAHOMEY	19	
39.7	1.7	20.5	GUINEA	17	
40.9	1.2	20.5	SOMALIA	17	
43.1	2.2	22.5	MALI	16	
43.9	0.8	22.5	TOGO	16	
54.8	10.9	24.0	ETHIOPIA	15	10
63.9	9.1	25.5	ZAIRE	14	
88.9	25.0	25.5	NIGERIA	14	
90.5	1.6	27.0	CHAD	11	
92.0	1.5	28.5	BURUNDI	9	
94.5	2.5	28.5	CAMEROON	9	
96.2	1.7	30.0	NIGER	8	
98.5	2.3	31.0	UPPER VOLTA	6	
100.0	1.5	32.0	RWANDA	4	

sources: *UN Statistical Yearbook 1969. Gambia, Mauritania: Statesman's Yearbook 1968–69.*

TABLE 6.6   Percent Change in the Number of Telephones per Capita, 1963–1967

```
RANGE =            248.00
MEAN =              47.75
STANDARD DEVIATION =            54.44
```

POPULATION PERCENT CUM.	COUNTRY	RANK	COUNTRY NAME	VALUE	RANGE DECILE
0.5	0.5	1.0	MAURITANIA	213	1
7.2	6.7	2.0	SUDAN	173	2
7.6	0.4	3.0	LESOTHO	150	3
7.8	0.2	4.5	GAMBIA	100	5
9.3	1.5	4.5	RWANDA	100	
9.6	0.3	6.0	BOTSWANA	92	
20.5	10.9	7.0	ETHIOPIA	88	6
22.4	1.9	8.0	IVORY COAST	79	
24.6	2.2	9.0	MALI	78	
26.3	1.7	10.0	NIGER	60	7
28.6	2.3	11.0	UPPER VOLTA	50	
28.8	0.2	12.5	GABON	41	
33.0	4.2	12.5	UGANDA	41	
34.6	1.6	14.0	CHAD	38	8
36.4	1.8	15.0	ZAMBIA	37	
37.6	1.2	16.0	DAHOMEY	36	
39.5	1.9	17.5	MALAWI	35	
45.2	5.7	17.5	TANZANIA	35	
46.9	1.7	19.0	GUINEA	31	
71.9	25.0	20.0	NIGERIA	27	
72.6	0.7	21.0	CAR	19	
73.7	1.1	22.0	SIERRA LEONE	17	
74.1	0.4	23.0	CONGO (BRA)	16	
75.6	1.5	25.0	BURUNDI	13	9
78.1	2.5	25.0	CAMEROON	13	
82.9	4.8	25.0	KENYA	13	
83.4	0.5	27.0	LIBERIA	11	
87.2	3.8	28.0	GHANA	0	
88.0	0.8	29.0	TOGO	-6	
89.7	1.7	30.0	SENEGAL	-7	
98.8	9.1	31.0	ZAIRE	-30	10
100.0	1.2	32.0	SOMALIA	-35	

source: *UN Statistical Yearbook 1969. Gambia, Mauritania: Statesman's Yearbook 1968–69.*

TABLE 6.7 Number of Movie Houses, ca. 1966

Definition: Includes both 16 mm and 35 mm cinemas.

```
RANGE =           97.00
MEAN =            22.41
STANDARD DEVIATION =        24.94
```

POPULATION PERCENT		RANK	COUNTRY NAME	VALUE	RANGE DECILE
CUM.	COUNTRY				
3.8	3.8	1.0	GHANA	99	1
8.6	4.8	2.0	KENYA	84	2
10.3	1.7	3.0	SENEGAL	77	3
11.5	1.2	4.0	SOMALIA	62	4
13.4	1.9	5.5	IVORY COAST	48	6
19.1	5.7	6.0	TANZANIA	41	
30.0	10.9	7.0	ETHIOPIA	29	8
55.0	25.0	8.0	NIGERIA	27	
64.1	9.1	9.0	ZAIRE	25	
66.6	2.5	10.5	CAMEROON	23	
73.3	6.7	10.5	SUDAN	23	
77.5	4.2	12.0	UGANDA	21	9
79.7	2.2	13.5	MALI	17	
81.5	1.8	13.5	ZAMBIA	17	
83.2	1.7	15.0	GUINEA	16	
83.6	0.4	16.0	CONGO (BRA)	12	
84.1	0.5	17.5	LIBERIA	10	10
85.2	1.1	17.5	SIERRA LEONE	10	
86.8	1.6	19.5	CHAD	8	
88.3	1.5	19.5	RWANDA	8	
88.6	0.3	23.5	BOTSWANA	7	
90.1	1.5	23.5	BURUNDI	7	
90.8	0.7	23.5	CAR	7	
91.0	0.2	23.5	GAMBIA	7	
92.9	1.9	23.5	MALAWI	7	
93.4	0.5	23.5	MAURITANIA	7	
95.7	2.3	27.0	UPPER VOLTA	5	
96.9	1.2	29.0	DAHOMEY	3	
97.1	0.2	29.0	GABON	3	
97.5	0.4	29.0	LESOTHO	3	
99.2	1.7	31.5	NIGER	2	
100.0	0.8	31.5	TOGO	2	

SOURCE: *UN Statistical Yearbook 1967.*

TABLE 6.8 Miles of Improved Roads per 1,000 Square Miles of Surface Area, 1967

```
RANGE =          238.00
MEAN =            54.78
STANDARD DEVIATION =         52.60
```

POPULATION PERCENT		RANK	COUNTRY NAME	VALUE	RANGE DECILE
CUM.	COUNTRY				
1.5	1.5	1.0	BURUNDI	239	1
2.6	1.1	2.0	SIERRA LEONE	160	4
27.6	25.0	3.0	NIGERIA	126	5
31.8	4.2	4.0	UGANDA	124	
40.9	9.1	5.5	ZAIRE	100	6
44.7	3.8	5.5	GHANA	100	
46.6	1.9	7.0	MALAWI	97	
48.1	1.5	8.0	RWANDA	90	7
48.3	0.2	9.0	GAMBIA	76	
49.5	1.2	10.0	DAHOMEY	67	8
51.4	1.9	11.0	IVORY COAST	65	
51.8	0.4	12.0	LESOTHO	54	
52.2	0.4	13.0	CONGO (BRA)	51	
53.0	0.8	14.0	TOGO	49	
57.8	4.8	15.0	KENYA	47	9
63.5	5.7	16.5	TANZANIA	35	
65.8	2.3	16.5	UPPER VOLTA	35	
66.3	0.5	18.0	LIBERIA	33	
68.0	1.7	19.5	GUINEA	32	
69.8	1.8	19.5	ZAMBIA	32	
70.0	0.2	21.5	GABON	28	
71.7	1.7	21.5	SENEGAL	28	
72.0	0.3	23.5	BOTSWANA	22	10
74.5	2.5	23.5	CAMEROON	22	
75.2	0.7	25.0	CAR	13	
86.1	10.9	26.0	ETHIOPIA	9	
88.3	2.2	27.0	MALI	8	
90.0	1.7	28.0	NIGER	4	
90.5	0.5	30.0	MAURITANIA	2	
91.7	1.2	30.0	SOMALIA	2	
98.4	6.7	30.0	SUDAN	2	
100.0	1.6	32.0	CHAD	1	

SOURCE: *AID Economic Data Book.*

TABLE 6.9 Commercial Vehicles per 100,000 Population and Number of Commercial Vehicles, 1966

RANGE = 776.00
MEAN = 249.06
STANDARD DEVIATION = 192.46

POPULATION PERCENT		RANK	COUNTRY NAME	VALUE	RANGE DECILE	TOTAL
CUM.	COUNTRY					
1.9	1.9	1.0	IVORY COAST	800	1	323
2.4	0.5	2.0	LIBERIA	625	3	68
2.8	0.4	3.0	CONGO (BRA)	556	4	47
3.0	0.2	4.0	GAMBIA	536		18
4.7	1.7	5.0	SENEGAL	526		188
4.9	0.2	6.0	GABON	448	5	21
7.4	2.5	7.0	CAMEROON	400	6	218
9.2	1.8	8.0	ZAMBIA	390		149
9.5	0.3	9.0	BOTSWANA	346		20
10.6	1.1	10.0	SIERRA LEONE	324	7	78
11.1	0.5	11.0	MAURITANIA	251	8	27
12.3	1.2	12.0	SOMALIA	240		63
16.1	3.8	13.0	GHANA	235		186
17.8	1.7	14.0	GUINEA	230		83
19.0	1.2	15.0	DAHOMEY	206		50
24.7	5.7	16.0	TANZANIA	200		236
25.4	0.7	17.0	CAR	183		26
34.5	9.1	18.0	ZAIRE	180		289
36.4	1.9	19.0	MALAWI	170	9	70
38.0	1.6	20.0	CHAD	160		54
42.8	4.8	21.0	KENYA	146		141
44.5	1.7	22.5	NIGER	128		44
51.2	6.7	22.5	SUDAN	128		178
53.4	2.2	24.0	MALI	119		55
55.7	2.3	25.0	UPPER VOLTA	103		51
59.9	4.2	26.0	UGANDA	77	10	60
84.9	25.0	27.0	NIGERIA	65		387
85.3	0.4	28.0	LESOTHO	58		5
86.8	1.5	29.0	BURUNDI	46		15
97.7	10.9	30.0	ETHIOPIA	39		89
99.2	1.5	31.0	RWANDA	31		10
100.0	0.8	32.0	TOGO	24		4

SOURCE: *UN Statistical Yearbook 1967.*

TABLE 6.10 Percent Change in Commercial Vehicles per 100,000 Population, 1958 to 1966

RANGE = 207.00
MEAN = 46.19
STANDARD DEVIATION = 52.87

POPULATION PERCENT		RANK	COUNTRY NAME	VALUE	RANGE DECILE
CUM.	COUNTRY				
1.9	1.9	1.0	IVORY COAST	173	1
4.4	2.5	2.0	CAMEROON	150	2
4.9	0.5	3.0	LIBERIA	146	
5.1	0.2	4.0	GAMBIA	122	3
6.2	1.1	5.0	SIERRA LEONE	120	
11.9	5.7	6.0	TANZANIA	108	4
13.1	1.2	7.0	DAHOMEY	104	
38.1	25.0	8.0	NIGERIA	87	5
38.6	0.5	9.0	MAURITANIA	68	6
40.1	1.5	10.0	BURUNDI	64	
41.3	1.2	11.0	SOMALIA	58	
41.6	0.3	12.0	BOTSWANA	57	
43.3	1.7	13.0	NIGER	44	7
44.9	1.6	14.0	CHAD	40	
47.2	2.3	15.0	UPPER VOLTA	37	
49.1	1.9	16.0	MALAWI	36	
51.3	2.2	17.0	MALI	30	
53.0	1.7	18.0	SENEGAL	18	8
53.4	0.4	19.0	CONGO (BRA)	13	
54.9	1.5	20.0	RWANDA	10	
61.6	6.7	21.5	SUDAN	9	
62.4	0.8	21.5	TOGO	9	
63.1	0.7	23.0	CAR	8	
72.2	9.1	24.5	ZAIRE	5	9
74.0	1.8	24.5	ZAMBIA	5	
78.8	4.8	26.0	KENYA	4	
89.7	10.9	28.0	ETHIOPIA	0	
93.5	3.8	28.0	GHANA	0	
93.9	0.4	28.0	LESOTHO	0	
98.1	4.2	30.0	UGANDA	-1	
99.8	1.7	31.0	GUINEA	-12	
100.0	0.2	32.0	GABON	-34	

SOURCE: *UN Statistical Yearbook 1967.*

TABLE 6.11 Passenger Cars per 10,000 Population and Number of Passenger Cars, 1966

```
RANGE     =     120.00
MEAN      =      37.91
STANDARD DEVIATION =        33.28
```

POPULATION PERCENT			COUNTRY		RANGE	
CUM.	COUNTRY	RANK	NAME	VALUE	DECILE	TOTAL
0.2	0.2	1.0	GABON	120	1	57
2.0	1.8	2.0	ZAMBIA	110		421
3.9	1.9	3.0	IVORY COAST	100	2	410
4.3	0.4	4.0	CONGO (BRA)	88	3	74
9.1	4.8	5.5	KENYA	80	4	750
10.8	1.7	5.5	SENEGAL	80		298
11.3	0.5	7.0	LIBERIA	70	5	75
11.5	0.2	8.5	GAMBIA	60	6	20
12.6	1.1	8.5	SIERRA LEONE	60		135
12.9	0.3	11.5	BOTSWANA	40	7	23
16.7	3.8	11.5	GHANA	40		303
18.4	1.7	11.5	GUINEA	40		140
22.6	4.2	11.5	UGANDA	40		312
25.1	2.5	14.0	CAMEROON	35	8	187
30.8	5.7	15.0	TANZANIA	30		360
31.5	0.7	16.0	CAR	25		36
32.7	1.2	17.0	DAHOMEY	24	9	59
41.8	9.1	18.0	ZAIRE	23		369
43.7	1.9	20.0	MALAWI	20		88
44.9	1.2	20.0	SOMALIA	20		50
51.6	6.7	20.0	SUDAN	20		260
62.5	10.9	22.0	ETHIOPIA	12	10	267
64.1	1.6	24.5	CHAD	10		33
64.6	0.5	24.5	MAURITANIA	10		16
66.8	2.2	24.5	MALI	10		54
91.8	25.0	24.5	NIGERIA	10		643
94.1	2.3	27.0	UPPER VOLTA	9		45
95.8	1.7	28.5	NIGER	8		27
97.3	1.5	28.5	RWANDA	8		28
98.8	1.5	30.0	BURUNDI	6		22
99.6	0.8	31.0	TOGO	5		8
100.0	0.4	32.0	LESOTHO	0		0

SOURCE: *UN Statistical Yearbook 1967.*

TABLE 6.12 Number of Miles of Railroad Track per 100,000 Square Miles Area, ca. 1965

```
RANGE     =     1318.00
MEAN      =      386.00
STANDARD DEVIATION =        380.32
```

POPULATION PERCENT			COUNTRY		RANGE
CUM.	COUNTRY	RANK	NAME	VALUE	DECILE
1.1	1.1	1.0	SIERRA LEONE	1318	1
1.9	0.8	2.0	TOGO	1241	
3.1	1.2	3.0	DAHOMEY	886	4
5.0	1.9	4.0	MALAWI	854	
9.8	4.8	5.0	KENYA	832	
13.6	3.8	6.0	GHANA	828	
17.8	4.2	7.0	UGANDA	792	
19.5	1.7	8.0	SENEGAL	788	5
44.5	25.0	9.0	NIGERIA	659	
45.0	0.5	10.0	LIBERIA	604	6
46.7	1.7	11.0	GUINEA	521	7
52.4	5.7	12.0	TANZANIA	445	
52.8	0.4	13.0	CONGO (BRA)	373	8
61.9	9.1	14.0	ZAIRE	352	
63.8	1.9	15.0	IVORY COAST	321	
66.1	2.3	16.0	UPPER VOLTA	313	
72.8	6.7	17.0	SUDAN	298	
74.6	1.8	18.0	ZAMBIA	218	9
85.5	10.9	19.0	ETHIOPIA	178	
85.8	0.3	20.5	BOTSWANA	177	
88.3	2.5	20.5	CAMEROON	177	
88.8	0.5	22.0	MAURITANIA	92	10
91.0	2.2	23.0	MALI	85	
92.5	1.5	28.0	BURUNDI	0	
93.2	0.7	28.0	CAR	0	
94.8	1.6	28.0	CHAD	0	
95.0	0.2	28.0	GABON	0	
95.2	0.2	28.0	GAMBIA	0	
95.6	0.4	28.0	LESOTHO	0	
97.3	1.7	28.0	NIGER	0	
98.8	1.5	28.0	RWANDA	0	
100.0	1.2	28.0	SOMALIA	0	

SOURCE: *Africa Report*, 10 (February 1965): back cover.

7. Political Regime Characteristics

This chapter presents data on aspects of the institutionalization of legislatures, executives, and judiciaries in African political systems, and data for some typologies describing African regimes. There is a paucity of systematic, comparable data on these subjects for black African nations, which in turn may reflect the lack of attention paid the subject in today's empirically and methodologically sophisticated comparative political science. Nevertheless, it is important to stimulate interest in the quantitative analysis of political regimes,[1] and we therefore offer some examples of the types of data (interval, ordinal, and nominal scales) that might prove useful in comparing African regimes.

Questions related to the analysis of political institutions are by no means absent in recent political theory, although they receive less emphasis than formerly. At the very least, political institutions are given the commanding status of "black boxes" in flow diagrams indicating the conversion of inputs into outputs by political systems whose basic components are political communities, regimes, and authorities.[2] The theoretical abstractions of functionalism have been used by some theorists to conceptualize political regimes as structural adaptations to the political functions of rule making, rule application, and rule adjudication.[3] This formulation hints at the discussion of the division of governmental power in the more ancient, but perhaps too prosaic language of Montesquieu, and seems to promote very direct, non-abstract and non-quantitative discussions of legislatures, bureaucracies, and legal systems when it is utilized for empirical analysis. The study of constitutional arrangements, once a staple of political science, has not entirely disappeared,[4] and for Africa is manifest most obviously in the sizable literature on federalism.[5] But perhaps the most insistent manifestation of the intellectual heritage of political science is to be seen in the proliferation of regime typologies. The Greek concern with the variants of oligarchy and democracy is paralleled in contemporary theory by typologies of political regimes that stress elitism and consti-

tutionalism,[6] the predominant characteristics of the ruling elite,[7] and multiple patterns of institutional and ideological development.[8]

Rule-Making Institutions

The characteristics of rule-making institutions that may be theoretically important are difficult to specify. The complexity of legislative organization may be related to the constitutional provision for federalism, the number of legislative chambers, and the size of legislative membership. Data on these aspects of African legislatures are given in Table 7.1. The coherence of legislative organization may be related to homogeneity in the background of legislative personnel, to party organization in legislatures, and —some have suggested—to such apparently uninteresting matters as the organization of seating accommodation within legislative chambers. We do not have background information on legislative personnel, but data on party fractionalization in African legislatures are given in Chapter 8. The representativeness of decision-making institutions is an important consideration, and we present, in Table 7.2, data on the representativeness of cabinets in Africa—representativeness being measured in terms of the correspondence between ethnic breakdowns in cabinet membership and in the population at large.

Rule-Application Institutions

The analysis of rule-application institutions properly focuses on aspects of bureaucratic organization, but again there is little guidance as to relevant variables in contemporary comparative theory. The three major theoretical interests in comparative analysis are: economic development, democracy, and modernization. In these terms attention is focused on efficiency and corruption, responsibility, specialization and centralization.[9] The problems of dealing adequately with efficiency, corruption, and responsibility seem to us too great to recommend coding by "experts" on ordinal scales and we believe that the critical evaluations are ultimately those of relevant publics rather than experts.[10] Patterns of bureaucratic institutionalization may, however, be discussed in terms of complexity and coherence. The complexity of bureaucratic organization may be indicated by the data in Table 7.3 on the percentage of the wage earning population employed in the public sector. Such data relate not only to the size and complexity of bureaucratic organization but also to the centralization of decision-making in the society. Coherence may be measured in terms of the data in Table 7.4 on the organization of local governments. This variable indicates the degree to which traditional values and institutions are recognized in bureaucratic organization, and in this way the measure relates to the coherence, centralization, and modernization of rule application. It should, of course, be noted that these data are based only on formal requirements for local government, and may be unrelated to the salience of traditional power and values in local and national decision-making.

Legal Systems

Knowledge of legal systems in Africa is an important element in understanding the operation and development of the social and political systems of the new African nations. Legal structures contribute to the integration of the social system and to the goal-attainment function of the political system. The central tasks of law relate to the solution of social conflicts and the development of conformity to authoritative decisions (rule adjudication).

The potential contribution of legal systems to the integration of the social systems of which they are a part may be conceptualized in terms of: (1) the dualism of the values and rules which structure the legal resolution of conflict; (2) the degree of professionalism and the size of the legal elite; and (3) the institutional controls which the judiciary maintains over the process of legislative decision-making.

A major dimension of variation in African legal systems is that of the coherence or dualism of the values or rules which become embodied in the structural mechanisms for conflict resolution.[11] The three basic sources of legal norms which have been embodied in dualistic or pluralistic African legal systems include: (1) law of European origin, applied in many countries as the dominant legal code during the colonial and post-independence periods; (2) Islamic law; and (3) systems of customary law. Structural adaptations of national legal systems in response to the existence of these multiple systems of law have been grouped into three basic categories. One approach to the development of post-independence legal systems adopted in many of the francophone countries was to abolish the parallel hierarchies of customary or Islamic law in favor of a single legal code based upon adaptations of common law or continental codified law. Another group of nations have maintained customary or Islamic legal structures at the lower levels of the system in the form of criminal and family law courts. In nations fitting this pattern, Islamic and customary law has been subordinated to general law courts at the higher appellate levels of the system. The third group of nations have fully institutionalized the basic dualism in their set of legal norms by establishing a structurally parallel hierarchy of courts for the application of customary or Islamic law. Data on legal dualism or coherence is given in Table 7.5. Again, it should be noted that this variable reflects formal constitutional requirements, and may be a very inadequate measure of the extent of variation in legal norms and practices at the local level in highly pluralistic nations.[12]

Measures of the size and level of professional development in national legal systems are one way of operationalizing the complexity of judicial institutions. Despite the major methodological problems involved in comparing professional qualifications across systems based on English, French, and Islamic law, a gross measure of the number of trained lawyers may be justified in terms of its relevance to elite socialization and the size of manpower pools. Contemporary analysts have stressed the impact of systematic legal education in inculcating a regularized approach to decision-making.[13] The size of the population with legal qualifications may also exceed the number of top level positions within the regime, and thereby contribute to the formation of a systematically trained opposition.

Unfortunately, there is no adequate means of assessing whether the academic requirements for admission to higher education in law are equal, or whether the levels of professional certification are comparable across systems. Furthermore, the basic indicators of the size of the pool of qualified lawyers within a system are extremely time bound. Many African nations have large numbers of law students who, when certified, will double or triple the size of that country's legal profession. For example, in 1962, Senegal is listed as having only 53 lawyers officially admitted to the bar, but it is also listed as having 764 students studying law within the country itself. In 1965, in Cameroon, there were only 15 certified members of the bar, while at the same time there were 328 students preparing for *la capacité en droit*.[14] This situation should be kept in mind when using Table 7.6, Lawyers and Legal Training.

Legal systems contribute to the development of political systems by encouraging conformity to administrative decisions. The extent to which legal systems make such a contribution is a function of the *autonomy* of legal structures as they relate to the legislative and executive structures. Unfortunately most cross-nationally valid measures of the relative level of judicial control over legislative decision-making processes are based upon the coder's interpretation of the national constitution. Without going into the actual decision records of the high courts, it is impossible to determine whether constitutional provisions for judicial review have actually been utilized. As Table 7.7 indicates, the majority of the African nations in our sample have no provision for judicial review of legislation. The analysis of the autonomy of different branches of African political regimes may in any event be less significant than an analysis of the autonomy of the regime as a whole. In these terms, neo-colonial influence may be evaluated from the data on foreign aid and foreign military assistance given in Chapters 10 and 12.

Typologies of African Regimes

The relevance of typological (nominal) categories for the analysis of political regimes is more often assumed than demonstrated, although it seems clear that theoretical concepts summarizing the relationships between different political institutions could be useful. Political scientists have sought to categorize the new African states according to varying criteria. Most have looked to the party system for indications of regime type, but implied scales of totalism and pluralism, or authoritarianism and democracy are common.

One of the earliest typologies is contained in Almond and Coleman's *The Politics of the Developing Areas*, in which observations by James Coleman were made for the period immediately prior to independence in most of Africa. In 1964, Coleman and Rosberg collaborated in establishing a typology which distinguished between two major categories of single party systems: Those which were highly centralized and revolutionary in their programs, in contrast to those which were pluralistic and pragmatic. This typology was developed in response to the fact that many African political systems were becoming single party systems, and yet a diversity of regime styles seemed to exist within them. The typology developed by the sociologist Morris Janowitz, also in 1964, combined two major criteria: The mass/patron party distinction utilized by Thomas Hodgkin in 1960, and an authoritarian/democratic distinction. Finally, David Apter has constructed a typology of four regime types based on pattern variables indicating the consummatory or instrumental character of political values, and the hierarchical or pyramidal character of political structure.

In Tables 7.8 and 7.9, we present data for two typologies constructed recently by Crawford Young.[15] Young has established two approximate time periods for observing and coding the political systems of Africa, and his typologies are based on the characteristics of the political formulas for independence, and the characteristics of the post-independence regime structure. Young's data can be compared with data for other typologies. It is possible on this basis to assess "inter-coder reliability" at the crudest level by comparing different typological codes for similar countries (although for different years), as in Figure 7.1.

Figure 7.1 Comparison of Coding: African Political Systems Typologies

	Almond-Coleman (1960)	Coleman-Rosberg (1964)	Janowitz (1964)	Adelman-Morris (1967)	Young (1970)
1. Ghana	one-party dominant	one-party revolutionary centralizing	authoritarian mass party	highly centralized low democratic low opposition freedom	mass party/ military regime
2. Nigeria	not classified	large-scale federation	democratic competitive	highly democratic high freedom of opposition	competitive party system/ military regime
3. Senegal	one-party dominant	single party pragmatic pluralistic	not coded	highly centralized moderately to low democratic	dominant patron party/ one party state
4. Tanzania	comprehensive nationalist	not coded (Zanzibar-historic oligarchy)	democratic competitive	moderate to high central, moderate to low democratic	mass party/ renewed mass party
5. Guinea	one-party dominant	single party revolutionary/ centralizing	authoritarian mass party	highly centralized low democratic	mass party/ renewed mass party

Data Quality

The data in this chapter should be used with some caution. We have emphasized the problems of conceptual validity in measures based on formal constitutional requirements, and have indicated the sensitivity of these measures to historical time. The reliability of the data is likewise difficult to assess. Using identical sources, which we have specified in the greatest detail possible, we are confident of inter-coder reliability, but the assessment of inter-source reliability has not been systematically undertaken. Though caution is necessary, it is to be hoped that the problems of data quality, and the difficulty of systematically operationalizing concepts related to the study of political regimes will not inhibit theoretical creativity and rigorous empirical analysis in future comparative study of African political systems.

Notes

[1] The word "regime" is used to connote a set of formal political institutions. See Harold D. Lasswell and Abraham Kaplan, *Power and Society* (New Haven, Conn.: Yale University Press, 1960) p. 130. The relevance of formal institutions has been questioned by contemporary political scientists, who have sought to analyze the regularities in behavior characteristics of individuals, groups, elites, and systems, rather than the formal prescriptions for behavior laid down by legal rules in legislatures, bureaucracies, and courts. This emphasis has stimulated the search for empirical descriptions of power structures as opposed to the analysis of formal regime characteristics, but such work has been confined for the most part to the study of community politics; and even in that field comparative analysis has been developed very little. For summaries of this power structure literature, and for affirmations of the need for comparative analysis, see William D. Hawley and Frederick M. Wirt, eds., *The Search for Community Power* (Englewood Cliffs, N.J.: Prentice-Hall, 1968) and Terry Clark, ed., *Community Structure and Decision-Making: Comparative Analysis* (San Francisco: Chandler Publishing Company, 1968). Our purpose in this chapter is not to demonstrate the relevance of formal institutions, but rather to suggest approaches to the measurement of regime characteristics which may provide a means to the comparative assessment of the role of political regimes in the development of other institutions such as political parties or the military, and in the development of economic growth and political order in the society as a whole.

[2] See David Easton, *A Framework for Political Analysis* (Englewood Cliffs, N.J.: Prentice-Hall, 1965), especially Chapters 7 and 8.

[3] This is part of the framework developed in the influential Gabriel A. Almond and James A. Coleman, eds., *The Politics of the Developing Areas* (Princeton, N.J.: Princeton University Press, 1960). The authors were aware of the limitations of their approach to the analysis of

political regimes. "While there is justification for having underplayed the governmental structures in this study, their neglect in the development of the theory of the functions of the polity represents a serious shortcoming in the present analysis. The threefold classification of governmental or output functions into rule-making, rule application, and rule adjudication will not carry us very far in our efforts at precise comparison of the performance of political systems," p. 55. See also the later developments in this work in Gabriel A. Almond and G. Bingham Powell, Jr., *Comparative Politics: A Developmental Approach* (Boston: Little, Brown and Company, 1966), especially Chapter VI.

4 The interest in institutional transfer, and the African adaptation to European constitutional models is well illustrated in David Apter, *Ghana in Transition* (New York: Atheneum, 1963). See also Carl J. Friedrich, "Some Reflections on Constitutionalism for Emergent Political Orders," in *Patterns of African Development*, ed. Herbert Spiro (Englewood Cliffs, N.J.: Prentice-Hall, 1967).

5 Important examples in the recent literature are William H. Riker, *Federalism* (Boston: Little, Brown and Company, 1964) and Obafemi Awolowo, *Thoughts on the Nigerian Constitution* (London: Oxford University Press, 1966) and *The People's Republic* (Ibadan: Oxford University Press, 1968).

6 J. P. Nettl, *Political Mobilization* (New York: Basic Books, 1967).

7 Lasswell distinguishes between patterns of rule based on the distribution of his eight base values, and classifies bureaucracy, aristocracy, ethocracy, democracy, virocracy, plutocracy, technocracy, and ideocracy, Lasswell and Kaplan, *Power and Society*, p. 209.

8 Compare the typology of political democracies, tutelary democracies, modernizing oligarchies, totalitarian oligarchies, and traditional oligarchies in Edward Shils, *Political Development in the New States* (New York: Humanities Press, 1962); the modificaton of Shils in Almond and Coleman, *Politics of the Developing Areas*; the typological pragmatic-pluralist and revolutionary-centralizing polities in James S. Coleman and Carl J. Rosberg, Jr., eds., *Political Parties and National Integration in Tropical Africa* (Berkeley: University of California Press, 1964); the distinctions between authoritarian-personal control, authoritarian-mass parties, democratic-competitive and semi-competitive systems, civil-military coalitions, and military oligarchies in Morris Janowitz, *The Military in the Political Development of New Nations* (Chicago: University of Chicago Press, 1964); and the pure-typical mobilization systems, theocracies, modernizing autocracies, and reconciliation systems described in David Apter, *The Politics of Modernization* (Chicago: The University of Chicago Press, 1965).

9 Compare Irma Adelman and Cynthia Taft Morris, *Society, Politics and Economic Development* (Baltimore, Md.: Johns Hopkins Press, 1967), pp. 76–78; Arthur Banks and Robert Textor, *A Cross-Polity Survey* (Cambridge: Massachusetts Institute of Technology Press, 1964), raw characteristic no. 53, "character of bureaucracy"; and the essays in Joseph La Palombara, ed., *Bureaucracy and Political Development* (Princeton, N.J.: Princeton University Press, 1963).

10 For important developments in the analysis of the relationships between bureaucracy and the mass public see the analysis of survey research in Gabriel Almond and Sidney Verba, *The Civic Culture* (Boston: Little, Brown Company, 1965), and Samuel J. Eldersveld, V. Jagannerdham, and A. P. Barnabas, *The Citizen and the Administrator in a Developing Democracy* (Glenview, Ill.: Scott, Foresman and Company, 1968).

11 See Thomas Lee Roberts, *Judicial Organization and Institutions of Contemporary West Africa: A Profile* (New York: Institute of Public Administration, 1966), for the discussion on which this paragraph is based.

12 "Any human society . . . does not possess a single consistent legal system, but as many such systems as there are functioning subgroups. Conversely, every functioning subgroup of a society regulates the relations of its members by its own legal system, which is of necessity different, at least in some respects, from that of the other groups." Leopold Pospisil, "Legal Levels and Multiplicity of Legal Systems in Human Societies," *Journal of Conflict Resolution*, 11 (March 1967): 3.

13 Peter C. Lloyd, ed., *The New Elites of Tropical Africa* (New York: Oxford University Press, 1966), p. 8.

14 UNESCO, *The Development of Higher Education in Africa* (New York, 1962), p. 230.

15 Crawford Young, "Political Systems Development," in *The African Experience*, eds. John N. Paden and Edward Soja (Evanston, Ill.: Northwestern University Press, 1970).

TABLE 7.1 Size of the Legislature

Definition: The number of legislators in the central government elected by universal suffrage in 1968, or prior to the first coup d'etat in countries where coups have occurred.

```
RANGE =            281.00
MEAN =              87.53
STANDARD DEVIATION =         60.47
```

POPULATION PERCENT		RANK	COUNTRY NAME	VALUE	RANGE DECILE
CUM.	COUNTRY				
25.0	25.0	1.0	NIGERIA	312	1
35.9	10.9	2.0	ETHIOPIA	250	3
42.6	6.7	3.0	SUDAN	173	5
47.4	4.8	4.0	KENYA	158	6
56.5	9.1	5.0	ZAIRE	137	7
57.7	1.2	6.0	SOMALIA	123	
63.4	5.7	7.0	TANZANIA	107	8
67.2	3.8	8.0	GHANA	104	
69.1	1.9	9.0	IVORY COAST	85	9
73.3	4.2	10.0	UGANDA	82	
75.5	2.2	11.0	MALI	80	
77.1	1.6	13.0	CHAD	75	
78.8	1.7	13.0	GUINEA	75	
80.6	1.8	13.0	ZAMBIA	75	
81.1	0.5	15.0	LIBERIA	70	
81.3	0.2	16.0	GABON	67	
82.8	1.5	17.0	BURUNDI	65	
83.9	1.1	18.0	SIERRA LEONE	62	
84.3	0.4	19.0	CONGO (BRA)	61	
85.5	1.2	21.5	DAHOMEY	60	
85.9	0.4	21.5	LESOTHO	60	
87.6	1.7	21.5	NIGER	60	
89.3	1.7	21.5	SENEGAL	60	
90.1	0.8	24.0	TOGO	56	10
92.6	2.5	26.5	CAMEROON	50	
93.3	0.7	26.5	CAR	50	
95.2	1.9	26.5	MALAWI	50	
97.5	2.3	26.5	UPPER VOLTA	50	
99.0	1.5	29.0	RWANDA	47	
99.5	0.5	30.0	MAURITANIA	34	
99.7	0.2	31.0	GAMBIA	32	
100.0	0.3	32.0	BOTSWANA	31	

SOURCES: *Statesman's Yearbook, 1968–1969. Burundi, CAR, Chad, Congo (Brazzaville), Zaire (Congo K.), Dahomey, Gabon, Ghana, Kenya, Mali, Nigeria, Sierra Leone, Togo, Uganda, Upper Volta*: Helen Kitchen, ed., *A Handbook of African Affairs* (New York: Praeger, 1964). *Sudan*: U.S. Department of the Army, *Area Handbook for the Sudan*, Pamphlet No. 550-27 (Washington, D.C.: Government Printing Office, 1964). *Cameroon, Zaire (Congo K.), Ethiopia, Nigeria, Tanzania, Uganda*: States which have had federal or quasi-federal constitutions during the period 1957 to 1967. *Botswana, Zaire (Congo K.), Ethiopia, Kenya, Lesotho, Liberia, Nigeria*: Countries which have bicameral legislatures. All others have unicameral legislatures.

TABLE 7.2 Cabinet Ethnic Representativeness at Independence

Definition: This index is a *C* coefficient,[1] measuring the extent to which ethnic proportions in cabinet membership *deviate* from proportions "expected" from the national ethnic population distributions. A high value on this index means the cabinet is unrepresentative of the ethnic composition of the population.

[1] The coefficient was calculated according to this formula:

$$C = \sqrt{\frac{x^2}{N + x^2}}; \quad x^2 = \sum_{i=1}^{N} \frac{(O_i - E_i)^2}{E_i}$$

Where N= the number of ethnic groups in a national population (see Part II)
O_i= the proportion of the cabinet membership belonging to the ith ethnic group
E_i= the proportion of the national population belonging to the ith ethnic group

```
RANGE =             0.84
MEAN =              0.23
STANDARD DEVIATION =          0.27
```

POPULATION PERCENT		RANK	COUNTRY NAME	VALUE	RANGE DECILE
CUM.	COUNTRY				
0.5	0.5	1.0	LIBERIA	0.84	1
2.1	1.6	2.0	CHAD	0.79	
5.9	3.8	3.0	GHANA	0.77	
6.6	0.7	4.0	CAR	0.72	2
9.1	2.5	5.0	CAMEROON	0.58	4
9.3	0.2	6.0	GAMBIA	0.55	
10.4	1.1	7.0	SIERRA LEONE	0.54	
10.6	0.2	8.0	GABON	0.51	
12.1	1.5	9.0	BURUNDI	0.37	6
17.8	5.7	10.0	TANZANIA	0.25	7
19.7	1.9	11.0	IVORY COAST	0.17	8
30.6	10.9	12.0	ETHIOPIA	0.17	9
32.3	1.7	13.0	NIGER	0.16	
34.1	1.8	14.0	ZAMBIA	0.11	
35.6	1.5	15.0	RWANDA	0.09	
39.8	4.2	16.0	UGANDA	0.08	
40.2	0.4	17.0	CONGO (BRA)	0.08	10
42.1	1.9	18.0	MALAWI	0.08	
48.8	6.7	19.0	SUDAN	0.08	
51.0	2.2	20.0	MALI	0.08	
51.8	0.8	21.0	TOGO	0.06	
53.5	1.7	22.0	SENEGAL	0.06	
62.6	9.1	23.0	ZAIRE	0.05	
63.1	0.5	24.0	MAURITANIA	0.05	
67.9	4.8	25.0	KENYA	0.05	
92.9	25.0	26.5	NIGERIA	0.03	
95.2	2.3	26.5	UPPER VOLTA	0.03	
96.9	1.7	28.0	GUINEA	0.03	
98.1	1.2	29.0	DAHOMEY	0.03	
99.3	1.2	30.0	SOMALIA	0.03	
99.6	0.3	31.0	BOTSWANA	0.00	
100.0	0.4	32.0	LESOTHO	0.0	

SOURCE: The sources and coding of ethnic units in national populations are detailed by country in Part II. The ethnicity of cabinet members was obtained from identifications made by country experts, nationals of particular countries, and various published reference works. Detailed information can be obtained by direct inquiry to the authors of this Handbook.

**TABLE 7.3 Percentage of the Wage and Salary Earners
Employed in the Public Sector, ca. 1965**

Definition: Definitions of wage and salary earners, and of the
"public sector" may vary from country to country. The measure
given here is reported directly from government economic
statistics, and we have no means of comparing their operationalizations.

```
RANGE =           54.00
MEAN =            30.79
STANDARD DEVIATION =            13.72
```

POPULATION PERCENT		RANK	COUNTRY NAME	VALUE	RANGE DECILE
CUM.	COUNTRY				
1.2	1.2	1.0	SOMALIA	60	1
7.9	6.7	2.0	SUDAN	57	
9.0	1.1	3.0	SIERRA LEONE	54	2
9.8	0.8	4.0	TOGO	48	3
11.0	1.2	5.0	DAHOMEY	46	
11.3	0.3	6.0	BOTSWANA	43	4
36.3	25.0	7.0	NIGERIA	41	
36.8	0.5	8.0	MAURITANIA	36	5
40.6	3.8	10.0	GHANA	35	
41.0	0.4	10.0	LESOTHO	35	
42.7	1.7	10.0	SENEGAL	35	
45.0	2.3	12.0	UPPER VOLTA	33	
50.7	5.7	13.0	TANZANIA	32	6
54.9	4.2	14.0	UGANDA	31	
56.5	1.6	15.5	CHAD	30	
58.7	2.2	15.5	MALI	30	
63.5	4.8	17.5	KENYA	29	
65.2	1.7	17.5	NIGER	29	
67.7	2.5	19.0	CAMEROON	28	
68.1	0.4	20.5	CONGO (BRA)	23	7
68.3	0.2	20.5	GABON	23	
69.0	0.7	22.0	CAR	21	8
70.9	1.9	23.0	MALAWI	19	
72.7	1.8	24.0	ZAMBIA	18	
74.4	1.7	25.0	GUINEA	16	9
74.9	0.5	26.0	LIBERIA	15	
76.8	1.9	27.0	IVORY COAST	14	
78.3	1.5	28.0	BURUNDI	6	10
79.8	1.5	29.0	RWANDA	6	

```
DATA NOT AVAILABLE FOR THE FOLLOWING COUNTRIES

ZAIRE          ETHIOPIA      GAMBIA
```

SOURCES: *Directory of Labor Organizations, Africa*, Vols. I and II
(Washington; D.C.: United States Department of Labor, May 1966).
Burundi, Rwanda, Somali: Estimate based on the figures given in
Directory of Labor Organizations; *Sudan*: Estimate based on the figures
given in *Directory of Labor Organizations*, and in *AID Economic Data
Handbook*; *Gabon, Liberia*: Unpublished data collected by George
Martens, Northwestern University; *Botswana*: In Basutoland in
1956 "the public sector, particularly the government, is the largest
employer," *Directory of Labor Organizations; Ghana, Tanzania*: Gio-
vanni Arrighi, "International Corporations, Labor Aristocracies
and Economic Development in Tropical Africa," in *Imperialism and
Underdevelopment*, ed. Robert I. Rhodes (New York: Monthly
Review Press, 1970), p. 232.

TABLE 7.4 Organization of Local Government Administration

Definition: Local government is here defined as the set of formally recognized decision-makers having specified competences (granted by the central government) within the administrative unit next in size to the national unit itself. In federal systems, local government is subordinate to state or regional governments, and for all nations this definition excludes municipalities as local government agencies. The data for this variable is applicable to 1968, or to the period preceding a coup d'etat in countries which had coups, and it is coded as follows:

1. Administrative officials salaried and appointed by the national government, but no provision for representative institutions at the local level.
2. Administrative officials salaried and appointed by the national government with local councils having elected membership.
3. Administrative officials salaried and appointed by the national government with local councils composed of some mixture of traditional and elected membership.

```
RANGE          =        2.00
MEAN           =        1.80
STANDARD DEVIATION =            0.75
```

POPULATION PERCENT CUM.	COUNTRY	RANK	COUNTRY NAME	VALUE	RANGE DECILE
0.3	0.3	3.5	BOTSWANA	3	1
0.5	0.2	3.5	GAMBIA	3	
25.5	25.0	3.5	NIGERIA	3	
26.6	1.1	3.5	SIERRA LEONE	3	
33.3	6.7	3.5	SUDAN	3	
35.1	1.8	3.5	ZAMBIA	3	
35.5	0.4	12.5	CONGO (BRA)	2	5
36.7	1.2	12.5	DAHOMEY	2	
38.4	1.7	12.5	GUINEA	2	
40.3	1.9	12.5	IVORY COAST	2	
45.1	4.8	12.5	KENYA	2	
47.0	1.9	12.5	MALAWI	2	
48.7	1.7	12.5	NIGER	2	
50.4	1.7	12.5	SENEGAL	2	
51.6	1.2	12.5	SOMALIA	2	
52.4	0.8	12.5	TOGO	2	
56.6	4.2	12.5	UGANDA	2	
58.9	2.3	12.5	UPPER VOLTA	2	
61.4	2.5	19.0	CAMEROON	1	10
62.1	0.7	20.0	CAR	1	
63.7	1.6	26.5	CHAD	1	
72.8	9.1	26.5	ZAIRE	1	
83.7	10.9	26.5	ETHIOPIA	1	
83.9	0.2	26.5	GABON	1	
87.7	3.8	26.5	GHANA	1	
88.1	0.4	26.5	LESOTHO	1	
88.6	0.5	26.5	LIBERIA	1	
89.1	0.5	26.5	MAURITANIA	1	
91.3	2.2	26.5	MALI	1	
97.0	5.7	26.5	TANZANIA	1	

```
DATA NOT AVAILABLE FOR THE FOLLOWING COUNTRIES

BURUNDI     RWANDA
```

sources: Gwendolen M. Carter, ed., *National Unity and Regionalism in Eight African States* (Ithaca, N.Y.: Cornell University Press, 1966). *Botswana: Bechuanaland: Report for the Year 1965* (London: Her Majesty's Stationery Office, 1966); *Gambia*: Harry A. Gailey, *A History of the Gambia* (New York: Praeger, 1965); *Sierra Leone*: Martin Kilson, *Political Change in a West African State* (Cambridge, Mass.: Harvard University Press, 1966); *Sudan*: U.S. Department of the Army, *Handbook for the Sudan*, 1964); *Zambia*: *Zambia* (London: British Information Services, 1964); *Dahomey, Senegal, Mauritania*: M. J. Campbell, T. G. Brierly, and L. F. Blitz, *The Structure of Local Government in West Africa* (The Hague, Netherlands: Martinus Nijhoff, 1965); *Ghana, Guinea, Ivory Coast*: Aristide R. Zolberg, *Creating Political Order* (Chicago, Ill.: Rand McNally, 1966); *Kenya*: S. Nyagah, *The Politicalization of Administration in East Africa*, Kenya Institute of Administra-tion, Occasional Paper No. 1 (Lower Kabek: 1968); *Malawi*: *Malawi* (London: British Information Service, April, 1964); *Somalia*: I. M. Lewis, *The Modern History of Somaliland* (New York: Praeger, 1965); *Cameroon*: Information from unpublished field research by Gene Larimore; *Zaire (Congo K.)*: Crawford Young, *Politics in the Congo* (Princeton, N.J.: Princeton University Press, 1965), *Lesotho*: *Statesman's Yearbook, 1968-1969*; *Liberia*: Gwendolen Carter, ed., *African One-Party States* (Ithaca, N.Y.: Cornell University Press, 1962); *Mali*: James S. Coleman and Carl G. Rosberg, Jr., eds., *Political Parties and National Integration in Tropical Africa* (Berkeley: University of California Press, 1966); *Tanzania*: Henry Bienen, *Tanzania: Party Transformation and Economic Development* (Princeton, N.J.: Princeton University Press, 1967).

**TABLE 7.5 Structural Dualism of the National
Legal System**

Definition: The structural heterogeneity of the national legal system is operationalized in terms of the existence of parallel hierarchies of Islamic or customary law. The three prototypes of legal systems include:

1. Unitary systems—i.e. national legal systems in which a separate and parallel hierarchy of courts for the administrators of Islamic or customary law is not present.

2. Unitary systems of higher courts with differentiated lower courts—i.e. nations maintaining Islamic and/or customary courts at lower levels, and integrating them with general law courts at the high court or appellate level.

3. Separate parallel hierarchy—i.e. national legal systems maintaining a separate hierarchy of courts for the application of Islamic or customary law.

```
RANGE  =          2.00
MEAN  =           1.84
STANDARD DEVIATION  =        0.72
```

POPULATION PERCENT			COUNTRY		RANGE
CUM.	COUNTRY	RANK	NAME	VALUE	DECILE
0.5	0.5	3.5	LIBERIA	3	1
1.0	0.5	3.5	MAURITANIA	3	
2.2	1.2	3.5	SOMALIA	3	
8.9	6.7	3.5	SUDAN	3	
9.7	0.8	3.5	TOGO	3	
12.0	2.3	3.5	UPPER VOLTA	3	
12.3	0.3	13.5	BOTSWANA	2	5
13.8	1.5	13.5	BURUNDI	2	
16.3	2.5	13.5	CAMEROON	2	
17.9	1.6	13.5	CHAD	2	
18.3	0.4	13.5	CONGO (BRA)	2	
27.4	9.1	13.5	ZAIRE	2	
27.6	0.2	13.5	GAMBIA	2	
31.4	3.8	13.5	GHANA	2	
36.2	4.8	13.5	KENYA	2	
36.6	0.4	13.5	LESOTHO	2	
38.5	1.9	13.5	MALAWI	2	
63.5	25.0	13.5	NIGERIA	2	
64.6	1.1	13.5	SIERRA LEONE	2	
66.4	1.8	13.5	ZAMBIA	2	
67.1	0.7	21.0	CAR	1	10
68.3	1.2	27.0	DAHOMEY	1	
79.2	10.9	27.0	ETHIOPIA	1	
79.4	0.2	27.0	GABON	1	
81.1	1.7	27.0	GUINEA	1	
83.0	1.9	27.0	IVORY COAST	1	
85.2	2.2	27.0	MALI	1	
86.9	1.7	27.0	NIGER	1	
88.6	1.7	27.0	SENEGAL	1	
94.3	5.7	27.0	TANZANIA	1	
98.5	4.2	27.0	UGANDA	1	

DATA NOT AVAILABLE FOR THE FOLLOWING COUNTRIES

RWANDA

sources: Thomas Lee Roberts, *Judicial Organization and Institutions of Contemporary West Africa: A Profile* (New York: Institute of Public Administration, 1966). *Burundi, Cameroon, Congo (Brazzaville), Zaire (Congo K.), Dahomey, Ethiopia, Gabon, Malawi, Mauritania, Somalia, Sudan, Togo: Law and the Judicial Systems of Nations* (Washington, D.C.: World Peace through Law Fund, 1965); *Botswana: Bechuanaland 1965*; *CAR, Chad*: Amos Peaslee, *Constitutions of Nations* (New York: Justice House, 1965); *Gambia*: Gailey, *History of the Gambia*; *Kenya: Statesman's Yearbook 1967–1968*; *Lesotho*: J. E. Spence, *Lesotho: The Problems of Independence* (London: Oxford University Press, 1968); *Guinea*: L. G. Cowan, "Guinea" in *African One-Party States*, ed. Carter; *Tanzania*: Personal communication, Professor Roland Young, Northwestern University; *Uganda*: Donald Rothchild and Michael Rogan, "Uganda" in *National Unity and Regionalism in Eight African States*, ed. Carter.

TABLE 7.6 Number of Practicing Lawyers and Form of Legal Training Requirement, ca. 1965

Definition: Number of lawyers are those officially admitted to the bar as qualified members of a regulated legal profession. Unofficial advisors and counsellors on legal matters are not included. The type of training required to qualify as an accredited, full member of the national legal profession are coded as follows:
0. Data unavailable.
1. Those requiring apprenticeship only.
2. Those having only requirements for formal schooling.
3. Those requiring both formal schooling and apprenticeship.
"Formal schooling" is defined as a specified number of years in a law school, and "apprenticeship" is defined as a specified number of years in a local law office or other form of practical local experience.

```
RANGE     =      1965.00
MEAN      =       226.71
STANDARD DEVIATION =          486.41
```

POPULATION PERCENT CUM.	COUNTRY	RANK	COUNTRY NAME	VALUE	RANGE DECILE	TOTAL
10.9	10.9	1.0	ETHIOPIA	1967	1	3
35.9	25.0	2.0	NIGERIA	1600	2	3
39.7	3.8	3.0	GHANA	400	8	3
44.5	4.8	4.0	KENYA	380	9	1
45.0	0.5	5.0	LIBERIA	315		0
51.7	6.7	6.0	SUDAN	176	10	2
57.4	5.7	7.0	TANZANIA	173		3
61.6	4.2	8.0	UGANDA	75		3
63.5	1.9	9.5	MALAWI	53		2
65.2	1.7	9.5	SENEGAL	53		3
65.6	0.4	11.0	CONGO (BRA)	40		0
66.7	1.1	12.0	SIERRA LEONE	38		3
68.2	1.5	14.0	BURUNDI	30		0
77.3	9.1	14.0	ZAIRE	30		2
79.2	1.9	14.0	IVORY COAST	30		3
80.8	1.6	16.0	CHAD	27		0
83.3	2.5	17.0	CAMEROON	15		2
84.8	1.5	18.0	RWANDA	8		0
86.0	1.2	19.0	DAHOMEY	7		3
88.2	2.2	20.5	MALI	6		0
89.0	0.8	20.5	TOGO	6		0
89.2	0.2	22.5	GABON	5		3
90.9	1.7	22.5	GUINEA	5		0
93.2	2.3	24.0	UPPER VOLTA	2		0

DATA NOT AVAILABLE FOR THE FOLLOWING COUNTRIES

BOTSWANA	CAR	GAMBIA	LESOTHO
MAURITANIA	NIGER	SOMALIA	ZAMBIA

sources: *Law and the Judicial Systems of Nations* (Washington, D.C.: World Peace through Law Fund, 1965). *Ghana, Ivory Coast, Mali, Senegal, Sierra Leone, Togo, Upper Volta*: Thomas Lee Roberts, *Judicial Organization and Institutions of Contemporary West Africa: A Profile* (New York: Institute of Public Administration, 1966): *Guinea*: U.S. Department of the Army, *Area Handbook for Guinea* (Washington, D.C.: Government Printing Office, 1961).

TABLE 7.7 The Presence of Institutional Provisions for Judicial Review of Legislation

Definition: Structural approaches to judicial review of legislation in the constitution are coded:
1. Systems in which judicial review of legislation exists in full.
2. Systems in which partial judicial review exists either because it applies to legislation or because the review process can only be started by certain bodies.
3. Systems in which there is no constitutional provision for judicial review of legislation.

```
RANGE     =      2.00
MEAN      =      2.63
STANDARD DEVIATION =          0.70
```

POPULATION PERCENT CUM.	COUNTRY	RANK	COUNTRY NAME	VALUE	RANGE DECILE
0.3	0.3	12.5	BOTSWANA	3	1
1.8	1.5	12.5	BURUNDI	3	
2.5	0.7	12.5	CAR	3	
2.9	0.4	12.5	CONGO (BRA)	3	
12.0	9.1	12.5	ZAIRE	3	
13.2	1.2	12.5	DAHOMEY	3	
24.1	10.9	12.5	ETHIOPIA	3	
24.3	0.2	12.5	GABON	3	
24.5	0.2	12.5	GAMBIA	3	
28.3	3.8	12.5	GHANA	3	
30.0	1.7	12.5	GUINEA	3	
34.8	4.8	12.5	KENYA	3	
35.2	0.4	12.5	LESOTHO	3	
37.1	1.9	12.5	MALAWI	3	
62.1	25.0	12.5	NIGERIA	3	
63.6	1.5	12.5	RWANDA	3	
64.7	1.1	12.5	SIERRA LEONE	3	
65.9	1.2	12.5	SOMALIA	3	
72.6	6.7	12.5	SUDAN	3	
78.3	5.7	12.5	TANZANIA	3	
79.1	0.8	12.5	TOGO	3	
83.3	4.2	12.5	UGANDA	3	
85.6	2.3	12.5	UPPER VOLTA	3	
87.4	1.8	12.5	ZAMBIA	3	
89.3	1.9	26.5	IVORY COAST	2	5
89.8	0.5	26.5	MAURITANIA	2	
92.0	2.2	26.5	MALI	2	
93.7	1.7	26.5	NIGER	2	
96.2	2.5	30.5	CAMEROON	1	10
97.8	1.6	30.5	CHAD	1	
98.3	0.5	30.5	LIBERIA	1	
100.0	1.7	30.5	SENEGAL	1	

source: Jean Blondel, *An Introduction to the Study of Comparative Government* (New York: Praeger, 1970). We are grateful to Mr. Blondel for permission to use his typology and basic data.

TABLE 7.8 Political Formula at Independence

Definition: 1. mass
2. dominant patron
3. competitive
4. revolutionary liberation
5. no party tradition

RANGE =   4.00
MEAN =   3.00
STANDARD DEVIATION =   1.27

| POPULATION PERCENT | | | | | |
CUM.	COUNTRY	RANK	COUNTRY NAME	VALUE	RANGE DECILE
0.3	0.3	2.5	BOTSWANA	5	1
0.5	0.2	2.5	GAMBIA	5	
5.3	4.8	2.5	KENYA	5	
5.7	0.4	2.5	LESOTHO	5	
8.2	2.5	9.5	CAMEROON	4	3
9.8	1.6	9.5	CHAD	4	
10.2	0.4	9.5	CONGO (BRA)	4	
11.4	1.2	9.5	DAHOMEY	4	
11.6	0.2	9.5	GABON	4	
36.6	25.0	9.5	NIGERIA	4	
37.7	1.1	9.5	SIERRA LEONE	4	
38.5	0.8	9.5	TOGO	4	
42.7	4.2	9.5	UGANDA	4	
45.0	2.3	9.5	UPPER VOLTA	4	
54.1	9.1	16.5	ZAIRE	3	5
56.0	1.9	16.5	MALAWI	3	
61.7	5.7	16.5	TANZANIA	3	
63.5	1.8	16.5	ZAMBIA	3	
64.2	0.7	23.5	CAR	2	8
68.0	3.8	23.5	GHANA	2	
69.7	1.7	23.5	GUINEA	2	
71.6	1.9	23.5	IVORY COAST	2	
72.1	0.5	23.5	LIBERIA	2	
72.6	0.5	23.5	MAURITANIA	2	
74.8	2.2	23.5	MALI	2	
76.5	1.7	23.5	NIGER	2	
78.2	1.7	23.5	SENEGAL	2	
79.4	1.2	23.5	SOMALIA	2	
80.9	1.5	30.5	BURUNDI	1	10
91.8	10.9	30.5	ETHIOPIA	1	
93.3	1.5	30.5	RWANDA	1	
100.0	6.7	30.5	SUDAN	1	

SOURCE: Crawford Young, "Political Systems Development," in *The African Experience*, eds. John Paden and Edward Soja (Evanston, Ill.: Northwestern University Press, 1970).

TABLE 7.9 Political Formula, Post-Independence as of Mid-1969

Definition: 1. renewed mass party
2. military
3. competitive party
4. no party tradition
5. party state

RANGE =   4.00
MEAN =   3.69
STANDARD DEVIATION =   1.47

| POPULATION PERCENT | | | | | |
CUM.	COUNTRY	RANK	COUNTRY NAME	VALUE	RANGE DECILE
0.3	0.3	9.0	BOTSWANA	5	1
2.8	2.5	9.0	CAMEROON	5	
4.4	1.6	9.0	CHAD	5	
4.8	0.4	9.0	CONGO (BRA)	5	
5.0	0.2	9.0	GABON	5	
6.7	1.7	9.0	GUINEA	5	
8.6	1.9	9.0	IVORY COAST	5	
13.4	4.8	9.0	KENYA	5	
13.8	0.4	9.0	LESOTHO	5	
14.3	0.5	9.0	LIBERIA	5	
16.2	1.9	9.0	MALAWI	5	
16.7	0.5	9.0	MAURITANIA	5	
18.4	1.7	9.0	NIGER	5	
19.9	1.5	9.0	RWANDA	5	
21.6	1.7	9.0	SENEGAL	5	
25.8	4.2	9.0	UGANDA	5	
27.6	1.8	9.0	ZAMBIA	5	
38.5	10.9	18.0	ETHIOPIA	4	3
38.7	0.2	19.5	GAMBIA	3	5
39.9	1.2	19.5	SOMALIA	3	
41.4	1.5	26.0	BURUNDI	2	8
42.1	0.7	26.0	CAR	2	
51.2	9.1	26.0	ZAIRE	2	
52.4	1.2	26.0	DAHOMEY	2	
56.2	3.8	26.0	GHANA	2	
58.4	2.2	26.0	MALI	2	
83.4	25.0	26.0	NIGERIA	2	
84.5	1.1	26.0	SIERRA LEONE	2	
91.2	6.7	26.0	SUDAN	2	
92.0	0.8	26.0	TOGO	2	
94.3	2.3	26.0	UPPER VOLTA	2	
100.0	5.7	32.0	TANZANIA	1	10

SOURCE: Young, "Political Systems Development," in *African Experience*, eds. Paden and Soja, p. 461.

8. Political Parties and Elections

If the work of political scientists is any indication of the relative importance of different concepts in the analysis of developing political systems, political parties and elections would surely be judged of great significance. Perhaps the greatest single scholarly investment in the study of African political systems has gone into the analysis of political parties.[1] The pay-off of this intensive work for the student of cross-national research, and for the evaluation of the utility of concepts relating to parties and elections, is, however, slight. The literature is rich in case study material, but lacking in theoretical content, conceptual sophistication, and testable propositions. The most well-refined tools of the American political scientist have been developed in the study of voting, but the difficulties in African settings of social survey research, in particular, have greatly limited the study of elections in African politics. American political scientists have rather devoted their energies to the study of African political parties—a subject in which theoretical and methodological tools are least well developed.[2] The data presented here are, therefore, intended more to stimulate the development of operational theory and generalizable research than to provide an adequate data base for the comparative analysis of parties and elections in the development of African political systems.

In one of his more pithy paragraphs, Max Weber explains the great interest parties hold for the political scientist by noting that, whereas class and status are concepts relating to the distribution of wealth and honor, party "lives in a house of power."[3] Party and electoral systems are institutions designed to regulate the distribution of political control, and they contribute to the integration and conflict management of the political system. The theoretical relevance of the study of political parties and elections is closely tied to the study of political order. The two phenomena are appropriately treated together since both parties and elections are critically concerned with the question of orderly *succession* in the development of political systems.[4] Within this general context, there are numerous refinements in the definition and conceptualization of party systems according to function and purpose.

Research on African Parties

Gabriel Almond in his early work focused upon the interest aggregation function of party structures;[5] more classical definitions stress the purpose of parties as the accretion of governmental power (particularly the winning of legislative office);[6] while more appropriate and flexible conceptualizations include socialization, integration, conflict management, mobilization, participation and the development of legitimacy as party functions.[7] Measures of functional performance on each of these dimensions need to be developed, as do measures of structural variation in party and electoral systems.

Since the publication of David Apter's *The Gold Coast in Transition* (1955), social scientists have increasingly addressed themselves to the question of the role of the party vis-à-vis democratic processes in African nations. With the passage of time and with the appearance of single party systems as the norm rather than as a transitional stage, the central issue of democracy within the one-party system came into clearer focus.[8] Aristide Zolberg suggests that pessimism directed toward African one-party systems can be traced to the conventional view of democratic theory based on Joseph Schumpeter's competitive model and on the tradition of pluralistic politics in the West.[9]

Prominent normative and empirical scholars have given critical attention to evaluation of African political parties. Writing in 1961, Ruth Schachter Morgenthau cited the widespread mass consent enjoyed by these parties, the recruitment of leadership from lower levels of the social scale, and the practice of debate and active opposition prior to decision-making within the party framework.[10] Thomas Hodgkin stressed the importance of objectives—the development of government open to the poorer masses as opposed to that controlled by aristocratic groups, and the transfer of government from foreign ruling elites to the indigenous populations—as the test of democracy in the new nations.[11] Aristide Zolberg voiced his preference for evaluation in light of performance or consequences—the dissemination of equality, modernization, mass participation—rather than form,[12] and Martin Kilson (1963) argued for a more systematic investigation of this question:

> Some would suggest that single party systems are capable of sustaining an important measure of democracy by which they mean widespread parties, active free discussion, etc.,— all of which constitutes influence by the *demos* upon the decision making process. The problem, however, has not been taken very much beyond the realm of assertion, still wanting empirical demonstration and conceptual definition. What kind of decisions, for instance, are influenced by participation and discussion in parties. . . .?[13]

Immanuel Wallerstein, writing in 1966, notes the decline of the party as a vehicle for mass participation in single-party states. This he states is due to several factors—the loss of revolutionary momentum after the establishment of full independence, the decreasing amount of time devoted to party work by leaders due to the assumption of official duties, and a decline in enthusiasm and participation at the local level.[14]

Measuring Party and Electoral Variables

No matter how we investigate the development of political parties and electoral systems, it is necessary to develop operational variables that can be used to test theories of political development which hypothesize the importance of parties and elections, and to evaluate the utility of typologies of party and regime characteristics.[15]

Organization theory offers useful conceptual categories for variable construction,[16] but available sources on African party organization and elections do not contain the information necessary to construct reliable indices of such concepts as party centralization, autonomy, and hierarchy. In particular, attempts to construct variables measuring membership and ideological characteristics of political parties failed for lack of data and reliability.

Despite this, we have attempted to measure some aspects of the institutionalization of party systems in African states.[17] Tables 8.1, 8.3, and 8.4, give measures of the *durability* of party systems in Africa in terms of the chronological experience of national party organization, change in the number of political parties with legislative representation, and the degree to which party organization is complicated by mergers and splits. The *complexity* of the party system may be measured simply by the data on the number of legal political parties in the post-independence period given in Table 8.2. Another measure of the complexity or coherence of the party system is that of the fractionalization of party representation in the legislatures, which is given in Table 8.5. The *autonomy* of political parties may be indicated by the measure of the number of parties banned given in Table 8.6. The *penetration* of the party system in terms of the degree to which political parties mobilize or aggregate support from the society is partially indicated by measures of voting turnout and electoral support for the ruling party given in Tables 8.7 and 8.8.

Reliability

The collection of data on parties and elections in Black Africa requires searching numerous sources, and raises severe problems of inter-coder and inter-source reliability. The problem is magnified by the difficulty of precisely defining a *party*. The data presented here are based on information on all organizations that call themselves political parties. On this basis, we get fairly high reliability between coders using similar sources: we found that the average inter-coder reliability for coding the number of parties in each year after independence is $r = .91$.

The critical problem in assessing the reliability of this information is the difficulty of assuring access to the relevant sources of information. Our data are based on an intensive search of case study materials for each country, and a systematic search of new sources and yearbooks. From these sources, we diagrammed the historical development of political parties, as shown in Part II of this Handbook, and had these diagrams checked by "experts" for many of the countries. The reliability of data gathered in this way is contingent not only on coder error, but more critically on the expectation that the universe of information can be utilized, or that researchers can be expected to reference the same sources. We expect that this goal was less satisfactorily accomplished for the French-speaking countries since we could not locate country experts who were available to read the manuscript for many of these countries.

Notes

1 Representative of this literature are: David Apter, *Ghana in Transition* (New York: Atheneum Press, 1963); Henry Bienen, *Tanzania: Party Transformation and Economic Development* (Princeton, N.J.: Princeton University Press, 1967); Gwendolen M. Carter, ed., *African One-Party Systems* (Ithaca, N.Y.: Cornell University Press, 1962); James S. Coleman and Carl G. Rosberg, eds., *Political Parties and National Integration in Tropical Africa* (Berkeley: University of California Press, 1966); Thomas Hodgkin, *African Political Parties* (London: Penguin Books, 1961); Ruth Schachter Morgenthau, *Political Parties in French-Speaking West Africa* (London: Oxford University Press, 1964); Richard Sklar, *Nigerian Political Parties* (Princeton, N.J.: Princeton University Press, 1963); Aristide R. Zolberg, *One-Party Government in the Ivory Coast* (Princeton, N.J.: Princeton University Press, 1964). Zolberg's *Creating Political Order* (Chicago: Rand McNally, 1966) is an interesting critique of party analysis indicating the symbiosis of party and state in Africa, and the institutional fragility of both.

2 For an interesting series of articles on the study of political parties which relates to bodies of social science theory, see William J. Crotty, ed., *Approaches to the Study of Party Organization* (Boston: Allyn and Bacon, 1967).

3 Max Weber, "Class, Status, Party," in *From Max Weber*, eds. H. H. Gerth and C. Wright Mills (New York: Oxford University Press, 1958).

4 See Carl Joachim Friedrich's discussion in *Man and His Government* (New York: McGraw-Hill, 1963), Chap. 28, "Succession and the Uses of Party," pp. 502–523.

5 Gabriel Almond and James A. Coleman, *The Politics of the Developing Areas* (Princeton, N.J.: Princeton University Press, 1960).

6 See the definition by Bernard Hennessy in Crotty, *Approaches to the Study of Party Organization*, p. 1.

7 Myron Weiner and Joseph La Palombara, eds., *Political Parties and Political Development* (Princeton, N.J.: Princeton University Press, 1964).

8 David Apter, *The Gold Coast in Transition* (Princeton, N.J.: Princeton University Press, 1955) p. vii.

9 Zolberg, *One-Party Government in the Ivory Coast*, p. 7. Joseph A. Schumpeter, *Capitalism, Socialism and Democracy*, 3rd ed. (New York: Harper and Brothers, 1950), p. 269. Schumpeter states "the democratic method is that institutional arrangement for arriving at political decisions in which individuals acquire the power to decide by means of a competitive struggle for the people's votes."

10 Ruth Schachter Morgenthau, "Single-Party Systems in West Africa," *American Political Science Review*, 55 (1961): 304–305.

11 Hodgkin, *African Political Parties*, pp. 155–159.

12 Zolberg, *One Party Government in the Ivory Coast*, p. 9.

13 Martin Kilson, "Authoritarian and Single-Party Tendencies in African Parties," *World Politics*, 15 (1963): p. 292.

14 Immanuel Wallerstein, "The Decline of the Party in Single-Party African States," in Weiner and La Palombara, *Political Parties and Political Development*, pp. 201–216.

15 See Chapter 7 for a discussion of typologies based on characteristics of the political party system.

16 See the essay by Lee F. Anderson in Crotty, ed., *Approaches to Party Organization*, and the work in progress by Professor Kenneth Janda and his staff on the International Comparative Political Parties Project at Northwestern University. The ICPP sample of nation-states includes eleven African nations.

17 Compare Samuel Huntington, *Political Order in Changing Societies* (New Haven, Conn.: Yale University Press, 1968), for a discussion of institutionalization and for hypotheses relating party institutionalization to aspects of political development, particularly political instability.

TABLE 8.1   Number of Years since the Establishment of the First Political Party Through 1970

Definition: Any organization open to African membership and either calling itself a political party, or having a specific program for changing the structure of territorial government, is considered as a political party.

```
RANGE  =        107.00
MEAN   =         25.25
STANDARD DEVIATION =          17.92
```

POPULATION PERCENT		RANK	COUNTRY NAME	VALUE	RANGE DECILE
CUM.	COUNTRY				
0.5	0.5	1.0	LIBERIA	107	1
0.7	0.2	2.5	GABON	47	6
5.5	4.8	2.5	KENYA	47	
30.5	25.0	4.0	NIGERIA	44	
36.2	5.7	5.0	TANZANIA	38	7
40.4	4.2	6.0	UGANDA	32	8
42.1	1.7	7.0	SENEGAL	31	
42.3	0.2	8.0	GAMBIA	26	
43.5	1.2	9.5	SOMALIA	24	
50.2	6.7	9.5	SUDAN	24	
52.1	1.9	11.0	MALAWI	23	
54.4	2.3	12.0	UPPER VOLTA	22	
55.1	0.7	18.0	CAR	21	9
56.7	1.6	18.0	CHAD	21	
57.1	0.4	18.0	CONGO (BRA)	21	
58.3	1.2	18.0	DAHOMEY	21	
60.0	1.7	18.0	GUINEA	21	
61.9	1.9	18.0	IVORY COAST	21	
62.4	0.5	18.0	MAURITANIA	21	
64.6	2.2	18.0	MALI	21	
66.3	1.7	18.0	NIGER	21	
67.1	0.8	18.0	TOGO	21	
68.9	1.8	18.0	ZAMBIA	21	
72.7	3.8	24.0	GHANA	20	
75.2	2.5	25.0	CAMEROON	19	
84.3	9.1	26.5	ZAIRE	17	
85.4	1.1	26.5	SIERRA LEONE	17	
85.8	0.4	28.0	LESOTHO	15	
86.1	0.3	30.0	BOTSWANA	8	10
87.6	1.5	30.0	BURUNDI	8	
89.1	1.5	30.0	RWANDA	8	
100.0	10.9	32.0	ETHIOPIA	0	

SOURCES: Ruth Schachter Morgenthau, *Political Parties in French-Speaking West Africa* (London: Oxford University Press, 1964). *Burundi, Congo (Brazzaville), Zaire (Congo K.), Liberia, Rwanda, Togo*: Ronald Segal, *Political Africa: A Who's Who of Personalities and Parties* (New York: Praeger, 1961); *CAR, Chad, Gabon*: Virginia Thompson and Richard Adloff, *The Emerging States of French Equatorial Africa* (London: Oxford University Press, 1960). (For Gabon, the actual date of the founding of *Jeune Gabonaise* is not given. Thompson and Adloff say it was founded in the post-World War I depression.) *Kenya, Malawi, Tanzania, Uganda, Zambia*: Stanley Diamond and Fred G. Burke, eds., *The Transformation of East Africa* (New York: Basic Books, 1966); *Nigeria*: Richard L. Sklar, *Nigerian Political Parties* (Princeton, N.J.: Princeton University Press, 1963); *Gambia*: Harry A. Gailey, *A History of the Gambia* (New York: Praeger, 1965); *Somalia*: I. M. Lewis, *The Modern History of Somaliland* (New York: Praeger, 1965); *Sudan*: P. M. Holt, *A Modern History of the Sudan* (New York: Grove Press, 1961); *Botswana, Ghana*: Colin Legum, ed., *Africa: A Handbook to the Continent* (London: Anthony Blond, 1961); *Cameroon*: Victor LeVine, *Cameroon: From Mandate to Independence* (Berkeley: University of California Press, 1964); *Sierra Leone*: James S. Coleman and Carl G. Rosberg, Jr., eds., *Political Parties and National Integration in Tropical Africa* (Berkeley: University of California Press, 1966); *Lesotho*: J. E. Spence, *Lesotho: The Politics of Dependence* (London: Oxford University Press, 1966); *Ethiopia*: No parties.

TABLE 8.2 Number of Political Parties, Independence to 1969

Definition: All political parties that were legal (and not banned) in this period are counted, whether or not they resulted from mergers or splits.

```
RANGE     =     17.00
MEAN      =      5.84
STANDARD DEVIATION =        3.99
```

POPULATION PERCENT CUM.	COUNTRY	RANK	COUNTRY NAME	VALUE	RANGE DECILE
9.1	9.1	1.0	ZAIRE	17	1
34.1	25.0	2.0	NIGERIA	14	2
37.9	3.8	3.0	GHANA	13	3
40.4	2.5	4.5	CAMEROON	11	4
47.1	6.7	4.5	SUDAN	11	
48.3	1.2	6.0	SOMALIA	9	5
49.5	1.2	7.5	DAHOMEY	8	6
49.9	0.4	7.5	LESOTHO	8	
51.0	1.1	9.0	SIERRA LEONE	7	
51.3	0.3	13.5	BOTSWANA	6	7
52.0	0.7	13.5	CAR	6	
52.4	0.4	13.5	CONGO (BRA)	6	
52.6	0.2	13.5	GABON	6	
52.8	0.2	13.5	GAMBIA	6	
53.3	0.5	13.5	MAURITANIA	6	
55.0	1.7	13.5	SENEGAL	6	
56.8	1.8	13.5	ZAMBIA	6	
58.3	1.5	20.0	BURUNDI	5	8
63.1	4.8	20.0	KENYA	5	
64.6	1.5	20.0	RWANDA	5	
65.4	0.8	20.0	TOGO	5	
69.6	4.2	20.0	UGANDA	5	
71.2	1.6	24.0	CHAD	3	9
73.1	1.9	24.0	MALAWI	3	
78.8	5.7	24.0	TANZANIA	3	
81.1	2.3	26.0	UPPER VOLTA	2	
82.8	1.7	29.0	GUINEA	1	10
84.7	1.9	29.0	IVORY COAST	1	
85.2	0.5	29.0	LIBERIA	1	
87.4	2.2	29.0	MALI	1	
89.1	1.7	29.0	NIGER	1	
100.0	10.9	32.0	ETHIOPIA	0	

SOURCES: *Europa Yearbook* and *Africa Research Bulletin* were consulted for all countries. The major sources for each individual country were: *Zaire (Congo K.)*: Crawford Young, *Politics in the Congo* (Princeton, N.J.: Princeton University Press, 1964) and *Congo: Les dosiers du C.R.I.S.P.*, Vol. 1 and *Congo, 1965* (Princeton: Princeton University Press, 1967). The 49 parties regrouped as CONACO for the 1965 election are counted as one; *Nigeria*: Sklar, *Nigerian Political Parties*, pp. 35–37. This figure represents parties which fought in elections from 1956 onwards and gained seats, or a proportion of the vote in sufficient number to be recorded by Sklar; *Cameroon*: LeVine, *Cameroon: from Mandate to Independence*; *Sudan*: U.S. Department of the Army, *Area Handbook for the Sudan*, 2nd ed. (Washington, D.C.: Government Printing Office, 1964); *Ghana*: Dennis Austin, *Politics in Ghana, 1946–61* (London: Oxford University Press, 1964); *Somalia*: Lewis, *Modern History of Somaliland*, and Saadia Touval, *Somali Nationalism* (Cambridge, Mass.: Harvard University Press, 1963); *CAR, Chad, Congo (Brazzaville), Gabon*: Thompson and Adloff, *Emerging States of French Equatorial Africa*; Gwendolen M. Carter, ed., *National Unity and Regionalism in Eight African States* (Ithaca, N.Y.: Cornell University Press, 1966); and unpublished research files of George Martens, Northwestern University; *Dahomey*: Segal, *Political Africa*, and Martens' unpublished files. *Guinea, Mali, Senegal, Sierra Leone*: Coleman and Rosberg, *Political Parties and National Integration in Tropical Africa*; *Botswana*: Helen Kitchen, ed., *A Handbook of African Affairs* (New York: Praeger, 1964); *Lesotho*: Spence, *Lesotho*; *Mauritania*: Segal, *Political Africa*, and Martens' unpublished files; *Burundi, Rwanda*: Segal, *Political Africa*, and Legum, *Africa*; *Togo*: Segal, *Political Africa*, and M. H. Dorsinville, "Report of the UN Commissioner for Supervision of Elections in Togoland under French Administration," UN Document T/1392, June 30, 1958; *Gambia, Zambia*: Richard Hall, *Zambia* (New York: Praeger, 1965); *Kenya, Tanzania*: Diamond and Burke, *Transformation of East Africa* (for Tanzania, Zanzibar's four parties are not included); *Uganda*: Carter, *National Unity in Eight African States*; *Malawi*: Lucy Mair, *The Nyasaland Elections of 1961* (London: Athlone Press, 1962); and John G. Pike, *Malawi: A Political and Economic History* (New York: Praeger, 1968); *Ivory Coast*: Aristide R. Zolberg, *One-Party Government in the Ivory Coast* (Princeton, N.J.: Princeton University Press, 1964), and Gwendolen M. Carter, ed., *African One-Party States* (Ithaca, N.Y.: Cornell University Press, 1962); *Liberia*: Carter, *African One-Party States*; *Niger, Upper Volta*: Information gathered by George Martens in Niger and Upper Volta for dissertation research, 1968–69; *Ethiopia*: Richard Greenfield, *Ethiopia: A New Political History* (New York: Praeger, 1965).

TABLE 8.3   Change in the Number of Parties, Independence to 1967

Definition: Number of parties with legislative representation in 1967 minus the number of parties with legislative representation at independence. Independents were counted as one party.

```
RANGE =            20.00
MEAN =             -1.40
STANDARD DEVIATION =        3.26
```

POPULATION PERCENT		RANK	COUNTRY NAME	VALUE	RANGE DECILE
CUM.	COUNTRY				
6.7	6.7	1.0	SUDAN	5	1
7.1	0.4	2.5	LESOTHO	1	3
7.9	0.8	2.5	TOGO	1	
8.2	0.3	8.5	BOTSWANA	0	
9.9	1.7	8.5	GUINEA	0	
11.8	1.9	8.5	IVORY COAST	0	
12.3	0.5	8.5	LIBERIA	0	
12.8	0.5	8.5	MAURITANIA	0	
15.0	2.2	8.5	MALI	0	
16.7	1.7	8.5	NIGER	0	
18.4	1.7	8.5	SENEGAL	0	
24.1	5.7	8.5	TANZANIA	0	
25.9	1.8	8.5	ZAMBIA	0	
27.4	1.5	18.5	BURUNDI	-1	4
29.9	2.5	18.5	CAMEROON	-1	
30.3	0.4	18.5	CONGO (BRA)	-1	
30.5	0.2	18.5	GABON	-1	
30.7	0.2	18.5	GAMBIA	-1	
35.5	4.8	18.5	KENYA	-1	
37.4	1.9	18.5	MALAWI	-1	
38.6	1.2	18.5	SOMALIA	-1	
42.8	4.2	18.5	UGANDA	-1	
45.1	2.3	18.5	UPPER VOLTA	-1	
45.8	0.7	24.5	CAR	-2	
47.4	1.6	24.5	CHAD	-2	
48.6	1.2	26.0	DAHOMEY	-3	5
73.6	25.0	27.5	NIGERIA	-5	6
74.7	1.1	27.5	SIERRA LEONE	-5	
78.5	3.8	29.0	GHANA	-7	7
87.6	9.1	30.0	ZAIRE	-15	

```
DATA NOT AVAILABLE FOR THE FOLLOWING COUNTRIES

ETHIOPIA      RWANDA
```

SOURCES: See Table 8.2.

TABLE 8.4   Organizational Discontinuity in the Party System, 1957 to 1969

Definition: Number of splits and mergers in the parties.
Mergers are calculated as the number of times there is either a formation of a new political party by two or more existing parties, or the joining of one existing party by another. *Splits* are calculated as the number of times a new party, formed by a breakaway faction of an existing party, continues in existence after the break.

```
RANGE =            7.00
MEAN =             2.66
STANDARD DEVIATION =        2.27
```

POPULATION PERCENT		RANK	COUNTRY NAME	VALUE	RANGE DECILE
CUM.	COUNTRY				
2.5	2.5	2.0	CAMEROON	7	1
4.2	1.7	2.0	SENEGAL	7	
5.3	1.1	2.0	SIERRA LEONE	7	
30.3	25.0	5.0	NIGERIA	6	2
31.5	1.2	5.0	SOMALIA	6	
33.8	2.3	5.0	UPPER VOLTA	6	
35.6	1.8	7.0	ZAMBIA	5	3
44.7	9.1	9.5	ZAIRE	4	5
44.9	0.2	9.5	GAMBIA	4	
49.7	4.8	9.5	KENYA	4	
53.9	4.2	9.5	UGANDA	4	
54.3	0.4	12.5	LESOTHO	3	6
55.1	0.8	12.5	TOGO	3	
55.4	0.3	16.0	BOTSWANA	2	8
57.0	1.6	16.0	CHAD	2	
57.2	0.2	16.0	GABON	2	
57.7	0.5	16.0	MAURITANIA	2	
63.4	5.7	16.0	TANZANIA	2	
64.9	1.5	23.0	BURUNDI	1	9
65.6	0.7	23.0	CAR	1	
66.8	1.2	23.0	DAHOMEY	1	
70.6	3.8	23.0	GHANA	1	
72.3	1.7	23.0	GUINEA	1	
74.2	1.9	23.0	IVORY COAST	1	
76.4	2.2	23.0	MALI	1	
78.1	1.7	23.0	NIGER	1	
79.6	1.5	23.0	RWANDA	1	
80.0	0.4	30.0	CONGO (BRA)	0	
90.9	10.9	30.0	ETHIOPIA	0	
91.4	0.5	30.0	LIBERIA	0	
93.3	1.9	30.0	MALAWI	0	
100.0	6.7	30.0	SUDAN	0	

SOURCES: These data are taken from the diagrammatic representations of party development in Part II. The data in those diagrams are based primarily on the sources given for Table 8.2.

TABLE 8.5   Legislative Fractionalization at Independence

Definition: The index is computed on the basis of seats won in the election closest to, but before, the date of independence by the various parties. The values of this index range from 0 to 1; the higher the value of the index,[1] the higher the party fractionalization of the legislature.

[1] $1-\Sigma(PR_i{}^2)$ where PR_i equals proportion of seats in the lower house held by the ith political party. Independents are treated as belonging to a single party.

```
RANGE  =         0.86
MEAN   =         0.35
STANDARD DEVIATION =        0.25
```

POPULATION PERCENT					
CUM.	COUNTRY	RANK	COUNTRY NAME	VALUE	RANGE DECILE
9.1	9.1	1.0	ZAIRE	0.86	1
13.3	4.2	2.0	UGANDA	0.71	2
15.8	2.5	3.0	CAMEROON	0.68	3
40.8	25.0	4.0	NIGERIA	0.66	
41.0	0.2	5.5	GABON	0.60	4
47.7	6.7	5.5	SUDAN	0.60	
48.9	1.2	7.0	DAHOMEY	0.59	
53.7	4.8	8.0	KENYA	0.57	
54.1	0.4	9.0	LESOTHO	0.56	
55.3	1.2	10.0	SOMALIA	0.53	
55.5	0.2	11.5	GAMBIA	0.52	
56.6	1.1	11.5	SIERRA LEONE	0.52	
58.2	1.6	13.5	CHAD	0.50	5
62.0	3.8	13.5	GHANA	0.50	
62.8	0.8	15.0	TOGO	0.45	
64.3	1.5	16.0	RWANDA	0.34	7
64.7	0.4	18.0	CONGO (BRA)	0.26	
67.0	2.3	18.0	UPPER VOLTA	0.26	
68.8	1.8	18.0	ZAMBIA	0.26	
69.1	0.3	20.5	BOTSWANA	0.18	8
70.8	1.7	20.5	NIGER	0.18	
72.3	1.5	22.0	BURUNDI	0.17	9
78.0	5.7	23.0	TANZANIA	0.15	
78.7	0.7	24.5	CAR	0.14	
80.4	1.7	24.5	GUINEA	0.14	
82.3	1.9	26.0	MALAWI	0.12	
93.2	10.9	29.5	ETHIOPIA	0.0	
95.1	1.9	29.5	IVORY COAST	0.0	
95.6	0.5	29.5	LIBERIA	0.0	
96.1	0.5	29.5	MAURITANIA	0.0	
98.3	2.2	29.5	MALI	0.0	
100.0	1.7	29.5	SENEGAL	0.0	

SOURCES: *Botswana: Africa Research Bulletin* (March 1965), p. 1079; *Burundi, Rwanda: Europa Yearbook 1962*; *Cameroon*: Willard R. Johnson, *The Cameroon Federation* (Princeton: Princeton University Press, 1970), appendix; *CAR*: Thompson and Adloff, *Emerging States of French Equatorial Africa*, p. 396 and a clipping file from French newspapers collected by George Martens; *Chad*: Michel Saint-Louis, "Le parti progressiste Tchadien dans le vie politique de Tchad (PPT-RDA)," unpublished doctoral dissertation, University of Paris; *Congo (Brazzaville)*: Jean M. Wagret, "L'assumption politique de l'UDDIA (Congo) et son prise du pouvoir (1956–1959)," *Revue juridique et politique d'outre-mer* (April–June, 1963); *Zaire (Congo K.)*: Young, *Politics in the Congo*, and *C.R.I.S.P.*; *Dahomey*: Hodgkin, *African Political Parties* and *Keesings Contemporary Archives, 1957*, p., 15587; *Ethiopia*: Greenfield, *Ethiopia*; *Gabon*: Thompson and Adloff, *Emerging States of French Equatorial Africa, Keesings Contemporary Archives, 1959–60*, p. 15587; *Gambia: The Gambia Echo*, and Gailey, *History of the Gambia*; *Ghana*: Austin, *Politics in Ghana, 1946–61*; *Guinea*,

Ivory Coast, Mali, Senegal, Sierra Leone: Coleman and Rosberg, *Political Parties and National Integration in Tropical Africa*; *Kenya*: Clyde Sange, and John Nottingham, "The Kenya General Election of 1963," *Journal of Modern African Studies*, 2 (1964): 342; *Lesotho*: Spencer *Lesotho*; *Liberia*: Carter, *African One-Party States*, p. 342 for May 1955 election; *Malawi*: Lucy Mair, *The Nyasaland Elections of 1961* (London: The Athlone Press, 1962), pp. 80–81; *Niger, Mauritania*: Martens' French newspaper clipping file; *Nigeria*: K. W. J. Post, *The Nigerian Federal Election of 1959* (London: Oxford University Press, 1963); *Somalia*: Touval, *Somali Nationalism*; *Sudan: Egyptian Gazette*, December 11, 1953, p. 1; *Tanzania*: Henry Bienen, *Tanzania: Party Transformation and Economic Development* (Princeton, N.J.: Princeton University Press, 1967); *Togo*: UN Report, June 30, 1958; *Uganda*: *Africa Diary*, May 11–18, 1962, p. 551; *Upper Volta*: Thomas Hodgkin, *African Political Parties* (Baltimore, Md.: Penguin Books, 1961); *Zambia*: David C. Mulford, "Some Observations on the Elections," *Africa Report* (February 1964): 14.

TABLE 8.6 Number of Illegal Parties, 1957–1969

Definition: Number of parties banned or proscribed during the period 1957 to 1969.

```
RANGE =          14.00
MEAN =            2.84
STANDARD DEVIATION =        3.57
```

POPULATION PERCENT					
CUM.	COUNTRY	RANK	COUNTRY NAME	VALUE	RANGE DECILE
25.0	25.0	1.0	NIGERIA	14	1
34.1	9.1	2.0	ZAIRE	13	
40.8	6.7	3.0	SUDAN	9	4
42.0	1.2	4.0	DAHOMEY	7	6
42.8	0.8	5.0	TOGO	5	7
44.3	1.5	8.5	BURUNDI	4	8
45.0	0.7	8.5	CAR	4	
45.4	0.4	8.5	CONGO (BRA)	4	
45.9	0.5	8.5	MAURITANIA	4	
47.0	1.1	8.5	SIERRA LEONE	4	
51.2	4.2	8.5	UGANDA	4	
53.7	2.5	12.0	CAMEROON	3	
57.5	3.8	14.0	GHANA	2	9
59.2	1.7	14.0	SENEGAL	2	
61.5	2.3	14.0	UPPER VOLTA	2	
63.1	1.6	19.0	CHAD	1	10
67.9	4.8	19.0	KENYA	1	
69.8	1.9	19.0	MALAWI	1	
72.0	2.2	19.0	MALI	1	
73.7	1.7	19.0	NIGER	1	
79.4	5.7	19.0	TANZANIA	1	
81.2	1.8	19.0	ZAMBIA	1	
81.5	0.3	23.0	BOTSWANA	0	
92.4	10.9	28.0	ETHIOPIA	0	
92.6	0.2	28.0	GABON	0	
92.8	0.2	28.0	GAMBIA	0	
94.5	1.7	28.0	GUINEA	0	
96.4	1.9	28.0	IVORY COAST	0	
96.8	0.4	28.0	LESOTHO	0	
97.3	0.5	28.0	LIBERIA	0	
98.8	1.5	28.0	RWANDA	0	

DATA NOT AVAILABLE FOR THE FOLLOWING COUNTRIES

SOMALIA

SOURCES: *Europa Yearbook* and *Africa Research Bulletin* were consulted for all countries. The data in this table are based on the party charts given in Part II, and sources correspond to those for Table 8.4. *Nigeria*: This figure is based on the data in Table 8.4. *Africa Research Bulletin* reports a statement to the effect that 81 political parties and alliances were banned by the 1966 coup; *Sierra Leone*: Coleman and Rosberg, *Political Parties and National Integration in Tropical Africa*. *Africa Research Bulletin* lists four Sierra Leone parties in 1967—SLPP, APC, National Council of Sierra Leone, and Sierra Leone Labor Party. The latter two have not been mentioned elsewhere, and it is unclear if they are new parties or continuations of others. In any case, the absolute number of bannings remains the same; *Liberia, Upper Volta, Zambia*: Segal, *Political Africa*. In Liberia there is "no 'legal' ban on the formation of legal parties"; *Cameroon*: Levine, *Cameroon: From Mandate to Independence*, and *Africa Diary*. The PTC became moribund when its leaders were arrested, and is coded as proscribed; *Chad*: Martens' unpublished data from French newspapers; *Ghana*: Austin, *Politics in Ghana, 1946–61*; *Senegal*: Morgenthau, *Political Parties in French-Speaking West Africa*; *Tanzania*: Diamond and Burke, eds., *The Transformation of East Africa*; *Gabon*: In Gabon, the PDID, though not banned, can hardly be said to have enjoyed an autonomous existence; *Lesotho*: Spence, *Lesotho*.

TABLE 8.7 Voting Turnout at Independence

Definition: Number of voters voting in the national legislative election closest to, but before, the date of independence, as a percentage of the population in that year.

```
RANGE =          51.00
MEAN =           23.13
STANDARD DEVIATION =       12.33
```

POPULATION PERCENT					
CUM.	COUNTRY	RANK	COUNTRY NAME	VALUE	RANGE DECILE
0.4	0.4	1.0	LESOTHO	52	1
1.9	1.5	2.0	RWANDA	46	2
3.8	1.9	3.0	IVORY COAST	45	
4.3	0.5	4.0	MAURITANIA	38	3
4.5	0.2	5.5	GAMBIA	37	
6.3	1.8	5.5	ZAMBIA	37	
6.7	0.4	7.5	CONGO (BRA)	34	4
6.9	0.2	7.5	GABON	34	
9.4	2.5	9.0	CAMEROON	30	5
11.1	1.7	10.0	SENEGAL	28	
11.6	0.5	11.0	LIBERIA	27	
13.1	1.5	12.0	BURUNDI	26	6
13.4	0.3	13.5	BOTSWANA	23	
14.2	0.8	13.5	TOGO	23	
15.9	1.7	16.0	GUINEA	22	
20.7	4.8	16.0	KENYA	22	
23.0	2.3	16.0	UPPER VOLTA	22	
32.1	9.1	19.0	ZAIRE	20	7
33.3	1.2	19.0	DAHOMEY	20	
34.5	1.2	19.0	SOMALIA	20	
36.1	1.6	21.0	CHAD	19	
38.3	2.2	22.0	MALI	18	
63.3	25.0	23.0	NIGERIA	16	8
67.5	4.2	24.0	UGANDA	15	
78.4	10.9	25.0	ETHIOPIA	13	
80.1	1.7	26.0	NIGER	12	
83.9	3.8	27.0	GHANA	11	9
90.6	6.7	28.0	SUDAN	10	
91.3	0.7	29.5	CAR	8	
92.4	1.1	29.5	SIERRA LEONE	8	
94.3	1.9	31.0	MALAWI	3	10
100.0	5.7	32.0	TANZANIA	1	

SOURCES: Same as those listed in Table 8.5 with the following additions: *Cameroon*: The first federal elections for President were held in 1965, and the data are based on that election. Members of the National Assembly are chosen by state legislators; *Congo (Brazzaville)*: *Le Monde*, June 16, 1959, p. 1; *Ethiopia*: *A Review of Elections 1961 and 1962* (London 1964), p. 77 for election in 1957, the first election ever held in Ethiopia; *Gambia*: *Gambia Echo*, June 4, 1962, p. 2; *Liberia*: In Liberia election results for 1959 seem less than credible; Tubman received 537,472 votes with 55 votes for his opponent. Data for the 1955 election is used here. See Carter, *African One-Party States*; *Malawi*: In Malawi the April 1964 elections were not held because the candidates of the M.C.P. were unopposed. The estimate of voters is based on the fact that 1,871,170 people were registered to vote; *Niger, Upper Volta*: These data are taken from the unpublished dissertation research files of George Martens, Northwestern University, who spent 1968–1969 doing field work in Niger and Upper Volta; *Somalia*: Touval, *Somali Nationalism*, gives 313,760 voting in the Trust Territory of Somalia but no data for British Somaliland. We estimate 400,000 voting in both Somali territories; *Sudan*: Data for the 1958 election from *Electoral Commissions Final Report, Parliamentary Elections 1957/8* (Khartoum: 1958), p. 59; *Tanzania*: In Tanzania the low turnout is partially explained by a large number of uncontested seats; *Uganda*: *East African Standard*, April 28, 1962.

TABLE 8.8 Percentage of the Vote Cast for the Winning Party in the Election Closest to, but before, the Date of Independence

Definition: The winning party is the party from which the government executive (cabinet), or head of government in a coalition is chosen.

```
RANGE  =        92.00
MEAN   =        63.25
STANDARD DEVIATION =          25.19
```

POPULATION PERCENT		RANK	COUNTRY NAME	VALUE	RANGE DECILE
CUM.	COUNTRY				
1.9	1.9	1.5	IVORY COAST	100	1
2.4	0.5	1.5	MAURITANIA	100	
2.9	0.5	3.5	LIBERIA	99	
4.8	1.9	3.5	MALAWI	99	
5.5	0.7	5.0	CAR	89	2
5.8	0.3	6.0	BOTSWANA	87	
7.5	1.7	7.5	SENEGAL	83	
13.2	5.7	7.5	TANZANIA	83	
14.7	1.5	9.0	BURUNDI	81	3
16.2	1.5	10.0	RWANDA	78	
17.9	1.7	11.5	GUINEA	77	
19.6	1.7	11.5	NIGER	77	
21.8	2.2	13.5	MALI	76	
23.0	1.2	13.5	SOMALIA	76	
24.8	1.8	15.0	ZAMBIA	70	4
26.4	1.6	16.0	CHAD	68	
26.6	0.2	18.0	GAMBIA	60	5
27.4	0.8	18.0	TOGO	60	
29.7	2.3	18.0	UPPER VOLTA	60	
30.1	0.4	20.0	CONGO (BRA)	58	
33.9	3.8	21.0	GHANA	57	
38.7	4.8	22.0	KENYA	54	6
42.9	4.2	23.0	UGANDA	52	
45.4	2.5	24.5	CAMEROON	50	
45.6	0.2	24.5	GABON	50	
46.7	1.1	26.0	SIERRA LEONE	46	
47.1	0.4	27.0	LESOTHO	42	7
72.1	25.0	28.0	NIGERIA	28	8
81.2	9.1	29.0	ZAIRE	25	9
82.4	1.2	30.0	DAHOMEY	16	10
93.3	10.9	31.0	ETHIOPIA	15	
100.0	6.7	32.0	SUDAN	8	

sources: The same as for Table 8.7 with the following additions: *Cameroon*: This figure is an estimate for the ruling coalition of Ahidjo and Foncha after federation. Ahidjo's party got 45 percent of the vote in the 1960 election in East Cameroon and Foncha's party got 55 percent of the vote in the 1961 West Cameroon election; *Zaire (Congo K.)*: *Congo: Les dossiers du C.R.I.S.P.* (1960), Vol. 1, pp. 257–266. This includes the alliance of MNC-L, MNC-K, COAKA, UNC. Alone, the MNC-L got 592,456 votes; *Ethiopia*: Since there are no political parties in Ethiopia, this is a mean for the rest of Black Africa; *Gambia*: This estimate is based on the fact that the ruling PPP got 64.5 percent of the Protectorate vote but, in alliance with the Democratic Congress, won only 46.5 percent of the Colony vote; *Somalia*: This figure is for the ruling SYL vote in the Trust Territory of Somalia 1959 election; *Sudan*: This is the mean for the other black African nations. The ruling National Unionist Party won nearly 60 percent of the seats.

9. Extent of Government Influence

In addition to the formal structure of governmental institutions and the nature of party and electoral systems, discussed in the last two chapters, it is useful to consider the relative impact of government in the different black African nations. The centralization of government influence is a major issue in theories of economic development and political integration.[1] Governments vary in the range and scope of their influence or, put otherwise, in their extensiveness and diffuseness.[2]

Impact of Central Government

Both the range and scope of governmental decision-making are related to: (1) the economic role of government in centralizing the collection and disbursement of resources for development planning and projects, and for recurrent expenses; and (2) the role of government in mobilizing support and centralizing political authority. These two roles are reinforcing in the sense that the legitimation of governmental power is generally necessary for effective systems of taxation, and, in turn, the effective functioning of a tax system may reinforce the legitimacy of governments. Without comparative survey data on public attitudes, the measurement of legitimacy and authority (the latter being the public legitimation of government power) is impossible. We can, nevertheless, consider the data on the size and growth of government budgets, spending, revenue, and income from taxation in this chapter, and the data on military and security systems in Chapter 10 as indicative of governmental influence.[3]

The economic role of the government includes policies regarding domestic revenue, and the attraction of foreign aid and investment.[4] The importance of taxation for the accomplishment of both these objectives is clear. At certain thresholds of direct taxation the national citizen-consumer may try harder to avoid paying taxes, with obvious negative effects on government revenue. Correspondingly, high levels of indirect taxation, particularly on imported goods, may discourage the consumption of such goods, and dissuade foreign governments and citizens from providing aid and investments in a given country. Although we have no data to evaluate different tax structures, the data in Tables 9.9 and 9.10 are based on the percentage of total government revenue obtained from direct taxes. This measure is relevant not only to an analysis of tax structure and effectiveness, but also to the measurement of the visibility of the government to the citizen, and its influence upon him.

Taxes provide government with revenue. Since the countries of sub-Saharan African are at a low level of economic development and subsistence incomes are widespread, it is generally difficult to increase revenue by taxing the population. Nevertheless, substantial increases in revenue have been achieved in most of these countries during and, in some cases, before the independence period (see Tables 9.8 and 9.11). No matter how great the increase in revenue has been, however, it is what governments *do* with revenue that is critically important in economic and political development.

The effects of government spending on the structure of demand for goods and services are related to: (1) the range of government control over investment—the degree to which domestic saving and investment is centralized in the hands of government; (2) the variety and emphasis of government investment; and (3) the predominance of government employees in the labor force, or the degree to which government "feeds" itself. These factors in part affect the rate of return on investment, the redistribution of income, and the productivity of the economy in general. The range of political control over investment can be indicated by the measures on government spending and the size of government budgets, particularly as they relate to GNP (see Tables 9.6 and 9.7). The range of central government influence may be isolated in the data relating to central government revenue and spending (Tables 9.1, 9.2, 9.11). The variety and emphasis of government spending is of considerable interest, but the detailed breakdowns of expenditure that are required for such analysis were not available for enough countries. An indication of the predominance of government employment in the labor force is given in Table 7.3.

Validity

The use of any of the measures given in this chapter as indicative of the potential contribution of government to economic development and political integration is subject to several qualifications. Governments, through the collection and spending of revenue, may make an important contribution to the shifting of resources from consumption to investment activities. But all government spending is not investment,[5] and the bureaucratic administration of investment is subject to important limitations in countries where the number and experience of skilled personnel is small. First, bureaucratic decision-making may require more of a general educational experience than is necessary or adequate for the evaluation of specific economic decisions. Second, bureaucracies may so obscure communications by loss of information through hierarchical decision chains that the range of inputs required for economic decisions is more confusing than optimal. Third, the dysfunctional consequences of bureaucratic inertia and unwillingness to take responsibility affect the efficiency of centralized decision-making.[6] The range of both economic and ideological arguments for and against the centralization of economic decision-making cannot be reviewed here,[7] nor do we present sufficient data to explore them fully. The evaluation of specific patterns of government influence in the economy must be related to the particular structural conditions pertaining in a given country or economic region.[8]

The suggested use of the data presented in this chapter for the analysis of the impact of government influence on patterns of political development has already been qualified by pointing to the impossibility of controlling for public attitudes towards government with our data. There is, nevertheless, justification for evaluating the effects of the centralization of government on political development. The

extension and centralization of governmental power in African nations is likely to accentuate conflict between central governments and the political authorities of sub-national communities, just as taxation is likely to produce disaffection in sectors of the population whose values are incompatible with those of the government that administers them. Political integration by the centralization of government in culturally plural societies may increase conflict and political instability.[9]

Reliability

Government budgets are the planned expenditures of all public agencies. Occasionally, some publicly owned corporations and some development expenditures are not included in the budget. This should not be significant in most of the nations considered here, however, and the figures reported by governments should have high reliability. The figures for actual expenditures and revenues may be subject to error caused by unreliable corrections for unpredictable occurrences such as crop failures, international price changes, and domestic cost changes, but we cannot make any estimate of such error.

Notes

[1] For a discussion of the role of government in economic development, see Ursula Hicks, *Development Finance: Planning and Control* (New York: Oxford University Press, 1965); Otto Eckstein, "A Summary of the Theory of Public Expenditures," in *Public Finances: Needs, Sources, and Utilization* (Princeton, N.J.: National Bureau and Princeton University Press, 1961); and A. R. Prest, *Public Finance in Underdeveloped Countries* (London: Weidenfeld and Nicolson, 1962). For discussions of the importance of the centralization of political authority in the process of political integration, see Myron Weiner, "Political Integration and Political Development," *The Annals*, 358 (March 1965): 52–64; and Amitai Etzioni, *Political Unification: A Comparative Study of Leaders and Forces* (New York: Holt, Rinehart and Winston, 1965).

[2] For a discussion of the terms "range" and "scope," see Harold D. Lasswell and Abraham Kaplan, *Power and Society* (New Haven, Conn.: Yale University Press, 1950), p. 225; and Karl W. Deutsch, *The Analysis of International Relations* (Englewood Cliffs, N.J.: Prentice-Hall, 1968), pp. 158–160.

[3] The word "influence" here is used to connote potential rather than actual power. "By influence is meant the value position and potential of a person or group," Lasswell and Kaplan, *Power and Society*, p. 55. In this sense, the measures we discuss in this chapter may be considered valid operationalizations of governmental influence.

4 This is obviously a restrictive statement of the economic role of government. The concern with fiscal policy and the neglect of monetary policy is, however, appropriate in the African context, where the ability of governments to control the value and availability of money is restricted by the absence of developed financial institutions, and by the external controls over African currency exercised by the governments of foreign countries, whose central banks control the international standards of exchange used in Africa.

5 The percentage of increased government revenue that goes into investment may be as low as 5–10 percent.

6 See Joseph J. Spengler, "Bureaucracy and Economic Development," in Joseph LaPalombara, ed., *Bureaucracy and Political Development* (Princeton, N.J.: Princeton University Press, 1963), especially pp. 223–232.

7 An important discussion is contained in Albert Waterson, *Development Planning: Lessons of Experience* (Baltimore, Md.: Johns Hopkins Press, 1966).

8 See the analysis of A. F. Ewing, *Industry in Africa* (London: Oxford University Press, 1968). It should be pointed out that the scope of government investment is not necessarily a simple function of political ideology. Table 9.4 on the percentage of GNP made up by government spending indicates that both Guinea and Ivory Coast, with pronounced differences in ideology and economic organization, are at the top of the distribution.

9 For empirical confirmation of this hypothesis, see Lynn Fischer, Donald G. Morrison, and Hugh M. Stevenson, "Modernization and Political Instability in Africa: An Empirical Assessment of Macro-Theory," a paper presented to the annual convention of the African Studies Association, Montreal, October 19, 1969.

TABLE 9.1 Per Capita Central Government Budget, in U.S. Dollars, 1951

```
RANGE    =      21.50
MEAN     =       6.40
STANDARD DEVIATION =              4.42
```

POPULATION PERCENT CUM.	COUNTRY	RANK	COUNTRY NAME	VALUE	RANGE DECILE
3.8	3.8	1.0	GHANA	23.30	1
6.3	2.5	2.0	CAMEROON	12.00	6
6.8	0.5	3.0	LIBERIA	11.10	
8.5	1.7	4.0	SENEGAL	9.90	7
10.2	1.7	5.0	GUINEA	9.30	
10.9	0.7	6.5	CAR	8.00	8
12.1	1.2	6.5	SOMALIA	8.00	
16.9	4.8	8.0	KENYA	7.40	
23.6	6.7	9.0	SUDAN	6.70	
27.8	4.2	10.0	UGANDA	6.40	
29.7	1.9	11.0	IVORY COAST	5.80	9
35.4	5.7	12.0	TANZANIA	5.70	
36.5	1.1	13.0	SIERRA LEONE	5.40	
38.2	1.7	14.0	NIGER	5.10	
63.2	25.0	15.0	NIGERIA	4.50	
64.8	1.6	16.5	CHAD	4.30	
66.0	1.2	16.5	DAHOMEY	4.30	
66.3	0.3	18.5	BOTSWANA	4.00	
67.1	0.8	18.5	TOGO	4.00	
76.2	9.1	20.5	ZAIRE	3.20	10
78.4	2.2	20.5	MALI	3.20	
80.7	2.3	22.0	UPPER VOLTA	2.40	
82.2	1.5	23.5	BURUNDI	2.10	
83.7	1.5	23.5	RWANDA	2.10	
94.6	10.9	25.0	ETHIOPIA	1.80	

DATA NOT AVAILABLE FOR THE FOLLOWING COUNTRIES

CONGO (BRA)	GABON	GAMBIA	LESOTHO
MALAWI	MAURITANIA	ZAMBIA	

SOURCES: *ECA Statistical Bulletin I. Cameroon*: French Cameroon only; *Botswana*: *Basutoland, Bechuanaland Protectorate, and Swaziland, Report of an Economic Survey Mission* (London: Her Majesty's Stationery Office, 1960).

TABLE 9.2 Average Annual Central Government Budget Growth per Capita, 1957 to 1959

```
RANGE    =      15.00
MEAN     =       8.63
STANDARD DEVIATION =              4.01
```

POPULATION PERCENT CUM.	COUNTRY	RANK	COUNTRY NAME	VALUE	RANGE DECILE
1.9	1.9	1.0	IVORY COAST	17	1
3.6	1.7	2.0	SENEGAL	15	2
12.7	9.1	3.0	ZAIRE	14	3
13.9	1.2	4.0	DAHOMEY	13	
17.7	3.8	5.5	GHANA	12	4
20.0	2.3	5.5	UPPER VOLTA	12	
20.5	0.5	8.0	LIBERIA	11	5
22.7	2.2	8.0	MALI	11	
23.8	1.1	8.0	SIERRA LEONE	11	
25.3	1.5	10.5	BURUNDI	10	
26.1	0.8	10.5	TOGO	10	
26.8	0.7	12.5	CAR	8	7
31.6	4.8	12.5	KENYA	8	
33.2	1.6	15.0	CHAD	7	
44.1	10.9	15.0	ETHIOPIA	7	
45.6	1.5	15.0	RWANDA	7	
48.1	2.5	18.0	CAMEROON	6	8
73.1	25.0	18.0	NIGERIA	6	
79.8	6.7	18.0	SUDAN	6	
81.5	1.7	20.0	NIGER	5	9
87.2	5.7	21.0	TANZANIA	4	
88.4	1.2	22.0	SOMALIA	3	10
90.1	1.7	23.0	GUINEA	2	
94.3	4.2	24.0	UGANDA	2	

DATA NOT AVAILABLE FOR THE FOLLOWING COUNTRIES

BOTSWANA	CONGO (BRA)	GABON	GAMBIA
LESOTHO	MALAWI	MAURITANIA	ZAMBIA

SOURCE: *ECA Statistical Bulletin I.*

TABLE 9.3   Per Capita Central Government Budget, in U.S. Dollars, 1961

```
RANGE           =        61.00
MEAN            =        15.97
STANDARD DEVIATION =            12.85
```

POPULATION PERCENT CUM.	COUNTRY	RANK	COUNTRY NAME	VALUE	RANGE DECILE
3.8	3.8	1.0	GHANA	63	1
5.5	1.7	2.0	SENEGAL	41	4
5.9	0.4	4.0	CONGO (BRA)	33	5
7.8	1.9	4.0	IVORY COAST	33	
8.3	0.5	4.0	LIBERIA	33	
8.8	0.5	6.0	MAURITANIA	26	7
11.3	2.5	7.5	CAMEROON	23	
13.1	1.8	7.5	ZAMBIA	23	
13.3	0.2	9.0	GAMBIA	20	8
18.1	4.8	10.0	KENYA	17	
18.8	0.7	11.5	CAR	16	
19.9	1.1	11.5	SIERRA LEONE	16	
21.1	1.2	13.0	DAHOMEY	13	9
30.2	9.1	15.5	ZAIRE	12	
32.4	2.2	15.5	MALI	12	
39.1	6.7	15.5	SUDAN	12	
39.9	0.8	15.5	TOGO	12	
41.6	1.7	18.0	GUINEA	11	
43.5	1.9	20.0	MALAWI	10	
45.2	1.7	20.0	NIGER	10	
46.4	1.2	20.0	SOMALIA	10	
48.0	1.6	23.5	CHAD	8	10
73.0	25.0	23.5	NIGERIA	8	
78.7	5.7	23.5	TANZANIA	8	
82.9	4.2	23.5	UGANDA	8	
84.4	1.5	27.0	BURUNDI	6	
84.6	0.2	27.0	GABON	6	
86.9	2.3	27.0	UPPER VOLTA	6	
87.3	0.4	29.0	LESOTHO	5	
98.2	10.9	30.5	ETHIOPIA	4	
99.7	1.5	30.5	RWANDA	4	
100.0	0.3	32.0	BOTSWANA	2	

SOURCES: *ECA Statistical Bulletin I*, Table 71, pp. 366–367. *Lesotho*: Estimated; similar to Botswana; *Somalia*: International Monetary Fund, *Surveys of African Economies*, Vol. 2.

TABLE 9.4   Government Spending as a Percent of GNP, 1961

```
RANGE           =        23.00
MEAN            =        16.47
STANDARD DEVIATION =            5.85
```

POPULATION PERCENT CUM.	COUNTRY	RANK	COUNTRY NAME	VALUE	RANGE DECILE
1.7	1.7	1.0	GUINEA	31	1
5.5	3.8	2.5	GHANA	26	3
7.4	1.9	2.5	IVORY COAST	26	
9.1	1.7	4.0	SENEGAL	24	4
9.5	0.4	6.0	CONGO (BRA)	23	
9.7	0.2	6.0	GAMBIA	23	
11.6	1.9	6.0	MALAWI	23	
12.1	0.5	8.0	LIBERIA	21	5
12.6	0.5	9.0	MAURITANIA	20	
14.8	2.2	11.0	MALI	19	6
15.9	1.1	11.0	SIERRA LEONE	19	
17.1	1.2	11.0	SOMALIA	19	
22.8	5.7	13.0	TANZANIA	18	
27.6	4.8	14.0	KENYA	17	7
28.8	1.2	16.0	DAHOMEY	16	
35.5	6.7	16.0	SUDAN	16	
39.7	4.2	16.0	UGANDA	16	
39.9	0.2	19.0	GABON	14	8
42.2	2.3	19.0	UPPER VOLTA	14	
44.0	1.8	19.0	ZAMBIA	14	
45.6	1.6	22.0	CHAD	13	
47.3	1.7	22.0	NIGER	13	
48.1	0.8	22.0	TOGO	13	
57.2	9.1	24.0	ZAIRE	12	9
58.7	1.5	26.0	BURUNDI	11	
59.4	0.7	26.0	CAR	11	
84.4	25.0	26.0	NIGERIA	11	
95.3	10.9	28.5	ETHIOPIA	10	10
96.8	1.5	28.5	RWANDA	10	
97.1	0.3	31.0	BOTSWANA	8	
99.6	2.5	31.0	CAMEROON	8	
100.0	0.4	31.0	LESOTHO	8	

SOURCES: *AID Economic Data Book* and *ECA Statistical Bulletin II*. *Zaire (Congo K.)*, *Senegal*: *Europa Yearbook 1961*; *CAR, Cameroon, Congo (Brazzaville)*, *Chad, Gabon*: International Monetary Fund, *Surveys of African Economies*, Vol. 1; *Kenya*: International Monetary Fund, *Surveys of African Economies*, Vol. 2; *Botswana*: *Bechuanaland Report 1965* (London: Her Majesty's Stationery Office, 1966); *Lesotho*: Estimated; similar to Botswana.

TABLE 9.5 Government Spending per Capita in U.S. Dollars and Total Government Expenditures, 1968

Definition: Total government expenditures are in millions of U.S. dollars.

```
RANGE     =        114.00
MEAN      =         29.44
STANDARD DEVIATION =              26.88
```

POPULATION PERCENT CUM. COUNTRY	RANK	COUNTRY NAME	VALUE	RANGE DECILE	TOTAL
1.8 1.8	1.0	ZAMBIA	118	1	498
2.0 0.2	2.0	GABON	92	3	46
2.4 0.4	3.0	CONGO (BRA)	71	5	64
4.3 1.9	4.0	IVORY COAST	64		263
4.8 0.5	5.0	LIBERIA	62		75
5.1 0.3	6.0	BOTSWANA	56	6	34
6.8 1.7	7.0	SENEGAL	51		200
10.6 3.8	8.0	GHANA	49	7	418
12.3 1.7	9.0	GUINEA	33	8	130
13.0 0.7	10.0	CAR	27		41
15.5 2.5	11.0	CAMEROON	26	9	149
20.3 4.8	12.0	KENYA	24		264
20.8 0.5	13.5	MAURITANIA	23		26
27.5 6.7	13.5	SUDAN	23		356
31.7 4.2	15.0	UGANDA	21		175
31.9 0.2	16.5	GAMBIA	20		8
33.0 1.1	16.5	SIERRA LEONE	20		51
42.1 9.1	18.0	ZAIRE	17		288
44.0 1.9	19.0	MALAWI	16		72
45.6 1.6	20.0	CHAD	15	10	51
46.8 1.2	21.0	SOMALIA	14		38
48.0 1.2	23.0	DAHOMEY	13		34
53.7 5.7	23.0	TANZANIA	13		172
54.5 0.8	23.0	TOGO	13		24
56.2 1.7	25.0	NIGER	11		43
56.6 0.4	26.0	LESOTHO	10		9
81.6 25.0	27.0	NIGERIA	9		450
83.8 2.2	28.0	MALI	8		40
94.7 10.9	29.0	ETHIOPIA	7		185
96.2 1.5	30.5	BURUNDI	6		22
98.5 2.3	30.5	UPPER VOLTA	6		33
100.0 1.5	32.0	RWANDA	4		15

SOURCE: *Africa Contemporary Record 1968–69. Botswana, Ivory Coast, Malawi, Somalia*: data for 1967; *Congo (Brazzaville), Liberia*: data for 1969.

TABLE 9.6 Ratio of Government Spending to GNP: Rate of Growth, 1963 to 1968

```
RANGE     =        235.00
MEAN      =         22.73
STANDARD DEVIATION =              45.67
```

POPULATION PERCENT CUM. COUNTRY	RANK	COUNTRY NAME	VALUE	RANGE DECILE	TOTAL
1.8 1.8	1.0	ZAMBIA	200	1	498
4.3 2.5	2.0	CAMEROON	90	5	149
5.9 1.6	3.0	CHAD	73	6	51
6.3 0.4	4.0	CONGO (BRA)	58	7	64
15.4 9.1	5.0	ZAIRE	57		288
16.6 1.2	6.0	SOMALIA	53		38
16.8 0.2	7.5	GABON	50		46
18.7 1.9	7.5	MALAWI	50		72
22.9 4.2	9.0	UGANDA	41		175
24.6 1.7	10.0	GUINEA	35	8	130
26.5 1.9	11.0	IVORY COAST	32		263
27.2 0.7	12.0	CAR	31		41
32.9 5.7	13.0	TANZANIA	25		172
37.7 4.8	14.0	KENYA	16		264
44.4 6.7	15.0	SUDAN	15		356
44.9 0.5	16.0	LIBERIA	11	9	75
55.8 10.9	17.0	ETHIOPIA	9		185
57.3 1.5	20.0	BURUNDI	0		22
61.1 3.8	20.0	GHANA	0		418
62.8 1.7	20.0	NIGER	0		43
64.3 1.5	20.0	RWANDA	0		15
66.0 1.7	20.0	SENEGAL	0		200
67.2 1.2	23.0	DAHOMEY	-5		34
68.3 1.1	24.0	SIERRA LEONE	-13	10	51
70.5 2.2	25.0	MALI	-14		40
95.5 25.0	26.0	NIGERIA	-20		450
95.7 0.2	27.0	GAMBIA	-22		8
96.5 0.8	28.0	TOGO	-25		24
97.0 0.5	29.0	MAURITANIA	-30		26
99.3 2.3	30.0	UPPER VOLTA	-35		33

DATA NOT AVAILABLE FOR THE FOLLOWING COUNTRIES

BOTSWANA   LESOTHO

SOURCES: See tables for government spending and GNP for relevant years.

TABLE 9.7 Government Revenue as a Percent of GNP, 1966

RANGE = 31.00
MEAN = 19.03
STANDARD DEVIATION = 7.19

POPULATION PERCENT			COUNTRY		RANGE
CUM.	COUNTRY	RANK	NAME	VALUE	DECILE
1.8	1.8	1.0	ZAMBIA	38	1
2.2	0.4	2.0	CONGO (BRA)	33	2
3.9	1.7	3.0	GUINEA	32	
13.0	9.1	4.0	ZAIRE	31	3
13.7	0.7	5.0	CAR	27	4
13.9	0.2	6.5	GABON	26	
14.1	0.2	6.5	GAMBIA	26	
16.0	1.9	9.0	IVORY COAST	22	6
16.5	0.5	9.0	LIBERIA	22	
17.7	1.2	9.0	SOMALIA	22	
18.0	0.3	11.0	BOTSWANA	21	
19.9	1.9	12.0	MALAWI	19	7
22.1	2.2	14.0	MALI	18	
23.8	1.7	14.0	SENEGAL	18	
30.5	6.7	14.0	SUDAN	18	
35.3	4.8	17.5	KENYA	17	
35.8	0.5	17.5	MAURITANIA	17	
41.5	5.7	17.5	TANZANIA	17	
45.7	4.2	17.5	UGANDA	17	
47.3	1.6	21.0	CHAD	16	8
48.5	1.2	21.0	DAHOMEY	16	
52.3	3.8	21.0	GHANA	16	
54.0	1.7	23.0	NIGER	15	
55.1	1.1	24.5	SIERRA LEONE	14	
57.4	2.3	24.5	UPPER VOLTA	14	
59.9	2.5	27.0	CAMEROON	13	9
60.3	0.4	27.0	LESOTHO	13	
61.1	0.8	27.0	TOGO	13	
62.6	1.5	29.5	BURUNDI	11	
73.5	10.9	29.5	ETHIOPIA	11	
98.5	25.0	31.0	NIGERIA	9	10
100.0	1.5	32.0	RWANDA	7	

SOURCES: *AID Economic Data Book*. *Congo (Brazzaville)*: International Monetary Fund, *Surveys of African Economies*, Vol. 1.

TABLE 9.8 Government Revenue, Percent Rate of Growth, 1963 to 1965

RANGE = 104.00
MEAN = 20.16
STANDARD DEVIATION = 22.68

POPULATION PERCENT			COUNTRY		RANGE
CUM.	COUNTRY	RANK	NAME	VALUE	DECILE
0.7	0.7	1.0	CAR	92	1
2.2	1.5	2.0	RWANDA	75	2
3.4	1.2	3.0	SOMALIA	57	4
12.5	9.1	4.0	ZAIRE	41	5
23.4	10.9	5.0	ETHIOPIA	37	6
25.0	1.6	6.0	CHAD	33	
30.7	5.7	7.0	TANZANIA	31	
33.2	2.5	8.5	CAMEROON	30	
33.4	0.2	8.5	GABON	30	
33.8	0.4	10.0	CONGO (BRA)	27	7
35.7	1.9	11.0	MALAWI	26	
36.0	0.3	12.0	BOTSWANA	25	
37.2	1.2	13.0	DAHOMEY	23	
42.0	4.8	14.0	KENYA	21	
44.2	2.2	15.0	MALI	20	
46.0	1.8	16.0	ZAMBIA	18	8
49.8	3.8	17.0	GHANA	14	
50.0	0.2	18.5	GAMBIA	13	
54.2	4.2	18.5	UGANDA	13	
79.2	25.0	20.5	NIGERIA	12	
85.9	6.7	20.5	SUDAN	12	
87.8	1.9	22.5	IVORY COAST	10	
88.2	0.4	22.5	LESOTHO	10	
89.9	1.7	24.0	GUINEA	7	9
90.4	0.5	25.0	MAURITANIA	6	
90.9	0.5	26.0	LIBERIA	4	
92.4	1.5	27.0	BURUNDI	0	
94.1	1.7	28.0	NIGER	-6	10
94.9	0.8	29.5	TOGO	-7	
97.2	2.3	29.5	UPPER VOLTA	-7	
98.9	1.7	31.0	SENEGAL	-10	
100.0	1.1	32.0	SIERRA LEONE	-12	

SOURCES: *AID Economic Data Book* and *ECA Statistical Bulletin II*. *Malawi*: Edwin S. Munger, *Bechuanaland* (London: Oxford University Press, 1965); *Lesotho*: Estimate.

TABLE 9.9 Direct Taxes as a Percent of Total Government Revenue, 1966

Definition: Direct taxes include income and profit taxes and all other taxes paid directly to the government without passing through an intermediary.

```
RANGE    =        41.00
MEAN     =        23.25
STANDARD DEVIATION =          11.07
```

POPULATION PERCENT CUM. COUNTRY		RANK	COUNTRY NAME	VALUE	RANGE DECILE
3.8	3.8	1.0	GHANA	43	1
12.9	9.1	2.5	ZAIRE	40	
14.7	1.8	2.5	ZAMBIA	40	
19.5	4.8	4.0	KENYA	37	2
30.4	10.9	5.5	ETHIOPIA	34	3
36.1	5.7	5.5	TANZANIA	34	
36.6	0.5	7.0	LIBERIA	33	
38.1	1.5	8.5	BURUNDI	31	
40.0	1.9	8.5	MALAWI	31	
41.7	1.7	10.0	NIGER	29	4
42.0	0.3	11.0	BOTSWANA	27	
67.0	25.0	12.5	NIGERIA	25	5
69.3	2.3	12.5	UPPER VOLTA	25	
70.0	0.7	14.0	CAR	24	
72.2	2.2	15.0	MALI	23	
73.3	1.1	16.5	SIERRA LEONE	22	6
77.5	4.2	16.5	UGANDA	22	
80.0	2.5	18.5	CAMEROON	20	
81.6	1.6	18.5	CHAD	20	
82.0	0.4	20.5	CONGO (BRA)	18	7
82.2	0.2	20.5	GABON	18	
83.7	1.5	22.0	RWANDA	11	8
85.6	1.9	23.0	IVORY COAST	10	9
86.4	0.8	24.0	TOGO	9	
87.6	1.2	25.5	DAHOMEY	8	
94.3	6.7	25.5	SUDAN	8	
95.5	1.2	27.0	SOMALIA	7	
97.2	1.7	28.0	GUINEA	2	10

DATA NOT AVAILABLE FOR THE FOLLOWING COUNTRIES

GAMBIA   LESOTHO   MAURITANIA   SENEGAL

sources: *AID Economic Data Book. Cameroon, CAR, Chad, Congo (Brazzaville), Gabon*: International Monetary Fund, *Surveys of African Economies*, Vol. 1; *Kenya, Somalia, Tanzania, Uganda: ibid.*, Vol. 2.

TABLE 9.10 Percent Growth of the Ratio of Direct Taxes to Total Government Revenue, 1963 to 1966

```
RANGE    =       101.00
MEAN     =         1.17
STANDARD DEVIATION =        22.57
```

POPULATION PERCENT CUM. COUNTRY		RANK	COUNTRY NAME	VALUE	RANGE DECILE
3.8	3.8	1.0	GHANA	59	1
12.9	9.1	2.0	ZAIRE	54	
15.2	2.3	3.0	UPPER VOLTA	25	4
15.9	0.7	4.5	CAR	20	
40.9	25.0	4.5	NIGERIA	20	
42.6	1.7	6.0	NIGER	8	6
42.8	0.2	7.0	GABON	6	
53.7	10.9	8.0	ETHIOPIA	3	
54.0	0.3	12.5	BOTSWANA	0	
56.5	2.5	12.5	CAMEROON	0	
56.9	0.4	12.5	LESOTHO	0	
57.4	0.5	12.5	LIBERIA	0	
59.3	1.9	12.5	MALAWI	0	
60.4	1.1	12.5	SIERRA LEONE	0	
61.6	1.2	12.5	SOMALIA	0	
67.3	5.7	12.5	TANZANIA	0	
72.1	4.8	17.0	KENYA	-8	7
72.5	0.4	18.0	CONGO (BRA)	-10	
76.7	4.2	19.0	UGANDA	-15	8
78.3	1.6	20.5	CHAD	-20	
79.5	1.2	20.5	DAHOMEY	-20	
81.4	1.9	22.0	IVORY COAST	-23	9
83.2	1.8	23.0	ZAMBIA	-29	
89.9	6.7	24.0	SUDAN	-42	

DATA NOT AVAILABLE FOR THE FOLLOWING COUNTRIES

| BURUNDI | GAMBIA | GUINEA | MAURITANIA |
| MALI | RWANDA | SENEGAL | TOGO |

source: Derived from *AID Economic Data Book.*

TABLE 9.11 Central Government Revenue, Percent Rate of Growth, 1963 to 1966

```
RANGE  =          88.00
MEAN  =           35.84
STANDARD DEVIATION =              18.66
```

POPULATION PERCENT		RANK	COUNTRY NAME	VALUE	RANGE DECILE
CUM.	COUNTRY				
1.8	1.8	1.0	ZAMBIA	88	1
2.5	0.7	2.0	CAR	76	2
11.6	9.1	3.0	ZAIRE	56	4
13.2	1.6	4.0	CHAD	54	
24.1	10.9	6.0	ETHIOPIA	50	5
25.3	1.2	6.0	SOMALIA	50	
29.5	4.2	6.0	UGANDA	50	
29.7	0.2	8.5	GABON	49	
31.6	1.9	8.5	IVORY COAST	49	
56.6	25.0	10.0	NIGERIA	47	
60.4	3.8	11.0	GHANA	46	
62.3	1.9	12.0	MALAWI	44	
68.0	5.7	13.0	TANZANIA	43	6
70.5	2.5	14.0	CAMEROON	42	
70.7	0.2	15.0	GAMBIA	40	
71.2	0.5	16.0	MAURITANIA	35	7
76.0	4.8	17.0	KENYA	34	
76.3	0.3	18.0	BOTSWANA	30	
77.5	1.2	19.0	DAHOMEY	28	
77.9	0.4	20.0	CONGO (BRA)	27	
78.4	0.5	21.0	LIBERIA	26	8
80.6	2.2	22.0	MALI	22	
82.3	1.7	24.0	GUINEA	21	
82.7	0.4	24.0	LESOTHO	21	
89.4	6.7	24.0	SUDAN	21	
91.1	1.7	26.5	NIGER	19	
92.8	1.7	26.5	SENEGAL	19	
93.6	0.8	28.0	TOGO	17	9
95.1	1.5	29.0	RWANDA	16	
97.4	2.3	30.0	UPPER VOLTA	15	
98.5	1.1	31.0	SIERRA LEONE	12	
100.0	1.5	32.0	BURUNDI	0	10

SOURCES: *AID Economic Data Book. Botswana*: Munger, *Bechuanaland*, p. 115; *Lesotho*: Estimate for years 1964 to 1966.

10. Military and Security Systems

The analysis of military and security systems has traditionally distinguished between the military as an institution for the protection of a society from external threats to its security,[1] and security (police and para-military) forces as agencies for the maintenance of internal order. In developing nations, however, this distinction has little relevance, and military and security forces may be seen as having largely overlapping functions in the internal politics of development.[2] Contemporary theory stresses two aspects of the role of the military: (1) as an autonomous agent of political development, and (2) as an agent responsible to autonomous political authorities.

The analysis of the military as an autonomous political institution has been characterized by two contrary themes. One stresses the authoritarian and undemocratic nature of military institutions; the other their rational and efficient character.[3] The argument for the modernizing and reformist character of the military in developing countries is based on the inference that technological skill, bureaucratic organization, national identification, and detachment from civilian and traditional power structures, predisposes the military towards the development of modern and technologically advanced societies.[4] A contrary position is argued to the effect that it is questionable that the use and maintenance, as opposed to the manufacture, of technically advanced equipment is sufficient to imbue the military with a passion for modernizing their countries.[5] Furthermore, it is argued, the very organizational and professional qualities that permit the military to accumulate political power limit their ability to adapt to the political skills of compromise and bargaining.[6]

The conception of the military as an agent of autonomous political authorities is often based on a normative commitment to constitutional, or civilian, rather than praetorian forms of government. In this view, the role of the military is to enforce the authoritative decisions of political leadership, and the size of the military and security system is used as an indicator of the "facilities" or "coercive potential" available to political authorities.[7] The utility of such approaches is empirically questionable as military intervention in Black Africa has become more common. Unless the conditions are clearly specified under which obedience rather than intervention is characteristic of the military, it may be more useful to consider military intervention as a norm rather than an aberration.[8]

Data on the Military

The likelihood of military intervention, and the results of such intervention in Black Africa, are empirical problems. Whatever the answers to such questions, it is clear, however, that the very possibility of military intervention, and the claim of the military on the scarce economic resources of developing nations, may have inhibiting effects on the decision latitudes of civilian regimes. Analysis of these questions about the role of the military in national development in Black Africa can be facilitated in part by the data in this chapter on the size, cost, institutionalization, and foreign support of military and security systems.

The coercive power potentially available to civilian governments for the repression of dissent and the maintenance of order is indicated by the data on the size of black African military and security forces (Tables 10.1 through 10.5). These data are equally relevant to the measurement of the potential for military intervention, although size itself is hardly a limiting factor in a continent where an army only 300 strong has carried out a successful *coup d'etat*.

The cost of military and security systems is indicated by the data on the percentage of GNP taken up by budgetary appropriations to the military (Table 10.6), and the percentage of government expenditures represented by military appropriations (Table 10.7). A measure of change in total military spending (Table 10.8) is particularly relevant to the analysis of the causes of military intervention.

Unfortunately the years for which these data are calculated sometimes include the increased expenditures resulting from military intervention, thus masking low rates of expenditure as a possible cause of intervention.

The analysis of the modernizing influence of the military, and its predisposition towards intervention, is best analyzed by detailed data on the organizational structure, cohesion, skill distribution, recruitment policy and ideology of particular military institutions.[9] We do not have sufficient data on these concepts to present in this chapter. However, a particularly important aspect of the institutionalization of the military in Black Africa is the "Africanization" of the officer corps, for which we present data in Table 10.9. In many black African nations, national armies were not established until after independence. Thus in both the pre- and immediate post-independence periods, many nations were dependent upon officers from metropole (colonial ruler) countries to fill a large proportion of the positions in their officer corps. The presence of a high proportion of expatriate officers during this period may have retarded the growth of a spirit of professionalism, and the development of a tradition of political non-involvement in the indigenous officer corps. The relatively recent independence of black African military institutions from colonial authority, and the relatively recent Africanization of their officer corps, has, therefore, left little time for the development of a cohesive national consciousness[10] on the part of the officers.

Finally, we present data on the amount of foreign military assistance available to black African countries (Tables 10.10 and 10.11). These data may be much more relevant to the analysis of the coercive potential of black African governments than data on the size of domestic forces. The critical role of foreign military forces in former French Africa (notably in Gabon), and in East Africa after the mutinies of 1964, is an indication of the need for including such information in any account of black African politics. However, it should be stressed that these data, like all the data in this chapter, are particularly sensitive to historical time, and foreign military assistance may be a consequence of, rather than a preventative antecedent to, military intervention.

Reliability

The size of the armed forces would appear, in principle, to be well defined. However, different sources provide considerably different information on this variable, even when reported for identical years. One analytic device which can be utilized to increase confidence in the figures is a comparison of a country's defense expenditures with the size of its armed forces. The value of this procedure is limited, however, unless detailed data can be obtained for a series of points in time. Where possible, we have followed this procedure to choose between conflicting sources.

Figures for the size of internal security forces suffer from similar problems of inter-source reliability. "Internal security forces are all those personnel whose primary function is the maintenance of internal order in the society," but sources disagree on whether or not to include military and paramilitary personnel in their figures on this variable. Since the available sources for information on internal security forces do not cite the sources of *their* information, it is impossible to speculate on reasons for differences in the original reporting of the data.

The figures for defense expenditures are taken from the national government budgets. Problems of reliability in these data arise because of the lack of comparability in the definition of fiscal years from country to country, and because of the possibility that certain military and para-military expenditures may not be reported as such in the budgets.

Dimensionality

In a factor analysis of 47 measures of military and security systems, six factors accounted for 80 percent of the total variance in the intercorrelation matrix. These factors represent dimensions of (1) overall size—e.g. military size, total budget, police size; (2) per capita size; (3) military aid from the metropole; (4) total military aid; (5) patterns of change in military expenditure; and (6) military appropriations per capita.

Notes

[1] Or, in the sense of Clausewitz, as an agency for the implementation of national policy in international relations.

[2] We shall, therefore, take "military" to mean military and security forces in what follows.

[3] See David C. Rapoport, "Military and Civil Societies: The Contemporary Significance of a Traditional Subject in Political Theory," *Political Studies* (June 1964): 178–201.

[4] For details of these arguments, see John J. Johnson, ed., *The Role of the Military in Underdeveloped Countries* (Princeton, N.J.: Princeton University Press, 1962), especially the articles by Pye and Shils, and Samuel P. Huntington, ed., *Changing Patterns of Military Politics* (New York: The Free Press, 1962). Also see the application of this argument to African politics in Harvey Glickman, "The Military in African Politics: A Bibliographic Essay," *African Forum*, 2 (Summer 1966): 73.

[5] See Keith Hopkins, "Civil-Military Relations in Developing Countries," *British Journal of Sociology*, 17 (1966): 165–182. "The political intervention of the military seems to me to proceed not so much from its prior attitudes to social change but from its strategic position within the arena of social dissensus, for its relatively large size and hierarchic organization facilitate a cohesion which no other elite group can match."

[6] See Morris Janowitz, *The Military in the Development of New Nations* (Chicago: The University of Chicago Press, 1964). Also, Kenneth Grundy, *Conflicting Images of the Army in Africa* (Nairobi: East Africa Publishing House, 1968); Henry Bienen, ed., *The Military Intervenes: Case Studies in Political Development* (New York: Russell Sage Foundation, 1968), and Ernest W. Lefever, *Spear and Scepter: Army, Police and Politics in Tropical Africa* (Washington, D.C.: The Brookings Institution, 1970). For a recent review of the African military which contains a thorough discussion of its role in the political community see J. M. Lee, *African Armies and Civil Order* (London: Chatto and Windus, 1969). This book presents a fair amount of data including information on the army commanders of twenty African countries in 1967. It also contains an excellent bibliographical note.

[7] See for example Ted Gurr, "A Causal Model of Civil Strife: A Comparative Analysis Using New Indices," *American Political Science Review*, 67 (December 1968): 1104–1124; and D. P. Bwy, "Political Instability in Latin America: The Cross-Cultural Test of a Causal Model," *Latin American Research Review*, 3 (Spring 1968): 17–66.

[8] See Pierre van den Berghe, "The Role of the Army in Contemporary Africa," *Africa Report*, 10 (March 1965): 12–17; and James O'Connell, "The Inevitability of Instability," *Journal of Modern African Studies*, 5 (1967): 181–191.

[9] See Janowitz, *Military in the Development of New Nations*.

[10] See the analysis in Ali A. Mazrui and Donald Rothchild, "The Soldier and the State in East Africa: Some Theoretical Conclusions on the Army Mutinies of 1964," *Western Political Quarterly*, 20 (March 1967): especially p. 83.

TABLE 10.1   Total Manpower in Armed Forces, in Hundreds, ca. 1967

```
RANGE  =        500.00
MEAN   =         70.88
STANDARD DEVIATION =          115.87
```

POPULATION PERCENT		RANK	COUNTRY NAME	VALUE	RANGE DECILE
CUM.	COUNTRY				
25.0	25.0	1.0	NIGERIA	500	1
34.1	9.1	2.0	ZAIRE	354	3
45.0	10.9	3.0	ETHIOPIA	350	4
51.7	6.7	4.0	SUDAN	185	7
55.5	3.8	5.0	GHANA	160	
56.7	1.2	6.0	SOMALIA	95	9
60.9	4.2	7.0	UGANDA	60	
62.6	1.7	8.0	SENEGAL	55	
64.3	1.7	9.5	GUINEA	50	10
70.0	5.7	9.5	TANZANIA	50	
74.8	4.8	11.0	KENYA	48	
76.7	1.9	12.0	IVORY COAST	45	
77.2	0.5	13.0	LIBERIA	41	
79.7	2.5	14.5	CAMEROON	35	
81.9	2.2	14.5	MALI	35	
83.7	1.8	16.0	ZAMBIA	30	
85.2	1.5	17.0	RWANDA	25	
86.3	1.1	18.0	SIERRA LEONE	19	
86.7	0.4	19.5	CONGO (BRA)	18	
87.9	1.2	19.5	DAHOMEY	18	
88.7	0.8	21.5	TOGO	15	
91.0	2.3	21.5	UPPER VOLTA	15	
92.7	1.7	23.0	NIGER	13	
94.2	1.5	24.5	BURUNDI	10	
94.7	0.5	24.5	MAURITANIA	10	
96.3	1.6	26.5	CHAD	9	
98.2	1.9	26.5	MALAWI	9	
98.4	0.2	28.0	GABON	8	
99.1	0.7	29.0	CAR	6	
99.4	0.3	31.0	BOTSWANA	0	
99.6	0.2	31.0	GAMBIA	0	
100.0	0.4	31.0	LESOTHO	0	

SOURCES: D. Wood, *The Armed Forces of African States*, Adelphi Papers, no. 27 (London: Institute for Strategic Studies, 1966). Robert C. Sellers, *Reference Handbook to the Armed Forces of the World*, 2nd ed. (Garden City, N.Y.: Robert C. Sellers and Assoc., 1968). *Nigeria*: Estimate—Nigerian armed forces were officially given as 12,500 in Sellers, but rapid expansion due to the civil war has escalated this figure to as much as 100,000 in 1968 and, some say, to 200,000 in 1970.

TABLE 10.2   Percent Change in Total Armed Forces Manpower, 1963 to 1967

```
RANGE  =        613.00
MEAN   =         72.34
STANDARD DEVIATION =          128.38
```

POPULATION PERCENT		RANK	COUNTRY NAME	VALUE	RANGE DECILE
CUM.	COUNTRY				
0.8	0.8	1.0	TOGO	569	1
25.8	25.0	2.0	NIGERIA	479	2
30.0	4.2	3.0	UGANDA	182	7
31.5	1.5	4.0	RWANDA	153	
31.9	0.4	5.0	CONGO (BRA)	143	
33.5	1.6	6.0	CHAD	117	8
35.2	1.7	7.0	SENEGAL	103	
35.7	0.5	8.0	MAURITANIA	90	
36.9	1.2	9.0	SOMALIA	85	
40.7	3.8	10.0	GHANA	83	
45.5	4.8	11.0	KENYA	71	9
46.7	1.2	12.0	DAHOMEY	64	
53.4	6.7	13.0	SUDAN	54	
55.7	2.3	14.0	UPPER VOLTA	43	
55.9	0.2	15.0	GABON	30	
58.4	2.5	16.0	CAMEROON	21	
59.9	1.5	17.0	BURUNDI	15	10
70.8	10.9	18.0	ETHIOPIA	14	
71.5	0.7	19.5	CAR	11	
77.2	5.7	19.5	TANZANIA	11	
86.3	9.1	21.5	ZAIRE	10	
86.8	0.5	21.5	LIBERIA	10	
89.0	2.2	23.0	MALI	6	
90.9	1.9	24.0	IVORY COAST	4	
92.0	1.1	25.0	SIERRA LEONE	1	
92.3	0.3	27.5	BOTSWANA	0	
92.5	0.2	27.5	GAMBIA	0	
92.9	0.4	27.5	LESOTHO	0	
94.6	1.7	27.5	NIGER	0	
96.3	1.7	30.0	GUINEA	-4	
98.1	1.8	31.0	ZAMBIA	-6	
100.0	1.9	32.0	MALAWI	-44	

SOURCES: Wood, *Armed Forces of African States*, and Sellers, *Reference Handbook to the Armed Forces of the World*.

TABLE 10.3   **Armed Forces Manpower per 100,000 Population, 1967**

```
RANGE      =      369.00
MEAN       =      100.50
STANDARD DEVIATION =          89.96
```

POPULATION PERCENT CUM.	COUNTRY	RANK	COUNTRY NAME	VALUE	RANGE DECILE
0.5	0.5	1.0	LIBERIA	369	1
1.7	1.2	2.0	SOMALIA	357	
10.8	9.1	3.0	ZAIRE	216	5
11.2	0.4	4.0	CONGO (BRA)	209	
15.0	3.8	5.0	GHANA	196	
15.2	0.2	6.0	GABON	169	6
16.9	1.7	7.0	SENEGAL	150	
27.8	10.9	8.0	ETHIOPIA	149	
29.5	1.7	9.0	GUINEA	135	7
36.2	6.7	10.0	SUDAN	129	
38.1	1.9	11.0	IVORY COAST	112	
38.6	0.5	12.0	MAURITANIA	91	8
39.4	0.8	13.0	TOGO	87	
64.4	25.0	14.0	NIGERIA	81	
65.5	1.1	15.0	SIERRA LEONE	78	
67.0	1.5	17.0	RWANDA	76	
71.2	4.2	17.0	UGANDA	76	
73.0	1.8	17.0	ZAMBIA	76	
75.2	2.2	19.0	MALI	74	
76.4	1.2	20.0	DAHOMEY	72	9
78.9	2.5	21.0	CAMEROON	64	
83.7	4.8	22.0	KENYA	48	
84.4	0.7	23.0	CAR	41	
86.1	1.7	24.0	NIGER	37	
87.6	1.5	25.5	BURUNDI	30	10
89.9	2.3	25.5	UPPER VOLTA	30	
91.5	1.6	27.0	CHAD	26	
93.4	1.9	28.0	MALAWI	22	
99.1	5.7	29.0	TANZANIA	16	
99.4	0.3	31.0	BOTSWANA	0	
99.6	0.2	31.0	GAMBIA	0	
100.0	0.4	31.0	LESOTHO	0	

SOURCES: Sellers, *Reference Handbook to the Armed Forces of the World.* Population data from Appendix 5.

TABLE 10.4   **Size of Internal Security Forces per 100,000 Population, 1967**

```
RANGE      =      166.00
MEAN       =       89.81
STANDARD DEVIATION =          47.16
```

POPULATION PERCENT CUM.	COUNTRY	RANK	COUNTRY NAME	VALUE	RANGE DECILE	TOTAL
0.2	0.2	1.0	GABON	190	1	9
1.4	1.2	2.0	SOMALIA	180		48
1.6	0.2	3.0	GAMBIA	175		6
2.0	0.4	4.0	CONGO (BRA)	174		15
3.8	1.8	5.0	ZAMBIA	157	2	62
5.7	1.9	6.0	MALAWI	143	3	59
16.6	10.9	7.0	ETHIOPIA	128	4	300
16.9	0.3	8.0	BOTSWANA	118	5	5
21.7	4.8	9.0	KENYA	116		115
25.5	3.8	10.0	GHANA	111		90
28.0	2.5	11.5	CAMEROON	103	6	59
28.7	0.7	11.5	CAR	103		15
37.8	9.1	13.0	ZAIRE	92		150
39.5	1.7	14.0	GUINEA	89	7	33
41.2	1.7	15.5	SENEGAL	82		30
42.3	1.1	15.5	SIERRA LEONE	82		20
43.1	0.8	17.0	TOGO	75		13
43.6	0.5	18.0	MAURITANIA	73	8	4
50.3	6.7	19.0	SUDAN	70		100
54.5	4.2	20.0	UGANDA	69		55
55.7	1.2	21.0	DAHOMEY	68		17
56.2	0.5	22.0	LIBERIA	63		7
57.8	1.6	23.0	CHAD	59		20
59.7	1.9	24.0	IVORY COAST	57	9	23
60.1	0.4	25.0	LESOTHO	56		5
61.8	1.7	26.0	NIGER	42		15
67.5	5.7	27.0	TANZANIA	41		50
92.5	25.0	28.0	NIGERIA	37	10	230
94.8	2.3	29.0	UPPER VOLTA	36		18
97.0	2.2	30.0	MALI	34		6
98.5	1.5	31.0	BURUNDI	27		9
100.0	1.5	32.0	RWANDA	24		7

SOURCES: See Table 10.3.

TABLE 10.5   Percent Change in Internal Security Forces per 100,000 Population, 1964 to 1967

```
RANGE  =        281.00
MEAN   =          6.28
STANDARD DEVIATION =        45.38
```

POPULATION PERCENT CUM.	COUNTRY	RANK	COUNTRY NAME	VALUE	RANGE DECILE
0.4	0.4	1.0	CONGO (BRA)	185	1
0.9	0.5	2.0	MAURITANIA	87	4
2.8	1.9	3.0	MALAWI	83	
4.3	1.5	4.0	BURUNDI	69	5
6.6	2.3	5.0	UPPER VOLTA	29	6
8.8	2.2	6.0	MALI	26	
10.3	1.5	7.0	RWANDA	20	
11.9	1.6	8.0	CHAD	0	7
12.7	0.8	9.0	TOGO	-1	
12.9	0.2	10.5	GABON	-3	
14.8	1.9	10.5	IVORY COAST	-3	
25.7	10.9	12.5	ETHIOPIA	-5	
26.8	1.1	12.5	SIERRA LEONE	-5	
27.0	0.2	14.5	GAMBIA	-6	
27.5	0.5	14.5	LIBERIA	-6	
27.8	0.3	16.5	BOTSWANA	-7	
36.9	9.1	16.5	ZAIRE	-7	
38.1	1.2	20.5	DAHOMEY	-8	
41.9	3.8	20.5	GHANA	-8	
43.6	1.7	20.5	GUINEA	-8	
68.6	25.0	20.5	NIGERIA	-8	
75.3	6.7	20.5	SUDAN	-8	
79.5	4.2	20.5	UGANDA	-8	
84.3	4.8	24.5	KENYA	-9	
90.0	5.7	24.5	TANZANIA	-9	
92.5	2.5	26.5	CAMEROON	-10	
92.9	0.4	26.5	LESOTHO	-10	
94.6	1.7	28.5	NIGER	-11	
95.8	1.2	28.5	SOMALIA	-11	
97.6	1.8	30.0	ZAMBIA	-20	8
99.3	1.7	31.0	SENEGAL	-31	
100.0	0.7	32.0	CAR	-96	

SOURCES: See Table 10.3.

TABLE 10.6   Defense Budget as Percent of GNP, ca. 1967

```
RANGE  =         5.90
MEAN   =         2.27
STANDARD DEVIATION =        1.42
```

POPULATION PERCENT CUM.	COUNTRY	RANK	COUNTRY NAME	VALUE	RANGE DECILE
9.1	9.1	1.0	ZAIRE	5.9	1
10.3	1.2	2.0	SOMALIA	5.0	2
10.7	0.4	3.0	CONGO (BRA)	4.7	3
12.4	1.7	4.0	GUINEA	4.3	
14.6	2.2	5.5	MALI	3.5	5
21.3	6.7	5.5	SUDAN	3.5	
21.8	0.5	7.0	MAURITANIA	3.4	
23.5	1.7	8.0	SENEGAL	3.1	
34.4	10.9	9.5	ETHIOPIA	2.9	6
38.6	4.2	9.5	UGANDA	2.9	
41.1	2.5	11.0	CAMEROON	2.7	
42.3	1.2	12.0	DAHOMEY	2.5	
43.9	1.6	14.0	CHAD	2.4	
45.6	1.7	14.0	NIGER	2.4	
47.4	1.8	14.0	ZAMBIA	2.4	
48.9	1.5	16.0	RWANDA	2.3	7
49.6	0.7	17.0	CAR	2.2	
53.4	3.8	18.0	GHANA	2.0	
55.7	2.3	19.0	UPPER VOLTA	1.9	
56.5	0.8	20.0	TOGO	1.8	
56.7	0.2	21.0	GABON	1.7	8
81.7	25.0	22.0	NIGERIA	1.6	
86.5	4.8	23.5	KENYA	1.4	
87.0	0.5	23.5	LIBERIA	1.4	
88.9	1.9	25.0	IVORY COAST	1.3	
94.6	5.7	26.0	TANZANIA	1.0	9
96.5	1.9	27.5	MALAWI	0.8	
97.6	1.1	27.5	SIERRA LEONE	0.8	
99.1	1.5	29.0	BURUNDI	0.7	
99.4	0.3	31.0	BOTSWANA	0.0	10
99.6	0.2	31.0	GAMBIA	0.0	
100.0	0.4	31.0	LESOTHO	0.0	

SOURCES: Defense: Sellers, *Reference Handbook to the Armed Forces of the World*; GNP: See GNP figures for 1965 in Table 4.1.

TABLE 10.7 Defense Budget as Percent of Government Expenditures, 1967

RANGE = 21.20
MEAN = 9.88
STANDARD DEVIATION = 5.62

POPULATION PERCENT CUM.	COUNTRY	RANK	COUNTRY NAME	VALUE	RANGE DECILE
2.2	2.2	1.0	MALI	21.2	1
4.7	2.5	2.0	CAMEROON	19.5	
5.9	1.2	3.0	SOMALIA	18.1	2
6.4	0.5	4.0	MAURITANIA	17.9	
13.1	6.7	5.0	SUDAN	17.7	
24.0	10.9	6.0	ETHIOPIA	17.0	
33.1	9.1	7.0	ZAIRE	14.5	4
35.4	2.3	8.0	UPPER VOLTA	14.1	
37.0	1.6	9.5	CHAD	13.5	
37.8	0.8	9.5	TOGO	13.5	
39.0	1.2	11.0	DAHOMEY	12.0	5
40.7	1.7	12.0	SENEGAL	11.6	
42.4	1.7	13.0	NIGER	10.8	
46.6	4.2	14.0	UGANDA	10.2	6
71.6	25.0	15.0	NIGERIA	9.9	
73.1	1.5	16.0	RWANDA	9.7	
73.5	0.4	17.0	CONGO (BRA)	8.9	
75.2	1.7	18.0	GUINEA	8.1	7
75.9	0.7	19.0	CAR	7.9	
76.1	0.2	20.0	GABON	7.6	
79.9	3.8	21.0	GHANA	7.4	
81.4	1.5	23.0	BURUNDI	6.9	
83.3	1.9	23.0	IVORY COAST	6.9	
88.1	4.8	23.0	KENYA	6.9	
88.6	0.5	25.0	LIBERIA	6.7	
90.4	1.8	26.0	ZAMBIA	5.7	8
91.5	1.1	27.0	SIERRA LEONE	4.9	
97.2	5.7	28.0	TANZANIA	3.8	9
99.1	1.9	29.0	MALAWI	3.3	
99.4	0.3	31.0	BOTSWANA	0.0	10
99.6	0.2	31.0	GAMBIA	0.0	
100.0	0.4	31.0	LESOTHO	0.0	

SOURCE: Sellers, *Reference Handbook to the Armed Forces of the World.*

TABLE 10.8 Percent Change in Defense Budget, 1963 to 1967

RANGE = 413.00
MEAN = 75.63
STANDARD DEVIATION = 90.70

POPULATION PERCENT CUM.	COUNTRY	RANK	COUNTRY NAME	VALUE	RANGE DECILE	TOTAL
4.2	4.2	1.0	UGANDA	400	1	20000
5.0	0.8	2.0	TOGO	350	2	2757
6.5	1.5	3.0	RWANDA	182	6	3500
12.2	5.7	4.0	TANZANIA	150	7	7600
37.2	25.0	5.0	NIGERIA	128		76000
46.3	9.1	6.0	ZAIRE	118		74900
48.1	1.8	7.0	ZAMBIA	110	8	20000
49.8	1.7	8.0	SENEGAL	107		21000
54.6	4.8	9.0	KENYA	100		14000
56.3	1.7	10.0	GUINEA	87		11000
57.0	0.7	11.0	CAR	83		3800
57.4	0.4	12.0	CONGO (BRA)	80		6500
59.1	1.7	13.0	NIGER	71		6000
65.8	6.7	14.0	SUDAN	67	9	49000
76.7	10.9	15.0	ETHIOPIA	45		34000
78.6	1.9	16.0	IVORY COAST	44		13000
78.8	0.2	17.0	GABON	41		3520
81.3	2.5	18.0	CAMEROON	35		18000
82.9	1.6	21.0	CHAD	33		5736
86.7	3.8	21.0	GHANA	33		45162
88.6	1.9	21.0	MALAWI	33		1305
89.7	1.1	21.0	SIERRA LEONE	33		2900
90.9	1.2	21.0	SOMALIA	33		7524
91.4	0.5	24.0	LIBERIA	28	10	3100
93.6	2.2	25.0	MALI	17		10400
94.8	1.2	26.0	DAHOMEY	15		4070
95.3	0.5	27.0	MAURITANIA	10		4339
95.6	0.3	29.5	BOTSWANA	0		0
95.8	0.2	29.5	GAMBIA	0		0
96.2	0.4	29.5	LESOTHO	0		0
98.5	2.3	29.5	UPPER VOLTA	0		2819
100.0	1.5	32.0	BURUNDI	-13		963

SOURCE: Sellers, *Reference Handbook to the Armed Forces of the World.*

TABLE 10.9 Africanization of the Army Officer Corps in 1965

Definition:

0. No army before or after independence.
1. Officer corps entirely foreign before independence. After independence foreign officers still served at most high-level positions in 1965.
2. No indigenous officer corps before independence. After independence a mixed white and indigenous officer corps, with Africanization nearly or totally completed by 1965.
3. No indigenous officer corps before independence. After independence a total Africanization program.
4. Indigenous officers before independence, but not at highest levels. After independence white officers continued to serve in some positions but had been entirely superseded by 1965.
5. (a) Never a colonial country, or (b) an indigenous officer corps existed at all levels by or shortly after independence.

```
RANGE     =        5.00
MEAN      =        2.59
STANDARD DEVIATION =          1.62
```

POPULATION PERCENT CUM.	COUNTRY	RANK	COUNTRY NAME	VALUE	RANGE DECILE
10.9	10.9	3.5	ETHIOPIA	5	1
14.7	3.8	3.5	GHANA	5	
16.4	1.7	3.5	GUINEA	5	
16.9	0.5	3.5	LIBERIA	5	
18.1	1.2	3.5	SOMALIA	5	
24.8	6.7	3.5	SUDAN	5	
26.3	1.5	9.0	BURUNDI	4	2
28.5	2.2	9.0	MALI	4	3
53.5	25.0	9.0	NIGERIA	4	
55.2	1.7	9.0	SENEGAL	4	
57.5	2.3	9.0	UPPER VOLTA	4	
66.6	9.1	13.0	ZAIRE	3	4
66.8	0.2	13.0	GABON	3	5
68.5	1.7	13.0	NIGER	3	
69.2	0.7	19.0	CAR	2	6
70.8	1.6	19.0	CHAD	2	7
71.2	0.4	19.0	CONGO (BRA)	2	
72.4	1.2	19.0	DAHOMEY	2	
74.3	1.9	19.0	IVORY COAST	2	
79.1	4.8	19.0	KENYA	2	
79.6	0.5	19.0	MAURITANIA	2	
80.7	1.1	19.0	SIERRA LEONE	2	
81.5	0.8	19.0	TOGO	2	
84.0	2.5	26.5	CAMEROON	1	8
85.9	1.9	26.5	MALAWI	1	9
87.4	1.5	26.5	RWANDA	1	
93.1	5.7	26.5	TANZANIA	1	
97.3	4.2	26.5	UGANDA	1	
99.1	1.8	26.5	ZAMBIA	1	
99.4	0.3	31.0	BOTSWANA	0	
99.6	0.2	31.0	GAMBIA	0	
100.0	0.4	31.0	LESOTHO	0	

SOURCES: William F. Guttridge, *Military Institutions and Power in the New States* (London: Pall Mall, 1965). George Weeks, "The Armies of Africa," *Africa Report*, 9 (January 1964). James Coleman and Belmont Brice, Jr., "The Role of the Military in Sub-Saharan Africa," in *The Role of the Military in Underdeveloped Countries*, ed. John Johnson (Princeton, N.J.: Princeton University Press, 1962).

TABLE 10.10 Number of Countries from which Military Aid Was Received, ca. 1964

```
RANGE     =        8.00
MEAN      =        2.66
STANDARD DEVIATION =          2.23
```

POPULATION PERCENT CUM.	COUNTRY	RANK	COUNTRY NAME	VALUE	RANGE DECILE
3.8	3.8	2.0	GHANA	8	1
28.8	25.0	2.0	NIGERIA	8	
34.5	5.7	2.0	TANZANIA	8	
43.6	9.1	5.5	ZAIRE	5	4
54.5	10.9	5.5	ETHIOPIA	5	
59.3	4.8	5.5	KENYA	5	
66.0	6.7	5.5	SUDAN	5	
67.2	1.2	8.5	SOMALIA	4	5
71.4	4.2	8.5	UGANDA	4	
73.3	1.9	10.0	IVORY COAST	3	7
75.8	2.5	16.0	CAMEROON	2	8
76.5	0.7	16.0	CAR	2	
76.9	0.4	16.0	CONGO (BRA)	2	
78.1	1.2	16.0	DAHOMEY	2	
79.8	1.7	16.0	GUINEA	2	
82.0	2.2	16.0	MALI	2	
83.7	1.7	16.0	NIGER	2	
85.4	1.7	16.0	SENEGAL	2	
86.5	1.1	16.0	SIERRA LEONE	2	
88.8	2.3	16.0	UPPER VOLTA	2	
90.6	1.8	16.0	ZAMBIA	2	
92.1	1.5	25.5	BURUNDI	1	9
93.7	1.6	25.5	CHAD	1	
93.9	0.2	25.5	GABON	1	
94.4	0.5	25.5	LIBERIA	1	
96.3	1.9	25.5	MALAWI	1	
96.8	0.5	25.5	MAURITANIA	1	
98.3	1.5	25.5	RWANDA	1	
99.1	0.8	25.5	TOGO	1	
99.4	0.3	31.0	BOTSWANA	0	10
99.6	0.2	31.0	GAMBIA	0	
100.0	0.4	31.0	LESOTHO	0	

SOURCE: M. J. V. Bell, *Military Assistance to Independent African States*, Adelphi Paper, no. 15 (London: Institute for Strategic Studies, 1964).

TABLE 10.11 Index of Total Military Aid, 1964

Definition: Various forms of aid were weighted as follows and summed: (1) training, minor facilities, (2) training, extensive facilities, experts; (1) equipment up to fitting out units, (2) equipment basic for all or most of armed service, (3) lavish equipment beyond need of internal security. High values are the result of more than one country giving military aid, since each country's contribution was scored and summed to get a total score.

```
RANGE  =          18.00
MEAN   =           6.69
STANDARD DEVIATION =          4.37
```

POPULATION PERCENT		RANK	COUNTRY NAME	VALUE	RANGE DECILE
CUM.	COUNTRY				
5.7	5.7	1.0	TANZANIA	18	1
14.8	9.1	2.5	ZAIRE	15	2
39.8	25.0	2.5	NIGERIA	15	
43.6	3.8	4.0	GHANA	14	3
54.5	10.9	5.5	ETHIOPIA	12	4
61.2	6.7	5.5	SUDAN	12	
62.4	1.2	7.0	SOMALIA	11	
64.1	1.7	8.5	GUINEA	8	6
68.9	4.8	8.5	KENYA	8	
70.8	1.9	11.5	IVORY COAST	7	7
72.5	1.7	11.5	NIGER	7	
74.2	1.7	11.5	SENEGAL	7	
78.4	4.2	11.5	UGANDA	7	
80.6	2.2	14.0	MALI	6	
83.1	2.5	18.0	CAMEROON	5	8
83.8	0.7	18.0	CAR	5	
84.2	0.4	18.0	CONGO (BRA)	5	
85.4	1.2	18.0	DAHOMEY	5	
86.5	1.1	18.0	SIERRA LEONE	5	
88.8	2.3	18.0	UPPER VOLTA	5	
90.6	1.8	18.0	ZAMBIA	5	
92.1	1.5	25.5	BURUNDI	4	
93.7	1.6	25.5	CHAD	4	
93.9	0.2	25.5	GABON	4	
94.4	0.5	25.5	LIBERIA	4	
96.3	1.9	25.5	MALAWI	4	
96.8	0.5	25.5	MAURITANIA	4	
98.3	1.5	25.5	RWANDA	4	
99.1	0.8	25.5	TOGO	4	
99.4	0.3	31.0	BOTSWANA	0	
99.6	0.2	31.0	GAMBIA	0	
100.0	0.4	31.0	LESOTHO	0	

SOURCES: Bell, *Military Assistance to Independent African States. Congo (Brazzaville), Kenya, Tanzania*: Uncertain whether Communist China actually gave aid.

11. Political Instability

From 1958 through December 1970, there have been twenty-four successful coups in thirteen different sub-Saharan states. In addition, there have been at least twelve major attempted but unsuccessful coups during this period. Many of these coups occurred during the period 1963–1966, i.e. during the early years of independence. In almost every case, the military assumed control in a relatively bloodless manner. In contrast, considerable violence has characterized threats to the governments of black African nations by disaffected communal or ethnic groups. The most widely publicized attempts at secession have been in Zaire (Katanga) and Nigeria (Biafra), but other instances have also occurred in Sudan (in the three southern provinces) and in Ethiopia (with the disaffection of Eritrea). The Tiv in Nigeria were in a state of armed rebellion from 1961 through 1965. The Baganda of Uganda strongly resisted the efforts of the central government to limit the powers of the Kabaka. The Lumpa of Zambia rebelled against the supremacy of national loyalties over religious loyalties. Finally, there have been significant instances of irredentism, in which ethnic groups have sought reunification across arbitrarily imposed boundaries. This has often led to communal violence or strong political pressure as with the Ewé (in Ghana and Togo), the Kongo (in Congo [Brazzaville], Zaire [Congo K.], and Angola), and the Somali (in Ethiopia and Kenya).

Although there is no lack of commentary on events like those just referred to, the analysis of such historical experience is encumbered by differences of value bias and conceptual terminology. In this chapter, we refer to these kinds of events as "political instability," which we mean to define in ways which assume no *a priori* evaluation of stability as a normal or preferable condition of political systems, and which we attempt to measure in theoretically meaningful ways.

Conceptualizations of Political Instability

In the long historical tradition of political theory, the analysis of the basis of order is closely tied to the central issues of clarifying the nature of the "good" society. Order, stability, and political development are often assumed to be identical in political research, and in common wisdom the identity is all but a hallowed truth. It is important, however, to distinguish between *development* and *stability* in political analysis.

Political development has meaning as a concept only in the sense of a political process that approximates a normative preference of some kind.[1] In this sense, most of the analysis of political development in contemporary political science is deficient because of a failure to specify the normative justification for the characteristics of political systems that are identified as "developed."[2] From our point of view, *political development* is a process of continuous change in the adaptation of political systems to conflicting demands for justice, which we conceptualize as the capacity of political systems to maximize the opportunity of individuals to live their lives in the way they wish. *Political instability*, in contrast, is defined as a condition in political systems in which the institutionalized patterns of authority break down, and the expected compliance to political authorities is replaced by violence intended to change the personnel, policies or sovereignty of the authorities through injury to persons or property. While it is clear that violence obstructs the opportunity of people to live their lives in the way they wish, it is also clear that established and stable patterns of political authority are no guarantee of justice, and that violence may well promote the opportunities for justice for some members of political systems. In the absence, therefore, of detailed historical analyses of incidents of political instability, the most we can say of the relationship between political instability and political development is that political systems are more developed the more they accommodate changing demands for justice without violent changes in their structure. This statement, of course, does not imply that political systems are more developed the more stable they remain.

Leaving aside the critical, but difficult, evaluations of the relationship between political instability and political development in concrete historical situations, political scientists have been interested in the no less relevant questions of the conditions under which the likelihood of political instability is increased or reduced. The terminology varies, but whether the subject matter is defined as political instability,[3] political violence,[4] conflict behavior,[5] internal war,[6] or civil strife,[7] the phenomena under investigation have included revolutions, rebellions, civil and guerrilla war, coups d'état and riots. This agreement on the richness of ordinary language in describing different kinds of events has, however, created one of the issues to which most attention has been given by political scientists: namely, how to systematically categorize and measure what we have chosen to refer to generically as political instability.

It has been assumed, perhaps too naively, that there is relatively little difficulty in recording the incidence of events in which political violence occurs, but there is little agreement as to how these events shall be classified or weighted as types or intensities of political instability. Factor analysis has been widely used as an inductive approach to typologies of political instability, and factor solutions of variables measuring the frequency in nations of revolts, civil wars, coups d'état, and so on, have been interpreted as revealing either two or three dimensions of political instability. These dimensions have been labelled variously as revolution, subversion and turmoil;[8] internal war and turmoil;[9] or organized and anomic violence;[10] and, on the basis of these results, more recent research is based on the direct coding of raw data as incidents of internal war, conspiracy, and anomic violence.[11] In response to this linguistic and empirical confusion, other political scientists have criticized the attempt to categorize types of political instability as being dependent more on statistical explanation than analytic needs,[12] and they have chosen to treat events described by different words in ordinary language as instances of a single behavioral phenomenon, which they define broadly as internal war,[13] or revolution.[14] Similarly, it has been suggested that a simple index of the number of persons killed in domestic group violence is the most satisfactory indication of political instability in nations.[15]

We believe that it *is* important to distinguish between types of political instability. In line with what we have said in defining political development and political instability, we suggest that political instability is the result of conflict between different groups over the values according to which justice is defined, and according to which rewards are allocated in the political system. Theoretically, therefore, we anticipate that the nature of political instability will vary according to the nature of the groups involved in political conflict, and that the processes that inhibit or intensify the likelihood of political instability will be different for different kinds of conflict in nations. In what follows, then, we categorize and measure political instability in terms of the organizational basis of the insurgent groups involved in political violence, and the structural alterations they intend to carry out in the political system.

Categorization and Data

We distinguish between three different kinds of social grouping or organization as distinctive actors in events involving political violence: elites, communal groups and mass movements. Depending on which of these three actors are the insurgents in an event involving political violence, we distinguish between elite, communal and mass instability. *Elites* are those relatively small groups who hold the command positions in social institutions, and elite instability is violent action by members of either the political elite, or some alternative elite, intended to remove persons from their positions in the government. *Communal groups* are large social groups in which membership is based on ascribed characteristics of ethnicity, language, religion or territory; communal instability is violent action by members of one or more communal groups who aim to restructure the distribution of authority or rewards amongst communal groups, or between communal groups and the national government. *Mass movements* are large social groups organized for the attainment of relatively specific political goals;

membership in mass movements is based on the associational or voluntary commitment of individuals to these goals. Mass instability is violent action by mass movements intended to reorganize the structure and policy of the national government. This typology[16] is elaborated in terms of the kinds of events we have coded and represented in quantitative indices of political instability.

Elite instability involves limited violence and structural reorganization. The characteristic behaviors involving elites in conflict are (1) the replacement or reorganization of elite personnel by dismissal, resignation, and reallocation of persons in elite office; and (2) coups d'état organized from within a single elite, or by an alternative functional elite, usually the military. Table 11.1 gives data on the extent of elite instability as measured by the frequency of dismissals and resignations of cabinet officials in African governments. Table 11.2 gives a composite index of the frequency of coups, attempted coups and plotted coups d'état.

Communal instability involves much more extensive violence than elite instability, and threatens more extensive change in the structure of the political system. The events coded as communal instability are: (1) civil wars, in which one or more communities engage in violence to alter their authority relationships within the national unit, mostly by attempted secession; (2) rebellions, in which a community seeks to gain a significant measure of autonomy from the elite controlling the wider political system of which it is a part; and (3) irredentism, in which a community seeks to change its political allegiance from one national political elite to another, or to a new political system, in which the members of the new polity have closer communal ties with the community involved than their fellow citizens have in the established system. We have also coded instances of inter-ethnic violence which are not aimed at secession, autonomy, or political re-alignment, but which nevertheless represent a breakdown of authority relationships within the political system. Table 11.3 gives a weighted measure of communal instability. The specific events incorporated in this measure, as in the elite instability measures, are given by country in Part II of this Handbook.

Mass instability involves revolts or revolutions in which agents and supporters of the established political authority are attacked by insurgents whose primary source of common identity is their associational membership in a political movement, rather than any ascriptive communal identity. Mass instability, in these terms, is very difficult to isolate in contemporary African nations[17]—the revolt in Zaire (Congo K.) coordinated by the Comité Nationale de Libération, the revolt in Malawi in support of Chipembere, the sporadic revolt in Niger led by the Sawaba party, and the revolt against the Sudanese military government in 1964, are the only instances of significant political violence in which associational rather than communal organization may have been a predominant characteristic of the insurgents.

Finally, we are unable to distinguish from available sources whether events such as riots, demonstrations, and strikes are based on communal rather than associational organization, and whether the intention of such activity is political reorganization or more restricted social change. We are loathe, therefore, to classify such phenomena as a form of political instability, and certainly disagree with the classification of such events as anomic or unorganized. Since there is no doubt a connection between such activity and forms of instability, however, and since measures of this kind are so frequently used in the study of political instability, we give a composite measure of turmoil in Table 11.4.

All forms of instability involve violence,[18] and in most extreme cases, death. Table 11.5 gives figures on the number of persons killed in domestic violence, which substantiate our reasoning that communal instability is more violent than elite instability. The correlations between the number of persons killed in domestic violence and measures of communal instability are uniformly higher than the comparable relationship with measures of elite instability.[19]

Dimensionality and Reliability

The theoretical distinctions between elite and communal instability are clearly supported by a factor analysis of forty-one political instability variables, including measures developed by other researchers. The factor analysis is also useful in assessing aspects of data quality control in the study of political instability in Africa. The data used by Ted Gurr, for example, tend to be weakly associated with our measures of elite and communal instability.[20] His measure of the magnitude of conspiracy, which includes coups d'état and government crises, is correlated $-.008$ with our weighted measure of elite instability, and $-.22$ with a simple scale of coups (3), attempted coups (2), plots (1), and none of these (0). His measure of internal war, which includes civil war and rebellion, is highly associated with our weighted measure of community instability ($r = .72$) as is his composite measure of civil strife with our general instability measure ($r = .82$). The correlation between Gurr's measure of turmoil and the variables reported here is $r = .40$. The evaluation of Gurr's data is not so much indicative of the reliability of his or our data, as it is a commentary on the validity of measures of political instability in use. It seems clear that if the correlations between conspiracy and coup behavior are low and in the wrong direction, there is some difficulty in making meaningful judgments and analyses about African political-systems development as effected by, or as a cause of, conspiracy.[21]

It does not seem to us acceptable to neglect the African experience in comparative analysis because of want of information. Although we have no estimates on inter-coder reliability for our measures of political instability, we are confident that the coding procedures are clear enough, and the data sources rich enough, to permit reliable measures of political instability in Africa. The most pressing difficulty is the lack of comparability in the coverage of events in different sources, and the need, therefore, to search out a sufficiently exhaustive set of information sources. The sources used in the compilation of this data suffer from three major defects in coverage. There is likely to be more detailed coverage for countries which are large rather than small; for those in which "dramatic" events are taking place; and our sources are likely to be better informed on English-speaking than on French-speaking areas. In addition to variation in geographical coverage, there is variation in coverage over

historical time. In particular the years from independence to 1962 suffer from poor documentation. Given these qualifications, the data presented here are intended to stimulate assessments of data reliability and theoretical analysis appropriate to the African context in the quest for understanding the relationship between political instability and political development.

Notes

[1] See the comparison of the concepts "change," "movement," and "development" in Adam Schaff's contribution to Raymond Aron, ed., *Symposium on Social Development* (Paris: UNESCO, 1961).

[2] Contemporary students of political development define their subject matter in terms of any, or all, of the following characteristics of nations: (1) structural differentiation, institutionalization, and autonomy within the political system; (2) the integration of formerly diverse cultural elements and the collective acquisition of national loyalties; (3) higher magnitudes of popular participation and equality of opportunity in political life; (4) greater centralization and distributive capacity in the political system; and (5) stability in the exercise of political authority. Details and variations in the definition of political development along these lines can be seen in the publications issued under the auspices of the Committee on Comparative Politics of the Social Science Research Council. For a useful summary of conceptualization and data collection in contemporary studies of political development, see Raymond F. Hopkins, "Aggregate Data and the Study of Political Development," *Journal of Politics*, 31 (1969), 71–94.

[3] Ivo K. Feierabend, Rosalind L. Feierabend, and Betty A. Nesvold, "Social Change and Political Violence: Cross-National Patterns," in *The History of Violence in America*, eds. Hugh Davis Graham and Ted Robert Gurr (New York: Bantam Books, 1969), pp. 632–687.

[4] Ted Gurr, "Psychological Factors in Civil Violence, "*World Politics*," 20 (1968): 245–278.

[5] R. J. Rummel, "Dimensions of Conflict Behavior within Nations, 1946–59," *Journal of Conflict Resolution*, 10 (1966): 65–73.

[6] Harry Eckstein, ed., *Internal War: Problems and Approaches* (New York: The Free Press of Glencoe, 1964).

[7] Ted Gurr, "A Causal Model of Civil Strife: A Comparative Analysis Using New Indices," *American Political Science Review*, 68 (1968): 1104–1124.

[8] Rummel, "Dimensions of Conflict Behavior within Nations."

[9] Raymond Tanter, "Dimensions of Conflict Behavior within and between Nations, 1957–60," *Journal of Conflict Resolution*, 10 (1966): 41–64.

[10] D. P. Bwy, "Political Instability in Latin America: The Cross-Cultural Test of a Causal Model," *Latin American Research Review*, 3 (1968): 17–66.

[11] Gurr, "A Causal Model of Civil Strife."

[12] See the discussion in Harry Eckstein, "On the Etiology of Internal War," *History and Theory*, 4 (1965), especially p. 135.

[13] Eckstein, "On the Etiology of Internal War."

[14] P. A. R. Calvert, "Revolution: The Politics of Violence," *Political Studies*, 15 (1967), 1–11.

[15] Bruce M. Russett, et al., *World Handbook of Political and Social Indicators* (New Haven: Yale University Press, 1964), 97–98.

[16] A comparable typology is sketched in James N. Rosenau, "Internal War as an International Event," in Rosenau, ed., *International Aspects of Civil Strife* (Princeton, N.J.: Princeton University Press, 1964), pp. 45–91. Rosenau speaks of personnel, authority and structural wars as types of internal war (pp. 63–64).

[17] Interestingly, colonial revolts such as those in Kenya and Cameroon were events in which the organizational basis of insurgency was a mass movement, involving associational rather than communal ties as the sources of primary identification. This is, of course, also true of liberation movements in Southern Africa.

[18] Violence, like instability, is variously defined, but includes behaviors ranging from activity intended to injure physically, to actions that flout institutionalized expectations of "proper" behavior.

See Chalmers Johnson, *Revolution* (Stanford: Hoover Institution, Stanford University, 1964), p. 8, and H. L. Nieburg, *Political Violence* (New York: St. Martin's Press, 1969), p. 13.

[19] The correlations are low, however, probably reflecting the lack of reliability in estimates of death in civil violence, as well as the wide variation in destruction during periods of political instability.

[20] We discuss Gurr's work ("A Causal Model of Civil Strife") not because his data are poor, but because he represents some of the most sophisticated work in the field, and because *he*, unlike most authors, has bothered to collect data on African nations.

[21] There is a problem of the comparability of the periods for which data are collected, but Gurr's data collected for 1961–1965 should be roughly comparable to our own. It should be further noted that the correlations expected here are based only on the sample of African countries for which Gurr has data—28 of our 32.

**TABLE 11.1 Cabinet Resignations and Dismissals,
Independence to 1967**

Definition: The number of resignations or dismissals have been coded for each year in the period from independence to 1967, and this number is standardized as a ratio of the largest size of the cabinet in each year. Changes in cabinet personnel as an immediate result of coups d'état or elections are not taken into account in these calculations. The index in this table is the *average* number of resignations and dismissals per annum for the period, taking the size of cabinets into account.

```
RANGE  =          0.80
MEAN   =          0.19
STANDARD DEVIATION =        0.16
```

POPULATION PERCENT		RANK	COUNTRY NAME	VALUE	RANGE DECILE
CUM.	COUNTRY				
9.1	9.1	1.0	ZAIRE	0.80	1
10.6	1.5	2.5	BURUNDI	0.38	6
11.8	1.2	2.5	SOMALIA	0.38	
13.7	1.9	4.0	MALAWI	0.37	
14.2	0.5	5.0	MAURITANIA	0.35	
14.4	0.2	6.0	GABON	0.34	
21.1	6.7	7.0	SUDAN	0.33	
22.7	1.6	8.5	CHAD	0.25	7
23.5	0.8	8.5	TOGO	0.25	
25.8	2.3	10.0	UPPER VOLTA	0.23	8
27.0	1.2	11.0	DAHOMEY	0.22	
28.9	1.9	12.0	IVORY COAST	0.21	
31.4	2.5	13.0	CAMEROON	0.19	
31.8	0.4	14.5	CONGO (BRA)	0.18	
35.6	3.8	14.5	GHANA	0.18	
37.3	1.7	16.0	SENEGAL	0.16	9
43.0	5.7	17.0	TANZANIA	0.14	
43.5	0.5	18.0	LIBERIA	0.13	
45.7	2.2	19.5	MALI	0.12	
47.2	1.5	19.5	RWANDA	0.12	
48.9	1.7	21.0	GUINEA	0.10	
50.0	1.1	22.0	SIERRA LEONE	0.09	
51.7	1.7	23.5	NIGER	0.08	10
76.7	25.0	23.5	NIGERIA	0.08	
77.4	0.7	26.0	CAR	0.07	
77.6	0.2	26.0	GAMBIA	0.07	
79.4	1.8	26.0	ZAMBIA	0.07	
84.2	4.8	28.5	KENYA	0.05	
88.4	4.2	28.5	UGANDA	0.05	
88.7	0.3	30.0	BOTSWANA	0.0	
89.1	0.4	31.5	LESOTHO	0.0	

DATA NOT AVAILABLE FOR THE FOLLOWING COUNTRIES

ETHIOPIA

SOURCES: *Africa Digest, Africa Report, Africa Diary, African Research Bulletin, Europa Yearbook,* and *Middle East Journal.* A compilation from French language newspapers prepared by George Martens at Northwestern University was used to supplement the general reference works, and Crawford Young's *Politics in the Congo* (Princeton, N.J.: Princeton Univ. Press, 1966) was used for *Zaire* (*Congo K.*).

TABLE 11.2   Elite Instability, Independence to 1969

Definition: A numerical weight was given to coups d'état (5), attempted coups (3), and plots (1).* The index here is a sum of the scores for all such events coded for a given country during the period from independence to December, 1969.

```
RANGE =           26.00
MEAN =             7.19
STANDARD DEVIATION =            7.34
```

POPULATION PERCENT CUM.	COUNTRY	RANK	COUNTRY NAME	VALUE	RANGE DECILE
1.2	1.2	1.0	DAHOMEY	26	1
7.9	6.7	2.0	SUDAN	22	2
17.0	9.1	3.5	ZAIRE	20	3
17.8	0.8	3.5	TOGO	20	
18.2	0.4	5.0	CONGO (BRA)	17	4
19.7	1.5	6.0	BURUNDI	16	
23.5	3.8	7.0	GHANA	13	5
48.5	25.0	8.0	NIGERIA	12	6
49.6	1.1	9.0	SIERRA LEONE	11	
50.3	0.7	11.0	CAR	8	7
51.5	1.2	11.0	SOMALIA	8	
55.7	4.2	11.0	UGANDA	8	
57.9	2.2	13.5	MALI	7	8
60.2	2.3	13.5	UPPER VOLTA	7	
60.7	0.5	15.5	LIBERIA	6	
62.4	1.7	15.5	SENEGAL	6	
64.0	1.6	17.0	CHAD	5	9
74.9	10.9	18.5	ETHIOPIA	4	
76.6	1.7	18.5	GUINEA	4	
76.8	0.2	20.0	GABON	3	
78.7	1.9	21.0	IVORY COAST	2	10
81.2	2.5	24.0	CAMEROON	1	
86.0	4.8	24.0	KENYA	1	
86.4	0.4	24.0	LESOTHO	1	
88.3	1.9	24.0	MALAWI	1	
90.0	1.7	24.0	NIGER	1	
90.3	0.3	29.5	BOTSWANA	0	
90.5	0.2	29.5	GAMBIA	0	
91.0	0.5	29.5	MAURITANIA	0	
92.5	1.5	29.5	RWANDA	0	
98.2	5.7	29.5	TANZANIA	0	
100.0	1.8	29.5	ZAMBIA	0	

SOURCES: The same as Table 11.1. In addition, reference was made to *Deadline Data* and *The New York Times Index.*

* A *coup d'état* is defined as an event in which the existing political regime is suddenly and illegally displaced by the action of relatively small elite groups without an overt mass participation in the event. The scope of change in the regime resulting from coups d'état may vary from the wholesale replacement of political decision-makers by instigators of the coup and their followers, to a dissolution of the constitutional relationships between different groups of decision-makers (e.g. the dissolution of legislatures) without any substantial replacement of decision-makers. The coup may be organized by members of the governing elite (palace revolution), or by members of an alternate elite (notably the military). The stated aims of the insurgent elite may vary from reaction to reform, and the degree of physical injury resulting from a coup may be negligible or pronounced.

Attempted coups are unsuccessful coups d'état, in which an insurgent elite fails to effect any lasting displacement of the political regime, but is known to have succeeded in some combination of the following: (a) the assassination, attempted assassination, or arrest of some members of the political elite; (b) the temporary (for less than a week) disruption, interruption, or take-over of government facilities; and (c) the sudden mutiny, mobilization of, or action by armed forces explicitly aimed at the take-over of government.

Plots are events in which an announcement or admission is made by the elite group in power that a plot to overthrow the government by violence has been discovered. Reported plots may take various forms ranging from a simple statement that a plot has been thwarted, without further elaboration, to the arrest, identification, and trial of alleged plotters. Plots may in fact be manufactured by the government as a pretext for the elimination of competing elites or for the imposition of extreme or coercive policies. Although there is no reliable means by which the researcher can clearly distinguish between bona fide plots and manufactured allegations, the "reported plot" may in any case be viewed as a political datum, indicative of elite instability.

TABLE 11.3 Communal Instability, Independence to 1969

Definition: A numerical weight was given to civil wars (5), rebellions (4), irredentism (3), and ethnic violence (1).* The index here was computed by multiplying the score for each event by the number of years in which it was reported in any country, and by summing the resultant scores. The computations are based on the period from independence to December, 1969.

```
RANGE  =        38.00
MEAN   =         6.75
STANDARD DEVIATION =              10.23
```

POPULATION PERCENT		RANK	COUNTRY NAME	VALUE	RANGE DECILE
CUM.	COUNTRY				
6.7	6.7	1.0	SUDAN	38	1
17.6	10.9	2.0	ETHIOPIA	30	3
26.7	9.1	3.5	ZAIRE	27	
51.7	25.0	3.5	NIGERIA	27	
53.3	1.6	5.0	CHAD	17	6
54.8	1.5	6.0	RWANDA	15	7
59.6	4.8	7.0	KENYA	14	
63.8	4.2	8.0	UGANDA	12	
66.0	2.2	9.0	MALI	6	9
67.5	1.5	11.0	BURUNDI	5	
71.3	3.8	11.0	GHANA	5	
73.2	1.9	11.0	IVORY COAST	5	
73.6	0.4	13.0	CONGO (BRA)	4	
74.8	1.2	14.5	SOMALIA	3	10
76.6	1.8	14.5	ZAMBIA	3	
77.1	0.5	16.0	MAURITANIA	2	
79.6	2.5	18.0	CAMEROON	1	
80.8	1.2	18.0	DAHOMEY	1	
81.9	1.1	18.0	SIERRA LEONE	1	
82.2	0.3	26.0	BOTSWANA	0	
82.9	0.7	26.0	CAR	0	
83.1	0.2	26.0	GABON	0	
83.3	0.2	26.0	GAMBIA	0	
85.0	1.7	26.0	GUINEA	0	
85.4	0.4	26.0	LESOTHO	0	
85.9	0.5	26.0	LIBERIA	0	
87.8	1.9	26.0	MALAWI	0	
89.5	1.7	26.0	NIGER	0	
91.2	1.7	26.0	SENEGAL	0	
96.9	5.7	26.0	TANZANIA	0	
97.7	0.8	26.0	TOGO	0	
100.0	2.3	26.0	UPPER VOLTA	0	

SOURCES: The same as Table 11.2. In addition, reference was made to Young, *Politics in the Congo*, and Jules Gerard-Libois, *Katanga Secession* (Madison: University of Wisconsin Press, 1966), for details of events in Congo (Kinshasa); and to John P. MacKintosh, *Nigerian Government and Politics* (Evanston, Ill.: Northwestern University Press, 1966), for details of the Tiv rebellion in Nigeria.

* *Civil war* is defined as an event in which an identifiable communal group (in which membership is based on ascribed characteristics of ethnicity, or combinations of common language, and/or religion, and/or territory) seeks by violence to form a new political system based on boundaries of ethnic community, or attempts by violence to monopolize political power for the communal group within the existing political system.

Rebellion is defined as an event in which an identifiable communal group seeks by violence to gain increased autonomy from the national political authorities, or attacks supporters or agents of the national government without aiming to secede from or monopolize power within the existing political system.

Irredentism is defined as an event in which an identifiable communal group seeks to change its political allegiance from the government of the territorial unit in which it resides to a political system, either existing or to be created, in which the authorities share the communal identification of the irredentist group concerned. Successful irredentism, therefore, involves the establishment of new political units transcending (rather than coinciding with or incorporated within) existing national boundaries.

Ethnic violence is defined as an event of short duration (no more than a few days) in which two identifiable communal groups are antagonists in violence to secure some short term goal, but not designed to secure independence, autonomy, or political realignment for the groups concerned.

TABLE 11.4   Turmoil, Independence to 1969

Definition: This index is calculated as the sum of all reported riots, demonstrations, strikes, terrorist events, and declarations of emergency* in the period from independence to December, 1969.

```
RANGE =          48.00
MEAN =           11.06
STANDARD DEVIATION =          10.36
```

POPULATION PERCENT					
CUM.	COUNTRY	RANK	COUNTRY NAME	VALUE	RANGE DECILE
25.0	25.0	1.0	NIGERIA	48	1
26.2	1.2	2.0	DAHOMEY	32	4
32.9	6.7	3.0	SUDAN	26	5
42.0	9.1	4.0	ZAIRE	25	
43.7	1.7	5.0	SENEGAL	21	6
47.5	3.8	6.0	GHANA	19	7
49.3	1.8	7.0	ZAMBIA	18	
50.9	1.6	8.0	CHAD	16	
61.8	10.9	9.0	ETHIOPIA	15	
66.6	4.8	10.0	KENYA	14	8
69.1	2.5	11.5	CAMEROON	12	
69.5	0.4	11.5	CONGO (BRA)	12	
70.0	0.5	13.5	LIBERIA	10	
70.5	0.5	13.5	MAURITANIA	10	
71.6	1.1	15.5	SIERRA LEONE	9	9
75.8	4.2	15.5	UGANDA	9	
77.3	1.5	17.0	BURUNDI	7	
79.2	1.9	18.5	IVORY COAST	6	
81.5	2.3	18.5	UPPER VOLTA	6	
82.7	1.2	20.5	SOMALIA	5	
83.5	0.8	20.5	TOGO	5	
83.7	0.2	23.5	GABON	4	10
85.4	1.7	23.5	GUINEA	4	
85.8	0.4	23.5	LESOTHO	4	
87.5	1.7	23.5	NIGER	4	
87.8	0.3	27.0	BOTSWANA	3	
89.7	1.9	27.0	MALAWI	3	
95.4	5.7	27.0	TANZANIA	3	
97.6	2.2	29.5	MALI	2	
99.1	1.5	29.5	RWANDA	2	
99.8	0.7	31.5	CAR	0	
100.0	0.2	31.5	GAMBIA	0	

SOURCES: The same as Tables 11.2 and 11.3.

* *Riots* are defined as events involving relatively spontaneous, unplanned, but violent activity, in which the generalized aim of the activity, or objects of aggression, are not coherently specified, but which is responded to by political authorities and their supporters as subversive of "law and order."

Demonstrations are defined as events involving relatively organized and nonviolent activity, in which the aim of the activity is to protest some specific action on the part of domestic political authorities. When demonstrations are counteracted by violence on the part of others (notably police), they become riots.

Strikes are defined as events involving organized disruptions of the economy by groups who refuse to work at their regular employment in order to react against, or bring pressure to bear on political or economic authorities. A strike event is identified in terms of the organizational unity of the strikers, not the economic or geographical differentiation of work locations. A strike of mine workers which begins at one mine on Monday and another mine on Wednesday is counted as one event not two, which accounts for disparities between our coding and figures reported for strikes by other sources, in Zambia particularly.

Terrorism is defined as events involving relatively highly organized and planned activity, on the part of small but cohesive groups, in which the aim of the activity is to damage, injure, or eliminate government property or personnel. These activities include bomb plants, sabotage of electrical and transportation facilities, assassinations (attempted and successful), and isolated guerrilla activities.

Declaration of emergency is defined as a formal declaration of emergency by the national government in response to real or presumed threats to public order.

TABLE 11.5 Intensity of Violence, Independence to 1969

Definition: This index is calculated as the $\log_{10}$ $(x+1)$ of the total number of deaths (per million population) reported in instability events of all kinds in the period from independence to December, 1969.* In cases of conflicting reports, we have used the highest figure given, since we had no independent means of assessing the reliability of different reports.

```
RANGE =          11.00
MEAN =            3.28
STANDARD DEVIATION =          2.76
```

POPULATION PERCENT		RANK	COUNTRY NAME	VALUE	RANGE DECILE
CUM.	COUNTRY				
25.0	25.0	1.0	NIGERIA	11	1
34.1	9.1	2.5	ZAIRE	8	3
35.6	1.5	2.5	RWANDA	8	
37.1	1.5	4.5	BURUNDI	7	4
38.7	1.6	4.5	CHAD	7	
39.1	0.4	6.0	CONGO (BRA)	6	5
50.0	10.9	8.0	ETHIOPIA	5	6
54.8	4.8	8.0	KENYA	5	
61.5	6.7	8.0	SUDAN	5	
64.0	2.5	11.5	CAMEROON	4	7
68.2	4.2	11.5	UGANDA	4	
70.5	2.3	11.5	UPPER VOLTA	4	
72.3	1.8	11.5	ZAMBIA	4	
73.5	1.2	16.5	DAHOMEY	3	8
73.7	0.2	16.5	GABON	3	
73.9	0.2	16.5	GAMBIA	3	
74.3	0.4	16.5	LESOTHO	3	
74.8	0.5	16.5	LIBERIA	3	
75.3	0.5	16.5	MAURITANIA	3	
76.4	1.1	20.5	SIERRA LEONE	2	9
77.2	0.8	20.5	TOGO	2	
81.0	3.8	24.0	GHANA	1	10
82.9	1.9	24.0	IVORY COAST	1	
84.8	1.9	24.0	MALAWI	1	
86.0	1.2	24.0	SOMALIA	1	
91.7	5.7	24.0	TANZANIA	1	
92.0	0.3	29.5	BOTSWANA	0	
92.7	0.7	29.5	CAR	0	
94.4	1.7	29.5	GUINEA	0	
96.6	2.2	29.5	MALI	0	
98.3	1.7	29.5	NIGER	0	
100.0	1.7	29.5	SENEGAL	0	

SOURCES: See Tables 11.2 and 11.3.

* We used this method because it reduces the distortions in raw and unreliable reports of death, and gives greater emphasis to the symbolic intensity of violence rather than to the incidence of death.

12. International Economic Aid

Aid from the industrial countries is a major aspect of international relations both among the industrial nations and between the industrial and under-developed nations. There are three major and several minor sources for this aid.[1] Major sources are the ex-metropole nations, the United States, and the Eastern-bloc nations. Other important sources include multi-national organizations, various European nations, Israel, and the Republic of China. The reasons for giving this aid range from the exigencies of cold war politics and maintenance of pre-independence economic dominance to more subtle international political goals. Nevertheless, most aid is nominally given for economic development projects and import maintenance.

Types of Aid

There are several components to aid as it is normally defined. The main categories are as follows:

1. *Grants*—an outright gift of money or resources, often for projects that are unlikely to have direct financial return. These grants may be tied to the country giving the aid, in the sense that they must be spent in the donor country. Generally, the French give grants. Some of the British aid is of this type, but increasingly less of the American aid is on a grant basis. The Eastern-bloc aid is a mixture of grants, loans, and subsidized trade.
2. *Loans.* Generally, intergovernmental loans are low-interest, have a long grace period, and some-times are repayable in local nonconvertible currencies. This is the most common form of American aid and, in contrast, is only a small part of French aid. The French policy may be the result of a realization that most of these countries will not be in a position to repay loans for a considerable time to come. The accumulation of debts through loans may involve the recipient countries in considerable drains on their foreign reserves for the future and the possibility of

financial crises.[2] This would occur whenever repayments become a substantial percentage of foreign-exchange earnings.
3. *Food for Peace.* American grain surpluses have stimulated massive exports of food under Public Law 480 by which the U.S. sells grain to develop-ing nations for local currencies.[3] These currencies can be used only in the recipient country with the governments' mutual consent. This program does not have direct counterparts in aid programs of other countries.
4. *Technical aid and cooperation.* These programs usually involve sending field experts to evaluate programs and policies or to train indigenous personnel for various technical functions. The smaller aid-giving countries often concentrate their aid in this area with agricultural experts, teachers, and organizations similar to the Peace Corps.
5. *Government bank loans.* Various governmental banks, like the U.S. Export-Import Bank, give loans on several bases to governments and private business. They often give market-interest loans on projects with the expectation that earnings generated over a 5- to 10-year period will repay the loan. Such institutions are closest to com-mercial banks in their criteria for loans.

All together the black African countries receive a considerable amount of aid. In 1967 former French colonies were receiving aid at the rate of approxi-mately $5.50 per capita, former British colonies at $1.70, and the rest at about $3.00 per capita.[4] This compares with India, for example, which received about $2.00 per capita in 1967.

Effect of Aid

The effect of aid on the recipients has both economic and political ramifications. First, it allows for the importation of specific resources to aid in economic development projects. The aid is generally used to import capital, both physical and human. Hence, machinery and technicians may be imported to build a dam or factory. Further, teachers may be imported to teach technical subjects at the secondary and university level. The aid is sometimes in the form of consumption items which are intended to release indigenous resources such as those necessary for buildings, and so on. This allows resources formerly devoted to consumption goods to shift to investment goods production. Other aid is used for general support of the governmental recurrent and development budgets and is intended to facilitate flexibility in development-planning decisions.

The second aspect of aid concerns its political implications. The aid may permit the recipient government's expenditures to be considerably greater than its revenues. This budget augmentation could be expected to lead to increased centralization of governmental authority and possibly increased integration. Of course aid may lead to dependence on the donor nation, with the potential for neo-colonial interference with the recipient nation's sovereignty. The effects of aid, however, often are counter to expectations. It is unfortunate that intensive analyses of the political and developmental effects of aid are not generally available.[5]

In the data presented, American aid per capita is given for 1968 (Table 12.2), as well as a percent rate of change of this measure (Table 12.3). Since American aid patterns have been irregular, they have been presented in more detail than the ex-metropole aid pattern. In fact, annual ex-metropole[6] aid patterns, both on a per capita basis and in total value (Table 12.7), are highly correlated over the five years 1960 through 1964. The U.S. aid patterns in contrast have low correlations from year to year and several distinct periods appear, namely the periods ca. 1963–64 (Table 12.5) and ca. 1967 (Table 12.6).[7]

Aid, in part, is given in order to maintain influence in the recipient country, both with respect to domestic and foreign policy. Data such as those included here should be useful for studies of neo-colonialism and cold war politics in sub-Saharan Africa. Darlington, a former American ambassador to Gabon, describes the operation of French and American aid to Gabon in just this context.[8]

Reliability and Dimensionality

Since the units of measurement are well defined,[9] reliability of these data are primarily a function of consistency of definition from source to source. We have used a single source which has apparently tried to present uniform and reliable measurements across donor countries. Nevertheless, its information was gathered by questionnaires sent to each donor country and may reflect different definitions. Except for this, the data should be highly reliable as an indicator of intergovernmental transfer payments.

In a factor analysis of fifty-nine measures of American, ex-metropole, and Eastern-bloc aid, six factors accounted for 85 percent of the variance. The factors can be characterized as follows: Factors 1–3 are ex-metropole aid, Eastern-bloc aid and U.S. per capita aid. The remaining three factors have various combinations of U.S. total aid and percent distribution of U.S. aid.

Notes

[1] We are considering only governmental and international organizations as sources of aid in what follows. Any comprehensive study of aid would have to take into account the activities of American foundations in Africa, especially the Ford and Rockefeller Foundations, and missionary organizations. Data on military aid will be found in Chapter 10.

[2] Charles and Alice Darlington, *African Betrayal* (New York: David McKay, 1968). The authors also give a case study of the bureaucratic and domestic political patterns in which U.S. aid is enmeshed.

[3] Known as "counterpart funds."

[4] Corresponding figures for 1962 are $11.00, $2.80, and $4.75, per capita. I. M. D. Little, *Aid to Africa* (Oxford: Pergamon, 1964), pp. ix–x; and Albert Waterson, *Lessons from Developing Countries* (Baltimore, Md.: Johns Hopkins Press, 1967).

[5] For an especially critical view of aid see Stanislaus Andreski, *African Predicament* (New York: Atherton, 1968). An Austrian scholar, Nikolaus Scherk, has written a study of France's neo-colonialism in Africa, *Dekolonisation und Souveränität* (Vienna: Braumüller, 1969).

[6] This includes *all* ex-metropole countries.

[7] In part, this may be the result of new nations being created over the period—although it should be noted that the U.S. was giving aid to most of these countries by fiscal year 1962.

[8] Darlington and Darlington, *African Betrayal*.

[9] Dollars, francs, pounds, etc.

TABLE 12.1 Total U.S. Economic Aid to Africa through 1968, in Millions of U.S. Dollars

Definition: Includes grants, loans, Food for Peace, and all other forms of U.S. economic aid. The time period covers all years in which the U.S. Government was giving aid.

```
RANGE    =       404.00
MEAN     =        66.38
STANDARD DEVIATION =          95.45
```

POPULATION PERCENT CUM.	COUNTRY	RANK	COUNTRY NAME	VALUE	RANGE DECILE
9.1	9.1	1.0	ZAIRE	405	1
9.6	0.5	2.0	LIBERIA	252	4
13.4	3.8	3.0	GHANA	240	5
24.3	10.9	4.5	ETHIOPIA	229	
49.3	25.0	4.5	NIGERIA	229	
56.0	6.7	6.0	SUDAN	107	8
57.7	1.7	7.0	GUINEA	74	9
58.9	1.2	8.0	SOMALIA	73	
60.8	1.9	9.0	IVORY COAST	67	
65.6	4.8	10.0	KENYA	63	
71.3	5.7	11.0	TANZANIA	62	
73.1	1.8	12.0	ZAMBIA	41	10
74.2	1.1	13.0	SIERRA LEONE	39	
75.9	1.7	14.0	SENEGAL	32	
80.1	4.2	15.0	UGANDA	30	
82.6	2.5	16.0	CAMEROON	27	
84.5	1.9	17.0	MALAWI	23	
86.7	2.2	18.0	MALI	19	
87.0	0.3	19.0	BOTSWANA	16	
88.7	1.7	20.0	NIGER	15	
89.5	0.8	21.0	TOGO	14	
90.7	1.2	22.5	DAHOMEY	11	
93.0	2.3	22.5	UPPER VOLTA	11	
94.6	1.6	24.5	CHAD	8	
94.8	0.2	24.5	GABON	8	
96.3	1.5	26.5	BURUNDI	7	
97.8	1.5	26.5	RWANDA	7	
98.5	0.7	28.0	CAR	5	
98.9	0.4	29.0	LESOTHO	4	
99.4	0.5	30.0	MAURITANIA	3	
99.8	0.4	31.0	CONGO (BRA)	2	
100.0	0.2	32.0	GAMBIA	1	

SOURCES: *AID Economic Data Book 1970. Cameroon: Africa Report* (June 1967): 8–15.

TABLE 12.2 U.S. Economic Aid per Capita in U.S. Dollars, 1968

Definition: Loans and grants by U.S. in fiscal year 1968 ending June 30.

```
RANGE    =         9.12
MEAN     =         1.13
STANDARD DEVIATION =          1.94
```

POPULATION PERCENT CUM.	COUNTRY	RANK	COUNTRY NAME	VALUE	RANGE DECILE
1.9	1.9	1.0	IVORY COAST	9.12	1
2.4	0.5	2.0	LIBERIA	6.83	3
6.2	3.8	3.0	GHANA	3.35	7
8.1	1.9	4.0	MALAWI	2.02	8
17.2	9.1	5.0	ZAIRE	1.97	
18.4	1.2	6.0	SOMALIA	1.82	9
19.5	1.1	7.0	SIERRA LEONE	1.56	
19.9	0.4	8.0	LESOTHO	1.33	
21.6	1.7	9.0	GUINEA	1.05	
21.8	0.2	10.0	GABON	1.00	
23.5	1.7	11.0	SENEGAL	0.92	
25.2	1.7	12.0	NIGER	0.54	10
25.4	0.2	13.0	GAMBIA	0.50	
31.1	5.7	14.5	TANZANIA	0.44	
31.9	0.8	14.5	TOGO	0.44	
56.9	25.0	16.0	NIGERIA	0.42	
61.7	9.1	17.0	KENYA	0.41	
62.9	1.2	18.0	DAHOMEY	0.36	
73.8	10.9	19.0	ETHIOPIA	0.35	
74.1	0.3	20.0	BOTSWANA	0.33	
78.3	4.2	21.0	UGANDA	0.30	
79.9	1.6	22.0	CHAD	0.29	
82.2	2.3	23.0	UPPER VOLTA	0.27	
84.0	1.8	24.0	ZAMBIA	0.26	
85.5	1.5	25.0	RWANDA	0.17	
86.2	0.7	26.0	CAR	0.13	
88.7	2.5	27.5	CAMEROON	0.04	
90.9	2.2	27.5	MALI	0.04	
92.4	1.5	29.0	BURUNDI	0.03	
92.8	0.4	31.0	CONGO (BRA)	0.0	
93.3	0.5	31.0	MAURITANIA	0.0	
100.0	6.7	31.0	SUDAN	0.0	

SOURCES: *AID Economic Data Book 1970. Cameroon: Africa Report* (June 1967): 8–15.

TABLE 12.3 Percent Change in U.S. Economic Aid per Capita, 1962–1968

```
RANGE =         1546.00
MEAN =            65.84
STANDARD DEVIATION =              263.30
```

POPULATION PERCENT CUM.	COUNTRY	RANK	COUNTRY NAME	VALUE	RANGE DECILE
1.9	1.9	1.0	IVORY COAST	1446	1
3.8	1.9	2.0	MALAWI	312	8
5.6	1.8	3.0	ZAMBIA	189	9
6.7	1.1	4.0	SIERRA LEONE	136	
7.0	0.3	7.0	BOTSWANA	100	
8.5	1.5	7.0	BURUNDI	100	
8.9	0.4	7.0	LESOTHO	100	
9.4	0.5	7.0	MAURITANIA	100	
10.9	1.5	7.0	RWANDA	100	
16.6	5.7	10.0	TANZANIA	83	
16.8	0.2	11.0	GAMBIA	50	10
18.5	1.7	12.5	NIGER	35	
20.8	2.3	12.5	UPPER VOLTA	35	
31.7	10.9	14.0	ETHIOPIA	21	
31.9	0.2	15.0	GABON	14	
33.1	1.2	16.0	DAHOMEY	13	
37.9	4.8	17.0	KENYA	8	
38.3	0.4	18.0	CONGO (BRA)	0	
40.0	1.7	19.0	SENEGAL	-1	
65.0	25.0	20.0	NIGERIA	-2	
65.7	0.7	21.0	CAR	-19	
66.2	0.5	22.0	LIBERIA	-35	
70.4	4.2	23.0	UGANDA	-42	
72.1	1.7	24.0	GUINEA	-44	
72.9	0.8	25.0	TOGO	-45	
82.0	9.1	26.0	ZAIRE	-57	
85.8	3.8	27.0	GHANA	-63	
87.0	1.2	28.0	SOMALIA	-65	
88.6	1.6	29.0	CHAD	-71	
90.8	2.2	30.0	MALI	-93	
93.3	2.5	31.0	CAMEROON	-98	
100.0	6.7	32.0	SUDAN	-100	

SOURCES: *AID Economic Data Book 1970*. Countries that had no aid in 1962 and received aid in 1968 were arbitrarily given 100 percent scores since the actual scores would be infinite and therefore misleading.

TABLE 12.4 Average Annual per Capita Net Official Aid from Developed Countries in U.S. Dollars, 1967–1969

```
RANGE =          29.83
MEAN =            9.02
STANDARD DEVIATION =            7.93
```

POPULATION PERCENT CUM.	COUNTRY	RANK	COUNTRY NAME	VALUE	RANGE DECILE
0.4	0.4	1.0	CONGO (BRA)	31.18	1
0.7	0.3	2.0	BOTSWANA	27.12	2
3.2	2.5	3.0	CAMEROON	27.00	
3.7	0.5	4.0	LIBERIA	21.53	4
3.9	0.2	5.0	GABON	21.00	
4.3	0.4	6.0	LESOTHO	15.47	6
6.0	1.7	7.0	SENEGAL	11.41	7
7.8	1.8	8.0	ZAMBIA	10.56	
8.5	0.7	9.0	CAR	10.19	8
10.4	1.9	10.0	IVORY COAST	8.96	
10.6	0.2	11.0	GAMBIA	8.91	
11.8	1.2	12.0	SOMALIA	8.78	
15.6	3.8	13.0	GHANA	8.66	
16.1	0.5	14.0	MAURITANIA	7.31	9
16.9	0.8	15.0	TOGO	6.77	
18.8	1.9	16.0	MALAWI	6.41	
20.5	1.7	17.0	NIGER	5.94	
25.3	4.8	18.0	KENYA	5.57	
26.5	1.2	19.0	DAHOMEY	5.50	
28.1	1.6	20.0	CHAD	5.16	
37.2	9.1	21.0	ZAIRE	4.50	
38.7	1.5	22.0	RWANDA	4.36	
41.0	2.3	23.0	UPPER VOLTA	3.48	10
42.1	1.1	24.0	SIERRA LEONE	3.42	
44.3	2.2	25.0	MALI	3.41	
45.8	1.5	26.0	BURUNDI	3.17	
51.5	5.7	27.0	TANZANIA	2.84	
53.2	1.7	28.0	GUINEA	2.73	
57.4	4.2	29.0	UGANDA	2.58	
68.3	10.9	30.0	ETHIOPIA	1.72	
93.3	25.0	31.0	NIGERIA	1.62	
100.0	6.7	32.0	SUDAN	1.35	

SOURCE: *Development Assistance: 1970 Review* (Paris: OECD, December 1970), pp. 194–196.

TABLE 12.5 Distribution of U.S. Economic Aid to Each Country as a Percent of Total U.S. Aid for 32 African Countries, 1964

RANGE =   34.80
MEAN =   3.12
STANDARD DEVIATION =   6.47

POPULATION PERCENT		RANK	COUNTRY NAME	VALUE	RANGE DECILE
CUM.	COUNTRY				
25.0	25.0	1.0	NIGERIA	34.80	1
34.1	9.1	2.0	ZAIRE	15.30	6
34.6	0.5	3.0	LIBERIA	9.40	8
36.3	1.7	4.0	GUINEA	5.40	9
38.2	1.9	5.5	IVORY COAST	4.60	
43.9	5.7	5.5	TANZANIA	4.60	
54.8	10.9	7.0	ETHIOPIA	3.50	
59.6	4.8	8.0	KENYA	2.50	10
60.0	0.4	9.5	CONGO (BRA)	2.20	
62.2	2.2	9.5	MALI	2.20	
63.4	1.2	11.0	SOMALIA	2.10	
67.6	4.2	12.0	UGANDA	1.90	
69.3	1.7	13.0	NIGER	1.60	
76.0	6.7	14.0	SUDAN	1.50	
77.7	1.7	15.0	SENEGAL	1.40	
80.2	2.5	16.0	CAMEROON	1.00	
80.9	0.7	17.5	CAR	0.80	
82.0	1.1	17.5	SIERRA LEONE	0.80	
82.2	0.2	19.5	GABON	0.60	
84.0	1.8	19.5	ZAMBIA	0.60	
85.6	1.6	21.0	CHAD	0.50	
87.1	1.5	23.5	BURUNDI	0.40	
88.3	1.2	23.5	DAHOMEY	0.40	
92.1	3.8	23.5	GHANA	0.40	
93.6	1.5	23.5	RWANDA	0.40	
95.5	1.9	26.0	MALAWI	0.30	
96.0	0.5	28.0	MAURITANIA	0.20	
96.8	0.8	28.0	TOGO	0.20	
99.1	2.3	28.0	UPPER VOLTA	0.20	
99.4	0.3	31.0	BOTSWANA	0.0	
99.6	0.2	31.0	GAMBIA	0.0	
100.0	0.4	31.0	LESOTHO	0.0	

SOURCE: *Economic Assistance Programs 1967.*

TABLE 12.6 Distribution of U.S. Economic Aid to Each Country as a Percent of Total U.S. Aid for 32 African Countries, 1968

RANGE =   13.30
MEAN =   2.08
STANDARD DEVIATION =   3.50

POPULATION PERCENT		RANK	COUNTRY NAME	VALUE	RANGE DECILE
CUM.	COUNTRY				
1.9	1.9	1.0	IVORY COAST	13.30	1
11.0	9.1	2.0	ZAIRE	12.00	
14.8	3.8	3.0	GHANA	10.00	3
39.8	25.0	4.0	NIGERIA	7.91	5
41.7	1.9	5.0	MALAWI	3.20	8
52.6	10.9	6.0	ETHIOPIA	3.10	
53.1	0.5	7.0	LIBERIA	2.91	
58.8	5.7	8.0	TANZANIA	2.02	9
60.0	1.2	9.0	SOMALIA	1.81	
64.8	4.8	10.0	KENYA	1.60	
66.5	1.7	11.0	GUINEA	1.50	
67.6	1.1	12.0	SIERRA LEONE	1.38	
69.3	1.7	13.0	SENEGAL	1.30	10
73.5	4.2	14.0	UGANDA	0.89	
75.2	1.7	15.0	NIGER	0.70	
77.5	2.3	16.0	UPPER VOLTA	0.50	
77.9	0.4	17.0	LESOTHO	0.43	
79.7	1.8	18.0	ZAMBIA	0.39	
81.3	1.6	19.0	CHAD	0.35	
82.5	1.2	20.0	DAHOMEY	0.30	
83.3	0.8	21.0	TOGO	0.28	
84.8	1.5	22.0	RWANDA	0.21	
85.0	0.2	23.0	GABON	0.20	
85.3	0.3	26.0	BOTSWANA	0.07	
87.8	2.5	26.0	CAMEROON	0.07	
88.5	0.7	26.0	CAR	0.07	
88.7	0.2	26.0	GAMBIA	0.07	
90.9	2.2	26.0	MALI	0.07	
92.4	1.5	29.0	BURUNDI	0.04	
92.8	0.4	31.0	CONGO (BRA)	0.0	
93.3	0.5	31.0	MAURITANIA	0.0	
100.0	6.7	31.0	SUDAN	0.0	

SOURCE: *AID Economic Data Book 1970.*

TABLE 12.7 Aid From Ex-Metropole per Capita in U.S. Dollars, 1969

Definition: Includes all forms of economic aid.

RANGE = 17.22
MEAN = 5.51
STANDARD DEVIATION = 4.60

POPULATION PERCENT CUM. COUNTRY		RANK	COUNTRY NAME	VALUE	RANGE DECILE
0.2	0.2	1.0	GABON	17.22	1
0.5	0.3	2.0	BOTSWANA	16.80	
0.9	0.4	3.0	CONGO (BRA)	13.26	3
2.6	1.7	4.0	SENEGAL	12.93	
3.1	0.5	5.0	LIBERIA	11.87	4
3.6	0.5	6.0	MAURITANIA	9.11	5
5.5	1.9	7.0	MALAWI	8.27	6
5.7	0.2	8.0	GAMBIA	8.04	
7.6	1.9	9.0	IVORY COAST	7.27	
8.0	0.4	10.0	LESOTHO	7.11	
8.7	0.7	11.0	CAR	7.02	
10.5	1.8	12.0	ZAMBIA	6.14	7
15.3	4.8	13.0	KENYA	5.65	
16.5	1.2	14.0	DAHOMEY	5.52	
25.6	9.1	15.0	ZAIRE	4.55	8
27.3	1.7	16.0	NIGER	3.68	
28.9	1.6	17.0	CHAD	3.52	
31.4	2.5	18.0	CAMEROON	3.50	
56.4	25.0	19.0	NIGERIA	3.38	9
57.6	1.2	20.0	SOMALIA	3.36	
58.7	1.1	21.0	SIERRA LEONE	2.42	
62.9	4.2	22.0	UGANDA	2.41	
68.6	5.7	23.0	TANZANIA	2.35	
69.4	0.8	24.5	TOGO	2.16	
71.7	2.3	24.5	UPPER VOLTA	2.16	
73.2	1.5	26.0	BURUNDI	1.90	
74.7	1.5	27.0	RWANDA	1.67	10
76.9	2.2	28.0	MALI	1.39	
80.7	3.8	29.0	GHANA	0.93	
91.6	10.9	30.0	ETHIOPIA	0.42	
98.3	6.7	31.0	SUDAN	0.27	
100.0	1.7	32.0	GUINEA	0.0	

SOURCES: Ministère de la Cooperation, *1959–64, Cinq ans de fonds d'aide et de cooperation* (Paris: 1965), pp. 49–53; *Special Commonwealth African Assistance Plan Report* (London: 1964). *Malawi*: *AID Economic Data Book*, 1962 figures; *Botswana*: Edwin S. Munger, *Bechuanaland* (London: Oxford University Press, 1965); *Gabon*: International Monetary Fund, *Surveys of African Economies*, Vol. 1.

TABLE 12.8 Aid from Ex-Colonial Power per Capita in U.S. Dollars, 1967

RANGE = 34.10
MEAN = 6.07
STANDARD DEVIATION = 7.52

POPULATION PERCENT CUM. COUNTRY		RANK	COUNTRY NAME	VALUE	RANGE DECILE
0.5	0.5	1.0	LIBERIA	33.70	1
0.8	0.3	2.0	BOTSWANA	27.00	2
1.0	0.2	3.0	GABON	16.10	6
1.4	0.4	4.0	LESOTHO	13.30	
3.2	1.8	5.0	ZAMBIA	10.90	7
3.9	0.7	6.0	CAR	10.60	
4.3	0.4	7.0	CONGO (BRA)	10.20	
6.0	1.7	8.0	SENEGAL	8.50	8
6.2	0.2	9.5	GAMBIA	7.30	
6.7	0.5	9.5	MAURITANIA	7.30	
8.6	1.9	11.0	IVORY COAST	6.40	9
10.5	1.9	12.0	MALAWI	5.90	
11.7	1.2	13.5	DAHOMEY	3.40	
13.4	1.7	13.5	NIGER	3.40	
15.9	2.5	15.0	CAMEROON	3.30	
17.5	1.6	16.5	CHAD	3.10	
26.6	9.1	16.5	ZAIRE	3.10	
27.4	0.8	18.5	TOGO	2.70	10
29.7	2.3	18.5	UPPER VOLTA	2.70	
54.7	25.0	20.0	NIGERIA	2.60	
56.2	1.5	21.0	RWANDA	2.50	
61.0	4.8	22.0	KENYA	2.20	
62.5	1.5	23.0	BURUNDI	2.10	
66.7	4.2	24.0	UGANDA	1.80	
68.9	2.2	25.0	MALI	1.70	
70.0	1.1	26.5	SIERRA LEONE	0.90	
71.2	1.2	26.5	SOMALIA	0.90	
82.1	10.9	28.0	ETHIOPIA	0.50	
87.8	5.7	29.0	TANZANIA	0.20	
91.6	3.8	30.5	GHANA	0.10	
98.3	6.7	30.5	SUDAN	0.10	
100.0	1.7	32.0	GUINEA	−0.40	

SOURCE: *Geographical Distribution of Financial Flows to Less Developed Countries 1966–1967* (Paris: OECD, 1969).

TABLE 12.9   Total Eastern-Bloc Foreign Aid, 1958 to 1965, in Millions of U.S. Dollars

Definition: Includes aid from Bulgaria, China, Cuba, Czechoslovakia, Hungary, Poland, Roumania, Soviet Union and Yugoslavia.

```
RANGE =        164.00
MEAN =          23.13
STANDARD DEVIATION =        42.31
```

POPULATION PERCENT					
CUM.	COUNTRY	RANK	COUNTRY NAME	VALUE	RANGE DECILE
3.8	3.8	1.0	GHANA	164	1
5.5	1.7	2.0	GUINEA	119	3
16.4	10.9	3.0	ETHIOPIA	114	4
17.6	1.2	4.0	SOMALIA	96	5
18.0	0.4	5.0	CONGO (BRA)	62	7
22.8	4.8	6.0	KENYA	55	
28.5	5.7	7.0	TANZANIA	51	
32.7	4.2	8.0	UGANDA	30	9
39.4	6.7	9.0	SUDAN	22	
64.4	25.0	10.0	NIGERIA	14	10
66.1	1.7	11.0	SENEGAL	7	
66.8	0.7	12.0	CAR	4	
69.0	2.2	13.0	MALI	2	
69.3	0.3	23.0	BOTSWANA	0	
70.8	1.5	23.0	BURUNDI	0	
73.3	2.5	23.0	CAMEROON	0	
74.9	1.6	23.0	CHAD	0	
84.0	9.1	23.0	ZAIRE	0	
85.2	1.2	23.0	DAHOMEY	0	
85.4	0.2	23.0	GABON	0	
85.6	0.2	23.0	GAMBIA	0	
87.5	1.9	23.0	IVORY COAST	0	
87.9	0.4	23.0	LESOTHO	0	
88.4	0.5	23.0	LIBERIA	0	
90.3	1.9	23.0	MALAWI	0	
90.8	0.5	23.0	MAURITANIA	0	
92.5	1.7	23.0	NIGER	0	
94.0	1.5	23.0	RWANDA	0	
95.1	1.1	23.0	SIERRA LEONE	0	
95.9	0.8	23.0	TOGO	0	
98.2	2.3	23.0	UPPER VOLTA	0	
100.0	1.8	23.0	ZAMBIA	0	

SOURCE: Ralph Meagher, *Bilateral Aid to Africa,* unpublished paper, (Evanston, Ill.: Africana Library, Northwestern University).

13. International Trade

In the post-World War II era, trade has increased far beyond the expectations of the Bretton Woods Conference, at which the basis for contemporary international trade and finance was established in 1944.[1] The major share of the increase has been among the industrialized nations, but considerable growth has also been experienced in sub-Saharan Africa. Changes in the number of nations traded with have been considerable, as has the mix of trading partners, which has resulted in substantial shifts in patterns of international interdependence and dependency.

The Importance of Trade

While trade is only a partial measure of economic integration and a questionable measure of incipient political integration, it does have a bearing on both phenomena. Economic integration is a process in which institutional arrangements such as custom unions, tariff regulations, common monetary and labor policy provide for the flow of goods and services between national economies in such a way that their comparative advantages are reciprocally rewarded and hindrances to economic transactions are minimized.[2] Trade is an indicator of such complimentary comparative advantage and a partial indicator of the potential for economic integration. However, other aspects such as capital and labor markets, monetary and tariff policy affect such a measure, as does the freedom to change trading partners without penalty. International trade is therefore a partial measure of integration as defined by Karl Deutsch.[3] It should be stressed, however, that trade is but one aspect of the range of cultural, social, political, and economic integration, and as such can be, at best, an incomplete indicator of those concepts.

Trade is also an important requirement for economic development. In exchange for exported goods, a country is able to import capital resources to speed development. We have included a wide range of measures covering data from the 1920s to the present. Trade as a percent of Gross Domestic Product is intended to give a measure of the country's dependence on foreign trade (Table 13.1). In the industrial countries this percentage varies from as low as 4 or 5 percent to 50 percent and more.[4] While this gives a gross measure of dependency, the principal export's share in the total gives a measure of dependence on one commodity (Table 13.2). In Africa this may range from over 90 percent to less than 25 percent, but generally one or two products constitute a much higher percentage than is common in the industrial countries. Another measure of dependence is the number of items making up a given percentage of exports. In this case we have taken 70 percent of exports over the period 1966 to 1968 (Table 13.3).

The composition of imports (e.g., equipment, Table 13.4) can be indicative of the usefulness of the imported resources to the country's development. Such figures must be treated carefully since aid may be used, partially, to offset the transfer of local labor from food-producing or other activities for which the aid-financed imports are replacements. Dependence on imports of a particular commodity *may not* indicate an incapacity to produce that commodity, but may indicate rather the comparative advantages to the country of employing labor in other sectors.

Neo-classical trade theory holds the view that goods and services are exchanged in order to increase the quantity and range of consumption and investment of the trading partners.[5] Further, some analysts view the size of the trade sector as the limiting factor governing capital accumulation, which in turn limits the rate of economic growth.[6] Other views, however, stress the adverse terms of trade for primary products in terms of industrial goods and the resultant adverse international income distribution.[7] Also, the internal structure of trade has important political and economic ramifications. Trade dependence on a few products increases the sensitivity of the country's foreign exchange to price changes beyond its control. This may lead to considerable variation from year to year in foreign exchange holdings and a resultant inability to pursue long-term development plans.

Since trade is a measure of interaction, data giving the trading partner breakdowns are quite relevant. First, the import and export trade with the rest of Black Africa are given for the year 1962[8] (Tables 13.5 and 13.6). Since political and economic dependence on the former colonial power (ex-metropole) are important politically and theoretically, we offer considerable data over the period from the 1920s to 1968 (Table 13.7 to Table 13.11). The first two tables are measures of import and export dependence on the colonial power about 1925. The trade roles of the ex-colonial powers have varied significantly over time and should reflect colonial and neo-colonial economic policies. Table 13.12 gives a qualitative measure of Eastern-bloc trade with tropical Africa. About half of the countries have over 1 percent of their trade with the Eastern bloc. This is still quite small, however, and increases in such trade should be expected. United States' trade with Africa (Tables 13.13 to 13.14) has increased considerably over the last two decades from relations with only a few countries in the early 1950s to an average of about 9 percent of each country's trade in 1968. This picture is quite varied since U.S. trade with the ex-French colonies is generally much lower than with the other black African countries. It is clear, however, that U.S. economic interests are on the increase in Black Africa.

The last trade measure offered is the cumulative balance of trade between 1963 and 1968 inclusive, as a percent of the nation's GNP (Table 13.15). Adverse balances of trade must be made up by using imported capital, or by a deflationary fiscal and monetary policy. Since the first depends on international credit somewhat difficult to obtain, and the second is politically undesirable, political instability may often occur during periods of prolonged trade deficits.[9] The ratio of cumulative trade balance to GNP is intended to measure each country's ability to sustain the deficit in terms of its total yearly production of goods and services. Other bases for standardization could be measures of total trade or exports instead of GNP.

Reliability

Generally, trade figures are estimated for all unregistered trade and these are added to the total figure. While the reliability of trade statistics is generally high, two problems in particular affect the accounting of several countries in this Handbook. (1) Countries like Sierra Leone that export small high-value items such as gold or diamonds often have considerable amounts smuggled out to avoid export taxes and control. Smuggling is also a problem however, with any commodity for which the structure of the market imposes substantial economic penalties for legal transactions within it, as for example in the cocoa market in Ghana and the coffee market in Guinea. (2) Another phenomenon affects coastal nations where goods are imported for export to land-locked interior countries. As a result, the trade figures for such countries are inflated and do not reflect the actual conditions of internal consumption. This does not necessarily diminish the relevance of the data, however, since importation for re-export allows for an increase in value added for the economy; nevertheless the trade figures given here should be considered in the light of these data problems.

In a factor analysis of 67 trade measures we found four factors accounting for 89 percent of the variance of the correlation matrix. These factors can be labeled as follows:

1. Volume of trade with U.S.; balance of trade
2. Trade distribution with respect to Africa and ex-metropole
3. Volume of trade with ex-metropole
4. Percent trade distribution with respect to the U.S.

We have tried to account for all these factors in our tables as well as to present important individual variables which did not fall on these factors such as exports, dominant export, trade with Eastern-bloc countries, and trade as a percent of GNP.

Notes

[1] The major institutional expression of the Bretton Woods deliberations is the International Monetary Fund.

[2] Bela Belasa, *Economic Integration* (Homewood, Ill.: Robert Irwin, 1962).

[3] See Karl W. Deutsch, *The Analysis of International Relations* (Englewood Cliffs, N.J.: Prentice-Hall, 1968). For introductions to the analysis of transaction flows, which should be distinguished from trade, see I. Richard Savage and Karl W. Deutsch, "A Statistical Model of the Gross Analysis of Transaction Flows," *Econometrica*, 28 (1960): 551–572. Also see Bruce Russett, *International Regions and the International System* (Chicago: Rand McNally, 1967).

[4] The U.S. averages about 4–5 percent while nations such as Britain average as much as 50 percent. See International Monetary Fund, *World Trade Statistics*, Washington, D.C., monthly.

[5] Major developments in this theory include Murray Kemp, *The Pure Theory of International Trade* (Englewood Cliffs, N.J.: Prentice-Hall, 1964); Jaroslav Vanek, *International Trade: Theory and Economic Policy* (Homewood, Ill.: Robert Irwin, 1962); Jacob Viner, *International Trade and Economic Development* (Oxford: Clarendon Press, 1953); James Meade, *Trade and Welfare* (New York: Oxford University Press, 1955).

[6] For a recent review of this point see John Chipman "A Survey of the Theory of International Trade, Part I, Classical Theory; Part II, Neo-Classical Theory," *Econometrica*, 33, nos. 3 and 4 (1965), 477–519, 685–760; and Richard Caves, *Trade and Economic Structure* (Cambridge: Harvard University Press, 1963).

[7] An outstanding exponent of this view is Gunnar Myrdal. For example, his *Economic Theory and Underdeveloped Regions* (Mystic, Conn.: Lawrence Verry, 1957). See also Gerald Meier and R. Baldwin, *Economic Development* (New York: John Wiley, 1957), and R. Prebisch, *Towards a Dynamic Development Policy for Latin America* (New York: UN, 1963).

[8] Data for other years are in the sources given in the tables.

[9] See O. H. Abdel-Salam, "Balance of Payments Problems of African Countries," *Journal of Modern African Studies*, 4 (1966): 155–176.

TABLE 13.1   Trade as Percent of GNP, ca. 1968

```
RANGE  =        102.00
MEAN  =          50.83
STANDARD DEVIATION =          28.38
```

CUM.	POPULATION PERCENT COUNTRY	RANK	COUNTRY NAME	VALUE	RANGE DECILE
0.5	0.5	1.0	LIBERIA	120	1
2.3	1.8	2.0	ZAMBIA	109	2
2.5	0.2	3.0	GABON	96	3
2.7	0.2	4.0	GAMBIA	95	
3.1	0.4	5.0	CONGO (BRA)	93	
4.3	1.2	6.0	DAHOMEY	71	5
6.2	1.9	7.0	IVORY COAST	69	6
6.7	0.5	8.0	MAURITANIA	65	
15.8	9.1	9.0	ZAIRE	63	
17.7	1.9	10.0	MALAWI	59	
23.4	5.7	11.0	TANZANIA	58	7
24.6	1.2	12.0	SOMALIA	55	
29.4	4.8	13.5	KENYA	51	
33.6	4.2	13.5	UGANDA	51	
36.1	2.5	15.5	CAMEROON	49	
37.2	1.1	15.5	SIERRA LEONE	49	
38.0	0.8	17.0	TOGO	42	8
38.7	0.7	18.0	CAR	39	
42.5	3.8	19.0	GHANA	37	9
44.2	1.7	20.0	SENEGAL	29	
45.9	1.7	21.0	GUINEA	27	10
47.4	1.5	22.0	RWANDA	26	
49.7	2.3	23.0	UPPER VOLTA	25	
51.3	1.6	24.0	CHAD	24	
52.8	1.5	25.5	BURUNDI	22	
59.5	6.7	25.5	SUDAN	22	
61.2	1.7	27.5	NIGER	21	
86.2	25.0	27.5	NIGERIA	21	
88.4	2.2	29.0	MALI	19	
99.3	10.9	30.0	ETHIOPIA	18	

```
DATA NOT AVAILABLE FOR THE FOLLOWING COUNTRIES

BOTSWANA      LESOTHO
```

SOURCE: *AID Economic Data Book 1970.*

TABLE 13.2   Principal Export as Percent of Total Exports, 1966–1968

Comment: Average over the three-year time span.

```
RANGE  =        78.00
MEAN  =         53.47
STANDARD DEVIATION =          20.76
```

CUM.	POPULATION PERCENT COUNTRY	RANK	COUNTRY NAME	VALUE	RANGE DECILE
0.3	0.3	1.0	BOTSWANA	96	1
2.1	1.8	2.0	ZAMBIA	94	
2.6	0.5	3.0	MAURITANIA	85	2
4.1	1.5	4.0	BURUNDI	84	
5.7	1.6	5.0	CHAD	80	3
7.4	1.7	6.0	SENEGAL	75	
7.9	0.5	7.0	LIBERIA	73	
9.6	1.7	8.0	NIGER	65	4
11.3	1.7	9.0	GUINEA	64	5
20.4	9.1	10.0	ZAIRE	61	
20.8	0.4	11.0	LESOTHO	60	
22.3	1.5	12.5	RWANDA	57	
23.4	1.1	12.5	SIERRA LEONE	57	
34.3	10.9	14.0	ETHIOPIA	56	6
38.1	3.8	15.5	GHANA	55	
44.8	6.7	15.5	SUDAN	55	
49.0	4.2	17.0	UGANDA	53	
49.7	0.7	18.5	CAR	51	
52.0	2.3	18.5	UPPER VOLTA	51	
53.2	1.2	20.0	DAHOMEY	49	7
53.6	0.4	21.0	CONGO (BRA)	48	
54.8	1.2	22.0	SOMALIA	47	
55.0	0.2	23.0	GAMBIA	45	
55.8	0.8	24.0	TOGO	37	8
56.0	0.2	25.5	GABON	35	
57.9	1.9	25.5	IVORY COAST	35	
60.4	2.5	27.0	CAMEROON	28	9
85.4	25.0	28.0	NIGERIA	27	
90.2	4.8	29.0	KENYA	26	
92.1	1.9	30.0	MALAWI	25	10
97.8	5.7	31.0	TANZANIA	19	
100.0	2.2	32.0	MALI	18	

SOURCE: *AID Economic Data Book 1970.*

TABLE 13.3   Number of Commodities Making Up 70 Percent of Exports, 1966–1968

```
RANGE =          5.00
MEAN =           2.59
STANDARD DEVIATION =        1.41
```

POPULATION PERCENT CUM.	COUNTRY	RANK	COUNTRY NAME	VALUE	RANGE DECILE
4.8	4.8	2.0	KENYA	6	1
7.0	2.2	2.0	MALI	6	
12.7	5.7	2.0	TANZANIA	6	
15.2	2.5	5.0	CAMEROON	4	4
17.1	1.9	5.0	MALAWI	4	5
42.1	25.0	5.0	NIGERIA	4	
51.2	9.1	10.5	ZAIRE	3	6
62.1	10.9	10.5	ETHIOPIA	3	7
62.3	0.2	10.5	GABON	3	
66.1	3.8	10.5	GHANA	3	
68.0	1.9	10.5	IVORY COAST	3	
74.7	6.7	10.5	SUDAN	3	
75.5	0.8	10.5	TOGO	3	
77.8	2.3	10.5	UPPER VOLTA	3	
78.5	0.7	20.0	CAR	2	8
78.9	0.4	20.0	CONGO (BRA)	2	9
80.1	1.2	20.0	DAHOMEY	2	
80.3	0.2	20.0	GAMBIA	2	
82.0	1.7	20.0	GUINEA	2	
82.4	0.4	20.0	LESOTHO	2	
84.1	1.7	20.0	NIGER	2	
85.6	1.5	20.0	RWANDA	2	
86.7	1.1	20.0	SIERRA LEONE	2	
87.9	1.2	20.0	SOMALIA	2	
92.1	4.2	20.0	UGANDA	2	
92.4	0.3	29.0	BOTSWANA	1	10
93.9	1.5	29.0	BURUNDI	1	
95.5	1.6	29.0	CHAD	1	
96.0	0.5	29.0	LIBERIA	1	
96.5	0.5	29.0	MAURITANIA	1	
98.2	1.7	29.0	SENEGAL	1	
100.0	1.8	29.0	ZAMBIA	1	

SOURCE: *AID Economic Data Book 1970.*

TABLE 13.4   Percent of Imports Composed of Equipment, 1962

Definition: All imports composed of machinery, vehicles, and other mechanical devices.

```
RANGE =          75.00
MEAN =           28.16
STANDARD DEVIATION =       14.02
```

POPULATION PERCENT CUM.	COUNTRY	RANK	COUNTRY NAME	VALUE	RANGE DECILE
0.5	0.5	1.0	MAURITANIA	80	1
1.0	0.5	2.0	LIBERIA	55	4
1.2	0.2	3.5	GABON	43	5
3.4	2.2	3.5	MALI	43	
3.8	0.4	5.0	CONGO (BRA)	42	6
5.5	1.7	6.0	GUINEA	40	
16.4	10.9	7.0	ETHIOPIA	38	
23.1	6.7	8.0	SUDAN	36	
25.0	1.9	9.0	IVORY COAST	32	7
26.2	1.2	10.0	DAHOMEY	31	
28.0	1.8	11.0	ZAMBIA	30	
28.8	0.8	12.5	TOGO	28	
33.0	4.2	12.5	UGANDA	28	
34.7	1.7	14.5	SENEGAL	26	8
40.4	5.7	14.5	TANZANIA	26	
42.3	1.9	16.5	MALAWI	25	
43.5	1.2	16.5	SOMALIA	25	
44.2	0.7	18.5	CAR	24	
69.2	25.0	18.5	NIGERIA	24	
69.4	0.2	20.0	GAMBIA	23	
78.5	9.1	21.5	ZAIRE	22	
82.3	3.8	21.5	GHANA	22	
83.9	1.6	23.0	CHAD	21	
88.7	4.8	24.0	KENYA	20	9
89.0	0.3	26.5	BOTSWANA	18	
90.5	1.5	26.5	BURUNDI	18	
92.0	1.5	26.5	RWANDA	18	
94.3	2.3	26.5	UPPER VOLTA	18	
96.8	2.5	29.0	CAMEROON	16	
97.9	1.1	30.0	SIERRA LEONE	15	
99.6	1.7	31.0	NIGER	9	10
100.0	0.4	32.0	LESOTHO	5	

SOURCES: *Étude Monographique*, Vol. 1, p. 27. *Ethiopia, Malawi, Sudan, Zambia*: Annual rate of change calculated and from that the 1962 figure estimated. *ECA Statistical Bulletin I*, Tables 50, 52; *Somalia*: Estimated from mean of Tanzania, Kenya and Uganda; *Botswana*: *Bechuanaland Report, 1965* (London: Her Majesty's Stationery Office, 1966), p. 173; *Burundi, Rwanda*: Burundi and Rwanda reported as a combined figure; *Lesotho*: Estimate assuming Lesotho has very low equipment imports; *Cameroon*: Twenty for East Cameroon, eight for West Cameroon. Population ratio 2 : 1 gives an average of sixteen.

TABLE 13.5 Percent of Import Trade with African States, ca. 1968

Definition: Excludes trade with South Africa, Egypt, and North Africa.

```
RANGE     =        33.00
MEAN      =         9.58
STANDARD DEVIATION =          7.98
```

POPULATION PERCENT					
CUM.	COUNTRY	RANK	COUNTRY NAME	VALUE	RANGE DECILE
2.3	2.3	1.0	UPPER VOLTA	34	1
6.5	4.2	2.0	UGANDA	25	3
8.4	1.9	3.5	MALAWI	24	4
9.9	1.5	3.5	RWANDA	24	
15.6	5.7	5.0	TANZANIA	17	6
17.3	1.7	6.0	NIGER	15	
19.0	1.7	7.0	SENEGAL	13	7
20.6	1.6	8.0	CHAD	12	
21.8	1.2	10.0	DAHOMEY	11	
26.6	4.8	10.0	KENYA	11	
27.8	1.2	10.0	SOMALIA	11	
29.3	1.5	13.5	BURUNDI	10	8
31.8	2.5	13.5	CAMEROON	10	
33.7	1.9	13.5	IVORY COAST	10	
35.5	1.8	13.5	ZAMBIA	10	
36.3	0.8	16.0	TOGO	9	
37.0	0.7	17.5	CAR	6	9
37.4	0.4	17.5	CONGO (BRA)	6	
37.7	0.3	20.0	BOTSWANA	5	
37.9	0.2	20.0	GABON	5	
38.3	0.4	20.0	LESOTHO	5	
47.4	9.1	22.5	ZAIRE	4	10
47.6	0.2	22.5	GAMBIA	4	
51.4	3.8	24.5	GHANA	3	
52.5	1.1	24.5	SIERRA LEONE	3	
53.0	0.5	27.5	LIBERIA	2	
53.5	0.5	27.5	MAURITANIA	2	
78.5	25.0	27.5	NIGERIA	2	
85.2	6.7	27.5	SUDAN	2	
96.1	10.9	30.0	ETHIOPIA	1	
97.8	1.7	31.5	GUINEA	1	

```
DATA NOT AVAILABLE FOR THE FOLLOWING COUNTRIES

MALI
```

SOURCE: *AID Economic Data Book 1970.*

TABLE 13.6 Percent of Export Trade with African States, ca. 1968

Definition: Excludes trade with South Africa, Egypt, and North Africa.

```
RANGE     =        70.60
MEAN      =        13.34
STANDARD DEVIATION =         18.65
```

POPULATION PERCENT					
CUM.	COUNTRY	RANK	COUNTRY NAME	VALUE	RANGE DECILE
2.3	2.3	1.0	UPPER VOLTA	71	1
3.8	1.5	2.0	RWANDA	67	
6.0	2.2	3.0	MALI	54	3
10.8	4.8	4.0	KENYA	39	5
12.5	1.7	5.0	NIGER	30	6
14.4	1.9	6.0	MALAWI	19	8
20.1	5.7	7.5	TANZANIA	18	
24.3	4.2	7.5	UGANDA	18	
25.5	1.2	9.0	DAHOMEY	17	
27.2	1.7	10.0	SENEGAL	12	9
28.8	1.6	11.0	CHAD	10	
31.3	2.5	12.5	CAMEROON	9	
33.0	1.7	12.5	GUINEA	9	
34.9	1.9	14.0	IVORY COAST	8	
35.1	0.2	15.0	GABON	7	10
35.4	0.3	17.5	BOTSWANA	5	
46.3	10.9	17.5	ETHIOPIA	5	
46.7	0.4	17.5	LESOTHO	5	
47.5	0.8	17.5	TOGO	5	
47.9	0.4	20.0	CONGO (BRA)	4	
48.4	0.5	21.0	MAURITANIA	3	
48.9	0.5	22.5	LIBERIA	2	
73.9	25.0	22.5	NIGERIA	2	
75.4	1.5	27.0	BURUNDI	1	
76.1	0.7	27.0	CAR	1	
85.2	9.1	27.0	ZAIRE	1	
85.4	0.2	27.0	GAMBIA	1	
89.2	3.8	27.0	GHANA	1	
90.4	1.2	27.0	SOMALIA	1	
92.2	1.8	27.0	ZAMBIA	1	
93.3	1.1	31.5	SIERRA LEONE	0	
100.0	6.7	31.5	SUDAN	0	

SOURCE: *AID Economic Data Book 1970.*

TABLE 13.7 Percent of Import Trade with Colonial Power, ca. 1925

Definition and Comments: Colonial power is either France, England or Belgium. Part II gives the colonial power for each country. Not applicable for Ethiopia.

```
RANGE    =        77.00
MEAN     =        45.29
STANDARD DEVIATION =           21.67
```

POPULATION PERCENT CUM.	COUNTRY	RANK	COUNTRY NAME	VALUE	RANGE DECILE
25.0	25.0	1.0	NIGERIA	77	1
29.8	4.8	2.5	KENYA	69	2
34.0	4.2	2.5	UGANDA	69	
37.8	3.8	4.0	GHANA	68	
38.9	1.1	5.0	SIERRA LEONE	67	
44.6	5.7	6.0	TANZANIA	64	
45.1	0.5	7.5	MAURITANIA	62	
46.8	1.7	7.5	NIGER	62	
47.0	0.2	9.0	GABON	59	3
49.2	2.2	10.5	MALI	51	4
55.9	6.7	10.5	SUDAN	51	
57.6	1.7	12.5	SENEGAL	49	
59.4	1.8	12.5	ZAMBIA	49	
61.9	2.5	14.0	CAMEROON	44	5
62.6	0.7	15.0	CAR	43	
63.0	0.4	16.5	CONGO (BRA)	42	
64.9	1.9	16.5	IVORY COAST	42	
66.6	1.7	18.0	GUINEA	36	6
68.2	1.6	19.0	CHAD	31	
69.4	1.2	20.0	DAHOMEY	26	7
70.2	0.8	21.0	TOGO	20	8
70.5	0.3	22.5	BOTSWANA	3	10
72.8	2.3	22.5	UPPER VOLTA	3	
73.2	0.4	24.0	LESOTHO	0	

```
DATA NOT AVAILABLE FOR THE FOLLOWING COUNTRIES

BURUNDI      ZAIRE       ETHIOPIA     GAMBIA
LIBERIA      MALAWI      RWANDA       SOMALIA
```

SOURCES: Raymond L. Buell, *The Native Problem in Africa* (New York: Macmillan, 1928). *Mauritania, Niger*: Total for all French West Africa; *Central African Republic, Congo (Brazzaville), Gabon*: Georges Bruel, *L'Afrique équatorial française* (Paris: Larose, 1935); *Botswana, Lesotho*: Estimate, assuming most trade must be with South Africa.

TABLE 13.8 Percent Export Trade with Colonial Power, ca. 1925

Definition and Comments: See Table 13.7.

```
RANGE    =        84.00
MEAN     =        41.83
STANDARD DEVIATION =           25.44
```

POPULATION PERCENT CUM.	COUNTRY	RANK	COUNTRY NAME	VALUE	RANGE DECILE
4.8	4.8	1.5	KENYA	84	1
9.0	4.2	1.5	UGANDA	84	
10.1	1.1	3.0	SIERRA LEONE	76	
11.8	1.7	4.0	SENEGAL	74	2
17.5	5.7	5.0	TANZANIA	69	
19.7	2.2	6.0	MALI	59	3
44.7	25.0	7.0	NIGERIA	56	4
46.4	1.7	8.5	GUINEA	52	
48.3	1.9	8.5	IVORY COAST	52	
55.0	6.7	10.0	SUDAN	47	5
55.5	0.5	11.5	MAURITANIA	45	
57.2	1.7	11.5	NIGER	45	
57.4	0.2	13.0	GABON	44	
58.2	0.8	14.0	TOGO	40	6
60.0	1.8	15.0	ZAMBIA	39	
61.2	1.2	16.0	DAHOMEY	38	
65.0	3.8	17.0	GHANA	35	
67.5	2.5	18.0	CAMEROON	28	7
67.9	0.4	19.0	CONGO (BRA)	23	8
68.6	0.7	20.0	CAR	8	10
68.9	0.3	21.5	BOTSWANA	3	
70.5	1.6	21.5	CHAD	3	
70.9	0.4	23.0	LESOTHO	0	
73.2	2.3	24.0	UPPER VOLTA	0	

```
DATA NOT AVAILABLE FOR THE FOLLOWING COUNTRIES

BURUNDI      ZAIRE       ETHIOPIA     GAMBIA
LIBERIA      MALAWI      RWANDA       SOMALIA
```

SOURCES: Buell, *The Native Problem in Africa. Liberia*: 1940 figure, *Handbook of Liberia*, p. 41; *Sudan*: 1938 figure, *Sudan Almanac 1956* (Khartoum: National Guidance Office, 1956), p. 91. *Mauritania, Niger*: Total figure for French West Africa; *Botswana, Lesotho*: Estimate assuming most trade must be with South Africa; *Ethiopia*: No metropole.

TABLE 13.9 Percent Export Trade with Colonial Power, 1955

Definition and Sources: See Table 13.7.

```
RANGE =          91.00
MEAN =           50.23
STANDARD DEVIATION =        25.77
```

POPULATION PERCENT		RANK	COUNTRY NAME	VALUE	RANGE DECILE
CUM.	COUNTRY				
1.2	1.2	1.0	DAHOMEY	93	1
2.9	1.7	2.5	NIGER	85	
3.7	0.8	2.5	TOGO	85	
4.4	0.7	4.0	CAR	83	2
6.6	2.2	5.0	MALI	81	
8.3	1.7	6.0	SENEGAL	80	
9.9	1.6	7.5	CHAD	73	3
11.0	1.1	7.5	SIERRA LEONE	73	
12.7	1.7	9.0	GUINEA	63	4
37.7	25.0	10.0	NIGERIA	62	
39.6	1.9	11.5	MALAWI	60	
41.4	1.8	11.5	ZAMBIA	60	
43.3	1.9	13.0	IVORY COAST	58	
43.5	0.2	14.5	GAMBIA	55	5
44.0	0.5	14.5	MAURITANIA	55	
46.5	2.5	16.5	CAMEROON	53	
55.6	9.1	16.5	ZAIRE	53	
55.8	0.2	18.0	GABON	51	
62.5	6.7	19.0	SUDAN	43	6
64.0	1.5	20.5	BURUNDI	37	7
65.5	1.5	20.5	RWANDA	37	
69.3	3.8	22.0	GHANA	36	
69.7	0.4	23.0	CONGO (BRA)	34	
75.4	5.7	24.0	TANZANIA	33	
80.2	4.8	25.0	KENYA	27	8
84.4	4.2	26.0	UGANDA	21	
86.7	2.3	27.0	UPPER VOLTA	6	10
87.0	0.3	28.0	BOTSWANA	5	
87.4	0.4	29.0	LESOTHO	3	
88.6	1.2	30.0	SOMALIA	2	

```
DATA NOT AVAILABLE FOR THE FOLLOWING COUNTRIES

ETHIOPIA     LIBERIA
```

SOURCES: Service des Statistiques d'Outre-mer, *Outre-mer, 1958* (Paris: Ministere de la France d'Outre-mer, 1960). *CAR*: 1958 figure, *AID Economic Data Book*; *Mali*: 1958 figure, *Europa Yearbook 1961*, p. 787; *Malawi*: Estimate based on 1964 data on Malawi of 48 percent and Zambia 1958 value of 60 percent. Expect 1955 figure to be higher than 1964 and of same order as Zambia's; *Chad*: 1959 figure, *Europa Yearbook 1961*, p. 376; *Zambia*: *Annual Statement of the Trade of Northern Rhodesia* (Lusaka: 1953); *Gambia, Mauritania*: 1962 figure; *Gabon*: International Monetary Fund, *Survey of African Economies*, Vol. 1, p. 330; *Cameroon*: 1959 figure, East Cameroon only, *Europa Yearbook 1961*, p. 307; *Sudan*: 1954 figure, *Sudan Almanac, 1956*, p. 91; *Burundi, Rwanda*: 1958 figure, *Europa Yearbook 1961*, p. 1012. Burundi and Rwanda combined figure. *Ghana*: 1958 figure, *Europa Yearbook 1961*, p. 535; *Congo (Brazzaville)*: 1959 figure, *Europa Yearbook 1961*, p. 376; *Tanzania*: Tanganyika only; *Lesotho*: Estimate, vast majority of trade with South Africa.

TABLE 13.10 Total Trade with Colonial Power or ex-Colonial Power as Percent of Total Trade, 1962

Definition: Total trade is the sum of exports and imports. For date of independence see Part II.

```
RANGE =          64.00
MEAN =           40.40
STANDARD DEVIATION =        17.59
```

POPULATION PERCENT		RANK	COUNTRY NAME	VALUE	RANGE DECILE
CUM.	COUNTRY				
1.7	1.7	1.0	SENEGAL	74	1
2.9	1.2	2.0	DAHOMEY	69	
4.5	1.6	3.0	CHAD	64	2
4.7	0.2	4.0	GABON	61	3
5.4	0.7	5.0	CAR	59	
7.9	2.5	6.0	CAMEROON	57	
8.1	0.2	7.5	GAMBIA	55	
8.6	0.5	7.5	MAURITANIA	55	
10.5	1.9	9.5	IVORY COAST	54	4
12.2	1.7	9.5	NIGER	54	
12.6	0.4	11.0	CONGO (BRA)	51	
14.9	2.3	12.0	UPPER VOLTA	47	5
16.0	1.1	13.0	SIERRA LEONE	46	
21.7	5.7	14.0	TANZANIA	45	
22.5	0.8	15.0	TOGO	41	6
47.5	25.0	16.0	NIGERIA	39	
48.7	1.2	17.0	SOMALIA	38	
50.6	1.9	18.0	MALAWI	34	7
54.4	3.8	19.0	GHANA	33	
63.5	9.1	20.0	ZAIRE	32	
65.0	1.5	21.0	RWANDA	31	
69.8	4.8	22.5	KENYA	30	
71.6	1.8	22.5	ZAMBIA	30	
78.3	6.7	24.0	SUDAN	21	9
79.8	1.5	25.5	BURUNDI	20	
84.0	4.2	25.5	UGANDA	20	
85.7	1.7	27.0	GUINEA	17	
87.9	2.2	28.0	MALI	15	10
88.2	0.3	29.0	BOTSWANA	10	
88.6	0.4	30.0	LESOTHO	10	

```
DATA NOT AVAILABLE FOR THE FOLLOWING COUNTRIES

ETHIOPIA     LIBERIA
```

SOURCES: *AID Economic Data Book* and *Europe-France Outre-mer* (Paris), March 1964. *Chad*: *Étude Monographique*, Vol. 1, p. 27.

TABLE 13.11 Total Trade with ex-Colonial Power as Percent of Total Trade, 1968

Definition: See Table 13.10.

```
RANGE =            72.00
MEAN =             33.37
STANDARD DEVIATION =            15.19
```

POPULATION PERCENT		RANK	COUNTRY NAME	VALUE	RANGE DECILE
CUM.	COUNTRY				
1.7	1.7	1.0	SENEGAL	77	1
3.4	1.7	2.0	NIGER	56	3
5.0	1.6	3.0	CHAD	51	4
5.7	0.7	4.0	CAR	50	
6.8	1.1	5.0	SIERRA LEONE	48	5
7.0	0.2	6.0	GAMBIA	47	
9.5	2.5	7.0	CAMEROON	46	
9.7	0.2	8.0	GABON	42	
11.6	1.9	9.0	IVORY COAST	41	6
12.8	1.2	10.0	SOMALIA	40	
14.0	1.2	11.0	DAHOMEY	38	
14.4	0.4	12.5	CONGO (BRA)	37	
23.5	9.1	12.5	ZAIRE	37	
24.3	0.8	14.0	TOGO	35	
26.6	2.3	15.0	UPPER VOLTA	34	
28.5	1.9	16.0	MALAWI	33	7
53.5	25.0	17.0	NIGERIA	30	
54.0	0.5	18.0	MAURITANIA	29	
57.8	3.8	19.5	GHANA	27	
60.0	2.2	19.5	MALI	27	
61.8	1.8	21.0	ZAMBIA	26	8
66.6	4.8	22.0	KENYA	24	
72.3	5.7	23.0	TANZANIA	23	
73.8	1.5	24.5	RWANDA	22	
78.0	4.2	24.5	UGANDA	22	
79.5	1.5	26.0	BURUNDI	21	
86.2	6.7	27.0	SUDAN	15	9
87.9	1.7	28.0	GUINEA	13	
88.2	0.3	29.0	BOTSWANA	5	
88.6	0.4	30.0	LESOTHO	5	

```
DATA NOT AVAILABLE FOR THE FOLLOWING COUNTRIES

ETHIOPIA     LIBERIA
```

SOURCE: *AID Economic Data Book 1970.*

TABLE 13.12 Index of Importance of Trade with Eastern-Bloc Countries, 1968

Definition: 1 = less than 1 percent, 2 = 1–10 percent, 3 = over 10 percent of trade. "Eastern bloc" includes Cuba, excludes Yugoslavia. Total trade is the sum of exports and imports.

```
RANGE =            2.00
MEAN =             1.81
STANDARD DEVIATION =            0.58
```

POPULATION PERCENT		RANK	COUNTRY NAME	VALUE	RANGE DECILE
CUM.	COUNTRY				
1.7	1.7	2.0	GUINEA	3	1
3.9	2.2	2.0	MALI	3	
10.6	6.7	2.0	SUDAN	3	
13.1	2.5	13.5	CAMEROON	2	5
14.7	1.6	13.5	CHAD	2	
15.1	0.4	13.5	CONGO (BRA)	2	
16.3	1.2	13.5	DAHOMEY	2	
27.2	10.9	13.5	ETHIOPIA	2	
31.0	3.8	13.5	GHANA	2	
32.9	1.9	13.5	IVORY COAST	2	
37.7	4.8	13.5	KENYA	2	
38.2	0.5	13.5	LIBERIA	2	
38.7	0.5	13.5	MAURITANIA	2	
40.4	1.7	13.5	NIGER	2	
65.4	25.0	13.5	NIGERIA	2	
66.9	1.5	13.5	RWANDA	2	
68.6	1.7	13.5	SENEGAL	2	
69.7	1.1	13.5	SIERRA LEONE	2	
70.9	1.2	13.5	SOMALIA	2	
76.6	5.7	13.5	TANZANIA	2	
77.4	0.8	13.5	TOGO	2	
81.6	4.2	13.5	UGANDA	2	
83.4	1.8	13.5	ZAMBIA	2	
83.7	0.3	28.0	BOTSWANA	1	10
85.2	1.5	28.0	BURUNDI	1	
85.9	0.7	28.0	CAR	1	
95.0	9.1	28.0	ZAIRE	1	
95.2	0.2	28.0	GABON	1	
95.4	0.2	28.0	GAMBIA	1	
95.8	0.4	28.0	LESOTHO	1	
97.7	1.9	28.0	MALAWI	1	
100.0	2.3	28.0	UPPER VOLTA	1	

SOURCE: *AID Economic Data Book 1970.*

TABLE 13.13 Total Trade with U.S. as Percent of Total Trade, 1962

Definition: Total trade is the sum of exports and imports.

```
RANGE  =          70.00
MEAN   =          10.06
STANDARD DEVIATION =        14.06
```

POPULATION PERCENT CUM.	COUNTRY	RANK	COUNTRY NAME	VALUE	RANGE DECILE
1.5	1.5	1.0	BURUNDI	70	1
2.0	0.5	2.0	LIBERIA	43	4
12.9	10.9	3.0	ETHIOPIA	28	6
22.0	9.1	4.0	ZAIRE	24	7
23.5	1.5	5.0	RWANDA	20	8
27.7	4.2	6.0	UGANDA	13	9
31.5	3.8	7.0	GHANA	12	
33.2	1.7	8.0	GUINEA	11	
35.1	1.9	9.0	IVORY COAST	10	
60.1	25.0	10.0	NIGERIA	9	
60.8	0.7	11.5	CAR	8	
65.6	4.8	11.5	KENYA	8	
71.3	5.7	13.0	TANZANIA	7	10
73.8	2.5	15.5	CAMEROON	6	
74.0	0.2	15.5	GABON	6	
74.2	0.2	15.5	GAMBIA	6	
74.7	0.5	15.5	MAURITANIA	6	
75.9	1.2	18.5	SOMALIA	5	
76.7	0.8	18.5	TOGO	5	
83.4	6.7	20.0	SUDAN	4	
85.0	1.6	23.0	CHAD	3	
86.7	1.7	23.0	NIGER	3	
87.8	1.1	23.0	SIERRA LEONE	3	
90.1	2.3	23.0	UPPER VOLTA	3	
91.9	1.8	23.0	ZAMBIA	3	
93.8	1.9	26.5	MALAWI	2	
95.5	1.7	26.5	SENEGAL	2	
96.7	1.2	28.5	DAHOMEY	1	
98.9	2.2	28.5	MALI	1	
99.2	0.3	31.0	BOTSWANA	0	
99.6	0.4	31.0	CONGO (BRA)	0	
100.0	0.4	31.0	LESOTHO	0	

SOURCES: *AID Economic Data Book*, and *Europe-France Outre-mer*. Zaire (*Congo K.*): Economist Intelligence Unit, *Annual Supplement 1962*, (London: The Economist, 1962).

TABLE 13.14 Total Trade with U.S. as Percent of Total Trade, 1968

Definition: Total trade is the sum of exports and imports.

```
RANGE  =          34.00
MEAN   =           9.28
STANDARD DEVIATION =         9.03
```

POPULATION PERCENT CUM.	COUNTRY	RANK	COUNTRY NAME	VALUE	RANGE DECILE
1.5	1.5	1.5	BURUNDI	34	1
12.4	10.9	1.5	ETHIOPIA	34	
12.9	0.5	3.0	LIBERIA	31	
16.7	3.8	4.0	GHANA	21	4
17.4	0.7	5.0	CAR	18	5
21.6	4.2	6.0	UGANDA	15	6
23.3	1.7	7.0	GUINEA	13	7
25.2	1.9	8.0	IVORY COAST	12	
34.3	9.1	9.0	ZAIRE	11	
34.5	0.2	10.0	GABON	10	8
37.0	2.5	11.0	CAMEROON	9	
62.0	25.0	13.0	NIGERIA	8	
63.1	1.1	13.0	SIERRA LEONE	8	
68.8	5.7	13.0	TANZANIA	8	
73.6	4.8	15.0	KENYA	7	
74.8	1.2	16.0	SOMALIA	6	9
76.4	1.6	18.5	CHAD	5	
77.6	1.2	18.5	DAHOMEY	5	
78.1	0.5	18.5	MAURITANIA	5	
79.9	1.8	18.5	ZAMBIA	5	
80.3	0.4	23.0	CONGO (BRA)	4	
82.2	1.9	23.0	MALAWI	4	
83.9	1.7	23.0	NIGER	4	
85.4	1.5	23.0	RWANDA	4	
92.1	6.7	23.0	SUDAN	4	
93.8	1.7	26.5	SENEGAL	3	10
96.1	2.3	26.5	UPPER VOLTA	3	
96.3	0.2	28.5	GAMBIA	2	
97.1	0.8	28.5	TOGO	2	
97.4	0.3	30.5	BOTSWANA	1	
97.8	0.4	30.5	LESOTHO	1	
100.0	2.2	32.0	MALI	0	

SOURCE: *AID Economic Data Book 1970*.

**TABLE 13.15   Cumulative Balance of Trade, 1963–1968, as
Percent of 1967 GNP**

Definition: The sum of the balance of trade for the years 1963
through 1968 divided by the GNP in 1967.

```
RANGE  =          229.00
MEAN   =            9.87
STANDARD DEVIATION =           45.49
```

POPULATION PERCENT		RANK	COUNTRY NAME	VALUE	RANGE DECILE
CUM.	COUNTRY				
0.2	0.2	1.0	GABON	130	1
2.0	1.8	2.0	ZAMBIA	98	2
2.5	0.5	3.0	LIBERIA	70	3
11.6	9.1	4.0	ZAIRE	47	4
12.1	0.5	5.0	MAURITANIA	44	
14.0	1.9	6.0	IVORY COAST	36	5
18.2	4.2	7.0	UGANDA	29	
23.9	5.7	8.0	TANZANIA	28	
25.0	1.1	9.0	SIERRA LEONE	25	
26.9	1.9	10.0	MALAWI	22	
31.7	4.8	11.5	KENYA	21	
32.9	1.2	11.5	SOMALIA	21	
34.6	1.7	13.5	SENEGAL	19	
35.4	0.8	13.5	TOGO	19	
42.1	6.7	15.0	SUDAN	16	
43.8	1.7	16.0	GUINEA	12	6
68.8	25.0	17.5	NIGERIA	11	
70.3	1.5	17.5	RWANDA	11	
72.0	1.7	19.0	NIGER	7	
74.2	2.2	20.0	MALI	3	
76.7	2.5	21.0	CAMEROON	-4	
77.4	0.7	22.0	CAR	-15	7
78.9	1.5	23.5	BURUNDI	-16	
89.8	10.9	23.5	ETHIOPIA	-16	
91.4	1.6	25.0	CHAD	-18	
95.2	3.8	26.0	GHANA	-19	
95.4	0.2	27.0	GAMBIA	-53	8
97.7	2.3	28.0	UPPER VOLTA	-56	9
98.9	1.2	29.0	DAHOMEY	-77	10
99.3	0.4	30.0	CONGO (BRA)	-99	

DATA NOT AVAILABLE FOR THE FOLLOWING COUNTRIES

BOTSWANA   LESOTHO

SOURCE: *AID Economic Data Book 1970.*

14. International Relations

In the era of the Vietnam war, there should be little question as to the relevance of international relations to the development of national political systems in "new" states. In the extreme case of such a war, international intervention and aggression may come close to the obliteration of a national population, the intensification of domestic conflict, and the drastic restructuring of the economic system of a new state. International relations in turn, are contingent on patterns of interaction within nations—the civil wars in Nigeria and Zaire (Congo K.), and the consequent introduction of foreign assistance, military technology and "advisers," are clear examples.[1] The analysis of political development in Africa requires information on patterns of international relations, although recent research on new nations is generally lacking in any systematic attention to the impact of intranational relations on international relations, or vice versa.[2]

Integration and conflict are relevant theoretical foci for the study of international as well as national behavior.[3] Neo-colonialism is also a concept of vital concern to Africans and merits more systematic attention by social scientists whose dated concern with cold-war alliances tends to dominate the study of African international relations.[4] More traditional concepts in the literature on international relations such as power and influence[5] are still relevant (and crucial probably to the study of neo-colonialism), and may be partially measured in terms of indication of wealth and coercive potential which are given in Chapters 3 and 4 of the Handbook. Other important aspects of the measurement of neo-colonialism are given in the sections on foreign aid and military variables, Chapters 12 and 10.

The Data

In this chapter, we first present data on international integration in the form of measures of diplomatic exchange (Tables 14.1 and 14.2). Like the economic transaction flows discussed in the chapters on aid and trade, Chapters 12 and 13, the inclusion of data on diplomatic exchange may be justified in terms of transaction-oriented approaches to international integration. Analysts such as Alger and Brams have recently begun to systematically evaluate the impact of the human transaction flows involved in bilateral and multilateral forms of international representation.[6] Alger and Brams point out that the structure of international diplomacy is changing through the reduction of the autonomy of the individual diplomat and the increase in the number of diplomats representing individual countries. These changes have affected the patterns of diplomacy within Black Africa in many of the same ways that they have affected diplomatic transactions among Western nations. For example, seventeen regionally specific international organizations operating within Africa provide an opportunity for additional exchange of diplomats beyond the range of bilateral relations. Within the African context, however, relative measures of diplomatic exchange may take on increasing importance because diplomatic representatives may not only represent their countries within the official diplomatic community, but may also assume roles within the relatively small national elite of the country in which they are stationed.

The number of diplomats sent overseas may also be an indicator of the amount of attention given to international affairs. This measure, of course, may or may not be highly correlated with government revenue and capacity to finance overseas missions. The number of foreign missions in a country is also a measure of outside interest in that country.

The second set of tables contain data on international organizations (Tables 14.3–14.6). The relevance of shared organizational memberships to a system's potential for international and intranational integration has been stressed by a number of authors. Analysts in the disciplines of anthropology, sociology, and international relations have pointed out that cohesion may be linked with the presence of conflict situations in which the actors are cross-pressured by their different loyalties or organizational affiliations.[7] Multiple memberships in international organizations may provide a cross-cutting system of alliances and loyalties, through which nations can relate to each other in a number of alternative roles.

Because of the relative recency with which national boundaries have been created, in disregard of traditional ethnic boundaries, some inter-ethnic conflicts will continue to transcend national boundaries (e.g., Somali irredentism in northern Kenya). Such conflict situations which continue to threaten the stability and internal unity of individual African countries can only be settled by dealing with other nations in the organizational structure of regional or international organizations.[8] The relative proportion of regional to broader organizational memberships may also be of interest in assessing the relative importance of regional organizations in international relations.[9] Time series data on the relative growth of memberships in regional organizations as compared with universal organizations would also be useful in analyzing the impact of global and regional organization on the intensity of international conflict.

Table 14.3 shows the total number of regional organizations in which a given country has membership, while Table 14.4 indicates the total number of memberships in multilateral economic organizations for each country. The interpretation of the impact of multiple organizational memberships upon the capacity of African nations for integration should be qualified in terms of the variables operationalizing the mutual relevance of their economic transactions in the chapters on aid and trade.

The next two tables, 14.5 and 14.6, present data on two different types of international organizations which have relationships with African countries. For a number of years the *Yearbook of International Organizations* has published extensive information about the numerous intergovernmental and international non-governmental non-profit organizations such as the various United Nations agencies, Red Cross and other humanitarian agencies, trade organizations, and so on. Using this source, Table 14.5 gives the total number of different non-profit organizations which have representatives in each country. This is a crude measure of international involvement.

The second type of organization is the multinational corporation. This is a profit-making corporation which has subsidiaries in one or more countries. A subsidiary is defined as "a foreign firm established under national law of the country, whose capital stock is 50 percent or more controlled by the parent company."[10] The growth of these corporations in the last decade has been very rapid and the prospects for their future growth are such that it has been estimated that within the next decade 75 percent of the world's productive capacity will be controlled by a group of three hundred multinational corporations.[11] The *Yearbook of International Organizations* in the latest edition available to us (1968–69) presents its first preliminary analysis of multinational business enterprises. Table 14.6 gives the total number of different multinational corporations active in each country from this source. This measures the breadth but not the depth of this form of international capitalism in the countries since one such corporation might dominate one nation's economy, while fifteen in another country might have only a marginal effect. The data source breaks the information down by country of origin of the multinational corporation and also lists the corporations and their addresses.

Tables 14.7 and 14.8 present quantitative information on international conflict. Measures of aggressive behavior and hostile communications directed towards each country are fairly obvious operationalizations of international conflict, while the measure of diplomatic representation in communist countries gives an indication of the extent of neutralism (since representation in "Western" countries is relatively invariant), and an indication of the relationship between African countries and the cold-war conflict.

In the analysis of the relationships between intranational and international behavior suggested earlier, data such as those presented here can be utilized to examine hypotheses regarding the conflict potential of inherited boundaries in Africa,[12] the effects of international organization, and the effects of patterns of unilateral influence and assistance on national systems development. Refinements of these data in the form of measures of interaction between pairs of countries would be especially fruitful for this kind of analysis.

Reliability and Dimensionality

The data presented here have not been checked for inter-coder reliability, but a factor analysis of a total set of 36 variables measuring aspects of international relations showed a sufficiently coherent factor structure to indicate that the coding of these measures over time was consistent, although not necessarily free of systematic error. In addition, variables that seem conceptually related, but were coded by different persons from different sources, clustered together in the factor solution, suggesting that the measures reported here are relatively reliable.

Notes

[1] For a short, but effective explication of the importance of international intervention in Biafra see Richard L. Sklar, "The United States and the Biafran War," *Africa Report*, 14 (November 1969): 22–23.

[2] Recent attempts to confront questions of this sort with quantitative evidence are John N. Collins, *Foreign Conflict Behavior and Domestic Disorder in Africa*, unpublished Ph.D. dissertation, Department of Political Science, Northwestern University, 1966; and Patrick McGowan, "Africa and Non-Alignment: A Comparative Study of Foreign Policy," *International Studies Quarterly*, 12 (1968): 262. A comprehensive discussion of the need for "systematic conceptual exploration of the flow of influence across the changing boundaries of national and international systems" is contained in James N. Rosenau, ed., *Linkage Politics: Essays on the Convergence of National and International Systems* (New York: The Free Press, 1969). See also articles by Carl J. Friedrich, George Blanksten, and Pablo Casanova, in R. Barry Farrell, ed., *Approaches to Comparative and International Politics* (Evanston, Ill.: Northwestern University Press, 1966).

[3] For analysis of integration of international communities using transaction flow data see: Karl W. Deutsch, et al., *Political Community in the North Atlantic Area* (Princeton, N.J.: Princeton University Press, 1957); Hayward Alker, Jr., and Donald Punchala, "Trends in Economic Partnership: The North Atlantic Area, 1928, 1963"; and Bruce M. Russett, "Delineating International Regions" in *Quantitative International Politics, Insights and Evidence*, ed. J. David Singer (New York: The Free Press, 1968), pp. 287–352. For a conflict-oriented approach, see: Rudolph J. Rummel, "The Relationship between National Attributes and Foreign Conflict Behavior" and Michael Haas, "Social Change and National Aggressiveness, 1900–1960," also in *Quantitative International Politics*, pp. 187–246; and Daniel Katz, "Nationalism and Strategies of International Conflict Resolution" and Robert A. LeVine, "Socialization, Social Structure and Intersocietal Images" in *International Behavior*, ed. Herbert C. Kelman (New York: Holt, Rinehart and Winston, 1965).

[4] One of the clearest statements of the problem of neo-colonialism in Africa is that of Kwame Nkrumah in his *Neo-Colonialism: The Last Stage of Imperialism* (London, Thomas Nelson & Sons, Ltd., 1965).

[5] For a clear conceptual and operational treatment of these concepts, see Karl W. Deutsch, *The Analysis of International Relations* (Englewood Cliffs, N.J.: Prentice-Hall, 1968).

[6] Chadwick F. Alger and Stephen S. Brams, "Patterns of Representation in National Capitals and Intergovernmental Organizations," *World Politics*, 19 (July 1967): 646–663.

[7] Max Gluckman, *Custom and Conflict in Africa*, (Glencoe, Ill.: The Free Press, 1955), pp. 4–7; Harold Guetzkow, *Multiple Loyalties: Theoretical Approach to a Problem in International Organization* (Princeton, N.J.: Center for Research on World Political Institutions, 1955); Lewis Coser, *The Functions of Social Conflict* (Glencoe, Ill., The Free Press, 1966).

[8] Chadwick F. Alger, "Comparison of Intranational and International Politics," *American Political Science Review*, 57 (1963): 406–419.

[9] See John W. Burton, *Peace Theory: Preconditions for Disarmament* (New York: Alfred Knopf, 1962).

[10] A. J. N. Judge, "Multinational Business Enterprises," in *Yearbook of International Organizations 1968–69*, ed. Evyind S. Tew (Brussels: Union of International Associations, 1969), p. 1190.

[11] *Ibid.*, p. 1189.

[12] See Ravi L. Kapil, "On the Conflict Potential of Inherited Boundaries in Africa," *World Politics*, 18 (1966): 656–673.

TABLE 14.1 Number of Diplomats Sent to Foreign Countries, 1963–1964

```
RANGE     =    210.00
MEAN      =     43.04
STANDARD DEVIATION =        46.56
```

POPULATION PERCENT CUM.	COUNTRY	RANK	COUNTRY NAME	VALUE	RANGE DECILE
3.8	3.8	1.0	GHANA	212	1
28.8	25.0	2.0	NIGERIA	151	3
35.5	6.7	3.0	SUDAN	93	6
46.4	10.9	4.0	ETHIOPIA	81	7
48.1	1.7	5.0	SENEGAL	72	
49.8	1.7	6.0	GUINEA	63	8
52.0	2.2	7.0	MALI	55	
52.5	0.5	8.0	LIBERIA	54	
55.0	2.5	9.0	CAMEROON	41	9
56.9	1.9	10.5	IVORY COAST	39	
58.1	1.2	10.5	SOMALIA	39	
59.2	1.1	12.0	SIERRA LEONE	35	
68.3	9.1	13.5	ZAIRE	33	
70.6	2.3	13.5	UPPER VOLTA	33	
71.0	0.4	15.0	CONGO (BRA)	22	10
72.2	1.2	16.0	DAHOMEY	19	
72.9	0.7	18.0	CAR	16	
74.5	1.6	18.0	CHAD	16	
75.3	0.8	18.0	TOGO	16	
77.0	1.7	20.0	NIGER	15	
78.5	1.5	21.5	BURUNDI	11	
79.0	0.5	21.5	MAURITANIA	11	
79.2	0.2	23.0	GABON	10	
84.9	5.7	24.0	TANZANIA	9	
86.4	1.5	25.0	RWANDA	8	
90.6	4.2	26.0	UGANDA	6	
95.4	4.8	27.0	KENYA	2	

DATA NOT AVAILABLE FOR THE FOLLOWING COUNTRIES

BOTSWANA   GAMBIA   LESOTHO   MALAWI
ZAMBIA

SOURCE: Stephen Brams, *Flow and Form in the International System*, unpublished Ph.D. dissertation, Department of Political Science, Northwestern University, 1966.

TABLE 14.2 Number of Foreign Diplomats Received, 1963–1964

```
RANGE     =    219.00
MEAN      =     95.36
STANDARD DEVIATION =        58.85
```

POPULATION PERCENT CUM.	COUNTRY	RANK	COUNTRY NAME	VALUE	RANGE DECILE
3.8	3.8	1.0	GHANA	242	1
28.8	25.0	2.0	NIGERIA	223	
30.5	1.7	3.0	SENEGAL	163	4
39.6	9.1	4.5	ZAIRE	158	
41.3	1.7	4.5	GUINEA	158	
48.0	6.7	6.0	SUDAN	153	5
58.9	10.9	7.0	ETHIOPIA	129	6
61.1	2.2	8.0	MALI	115	
66.8	5.7	9.0	TANZANIA	104	7
67.3	0.5	10.5	LIBERIA	99	
69.2	1.9	11.0	IVORY COAST	98	
70.4	1.2	12.0	SOMALIA	92	
72.7	2.3	13.0	UPPER VOLTA	82	8
75.2	2.5	14.0	CAMEROON	80	
80.0	4.8	15.0	KENYA	75	
80.4	0.4	16.0	CONGO (BRA)	60	9
84.6	4.2	17.0	UGANDA	52	
85.8	1.2	18.5	DAHOMEY	50	
86.9	1.1	18.5	SIERRA LEONE	50	
87.7	0.8	20.0	TOGO	45	
89.3	1.6	21.0	CHAD	40	10
91.0	1.7	22.0	NIGER	38	
91.7	0.7	23.0	CAR	29	
92.2	0.5	24.0	MAURITANIA	26	
92.4	0.2	25.0	GABON	23	

DATA NOT AVAILABLE FOR THE FOLLOWING COUNTRIES

BOTSWANA   BURUNDI   GAMBIA   LESOTHO
MALAWI   RWANDA   ZAMBIA

SOURCE: Brams, *Flow and Form in the International S stem*.

TABLE 14.3 Total Number of Memberships in Principal Regional and International Organizations and Conferences

Definition: The eighteen organizations listed by the source include the United Nations, Organization of African Unity, organizations such as the Commonwealth and French Community, the Monrovia and Brazzaville Groups, the Belgrade and Bandung Conferences, Casablanca Powers and the East African Common Services Organization. The data are for ca. 1967.

RANGE = 7.00
MEAN = 6.59
STANDARD DEVIATION = 2.26

POPULATION PERCENT CUM.	COUNTRY	RANK	COUNTRY NAME	VALUE	RANGE DECILE
0.4	0.4	2.5	CONGO (BRA)	10	1
2.3	1.9	2.5	IVORY COAST	10	
4.0	1.7	2.5	NIGER	10	
5.7	1.7	2.5	SENEGAL	10	
8.2	2.5	7.5	CAMEROON	9	2
8.9	0.7	7.5	CAR	9	
10.5	1.6	7.5	CHAD	9	
11.7	1.2	7.5	DAHOMEY	9	
11.9	0.2	7.5	GABON	9	
14.2	2.3	7.5	UPPER VOLTA	9	
16.4	2.2	11.5	MALI	8	3
17.2	0.8	11.5	TOGO	8	
21.0	3.8	13.5	GHANA	7	5
27.7	6.7	13.5	SUDAN	7	
36.8	9.1	18.0	ZAIRE	6	6
47.7	10.9	18.0	ETHIOPIA	6	
52.5	4.8	18.0	KENYA	6	
77.5	25.0	18.0	NIGERIA	6	
79.0	1.5	18.0	RWANDA	6	
80.1	1.1	18.0	SIERRA LEONE	6	
81.3	1.2	18.0	SOMALIA	6	
81.5	0.2	23.5	GAMBIA	5	8
83.2	1.7	23.5	GUINEA	5	
83.7	0.5	23.5	LIBERIA	5	
87.9	4.2	23.5	UGANDA	5	
89.8	1.9	27.5	MALAWI	4	9
90.3	0.5	27.5	MAURITANIA	4	
96.0	5.7	27.5	TANZANIA	4	
97.8	1.8	27.5	ZAMBIA	4	
98.1	0.3	31.0	BOTSWANA	3	
99.6	1.5	31.0	BURUNDI	3	
100.0	0.4	31.0	LESOTHO	3	

SOURCE: Abdul O. Said, *The African Phenomenon* (London: Allyn and Bacon, 1968), pp. 164–167.

TABLE 14.4 Total Number of Memberships in Major African Multilateral Economic Organizations, 1967

Definition: These include all-African organizations such as the UN Economic Commission for Africa, regional organizations such as the Economic Community of West Africa and the Chad Basin Commission, and limited purpose organizations such as Air Afrique, an airline supported by most of the former-French colonies. The source lists a total of 25 organizations.

RANGE = 14.00
MEAN = 7.44
STANDARD DEVIATION = 4.22

POPULATION PERCENT CUM.	COUNTRY	RANK	COUNTRY NAME	VALUE	RANGE DECILE
1.9	1.9	1.0	IVORY COAST	15	1
4.4	2.5	3.0	CAMEROON	14	
5.6	1.2	3.0	DAHOMEY	14	
7.3	1.7	3.0	NIGER	14	
7.7	0.4	6.5	CONGO (BRA)	12	3
9.4	1.7	6.5	SENEGAL	12	
10.2	0.8	6.5	TOGO	12	
12.5	2.3	6.5	UPPER VOLTA	12	
13.2	0.7	9.5	CAR	11	
14.8	1.6	9.5	CHAD	11	
15.0	0.2	11.5	GABON	10	4
40.0	25.0	11.5	NIGERIA	10	
40.5	0.5	13.0	MAURITANIA	9	5
42.7	2.2	14.5	MALI	8	6
48.4	5.7	14.5	TANZANIA	8	
57.5	9.1	17.0	ZAIRE	6	7
62.3	4.8	17.0	KENYA	6	
63.8	1.5	17.0	RWANDA	6	
74.7	10.9	20.5	ETHIOPIA	5	8
78.5	3.8	20.5	GHANA	5	
79.6	1.1	20.5	SIERRA LEONE	5	
83.8	4.2	20.5	UGANDA	5	
85.3	1.5	24.5	BURUNDI	4	
87.0	1.7	24.5	GUINEA	4	
87.5	0.5	24.5	LIBERIA	4	
88.7	1.2	24.5	SOMALIA	4	
90.6	1.9	27.5	MALAWI	3	9
92.4	1.8	27.5	ZAMBIA	3	
92.6	0.2	29.5	GAMBIA	2	10
99.3	6.7	29.5	SUDAN	2	
99.6	0.3	31.5	BOTSWANA	1	
100.0	0.4	31.5	LESOTHO	1	

SOURCE: *Africa Report*, 12 (June 1967): 24.

TABLE 14.5 Total Number of International Non-profit Organizations with Representatives in Each Country, 1968

Definition: These include intergovernmental and international non-governmental, non-profit organizations.

```
RANGE     =    212.00
MEAN      =    125.24
STANDARD DEVIATION =         51.87
```

POPULATION PERCENT CUM.	COUNTRY	RANK	COUNTRY NAME	VALUE	RANGE DECILE
25.0	25.0	1.0	NIGERIA	263	1
28.8	3.8	2.0	GHANA	217	3
33.6	4.8	3.0	KENYA	185	4
35.3	1.7	4.0	SENEGAL	168	5
44.4	9.1	5.0	ZAIRE	160	
48.6	4.2	6.0	UGANDA	157	6
51.1	2.5	7.0	CAMEROON	141	
56.8	5.7	8.0	TANZANIA	140	
63.5	6.7	9.0	SUDAN	131	7
65.4	1.9	10.0	IVORY COAST	123	
76.3	10.9	11.0	ETHIOPIA	109	8
78.1	1.8	12.0	ZAMBIA	107	
79.2	1.1	13.0	SIERRA LEONE	105	
79.7	0.5	14.0	LIBERIA	96	
79.9	0.2	15.0	GABON	90	9
80.3	0.4	16.0	CONGO (BRA)	89	
82.2	1.9	17.0	MALAWI	85	
83.0	0.8	18.0	TOGO	83	
83.7	0.7	19.0	CAR	79	
85.2	1.5	20.0	BURUNDI	51	
86.9	1.7	21.0	GUINEA	51	

DATA NOT AVAILABLE FOR THE FOLLOWING COUNTRIES

BOTSWANA	CHAD	DAHOMEY	GAMBIA
LESOTHO	MAURITANIA	MALI	NIGER
RWANDA	SOMALIA	UPPER VOLTA	

SOURCE: Eyvind S. Tew, ed., *Yearbook of International Organizations 1968–69* (Brussels: Union of International Associations, 1969), p. 1200.

TABLE 14.6 Number of Multinational Corporations with Subsidiaries in Each Country, ca. 1968

Definition and Comments: Multinational corporations in this context are corporations in Austria, Belgium, Denmark, France, German Federal Republic, Italy, Luxemburg, Netherlands, Norway, Portugal, Spain, Sweden, Switzerland, United Kingdom and the United States (data on Canada and Japan were unavailable) which have one or more subsidiaries in each country. The European data is for 1968 while the American data is for 1966. The American data available to the source did not distinguish between subsidiaries, associates and branches, which may result in slight overestimates.

```
RANGE     =    212.00
MEAN      =     59.00
STANDARD DEVIATION =         55.52
```

POPULATION PERCENT CUM.	COUNTRY	RANK	COUNTRY NAME	VALUE	RANGE DECILE
25.0	25.0	1.0	NIGERIA	222	1
29.8	4.8	2.0	KENYA	160	3
38.9	9.1	3.0	ZAIRE	138	4
40.7	1.8	4.0	ZAMBIA	128	5
44.5	3.8	5.5	GHANA	66	8
46.4	1.9	5.5	IVORY COAST	66	
52.1	5.7	7.0	TANZANIA	59	
52.6	0.5	8.0	LIBERIA	56	
54.3	1.7	9.0	SENEGAL	52	9
58.5	4.2	10.0	UGANDA	51	
61.0	2.5	11.0	CAMEROON	47	
62.9	1.9	12.0	MALAWI	38	
73.8	10.9	13.0	ETHIOPIA	31	10
74.9	1.1	14.0	SIERRA LEONE	28	
81.6	6.7	15.0	SUDAN	23	
83.3	1.7	16.0	GUINEA	19	
84.8	1.5	17.0	BURUNDI	12	
85.5	0.7	19.0	CAR	11	
85.9	0.4	19.0	CONGO (BRA)	11	
86.1	0.2	19.0	GABON	11	
86.9	0.8	21.0	TOGO	10	

DATA NOT AVAILABLE FOR THE FOLLOWING COUNTRIES

BOTSWANA	CHAD	DAHOMEY	GAMBIA
LESOTHO	MAURITANIA	MALI	NIGER
RWANDA	SOMALIA	UPPER VOLTA	

SOURCE: Eyvind S. Tew, ed., *Yearbook of International Organizations 1968–69* (Brussels: Union of International Associations, 1969), p. 1200.

TABLE 14.7 Experience of External Aggression and Threats, 1963–1965

Definition and Comments: The index is the average number of times the country was the object of aggressive behavior and aggressive communication originating from another country in the years 1963–1965. Behavior and communication (broadcast threats, etc.) were combined because this procedure avoids some of the difficulty of distinguishing between actual border clashes and those which are falsely claimed by one of the two parties and recognizes that threats may have as much of an effect on the situation as behavior.

```
RANGE     =       140.00
MEAN  =           28.94
STANDARD DEVIATION =        37.64
```

POPULATION PERCENT CUM. COUNTRY		RANK	COUNTRY NAME	VALUE	RANGE DECILE
1.2	1.2	1.0	SOMALIA	140	1
5.0	3.8	2.0	GHANA	120	2
15.9	10.9	3.0	ETHIOPIA	117	
25.0	9.1	4.0	ZAIRE	103	3
26.5	1.5	5.0	BURUNDI	47	7
31.3	4.8	6.0	KENYA	43	
31.7	0.4	7.5	CONGO (BRA)	40	8
35.9	4.2	7.5	UGANDA	40	
42.6	6.7	9.0	SUDAN	37	
44.3	1.7	10.5	NIGER	33	
45.1	0.8	10.5	TOGO	33	
50.8	5.7	12.0	TANZANIA	30	
52.3	1.5	13.0	RWANDA	23	9
77.3	25.0	14.0	NIGERIA	20	
78.0	0.7	15.5	CAR	17	
79.2	1.2	15.5	DAHOMEY	17	
81.1	1.9	17.5	MALAWI	13	10
81.6	0.5	17.5	MAURITANIA	13	
83.3	1.7	19.0	GUINEA	10	
85.2	1.9	21.0	IVORY COAST	7	
85.7	0.5	21.0	LIBERIA	7	
88.0	2.3	21.0	UPPER VOLTA	7	
90.5	2.5	24.0	CAMEROON	3	
92.7	2.2	24.0	MALI	3	
94.5	1.8	24.0	ZAMBIA	3	
94.8	0.3	29.0	BOTSWANA	0	
96.4	1.6	29.0	CHAD	0	
96.6	0.2	29.0	GABON	0	
96.8	0.2	29.0	GAMBIA	0	
97.2	0.4	29.0	LESOTHO	0	
98.9	1.7	29.0	SENEGAL	0	
100.0	1.1	29.0	SIERRA LEONE	0	

SOURCE: John Collins, *Foreign Conflict Behavior and Domestic Disorder in Africa 1963–1965*, unpublished Ph.D. dissertation, Department of Political Science, Northwestern University, 1966. Collins coded his data from *Africa Report*, *Africa Diary*, *Africa Research Bulletin* and *Deadline Data*.

TABLE 14.8 Index of Representation from Eastern-Bloc Countries, 1967

Definition: Countries include Bulgaria, China, Czechoslovakia, Hungary, North Korea, North Vietnam, Poland, Roumania, the Soviet Union, and Yugoslavia. Each country's representation is weighted as follows: 3 = Embassy; 2 = Consulate; 1 = Diplomatic representation without 3 or 2; 0 = No representation. The index gives the total score.

```
RANGE   =        30.00
MEAN  =          10.72
STANDARD DEVIATION =          9.40
```

POPULATION PERCENT CUM. COUNTRY		RANK	COUNTRY NAME	VALUE	RANGE DECILE
2.2	2.2	1.5	MALI	30	1
7.9	5.7	1.5	TANZANIA	30	
9.6	1.7	3.0	GUINEA	29	
10.0	0.4	4.0	CONGO (BRA)	23	3
13.8	3.8	5.0	GHANA	21	4
15.0	1.2	8.0	DAHOMEY	18	5
25.9	10.9	8.0	ETHIOPIA	18	
30.7	4.8	8.0	KENYA	18	
55.7	25.0	8.0	NIGERIA	18	
59.9	4.2	8.0	UGANDA	18	
60.4	0.5	11.5	MAURITANIA	16	
67.1	6.7	11.5	SUDAN	16	
76.2	9.1	13.0	ZAIRE	13	6
78.0	1.8	14.0	ZAMBIA	12	7
79.2	1.2	15.0	SOMALIA	11	
80.9	1.7	16.5	SENEGAL	9	8
81.7	0.8	16.5	TOGO	9	
82.8	1.1	18.0	SIERRA LEONE	7	
83.5	0.7	19.5	CAR	6	9
84.0	0.5	19.5	LIBERIA	6	
86.5	2.5	21.0	CAMEROON	4	
88.0	1.5	23.0	BURUNDI	3	10
89.6	1.6	23.0	CHAD	3	
91.1	1.5	23.0	RWANDA	3	
91.3	0.2	25.0	GAMBIA	2	
91.6	0.3	29.0	BOTSWANA	0	
91.8	0.2	29.0	GABON	0	
93.7	1.9	29.0	IVORY COAST	0	
94.1	0.4	29.0	LESOTHO	0	
96.0	1.9	29.0	MALAWI	0	
97.7	1.7	29.0	NIGER	0	
100.0	2.3	29.0	UPPER VOLTA	0	

SOURCE: *Bulletin of the African Institute*, 1968, p. 58, and *Europa Yearbook*, 1967.

15. Urban Patterns

Africa is at once the least urbanized and the fastest urbanizing of the world's continents. According to United Nations data for the entire continent (including North Africa and South Africa), the percent of the population residing in localities of 20,000 and more inhabitants in 1960 was 13 percent, as compared with Asia's 17 percent and Latin America's 32 percent.[1] In terms of urban growth, however, African cities have been growing at a very high rate. One hundred years ago there were only two cities approaching 100,000 in population in the thirty-two countries considered in this Handbook,[2] while by 1965 there were fifty-seven cities of this size or greater, and some eighteen million black Africans resided in towns of 20,000 or more.[3]

The recency of the growth of large settlements should not obscure the fact that cities have been an important aspect of African history for a thousand years or more. Although relatively small by present-day standards, cities such as Kano, Timbuktu, Gao, Oyo, and Mombasa developed as important centers of trade and political power at various times from the eleventh through the nineteenth centuries.[4]

Contemporary urbanization in Africa is one of the key components of the modernization process and an important aspect of political development.[5] Cities require a societal level of agricultural production adequate to produce a surplus to support the non-agricultural urban population.[6] Large cities are typically the center of international trade, communication, and local manufacture. The major or capital city may stand both as a referent or symbol of national identity, and as a source of mass media dissemination which operates to instill nationalistic sentiments and values.

The city exerts its influence on and through its inhabitants. African urban residents, relatively independent as they are from the land and from their traditional social matrix, tend to acquire aspects of a new way of life and to modify their traditional world view.[7] The effect of urban life on the society as a whole is multiplied by the close ties African city dwellers maintain with their villages or homesteads.

Most African city dwellers are first-generation migrants who participate in urban associations made up of people from the same village or area; they return "home" regularly, and provide hospitality for fellow villagers who visit the city. Through these influences African cities exert an influence far beyond their administrative boundaries.

The effect of urban life upon city dwellers should not be exaggerated, however. In earlier writings on African urbanization there was a tendency to suppose that the change to urban living by tribesmen brought about an extreme individualism, a loss of tribal identity or "detribalization," and thus a tendency to feel normless or rootless.[8] Recent studies show that this analysis of the effects of urban living was distorted. There certainly are serious social problems in many overcrowded African cities and these will become more serious in the next decade as the ranks of the unemployed school dropouts increase and concentrate in the cities. Nevertheless, the resiliency of African culture has led to the spontaneous development of new forms of urban social organization, such as friendly societies and tribal associations, which mitigate the harshness of the new environment and relate the newcomers to their ethnic group in powerful new ways.[9] The extended family, moreover, has tended to retain its importance despite the relative dispersion of its members both geographically and socially.[10]

African cities may be differentiated in terms of function (administrative, mining, port, etc.), history (traditional, colonial, post-colonial), location (West Africa, East Africa, etc.), as well as size. The variables presented in this chapter treat all cities as alike, however, taking account only of size and that in a relatively limited manner. Nevertheless, the recent founding of most African cities and their general characteristic of serving as loci for rapidly expanding economic and/or political and administrative activities suggests that they share important underlying uniformities. This homogeneity is evidenced by the failure of the few modern African cities built upon traditional urban bases, such as Kumasi or Ibadan, to develop into what Bert Hoselitz has called "parasitic cities." This type of city, common in Asia, has a traditional foundation and tends in the modern era to live off the areas surrounding it and to resist reorganization of any kind. Brian Berry studied Kumasi, a large city in Ghana that might be expected by Hoselitz's notions to develop parasitic characteristics. He found that even Kumasi had made a "smooth rapid transition" to a specialized commercial economy which was more generative than parasitic.[11]

Concepts and Definitions

What criterion shall be evoked for defining one population agglomeration in Africa as an "urban unit" and another as "not an urban unit"? Arguments can be offered that the distinctive thing about a city is not its size but its style of life or its mode of social organization. Given the limited availability of data on African cities, the criterion for our purposes will have to be one of size only. But what population size is the most appropriate urban cut-off point? Kingsley Davis used a population of 100,000 as his operational definition for a metropolitan area in an examination of world urban patterns,[12] while the UN has used 20,000 as the urban cut-off point in comparative studies. Individual countries, of course, vary widely in the size definition of "urban" used in their statistical reports. Davis' criterion is too large to be useful for Africa, where seven of our thirty-two countries have no urban units as large as 100,000, while the official criterion of the countries themselves is too variable to be of comparative value. We have decided for purposes of reliability and comparability to use the UN cut-off point of 20,000 in calculating the index of urban population as percent of total population. By contemporary American standards a non-suburban town of 20,000 may seem more village than urban in character, but in Africa today most towns with populations of 20,000 exhibit a distinctly non-traditional way of life.

Having decided upon a population of 20,000 as the lower limit of our definition of urban, the problem that next presents itself is the basis for defining the boundary of the urban unit. According to the 1959 Uganda census, the population of the administratively defined area of Kampala City was only 46,735, while the population of the larger urban area including the contiguous, densely populated areas such as Mengo was actually about 122,000. Sometimes the opposite situation occurs in Africa. Kumasi was reported by the *UN Demographic Yearbook* to have a population of 249,000 in 1966, but according to information from a specialist on Ghanaian urbanization this figure is for an administrative unit, the Kumasi Municipal Council area, which contains a considerable rural area. This source suggested a figure of 180,000 as more representative of the actual population of what we might call the Kumasi urban agglomeration.

Our approach to the boundary problem has been to use the existing definitions of urban places, with the following exceptions: (1) When UN data differentiates between cities and urban agglomeration[13] figures for the largest city in a country, we use the latter figure on the supposition that this reflects the reality of an urbanized area spreading beyond city administrative boundaries in a way similar to the use of the Metropolitan Area definition in the United States. The cities affected in this manner are Bathurst, Accra, Conakry, Abidjan, Nairobi, Bamako, Lomé, and Kampala. (2) Where experts suggest that the administrative definition is inappropriate for comparative purposes, we have taken their advice. This occurred in the cases of Kampala, Kumasi, and Lagos.

The various indexes of urbanization which are presented here are chosen from a larger number of possible indexes as those most appropriate, given the data available. With the exception of primacy their meaning is self-evident. Primacy indicates the size dominance of the largest city in a country (Table 15.6). Size dominance is often related to administrative, political, and economic dominance, thus it is not surprising that most of the primate cities are also the capital cities.[14] Since the capital city and its relation to the country as a whole is of particular political importance in the newly independent nations, we present another primacy index (Table 15.7) giving the capital city's dominance (or nondominance) in the urban hierarchy.

There are various ways to calculate primacy

indexes. The method used here gives the population of the city (largest and/or capital) as a percentage of the total population of the four largest cities.[15] In the cases where there were fewer than four cities over 20,000 in population, the index was calculated using the population of the two or three cities which reached this size.

Reliability

Reliability is a serious problem for African urban data. The ideal data source is a modern census taken the year for which our data are presented—i.e. 1955 or 1965 for the variables on cities 20,000 or more (Tables 15.1–15.4). Rarely have our model year and a modern census come into juxtaposition in such a fortuitous way, however. Failing a modern census, a sophisticated and well executed sample survey in the same year would be virtually as reliable, but again these have rarely coincided with our years. Thus we have had to do our own interpolations or extrapolations from the latest available data on urban populations, or had to rely on other scholars' estimates. Since our approach for the 1955 and 1965 urbanism variables has varied, we will discuss each in turn in order to give the reader a sense of the reliability of the data and information regarding an alternate data source.

1955 Urban Population (Table 15.1)

For this variable we have relied upon two existing data sources. The first is the Ginsburg *Atlas of Economic Development*, which gives data on this variable for the entire world, including all of Africa. The Ginsburg data is derived from work done for the Berkeley International Population and Urban Research Center. These data have the advantage of providing estimates for a single year. Unfortunately the Ginsburg atlas presents data for the French African federations as a whole instead of for their constituent countries. It was necessary to consult a second data source, the extremely helpful French publication *Démographie Comparée*, for comparable data for each of the former French African countries. This invaluable source presents a table showing the

growth of every city of 10,000 and above for French Africa from 1915 to 1960. This source does not extrapolate between estimates, however. Thus Abidjan is shown as having a population of 121,000 for 1955–1959 and then in 1960 the population jumps to 180,000. Where necessary, we have interpolated between points in arriving at our 1955 urban estimates.[16] The reliability of these data cannot be stated with any degree of precision but, since the census and sample survey data for the 1950s is generally not up to modern standards, it must be assumed to be rather low and all the data for this variable should be regarded as estimates.

1965 Urban Population (Table 15.2)

Data for this variable were gathered from a wide variety of sources, country by country, including wherever possible the most recent census or sample survey which provided urban population data. These sources are presented in Part II for each country. In general the reliability of this variable should be significantly greater than for the earlier variable, because many of the countries have had modern censuses or special sample surveys of urban populations in recent years. But this has been less true of the former French countries, thus introducing a possible source of systematic error. Furthermore, given the extremely rapid growth rate of African cities, attempts to estimate the population of a city from census data three or even two years old can be a hazardous business. This is why the variable is given as "ca. 1965." Data available only for 1966, for example, were calculated on the basis of 1966 population estimates rather than trying to estimate from there the 1965 urban population. Given these problems, the data on this variable also should be considered as estimates.

The existence of an alternative data source for some of the countries allows a partial check on our data which suggests that our cautionary statements on reliability are well founded. This source is a preliminary version of a report by the United Nations Economic Commission for Africa (EAC).[17] It contains data on percentage of population in cities 20,000 or more for a variety of years, the years chosen being based upon the availability of data. Thus

Dahomey has data for 1955 and 1961, while Gambia's data is for 1951 and 1964. The ECA estimates are based upon the *UN Demographic Yearbooks* and "national publications," and individual city totals are not given, making a detailed comparison impossible. Of the seven possible comparisons of ECA data with our 1955 data, all on former French countries, six show our estimates to be lower than the ECA estimate, the average difference being 30 percent. For the three possible 1965 comparisons, none involving former French countries, our estimates were higher in two of the three cases by an average of 20 percent. There are a variety of possible explanations for these differences, involving conjectures about the ECA methodology, which could account for the difference, apart from the obvious explanation that one is based on inaccurate data.[18] None of these can be proved without further information about the ECA data which is unavailable to us at the present time.

Notes

[1] United Nations Economic Commission for Africa, "Size and Growth of Urban Population in Africa," in *The City in Newly Developing Countries*, ed. Gerald Breese (Englewood Cliffs, N.J.: Prentice-Hall, 1969), pp. 128–145.

[2] All further references to Africa in this chapter are restricted to the thirty-two countries unless otherwise indicated.

[3] Africa has experienced a 30 percent increase in population in localities of 20,000 or more (1950–1960) as compared with the world (19 percent) and North America (14 percent). ECA, "Urban Population in Africa," p. 128.

[4] We cannot assume that urbanization in some form would not have continued without exogenous influences. Some difference of opinion exists among scholars, however, as to whether these population centers can qualify as "cities" since while the criteria of size and density were met, social heterogeneity and functional specialization were not characteristic of some, and unified political authority and common institutions were not present in others. For discussions of traditional urbanism in Africa see Hilda Kuper, ed., *Urbanization and Migration in West Africa* (Berkeley: University of California Press, 1965), pp. 1–22; William Bascom, "Urbanization among the Yoruba," *American Journal of Sociology*, 60 (1955): 445–454; Horace Miner, *The Primitive City of Timbuctoo* (Princeton: Princeton University Press, 1953), and "The Folk Urban Continuum," *American Sociological Review*, 17 (1952): 529–537; P. C. Lloyd, A. L. Mabogunje, and B. Awe, eds., *The City of Ibadan* (Cambridge: Cambridge University Press, 1967); Eva Krapf-Askari, *Yoruba Towns and Cities* (Oxford: Clarendon Press, 1969).

[5] Daniel Lerner, *The Passing of Traditional Society* (New York: Free Press, 1958): pp. 54–65. Karl W. Deutsch has suggested measures of urbanization to assess rates of social mobilization, the process

in which traditional "economic and psychological commitments are eroded or broken and people become available for new patterns of socialization and behavior." Karl W. Deutsch, "Social Mobilization and Political Development," *American Political Science Review*, 55 (1961): 493–514. See also Akin Mabogunje, "Urbanization and Change" in *The African Experience*, eds. John Paden and Edward Soja (Evanston, Ill.: Northwestern University Press, 1970).

[6] For additional discussion of the pre-conditions for urbanization see Gideon Sjoberg, *The Preindustrial City* (New York: Free Press, 1960): pp. 25–49. Two additional prerequisites cited by Sjoberg are a favorable ecological base and a complex social organization. Serious problems exist and may intensify in the next decade should the rate of urbanization outstrip the capacity of developing economies to absorb non-agricultural manpower.

[7] In addition to contributions by Breese and Kuper, the following are some of the major works on urbanization in Africa: A. L. Epstein, "Urbanization and Social Change in Africa," *Current Anthropology*, 8 (1967): 275–296; Horace Miner, ed., *The City in Modern Africa* (New York: Praeger, 1967); Kenneth Little, *West African Urbanization* (Cambridge: Cambridge University Press, 1965); Philip M. Hauser and Leo F. Schnore, eds., *The Study of Urbanization* (New York: John Wiley, 1967); Leo Van Hoey, "The Coercive Process of Urbanization: The Case of Niger," pp. 15–32; Dennis McElrath, "Societal Scale and Social Differentiation: Accra, Ghana," pp. 33–52, in *The New Urbanization*, eds. Scott Greer et al. (New York: St. Martin's Press, 1968); and William A. Hance, *Population, Migration, and Urbanization in Africa* (New York: Columbia University Press, 1970). Studies of specific cities in the modern time frame include Richard J. Peterec, *Dakar and West African Economic Development* (New York: Columbia University Press, 1967); Claude Meillassoux, *Urbanization of an African Community, Voluntary Associations in Bamako* (Seattle: University of Washington Press, 1968); Valdo Pons, *Stanleyville, An African Urban Community under Belgian Administration* (London: Oxford University Press, 1969); and Harm J. de Blij, *Mombasa, an African City* (Evanston, Ill.: Northwestern University Press, 1968). A recent study of the urbanization of a particular country is Akin L. Mabogunje, *Urbanization in Nigeria* (New York: Africana, 1969). William J. Hanna and Judith Hanna, *Urban Dynamics in Black Africa*, (Chicago, Ill.: Aldine Press, 1971) is a most useful synthesis of the literature which includes a 169-page bibliography.

[8] For an example of this perspective see G. Malengrean, "Observations on the Orientations of Sociological Researches in African Urban Centers, with Reference to the Situation in the Belgian Congo" in *Social Implications of Industrialization and Urbanization in Africa South of the Sahara*, International African Institute (Paris, UNESCO, 1956): pp. 624–638.

[9] Peter Marris, *Family and Social Change in an African City* (Evanston, Ill.: Northwestern University Press, 1961); Kenneth Little, *West African Urbanization: A Study of Voluntary Associations in Social Change* (London: Cambridge University Press, 1965).

[10] Peter C. W. Gutkind, "African Urban Family Life and the Urban System" in *Urbanism, Urbanization, and Change: Comparative Perspectives*, eds. Paul Meadows and Ephraim Mizruchi (Reading, Mass.: Addison-Wesley, 1969), pp. 215–222; Joan Aldous, "Urbanization, the Extended Family and Kinship Ties in West Africa," *Social Forces*, 51 (October 1962): 6–12.

[11] Brian J. L. Berry, "Urban Growth and the Economic Development of Ashanti" in *Urban Systems and Economic Development*, ed. Forrest R. Pitts (Eugene: University of Oregon School of Business Administration, 1962), pp. 53–64.

[12] The original study by Davis was International Urban Research,

The World's Metropolitan Areas (Berkeley: University of California Press, 1959). The most recent volume which contains much data on Africa, all compiled independently of our data-gathering effort, is Kingsley Davis, *World Urbanization 1950–1970. Volume I: Basic Data for Cities, Countries, and Regions*. Population Monograph Series No. 4. (Berkeley, Calif.: Institute of International Studies, 1969).

[13] "The urban agglomeration has been defined as including the suburban fringe or thickly settled territory lying outside of, but adjacent to, the city boundaries." *UN Demographic Yearbook 1966*, p. 24.

[14] For example, Dakar, Senegal, with 16 percent of the country's population, has over 70 percent of the country's commercial workers, consumes 35 percent of the country's electric power production, etc. Hance, *Population, Migration and Urbanization*, p. 209. See on primate cities: Arnold S. Linsky, "Some Generalizations Concerning Primate Cities," *Annals of the Association of American Geographers*, 55 (1965): 506–513. Surrinder K. Mehta, "Some Demographic and Economic Correlates of Primate Cities: A Case for Revaluation" in *The City in Newly Developing Countries*, ed. Gerald Breese, pp. 295–308. The Mehta paper in Breese's volume is somewhat expanded from its original published form in the journal, *Demography*.

[15] This is the method used in Norton Ginsburg, ed., *Atlas of Economic Development* (Chicago: University of Chicago Press, 1961). For an alternative method see Harley L. Browning and Jack P. Gibbs, "Some Measures of Demographic and Spatial Relationships Among Cities," in *Urban Research Methods*, ed. Jack P. Gibbs (New York: Van Nostrand, 1961), pp. 436–461.

[16] A difference in procedure which may account for some systematic variation between the two data sources is the fact that we used our own national population estimates for 1955 in computing the percentage figure for the former French countries while the Ginsburg data were already in percent form. Since our national population estimates are calculated on the most recent data available, and since the earlier estimates of many African nations' populations are regarded as underestimates, the result may be an overestimation of the level of urbanism in the non-French countries. This is predicated on the assumption that the urban counts in the earlier censuses were more accurate than the total counts, thus a relatively "true" count of the cities was used with an underestimated population base. It is not possible to know the extent to which this may in fact have been the case.

[17] United Nations, Economic Commission for Africa, "Urban Population in Africa."

[18] For the 1955 discrepancies, the effect of using different population bases in calculating the percent figures may have lowered our estimates in the way outlined in footnote 16. The largest differences for 1955 were for Guinea (60 percent) and Congo (Brazzaville) (34 percent). The 1965 differences may in part be attributed to the fact that the ECA data for Botswana and Gambia are for the year preceding our estimates.

TABLE 15.1 Estimated Percent of Population in Cities of 20,000 and More, ca. 1955

Definition: We cannot tell whether the populations for the largest cities are for urban agglomerations or not; presumably they are not.

```
RANGE =          17.70
MEAN =            4.44
STANDARD DEVIATION =        4.18
```

POPULATION PERCENT					RANGE
CUM.	COUNTRY	RANK	COUNTRY NAME	VALUE	DECILE
0.4	0.4	1.0	CONGO (BRA)	17.7	1
2.1	1.7	2.0	SENEGAL	14.8	2
3.9	1.8	3.0	ZAMBIA	11.4	4
28.9	25.0	4.0	NIGERIA	9.4	5
29.1	0.2	5.0	GAMBIA	8.3	6
38.2	9.1	6.0	ZAIRE	8.0	
38.9	0.7	7.0	CAR	7.4	
42.7	3.8	8.0	GHANA	6.4	7
44.6	1.9	9.0	IVORY COAST	5.3	8
51.3	6.7	10.0	SUDAN	5.0	
53.8	2.5	11.5	CAMEROON	4.7	
54.0	0.2	11.5	GABON	4.7	
54.3	0.3	13.0	BOTSWANA	4.5	
55.5	1.2	14.0	DAHOMEY	4.2	
56.7	1.2	15.0	SOMALIA	3.9	
61.5	4.8	16.0	KENYA	3.8	
62.6	1.1	17.0	SIERRA LEONE	3.1	9
63.4	0.8	18.0	TOGO	2.8	
63.9	0.5	19.5	LIBERIA	2.2	
66.1	2.2	19.5	MALI	2.2	
67.8	1.7	21.0	GUINEA	2.1	
69.4	1.6	22.5	CHAD	2.0	
71.7	2.3	22.5	UPPER VOLTA	2.0	
82.6	10.9	24.0	ETHIOPIA	1.7	10
88.3	5.7	25.0	TANZANIA	1.5	
92.5	4.2	26.0	UGANDA	0.9	
94.2	1.7	27.0	NIGER	0.8	
95.7	1.5	28.0	BURUNDI	0.7	
97.6	1.9	29.0	MALAWI	0.6	
98.0	0.4	31.0	LESOTHO	0.0	
98.5	0.5	31.0	MAURITANIA	0.0	
100.0	1.5	31.0	RWANDA	0.0	

sources: Leo F. Schnore, "Economic Development and Urbanization: An Ecological Approach," data republished in N. Ginsburg, *Atlas of Economic Development* (Chicago: University of Chicago, 1961), p. 34. The Schnore data uses his own population estimates while the *Démographie Comparée* data was used with the 1955 population estimates given in Appendix 5. *Cameroon, Chad, Congo (Brazzaville), Dahomey, Gabon, Guinea, Ivory Coast, Mali, Niger, Senegal, Togo, Upper Volta*: *Démographie Comparée* (1966); *Nigeria*: Schnore figure adjusted by population estimate for Nigeria in Appendix 5.

TABLE 15.2 Estimated Percent of Population in Cities of 20,000 and More, ca. 1965

Definition: Largest cities' population is for urban agglomeration if this figure is given in the *UN Demographic Yearbook*. Estimates are not always for the same year owing to the unavailability of data. Cities whose population is close to 20,000 according to earlier data are sometimes included. The complete list of cities is given by country in Part II.

```
RANGE =          29.00
MEAN =           10.19
STANDARD DEVIATION =        7.41
```

POPULATION PERCENT					RANGE
CUM.	COUNTRY	RANK	COUNTRY NAME	VALUE	DECILE
0.4	0.4	1.0	CONGO (BRA)	30	1
1.1	0.7	2.5	CAR	24	3
2.8	1.7	2.5	SENEGAL	24	
3.1	0.3	4.0	BOTSWANA	21	4
4.9	1.8	5.0	ZAMBIA	20	
5.1	0.2	6.0	GABON	18	5
8.9	3.8	7.0	GHANA	16	
10.8	1.9	9.0	IVORY COAST	14	6
35.8	25.0	9.0	NIGERIA	14	
37.0	1.2	9.0	SOMALIA	14	
37.2	0.2	11.0	GAMBIA	13	
46.3	9.1	12.0	ZAIRE	12	7
47.5	1.2	13.0	DAHOMEY	10	
50.0	2.5	14.5	CAMEROON	9	8
50.5	0.5	14.5	LIBERIA	9	
51.3	0.8	16.0	TOGO	8	
53.0	1.7	18.5	GUINEA	7	
57.8	4.8	18.5	KENYA	7	
58.9	1.1	18.5	SIERRA LEONE	7	
65.6	6.7	18.5	SUDAN	7	
67.2	1.6	21.5	CHAD	6	9
69.4	2.2	21.5	MALI	6	
80.3	10.9	23.5	ETHIOPIA	5	
86.0	5.7	23.5	TANZANIA	5	
87.7	1.7	25.5	NIGER	4	
90.0	2.3	25.5	UPPER VOLTA	4	
91.9	1.9	27.5	MALAWI	3	10
96.1	4.2	27.5	UGANDA	3	
97.6	1.5	29.5	BURUNDI	2	
98.0	0.4	29.5	LESOTHO	2	
98.5	0.5	31.5	MAURITANIA	1	
100.0	1.5	31.5	RWANDA	1	

sources: *UN Demographic Yearbook 1967* and various other sources listed in Part II by country, with population estimates from Appendix 5. *Zaire (Congo K.)*: Rough estimate, recent data unavailable.

TABLE 15.3   Estimated Percent Increase in Percent Population in Cities 20,000 and More, 1955–ca. 1965

```
RANGE               =   360.00
MEAN                =   178.75
STANDARD DEVIATION  =           100.84
```

POPULATION PERCENT CUM.	COUNTRY PERCENT	RANK	COUNTRY NAME	VALUE	RANGE DECILE
1.9	1.9	1.5	MALAWI	400	1
3.6	1.7	1.5	NIGER	400	
3.9	0.3	3.0	BOTSWANA	367	
4.4	0.5	4.0	LIBERIA	309	3
4.6	0.2	5.0	GABON	283	4
6.1	1.5	6.0	RWANDA	275	
7.3	1.2	7.0	SOMALIA	259	
9.0	1.7	9.0	GUINEA	233	5
14.7	5.7	9.0	TANZANIA	233	
18.9	4.2	9.0	UGANDA	233	
19.6	0.7	11.0	CAR	224	
21.2	1.6	12.5	CHAD	200	6
21.7	0.5	12.5	MAURITANIA	200	
32.6	10.9	14.0	ETHIOPIA	194	
34.1	1.5	15.5	BURUNDI	186	
34.9	0.8	15.5	TOGO	186	
37.1	2.2	17.0	MALI	173	7
39.0	1.9	18.0	IVORY COAST	164	
42.8	3.8	19.0	GHANA	150	
44.0	1.2	20.0	DAHOMEY	138	8
45.1	1.1	21.0	SIERRA LEONE	126	
45.5	0.4	22.5	LESOTHO	100	9
47.8	2.3	22.5	UPPER VOLTA	100	
50.3	2.5	24.0	CAMEROON	95	
55.1	4.8	25.0	KENYA	84	
56.9	1.8	26.0	ZAMBIA	75	10
57.3	0.4	27.0	CONGO (BRA)	69	
57.5	0.2	28.0	GAMBIA	63	
59.2	1.7	29.0	SENEGAL	62	
68.3	9.1	30.0	ZAIRE	50	
93.3	25.0	31.0	NIGERIA	49	
100.0	6.7	32.0	SUDAN	40	

SOURCE: Tables 15.1 and 15.2. *Lesotho, Mauritania, Rwanda*: Population increase calculated on the basis of the growth of one city; data for these is given in Part II.

TABLE 15.4   Number of Cities, 20,000 or More in Population, per Million National Population, ca. 1965

```
RANGE               =   6.20
MEAN                =   1.54
STANDARD DEVIATION  =           1.39
```

POPULATION PERCENT CUM.	COUNTRY PERCENT	RANK	COUNTRY NAME	VALUE	RANGE DECILE
0.3	0.3	1.0	BOTSWANA	6.4	1
1.0	0.7	2.0	CAR	4.6	3
1.2	0.2	3.0	GABON	4.1	4
1.6	0.4	4.0	CONGO (BRA)	3.4	5
1.8	0.2	5.0	GAMBIA	2.8	6
26.8	25.0	6.0	NIGERIA	2.7	
28.0	1.2	7.5	SOMALIA	2.2	7
29.8	1.8	7.5	ZAMBIA	2.2	
31.5	1.7	9.0	SENEGAL	1.9	8
35.3	3.8	10.0	GHANA	1.6	
36.5	1.2	11.0	DAHOMEY	1.5	
38.4	1.9	12.0	IVORY COAST	1.4	9
40.9	2.5	13.0	CAMEROON	1.2	
42.5	1.6	14.5	CHAD	1.1	
42.9	0.4	14.5	LESOTHO	1.1	
45.1	2.2	16.5	MALI	1.0	
46.8	1.7	16.5	NIGER	1.0	
47.3	0.5	19.5	LIBERIA	0.9	
47.8	0.5	19.5	MAURITANIA	0.9	
54.5	6.7	19.5	SUDAN	0.9	
60.2	5.7	19.5	TANZANIA	0.9	
61.9	1.7	22.5	GUINEA	0.8	10
63.0	1.1	22.5	SIERRA LEONE	0.8	
72.1	9.1	24.0	ZAIRE	0.7	
72.9	0.8	25.5	TOGO	0.6	
75.2	2.3	25.5	UPPER VOLTA	0.6	
77.1	1.9	27.0	MALAWI	0.5	
88.0	10.9	28.5	ETHIOPIA	0.4	
92.8	4.8	28.5	KENYA	0.4	
94.3	1.5	30.5	BURUNDI	0.3	
95.8	1.5	30.5	RWANDA	0.3	
100.0	4.2	32.0	UGANDA	0.2	

SOURCES: Cities are listed with sources by country in Part II.

TABLE 15.5   Population of Largest City in Thousands, ca. 1966

Definition: Population is given, where applicable, for urban agglomeration. Data for 1965 or 1967 are presented here without change, while data from earlier or later years were adjusted to make a 1966 estimate.

```
RANGE    =        985.00
MEAN     =        231.50
STANDARD DEVIATION =        251.59
```

POPULATION PERCENT CUM.	COUNTRY	RANK	COUNTRY NAME	VALUE	RANGE DECILE
9.1	9.1	1.5	ZAIRE	1000	1
34.1	25.0	1.5	NIGERIA	1000	
45.0	10.9	3.0	ETHIOPIA	640	4
48.8	3.8	4.0	GHANA	600	5
50.5	1.7	5.0	SENEGAL	500	6
55.3	4.8	6.0	KENYA	396	7
57.2	1.9	7.0	IVORY COAST	320	
62.9	5.7	8.0	TANZANIA	273	8
65.4	2.5	9.0	CAMEROON	200	9
72.1	6.7	10.0	SUDAN	198	
73.8	1.7	11.0	GUINEA	197	
78.0	4.2	12.0	UGANDA	175	
80.2	2.2	14.0	MALI	170	
81.4	1.2	14.0	SOMALIA	170	
83.2	1.8	14.0	ZAMBIA	170	
83.9	0.7	16.5	CAR	150	
84.3	0.4	16.5	CONGO (BRA)	150	
85.4	1.1	18.0	SIERRA LEONE	148	
86.2	0.8	19.0	TOGO	129	
87.4	1.2	20.0	DAHOMEY	111	10
89.0	1.6	21.5	CHAD	110	
90.9	1.9	21.5	MALAWI	110	
91.4	0.5	23.0	LIBERIA	100	
93.7	2.3	24.0	UPPER VOLTA	78	
95.2	1.5	25.0	BURUNDI	71	
96.9	1.7	26.0	NIGER	60	
97.1	0.2	27.0	GABON	57	
97.3	0.2	28.0	GAMBIA	43	
97.6	0.3	29.0	BOTSWANA	34	
98.0	0.4	30.0	LESOTHO	18	
98.5	0.5	31.5	MAURITANIA	15	
100.0	1.5	31.5	RWANDA	15	

SOURCES: *UN Demographic Yearbook 1967* and other sources. See Part II for information on individual cities and sources.

TABLE 15.6   Primacy of Largest City, ca. 1965

Definition: Population of the largest city divided by the sum of the population of the four largest cities (including the largest): or where fewer than four cities are 20,000 or above in population, by the population of the two or three largest cities. In countries where only one city had a population of 20,000 or more, the index is arbitrarily given as 1.00. Where urban agglomeration data is available, it is used. The higher the number, the greater the primacy.

```
RANGE    =         71.00
MEAN     =         67.59
STANDARD DEVIATION =         21.46
```

POPULATION PERCENT CUM.	COUNTRY	RANK	COUNTRY NAME	VALUE	RANGE DECILE
1.5	1.5	4.0	BURUNDI	100.00	1
1.7	0.2	4.0	GAMBIA	100.00	
2.1	0.4	4.0	LESOTHO	100.00	
2.6	0.5	4.0	LIBERIA	100.00	
3.1	0.5	4.0	MAURITANIA	100.00	
4.6	1.5	4.0	RWANDA	100.00	
5.4	0.8	4.0	TOGO	100.00	
7.3	1.9	8.5	MALAWI	85.00	3
8.4	1.1	8.5	SIERRA LEONE	85.00	
10.1	1.7	10.0	GUINEA	78.00	4
14.3	4.2	11.0	UGANDA	75.00	
16.0	1.7	12.0	SENEGAL	73.00	
26.9	10.9	13.0	ETHIOPIA	69.00	5
27.1	0.2	14.5	GABON	66.00	
29.0	1.9	14.5	IVORY COAST	66.00	
32.8	3.8	16.0	GHANA	64.00	6
35.0	2.2	17.0	MALI	63.00	
44.1	9.1	18.0	ZAIRE	61.00	
44.5	0.4	19.0	CONGO (BRA)	60.00	
45.2	0.7	20.5	CAR	59.00	
50.9	5.7	20.5	TANZANIA	59.00	
55.7	4.8	22.0	KENYA	58.00	
57.3	1.6	23.0	CHAD	56.00	7
58.5	1.2	24.0	SOMALIA	55.00	
61.0	2.5	25.0	CAMEROON	51.00	
62.2	1.2	26.0	DAHOMEY	48.00	8
64.5	2.3	27.0	UPPER VOLTA	46.00	
66.2	1.7	28.0	NIGER	44.00	
91.2	25.0	29.0	NIGERIA	43.00	9
97.9	6.7	30.0	SUDAN	37.00	
99.7	1.8	31.0	ZAMBIA	33.00	10
100.0	0.3	32.0	BOTSWANA	29.00	

SOURCES: *UN Demographic Yearbook 1967* and other sources. See Part II for detailed information by country. *Congo (Brazzaville), Guinea, Upper Volta*: index calculated on three cities; *Gabon, Malawi, Sierra Leone, Uganda*: index calculated on two cities; *Sudan*: it may be more appropriate to consider Khartoum, Khartoum North and Omdurman as a single primate city.

TABLE 15.7   Primacy of Capital City, ca. 1965

Definition: Population of capital city divided by the sum of the populations of the four largest cities (including the capital city, but only if it is one of the four largest cities). See the definition for Table 15.6 for further details.

```
RANGE =          96.00
MEAN =           65.53
STANDARD DEVIATION =        24.69
```

POPULATION PERCENT					
CUM.	COUNTRY	RANK	COUNTRY NAME	VALUE	RANGE DECILE
1.5	1.5	4.0	BURUNDI	100.00	1
1.7	0.2	4.0	GAMBIA	100.00	
2.1	0.4	4.0	LESOTHO	100.00	
2.6	0.5	4.0	LIBERIA	100.00	
3.1	0.5	4.0	MAURITANIA	100.00	
4.6	1.5	4.0	RWANDA	100.00	
5.4	0.8	4.0	TOGO	100.00	
7.3	1.9	8.5	MALAWI	85.00	2
8.4	1.1	8.5	SIERRA LEONE	85.00	
10.1	1.7	10.0	GUINEA	78.00	3
14.3	4.2	11.0	UGANDA	75.00	
16.0	1.7	12.0	SENEGAL	73.00	
26.9	10.9	13.0	ETHIOPIA	69.00	4
27.1	0.2	14.5	GABON	66.00	
29.0	1.9	14.5	IVORY COAST	66.00	
32.8	3.8	16.0	GHANA	64.00	
35.0	2.2	17.0	MALI	63.00	
44.1	9.1	18.0	ZAIRE	61.00	5
44.5	0.4	19.0	CONGO (BRA)	60.00	
45.2	0.7	20.5	CAR	59.00	
50.9	5.7	20.5	TANZANIA	59.00	
55.7	4.8	22.0	KENYA	58.00	
57.3	1.6	23.0	CHAD	56.00	
58.5	1.2	24.0	SOMALIA	55.00	
60.8	2.3	25.0	UPPER VOLTA	46.00	6
62.5	1.7	26.0	NIGER	44.00	
87.5	25.0	27.0	NIGERIA	43.00	
94.2	6.7	28.0	SUDAN	38.00	7
96.0	1.8	29.0	ZAMBIA	33.00	
97.2	1.2	30.0	DAHOMEY	31.00	8
99.7	2.5	31.0	CAMEROON	26.00	
100.0	0.3	32.0	BOTSWANA	4.00	10

SOURCES: *UN Demographic Yearbook 1967* and other sources, see Part II. *Congo (Brazzaville), Guinea, Malawi, Upper Volta*: index calculated on three cities; *Gabon, Sierra Leone, Uganda*: index calculated on two cities; *Sudan*: it may be more appropriate to consider Khartoum, Khartoum North and Omdurman as a single primate city.

TABLE 15.8   Percent Increase Capital City Population, ca. 1950–1967

Definition: Population of capital city in 1967, which includes urban agglomeration data where applicable, divided by the population of the capital city in 1950 (which presumably does not include urban agglomeration data) times 100.

```
RANGE =         534.00
MEAN =          186.97
STANDARD DEVIATION =        117.79
```

POPULATION PERCENT					
CUM.	COUNTRY	RANK	COUNTRY NAME	VALUE	RANGE DECILE
1.7	1.7	1.0	NIGER	567	1
3.4	1.7	2.0	GUINEA	405	4
7.2	3.8	3.0	GHANA	344	5
7.4	0.2	4.0	GABON	338	
8.9	1.5	5.0	BURUNDI	318	
9.7	0.8	6.0	TOGO	290	6
11.6	1.9	7.0	IVORY COAST	264	
12.0	0.4	8.0	LESOTHO	260	
13.6	1.6	9.0	CHAD	253	
17.8	4.2	10.0	UGANDA	224	7
42.8	25.0	11.0	NIGERIA	189	8
48.5	5.7	12.0	TANZANIA	176	
53.3	4.8	13.0	KENYA	167	
60.0	6.7	14.0	SUDAN	160	
62.5	2.5	15.0	CAMEROON	152	
63.2	0.7	17.0	CAR	138	9
64.4	1.2	17.0	DAHOMEY	138	
66.7	2.3	17.0	UPPER VOLTA	138	
75.8	9.1	19.0	ZAIRE	130	
76.0	0.2	20.0	GAMBIA	126	
77.2	1.2	21.0	SOMALIA	118	
79.0	1.8	22.0	ZAMBIA	117	
80.9	1.9	23.0	MALAWI	111	
81.4	0.5	24.0	LIBERIA	93	
83.6	2.2	25.0	MALI	91	
94.5	10.9	26.0	ETHIOPIA	87	
95.6	1.1	27.0	SIERRA LEONE	74	10
96.0	0.4	28.0	CONGO (BRA)	62	
97.7	1.7	29.0	SENEGAL	46	
99.2	1.5	30.0	RWANDA	33	

DATA NOT AVAILABLE FOR THE FOLLOWING COUNTRIES

BOTSWANA   MAURITANIA

SOURCES: *UN Demographic Yearbook 1967* and other sources listed in Part II by country.

16. Ethnic Pluralism

Ethnic pluralism, in the most simple conceptual terms, refers to the number and diversity of ethnic groups in a national population. The more commonly used term—cultural pluralism—has the disadvantage of failing to make explicit the social entities to which pluralism refers, although that is understandable given the considerable conceptual and empirical confusion involved in the identification of ethnic, or culturally distinctive, groups in national populations. We *are* concerned, however, with the core conceptual meaning of the term "cultural pluralism," which is the extent to which a population is divided into groups with distinctive cultures and mutually exclusive institutions.[1] It is the purpose of this chapter to provide some preliminary indices of cultural pluralism in black African nations.

The need to develop comparative measurements of cultural pluralism in Black Africa is related to a number of theoretical interests. In the first place, the extent of cultural pluralism can be seen as an indicator of the absence of national integration, and we discuss the collection of the data in this chapter in the context of integration theory in Chapters 2 and 3 of Part III of this Handbook. From somewhat different theoretical perspectives, cultural pluralism has been seen as a major source of social and political conflict in the black African nations,[2] and there is a considerable body of political theory that suggests that modernization and social mobilization tend to produce social and political disruption and instability by exacerbating the latent conflicts between segments of culturally plural populations,[3] and by reinforcing lines of cultural segregation with overlapping cleavages based on new patterns of economic stratification.[4]

Definition and Coding of Variable

The basic operational definition of cultural pluralism used in this chapter is *the degree of variation in the cultural characteristics of ethnic groups in a nation.* The critical empirical problems in this definition are the identification of what we call "ethnic units" (not to be confused with identity groups or "tribes"), and the description of their cultural characteristics in quantitative form.[5] Because of the complexity and novelty of our ethnic unit approach, we include a full discussion of the rationale and procedure used in identifying the ethnic units in Chapter 4 of Part III of this Handbook. In addition, a list of ethnic units, with a description of their constituent identity groups or "tribes," and their population size, is given by nation in the sections entitled "Ethnic Patterns" in Part II of the Handbook. In this chapter we assume a familiarity with these other sections of the Handbook.

It was necessary, both for the identification of ethnic units, and for the measurement of cultural pluralism as we have operationally defined it, to specify dimensions of cultural variation in human populations, and to construct measures, relating to these dimensions, which could describe the specific cultural characteristics of each of our ethnic units. Initially the dimensions that were selected were: (a) *marriage*[6] (variables which indicate processes of intergroup alliances based on marriage, also those variables which indicate the composition of family groups); (b) *descent* (variables which indicate how kinship and lineage establish obligations and loyalties which may have implications for community formation); (c) *community organization*[7] (variables such as stratification and settlement patterns); and (d) *authority*[8] (variables which indicate the nature of authority and the levels at which it exists within the political community; also processes by which authority changes hands).

In addition, because of the close correlation between environmental constraints (or ecological factors) and social behavior, we selected certain variables which indicated the basic *economic structure*[9] of the ethnic units. Levels of agricultural development and/or animal husbandry have frequently been used by anthropologists to typologize ethnic units, (e.g., "hunters and gatherers," "pastoralists," settled agriculturalists, etc.).

On the basis of these guidelines, eighteen variables

were formulated to reflect the above dimensions. These measures were structured as ordinal scales[10] which are summarized in Figure 16.1.

Figure 16.1 Summary Definitions of Selected Variables

I. *Descent*
1. MARREV: Marital residence refers to the prevailing pattern of *location* of spouses after marriage, ranging from location near female side to location near male side.
2. PAKINV: Patrilineal kin groups refers to the *scale* or size of patrilineal groups.
3. MAKINV: Matrilineal kin groups refers to the *scale* or size of matrilineal groups.
*4. DESCEV: Principles of reckoning *descent* assumes continuum from matrilineality through double descent to patrilineality.

II. *Economic Structure*
5. DEPAHV: Dependence on animal husbandry refers to the percentage of time devoted to this activity. (0–100 percent)
6. DEPAGV: Dependence on agriculture refers to the percentage of time devoted to this activity. (0–100 percent)
*7. SETPAV: Settlement patterns refers to the *permanence* and complexity of community settlements, ranging from migratory to permanent/complex.

III. *Social Stratification*
*8. HIEAFV: Hierarchy above family refers to the number of *levels of community structure* above the family, ranging from stateless groupings, to petty chiefdoms, to tribal chiefdoms.
9. CLASTV: Class stratification refers to the *degree and type of class differentiation*, ranging from absence of class to complex stratification.
10. CASSTR: Caste stratification refers to the *degree and type of caste differentiation*, ranging from absence of caste to complex stratification.

IV. *Social Scale*
11. FAMORV: Family organization refers to the *scale of the prevailing unit* of domestic or familial organization, ranging from large extended families to nuclear families.
*12. LEVHIV: Number of levels of hierarchy in local community refers to the *levels of relationship* between family units and local community organization.
13. CLANSV: Number of clans per local community refers to the *complexity* of communities, ranging from no clans to many clans.

V. *Complexity of Settlement*
14. AGRICV: Level of development and intensity of agriculture refers to the *complexity and sophistication of agriculture systems*.
*15. INHERI: Inheritance of real property refers to the rules for the *transmission and disposition of real property* (i.e., land). Scaling ranges from distant heir to close son.

VI. *Family Organization*
*16. MOMARV: Mode of marriage refers to the *prevailing mode of obtaining a wife*, ranging from situations where groom gives resources to bride's family, to where bride's family gives resources to groom.
17. POLYGV: Polygyny refers to the *degree to which polygyny* is present in society.

VII. *Authority Patterns*
*18. AUTHOR: Refers to *structure of decision-making power* ranging from segmental, to pyramidal, to hierarchical.

* Variables presented in this chapter's tables.

An example of the construction of these variables is the measure of *Patterns of Inheritance of Real Property* (See Table 16.5). George Peter Murdock in his *Ethnographic Atlas* has seven classifications regarding inheritance of real property. They are listed in Figure 16.2 in alphabetical order.

Figure 16.2 Murdock Classification of Real-Property Inheritance

Murdock Symbol	Variable Name
C	Inheritance by children of either sex or both.
D	Inheritance by children but daughter receives less than sons.
M	Matrilineal inheritance by sister's son or sons.
N	Inheritance by matrilineal heirs who take precedence over sister's sons.
O	Absence of individual property rights in land or any rule of inheritance governing the transmission of such rights.
P	Patrilineal inheritance by a son or sons.
Q	Inheritance by patrilineal heirs who take precedence over sons.

These classifications were then reordered on the basis of a scale measuring an ordinal progression of rules for the transmission of land and material goods ranging from relatives other than children to inheritance by a son or sons. This was accomplished by assigning numbers to each of the above categories such that the numeric designation reflects a ranking on the scale continuum defined above. The correspondence is as follows:

Murdock Code	O	N Q	C	D	M	P
Assigned Number	1	2	3	4	5	6

No Inheritance ←————————————→ Patrilineal Inheritance by son or sons

Once ethnic units had been decided upon and coded on these variables, factor analysis was used to refine and differentiate these measures for dimensionality. Some of the results of this factor analytic work are included in Figure 16.3. Six dimensions emerge which closely approximate our original guidelines. These dimensions are all relevant to

Figure 16.3 Culture Dimensionality: Factor Loadings for Each Variable on Its Principal Factor*

(Varimax Rotation)

Factor	Variable	Loading
I. *Descent*		
	1. Marital Residence	.888
	2. Patrilineal kinship	.805
	3. Matrilineal kinship	−.899
	4. Descent principles	.913
II. *Economic Structure*		
	5. Dependence on animal husbandry	−.895
	6. Dependence on agriculture	.809
	7. Settlement complexity	.764
III. *Social Stratification*		
	8. Hierarchy above family	−.699
	9. Class stratification	−.842
	10. Caste stratification	−.606
IV. *Social Scale*		
	11. Scale of domestic organization	.739
	12. Levels of organization above family	−.815
	13. Number of clans in community	−.602
V. *Complexity of Settlement*		
	14. Complexity of agricultural systems	.549
	15. Land inheritance	.696
VI. *Family Organization*		
	16. Mode of marriage	−.743
	17. Degree of polygyny	.651

* Variable 18, AUTHOR, was added after the factor analysis was run.

community formation and there is no significance to the order of listing since there were no predominant factors. Six variables representative of these dimensions were used to construct measures of cultural pluralism which are given in this chapter's tables.

Measures of Cultural Pluralism

The data in this chapter are intended to indicate *within-country* variance with respect to traditional cultural patterns across each country's ethnic units. Codings were made on the aforementioned variables for each ethnic unit through the use of a representative group for that ethnic unit. For instance, codings were made using the Makonde as representative of Tanzania's Central Bantu cluster. Standard deviations across ethnic units were calculated for each country. The assumption behind this relatively crude procedure is that the greater the standard deviation, the greater the cultural pluralism within a country.[11] Countries with only one ethnic unit will have no variance of course. But it is also possible that a country with several ethnic units would have no variance since all ethnic units might have the same codings on a particular variable. This is the case for Ghana on the *Agricultural Development* measure where all four units have the same patterns of shifting cultivation.

Each table also includes the mean or average score on the index for each country. The mean reflects the national average for that variable, and for this reason may be of interest in cross-national comparisons. It must be noted here that neither the mean nor the standard deviation take into account the *size* of the groups involved, however. Thus the "predominant level" must be interpreted in terms of units, not individuals. If one group comprising 60 percent of the population of a country ranks high on a particular index while the remaining four groups (20 percent of the population) have low values, the mean will not reflect the fact that three-fourths of the people coded have the high value.[12]

Reliability

The definition of ethnic units is treated at length in

Part III of this book and will not be discussed further here. Once the units have been defined, there remains the difficulty of coding our variables, and the accompanying source and coder reliability problems. The primary data and coding sources were Murdock's *Ethnographic Atlas*,[13] *Cultural Summaries*,[14] and the periodical *Ethnology*.[15] Coder error, therefore, is restricted almost exclusively to the errors that may have occurred in the coding of ethnographies into the classification used by Murdock in his works cited above. We have no assessment of this error, although periodically issues of *Ethnology* update and correct codings that originally appeared in the *Ethnographic Atlas* or previous issues of *Ethnology*.

The major reliability problem appears to be with the data sources, that is the ethnographies themselves. Many of the sources are not written by modern professional anthropologists and the time period in which the works were written shows considerable variance. Furthermore, even the professional ethnographers vary widely in their intentions and fieldwork methods,[16] and their descriptions can be expected to vary depending on how adequate their sampling of the population in a particular ethnic group has been. Finally, given the timing of ethnographic fieldwork, and given the knowledge that the structure of ethnic groups is not static, but varies in time with the incorporation of new populations and the assimilation of new values,[17] these data are, at best, a reliable picture of ethnic pluralism in Black Africa only for a period approximately twenty to forty years *before* independence. It is our hope, therefore, that these data will stimulate, and be superseded by, measures of cultural pluralism based on more systematic survey research, replicated at different time periods in the black African nations.

Notes

[1] Like many other widely used concepts in social science, cultural pluralism enjoys no universally accepted definition. The term was introduced in J. S. Furnivall, *Colonial Policy and Practice* (Cambridge: Cambridge University Press, 1948) to describe the peculiarities of tropical colonies in which historically and culturally segregated races, societies or tribes were brought into limited contact by the extension of the colonial economic market, but retained separate identities and organization for all but economic activity. In subsequent usage, definitions of cultural pluralism have attempted to distinguish the term from the more general notion of cultural heterogeneity by stressing the rigidity and institutional incompatibility of cultural cleavages in the populations of culturally plural societies. See the somewhat different discussions in M. G. Smith, "Social and Cultural Pluralism," *Annals of the New York Academy of Sciences*, 83 (January 1960), 763–777; Leo A. Despres, *Cultural Pluralism and Nationalist Politics in British Guiana* (Chicago: Rand McNally, 1967); and Pierre van den Berghe, "Towards a Sociology for Africa," *Social Forces*, 43 (October 1964), 11–18. Another specification of the meaning of cultural pluralism, which we think too limiting and which we do not make use of, is the suggestion that cultural pluralism is distinctively different from cultural heterogeneity because of the political subjugation of one cultural group by another that is a condition of cultural pluralism. See the articles by the editors in Leo Kuper and M. G. Smith, eds., *Pluralism in Africa* (Berkeley: University of California Press, 1969).

[2] See van den Berghe, "Towards a Sociology for Africa."

[3] Notable examples of this argument are contained in Karl W. Deutsch, "Social Mobilization and Political Development," *American Political Science Review*, 55 (September 1961), 493–514; and S. N. Eisenstadt, *Modernization: Protest and Change* (Englewood Cliffs, New Jersey: Prentice-Hall, 1966).

[4] See Robert Melson and Howard Wolpe, "Modernization and the Politics of Communalism: A Theoretical Perspective," *American Political Science Review*, 64 (December 1970), 1112–1130. Also, the general discussion of ethnic stratification in Tamotsu Shibutani and Kian M. Kwan, *Ethnic Stratification: A Comparative Approach* (New York: Macmillan, 1965).

[5] For two succinct discussions of the problems of ethnic unit classification or identification, see Raoul Naroll, "On Ethnic Unit Classification," *Current Anthropology*, 5 (1964): 282–312, and Alan Merriam, "The Concept of Culture Clusters Applied to the Belgian Congo," *Southeastern Journal of Anthropology*, 15 (1959): 373–395.

[6] For a discussion of marriage concepts, see Jack Goody, *Comparative Studies in Kinship* (Stanford: Stanford University Press, 1969); George Peter Murdock, *Social Structure* (New York: Free Press, 1949).

[7] For a discussion of ethnic stratification theory, see Tamotsu Shibutani and Kian Kwan, *Ethnic Stratification: A Comparative Approach* (New York: Macmillan, 1965); Arthur Tuden and Leonard Plotnicov, eds., *Social Stratification in Africa* (New York: Free Press, 1970).

[8] For a discussion of ethnic political authority patterns, see Ronald Cohen and A. Schlegel, "The Tribe as a Socio-Political Unit—A Cross-Cultural Examination," in *Essays on the Problem of Tribe*, ed. June Helm (Seattle: University of Washington Press, 1968), pp. 120–149; Ronald Cohen and John Middleton, eds., *Comparative Political Systems* (Garden City, N.Y.: The Natural History Press, 1967); John Middleton and David Tait, eds., *Tribes without Rulers* (London: Routledge and Kegan Paul, 1958); Marc J. Swartz, Victor W. Turner, Arthur Tuden, eds., *Political Anthropology* (Chicago: Aldine, 1966); Max Gluckman, *Politics, Law and Ritual in Tribal Society* (Oxford: Blackwell, 1965); Michael Banton, ed., *Political Systems and the Distribution of Power* (Edinburgh: Tavistock Publications, 1965).

[9] For a discussion of economic factors in ethnic society, see George Dalton, "Traditional Economic Systems," in *The African Experience*, *Vol. I*, eds. John N. Paden and Edward W. Soja (Evanston, Ill.: Northwestern University Press, 1970); George Dalton, ed., *Tribal and Peasant Economies: Readings in Economic Anthropology* (New York: Doubleday, 1967).

[10] These scales were constructed for the most part from the nominal

classifications used in George P. Murdock, *Ethnographic Atlas* (Pittsburgh: University of Pittsburgh Press, 1967). Complete operational definitions of the ordinal scales used in the measures of cultural pluralism given in this chapter are provided in the tables. The full definitions of other variables summarized in Figure 16.1 are contained in a machine-readable codebook which can be consulted upon request to the authors.

[11] Because the data is ordinal, this is, at best, only an approximation of an ideal measure of pluralism. It is offered here to encourage other measures that might be more accurate indicators.

[12] The choice of weighting depends on the view of the researcher as to the main interacting units in his own research (i.e., individuals or groups of individuals).

[13] George Peter Murdock, *Ethnographic Atlas* (Pittsburgh: University of Pittsburgh Press, 1967).

[14] George Peter Murdock, *Cultural Summaries: Africa*, 6 volumes, unpublished. Available at Africana Library, Northwestern Univ.

[15] Additional sources that were consulted where necessary were the *Human Relations Area Files* (HRAF), recently indexed by computer at Northwestern University (see Donald G. Morrison, "An Index to the Human Relations Area Files," *American Behavioral Scientist*, 10 (February 1967): 27–30; George Peter Murdock, *Outline of Cultural Materials* (New Haven, Conn.: HRAF Press, 1962), and *Outline of World Cultures*, 3rd ed. (New Haven, Conn.: HRAF Press, 1965); and Robert B. Textor, *A Cross-Cultural Summary* (New Haven, Conn.: HRAF Press, 1967). For a discussion of the above, see Robert B. Textor "Computer Summarization of Coded Cross-Cultural Literature," in *Comparative Research across Cultures and Nations*, ed. Stein Rokkan (The Hague: Mouton, 1968), pp. 54–63.

[16] For a discussion of cross-cultural reliability, see Robert M. Marsh, *Comparative Sociology* (New York: Harcourt, Brace and World, 1967); Frank W. Moore, ed., *Readings in Cross-Cultural Methodology* (New Haven, Conn.: HRAF Press, 1961), pp. 261–279; and Raoul Naroll, *Data Quality Control* (New York: Free Press, 1962).

[17] For a discussion of incorporation and integration in ethnic groups over time, see Ronald Cohen and John Middleton, *From Tribe to Nation in Africa: Studies in Incorporation Processes* (Scranton, Pa.: Chandler Publishing Company, 1970).

TABLE 16.1 Principles of Reckoning Descent: Mean and Standard Deviation

Definition: Scaling assumes an ordinal continuum ranging from matrilineality, through double descent, to exclusive patrilineality.
(1) *Matrilineal exclusive* (individuals affiliate with kin groups exclusively on the basis of relationships through the female line of descent).
(2) *Matrilineal mixed* (individuals affiliate with kin groups bilaterally, though the female line predominates).
(3) *Ambilineal* (individuals affiliate optionally with either matrilineal or patrilineal kin groups).
(4) *Double Descent* (individuals affiliate with specified kin groups through matrilineal descent and specified kin groups through patrilineal descent).
(5) *Patrilineal mixed* (individuals affiliate with kin groups bilaterally, though the male line predominates).
(6) *Patrilineal exclusive* (individuals affiliate with kin groups exclusively on basis of relationships through the male line of descent).

Coding is on each nation's ethnic units (not tribes). The greater the standard deviation, the greater the cultural pluralism on this variable.

RANGE = 2.36
MEAN = 1.01
STANDARD DEVIATION = 0.72

POPULATION PERCENT CUM.	COUNTRY	RANK	COUNTRY NAME	VALUE	RANGE DECILE	TOTAL
9.1	9.1	1.0	ZAIRE	2.36	1	3.42
14.8	5.7	2.0	TANZANIA	2.15		3.78
15.2	0.4	3.5	CONGO (BRA)	1.96	2	2.60
15.4	0.2	3.5	GABON	1.96		2.60
17.3	1.9	5.0	IVORY COAST	1.81	3	3.86
18.1	0.8	6.0	TOGO	1.77		4.83
20.4	2.3	7.0	UPPER VOLTA	1.73		4.38
27.1	6.7	8.0	SUDAN	1.61	4	4.50
29.0	1.9	9.0	MALAWI	1.60		2.20
31.2	2.2	10.0	MALI	1.53		4.00
32.9	1.7	11.0	NIGER	1.50		3.40
34.7	1.8	12.0	ZAMBIA	1.46		2.17
59.7	25.0	13.0	NIGERIA	1.30	5	3.75
60.8	1.1	14.0	SIERRA LEONE	1.09	6	4.75
64.6	3.8	15.5	GHANA	1.00		4.00
66.3	1.7	15.5	SENEGAL	1.00		4.00
66.5	0.2	17.0	GAMBIA	0.98		4.20
67.0	0.5	18.0	MAURITANIA	0.94	7	4.33
68.6	1.6	19.0	CHAD	0.90		4.83
79.5	10.9	20.0	ETHIOPIA	0.83		4.86
80.0	0.5	21.0	LIBERIA	0.80		4.60
82.5	2.5	22.0	CAMEROON	0.75		4.67
87.3	4.8	23.5	KENYA	0.69	8	5.17
91.5	4.2	23.5	UGANDA	0.69		5.17
91.8	0.3	28.5	BOTSWANA	0.0		3.00
93.3	1.5	28.5	BURUNDI	0.0		5.00
94.0	0.7	28.5	CAR	0.0		5.00
95.2	1.2	28.5	DAHOMEY	0.0		5.00
96.9	1.7	28.5	GUINEA	0.0		5.00
97.3	0.4	28.5	LESOTHO	0.0		5.00
98.8	1.5	28.5	RWANDA	0.0		5.00
100.0	1.2	28.5	SOMALIA	0.0		5.00

SOURCE: Murdock, *Ethnographic Atlas.*

TABLE 16.2 Settlement Patterns: Mean and Standard Deviation

Definition: Refers to the permanence and complexity of community settlements. Scaling assumes an ordinal continuum extending from migratory bands with small non-complex settlement patterns to systems with permanent and complex bases.
(1) *Fully migratory* or nomadic bands.
(2) *Seminomadic* (communities whose members wander in bands for at least half the year, but occupy fixed settlement for some seasons).
(3) *Semisedentary* (communities whose members shift from one to another fixed settlement at different seasons, or who occupy a relatively permanent single settlement as a base from which shifting camps are set up).
(4) *Compact but impermanent settlements* (villages whose location is shifted every few years).
(5) *Neighborhoods* of dispersed family homesteads.
(6) *Separated hamlets* which form a relatively permanent single community.
(7) *Compact and relatively permanent settlements* (e.g. nucleated towns).
(8) *Complex settlements* (consisting of nucleated villages or towns with outlying homesteads).

Coding is on each nation's ethnic units (not tribes). The greater the standard deviation, the greater the cultural pluralism on this variable.

RANGE = 2.53
MEAN = 1.07
STANDARD DEVIATION = 0.85

POPULATION PERCENT CUM.	COUNTRY	RANK	COUNTRY NAME	VALUE	RANGE DECILE	TOTAL
1.7	1.7	1.0	NIGER	2.53	1	5.00
12.6	10.9	2.0	ETHIOPIA	2.50		4.43
14.2	1.6	3.0	CHAD	2.49		4.67
16.4	2.2	4.0	MALI	2.43		5.33
23.1	6.7	5.0	SUDAN	2.27	2	3.83
23.6	0.5	6.0	MAURITANIA	2.16		4.00
28.4	4.8	7.0	KENYA	2.13		5.33
28.6	0.2	8.0	GAMBIA	1.74	4	5.60
30.3	1.7	9.0	SENEGAL	1.61		5.50
32.1	1.8	10.0	ZAMBIA	1.60		5.67
34.6	2.5	11.0	CAMEROON	1.49	5	5.67
59.6	25.0	12.5	NIGERIA	1.32		6.00
61.9	2.3	12.5	UPPER VOLTA	1.32		5.50
71.0	9.1	14.0	ZAIRE	1.14	6	6.17
71.7	0.7	15.0	CAR	1.00	7	6.00
72.9	1.2	16.5	DAHOMEY	0.94		6.33
78.6	5.7	16.5	TANZANIA	0.94		6.00
80.5	1.9	18.0	MALAWI	0.80		6.40
84.7	4.2	19.0	UGANDA	0.75	8	5.33
86.6	1.9	20.0	IVORY COAST	0.70		6.71
87.4	0.8	21.0	TOGO	0.69		6.83
91.2	3.8	22.0	GHANA	0.50	9	7.50
91.7	0.5	23.0	LIBERIA	0.49		7.40
93.4	1.7	24.5	GUINEA	0.43		7.25
94.5	1.1	24.5	SIERRA LEONE	0.43		7.75
94.8	0.3	29.0	BOTSWANA	0.0	10	8.00
96.3	1.5	29.0	BURUNDI	0.0		5.00
96.7	0.4	29.0	CONGO (BRA)	0.0		7.00
96.9	0.2	29.0	GABON	0.0		7.00
97.3	0.4	29.0	LESOTHO	0.0		6.00
98.8	1.5	29.0	RWANDA	0.0		5.00
100.0	1.2	29.0	SOMALIA	0.0		1.00

SOURCE: Murdock, *Ethnographic Atlas.*

TABLE 16.3   Hierarchy above Family: Mean and Standard Deviation

Definition: Refers to the number of levels of community structure above the family. Scaling assumes an ordinal continuum of increasing structural inclusion above the family.
(1) Stateless or segmentary societies.
(2) Petty and paramount chiefdoms.
(3) Tribal chiefdoms.
Coding is on each nation's ethnic units (not tribes). The greater the standard deviation, the greater the cultural pluralism on this variable.

```
RANGE =            1.09
MEAN =             0.52
STANDARD DEVIATION =            0.32
```

POPULATION PERCENT						
CUM.	COUNTRY	RANK	COUNTRY NAME	VALUE	RANGE DECILE	TOTAL
1.1	1.1	1.0	SIERRA LEONE	1.09	1	2.25
3.4	2.3	2.0	UPPER VOLTA	0.97	2	1.25
12.5	9.1	3.0	ZAIRE	0.93		1.71
16.7	4.2	4.0	UGANDA	0.90		1.83
27.6	10.9	5.0	ETHIOPIA	0.83	3	1.86
29.2	1.6	6.5	CHAD	0.82		2.00
34.9	5.7	6.5	TANZANIA	0.82		1.67
35.4	0.5	8.0	LIBERIA	0.80		2.40
37.9	2.5	9.0	CAMEROON	0.76	4	1.50
39.6	1.7	10.0	NIGER	0.75		2.20
43.4	3.8	11.0	GHANA	0.71		2.00
48.2	4.8	12.0	KENYA	0.69		1.83
73.2	25.0	13.0	NIGERIA	0.66		2.25
75.4	2.2	15.0	MALI	0.58	5	2.00
82.1	6.7	15.0	SUDAN	0.58		2.00
83.9	1.8	15.0	ZAMBIA	0.58		2.00
84.3	0.4	17.5	CONGO (BRA)	0.49	6	1.40
84.5	0.2	17.5	GAMBIA	0.49		1.60
85.2	0.7	21.0	CAR	0.47		1.33
86.4	1.2	21.0	DAHOMEY	0.47		2.67
86.9	0.5	21.0	MAURITANIA	0.47		1.67
88.6	1.7	21.0	SENEGAL	0.47		1.67
89.4	0.8	21.0	TOGO	0.47		1.33
91.3	1.9	24.0	IVORY COAST	0.45		1.71
93.2	1.9	25.0	MALAWI	0.40	7	1.80
93.5	0.3	29.0	BOTSWANA	0.0		2.00
95.0	1.5	29.0	BURUNDI	0.0		3.00
95.2	0.2	29.0	GABON	0.0		1.00
96.9	1.7	29.0	GUINEA	0.0		2.00
97.3	0.4	29.0	LESOTHO	0.0		3.00
98.8	1.5	29.0	RWANDA	0.0		3.00
100.0	1.2	29.0	SOMALIA	0.0		2.00

SOURCE: Murdock, *Ethnographic Atlas.*

TABLE 16.4   Number of Levels of Hierarchy in Local Community Organization: Mean and Standard Deviation

Definition: Refers to the levels of relationship between family units and local community organization. Scaling assumes an ordinal continuum ranging from situations in which the nuclear family itself is the highest level of authority, to situations in which the village is the significant level of authority.
(1) *Nuclear family* highest level of authority.
(2) *Extended family* highest level of authority.
(3) *Clan/barrio* highest level of authority.
(4) *Village* highest level of authority.
Coding is on each nation's ethnic units (not tribes). The greater the standard deviation, the greater the cultural pluralism on this variable.

```
RANGE =        0.75
MEAN =         0.44
STANDARD DEVIATION =            0.22
```

POPULATION PERCENT						
CUM.	COUNTRY	RANK	COUNTRY NAME	VALUE	RANGE DECILE	TOTAL
1.6	1.6	1.5	CHAD	0.75	1	2.67
2.1	0.5	1.5	LIBERIA	0.75		3.20
27.1	25.0	3.0	NIGERIA	0.71		3.50
29.3	2.2	4.5	MALI	0.69		3.17
30.1	0.8	4.5	TOGO	0.69		2.83
32.0	1.9	6.0	MALAWI	0.63	2	3.00
34.3	2.3	7.0	UPPER VOLTA	0.60	3	3.13
43.4	9.1	8.0	ZAIRE	0.54		2.71
47.2	3.8	10.5	GHANA	0.50	4	3.50
48.9	1.7	10.5	GUINEA	0.50		3.50
50.0	1.1	10.5	SIERRA LEONE	0.50		3.50
55.7	5.7	10.5	TANZANIA	0.50		2.56
56.1	0.4	14.5	CONGO (BRA)	0.49		3.40
67.0	10.9	14.5	ETHIOPIA	0.49		2.57
67.2	0.2	14.5	GABON	0.49		3.60
69.1	1.9	14.5	IVORY COAST	0.49		3.43
69.8	0.7	19.0	CAR	0.47		2.67
71.0	1.2	19.0	DAHOMEY	0.47		3.67
71.5	0.5	19.0	MAURITANIA	0.47		2.67
75.7	4.2	19.0	UGANDA	0.47		2.67
77.5	1.8	19.0	ZAMBIA	0.47		2.67
77.7	0.2	22.5	GAMBIA	0.40	5	2.80
79.4	1.7	22.5	NIGER	0.40		2.80
81.9	2.5	25.5	CAMEROON	0.37	6	2.83
86.7	4.8	25.5	KENYA	0.37		2.83
88.4	1.7	25.5	SENEGAL	0.37		2.83
95.1	6.7	25.5	SUDAN	0.37		3.17
95.4	0.3	30.0	BOTSWANA	0.0		3.00
96.9	1.5	30.0	BURUNDI	0.0		3.00
97.3	0.4	30.0	LESOTHO	0.0		3.00
98.8	1.5	30.0	RWANDA	0.0		3.00
100.0	1.2	30.0	SOMALIA	0.0		3.00

SOURCE: Murdock, *Ethnographic Atlas.*

TABLE 16.5 Inheritance of Real Property: Mean and Standard Deviation

Definition: Refers to the rules for the transmission and disposition of real property (especially land), ranging from relatives other than children to inheritance by a son or sons.
(1) *Absence of individual property rights,* i.e. systems lacking any consistent rules of inheritance.
(2) Inheritance by matrilineal heirs takes precedence over sisters' sons; or, inheritance by patrilineal heirs takes precedence over sons.
(3) Inheritance by children of either sex.
(4) Inheritance by children with daughters receiving less than sons.
(5) Matrilineal inheritance by sisters' sons or son.
(6) Patrilineal inheritance by a son or sons.
Coding is on each nation's ethnic units (not tribes). The greater the standard deviation, the greater the cultural pluralism on this variable.

```
RANGE =          2.36
MEAN =           1.39
STANDARD DEVIATION =        0.87
```

POPULATION PERCENT		RANK	COUNTRY NAME	VALUE	RANGE DECILE	TOTAL
CUM.	COUNTRY					
2.5	2.5	2.0	CAMEROON	2.36	1	4.33
3.0	0.5	2.0	MAURITANIA	2.36		4.33
9.7	6.7	2.0	SUDAN	2.36		3.67
34.7	25.0	4.0	NIGERIA	2.18		4.00
35.2	0.5	5.0	LIBERIA	2.06	2	3.60
40.9	5.7	6.0	TANZANIA	2.05		4.00
44.7	3.8	8.5	GHANA	2.00		4.00
46.4	1.7	8.5	GUINEA	2.00		4.00
47.2	0.8	8.5	TOGO	2.00		4.00
49.5	2.3	8.5	UPPER VOLTA	2.00		3.50
60.4	10.9	11.0	ETHIOPIA	1.99		4.43
60.8	0.4	12.0	CONGO (BRA)	1.96		4.40
69.9	9.1	13.0	ZAIRE	1.88	3	3.25
70.1	0.2	14.0	GABON	1.85		2.40
72.0	1.9	15.0	MALAWI	1.83		4.20
74.2	2.2	16.0	MALI	1.80		3.33
74.4	0.2	17.0	GAMBIA	1.79		3.00
76.1	1.7	18.5	NIGER	1.67		4.00
77.8	1.7	18.5	SENEGAL	1.67		2.83
78.9	1.1	20.0	SIERRA LEONE	1.64	4	3.25
80.5	1.6	21.0	CHAD	1.61		3.50
85.3	4.8	22.5	KENYA	1.49		5.33
87.1	1.8	22.5	ZAMBIA	1.49		2.67
89.0	1.9	24.0	IVORY COAST	0.53	8	2.00
89.3	0.3	28.5	BOTSWANA	0.0		6.00
90.8	1.5	28.5	BURUNDI	0.0		6.00
91.5	0.7	28.5	CAR	0.0		6.00
92.7	1.2	28.5	DAHOMEY	0.0		6.00
93.1	0.4	28.5	LESOTHO	0.0		1.00
94.6	1.5	28.5	RWANDA	0.0		6.00
95.8	1.2	28.5	SOMALIA	0.0		4.00
100.0	4.2	28.5	UGANDA	0.0		6.00

SOURCE: Murdock, *Ethnographic Atlas.*

TABLE 16.6 Mode of Marriage: Mean and Standard Deviation

Definition: Assume an ordinal continuum extending between systems having a system of brideprice or bridewealth in which the woman is regarded as an asset which is being lost by her lineage, and the systems of the opposite type in which dowry payment represents a compensation by the bride's kin group in exchange for the less productive female role.
(1) *Brideprice or bridewealth* is prevailing pattern, i.e. societies in which money, livestock, or other goods are transferred from the groom or his kin group to the relatives of the bride.
(2) *Brideservice,* e.g. systems in which labor or other services are rendered by the groom to the bride's kinsmen.
(3) *Token brideprice,* e.g. systems in which a small or symbolic payment is required.
(4) *Reciprocal gift exchange,* e.g. systems in which gifts of substantial value are exchanged between the family of the groom and the family of the bride.
(5) *Exchange of siblings,* e.g. systems in which there is a transfer of a female relative of the groom in exchange for the bride.
(6) *Absence* of any significant exchange or consideration.
(7) *Dowry,* e.g. systems in which there is institutionalized transfer of property from the bride's relatives to the married couple or kinsmen of the groom.
Coding is on each nation's ethnic units (not tribes). The greater the standard deviation, the greater the cultural pluralism on this variable.

```
RANGE =          2.24
MEAN =           0.55
STANDARD DEVIATION =        0.78
```

POPULATION PERCENT		RANK	COUNTRY NAME	VALUE	RANGE DECILE	TOTAL
CUM.	COUNTRY					
4.8	4.8	1.0	KENYA	2.24	1	2.00
5.9	1.1	2.0	SIERRA LEONE	2.17		2.25
16.8	10.9	3.0	ETHIOPIA	2.05		2.29
17.3	0.5	4.0	LIBERIA	2.00	2	2.00
19.2	1.9	5.0	MALAWI	1.72	3	2.80
19.9	0.7	6.0	CAR	1.49	4	1.67
20.7	0.8	7.0	TOGO	1.46		2.17
45.7	25.0	8.0	NIGERIA	1.32	5	1.63
47.5	1.8	9.0	ZAMBIA	0.82	7	2.00
49.4	1.9	10.0	IVORY COAST	0.73		1.43
51.7	2.3	11.0	UPPER VOLTA	0.71		1.50
60.8	9.1	12.0	ZAIRE	0.61	8	1.29
66.5	5.7	13.0	TANZANIA	0.31	9	1.11
66.8	0.3	23.0	BOTSWANA	0.0		1.00
68.3	1.5	23.0	BURUNDI	0.0		3.00
70.8	2.5	23.0	CAMEROON	0.0		1.00
72.4	1.6	23.0	CHAD	0.0		1.00
72.8	0.4	23.0	CONGO (BRA)	0.0		1.00
74.0	1.2	23.0	DAHOMEY	0.0		1.00
74.2	0.2	23.0	GABON	0.0		1.00
74.4	0.2	23.0	GAMBIA	0.0		1.00
78.2	3.8	23.0	GHANA	0.0		1.00
79.9	1.7	23.0	GUINEA	0.0		1.00
80.3	0.4	23.0	LESOTHO	0.0		1.00
80.8	0.5	23.0	MAURITANIA	0.0		1.00
83.0	2.2	23.0	MALI	0.0		1.00
84.7	1.7	23.0	NIGER	0.0		1.00
86.2	1.5	23.0	RWANDA	0.0		1.00
87.9	1.7	23.0	SENEGAL	0.0		1.00
89.1	1.2	23.0	SOMALIA	0.0		1.00
95.8	6.7	23.0	SUDAN	0.0		1.00
100.0	4.2	23.0	UGANDA	0.0		1.00

SOURCE: Murdock, *Ethnographic Atlas.*

TABLE 16.7   Type of Authority System: Mean and Standard Deviation

Definition: Refers to the locus of decision-making authority within total community. Scaling assumes ordinal continuum ranging from lesser to greater centralization and institutionalization of authority.

(1) *Segmental authority*, e.g. acephalous, kinship-based societies lacking governmental organs, legal institutions, and centralized leadership. Decisions made by the group as a whole or on ad hoc basis.

(2) *Pyramidal authority*, e.g. that of segmentary societies in which there is a vertical distribution of power which is largely upward. The powers exercised in this way are approximately of the same type at the several different levels of the pyramidal segmentary structure. At highest level, frequently a council of paramount chiefs who make joint decisions.

(3) *Hierarchical authority*, e.g. that of centralized societies. This system is patterned along bureaucratic or military lines. At the top is a central command figure—a ruler, chief, king, commander, etc. He combines in his role symbolic, integrational, ethnic, and sanctioned functions. Power by subordinates devolves from the central leader.

Coding is on each nation's ethnic units (not tribes). The greater the standard deviation, the greater the cultural pluralism on this variable.

```
RANGE =             1.30
MEAN =              0.68
STANDARD DEVIATION =            0.41
```

POPULATION PERCENT CUM.	COUNTRY	RANK	COUNTRY NAME	VALUE	RANGE DECILE	TOTAL
1.1	1.1	1.0	SIERRA LEONE	1.30	1	2.25
2.8	1.7	2.0	SENEGAL	1.21		2.17
4.4	1.6	3.0	CHAD	1.15	2	2.00
6.6	2.2	4.0	MALI	1.11		2.33
8.3	1.7	5.0	NIGER	1.10		2.00
17.4	9.1	6.0	ZAIRE	1.04		0.46
21.6	4.2	7.0	UGANDA	1.00	3	2.00
22.0	0.4	8.0	CONGO (BRA)	0.98		1.80
24.5	2.5	10.0	CAMEROON	0.94		1.67
25.2	0.7	10.0	CAR	0.94		1.67
26.4	1.2	10.0	DAHOMEY	0.94		1.33
28.7	2.3	12.0	UPPER VOLTA	0.93		1.88
30.6	1.9	13.0	IVORY COAST	0.90	4	2.43
32.3	1.7	14.5	GUINEA	0.87		2.50
57.3	25.0	14.5	NIGERIA	0.87		2.00
57.5	0.2	17.0	GAMBIA	0.80		2.60
58.0	0.5	17.0	LIBERIA	0.80		2.60
59.9	1.9	17.0	MALAWI	0.80		2.40
66.6	6.7	19.0	SUDAN	0.76	5	2.50
68.4	1.8	20.0	ZAMBIA	0.75		2.33
69.2	0.8	21.0	TOGO	0.69		2.17
74.9	5.7	22.0	TANZANIA	0.67		2.67
78.7	3.8	23.5	GHANA	0.50	7	2.50
83.5	4.8	23.5	KENYA	0.50		1.50
94.4	10.9	25.0	ETHIOPIA	0.35	8	2.14
94.7	0.3	29.0	BOTSWANA	0.0	10	3.00
96.2	1.5	29.0	BURUNDI	0.0		3.00
96.4	0.2	29.0	GABON	0.0		1.00
96.8	0.4	29.0	LESOTHO	0.0		2.00
97.3	0.5	29.0	MAURITANIA	0.0		3.00
98.8	1.5	29.0	RWANDA	0.0		3.00
100.0	1.2	29.0	SOMALIA	0.0		2.00

SOURCE: David Apter, *The Politics of Modernization.*

Part II
Country Profiles

Introduction

The nature of the aggregate indicators on dimensions such as ethnic pluralism, language, urbanization, political patterns, and political instability in Part I was, in many cases, dependent on the judgments of the authors. Part II provides specific information about the basis of some of our judgments. Part II consists of 32 chapters, one for each country discussed. Each chapter contains eight parts: (1) country map, (2) summary of basic information, (3) ethnic patterns, (4) language patterns, (5) urban patterns, (6) political patterns, (7) national integration and stability, (8) selected references.

It should be emphasized that the data presented in Part II does *not* provide a comprehensive profile of the countries included. There are sources which do this, such as Colin Legum's *Africa: A Handbook to the Continent* and the Jeune Afrique Yearbooks, *Africa 69/70*, etc., and the reader is referred to these for further information. Our purpose is to give comparable, detailed data on a relatively few dimensions. The brief descriptions that follow discuss the nature of the data, our definitions and intentions, and the basic sources used. The reliability of these data are similar to those presented in the other parts of this book. Wherever possible we had these sections checked by country experts of our acquaintance. In general, less information was available to us for the former French colonies.

Country Map

Each map has been drawn to show the location of the country's ethnic units, and cities with a population of 20,000 or over. These cities are called "major cities" on the map's legend and are indicated by a small circle. We also give the locations of a number of the smaller population centers, which are shown by black dots, but only rarely have we named these centers. The map also shows the country's major communication linkages in the form of roads, railroads, and major rivers. Special attention has been given to the places where these linkages cross the country's boundaries. The principal sources for urban locations, spelling, and major transport networks, were P. Ady, *Oxford Regional Economic Atlas: Africa* (Oxford: Clarendon Press, 1965), and *Africa 69/70*. The sources for the ethnic unit locations are the various works cited in the ethnic patterns sections and George Peter Murdock, *Africa: Its Peoples and Their Culture History* (New York: McGraw-Hill, 1959). The locations of the ethnic units should be considered as rough approximations. The reader should note that these units are not usually coterminous with ethnic identity groups or "tribes" (see II below).

I. Basic Information

The population and size data are from the *United Nations Demographic Yearbook 1971*. The major exports are given for 1968 when available, otherwise they are for 1967. The sources for the export data are *AID Economic Data Book* (1970), and *Africa 69/70* (1967).

II. Ethnic Patterns

In this section we list every *ethnic unit* (not identity group or tribe) which has 5 percent or more of the total country population. An introductory paragraph discusses the country's ethnic patterns and Table 1 gives the following information: (a) name of the ethnic unit with alternative ethnic names in parentheses; (b) constituent groups (tribes) which are included in the ethnic unit; (c) estimated size of the ethnic unit in 1967 and, wherever possible, the size of all the important constituent identity groups; and (d) percentage of the total 1967 country population accounted for by each ethnic unit.

The concept, "ethnic unit," is discussed at length in an essay in Part III, Chapter 4. Briefly, ethnic units are analytic constructions which are meant to represent culturally distinctive and numerically significant segments of national populations whose members have similar values and practices. We constructed these ethnic units for the special purpose of cross-national research on national integration and do not claim that they represent the only way to group African populations into larger units. Sometimes an ethnic unit will be coterminus with a single identity group or "tribe," but generally the ethnic unit is made up of *two or more tribes* whose individuals have values, practices, and institutions in common (ethnic types), or only values and prac-

tices in common (ethnic clusters). The organization of identity groups or tribes into ethnic units has been done *separately* for each country using the criteria described in Part III. Thus ethnic groups which are found in more than one country may be placed in different kinds of ethnic units (a *type* in one country and a *cluster* in another) because of the differing range of cultural variance that appears in each country.

The sources used in the ethnic unit classifications are indicated in Table 1, further references to the comparative literature will be found in Part III, Chapter 4, on ethnic unit classification. The availability of recent data on the size of ethnic groups is variable; the 1967 estimates are often extrapolations from earlier figures. In making these extrapolations we have had to operate on the assumption that the ethnic units in each country have all grown at the same rate.

III. Language Patterns

The brief descriptive statement discusses the language families found within the country following Joseph Greenberg's seminal work, *The Languages of Africa* (Bloomington: Indiana University Press, 1966). We also consider the various estimates on which language is most widely spoken within the country by speakers using it as a first language or as a *lingua franca*, and indicate our own estimates. There are three works which provide estimates for most of our countries: Duncan MacDougald, Jr.'s *The Languages and Press of Africa* (Philadelphia: University of Pennsylvania Press, 1944); Jan Knappert's "Language Problems of the New Nations of Africa," *Africa Quarterly*, 5 (1965): 95–105; and Dankwart Rustow's chapter, "Language, Modernization and Nationhood—An Attempt at Typology," in *Language Problems of Developing Nations*, eds. Joshua A. Fishman, et al. (New York: Wiley, 1968).

These authors' estimates vary widely. Our own estimates are based on recent information in some cases, but often amount to our own "educated" guesses.

Table 2 summarizes the language pattern of the country in four dimensions: (1) Primacy or the percent of the population that speaks the first and second most widely used language; (2) Greenberg's classification for all ethnic units over 5 percent; (3) the names of the indigenous *lingua franca(s)* which are defined as languages spoken by 5 percent or more of the population as a second or third language; and (4) the official language(s) in the country, including languages which are used officially in regions within a country. A fuller discussion of the issues and definitions involved in language classification including a summary table of Greenberg's African language families will be found in Part I, Chapter 2.

IV. Urban Patterns

This section presents the data on all cities of 20,000 or more population from which the urban variables

presented in Part I, Chapter 15, were derived. Table 3 gives the population figures by decade from approximately 1920 to the present for the capital city and also, in cases where the capital city is not the largest city, for the largest city as well. UA after the population indicates that the figure is for the urban agglomeration and not just the central city. These data should be treated as rough estimates. The dominant ethnicity and name of major vernacular is coded for the capital city and, when available, a figure is given for the percent of the capital's population of the major ethnic group. In a number of cases these data are out of date, and recent population growth in the capital may have changed the situation.

Table 4 gives the names and populations of all cities of 20,000 and over (Nigeria's list is restricted to cities of 50,000 and over because of the number of large Nigerian cities). The target date for the urban figures is 1966 as this was thought to be the latest date for which comparable data might be available for most of the countries. Most of the data are, in fact, for one of the years 1965–1967, but in certain cases older data were all that was available. In every case the latest census data are given. When data for a city were available for either the central city or the urban agglomeration, the latter were used as better representing the urban reality. For the details of this procedure see Part I, Chapter 15. The sources of the urban data are given in the table footnotes.

V. Political Patterns

There are two segments in this section: (A) Political Parties and Elections; and (B) Political Leadership. In (A) there is a brief descriptive statement regarding the development of political parties and the results of national elections during the period 1957 through 1970. Where military coups have suspended the political party system, this is noted. Figure 1 shows party and election data in time sequence. Minor parties as well as major parties are diagrammed in most cases in order to more adequately reflect the complexity of African political life (even in "one-party" states). A time grid scaled by years allows for an assessment of changes in the party system at any point in time, and also for an overview of the emergence of the party system. There is clearly a difference among one-party systems which are based on an original unity, those resulting from the banning of all other parties, those which have come about through voluntary mergers, those which are the result of the military assuming power and becoming a party, those in which small minority parties may operate legally, coalition systems of "national" government, two-party competitive systems, multiparty competitive systems, and multi-party systems based on large numbers of minority parties. All these different patterns are represented in the Black African countries, and are illustrated in the diagrams.

A number of symbols and abbreviations used in Figure 1 are listed below:

1.   ⟶   governing party or parties
2.   ⟶   active opposition party
3.   ---⟶ party whose exact date of origin is unknown
4.   -----⟶ party whose existence is unascertainable
5.   ⟹   coalition between parties
6.   ⟹⟶ merger of parties
7. OPS   one-party state instituted officially
8. coup   coup d'état against the governing party
9. b   party banned
10. d   Party has dissolved itself

The discipline of codifying these data and drawing them on the chart in an unambiguous way was enlightening since it revealed the relatively unsystematic character of many of the sources' coverage of these events and the not infrequent disagreements among the sources on dates and other matters. We used various country political sources which may be found in the selected references section at the end of each chapter, and several comparative works, the most important of which were *Africa 69/70*; Colin Legum, ed., *Africa: A Handbook to the Continent* (New York: Praeger, 1966); and Colin Legum and John Drysdale, eds., *Africa Contemporary Record* (London: Africa Research Ltd., 1969, 1970, 1971). Although we have tried to record all referendums and general elections, the election data are still somewhat incomplete and are included only because we felt they might be of some use in their present form

The Political Leadership section (B) contains information about the head of government plus cabinet-level leadership. Table 5 lists all the *post-independence* heads of government or occasionally, where the head of state is especially politically relevant (e.g., the Emperor in Ethiopia), the head of state. The cutoff date is July of 1971. The ethnic data on the political leadership is given by ethnic *unit* except for those heads of government whose identity group is not a part of one of the country ethnic units. The age of the present head of government is from *The New York Times Encyclopedic Almanac 1971* (New York: New York Times, 1970), and *Africa South of the Sahara 1971* (London: Europa

Publications, 1971) which contains a useful "Who's Who."

Table 6 delineates the distribution of the cabinet membership by ethnic unit for two or three time periods: at independence, in 1967, and/or—in countries with coups prior to 1969—immediately prior to the first coup. The data are given as of December of each year. This information was gathered from published lists of cabinet members, published country materials, *Who's Whos*, and, in certain cases, communication with scholars who were familiar with the particular countries.

VI. National Integration and Stability

A brief descriptive statement summarizes the major *post-independence* events we have coded as elite instability (coups d'état, attempted coups); communal instability (civil wars, rebellions, irredentism); and mass instability (revolts or revolutions). The cut off date is March 1971 for these events. The reader may consult Part I, Chapter 11, for the detailed conceptual definitions of these events and for the general sources used. We explicitly exclude from consideration such events as strikes, riots, arrests, terrorist events, etc., because of the difficulty of ascertaining the identity of the participants (e.g., ethnic or class primacy identification) and of obtaining accurate information cross-nationally. In the tabular summaries, we have arranged the information in three broad categories: (a) description of

the event, (b) characteristics of the participants, and (c) apparent (and/or stated) causes of the event. The accuracy of these summaries and the reliability of the coding depends on the availability of published information on each event. The "dramatic" cases of coups d'état and civil war are generally well-documented, but attempted coups, rebellions, irredentism, and particularly those events we have coded as revolts, are less well-documented, and therefore may be less reliably coded. We relied upon *Africa Research Bulletin*, *Africa Confidential*, *Africa Contemporary Record*, *Africa Report* and *The New York Times*, as well as upon numerous articles or books on particular events; the specific sources are listed below Tables 7, 8, and 9.

VII. Selected References

An effort was made to include recent, English language (if possible) references which would give the reader access to the best available information on each country. The references are highly selective and preference was given to those which treat the country, and which would provide coverage on bibliographical, general, political, economic, and social topics.

Regrettable as their auspices may be, the U.S. Army series of handbooks are often very useful summaries of the literature on African countries. Cornell University Press is bringing out a series of country books, primarily by political scientists,

which we have listed even if they were only forthcoming at the time we completed our manuscript. The Boston University bibliography series is extremely useful, as is the International Monetary Fund economic series. The former French African countries posed special bibliographic problems because of the relative unavailability of literature in English on them. We tried to compensate for this by referencing the appropriate sections of the comprehensive books by Virginia Thompson and Richard Adloff, and the somewhat less satisfactory book by Guy de Lusignan, *French-Speaking Africa since Independence* (London: Pall Mall, 1969).

1. Botswana

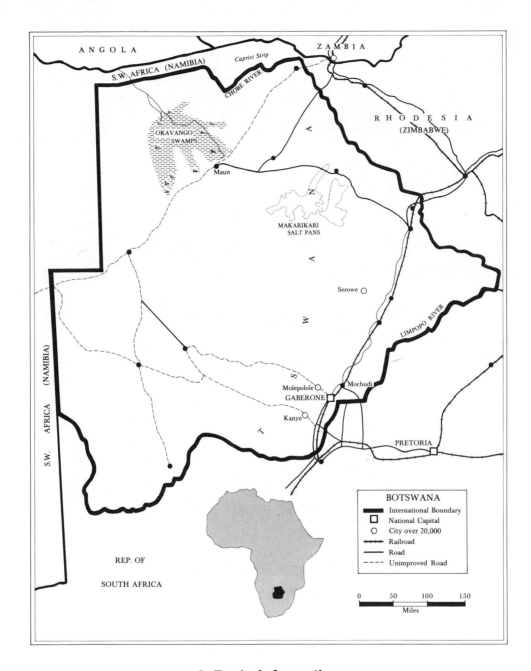

I. Basic Information

Date of Independence: September 30, 1966
Former Colonial Ruler: United Kingdom
Former Name: Bechuanaland
Estimated Population (1970): 650,000

Area Size (equivalent in U.S.): 222,000 sq. mi. (twice Arizona)
Date of Last Census: 1964 (Census planned for 1971)
Major Exports 1967 as Percent of Total Exports: cattle and products—90 percent

II. Ethnic Patterns

The Tswana (Batswana or Bechuana) share a common language (Sechuana) and a common culture, and regard themselves to be part of a single identity group. Within this larger ethnicity, however, are a number of distinct sub-groups which are distinguished primarily by lineage patterns. The largest of these, according to the 1964 census, are the Bamangwato (201,000), the Bakwena (73,000), the Banwaketse (71,300), the Batawana (42,400), the Bakgatla (32,100), the Bamalete (13,850), the Barolong (10,700), and the Batlokwa (3,700). Under colonial rule these sub-group identities were encapsulated by means of regional boundaries. Minority ethnic groups, such as the Koba, Herero, Kgalagadi, and Bushman are dispersed throughout the Tswana territories. These, with 7,500 Europeans and Afro-Europeans, constitute the 10 percent of the population which are not of Tswana ethnicity.

TABLE 1.1   Ethnic Units Over 5 Percent of Country Population

Ethnic Units	Estimated Ethnic Population 1967	Estimated Ethnic Percentage
a. Tswana	533,700	*90%*

SOURCE: *Bechuanaland, Report for the Year 1965* (London: Her Majesty's Stationery Office, 1966), including 1964 Census Report, pp. 25–26.

III. Language Patterns

Botswana is a state based primarily on a single language group: Tswana (Sechuana). Approximately 90 percent of the population speak Tswana as a first language, and Denny (1963) suggests that it is a *lingua franca* throughout the country. Knappert estimates 100 percent of the population are Tswana-speaking. The estimate of Tswana speakers as 69 percent by Rustow (who suggests Shona is spoken by 9 percent of the population) is clearly too low. So as not to imply complete homogeneity, we have estimated that 99 percent of the population speak Tswana. English remains an official language.

TABLE 1.2   Language Patterns

1. Primacy
1st language	Tswana	(99%)
2nd language	Shona	(1%)
2. Greenberg classification   Tswana   IA5
   (all ethnic units in country over 5%)
3. *Lingua franca*   Tswana
4. Official languages   English, Setswana

SOURCE: Neville Denny, "Languages and Education in Africa" in *Language in Africa*, ed. John Spencer (London: Cambridge University Press, 1963), pp. 40–52.

IV. Urban Patterns

Capital: Gaberone
Largest city: Serowe
Dominant ethnicity/language of capital
    Major vernacular: Tswana
    Major ethnic group: Tswana
    Major ethnic group as percent of capital's population:
        Nearly 100 percent

TABLE 1.3   Growth of Capital and Largest City

Date	Gaberone*	Serowe
1950	—	23,000
1960	—	32,000
1964	6,000	34,000
1969	13,000	—

* Gaberone is a new city.

SOURCES: Various editions of the *Statesman's Yearbook*, and *UN Demographic Yearbook 1969*.

TABLE 1.4   Cities of 20,000 and Over

City	Size	Date
Serowe	34,182	1964
Kanye	34,045	1964
Molepolole	29,625	1964
Mochudi	17,700	1964

SOURCE: Census.

V. Political Patterns

A. Political Parties and Elections

A legislative council was established in Bechuanaland in June 1961, with an equal number of European and African members. The general election in March 1965 was a prelude to independence. Two major African parties in competition were the *Bechuanaland People's Party* (BPP) formed in 1961, and the *Bechuanaland Democratic Party* (BDP) founded in 1962. The BDP, under the leadership of Seretse Khama, won a decisive victory (28 out of 31 seats) and has continued to govern to the present time. In the October 1969 election the BDP won re-election, with 68.6 percent of the vote, but lost four of its 28 seats.

Figure 1.1 **Political Parties and Elections**

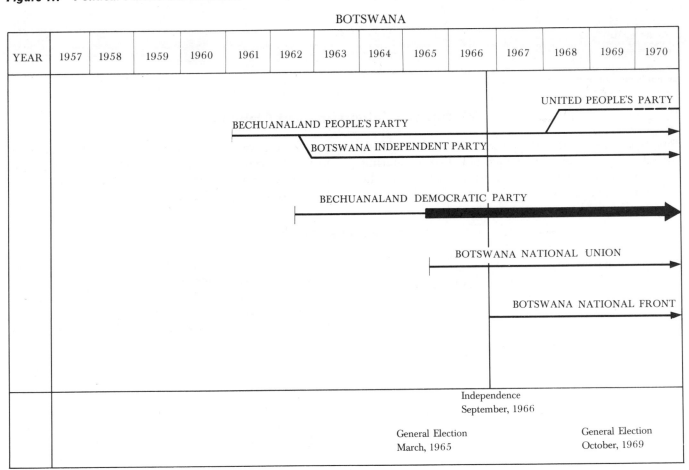

BOTSWANA

B. Political Leadership

The government, led by Sir Seretse Khama, has remained unchanged since independence, except for the departure of the former Minister of Finance, B. C. Thema. The cabinet, like the country, is ethnically homogeneous. A single European member in the cabinet is the only non-Tswana.

TABLE 1.5   Head of Government (Post Independence)

Name	Dates in Office	Age (1971)	Ethnicity	Education	Former Occupation
1. Sir Seretse Khama (President)	1966– present	50	Tswana (Bamangwato)	Fort Hare, Univ. of Witwatersrand, Oxford	Read law

TABLE 1.6   Cabinet Membership: Distribution by Ethnic Unit*

Ethnicity*	Independence Cabinet	1967 Cabinet
1. Tswana (90%)	88%	86%
2. Others (10)	12	14
N =	8	7

* Ethnic units arranged in rank order of size within country with the unit's percent of national population in parentheses.

VI. National Integration and Stability

Botswana has been independent only since 1966, preceded by a year and a half of self-rule. During this short period there has been little political mobilization and no apparent political conflict. The stability of the government and the country as a whole is probably reinforced by cultural, linguistic, and ecological homogeneity. As of 1972 we have coded no instances of political instability.

VII. Selected References

BIBLIOGRAPHY

Middleton, Coral. *Bechuanaland: A Bibliography.* Cape Town: University of Cape Town School of Librarianship, 1965.

Mohome, Paulus, and John B. Webster. *A Bibliography of Bechuanaland.* Occasional Bibliography No. 5. Syracuse, N.Y.: Syracuse University Program of Eastern African Studies, 1966.

Webster, John B., et al. *A Supplement to a Bibliography on Bechuanaland.* Occasional Bibliography No. 12. Syracuse, N.Y.: Syracuse University Program of Eastern African Studies, 1968.

GENERAL

Munger, E. S. *Bechuanaland, Pan-African Outpost or Bantu Homeland?* London: Oxford University Press, 1965.

Schapera, Isaac. *The Tswana.* London: International African Institute, 1953.

Sillery, A. *The Bechuanaland Protectorate.* New York: Oxford University Press, 1952.

Stevens, Richard. *Lesotho, Botswana and Swaziland.* London: Pall Mall Press, 1967.

Young, B. A. *Bechuanaland.* London: Her Majesty's Stationery Office, 1966.

POLITICAL

Macartney, W. A. J. "Botswana Goes to the Polls." *Africa Report,* 14 (December 1969): 28–30.

Stevens, Richard P. "The New Republic of Botswana." *Africa Report,* 11 (October 1966): 15–20.

SOCIAL

Rose, Brian. "Education in Botswana, Lesotho and Swaziland." In *Education in Southern Africa,* ed. B. Rose. London: Collier-Macmillan, 1970.

Schapera, Isaac. *Migrant Labour and Tribal Life.* New York: Oxford University Press, 1947.

2. Burundi

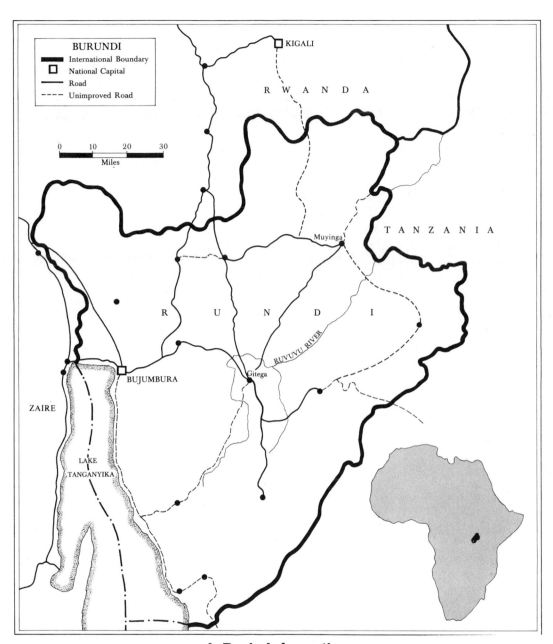

I. Basic Information

Date of Independence: July 1, 1962
Fomer Colonial Ruler: Belgium
Change in Boundaries: Split from pre-independence Trust territory of Ruanda-Urundi in 1962
Former Name: Urundi (in Ruanda-Urundi)
Estimated Population (*1970*): 3,600,000

Area Size (*equivalent in U.S.*): 11,000 sq. mi. (New Hampshire and Delaware)
Date of Last Census: 1965
Major Export 1967 as Percent of Total Exports: coffee— 82 percent

185

II. Ethnic Patterns

Burundi is an ethnically stratified society in which the Tutsi have formed the nobility and the Hutu the common peasantry. These two groups originally represented divergent racial, cultural, and linguistic patterns (Nilotic and Bantu respectively), yet today they comprise a more or less unitary society. Considerable intermixing has taken place between the two groups. They have come to share a common language (Rundi) and social system in most areas; but, significant numbers of Hutu are geographically isolated from the mainstream of Burundi culture, and therefore retain a certain degree of distinctiveness. Estimates of Tutsi population range up to 17 percent. Because of the influx of refugees from Rwanda (approximately 60,000 according to *Europa Yearbook 1967*), an increase in the Tutsi population is likely. The Mwami and the *ganwa* (princes of royal blood)

were Tutsi but were considered a group set apart. In addition to the Tutsi and Hutu, there is a minimal (less than 1 percent) representation of pygmy people known as Twa. In 1965 (according to *Europa Yearbook 1967*), there was a foreign population of 32,000 Africans, Europeans, Asians, and Arabs.

TABLE 2.1 Ethnic Units Over 5 Percent of Country Population

Ethnic Units	Estimated Ethnic Population 1967	Estimated Ethnic Percentage
a. Rundi	3,270,000	*98%*
1. Hutu (Bahutu, Wakhutu)	(2,800,000)	(84%)
2. Tutsi (Tussi, Batusi, Watutsi)	(470,000)	(14%)

SOURCE: "Burundi at Close Range," *Africa Report*, 10 (March 1965): 19–24.

III. Language Patterns

By ethnic identity, the population of Burundi is 84 percent Hutu and 14 percent Tutsi. However, they have come to share a common language— Rundi, the Hutu Bantu language. MacDougald estimates that 84 percent of the people speak Rundi; Knappert suggests 100 percent (Rustow estimates only 28 percent). Maquet (1960) suggests that Rundi is universal. We estimate that at least 90 percent of the population speak Rundi. The second language is Swahili, which Rustow estimates as understood by 17 percent of the population. Our estimate is 10 percent. French continues to be used in government and

secondary schools. Rundi became an official language in Burundi after 1965.

TABLE 2.2 Language Patterns

1. Primacy		
1st language	Rundi	(90%)
2nd language	Swahili	(10%)
2. Greenberg classification (all	Hutu	IA5
ethnic units in country over 5%)	Tutsi	IIEI
3. *Lingua francas*	Rundi, Swahili	
4. Official languages	Rundi, French	

SOURCES: J. J. Maquet, *The Premise of Inequality* (London: Oxford University Press, 1960). U.S. Department of the Army, *Handbook for Burundi* (Washington: Government Printing Office, 1969), pp. 43–44.

IV. Urban Patterns

Capital/largest city: Bujumbura (founded ca.1892)
Dominant ethnicity/language of capital
    Major vernacular: Rundi
    Major ethnic group: Rundi
    Major ethnic group as percent of capital's population:
        Nearly 100 percent

TABLE 2.3 Growth of Capital/Largest City

Date	Bujumbura
1930	6,000
1940	8,000[a]
1950	18,000[b]
1960	42,000[c]
1965	71,000[c]

SOURCES:
[a] Estimated from 1935 and 1945 figures in Denis, *Le Phénoméne urbain*.
[b] *Zaire*, 10 (1956): 115–145.
[c] *UN Demographic Yearbook 1967*.

TABLE 2.4 Cities of 20,000 and Over*

City	Size	Date
Bujumbura	71,000	1965

* The second largest town appears to be the Mwamis' traditional headquarters, Gitega (formerly Kitega), with a population (1963) of 5,000. Bujumbura was formerly named Usumbura and, before that, Costermansville.

SOURCE: *UN Demographic Yearbook 1967.*

V. Political Patterns

A. Political Parties and Elections

The pre-independence struggle in Burundi centered largely around the Belgian backed *Parti Démocrate* *Chrétien* (PDC) and the more nationalistic *Unité et Progrés National* (UPRONA). PDC received a majority in the communal elections held in 1960 and governed until the legislative elections in September

Figure 2.1 **Political Parties and Elections**

BURUNDI*

| YEAR | 1957 | 1958 | 1959 | 1960 | 1961 | 1962 | 1963 | 1964 | 1965 | 1966 | 1967 | 1968 | 1969 | 1970 |

PARTI de l'UNITÉ et PROGRÉS NATIONAL

"CASABLANCA"
"MONROVIA" [b]

FRONT** COMMUN PARTI DÉMOCRATE CHRÉTIEN [b]

PARTI du PEOPLE [b]

PARTI DÉMOCRATE RURAUX [b]

**COALITION OF SEVEN SMALLER PARTIES

Independence
July, 1962

Coups
July and November, 1966

General Election
September, 1961

General Election
May, 1965

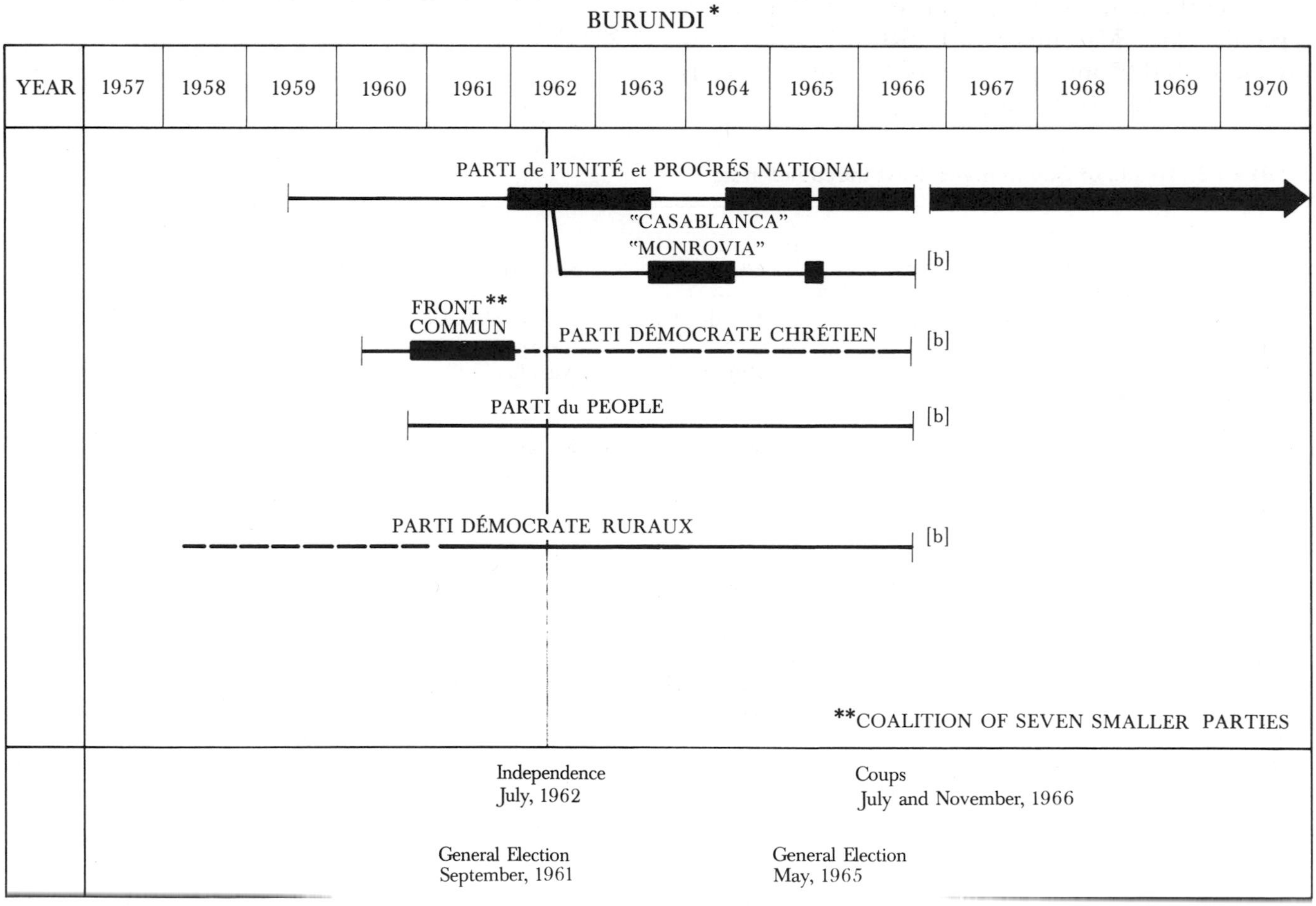

* On the eve of independence there were 24 political parties listed by *Europa Yearbook 1961*. However, according to the 1961 election results "other" parties won no seats and only 1.2 percent of the total vote.

1961 when UPRONA received an overwhelming majority. In the following month UPRONA Prime Minister Prince Louis Rwagasore was assassinated, and the prime ministership passed to André Muhirwa who held office until June of 1963. In 1962 UPRONA split into two factions, the Muhirwa faction became known as the "Casablanca" group and the Mirere-kano faction, the "Monrovia" group. Muhirwa was succeeded by Pierre Ngendandumwe, who was then followed by Albin Nyamoya in April 1964. In July 1966 Prince Ndizeye deposed the king (Mwambutsa IV) and dismissed the UPRONA prime minister, Mr. Biha. Michael Micombero was appointed to be the new UPRONA prime minister and Prince Charles was proclaimed King Mwami Ntare V. The following November Captain Micombero ousted the newly enthroned king and proclaimed Burundi a republic. Mr. Micombero's UPRONA party was proclaimed the only political party and has continued to govern Burundi.

B. Political Leadership

The government of Burundi has changed frequently since independence. Until 1966 the head of state was the Mwami. The six heads of government since independence have presided over ethnically mixed cabinets, in which Hutu and Tutsi ministers have been carefully selected so as to maintain representativeness. Since the 1966 coup d'état, led by the current prime minister, Micombero, ethnic distinctions have been officially proscribed, and the membership of the cabinet has become more stable. Micombero dissolved the monarchy and Burundi became a republic in November 1966. In January 1968 Micombero dissolved the National Council of the Revolution which had been established following the 1966 coup. Muhirwa and Biha are members of the *ganwa* clan.

TABLE 2.5 Heads of Government (Post Independence)

Name	Dates in Office	Age (1971)	Ethnicity	Education	Former Occupation
1. André Muhirwa (Prime Minister)	1962–1963		Rundi (Tutsi)	Cercle scholaire d'Astrida	
2. Pierre Ngendandumwe (Prime Minister)	1963	39	Rundi (Hutu)	Astrida	
3. Albin Nyamoya (Prime Minister)	1964–1965		Rundi (Tutsi)	Astrida	
4. Pierre Ngendandumwe (Prime Minister)	1965	Assassinated June, 1965			
5. Joseph Bamina (Prime Minister)	1965		Rundi (Hutu)		
6. Leopold Biha (Prime Minister)	1965		Rundi (Tutsi)	Astrida	
7. Michael Micombero (Prime Minister-President)	1966–present	31	Mixed (Hutu-Tutsi)	Catholic College of St. Esprit (Burundi)	Military Officer

TABLE 2.6 Cabinet Membership: Distribution by Ethnic Unit*

Ethnicity*	Independence Cabinet	Immediate Pre-Coup Cabinet	1967 Cabinet
1. Rundi (Hutu) (84%)	50%	50%	56%
2. Rundi (Tutsi) (14%)	50	50	44
3. Other	0	0	0
N =	8	13	11

* Ethnic units arranged in rank order of size within country with the unit's percent of national population in parentheses.

VI. National Integration and Stability

Problems of national integration in Burundi centered initially on rivalry between the major *ganwa* (princely) clans and then on the unresolved cleavage between two ethnic groups: the Hutu (who, although a majority of the population have not held political power until recently) and the Tutsi (who dominated the political life of Burundi for 400 years —until November 1966). Initially Hutu partisans tried to achieve power through a violent, unsuccessful revolution. Later, when they had achieved political power through electoral means, they were resisted by the Tutsi monarchy, which was finally overthrown by military elements led by Colonel Micombero (of mixed Hutu-Tutsi parentage).

TABLE 2.7 Elite Instability

Event and Date	Characteristics
1. Assassination January 15, 1965	a. *Description*: Prime Minister Pierre Ngendandumwe was killed in Bujumbura three days after he had been asked to form a national government by Mwami Mwambutsa IV. b. *Participants*: About a dozen men were eventually arrested for conspiracy against the security of the state, including: Albin Nyamoya, the outgoing prime minister; Augustin Ntamagara, president of the Fédération des Travailleurs du Burundi (FTB); Prim Nyongabo, president of Jeunesse Nationaliste Rwagasore (JNR), Zenon Nicayenzi and Pierre Ngunzu, former members of the Nyamoya government. The assassination was closely followed by the dismissal of gendarmerie commander Pascal Magenge, the banning of the FTB and JNR, and the severing of relations with mainland China. c. *Apparent Causes*: A few days before the assassination the Mwami had withdrawn support of the Nyamoya government after persistent rumors of an impending coup d'état by pro-Chinese elements. Nyamoya had apparently sought Chinese support to offset "loss of domestic support." The connection between these events and the assassination is not clear.
2. Coup Attempt October 18, 1965	a. *Description*: Dissident Hutu members of the army and gendarmerie attacked the royal palace, but were eventually driven off by loyal troops under the command of Colonel Michael Micombero; Hutu troops also attacked the home of Prime Minister Biha who was seriously wounded. b. *Participants*: Members of the army and gendarmerie, mostly Hutu, led by Antoine Serukwavu, secretary of state for the gendarmerie. c. *Apparent Causes*: Continued attempts by Mwami Mwambutsa IV to transfer power from parliament to himself after Hutu members, for the first time since independence, had gained a parliamentary majority.
3. Coup d'Etat July 8, 1966	a. *Description*: Tutsi nationalists took over power. Prince Ndizeye (age 19) deposed his father, and transferred the premiership from Leopold Biha to Colonel Michael Micombero. On September 1, 1966, Ndizeye was proclaimed King (Mwami Ntare V), and the constitution was suspended. b. *Participants*: Prince Charles Ndizeye, Crown Prince of Burundi, supported by a number of young Tutsi politicians and army officers.

Event and Date	Characteristics
4. Coup d'Etat November 28, 1966	c. *Apparent Cause*: Prince Charles said he took power in order to "safeguard the country's institutions and make the development of a national economy possible." Colonel Michael Micombero was named prime minister and the cabinet was staffed by young intellectuals. a. *Description*: Prime Minister Micombero declared himself president while Ntare V was out of the country. b. *Participants*: Young Tutsi army officers led by Captain Micombero deposed Ntare V and abolished the monarchy. c. *Apparent Causes*: Ntare V and those whose interests he represented had been vying for power with the military and government bureaucrats. Micombero accused Ntare of being influenced by criminals, practicing nepotism, and plotting to destroy the army.

TABLE 2.8   Communal Instability

Event and Date	Characteristics
1. Civil War: Attempted Take Over Oct. 20–Nov. 1965	a. *Description*: On October 19, 1965, a putsch by Hutu army and gendarmerie officers was thwarted by loyal army troops under Colonel Micombero. The king declared martial law. On October 20, Hutu peasants in Muramvya province and near the Rwanda border killed about 500 Tutsi. On October 23 Hutu began burning houses of Tutsi near the capital city. Shortly thereafter Tutsi reprisals took place. Almost all Hutu gendarmerie and army officers were executed and most of the Hutu political leaders were also killed. An estimated 5,000 Hutu were killed. Martial law was lifted in February 1966. b. *Participants*: It is difficult to specify leaders on either side for the duration of the war. The Hutu outburst seems to have been uncoordinated and the Tutsi retaliation was organized by the army. Antoine Serukwavu, secretary of state for the gendarmerie, led the original coup attempt (October 18, 1965), and is alleged to have incited Hutu peasants to attack Tutsi during his escape to Rwanda. c. *Apparent Causes*: Precipitated by the Hutu putsch, the civil war gave vent to the Hutu-Tutsi animosity which had been developing since independence. The Hutu, influenced by events in Rwanda and aware of the advantages of democratic processes, were expecting to take advantage of the newly created opportunities in the social and political structures. The Tutsi saw democratic rule as a threat to their dominant position; by attempting to subvert further development of such institutions they incurred the hostility of the Hutu.

VII. Selected References

BIBLIOGRAPHY

Clement, Joseph R. A. M. *Essai de Bibliographie de Ruanda-Urundi*. Usumbura: n.p., 1959.

GENERAL

Harroy, Jean Paul, et al. *Le Ruanda-Urundi: Ses Ressources Naturelles, Ses Populations*. Brussels: Les Naturalistes Belges, 1956.

Lemarchand, René. *Rwanda and Burundi*. New York: Praeger, 1970.

Office de l'Information et des Relations Publiques du Congo Belge et du Ruanda-Urundi. *Ruanda-Urundi, Geography and History*. Brussels: 1960.

U.S. Department of the Army. *Area Handbook for Burundi*. Pamphlet No. 550–83. Washington, D.C.: G.P.O., 1969.

POLITICAL

Chronique de Politique Étrangère. *Décolonisation et Indépendence de Rwanda et du Burundi*. Brussels: Institut Royal des Relations Internationales, 1963.

Lemarchand, René. "Political Instability in Africa: The Case of Rwanda and Burundi." *Civilisations*, 16 (1966): 307–337.

Lemarchand, René. "Social Change and Political Modernisation in Burundi." *Journal of Modern African Studies*, 4 (1966): 401–433.

Lemarchand, René. "The Passing of Mwamiship in Burundi." *Africa Report*, 12 (January 1967): 14–24.

ECONOMIC

Leurquin, Philippe P. *Agricultural Change in Ruanda-Urundi 1945–1960*. Stanford: Stanford University Food Research Institute, 1963.

SOCIAL

Baeck, L. *Étude Socio-Économique du Centre Extra Coutumier d'Usumbura*. Brussels: Académie Royale des Sciences Coloniales, 1957.

Bourgeois, R. *Banyarwanda et Barundi*. Académie royale des sciences coloniales. Classe des sciences morales et politiques. Mémoires in-8°. Brussels: 1954.

Liège Université. Fondation pour les recherches scientifiques au Congo belge et au Ruanda-Urundi. *Le problème de l'enseignement dans le Ruanda-Urundi*. Elizabethville: C.E.P.S.I., 1958.

3. Cameroon

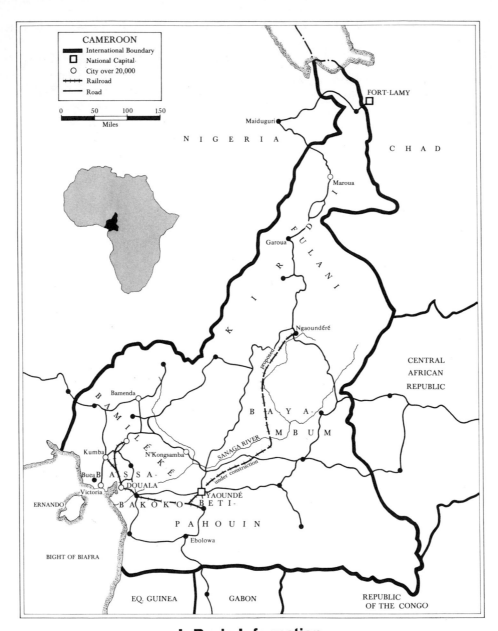

CAMEROON
- ▬ International Boundary
- □ National Capital
- ○ City over 20,000
- ┼┼┼ Railroad
- — Road

0   50   100   150
Miles

NIGERIA

CHAD

FORT-LAMY

Maiduguri

Maroua

K I R D I

F U L A N I

Garoua

Ngaoundéré

CENTRAL
AFRICAN
REPUBLIC

Bamenda

B A Y A -

B A M I L E K E

M B U M

Kumba

N'Kongsamba

SANAGA RIVER

Buea

Victoria

DOUALA

B A S S A -

B A K O K O

B E T I -

YAOUNDÉ

ERNANDO

P A H O U I N

BIGHT OF BIAFRA

Ebolowa

EQ. GUINEA   GABON   REPUBLIC
OF THE CONGO

I. Basic Information

Date of Independence: January 1, 1960 (West Cameroon became independent in October, 1961)

Former Colonial Rulers: France and United Kingdom

Changes in Boundaries: The Southern Cameroons (British) voted to become part of the Cameroon Republic (French) on February 11, 1961

Former Names: Cameroun (Fr.), Kamerun (Ger.)

Estimated Population (1969): 5,736,000

Area Size (equivalent in U.S.): 178,000 sq. mi. (Oregon and Washington)

Date of Last Census: 1960–65 (national survey)

Major Exports 1968 as Percent of Total Exports: coffee—27 percent, cocoa and derivatives—23 percent, aluminum—10 percent, wood—6 percent

192

II. Ethnic Patterns

The Cameroon is a country of great ethnic heterogeneity. To classify such diversity demands a rather high level of abstraction. In judging greater or lesser cultural similarity between groups, it is necessary to ignore variation on specific cultural variables and to define an acceptable *range* of variation at a level of relatively high generalization.

The ethnic clusters we have selected are based primarily on cultural similarities, with additional weight given to linguistic criteria, common ecological adaptations, and historical relatedness. In most, but not all, cases these similarities are recognized locally as bases for group identity. The Fulani are clearly an identity group. The large majority of the Equatorial Bantu cluster (i.e., the Beti-Pahouin) recognize a vague sense of common identity. The Bamiléké are beginning to develop a sense of identity largely through outgroup ascription in the large cities of southern Cameroon. The other broad groupings (e.g., Bassa-Bakoko, Baya-Mbum) include peoples who have not necessarily translated their cultural similarity (and proximity) into an explicit notion of shared identity.

The Kirdi (the term is the Kanuri word for "pagan") raise particular problems. These peoples are in reality rather culturally diverse and represent what could be termed an "ethnic shatter belt." They are, however, identified for administrative purposes and by other peoples in Cameroon as an ethnic group. Historically, they are peoples in northern Cameroon who resisted the Fulani Jihad of the early nineteenth century. Their isolation, stemming from this early resistance, has resulted in a uniformly low level of socio-economic development. There appears to be some sense of common ethnicity and polity which is developing among these peoples. (It should be noted that population estimates for the Kirdi range from 13–17 percent.)

TABLE 3.1   Ethnic Units Over 5 Percent of Country Population

Ethnic Units	Estimated Ethnic Population 1967	Estimated Ethnic Percentage
a. Highland Bantu Cluster (Bamiléké)	1,480,000	27%
1. Bamiléké, 2. Tikar, 3. Widekum, 4. Bamenda, 5. Bamoun, 6. Banen, 7. Yanbasa, 8. Meta		
b. Equatorial Bantu Type (Beti-Pahouin)	985,000	18%
1. Ewondo, 2. Eton, 3. Bane, 4. Fond, 5. Bulu, 6. Fang, 7. Maka, 8. Djem		
c. Northern Animist Type (Kirdi)	820,500	15%
1. Masa, 2. Tupur, 3. Matakam, 4. Musgum, 5. Mofu, 6. Gisiga, 7. Fali, 8. Kapsigi, 9. Daba, 10. Mundang		
d. Fulani (Peul)	520,000	9.5%
e. Bassa-Bakoko Type (Northwestern and Coastal Bantu)	430,000	8%
1. Bassa-Bakoko, 2. Douala, 3. Mbo, 4. Bakwiri-Mboko, 5. Bakossi		
f. Eastern Nigritic Type (Baya-Mbum)	320,000	6%
1. Baya, 2. Mbum, 3. Duru-Verre, 4. Vute, 5. Namchi, 6. Chamba		

SOURCE: Victor T. LeVine, *The Cameroons from Mandate to Independence* (Berkeley: University of California Press, 1964), pp. 12–14.

Smaller ethnic groupings found within Cameroon are the Shuwa Arabs, Kanuri, Hausa, Mandara, and Kotoko of the far north; sizable populations of Southern Nigerians (Ibo, Ibibio, etc.) and Plateau Nigerians (Mambilla, Tigon, Jukun, etc.) in the western region; and a small population of Pygmies in the south. In addition to these indigenous peoples and Nigerian migrants, there are several hundred thousand other African migrants living in the country.

III. Language Patterns

Although Fulani (Fulfulde) is widely spoken throughout the north, even by Kirdi, the two major language groups are in southern Cameroon and are Bantu: Bamiléké (27 percent) and Beti-Pahouin (Bulu) (18 percent). Rustow estimates that Fang (Bulu) is the major language (19 percent) and puts Bamiléké second with 18 percent. Since Bamiléké is an outgroup ascription of several different peoples, with at least seventeen dialects (some of which are mutually unintelligible), it is realistic to recognize its limitations as a language group. Beti-Pahouin (Pahouin is a European ascription of ethnicity) includes variations on Bulu and Ewondo which have come to be limited *lingua francas* in southern Cameroon. Pidgin English is also used as a *lingua franca* in southern Cameroon.

In terms of official language policy, Cameroon requires government to be conducted in both French and English. (Cameroon is the only state in Africa which is officially bilingual in French and English.)

TABLE 3.2   Language Patterns

1. Primacy		
1st language	Beti-Pahouin	(24%)
2nd language	Bamiléké	(18%)
2. Greenberg classification	Beti-Pahouin	IA5
(all ethnic units in	Bamiléké	IA5
country over 5%)	Kirdi	IIIE
	Fulani	IA1
	Bassa-Bakoko	IA4
	Baya-Mbum	IA6
3. *Lingua francas*	Beti-Pahouin (including Bulu des Cheffeurs and Ewondo Populaire); Fulfulde (Fulani); Pidgin English	
4. Official languages	French and English	

SOURCES: Pierre Alexandre, "Aperçu sommaire sur le pidgin A 70 du Cameroun," *Colloque sur le Multilinguisme* (1962): 251–256. Willard R. Johnson, "African-Speaking Africa: Lessons from the Cameroon," *African Forum*, 1 (1965): 65–77.

IV. Urban Patterns

Capital: Yaoundé (founded 1889)
Largest city: Douala (founded ca.1600–1650)
Dominant ethnicity/language of capital
  Major vernacular: Ewondo[1]
  Major ethnic group: Ewondo
  Major ethnic group as percent of capital's population:
    14.42 percent (1957)

[1] Victor LeVine, *The Cameroons: From Mandate to Independence* (Berkeley and Los Angeles: University of California Press, 1964), p. 64.

TABLE 3.3   Growth of Capital and Largest City

Date	Yaoundé	Douala
1920	—	ca. 15,000
1930	—	26,000
1940	—	42,000
1950	—	102,000
1960	74,000	ca. 140,000
1965	110,000	200,000 UA
1969	165,000	—

SOURCES: LeVine, *The Cameroons*, extrapolated to our time points and, for 1965 and 1969, sample survey data. It is not known whether the United Nations' urban agglomeration figure is comparable with the earlier data for Douala.

TABLE 3.4 Cities of 20,000 and Over

City	Size	Date
Douala[a]	200,000 UA	1965
Yaoundé[b]	110,000	1965
N'Kongsamba[c]	50,000	ca. 1965
Bamenda[c]	40,000	ca. 1965
Maroua[c]	32,000	ca. 1965
Kumba[d]	31,000	1964
Victoria[d]	22,000	1964

SOURCES:
[a] *UN Demographic Yearbook 1967.*
[b] Survey.
[c] *Statesman's Yearbook 1967–68.*
[d] *Europa Yearbook 1967* and sample survey data.

V. Political Patterns

A. Political Parties and Elections

The Federal Republic of Cameroon was formed in October 1961, comprised of the former French trust territory and part of the former British trust territory. One of the informal arrangements of this federation was that the President (Ahidjo) would come from the French-speaking region and the Vice-President (Foncha) would come from the English-speaking region. This formula has continued until the present. The dominant party of the French-speaking area, the *Union Camerounaise* (UC) led by Ahidjo, and the dominant party of the English-speaking area, the *Kamerun National Democratic Party* (KNDP) led by Foncha, merged into a single national party, the *Union Nationale Camerounaise* (UNC) in 1966. This party continued to govern Cameroon as a one-party state. Although elections were due in 1969, the National Assembly extended its term by fifteen months and the elections were not held until June 1970.

B. Political Leadership

Since the Federation of former East and West Cameroons, the government has been led by President Ahmadou Ahidjo. There have been several cabinet reshuffles, most recently in January and August 1968, and June 1970.

TABLE 3.5 Head of Government (Post Independence)

Name	Dates in Office	Age (1971)	Ethnicity	Education	Former Occupation
1. Ahmadou Ahidjo (President)	1961–present	47	Fulani	Technical-secondary Yaoundé	Radio technician

TABLE 3.6 Cabinet Membership: Distribution by Ethnic Unit*

Ethnicity*	Independence Cabinet	1967 Cabinet
1. Bamiléké (27%)	40%	40%
2. Beti-Pahouin (18)	20	7
3. Kirdi (15)	0	0
4. Fulani (9.5)	20	20
5. Bassa-Bakoko (8)	10	27
6. Baya-Mbum (6)	10	7
7. Others (17)	0	0
N =	10	17

* Ethnic units arranged in rank order of size within country with the unit's percent of national population in parentheses.

Figure 3.1 **Political Parties and Elections**

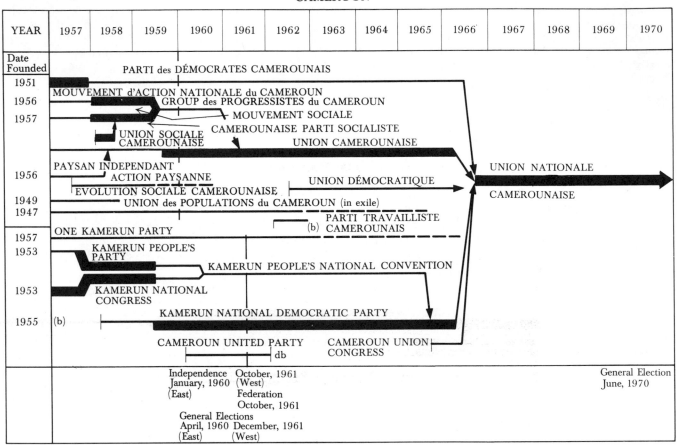

CAMEROON

YEAR	1957	1958	1959	1960	1961	1962	1963	1964	1965	1966	1967	1968	1969	1970

Date Founded

1951   PARTI des DÉMOCRATES CAMEROUNAIS

1956   MOUVEMENT d'ACTION NATIONALE du CAMEROUN
        GROUP des PROGRESSISTES du CAMEROUN

1957   MOUVEMENT SOCIALE
        CAMEROUNAISE PARTI SOCIALISTE
        UNION SOCIALE
        CAMEROUNAISE   UNION CAMEROUNAISE

1956   PAYSAN INDEPENDANT
        ACTION PAYSANNE   UNION DÉMOCRATIQUE   UNION NATIONALE
        EVOLUTION SOCIALE CAMEROUNAISE   CAMEROUNAISE

1949   UNION des POPULATIONS du CAMEROUN (in exile)
1947   PARTI TRAVAILLISTE
        (b) CAMEROUNAIS

1957   ONE KAMERUN PARTY

1953   KAMERUN PEOPLE'S
        PARTY   KAMERUN PEOPLE'S NATIONAL CONVENTION

1953   KAMERUN NATIONAL
        CONGRESS

1955   (b)   KAMERUN NATIONAL DEMOCRATIC PARTY

        CAMEROUN UNITED PARTY   CAMEROUN UNION
        db   CONGRESS

Independence October, 1961
January, 1960 (West)
(East)   Federation
        October, 1961
    General Elections
    April, 1960 December, 1961
    (East)   (West)

General Election
June, 1970

VI. National Integration and Stability

Cameroon experienced an extended period of mass instability in the years immediately prior to independence, related to demands for self-government. Outlawed in July 1955 for nationalist activities unacceptable to French authorities, the *Union des Populations du Cameroun* (UPC) carried on a war of resistance which denied control by the central government over most of two provinces. Part of the unrest at the time was related to urban unemploy-

ment. While Bamiléké and Bassa communalism were evident in the movement, we have coded it as a "mass" phenomenon because of its multi-ethnic nature and ideological orientation.

Since independence, the northern (Fulani/Islamic) based government has worked cautiously to avoid a north/south split which might occur along ethnic/religious/ecological lines. Although the Fulani are a minority in the north itself, they have ruled most of the area since the time of the Sokoto Jihad in the early 19th century. (Almost all of northern Cameroon was formerly under the influence of Adamawa—now in northern Nigeria; Apamawa in turn, paid allegiance to Sokoto.) Recently, the numerous non-Muslim Kirdi in the north have begun to immigrate to northern urban centers, raising the problem of integration within the north itself.

In the south, there has been an intensification of rivalry between the English-speaking western region and the French-speaking eastern region since 1961. Within the eastern region, the role of the Bamiléké vis-à-vis the Beti-Pahouin groups and others has remained precariously balanced. Since independence Cameroon has avoided elite instability and there has been only one minor instance of ethnic violence.

TABLE 3.8 Communal Instability

Event and Date	Characteristics
1. Ethnic Violence January 1, 1967	a. *Description*: Ethnic violence occurred between the Bakossi (Bassa-Bakoko Type) and the Bamiléké which resulted in 236 dead (mainly Bamiléké). A total of 143 Bakossi were arrested. b. *Participants*: Bamiléké and Bakossi members. c. *Apparent Causes*: Not ascertainable.

TABLE 3.9 Mass Instability

Event and Date	Characteristics
1. Attempted Revolution, 1955–November, 1962	a. *Description*: In 1955, prior to independence, the *Union des Populations du Cameroun* (UPC) was dissolved after it became apparent that revolutionary means were being used to take over control of government. Major fighting ended in September 1958 with death of rebel leader Um Nyobé. The UPC, however, remained in exile and conducted sporadic attacks. According to UPC sources-in-exile, 175 pro-government persons were killed by guerrillas, and several steam tugs and barges were destroyed during the period October 1, 1961 to December 23, 1961. On January 23, 1962, the Cameroon government restated its ban of the National Congress of the UPC. From February to November many of the major leaders of the UPC (Emah Otu, Mayi-Matep, Prince Deka Akwa Nya) were arrested (or killed), and condemned to death or long prison terms. b. *Participants*: Major support for the UPC came from members of the Bassa and Bamiléké ethnic groups, especially those living in south and southwestern urban centers where trade union activity was strong. The original leadership included Felix Moumié and Reuben Um Nyobé, both of whom were killed. c. *Apparent Causes*: Initially, the UPC focused on two major issues: immediate independence and free elections. Implicit in Bamiléké and Bassa mass participation was concern over Northern Muslim domination. Government justified harsh measures in terms of national unity, including need for ethnic and religious cooperation.

SOURCES: Victor T. LeVine, "Cameroun," in *Political Parties and National Integration in Tropical Africa*, eds. James S. Coleman and Carl G. Rosberg, Jr. (Berkeley: University of California Press, 1966), pp. 132–147. Victor T. LeVine, *The Cameroons from Mandate to Independence* (Berkeley: University of California Press, 1964), pp. 141–215. Willard Johnson, "The Union des Populations du Cameroun in Rebellion: The Integrative Backlash of Insurgency," in *Protest and Power in Black Africa*, eds. Robert I. Rotberg and Ali A. Mazrui (New York: Oxford University Press, 1970), pp. 671–692.

VII. Selected References

GENERAL

LeVine, Victor T. *Cameroun.* Ithaca, N.Y.: Cornell University Press, 1971.

LeVine, Victor T. *The Cameroons; From Mandate to Independence.* Berkeley and Los Angeles: University of California Press, 1964.

POLITICAL

Ardener, Edwin. "The Nature of Reunification of Cameroon." In *African Integration and Disintegration,* ed. A. Hazelwood. London: Oxford University Press, 1967.

Gardinier, David E. *Cameroon: United Nations Challenge to French Policy.* London: Oxford University Press, 1963.

de Lusignan, Guy. *French-Speaking Africa since Independence,* pp. 121–132. London: Pall Mall Press, 1969.

Johnson, Willard R. *The Cameroon Federation: Political Integration in a Fragmentary Society.* Princeton, N.J.: Princeton University Press, 1970.

LeVine, Victor T. "Cameroon." In *Political Parties and National Integration in Tropical Africa,* eds. J. S. Coleman and C. G. Rosberg. Los Angeles: University of California Press, 1964.

LeVine, Victor T. "The Cameroon Federal Republic." In *Five African States: Responses to Diversity,* ed. G. M. Carter. Ithaca, N.Y.: Cornell University Press, 1963.

ECONOMIC

Green, R. H. "The Economy of Cameroon Federal Republic." In *The Economies of Africa,* eds. P. Robson and D. A. Lury, pp. 136–186. Evanston, Ill.: Northwestern University Press, 1969.

Hugon, Philippe. *Analyse du sous-développement en Afrique Noire: l'exemple de l'économie du Cameroun.* Paris: Presses Universitaires de France, 1968.

International Monetary Fund. "Federal Republic of Cameroon." In *Surveys of African Economies,* Vol. 1. Washington, D.C.: I.M.F., 1968.

Wells, Frederick A. *Studies in Industrialization: Nigeria and the Cameroons.* London: Oxford University Press, 1962.

SOCIAL

Ardener, Edwin, et al. *Plantation and Village in the Cameroons: Some Economic and Social Studies.* London: Oxford University Press, 1960.

Vernon-Jackson, H. O. H. *Language, Schools and Government in Cameroon.* New York: Teachers College Press, 1967.

4. Central African Republic (CAR)

I. Basic Information

Date of Independence: August 13, 1960
Former Colonial Ruler: France
Change in Boundaries: Formerly part of French Equatorial Africa
Former Names: Ubangi-Shari, Oubangui-Chari
Estimated Population (1970): 1,520,000

Area Size (equivalent in U.S.): 238,000 sq. mi. (Texas and Minnesota)
Date of Last Census: 1959–1960
Major Exports 1968 as Percent of Total Exports: Diamonds—53 percent; coffee—14 percent; cotton —24 percent

II. Ethnic Patterns

The ethnic classification for CAR is done at a low level of abstraction and the cultural groups selected correspond in most cases to real identity groups. However, the Yakoma, Sango, and Gbanziri are clustered together because they share a similar ecological adaptation to a riverine environment. In addition to these peoples, CAR has smaller populations such as the N'Zakara (3 percent), the Azandé (1 percent) and a small number of Pygmies. In the extreme north there are also small groups of Waddaiens (Rounga, Goula, Kara, Youla) and Sara (Kaba, Dagba).

TABLE 4.1 Ethnic Units Over 5 Percent of Country Population

Ethnic Units	Estimated Ethnic Population 1967	Estimated Ethnic Percentage
a. Banda	452,300	31%
1. Linda, 2. Kreich, 3. Langba, 4. Yakpa, 5. N'Gao, 6. Togbo, 7. N'Di, 8. Dakpa		
b. Baya (Baja)	423,100	29%
c. Mandjia (Mandja)	124,000	8.5%
d. Riverine Type	116,700	8%
1. Yakoma, 2. Sango, 3. Gbanziri		
e. Mbum (Bum)	102,100	7%
f. Mbaka (or Bwaka)		6.5%

SOURCE: Percentages based on 1959–1960 *Enquête Démographique en République Centrafricaine*. Note that this census excluded the Eastern Region (ca. 58,000 people; mainly of Azandé ethnicity). Total country population at that time was ca. 1,200,000.

III. Language Patterns

All major languages of CAR are of the Adamawa (Eastern) sub-branch of the Niger-Congo family. Such languages include Banda, Baya, Mandjia, Sango, Mbum, and Ngbaka. The major ethnic group, Banda, constitutes 31 percent of the population, and the Baya 29 percent. Rustow estimates the major languages to be Banda (47 percent) and Gbaya (Baya) (27 percent). Since Banda does not serve as a *lingua franca*, we limit our estimate to 31 percent. Rather, the role of *lingua franca* is performed by Sango, which is a pidgin of limited vocabulary based mainly on Ngbandi, which has not only come to be the major *lingua franca* but also the official national language of CAR (although French continues as the working language of government). Knappert suggests that Sango is the major language of CAR, although his estimate of 10 percent is probably low. Our own estimates would be Banda 31 percent, Baya 29 percent, and Sango 25 percent.

TABLE 4.2 Language Patterns

1. Primacy		
1st language	Banda	(31%)
2nd language	Baya	(29%)
2. Greenberg classification	Banda	IA6
(all ethnic units in country	Baya	IA6
over 5%)	Mandjia	IA6
	Riverine	IA6
	Mbum	IA6
	Mbaka	IA6
3. *Lingua franca*	Sango	
4. Official languages	Sango and French	

SOURCE: William J. Samarin, "Une lingua franca centrafricaine," in *Colloque sur le Multilinguisme*, Brazzaville (1962), pp. 257–266.

IV. Urban Patterns

Capital/largest city: Bangui (founded 1899)
Dominant ethnicity/language of capital
 Major vernacular: Sango[1]

Major ethnic group: —
Major ethnic group as percent of capital's population: —

[1] Jan Knappert, "Language Problems of the New Nations of Africa," *African Quarterly*, 5 (1965): 95–105.

TABLE 4.3   **Growth of Capital/Largest City**

Date	Bangui
1930	20,000[a]
1940	33,000[b]
1950	60,000[c]
1960	90,000[d]
1965	150,000[e] UA

SOURCES:
[a] *Démographie Comparée.*
[b] *Ibid.* and *Encyclopédie d'Outre Mer*, Vol. 2, p. 145.
[c] Thomas Hodgkin, *Nationalism in Colonial Africa* (London: Penguin, 1961).
[d] *Statesman's Yearbook, 1960.*
[e] *UN Demographic Yearbook 1967. Africa 1968* and *Europa Yearbook 1967* give a population figure of 238,000 with no date specified, but presumably for no later than 1966. We have arbitrarily adopted the lower UNDYB figure.

TABLE 4.4   **Cities of 20,000 and Over**

City	Size	Date
Bangui[a]	150,000 UA	1965
Berbérati[b]	38,000	1965
Bossangoa[b]	35,000	1965
Bambari[b]	31,000	1965
Bouar[b]	28,000	1965
Bangassou[b]	28,000	1965
Bria[b]	25,000	1965

SOURCES:
[a] *UN Demographic Yearbook 1967.*
[b] *Africa 1968.* These estimates may not be comparable with UN figures.

V. Political Patterns

Figure 4.1   **Political Parties and Elections**

CENTRAL AFRICAN REPUBLIC

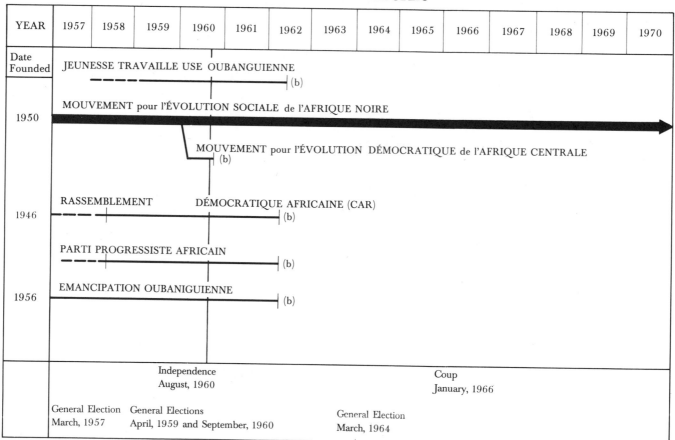

A. Political Parties and Elections

Formed in 1946, the *Mouvement pour l'Évolution Sociale de l'Afrique Noire* (MESAN) has been the dominant party in the Central African Republic. The *Mouvement pour l'Évolution Démocratique de l'Afrique Centrale* (MEDAC) emerged as the major opposition party for a short time after independence until it was suppressed. From 1962 to 1966 MESAN, under M. David Dacko, was the only party in what evolved into a one-party state. In January 1966 there was a military coup and the CAR Chief of Staff, Colonel Jean-Bedel Bokassa took power and declared himself president. The military continues to rule in the CAR with no legal opposition.

B. Political Leadership

From independence until the coup d'état in 1966, the government of the CAR remained substantially unchanged. Since the coup, although the government has become more representative of the ethnic diversity of the country, there appears still to be considerable "malapportionment" in the recruitment to cabinet positions, although different groups are more prominent in the pre- and post-coup government. There were major cabinet reshuffles in April and October 1968.

TABLE 4.5   Heads of Government (Post Independence)

Name	Dates in Office	Age (1971)	Ethnicity	Education	Former Occupation
1. David Dacko (President)	1960–1966	41	Baya	Technical-secondary in Africa (Congo-Br)	Schoolteacher
2. Jean-Bédel Bokassa (President)	1966– present	49	Mbaka	Mission school in CAR and Brazzaville	Soldier

TABLE 4.6   Cabinet Membership: Distribution by Ethnic Unit*

Ethnicity*	Independence Cabinet	Immediate Pre-Coup Cabinet	1967 Cabinet
1. Banda (31%)	0%	11%	0%
2. Baya (29)	14	11	15
3. Mandjia (8.5)	0	11	8
4. Riverine (8)	43	44	15
5. Mbum (7)	0	0	8
6. Mbaka (6.5)	0	0	23
7. Others (10)	43	22	31
N =	8	11	15

* Ethnic units arranged in rank order of size within country with the unit's percent of national population in parentheses.

VI. National Integration and Stability

Political instability in the CAR has been characterized by conflict between elites. In January 1966, Dacko was overthrown in a military coup led by Jean Bokassa who has subsequently maintained control. In mid-1968 Bokassa reported the discovery of a coup plot backed by an unnamed foreign power.

The CAR is a relatively homogeneous country in terms of language and cultural criteria. Although refugees from the Sudan civil war have migrated to CAR, this has not affected ethnic relations in CAR. We have coded no instances of communal or mass instability.

TABLE 4.7 Elite Instability

Event and Date	Characteristics
1. Coup d'Etat January 1, 1966	a. *Description*: A bloodless coup d'état staged by military officers replaced the elected civilian regime of David Dacko. b. *Participants*: High level officers of the 450-man army led by Colonel Jean-Bédel Bokassa (Army Chief of Staff). c. *Apparent Causes*: According to the military regime, Dacko's aides were concealing errors, wasting public funds, and losing touch with the masses. Other reasons may have been discontent with military appropriations, rumors that Bokassa was to be dismissed, and unrest over an austerity program which reduced government salaries by 20 percent. Immediately after the coup (January 5) Bokassa also stated that the coup forestalled a plot organized by pro-Chinese extremists in cooperation with the Chinese Embassy which involved the Gendarmerie which was being transformed into a Presidential Guard.

SOURCE: *Africa Report*, 11 (February, 1966), pp. 12–13.

VII. Selected References

GENERAL

Ballard, John A. "Four Equatorial States: Congo, Gabon, Ubangi-Shari, Chad." In *National Unity and Regionalism in Eight African States*, ed. Gwendolen M. Carter, pp. 231–329. Ithaca, N.Y.: Cornell University Press, 1966.

Thompson, Virginia, and Richard Adloff. *The Emerging States of French Equatorial Africa*, pp. 385–425. Stanford, Calif.: Stanford University Press, 1960.

POLITICAL

de Lusignan, Guy. *French-Speaking Africa since Independence*, pp. 108–114. London: Pall Mall Press, 1969.

LeVine, Victor T. "The Central African Republic: Insular Problems of an Inland State." *Africa Report*, 10 (November 1965): 17–23.

LeVine, Victor T. "The Coups in Upper Volta, Dahomey and the Central African Republic." In *Power and Protest in Black Africa*, eds. Robert I. Rotberg and Ali A. Mazrui, pp. 1035–1071. New York: Oxford University Press, 1970.

ECONOMIC

International Monetary Fund. "The Central African Republic." In *Surveys of African Economies*, Vol. 1. Washington, D.C.: I.M.F., 1968.

SOCIAL

Lebeuf, Jean-Paul. *Bangui*. Paris, 1954.

5. Chad

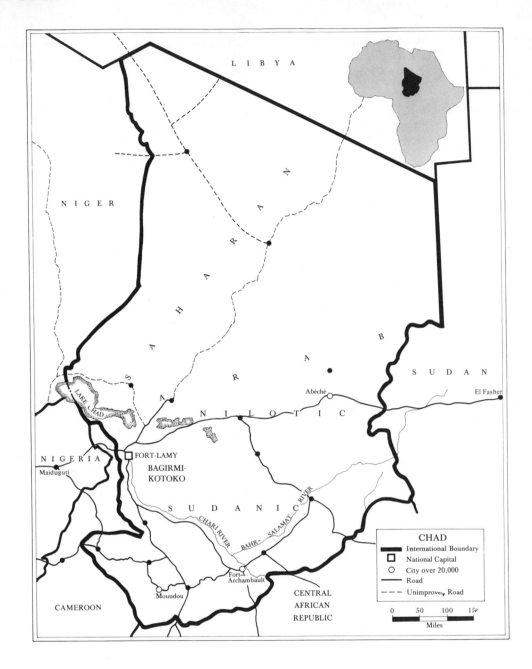

I. Basic Information

Date of Independence: August 11, 1960
Former Colonial Ruler: France
Change in Boundaries: Formerly part of French Equatorial Africa
Estimated Population (*1970*): 3,710,000

Area Size (*equivalent in U.S.*): 496,000 sq. mi. (Texas, New Mexico, and Oklahoma)
Date of Last Census: 1963–64 (sample survey)
Major Exports 1967 as Percent of Total Exports: cotton—80 percent

II. Ethnic Patterns

Classification of the peoples of Chad is quite difficult since this area has a long history of migrations and culture contact. Arab peoples constitute almost half the population, and are distinctive in language, culture, and identity. The Sudanic peoples bridge the zone between the rain forest and savannah area and are culturally similar to many of the Bantu peoples. The Saharan peoples live in the Sahara Desert, and are culturally similar to many of the Chado-Hamitic peoples. The term "Nilotic" is not satisfactory as a cultural label but essentially refers to peoples who are historically related to groups in southern Sudan. Ethnic units less than 5 percent of the population include the Bagirmi-Kotoko type (Bagirmi, Somrai, Gaberi, Bua, Fanyan, Sokoro, Kotoko).

TABLE 5.1 Ethnic Units Over 5 Percent of Country Population

Ethnic Units	Estimated Ethnic Population 1967	Estimated Ethnic Percentage
a. Arab Type	1,570,000	46%
1. Hassauna or Shuwa (Western Arabs)		
i. Assale, ii. Dagana, iii. Ouled Mehareb, iv. Ouled Mansour, v. Ben Wail		
2. Djoheina (Eastern Arabs)		
i. Hemat, ii. Salamat, iii. Rachid, iv. Myssirie, v. Djadne, vi. Khozzam, vii. Rizegat (Mahamid, Maharge, Mararit)		
b. Sudanic Cluster	955,000	28%
1. Sara		
i. Sara, ii. Barma, iii. Dindje, iv. Kaba, v. Mbai, vi. Kumra, vii. Djioko		
2. Runga, Gula, Kara, Nduka		
3. Kirdi	(170,000)	(5%)
i. Masa, ii. Musgum, iii. Tupuri, iv. Mundang		
c. Nilotic Cluster	324,000	9.5%
1. Wadaians (Maba)		
i. Wadai Kodoi, ii. Malanga, iii. Madaba, iv. Debba, v. Abissa, vi. Dekker, vii. Djema		
2. Masalit		
3. Lisi		
i. Bulala, ii. Kuka, iii. Midogo, iv. AbuSemen		
4. Mubi and Karbo		
5. Mesmedjé, Kenga, Babalia, Diongor, Saba		
6. Yalna, Toundjour, Torom		
d. Saharan Cluster	239,000	7%
1. Kanembu	(78,400)	(2.3%)
2. Tubu	(150,000)	(4.4%)
i. Teda, ii. Daza, iii. Kreda, iv. Bulgeda		

SOURCES: Pierre Hugot, *Le Tchad* (Paris: Nouvelles Editions Latines, 1965), pp. 26–27. J-C. Lebeuf, *Afrique Centrale* (Guide Bleu, 1962). G. P. Murdock, *African Summaries*, unpublished manuscript.

III. Language Patterns

The Arab population of Chad is approximately 46 percent, while Sudanic peoples constitute 28 percent. Knappert and Rustow seem to underestimate both the Arabic-speaking population (at 40 percent and 33 percent respectively) and also the use of Arabic as a *lingua franca*. Although not encouraged by the government, Arabic would probably be understood by at least 55 percent of the population. Sara is probably the second largest of the languages in Chad and because it serves as a limited *lingua franca* we estimate it at 28 percent. (Rustow suggests Bongo-Bagirmi as the second largest language—25 percent —although there is no apparent basis to this assertion.) French is the official language.

TABLE 5.2 Language Patterns

1. Primacy		
1st language	Arabic	(55%)
2nd language	Sara	(28%)
2. Greenberg classification	Arabic	IIIA
(all ethnic units in country	Sara	IIE2
over 5%)	Nilotic	IIC
	Saharan	IIB
3. *Lingua francas*	Arabic, Sara	
4. Official language	French	

IV. Urban Patterns

Capital/largest city: Fort-Lamy (founded 1900)
Dominant ethnicity/language of capital
   Major vernacular: Arabic[1]
   Major ethnic group: Arab
   Major ethnic group as percent of capital's population:
     47 percent (1950)[2]

[1] Jan Knappert, "Language Problems of the New Nations of Africa," *African Quarterly*, 5 (1965): 95–105.
[2] *Encyclopédie des Pays d'Outre-Mer.*

TABLE 5.3   Growth of Capital/Largest City

Date	Fort-Lamy
1940	15,000
1950	28,000
1960	80,000
1965	110,000 UA

SOURCE: *Démographie Comparée.*

TABLE 5.4   Cities of 20,000 and Over

City	Size	Date
Fort-Lamy	110,000 UA	ca. 1964
Fort Archambault	34,000	ca. 1964
Moundou	29,000	ca. 1964
Abéché	24,000	ca. 1964

SOURCE: *Africa 1968.*

Figure 5.1   **Political Parties and Elections**

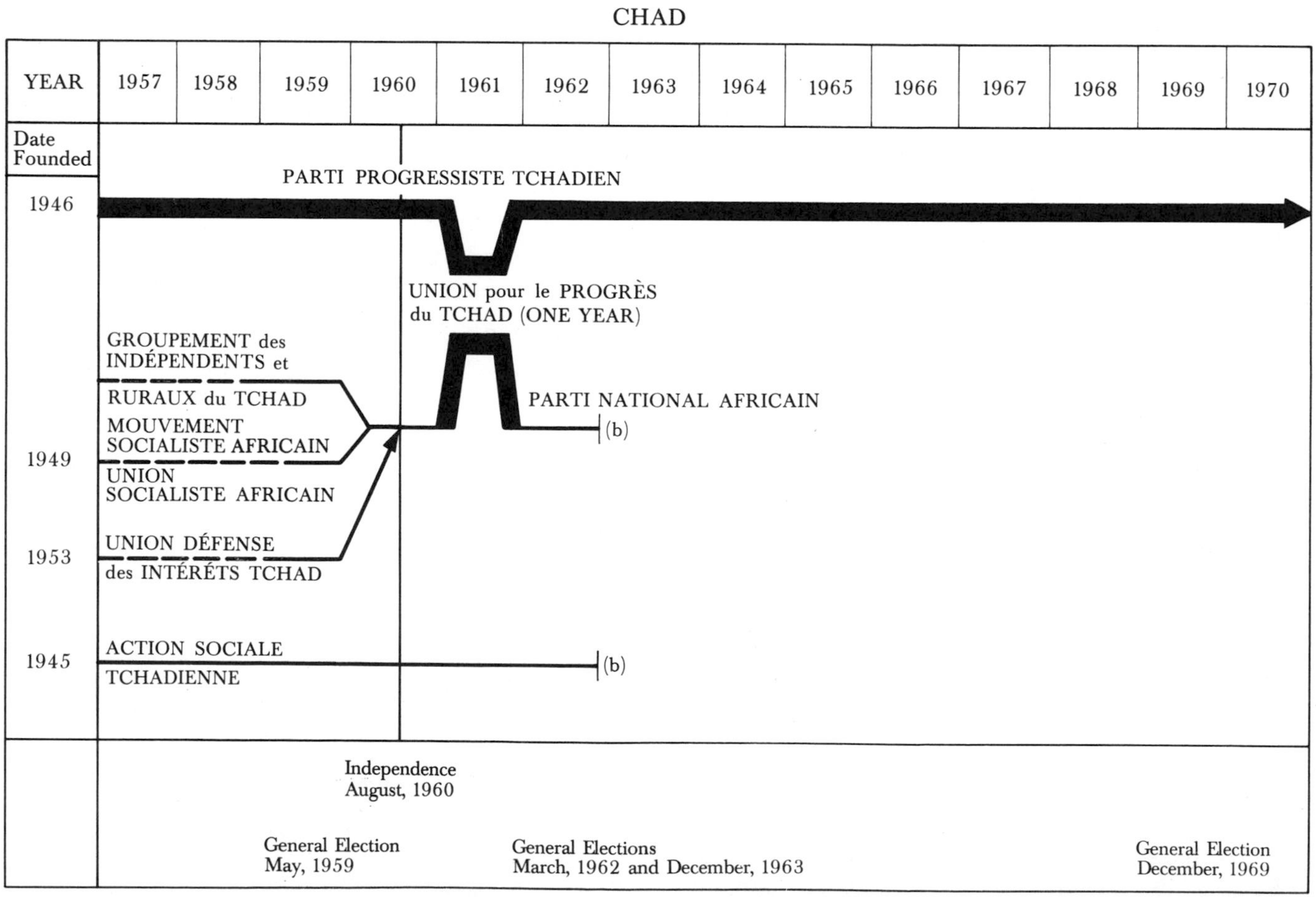

CHAD

V. Political Patterns

A. Political Parties and Elections

Since its formation in 1946, the *Parti Progressiste Tchadien* (PPT), a section of the *Rassemblement Démocratique Africain* (RDA), has been the dominant party in Chad. Opposition was supplied by the *Groupement des Indépendents et Ruraux du Tchad* (GIRT) and the *Mouvement Socialiste Africain* (MSA) which merged to form the *Parti National Africain* (PNA) in 1960. After independence in 1960 the PPT and the newly formed PNA formed a coalition government known as the *Union pour le Progrès du Tchad* (UPT). This coalition, however, lasted only a year and was followed by the banning of the PNA in 1962. The only other opposition party, the *Action Sociale Tchadienne* (AST), was also banned in 1962. In 1963, after the elections, President François Tombalbaye of the PPT declared Chad to be a one-party state. At present, M. Tombalbaye continues as president with the support of an assembly elected in 1963.

B. Political Leadership

The government of Chad has been led by President François Tombalbaye from independence until the present. During this period there have been numerous changes in the personnel occupying individual portfolios, and a number of new members have been brought into government office. Recruitment to office seems to be broadly based by design, although the Sudanic peoples have become increasingly prominent in the cabinet.

TABLE 5.5   Head of Government (Post Independence)

Name	Dates in Office	Age (1971)	Ethnicity	Education	Former Occupation
1. François Tombalbaye (President)	1960– present	53	Sudanic (Sara)	Primary	Assistant Teacher, Trade-Unionist

TABLE 5.6   Cabinet Membership: Distribution by Ethnic Unit*

Ethnicity*	Independence Cabinet	1967 Cabinet
1. Arab (46%)	38%	43%
2a. Sudanic (Sara) (28)	38	50
2b. Sudanic (Kirdi) (5)	0	0
3. Nilotes (9.5)	0	0
4. Saharan Cluster (7)	0	0
5. Others (4)	25	7.2
N =	10	16

* Ethnic units arranged in rank order of size within country with the unit's percent of national population in parentheses.

VI. National Integration and Stability

The Tombalbaye regime has dominated the political scene since independence and during this period the major problem of national integration has been to link northern/Muslim peoples with southern/non-Muslim peoples. Plots by northern elements to overthrow the government (Tombalbaye is a southern Christian), were reported in 1963, 1965, and 1967, and were followed by arrests of northern politicians. Incidents in the east and north that began in 1965 had expanded by 1968–69 into large-scale fighting between northern Muslims, and government forces (reinforced by French forces called in under the Mutual Defense Treaty).

TABLE 5.7   Elite Instability

Event and Date	*Characteristics*
1. Attempted coup August 27, 1971	a. *Description*: Plotters were accused of trying to overthrow President Tombalbaye in order to set up their own government. b. *Participants*: Only Ahmed Abadallah of the plotters was named in the news dispatches, and he was described as a former deputy. He and his fellow plotters were arrested, and it was reported that he committed suicide soon after his arrest. c. *Apparent Causes*: Chad broke off diplomatic relations with Egypt immediately after the attempted coup, and accused her of being behind the plot which presumably was a move by northerners against the southerners in charge of the government.

TABLE 5.8   Communal Instability

Event and Date	*Characteristics*

1. Rebellion mid-1965 to 1968, Civil War 1968–	a. *Description*: Despite long-standing official reticence concerning the rebellion, evidence indicates significant military action began in mid-1965 after a period of "simple banditry." At that time President Tombalbaye threatened to expel all Sudanese citizens from Chad if Sudan did not stop giving sanctuary to rebels living in Khartoum and calling themselves the "Gouvernement de la République Islamique de Tchad." The first notable incidents occurred in November 1965 at Mangolme (central Chad) where two high government officials were among eight killed, and at Asbel, a frontier post attacked by an armed band from the Sudan.
	    Clashes between government and rebel forces became more frequent and intense in 1966; by Aug. 1, 231 had been killed. Much of this fighting took place near the Chad-Sudan frontier in Wadai (Ouaddai) Province. This prompted the government to restrict all Sudanese in Chad to within 5 kilometers of their residences. Nevertheless, insurgents battled government troops on at least two occasions (16 dead) before the end of the year.
	    Events of February 1967 presaged further intensification of the conflict; political arrests became more common and after a serious battle at Am Timon (50 dead) in which the Prefet of Salamot and his deputy were killed, all news dispatches by foreign correspondents were censored. Thus, information on specific incidents became scarce. By the fall of 1969 the rebellion was a continued and growing threat to the national government; opposition was no longer confined to the Chad-Sudan frontier but occurred sporadically in the north and in the southeast. Cotton crops were burned and government vehicles ambushed.
	 b. *Participants*: Rebel forces consist almost entirely of Muslim northerners who comprise about 46 percent of Chad's population. Their spokesman since 1968 is a non-northerner, Dr. Abba Sidick, secretary general of the Chad National Liberation Front (FROLINAT). Dr. Sidick has said that rebel troops number about 2,000.
	    The national government, headed by François Tombalbaye, a Protestant, is dominated by

southerners. French troops have been supporting government forces since 1968. In the fall of 1969, approximately 2,500 French Foreign Legion troops were sent to assist the government.

    c. *Apparent Causes*: In 1962 President Tombalbaye banned all political parties in Chad except his own *Union pour le Progrès du Tchad* (UPT). Among the dissolved parties was the Muslim dominated *Parti National Africain*. It was apparently at this point that northern politicians called for extra-constitutional support from their followers who were dissatisfied as a result of the government's strong-arm methods of collecting taxes. The insurgent movement apparently includes a range of elements from bandits to genuine rebels with a corresponding range of motivations.

SOURCE: Robert Pledge, "France at War in Africa." *Africa Report*, 15 (June 1970): 16–19.

VII. Selected References

GENERAL

Diguimbaye, Georges, and Robert Langue. *L'Essor du Tchad*. Paris: Presses Universitaires de France, 1969.

Hugot, Pierre. *Le Tchad*. Paris: Nouvelles Editions Latines, 1965.

Thompson, Virginia, and Richard Adloff. *The Emerging States of French Equatorial Africa*, pp. 426–475. Stanford: Stanford University Press, 1960.

POLITICAL

Ballard, John A. "Four Equatorial States: Congo, Gabon, Ubangi-Shari, Chad." In *National Unity and Regionalism in Eight African States*, ed. Gwendolen M. Carter, pp. 231–329. Ithaca, N.Y.: Cornell University Press, 1966.

Le Cornec, Jacques. *Histoire Politique du Tchad de 1900 à 1962*. Paris: R. Pichon et R. Durand-Auzias, 1963.

Decraene, Philippe. "Chad at World's End." *Africa Report*, 13 (January 1968): 54.

de Lusignan, Guy. *French-Speaking Africa since Independence*, pp. 114–121. London: Pall Mall Press, 1969.

ECONOMIC

International Monetary Fund. "Chad." In *Surveys of African Economies*, Vol. 1. Washington, D.C.: I.M.F., 1968.

SOCIAL

International Labour Organization. "Employment Position and Problems in Chad." *International Labour Review*, 85 (1962): 500–507.

Lebeuf, Annie. *Les Populations du Tchad*. Paris: Presses Universitaires de France, 1959.

6. Congo (Brazzaville)

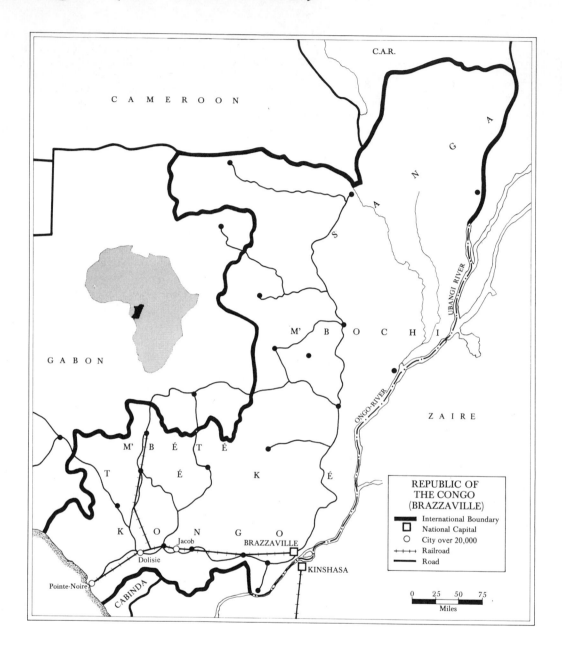

I. Basic Information

Date of Independence: August 15, 1960
Former Colonial Ruler: France
Change in Boundaries: Formerly part of French Equatorial Africa
Former Name: Moyen Congo
Estimated Population (1970): 940,000

Area Size (equivalent in U.S.): 132,000 sq. mi. (Montana)
Date of Last Census: 1960–61
Major Exports 1968 as Percent of Total Exports: wood—51 percent; diamonds—31 percent (originate mainly from Zaire [Congo K.])

II. Ethnic Patterns

The ethnic classifications selected for Congo (Brazzaville), as well as being based on cultural criteria, are based on locally recognized identity groups. The Kongo grouping, which constitutes nearly half the total population, is a broad group of culturally similar peoples who have historically come under the dominance of the Kongo kingdom and who speak Kikongo. They are also an important group in Congo (Kinshasa). It should be noted that the numerically and politically significant Lali (or Lari), although considered a Kongo group today, are of Téké origin and have formerly been classified as such. In addition to the major groups there are also Eshira peoples (4 percent), Maka (3 percent), and Kota (1 percent). Scattered Pygmy populations exist in the north. (Note: the term "M'bochi" is used in Congo (Brazzaville) census reports, but is not used by Murdock.)

TABLE 6.1 Ethnic Units Over 5 Percent of Country Population

Ethnic Unit	Estimated Ethnic Population 1967	Estimated Ethnic Percentage
a. Kongo (Bakongo)	400,000	47%
1. Lali (Lari),	(180,000)	(21%)
2. Kongo, 3. Sundi, 4. Vili,		
5. Yombe, 6. Bembe, 7. Kamba,		
8. Dondo		
b. Téké	170,000	20%
1. Téké, 2. Bakoukouya		
c. M'bochi Type	95,000	11%
1. Bangi, 2. M'bochi, 3. Kuyu,		
4. Maku, 5. Furu, 6. Irébu,		
7. Likuba, 8. Linga, 9. Loi,		
10. Mboko, 11. Ngiril		
d. M'bété (M'béti)	60,000	7%
e. Sanga (Bosanga)	43,000	5%
1. Bassanga, 2. Mbimu, 3. Bombo,		
4. Konambembe, 5. Besom		

SOURCE: *Enquête Démographique de la République du Congo* (Brazzaville: 1960).

III. Language Patterns

All language groups in Congo (Brazzaville) are Bantu. The largest are Kongo (47 percent) and Téké (20 percent). Rustow estimates the two major languages are Kongo (50 percent) and Téké (25 percent); (Knappert puts Kongo at 40 percent, which is clearly too low, especially since Kongo has become a trade language at the mouth of the Congo River). Our own estimate is Kongo 52 percent; Téké 20 percent. French is the official language.

TABLE 6.2 Language Patterns

1. Primacy		
1st language	Kongo (52%)	
2nd language	Téké (20%)	
2. Greenberg classification	Kongo	IA5
(all ethnic units in	Téké	IA5
country over 5%)	M'bochi	IA5
	M'bété	IA5
	Sanga	IA5
3. *Lingua francas*	Kongo, Lingala, Monokutuba	
4. Official language	French	

SOURCE: U.S. Department of the Army, *Area Handbook for the People's Republic of the Congo (Congo Brazzaville)* (Washington, D.C.: Government Printing Office, 1971), pp. 59–62.

IV. Urban Patterns

Capital/largest city: Brazzaville (founded 1883)
Dominant ethnicity/language of capital
   Major vernacular: Kongo[1]

[1] Jan Knappert, Language Problems of the New Nations of Africa," *African Quarterly*, 5 (1965): 95–105.

Major ethnic group: Kongo
Major ethnic group as percent of capital's population: 60 percent (1959)[2]

[2] Marcel Soret, *Les Kongo Nord-occidentaux* (Paris: Presse Universitaires de France, 1959), p. 2.

TABLE 6.3   Growth of Capital/Largest City

Date	Brazzaville
1930	17,000
1940	45,000
1950	84,000
1960	130,000
1965	150,000 UA

SOURCES: *Démographie Comparée*, with the exception of 1940, which is from *Encyclopédie des pays d'Outre Mer*, Vol. 2, p. 145.

TABLE 6.4   Cities of 20,000 and Over

City	Size	Date
Brazzaville[a]	150,000 UA	1965
Pointe-Noire[b]	79,000	ca. 1966
Dolisie[c]	20,000	ca. 1965
Jacob[d]	19,000	1964

SOURCES:
[a] *Statesman's Yearbook 1967–68*.
[b] *Europa Yearbook 1967*. Pointe-Noire is the main port for Francophone Equatorial Africa.
[c] *Africa 1969–70*.
[d] Jacob is included because by 1965 its population probably approached 20,000. *Economie et Plan Developpement*, République de Congo-Brazzaville (Paris: Ministère de Cooperation, Dec. 1965).

V. Political Patterns

Figure 6.1 **Political Parties and Elections**

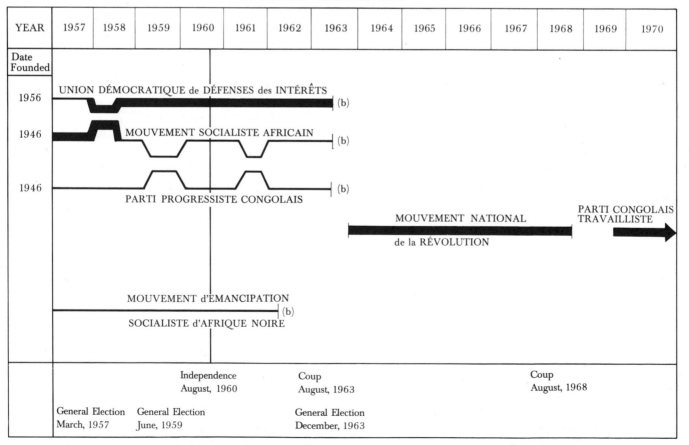

CONGO - BRAZZAVILLE

A. Political Parties and Elections

The dominant political parties in the pre-independence French Congo were: the *Mouvement Socialiste Africain* (MSA) led by Jacques Opangault which governed from 1957 to late 1958, and the *Union Démocratique de Défenses des Intérêts* (UDDI) under Abbé Fulbert Youlou which governed from 1958 until a civilian/military coup forced Youlou to resign in August 1963. Following the coup, the *Mouvement National de la Révolution* (MNR) was formed, and selected Alphonse Massemba-Débat to form the government. Massemba-Débat continued to govern until August 1968 when his government was replaced by a military coup. The newly formed *National Council of the Revolution* (CNR) banned political activity. In December 1969 a People's Republic was declared, guided by Marxist-Leninist principles, and the MNR was renamed the *Congolese Labor Party* (PCT).

B. Political Leadership

The 1963 constitution gives strong executive power to the president, so only heads of state are given here and not the prime ministers. In a highly pluralistic society, the cabinets of Presidents Youlou and Massemba-Débat were fairly broadly based in terms of recruitment from the largest ethnic communities. In 1968 Alfred Raoul, the prime minister, became head of state for a short period before Marien Ngouabi assumed power as the first northern president, with Raoul as vice president. Cabinet reshuffles in this period led to more northern representation than before. On December 30, 1969 a new constitution was adopted.

TABLE 6.5 Heads of State (Post Independence)

Name	Dates in Office	Age (1971)	Ethnicity	Education	Former Occupation
1. Abbé Fulbert Youlou (President)	1960–1963	54	Kongo (Lari)	Seminary in Akono (Fr. Cameroon)	Catholic Priest
2. Alphonse Massemba-Débat (President)	1963–1968	50	Kongo (Lari)	University "training college" for civil service in Fr. Equatorial Africa	Civil Servant
3. Alfred Raoul, (Prime Minister and President)	1968–1969			St. Cyr (France)	Soldier
4. Marien Ngouabi (President)	1969–	34	M'bochi (Kuyu)	French Military Academy	Soldier

TABLE 6.6 Cabinet Membership: Distribution by Ethnic Unit*

Ethnicity*	Independence Cabinet	Immediate Pre-Coup Cabinet	1967 Cabinet
1. Kongo (47%)	43%	57%	50%
2. Téké (20)	7.1	7.1	10
3. M'bochi (11)	21	21	10
4. M'bété (7)	0	0	10
5. Sanga (5)	7.1	7.1	0
6. Others (10)	23	7.1	20
N =	11	15	11

* Ethnic units arranged in rank order of size within country with unit's percent of national population in parentheses.

VI. National Integration and Stability

Marked by two successful coups d'état and numerous reported plots since independence in 1960, the political life of the Republic of Congo has been profoundly complicated by external forces and influences, particularly from its neighbor to the south, Zaire (Congo K.). Of seven reported plots to overthrow the government, five can be linked to external involvement (including Portuguese, Belgian, and Zairese). The two successful coups both in-

volved military action. The second, occurring in August, 1968, appears to have been precipitated by ethnic violence; however, the pattern of instability has been generally characterized by elite competition. This coup was not fully realized for several weeks despite the immediate diminution of Massemba-Débat's power.

Part of the problem of national integration in Congo (Brazzaville) has been that the major ethnic

TABLE 6.7   Elite Instability

Event and Date	*Characteristics*
1. Coup d'État August 15, 1963	a. *Description*: After a three-day general strike and sporadic violence, the army forced civilian President Abbé Fulbert Youlou to resign. It then supported the Christian and Communist labor leaders in their choice of a provisional government headed by Massemba-Débat and composed of radical young technician-ministers. b. *Participants*: Trade unions, with the cooperation of the army. c. *Apparent Causes*: The unions cited unemployment and regime incompetence in the face of a growing economic crisis. Once in power, Massemba-Débat said the coup had taken place to put an end to fiscal mismanagement, extravagance in high places, despotism, tribalism, and moral corruption.
2. Coup d'État August 3, 1968	a. *Description*: Captain Marien Ngouabi, commander of the army's paratroop batallion, was arrested by Massemba-Débat. Elements of the army overthrew the government and rescued Ngouabi from prison. Massemba-Débat, who had fled occupied Brazzaville, was recalled to limited power by the newly constituted National Council of the Revolution. Further conflict within a couple of weeks led to Massemba-Débat's resignation and Ngouabi's eventual assumption of full power in December 1968. b. *Participants*: The coup d'état was organized by Captain Ngouabi, whose control of the paratroops was reinforced by ideological support from left-wing factions in the party and labor organizations, and by disadvantaged northerners in these institutions. The government of Massemba-Débat was brought down by the coup, and the influence of moderate and southern politicians who supported the former president was substantially reduced. c. *Apparent Causes*: Massemba-Débat referred to the elections proposed for December, 1968, as a factor contributing to the political conflicts in the middle of that year. These conflicts appear to be related to both ideology and ethnicity. Massemba-Débat's appointment of moderate ministers, his dismissal or demotion of leading left-wing politicians, and his imprisonment of Ngouabi (a left-wing northerner) intensified these conflicts and precipitated the coup.
3. Coup Attempt March 22–23, 1970	a. *Description*: A commando unit led by Lieutenant Kikanga took over the radio station in Brazzaville. Within a few hours troops led by President Ngouabi defeated the rebels, killing their leader. On March 29, 1970, Captain Albert Miaouma, Adjutant-in-Chief of the Gendarmerie, André Nkoutou, and Sergeant Jean-Marie Mengo were executed for their part in the coup attempt. b. *Participants*: A small group of dissidents in the army. Kikanga, according to *Africa Digest*, had taken part in an earlier coup attempt in November 1969. c. *Apparent Causes*: Kikanga's grievances and political program are not known. According to *Africa Digest* the earlier coup attempt in which he participated was supported by ex-President Fulbert Youlou who was in exile in Spain.

sources: *Africa Diary* (1963): 1327–1329; *Africa Contemporary Record 1968–69*, pp. 454–457; *Africa Digest*, 17 (1970): 56–57.

group, the Kongo, is split between three countries—Congo (Brazzaville), Zaire (Congo K.), and Angola—and there has been some continuing quasi-irredentism. Tension between the Kongo and the northern peoples, most notably the M'bochi, has been an important source of strain behind events since 1968, as has been an ideological left-right struggle.

TABLE 6.8 Communal Instability

Event and Date	Characteristics
1. Ethnic Violence February 7–11, 1963	a. *Description*: An uprising of Lali partisans of Youlou took place in Brazzaville; despite military intervention the outbreak lasted three days. b. *Participants*: Lali ethnic members who were opposed by members of revolutionary youth groups. The government accused Catholic and Western embassies of inciting the uprising. c. *Apparent Causes*: Continuing discontent of Youlou supporters, many of whom were dissatisfied with the results of an election held earlier in February.
2. Rebellion August 29– September 1, 1968	a. *Description*: Following the coup d'état of August 16, 1968, resistance to the new government of Captain Ngouabi was organized by leading civilian politicians and a faction of the youth wing of the ruling party, who were armed as members of the civil militia and in training at a meteorological camp near Brazzaville. Fighting between these elements and the regular army lasted from August 29 to September 1, when the leaders of the rebellion were arrested, and their fellow insurgents disarmed. b. *Participants*: The leaders of this rebellion were leading members of the ruling party (MNR) and of its youth wing (JMNR), notably André Hombessa and Michel Bindi. The insurgents appear to have identified themselves as an ethnically cohesive group, as evidenced by their adoption of the name "Biafrans," and by the fact that Hombessa and Bindi were leading Lari politicians. But it is not clear what aims the insurgents pursued, and to what degree they represented a communal or ethnically homogeneous, rather than an ideological and associational grouping. c. *Apparent Causes*: The rebellion was a reaction to the coup d'état, and the recognition of the supremacy of Captain Ngouabi and the subordination of Massemba-Débat.

SOURCES: (for #1 Ethnic Violence): John A. Ballard, "Four Equatorial States," in *National Unity and Regionalism in African States*, ed. Gwendolen M. Carter (Ithaca, N.Y.: Cornell University Press, 1966), pp. 231–335. Philippe Decraene and Mohammed Bahri, "Two Views of Congo-Brazzaville," *Africa Report*, 10 (October 1965): 35–37.

VII. Selected References

GENERAL

Thompson, Virginia, and Richard Adloff. *The Emerging States of French Equatorial Africa*, pp. 476–526. Stanford, Calif.: Stanford University Press, 1960.

U.S. Department of the Army. *Area Handbook for People's Republic of the Congo (Congo Brazzaville)*. Pamphlet No. 550–91. Washington, D.C.: G.P.O., 1971.

Wagret, Jean Michel. *Histoire et Sociologie Politiques de la République du Congo (Brazzaville)*. Paris: R. Ichon et R. Durand-Auzias, 1963.

POLITICAL

Ballard, John A. "Four Equatorial States: Congo, Gabon, Ubangi-Shari, Chad." In *National Unity and Regionalism in Eight African States*, ed. Gwendolen M. Carter, pp. 231–329. Ithaca, N.Y.: Cornell University Press, 1966.

de Lusignan, Guy. *French-Speaking Africa since Independence*, pp. 91–100. London: Pall Mall Press, 1969.

"Two Views of Congo-Brazzaville." *Africa Report*, 10 (October 1965); 35–37.

ECONOMIC

Amin, S., and Coquery-Victrovich, *Histoire économique du Congo, 1888–1968.* Paris: Editions Anthropos, 1969.

International Monetary Fund. "Congo-Brazzaville." In *Surveys of African Economies*, Vol. 1. Washington, D.C.: I.M.F., 1968.

SOCIAL

Andersson, Efrain. *Churches at the Grass Roots: A Study of Congo-Brazzaville.* London: Lutterworth, 1968.

Balandier, Georges. *Sociologie actuelle de L'Afrique Noire*, 2nd ed. Paris: Presses Universitaires de France, 1963.

Balandier, Georges. *Sociologie des Brazzavilles Noires.* Paris: Colon, 1955.

Frey, Roger. *Brazzaville, Capitale de A.E.F.* Paris: Encyclopédie mensuelle d'Outre mer, 1954.

Lucas, Gerard. *Formal Education in the Congo-Brazzaville: A Study of Educational Policy and Practice.* Stanford: California Comparative Education Center, School of Education, Stanford University, 1964.

Vennetier, Pierre. "L'Urbanisation et ses Consequences au Congo (Brazzaville)." *Les Cahiers d'Outre Mer*, 16 (1963): 263–280.

7. Zaire (Congo-Kinshasa)

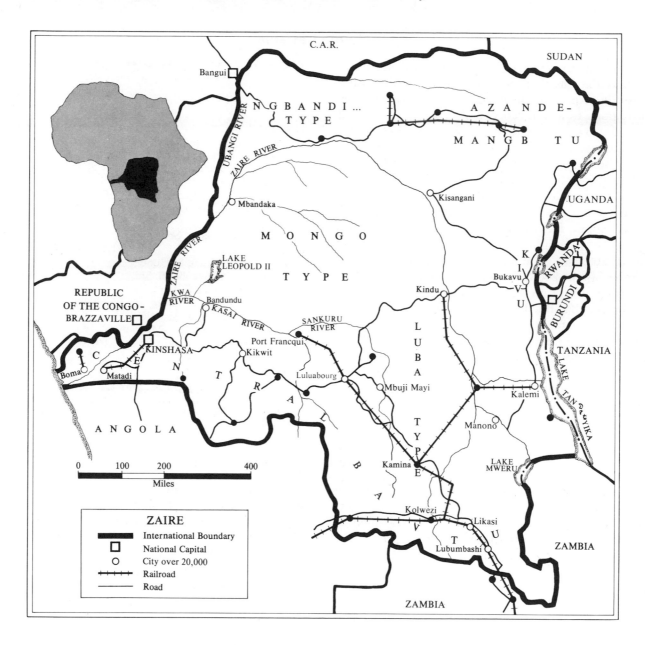

I. Basic Information

Date of Independence: June 30, 1960
Former Colonial Ruler: Belgium
Former Names: Belgian Congo, Congo (Leopoldville), Congo (Kinshasa)
Population (1970): 21,637,876 (Census Results)[1]

[1] *Africa Contemporary Record, 1970–1971*, p. B 303.

Area Size (equivalent in U.S.): 906,000 sq. mi., (Alaska, Texas, and Colorado)
Date of Last Census: 1969–70 (provisional census)
Major Exports 1967 as Percent of Total Exports: copper —60 percent; palm oil—7 percent; coffee—6 percent; diamonds—5 percent

II. Ethnic Patterns

Vansina's Zaire (Congo K.) ethnic classification, which is the basis of our categories, distinguishes identity groups and clusters there into broad regions. The regions, however, reflect a high degree of internal cultural variation. The identity groups which we have clustered together are judged to be culturally similar and Q-factor analytic techniques have been used in this determination (for details, see essay in Part III). In addition to cultural criteria, we have also tried to assess linguistic, ecological, historical, and economic factors. Prominent groups which do not satisfy the minimum size requirement are Téké (about 200,000), the Pende (about 200,000), the Luimbe (about 200,000) and smaller groups such as the Yeke, the Lunda, the Yaka, the Kuba, the Hemba-Bemba, the Boa, and the Binza. Beginning in the 1880s those peoples who shared Lingala, a common trade language, have been referred to as if they constituted an ethnic group called the Bangala. President Mobutu, while born into the Ngwandi ethnic group, now claims this wider Bangala ethnicity. Population data on the ethnic units are based on 1962 data cited in the *Area Handbook for the Congo*.

TABLE 7.1   Ethnic Units Over 5 Percent of Country Population

Ethnic Unit	Estimated Ethnic Population 1967	Estimated Ethnic Population Percentage
a. Central Bantu Type (Kongo) Kongo, 2. Kunda, 3. Lala, 4. Ndembu, 5. Sakata, 6. Yaka, 7. Yanzi	5,560,000	34%
b. Mongo Type Kasai Luba, 2. Mongo	2,610,000	16%
c. Luba Type 1. Katanga Luba, 2. Songye	1,960,000	12%
d. Kivu Peoples 1. Furiiru, 2. Havu, 3. Hunde, 4. Nyanga, 5. Rwanda, 6. Shi, 7. Yira (Nande or Kongo)	1,470,000	9%
e. Azandé-Mangbetu Cluster 1. Alur, 2. Amba, 3. Azandé, 4. Manbetu, 5. Mamvu-Mangutu	1,140,000	7%
f. Ngbandi-Nbaka-Mbandja Type 1. Ngbandi, 2. Ngbaka, 3. Mbandja	980,000	6%

SOURCES: Jan Vansina, *Introduction à l'Ethnographe du Congo* (Editions Universitaires du Congo, 1966). U.S. Department of the Army, *Area Handbook for the Congo* (Washington, D.C.: Government Printing Office, 1962).

III. Language Patterns

Almost all in Zaire speak one or more of the Bantu languages (i.e., the Central sub-stock of the Niger-Congo family). A few groups may be classified as part of the Adamawa (eastern) branch of the Niger-Congo family (e.g., Pazande and Ngbandi); and a few groups represent the Central Sudanic language family (e.g., the Moru-Mangbetu). Within the Bantu language family, there are fourteen important sub-stocks in Zaire, including Kongo, Luba, Mongo, Bira-Kumu and Lega.

There are four *lingua francas* in Zaire: Lingala, Swahili (Kingwana), Tshiluba (Luba or Kiluba), and Kongo (Kikongo). Lingala is used along the river between Ubangi-Uele and Kisangani. Lingala developed in the 1880s when the commercial people on the middle Zaire River, who came to be called Bangala, developed Lingala as a trading language. Lingala later became the language of the Zairese army. Kingwana—a dialect of Swahili—developed

in eastern Zaire in the late nineteenth century as a result of trade contact with East Africa. It is now spoken mainly in the eastern provinces of Katanga, Kivu, Kasai, and Orientale. Tshiluba, while based on the language of the Luba people of Kasai, is now widely used as a *lingua franca* in southeastern Zaire (spoken in the area between Angola and Lake Mwero). Kongo is the language of the Kongo peoples. It is widely used as a *lingua franca* in Kinshasa Province, Lower Congo, and Kwango in the form of a simplified dialect, Kileta (or Kituba).

In order to estimate the percentage of population who speak the above languages, it is necessary to review language policy in Zaire. During the colonial period, there was no consistent linguistic planning, and vernacular languages were used in the elementary schools. Originally the armed forces (the Force Publique) used Hausa, surprisingly, and Swahili, but later adopted Lingala. Many of the missionaries, such as the White Fathers, used Swahili as the language of evangelization.

Under the Belgian colonial regime, the two official languages were French (Walloon dialect) and Dutch (Flemish dialect), although French was clearly predominant and was the language of secondary school. In the post-colonial era, French has continued to be the official language, but four Zairese languages have official status: Lingala, Swahili, Luba, and Kongo. Since 1961, English has been encouraged in the schools.

Estimates vary as to which language is spoken and understood by the largest percent of the population. Knappert suggests Kongo (30 percent); Mac-Dougald suggests Swahili (24 percent). Rustow, apparently looking only at first-language speakers, suggests Rwanda and Luba/Lulua are co-equal at 17 percent. Our own estimate would be Kongo (30 percent), with Swahili and Lingala each 25 percent. These estimates are extremely tentative, and are based partly on conversations with persons familiar with Zaire.

TABLE 7.2 Language Patterns

1. Primacy		
1st language	Kongo (30%)	
2nd language	Swahili (25%)	
2. Greenberg classification (all ethnic units in country over 5%)	Central Bantu	IA5
	Mongo	IA5
	Luba	IA5
	Kivu	IA5
	Azandé-Mangbetu	IA6
	Ngbandi-Ngbaka-Mbandja	IA6
3. *Lingua francas*	Swahili, Tshiluba, Kongo, Lingala	
4. Official language	French	

SOURCE: Edgar Polome, "The Choice of Official Languages in the Democratic Republic of the Congo," in *Language Problems of Developing Nations*, eds. Joshua Fishman, Charles Ferguson, and Jyotirindra Das Gupta (New York: John Wiley, 1968), pp. 295–312.

IV. Urban Patterns

Capital/largest city: Kinshasa (founded 1881)
Dominant ethnicity/language of capital
   Major vernacular: Lingala[1]
   Major ethnic group: Kongo[2]
   Major ethnic group as percent of capital's population: 63 percent (1955)

TABLE 7.3 Growth of Capital/Largest City

Date	Kinshasa
1920	18,000
1930	36,000
1940	47,000
1950	222,000
1960	380,000
1965	1,000,000 UA

SOURCES: From Jacques Denis, *Le Phénomène Urbain* (for 1920 and 1930), and from Thomas Hodgkin, *Nationalism in Colonial Africa* (New York: New York University Press, 1957), p. 67.

TABLE 7.4 Cities of 20,000 and Over

City	Former Name	Size	Date
Kinshasa	Leopoldville	1,323,000	1970
Luluabourg		428,000	1970
Lubumbashi	Elizabethville	318,000	1970
Mbuji Mayi	Bakwanga	256,000	1970
Kisangani	Stanleyville	230,000	1970
Likasi	Jadotville	146,000	1970
Bukavu		135,000	1970
Kikwit		112,000	1970
Matadi		110,000	1970
Mbandaka	Coquilhatville	108,000	1970
Bandundu		74,000	1970
Kalemie	Albertville	29,000	1958
Boma		26,000	1958
Manono		20,000	1958
Kindu		19,000	1958
N'Djili		19,000	1958

SOURCES: Recent population estimates for Zaire's cities have been among the poorest in Black Africa. In 1970, however, a census was carried out which gives the data reproduced here for eleven "villes." We include these because there seemed to be no valid way to extrapolate between the 1958 census and the 1970 census, given the dynamics of recent Zaire history. The 1970 data were reported in a series of issues of *L'Etoile* (August 1970) and reprinted in Leon de Saint Moulin, "Les statistiques démographiques en République Démocratique du Congo" *Congo-Afrique*, 47 (1970): 377–385. For those towns whose population was not reported for 1970 we give data from the 1958 census. *Rapport sur l'administration du Congo Belge pendant l'anee 1958 presente aux Chambres legislatives* (Brussels: 1959), pp. 63–69.

[1] Jan Knappert, "Language Problems of the New Nations of Africa," *African Quarterly*, 5 (1965): 95–105.
[2] L. Baeck, "Leopoldville," *Zaire*, 10 (1956): p. 623.

V. Political Patterns

A. Political Parties and Elections

Political parties developed at a late stage in Zaire (Congo K.), during the 1958–59 period, just prior to independence in June 1960. By 1960 there were an estimated 100 parties. The first national elections were held in May 1960 when the *Mouvement National Congolais* (MNC), led by Patrice Lumumba, won a plurality. A government was formed with the MNC in coalition with *Alliance des Ba-Kongo* (ABAKO), led by Joseph Kasavubu, who was elected president in June 1960. Although the army mutinied in July, the government continued until September, when a constitutional crisis resulted in the army—*Armée*

Nationale Congolaise (ANC) led by Colonel Joseph Mobutu—taking over the government and then turning it over to a set of civil servants and university graduates. In November 1960, the ABAKO party was drawn into the government, although the MNC challenged the legitimacy of the regime. Between 1960 and 1965 the cabinets included ministers from various political parties. In March–May of 1965 elections were held, but the results were questioned by all sides, and in November the army again took over control of the country. In April 1967 Mobutu founded the *Mouvement Populaire de la Révolution* (MPR) from which the army was excluded.

Figure 7.1   **Political Parties and Elections**

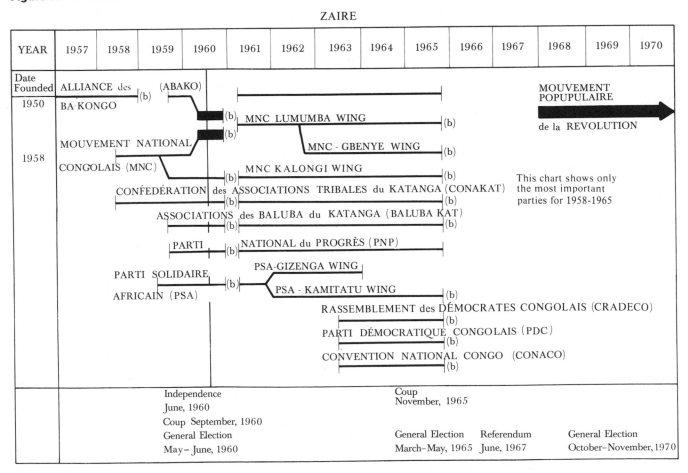

ZAIRE

B. Political Leadership

The president and also head of state until 1965 was Joseph Kasavubu. Following the first coup d'état in the first year of independence, the prime minister-ship changed hands continuously until the second coup in 1965, since which time the government appears to have become much more stable. General Mobutu ruled at first, with Léonard Mulamba as his

prime minister, but on October 26, 1966 he dismissed Mulamba and assumed the functions of prime minister himself. In a country of the greatest cultural complexity, recruitment to governmental leadership has been considerably diversified in terms of the regional and ethnic background of cabinet members.

TABLE 7.5 Heads of Government (Post Independence)

Name	Dates in Office	Age (1971)	Ethnicity	Education	Former Occupation
1. Patrice Lumumba (Prime Minister)	June 1960–Sept. 5, 1960	Died 1961 age 36	(Tetela)	Mission School, Kasai	Tax clerk, Postmaster
2. Joseph Ileo (Prime Minister)	Sept. 5–30, 1960 Feb.–Aug. 1961	49	Mongo	Catholic Missions & Night School	Accountant
3. Cyril Adoula (Prime Minister)	Aug. 1961–July 1964	50	(Bulya)	Roman Catholic Secondary	Trade unionist
4. Moise Tshombe (Prime Minister)	July 1964–Oct. 1965	Died 1969 age 49	(Lunda)	American Methodist Missions	Businessman
5. E. Kimba (Prime Minister)	Oct. 1965–Nov. 1965		Luba		
6. Joseph Mobutu (President)	1965–	41	(Ngwandi)	Secondary and Ecole des Cadres, Force Publique, Luluaborg	Journalist, Soldier

Table 7.6 Cabinet Membership: Distribution by Ethnic Unit*

Ethnicity	Independence Cabinet	Immediate Pre-Coup Cabinet	1967 Cabinet
1. Central Bantu (34%)	18%	26%	17%
2. Mongo (16)	18	26	13
3. Luba (12)	14	11	34
4. Kivu (9)	18	5.3	0
5. Azandé-Mangbetu (7)	0	5.3	0
6. Ngbandi-Ngbaka-Mbanja (6)	0	0	0
7. Others (16)	32	21	39
N =	23	19	23

* Ethnic units arranged in rank order of size within country with the unit's percent of national population in parentheses.

VI. National Integration and Stability

In no African state except perhaps Sudan does the combined magnitude of elite, communal, and mass instability approach that of Zaire (formerly Congo [Kinshasa]); we cannot give an adequate summary of the over-all pattern of events here. Two successful coups d'état (September 1960 and November 1965), along with a large number of attempted coups and (reported) plots, have been organized. In addition to elite instability, there has been a major civil war and a series of loosely coordinated rebellions marked by high levels of violence that have been potentially destructive of territorial integrity. The civil war resulted from the Katanga secession (July 1960–January 1963) and the attempted revolution was led by the *Conseil National de Libération* (mainly from January 1964 to late 1965). Domestic insurgency was successfully resisted by the Mobutu government by 1966, and the only major threat thereafter was that of the exiled former Prime Minister Tshombe and mercenaries operating from Angola. The Congolese army defeated the mercenaries led by Colonel Schramme in October 1967. In June 1969 demonstrating students from Louvanium University were fired upon by the army and an estimated 40–50 were killed. In June 1971 the university was closed.

TABLE 7.7   Elite Instability

Event and Date	Characteristics
1. Coup d'État September 14, 1960	a. *Description*: A military **coup**, led by Colonel Joseph Mobutu. Control was placed in the hands of a College of Commissioners, who served until February 9, 1961. b. *Participants*: Military forces, under the leadership of Mobutu. c. *Apparent Causes*: The breakdown of the constitutional regime. Kasavubu and Lumumba attempted to remove each other from office.
2. Unsuccessful Coup November 19, 1963	a. *Description*: General Mobutu and the chief of the security police Victor Nendaka were kidnapped by plotters, but later escaped. The *Comité National de Libération* (CNL) hoped to overthrow the Adoula regime and attempted to do so by kidnapping its most powerful supporters. b. *Participants*: The coup was organized by the CNL which was headed by C. Gbenye. c. *Apparent Causes*: Factionalism within the CNL prevented a clear statement of goals. Most, however, claimed to favor a Lumumbist type of radical nationalism.
3. Coup d'État November 25, 1965	a. *Description*: General Mobutu displaced Joseph Kasavubu and named himself president; Brigadier General Leonard Molamba became prime minister. b. *Participants*: General Joseph Mobutu, commander in chief of the *Armée National Congolaise*. c. *Apparent Causes*: Mobutu said that he wanted to put an end to the parliamentary power struggle between supporters of Kasavubu and Tshombe: the army was reputed to fear that Kasavubu was moving away from a pro-Western position and that he was willing to negotiate with Gbenye's CNL.

TABLE 7.8 Communal Instability

Event and Date	Characteristics
1. Civil War: Unsuccessful Secession 1960–1963	a. *Description*: Katanga province had been almost completely autonomous in the pre-independence period and local administration was largely in the hands of Belgian mining companies. During the disorder following the July mutiny of the Zairese army against their Belgian officers, the mineral-wealthy province of Katanga under Moise Tshombe attempted to secede from Zaire. Secession was eventually defeated by combined Zairese and United Nations forces. b. *Participants*: The major ethnic group in Katanga (the Lunda) fully supported secession and many minority groups also appeared supportive. Moïse Tshombe, the Katanga secessionist leader, had built up a solid following in Katanga prior to independence. Although he was not a traditional ruler himself, his following depended partly on the influence and claim of his father to such authority among the Lunda. European mercenaries participated in the leadership of the attempted secession. This was essentially a soldiers' war, not a civilian war. On the government side, 6,000 UN troops participated from five African countries and India. On the secessionist side Belgian, French, Rhodesian, and South African mercenaries participated. In all, an estimated 20,000 government troops and 12,000 secessionist troops were involved. Both sides had heavy casualties. c. *Apparent Causes*: The government feared the threat to national unity, loss of natural resources in Katanga, and predominance of foreign influence in Katanga. On the other hand, secessionists wanted to use local resources to develop Katanga and not the entire country; also there was a personality and ideological clash between Tshombe and Zairese leaders. At the ethnic level, Lunda masses feared the economic consequences of increasing immigration of Luba and other ethnic groups into the urban centers of Katanga.
2. Civil War 1967	a. *Description*: In August 1967, Colonel Mongax, who had been named by the exiled Moise Tshombe as his chief of staff in exile, proclaimed a "Government of Public Safety" in Bukavu, which had been occupied by a force of 300 white mercenaries and 2,000 former Katangese gendarmes led by Colonel "Black Jack" Schramme. The military operation was apparently directed initially from Angola. The Congolese Army recaptured Bukavu on November 5, and most of the insurgents fled to Rwanda. b. *Participants*: The mercenaries and Katangese insurgents were presumably in the pay of, and acting in the interests of Tshombe, the leader of the Kantanga secession, 1960–1963, at this time in exile in Europe. c. *Apparent Causes*: The insurgents aimed to depose the existing government of Zaire in the interests of M. Tshombe's political ambitions. Although they referred to widespread resistance to the Mobutu government and the Zaïre Army, there is no evidence that their support extended beyond Bukavu.
3. Ethnic Violence January and May, 1963.	a. *Description*: Two distinguishable outbreaks of inter-ethnic violence occurred in 1963 in areas in which the Katanga secession was practically at an end. In January, fighting between tribes in the Kasai province caused deaths estimated between 400 and 4000. In May, inter-ethnic violence in the African quarters of Elizabethville and Jadotville caused over 50 deaths. b. *Participants*: Lulua tribesmen in the Kakenge area north of Luluabourg were involved in the clashes in January, and the fighting in May was between Luba and Lunda tribesmen. c. *Apparent Causes*: The Kasai events were caused by rival claims to land on which a Belgian timber company operated a concession, and the Jadotville violence apparently started as the result of a rape involving two youths from different tribes.

TABLE 7.9   Mass Instability

Type of Event	Characteristics
1. Unsuccessful Revolt 1960–1966	a. *Description*: A series of revolts have disrupted political authority in Zaire from 1960 to 1966. After the dismissal of Lumumba by President Kasavubu in September 1960, the vice-prime minister, Antoine Gizenga, set up a rival government in Stanleyville in October. The revolt, led by Gizenga and other former ministers in Lumumba's cabinet (including Mulele as representative to Cairo), succeeded in gaining control of Orientale province, proclaimed a North Katanga province, controlled the Sankuru district of Kasai, and briefly took the Luluabourg garrison. Lumumba attempted to escape to Stanleyville in November 1960, but was captured, and murdered en route to Elizabethville. The Stanleyville revolt came to an end in January 1962, when Gizenga was arrested and sent to prison on the island of Bula-Bemba. From 1963 to 1966, a number of loosely coordinated revolts were organized in the northeast and southwest of Zaire. "Only superficially could these events be considered a single movement; on close examination, the rebellion dissolved into a series of revolts, strongly influenced by local contingencies, bound together by a shifting coalition of leaders, certain common grievances on the part of the population, and common external support." (Young, 1965) The Kwilu rebellion, led by Mulele, began in January 1964, when schools, government offices, a Portuguese palm oil factory, and a mission were destroyed. In May 1964, urban terrorism was launched in Leopoldville, but was easily contained by government forces. Also in May, on the eastern borders of Zaire, Soumialot coordinated a revolt in which two ANC battalions were defeated, and he established a provisional government in Albertville. Government forces had retaken this area by August 1964, but the revolt gained new impetus from the Simba organization of Olenga, which took Stanleyville in that month, and a Peoples' Republic of the Congo was proclaimed led by Gbenye. Over 20,000 people are estimated to have been killed in this period. The Stanleyville insurgency was ended by a United States airlift of Belgian paratroops into the city in advance of regular ANC units in November 1964. For two more years there was scattered, but violent, resistance to the Congolese army and, after November 1965, to its soldier-president Mobutu. An amnesty was announced in October 1966, when 1500 rebels were reported to have surrendered, and after which date the revolt was contained by government forces.
	b. *Participants*: In October 1963, the *Conseil National de Liberation* was formed by former colleagues of Lumumba and Gizenga. Never a cohesive leadership, the CNL represented factions of the MNC and PSA political parties in Zaire. In the field, the insurgents were tightly organized by Mulele and Olenga, and ideological training and programs synthesizing elements of nationalist, Marxist, and syncretic religious thought were developed by the movement. Ethnic identities seem to have been less distinctive of the insurgents than organizational affiliations to individual leaders (Mulelests), parties (PSA and MNC) and movements (Simba).
	c. *Apparent Causes*: The government feared the threat to national unity and also foreign interference (i.e., Chinese) in Zaire's internal affairs. The revolutionaries who identified themselves as "socialist" emphasized four issues: (1) Inequities in the distribution of the rewards of independence; (2) decline in material well-being of most Zairese since independence; (3) corrupt practices of the politicians and civil servants; and (4) the unpopularity of the *Armée Nationale Congolaise* (ANC).

SOURCES: (for #1 Unsuccessful Revolt): Renée C. Fox, Willy de Craemer, and Jean-Marie Ribeaucourt, " 'The Second Independence': A Case Study of the Kwilu Rebellion in the Congo," *Comparative Studies in Society and History*, 7 (October 1965), 78–109. Crawford Young, "Rebellion and the Congo," in *Power and Protest in Black Africa*, eds. Robert I. Rotberg and Ali A. Mazrui (New York: Oxford University Press, 1970), pp. 969–1011.

VII. Selected References

BIBLIOGRAPHY

Bustin, Edouard. *A Study Guide for Congo-Kinshasa.* Boston: Development Program, African Studies Center, Boston University, 1970.

GENERAL

Anstey, Roger. *King Leopold's Legacy: the Congo under Belgian Rule, 1908–1960.* London: Oxford University Press, issued under the auspices of the Institute of Race Relations, 1966.

Biebuyck, Daniel, and Mary Douglas. *Congo Tribes and Parties.* Royal Anthropological Institute Pamphlet no. 1. London: Royal Anthropological Institute, 1961.

Cornevan, Robert. *Histoire de Congo (Leopoldville).* Paris: Bergere-Levrault, 1963.

Merlier, M. *Le Congo de la colonisation belge à l'indépendence.* Paris: Maspero, 1962.

Slade, Ruth M. *The Belgian Congo,* 2nd ed. New York, Oxford University Press, 1961.

U.S. Department of the Army. *Area Handbook for the Congo,* 2nd ed. Pamphlet No. 550–67. Washington, D.C.: Government Printing Office, (1962), 1971.

Vansina, Jan. *Kingdoms of the Savannah.* Madison, Wisc.: University of Wisconsin Press, 1968.

POLITICAL

Bustin, Edouard. "Congo." In *Five African States: Responses to Diversity,* ed. G. M. Carter. Ithaca, N.Y.: Cornell University Press, 1963.

Bustin, Edouard. "The Quest for Political Stability in the Congo: Soldiers, Bureaucrats and Politicians." In *Africa: The Primacy of Politics,* ed. Herbert J. Spiro. New York: Random House, 1966.

Gerard-Libois, J. *Katanga Secession.* Madison: University of Wisconsin Press, 1966.

Hoskyns, Catherine. *The Congo since Independence: January 1960–December 1961.* London: Oxford University Press, 1965.

Lemarchand, René. "Congo." In *Political Parties and National Integration in Tropical Africa,* eds. J. S. Coleman and C. G. Rosberg. Los Angeles: University of California Press, 1964.

Lemarchand, René. *Political Awakening in the Congo.* Berkeley: University of California Press, 1964.

Lumumba, Patrice. *Congo, My Country.* New York: Praeger, 1962.

Weiss, Herbert. *Political Protest in the Congo: The Parti Solidaire Africain During the Independence Struggle.* Princeton, N.J.: Princeton University Press, 1967.

Willame, Jean-Claude. "Military Intervention in the Congo." *Africa Report,* 11 (December 1966): 41–45.

Young, Crawford. *Politics in the Congo: Decolonization and Independence.* Princeton, N.J.: Princeton University Press, 1965.

ECONOMIC

International Monetary Fund. "Democratic Republic of the Congo." In *Surveys of African Economies,* Vol. 4. Washington, D.C.: I.M.F., 1971.

Lacroix, Jean Louis. *Industrialisation au Congo: La transformation des structures économiques.* Paris: Mouton, 1967.

"La République Démocratique du Congo: Économie et Développement." *Marches Tropicaux et Mediterranées,* No. 1269 (March, 7, 1970): p. 195. [Special issue on Congo-Kinshasa's economic development.]

Miracle, Marvin P. *Agriculture in the Congo Basin.* Madison: University of Wisconsin Press, 1967.

SOCIAL

Andersson, Efraim. *Messianic Popular Movements in the Lower Congo.* Uppsala: Almqvist & Wiksells, 1958.

Ceulemans, P. "Introduction de l'influence de l'Islam au Congo." In *Islam in Tropical Africa,* ed. I. M. Lewis, pp. 174–192. London: Oxford University Press, 1966.

Mabusa, Basile. "Post-Independence Education in the Congo." *Africa Report,* 11 (June 1966): 24–28.

Polome, Edgar. "The Choice of Official Languages in the Democratic Republic of the Congo." In *Language Problems of Developing Nations,* eds. Joshua A. Fishman, Charles A. Ferguson and Jyotirindra Das Gupta, pp. 295–312. New York: John Wiley, 1968.

Pons, V. G. *Stanleyville: An African Urban Community under Belgian Administration.* London: Oxford University Press, 1969.

Reardon, Ruth Slade. "Catholics and Protestants in the Congo." In *Christianity in Tropical Africa*, ed. C. G. Bacta, pp. 83–100. London: Oxford University Press, 1968.

United Nations Economic Commission for Africa. "Leopoldville and Lagos: Comparative Study of Conditions in 1960." In *The City in Newly Developing Countries*, ed. Gerald Breese, pp. 436–460. Englewood Cliffs, N.J.: Prentice-Hall, 1969.

8. Dahomey

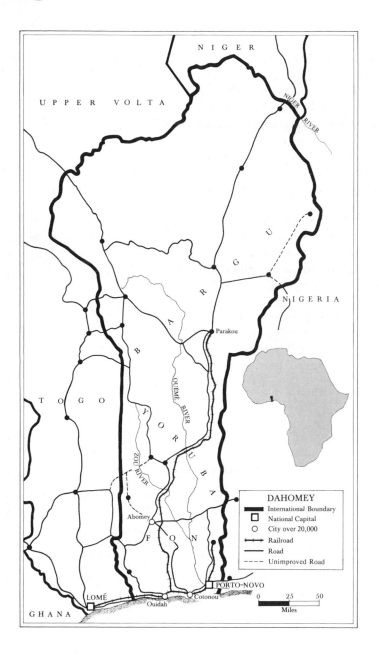

I. Basic Information

Date of Independence: August 1, 1960
Former Colonial Ruler: France
Change in Boundaries: Formerly part of the French West Africa Federation
Estimated Population (*1970*): 2,690,000

Area Size (*equivalent in U.S.*): 43,000 sq. mi. (Tennessee)
Date of Last Census: 1961
Major Exports 1967 as Percent of Total Exports: oil (palm, palmetto, and oil cake)—40 percent; cotton—11 percent; groundnuts—6 percent

II. Ethnic Patterns

The three major ethnic groupings we have selected for Dahomey are rather inclusive. The groups of the Fon type share a more or less common culture except for the coastal fishing groups (i.e., Mina and Gun). The Yoruba groups are linguistically similar, and these peoples also share a very similar life-style. The northern peoples, or Bargu cluster, are also culturally similar, although there is some justification for distinguishing the Kilinga and Somba from the Bariba inasmuch as they were indigenous people who acculturated to the intrusive Bariba. (Their general level of socio-economic development is also lower than that of the Bariba.) In addition to these peoples there are smaller populations of Sudanic peoples such as the Dendi and Tienga (2 percent), Gurmanche, and Boko. Also significant are the Fulani or Peul (2.4 percent) who are migratory and who live as a social segment within the Bariba kingdom. Note that the ethnic figures given by Thompson (in Carter, 1963, p. 201) yield different percentages: i.e., Fon—51 percent, Bargu (Bariba)—13 percent, Yoruba—9 percent.

TABLE 8.1 Ethnic Units Over 5 Percent of Country Population

Ethnic Unit	Estimated Ethnic Population 1967	Estimated Ethnic Percentage
a. Fon Type	1,395,000	*55.5%*
1. Fon (Dahomeans, Fonn)	(636,000)	(25.4%)
i. Fon, ii. Mahi, iii. Agonlinu		
2. Gun	(302,000)	(12%)
i. Gun, ii. Guemenu, iii. Tofinu		
3. Adja-Wachi	(272,000)	(10.8%)
4. Aizo	(113,000)	(4.5%)
5. Mina (Popo)	(71,000)	(2.8%)
b. Bargu Cluster (Bariba, Barba, Borgawa)	565,000	*22.5%*
1. Bariba	(309,000)	(12.3%)
2. Somba	(145,000)	(5.7%)
i. Berba, ii. Natimba, iii. Niendé, iv. Woaba, v. Soruba, vi. Dye		
3. Kilinga	(110,000)	(4.5%)
i. Dompago, ii. Pila-Pila (Yowa)		
c. Yoruba (Egba)	341,000	*13.6%*
1. Holli, 2. Dassa, 3. Ketu, 4. Manigri, 5. Itsha, 6. Chabe, 7. Anago		

SOURCE: *Enquête Démographique au Dahomey, 1961* (Paris: Ministère de la Coopération, 1964).

III. Language Patterns

The major language groups of Dahomey are Fon (Ewé), Bariba, and Yoruba. Estimates on Fon (Ewé) speakers as percent of total population are in relatively close agreement (Knappert, 50 percent; MacDougald, 51 percent; and Rustow, 58 percent). Our own estimate would be 60 percent. The Yoruba and Bariba language groups are in second and third place with approximately 13 and 12 per cent respectively. French is the official language of Dahomey.

TABLE 8.2 Language Patterns

1. Primacy		
1st language	Fon-Ewé	(60%)
2nd language	Yoruba	(13%)
2. Greenberg classification	Fon-Ewé	IA4
(all ethnic units in	Bargu	
country over 5%)	(Bariba)	IA3
	Yoruba	IA4
3. *Lingua franca*	Fon-Ewé	
4. Official language	French	

IV. Urban Patterns

Capital: Porto-Novo (founded early 18th century)
Largest City: Cotonou (founded 1868)
Dominant ethnicity/language of largest city (Cotonou)
  Major vernacular: Fon[1]

[1] Jan Knappert, "Language Problems of the New Nations of Africa," *African Quarterly*, 5 (1965): 95–105.

Major ethnic group: Fon[2]
Major ethnic group as percent of Cotonou's population:
  49 percent (1955)

[2] Professor Dov Ronen suggests that contemporary Cotonou has a largely mixed population, ethnically, and that French is widely spoken in the city.

TABLE 8.3 Growth of Capital and Largest City

Date	Porto-Novo	Cotonou
1920	20,000	4,000
1930	26,000	9,000
1940	28,000	7,000
1950	29,000	20,000
1960	60,000	70,000
1964	71,000	111,000

SOURCE: *Démographie Comparée.*

TABLE 8.4 Cities of 20,000 and Over

City	Size	Date
Cotonou	111,000	ca. 1966
Porto-Novo	71,000	ca. 1966
Abomey	29,000	ca. 1966
Ouidah	20,000	ca. 1966

SOURCE: *Africa 1968.* According to *Africa Contemporary Record 1968–69,* p. 477, Parakou had 25,000 population for an unspecified year, presumably ca. 1966; but *Africa 1969–70* gives a population of only 16,000 for Parakou.

V. Political Patterns

Figure 8.1 **Political Parties and Elections**

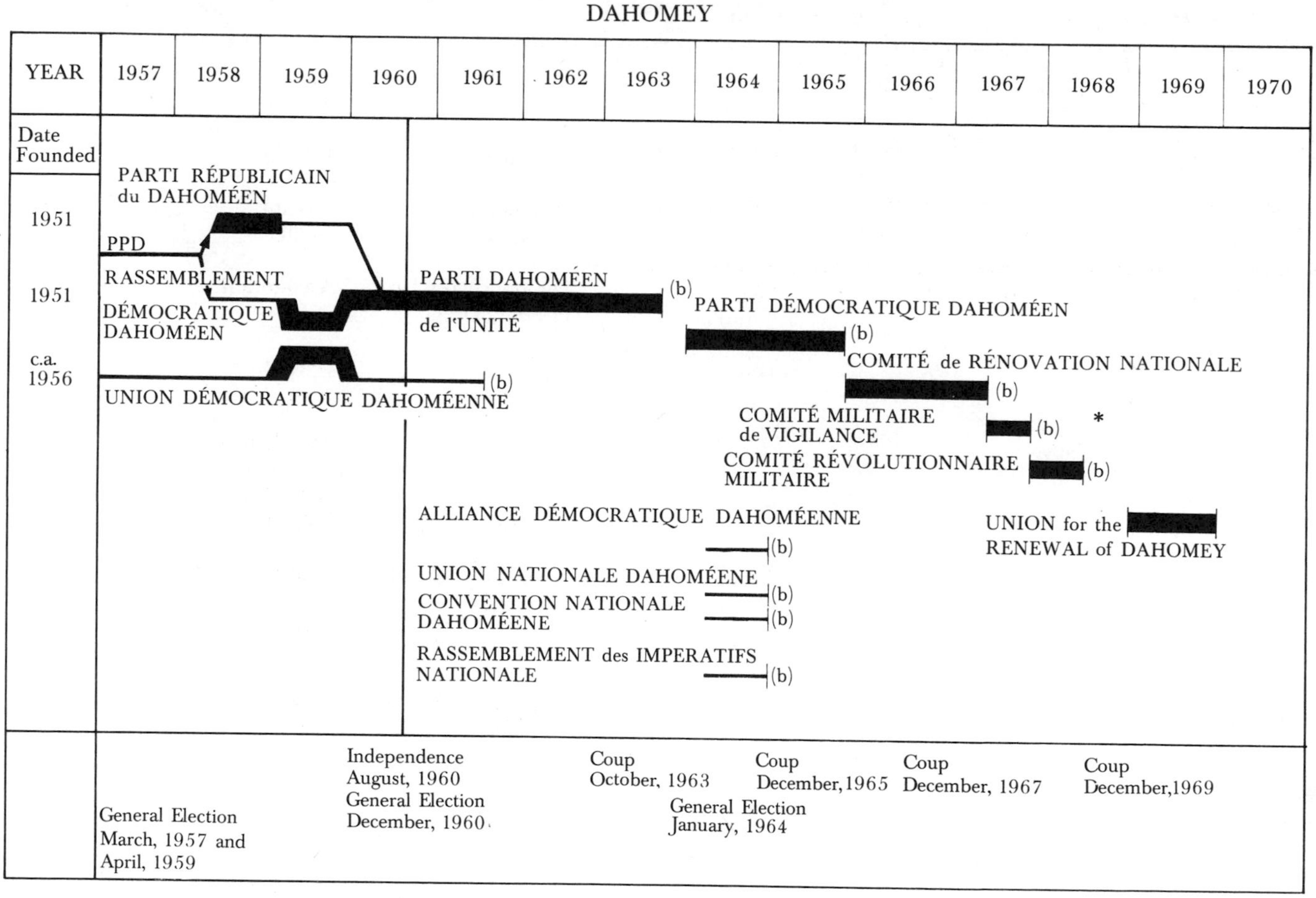

DAHOMEY

YEAR	1957	1958	1959	1960	1961	1962	1963	1964	1965	1966	1967	1968	1969	1970

Date Founded

1951 PARTI RÉPUBLICAIN du DAHOMÉEN

PPD

1951 RASSEMBLEMENT DÉMOCRATIQUE DAHOMÉEN — PARTI DAHOMÉEN de l'UNITÉ (b) PARTI DÉMOCRATIQUE DAHOMÉEN (b)

c.a. 1956 UNION DÉMOCRATIQUE DAHOMÉENNE (b)

COMITÉ de RÉNOVATION NATIONALE (b)

COMITÉ MILITAIRE de VIGILANCE (b) *

COMITÉ RÉVOLUTIONNAIRE MILITAIRE (b)

ALLIANCE DÉMOCRATIQUE DAHOMÉENNE (b)

UNION for the RENEWAL of DAHOMEY

UNION NATIONALE DAHOMÉENE (b)

CONVENTION NATIONALE DAHOMÉENE (b)

RASSEMBLEMENT des IMPERATIFS NATIONALE (b)

Independence August, 1960
General Election December, 1960

Coup October, 1963

Coup December, 1965

Coup December, 1967

Coup December,1969

General Election January, 1964

General Election March, 1957 and April, 1959

* The CRN, CMV and CRM were not political parties, but ruling military committees. They have been included to show shifts in the composition of the military rule.

A. Political Parties and Elections

Dahomey's complex political history revolves around three dominant civilian figures: S. M. Apithy, Hubert Maga, and Justin Ahomadegbe, and a general: Christophe Soglo. Sourou Migan Apithy supported by his _Parti Républicain du Dahoméen_ (PRD) was vice-premier* from 1957 until 1959. Hubert Maga then served as the first prime minister from 1959 until 1960 at the head of a coalition of his party, the _Rassemblement Démocratique Dahoméen_ (RDD), and the _Union Démocratique Dahoméenne_ (UDD). After independence in 1960, he and Apithy

* As a colony, Dahomey was ruled by a French Governor who held the title Premier.

formed a coalition party, the _Parti Dahoméen de l'Unité_ (PDU), and he served as president until the military coup of October 1963. With the coup, General Christophe Soglo banned the PDU and called for elections in January 1964. The newly formed _Parti Démocratique Dahoméen_ (PDD) came into power and, with Mr. Apithy as president and Justin Ahomadegbe (former leader of the UDD) as prime minister, governed until they were overthrown by General Soglo in November 1965. To replace the banned political parties, a committee—largely civilian—was then formed, the _Comité de Rénovation Nationale_ (CRN) with Gen. Soglo at its head. In April 1967 the CRN was replaced, by Gen. Soglo, by the _Comité Militaire de Vigilance_ (CMV), composed

TABLE 8.5   Heads of Government (Post Independence)

Name	Dates in Office	Age (1971)	Ethnicity	Education	Former Occupation
1. Hubert Maga (President)	1960– Oct. 1963	61	Fon (Gurma)	Technical-secondary (Dahomey)	Teacher, Civil Servant
2. Gen. Christophe Soglo (President)	Oct. 1963– Jan. 1964	62	Fon	In France	Soldier
3. Sourou Migan Apithy (President)	Jan. 1964– Nov. 1965	58	Fon (Gun)	Diploma Paris Inst. of Political Sci.	Accountant
and Dr. Justin Ahomadegbe (Vice President)		54	Fon	Dental	Dentist
4. Tahirou Congacou (President)	Nov.– Dec. 1965				President of National Assembly
5. Gen. Christophe Soglo (President)	1965– Dec. 1967	62	Fon	In France	Soldier
6. Lt. Col. Alphonse Alley (President)	Dec. 1967– Aug. 1968	41	Other (Basila) ("Northern")	Secondary School (Senegal)	Soldier
and Col. Maurice Kouandété (Prime Minister)		32			Soldier
7. Dr. Émile-Derin Zinsou (President)	Aug. 1968– Dec. 1969	53	Fon (Mina)	Graduate School, Paris	Doctor (M.D.)
8. Lt. Col. Paul Émile de Souza (Head of three-man directorate)	1969– May 1970				
9. Hubert Maga (President)	1970–	61	Fon (Gurma)	Technical-Secondary	Teacher, Civil Servant

of younger generation military. In December 1967 after a coup, Gen. Soglo and the CMV were replaced by a ruling military committee, the *Comité Révolutionnaire Militaire* (CRM) under the direction of Lt. Col. Alley, who became president, and Col. Maurice Kouandété, who eventually became prime minister. In June 1968, after a boycotted election, the military chose a civilian, Dr. Émile Derlin Zinsou to become president and form a government. This government was removed by the military in December 1969. The presidential election held in March 1970 had to be suspended before its completion owing to violence.

B. Political Leadership

The government of Dahomey has changed a great deal since independence. Several coups d'etat have introduced change from civilian to military rule, and vice versa. The civilian governments replaced by coups in 1963 and 1965 were characterized by fairly marked changes in the membership of cabinets, although patterns of recruitment to executive office appear to have remained similar throughout the

post-independence period, with the continued predominance of the Fon. Twice the leadership was sufficiently shared to justify the inclusion of two leaders as "heads of government." In both instances the situations contributed to political instability. Shortly after the most recent coup (December 1969), the establishment of a three–man directorate was announced whose President was Paul Émile de Souza and whose other members were Col. Maurice Kouandété and Lt. Col. Benoit Sinzogan. In May 1970 civilian rule was re-established. President Maga heads a three-man presidential commission, with the presidency rotating every two years.

TABLE 8.6 Cabinet Membership: Distribution by Ethnic Unit*

Ethnicity*	Independence Cabinet	Immediate Pre-Coup Cabinet	1967 Cabinet
1. Fon (56%)	70%	92%	73%
2. Bargu (25)	20	8.3	18
3. Yoruba (14)	10	0	9.1
4. Others (8)	0	0	0
N =	12	14	12

* Ethnic units arranged in rank order of size within country with the unit's percent of national population in parentheses.

VI. National Integration and Stability

The regionalism of Dahomey has contributed to political instability at the elite level; four coups have occurred since independence. The three significant regions in Dahomey are the north, the southeast, and the southwest. Within this framework, the three leading politicians came to represent each of the three regions respectively: Maga (from Parakou), Apithy (from Porto-Novo) and Ahoma-degbe (from Abomey). The city of Cotonou stands apart from such regionalism, but has come to be identified with trade union and commercial interests. Military intervention under Soglo was undertaken as a stop-gap measure since, in most cases, power was returned voluntarily to civilians. The army suffers from regional and generational differences, however.

TABLE 8.7 Elite Instability

Event and Date	Characteristics
1. Coup d'Etat October 28, 1963	a. *Description*: Union and worker dissatisfaction with the government led to violent demonstrations in Parakou and Porto-Novo. Despite the presence of troops and a curfew, the demonstrations continued for several days. Various civilian factions failed to pacify the demonstrators and on October 28, Colonel Christophe Soglo intervened. Popular approval and support for the military facilitated the takeover. On October 20, a provisional government was formed with Soglo as president, and the three major civilian leaders (Apithy, Ahomadegbe, and Maga) as the only members of his cabinet.

TABLE 8.7 Elite Instability *(cont.)*

Event and Date	*Characteristics*

b. *Participants*: Events preceding the coup were organized by labor unions and supported by many southerners, who accused President Maga (a northerner) of regional discrimination. The coup was carried out without violence by members of the military and their commander, Colonel Soglo.

c. *Apparent Causes*: Worker dissatisfaction with government activity and southern antipathy for the government due to alleged discrimination by the former president seem to have been the major causes. The unions had been disturbed over the 10 percent cut in service wages. Soglo stated that the coup "preserved national unity and cohesion." Military spokesmen also cited other reasons for the coup: the high style of living of those in government (e.g., a 3.5 million dollar presidential palace; an unnecessary increase in the number of ministers; and various anti-democratic measures by the government). The military leaders returned power to civilians (Apithy and Ahomadegbe) through elections, January 1964.

2. Coup d'Etat
December 22, 1965

a. *Description*: On the evening of November 27, 1965, there were violent demonstrations in Porto-Novo in support of President Apithy, whose resignation was demanded by "l'Assemble du Peuple," a group favoring Vice-President Ahomadegbe. On November 29, General Soglo obtained the resignation of both men, and in accordance with the constitution, Tahirou Congacou (president of the National Assembly) was appointed to head a civilian provisional government. A political impasse developed and Soglo once again stepped into the breach by dismissing the government, suspending the constitution, banning all political parties, and naming himself head of state.

b. *Participants*: General Soglo, the army chief of staff, and military elements.

c. *Apparent Causes*: According to official sources, "Before the spectacle of the struggling political leaders, and . . . after having seen that their replacements did not extinguish those passions, General Soglo decided to suspend the constitution, dissolve the National Assembly, and political parties." The conflicts between the head of state and the head of government were a big factor.

3. Coup d'Etat
December 17, 1967

a. *Description*: Two commando units, led by Major Kerakou and Colonel Kouandété surrounded the residences of General Soglo, Colonel Alley, Lieutenant Colonel Aho, and Major Sinzogan. After four days, Army Chief of Staff Alley was asked to become head of state, apparently because he was satisfactory to the labor unions and to France, and had not been identified with any particular region. The cabinet eventually named consisted of an even number of northerners and southerners.

b. *Participants*: Major Kerakou and Colonel Kouandété were northerners but they received support from many junior officers of southern origins. All the military men involved were younger than their predecessors.

c. *Apparent Causes*: According to official sources, "Weakness and deficiency shown by an increasingly condemned leader"; the fact that decisions were made by a "family circle"; and the feeling that the army was threatened by internal cleavage from which "we could not retrace our steps." Northern elements in the army also complained that Soglo had given in too often to trade-union demands.

4. Coup d'Etat
December 10, 1969

a. *Description*: President Émile-Derin Zinsou was seized by elements of the army and the military assumed control of the government. A three-man directorate, consisting of Lt. Col. Paul Émile de Souza, who was given the presidency of the directorate, Lt. Col. Benoit Sinzogan, and Col. Maurice Kouandété, was chosen to hold power.

b. *Participants*: The coup was engineered by Kouandété, a senior officer and army chief of staff, and by younger officers of the "third generation."

c. *Apparent Cause*: Internal conflict in the army between the followers of Lt. Col. Alphonse Alley and Kouandété, following supposed attacks on Kouandété. Alley was sentenced to jail for one of these attacks. These apparently led Kouandété to suspect President Zinsou of being involved in a plot to limit his power.

SOURCES: René Lemarchand, "Dahomey: Coup within a Coup," *Africa Report*, 13 (June 1968): 46–54. W. A. F. Skurnik, "Political Instability and Military Intervention in Dahomey and Upper Volta" in *Soldier and State in Africa*, ed. Claude Welch (Evanston, Ill.: Northwestern University Press, 1970). Claude Garin, "Dahomey: Another Coup," *Africa Report*, 15 (January 1970): 3–4.

TABLE 8.8 Communal Instability

Event and Date	Characteristics
1. Ethnic Violence March 13, 1964	a. *Description*: In the town of Parakou, hometown of deposed President Maga, northern ethnic groups attacked local southerners. Several persons were killed and homes were burned. The army put down the dissidents. b. *Participants*: Chabi Mama, secretary general of Maga's *Parti Dahoméen de l'Unité* was arrested and sentenced to prison. c. *Apparent Cause*: Northern resentment at southern treatment of their political leader.

SOURCE: René Lemarchand, "Dahomey: Coup within a Coup" *Africa Report*, 13 (June 1968): 46–54.

VII. Selected References

GENERAL

Cornevan, Robert. *Histoire du Dahomey*. Paris: Bergere-Levrault, 1962.

Thompson, Virginia, and Richard Adloff. *French West Africa*, pp. 139–145. Stanford, Cal.: Stanford University Press, 1957.

POLITICAL

Glélé, Maurice-A. *Naissance d'un état noir*. Paris: Librairie Générale de Droit, 1969. [Dahomey through the coup of December 1965.]

de Lusignan, Guy. *French-Speaking Africa since Independence*, pp. 159–169. London: Pall Mall Press, 1969.

Lemarchand, René. "Dahomey: Coup Within a Coup." *Africa Report*, 13 (June 1968): 46–54.

LeVine, Victor T. "The Coups in Upper Volta, Dahomey and the Central African Republic." In *Power and Protest in Black Africa*, eds. Robert I. Rotberg and Ali A. Mazrui, pp. 1035–1071. New York: Oxford University Press, 1970.

Ronen, Dov. "The Two Dahomeys." *Africa Report*, 13 (June 1968): 55–56.

Thompson, Virginia. "Dahomey." In *Five African States: Responses to Diversity*, ed. G. M. Carter. Ithaca, N.Y.: Cornell University Press, 1963.

ECONOMIC

International Monetary Fund. "Dahomey." In *Surveys of African Economies*, Vol. 3. Washington, D.C.: I.M.F., 1970.

Serreau, Jean. *Le Développement à la base au Dahomey et au Sénégal*. Paris: Librairie Générale de Droit et de Jurisprudence, 1966.

SOCIAL

Tardits, Claude. *Porto Novo: Les nouvelles générations africaines entre leur traditions et l'Occident*. Paris and The Hague: Mouton, 1958.

9. Ethiopia

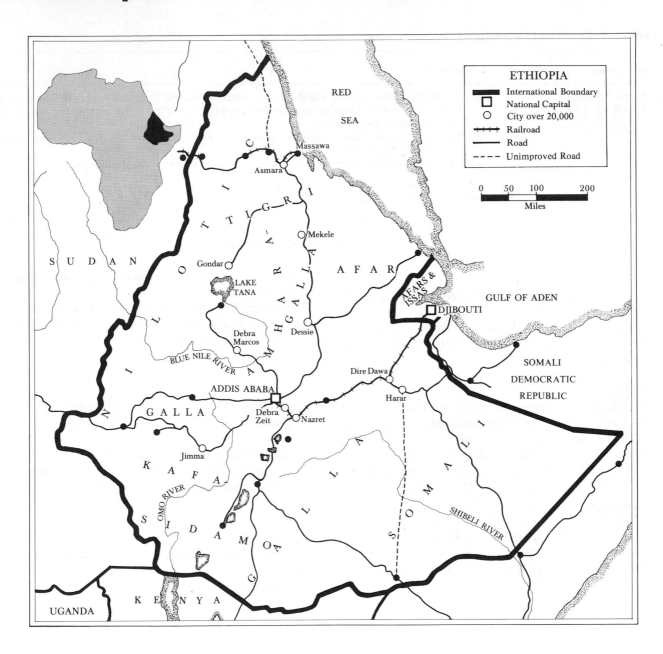

I. Basic Information

Date of Independence: Ancient kingdom
Former Colonial Ruler: None
Change in Boundaries: Eritrea added in 1952
Former Name: Both Ethiopia and Abyssinia are ancient names for the nation
Estimated Population (1970): 25,050,000

Area Size (equivalent in U.S.): 457,000 sq. mi. (Texas and Montana)
Date of Last Census: None
Major Exports 1968 as Percent of Total Exports: coffee—57 percent; hides and skins—9 percent; vegetables—9 percent

II. Ethnic Patterns

The ethnic categories for Ethiopia are on mixed levels. In each case the groups comprising the categories are culturally and linguistically related. The Galla, Somali, and Afar are also identity groups, as are the Amhara-Tigre (excluding the related Gurage and Harari). It should be noted that the Galla, Somali, and Afar have considerable cultural and linguistic similarities and can be subsumed under a more general category, Eastern Cushitic. In addition to these major groups there are populations of Agans (75,000), Saho-speaking peoples of Eritrea (43,000—1943 estimate), and the nomadic Beni-Amer.

TABLE 9.1 Ethnic Units Over 5 Percent of Country Population

Ethnic Unit	Estimated Ethnic Population 1967	Estimated Ethnic Percentage
a. Galla (Oromo)	9,400,000	40%
1. Borana, 2. Jima, 3. Kosa, 4. Gera, 5. Guma, 6. Arushi, 7. Walaga, 8. Wallo, 9. Yaju, 10. Raya		
b. Amhara-Tigre (Abyssinian)	7,030,000	30%
1. Amhara, 2. Tigre, Related groups: 3. Gurage, 4. Harari		
c. Kafa-Sidamo Type	2,100,000	9%
1. Bako, 2. Gibe, 3. Gimira, 4. Janjero, 5. Kafa, 6. Kambatta, 7. K'onso, 8. Maji, 9. Ometo, 10. Sidamo		
d. Somali	1,400,000	6%
e. Nilotic Cluster	1,400,000	6%
1. K'unama and Barya 2. Beni-Sciangul i. Guma, ii. Berta, iii. Koma, iv. Mao 3. Annuak		
f. Afar (Danakil)	1,100,000	5%

SOURCE: G. F. Lipsky, *Ethiopia: Its People, Its Society, Its Culture* (New Haven, Conn.: HRAF Press, 1962), pp. 34–51; modified according to suggestions from Professor Asmaron Legesse, Boston University.

III. Language Patterns

All the major languages of Ethiopia belong to the Afro-Asiatic language family. The two main substocks in Ethiopia are (1) Semitic (e.g., Amharic, Tigrinya, Tigre, Gurage, Harari); (2) Cushitic (e.g., Gallinya, Beja, Somali, Afar, Agau). The two major languages of Ethiopia are Amharic and Gallinya. Amharic is closely related to the ancient language of the Kingdom of Axum—called Ge'ez—which still serves as the liturgical language of the Ethiopian Coptic Church. Amharic itself has few dialectical variations. Gallinya, by contrast, has a number of dialects: (1) Macha (spoken by ethnic groups such as the Macha, Kaffas, Kasas, and Gibes—all in the west and southwest); (2) Tulama (the dialect of Shoa); (3) Eastern Gallinya (spoken by Galla groups in Harar and Arusi); (4) Southern Gallinya (spoken by the Borana). An extensive literature exists in Amharic and Tigrinya. Because of the increased use of Amharic as a *lingua franca* it is difficult to estimate its actual distribution. Kloss (1968) puts the figure at 32 percent; Demoz (1968) puts the figure at 35 percent (of whom one-third are non-Amharic peoples); Rustow puts the figure at 49 percent; whereas Knappert goes as high as 71 percent. Part of the discrepancy is ambiguity over the level, or standard, of proficiency. Likewise, with regard to Gallinya, Rustow puts the figure at 23 percent, while Kloss puts it at 44 percent. In assessing these and other sources, we have put the Amharic-speaking population at 40 percent and the Gallinya-speaking population at approximately 50 percent.

Amharic (or Amharinya) is the official language, and English is the primary foreign language. Amharic is used in government and trade throughout most of Ethiopia, although Tigrinya (and Arabic) is used in government and trade in Eritrea. English has recently been replaced by Amharic as the medium of instruction through the sixth grade, and it is likely that Amharic will soon be used in secondary schools as well. Tigrinya is the only vernacular other than Amharic which has a script, although Gallinya and Tigre have been written in the Ethiopic script. At present, the only vernacular (other than Amharic) used in radio broadcasting is the Somali language. On the other hand, Radio Mogadiscio (Somalia) broadcasts into Ethiopia in Gallinya.

TABLE 9.2 Language Patterns

1. Primacy		
1st language	Amharic	(40%)
2nd language	Gallinya	(50%)
2. Greenberg classification	Galla	IIID3
(all ethnic units in	Amhara-Tigre	IIIA
country over 5%)	Kafa-Sidamo	IIID3
	Somali	IIID3
	Nilotic	IIIE3
	Afar	IIID3
3. *Lingua francas*	Amharic, Gallinya, Tigrinya	
4. Official language	Amharic	

SOURCES: Abraham Demoz, "Amharic for Modern Use," *Journal of the Faculty of Education*, Haile Selassie University (1968), pp. 15–20. Heinz Kloss, "Notes Concerning a Language-Nation Typology," in *Language Problems of Developing Nations*, eds. Joshua Fishman, Charles Ferguson, and Jyotirindra Das Gupta (New York: John Wiley, 1968), pp. 69–88.

IV. Urban Patterns

Capital/largest city: Addis Ababa (founded 1886)
Dominant ethnicity/language of capital
  Major vernacular: Amharic[1]
  Major ethnic group: Galla[2]
  Major ethnic group as percent of capital's population: 53 percent (1952)

TABLE 9.3 Growth of Capital/Largest City

Date	Addis Ababa
1920	ca. 50,000
1930	ca. 70,000
1940	ca. 150,000
1950	ca. 300,000
1966	640,000

SOURCE: Various editions of the *Statesman's Yearbook*.

TABLE 9.4 Cities of 20,000 and Over*

City	Size	Date
Addis Ababa	644,000	1966
Asmara	179,000	1965
Dire-Dawa	51,000	1965
Harar	43,000	1965
Dessie	41,000	1965
Gondar	31,000	1965
Jimma	31,000	ca. 1965
Nazret	28,000	1965
Mekele	23,000	1965
Debra Zeit	22,000	1965
Debra Marcos	22,000	1965

* Current populations for Ethiopian cities, other than Addis Ababa, were unavailable until the Ethiopian government began a series of sample surveys aimed at establishing the *de facto* civil population of all cities over 5,000. In 1965 21 towns with populations of over 10,000 were covered and Addis Ababa was surveyed in 1966. For a brief report of these surveys see *Sample Surveys of Current Interest*, Statistical Papers Series C, No. 12 (New York: United Nations, 1967), pp. 80–84. Population for Jimma is taken from *Africa 1968*.

V. Political Patterns

A. Political Parties and Elections

There are no political parties in Ethiopia. Political pressures are expressed through factions within and without the government which are manipulated by

[1] Jan Knappert, "Language Problems of the New Nations of Africa," *African Quarterly*, 5 (1965), 95–105.
[2] *African Urban Notes*, May 1967.

the Emperor. Popular elections to the Ethiopian Chamber of Deputies were introduced in an Electoral Law Proclamation of 1956, and elections have been held every four years since 1957.

B. Political Leadership

The government of Ethiopia is difficult to compare

to the governments of other African countries. The personal rule of the Emperor, Haile Selassie, has changed little for many years, although the prominence of different formal agencies—the Ministry of the Pen, His Imperial Majesty's Private Cabinet, the Crown Council, and the Council of Ministers—has changed over time. The Council of Ministers has been particularly important since the attempted coup d'etat in 1960. In 1966, the Prime Minister was given the authority to "propose" ministerial appointments, and the Council obtained the ambiguous power to make decisions which do not effect "matters of policy." With the addition of two new portfolios in 1966, the membership of the Council stood at nineteen; office-holders have always been overwhelmingly representative of the Amhara people.

TABLE 9.5   Head of Government

Name	Dates in Office	Age (1971)	Ethnicity	Education
His Imperial Majesty Haile Selassie I (Emperor)	1930–	80	Amhara-Tigre (Amhara)	Private tutors

TABLE 9.6   Cabinet Membership: Distribution by Ethnic Unit*

Ethnicity*	Independence Cabinet†	1967 Cabinet†
1. Galla (40%)	13%	8.7%
2. Amhara-Tigre (30)	88	91
3. Kafa-Sidamo (9)	9	0
4. Somali (6)	0	0
5. Nilotic (6)	0	0
6. Afar (5)	0	0
7. Other (4)	0	0
N =	8	23

* Ethnic units arranged in rank order of size within country with the unit's percent of national population in parentheses.

† The "Cabinet" is taken to be the Council of Ministers and "Independence" is treated for comparable purposes as 1960.

VI. National Integration and Stability

The ancient empire of Ethiopia is ruled by a monarchy which traces its descent from King Solomon. The Amhara people, who have produced the Emperor, are only one of several major ethnic groups in Ethiopia, however. Furthermore, the fact that the Amhara are Christian, and several of the other major groups (e.g., Galla and Somali) are predominantly Muslim has been a potential source of cleavage for years. Yet, until the United Nations arranged the merger of Eritrea with Ethiopia (1952) and the birth of the Somali Republic (early 1960s), there was relatively little communal instability in Ethiopia. In this Handbook, we have coded an attempted secession movement in Eritrea and an irredentist movement of Somalis.

Successful elite coups (drawing on members of the royal family) have been a part of Ethiopian history. In modern times, the perseverance of the Emperor,

Haile Selassie I, has been legendary. There was one unsuccessful coup attempt in 1960. The Ethiopian press has reported several coup "plots" since this time, but details of their magnitude are unavailable. In recent years opposition to Haile Selassie from the university students has grown to major proportions.

In 1969 the university and secondary-school students boycotted classes and the university was closed. In December 1969 a number of university students were killed in clashes with the police in Addis Ababa.

TABLE 9.7   Elite Instability

Event and Date	Characteristics
1. Unsuccessful Coup December 14–17, 1960	a. *Description*: Brigadier-General Mengistu Neway, Commander of the Imperial Body Guard, and his brother Germame Neway, governor of Jijiga, were the organizers of the coup. The Emperor was out of the country at the time, but returned, and—with the aid of loyal army and air force troops—ousted the rebels after a three-day battle. b. *Participants*: Imperial Body Guard, plus various younger elements in the army, government, and police. c. *Apparent Causes*: According to the Revolutionary Proclamation which was drawn up by the leaders of the coup and proclaimed over the national radio, apparently by the Crown Prince, "There has been no progress. . . . A few self-centered persons . . . have chosen to indulge in selfishness and nepotism. The Ethiopia people hope to be freed from . . . ignorance, illiteracy and poverty." The proclamation promised land redistribution.

SOURCES: Richard Greenfield, *Ethiopia* (New York: Praeger, 1965), pp. 337–452. See also Christopher Clapham, "The Ethiopian Coup d'État of December 1960," *Journal of Modern African Studies*, 6 (1968): 495–508.

TABLE 9.8   Communal Instability

Event and Date	Characteristics
1. Civil War and Unsuccessful Secession ca. 1955 to present	a. *Description*: Eritrea was an Italian colony until 1941; a British-administered territory (1941–1952); a semi-autonomous state federated with Ethiopia (1952–1962); and a province of Ethiopia (1962–present). An Eritrean Secessionist Movement started a few years after the federation of Eritrea with Ethiopia in 1952 and has continued in sporadic form. Although the secessionist movement has not yet become an all-out campaign on the scale of the Katanga or the Biafra civil wars, widespread disturbances have occurred in the northern regions. In 1962 the Ethiopian government abolished the federal status of Eritrea. From this point (1962), Eritrea has been a province under the centralized administration of the Ethiopian government. The *Eritrean Liberation Front* (ELF) has received help from a number of Arab states including Syria, and periodically releases press dispatches of clashes between the ELF and the Ethiopian government. (The latter government usually contests the substance of the ELF news reports.) ELF tactics have included the hijacking of an Ethiopian commercial airliner in September 1969. b. *Participants*: Initially, mainly the Muslim ethnic groups in Eritrea (e.g. Bani Amer, Danakil). Now many Christians are to be found among the ELF and at least one of the top leaders is a Tigre Christian. c. *Apparent Causes*: From the government's point of view, secession poses a threat to national unity and is interpreted as foreign (Arab) interference in Ethiopian internal affairs. Eritrea also offers Ethiopia two important seaports at Massawa and Assab. The secessionists, on the other hand, are concerned with denial of self-determination for Eritreans, and domination of Muslims by Christians. Many felt that the Federation was a failure because Eritrea was in fact governed just like another province.

TABLE 9.8 Communal Instability *(cont.)*

Event and Date	Characteristics
2. Irredentism 1960–present	a. *Description*: Somali ethnic segments in Ethiopia, and Somali troops and "raiders" (*shifta*) long have been engaged in intermittent clashes with Ethiopian military forces. Since 1960 this situation has become a widely publicized issue between the two countries. Conservative estimates put the total number killed in the first five years of fighting at 1,300. A cease fire was agreed upon in July 1964, and relative peace prevailed until March 1965. Hostilities were renewed, and in the next six months of fighting 250 persons were killed. The efforts of the Organization for African Unity were successful at quelling any major activity during 1966–67, and the Somali government prior to the 1969 Somalia coup was apparently interested in a peaceful settlement. As of December 1969 it was not clear what the position of the new military regime in Somalia will be. b. *Participants*: The three parties to the dispute include the Ethiopian government, the Somali government, and the Somali pastoralists inside Ethiopia. The Somali irredentist groups have strong kinship and religious (Islamic) ties with Somalia. There are no predominant leaders of the Somali irredentist movement, although the civilian governments of Somalia have been deeply committed to reunification. c. *Apparent Causes*: Ethiopia contends that the border with Somalia has been internationally recognized since 1897, and also claims that self-determination by Somalis in Ethiopia would be contrary to the OAU resolution of 1964. Somalis claim the border is not valid in law and that on ethnic, cultural, and historical grounds all Somalis should be incorporated into a nation-state.

VII. Selected References

BIBLIOGRAPHY

Sommer, John. *A Study Guide for Ethiopia.* Boston: Development Program, African Studies Center, Boston University, forthcoming.

GENERAL

Buxton, D. R. *The Abyssinians.* New York: Praeger, 1970.

Hess, Robert. *Ethiopia: The Modernization of Autocracy.* Ithaca, N.Y.: Cornell University Press, 1970.

Lipsky, George. *Ethiopia.* New Haven, Conn.: HRAF Press, 1962.

Luther, Ernest W. *Ethiopia Today.* London: Oxford University Press, 1958.

Ullendorff. E. *The Ethiopians.* London: Oxford University Press, 1960.

U.S. Department of the Army. *Area Handbook for Ethiopia.* 2nd ed. Pamphlet No. 550–28. Washington, D.C.: Government Printing Office, 1964.

POLITICAL

Greenfield, Richard. *Ethiopia: A New Political History.* New York: Praeger, 1965.

Hess, Robert. "Ethiopia." In *National Unity and Regionalism in Eight African States,* ed. G. M. Carter. Ithaca, N.Y.: Cornell University Press, 1966.

Levine, Donald. "Class Consciousness and Class Solidarity in the New Ethiopia Elites." In *The New Elites of Tropical Africa,* ed. P. Lloyd, pp. 212–327. London: Oxford University Press, 1966.

Markakis, John, and Asmelash Beyene. "Representative Institutions in Ethiopia." *Journal of Modern African Studies,* 5 (1967): 193–219.

Perham, Margery. *The Government of Ethiopia.* London: Faber, 1948.

ECONOMIC

Bequele, A., and E. Chole. *A Profile of the Ethiopian Economy.* Nairobi: Oxford University Press, 1969.

Ginzberg, Eli, and Herbert A. Smith. *Manpower Strategy for Developing Countries: Lessons from Ethiopia.* New York: Columbia University Press, 1967.

U.S. Department of Agriculture, Economic Research Service, Foreign Regional Analysis Division. *A Survey of Agriculture in Ethiopia.* ERS-Foreign 254. Washington, D.C.: Government Printing Office, 1969.

SOCIAL

Comhaire, Jean. "Urban Growth in Relation to Ethiopian Development." *Cultures et Developpement,* 1 (1968): 25–40.

Derus, Jacques. "Addis Ababa—Genese d'un Capitale Imperiale." *Revue Belge de Geographie,* 88 (1965): 283–314.

Levine, Donald. *Wax and Gold: Tradition and Innovation in Ethiopian Culture.* Chicago: University of Chicago Press, 1966.

Pankhurst, Richard. "The Foundation and Growth of Addis Ababa." *The Ethiopian Observer,* 6 (1962): 33–61.

Powne, Michael. *Ethiopian Music: An Introduction.* London: Oxford University Press, 1968.

Trimingham, John S. *Islam in Ethiopia.* London: Oxford University Press, 1952.

Ullendorff, Edward. *The Semitic Languages of Ethiopia: A Comparative Phonology.* London: Taylor's (Foreign) Press, 1955.

10. Gabon

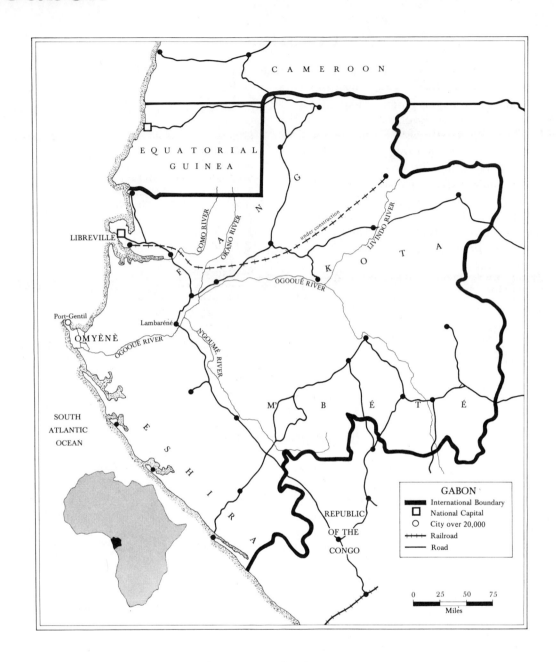

I. Basic Information

Date of Independence: August 17, 1960

Former Colonial Ruler: France

Change in Boundaries: Formerly part of French Equatorial Africa

Estimated population (1970): 500,000

Area Size (equivalent in U.S.): 703,000 sq. mi. (Colorado)

Date of Last Census: 1960–61 (sample survey)

Major Exports 1968 as Percent of Total Exports: wood and wood products—35 percent; petroleum—34 percent; manganese—21 percent

241

II. Ethnic Patterns

The Gabonese ethnic groups are clustered at a fairly low level of abstraction. All have essentially similar levels of socio-economic development. The major cultural variation is that the southern groups are transitional between the patrilineal belt to the north and the matrilineal belt of the Congo region. Each of the ethnic clusters is locally recognized as an identity group to some extent. In addition to the major units, there are smaller populations of Bakèlè (4 percent), Okandé (4 percent: Bapindji, Mitsogo, Pové, Bassimba, Okandé, Baveya), Séké (4 percent: Séké and Benga), and Pygmies.

TABLE 10.1 Ethnic Units Over 5 Percent of Country Population

Ethnic Unit	Estimated Ethnic Population 1967	Estimated Ethnic Percentage
a. Fang (Fan, Fanwe, Mfang, Mpangwe)	141,000	30%
1. Fang, 2. Ntoumou, 3. Mvaé, 4. Okak		
b. Eshira Type (Shira, Echira)	94,000	20%
1. Bapounou, 2, Eshira, 3. Ngowé 4. Bavarma, 5. Bavoungou, 6. Baloumbou, 7. Babuissi, 8. Massango		
c. M'Bété Type (M'Béti)	71,000	15%
1. Bandjabi, 2. Badouma, 3. Ambamba, 4. Bambana, 5. Mindoumou, 6. Bakaniqui, 7. Batsangui, 8. Bawandji.		
d. Kota Type (Bakota, Bandjambi, Ikota)	61,000	13%
1. Bakota, 2. Mahongwe, 3. Shake, 4. Dambomo, 5. Shamaye, 6. Mindassa, 7. Voumbou, 8. Mahouin		
e. Omyènè Type	23,000	5%
1. Mpongwe, 2. Adyumba, 3. Enenga, 4. Galoa, 5. Orungou, 6. Nkomi		

SOURCES: Brian Weinstein, *Nation Building on the Ogooué* (Cambridge: Massachusetts Institute of Technology Press, 1966), pp. 30–33. Census reported in *Europa Yearbook 1967*, p. 462.

III. Language Patterns

All of the languages of Gabon are Bantu. Fang is the predominant language and ethnic group. It is increasing both as an ethnic group (due to processes of assimilation and government support), and as a *lingua franca*. Knappert estimates the Fang-speaking population at 40 percent. Rustow suggests, however, that those who speak Fang as a first language are only 30 percent. Our own estimate of Fang-speakers is 50 percent. We consider the second largest group to be Eshira (20 percent), although this language seems confined to those who use it as a first language. French continues as the official language.

TABLE 10.2 Language Patterns

1. Primacy		
1st language	Fang	(50%)
2nd language	Eshira	(20%)
2. Greenberg classification	Fang	IA5
(all ethnic units in	Eshira	IA5
country over 5%)	M'Bété	IA5
	Kota	IA5
	Omyènè	IA5
3. *Lingua franca*	Fang	
4. Official language	French	

IV. Urban Patterns

Capital/largest city: Libreville (founded 1843)
Dominant ethnicity/language of capital
  Major vernacular: Fang[1]

[1] Jan Knappert, "Language Problems of the New Nations of Africa," *Africa Quarterly*, 5 (1965): 95–105.

Major ethnic group: Fang[2]
Major ethnic group as percent of capital's population:
  30 percent (1960–61)

[2] Report of 1960–61 survey of Libreville.

TABLE 10.3   Growth of Capital/Largest City

Date	Libreville
1920	3,000
1930	7,000
1940	11,000
1950	13,000
1960	28,000
1967	57,000 UA

SOURCE: *Démographie Comparée.*

TABLE 10.4   Cities of 20,000 and Over

City	Size	Date
Libreville[a]	57,000 UA	1967
Port-Gentil[b]	30,000	ca. 1966

SOURCES:
[a] *UN Demographic Yearbook 1967.* Libreville is a port as well as the capital of Gabon.
[b] *Africa 1968.*

V. Political Patterns

Figure 10.1 **Political Parties and Elections**

GABON

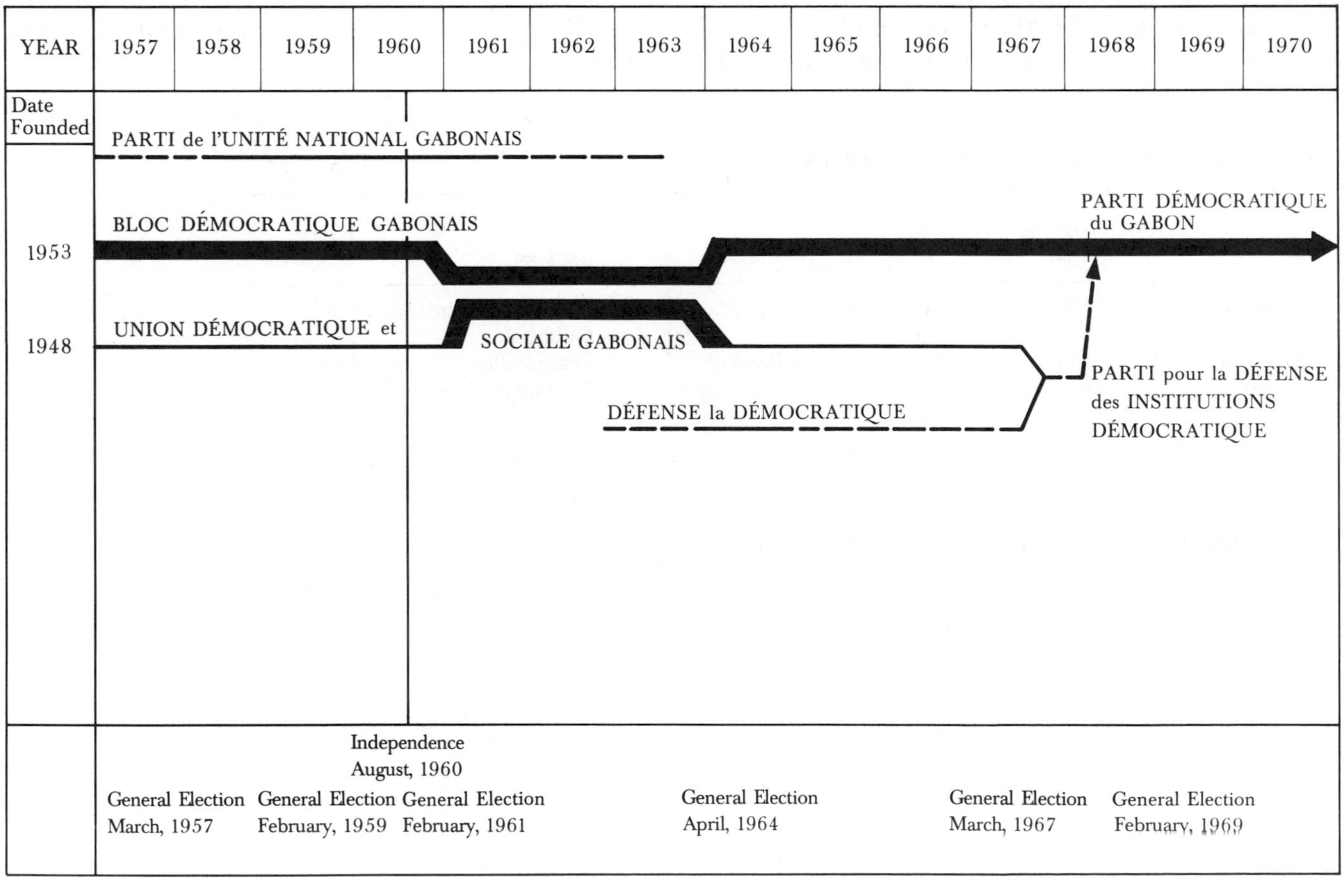

| YEAR | 1957 | 1958 | 1959 | 1960 | 1961 | 1962 | 1963 | 1964 | 1965 | 1966 | 1967 | 1968 | 1969 | 1970 |

Date Founded

PARTI de l'UNITÉ NATIONAL GABONAIS

1953   BLOC DÉMOCRATIQUE GABONAIS

PARTI DÉMOCRATIQUE du GABON

1948   UNION DÉMOCRATIQUE et SOCIALE GABONAIS

DÉFENSE la DÉMOCRATIQUE

PARTI pour la DÉFENSE des INSTITUTIONS DÉMOCRATIQUE

Independence
August, 1960

General Election March, 1957   General Election February, 1959   General Election February, 1961   General Election April, 1964   General Election March, 1967   General Election February, 1969

A. Political Parties and Elections

The dominant party, *Bloc Démocratique Gabonais* (BDG) was formed in the early 1950s as a territorial branch of the *Rassemblement Démocratique Africain* (RDA), and the leader of the BDG, Leon M'Ba, was a close supporter of Houphouet-Boigny (Ivory Coast). In 1961, the BDG joined the major opposition party, *Union Démocratique et Sociale Gabonaise* (UDSG) in what (in retrospect) appears to have been a *coalition*, although some scholars suggest it was a *merger*. This coalition lasted until the national elections in April 1964, when the UDSG broke away from the BDG, and along with several splinter parties (e.g., the *Défense la Démocratique* [DD]) contested the elections. The BDG gained 31 seats, and the opposition 16 seats. During the elections, the leader of the UDSG (M. Aubame) was arrested. In Libreville, the Government received 20,556 votes, and opposition parties received 19,503 votes.

On March 19, 1967, there was another national election, in which a single list was presented. The BDG won 100 percent of the seats, and M'Ba continued as president (as well as secretary general of the BDG). Opposition groups, not being represented in parliament, joined in a loose coalition called *Parti pour la Défense des Institutions Démocratique* (PDID). In 1968 President Bongo declared Gabon a one-party state.

B. Political Leadership

The leadership of the government of Gabon after Leon M'Ba's death in 1967 passed to his chosen successor, President Bongo. There has been considerable change in the composition of the cabinet since independence, with a significant rise in the number of resignations and dismissals from the cabinet following the attempted coup d'etat in 1964. Although the size of the cabinet has been expanded since independence, its members have become less representative of the cultural pluralism in Gabon as the Fang have become more prominent in government.

TABLE 10.5 Heads of Government (Post Independence)

Name	Dates in Office	Age (1971)	Ethnicity	Education	Former Occupation
1. Leon M'Ba (President)	1960–1967	Died 1967 Age 65	Fang	Catholic Secondary, Gabon	Civil Servant
2. Albert-Bernard Bongo (President)	1967– present	36	Bateke	Brazzaville Technical College	Civil Servant

TABLE 10.6 Cabinet Membership: Distribution by Ethnic Unit*

Ethnicity*	Independence Cabinet	1967 Cabinet
1. Fang (30%)	33%	70%
2. Eshira (20)	11	0
3. M'bété (15)	11	12
4. Kota (13)	0	0
5. Omyènè (5)	0	5.9
6. Others (17)	44	12
N =	9	17

* Ethnic units arranged in rank order of size within country with the unit's percent of national population in parentheses.

VI. National Integration and Stability

The general pattern in Gabon has been one of political stability, despite some tensions at the elite level. According to Weinstein (1966), even during the time of the unsuccessful coup, there was no evidence of communal violence. In general, the Fang in Gabon have dominated the national life of the country, but have been "assimilative" regarding other ethnic cultures. Under the presidency of de Gaulle, France maintained especially close relations with Gabon, and the threat of French intervention undoubtedly contributed to regime stability in Gabon.

TABLE 10.7 Elite Instability

Event and Date	Characteristics
1. Attempted Coup February 18–20, 1964	a. *Description*: Military coup led by Daniel M'bane temporarily deposed Leon M'Ba in favor of Jean-Hilare Aubame, the opposition leader. Less than 24 hours after the attempted coup began, French troops were flown from Chad and Congo (Bra) to restore M'Ba to power. In heavy fighting, 19 Gabonese and 2 French soldiers were killed. b. *Participants*: M'bane and junior army officers. c. *Apparent Causes*: Army discontent with low pay and the retention of French officers in command positions. Aubame had criticized M'Ba for being authoritarian, and had objected to the slow pace of Africanization of the army and administration.

SOURCES: "Gabon: Putsch or Coup d'état?" *Africa Report*, 9 (March 1964): 12–15. Charles and Alice Darlington, *African Betrayal*, (New York: David McKay, 1967), pp. 123–141. Brian Weinstein, *Nation Building on the Ogooué* (Cambridge: Massachusetts Institute of Technology Press, 1966).

VII. Selected References

BIBLIOGRAPHY

Weinstein, Brian. "Gabon: A Bibliographic Essay." *Africana Newsletter*, 1, no. 4, 1963.

GENERAL

Charbonnier, F. *Gabon, terre d'avenir*. Paris: Encyclopédie d'Outre mer, 1957.

Thompson, Virginia, and Richard Adloff. *The Emerging States of French Equatorial Africa*, pp. 343–384. Stanford, Cal.: Stanford University Press, 1960.

Weinstein, Brian. *Gabon: Nation Building on the Ogooué*. Cambridge: Massachusetts Institute of Technology Press, 1966.

POLITICAL

Ballard, John A. "Four Equatorial States: Congo, Gabon, Ubangi-Shari, Chad." In *National Unity and Regionalism in Eight African States*, ed. Gwendolen M. Carter, pp. 231–329. Ithaca, N.Y.: Cornell University Press, 1966.

de Lusignan, Guy. *French-Speaking Africa since Independence*, pp. 100–108. London: Pall Mall Press, 1969.

"Gabon: Putsch or Coup d'État." *Africa Report*, 9 (March 1964): 12–15.

ECONOMIC

"Gabon: une expansion rapide." *Europe-Franco-Outremer* (October 1969): 12–62.

Hilling, D. "The Changing Economy of Gabon: Developments in a New African Republic." *Geography*, 48 (1963): 155–165.

International Monetary Fund. "Gabon." In *Surveys of African Economies*, Vol. 1. Washington, D.C.: I.M.F., 1968.

SOCIAL

Balandier, Georges. *Sociologie actuelle de l'Afrique noire*, 2nd ed. Paris: Presses Universitaires de France, 1963.

Lasserre, Guy. *Libreville, la ville et sa région (Gabon, A.E.F.)*: étude de géographie humaine. Paris: Colin, 1958.

11. Gambia

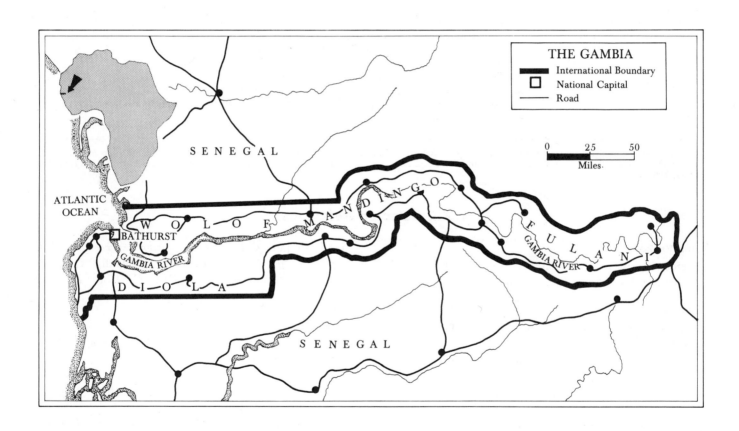

I. Basic Information

Date of Independence: February 18, 1965
Former Colonial Ruler: United Kingdom
Estimated Population (*1970*): 360,000
Area Size (*equivalent in U.S.*): 4,000 sq. mi. (twice
   Delaware)

Date of Last Census: 1963
Major Exports 1967 as Percent of Total Exports: groundnuts (peanuts) and derivatives—80 percent

II. Ethnic Patterns

The ethnic classification of Gambia is done at a low level of abstraction. All the ethnic categories correspond to functioning identity groups. All speak different languages and have different cultural and historical backgrounds. Most probably entered the region within the last 600 years as a result of pressures exerted in their former homelands in Mali. (Note that the ethnic group "Diola" is not the same as the broader term "Dyula," which refers to Mandé-speaking Muslim traders.) Distribution percentages are calculated from 1967 UN population estimate.

TABLE 11.1   Ethnic Units Over 5 Percent of Country Population

Ethnic Unit	Estimated Ethnic Population 1967	Estimated Ethnic Percentage
a. Mandingo (Malinké, Manding, Wangara)	140,000	41%
b. Fulani (Fula, Peul)	46,000	13.5%
c. Wolof (Jolof, Ouolof, Wollof)	44,000	13%
d. Diola (Jola, Dyola, Yola)	24,000	7%
e. Serahuli (Soninké, Sarakolé)	22,000	6.5%

SOURCES: *Report on the Census of Population of the Gambia Taken on 17th/18th April 1963* by H. A. Oliver, Census Controller. Sessional Paper no. 13 of 1965 (Bathurst: Government Printer, 1965), p. 50. H. A. Gailey, Jr., *A History of the Gambia* (London: Routledge & Kegan Paul, 1964).

III. Language Patterns

According to Weil (1968) there are three language groups in the Gambia: (1) Mandé (Western Division) (including Mandingo/Malinké, Soninké, Bambara, Dialonke, and Koranko); (2) West Atlantic (including Wolof, Serer, Diola, Fulani, Manyak, Banyun, Temne, and Mansuanka); (3) Other languages (mainly Creole and pidgin). Weil estimates that 40 percent of the population speak Mandingo as a first language, and that it is spoken as a second language by members of most other ethnic groups. (Knappert estimates 100 percent speak Mandingo; Rustow estimates 46 percent.) We estimate 60 percent of the population speak Mandingo. With regard to the second largest language, Weil estimates that about 16 percent of the population speak Fulani as a first language. There are seven dialects of Fulani found in Gambia: Tukulor, Futa Toro, Jombonko, Futa Jalonke, Fuladugu, Lorobo, and Aamanabi. Finally, Wolof is spoken as a first language by about 13 percent of the population. English is the official language of Gambia and is used in administration, law, education, and commerce. French is spoken by Wolof and Serer groups along the Senegal borders; Arabic is used as a religious language.

TABLE 11.2   Language Patterns

1. Primacy		
1st language	Mandingo	(60%)
2nd language	Fulani	(16%)
2. Greenberg classification	Mandingo	IA2
(all ethnic units in	Fulani	IAI
country over 5%)	Wolof	IA1
	Diola	IA1
	Serahuli (Soninké)	IA2
3. *Lingua franca*	Mandingo	
4. Official language	English	

SOURCE: Peter M. Weil, "Language Distribution in the Gambia: 1966–67," *African Language Review*, 7 (1968): 101–106.

IV. Urban Patterns

Capital/largest city: Bathurst (founded 1816)
Dominant ethnicity/language of capital
   Major vernacular: Creole[1]

[1] Jan Knappert, "Language Problems of the New Nations of Africa," *African Quarterly*, 5 (1965): 95–105.

Major ethnic group: Wolof[2]
Major ethnic group as percent of capital's population: 41 percent (1963)

[2] Census.

TABLE 11.3   Growth of Capital/Largest City

Date	Bathurst
1920[a]	9,000
1930[a]	11,000
1940	—
1950[b]	20,000
1960	26,000
1966	43,000 UA

SOURCES:
[a] O. Martens and O. Karstedt, *The African Handbook*, 2nd ed. (London: Allen and Unwin, 1938).
[b] Michael Banton, *West African City* (London: Oxford University Press, 1957).

TABLE 11.4   Cities of 20,000 and Over

City	Size	Date
Bathurst	43,000 UA	1966

SOURCE: *UN Demographic Yearbook 1967*. According to the census report: "To be accurate, there is no town in the Gambia except that of Bathurst." In 1963 the next largest town, Brikama, had a population of 4,000.

V. Political Patterns

Figure 11.1   **Political Parties and Elections**

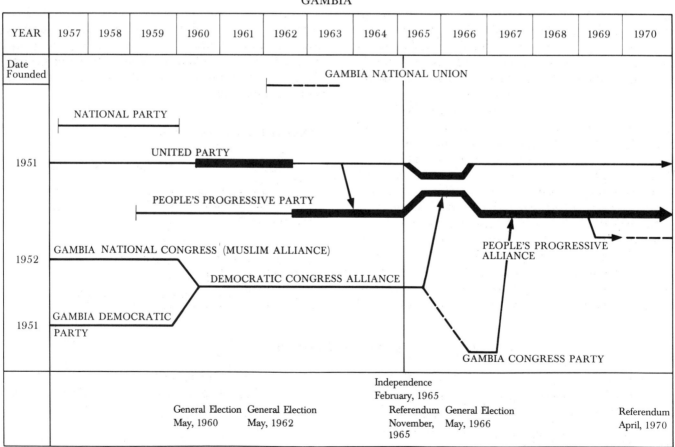

A. Political Parties and Elections

After the first Gambian elections held in May 1960, Pierre S. N'Jie was made Chief Minister. N'Jie's party, the *United Party* (UP) continued to govern Gambia until 1962 when the party was defeated by the *People's Progressive Party* (PPP) under the leadership of Dauda Jawara. In 1965 the PPP and the UP joined in a coalition government which lasted only until 1966 when the PPP assumed the sole leadership of the government. In the May 1966 election the PPP won 24 seats, and the UP/Congress won 8. The *Democratic Congress Alliance* (DCA), formed by a merger of the *Gambia Muslim Congress* (GMC) and the *Gambia Democratic Party* (GDP) in 1960, served as an opposition party until it merged with the PPP in 1966. Two referenda were held over the issue of declaring Gambia a republic. The issue was defeated in 1965, but succeeded in 1970 with a 70 percent affirmative vote.

B. Political Leadership

The Gambia became an independent nation in 1965, and since that time the government of President Jawara has remained in power. In a relatively small cabinet, the number of persons of Wolof background is greater than would be expected from the proportion of Wolof in the Gambian population.

TABLE 11.5   Head of Government (Post Independence)

Name	Dates in Office	Age (1971)	Ethnicity	Education	Former Occupation
1. Sir Dauda Jawara (Prime Minister/ President)	1965–	47	Mandingo	Veterinary (England)	Veterinarian, Party Organizer

TABLE 11.6   Cabinet Membership: Distribution by Ethnic Unit*

Ethnicity	Independence Cabinet	1967 Cabinet
1. Mandingo (41%)	43%	44%
2. Fulani (13.5)	15	11
3. Wolof (13)	43	33
4. Diola (7)	0	0
5. Serahuli (6.5)	0	0
6. Others (19)	0	11
N =	7	10

* Ethnic units arranged in rank order of size within country with the unit's percent of national population in parentheses.

VI. National Integration and Stability

Through 1969, Gambia has had no evidence of any type of elite, communal, or mass instability. The issues of national integration are far from solved, however, and the primary question is whether the thin sliver of territory, surrounded by Senegal on three sides, will at some future point join with Senegal in forming a new union: Senegambia. There are close ethnic links between the two countries, and if their borders were ever restricted, the potential for irredentism would be high.

VII. Selected References

BIBLIOGRAPHY

Gamble, D. P. *Bibliography of the Gambia*. Bathurst: Government Printer, 1967.

United States Library of Congress. General Reference and Bibliography Division. African Section. *Official Publications of Sierra Leone and Gambia*. Washington, D.C.: Government Printing Office, 1963.

GENERAL

Gailey, Harry A. *A History of the Gambia*. London: Routledge and Kegan Paul, 1964.

Teague, Michael. "The Gambia." *Geographical Magazine* (London), 34 (November 1961): 380–392.

POLITICAL

Robson, Peter. "The Problems of Senegambia." *Journal of Modern African Studies*, 3 (1965): 393–407.

Robson, Peter. "Problems of Integration between Senegal and Gambia." In *African Integration and Disintegration*, ed. Arthur Hazlewood, pp. 115–128. London: Oxford University Press, 1967.

Welch, Claude E., Jr. "Unlikely Gambia." *Africa Report*, 10 (February 1965): 5–9.

12. Ghana

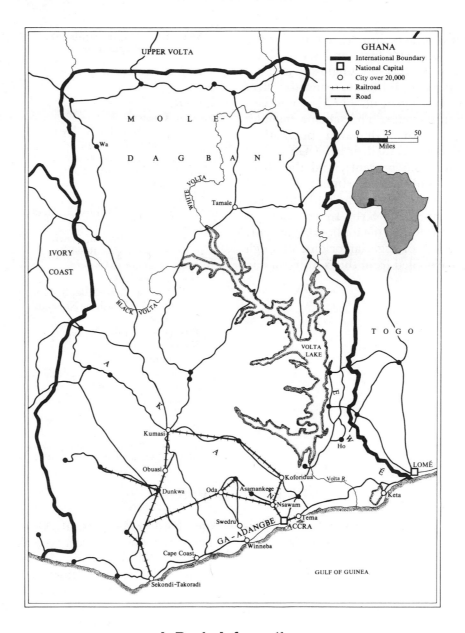

I. Basic Information

Date of Independence: March 6, 1957
Former Colonial Ruler: United Kingdom
Change in Boundaries: Addition of UN Trust Territory "British Togoland" on December 13, 1956
Former Name: Gold Coast
Estimated Population (*1970*): 8,545,561 (provisional census results)

Area Size (equivalent in U.S.): 92,000 sq. mi. (Wyoming)
Date of Last Census: 1970
Major exports 1968 as percent of total exports: cocoa—62 percent; timber—8 percent; aluminum—7 percent

II. Ethnic Patterns

This ethnic classification is essentially that used in the 1960 Ghanaian census. The first- and second-level groupings are based largely on linguistic affinity. This basis of classification, however, seems to reflect general cultural patterns as well. The Ewé and Ga-Adangbe are identity groups. The schema includes about 82 percent of the Ghanaian population. Significant groups not included are the Guan (3.7 percent), the Gurma (3.5 percent), and the Grusi (3.5 percent). There is also an assortment of Central Togo groups, as well as Tem (Kotokoli), Songhai, Mandé, Hausa, Fulani, and Kru. In addition, in 1967 there were about a quarter million (3 percent) foreign Africans, mainly of Nigerian origin, although many of these were expelled from the country in late 1969.

TABLE 12.1   Ethnic Units Over 5 Percent of Country Population

Ethnic Unit	Estimated Ethnic Population 1967	Estimated Ethnic Percentage
a. Akan Cluster	3,583,000	*44%*
1. Ashanti (Twi-Fanti, Twi)	(2,296,000)	(28.2%)
i. Ashanti, ii. Boron, iii. Akuapem, iv. Kwawu, etc.		
2. Fante (Twi-Fante, Fante)	(912,000)	(11.2%)
i. Fante, ii. Agona		
3. Nzema (Nzima)	(211,000)	(2.6%)
i. Nzema, ii. Evalue, iii. Ahanta		
4. Anyi-Bawle	(122,000)	(1.5%)
i. Sahwi (Sefwi), ii. Aowin, iii. Kyokoshi, iv. Bawle		
b. Mole-Dagbani (Mossi-Dagomba) Cluster	1,302,000	*16%*
1. Dagomba, 2. Dagaba, 3. Mosi, 4. Frafra, 5. Kusasi, 6. Nankansi, 7. Talensi		
c. Ewé (Ehoué, Eibe, Ephe, Krepe)	1,058,000	*13%*
d. Ga-Adangbe	692,000	*8.5%*
1. Ga (Gan)	(285,000)	(3.5%)
2. Adangbe (Adangme, Adampa)	(285,000)	(3.5%)
i. Ada, ii. Shai (Siade), iii. Krobo		

SOURCE: *1960 Population Census of Ghana*, Special Report "E," Tribes in Ghana, (Accra Census Office, 1964), pp. 1–5.

III. Language Patterns

Most of the languages of Ghana are part of the Niger-Congo family. Within this family there are two major sub-stock language groups: (1) Voltaic, or Gur (spoken mainly in the north); (2) Kwa (e.g., Akan, Ga, Ewé, spoken mainly in the south). The dominant northern language is Mole-Dagbani, and is spoken by a number of ethnic groups: Dagomba, Mamprusi, Nanumba, Gbanyang, Nankanse, Kusasi, Talensi, Wala, Dagaba, Birifor, Namnam. The dominant southern language group is Akan, including Twi (Ashanti, Fanti, Akim, Akwapim), Anyi-Baule (Nzima, Ahanta, Sefwi, Aowin, Anufo), and Guang (Gonja, Brong, Nawuri, Atyoti, Anyanga, Nchumuru, Nkunya, Late, Afutu). Knappert estimates that 57 percent of the Ghanaian population speak "Akan"; MacDougald estimates 62 percent;

and Rustow 44 percent. Our own estimate is 44 percent, with 16 percent speaking the second language (Mole-Dagbani). It should be noted that Fanti and Twi are distinctive but mutually intelligible. (About 35 years ago an attempt was made to blend them into a new language, Akan; this was not successful; see Owiredu, 1964.) Hausa is spoken as a *lingua franca* not only in the north, but in many of the southern cities as well.

The Ghana government after independence discouraged the use of vernacular languages in the schools (English was used from grade one), but it did extensive radio broadcasting in vernacular languages, and extensive international broadcasting in Hausa. English is the official language of Ghana. During the Nkrumah regime, French also was encouraged, and the eventual hope was to have a bilingual (French-English) state, to facilitate communications with Ghana's French-speaking neighbors. The major administrative regions within Ghana continue to be demarcated according to linguistic criteria. In 1960, the Nationality Act required that all would-be citizens of Ghana be proficient in an indigenous language.

TABLE 12.2   Language Patterns

1. Primacy		
1st language	"Akan"	(44%)
2nd language	Mole-Dagbani	(16%)
2. Greenberg classification	"Akan"	IA4
(all ethnic units in	Mole-Dagbani	IA3
country over 5%)	Ewé	IA4
	Ga-Adangbe	IA4
3. *Lingua franca*	Hausa	
4. Official language	English	

SOURCES: R. F. Amonoo, "Problems of Ghanaian Lingue Franche," in *Language in Africa*, ed. John Spencer (London: Cambridge University Press, 1963), pp. 78–85. P. A. Owiredu, "Proposals for a National Language in Ghana," *African Affairs*, 64 (1964): 142–145.

IV. Urban Patterns

Capital/largest city: Accra (founded ca.1550)
Dominant ethnicity/language of capital
   Major vernacular: Ga[1]
   Major ethnic group: Ga[2]
   Major ethnic group as percent of capital's population: 49 percent (1960)

TABLE 12.3   Growth of Capital/Largest City

Date	Accra
1920[a]	38,000
1930[b]	61,000
1940[a]	100,000
1950	135,000
1960	338,000
1966[c]	600,000 UA

SOURCES:
[a] Michael Banton, *West African City* (London: Oxford University Press, 1957).
[b] Gold Coast census (1931).
[c] *UN Demographic Yearbook 1967*.

[1] Jan Knappert, "Language Problems of the New Nations of Africa," *African Quarterly*, 5 (1965): 95–105.
[2] Census.

TABLE 12.4   Cities of 20,000 and Over*

City	Size	Date
Accra[a]	600,000 UA	1966
Kumasi[b]	180,000	ca. 1965
Tema[c]	84,000	1964
Sekondi-Takoradi[b]	75,000	ca. 1965
Cape Coast[b]	41,000	ca. 1965
Tamale[d]	40,000	1960
Koforidua[d]	34,000	1960
Obuasi[d]	26,000	1960
Winneba[d]	25,000	1960
Swedru[d]	20,000	1960
Nsawam[d]	20,000	1960
Oda[d]	20,000	1960
Keta[d]	18,000	1960

* Data for 1965–66 are not available, even in estimates, for many of the smaller Ghanaian cities over 20,000 in population. The populations of Kumasi and Tema given here differ from those reported by the UN; a country expert has reported that more reasonable estimates would be 180,000 and 84,000 for the towns themselves. In calculating the percent of country population in cities 20,000 or more for Part I, Keta (1960 population 18,000), was included.

SOURCES:
[a] *UN Demographic Yearbook 1967*.
[b] *Europa Yearbook 1967*.
[c] Tema, the new port city near Accra has grown rapidly. The estimate presented here is based on the results of a sample survey (Margaret Piel, personal communication).
[d] Census.

V. Political Patterns

A. Political Parties and Elections

The Convention People's Party (CPP) was founded in 1949 by Kwame Nkrumah, and was the dominant party in Ghana until the military coup in February 1966. During the pre-independence period there were a number of splinter parties. These merged together in 1957 into the *United Party* (UP), which was led by Dr. Kofi Busia. The UP served as the "opposition" party until Ghana officially became a one-party state in early 1964. However, the country had been essentially a one-party state since the plebiscite election in April 1960, which established the republican constitution (with 89 percent of the vote), and Nkrumah as president. After the military coup, all parties were banned, and a National Liberation Council was established to govern the country. The military government scheduled elections for August 31, 1969, with the intention of returning the country to civilian rule. During the summer of 1969 a number of political parties were formed in preparation for the election, but the CPP was still banned. These parties seemed to regroup into two major parties, the *Progress Party* (PP), led by Dr. Busia, and the *National Alliance of Liberals* (NAL), led by K. A.

Gbedemah. The results of the August 1969 elections gave control of the government to Dr. Busia. The PP won 105 of 140 seats. In October 1970 the three opposition parties, the NAL, *the United Nationalist Party* and the *All People's Republican Party*, merged to form the *Justice Party*.

B. Political Leadership

A coup d'état in 1966 brought an end to the government of President Nkrumah, who was succeeded by two senior military officers as head of state. Recruitment to cabinet positions after the coup was broadly based, although the cabinets of President Nkrumah reflected the cultural pluralism of the Ghanaian

Figure 12.1 **Political Parties and Elections**

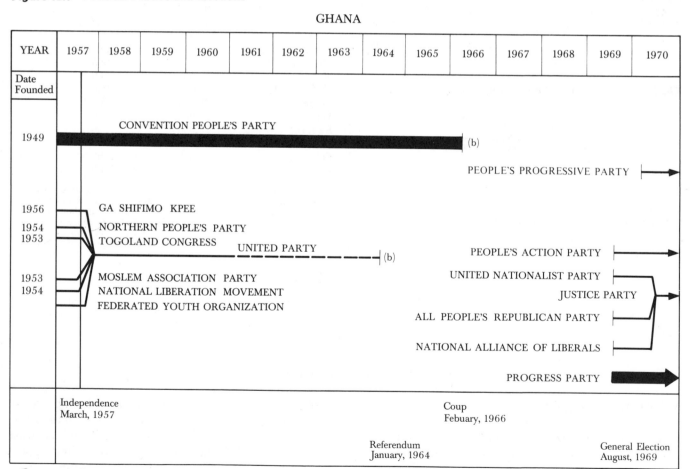

GHANA

people. Dr. Busia at first ruled at the sufferance of the National Liberation Council but on August 7, 1970 the Army's Presidential Commission dissolved itself thereby completing the return to civilian rule. In January 1972 the Busia government was ousted by a military coup.

TABLE 12.5   Heads of Government (Post Independence)

Name	Dates in Office	Age (1971)	Ethnicity	Education	Former Occupation
1. Dr. Kwame Nkrumah (President)	1957–1966	Died 1972 age 62	Akan (Nzima)	University & post-grad. work (United States)	Party Organizer
2. Lt. Gen. Joseph Ankrah (Chairman, NLC)	1966–1969	56	Ga	Wesleyan School	Teacher, Soldier
3. Brig. Gen. A. A. Afrifa (Chairman, NLC)	1969	35	Akan (Ashanti)	Sandhurst (England) & other Military Courses	Soldier, Infantry
4. Dr. Kofi Busia (Prime Minister)	Sept. 1969–	58	Akan (Ashanti)	Oxford Ph.D.	Univ. Prof.
5. Col. Ignatius Kutu Acheampong (Chairman, NRC)	Jan. 1972–	40	Akan (Ashanti)	Officer Cadet School (England)	Teacher, Soldier

TABLE 12.6   Cabinet Membership: Distribution by Ethnic Unit*

Ethnicity*	Independence Cabinet	Immediate Pre-Coup Cabinet	1967 Cabinet
1. Akan (44%)	62%	71%	25%
2. Mole-Dagbani (16)	23	12	13
3. Ewé (13)	7.7	12	38
4. Ga (8.5)	7.7	5.9	25
5. Others (18)	0	0	0
N =	13	17	8

* Ethnic units arranged in rank order of size within country with the unit's percent of national population in parentheses.

VI. National Integration and Stability

Except for Ewé irredentism in the early years following independence, there has been no evidence of communal instability. Elite instability, in the form of the 1966 coup and subsequent political activity, however, has been linked to communal tension. In his autobiography, A. A. Afrifa states that the coup against Nkrumah (Nzima) was partly based on the alliance of the Ashanti and Ewé peoples.

TABLE 12.7   Elite Instability

Event and Date	Characteristics
1. Coup d'Etat February 24, 1966	a. *Description*: While President Nkrumah was on a state visit to the Chinese Peoples' Republic, he was replaced by an army and police coup. In all, 27 Ghanaians were killed in the coup (including Major-General Charles Baruch who was shot when he refused to support the coup). General Ankrah (retired) was asked to head a new government by the coup leaders. Dr. Nkrumah took up residence in Guinea. b. *Participants*: Colonel F. K. Kotoka, commander of the second brigade, and T. W. K. Harley, commander of the police, along with junior officers such as A. A. Afrifa. About 3000 members of the army occupied Accra at the time of the takeover. c. *Apparent Causes*: The reasons for the coup were announced by the new regime during a broadcast on February 24: "... This act has been necessitated by the political and economic situation in the country. The concentration of power in the hands of one man has led to the abuse of individual rights and duties. He ... runs the country as his own personal property. The economic situation ... is chaotic."
2. Attempted Coup April 17, 1967	a. *Description*: General Ankrah reported that a plan to assassinate all senior officers was undertaken on April 17 when an army detachment on training maneuvers attacked a number of buildings in Accra. In the ensuing battle, General Kotoka and two other government officers were killed. b. *Participants*: An army reconnaissance team of 120 men, commanded by Lt. Sam Arthur. An additional squadron was also said to be involved. Lt. Arthur and Lt. Yeboah were tried, found guilty, and hanged. A third junior officer was sentenced to 20 years in prison. c. *Apparent Causes*: This appears to have been a counter-coup by troops who remained loyal to Nkrumah.
3. Coup d'Etat January 13, 1972	a. *Description*: A group of army officers led by Col. I. K. Acheampong, commander of the 1st Infantry Brigade based in Accra, seized power in a bloodless coup while Prime Minister Busia was in London for medical treatment. Cabinet ministers and two top-ranking officers were jailed. A National Redemption Council was set up headed by Col. Acheampong, parliament was disbanded, and all political parties were banned. b. *Participants*: Army officers led by Col. Acheampong. c. *Apparent Causes*: Discontent with the country's economic situation, especially the 44 percent devaluation of the *cedi* in December 1971, seems to have been the major cause. Busia's austerity budget involved cuts in military expenditures as well. Col. Acheampong accused Busia's government of extravagance and permitting widespread official corruption.

SOURCES: A. A. Afrifa, *The Ghana Coup: 24th February 1966* (New York: Humanities Press, 1966). Henry L. Bretton, *The Rise and Fall of Kwame Nkrumah: A Study of Personal Rule in Africa* (New York: Praeger, 1966). Robert Fitch and Mary Oppenheimer, *Ghana: End of an Illusion* (New York: Monthly Review Press, 1966). Jon Kraus, "The Men in Charge," *Africa Report*, 11 (April 1966): 16–20.

TABLE 12.8   Communal Instability

Event and Date	Characteristics
1. Irredentism ca. 1957–1963 (sporadic)	a. *Description*: Certain Ewé ethnic members of the Trans-Volta region in Ghana and kinsmen in the neighboring state of Togo demanded re-unification following the UN plebiscite which placed the Trans-Volta region under Ghanaian control. Ewé irredentists from Ghana were reputed to have taken refuge in Togo. There were a series of border incidents and border closings at the Ghana-Togo border. b. *Participants*: Ewé ethnic members. c. *Apparent Cause*: Ewé irredentism.

TABLE 12.8 Communal Instability *(cont.)*

Event and Date	Characteristics
2. Rebellion 1969	a. *Description*: Following a dispute over the appointment of the Ya Na (Paramount Chief) of Dagomba in November 1968, the National Liberation Council appointed a Committee of Enquiry which reported that the installation of one of the rival candidates had been unduly influenced by Government officials, army and police in the area. The Government's order for the installation of the other contending candidate resulted in riots in Yendi in September 1969, and a state of emergency was declared. Army and police personnel stationed in Yendi killed 23 and seriously injured 40 people in a confrontation with an armed crowd. Seven hundred were arrested and 4 Dagomba chiefs were banned from Yendi in connection with this disturbance. b. *Participants*: Partisans of Dagomba royal families. c. *Apparent Causes*: Opposition to a central government decision reversing a controversial appointment to the office of Ya Na made by the traditional authorities.

SOURCES: Claude Welch, *Dream of Unity* (Ithaca, N.Y.: Cornell University Press, 1966). Dennis Austin, "The Ghana-Togo Frontier," *Journal of Modern African Studies*, (1963): 139–146.

VII. Selected References

BIBLIOGRAPHY

Adams, Cynthia. *A Study Guide for Ghana.* Boston: Development Program, African Studies Center, Boston University, 1966.

Chand, Attar. "Ghana Since the Coup: A Select Bibliography." *Africa Quarterly*, 9 (1969): 310–315.

Johnson, A. F. *A Bibliography of Ghana, 1930–1961.* London: Longmans for Ghana Library Board, 1964.

GENERAL

Apter, David E. *Ghana in Transition.* New York: Atheneum, 1962.

Bourret, F. M. *Ghana: The Road to Independence 1919–1957.* London: Oxford University Press, 1960.

Dickson, Kwamina B. *An Historical Geography of Ghana.* London: Cambridge University Press, 1969.

Fage, John D. *Ghana: A Historical Interpretation.* Madison, Wis.: University of Wisconsin Press, 1959.

Genoud, Roger. *Nationalism and Economic Development in Ghana.* New York: Praeger, 1969.

U.S. Department of the Army. *Area Handbook for Ghana.* Washington, D.C.: Government Printing Office, 1971.

Ward, William E. F. *A History of Ghana.* London: Allen and Unwin, 1966.

Wright, Richard. *Black Power.* London: Dobson, 1954.

POLITICAL

Afrifa, A. A. *The Ghana Coup, 24th February, 1966.* London: Frank Cass, 1966.

Apter, David. "Ghana." In *Political Parties and National Integration in Tropical Africa*, eds. J. S. Coleman and C. G. Rosberg. Los Angeles: University of California Press, 1964.

Austin, Dennis. *Politics in Ghana 1946–1960.* London: Oxford University Press, 1964.

Bretton, Henry L. *The Rise and Fall of Kwame Nkrumah.* New York: Praeger, 1966.

Card, Emily, and Barbara Callaway. "Ghanaian Politics: The Elections and After." *Africa Report*, 15 (1970): 10–15.

Dubois, S. G. "What Happened in Ghana: The Inside Story." *Freedomways*, 6 (1966): 201–223.

Fitch, Bob, and Mary Oppenheimer. *Ghana: End of an Illusion.* New York: Monthly Review Press, 1966.

"Ghana without Nkrumah." *Africa Report*, 11 (April 1966): 10–20.

Omari, T. Peter. *Kwame Nkrumah: The Anatomy of an African Dictatorship.* New York: Africana Publishing Corporation, 1970.

Wallerstein, Immanuel. *The Road to Independence: Ghana and the Ivory Coast.* The Hague: Mouton, 1964.

ECONOMIC

Anyand, S. La. *Ghana Agriculture*. London: Oxford University Press, 1963.

Birmingham, Walter, et al., eds. *A Study of Contemporary Ghana*. Vol. 1. The Economy of Ghana. London: Allen and Unwin, 1966.

Hance, William A. "The Volta River Project: A Study in Industrial Development." In *African Economic Development*, rev. ed., by William A. Hance, pp. 87–114. New York: Praeger, 1967.

Killick A. and Szereszewski, R. "The Economy of Ghana," *The Economies of Africa*, eds. P. Robson and D. A. Lury, pp. 79–126. Evanston: Northwestern University Press, 1969.

Wills, J. Brian, ed. *Agriculture and Land Use in Ghana*. London: Oxford University Press for Ghana Ministry of Food and Agriculture, 1962.

SOCIAL

Acquah, I. *Accra Survey*. London: University of London Press, 1958.

Baeta, C. G. *Prophetism in Ghana: A Study of some "Spiritual" Churches*. London: S.C.M. Press, 1962.

Birmingham, Walter, et al., eds., *A Study of Contemporary Ghana*: Vol. 2, Some Aspects of Social Structure. London: Allen and Unwin, 1967.

Boateng, E. A. *A Geography of Ghana*. New York: Cambridge University Press, 1966.

Brokensha, David. *Social Change at Larteh, Ghana*. Oxford: Clarendon Press, 1966.

Caldwell, John C. *African Rural-Urban Migration: The Movement to Ghana's Towns*. New York: Columbia University Press, 1969.

Field, M. J. *Search for Security: An Ethno-Psychiatric Study of Rural Ghana*. London: Faber and Faber, 1960.

Foster, Philip. *Education and Social Change in Ghana*. Chicago: University of Chicago Press, 1965.

Hill, Polly. *The Migrant Cocoa Farmers of Southern Ghana*. Cambridge, Eng.: Cambridge University Press, 1963.

Kay, B. *Bringing up Children in Ghana*. London: Allen and Unwin, 1962.

Parsons, Robert T. *The Churches and Ghana Society*. Leiden: E. J. Brill, 1967.

Rouch, Jean. "Migrations au Ghana." *Journal de la Société des Africanistes*, 16 (1956): 33–96.

13. Guinea

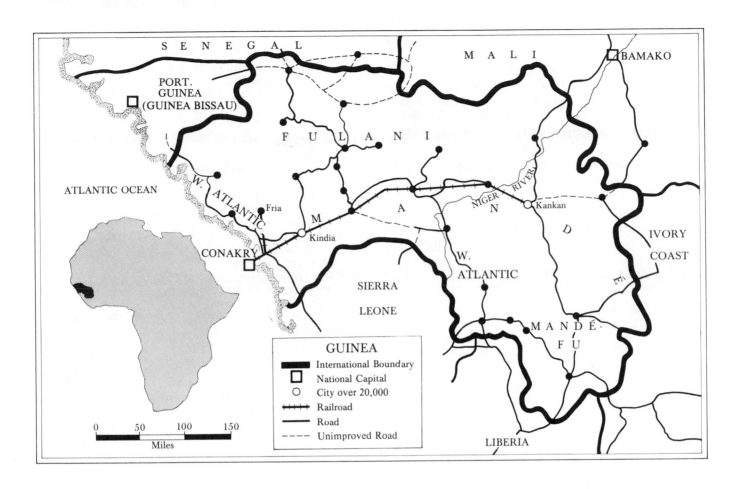

I. Basic Information

Date of Independence: October 2, 1958

Former Colonial Ruler: France

Change in Boundaries: Formerly part of the French West African Federation

Former Name: French Guinea

Estimated Population (1970): 3,920,000*

Area Size (equivalent in U.S.): 95,000 sq. mi (Oregon)

Date of Last Census: 1955

Major Exports 1966 as Percent of Total Exports: alumina—62 percent; bananas—8 percent; iron ore—6 percent

* According to a report in *The New York Times* (December 1968), between 500,000 and 1,000,000 Guineans have left the country since

independence. *Africa Contemporary Record 1969–70*, p. B 496, says that a population figure "in the region of 3,500,000 has been mentioned for 1967." The UN figure may represent an over-assessment.

II. Ethnic Patterns

The ethnic classification of Guinea is primarily based on linguistic criteria and not on identity groups (except for the Fulani). It will be noticed that our classification deviates from the standard rendering of ethnic proportionality in Guinea. Most sources have regarded the Fulani as the largest ethnic group, and the Malinké second largest. Thus, the *Area Handbook on Guinea* gives the following percentages: Foulah (Fulani) 37 percent; Malinké 19 percent; Soussou 8 percent; Kissi 6 percent; Guerzé 5 percent. We have, however, relied on the results of a sample survey done in 1964. This is an arbitrary choice, but there is no evidence that the survey is inaccurate.

TABLE 13.1 Ethnic Units Over 5 Percent of Country Population

Ethnic Unit	Estimated Ethnic Population 1967	Estimated Ethnic Percentage
a. Mandé Cluster	1,777,000	*48%*
1. Malinké	(1,111,000)	(30%)
i. Malinké, ii. Ouassoulonké, iii. Mikiforé, iv. Toubacaye (Diaknanké), v. Kouranko, vi. Lelé, vii. Konianke, viii. Sarakolé (Marka, Soninké)		
2. Soussou (Susu)	(592,000)	(16%)
i. Soussou, ii. Djallonké		
3. Bambara and others		
b. Fulani (Foula, Peul)	1,037,000	*28%*
1. Foula (Foula Djallon), 2. Pouli (Foulacounda), 3. Toucouleur		
c. Mandé-fu Type	407,000	*11%*
1. Guerzé (Kpellé), 2. Toma, 3. Manon (G'Bema), 4. Manon, 5. Kono		
d. West Atlantic Cluster	370,000	*10%*
1. Kissi	(259,000)	(7%)
2. Temne, 3. Baga, 4. Landouman (Tiapi), 5. Bagafore, 6. Mnami		

SOURCES: *Étude démographique* (Paris: Ministère de la France d'outremer. Service des statistiques, 1956), Vol. 1. Étude démographique par sondage en Guinée, 1954–55. U.S. Department of the Army, *U.S. Army Area Handbook for Guinea* (Washington, D.C.: Government Printing Office, 1961).

III. Language Patterns

The three major ethnic groups in Guinea are Malinké (in upper Guinea), Fulani (in middle Guinea), and Soussou (in coastal Guinea). Although Malinké and Soussou are part of the same language family (Mandé), they are distinct languages. Each of the three major ethnic languages serves as a *lingua franca*, to varying degrees, in the region where it is predominant. Malinké, however, seems to be emerging as a broader *lingua franca* in the country. The local term for Malinké is Maninka. Dyula is a simplified form of Malinké.

We differ with the existing estimates as to which of the languages in Guinea is most widely spoken. Knappert estimates Fulani (33 percent), MacDougald estimates Fulani (62 percent), and Rustow estimates Fulani (39 percent) with Malinké-Bambara-Dyula second at 26 percent. Our own estimate puts Malinké first with approximately 30 percent native speakers and an additional 18 percent of second

TABLE 13.2 Language Patterns

1. Primacy		
1st language	Malinké	(48%)
2nd language	Fulani	(33%)
2. Greenberg classification	Malinké	IA2
(all ethnic units in	Fulani	IA1
country over 5%)	Mandé-fu	IA2
	West Atlantic cluster (Kissi)	IA1
3. *Lingua francas*	Malinké, Fulani	
4. Official language	French	

language speakers (total 48 percent). Fulani native speakers probably comprise 28 percent; and perhaps an additional 5 percent of second-language speakers (total 33 percent).

The official language is French, which is used in government, education, and mass media. However, broadcasting is also conducted in Fulani, Malinké, Soussou, Kissi, Toma and Guerzé. It is official policy to encourage English as a second national language. Arabic is widely used as a language of religion.

IV. Urban Patterns

Capital/largest city: Conakry (founded 1885)
Dominant ethnicity/language of capital
  Major vernacular: Soussou[1]
  Major ethnic group: Soussou[2]
  Major ethnic group as percent of capital's population: 45 percent (1952)

TABLE 13.3   Growth of Capital/Largest City

Date	Conakry
1920	9,000
1930	7,000
1940	20,000
1950	39,000
1960	90,000
1967	197,000 UA

SOURCE: *Démographie Comparée.*

[1] Jan Knappert, "Language Problems of the New Nations of Africa," *African Quarterly*, 5 (1965): 95–105.
[2] O. Collfus, "Conakry en 1951–52: Étude Humaine et Economique," *Etudes Guineennes* 10/11 (1952); pp. 16–17.

TABLE 13.4   Cities of 20,000 and Over*

City	Size	Date
Conakry[a]	197,000 UA	1967
Kankan[b]	30,000	1960
Kindia[c]	25,000	1964

* Current urban data are generally unavailable for Guinea, making the assessment of Guinean urbanization an especially hazardous undertaking. Other main towns are: Labé, Boké, Macenta, Nzerekore and Kissidougou.

SOURCES:
[a] *UN Demographic Yearbook 1967.*
[b] *Démographie Comparée.*
[c] *Statesman's Yearbook 1967–68.*

V. Political Patterns

A. Political Parties and Elections

Since independence Guinea has been a one-party state. Founded in 1947 as a branch of the *Rassemblement Démocratique Africain* (RDA), the *Parti Démocratique de Guinée* (PDG) was Guinea's dominant party. Sékou Touré, the president of Guinea and the secretary-general of PDG, has held both positions, without opposition, since Guinea's independence in 1958. All members of the National Assembly (elected in 1963) belong to the PDG.

B. Political Leadership

Since independence in 1958, the government of Guinea has been led by President Sékou Touré. He has considerably enlarged his cabinet since that time and, except for the period 1963–64, there have been very few resignations and dismissals from the executive body. Mandé people tend to be rather more prominent in government than the Mandé proportion of the population would suggest, but cabinet membership is, nonetheless, ethnically diversified. Kwame Nkrumah, after being deposed from power in Ghana in 1966, was invited by Touré to become the co-president of Guinea, a largely symbolic arrangement.

Figure 13.1   **Political Parties and Elections**

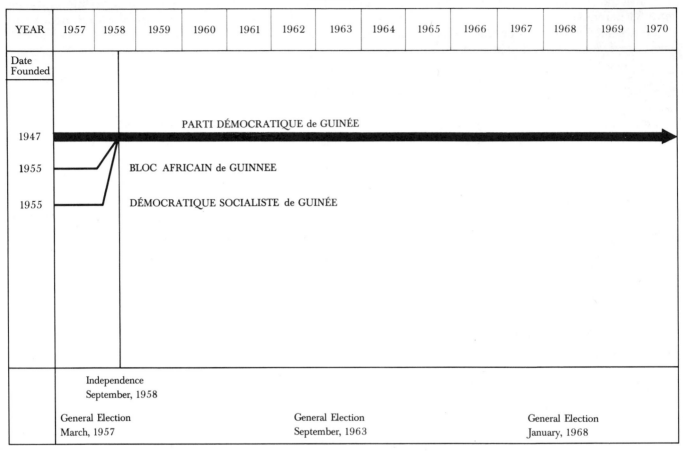

GUINEA

YEAR	1957	1958	1959	1960	1961	1962	1963	1964	1965	1966	1967	1968	1969	1970

Date Founded

1947   PARTI DÉMOCRATIQUE de GUINÉE

1955   BLOC AFRICAIN de GUINNEE

1955   DÉMOCRATIQUE SOCIALISTE de GUINÉE

Independence
September, 1958

General Election
March, 1957

General Election
September, 1963

General Election
January, 1968

TABLE 13.5   Head of Government (Post Independence)

Name	Dates in Office	Age (1971)	Ethnicity	Education	Former Occupation
1. Sékou Touré (President)	1958–	49	Mandé (Malinké)	Technical-Secondary (Guinea)	Clerk

TABLE 13.6   Cabinet Membership: Distribution by Ethnic Unit*

Ethnicity*	Independence Cabinet	1967 Cabinet
1. Mandé (48%)	60%	65%
2. Fulani (28)	30	27
3. Mandé-Fu (11)	0	0
4. West Atlantic (10)	10	3.8
5. Others (3)	0	3.8
N =	10	26

* Ethnic units arranged in rank order of size within country with the unit's percentage of national population in parentheses.

VI. National Integration and Stability

The regime of Sékou Touré has served continuously since the mid-1950s. To some extent, the "charisma" of Touré has continued up to the present, and his broad-based political party has been successful in linking masses with elites. Tension among the various ethnic groups is carefully handled by Guinean leaders and an effort is made to represent every ethnic group in the political life of Guinea. The role of ideology and widespread Islamic culture seem to be of special importance in achieving a substantial degree of national integration. There were reports of plots in 1960, 1965, and 1969 and an assassination attempt against Touré occurred in 1969. In November 1970, the government reported a "Portuguese invasion" attempt which was repulsed. *The New York Times* reported that the invaders included dissident Guineans.

VII. Selected References

BIBLIOGRAPHY

Organisation for Economic Cooperation and Development. *Bibliographie sur la Guinée*. Paris: O.E.C.D., 1965.

GENERAL

Ameillon, B. *La Guinée: bilan d'une indépendance*. Paris: Maspero, 1964.

Cowan, L. Gray, and Victor DuBois. *Guinea*. Ithaca, N.Y.: Cornell University Press, forthcoming.

Suret-Canale, J. *La République de Guinée*. Paris: Seghers, 1970.

Thompson, Virginia, and Richard Adloff. *French West Africa*, pp. 132–138. Stanford, Cal.: Stanford University Press, 1957.

U.S. Department of the Army. *Area Handbook for Guinea*. Washington, D.C.: G.P.O., 1961.

POLITICAL

Cowan, L. Gray. "Guinea." In *African One-Party States*, ed. G. M. Carter. Ithaca, N.Y.: Cornell University Press, 1962.

de Lusignan, Guy. *French-Speaking Africa since Independence*. pp. 180–198. London: Pall Mall Press, 1969.

DuBois, Victor David. *The Independence Movement in Guinea: A Study in African Nationalism*. Princeton, N.J.: Ph.D. Thesis available from University Microfilms, 1963.

DuBois, Victor. "Guinea." In *Political Parties and National Integration in Tropical Africa*, eds. J. S. Coleman and C. G. Rosberg. Los Angeles: University of California Press, 1964.

Zartman, William I. "Guinea: The Quiet War Goes on." *Africa Report*, 12 (November 1967): 67–72.

ECONOMIC

Amin, Samir. *Trois Expériences Africaines de Développement: Le Mali, la Guinée et le Ghana*. Paris: Presses Universitaires de France, 1965.

SOCIAL

Berg, Elliot. "Education and Manpower in Senegal, Guinea, and the Ivory Coast." In *Manpower and Education: Country Studies in Economic Development*, eds. F. B. Harbison and C. Myers. New York: McGraw-Hill, 1965.

Stern, T. N. "Political Aspects of Guinean Education." *Comparative Education Review*, 8 (June 1964): 98–103.

14. Ivory Coast

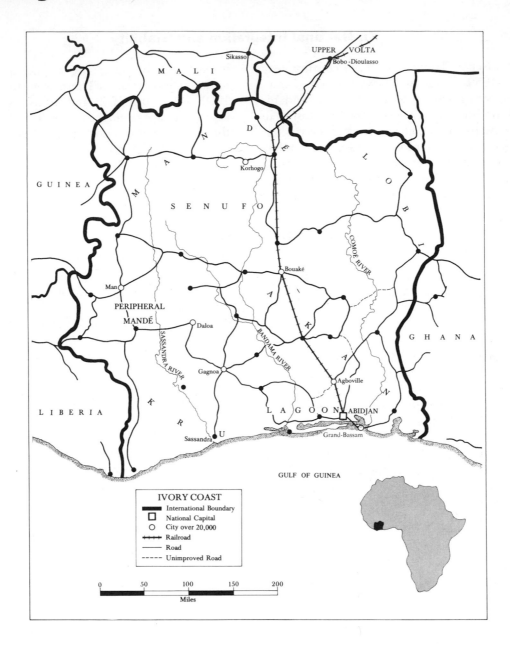

I. Basic Information

Date of Independence: August 7, 1960
Former Colonial Ruler: France
Change in Boundaries: Formerly part of the French West African Federation
Estimated Population (*1970*): 4,310,000

Area size (*equivalent in U.S.*): 725,000 sq. mi. (New Mexico)
Date of Last Census: 1957–58 (sample survey)
Major Exports 1968 as Percent of Total Exports: coffee—36 percent; wood—29 percent; cocoa—20 percent

II. Ethnic Patterns

This classification is at a relatively high level of abstraction. It is based primarily on linguistic criteria, as well as historical, ecological, and cultural factors. These seem to be the locally accepted ethno-cultural clusters, and the classification is used both by the Ivory Coast government in official sources, and by Zolberg (1963). The extent to which these clusters form identity groups is unknown.

TABLE 14.1 Ethnic Units Over 5 Percent of Country Population

Ethnic Unit	Estimated Ethnic Population 1967	Estimated Ethnic Percentage
a. Akan Cluster	1,000,000	25%
1. Baule (Baoulé)	(760,000)	(19%)
2. Agni (Anyi)	(236,000)	(6%)
i. Agni, ii. Nzima,		
iii. Ehotile, iv. Abouré,		
v. Abron		
b. Kru Type (Crau, Krao, Krawi, Nana)	732,000	18%
1. Bété	(372,000)	(9.3%)
i. Kru, ii. Dida, iii. Gueré, iv. Wobé, v. Godie, vi. Neyho		
c. Mandé Cluster	600,000	15%
1. Malinké, 2. Bambara, 3. Dyula, 4. Mahon		
d. Senufo Type (Senoufo, Sene, Siena)	520,000	13%
1. Senufo, 2. Minianka		
e. Peripheral Mandé Cluster	440,000	11%
1. Dan, 2. Yacouba, 3. Gouro, 4. Gagon		
f. Lagoon Type	292,000	7%
1. Abidji, 2. Abjukru, 3. Ebrie, 4. Attie, 5. Abe, 5. Alladian, 7. Avikam		
g. Lobi Type	236,000	6%
1. Lobi, 2. Djimini, 3. Tagouana, 4. Kulango		

SOURCES: Ivory Coast, Ministère du Plan, *Inventaire économique de la Côte d'Ivoire 1947–1956* (Abidjan, 1958), p. 26. Aristide P. Zolberg, *One-Party Government in the Ivory Coast* (Princeton, N.J.: Princeton University Press, 1963).

III. Language Patterns

There are four major language groupings in the Ivory Coast: (1) Kwa (including Akan and Kru), (2) Voltaic, (3) Mandé, and (4) Atlantic. The largest language group—the Akan—includes the Agni and Baoulé. The second largest language group—the Kru—includes Bété and Bakoué. Baoulé and Agni dialects are to some extent mutually intelligible. The Baoulé and Agni are also the two major ethnic groups in Ivory Coast, 25 percent and 18 percent respectively. Knappert estimates 30 percent for the Akan percentage of total language population, while Rustow estimates 24 percent for the Agni-Baoulé cluster within the Akan. (MacDougald's suggestion that Mossi was the major language of Ivory Coast reflects the fact that at the time of his writing, Upper Volta was part of Ivory Coast.) Rustow estimates Bété as the second language at 18 percent. This is in close agreement with our own estimate of Akan 25 percent, Bété/Kru 18 percent. It is important to note that Dyula, a Mandé language, is a trade language (*lingua franca*) in Ivory Coast.

The official language of Ivory Coast is French, and all education from grade one is conducted in French. There are no vernacular newspapers, but there is a limited amount of vernacular broadcasting. Most of the administrative units within Ivory Coast are linguistically mixed.

TABLE 14.2 Language Patterns

1. Primacy		
1st language	Akan (25%)	
2nd language	Kru-Bété (18%)	
2. Greenberg classification (all ethnic units in country over 5%)	Akan	IA4
	Kru	IA4
	Mandé	IA2
	Peripheral Mandé	IA2
	Senufo	IA3
	Lagoon Type	IA4
	Lobi	IA3
3. *Lingua franca*	Malinké/Dyula	
4. Official language	French	

IV. Urban Patterns

Capital/largest city: Abidjan (founded 1903)
Dominant ethnicity/language of capital
  Major vernacular: —
  Major ethnic group: Akan[1]
  Major ethnic group as percent of capital's population:
    15.5 percent (1965)

TABLE 14.3   Growth of Capital/Largest City

Date	Abidjan
1920	5,000
1930	10,000
1940	34,000
1950	69,000
1960	180,000
1965	360,000 UA

SOURCE: *Démographie Comparée.*

[1] Ministère des Finances, des Affaires Economiques et du Plan, *Cote d'Ivoire 1965: Population, Études Regionales 1962–1965, Synthese* (Abidjan: Ministère du Plan, July 1967).

TABLE 14.4   Cities of 20,000 and Over

City	Size	Date
Abidjan	360,000	1965
Bouaké	121,000	1965
Man	37,000	1965
Daloa	26,000	1963
Korhogo	24,000	1963
Grand-Bassam	23,000	1963

SOURCE: *Allgemeine Statistik Des Auslandes Lönderkurzberichte Elfenbeinküsk* (Stuttgart und Mainz: W. Kohlhammer, 1969), p. 10.

V. Political Patterns

A. Political Parties and Elections

In 1946, Felix Houphouet-Boigny formed the *Parti Démocratique de la Côte d'Ivoire* (PDCI) which has continued to be the dominant party until the present time. Houphouet-Boigny was also instrumental in founding the *Rassemblement Démocratique Africain* (RDA), and has been the only president of the RDA. Post-independence elections were held in November 1960, and April 1965, but the PDCI has always controlled 100 percent of the 70 seats in the Legislative Assembly. (The March 1957 national and territorial election was the last one marked by competition. The PDCI received 80 percent of the vote, and 58 out of 60 seats in the Territorial Assembly.) In the 1965 presidential election, Houphouet-Boigny received 1,723,058 (99.98 percent) of the votes. Splinter groups have developed periodically, but the Ivory Coast is a *de facto* one-party state.

B. Political Leadership

The government of President Houphouet-Boigny has been in power in the Ivory Coast continuously since independence. The composition of the cabinet has been enlarged in the post-independence period.

TABLE 14.5   Head of Government (Post Independence)

Name	Dates in Office	Age (1971)	Ethnicity	Education	Former Occupation
1. Felix Houphouet-Boigny (President)	1960–	66	Akan (Baoulé)	University (Dakar)	Doctor (M.D.)

Figure 14.1 **Political Parties and Elections**

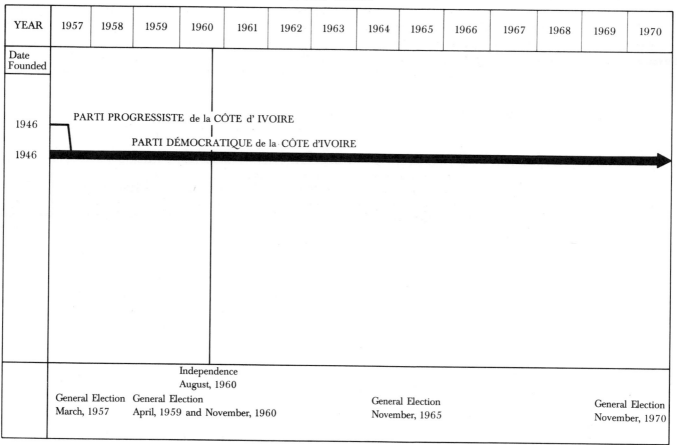

IVORY COAST

YEAR	1957	1958	1959	1960	1961	1962	1963	1964	1965	1966	1967	1968	1969	1970

Date Founded

1946   PARTI PROGRESSISTE de la CÔTE d' IVOIRE

1946   PARTI DÉMOCRATIQUE de la CÔTE d'IVOIRE

Independence
August, 1960

General Election   General Election
March, 1957   April, 1959 and November, 1960

General Election
November, 1965

General Election
November, 1970

Except for the marked internal reorganization and a number of dismissals from the cabinet in 1963, the government of the Ivory Coast has been little changed. Recruitment to executive office is broadly based, although persons of Akan background have become increasingly prominent in government.

TABLE 14.6 Cabinet Membership: Distribution by Ethnic Unit*

*Ethnicity**	*Independence Cabinet*	*1967 Cabinet*
1. Akan (25%)	33%	47%
2. Kru (18)	8.3	12
3. Mandé (15)	8.3	24
4. Senufo (13)	0	0
5. Peripheral Mandé (11)	0	0
6. Lagoon Type (7)	25	12
7. Lobi (6)	0	5.9
8. Others (5)	25	0
N =	12	17

* Ethnic units arranged in rank order of size within country with the unit's percent of national population in parentheses.

VI. National Integration and Stability

The regime of Houphouet-Boigny has continued since independence. The only evidence of elite instability was a major plot in 1963 and a number of rumored plots since. Economic prosperity seems to have alleviated some of the usual tensions of communal competition. Important sub-national identities exist, however, including a north/south regionalism which is reinforced by religious and cultural ties. Attempts to secede were made by the Agni in 1959; these were supported by Kwame Nkrumah, and they broke out again at the end of 1969.

TABLE 14.8   Communal Instability

Event and Date	Characteristics
Civil War December 1969	a. *Description*: A short-lived civil war was fought in the Aboisso region in the southeast of the Ivory Coast in December 1969. The insurgents were reported to be armed, and to have been provided with shirts thought to make them invulnerable to bullets. The army of the Ivory Coast, however, succeeded in killing and wounding several people, and brought the war to an end. How severe the military action was, and how long the civil war lasted is not known since the army operation was conducted in secret. b. *Participants*: The insurgents were members of the Agni tribe, and were organized by the Sanwi Liberation Movement. c. *Apparent Causes*: The Ivory Coast Minister of Interior said that the Sanwi movement believed that because the government had recognized Biafra, it should also grant independence to the Sanwi. According to the *New York Times* the Agni resented being ruled by a member of the Baoulé tribe and the Agni chiefs told their people that the Baoulé were going to massacre them.

VII. Selected References

BIBLIOGRAPHY

Organization for Economic Cooperation and Development. Development Center. *Essai d'une Bibliographie sur la Côte d'Ivoire*. Paris: O.E.C.D., 1964.

GENERAL

DuBois, Victor. *Ivory Coast*. Ithaca, N.Y.: Cornell University Press, forthcoming.

Foster, Philip, and Aristide R. Zolberg. *Ghana and the Ivory Coast: Perspectives on Modernization*. Chicago, Ill.: University of Chicago Press, 1971.

Siegel, Efrem. "Ivory Coast: Booming Economy, Political Calm." *Africa Report*, 15 (April 1970): 18–21.

Thompson, Virginia, and Richard Adloff. *French West Africa*, pp. 117–131. Stanford, Cal.: Stanford University Press, 1957.

U.S. Department of the Army. *Area Handbook for the Ivory Coast*. Washington, D.C.: Government Printing Office, 1962.

POLITICAL

de Lusignan, Guy. *French-Speaking Africa since Independence*, pp. 135–145. London: Pall Mall Press, 1969.

Thompson, Virginia. "Ivory Coast." In *African One-Party States*, ed. G. M. Carter. Ithaca, N.Y.: Cornell University Press, 1962.

Wallerstein, Immanuel. *The Road to Independence: Ghana and the Ivory Coast*. The Hague: Mouton, 1964.

Zolberg, Aristide. "Ivory Coast." In *Political Parties and National Integration in Tropical Africa*, eds. J. S. Coleman and C. G. Rosberg. Los Angeles: University of California Press, 1964.

Zolberg, Aristide. *One-Party Government in the Ivory Coast*. Princeton, N.J.: Princeton University Press, 1964, new ed. 1969.

ECONOMIC

Amin, Samir. *Le Développement du Capitalisme en Côte d'Ivoire*. Paris: Éditions de Minuit, 1967. [See review in the *Journal of Modern African Studies*, 6 (December 1966): 590–593.]

Due, Jean M. "Agricultural Development in the Ivory Coast and Ghana." *The Journal of Modern African Studies*, 7 (1969): 637–660.

EDIAFRIC. *L'Economie Ivorienne*. Paris: 1970.

International Monetary Fund. "Ivory Coast." In *Surveys of African Economies*, Vol. 3. Washington, D.C.: I.M.F., 1970.

Miracle, Marvin. "The Economy of the Ivory Coast." In *The Economies of Africa*, eds. P. Robson and D. A. Lury, pp. 195–235. Evanston, Ill.: Northwestern University Press, 1969.

SOCIAL

Berg, Elliot. "Education and Manpower in Senegal, Guinea, and the Ivory Coast," In *Manpower and Education: Country Studies in Economic Development*, eds. F. B. Harbison and C. Myers. New York: McGraw-Hill, 1965.

Clignet, Remi, and Philip Foster. *The Fortunate Few: A Study of Secondary Schools and Students in the Ivory Coast*. Evanston, Ill.: Northwestern University Press, 1966.

Holas, Bohumil. *Changements sociaux en Côte d'Ivoire*. Paris: Presses Universitaires de France, 1961.

Holas, Bohumil. *Le séparatisme religieux en Afrique noire: L'exemple de la Côte d'Ivoire*. Paris: Presses Universitaires de France, 1965.

15. Kenya

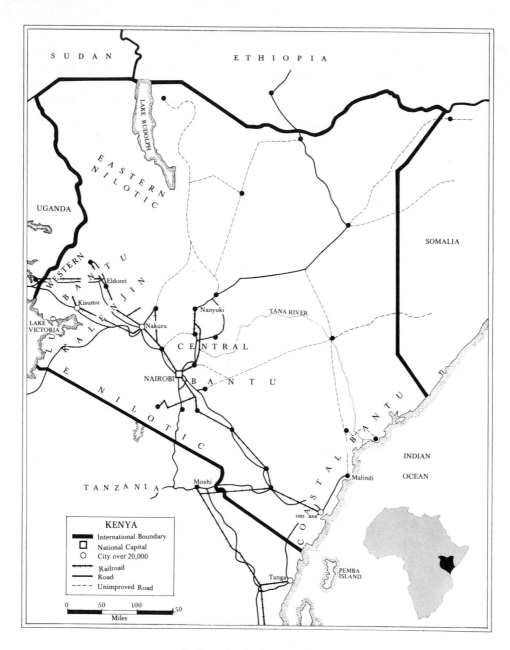

I. Basic Information

Date of Independence: December 12, 1963
Former Colonial Ruler: United Kingdom
Estimated Population (1969): 10,890,000 (census)
Area Size (equivalent in U.S.): 225,000 sq. mi. (Nevada and New Mexico)

Date of Last Census: 1969
Major Exports 1968 (excluding Uganda and Tanzania) as Percent of Total Exports: coffee—20 percent; tea—14 percent; petroleum products—9 percent

II. Ethnic Patterns

The ethnic classification selected for Kenya is that used by the Kenya census (1962), which states that the groupings were made on the basis of "ethnic, linguistic, and geographical considerations" and involves "somewhat arbitrary" groupings in certain cases. Thus, the Boni and Sanye, who are said to be among the oldest hunting tribes of Kenya, have been placed in their respective groups on account of linguistic and geographical considerations. None of the ethnic units are themselves identity groups except for the Luo, a Nilotic people. The sub-groups are all identity groups, although the Luhya is an emerging identity group whose sub-groups have a significant sense of self-identity. Excluded here are two northern clusters: Somali-speaking Eastern Hamatic groups (Gosha, Hawiyah, Ogaden, Ajuran, Gurreh), 3 percent; and Rendille and Galla-speaking Western Hamitic groups (Rendille, Boran, Gabbra, Sakakuya, Orma), 1 percent.

TABLE 15.1 Ethnic Units Over 5 Percent of Country Population

Ethnic Unit	Estimated Ethnic Population 1967	Estimated Ethnic Percentage
a. Central Bantu Cluster	3,780,000	38%
1. Kikuyu	(1,890,000)	(19%)
2. Kamba	(1,094,000)	(11%)
3. Meru	(497,000)	(5%)
4. Embu	(100,000)	(1%)
5. Mbere, 6. Tharaka, 7. Chuka,		
8. Igoji, 9. Miutini, 10. Mwimbi,		
11. Muthambi		

b. Western Bantu (Kavirondo) Cluster		19%
1. Luhya	(1,293,000)	(13%)
i. Isukka, ii. Idakho, iii. Kabras, iv. Nyala, v. Tsotso, vi. Wanga, vii. Marama, viii. Kisa, ix. Nyore, x. Maragoli, xi. Tiriki, xii. Bakhayo, xiii. Tachoni, xiv. Marach, xv. Samia, xvi. Bukusu		
2. Kisii (Gusii)	(597,000)	(6%)
3. Kuria		
c. Luo	1,393,000	14%
d. Kalenjin-Speaking Cluster	1,094,000	10%
1. Kipsigis	(398,000)	(4%)
2. Nandi	(199,000)	(2%)
3. Tugen	(115,000)	(1.1%)
4. Elgeyo	(100,000)	(1%)
5. Pokot (Suk), 6. Marakwet, 7. Sabaot		
e. Coastal Bantu Cluster		5%
1. Mijikenda	(500,000)	(5%)
i. Digo, ii. Duruma, iii. Chonyi, iv. Giriama, v. Rabai, vi. Ribe, vii. Jibana viii. Kauma, ix. Kambe		
2. Pokomo/Riverine, 3. Bajun, 4. Swahili/Shirazi, 5. Taveta, 6. Boni/Sanye		
f. Other Eastern Nilotic Groups		4.5%
1. Turkana	(230,000)	(2.1%)
2. Masai	(200,000)	(2%)
3. Iteso (Wamia, Elgumi)		
4. Samburu (Burkeneji)		
5. Nderobo, 6. Njemps		

SOURCE: *Kenya Population Census, 1962, Advance Report of Volumes I and II* (Nairobi: Economics and Statistics Division, Ministry of Finance and Economic Planning, January 1964): pp. 2–3, 45.

III. Language Patterns

The two major language families of Kenya are Bantu and Chari-Nile (especially the Nilotic sub-branch). The two major languages, Swahili and Kikuyu are both Bantu. Estimates of percent total speakers of these languages varies. For Swahili, Knappert suggests 25 percent; however, many recent estimates go as high as 85 percent. Since December 31, 1971 has been set as the date for Swahili to become the national language in Kenya, we have chosen a high estimate of 65 percent which is expected to increase rapidly. Kikuyu is part of the Central Bantu cluster, but as a distinct language probably has only 25 percent of total population as speakers. (MacDougald estimates 21 percent; Rustow 29 percent).

TABLE 15.2   Language Patterns

1. Primacy
1st language	Swahili	(65%)
2nd language	Kikuyu	(25%)
2. Greenberg classification
   (all ethnic units in
   country over 5%)
	Central Bantu	IA5
	Western Bantu	IA5
	Luo	IIE1
	Kalenjin	IIE1
	Coastal Bantu	IA5
	Eastern Nilotic (Masai)	IIE1
3. *Lingua franca*   Swahili
4. Official language   English*

* On December 31, 1971, Swahili replaced English as the official language of Kenya.

SOURCE: Lyndon Harries, "Swahili in Modern East Africa," in *Language Problems of Developing Nations*, eds. Joshua A. Fishman, Charles A. Ferguson, and Jyotirindra Das Gupta (New York: John Wiley, 1968), pp. 119–127.

IV. Urban Patterns

Capital/largest city: Nairobi (founded 1899)

Dominant ethnicity/language of capital

   Major vernacular: Kikuyu[1]

   Major ethnic group: Kikuyu[2]

   Major ethnic group as percent of capital's population:
   42 percent (1962)

TABLE 15.3   Growth of Capital/Largest City

Date	Nairobi
1920	14,000
1930	52,000
1940	65,000
1950	119,000
1960	267,000
1962	314,000 UA
1969	478,000 UA

SOURCES: Various editions of the *Statesman's Yearbook*, except for the 1950 figure which is from *East African High Commission Statistical Bulletin*, 2, No. 19: 14.

TABLE 15.4   Cities of 20,000 and Over

City	Size	Date
Nairobi	478,000 UA	1969
Mombasa	246,000 UA	1969
Nakuru	47,800	1969
Kisumu	30,700	1969

SOURCE: Provisional census results.

[1] Jan Knappert, "Language Problems of the New Nations of Africa," *African Quarterly*, 5 (1965): 95–105.

[2] Census (1962).

V. Political Patterns

A. Political Parties and Elections

Political party life in Kenya during this decade has been dominated by two major parties, both founded in 1960 by mergers of smaller parties. The *Kenya African National Union* (KANU) was originally led by James Gichuru and was based primarily on support from Kikuyu and Luo ethnic groups. The *Kenya African Democratic Union* (KADU) was comprised mainly of smaller ethnic groups and was led by Ronald Ngala. Although KANU won a majority in the 1961 elections, they refused to take office as long as Jomo Kenyatta was not allowed to form the government. KADU thus became the governing party until 1962 when a coalition between KANU and KADU was formed. The elections in May 1963 again gave Kenyatta and KANU a majority and he became prime minister. After independence, KANU continued to govern; in 1964 KADU merged with KANU. Kenyatta continued as president with Oginga Odinga as vice-president. Significant opposition to KANU emerged in 1966 with the defection from the ruling party of Oginga Odinga and some of his parliamentary followers and the formation of the *Kenya People's Union* (KPU). The significance of this opposition may be indicated by Odinga's subjection to house arrest and the banning of his party prior to the general election of December 1969. This election appears to have been a setback to the Kenyatta regime, since 96 incumbents (including five ministers) were defeated by other KANU candidates.

B. Political Leadership

The government of Kenya, under President Jomo Kenyatta, has been continuously in power since independence in 1963. The cabinet has been enlarged, and, except for a notable increase in dismissals and resignations in 1966, cabinet membership has remained fairly stable. Recruitment to cabinet positions is broadly based, although the Central Bantu peoples of Kenya are very prominently represented in the cabinet.

Figure 15.1 **Political Parties and Elections**

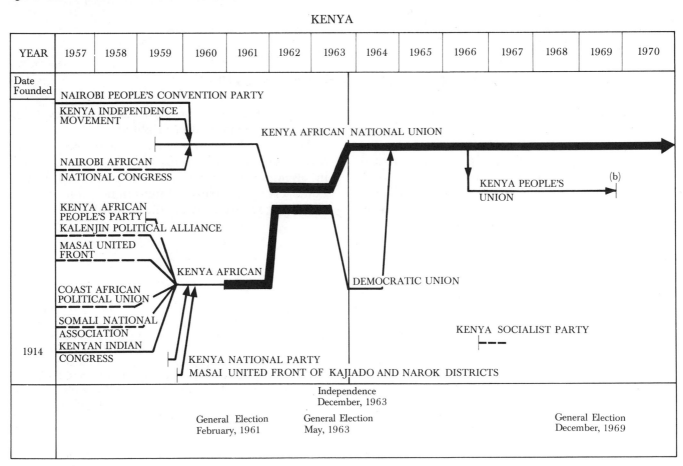

TABLE 15.5 Head of Government (Post Independence)

Name	Dates in Office	Age (1971)	Ethnicity	Education	Former Occupation
1. Jomo Kenyatta (President)	1963–	80	Central Bantu (Kikuyu)	London School of Economics	Politician

TABLE 15.6 Cabinet Membership: Distribution by Ethnic Unit*

Ethnicity*	Independence Cabinet	1967 Cabinet
1. Central Bantu (38%)	50%	52%
2. Western Bantu (13)	13	19
3. Luo (14)	25	14
4. Kalenjin-speaking (10)	0	4.8
5. Coastal Bantu (5)	0	4.8
6. Other Eastern Nilotic (4)	6.3	0
7. Others (16)	6.3	4.8
N =	16	21

* Ethnic groups arranged in rank order of size within country with the unit's percent of national population in parentheses.

VI. National Integration and Stability

Although there has been no instance of elite instability under the regime of Jomo Kenyatta, the assassination of Tom Mboya (Luo), and the imprisonment of Oginga Odinga (Luo) have created an atmosphere of inter-elite tension between Kikuyu and non-Kikuyu leaders and, within the Kikuyu, between the various clans. Despite the riots following the death of Mboya, the government of Kenya— as of July 1971—has been successful in preventing widespread communal instability.

The isolated instances of instability in Kenya have involved communal groups that have been engaged in attempted rebellion (the Kikuyu-based Kenya Land Freedom Army), inter-ethnic violence (the Turkana), or irredentism (the Somali).

TABLE 15.8 Communal Instability

Event and Date	Characteristics
1. Rebellion July 1961–1965	a. *Description*: With the formal ending of the state of emergency which existed in Kenya during most of the 1950s as a result of the Mau Mau revolution, a remnant of the Mau Mau forces continued to rebel against government forces, even after the governmental power shifted out of British hands. The so-called Kenya Land Freedom Army continued to make sporadic attacks on European, Kikuyu, Meru, Embu, and Somali settlements. In 1961 and 1962 more than 200 persons were arrested for Land Freedom Army activities in the Rift Valley. In May 1964, 200 members of the KLFA battled the Kenya police 30 miles south of Meru. The government eventually granted amnesty to the KLFA, and most surrendered.
	b. *Participants*: Leadership included Gatutu Gatuthuri (arrested in July 1961) and Cheze Mwanzo (arrested in March 1962). In January 1965, the two subsequent major leaders were killed, namely Baimungi and Chui. General China has written an autobiographical account of his own involvement in the KLFA.

TABLE 15.8 Communal Instability *(cont.)*

Event and Date	Characteristics
	c. *Apparent Causes*: Minority elements within the predominantly Kikuyu Mau Mau movement were dissatisfied with lack of comprehensive expropriation of European land and alleged government inequity in redistribution.
2. Ethnic Violence; January 1960–August 1964	a. *Description*: From January 1960–November 30, 1961, there were approximately 77 border incidents involving the Turkana in which 38 people were killed. In March 1962 the Kenya Ministry of Defense deployed 1000 troops and police who tried to disarm the Turkana tribesmen. In August 1964 about 200 Merille and Dongiro tribesmen on the Ethiopia–Kenya border retaliated against the Turkana, killing 121. On November 13, 1964, the Kenya-Ethiopia Consultative Council discussed border raids from Ethiopia and both governments promised action against persons involved.
	b. *Participants*: Turkana tribesmen attacked groups in Kenya and Ethiopia.
	c. *Apparent Causes*: Traditional animosity.
3. Irredentism ca. 1962–1968	a. *Description*: In 1962 Somali tribesmen in the Northeastern Region, of Kenya which borders on Somalia, declared before an Independent Commission that they wished to secede from Kenya and join Somalia. On November 13, 1963, Somali insurgents began a series of armed raids. On December 25, 1963, the Kenya government declared a state of emergency in the Northeastern Region. The Kenya Rifles subsequently patrolled the area, resulting in a series of armed clashes between the insurgents and the Kenya Rifles. In July 1966 large sections of the Kenya army were deployed in the area. During the 1963–1966 period approximately 1600 insurgents were killed.
	b. *Participants*: Somali ethnic groups in Northeastern Kenya, Somali insurgents from Somalia and the government of Kenya. There were no noticeable leaders of the Kenyan Somali groups. Several Somali traditional leaders who supported the Kenya government were abducted.
	c. *Apparent Causes*: Somali tribesmen's claims for reunion with kinsmen in Somalia. Kenya government's demands for national unity.

SOURCES: A. A. Castagno, "The Somali-Kenya Controversy," *Journal of Modern African Studies*, 2 (1964): 165–188. Waruhiu Itote (General China), "*Mau Mau*" *General* (Nairobi: East African Publishing House, 1967).

VII. Selected References

BIBLIOGRAPHY

Hakes, Jay E. *A Study Guide for Kenya*. Boston: Development Program, African Studies Center, Boston University, 1969.

United States Library of Congress. General Reference and Bibliography Division. African Section. *Official Publications of British East Africa. Part III. Kenya and Zanzibar*. Washington, D.C.: Government Printing Office, 1963.

Webster, J. B., et al. *A Bibliography on Kenya*. Eastern African Bibliographical Series no. 2. Syracuse, N.Y.: Syracuse Eastern African Studies Program, 1967.

GENERAL

Carey Jones, N. S. *The Anatomy of Uhuru: Dynamics and Problems of African Independence in an Age of Conflict*. New York: Praeger, 1967.

MacPhee, A. Marshall. *Kenya*. New York: Praeger, 1968.

Rosberg, Carl. *Kenya*. Ithaca, N.Y.: Cornell University Press, forthcoming.

U.S. Department of the Army. *Area Handbook for Kenya*. Pamphlet No. 550–56. Washington: Government Printing Office, 1967.

POLITICAL

Bennett, George. *Kenya: A Political History—The Colonial Period*. Students Library, no. 1. London: Oxford University Press, 1963.

Burke, Fred G. "Political Evolution in Kenya." In *The Transformation of East Africa*, eds. Stanley Diamond and Fred G. Burke. New York: Basic Books, 1966.

Gertzel, Cherry. *The Politics of Independent Kenya 1963–1968*. London: Heinemann, 1970.

Kenyatta, Jomo. *Suffering without Bitterness: The Founding of the Kenya Nation*. Nairobi: East African Publishing House, 1968.

Odinga, Oginga. *Not Yet Uhuru*. New York: Hill and Wang, 1967.

Rosberg, Carl G., and John Nottingham. *The Myth of Mau-Mau: Nationalism in Kenya*. N.Y.: Praeger, 1966.

ECONOMIC

International Bank for Reconstruction and Development. *The Economic Development of Kenya*. Baltimore, Md.: Johns Hopkins Press, 1963.

International Monetary Fund. "Kenya." In *Surveys of African Economies*, Vol. 2, pp. 137–209. Washington, D.C.: I.M.F., 1968.

Oser, Jacob. *Promoting Economic Development: With Illustrations from Kenya*. Evanston, Ill.: Northwestern University Press, 1967.

SOCIAL

Cowan, L. Gray. *The Costs of Learning: The Politics of Primary Education in Kenya*. New York: Columbia Teachers College Press, 1970.

de Blij, Harm J. *Mombasa: An African City*. Evanston, Ill.: Northwestern University Press, 1968.

Forrester, Marion W. *Kenya Today, Social Prerequisites for Economic Development*. The Hague: Mouton, 1962.

Morgan, W. T. W. *Nairobi: City and Region*. London: Oxford University Press, 1967.

Ominde, S. H. *Land and Population Movements of Kenya*. Evanston, Ill.: Northwestern University Press, 1968.

Soja, Edward W. *The Geography of Modernization in Kenya; A Spatial Analysis of Social, Economic and Political Change*. Syracuse, N.Y.: Syracuse University Press, 1968.

Weeks, Sheldon. *Divergence in Educational Development: The Case of Kenya and Uganda*. New York: Columbia Teachers College Press, 1967.

16. Lesotho

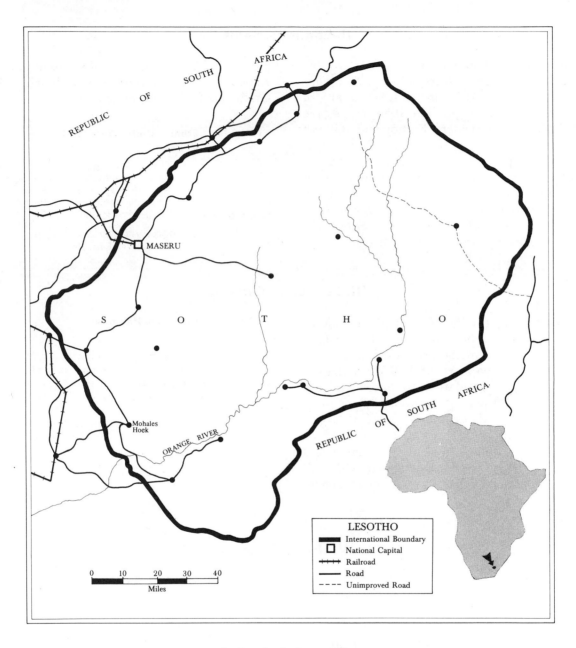

I. Basic Information

Date of Independence: October 4, 1966
Fomer Colonial Ruler: United Kingdom
Fomer Name: Basutoland
Estimated Population (1970): 1,040,000*
Area Size (equivalent in U.S.). 12,000 sq. mi. (New Hampshire and Delaware)

Date of Last Census: 1966
Major Exports 1967 as Percent of Total Exports: wool and mohair—30 percent; cattle—29 percent; diamonds—24 percent

* Includes absentee workers (approximately 12 percent of population).

II. Ethnic Patterns

The Sotho, who predominate in Lesotho, are distinguished by language, culture, history, and common identity. Other Africans in Lesotho are of Ngoni (Central Bantu) origin. The 1956 census gave only the figure of 83 percent Sotho, and did not break down the rest of the African population. It is probable that 83 percent is a low figure. Of central importance, Sotho is a kingdom and not just a kinship group. "Non-Sotho" peoples in the Sotho kingdom, have come to be regarded as Sotho. The 1966 census showed that about 117,000 Sotho had migrated temporarily to South Africa for work purposes. This would bring the population to about 1,000,000. In 1956 about 4.3 percent of the population was European, mixed, or Asian.

TABLE 16.1   Ethnic Units Over 5 Percent of Country Population

Ethnic Units	Estimated Ethnic Population 1967	Estimated Ethnic Percentage
a. Sotho (Basotho, Basuto)	734,600	95%

SOURCES: *1956 Basutoland Population Census*. J. E. Spence, *Lesotho, the Politics of Dependence* (London: Oxford, 1968).

III. Language Patterns

Lesotho consists essentially of a single kingdom: Sotho (95 percent). There are no other ethnic groups of over 5 percent. Sotho is used as a *lingua franca*, and both Knappert and Rustow regard virtually the entire population as Sotho-speaking (100 percent and 99 percent respectively). Rustow suggests that Zulu-Xhosa is the second largest language, with only 1 percent. Our own estimate is Sotho 99 percent; Zulu 1 percent. Both languages are Bantu. English is the official language, although since independence Sotho has also become an official language.

TABLE 16.2   Language Patterns

1. Primacy			
	1st language	Sotho	(99%)
	2nd language	Zulu	(1%)
2. Greenberg classification		Sotho	IA5
	(all ethnic units in	Zulu	IA5
	country over 5%)		
3. *Lingua franca*		Sotho	
4. Official languages		English, Sotho	

IV. Urban Patterns

Capital/largest city: Maseru (founded 1869)
Dominant ethnicity/language of capital
    Major vernacular: Sotho
    Major ethnic group: Sotho
    Major ethnic group as percent of capital's population:
      Nearly 100%

TABLE 16.3   Growth of Capital/Largest City

Date	Maseru
1920	2,000
1950	6,000
1960	9,000
1966	18,000 UA

SOURCES: Various editions of the *Statesman's Yearbook*.

TABLE 16.4   Cities of 20,000 and Over

City	Size	Date
Maseru*	18,000 UA	1966

* Although Maseru was under 20,000 in 1966, it is included since it is the only sizable town in Lesotho.
SOURCE: Census.

V. Political Patterns

A. Political Parties and Elections

Until 1970, political life in Lesotho was marked by the competition of three major parties. The *Basuto Congress Party* (BCP) was dominant from 1960 to 1965. The *Marema Tlou Freedom Party* (MFP) was formed in 1963 by a merger of the *Marema Tlou Party* (MTP) and the *Basuto Freedom Party* (BFP) under Bennet Khaketla. Along with the *Basuto National Party* (BNP), it served as opposition. In the election prior to independence the more conservative BNP, led by Chief Leabua Jonathan, won a narrow victory and elected 31 members to the National Assembly, while the BCP elected 25 and the MFP elected 4 members. In January 1970, after his leading political opponent, Ntsu Mokhehle of the BCP, had claimed victory in the general elections, Chief Jonathan suspended the constitution and took control of the government. At this time, according to *Africa South of the Sahara, 1971* (Europa Publications, 1971), all the opposition parties were banned.

B. Political Leadership

The government of Prime Minister Jonathan has remained unchanged since independence in 1966, and the cabinet, like the country itself, is ethnically homogeneous. The head of state is the young, Oxford-educated Paramount Chief, Motlotlehi Moshoeshoe II, who became a constitutional monarch in 1967 and who was placed under arrest after Chief Jonathan's coup in 1970.

Figure 16.1 **Political Parties and Elections**

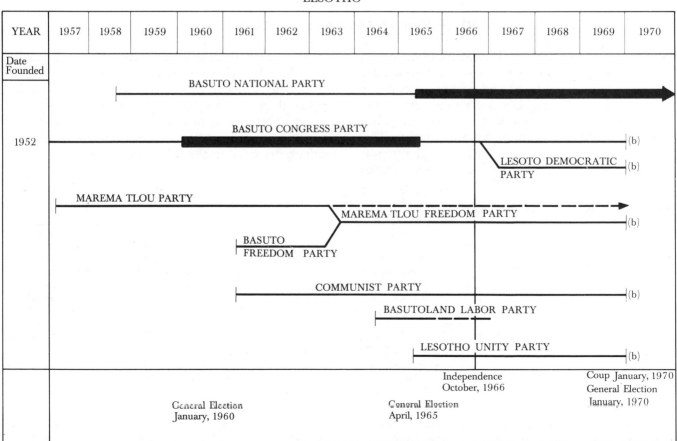

TABLE 16.5   Head of Government (Post Independence)

Name	Dates in Office	Age (1971)	Ethnicity	Education	Former Occupation
1. Chief Leabua Jonathan (Prime Minister)	1966–	57	Sotho	Primary, Mission School	Clerk, Storekeeper

TABLE 16.6   Cabinet Membership: Distribution by Ethnic Unit*

Ethnicity*	Independence Cabinet	1967 Cabinet
1. Sotho (95%)	100%	100%
2. Others (5)	0	0
N =	10	10

* Ethnic units arranged in rank order of size within country with the unit's percent of national population in parentheses.

VI. National Integration and Stability

There are personal and ideological conflicts among the major political leaders of the country which are complicated by its political and economic situation vis-à-vis South Africa. On December 30, 1966, supporters of King Moshoeshoe attacked the police station at Butha Buthe in northern Lesotho. This action, which was followed by other incidents, was reputedly part of the effort of the *Basuto Congress Party* (BCP) to shift power from Prime Minister Jonathan to King Moshoeshoe which resulted in Jonathan's moving against the king and limiting his political power. In January 1970 Chief Jonathan assumed extra-constitutional control following an apparent election defeat. A number of violent incidents occurred in the following months.

TABLE 16.7   Elite Instability

Event and Date	Characteristics
1. Coup d'État January 30. 1970	a. *Description*: Following an election in which his party, the Basutoland National Party, was apparently defeated, the prime minister, Chief Jonathan, proclaimed a state of emergency and suspended the constitution. He arrested all the executive members and many candidates of the rival Basutoland Congress Party and placed restrictions on the head of state, King Moshoeshoe II. b. *Participants*: The prime minister, counseled by "hard men in his party, together with some of the political appointees amongst the top civil servants." c. *Apparent Causes*: It seems that the Basutoland National Party only won 23 seats to the Basutoland Congress Party's 36 (Chief Jonathan is a strong advocate of close ties with South Africa while Ntsu Mokhehle, the head of the Congress Party, favors greater independence from South Africa). Chief Jonathan acted to continue himself in power.

SOURCES: "Lesotho Crisis," *Africa Digest*, 17 (1970): 27–28. "Lesotho Coup," *Africa Report*, 15 (March 1970): 3–4.

VII. Selected References

BIBLIOGRAPHY

Gordon, Loraine. *Lesotho: A Bibliography*. Johannesburg: University of the Witwatersrand, Department of Bibliography, Librarianship and Typography, 1970.

GENERAL

Ashton, Hugh. *The Basuto: A Social Study of Traditional and Modern Lesotho*, 2nd ed. London: Oxford, 1967.

Central Office of Information Reference Pamphlet. *Lesotho*. London: Her Majesty's Stationery Office, 1966.

Coates, Austin. *Basutoland*. London: Her Majesty's Stationery Office, 1966.

Stevens, Richard. *Lesotho, Botswana, and Swaziland*. London: Pall Mall Press, 1967.

POLITICAL

Spence, J. E. *Lesotho: The Politics of Independence*. London: Oxford University Press, 1968.

Weisfelder, Richard. "Power Struggle in Lesotho." *Africa Report*, 12 (January 1967): 5–13.

ECONOMIC

Ward, Michael. "Economic Independence for Lesotho?" *Journal of Modern African Studies*, 5 (1967): 355–368.

Leistner, J. M. E. *Lesotho: Economic Structure and Growth*. Pretoria: Africa Institute, 1966.

SOCIAL

Gerard, Albert S. "Literature of Lesotho." *Africa Report*, 11 (October 1965): 68–70.

Rose, Brian. "Education in Botswana, Lesotho and Swaziland." In *Education in Southern Africa*, ed. B. Rose. London: Collier-Macmillan, 1970.

Sheddick, Vernon G. J. *The Southern Sotho*. Ethnographic Survey of Africa. Southern Africa, pt. 2. London: International African Institute, 1953.

17. Liberia

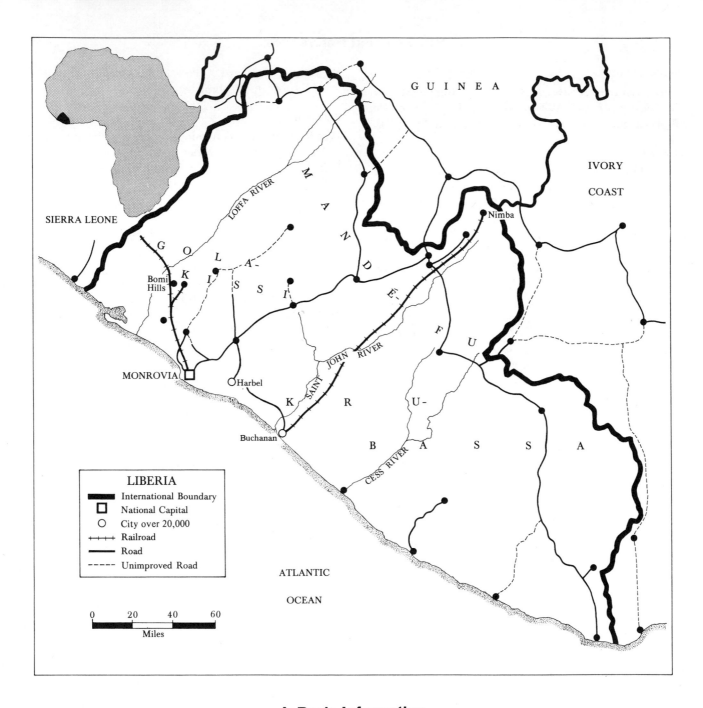

LIBERIA
- ▬ International Boundary
- ☐ National Capital
- ○ City over 20,000
- ┼┼┼ Railroad
- ── Road
- ---- Unimproved Road

0   20   40   60
Miles

GUINEA

IVORY
COAST

SIERRA LEONE

LOFFA RIVER

M A N D E

G O L A K I S S I

Nimba

Bomi
Hills

K P E L L E

MONROVIA

Harbel

SAINT JOHN RIVER

K R U - B A S S A

Buchanan

CESS RIVER

ATLANTIC

OCEAN

I. Basic Information

Date of Independence: 1847
Estimated Population (*1970*): 1,170,000
Area Size (*equivalent in U.S.*): 43,000 sq. mi. (Ohio)

Date of Last Census: 1962
Major Exports 1968 as Percent of Total Exports: iron ore—70 percent; rubber—15 percent

II. Ethnic Patterns

Liberia is an especially difficult country to classify into ethnic units. Pending the forthcoming publication in the Liberian Studies Working Papers Series (Department of Anthropology, University of Delaware) of a series of ethnographic and linguistic maps of Liberia, we have adopted, for the most part, the categories used by the Liberian government. These are based mainly on linguistic criteria. As an example of the complexity in individual cases, the Vai may be cited. They are close linguistically to the Mandingo, but many were Gola. In addition to the units listed, there is a small intrusive population of Mandingos (about 3 percent), as well as an even smaller population of Fanti fishermen from Ghana. Some writers on Liberia refer to the descendants of the original settlers from America as "Americo-Liberians." With increasing intermarriage between the descendants of the settlers and the growth of the Westernized urban population, this sharp a distinction now seems inappropriate. Locally, the urban Westernized people (including the settler descendants) are now referred to as the "Kwi" and there is an increasing tendency on the part of the settler descendants to emphasize "tribal" names and identities.

TABLE 17.1 Ethnic Units Over 5 Percent of Country Population

Ethnic Units	Estimated Ethnic Population 1967	Estimated Ethnic Percentage
a. Mandé-Fu Type	488,000	*44%*
1. Kpellé (Guerzé)	(230,000)	(21%)
2. Gio (Dan)	(91,000)	(8%)
3. Mano (Manon)	(78,000)	(7%)
4. Lorma (Buzzi, Loma, Toma)	(58,000)	(5%)
5. Ghandi (Bandi)	(31,000)	(3%)
6. Mendé		
b. Kru-Bassa Type (Coastal Cluster)	410,000	*37%*
1. Bassa (Basa, Basso, Gbasa)	(180,000)	(16%)
2. Kru (Crau, Krao, Nana)	(87,000)	(8%)
3. Grebo	(84,000)	(8%)
4. Krahn (Gueré)	(57,000)	(5%)
5. Dei		
c. Gola-Kissi Cluster (Mel, West Atlantic)	88,000	*8%*
1. Gola		
2. Kissi (Ghizi, Gissi, Kisi)		
d. Vai (Northern Mandé, Mandé-tan)		*3%*

SOURCES: *Liberia, Basic Data and Information* (Monrovia: Government Printer, 1966), p. 10; Colin Legum, *Africa* (New York: Praeger, 1966), pp. 231–232.

III. Language Patterns

The discussion of Liberia's language classification has centered on the distinction between various branches of Mandé which Welmers has now resolved. The current discussion centers on the classification of the Kru-speaking peoples. Westermann and Bryan (1952) used the distinction between Mandé-tan (including Soninké, Maninka-Bambara-Dyula, Khasonke, Vai) and Mandé-Fu (Susu-Yalunka, Mendé, Loko, Kpellé, Loma, Bandi, Mano, Gio-Dan). Welmers now suggests four categories: (1) Northern (including Susu-Yalunka, Soninké, Vai, Khasonke, Maninke-Bambara-Dyula), (2) Southwestern (Mandé, Loko, Bandi, Loma, Kpellé), (3) Southern (Mano, Gio-Dan, Tura, Mwa, Nwa, Gan, Kweni-Guro), (4) Eastern (Sya, Samo, Bisa, Busa). Westermann did see the close relationship between the Mandé-Fu (Welmers' Southwestern group) and the Mano and Gio, calling them collectively the "Mendé-Kpellé" group. We have decided to adopt the Mandé-Fu/Kpellé group as a language class (Mandé speakers) even though Rustow estimates that only 25 percent of the population understand Kpellé. The Mandé speakers are probably slightly larger in number than the Kru group (including Bassa). (MacDougald estimates Kru at 26 percent; Rustow, Kru-Bassa at 30 percent.)

The Vai language has a script and a literature, which is apparently used by other groups in addition to the Vai ethnic group. The settlers from America in Liberia used English, which is now related to other coastal English creole languages. English is the official language of Liberia.

TABLE 17.2 Language Patterns

1. Primacy

1st language	Mandé	(44%)
2nd language	Kru-Bassa	(37%)

2. Greenberg classification (all ethnic units in country over 5%)

Mandé-Fu	IA2
Kru-Bassa	IA4
Gola-Kissi	IA1

3. *Lingua franca*   English
(English is the first language of the settler descendants and is regarded as indigenous in this case)

4. Official language   English

IV. Urban Patterns

Capital/largest city: Monrovia (founded 1822)

Dominant ethnicity/language of capital

Major vernacular: English[1]

Major ethnic group: Kru-speaking peoples[2]

Major ethnic group as percent of capital's population: 45% (1959)

TABLE 17.3 Growth of Capital/Largest City

Date	Monrovia
1920	4,000
1930	10,000
1940	12,000
1950	42,000
1960	62,000
1965	ca. 100,000

SOURCE: Merran Fraenkel, *Tribe and Class in Monrovia* (London: Oxford University Press, 1964). The 1962 Liberian Census gave 81,000 as the population of Monrovia.

TABLE 17.4 Cities of 20,000 and Over

City	Size	Date
Monrovia	ca. 100,000	1965

SOURCE: *Africa 1968*.

[1] Jan Knappert, "Language Problems of the New Nations of Africa," *African Quarterly*, 5 (1965): 95–105.

[2] Merran Fraenkel, *Tribe and Class in Monrovia* (London: Oxford University Press, 1964), p. 36.

V. Political Patterns

A. Political Parties and Elections

Founded in 1860, the *True Whig Party* (TWP) has governed Liberia continuously since 1870. The leader of the True Whigs and the President of Liberia since 1944, William V. S. Tubman, governed with the aid of a Senate (six-year term) and a House of Representatives (four-year term). Elections are held every two years for part of the legislators. Presidential elections are held at the end of a first term of eight years, and every four years thereafter. Opposition to the *True Whig Party* is sporadic and disorganized, with no stable opposition party existing in Liberia.

B. Political Leadership

The government of Liberia was led by President William Tubman without notable change from 1944 to July 1971. The composition of the cabinet changed quite frequently, notably in the periods 1957–60 and 1964–65, when the rate of dismissal and resignation was high. These changes in personnel have not, however, changed the predominance of the minority settler-descended group in government.

Figure 17.1 **Political Parties and Elections**

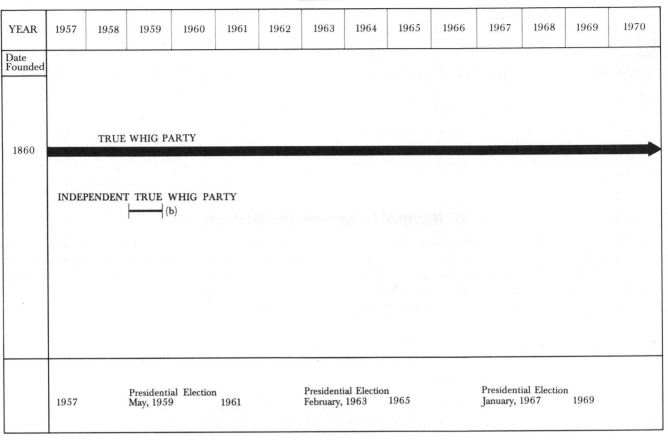

LIBERIA

YEAR	1957	1958	1959	1960	1961	1962	1963	1964	1965	1966	1967	1968	1969	1970

Date Founded

1860   TRUE WHIG PARTY

INDEPENDENT TRUE WHIG PARTY
(b)

1957   Presidential Election 1961   Presidential Election 1965   Presidential Election 1969
        May, 1959   February, 1963   January, 1967

TABLE 17.5 **Heads of Government**

Name	Dates in Office	Age (1971)	Ethnicity	Education	Former Occupation
1. William V. S. Tubman (President)	1944– 1971	Died 1971 age 75	"Settler"	Cuttington College	Lawyer
2. William R. Tolbert, Jr. (President)	1971–	58	"Settler"	Liberia College	Ordained Minister, Vice-President

TABLE 17.6 Cabinet Membership: Distribution by Ethnic Unit*

*Ethnicity**	*Independence†* *Cabinet*	*1967* *Cabinet*
1. Mandé-Fu (44%)	0	0
2. Kru-Bassa (37)	0	0
3. Gola-Kissi (8)	0	0
4. "Settler" (2)	100	93
5. Vai (3)	0	6.7
6. Others (6)	0	0
N =	12	15

* Ethnic units arranged in rank order of size within country with the unit's percent of national population in parentheses.

† For purposes of comparability, "independence" is treated as 1960 although Liberia has been an independent nation for more than a century.

VI. National Integration and Stability

Under the Tubman regime, with its policy of national integration, the tribal peoples have dramatically increased their participation in the government, although a relatively small elite group has held the great majority of the cabinet posts. There is continuing evidence of tension between the descendants of the settlers and the up-country groups, which until recently had been excluded from the country's political and economic life.

TABLE 17.7 Elite Instability

Event and Date	*Characteristics*
1. Attempted Coup June 24, 1955	a. *Description*: President Tubman was unharmed after an assassination attempt during the celebration of his election victory; the political assassin was seized.
	b. *Participants*: In all, 30 persons were charged with treason and sedition. All were reputed to be unsuccessful political candidates.
	c. *Apparent Causes*: The participants were associated with former President Barclay. They may have been motivated by opposition to Tubman's integrationist policies regarding the "tribal" peoples.

VII. Selected References

BIBLIOGRAPHY

Holsoe, S. *A Bibliography of Liberia*. Part I. Books. Newark, Del.: Liberian Studies Association, 1971.

Holsoe, S. "A Bibliography of Liberian Government Documents." *African Studies Bulletin*, 11 (April and September, 1968): 39–62, 149–194.

Holsoe, S. *A Study Guide for Liberia*. Boston: Development Program, African Studies Program, Boston University, 1967.

GENERAL

"A Second Look at Liberia." *Africa Report*, 11 (October 1966): 21–24.

Buell, Raymond L. *Liberia: A Century of Survival, 1847–1947*. Philadelphia: University of Pennsylvania Press, 1947.

Liberian Studies Journal. Newark, Del.: University of Delaware, Department of Anthropology.

U.S. Department of the Army. *Area Handbook for Liberia*.

Pamphlet No. 550–38. Washington, D.C.: Government Printing Office, 1964.

Wilson, Charles M. *Liberia: Black Africa in Microcosm.* New York: Harper, 1971.

POLITICAL

Liebenow, J. Gus. "Liberia." In *African One-Party States*, ed. G. M. Carter. Ithaca, N.Y.: Cornell University Press, 1962.

Liebenow, J. Gus. "Liberia." In *Political Parties and National Integration in Tropical Africa*, eds. J. S. Coleman and C. G. Rosberg. Los Angeles: University of California Press, 1964.

Liebenow, J. Gus, *Liberia, The Evolution of Privilege.* Ithaca, N.Y.: Cornell University Press, 1969.

ECONOMIC

Clower, Robert, et al. *Growth without Development: An Economic Survey of Liberia.* Evanston, Ill.: Northwestern University Press, 1966.

Dalton, George. "History, Politics and Economic Development in Liberia." *Journal of Economic History*, 25 (1965): 586–591.

Dalton, George and A. A. Walters. "The Economy of Liberia." In *The Economics of Africa*, eds. P. Robson and D. A. Lury, pp. 287–315. Evanston, Ill.: Northwestern University Press, 1969.

Hance, William A. "Iron Ore in Liberia: A Study of the Impact of Mining on a Developing Economy." In *African Economic Development*, rev. ed., pp. 54–86. New York: Praeger, 1967.

Quershi, Moeen A., et al. "The Liberian Economy," *International Monetary Fund Staff Papers*, 11 (1964): 285–326.

SOCIAL

Fraenkel, Merran. *Tribe and Class in Monrovia.* London: Oxford University Press, 1964.

Fraenkel, Merran. "Social Change on the Kru Coast of Liberia." *Africa*, 36 (1966): 154–172.

Hodgkin, Thomas. "Education and Social Change in Liberia." *West Africa*, nos. 1907–11 (1953), pp. 847, 871–872, 895, 918–919, 940–941.

Study Committee on Manpower Needs and Educational Capabilities in Africa. *Liberia: Study of Manpower Needs, Educational Capabilities and Overseas Study*, Report 5. New York: Education and World Affairs, 1965.

18. Malawi

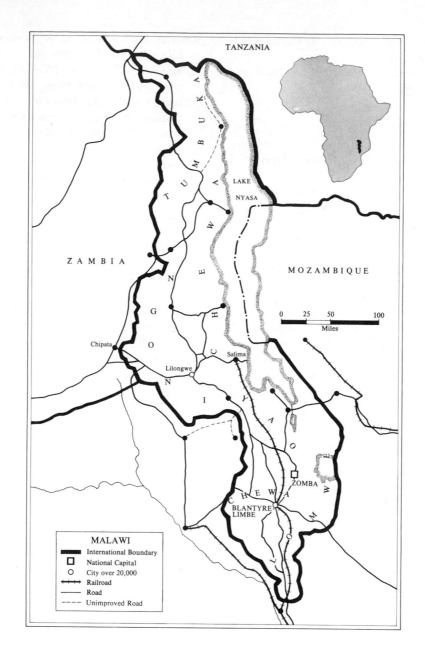

I. Basic Information

Date of Independence: July 6, 1964
Former Colonial Ruler: United Kingdom
Change in Boundaries: Formerly part of Central African Federation, 1953–1963
Former Name: Nyasaland
Estimated Population (*1970*): 4,530,000

Area Size (*equivalent in U.S.*): 46,000 sq. mi. (Louisiana)
Date of Last Census: 1966
Major Exports 1968 as Percent of Total Exports: tobacco—26 percent; tea—23 percent; peanuts—11 percent; corn—7 percent

II. Ethnic Patterns

As with Zambia, we have used Clyde Mitchell's classification of the Bantu of Southern Africa (1946). These are inclusive categories based on cultural and linguistic considerations. The Lomwe, Yao, and Ngoni are identity groups. In the north, there is a small Nyakyusa-type population (3 percent), consisting of Sukwa and Ngonde peoples. Other small groups are the Wandya and Lambya. It should be noted that our ethnic percentages are taken from the 1945 census, although they are assumed to be representative of the contemporary situation.

TABLE 18.1   Ethnic Units Over 5 Percent of Country Population

Ethnic Units	Estimated Ethnic Population 1967	Estimated Ethnic Percentage
a. Chewa Cluster	1,899,000	46%
1. Chewa (Achewa, Ancheya, Cewa, Masheba)	(1,156,000)	(28%)
2. Nyanja, 3. Lakeside Tonga	(619,000)	(15%)
b. Lomwe (Acilowe, Alomwe, Nguru)	784,000	19%
c. Yao (Achawa, Adjao)	578,000	14%
d. Ngoni Conquest States	371,000	9%
1. Mbelwe's Ngoni (Angoni, Mangoni, Wangoni), 2. Gomani's Ngoni, 3. Chiwere's Ngoni		
e. Tumbuka Type	247,000	6%
1. Tumbuka (Batumbuka, Matumboka), 2. Wenya, 3. Fungwe, 4. Phoka, 4. Fulilwa, 6. Henga, 7. Yombe, 8. Hewe, 9. Nthali, 10. Sisya		

SOURCES: *Report on the Census of 1945, Nyasaland Protectorate* (Blantyre: Government Printer, 1946), p. 15. Clyde Mitchell, *African Tribes and Languages of the Federation of Rhodesia and Nyasaland* (Salisbury: Federal Government Printer, 1964).

III. Language Patterns

All language groups in Malawi are Bantu. The Chewa group of peoples constitute approximately 28 percent of the population. Nyanja, the second largest component of the Chewa, constitutes a distinct language. Knappert estimates that as many as 83 percent of the population use Nyanja as either a *lingua franca*, or a mother tongue. Rustow estimates the figure at 36 percent. Nyanja is a *lingua franca*, and we have estimated that 51 percent of the population are able to use the language. Rustow suggests that Nguru (Lomwe) and Yao are the second largest language groups, each with 14 percent of the population. We estimate Lomwe at 19 percent. The official language of Malawi is English, and most trade and governmental functions are conducted in English.

TABLE 18.2   Language Patterns

1. Primacy		
1st language	Nyanja	(51%)
2nd language	Lomwe	(19%)
2. Greenberg classification (all ethnic units in country over 5%)	Nyanja	IA5
	Lomwe	IA5
	Ngoni	IA5
	Yao	IA5
	Tumbuka	IA5
3. *Lingua franca*	Nyanja	
4. Official language	English	

IV. Urban Patterns

Capital: Zomba (founded 1890)
Largest city: Blantyre (founded 1876)
Dominant ethnicity/language of largest city (Blantyre)
   Major vernacular: Nyanja[1]
   Major ethnic group: Nyanja[2]
   Major ethnic group as percent of Blantyre's population:
   36% (1957)

[1] Jan Knappert, "Language Problems of the New Nations of Africa," *African Quarterly*, 5 (1965): 95–105.
[2] D. G. Bettison and P. J. A. Rigby, *Patterns of Income and Expenditure in Blantyre-Limbe, Nyasaland* (Lusaka: Rhodes-Livingstone Institute, 1961), p. 18.

TABLE 18.3   Growth of Capital and Largest City

Date	Zomba	Blantyre
1940	3,000	
1950	10,000	41,000
1960	13,000	95,000
1966	20,000	110,000

SOURCE: *Federation of Rhodesia and Nyasaland Census, 1956*, and staff estimates. Blantyre had its name changed from Blantyre-Limbe in 1966. The capital is to be transferred from Zomba in the low-lying southern region to centrally located Lilongwe.

TABLE 18.4   Cities of 20,000 and Over

City	Size	Date
Blantyre	110,000	1966
Zomba	20,000	1966

SOURCE: Census.

V. Political Patterns

A. Political Parties and Elections

The Federation of Rhodesia and Nyasaland was set up in 1953, and was dissolved in 1963, at which point Nyasaland took the name Malawi, becoming independent in July 1964. In 1944 the *Malawi Congress Party* (MCP) was founded (as the *Nyasaland African Congress*), and in August 1961 it won 23 out of 28 seats in the Nyasaland Legislature. The *United Federal Party* (UFP), predominantly European, won 5 seats. The MCP has been the dominant party in Malawi since that time. The *Convention African National Union* (CANU) was established in 1962 to provide opposition to the MCP, but it was banned in 1966 when Malawi became a one-party state.

B. Political Leadership

The government of Malawi has been led by President Hastings Banda without notable change since independence in 1964. There have been marked changes in the composition of the cabinet, however, especially in 1964 when all but three ministers in the independence cabinet were dismissed. The ethnic representativeness of the cabinet has been increased by the new members, although ministers of Chewa background still predominate.

Figure 18.1 **Political Parties and Elections**

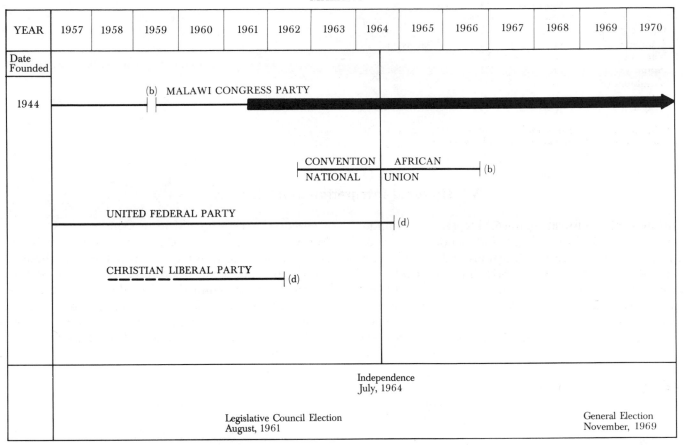

TABLE 18.5 **Head of Government (Post Independence)**

Name	Dates in Office	Age (1971)	Ethnicity	Education	Former Occupation
1. Dr. Hastings Kamuzu Banda (President)	1964–	65	Chewa	Medical (United States)	Doctor (M.D.)

TABLE 18.6 Cabinet Membership: Distribution by Ethnic Unit*

Ethnicity*	Independence Cabinet	1967 Cabinet
1. Chewa (46%)	78%	56%
2. Lomwe (19)	11	0
3. Yao (14)	0	22
4. Ngoni (9)	11	22
5. Tumbuka (6)	0	0
6. Others (6)	0	0
N =	10	9

* Ethnic units arranged in rank order of size within country with the unit's percent of national population in parentheses.

VI. National Integration and Stability

Although the political regime of Dr. Hastings Banda has continued since the pre-independence period, there have been severe dislocations within the ruling party, which later developed into a revolt. In September 1964 Dr. Banda emerged successful from an internal power struggle in the party, and a number of important ministers were dismissed for plotting to overthrow the government (and were accused of accepting aid from Communist China). Many of the more radical former ministers have gone into exile in Zambia and Tanzania. Dr. Banda refuses to support more severe sanctions against the white-dominated countries of southern Africa, arguing that the geographic and economic position of Malawi makes it suicidal for Malawians to be belligerent toward these powerful neighbors.

TABLE 18.9 Mass Instability

Event and Date	Characteristics
1. Revolt September 1964–October 1967	a. *Description*: In early September 1964, a number of ministers resigned (or were dismissed) after Dr. Banda refused to accede to their policy demands. These ministers included Henry Chipembere, Yatuta Chisiza, Manoah Chirwa, Kanyama Chiume, Willie Chokani, Augustine Bwanausi. On September 28, the district headquarters of the Malawi Congress Party was attacked. In February of 1965, the supporters of the ex-ministers, led by Henry Chipembere, took control of the Fort Johnson area and launched an unsuccessful drive on the capital city—Zomba. By July of 1966 most of the dissident leaders had left the country and Dr. Banda seemed to be tightening his control. The calm was broken when Yatuta Chisiza led a rebel band into the country in October 1967. In a battle with security forces Chisiza was killed and the remaining rebels scattered. b. *Participants*: All of the ministers mentioned above were considerably younger than Dr. Banda. Support seems to have coalesced around the program and personality of Chipembere. Ethnicity does not seem to be a prime factor in this conflict. c. *Apparent Causes*: The leaders of the revolt stated their demands as follows: quicker Africanization of the civil service; abolishment of hospital fees; recognition of China. They objected to Malawian trade agreements with Portugal and to Banda's positive foreign policy toward white-dominated countries to the south.

SOURCE: John G. Pike, *Malawi—A Political and Economic History* (New York: Praeger, 1968), p. 169.

VII. Selected References

BIBLIOGRAPHY

Brown, Edward E., et al. *A Bibliography of Malawi*. Eastern African Bibliographic Series, no. 1. Syracuse, N.Y.: Syracuse University, Program of Eastern African Studies, 1965.

Webster, John B., and Paulus Mohome. *A Supplement to a Bibliography on Malawi*. Occasional Bibliography no. 13. Syracuse, N.Y.: Syracuse University, Program of Eastern African Studies, 1969.

GENERAL

Debenham, F. *Nyasaland, the Land of the Lake*. London: Her Majesty's Stationery Office, 1955.

Pike, John G. *Malawi: A Political and Economic History*. New York: Praeger, 1968.

Pike, John G., and G. T. Rimmington. *Malawi, A Geographical Study*. London: Oxford University Press, 1965.

Rotberg, Robert I. *The Rise of Nationalism in Central Africa: The Making of Malawi and Zambia, 1873–1964*. Cambridge: Harvard University Press, 1966.

POLITICAL

Jones, Griff. *Britain and Nyasaland*. London: Allen and Unwin, 1964.

Liebenow, J. Gus. "Federalism in Rhodesia and Nyasaland." In *Federalism in the Commonwealth*, ed. William S. Livingston. London: Cassell, 1963.

Mair, Lucy P. *The Nyasaland Elections of 1961*. London: Oxford University Press, 1963.

Spiro, Herbert. "The Rhodesias and Nyasaland." In *Five African States: Responses to Diversity*, ed. G. M. Carter. Ithaca, N.Y.: Cornell University Press, 1963.

ECONOMIC

Hazelwood, Arthur and P. O. Henderson, eds. *Nyasaland: The Economics of Federation*. Oxford: Blackwell, 1960.

International Monetary Fund. "Malawi." In *Surveys of African Economies*, Vol. 4. Washington, D.C.: I.M.F., 1971.

SOCIAL

Rimmington, Gerald T. "Education for Independence. A Study of Changing Educational Administration in Malawi." *Comparative Education*, 2 (1966): 217–223.

Seltzer, George. "High Level Manpower in Nyasaland's Development." In *Manpower and Education: Country Studies in Economic Development*, eds. F. B. Harbison and C. Myers. New York: McGraw-Hill, 1965.

Wishlade, R. L. *Sectarianism in Southern Nyasaland*. London: Oxford University Press, 1965.

19. Mali

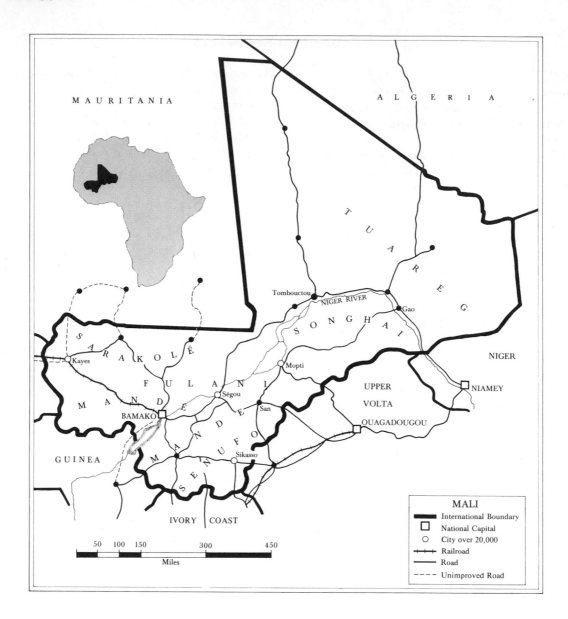

I. Basic Information

Date of Independence: September 22, 1960 (June 20, 1960 as Mali Federation)

Former Colonial Ruler: France

Change in Boundaries: Formerly part of French West African Federation. Part of the Mali Federation (formed with Senegal) from April 4, 1959, to August 20, 1960, when Senegal seceded.

Former Name: Soudan

Estimated Population (1970): 5,020,000

Area Size (equivalent in U.S.): 464,000 sq. mi. (Texas, Colorado and Nevada)

Date of Last Census: 1960–61

Estimated Major Exports 1968 as Percent of Total Exports: livestock, hides and skins—26 percent; fish—20 percent; cotton lint—19 percent; peanuts—9 percent

II. Ethnic Patterns

The ethnic classification selected for Mali is fairly inclusive. It is largely based on linguistic criteria, although cultural and identity factors strongly reinforce these criteria. The Fulani, Tuareg, and Songhai are identity groups. Within the Mandé family, the Dyula are probably of Senufo origin. They have been placed with the Mandé (as was done in the Ivory Coast classification), however, for reasons of language and culture (Muslim). Mali also contains a small (2.9 percent) Moorish population.

TABLE 19.1 Ethnic Units Over 5 Percent of Country Population

Ethnic Units	Estimated Ethnic Population 1967	Estimated Ethnic Percentage
a. Mandé Type	2,040,000	*43%*
1. Bambara	(1,471,000)	(31%)
2. Malinké	(251,000)	(5%)
3. Dyula (Diula)	(303,000)	(6%)
b. Fulani (Peul)	949,000	*20%*
c. Senufo (Sene, Siena) Type	712,000	*15%*
1. Senufo, 2. Minianka		
d. Sarakolé (Seraculeh, Soninké) Type	380,000	*8%*
1. Sarakolé		
2. Marka		
e. Tuareg (Touareg)	303,000	*6%*
f. Songhai (Songhoi, Sonhray)	289,000	*6%*

SOURCES: *Allgemeine Statistik des Auslandes, Landerberichte, Mali*, 1966. G. P. Murdock, *Africa* (New York: McGraw-Hill, 1959), p. 80.

III. Language Patterns

The two major languages in Mali are Bambara (of the Mandé family) and Fulani (of the West Atlantic family). Those who speak Bambara as a first language are probably 31 percent of the total population. However, Malinké- and Dyula-speakers (11 percent) would understand Bambara, and probably another 8 percent of the population understand it as a second language. Thus, our estimate of Bambara-speakers would be 50 percent. Rustow estimates the Malinké-Bambara-Dyula speakers to be 40 percent; Knappert suggests Bambara alone consists of 23 percent; and MacDougald suggests the broader category of Mandingo at 31 percent. The second largest language is Fulani—Rustow estimates 14 percent; our estimate is 20 percent based on ethnic figures alone.

French is the official language. Arabic is the language most widely used in religious matters.

TABLE 19.2 Language Patterns

1. Primacy		
1st language	Bambara	(50%)
2nd language	Fulani	(20%)
2. Greenberg classification	Malinké-Bambara-Dyula	IA2
(all ethnic units in	Fulani	IA1
country over 5%)	Senufo	IA3
	Sarakolé	IA2
	Tuareg	IIIC
	Songhai	IIA
3. *Lingua franca*	Bambara (Malinké-Dyula)	
4. Official language	French	

IV. Urban Patterns

Capital/largest city: Bamako (founded 1883)
Dominant ethnicity/language of capital
  Major vernacular: Bambara[1]

Major ethnic group: —
Major ethnic group as percent of capital's population: —

[1] Jan Knappert, "Language Problems of the New Nations of Africa," *African Quarterly*, 5 (1965): 95–105.

TABLE 19.3 Growth of Capital/Largest City

Date	Bamako
1920	14,000
1930	19,000
1940	26,000
1950	86,000
1960	130,000
1965	170,000 UA
1967	182,000 UA

SOURCE: *Démographie Comparée*. The various population estimates for Bamako for ca. 1965 illustrate the variability of the size estimates of African cities. These range from 150,000 (*Africa 68*) to 200,000 (*Europa Yearbook 1967*). The *Statesman's Yearbook 1967* estimate is in between at 170,000.

TABLE 19.4 Cities of 20,000 and Over

City	Size	Date
Bamako[a]	170,000 UA	1965
Kayes[b]	32,000	ca. 1965
Ségou[b]	32,000	ca. 1965
Mopti[c]	32,000	ca. 1965
Sikasso[c]	22,000	ca. 1965

SOURCES:
[a] *UN Demographic Yearbooks 1967, 1969.*
[b] *Africa 1969–70.*
[c] *Statesman's Yearbook 1967.*
Tombouctou's (Timbuctu) population is about 10,000 (*Africa 1969–70*).

V. Political Patterns

Figure 19.1 **Political Parties and Elections**

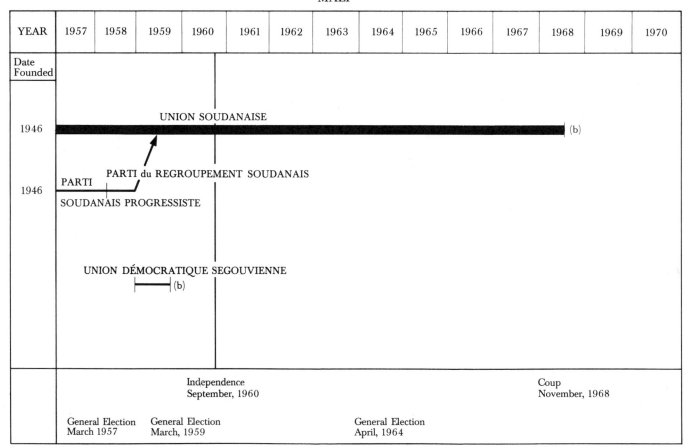

A. Political Parties and Elections

The *Union Soudanaise* (US) was founded in 1946 as a territorial branch of the *Rassemblement Démocratique Africain* (RDA). From 1946 until 1959, there was a two-party system in Mali. The *Parti du Regroupement Soudanais* (PRS) was founded in March 1958 from the *Parti Soudanais Progressiste* (PSP), but merged with the US in March 1959. Thus, from 1959 until the military coup in December 1968, Mali has been a one-party state. It should be noted that the US broke with the RDA in 1958, and in 1959 joined with the Senegalese leaders in the Federation of Mali creating a new party, the *Parti de la Federation*

Africaine, which dissolved when the Federation broke up in summer 1960.

B. Political Leadership

The government of Mali was led by President Mobido Keita from independence until the coup d'état in 1968. The arrangements following the coup have Lt. Moussa Traoré as Head of State and Capt. Yoro Diakité as Head of Government. As Traoré is also the Chairman of the Military Committee of National Liberation we include him here as "Head of Government."

TABLE 19.5 **Heads of Government (Post Independence)**

Name	Dates in Office	Age (1971)	Ethnicity	Education	Former Occupation
1. Mobido Keita (President)	1960–1968	56	Mandé (Malinké)	University (Dakar)	Teacher, Civil Servant (School Inspector)
2. Lt. Moussa Traoré (President of the Military Committee of National Liberation and Head of State)	1968–	35	Mandé	Frejus Training College in France	Soldier

TABLE 19.6 **Cabinet Membership: Distribution by Ethnic Unit***

Ethnicity*	Independence Cabinet	1967 Cabinet
1. Mandé (43%)	43%	33%
2. Fulani (20)	43	40
3. Senufo (15)	7.1	0
4. Sarakolé (8)	0	0
5. Tuareg (6)	0	0
6. Songhai (6)	7.1	0
7. Others (2)	7.1	20
N =	15	15

* Ethnic units arranged in rank order of size within country with the unit's percent of national population in parentheses.

VI. National Integration and Stability

Mali is a relatively homogenous country in terms of basic cultural orientation. One exception has been the minority nomadic tribes, who have insisted on continuing autonomy. Tensions between Mali and

France seem to have been reflected in the conflict between elites within Mali. The regime of Modibo Keita maintained power until the November 1968 coup. Signs of the tension, however, were apparent by 1962 when (on July 20) the government announced that it had discovered a plot organized by merchants and supported by the French Embassy (91 persons were accused of complicity). The plot was the result of the introduction of the Malian franc in conjunction with the declining economic situation (which also precipitated large demon-

strations in Bamako). The officers who led the 1968 coup have since turned to France, as well as Eastern-bloc countries, for aid though they have left intact most of the previous regime's structures. On August 12, 1969, 33 soldiers were arrested on suspicion of conspiring to overthrow the government. In December 1969 Captains Diby Diarra and Alassane Diarra and Sergeant Boubaear Traore were sentenced to hard labor for life for their leadership of the coup attempt. It is not known how far the plot had progressed before the arrests were made.

TABLE 19.7   Elite Instability

Event and Date	Characteristics
1. Coup d'État November 19, 1968	a. *Description*: The main targets of the military forces were Seydou Kouyate (a former minister with a "pro-China" reputation) and other ministers including the prime minister, several labor leaders, and certain persons affiliated with the militia. b. *Participants*: Lt. Moussa Traoré and Captains Malik Diallo, Charles Sissoko, and Mamadou Sissoko. Officers opposing the take-over (including the chief of staff) were arrested. c. *Apparent Causes*: The economic situation had badly deteriorated; according to Moussa Traoré "the state has been living far beyond its means" and the "demagogic and sterile radicalism" of the Keita regime has frightened away foreign investors.

TABLE 19.8   Communal Instability

Event and Date	Characteristics
1. Rebellion August 1963–August 1964	a. *Description*: On August 14, 1964, the government of Mali announced that for over a year an "insidious foreign power" had encouraged subversion and rebellion among the northern nomadic desert tribes. The government said that a major offensive occurred July 16, 1964, against the "last rebel stronghold," and order was restored. The government claimed that rebel elements intimidated loyal nomads by terrorism and by seizing thousands of domestic animals. b. *Participants*: Nomadic Tuareg groups. c. *Apparent Causes*: Opposition to taxes and administrative control. While Malian officials tended to minimize the importance of the rebellion, it was a strain on the economic resources of the government.

SOURCES: William I. Jones, "Economics of the Coup," *African Report*, 14 (1969): 23–26, 51–53. Francis G. Snyder, "An Era Ends in Mali," *ibid.*, 16–22.

VII. Selected References

BIBLIOGRAPHY

Brasseur, Paule. *Bibliographie générale du Mali (Anciens Soudan Français et Haut-Sénégal-Niger)*. I.F.A.N. catalogues et documents, 16. Dakar: I.F.A.N., 1964.

Cutter, C. H. "Mali: A Bibliographic Introduction." *African Studies Bulletin*, 9 (1966): 74–87.

GENERAL

Thompson, Virginia, and Richard Adloff. *French West Africa*, pp. 146–154. Stanford, Cal.: Stanford University Press, 1957.

POLITICAL

de Lusignan, Guy. *French-Speaking Africa since Independence*, pp. 231–249. London: Pall Mall Press, 1969.

Foltz, William J. *From French West Africa to the Mali Federation*. New Haven, Conn.: Yale University Press, 1965.

Hodgkin, Thomas, and Ruth Schachter Morgenthau. "Mali." In *Political Parties and National Integration in Tropical Africa*, eds. J. S. Coleman and C. G. Rosberg. Los Angeles: University of California Press, 1964.

Snyder, Francis G. *One-Party Government in Mali: Transition toward Control*. New Haven, Conn.: Yale University Press, 1965.

Zolberg, Aristide R. "Political Revival in Mali." *Africa Report*, 11 (July 1965): 15–20.

ECONOMIC

Amin, Samir. *Trois Expériences Africaines de Développement: Le Mali, la Guinée et le Ghana*. Paris: Presses Universitaires de France, 1965.

SOCIAL

Meillassoux, Claude. *Urbanisation of an African Community: Voluntary Associations in Bamako*. Seattle, Wash.: University of Washington Press, 1968.

20. Mauritania

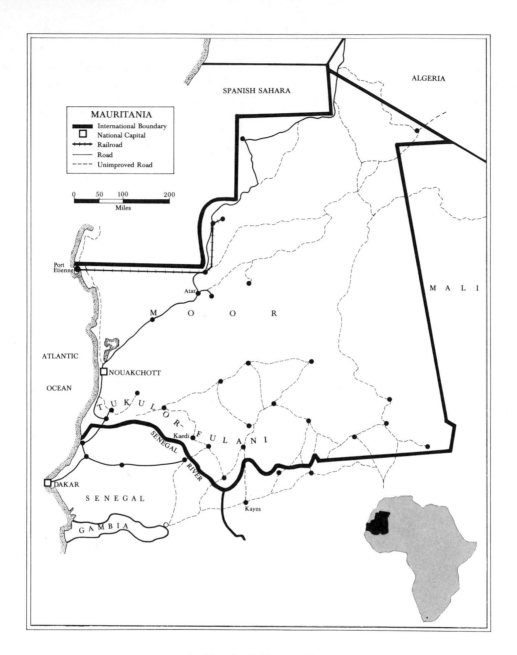

I. Basic Information

Date of Independence: November, 1960

Former Colonial Ruler: France

Change in Boundaries: Formerly part of French West Africa Federation (often grouped with Senegal for census purposes during the colonial period)

Estimated Population (1970): 1,170,000

Area Size (equivalent in U.S.): 410,000 sq. mi. (Texas, Colorado and Nevada)

Date of Last Census: 1964–65 (sample survey)

Major Exports 1968 as Percent of Total Exports: iron ore—89 percent

II. Ethnic Patterns

The many Moorish tribes represent various mixings of Berber and Arab stock. Although the distinction is made in the Mauritanian census between White Moors (54 percent) and Black Moors (28 percent), this is no longer so much a question of color, as of patrilineal descent and status difference. The Tukulor and Fulani maintain distinct identities, but share a common language and culture.

TABLE 20.1 Ethnic Units Over 5 Percent of Country Population

Ethnic Units	Estimated Ethnic Population 1967	Estimated Ethnic Percentage
a. Moor (Maure)	902,000	*82%*
1. Maaquil, 2. Lemtouna, Masoufa, 4. Tolbas, 5. Zenaga, 6. Nemadi, 7. Imraquen, 8. Azarzir, 9. Duaish, 10. Regeibat		
b. Tukulor-Fulani Type	143,000	*13%*
1. Tukulor (Takruri, Tekarir, Torodo, Toncouleur, Tukri)	(88,000)	(8%)
2. Fulani (Peul)	(55,000)	(5%)

SOURCES: Mauritania, Direction de l'information, *République islamique de Mauretanie* (Dakar: Grande impr. africaine, 1963). G. P. Murdock, *Africa* (New York: McGraw-Hill, 1959).

III. Language Patterns

The two major language groups in Mauritania are Arabic (of the Semitic group) and Fulani (of the West Atlantic group). Most of the Moorish peoples speak Arabic (although some, such as the Zenaga, retain the use of Berber). The Fulani and Tukulor both speak and write the same language (Fulfulde). Our estimate is that 87 percent of the total population speaks Arabic. (Rustow estimates Arabic at 82 percent; Knappert considers the Arabic-speaking population to be 100 percent.) Thirteen percent of the population are Fulani-speaking (Rustow estimates 12 percent). Arabic is being encouraged as a *lingua franca* by the government. In 1966, when Arabic was required in government and higher education, however, significant language riots resulted (see Table 20.8). French continues as an official language.

TABLE 20.2 Language Patterns

1. Primacy
   - 1st language   Arabic   (87%)
   - 2nd language   Fulani   (13%)
2. Greenberg classification   Arabic   IIIA
   (all ethnic units in   Fulani   IA1
   country over 5%)
3. *Lingua franca*   Arabic
4. Official languages   French, Arabic

IV. Urban Patterns

Capital/largest city: Nouakchott (new city)
Dominant ethnicity/language of capital
   Major vernacular: Arabic[1]
   Major ethnic group: Arab
   Major ethnic group as percent of capital's population: —

[1] Jan Knappert, "Language Problems of the New Nations of Africa," *African Quarterly*, 5 (1965): 95–105.

TABLE 20.3 Growth of Capital/Largest City

Date	Nouakchott
1961	6,000[a]
1965	15,000[b]

SOURCES:
[a] *UN Demographic Yearbook 1963.*
[b] *UN Demographic Yearbook 1967.*

TABLE 20.4 Cities of 20,000 and Over

City	Size	Date
Nouakchott	15,000	1965

SOURCE: *UN Demographic Yearbook 1967.* Despite the fact that its population is less than 20,000, Nouakchott is the largest city in Mauritania.

V. Political Patterns

A. Political Parties and Elections

Prior to independence the dominant party in Mauritania was the *Parti du Regroupement Mauritanien* (PRM), while the opposition parties were the *Parti de la Renaissance Nationale Mauritanienne* (LeNaddah) and the *Union Nationale Mauritanienne* (UNM). On the eve of independence in 1960 LeNaddah and UNM were banned by the PRM. After independence the newly revived LeNaddah and UNM merged into the PRM to form the *Parti du Peuple Mauritanien* (PPM). Mauritania is now a one-party state under the leadership of Moktar Ould Daddah, while all members of the National Assembly are members of the PPM.

Figure 20.1 **Political Parties and Elections**

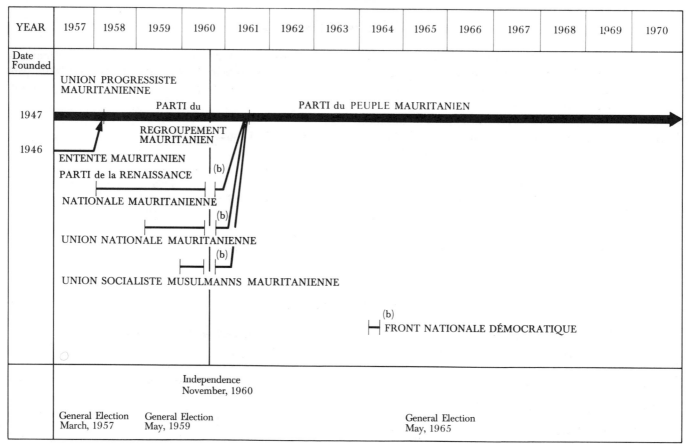

MAURITANIA

B. Political Leadership

The government of Mauritania has been led by President Moktar Ould Daddah since independence. There have, however, been substantial changes in the composition of the cabinet, particularly in the periods 1962–63 and 1965–66. New members of the cabinet have increased the representation of the Tukulor in the executive.

TABLE 20.5   Head of Government (Post Independence)

Name	Dates in Office	Age (1971)	Ethnicity	Education	Former Occupation
1. Moktar Ould Daddah (President)	1960–	47	Moor	Post-grad. professional (France)	Lawyer, Interpreter

TABLE 20.6   Cabinet Membership: Distribution by Ethnic Unit*

Ethnicity*	Independence Cabinet	1967 Cabinet
1. Moor (82%)	100%	83%
2. Tukulor-Fulani (13)	0	17
3. Others (5)	0	0
N =	10	12

* Ethnic units arranged in rank order of size within country with the unit's percent of national population in parentheses.

VI. National Integration and Stability

The government of Mauritania is led by educated Arabic-speaking elites. The government has tried to develop a multiracial society and an acceptance of the inherited state boundaries. The major internal problem of national integration is the question of linkages between northern/Moorish/Arabic-speaking/"light-skinned" elements and southern/non-Moorish/non-Arabic-speaking/dark-skinned elements. The language riots in 1966 manifested such tensions.

While there may be some irredentist sentiment in northern Mauritania for linkage with Morocco, we have not coded this as irredentism because the confrontation has been almost entirely at the governmental level rather than the popular level. It may be useful, however, to briefly review the situation. During the period 1960–1965, there were acute inter-state tensions resulting from the claims of Morocco to *all* of Mauritania on the basis of pre-colonial allegiance patterns. The Mauritanian government resisted such claims and the major connective road between the two states was closed. On August 13, 1963, four Mauritanian political leaders who had returned from self-imposed exile in Morocco were arrested on charges of subversion. In July 1965, three Mauritanians and a Moroccan were charged with treason on matters related to the Mauritanian-Moroccan dispute. The Organization of African Unity has tried to help settle the dispute.

TABLE 20.8 Communal Instability

Event and Date	Characteristics
1. Ethnic Violence January 1966–April 1966	a. *Description*: In January 1966, there were widespread demonstrations in several parts of Mauritania following a new regulation establishing compulsory teaching of Arabic in secondary schools. On February 9, riots occurred in Nouakchott following the creation of a commission to study language problems in Mauritania. On February 11, fighting continued in the capital city between Arabic-speaking and non-Arabic-speaking ethnic groups. With the establishment of Arabic (in addition to French) as an official language, certain ethnic groups felt that administrative and governmental posts were less accessible. On February 16, President Ould Daddah forbade any discussion of "racial" problems in Mauritania. On March 2, certain "black" government officials were arrested for attempting to create discord between "the Negroes and the Whites." By March 7, there were 6 deaths and 70 injuries. On April 3, fighting occurred between light-skinned and dark-skinned students at the government secondary school in Nouakchott. These "school riots" resulted in many injured. b. *Participants*: Arabic-speaking Moors vs. Tukulor-Fulani/Wolof and other ethnic minorities. There was no apparent leadership, although "dark-skinned" secondary-school students and government officials were involved. c. *Apparent Causes*: Ethnic/racial/language tensions were focused on the issue of language policies.
2. Ethnic Violence May 12, 1967	a. *Description*: Violence occurred between Sarakolé and Haratin near Selibaby (in the southeast). According to reports, 6 were killed and 20 wounded. b. *Participants*: Sarakolé and Haratin ethnic members. c. *Apparent Causes*: Not ascertainable.

SOURCE: Anthony S. Reyner, "Morocco's International Boundary," *Journal of Modern African Studies*, 1 (September 1963): 293–312.

VII. Selected References

GENERAL

Gerteiny, Alfred G. *Mauritania*. New York: Praeger, 1967.

Thompson, Virginia, and Richard Adloff. *French West Africa*, pp. 162–170. Stanford, Cal.: Stanford University Press, 1957.

POLITICAL

de Lusignan, Guy. *French-Speaking Africa since Independence*, pp. 218–230. London: Pall Mall Press, 1969.

Moore, Clement H. "One-Partyism in Mauritania." *Journal of Modern African Studies*, 3 (1965): 409–420.

Watson, J. H. A. "Mauritania: Problems and Prospects." *Africa Report*, 8 (February 1963).

ECONOMIC

International Monetary Fund. "Mauritania." In *Surveys of African Economies*, Vol. 3. Washington, D.C.: I.M.F., 1970.

Westebbe, Richard M. *The Economy of Mauritania*. New York: Praeger Special Study, 1971.

21. Niger

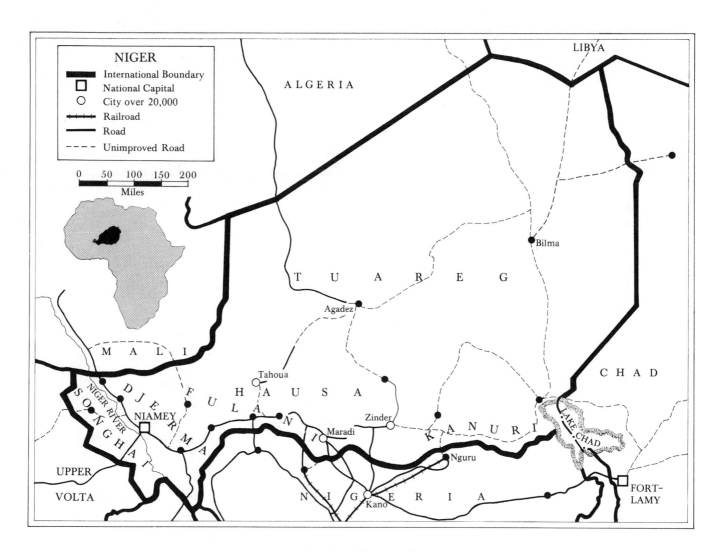

I. Basic Information

Date of Independence: August 3, 1960
Former Colonial Ruler: France
Change in Boundaries: Formerly part of the French West Africa Federation
Estimated Population (1970): 4,020,000

Area Size (equivalent in U.S.): 489,000 sq. mi. (Texas, Nevada, and New Mexico)
Date of Last Census: 1959–60 (sample survey)
Major Exports 1968 as Percent of Total Exports: peanuts and products 64 percent; livestock 15 percent

II. Ethnic Patterns

Although the ethnic groupings for Niger are widely inclusive, they correspond to real identity and language groups. These are also the categories recognized by the Niger government. Culturally, all of the groups are relatively similar, since they have all been Muslim for several centuries. There are important ecological differences, however, especially with regard to Fulani pastorialism and Tuareg nomadism.

TABLE 21.1 Ethnic Units Over 5 Percent of Country Population

Ethnic Units	Estimated Ethnic Population 1967	Estimated Ethnic Percentage
a. Hausa (Haoussa)	1,631,000	46%
1. Hausa, 2. Adarawa, 3. Kurfei		
b. Djerma-Songhai	674,000	19%
1. Djerma (Zerma, Zaberma)		
2. Songhai (Songhay)		
c. Fulani	461,000	13%
d. Tuareg	355,000	10%
1. Asben, 2. Aulliminden		
e. Kanuri (Beriberi)	177,000	5%

SOURCE: *Basic Data on the Republic of Niger, 1967.*

III. Language Patterns

The major languages of Niger are Hausa (of the Chadic family), Djerma-Songhai (of the Songhai family), Fulani (of the West Atlantic family), Tuareg or Tamashek (of the Berber family), and Kanuri (of the Saharan family). Although the percentage of total population who speak Hausa as a first language is 46 percent, at least another 24 percent (especially Fulani, Kanuri, Tuareg) speak it as a second language. Our estimate of Hausa-speakers is thus 70 percent. (Knappert, Mac-Dougald, and Rustow estimate 32 percent, 34 percent, and 43 percent respectively.) The second largest language is Djerma-Songhai, which is spoken as a first language by 19 percent of the total population (Rustow estimates 18 percent). It is concentrated in the capital city area around Niamey, and because of the influence of French and Hausa does not really serve as a *lingua franca*. French continues as the official language although, since about 1963, radio broadcasting and adult literacy campaigns have been conducted in all major vernacular languages.

TABLE 21.2 Language Patterns

1. Primacy		
1st language	Hausa	(70%)
2nd language	Songhai	(19%)
2. Greenberg classification	Hausa	IIIE
(all ethnic units in	Djerma-Songhai	IIA
country over 5%)	Fulani	IA1
	Tuareg	IIIC
	Kanuri	IIB
3. *Lingua franca*	Hausa	
4. Official language	French	

SOURCE: Petr Zima, "Hausa in West Africa: Remarks on Contemporary Role and Function," in *Language Problems of Developing Nations*, eds. Joshua A. Fishman, Charles A. Ferguson, and Jyotirindra Das Gupta (New York: John Wiley, 1968), pp. 365–378.

IV. Urban Patterns

Capital/largest city: Niamey
Dominant ethnicity/language of capital
  Major vernacular: Hausa[1]

Major ethnic group: Djerma
Major ethnic group as percent of capital's population: —

[1] Jan Knappert, "Language Problems of the New Nations of Africa," *African Quarterly*, 5 (1965): 95–105.

TABLE 21.3   Growth of Capital/Largest City

Date	Niamey
1920	2,000
1930	2,000
1940	6,000
1950	9,000
1960	30,000
1967	60,000
1968	79,000

SOURCES: *Démographie Comparée*, except for the 1929 (1,000) and 1931 (3,400) figures which are given in Niger Government, *Etude Demographique de la Ville de Niamey et des Besoins Solvables en Logements*, SCET/SONUCI, 1962. All figures exclude white population.

TABLE 21.4   Cities of 20,000 and Over

City	Size	Date
Niamey[a]	60,000	1967
Zinder[b]	30,000	1967
Maradi[b]	23,000	1967
Tahoua[b]	22,000	1967

SOURCES:
[a] *UN Demographic Yearbook 1967.*
[b] *Africa 1967.*

V. Political Patterns

Figure 21.1   **Political Parties and Elections**

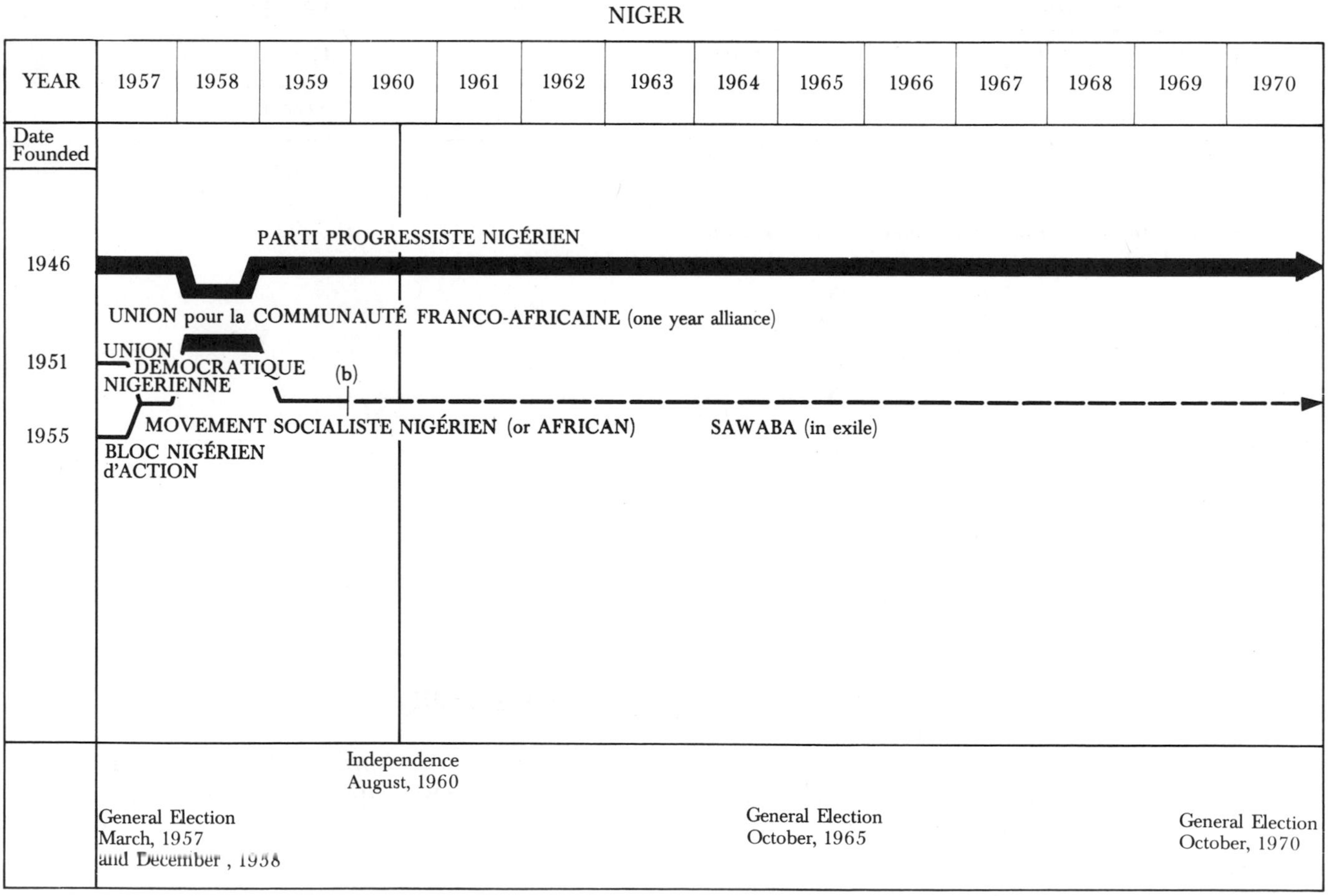

NIGER

YEAR	1957	1958	1959	1960	1961	1962	1963	1964	1965	1966	1967	1968	1969	1970

Date Founded

1946   PARTI PROGRESSISTE NIGÉRIEN

UNION pour la COMMUNAUTÉ FRANCO-AFRICAINE (one year alliance)

UNION
1951   DÉMOCRATIQUE   (b)
NIGERIENNE

1955   MOVEMENT SOCIALISTE NIGÉRIEN (or AFRICAN)   SAWABA (in exile)
BLOC NIGÉRIEN
d'ACTION

Independence
August, 1960

General Election
March, 1957
and December, 1958

General Election
October, 1965

General Election
October, 1970

A. Political Parties and Elections

Since the 1958 vote on General de Gaulle's constitution, the *Parti Progressiste Nigérien* (PPN), which recommended a "yes" vote, has been the dominant party in Niger. Prior to the referendum, the *Bloc Nigérien d'Action* (BNA), much better known by its Hausa name "SAWABA," was dominant. Once a "yes" vote had been achieved on the Referendum, the temporary PPN/BNA coalition was dissolved, and in 1959 under the leadership of Hamani Diori and the PPN, Niger became a one-party state. The SAWABA party was declared illegal and its leader,

Bakary Djibo, forced into exile. With no legal opposition, Diori continued as president, with all seats in the Legislative Assembly held by members of the PPN.

B. Political Leadership

Hamani Diori has been head of state throughout the entire independence period. Although the initial cabinet tended to be over-balanced in favor of the Djerma-Songhai, the balance had been redressed with an increase in the number of Hausa ministers by 1967.

TABLE 21.5　Head of Government (Post Independence)

Name	Dates in Office	Age (1971)	Ethnicity	Education	Former Occupation
1. Hamani Diori (President)	1960–	55	Djerma-Songhai	Secondary (Dahomey)	Civil Servant, Teacher

TABLE 21.6　Cabinet Membership: Distribution by Ethnic Unit*

Ethnicity*	Independence Cabinet	1967 Cabinet
1. Hausa (46%)	9.1%	40%
2. Djerma-Songhai (19)	55	33
3. Fulani (13)	18	6.7
4. Tuareg (10)	0	6.7
5. Kanuri (5)	9.1	6.7
6. Others (7)	9.1	6.7
N =	11	15

* Ethnic units arranged in rank order of size within country with the unit's percent of national population in parentheses.

VI. National Integration and Stability

The regime of Hamani Diori has survived a series of efforts by the SAWABA party to take over the government. SAWABA maintained itself in exile (in Ghana and Nigeria), and attracted younger educated elements as well as large numbers of

Hausa along the border from Birnin Konni to Zinder. SAWABA supporters assert that the Diori regime is too closely linked with Ivory Coast and France.

TABLE 21.9 Mass Instability

Event and Date	Characteristics
1. Revolt 1960 to present (most intensively 1964–1965)	a. *Description*: With the outlawing of the SAWABA political party prior to independence, many members went underground or migrated to Ghana or Nigeria. The SAWABA party, led by Djibo Bakary, engaged in sporadic terrorist attacks into Niger. The SAWABA movement was ideologically radical and closely allied to the CCP in Ghana (where Djibo Bakary came to maintain a government-in-exile until late 1965). (The coup d'état against President Nkrumah in Ghana undermined the strength of SAWABA throughout West Africa.) In September and October 1964, SAWABA raids were undertaken into Niger, allegedly from Kano (Nigeria), and armed attacks were made on administrative posts and customs stations. Also in April 1965, grenades were thrown at a public meeting in Niamey. In both cases the insurgents were caught and publicly executed. b. *Participants*: Djibo Bakary (former Prime Minister of Niger) and many young intellectuals dissatisfied with the conservative Diori regime. There was also some support from Hausa citizens. c. *Apparent Causes*: There were ideological motivations which encouraged SAWABA to try to take over the government in Niger. At a popular level, however, Djibo Bakary (who is a Djerma and in fact related to President Hamani Diori) attracted support from many Hausa peoples who felt they were underrepresented in the Niger government.

SOURCE: Virginia Thompson, "Niger," in *National Unity and Regionalism in Eight African States,"* ed. Gwendolen M. Carter (Ithaca, N.Y.: Cornell University Press, 1966), pp. 159–173.

VII. Selected References

GENERAL

Bonardi, Pierre, *La République du Niger: Naissance d'un État*. Paris: Agence Parisienne de Distribution, 1960.

Riveieres, Edmond Sere de. *Histoire du Niger*. Paris: Bergere-Levrault, 1965.

Thompson, Virginia, and Richard Adloff. *French West Africa*, pp. 155–161. Stanford, Cal.: Stanford University Press, 1957.

POLITICAL

de Lusignan, Guy. *French-Speaking Africa since Independence*, pp. 151–159. London, Pall Mall Press, 1969.

Thompson, Virginia. "Niger." In *National Unity and Regionalism in Eight African States*, ed. G. M. Carter. Ithaca, N.Y.: Cornell University Press, 1966.

ECONOMIC

International Monetary Fund. "Niger." In *Surveys of African Economies*, Vol. 3. Washington, D.C.: I.M.F., 1970.

SOCIAL

Van Hoey, Leo F. "The Coercive Process of Urbanization: The Case of Niger." In *The New Urbanization*, eds. Scott Greer, et al. New York: St. Martin's Press, 1968.

22. Nigeria

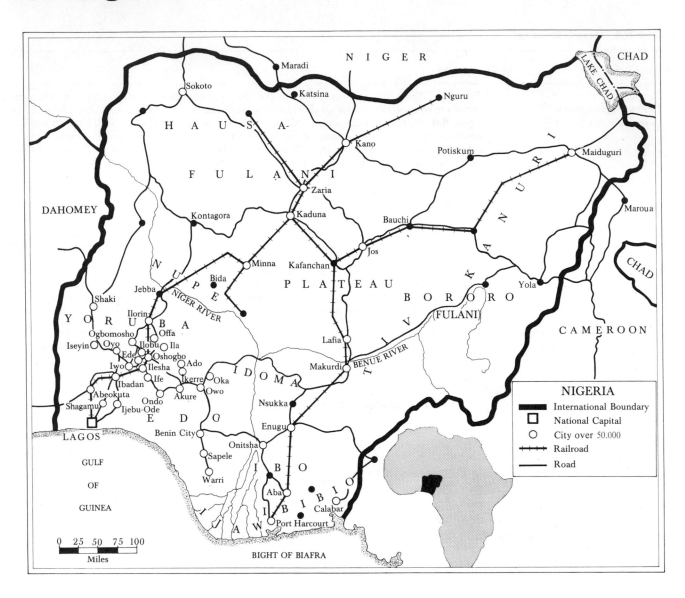

I. Basic Information

Date of Independence: October 1, 1960
Former Colonial Ruler: United Kingdom
Change in Boundaries: Addition of UN Trust Territory of Northern Cameroons on June 1, 1961
Estimated Population (1970): 55,070,000*
Area Size (equivalent in U.S.): 357,000 sq. mi. (Texas and Colorado)

Date of Last Census: 1963
Major Exports 1968 as Percent of Total Exports: cocoa—24 percent; peanuts and oil—22 percent; crude petroleum—12 percent;† palm kernels and oil—5 percent

* Latest UN estimate which does not accept the 1963 census results. See see Appendix 5 for another estimate.

† Production in 1968 dropped to almost one-third of the 1966 figure as a result of the civil war.

II. Ethnic Patterns

Although Nigeria is one of the most culturally diverse states in Africa, the far northern and southern areas of the country presented few problems of ethnic classification. For the most part the northern and southern groupings have attained the state level of socio-political development, and were thus clearly bounded units. They are also locally recognized identity units and have been characterized by distinctive cultural patterns. We have grouped the urban and settled Fulani with the Hausa (as Hausa-Fulani) because of the high degree to which the Fulani have been assimilated into Hausa culture and the fact that most of them use Hausa as a first language.

The middle belt, however, is a "scatter belt" of diverse peoples who are usually called the Plateau Peoples. We have retained this clustering, though we recognize its inadequacy. The Tiv are at least a million in population. Murdock subdivides these middle-belt people into three groups, but this

TABLE 22.1 Ethnic Units Over 1 Percent of Country Population

Ethnic Units	Estimated Ethnic Population 1967	Estimated Ethnic Percentage
a. Hausa-Fulani Type (plus Hausa-Fulani dominated or assimilated peoples)	15,370,000	29%
1. Hausa i. Daurawa, ii. Gobir, iii. Kanawa, iv. Katsenawa, v. Kebbawa, vi. Zamfara, vii. Zazzagawa, viii. Auyokawa 2. Fulani, 3. Jaba, 4. Kuturmi, 5. Kagoro, 6. Janji, 7. Ninzo, 8. Kwatawa, 9. Kagoma, 10. Bugaje, 11. Kambari, 12. Dakarkari, 13. Dukkawa, 14. Fakkawa, 15. Zabarma, 16. Gungawa, 17. Shangawa, 18. Lopawa, 19. Busawa, 20. Waja, 21. Bade, 22. Kudawa		
b. Yoruba	10,800,200	20%
1. Ahori, 2. Egba-Awori, 3. Ekiti, 4. Eko, 5. Ijebu, 6. Iiesha, 7. Jekri, 8. Oyo, 9. Ife, 10. Bune, 11. Ondo, 12. Akoko.		
c. Ibo	9,180,000	17%
1. Abadja, 2. Abaja, 3. Abam, 4. Alensaw, 5. Aro, 6. Awhawfia, 7. Awhawzara, 8. Awtanzu, 9. Edda, 10. Ekkpahia, 11. Etche, 12. Eziama, 13. Ezza, 14. Ihe, 15. Iji, 16. Ika, 17. Ikwerri, 18. Ikwo, 19. Ishielu (or Eshielu), 20. Isu, 21. Isu-Ochi, 22. Ndokki, 23. Ngbo, 24. Ngwa, 25. Nkalu, 26. Nkanu, 27. Okoba (or Okogba), 28. Onitsha-Awka, 29. Oratta, 30. Oru, 31. Ubani, 32. Ututu		
d. Tiv and Plateau Cluster	4,860,000	9%
1. Tiv, 2. Gwari (Gbari), 3. Mumuye, 4. Higgi (Kipsiki), 5. Bura, 6. Chamba, 7. Kaje, 8. Jari, 9. Eggan, 10. Kobchi, 11. Angas, 12. Birom, 13. Yergan, 14. Pangu, 15. Koro, 16. Basa, 17. Bokoro, 18. Bankal, 19. Gwandara, 20. Mada, 21. Afunu, 22. Gade, 23. Bassa Komo, 24. Burmawa, 25. Ankwai, 26. Ron, 27. Mirriam, 28. Mama Plateau, 29. Rukuba, 30. Njai, 31. Gude, 32. Komma Vomni, 33. Ndorawa, 34. Glavuda, 35. Jubu, 36. Tigon, 37. Mara		
e. Ibibio and Semi-Bantu Type	3,240,000	6%
1. Ibibio, 2. Anang, 3. Ogoni, 4. Efik, 5. Ejagham, 6. Boki, 7. Ekoi, 8. Yako, 9. Ekuri, 10. Akunakuna, 11. Mbembe, 12. Ododop, 13. Orri (Ukelle)		
f. Kanuri and Kanuri dominated peoples Type	2,484,000	5%
1. Kanuri, 2. Tera, 3. Bolewa, 4. Karekare, 5. Bede, 6. Manga, 7. Mober, 8. Koyam, 9. Ngizim, 10. Mandara		
g. Edo Type	1,784,000	3.3%
1. Edo (Bini), 2. Esa, 3. Kukuruku, 4. Sobo, 5. Urhobo, 6. Jsoko		
h. Idoma-Igala-Igbirra Type	1,404,000	2.6%
1. Arago, 2. Afu, 3. Akweya-Yachi, 4. Egede, 5. Idoma, 6. Igala, 7. Nkum, 8. Nikim, 9. Etulo (Utor)		
i. Ijaw	1,083,000	2.0%
j. Bororo (pastoral Fulani)	957,000	1.5%
k. Nupe	682,000	1.2%

SOURCES: G. P. Murdock, *Africa* (New York: McGraw-Hill, 1959). P. A. Talbot, *The Peoples of Southern Nigeria* (London: Oxford University Press, 1926), Vol. 3. 1963 Official Nigerian Census for Lagos, Midwestern Region, Western, Eastern and Northern Regions.

division does not seem to have been based on culture clustering. Information is lacking to allow a more rigorous and meaningful classification at this time. Because of the large size of Nigeria, there are several ethnic groups that are less than 5 percent of the total population yet have memberships of more than half a million persons; they are included in Table 22.1. The estimated ethnic populations are based on a 1967 total population estimate for Nigeria of 54,000,000 (see Appendix 5).

III. Language Patterns

Following the Greenberg classification (1963), the three major language families of Africa are all represented in Nigeria, and within each family a wide variety of language sub-stocks exist. Nigeria is thus perhaps the most linguistically diverse state in Africa. The major Nigerian language of the Afro-Asiatic family is Hausa, but others exist such as Shuwa Arabic, and Tamashek (the language of the Tuareg). All seven of the sub-stocks of the Niger-Congo family are represented in Nigeria: (1) Kwa (including Ibo, Yoruba, Edo, Nupe); (2) Ijaw; (3) Benue-Niger (including Ibibio, Tiv, Jukun, and Birom); (4) Adamawa-Eastern; (4) Voltaic (including the Bargu languages of the Borgu state); (6) Mandingo (including the Bussa); (7) Atlantic groups (primarily Fulani). Within the Sudanic language family, Kanuri and—to a much lesser extent—Songhai exist.

The major languages of Nigeria are Hausa, Yoruba, and Ibo. Of these, only Hausa has come to serve as a wider *lingua franca*, not only in Nigeria, but in other parts of West Africa. Thus, while all scholars are agreed that Hausa is the major language of Nigeria, it is difficult to estimate the exact percentage of distribution, since there are no data available on multi-lingualism. It is significant that Hausa in the twentieth century has come to be a language grouping rather than an ethnic grouping, and that a considerable number of persons have "become" Hausa through the continued use of the Hausa language. Knappert estimates the percentage of persons in Nigeria who understand Hausa at 55 percent; MacDougald estimates 36 percent; Rustow 21 percent. Kirk-Greene (1967, p. 89) estimates that 20 million persons in Northern Nigeria speak Hausa. Our estimate for the whole of Nigeria would be about 50 percent, of whom about half use Hausa as a first language. The second language, Yoruba, is probably understood by about 20 percent of the population, primarily those of Yoruba ethnicity, although some Ibo and Hausa living in Western State speak Yoruba. English continues to be a *lingua franca*, and the official language of Nigeria. During the first civilian regime Hausa was co-equal with English as the official language of the Northern Region. With the break-up of the Northern Region, Hausa has come to be used even more extensively in some states (e.g., Kano), and less so in other states (e.g., Kwara). During the early colonial period, Hausa was the medium of instruction in the north in both primary and secondary schools. Subsequently, English was made mandatory after the fourth grade throughout Nigeria.

TABLE 22.2 Language Patterns

1. Primacy		
1st language	Hausa	(50%)
2nd language	Yoruba	(20%)
2. Greenberg classification	Hausa	IIIE
(all ethnic units in	Yoruba	IA4
country over 5%)	Ibo	IA4
	Tiv	IA5
	Fulani	IA1
	Ibibio	IA5
	Kanuri	IIB
3. *Lingua franca*	Hausa	
4. Official language	English (Hausa in former Northern Region)	

SOURCES: John N. Paden, "Language Problems of National Integration in Nigeria: The Special Position of Hausa," in *Language Problems of Developing Nations*, eds. Joshua A. Fishman, Charles A. Ferguson, and Jyotirindra Das Gupta (New York: John Wiley, 1968), pp. 199–214. Hans Wolff, "Language, Ethnic Identity, and Social Change in Southern Nigeria," *Anthropological Linguistics*, 9 (1967): 18–25. A. H. M. Kirk-Greene, "The Linguistic Statistics of Northern Nigeria: A Tentative Presentation," *African Language Review*, 6 (1967), 75–101.

IV. Urban Patterns

Capital/largest city: Lagos (founded 1630)
Dominant ethnicity/language of capital
    Major vernacular: Yoruba[1]
    Major ethnic group: Yoruba
    Major ethnic group as percent of capital's population:
    59.5% (1963–64)[2]

[1] Jan Knappert, "Language Problems of the New Nations of Africa," *African Quarterly*, 5 (1965): 95–105.
[2] J. C. Caldwell and C. Okonjo, eds., *Population of Tropical Africa* (London: Longmans, 1968), p. 322.

TABLE 22.3 Growth of Capital/Largest City

Date	Lagos
1920	100,000
1930	126,000
1940	167,000
1950	320,000
1960	560,000
1965	1,000,000 UA

SOURCES: The growth data for 1940–1960 represent staff estimates extrapolating from various sources including the 1953 Nigerian census. Metropolitan Lagos goes far beyond the administrative boundary of Lagos City into the Western State. The estimate given here for the Lagos urban agglomeration therefore includes Mushin. This estimate is that of Pauline Baker in *African Urban Notes*, 2 (1967): p. 18.

TABLE 22.4 Cities of 50,000 and Over

City	Size	Source
Lagos	ca. 1,000,000 UA	
(Agege)	(46,000)	in Lagos Urban Agglomeration (ca. 1965)
(Ikorodu)	(95,000)	
(Mushin)	(352,000)	
		*1963 Census Enum. Area**
Ibadan	627,000	Ibadan (W)
Ogbomosho	343,000	Ogbomosho (W)
Kano	295,000	Kano (N)
Ilorin	208,000	Ilorin Central (N)
Oshogbo	208,000	(W)
Abeokuta	187,000	(W)
Port Harcourt	179,000	Ahoada Central (E)
Zaria	166,000	Zaria NA (Sabon Gari, Zaria City) (N)
Ilesha	165,000	Ilesha Urban (W)
Onitsha	163,000	Onitsha Urban (E)
Iwo	158,000	(W)
Ado	158,000	Ekiti NE (W)
Kaduna	149,000	Kaduna (N)

Enugu	138,000	Enugu (Urban) (E)
Ede	134,000	Ede Ejigbo (W)
Aba	131,000	Aba Urban (E)
Ife	130,000	Ife Town (W)
Ila	115,000	Ife Illa (W)
Oyo	112,000	Oyo East (W)
Ikerre	107,000	Ekiti SE (W)
Benin City	101,000	Benin Central (NW)
Iseyin	95,000	Oyo Central (W)
Jos	94,000	Jos Central (N)
Sokoto	90,000	Sokoto (N)
Ilobu	87,000	Oshogbo North
Offa	86,000	Ilarih South (N)
Ilawe	81,000	Ekiti SE (W)
Owo	80,000	Owo South (W)
Ikirun	80,000	Oshun North East (W)
Shaki	76,000	Oyo NW (W)
Calabar	76,000	Calabar (E)
Ondo	74,000	Ondo West (W)
Akure	71,000	Ondo North East (W)
Ijebu-Ode	69,000	Ijebu Central (W)
Shagamu (Offin, Makun)	68,000	Ijebu Remo (W)
Efon	67,000	Ekiti NW (W)
Komo	65,000	Ako (N)
Oka	63,000	Owo South (W)
Ikerre	62,000	Owo North (W)
Sapele	61,000	Urhobo West (MW)
Minna	60,000	Minna South (N)
Warri	55,000	Warri (MW)
Lafia	54,000	Lafia (N)
Ikire	54,000	Oshun South East (W)
Inisha	52,000	Oshun North East (W)

(Plus 109 cities 20,000–50,000 in size)

* 1963 Census Enumeration Areas Key: N: Northern Region; E: Eastern Region; W: Western Region; MW: Mid-Western Region.
    The urban data for cities over 50,000 are taken from the mimeographed reports of the 1963 Nigerian census. The 109 cities that are 20,000–50,000 in size were left out for lack of space. We have identified sources by citing appropriate sections of the census reports. The reports available to us do not list cities as such, but give the population of various levels of enumeration units such as urban councils, clans (in the Mid-West), rural councils, etc. The process of identifying cities from the census results in this format is open to error and it may be that a few cities over 50,000 may be left out or places which are not really cities over 50,000 may be added. The reliability of the Nigerian 1963 census is also a matter to be taken into account. Overall, the critics of the census argue that it is 5–10 percent overcount. Since political factors were involved in this situation, it may be that the results for certain cities, such as Ogbomosho which was the home of the late premier of the Western Region and which showed a vast increase in population from 1953 to 1963, may reflect certain biases. It must be emphasized, however, that we do not have evidence that this is the case and for all we know Ogbomosho may indeed have been badly undercounted in 1953 or have experienced a big upsurge in population in the intervening years. Akin Mabogunje's *Urbanization in Nigeria* is based on the 1952–53 census and contains a list of the cities and populations for that date.

V. Political Patterns

A. Political Parties and Elections

The pre-independence election of 1959 was based on direct sufferage in all regions. The *Northern People's Congress* (NPC) won a plurality of seats but not a majority. Hence they formed a coalition with the *National Council of Nigerian Citizens* (NCNC) which was in coalition with the *Northern Elements Progressive Union* (NEPU), the Northern opposition party. This coalition governed until early 1964. Just prior to the federal elections in December 1964, the coalition split and a major realignment occurred within the country. Two national coalitions emerged: The *Nigerian National Alliance* (NNA) comprised primarily

of the NPC and the Western Region-based *Nigerian National Democratic Party* (NNDP); and the *United Progressive Grand Alliance* (UPGA) comprised primarily of the NCNC, NEPU, and the Western Region opposition party *Action Group* (AG). As a result of the turmoil created when certain segments of the UPGA boycotted the elections, the NNA, although they won a majority of the seats in the federal election, decided to form a national coalition by incorporating certain representatives of the UPGA (mainly former members of the NCNC) into the government. The military regime which took office in early 1966 banned all political parties in Nigeria (there were a total of 81 parties listed by

Figure 22.1   Political Parties and Elections

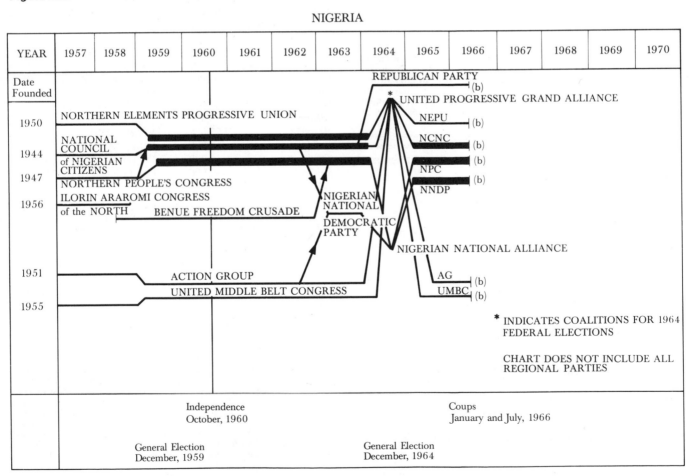

name in the military decree). Return to civilian rule has been scheduled for 1976, although General Gowon has administered the country with the aid of civilian commissioners, mainly former politicians identified with the UPGA.

B. Political Leadership

The government of Abubakar Balewa held office until 1966, after which time the leadership has been from the military. There do not appear to have been significant shifts in the cabinet ethnic balance between 1960 and 1966, but the cabinet turnover pattern fluctuates markedly from 1963 to 1966.

TABLE 22.5   Heads of Government (Post Independence)

Name	Dates in Office	Age (1971)	Ethnicity	Education	Former Occupation
1. Sir Abubakar Balewa (Prime Minister)	1960–1966	Died 1966, age 64	Hausa-Fulani (Hausa/Gerawa)	Katsina College, London School of Economics	Teacher
2. Maj. Gen. Johnson Aguiyi-Ironsi (Head, Federal Military Government)	1966	Died 1966, aged 41	Ibo	School of Infantry (England)	Soldier
3. Gen. Yakubu Gowon (Head, Federal Military Government)	1966–	37	Plateau Cluster (Angas)	Government College, Zaria Sandhurst (England)	Soldier

TABLE 22.6   Cabinet Membership: Distribution by Ethnic Unit*

Ethnicity*	Independence Cabinet	Immediate Pre-Coup Cabinet
1. Hausa-Fulani (29%)	39%	31%
2. Yoruba (20)	26	34
3. Ibo (17)	17	19
4. Tiv/Plateau (9)	4.3	3.1
5. Ibibio (6)	4.3	0
6. Kanuri (5)	4.3	9.8
7. Others (14)	4.3	3.1
N =	23	32

* Ethnic units arranged in rank order of size within country with the unit's percent of national population in parentheses.

VI. National Integration and Stability

Nigeria has experienced both elite and communal types of instability: the Tiv rebellion (1960–64), the first coup (January 1966), the ethnic violence (killings of Ibos) in the north (May–October 1966), the second coup (July 1966), and the civil war with Biafra (May 1967–January 1970).

Nigeria is by far the most populous state in Africa, and the problems of national integration span the entire spectrum of African experience. Mass-elite integration was a continuing problem throughout the civilian regime, as political leaders became increasingly out of touch with local people. Inter-ethnic integration was a problem both with regard to the three major groups—Hausa, Yoruba, Ibo— and with the multitude of minority tribes. Territorial malintegration in its primary form, was reflected in north/south regionalism. Although the problems of Nigeria have been formidable, the new twelve-state system provides some accommodation of subnational sentiment.

TABLE 22.7   Elite Instability

Event and Date	Characteristics
1. Coup d'Etat January 15, 1966	a. *Description*: Junior army officers in Kaduna, Ibadan, and Lagos killed the premier of the Northern Region (Sir Ahmadu Bello, Sardauna of Sokoto), the premier of the Western Region (Chief Akintola), and two of the major federal ministers: the prime minister, Sir Abubakar Tafawa Balewa, and the finance minister, Chief Festus Okotie-Eboh. The remaining federal ministers turned over control of the government to a senior military officer, General Aguiyi-Ironsi, an Ibo, who suspended the constitution, and maintained order (arresting several junior officers involved in the coup).
	b. *Participants*: Most of the junior officers involved were Ibo, and most of the government officials killed were non-Ibo. However, there was also a generation gap and ideological differences reflected in the coup.
	c. *Apparent Causes*: The junior officers involved insisted that there was no ethnic basis to the coup, but that they were trying to replace a corrupt regime, and trying to prevent politicians from using the army for political purposes.
2. Coup d'Etat July 29, 1966	a. *Description*: Northern army officers killed the military governor of the Western Region (Fajuyi) and General Aguiyi-Ironsi, and assumed control of the country.
	b. *Participants*: Troops from both the Middle Belt and from the Far North took control from national military officers and civilian advisors. Colonel Yakubu Gowon was asked to head the new regime.
	c. *Apparent Causes*: The coup was partly a reaction by Northerners against rapid centralization, and alleged exclusion of Northerners from the government.

SOURCES: James O'Connell "The Fragility of Stability: The Fall of the Nigerian Federal Government, 1966," In *Power and Protest in Black Africa*, eds. Robert I. Rotberg and Ali A. Mazrui (New York: Oxford University Press, 1970), pp. 1012–1034. Walter Schwartz, *Nigeria* (London: Pall Mall Press, 1968), pp. 191–231.

TABLE 22.8   Communal Instability

Event and Date	Characteristics
1. Rebellion August–October 1960; 1964	a. *Description*: In mid-1960, groups of Tiv ranging in number from 50 to 500 persons burned the houses of Chiefs and NPC members in the Benue Plateau area. By the time order was restored, thousands of people had been arrested, although not more than 25 were killed in all. In February 1964, with federal elections impending, there were renewed attacks by Tiv members on government facilities and supporters. The Nigerian army engaged in a counter-attack throughout the rest of 1964, and several hundred people were killed.
	b. *Participants*: Tiv traditional elements with a long history of "chiefless" society and local autonomy resisted both the regional and national governments, and the government-appointed Tiv chiefs. The rebellion had no predominant leadership. Although Joseph Tarka and the *United Middle Belt Congress* (UMBC) were identified with the demand for greater autonomy, there is no evidence as to their direct involvement in the rebellion (even though some UMBC supporters may have participated).
	c. *Apparent Causes*: Tiv elements demanded greater autonomy in the Northern Region. Much of the dissatisfaction was directed against the Native Authority and the NPC. There was no attempt to secede or take over the government.

TABLE 22.8 Communal Instability *(cont.)*

Event and Date	Characteristics
2. Ethnic Violence May–October 1966	a. *Description*: On May 29, 1966, in most of the major far northern cities, there were riots between northerners and Ibos/easterners. The riots lasted for about three days. Shortly thereafter with the successful northern counter-coup (late July), many easterners in the north began to leave for the Eastern Region. In late September and early October many of those who remained (or were in process of emigration) were killed by northern army elements. The estimate of persons killed in both May and October was put at 30,000 by the former Biafran government and around 5,000 by the Nigerian government. b. *Participants*: Ibos who had been living in the north were attacked in May primarily by Hausa urban dwellers. In October, elements of the army were clearly involved. c. *Apparent Causes*: The May riots were partly the result of northern frustration with the Ironsi regime and resentment against the dominant position of the educated Ibos in the north. The October killings are interpreted by many as the actual origins of the civil war, since the army had been broken up by region-of-origin after the July coup.
3. Secession May 1967–January 1970	a. *Description*: In May 1967 the former Eastern Region of Nigeria was declared to be a sovereign state, "Biafra." In July, Biafran troops crossed through the Mid-West Region and into the Western Region in an attempted attack on Lagos. Federal troops began major attacks on Biafra from the north and west and through naval blockade from the south. By the summer of 1968 most major towns in Biafra plus most non-Ibo areas were in federal control, although a number of important cities changed hands regularly. In summer 1969 Biafran counter-attacks were extended to the Mid-West Region. The civil war continued despite immense casualties and various attempts at negotiation, until Biafra's surrender in January 1970. b. *Participants*: Biafrans were predominantly Ibo but received some support from minority groups (e.g., Ibibio). The Biafran leader was Lt. Col. Odumegwu Ojukwu. Nigeria had approximately a 100,000-man army; Biafrans regarded this as a total war and mobilized the entire population. Material support to the federal government came from Britain and the USSR; material support for Biafra came from France. Military casualties were estimated to be very high (over 100,000), but most deaths were a result of population starvation in Biafra (estimates of such deaths range from half a million to two million). c. *Apparent Causes*: Biafra demanded self-determination in a state which could protect the lives and properties of its citizens. Nigeria demanded national unity as a preliminary to negotiations regarding the form of civilian government (including inter-regional relations).

SOURCES: John P. Mackintosh et al., eds., *Nigerian Government and Politics* (Evanston, Ill.: Northwestern University Press, 1966), pp. 498–501. *Africa Report* had a number of articles on the civil war between 1967 and 1970.

VII. Selected References

BIBLIOGRAPHY

African Bibliographic Center, Washington, D.C. *Prelude—Coup d'État—Military Government: Politics and Government in Nigeria, 1965 to February 1966.* Biblio-Research No. 1. Special Bibliographic Series, Vol. 4, No. 1, 1966.

Dipeolu, J. O. *Bibliographical Sources for Nigerian Studies.* Evanston, Ill.: Northwestern University Press, 1966.

Ita, Nduntuei O. *Bibliography of Nigeria: A Survey of Anthropological and Linguistic Writings from the Earliest Times to 1966.* New York: Africana, 1971.

U.S. Library of Congress. General Reference and Bibliography Division. African Section. *Nigeria: A Guide to Official Publications.* Washington, D.C.: Government Printing Office, 1966.

Wolpe, Howard. *A Study Guide for Nigeria.* Boston: Development Program, African Studies Center, Boston University, 1966.

GENERAL

Arikpo, Okoi. *The Development of Modern Nigeria.* Baltimore, Md.: Penguin, 1967.

Coleman, James S. *Nigeria, Background to Nationalism.* Berkeley: University of California Press, 1958.

Crowder, Michael. *The Story of Nigeria*, rev. ed. London: Faber, 1966.

Schwartz, Frederick A. O., Jr. *Nigeria: The Tribes, the Nations, or the Race—The Politics of Independence.* Cambridge: Massachusetts Institute of Technology Press, 1965.

Schwartz, Walter. *Nigeria.* New York: Praeger, 1968.

U.S. Department of the Army. *Area Handbook for Nigeria*, 2nd ed. Washington, D.C.: Government Printing Office, 1964.

Udo, Reuben K. *Geographical Regions of Nigeria.* Berkeley: University of California Press, 1970.

POLITICAL

Blitz, L. Franklin, ed. *The Politics and Administration of Nigerian Government.* New York: Praeger, 1965.

Dillon, W. "Nigeria's Two Revolutions." *Africa Report*, 11 (March 1966): 8–14, and following articles.

Mackintosh, John P., ed. *Nigerian Government and Politics.* Evanston, Ill.: Northwestern University Press, 1966.

Melson, Robert, and Howard Wolpe, eds. *Nigeria: Modernization and the Politics of Communalism.* East Lansing, Mich.: Michigan State University Press, 1971.

O'Connell, James. "Political Integration: The Nigerian Case." In *African Integration and Disintegration*, ed. Arthur Hazlewood, pp. 129–184. London: Oxford University Press, 1967.

Sklar, Richard L. *Nigerian Political Parties: Power in an Emergent African Nation.* Princeton, N.J.: Princeton University Press, 1963.

Sklar, Richard L., and C. S. Whitaker, "Nigeria." In *National Unity and Regionalism in Eight African States*, ed. G. M. Carter. Ithaca, N.Y.: Cornell University Press, 1966.

Whitaker, C. S. *The Politics of Tradition: Continuity and Change in Northern Nigeria, 1946–1966.* Princeton, N.J.: Princeton University Press, 1969.

ECONOMIC

Aboyade, Ojetunji. *Foundations of an African Economy.* New York: Praeger, 1966.

Aboyade, Ojetunji. "The Economy of Nigeria." In *The Economies of Africa*, eds. P. Robson and D. A. Lury, pp. 127–193. Evanston, Ill.: Northwestern University Press, 1969.

Eicher, Carl K., and Carl Liedholm, eds. *Growth and Development of the Nigerian Economy.* East Lansing: Michigan State University Press, 1970.

Food and Agriculture Organization of the United Nations. *Agricultural Development in Nigeria 1964–1980.* Rome: FAO, January 1965.

Kilby, Peter. *Industrialization in an Open Economy: Nigeria 1945–1966.* London: Cambridge University Press, 1969.

SOCIAL

Abernethy, David B. *The Political Dilemma of Popular Education: An African Case.* Stanford, Cal.: Stanford University Press, 1970.

Buchanan, Keith M., and J. C. Pugh. *Land and People in Nigeria: The Human Geography of Nigeria and its Environmental Background.* London: University of London Press, 1955.

Education and World Affairs, Nigeria Project Task Force. *Nigerian Human Resource Development and Utilization.* New York: Education and World Affairs, 1967.

Fagg, William. *Nigerian Images.* New York: Praeger, 1963.

Grimley, John B. and Gordon E. Robinson. *Church Growth in Central and Southern Nigeria.* Grand Rapids, Michigan: Eerdmans Publishing Co., 1966.

LeVine, Robert A. *Dreams and Deeds: Achievement Motivation in Nigeria.* Chicago: University of Chicago Press, 1966.

Lloyd, P. C., A. L. Mabogunje, and B. Awe. *The City of Ibadan.* London: Cambridge University Press, 1967.

Mabogunje, Akin L. *Urbanization in Nigeria.* New York: Africana, 1969.

Marris, P. *Family and Social Change in an African City.* Evanston, Ill.: Northwestern University Press, 1962. (Lagos).

23. Rwanda

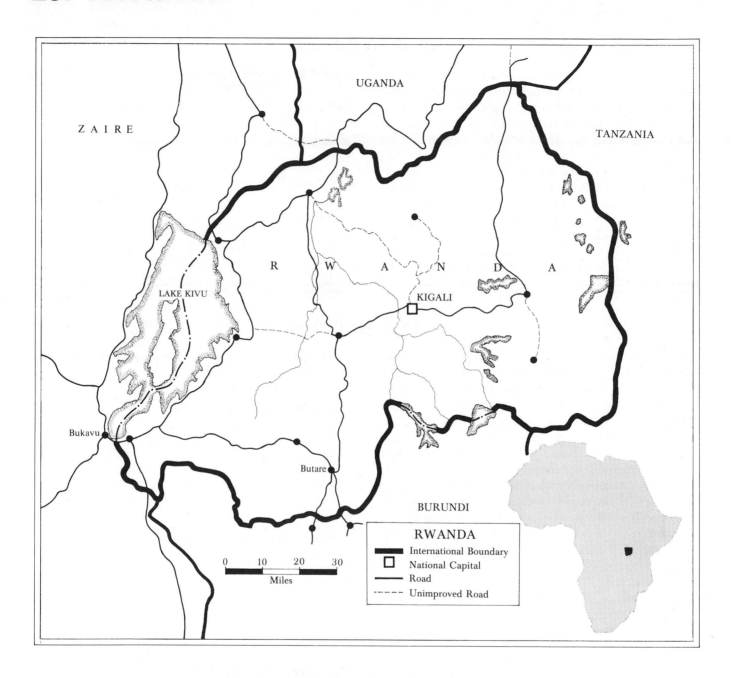

I. Basic Information

Date of Independence: July 1, 1962
Former Colonial Ruler: Belgium
Change in Boundaries: Pre-independence it was part of
   UN trust territory of Ruanda Urundi
Former Name: Ruanda

Estimated Population (1970): 3,590,000
Area Size (equivalent in U.S.): 10,000 sq. mi. (Vermont)
Date of Last Census: 1952
Major Exports 1968 as Percent of Total Exports:
   coffee—57 percent; cassiterite (tin)—22 percent

II. Ethnic Patterns

The ethnic situation in Rwanda is much like that in Burundi, with Hutu forming the bulk of the population and the Tutsi formerly serving as the aristocracy. In light of the Hutu/Tutsi conflict and the resultant Tutsi emigration, the Tutsi population is estimated at 4 percent at the end of 1969. We have adjusted the Tutsi and the total population estimates here to reflect this estimate. In all other places in the Handbook we continue to use the larger UN population estimates (for 1967, 3,306,000), however, because of the lack of official confirmation of the nature and magnitude of the Tutsi emigration. The Twa (Pygmies) represent less than one percent of the population.

TABLE 23.1   Ethnic Units Over 5 Percent of Country Population

Ethnic Units	Estimated Ethnic Population 1967	Estimated Ethnic Percentage
a. Rwanda type	2,874,000	99%
1. Hutu (Bahutu, Wakhutu)	(2,744,000)	(95%)
2. Tutsi (Tussi, Batusi, Watutsi)	(130,000)	(4%)

SOURCE: J. J. Maquet, *The Premise of Inequality* (London, International African Institute, Oxford University Press, 1960), p. 10.

III. Language Patterns

The ethnic composition of Rwanda is sometimes viewed as Hutu (of the Bantu language family), and Tutsi (of the Nilotic language family). It is also viewed by some (see Murdock, 1959; Maquet, 1960; d'Hertefelt, 1965) as a single society—"Rwanda." In either case, both "segments" of Rwanda society share a common Bantu language, Kinyarwanda (usually referred to as Rwanda). It is clear that this language is used most widely by Hutu/Tutsi peoples who have had close contact with each other. Knappert suggests that 100 percent of the population speaks Rwanda. MacDougald suggests 79 percent. There are still groups of isolated Hutu who do not use this language, hence our estimate of Rwanda speakers is 90 percent. Swahili is increasingly being used in the eastern portions of Rwanda, and our estimate of 10 percent may be low. French continues as the official language along with Rwanda.

TABLE 23.2   Language Patterns

1. Primacy		
1st language	Rwanda	(90%)
2nd language	Swahili	(10%)
2. Greenberg classification	Rwanda	IA5
(all ethnic units in	(Hutu	IA5)
country over 5%)	(Tutsi	IIE1)
	Swahili	IA5
3. *Lingua francas*	Rwanda, Swahili	
4. Official languages	Rwanda, French	

SOURCES: Marcel d'Hertefelt, "The Rwanda of Rwanda" in *Peoples of Africa*, ed. James L. Gibbs, Jr. (New York: Holt, Rinehart and Winston, 1965), pp. 403–440. J. J. Maquet, *The Premise of Inequality* (London: International African Institute, Oxford University Press, 1961).

IV. Urban Patterns

Capital/largest city: Kigali (founded ca. 14th century)
Dominant ethnicity/language of capital
    Major vernacular: Rwanda[1]
    Major ethnic group: Rwanda
    Major ethnic group as percent of capital's population:
        Nearly 100%

[1] Jan Knappert, "Language Problems of the New Nations of Africa," *African Quarterly*, 5 (1965): 95–105.

TABLE 23.3   Growth of Capital/Largest City

Date	Kigali
1950	ca. 3,000
1960	5,000*
1965	15,000

* *UN Demographic Yearbook 1963.*

TABLE 23.4   Cities of 20,000 and Over

City	Size	Date
Kigali	15,000	1965

SOURCE: *Africa 1968.* Despite the fact that its population is less than 20,000, Kigali is the largest city in Rwanda.

V. Political Patterns

A. Political Parties and Elections

Political parties in Rwanda are drawn along ethnic lines, with the dominant Hutu controlling the *Parti Républicain du Mouvement d'Émancipation des Hutus* (PARMEHUTU) and the *Association pour la Promo-* *tion Sociale de la Masse* (APROSOMA). The *Union Nationale Rwandaise* (UNAR) has served as the opposition voice for the minority Tutsi. By 1969 PARMEHUTU was the only active party. The 1969 election gave PARMEHUTU all 47 members of the

Figure 23.1   **Political Parties and Elections**

RWANDA

| YEAR | 1957 | 1958 | 1959 | 1960 | 1961 | 1962 | 1963 | 1964 | 1965 | 1966 | 1967 | 1968 | 1969 | 1970 |

PARTI RÉPUBLICAIN du MOUVEMENT d'ÉMANCIPATION des HUTUS*

ASSOCIATION pour la PROMOTION SOCIALEi de la MASSE

UNION NATIONALE RWANDAISE

RASSEMBLEMENT DÉMOCRATIQUE RWANDAISE

Independence
July, 1962

General Election
September, 1961

General Election
October, 1965

General Election
September, 1969

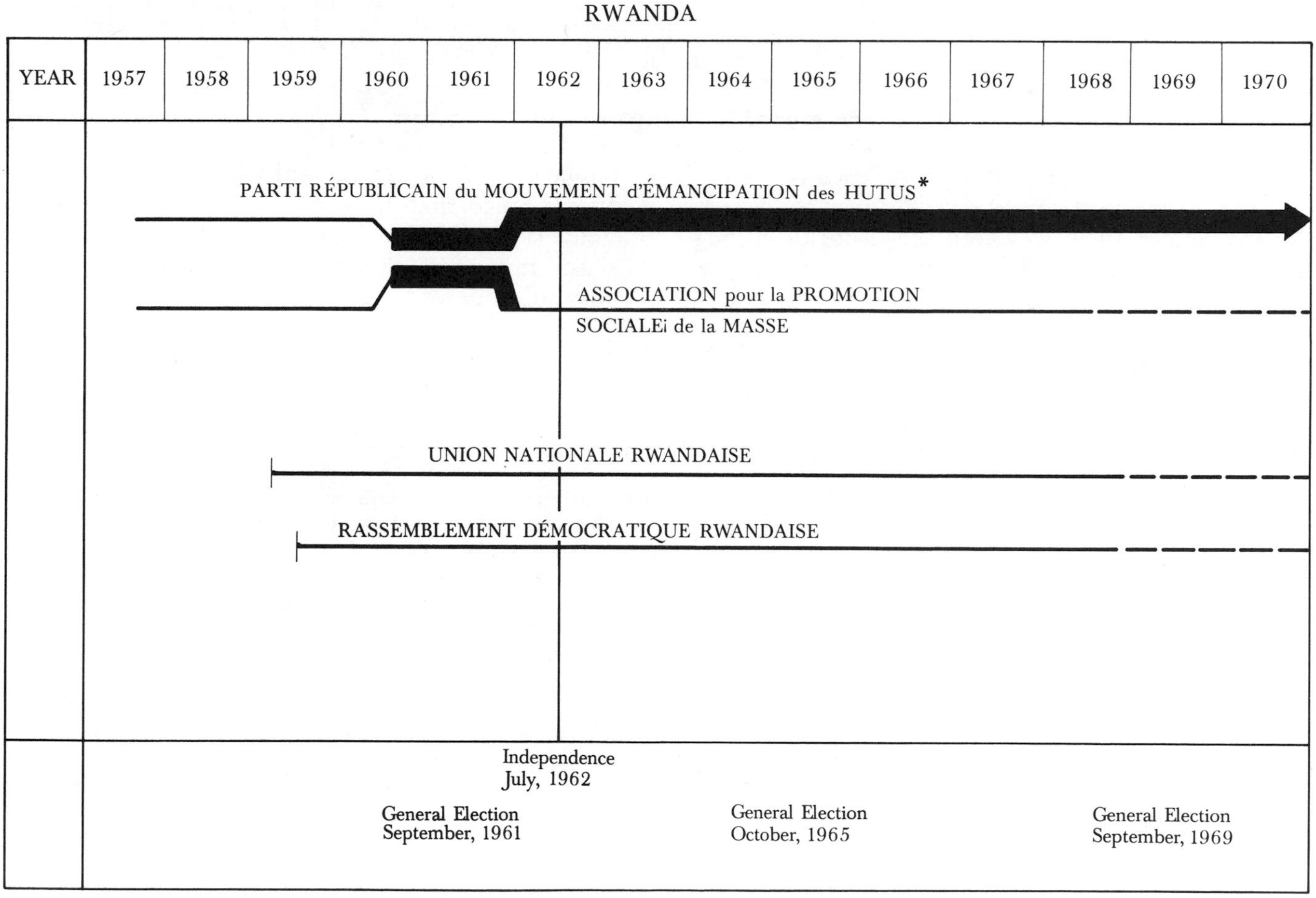

* Now known as the MDR-Parmehutu (*Mouvement Démocratique Républicain Parmehutu*).

TABLE 23.5   Head of Government (Post Independence)

Name	Dates in Office	Age (1971)	Ethnicity	Education	Former Occupation
1. Grégoire Kayibanda (President)	1962–	47	Mixed Hutu/ Congolese	Grand Seminary of Nyakibanda	Teacher

National Assembly and President Kayibanda 99.7 percent of the vote.

B. Political Leadership

Grégoire Kayibanda has been head of government since independence. The cabinet is entirely Hutu, with frequent turnovers in membership from 1964 to 1967.

TABLE 23.6   Cabinet Membership: Distribution by Ethnic Unit*

Ethnicity*	Independence Cabinet	1967 Cabinet
1. Hutu (95%)	80%	100%
2. Tutsi (4)†	20	0
3. Others (1)	0	0
N =	12	13

* Ethnic units arranged in rank order of size within country with the unit's percent of national population in parentheses.

† At the time of independence the Tutsi amounted to some 16 percent of the population.

VI. National Integration and Stability

Political instability in post-independence Rwanda is a legacy of the intensive and revolutionary civil war fought in late 1959, in which the historically long-subjected Hutu majority overthrew the minority Tutsi aristocracy in the *coup d'état* at Gitarama, January 28, 1961, a year and a half before independence. Since that time there have been renewed conflicts between the Hutu, now governing, and the Tutsi, many of whom have become refugees in Burundi.

TABLE 23.8   Communal Instability

Event and Date	Characteristics
1. Civil War 1963–64, 1966	a. *Description*: In an aftermath of the revolutionary civil war of 1959, civil war again broke out in Rwanda in 1963, initiated and intensified by a series of invasions from Burundi led by Tutsi refugees. The refugees and some of their fellow-Tutsi still residing in Rwanda attempted to overthrow the government of their former Hutu subjects. Successive invasions on November 25, December 20 and 27, 1963, were counteracted by Rwandese forces, and resulted in extensive mass reprisals during the following year. Between 5,000 and 14,000 people are estimated to have been killed at this time. Evidence of continuing civil war is obtainable from reports of Tustsi-Hutu clashes in 1966 in which 200 were estimated to have been killed. b. *Participants*: Although the initial action was a war between the government forces and a "foreign" invader, most of the serious violence and killing was the result of local action against Tutsi in Rwanda by Hutu officials and citizens, acting only under general instructions to take measures for their own security. c. *Apparent Causes*: There are no apparent causes apart from the desire of certain Tutsi refugees, identified only as "agitators" by a UN investigating commission, to regain their former political status in Rwanda.

SOURCES: Aaron Segal, "Rwanda—The Underlying Causes," *Africa Report*, 9 (April 1964): 3–6; and "United Nations Findings on Rwanda and Burundi," in the same issue, pp. 7–8.

VII. Selected References

BIBLIOGRAPHY

Clement, Joseph R. A. M. *Essai de Bibliographie de Ruanda-Urundi*. Usumbura: n. p., 1959.

GENERAL

Lemarchand, René. *Rwanda and Burundi*. New York: Praeger, 1970.

Office de l'Information et des Relations Publiques du Congo Belge et du Ruanda-Urundi. *Ruanda-Urundi, Geography and History*. Brussels: 1960.

U.S. Department of the Army. *Area Handbook for Rwanda*. Pamphlet No. 550–84. Washington, D.C.: Government Printing Office, 1969.

POLITICAL

Chronique de Politique Étrangère. *Décolonisation et Indépendence de Rwanda et du Burundi*. Brussels: Institut Royal des Relations Internationales, 1963.

Codere, Helen. "Power in Rwanda." *Anthropologica*, 4 (1962): 45–85.

Lemarchand, René. "Political Instability in Africa: The Case of Rwanda and Burundi." *Civilisations*, 16 (1966): 307–337.

Lemarchand, René. "The Coup in Rwanda." In *Power and Protest in Black Africa*, eds. Robert I. Rotberg and Ali A. Mazrui, pp. 877–923. New York: Oxford University Press, 1970.

Segal, Aaron. "Rwanda, The Underlying Causes: A Behind-the-Headlines Report on Bahutu-Batutsi Warfare." *Africa Report*, 9 (April 1964): 3–8.

ECONOMIC

Leurquin, Philippe P. *Agricultural Change in Ruanda-Urundi 1945–1960*. Stanford, Cal.: Stanford University Food Research Institute, 1963.

SOCIAL

d'Hertefelt, Marcel. "The Rwanda of Rwanda." In *Peoples of Africa*, ed. James L. Gibbs, Jr., pp. 403–440. New York: Holt, Rinehart and Winston, 1965.

Harroy, Jean Paul, et al. *Le Ruanda-Urundi: Ses Ressources naturelles, ses populations*. Brussels: Les Naturalistes Belges, 1956.

Liège Université. Fondation pour les recherches scientifiques au Congo belge et au Ruanda-Urundi. *Le problème de l'enseignement dans le Ruanda-Urundi*. Elizabethville: C.E.P.S.I., 1958.

Maquet, J. J. *The Premise of Inequality in Ruanda: A Study of Political Relations in a Central African Kingdom*. London: Oxford University Press, 1961.

24. Senegal

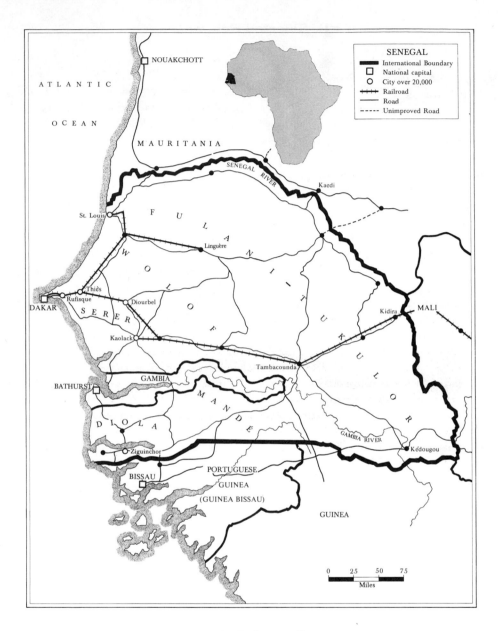

I. Basic Information

Date of Independence: August 29, 1960 (June 20, 1960 as Mali Federation)

Former Colonial Ruler: France

Change in Boundaries: Formerly part of French West African Federation. Part of Federation of Mali (formed with Mali) from April 4, 1959 to August 20, 1960, when Senegal seceded.

Estimated Population (*1969*): 3,780,000

Area Size (*equivalent in U.S.*): 76,000 sq. mi. (Nebraska)

Date of Last Census: 1961

Major Exports 1968 as Percent of Total Exports: peanuts and oil—73 percent; aluminum phosphate—8 percent

II. Ethnic Patterns

The ethnic classification of Senegal is done at a middle level of inclusion. The Wolof and the Serer might be grouped together in a more abstract schema. It should also be noted that although the Lebou are traditionally considered a branch of the Serer, they are mixed among and assimilating into the Wolof society. All of the ethnic groups in Senegal are predominantly Muslim and there is a high degree of cultural similarity between the groups.

The percentages used by Verrière (1963) diverge somewhat from other sources (see Foltz, 1964). Most notably, Verrière considers the Fulani to be only 7 percent of the population. (It will be noted that although we have grouped the Fulani and Tukulor together—since they share a common language and culture while retaining separate identities—we consider the Fulani component to be 15 percent of the total population.) Other small groups found in Senegal are the Sarakolé, Moors, and Bassari. About 2 percent of the population is European.

TABLE 24.1 Ethnic Units Over 5 Percent of Country Population

Ethnic Units	Estimated Ethnic Population 1967	Estimated Ethnic Percentage
a. Wolof Type (Jolof, Ouolof, Wolof)	1,358,000	37%
1. Wolof, 2. Lebou		
b. Fulani-Tukulor Type	880,000	24%
1. Fulani (Peul)	(550,000)	(15%)
2. Tukulor (Toucouleure)	(330,000)	(9%)
c. Serer (Serère, Sarer, Kegueme)	587,000	16%
d. Diola Type (Jola, Dyola, Yola)	330,000	9%
1. Diola, 2. Bainouk, 3. Balanté		
e. Mandé Type	257,000	7%
1. Malinké, 2. Bambara		

SOURCES: W. J. Foltz, "Senegal," in *Political Parties and National Integration in Tropical Africa*, eds. J. S. Coleman and C. G. Rosberg (Berkeley: University of California Press, 1964), p. 30. From SERESA, Rapport General (Dakar, 1960). H. Deschamps, *Le Sénégal et le Gambie* (Paris: Presses Universitaires de France, 1964), pp. 26–40. L. Verrière, *Où en est, où va la Population du Sénégal?* (Paris: Institut de Science Economique Appliqué, 1963).

III. Language Patterns

The languages of Senegal fall into two categories: (1) West Atlantic (including Wolof, Serère-Siné, Serère-Non, Diola, Fulani, Mandjaque, Mancagne, Balanté, Bassari); (2) Mandé (Malinké, Bambara, Sarakolé/Soninké). Wolof is spoken by about one-third of the population as a first language (Knappert estimates 33 percent; MacDougald 38 percent; Rustow 42 percent). However, another third of the population probably speak Wolof as a second or third language. Wolof has no official status in the country, and French continues as the official language. Arabic is widely used as a religious language.

TABLE 24.2 Language Patterns

1. Primacy		
1st language	Wolof	(60%)
2nd language	Fulani	(24%)
2. Greenberg classification	Wolof	IA1
(all ethnic units in	Fulani-Tukulor	IA1
country over 5%)	Serer	IA1
	Diola	IA2
	Mandé (Malinké)	IA2
3. *Lingua franca*	Wolof	
4. Official language	French	

IV. Urban Patterns

Capital/largest city: Dakar (founded 1840)
Dominant ethnicity/language of capital
   Major vernacular: Wolof[1]
   Major ethnic group: Wolof

[1] Jan Knappert, "Language Problems of the New Nations of Africa," *African Quarterly*, 5 (1965): 95–105.

Major ethnic group as percent of capital's population: 35% (1955)[2]

[2] Senegal Service de la Statistique Général, *Recensement Démographique de Dakar (1955)* (Paris: Haut Commissariat de la République en Afrique Occidental Française, 1958), p. 17.

TABLE 24.3   Growth of Capital/Largest City

Date	Dakar
1920	30,000
1930	69,000
1940	125,000
1950	257,000
1960	375,000 UA
1965	500,000 UA
1969	581,000 UA

SOURCE: *Démographié Comparée.*

TABLE 24.4   Cities of 20,000 and Over

City	Size	Date
Dakar[a]	400,000	1969
Kaolack[a]	95,000	1969
Thiès[a]	90,000	1969
Rufisque[a]	58,200	1969
Saint-Louis[a]	57,900	1969
Zinguinchor[b]	30,000	1960
Diourbel[b]	29,000	1960

SOURCES:
[a] Results of 1969 census as reported in *Africa South of the Sahara 1971* (London: Europa Publications, 1971), p. 645.
[b] *Démographie Comparée.*

V. Political Patterns

Figure 24.1   **Political Parties and Elections**

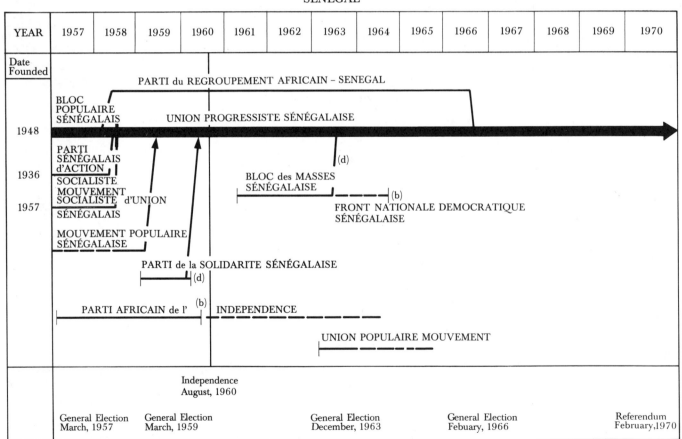

A. Political Parties and Elections

Since its formation in 1948 the *Union Progressiste Sénégalaise* (UPS), formerly known as the *Bloc Démocratique Sénégalais* (BDS) and then as the *Bloc Populaire Sénégalais* (BPS), has been the main political force in Senegal. Opposition to the UPS has existed in the past but the parties have either been absorbed or banned by the dominant UPS, and Senegal became a one-party state in 1967. Among the absorbed opposition parties were the *Bloc des Masses Sénégalaise* (BMS) and the *Parti du Regroupement Africain-Sénégal* (PRA-S). The *Parti Africain de l'Indépendance* (PAI), was banned in 1960. Léopold Sédar Senghor is both President of Senegal and the Secretary-General of the UPS; all seats in the Legislative Assembly are held by members of the UPS.

B. Political Leadership

Léopold Senghor has been head of government since independence. The new constitution, approved by the electorate in February 1970, created the office of prime minister but the president retains the predominant share of power. There has been little shift in the cabinet ethnic balance which tends to reflect the general population. There was marked cabinet turnover in the 1962–64 period, partly reflecting the ouster of Mamadou Dia.

TABLE 24.5 Head of Government (Post Independence)

Name	Dates in Office	Age (1971)	Ethnicity	Education	Former Occupation
1. Léopold Sédar Senghor (President)	1960–	65	Serer	University of Paris (France)	Teacher, Professor

TABLE 24.6 Cabinet Membership: Distribution by Ethnic Unit*

Ethnicity*	Independence Cabinet	1967 Cabinet
1. Wolof (37%)	42%	44%
2. Fulani-Tukulor (24)	17	28
3. Serer (16)	17	5.6
4. Diola (9)	8.3	5.6
5. Mandé (7)	9	5.6
6. Others (7)	17	11
N =	12	18

* Ethnic units arranged in rank order of size within country with the unit's percent of national population in parentheses.

VI. National Integration and Stability

Until recent years Senegal had experienced little political instability. The conspicuous exceptions were the ambiguous clash between President Senghor and Mamadou Dia in 1962 and the assassination attempt in 1967, which was attributed to Mamadou Dia's supporters by an official inquiry.

There have also been rumors of further plots against the President. The split between Dia and Senghor in 1962 may have resulted from preferences for "radical" vs. "conservative" policies respectively. Dia's (Muslim) and Senghor's (Catholic) religions also represent a potential source of conflict in Senegal, although the important traditional Muslim leaders have tended to support Senghor. To date, however, there has been no real evidence of communal in-

stability. In 1968 and 1969, however, both unions and students staged serious protests which caused the government much concern.

TABLE 24.7 Elite Instability

Event and Date	Characteristics
1. Attempted Coup December 17, 1962	a. *Description*: Prime Minister Mamadou Dia sent troops and police to evict the legislature in order to forestall a censure motion. The turning point seems to have been the loyalty of the parachutists who captured and isolated Dia and his ministers and who put a radio transmitter at Senghor's disposal. No injuries were reported. Dia stood trial and was imprisoned.
	b. *Participants*: President Senghor and Prime Minister Dia. One of Dia's major supporters was General Fall, Chief of the General Staff.
	c. *Apparent Causes*: Personal and ideological rivalry between Dia and Senghor.

SOURCE: Victor DuBois, "The Trial of Mamadou Dia," *American Universities Field Staff*, *Report Service*, West Africa Series, 6 (June 1963): 4–8.

VII. Selected References

BIBLIOGRAPHY

Abi-Saab, Rosemary. "Éléments de Bibliographie. Le Sénégal, des origines à l'indépendence." *Genva-Afrique*, 3 (1964): 288–297.

GENERAL

Crowder, Michael. *Senegal: A Study in French Assimilation Policy*, rev. ed. London: Methuen, 1967.

Deschamps, H. *Le Sénégal et la Gambie*. Paris: Presses Universitaires de France, 1964.

Klein, Martin A. *Islam and Imperialism in Senegal*. Stanford, Cal.: Stanford University Press, 1967.

Thompson, Virginia, and Richard Adloff. *French West Africa*, pp. 108–116. Stanford, Cal.: Stanford University Press, 1957.

U.S. Department of the Army. *Area Handbook for Senegal*. Washington, D.C.: Government Printing Office, 1963.

POLITICAL

Behrman, Lucy. *Muslim Brotherhoods and Politics in Senegal*. Cambridge, Mass.: Harvard University Press, 1970.

de Lusignan, Guy. *French-Speaking Africa since Independence*, pp. 199–217. London: Pall Mall Press, 1969.

Foltz, William J. "Senegal." In *Political Parties and National Integration in Tropical Africa*, eds. J. S. Coleman and C. G. Rosberg. Los Angeles: University of California Press, 1964.

Foltz, William J. *From French West Africa to the Mali Federation*. New Haven, Conn.: Yale University Press, 1965.

Foltz, William J. "Social Structure and Political Behavior of Senegalese Elites." *Behavior Science Notes*, 4 (1969): 145–163.

Markowitz, Irving L. *Leopold Senghor and the Politics of Negritude*. New York: Atheneum, 1969.

Milcent, E. "Senegal." In *African One-Party States*, ed. G. M. Carter, pp. 87–148. Ithaca, N.Y.: Cornell University Press, 1962.

Mortimer, Robert. "Senegal Seeks to Broaden Political Base." *Africa Report*, 15 (June 1970): 24–27.

Robson, Peter. "The Problems of Senegambia." *Journal of Modern African Studies*, 3 (1965): 393–407.

Senghor, Léopold Sédar. *On African Socialism*. New York: Praeger, 1964.

ECONOMIC

International Monetary Fund. "Senegal." In *Surveys of African Economies*, Vol. 3. Washington, D.C.: I.M.F., 1970.

Peterec, Richard J. *Dakar and West African Economic*

Development. New York: Columbia University Press, 1967.

Serreau, Jean. *Le Développement à la Base au Dahomey et au Sénégal.* Paris: Librarie Générale de Droit et de Jurisprudence, 1966.

SOCIAL

Berg, Elliot. "Education and Manpower in Senegal, Guinea, and the Ivory Coast." In *Manpower and Education: Country Studies in Economic Development*, eds. F. B. Harbison and C. Myers. New York: McGraw-Hill, 1965.

Collomb, Henri and Henry Ayats. "Migration in Senegal: A Psychopathological Study." In *Readings in African Psychology From French Language Sources*, ed. Frederic R. Wickert, pp. 335–356. East Lansing: African Studies Center, Michigan State University, 1967.

Costa, E. "Employment Problems and Policies in Senegal." *International Labor Review*, 95 (May 1967): 417–451.

Mercier, Paul. "Evolution of Senegalese Elites." *International Social Science Bulletin*, 8 (1956): 441–452.

Pfeffermann, G. *Industrial Labor in the Republic of Senegal.* New York: Praeger Special Study, 1968.

Sankalé, M., L. V. Thomas, and P. Fougeyrollas. *Dakar en devenir.* Paris: Présence africaine 1968.

Sy, Cheikh Tidiana. *La confrerie senegalaise des Mourides.* Paris: Présence africaine 1969.

25. Sierra Leone

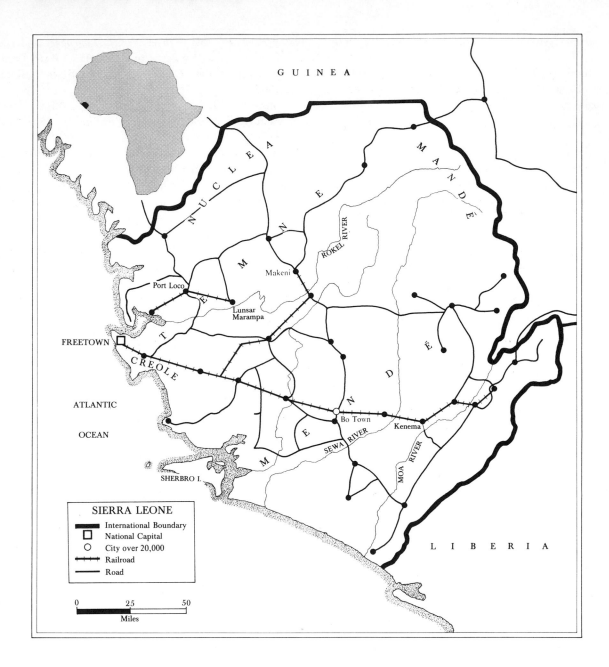

I. Basic Information

Date of Independence: April 27, 1961
Former Colonial Ruler: United Kingdom
Estimated Population (*1970*): 2,550,000
Area Size (*equivalent in U.S.*): 28,000 sq. mi. (South
Carolina)

Date of Last Census: 1963
Major Exports 1968 as Percent of Total Exports:
diamonds—59 percent; iron ore—13 percent

II. Ethnic Patterns

The ethnic classification of Sierra Leone is done according to the same principles used in the Ivory Coast and Liberia: the groups listed within each of the three major types are identity groups. In addition to these peoples, there are Fulani (3 percent), Lolo (3 percent), and Creole. There are also European and Asian populations of 3,000 and 5,000 respectively.

TABLE 25.1 Ethnic Units Over 5 Percent of Country Population

Ethnic Units	Estimated Ethnic Population 1967	Estimated Ethnic Percentage
a. Temne Type (West Atlantic)	1,098,000	*45%*
1. Temne (Timne)	(731,000)	(30%)
2. Limba	(195,000)	(8%)
3. Sherbro		
4. Kissi		
5. Krim		
6. Gola		
b. Mendé Type (Peripheral Mandé)	878,000	*36%*
1. Mendé (Kossa, Mendi)	(756,000)	(31%)
2. Kono		
3. Vai (Gallinas)		
c. Nuclear Mandé Type	195,000	*8%*
1. Koranko, 2. Susu,		
3. Malinké		
4. Yalunka (Jalonké)		
d. Creole	27,000	*1%*

SOURCES: J. I. Clarke, *Sierra Leone in Maps* (London: University of London Press, 1966). G. P. Murdock, *Africa* (New York: McGraw-Hill, 1959).

III. Language Patterns

According to Dalby (1962) there are five major language groups in Sierra Leone: (1) The Mandé languages (including Susu, Yalunka, Mendé, Loko, Bandi, Loma, Comendi, Mandinka, Koranko, Kono, and Vai or Gallinas); (2) West Atlantic languages (Temne, Banta, Bullom, Bum, Krim, Kissi, Limba); (3) the Kwa languages (Yoruba and Fante); (4) the Kru languages (Kru and Bassa); (5) other languages (Krio—i.e. Creole—and Pidgin). Dalby notes that in the southwestern part of the country a number of distinct ethnic groups (the Sherbo, Krim, Vai, and Gola) speak Mendé as a first language. Within Temne, there are five dialects: Western, Yoni, Bombali, Western Kuniké, Eastern Kuniké. The related language of Limba has seven major dialects: Tonko, Sela, Kamuke, Wara-Wara, Keleng, Biriwa, Safronko.

Several scholars suggest Mendé is the largest language group (Knappert suggests 31 percent, MacDougald 45 percent). Rustow links Temne, Bulom, and Limba together to form 52 percent. Because of linguistic similarities, we have grouped Temne and Limba together as the largest language zone comprising 45 percent of the population, although, as mentioned above, Mendé serves as a *lingua franca* in many areas. English is the official language of Sierra Leone, and French is used frequently as a trading language along the Guinea border. Arabic serves as the language of Islam within Sierra Leone.

TABLE 25.2 Language Patterns

1. Primacy		
1st language	Temne-Limba	(45%)
2nd language	Mendé	(36%)
2. Greenberg classification	Temne	IA1
(all ethnic units in country over 5%)	Mendé	IA2
3. *Lingua francas*	Krio, Mendé	
4. Official language	English	

SOURCE: T. D. P. Dalby, "Language Distribution in Sierra Leone: 1961–1962," *Sierra Leone Language Review*, No. 1 (1962): 62–67.

IV. Urban Patterns

Capital/largest city: Freetown (founded 1787)
Dominant ethnicity/language of capital
    Major vernacular: Krio[1]
    Major ethnic group: Creole
    Major ethnic group as percent of capital's population: —

TABLE 25.3   Growth of Capital/Largest City

Date	Freetown
1920	44,000
1930	56,000
1940	64,000
1950	85,000
1960	120,000
1966	148,000

SOURCE: Michael Banton, *West African City: A Study of Tribal Life in Freetown* (London: Oxford University Press, 1957).

TABLE 25.4   Cities of 20,000 and Over

City	Size	Date
Freetown[a]	148,000	1966
Bo Town[b]	27,000	1963

[1] Jan Knappert, "Language Problems of the New Nations of Africa," *African Quarterly*, 5 (1965): 95–105.

SOURCES:
[a] *UN Demographic Yearbook 1967.*
[b] Census.

V. Political Patterns

A. Political Parties and Elections

The 1957 general election in Sierra Leone was contested primarily by the *Sierra Leone People's Party* (SLPP) led by Albert Margai, and the *United Progressive Party* (UPP) led by Cyril Rogers-Wright. After the SLPP victory Sir Milton Margai, Albert Margai's brother, became prime minister and led the government until the constitutional conference in 1960. Opposition to his government came from the UPP and the *People's National Party* (PNP), formed in 1958 by dissident members of the SLPP and the UPP. All parties joined in coalition in 1960, except for Siaka Stevens the leader of PNP who again formed a new opposition party, the *All People's Congress* (APC). The coalition called the *United National Front* (UNF) was dominated by the SLPP.

In the 1962 general elections the SLPP won 28 seats, the APC won 16 seats, the SLPIM won 4 seats and the Independents won 14 seats. The general election in March 1967 was won by the APC but was followed by a coup the same month at which time all political activity was banned. The military govern-ment of Col. Juxton-Smith was then overthrown by another military coup in April 1968 led by support-ers of Siaka Stevens. At present Siaka Stevens and the APC govern with the support of the military. In 1970 an opposition party, the *National Democratic Party* (NPD), was formed by two young cabinet ministers who quit to go into opposition. The new party was banned in September 1970.

B. Political Leadership

Leadership in post-independence Sierra Leone was initially identified with the brothers Milton and Albert Margai. As a result of the 1967 election there was a sequence of military regimes which eventually resulted in the civilian government of Siaka Stevens. Creole representation in the cabinet has tended to be much greater than their percentage of the popula-tion. In April, 1971, Parliament rewrote the con-stitution, declaring the country a republic and changing Stevens' title to president. He began a second five-year term automatically without a new election.

Figure 25.1 **Political Parties and Elections**

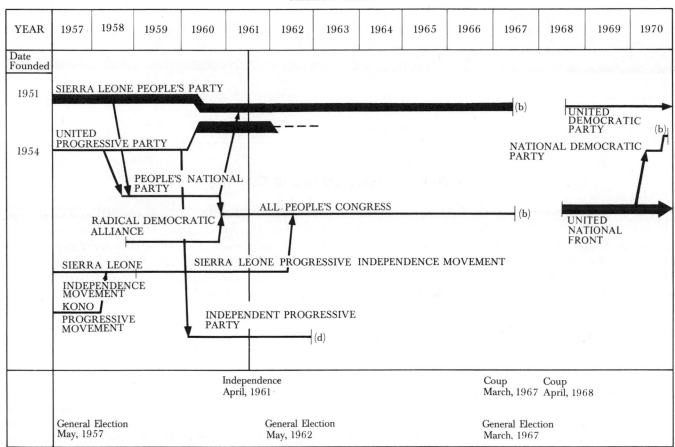

SIERRA LEONE

TABLE 25.5 **Heads of Government (Post Independence)**

Name	Dates in Office	Age (1971)	Ethnicity	Education	Former Occupation
1. Sir Milton Margai (Prime Minister)	1961–1964	Died 1964 age 69	Mendé	Medical degree, Durham (England)	Government Medical Service
2. Sir Albert Margai (Prime Minister)	1964–1967	61	Mendé	Middle Temple, London	Lawyer
3. Lt. Col. Andrew Juxon-Smith (NRC Secretariat)	1967–1968	40	Creole (Mixed)	Secondary (Sierra Leone)	Soldier
4. Siaka Stevens (Prime Minister, President)	1968–	66	Limba	Oxford	Policeman

TABLE 25.6 Cabinet Membership: Distribution by Ethnic Unit*

*Ethnicity**	*Independence Cabinet*	*Immediate Pre-Coup Cabinet*
1. Temne (45%)	29%	13%
2. Mendé (36)	36	62
3. Nuclear Mendé (8)	0	0
4. Creole (1)	36	25
5. Others (10)	0	0
N =	14	16

* Ethnic units arranged in rank order of size within country with the unit's percent of national population in parentheses.

VI. National Integration and Stability

There have been continuing tensions between the ethnic groups in Sierra Leone, both in the urbanized coastal areas and the interior, with occasional riots. The patterns of elite instability which resulted from the election of Stevens in 1967, however, are related in part to Mendé–Temne rivalry. On September 14, 1970, Prime Minister Stevens reacted to a challenge from two young Cabinet Ministers who quit and formed their own *National Democratic Party* by declaring a state of emergency. Stevens reported a plot by disloyal Army officers and began weeding out Temne army officers.

TABLE 25.7 Elite Instability

Event and Date	*Characteristics*
1. Coup d'Etat March 21, 1967	a. *Description*: The general elections of 1967 were won by Siaka Stevens (Limba), who was arrested shortly after he was sworn in as prime minister by Brigadier Lansana (Mendé). In the riots which followed this arrest, four persons were killed. Two days later, Brigadier Lansana and the former prime minister, Sir Albert Margai, were arrested by junior army officers, who also suspended the constitution, dissolved all political parties, and banned political activity. The control of the government was then offered to Lt. Col. Andrew Juxton-Smith of the NRC Secretariat. b. *Participants*: Junior army officers headed by Majors Jumu Blake and Kaisamba, plus Mr. William Leigh, Commissioner of Police, and units of the army and gendarmerie. c. *Apparent Causes*: According to Major Blake: "We can't stress too much that we acted only to avert civil war. This was an election clearly along tribal lines, west and north against south and east. Neither party and no one tribe could command the whole country's loyalty." Another factor was the class fears of the officers who were linked to the traditional ruling families. The junior officers added that they wished to prevent Brigadier Lansana from imposing Sir Albert Margai on the country.
2. Coup d'Etat April 18, 1968	a. *Description*: Military and police took control and established a National Interim Council (NIC) led by army officers loyal to Siaka Stevens. The NIC was formed to return the country to civilian authority. Their work culminated in the appointment of Siaka Stevens as prime minister on April 29, 1968. b. *Participants*: Army and police elements led by two warrant officers—Sergeants Major Patrick Contch and Amadu Rogers. c. *Apparent Causes*: Sergeant Rogers charged that the leaders of the National Reconstruction Council (NRC—formed after the March 1967 coup d'état) had become "more corrupt and selfish than the civilian regime," that they had ignored the rank and file of the army and police, and had failed to return the government to civilian rule.

TABLE 25.7 Elite Instability *(cont.)*

Event and Date	Characteristics
3. Attempted Coup March 23, 1971	a. *Description*: Prime Minister Stevens was briefly held captive by the army commander after a gunbattle outside the prime minister's home. Other senior army officers arrested the commander and restored Stevens to power. b. *Participants*: Brig. John Bangurah, the army commander, and his supporters. c. *Apparent Causes*: Coup attempt followed several months of political unrest. The coup participants opposed the proposed change in the constitution. It is reported that they were also opposed to Stevens' use of Guinaian troops in Sierra Leone.

SOURCE: John Cartwright, "Shifting Forces in Sierra Leone," *Africa Report*, 13 (December 1968): 26–30.

TABLE 25.8 Communal Instability

Event and Date	Characteristics
Ethnic Violence December, 1968	a. *Description*: Violent clashes between Mendé and Temne workers broke out at the Marampa iron mines, the Mokanji Hills bauxite mines, and the rutile mines in Bonthe district. In other southern towns, attacks against non-Mendé people were reported. Elections had been held the previous month, at which time there were numerous reports of ethnic clashes. b. *Participants*: The Mendé secret society was reportedly involved in organizing attacks against non-Mendé, but this is the only evidence of organizational control in this inter-ethnic violence. c. *Apparent Causes*: The clashes between Mendé and Temne do not appear to have been directed towards any immediate program for political change, although they reflected Mendé dissatisfaction with the post-coup government of Siaka Stevens, which was largely non-Mendé in composition, in contrast to the pre-coup governments led by the Mendé brothers—Sir Milton and Sir Albert Margai.

SOURCE: John Cartwright, "Shifting Forces in Sierra Leone," *Africa Report*, 13 (December 1968): 26–30.

VII. Selected References

BIBLIOGRAPHY

United States Library of Congress. General Reference and Bibliography Division. African Section. *Official Publications of Sierra Leone and Gambia.* Washington, D.C.: Government Printing Office, 1963.

Williams, Geoffrey J. *A Bibliography of Sierra Leone, 1925–1967.* New York: Africana, 1970.

GENERAL

Clarke, J. I., ed. *Sierra Leone in Maps.* London: University of London, 1969.

Collier, Gershon. *Sierra Leone: Experiment in Democracy in an African Nation.* New York: New York University Press, 1970.

Fyfe, C. *A History of Sierra Leone.* London: Oxford University Press, 1962.

Riddell, J. Barry. *The Spatial Dynamics of Modernization in Sierra Leone: Structure, Diffusion and Response.* Evanston: Northwestern University Press, 1970.

POLITICAL

Cartwright, John R. *Politics in Sierra Leone 1947–1967.* Toronto: University of Toronto Press, 1970.

Fisher, Humphrey J. "Elections and Coups in Sierra Leone, 1967." *The Journal of Modern African Studies,* 7 (1969): 611–636.

Kilson, Martin L. *Political Change in a West African State: A Study of the Modernization Process in Sierra Leone.*

Cambridge, Mass.: Harvard University Press, 1966.

Kilson, Martin L. "Sierra Leone." In *Political Parties and National Integration in Tropical Africa*, eds. J. S. Coleman and C. G. Rosberg. Los Angeles: University of California Press, 1964.

ECONOMIC

Saylor, Ralph Gerald. *The Economic System of Sierra Leone.* Durham, N.C.: Duke University Press, 1968.

SOCIAL

Banton, M. P. *West African City: A Study of Tribal Life in Freetown.* London: Oxford University Press, 1957.

Fyfe, Christopher, and Eldred Jones, eds. *Freetown: A Symposium.* Freetown: Sierra Leone University Press, 1968.

Little, Kenneth. "Structural Change in the Sierra Leone Protectorate." *Africa*, 25 (1955): 217–234.

Porter, A. T. *Creoledom: A Study of the Development of Freetown Society.* London: Oxford University Press, 1963.

Summer, D. L. *A History of Education in Sierra Leone.* London: Jarrold, 1963.

26. Somalia

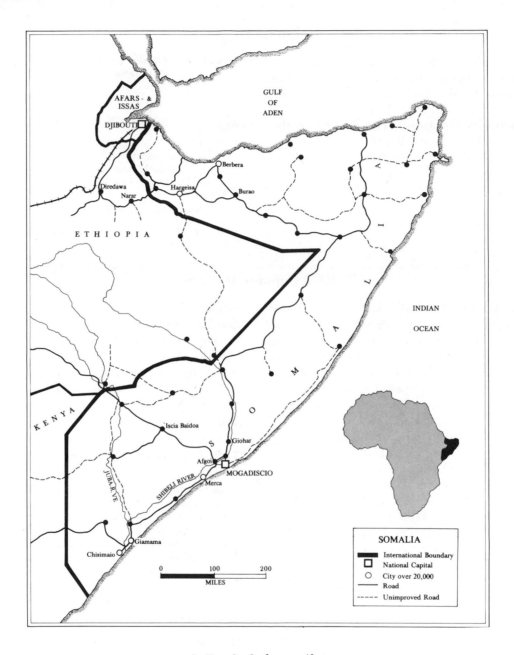

I. Basic Information

Date of Independence: July 1, 1960
Former Colonial Rulers: Italy and United Kingdom
Change in Boundaries: At independence, merger of UN Trust Territory of Somaliland and British Somaliland
Former Name: Somaliland, British Somaliland

Estimated Population (1970): 2,790,000
Area Size (equivalent in U.S.): 246,000 sq. mi. (Texas)
Date of Last Census: None
Major Exports 1967 as Percent of Total Exports: livestock, hides and skins—53 percent; bananas—35 percent

II. Ethnic Patterns

The Somali peoples of Somalia share a common language and a common culture (although the Sab are more agricultural than the Samaale). The Samaale and Sab are large-scale clans within the broader Somali identity group. In addition to the Somali there are about 80,000 Bantu who have come to be culturally similar to the Somali, about 42,000 Arabs and Asians, and 6,000 Europeans.

TABLE 26.1   Ethnic Units Over 5 Percent of Country Population

Ethnic Units	Estimated Ethnic Population 1967	Estimated Ethnic Percentage
a. Somali	2,534,000	95%
1. Samaale (Somal)	(2,022,000)	(76%)
i. Darod, ii. Ishaak, iii. Hawiye, iv. Dir		
2. Sab	(505,000)	(19%)
i. Rahanwein, ii. Dighil		

SOURCE: I. M. Lewis, *The Modern History of Somaliland* (New York: Praeger, 1965).

III. Language Patterns

The major language of Somalia is Somali (of the Cushitic family) which is closely related to Afar and Gallinya. It is spoken by 95 percent of the population as a first language. The three major Somali dialects include that of the Samaale nomads, that of the Sab farmers, and that spoken along the coastal area. All dialects are mutually intelligible. Somali has never been a written language, and there is continuing controversy as to whether Roman script, Arabic script, or an invented script called Usmaniya, should be used. In June 1971, a special commission set up to choose the script was urged to make a speedy decision by General Mohammed Siad Bare, president of the Supreme Military Council.

Knappert suggests that 100 percent of the population speak Somali; Rustow estimates 95 percent. Approximately 1–2 percent of the population speak Arabic as a first language, and probably 3 percent of the population uses Swahili as a *lingua franca*. Our estimate is that 97 percent of the population speaks Somali. We suggest that Swahili should be considered the second language (3 percent), although the *Area Handbook for Somalia* says English is gradually becoming the most common second language.

There are four official languages in Somalia: Somali, Arabic, English, and Italian. English and Italian, however, are used only in official situations.

TABLE 26.2   Language Patterns

1. Primacy
   1st language   Somali   (97%)
   2nd language   Swahili   (3%)
2. Greenberg classification   Somali   IIID3
   (all ethnic units in   Swahili   IA5
   country over 5%)   Arabic   IIIA
3. *Lingua franca*   Somali
4. Official languages   Somali, English, Arabic, Italian

SOURCE: U.S. Department of the Army, *Area Handbook for Somalia* (Washington, D.C.: Government Printing Office, 1970), pp. 65–76.

IV. Urban Patterns

Capital/largest city: Mogadiscio
Dominant ethnicity/language of capital
   Major vernacular: Somali
   Major ethnic group: Somali
   Major ethnic group as percent of capital's population: Nearly 100%

TABLE 26.3   Growth of Capital/Largest City

Date	Mogadiscio
1920	16,000
1930	32,000
1940	55,000
1950	78,000
1960	130,000
1966	170,000

SOURCE: Various editions of the *Statesman's Yearbook*.

TABLE 26.4 Cities of 20,000 and Over

City	Size	Date
Mogadiscio[a]	170,000	1966
Merca[b]	56,000	ca. 1966
Hargeisa[c]	50,000	ca. 1966
Chisimaio[d]	30,000	ca. 1966
Giamama[e]	22,000	1964
Berbera[d]	20,000	ca. 1966

SOURCES:
[a] *UN Demographic Yearbook 1967.*
[b] *Europa Yearbook 1967.*
[c] *Africa 1968.*
[d] *Statesman's Yearbook 1967–68.*
[e] *Europa Yearbook 1968.*
   These figures are very rough estimates since no reliable urban data are available.

V. Political Patterns

Figure 26.1 **Political Parties and Elections**

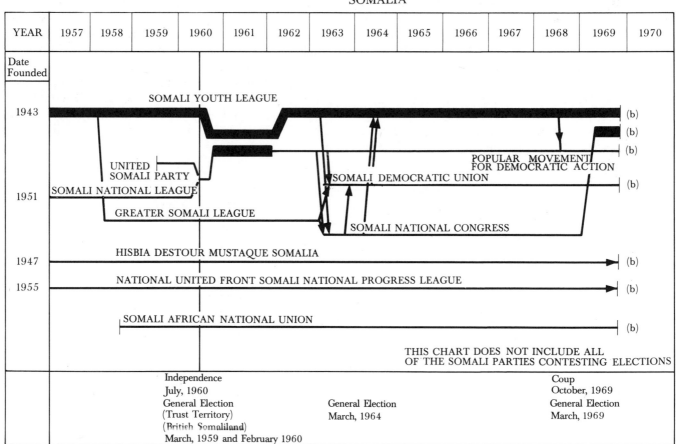

SOMALIA

YEAR	1957	1958	1959	1960	1961	1962	1963	1964	1965	1966	1967	1968	1969	1970

Date Founded

1943   SOMALI YOUTH LEAGUE   (b)
    (b)
    (b)

UNITED SOMALI PARTY
POPULAR MOVEMENT FOR DEMOCRATIC ACTION
SOMALI DEMOCRATIC UNION   (b)

1951   SOMALI NATIONAL LEAGUE
    GREATER SOMALI LEAGUE
    SOMALI NATIONAL CONGRESS

1947   HISBIA DESTOUR MUSTAQUE SOMALIA   (b)

1955   NATIONAL UNITED FRONT SOMALI NATIONAL PROGRESS LEAGUE   (b)

    SOMALI AFRICAN NATIONAL UNION   (b)

THIS CHART DOES NOT INCLUDE ALL OF THE SOMALI PARTIES CONTESTING ELECTIONS

Independence
July, 1960
General Election
(Trust Territory)
(British Somaliland)
March, 1959 and February 1960

General Election
March, 1964

Coup
October, 1969
General Election
March, 1969

A. Political Parties and Elections

Prior to independence and merger with the Somaliland Protectorate in July 1960, the dominant party in Somalia was the *Somali Youth League* (SYL), founded in 1943 as the Somali Youth Club. Opposition to the SYL came from the *United Somali Party* (USP) and the *Somali National League* (SNL). After independence a coalition government was formed between the SYL, and a combined USP and SNL. Adan Abdulla Osman served as president and Dr. Abdirashid Ali Shermarke as vice-president. The former prime minister of the Somaliland Protectorate, Mohammed Ibrahim Egal, became the minister of education. The coalition continued to govern until the March 1964 general elections (a victory for the SYL) when President Osman asked Abdirazak Hussein to form a new government. After considerable difficulty in organizing his cabinet, Hussein began his government in September 1964. Hussein's government was opposed by the USP, the *Somali Democratic Union* (SDU) formed by a merger of splinter groups from the USP/SNL coalition and the *Greater Somali League* (GSL), and the *Somali National Congress* (SNC) also formed from splinter groups of the SYL, USP, and SNL. In 1967 a new government was formed after Abdirashid Ali Shermarke was elected president. Mohammed Ibrahim Egal was chosen prime minister. More than sixty parties, based mainly on clan lines, contested the 1969 election, but the SYL won a substantial majority of the seats with about 40 percent of the vote. Egal remained as prime minister until the assassination of the president in October, 1969. The assassination was followed by a coup, after which all parties were banned.

B. Political Leadership

The Somali constitution gives executive power to the prime minister. The role of the president evolved into something far more than a figurehead, however, so we present in Table 26.5 the heads of state rather than the heads of government. During the 1967–1969 regime of President Abdirashid Shermarke, he, Prime Minister Mohammed Ibrahim Egal and Minister of Interior Yassin shared power, and Egal asserted his right to control the party. The new military regime which took power in 1969 set up a *Supreme Revolutionary Council* (SRC) composed of 25 officers under General Siad's presidency. Siad is a northerner and the Council has a northern–southern balance. The fourteen-man government appointed by the SRC is composed of young, well-educated civilians and the Police Commandant, General Jama Ali Korshel, who holds the post of minister of interior.

TABLE 26.5 Heads of State (Post Independence)

Name	Dates in Office	Age (1971)	Ethnicity	Education	Former Occupation
1. Aden Abdulla Osman (President)	1960–1967	63	Somali	No formal education	Administrator
2. Abdirashid Ali Shermarke (President)	1967–1969	Died 1969, age 50	Somali	Ph.D.	Civil Servant
3. Maj. Gen. Mohammed Siad Bare (President, Supreme Revolutionary Council)	1969–	52	Somali		Soldier

TABLE 26.6 Cabinet Membership: Distribution by Ethnic Unit*

Ethnicity*	Independence Cabinet	1967 Cabinet
1. Somali (95%)	100%	100%
2. Others (5)	0	0
N =	21	18

* Ethnic units arranged in rank order of size within country with the unit's percent of national population in parentheses.

VI. National Integration and Stability

In the context of Somalia's ethnic homogeneity, the potentially divisive identities are those of the various clans and the regionalism of a mixed colonial heritage—northern vs. southern Somali. Until 1969 the governments were successful in balancing the various groups in the country, and the most threatening conflicts were the border disputes with Ethiopia and Kenya. The president was assassinated in October 1969, however, and the army took power a week later.

TABLE 26.7 Elite Instability

Event and Date	Characteristics
1. Attempted Coup December 10, 1961	a. *Description*: On December 6, the Minister of Health, Suk Ali Guimale, was dismissed from the government by presidential decree. He was a powerful political opponent of President Osman. On December 10, twenty-three military officers failed in an attempt to seize command of an army unit in the north. The plan included seizure of local administration. All were brought to trial in Mogadiscio on December 13, and were imprisoned until January 1965. b. *Participants*: Young northern military officers. c. *Apparent Causes*: Reports of the attempted coup mention the removal of Suk Ali Guimale as a contributing factor to army discontent, but this seems to be conjecture. I. M. Lewis suggests the young British-trained junior officers were angered when they were placed under the command of Italian-trained officers from the south. The officers urged a separation of north and south.
2. Coup d'Etat October 21, 1969	a. *Description*: Following the assassination of President Abdirashid Ali Shermarke on October 15, and conflictful debate over the choice of his successor, the army took power. A National Revolutionary Council, led by the Army Commander, Major-General Mohammed Siad Bare, arrested all members of the deposed government, dissolved the National Assembly, and suspended the constitution. The coup was bloodless, and was followed by popular demonstrations supporting the new regime. b. *Participants*: Four army colonels organized the coup, and they obtained the support of the army commander and the police commissioner. These two senior officers came from the south and north respectively, and the Supreme Revolutionary Council gave balanced representation to these regions and to Somali clans. c. *Apparent Causes*: Apart from the leadership crisis brought about by the assassination of President Shermarke, the military government stressed its opposition to tribalism and corruption, and it seems that the major conflicts between Somali elites were intensified by the elections of March 1969, in which there were serious allegations of government rigging, and in which the ruling party received only 40 percent of the vote, split as it was between 64 clan-based parties.

SOURCE: A. A. Castagno, "Somalia Goes Military," *Africa Report*, 15 (February 1970): 25–27.

TABLE 26.8   Communal Instability

Event and Date	Characteristics
1. Rebellion April and May 1963	a. *Description*: Hergeisa is the capital of former British Somalia (now the northern province of Somalia). Demands for local autonomy and sporadic attacks had been increasing since independence in 1960. On May 2, 1963, authorities declared a state of siege in Hergeisa. In the resultant clash, many government forces and civilians were injured. According to Radio Djibouti, traditional leaders in Hergeisa demanded that new tax measures be rescinded or they would support a secession movement of Northern Somalia from Southern Somalia. The governor of Hergeisa and the local police reportedly supported the rebels. In January 1965, several persons connected with the rebellion were given amnesty after order was apparently restored. b. *Participants*: Northern Somalia clans, the local police, and the Northern Administration. c. *Apparent Causes*: Riots started soon after the central government had imposed a number of new taxes, although underlying factors include demands for local autonomy.

SOURCE: I. M. Lewis, *The Modern History of Somaliland* (New York: Praeger, 1965), pp. 173–175.

VII. Selected References

BIBLIOGRAPHY

African Bibliographic Center, Washington. *The Somali Republic*. Current Reading List Series, Vol. 1, no. 3, 1963.

Conover, Helen Field. *Official Publications of Somaliland, 1949–1959: A Guide*. Washington, D.C.: Library of Congress, 1960.

GENERAL

Castagno, A. A. *Somalia*. International Conciliation no. 522. New York: Carnegie Endowment for International Peace, 1959.

Hunt, John A. *A General Survey of the Somaliland Protectorate 1944–1950*. Colonial Development and Welfare Scheme D. 484. London: Crown Agents for the Colonies, 1951.

Lewis, I. M. *The Modern History of Somaliland: From Nation to State*. New York: Praeger, 1965.

Syad, William J. F., et al. "Independent Somali." *Présence Africaine*, 10 (1962): 68–219.

U.S. Department of the Army. *Area Handbook for Somalia*. D.A. Pamphlet 550–86. Washington, D.C.: Government Printing Office, 1970.

POLITICAL

Castagno, A. A. "Somali Republic." In *Political Parties and National Integration in Tropical Africa*, eds. J. S. Coleman and C. G. Rosberg. Berkeley: University of California Press, 1964.

Castagno, A. A. "Somalia Goes Military." *Africa Report*, 15 (Feb. 1970): 25–27.

Lewis, I. M. "Integration in the Somali Republic." In *African Integration and Disintegration*, ed. A. Hazelwood. London: Oxford University Press, 1967.

Touval, Saadia. *Somali Nationalism: International Politics and the Drive for Unity in the Horn of Africa*. Cambridge, Mass.: Harvard University Press, 1963.

ECONOMIC

International Monetary Fund. "Somalia." In *Surveys of African Economies*, Vol. 2, pp. 366–420. Washington, D.C.: I.M.F., 1968.

SOCIAL

Dawson, E. G. "Education in Somalia." *Comparative Education Review*, 8 (1964): 199–214.

Lewis, I. M. *A Pastoral Democracy: A Study of Pastoralism and Politics among the Northern Somali of the Horn of Africa*. London: Oxford University Press, 1961.

Lewis, I. M. "Conformity and Contrast in Somali Islam." In *Islam in Tropical Africa*, ed. I. M. Lewis, pp. 252–265. London: Oxford University Press, 1966.

Lewis, I. M. *Peoples of the Horn of Africa, Somali, Afar and Saho*. Ethnographic Survey of Africa: North Eastern Africa, pt. 1. London: International African Institute, 1955.

Trimingham, J. Spencer. *Islam in Ethiopia*. London: Oxford University Press, 1952. [Covers Somalia too.]

27. Sudan

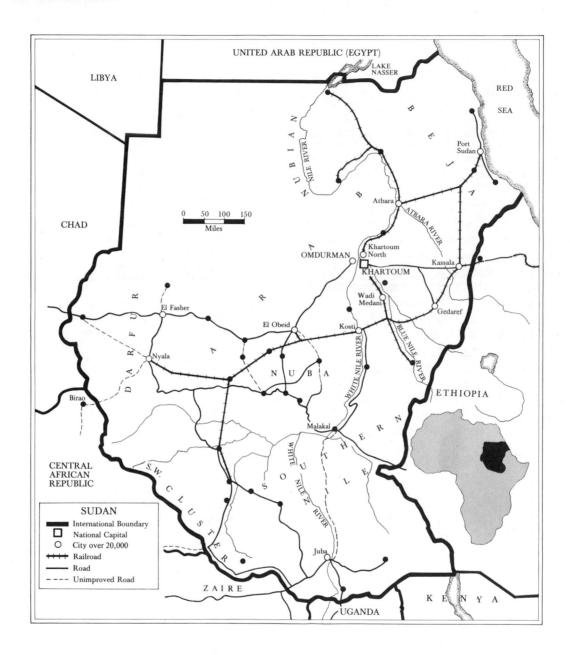

I. Basic Information

Date of Independence: January 1, 1956
Former Colonial Rulers: United Kingdom and Egypt
Former Name: Anglo-Egyptian Sudan
Estimated Population (*1971*): 15,700,000
Area Size (*equivalent in U.S.*): 967,000 sq. mi. (Alaska, Texas, and Colorado)

Date of Last Census: 1956
Major Exports 1968 as Percent of Total Exports: cotton— 60 percent; gum arabic—11 percent; peanuts— 7 percent

II. Ethnic Patterns

The Sudan has a large and ethnically heterogeneous population. The ethnic categories selected are widely inclusive, and are based on cultural and linguistic similarity, and to a certain degree on geographic proximity. They do not represent identity groups with the exception of the Beja. The northern Arabized peoples of Sudan are Muslim and are sharply distinguished by all criteria from the southern animist peoples. The percentages we have used are taken from the 1955–1956 Sudan census.

In addition to the major groups listed, about 3 percent of the population is made up of various peoples of West African origin (especially Hausa) who have settled in the Sudan while travelling to Mecca. Two percent of the population are Nubians (Halfa, Sukkot, Mahas, Dongolawis, Bedeiriya, Dilling, Nyima, Midobi, and Birked), and one percent are Fung (Fung, Ingassana, Gule, Berta, Koma, Udok, and Burun). Of these latter groups the last four Nubian groups are included in Barbour's calculation of the Nuba group percentage although we have chosen to classify them with the northern Nubians. The *Area Handbook for Sudan* deviates on a number of points from the Barbour classification, e.g., including the Burun with the Fung rather than the Nilotes.

TABLE 27.1 Ethnic Units Over 5 Percent of Country Population

Ethnic Units	Estimated Ethnic Population 1967	Estimated Ethnic Percentage
a. Arab	7,378,000	51%

  1. Ja'aliyin (Gaaliin) Arab
    i. Danagla Arabs, ii. Hassaniya,
    iii. Kawahla, iv. Gima, v. Husaynat
  2. Guhayna Arab
    i. Jamala
      (Kababish), (Shukriya)
    ii. Baggara
      (Seleim), (Hawazma), (Mesiriya),
      (Humr), (Rizeiqat), (Ta'aisha),
      (Beni Rashid), (Rashaida),
      (Habaniya)
    iii. Gezira
      (Messellimiya), (Halawin),
      (Rufa'a)

  3. Kawahla Arab (Fezara)
    i. Kawahla, ii. Hamid, iii. Hamar,
    iv. Bedeiriya, v. Gawama'a
  4. Zebaydiya Arabs
  5. Hawawir (Berber stock)
    i. Hawawir, ii. Jellaba,
    iii. Hawara, iv. Korobat
  6. Mixed Arab-Nubian
    i. Shaiqiya, ii. Manasir,
    iii. Rubatab, iv. Mirifab

b. Southern Nile Cluster	3,244,000	23%

  1. Western Nilotic (Nilote)
    i. Dinka, ii. Nuer,
    iii. Shilluk, iv. Anuak, v. Acholi,
    vi. Bor Belanda, vii. Jur (Jo Luo),
    viii. Shilluk Luo (Dembo, Shatt),
    ix. Pari
  2. Eastern Nilotic (Nilo-Hamite)
    i. Bari, ii. Mandari, iii. Nyangbara,
    iv. Pojulu (Fajelu), v. Kakwa,
    vi. Kuku, vii. Nyeyu, viii. Lokoya,
    ix. Luluba, x. Latuka, xi. Logit,
    xii. Lango, xiii. Toposa,
    xiv. Donyiro, xv. Jiye
  3. Murle type
    i. Boma Murle, ii. Beir, iii. Didinga

c. Darfur Type	789,000	6%

  1. Fur (Keira), 2. Daju and
  Beigo, 3. Zaghawa and Berti,
  4. Masalit, Gimr, and Tama

d. Nuba Type	674,000	5%

  1. Katla and Gulud, 2. Koalib,
  3. Tegali, 4. Talodi,
  5. Tumtum, 6. Temein,
  Keiga-Girru, and
  Teis-um-Danab, 7. Kadugli,
  8. Heiban

e. Southwestern Cluster	674,000	5%

  1. Azandé type
    i. Azandé, ii. Ndogo,
    iii. Sere, iv. Mundo, v. Biri
  2. Moru type
    i. Moru, ii. Madi, iii. Bongo,
    iv. Baka
  3. Fertit type
    i. Fertit (Mandala), ii. Feroge

f. Beja (Bega)	674,000	5%

  1. Beni Amer, 2. Amarar,
  3. Bisharin, 4. Hadendowa

SOURCES: K. M. Barbour, *The Republic of the Sudan* (London: University of London Press, 1961), pp. 74–87. U.S. Department of the Army, *Area Handbook for the Republic of the Sudan*, Pamphlet No. 550–27 (Washington, D.C., Government Printing Office, 1960), pp. 51–74. A. J. Butt, *The Nilotes of the Sudan and Uganda* (London: International African Institute, Oxford University Press, 1952).

III. Language Patterns

Arabic is the first language for about half of the population in Sudan. (Knappert estimates 60 percent; Rustow 48 percent.) In addition, there are probably over 100 non-Arabic languages in Sudan (Knappert, 1965). The Nilotic languages (including Nubian, Jii, Dinka, and Lango) are predominant in the central non-Arab areas. In the southwest, Azandé is spoken. In the Nuba Mountains of Kordofan, a number of Kordofanian languages exist. Finally, in the northeast, a number of persons speak Cushitic languages, especially Beja. According to the Sudan census of 1955–56, about 5,276,000 persons speak Arabic as a first language, 1,591,000 speak Dinka-Nuer, 570,000 speak Darfurian.

Arabic is spoken as a second language by most of the non-Arabic populations, except in the three southern provinces where probably only 1 percent is Arabic speaking. Sudanese Arabic is a distinct dialect of classical Arabic. Even within Sudanese Arabic there are sub-dialects spoken in Dongola,

Omdurman, Gezira, and Darfur areas, plus the Baggara ethnic dialects. In the far south, pidgin English is also used as a *lingua franca*.

TABLE 27.2   Language Patterns

1. Primacy		
1st language	Arabic	(60%)
2nd language	Dinka	(12%)
2. Greenberg classification	Arab	IIIA
(all ethnic units in	Southern Nile cluster	IIE1
country over 5%)	Darfur type	IID
	Nuba type	IB5
	Southwestern cluster	IA6
	Beja	IIID1
3. *Lingua franca*	Arabic	
4. Official language	Arabic	

SOURCES: Bjorn Jernudd, "Linguistic Integration and National Development: A Case Study of the Jebel Marra Area, Sudan," in *Language Problems of Developing Nations*, eds. Joshua A. Fishman, Charles A. Ferguson, and Jyotirindra Das Gupta (New York: John Wiley, 1968): pp. 167–182. Republic of the Sudan, Ministry for Social Affairs, Population Census Office, *First Population Census of Sudan*, 1955–56, p. 7.

IV. Urban Patterns

Capital: Khartoum (founded 1823)
Largest City: Omdurman (founded 1885)
Dominant ethnicity/language of capital
   Major vernacular: Arabic[1]
   Major ethnic group: Arab[2]
   Major ethnic group as percent of capital's population:
   42% (1955)

TABLE 27.3   Growth of Capital and Largest City

Date	Khartoum	Omdurman
1920	30,000	78,000
1930	42,000	103,000
1940	76,000	116,000
1950	71,000	130,000
1960	140,000	140,000
1966	185,000	198,000

SOURCES: Various editions of the *Statesman's Yearbook*; the most recent figures are from the *UN Demographic Yearbook* 1969.

[1] Jan Knappert, "Language Problems of the New Nations of Africa," *African Quarterly*, 5 (1965): 95–105.
[2] Census (1955).

TABLE 27.4   Cities of 20,000 and Over

City	Size	Date
Omdurman[a]	198,000	1966
Khartoum[a]	185,000	1966
Khartoum North[b]	80,000	ca. 1964–65
Port Sudan[b]	79,000	ca. 1964–65
Wadi Medani[b]	64,000	ca. 1964–65
El Obeid[b]	62,000	ca. 1964–65
Atbara[b]	48,000	ca. 1964–65
Kassala[c]	41,000	1956
El Fasher[b]	41,000	ca. 1964–65
Kosti[b]	30,000	ca. 1964–65
Nyala[b]	26,000	ca. 1964–65
Geneina[b]	20,000	ca. 1964–65
Gedaref[c]	18,000	1956

SOURCES:
[a] *UN Demographic Yearbook 1967*. [b] Survey. [c] Census.

Ever since 1964 the government of the Sudan has undertaken 10 percent sample surveys in many towns, and these data have been used whenever available. The definition of "urban place" by the government does *not* include all settlements over 20,000 in population. Villages of more than 35,000 population were omitted from the 1955/56 Census of Towns (Michael W. Kuhn, personal communication). Thus the list of cities given here should be regarded as incomplete.

Khartoum, Khartoum North, and Omdurman each have separate town councils although they form a conurbation at the confluence of the Blue and White Niles. The founding date of Khartoum (1823) is when Egyptians established a military post on the site.

V. Political Patterns

A. Political Parties and Elections

The complex history of Sudanese political parties since independence has centered on many cleavages. Ethnic, religious, and regional divisions have all had an effect of the formation of political parties. The first prime minister of independent Sudan, Ismail el-Azhari, and his *Nationalist Unionist Party* (NUP) were defeated in 1956 by a coalition of the Mirghanist-based *Popular Democratic Party* (PDP), the pro-Western *Umma Party* (UMMA), and the southern-based *Liberal Party* (LP). The new coalition, and its prime minister, Abdallah Khalil (UMMA),

continued to govern until the March 1958 elections, when the NUP, under el-Azhari received a plurality and went into an unstable coalition with the *Umma Party*. With the aid of Mr. Khalil (UMMA), the military (under General Abboud) assumed control in November 1958 and continued to rule until the revolt in November 1964. General Abboud was removed from office, and a new government led by el-Khatim el-Khalifah, a non-partisan civil servant, was formed. The cabinet was largely made up of NUP and UMMA members. Attempts were made to reconcile southern and northern partisans in 1967 and 1968 and, after having little success, the PDP

Figure 27.1 Political Parties and Elections

SUDAN *

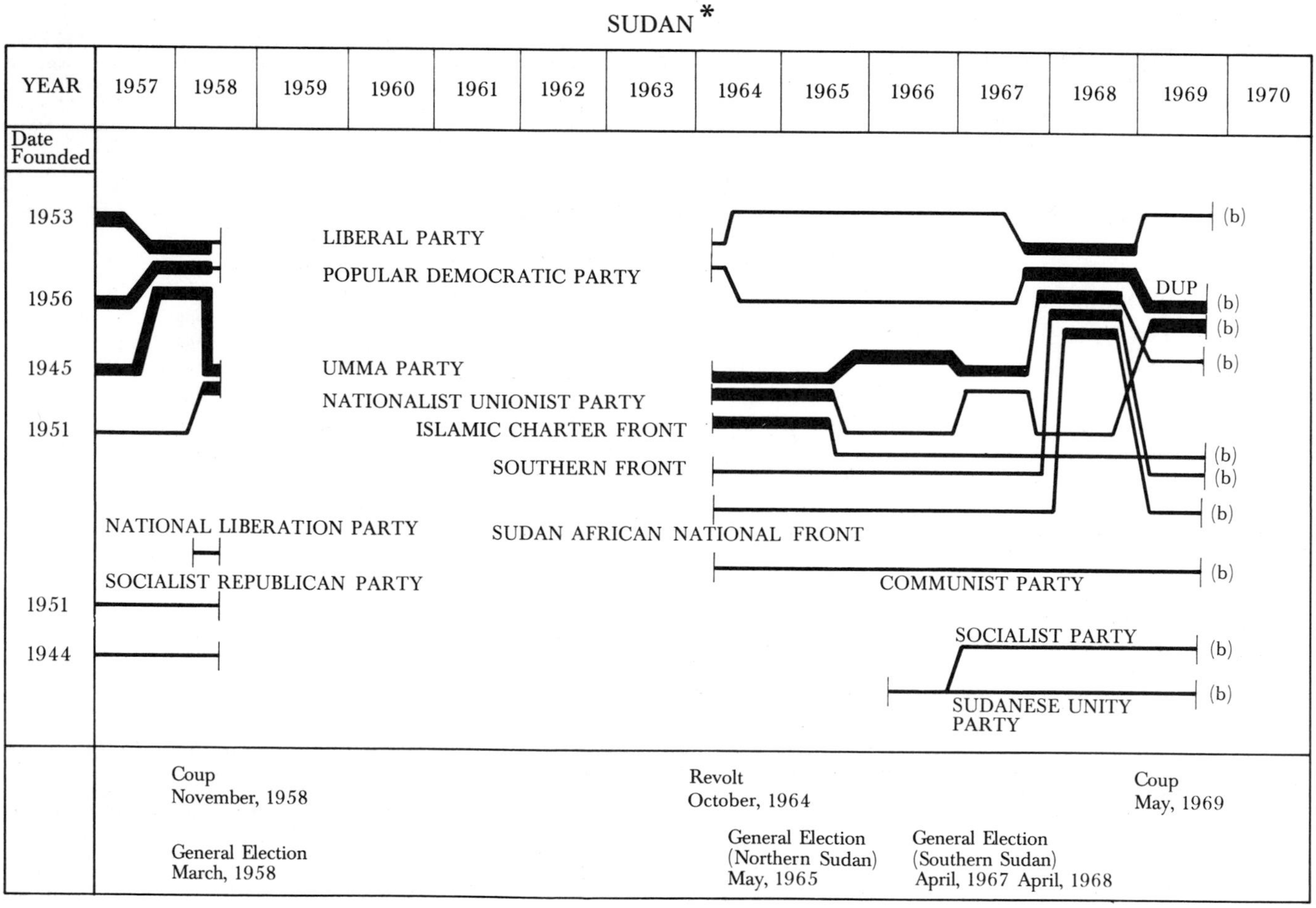

* Independence—January 1956.

TABLE 27.5   Heads of Government (Post Independence)

Name	Dates in Office	Age (1971)	Ethnicity	Education	Former Occupation
1. Ismail el-Azhari (Prime Minister)	1956	Died 1969, age 71	Arab	American University (Beirut)	Teacher
2. Abdallah Khalil (Prime Minister)	1956–58	Died 1970, age 78	Darfur	Military School, Khartoum	Soldier
3. Lt. General Ibrahim Abboud (Prime Minister)	1958–64	72		Engineering (Sudan)	Soldier
4. Sir el-Khatim el-Khalifah (Prime Minister)	1964–65	51			Civil Servant
5. Muhammad Ahmad Mahgoub (Prime Minister)	1965–66	63	Arab	Law and Engineering (Sudan)	Lawyer
6. Sayed Siddik El Mahdi (Prime Minister)	1966–67	35	Arab	Oxford	
7. Muhammad Ahmad Mahgoub (Prime Minister)	1967–69				
8. Abubakr Awadallah (Prime Minister)	1969	56		Law (England)	Lawyer
9. Maj. General Gaafar al Nimeiry (Prime Minister and President of the Revolutionary Council)	1969–	41		Sudan Military College	Soldier

and the NUP formed a coalition government—the *Democratic Unionist Party* (DUP)—in early 1969. The military coup in May 1969 resulted in the banning of all political parties. The *Communist Party* of the Sudan is reputed by *The New York Times* (October 29, 1969) to be the largest in Africa, with around 50,000 members, but it is split. In November 1970, following the death of Egypt's President Nasser, Egypt, Libya, Syria and Sudan announced their intention to move towards a federation.

B. Political Leadership

There has been high turnover of political leadership in Sudan, both military and civilian. Cabinet turnover was particularly high in 1965. Cabinet ethnic balance has remained constant. The 1955 constitution replaced the British governor general by a

five-man Supreme Council which held collective responsibility for governing the state so that, strictly speaking, the prime minister is not the head of government.

TABLE 27.6   Cabinet Membership: Distribution by Ethnic Unit*

Ethnicity*	Independence Cabinet	1967 Cabinet
1. Arab (51%)	56%	47%
2. Southern Nile (23)	25	20
3. Darfur (6)	0	7
4. Nuba (5)	19	27
5. Southwestern (5)	0	0
6. Beja (5)	0	0
7. Others	0	0
N =	16	16

* Ethnic units arranged in rank order of size within country with the unit's percent of national population in parentheses.

VI. National Integration and Stability

The Sudan has experienced instability at the elite, communal, and mass levels. Political elite turn-over seems to be related to ideological as well as religious and regional factors, although the most recent coup (May 1969) may be related to Arab World politics as well. Communal instability is partly the result of the colonial legacy in the south, whereby many small-scale societies of Nilotic peoples (who have resisted the Arabization of the northern Sudan) were attached to the predominantly Arab north. The revolt in 1964 was largely the result of an urban coalition of workers, students, and civil servants.

TABLE 27.7 Elite Instability

Event and Date	Characteristics
1. Coup d'Etat November 17, 1958	a. *Description*: During the night of November 17, four thousand troops under the command of General Ibrahim Abboud occupied Khartoum and arrested all the members of Prime Minister Khalil's cabinet. b. *Participants*: Lieutenant General Ibrahim Abboud (Commander-in-Chief of the Armed Forces) and several senior army officers. According to some reports the incumbent Prime Minister Khalil consulted with the military and suggested they take over to preserve order and stability. c. *Apparent Causes*: The army was apparently invited by Abdallah Khalil to take power to fore-stall pro-Egyptian elements who were gaining strength. According to a Sudanese broadcast: "The aim of the revolution is to maintain the independence of the Sudan and to raise the standard of living. Former politicians failed to do that in view of the fact that no one party had a clear majority."
2. Coup Attempt May 21–22, 1959	a. *Description*: Army elements marched on Khartoum with the intention of supporting Brigadiers Muyhi al-Din 'Abdallah, and 'Abdal-Rahim Shannan in a confrontation with Hasan Bashir Nasr, the army's deputy-commander-in-chief and minister for presidential affairs. They retreated when advised to do so by Muyhi al-Din. Muyhi al-Din and Shannan were arrested and charged with inciting to mutiny with the object of overthrowing the regime. b. *Participants*: Two platoons of troops from the eastern area (Muyhi al-Din was their former commander), several other officers, and a member of the Supreme Council. The two brigadiers had been in contact with many of the younger officers and politicians. c. *Apparent Causes*: Muyhi al-Din 'Abdallah and 'Abdal-Rahim Shannan supported the National Unionist Party (NUP) and were, therefore, not politically popular with other members of the Supreme Council. They were apparently opting for the removal of Bashir from the Council.
3. Coup Attempt November 9, 1959	a. *Description*: A mutiny at the Infantry School in Omdurman failed when expected support from the rest of the army and the populace did not develop. b. *Participants*: Young officers, mainly majors and captains, who were reportedly influenced by the "Muslim Brothers." c. *Apparent Causes*: Not ascertainable. The officers were reputedly connected with the Communists and/or the Muslim Brothers.
4. Coup Attempt December 18, 1966	a. *Description*: Soon after the High Court ruled the government's ban on the Communist Party was unconstitutional, riots between pro- and anti-communist demonstrators erupted. In the wake of these events the government announced that it had averted a coup attempt by the armed forces. b. *Participants*: Approximately 300 trainees from the Gordon Training School led by 2nd Lieutenant Khalid Hussein. Six other officers, including the commanding officer of the Eastern Sudan Military Command, were eventually arrested. Following the announcement of the coup the leading members of the Communist Party were arrested, but their connection with the coup attempt was never made clear. c. *Apparent Causes*: No explanations for the military action were offered. The arrests of leading communists appeared to some sources to be the influence of traditional religious elements.

TABLE 27.7 Elite Instability *(cont.)*

Event and Date	*Characteristics*
5. Coup d'Etat May 25, 1969	a. *Description*: A group of middle-ranking army officers commanding two parachute units, an infantry unit, and an armored unit, totalling some 400 soldiers, cut off communications in the Sudanese capital, arrested senior army officers, and placed President el-Azhari and the cabinet of Mr. Mahgoub under house arrest. The provisional constitution was dissolved, public meetings were banned, and a military revolutionary council and civilian cabinet were appointed. The coup was led by Col. Gaafar al Nimeiry, who became President of the Revolutionary Council.
	b. *Participants*: The government displaced by this coup had been formed after the elections of April 1968, in which a complicated alliance between three parties produced a government headed by the pre-election prime minister (Mahgoub) and by the president (el-Azhari). In contrast to the intricate coalition before the coup, the new regime was homogeneous. The organizers of the coup were a group of army majors and colonels who were members of a 10-year-old underground organization with an articulate socialist and pan-Arab orientation. These officers formed the new Revolutionary council, and the civilian council led by Abubakr Awadallah, a former Presidential candidate of the leftist bloc, included at least three other well-known Sudanese Marxists. (Awadallah, a communist sympathizer although not a communist, was put out of office by al Nimeiry, a self-proclaimed Nasserist, five months later.)
	c. *Apparent Causes*: The new regime, as reasons for the coup, cited the failure of the governments appointed by former President el-Azhari to solve the country's economic and political problems. In particular, they referred to the continuing civil war in the south, the failures in Sudanese agricultural policy, corruption and disorganization in civilian party politics, and the failure of the Sudan to take an aggressive posture against imperialism in the Arab world, and against Zionism in Palestine.
6. Coup Attempt July 20–22, 1971	a. *Description*: A group of reputedly leftist army officers seized power for two days, imprisoning Prime Minister al Nimeiry and other government officials. They created a seven-member command council with Lieutenant Colonel Bubakr al-Nur Osman, age 37, as chairman. Iraq immediately recognized the new government, which quickly lifted restrictions on the country's communist movement and announced a policy of regional autonomy for the south. On July 22 troops loyal to Prime Minister al Nimeiry staged a countercoup which was successful after severe fighting in which 30 loyalist soldiers and officers were killed. Just prior to the countercoup, neighboring Libya forced down a British airliner which was carrying two of the coup leaders, Lieut. Col. al-Nur Osman and Major Farouk Osman Hamadallah, from London, where al-Nur Osman had been undergoing a medical checkup, back to the Sudan. The coup leaders were executed.
	b. *Participants*: The coup leaders were Major Hashem al-Ata, who led the military attack; Colonel Abdel Moneim Ahmed, commander of the Third Armored Brigade; Lieutenant Colonel Osman Hussein, commander of the Republican Guards; and Captain Muaweya Abdel Hai. Lieut. Col. al-Nur Osman and Maj. Hamadallah, although part of the plot, were in London during the coup attempt.
	c. *Apparent Causes*: In November 1970, al-Nur Osman, Hamadallah and al-Ata had been ousted by Prime Minister al Nimeiry in a quarrel over plans to link the Sudan with Egypt and Libya in a federation. "General Nimeiry charged that the ousted officers had fought the federation plan at the instigation of a Communist faction headed by Muhammad Mahgoub, secretary of the ostensibly banned Communist party." General al Nimeiry is closely allied politically with Egypt and Libya.

SOURCES: Helen Kitchen, "The Sudan in Transition," *Current History*, 37 (1959): 35–40. P. M. Holt, *A Modern History of the Sudan* (New York: Grove Press, 1961), pp. 18–90. Tariq Ismael, "Sudan Joins the Arabs," *Africa Report*, 15 (January 1970): 12–13. *The New York Times*, July 21–24, 1971.

TABLE 27.8 Communal Instability

Event and Date	*Characteristics*
1. Civil War: Attempted Secession 1963–present	a. *Description*: The south has been in rebellion since 1955. Military action in the south developed during 1963 when General Abboud's regime chose force as the most likely method of national unification. Combatant deaths for 1963–1967 were reported to be over 1500 although figures as high as 500,000 have recently been cited. The secessionists cannot match the armament of the central government and therefore have depended on sabotage and small scale forays. b. *Participants*: The three southern provinces of Sudan (which are non-Arab) have demanded separation from the Arab-dominated northern portions of Sudan. Southern distrust of northerners has its roots in 19th-century Arab slave trading. Secessionist leadership has been fragmented and prone to feuds. The rebels refer to their movement as "*Anya nya*," but the degree to which they are organized cannot be ascertained. Some estimates place southern troop strength at 12,000; the north is said to have 18,000 troops in the south. c. *Apparent Causes*: Secessionists who are drawn from black non-Muslim identity groups claim four major grievances: (1) political domination by the Arab north; (2) attempts by the north to Arabize the south; (3) discrimination in jobs, salaries, educational opportunities; and (4) discrimination in the allocation of funds and projects for general regional development.
2. Rebellion June 1966	a. *Description*: Security forces raided the offices of the Sony Liberation Movement. The Sudanese Minister of Information said that guns, money, and anti-Sudan unity literature were found. b. *Participants*: In all, 20 persons were arrested; no mention of the extent of their support was ever made. The movement, said the government, was taking place in Kordofan and Darfur provinces. c. *Apparent Causes*: Not ascertainable.
3. Rebellion March 1970	a. *Description*: Following an unsuccessful attempt to assassinate Premier al Nimeiry on March 27, 1970, supporters of Imam el-Hadi Ahmed el-Mahdi revolted in the city of Omdurman and on Aba Island, 150 miles south of Khartoum. Within a week the government crushed the rebellion and the Imam was killed in an assault on his headquarters at Aba Island. b. *Participants*: The followers of the Imam comprise the Ansar Muslim sect and number nearly two million. Some reports indicated that 1,000 or more persons died in the fighting in Omdurman and another 1,000 on Aba Island. A retired army officer, Brigadier Mohammed Abdullah Hamed was arrested and charged with training members of the Ansar sect in modern weapons, and the Imam's nephew and potential successor, Sadik al-Mahdi, was expelled from the country. c. *Apparent Causes*: The Ansar sect represents a serious threat to the present Sudan government because of their size, the fact that they are influential in the army and civil service, and their opposition to government policies which they interpret as encouraging Nasserism, communism, growing secularism and the secession of the southern provinces. The government did not back away from a direct confrontation with what they regarded as a "reactionary stronghold," and it appears likely that it precipitated the conflict. This event is coded as a rebellion, although if the Ansar sect was attempting to monopolize the existing political system it would be a civil war by our definitions.

SOURCES: *Africa Digest*, 17 (July 1970): 52–53, *Africa Contemporary Record* 1970–71, B 44–45.

TABLE 27.9 Mass Instability

Event and Date	Characteristics
1. Revolt October 20–30, 1964	a. *Description*: Civilian demonstrators forced the military government to abdicate. Reported casualties for the duration of the disorders were 36 dead and more than 100 wounded. b. *Participants*: Several thousand demonstrators from the working population of Khartoum. The judiciary and the civil service went on a general strike. Students and teachers were the first to openly defy government authority. The former political parties (Umma, NUP, Communist Party), together with the Muslim Brothers formed the United National Front to coordinate their activities for the duration of the revolt. c. *Apparent Causes*: Discontent with the military regime was pervasive. Students resented government encroachment into university affairs; workers were burdened with tax increases; and government restrictions on political expression were generally unpopular. The military regime was also charged with nepotism and misuse of government funds. Because of the ideological foundation of the coalition, it might be coded as revolution.

SOURCES: Mohammed O. Beshir, "The Sudan: A Military Surrender," *Africa Report*, 9 (December 1964): 3–6. Yusuf Fadl Hasan, "The Sudanese Revolution of October 1964," *Journal of Modern African Studies*, 5 (1967): 491–510.

VII. Selected References

BIBLIOGRAPHY

African Bibliographic Center, Washington. *A Current Bibliography on Sudanese Affairs, 1960–64*. Special Bibliographic Series, Vol. 3, No. 4, 1965. Westport, Conn.: Greenwood, 1965.

El Nasri, Abdal Rahman. *A Bibliography of the Sudan 1938–1958*. London: Oxford University Press for the University of Khartoum, 1962.

GENERAL

Barbour, K. M. *The Republic of the Sudan: A Regional Geography*. London: University of London Press, 1961.

El-Mahdi, Mandour. *Short History of the Sudan*. London: Oxford University Press, 1965.

Henderson, K. D. D. *Sudan Republic*. New York: Praeger, 1965.

Holt, P. M. *A Modern History of the Sudan*. New York: Grove Press, 1961.

Kitchen, Helen. Special Sudan Issue. *Africa Report*, 4 (January 1959).

Kitchen, Helen. *Sudan*. Ithaca, N.Y.: Cornell University Press, forthcoming.

Oduho, J., and W. Deng. *The Problem of the Southern Sudan*. London: Oxford University Press, 1963.

U.S. Department of the Army. *Area Handbook for Sudan*. Pamphlet No. 550–27. Washington, D.C.: Government Printing Office, 1964.

POLITICAL

Albino, O. *The Sudan: A Southern Viewpoint*. New York: Oxford University Press, 1970.

Al-Rahim, Muddathir. *Imperialism and Nationalism in the Sudan: A Study in Constitutional and Political Development, 1899–1956*. London: Oxford University Press, 1969.

Hasan, Yusuf Fadl. "The Sudanese Revolution of October 1964." *Journal of Modern African Studies*, 5 (1967): 491–509.

ECONOMIC

Hance, William A. "The Gezira Scheme: A Study in Agricultural Development." In *African Economic Development*, rev. ed., pp. 31–53. New York: Praeger, 1967.

Osman, Omar, and A. A. Suleiman. "The Economy of Sudan." In *The Economies of Africa*, eds. P. Robson and D. A. Lury, pp. 436–470. Evanston, Ill.: Northwestern University Press, 1969.

Tothill, J. D., ed. *Agriculture in the Sudan*. London: Oxford University Press, 1948.

SOCIAL

Beshir, Mohammed Omer. *Educational Development in the Sudan, 1898–1956*. London: Oxford University Press, 1969.

Gannon, E. J. "Education in the Sudan." *Comparative Education Review*, 9 (October 1965): 323–330.

McLoughlin, J. "The Sudan's Three Towns: A Demographic and Economic Profile of an African Urban Complex." *Economic Development and Cultural Change*, 12: Pt. 1 (October 1963), pp. 70–83; Pt. 2 (January 1964), pp. 158–173; Pt. 3 (April 1964), pp. 286–304.

Trimingham, J. S. *Islam in the Sudan*. London: Oxford University Press, 1949.

United Nations. *Population Growth and Manpower in the Sudan*. New York: United Nations, 1964.

28. Tanzania

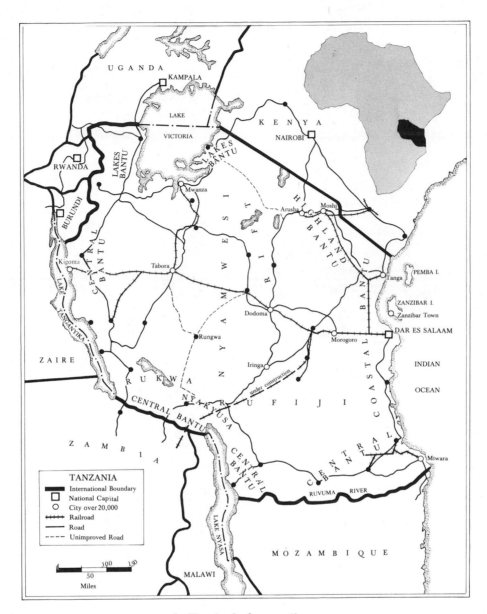

I. Basic Information

Date of Independence: December 9, 1961
Former Colonial Ruler: United Kingdom
Change in Boundaries: April 26, 1964, Tanganyika and Zanzibar became the United Republic of Tanganyika and Zanzibar; October 29, 1964, name became Tanzania.
Former Names: Tanganyika and Zanzibar
Estimated Population (1970): 13,270,000

Area Size (equivalent in U.S.): 363,000 sq. mi. (Texas and Colorado)
Date of Last Census: 1967
Major Exports 1968 as Percent of Total Exports (including Kenya and Uganda): cotton—17 percent; coffee—16 percent; sisal—10 percent; diamonds—8 percent

II. Ethnic Patterns

The ethnic classification of Tanzania is adapted from Murdock (1959) and draws heavily on Moffett (1958). Because of the relative homogeneity in language and culture, yet the considerable number of identity groups, we have used geographical criteria more than usual in combining identity groups into clusters and types at a high level of abstraction.

In addition to the major clusters, other Tanzanian groups include: Southern Cushitic peoples—2 percent (Iraqw, Mbulu, Gorowa, Fiome, Burungi, Mbugu, Wasi or Alawa); Interlacustrine Hamites— 3 percent (Hima, Tutsi, Rundi, and Rwanda); "Nilo-Hamites"—2 percent (Masai, Kwavi or

TABLE 28.1   Ethnic Units Over 5 Percent of Country Population

Ethnic Units	Estimated Ethnic Population 1967	Estimated Ethnic Percentage
a. Nyamwesi Type	2,260,000	*19%*
1. Sukuma	(1,411,000)	(12%)
i. Sukuma, ii. Rongo, iii. Shashi		
2. Nyamwesi (Banyamwesi)	(584,000)	(5%)
i. Nyamwese, ii. Gala, iii. Galaganza, iv. Irwana, v. Nankwili		
3. Sumbwa, 4. Kimbu, Yanzi, Konongo, 5. Bende, Tongwe		
b. Interlacustrine Bantu (Lakes Bantu) Type	1,676,000	*14%*
1. Ha	(470,000)	(4%)
i. Ha, ii. Vinza, iii. Jiji		
2. Haya	(438,000)	(4%)
i. Haya, ii. Nyambo, iii. Mwani, v. Ziba		
3. Zinza, 4. Subi, Hangaza, 5. Suba, 6. Ikizu, 7. Ikoma, 8. Jita, Kwaya and Ruri, 9. Nguruimi, 10. Zanaki, 11. Kerewe and Redi, 12. Issenye and Nata, 13. Kisii (Gusii), 14. Kuriya (Tende, Kulya)		
c. Northeast Coastal Bantu Type	1,381,000	*11%*
1. Zigula	(692,000)	(6%)
i. Zigula, ii. Luguru, Kami, Kutu, iii. Bondei, iv. Kwere and Doe, v. Nguru, Kilindi, Shambala (Sambaa)		

2. Swahili	(636,000)	(5%)
i. Shirazi (Hadimu, Tumbatu, Pemba, Mbwera), ii. Zaramo and Nyagtwa, iii. Ndengereko, iv. Segeju		
3. Digo		
d. Central Bantu Cluster	1,315,000	*11%*
1. Yao	(1,225,000)	(10%)
i. Yao, ii. Mwera and Kiturika, iii. Makua, iv. Makonde, Matambwe and Mawia, v. Ngindo, vi. Ndonde, vii. Machinga and Songo		
2. Nyasa (Maravi cluster)		
3. Bemba		
i. Holoholo, ii. Mambwe		
e. Rift Cluster	1,188,000	*10%*
1. Gogo	(438,000)	(4%)
2. Iramba, Irambi and Izanzu, 3. Nyaturu, 4. Rangi and Mbugwe,		
f. Rufiji Cluster	1,137,000	*9%*
1. Bena, Sowe, and Vemba, 2. Hehe, Kosishamba and Zungwa, 3. Matumbi-Ndendehule, 4. Mbunga, 5. Ndamba and Pogoro, 6. Sagara, Kaguru, Kinongo and Vidunda, 7. Sangu and Poroto, 8. Rufiji and Mawanda, 9. Wungu		
g. Nyakyusa Cluster	727,000	*6%*
1. Nyakyusa (Niabiussa, Sochile, Sokile)	(337,000)	(3%)
i. Nyakyusa and Kukwe, ii. Mwamba, iii. Ngonde, iv. Selya, v. Sukwa		
2. Nyasa group	(390,000)	(3%)
i. Matengo, ii. Kinga, Panga, and Wanji		
h. Rukwa Cluster	635,000	*5%*
1. Fipa, Nyika and Rungu, 2. Iwa (Nyamwanga), 3. Lambya, Malila, Ndali, Tambo and Wandya, 4. Pimbwe and Rungwa, 5. Safwa, Guruka, Mbwila, Songwe		
i. Kenya Highland Bantu Cluster	572,000	*5%*
1. Chagga and Kahe	(377,000)	(3%)
2. Pare and Taveta, 3. Meru		

SOURCES: J. P. Moffett, ed., *Handbook of Tanganyika*, 2nd ed. (Dar es Salaam: Government Printer, 1958), pp. 283–297. G. P. Murdock, *Africa* (New York: McGraw-Hill, 1959). M. Lofchie, "Party Conflict in Zanzibar," *Journal of Modern African Studies*, 1 (1963): 185–207.

Lumbwa, Arusha, Barabaig, Tatog, Mangati, Kismajend, Taturu); Nguni—1 percent; Nilotic-Kavirondo or Luo—0.7 percent; and Bushman-like peoples—0.4 percent (Dorobo, Kindiga, and Sandawe). It should be noted that many of the Interlacustrine (Lakes) Bantu have come under the

political domination of the Interlacustrine Hamites (e.g. Rwanda). It should also be noted that in many previous classifications, eastern and western portions of the Lakes Bantu are not regarded as part of the same cluster. On the basis of increasing cultural similarity, however, this now seems appropriate.

III. Language Patterns

All of the major languages of Tanzania are Bantu. Swahili has emerged as the *lingua franca* throughout the country. In 1942, MacDougald estimated that 52 percent of the population spoke Swahili. Knappert estimated 89 percent in 1965. In a sense, the entire country might be regarded as understanding some level of Swahili. However, Swahili has become a national language (strenuously encouraged by the government) only since the mid-1960s. It is reasonable to assume that given the age structure of the country, there are some groups (very young, or very old) who do not speak Swahili. We therefore estimate 88 percent of the population to be Swahili-speaking. The second largest language is Sukuma, spoken as a first language by 12 percent of the population. English is still widely used in Tanzania in government and higher education.

TABLE 28.2   Language Patterns

1. Primacy		
1st language	Swahili	(88%)
2nd language	Sukuma	(12%)
2. Greenberg classification	Swahili	IA5
(all ethnic units in	Nyamwesi (Sukuma)	IA5
country over 5%)	Interlacustrine Bantu	IA5
	Northeast Coastal Bantu	IA5
	Central Bantu	IA5
	Rift Cluster	IA5
	Rufiji Cluster	IA5
	Nyakyusa Cluster	IA5
	Rukwa Cluster	IA5
	Kenya Highland Bantu Cluster	IA5
3. *Lingua franca*	Swahili	
4. Official language	Swahili	

SOURCE: Lyndon Harries, "Swahili in Modern East Africa," in *Language Problems of Developing Nations*, eds. Joshua A. Fishman, Charles A. Ferguson, and Jyotirindra Das Gupta (New York: John Wiley, 1968), pp. 119–127.

IV. Urban Patterns

Capital/largest city: Dar es Salaam (founded 1862)
Dominant ethnicity/language of capital
   Major vernacular: Swahili
   Major ethnic group: —
   Major ethnic group as percent of capital's population: —

TABLE 28.3   Growth of Capital/Largest City

Date	Dar es Salaam
1930	25,000[a]
1940	65,000
1950	99,000[b]
1960	150,000
1967	273,000

SOURCES:
[a] O. Martens and O. Karstedt, *The African Handbook*, 2nd ed. (London: Allen and Unwin, 1938)
[b] East African High Commission, *Statistical Bulletin*, 2 (19), p. 4.

TABLE 28.4   Cities of 20,000 and Over

City	Size	Date
Dar es Salaam	273,000	1967
Zanzibar Town	68,000	1967
Tanga	61,000	1967
Mwanza	35,000	1967
Arusha	32,000	1967
Moshi	27,000	1967
Morogoro	25,000	1967
Dodoma	24,000	1967
Iringa	22,000	1967
Tabora	21,000	1967
Kigoma/Ujiji	21,000	1967
Mtwara/Mikindani	20,000	1967

SOURCE: Census.

V. Political Patterns

A. Political Parties and Elections

In elections just prior to independence the *Tanganyika African National Union* (TANU), under the direction of Julius Nyerere, achieved an overwhelming victory and continued to govern Tanganyika until 1964. At that time, a federation was formed with Zanzibar, and TANU joined with the *Afro-Shirazi Party* (ASP) of Zanzibar. Opposition to TANU came mainly from the *African National Congress* (ANC) which split from TANU in 1957.

In Zanzibar, the ASP governed from 1957 to 1960 when they lost their majority. Political control then passed to a caretaker government until mid-1960 when the *Zanzibar and Pemba People's Party* (ZPPP) and the *Zanzibar Nationalist Party* (ZNP) formed a coalition government, with Sheikh Muhammed Shamte (ZPPP) as chief minister. A revolution in January 1964 ended the ZNP/ZPPP coalition and returned the ASP and Sheikh Abeid Karume to power as president of Zanzibar and first vice-president of Tanzania.

Union between Tanganyika and Zanzibar took place in April 1964 and the ruling parties of both

Figure 28.1   Political Parties and Elections

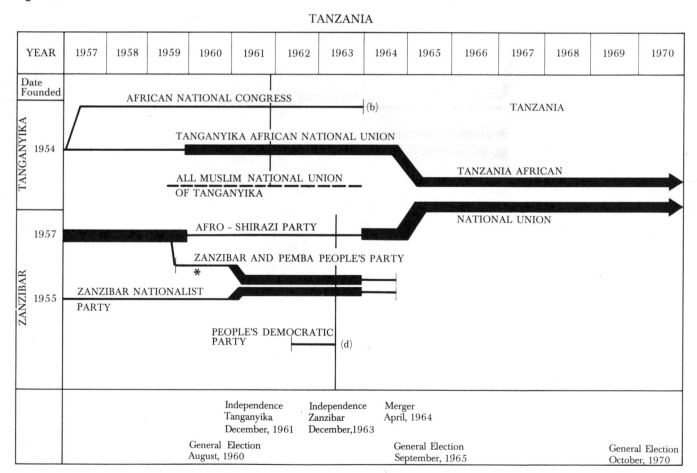

* A caretaker government was formed in early 1960 when no party won a clear majority. The deadlock was broken in July 1960 with the coalition between ZPPP and ZNP.

TABLE 28.5   Head of Government (Post Independence)

Name	Dates in Office	Age (1971)	Ethnicity	Education	Former Occupation
1. Julius Nyerere (President)	1961–	49	Interlacustrine Bantu (Zanaki)	M.A., Edinburgh	Civil Servant, Teacher

countries joined together under the name of TANU with Dr. Nyerere as president of the Republic, Abeid Karume as first vice-president, and Rashidi Kawawa (TANU) as second vice-president. In the 1965 general elections, TANU was the only party to offer candidates. Within each of the electoral districts, however, a number of TANU candidates competed with each other. TANU was confirmed in power in the 1970 elections.

B. Political Leadership

Julius Nyerere has been head of government during the post-independence period. Cabinet turnover was high in 1964, reflecting the federation with Zanzibar.

TABLE 28.6   Cabinet Membership: Distribution by Ethnic Unit*

Ethnicity*	Independence Cabinet	1967 Cabinet
1. Nyamwezi (19%)	9.1%	11%
2. Interlacustrine Bantu (14)	9.1	11
3. N. E. Coastal Bantu (11)	0	26
4. Central Bantu (11)	0	11
5. Rift Cluster (10)	9.1	5.3
6. Rufiji Cluster (9)	0	0
7. Nyakyusa (6)	0	0
8. Rukwa (5)	0	0
9. Kenya Highland Cluster (5)	9.1	16
10. Others (10)	64	21
N =	12	19

* Ethnic units arranged in rank order of size within country with the unit's percent of national population in parentheses.

VI. National Integration and Stability

Tanzania has experienced neither elite nor communal types of instability. In January 1964, however, there was an attempted mutiny by the 1st Battalion of the Tanganyika Rifles, who took control of Dar es Salaam while protesting pay conditions and of the continued presence of British officers in their army. The 2nd Battalion mutinied at Tabora on January 21. On January 25, six hundred British Royal Marines were called in by the Tanganyikan government and the mutiny was forcibly suppressed. This event has not been classified as an attempted coup since we have no evidence that the regime itself was threatened by the army demands. Prior to its union with Tanganyika to form Tanzania, Zanzibar had a revolution.

Tanzania has developed a remarkable degree of national unity among a very large number of small ethnic groups. There is no single ethnic group which is in a position to dominate the country. The ideological position of the government, which tries to minimize the "mass-elite" gap, and the use of Swahili as a national language seem to have a consolidating effect on the country. In October 1969 two civilians and four army officers were arrested for plotting a coup.

VII. Selected References

BIBLIOGRAPHY

Bates, Margaret. *A Study Guide for Tanzania*. Boston: Development Program, African Studies Center, Boston University, 1969.

Kuria, Lucas, and John Webster, comps. *A Bibliography on Anthropology and Sociology in Tanzania and East Africa*. Occasional Bibliography no. 4. Syracuse, N.Y.: Syracuse University Program of Eastern African Studies, 1966.

United States Library of Congress. General Reference and Bibliography Division. African Section. *Official Publications of British East Africa*. Part II. Tanganyika. Washington, D.C.: Government Printing Office, 1962.

GENERAL

Bienen, Henry. *Tanzania: Party Transformation and Economic Development*. Expanded edition. Princeton, N.J.: Princeton University Press (1967), 1970.

Cliffe, Lionel. *Tanzania*. London: Pall Mall Press, 1970.

Kimambo, I. M., and A. J. Temu, eds. *A History of Tanzania*. Nairobi: East African Publishing House for the Historical Association of Tanzania, 1969.

Middleton, John, and Jane Campbell, *Zanzibar: Its Society and Its Policies*. London: Oxford University Press, 1965.

Pratt, Crawford. *Tanzania*. Ithaca, N.Y.: Cornell University Press, forthcoming.

U.S. Department of the Army. *Area Handbook for Tanzania*. Pamphlet No. 550–62. Washington, D.C.: Government Printing Office, 1968.

POLITICAL

Bates, M. L. "Tanganyika." In *African One-Party States*, ed. G. M. Carter. Ithaca, N.Y.: Cornell University Press, 1962.

Cliffe, Lionel. *One-Party Democracy: The 1965 General Elections*. Nairobi: East African Publishing House, 1967.

Friedland, William H. "The Evolution of Tanganyika's Political System." In *The Transformation of East Africa*, eds. Stanley Diamond and Fred G. Burke, pp. 241–311. New York: Basic Books, 1966.

Glickman, Harvey. "Traditional Pluralism and Democratic Processes in Mainland Tanzania." In *Asian and African Studies*, 5 (1969): 165–201.

Lofchie, M. *Zanzibar: Background to Revolution*. Princeton, N.J.: Princeton University Press, 1965.

Lofchie, M. "The Zanzibari Revolution: African Protest in a Racially Plural Society." In *Power and Protest in Black Africa*, eds. Robert I. Rotberg and Ali A. Mazrui, pp. 924–968. New York: Oxford University Press, 1970.

Lowenkopf, Martin. "Socialism and Self Reliance: The Meaning of Arusha." *Africa Report*, 12 (March 1967): 8–13.

Mazrui, Ali A. "Socialism as a Mode of International Protest: The Case of Tanzania." In *Power and Protest in Black Africa*, eds. Robert I. Rotberg and Ali A. Mazrui, pp. 1139–1152. New York: Oxford University Press, 1970.

Nyerere, Julius K. *Freedom and Socialism: Uhuru na Ujamaa*. London: Oxford University Press, 1969.

ECONOMIC

Fuggles-Couchman, N. R. *Agricultural Change in Tanganyika 1945–1960*. Stanford, Cal.: Stanford University Food Research Institute, 1964.

International Bank for Reconstruction and Development. *The Economic Development of Tanganyika*. Baltimore, Md.: Johns Hopkins Press, 1961.

International Monetary Fund. "Tanzania." In *Surveys of African Economies*, Vol. 2, pp. 210–292. Washington, D.C.: I.M.F., 1968.

Smith, Hadley E. *Agricultural Development in Tanzania*. Institute of Public Administration, Dar es Salaam, Study 2. London: Oxford University Press, 1965.

SOCIAL

Cameron, J., and W. A. Dodd. *Society, Schools and Progress in Tanzania*. New York: Pergamon, 1970.

De Blij, Harm J. *Dar es Salaam: A Study in Urban Geography*. Evanston, Ill.: Northwestern University Press, 1963.

Hunter, Guy. *Manpower, Employment and Education in the Rural Economy of Tanzania*. African Research Monographs No. 9. Paris: UNESCO, 1966.

Leslie, J. A. K. *A Survey of Dar es Salaam*. London: Oxford University Press for the East African Institute of Social Research, 1963.

Ranger, T. O. *The African Churches of Tanzania*. Nairobi: East African Publishing House, 1969.

Resnick, Idrian, ed. *Tanzania: Revolution by Education*. New York: Humanities Press, 1969.

Sutton, J. E. G., ed. "Dar es Salaam: City, Port and Region." *Tanzania Notes and Records*, 71 (1970).

Tordoff, W. "Trade Unions in Tanzania." *Journal of Development Studies*, 2 (1966): 408–430.

29. Togo

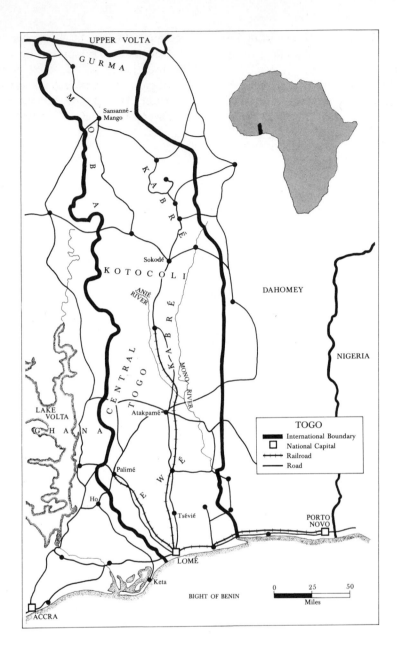

I. Basic Information

Date of Independence: April 27, 1960
Former Colonial Ruler: France
Former Name: Togoland
Population (*1970*): 1,955,916 (Census results)
Area Size (*equivalent in U.S.*): 22,000 sq. mi. (West Virginia)

Date of Last Census: 1970
Major Exports 1968 as Percent of Total Exports: phosphates—34 percent; cocoa—24 percent;* coffee—17 percent

  * Perhaps one-third of the cocoa is smuggled to Togo by Ghanaian farmers for better prices.

II. Ethnic Patterns

The ethnic classification of Togo is fairly inclusive and is at a level of abstraction just above recognized identity groups. It classifies with the major identity groups a number of smaller groups which are related culturally. The Central Togo cluster, however, is an example of an "ethnic shatter belt," although these people are tending to assimilate to the culture of the northern Voltaic peoples. In addition to the major groups, about 3 percent of the population are Yoruba-related peoples (Ana and Nago); 2 percent are Hausa and Fulani; and 1 percent Chokosi (a people of Akan descent, but assimilating to Voltaic peoples).

TABLE 29.1 Ethnic Units Over 5 Percent of Country Population

Ethnic Units	Estimated Ethnic Population 1967	Estimated Ethnic Percentage
a. Ewé Type	753,000	44%
1. Ewé (Ehoué, Eibe, Ephe, Krepe)	(362,000)	(21%)
2. Ouatchi, 3. Mina, 4. Fon, 5. Ehoué, 6. Adja, 7. Pedah, 8. Pla		
b. Kabré Type	399,000	23%
1. Kabré (Cabrai, Bekaburum, Kabure, Kaure)	(241,000)	(14%)
2. Losso, 3. Lamba, 4. Tamberma, 5. Mossi, 6. Logba		
c. Moba Type	122,000	7%
1. Moba (Bmoba, Moab, Moare, Mwan) 2. Konkomba, 3. Ngangan (Bou Bankam)		
d. Kotocoli Type	122,000	7%
1. Kotocoli (Cotocoli, Tem, Chaucho, Temba, Timn) 2. Bassari, 3. Tchamba		
e. Central Togo Cluster	77,000	5%
1. Akposso, 2. Akebou, 3. Agnagan, 4. Adele, 5. Ahlon, 6. Bassila, 7. Buem		
f. Gurma (Gourmantche, Gourma)	76,000	5%

SOURCES: H. Attignon, *Géographie du Togo*, mimeographed text, 1965, p. 22. J. C. Froelich, *Les Populations du Nord-Togo* (Paris: Presses Universitaires de France, 1963). G. P. Murdock, *Africa* (New York: McGraw-Hill, 1959).

III. Language Patterns

The two major language groups in Togo are Ewé (of the Kwa family) and Kabré (of the Voltaic family). Probably 44 percent of the total population speak Ewé as a first language (Rustow suggests 41 percent; Knappert and MacDougald suggest 32 percent). Since Ewé is spoken as a *lingua franca* in southern Togo, our estimate of total speakers is 50 percent. Kabré is probably the second largest language group. As a rough estimate, perhaps 20 percent of the population speak Kabré as a first language (Rustow estimates 22 percent). However, in the northern part of Togo where Kabré is to be found, Hausa serves as more of a *lingua franca* than Kabré. French continues to be the official language, but many Togolese speak English or German. Until 1963 Ewé and Hausa also served as official languages.

TABLE 29.2 Language Patterns

1. Primacy		
1st language	Ewé	(50%)
2nd language	Kabré	(20%)
2. Greenberg classification	Ewé	IA4
(all ethnic units in	Kabré	IA3
country over 5%)	Moba	IA3
	Kotocoli	IA3
	Central Togo cluster	IA4
	Gurma	IA3
3. *Lingua francas*	Ewé, Hausa	
4. Official language	French	

IV. Urban Patterns

Capital/largest city: Lomé
Dominant ethnicity/language of capital

Major vernacular: Ewé[1]

[1] Jan Knappert, "Language Problems of the New Nations of Africa," *African Quarterly*, 5 (1965): 95–105.

Major ethnic group: Ewé[2]
Major ethnic group as percent of capital's population: 24% (1951)

TABLE 29.3   Growth of Capital/Largest City

Date	Lomé
1920	6,000
1930	8,000
1940	38,000
1950	33,000
1960	100,000
1966	129,000 UA
1968	135,000 UA

SOURCE: *Démographie Comparée.*

[2] *Encyclopédie Afrique Française*, Vol. 6, p. 435.

TABLE 29.4   Cities of 20,000 and Over

City	Size	Date
Lomé	129,000 UA	1966

SOURCE: *UN Demographic Yearbook 1967.* The second largest town, according to *Africa 1968*, is Sokodé with a population of 17,000.

V. Political Patterns

Figure 29.1   **Political Parties and Elections**

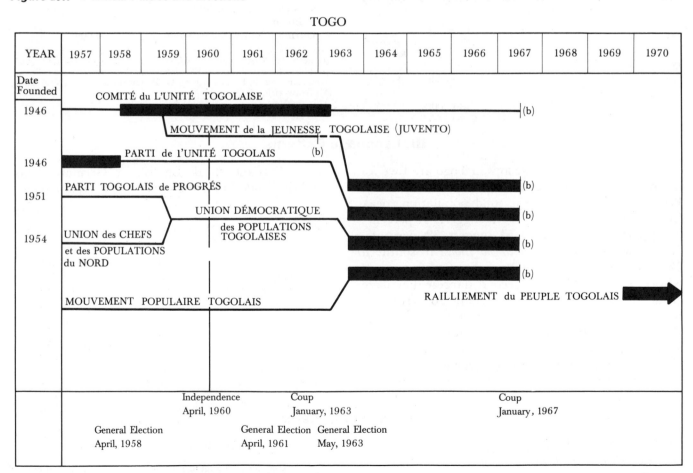

TOGO

* The election list for 1963 was drawn equally from UDPT, JUVENTO, PUT and MPT. Mr. Grunitsky was elected President.

A. Political Parties and Elections

In 1957 Togo elected its first prime minister, Nicholas Grunitsky of the *Parti de l'Unité Togolaise* (PUT), who governed until his defeat in 1958 by the *Comité du l'Unité Togolaise* (CUT). The newly elected prime minister, Sylvanus Olympio, served until assassinated by the army in January 1963. A provisional government elected in 1963 from a single slate of electors—equal numbers from the *Mouvement de la Jeunesse Togolaise* (JUVENTO), the *Union Démocratique des Populations Togolaises* (UDPT), the *Mouvement Populaire Togolais* (MPT) and the *Parti de l'Unité Togolaise* (PUT)—chose Grunitsky to head the government. Olympio's party, led by Theophile Mally, went into exile. The grand coalition continued to govern until January 1967 when a military coup, led by Lt. Col. Etiénne Eyadema, removed Grunitsky and instituted military rule. In 1969 the military instituted the *Ralliement du Peuple Togolais* (RPT).

B. Political Leadership

Since the assassination of Sylvanus Olympio (1963) there has been an alternation of military and civilian rule. Cabinet ethnic balance has shifted from the Ewé at the time of independence, to the Kabré at present. There was a particularly high turnover in cabinet membership in 1966 prior to the military coup.

TABLE 29.5   Heads of Government (Post Independence)

Name	Dates in Office	Age (1971)	Ethnicity	Education	Former Occupation
1. Sylvanus Olympio (Prime Minister/ President)	1960–1963	Died 1963, age 67	Ewé	Univ. of London (England)	Business Entrepreneur
2. Nicholas Grunitsky (President)	1963–1967	Died 1969, age 56	Kabré/German	Engineering	Transport Business Owner
3. Col. Kleber Dadjo (Chairman, Comité de Reconciliation Nationale)	1967	57	Kabré (Losso)	Secondary (Togo)	Soldier
4. Gen. Etiénne Eyadema (President)	1967–	36	Kabré	Sixth grade (Togo)	Soldier

TABLE 29.6   Cabinet Membership: Distribution by Ethnic Unit*

Ethnicity*	Independence Cabinet	Immediate Pre-Coup Cabinet	1967 Cabinet
1. Ewé (44%)	67%	70%	25%
2. Kabré (23)	22	20	42
3. Moba (7)	0	0	8.3
4. Kotocoli (7)	0	10	17
5. Central Togo Cluster (5)	11	0	0
6. Gurma (5)	0	0	0
7. Others (9)	0	0	8.3
N =	9	12	12

* Ethnic units arranged in rank order of size within country with the unit's percent of national population in parentheses.

VI. National Integration and Stability

The assassination of President Olympio in 1963 began a pattern of elite instability which has continued to the present day, with the army intervening and withdrawing on various occasions. The Ewé irredentist movement in Ghana has widespread support among the Ewé in Togo.

TABLE 29.7   Elite Instability

Event and Date	Characteristics
1. Coup d'Etat January 13, 1963	a. *Description*: President Olympio was killed by non-commissioned army officers. A provisional civilian government was set up with Nicholas Grunitsky (president) and Antoine Meatchi (vice-president). b. *Participants*: Army elements, including former sergeants in the French army. Sergeants Bodjillo and Eyadema led the revolt of about 700 Togolese, recently mustered out of the French army. c. *Apparent Causes*: About 700 Togolese who had fought in the French army returned to their country in late 1962. Olympio refused to reintegrate them into the Togolese army. After the coup the size of the army increased from 250 to 1200 men.
2. Attempted Coup November 21, 1966	a. *Description*: Noe Kutuklui called for demonstrations against Grunitsky in a radio broadcast. More than 5000 people took to the streets in the city of Lomé, but the coup attempt was aborted by the army without violence. b. *Participants*: Noe Kutuklui, Secretary General of the Union Togolaise party, and a leading Ewé politician. He was supported by many members of his party. Support for the attempt seemed to be widespread, but civilian crowds were unable to cope with the military. c. *Apparent Causes*: Ewé dissastisfaction with military rule.
3. Coup d'Etat January 13, 1967	a. *Description*: The coup was preceded by a power struggle between President Grunitsky and Vice-president Meatchi. Grunitsky was deposed by the military. b. *Participants*: Lt. Col. Etiénne Eyadema, Chief of Staff, and the Togolese Army. c. *Apparent Causes*: Eyadema's dissatisfaction with Grunitsky and Meatchi's performance. Grunitsky had called for the resignation of the junta after the November 1966 coup attempt. There had also been reductions in army appropriations. Eyadema decided to assume direct control instead of using civilian ministers.

SOURCE: Russell Warren Howe, "Togo: Four Years of Military Rule," *Africa Report*, 12 (May 1967): 6–12.

VII. Selected References

GENERAL

Coleman, James S. *Togoland*. International Conciliation, September 1956. no. 509. New York: Carnegie Endowment for International Peace, 1956.

Cornevin, Robert. *Histoire du Togo*, 2nd ed. Paris: Bergère-Levrault, 1962.

Cornevin, Robert. *Le Togo, Nation-Pilote*. Paris: Nouvelles Editions Latines, 1963.

Lewis, William H. "Togo: Africa's New Pressure Point." *Africa Report*, 5 (April 1960): 3–6, 12, 15.

POLITICAL

de Lusignan, Guy. *French-Speaking Africa since Independence*, pp. 170–179. London: Pall Mall Press, 1969.

Howe, Russell W. "Togo: Four Years of Military Rule." *Africa Report*, 12 (May 1967): 6–12.

ECONOMIC

International Monetary Fund. "Togo." In *Surveys of African Economies*, Vol. 3. Washington, D.C.: I.M.F., 1970.

SOCIAL

Debrunner, H. *A Church Between Colonial Powers: The Church in Togo*. London: Lutterworth Press, 1965.

30. Uganda

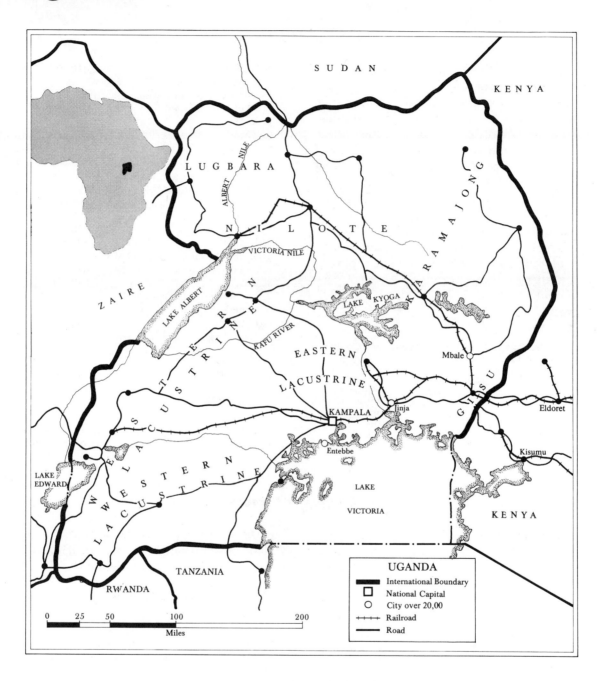

I. Basic Information

Date of Independence: October 9, 1962
Former Colonial Ruler: United Kingdom
Population (1970): 9,760,000 (Census results)
Area Size (equivalent in U.S.): 91,000 sq. mi. (Oregon)

Date of Last Census: 1969
Major Exports 1968 as Percent of Total Exports: coffee—
54 percent; cotton—23 percent; copper—8 percent

II. Ethnic Patterns

The ethnic classification for Uganda is at a high level of abstraction and does not represent identity groups. In the case of the Eastern and Western Lacustrine clusters geography is the basic differentiating criterion: it would be possible to combine the groups into the Interlacustrine Bantu. Likewise a Nilotic cluster could be devised at an even higher level of abstraction which would include the Nilote Type, Karamajong Cluster, Gisu Cluster, and Lugbara Types. The sub-categories under each type are generally identity groups. In addition to these major types and clusters, there are small populations of Nandi-like Suk and Sebei (1 percent), plus a fractional number of Twa (Pygmies). About 2 percent of the population is made up of Indians (83,000) and Europeans.

TABLE 30.1 Ethnic Units Over 5 Percent of Country Population

Ethnic Units	Estimated Ethnic Population 1967	Estimated Ethnic Percentage
a. Eastern Lacustrine Cluster	2,135,000	27%
1. Ganda (Baganda, Waganda)	(1,270,000)	(16%)
2. Soga	(610,000)	(8%)
3. Gwere, 4. Nyuli		
b. Western Lacustrine Cluster	1,950,000	25%
1. Nkole (Nyankole)	(610,000)	(8%)
2. Kiga	(560,000)	(7%)
3. Toro	(255,000)	(3.2%)
4. Nyoro	(230,000)	(2.9%)
5. Konjo	(135,000)	(1.7%)
6. Rwanda, 7. Rundi, 8. Ambo		
c. Nilote Type (Luo, Lwoo)	1,175,000	15%
1. Lango	(444,000)	(6%)
2. Acholi	(350,000)	(4%)
3. Alur	(150,000)	(1.9%)
4. Padhola	(125,000)	(1.6%)
5. Kuman, 6. Jonam, 7. Paluo		
d. Karamajong Cluster	870,000	11%
1. Teso	(640,000)	(8%)
2. Karamajong, 3. Dodoth, 4. Jie, 5. Tepeth, 6. Nyakwai		
e. Gisu Cluster	450,000	6%
1. Gisu (Bageshu, Bagish, Geshu, Masaba, Sokwia)	(405,000)	(5.1%)
2. Nyole, 3. Samia		
f. Lugbara Type	390,000	5%
1. Lugbara	(285,000)	(3.6%)
2. Madi, 3. Lendu		

SOURCE: U.S. Department of the Army, *Area Handbook for Uganda* (Washington, D.C.: Government Printing Office, 1969), pp. 77–90

III. Language Patterns

The two major language families in Uganda are Bantu (including Ganda, Swahili, Soga, Toro, Nyoro, Rwanda, and Gisu) and Nilotic (including Lango, Acholi, Alur, Iteso, Karamajong, Lugbara). Ganda (Luganda) is probably the largest single language in Uganda, including about 13 percent of the total population who speak it as a first language, and another 20 percent who speak it as a second language, mainly from the Ganda-related language groups. (Knappert estimates that 33 percent speak Luganda: MacDougald 28 percent; Rustow 28 percent.) The second most widely distributed language is probably Swahili, with a minimum of 20 percent population who speak it as a second or third language. (The preliminary reports of the UNESCO language survey in East Africa are not yet publicly available, but the consensus seems to be that Swahili is more widely spoken than had been anticipated.) English is the official language of Uganda.

TABLE 30.2 Language Patterns

1. Primacy		
1st language	Ganda	(33%)
2nd language	Swahili	(20%)
2. Greenberg classification (all ethnic units in country over 5%)	Eastern Lacustrine	IA5
	Western Lacustrine	IA5
	Nilote	IIE1
	Karamajong	IIE1
	Gisu	IA5
	Lugbara	IE11
3. *Lingua francas*	Ganda, Swahili	
4. Official language	English (Ganda was formerly the official language of the region of Buganda)	

IV. Urban Patterns

Capital/largest city: Kampala (1890)
Dominant ethnicity/language of capital
    Major vernacular: Ganda[1]
    Major ethnic group: Ganda[2]
    Major ethnic group as percent of capital's population:
    42% (1952)

TABLE 30.3　Growth of Capital/Largest City

Date	Kampala
1930	10,000
1940	24,000
1950	38,000
1960	120,000
1966	175,000 UA

SOURCE: Southall and Gutkind, *Townsmen in the Making* (Kampala: East Africa Institute of Social Research, 1957).

TABLE 30.4　Cities of 20,000 and Over

City	Size	Date
Kampala[a]	331,000	1970
Jinja[a]	100,000	1970
Mbale[b]	23,539	1969
Entebbe[b]	21,176	1969

[1] Jan Knappert, "Language Problems of the New Nations of Africa," *African Quarterly*, 5 (1965): 95–105.

[2] Aiden Southall and P. G. Gutkind, *Townsmen in the Making*, (Kampala: East African Institute of Social Research, 1957), p. 26.

SOURCES:
[a] Estimated from *Africa South of the Sahara 1971* (London: Europa Publications, 1971).
[b] From 1969 provisional census results. Gulu is the next largest town, with a population of 19,707.

V. Political Patterns

A. Political Parties and Elections

Uganda had its first direct elections for African representatives on the Legislative Council in 1958. In March 1961, elections were held in which the *Democratic Party* (DP) won 43 seats, and the *Uganda People's Congress* (UPC), led by Dr. Milton Obote, won 35 seats. The Buganda region, however, boycotted this election, even though the *Democratic Party* originated inside Buganda (reflecting the Catholic groups, as distinct from the majority Protestants). In October of 1961, the majority of the Buganda peoples formed a party called *Kabaka Yekka*, which allied with the UPC, and this coalition won the national elections in April 1962. (The UPC won 43 out of 91 seats). In November 1964 there was another election—the "lost counties" referendum, and by December 1965 the UPC majority had increased to 67 out of 91 seats. In February 1966 Prime Minister Obote deposed the president, Sir Edward

TABLE 30.5　Heads of Government (Post Independence)

Name	Dates in Office	Age (1971)	Ethnicity	Education	Former Occupation
1. Apollo Milton Obote (Prime Minister/ Executive President)	1962–1971	47	Nilote Cluster (Lango)	Makerere College	Business Entrepreneur
2. Major-General Idi Amin	Jan. 1971–	45	Karamajong Cluster (Kakwa)	Army Training Schools	Army officer

Figure 30.1 **Political Parties and Elections**

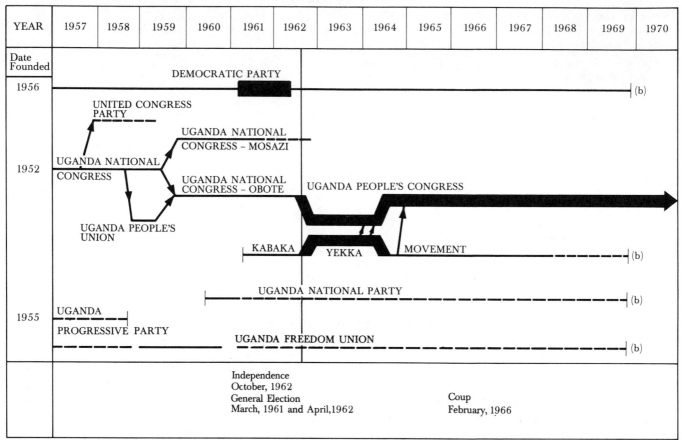

UGANDA

| YEAR | 1957 | 1958 | 1959 | 1960 | 1961 | 1962 | 1963 | 1964 | 1965 | 1966 | 1967 | 1968 | 1969 | 1970 |

Date Founded

1956 — DEMOCRATIC PARTY ————— (b)

UNITED CONGRESS PARTY

UGANDA NATIONAL CONGRESS – MOSAZI

1952 — UGANDA NATIONAL CONGRESS

UGANDA NATIONAL CONGRESS – OBOTE — UGANDA PEOPLE'S CONGRESS

UGANDA PEOPLE'S UNION

KABAKA YEKKA MOVEMENT ————— (b)

UGANDA NATIONAL PARTY ————— (b)

1955 — UGANDA PROGRESSIVE PARTY

UGANDA FREEDOM UNION ————— (b)

Independence
October, 1962
General Election
March, 1961 and April, 1962

Coup
February, 1966

Mutesa II, the Kabaka of Buganda, and has tried to put an end to Buganda autonomy. The Kabaka died in exile in November 1969. Following the attempted assassination of Dr. Obote in December 1969, all the opposition parties were banned. The military government banned all parties after the January 1971 coup.

B. Political Leadership

Milton Obote was head of government from independence to January 1971. There was a rapid cabinet turnover in 1966 following the deposition of the president, Edward Mutesa (the Kabaka of Buganda). As of 1969 cabinet ethnicity remained relatively constant with a slight decrease in Ganda members and an increase in Gisu members.

TABLE 30.6 Cabinet Membership: Distribution by Ethnic Unit*

Ethnicity*	Independence Cabinet	Immediate Pre-Coup Cabinet	1967 Cabinet
1. Eastern Lacustrine (27)	41%	50%	37%
2. Western Lacustrine (25)	0	6.3	0
3. Nilote (15)	24	13	26
4. Karamajong (11)	5.9	13	0
5. Gisu (6)	18	6.3	32
6. Lugbara (5)	0	6.3	5.3
7. Others (6)	12	0	0
N =	17	16	19

* Ethnic units arranged in rank order of size within country with the unit's percent of national population in parentheses.

VI. National Integration and Stability

The major problem of national integration in Uganda, both in terms of elite and communal stability, has been the question of the role of the powerful and formerly autonomous kingdom of Buganda. In 1966, the power of Buganda was successfully challenged by removing the Kabaka and establishing a unitary state. (The Kabaka died in exile in 1969.) On December 19, 1969, there was an attempted assassination of President Obote, who was overthrown by an army coup a little over a year later.

TABLE 30.7   Elite Instability

Event and Date	Characteristics
1. Coup d'Etat February 22, 1966	a. *Description*: Prime Minister Obote suspended the constitution, relieved the President, Sir Edward Mutesa (the Kabaka of Buganda), and declared himself Executive President. He ordered the arrest of five cabinet ministers.
	b. *Participants*: Prime Minister Obote, with the support of various police and military elements.
	c. *Apparent Causes*: Obote was challenged by the Kabaka Yekka Party and elements in his own party. Parliament voted to establish a commission to investigate allegations that he was involved in illegal activities in connection with the transfer of gold from the Congo (Kinshasa). He preempted his opponents by moving first.
2. Coup d'Etat January 25, 1971	a. *Description*: The army seized power while President Obote was in Asia attending the Commonwealth Conference. Scattered shooting was reported in Kampala and some continuing resistance was reported in other areas of the country for a time after the coup. All political prisoners were immediately released.
	b. *Participants*: The army, led by Major General Idi Amin, who had risen from the ranks to become its commander in 1966.
	c. *Apparent Causes*: Amin stated at the time of the coup that the government's economic policies were benefiting "the rich, big men" and that Obote had developed his own home region in the north at the expense of other parts of the country. There was rivalry and infighting between officers of Obote's Lango tribe and the Acholi and other tribes culturally related to Amin's Kakwa tribe. Apparently Obote had planned to dismissal Amin from his army command.

SOURCES: Crawford Young, "The Obote Revolution," *Africa Report*, 11 (June 1966): 8–15. Ali A. Mazrui, "Privilege and Protest as Integrative Factors: The Case of Buganda's Status in Uganda," in *Power and Protest in Black Africa*, eds. Robert I. Rotberg and Ali A. Mazrui (New York: Oxford University Press, 1970).

TABLE 30.8   Communal Instability

Event and Date	Characteristics
1. Ethnic Violence February 15– March 30, 1963	a. *Description*: On February 15 a state of emergency was declared in the counties of Busongora and Bwanba, in Toro District (West Uganda). On March 30, 1963, Buyaga county of the so-called "Lost Counties" was declared a "disturbed" area. In early March there were 43 incidents of violence; most were directed against Buganda chiefs.
	b. *Participants*: Bunyoro ethnic members and Buganda chiefs.
	c. *Apparent Causes*: Bunyoro spokesmen claimed that the "Lost Counties" in the Buganda kingdom should be returned to Bunyoro.

TABLE 30.8 Communal Instabilty *(cont.)*

Event and Date	Characteristics
2. Rebellion 1962–1963	a. *Description*: Amba and Konjo people demanded autonomy from their historical overlords, the Toro. This protest was organized by the Rwenzururu movement, which demanded a separate status within Toro district, and later established a secessionist government. Ugandan troops and police were sent to the area by the central government which supported the Toro District administration. Konjo and Amba attacks on Toro chiefs were brought to an end in 1964 by a ten-day attack by Toro. Hundreds of Konjo were killed, and many others fled into the Rwenzururu mountains, before order was effectively restored in the area by the police and army. b. *Participants*: Members of the Konjo, Amba and Toro ethnic groups. c. *Apparent Causes*: The feeling by Amba and Konjo of historical exploitation by Toro, and of increased political deprivation after Uganda's independence when administrative offices remained concentrated in Toro hands.
3. Rebellion March 24–July 1966	a. *Description*: The Buganda rebellion was caused essentially by the demand of the Buganda people to maintain strong kingship (Kabakaship) and regional autonomy in the face of national government efforts to create a centralized state. After the constitution was suspended in February 1966 tension arose between Obote and Sir Edward Mutesa, the Kabaka of Buganda and former President of Uganda. Buganda demanded that the central government leave Kampala. The government attacked the Kabaka's place on May 24 and the Kabaka fled to exile, although rebellion in rural areas continued for several days thereafter. b. *Participants*: The Buganda region which is ethnically homogeneous (Baganda) was almost completely autonomous in the colonial era and functioned under its traditional ruler, the Kabaka, who at the time of independence became the President of Uganda. Buganda has been the most developed region in Uganda. c. *Apparent Causes*: The Buganda perceived the central government to be dominating them, and were striving for a return to "local autonomy."

SOURCES: Martin R. Doornbos, "Kumanyana and Rwenzururu," in *Protest and Power in Black Africa*, eds. Robert I. Rotberg and Ali A. Mazrui (New York: Oxford University Press, 1970), pp. 1088–1138. Terence Hopkins, "Politics in Uganda: The Buganda Question," in *Transition in African Politics*, eds. Jeffrey Butler and A. A. Castagno (New York: Praeger, 1967). Crawford Young, "The Obote Revolution," *Africa Report*, 11 (June 1966): 8–15.

VII. Selected References

BIBLIOGRAPHY

Hopkins, T. K. *A Study Guide for Uganda.* Boston: Development Program, African Studies Center, Boston University, 1969.

Kuria, Lucas, et al., comps. *A Bibliography on Politics and Government in Uganda.* Occasional Bibliography no. 2. Syracuse, N.Y.: Syracuse University Program of Eastern African Studies, 1965.

Peckham, Robert, et al., comps. *A Bibliography on Anthropology and Sociology in Uganda.* Occasional Bibliography no. 3. Syracuse, N.Y: Syracuse University Program of Eastern African Studies, 1965.

United States Library of Congress. General Reference and Bibliography Division. African Section. *Official Publications of British East Africa.* Part III. Uganda. Washington, D.C.: Government Printing Office, 1963.

GENERAL

Gertzel, Cherry. *Uganda.* London: Pall Mall Press, 1970.

Rothchild, Donald. *Uganda.* Ithaca, N.Y.: Cornell University Press, forthcoming.

Uganda Government. *Atlas of Uganda.* Entebbe: Department of Lands and Surveys, 1962.

U.S. Department of the Army. *Area Handbook for Uganda.* Pamphlet No. 550–74. Washington, D.C.: Government Printing Office, 1969.

POLITICAL

Apter, David F. *The Political Kingdom in Uganda: A Study in Bureaucratic Nationalism*, 2nd ed. Princeton, N.J.: Princeton University Press, 1967.

Rothchild, Donald, and M. Rogin. "Uganda." In *National Unity and Regionalism in Eight African States*, edited by G. M. Carter. Ithaca, N.Y.: Cornell University Press, 1966.

Shepherd, George W., Jr. "Modernization in Uganda: The Struggle for Unity." In *The Transformation of East Africa*, eds. Stanley Diamond and Fred G. Burke, pp. 313–335. New York: Basic Books, 1966.

"The Uganda Army: Nexus of Power." *Africa Report*, 11 (December 1966): 37–39.

Young, Crawford, "The Obote Revolution." *Africa Report*, 11 (June 1966): 8–14.

ECONOMIC

Elkan, Walter, *Migrants and Proletarians: Urban Labour in the Economic Development of Uganda*. London: Oxford University Press, 1960.

International Bank for Reconstruction and Development. *The Economic Development of Uganda*. Baltimore, Md.: Johns Hopkins Press, 1962.

International Monetary Fund. "Uganda." In *Surveys of African Economies*, Vol. 2., pp. 293–365. Washington, D.C.: I.M.F., 1968.

Masefield, G. B. *Agricultural Change in Uganda 1945–1960*. Stanford, Cal.: Stanford University, Food Research Institute, 1962.

SOCIAL

Chesswas, J. D. *Educational Planning and Development in Uganda*. African Research Monograph No. 1. Paris: UNESCO, International Institute for Educational Planning, 1966.

Fallers, Lloyd A., ed. *The King's Men: Leadership and Status in Buganda on the Eve of Independence*. New York: Oxford University Press, 1964.

Parkin, David. *Neighbors and Nations in an African City Ward*. Berkeley and Los Angeles: University of California Press, 1969. (Kampala).

Scanlon, David. *Education in Uganda*. Washington, D.C.: Government Printing Office, 1964.

Scott, Roger. *The Development of Trade Unions in Uganda*. Nairobi: East African Publishing House, 1966.

Southall, A. W. "Kampala-Mengo." In *The City in Modern Africa*, ed. Horace Miner. New York: Praeger, 1967.

Southall, Aiden W. "The Concepts of Elites and Their Formation in Uganda." In *The New Elites in Tropical Africa*, ed. P. C. Lloyd. New York: Oxford University Press, 1966.

Southall, A. W., and P. G. Gutkind. *Townsmen in the Making: Kampala and Its Suburbs*. London: Routledge and Kegan Paul, 1957.

Weeks, Sheldon. *Divergence in Educational Development: The Case of Kenya and Uganda*. New York: Columbia Teachers College Press, 1967.

31. Upper Volta

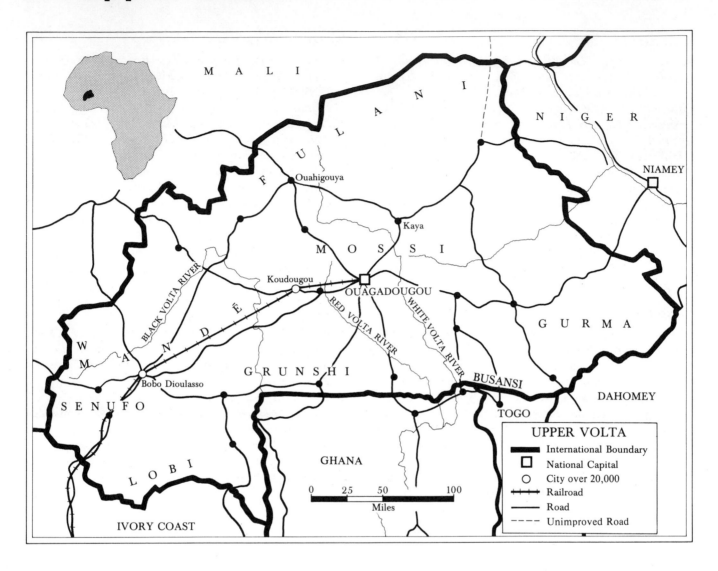

I. Basic Information

Date of Independence: August 5, 1960

Former Colonial Ruler: France

Change in Boundaries: Formerly part of French West African Federation; administered as part of the Ivory Coast after conquest; administered separately from 1919–1932; administered as part of Mali and Ivory Coast until 1947

Estimated Population (*1970*): 5,380,000

Area Size (*equivalent in U.S.*): 106,000 sq. mi. (Colorado)

Date of Last Census: 1960–61 (sample survey)

Major Exports 1967 as Percent of Total Exports: livestock, hides and skins—60 percent; cotton—17 percent

II. Ethnic Patterns

The ethnic classification of Upper Volta is done at a middle level of inclusion and abstraction. It follows the schema used by the government of Upper Volta, who state their main criterion as follows (our translation): "The classification given here is primarily based on cultural characteristics which are likely to have an influence on demographic traits." The Mossi, Fulani, Gurma, and Busansi are identity groups.

TABLE 31.1 Ethnic Units Over 5 Percent of Country Population

Ethnic Units	Estimated Ethnic Population 1967	Estimated Ethnic Percentage
a. Mossi (Mole, Moshi)	2,542,000	50%
1. Ouagadougou, 2. Tengkedogo, 3. Yatenga		
b. Western Mandé Type	880,000	16%
1. Bobo, 2. Barka, 3. Samo, 4. Dyula		
c. Senufo Type (Sene, Siena)	363,000	7%
1. Senufo-Minianka, 2. Karakora, 3. Toussian, 4. Tourka, 5. Gouin		
d. Grunshi Type (Gourounsi, Gorisè, Grussi, Grunsi)	341,000	6%
1. Grunshi, 2. Koussassis, 3. Kassena, 4. Sissala, 5. Nounoumas, 6. Kos, 7. Lelas		
e. Fulani (Peul)	313,000	6%
1. Fulani, 2. Rimibes (serfs)		
f. Lobi Type	291,000	5%
1. Lobi, 2. Vigne, 3. Dian, 4. Gan, 5. Dorossie, 6. Komono, 7. Birifor, 8. Dagari, 9. Wile		
g. Gurma (Gourmantche)	275,000	5%
h. Busansi (Bisa, Bisano, Bisapele, Bousanou, Bouzantchi, Busanga)	242,000	5%

SOURCE: Upper Volta, Direction de la statistique et des études économiques. *La situation démographique en Haute-Volta; résultats partiels de l'enquête démographique 1960–61* (Paris: Ministère de la Cooperation 1962).

III. Language Patterns

All of the languages of Upper Volta are in the Niger-Congo family, including the Voltaic sub-branch (Mossi, Senufu, Grunshi, Lobi, and Gurma), plus Dyula and Fulani. The major language in Upper Volta is Mossi, which is spoken by 50 percent of the population as a first language and probably by another 5 percent as a *lingua franca*. (Knappert estimates Mossi speakers at 50 percent; Rustow 54 percent.) The second largest language group is Dyula, a simplified form of Malinké (of the Mandé family). Probably 16 percent of the population speak Dyula as a first language, and probably 5 percent as a *lingua franca*. French is the official language.

TABLE 31.2 Language Patterns

1. Primacy		
1st language	Mossi	(55%)
2nd language	Dyula	(21%)
2. Greenberg classification	Mossi	IA3
(all ethnic units in	Western Mandé	IA2
country over 5%)	Senufo	IA3
	Grunshi	IA3
	Fulani	IA1
	Lobi	IA3
	Gurma	IA3
	Busansi	IA2
3. *Lingua francas*	Mossi, Dyula	
4. Official language	French	

IV. Urban Patterns

Capital/largest city: Ouagadougou
Dominant ethnicity/language of capital
  Major vernacular: Mossi[1]

Major ethnic group: Mossi[2]
Major ethnic group as percent of capital's population: 66% (1968)

[1] Jan Knappert, "Language Problems of the New Nations of Africa," *African Quarterly*, 5 (1965): 95–105.

[2] "Enquête Démographique Ouagadougou 1968," *Bulletin Mensuel l'Information Statistique et Economique*, New series, 1969.

TABLE 31.3 Growth of Capital/Largest City

Date	Ouagadougou
1920	12,000
1930	16,000
1940	24,000
1950	37,000
1960	55,000
1966	78,000

SOURCE: *Démographie Comparée, UN Demographic Yearbook*, 1969.

TABLE 31.4 Cities of 20,000 and Over

City	Size	Date
Ouagadougou[a]	78,000	ca. 1966
Bobo-Dioulasso[a]	68,000	ca. 1966
Koudougou[b]	25,000	1961

SOURCES:
[a] *UN Demographic Yearbook*, 1969.
[b] *Démographie Comparée.*

V. Political Patterns

A. Political Parties and Elections

The political structure and constitution of Upper Volta have been almost identical to the one-party system of Ivory Coast. The dominant party has been the *Union Démocratique Voltaique* (UDV), led by Maurice Yaméogo. This party was a branch of the *Rassemblement Démocratique Africain* (RDA) of Felix Houphouet-Boigny of the Ivory Coast. In the 1959 election the UDV won 71 out of 75 seats and subse-

Figure 31.1 **Political Parties and Elections**

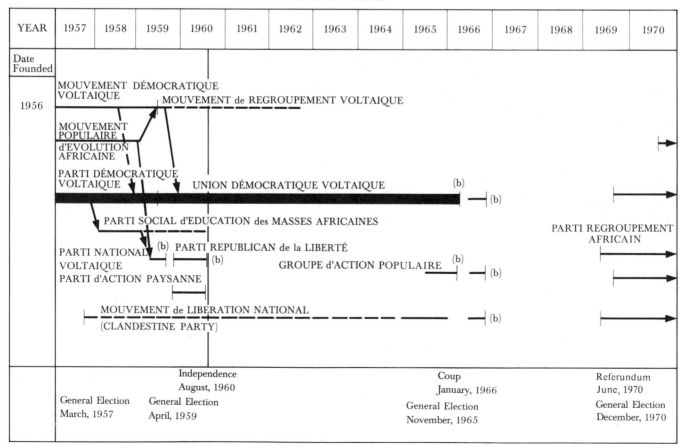

TABLE 31.5 Heads of Government (Post Independence)

Name	Dates in Office	Age (1971)	Ethnicity	Education	Former Occupation
1. Maurice Yaméogo (President)	1960–1966	50	Mossi	Secondary	Civil Servant
2. Gen. Sangoulé Lamizana (President)	1966–	55	W. Mandé	Secondary	Soldier

quently gained control of the remaining four seats. There were, prior to independence, a variety of opposition parties, although many of them were banned or merged with the UDV. In 1966 the military led by Lt. Colonel Sangoulé Lamizana took control of the government and suspended all parties for four years (except for a brief period later in that year). The UDV won 37 of 57 seats in the December 1970 election, the PRA 12, the MLN 6 and Independents 2.

B. Political Leadership

Maurice Yaméogo led the government until the military coup of 1966. More than half of the cabinet members have continued to be Mossi, reflecting the general population. There were rapid changes in cabinet membership in 1962 and 1966. The new 1970 constitution provides for a mixed military-civilian government for a four-year interim period. Lamizana continues as military president and, following the December 1970 elections, Gerard Kango Ouedraogo, a 46-year-old Mossi politician, became prime minister.

TABLE 31.6 Cabinet Membership: Distribution by Ethnic Unit*

Ethnicity*	Independence Cabinet	Immediate Pre-Coup Cabinet	1967 Cabinet
1. Mossi (50%)	57%	54%	54%
2. Western Mandé (16)	21	15	31
3. Senufo (7)	0	7.7	0
4. Grunshi (6)	7.1	7.7	7.7
5. Fulani (6)	0	0	0
6. Lobi (5)	0	7.7	0
7. Gurma (5)	0	7.7	0
8. Busansi (5)	0	0	7.7
9. Others (.1)	14	0	0
N =	14	13	13

* Ethnic units arranged in rank order of size within country with the unit's percent of national population in parentheses.

VI. National Integration and Stability

Upper Volta has had one coup d'état which developed out of a labor–government dispute.

TABLE 31.7 Elite Instability

Event and Date	Characteristics
1. Coup d'Etat January 3, 1966	a. *Description*: Labor unions sponsored a general strike after the National Assembly, on December 30, had approved a government-backed austerity program. President Maurice Yaméogo declared a state of emergency and banned the proposed strike. Nevertheless, the strike took place as large crowds surrounded the presidential palace shouting for the army to take power. On January 3, Sangoulé Lamizana, Army Chief of Staff, took power, and on January 5 he suspended the constitution and dissolved the assembly.
	b. *Participant*: Colonel Lamizana (Army Chief of Staff).
	c. *Apparent Causes*: Labor unions led by Joseph Ovedraogo, President of the *Confederation africaine des travailleurs croyants*, promoted the demonstrations to protest legislation by the National Assembly which had cut the salaries of government employees by 20 percent. The austerity budget included no reductions in the president's salary. Colonel Lamizana said that he had assumed power "to safeguard republican and democratic institutions and avoid all bloodshed."

VII. Selected References

GENERAL

Geradin, B. *Le Développement de la Haute-Volta.* Paris: Isea, 1964.

Guilhem, Marcel. *Histoire de la Haute-Volta, l'Afrique le Monde; cours moyens.* Paris: Ligel, 1964.

Thompson, Viriginia, and Richard Adloff. *French West Africa,* pp. 171–178. Stanford, Cal.: Stanford University Press, 1957.

POLITICAL

de Lusignan, Guy. *French-Speaking Africa since Independence,* pp. 145–151. London: Pall Mall Press, 1969.

LeVine, Victor T. "The Coups in Upper Volta, Dahomey and the Central African Republic." In *Power and Protest in Black Africa,* eds. Robert I. Rotberg and Ali A.

Mazrui, pp. 1035–1071. New York: Oxford University Press, 1970.

ECONOMIC

International Monetary Fund. "Upper Volta." In *Surveys of African Economies,* Vol. 3. Washington, D.C.: I.M.F., 1970.

SOCIAL

Levtzion, Nehemia. *Muslims and Chiefs in West Africa.* Oxford: Clarendon Press, 1968.

Rouch, Jean. "Migrations au Ghana." *Journal de la Société des Africanistes,* 26 (1956): 33–96.

Skinner, Elliott P. *The Mossi of the Upper Volta: The Political Development of a Sudanese People.* Stanford, Cal.: Stanford University Press, 1964.

32. Zambia

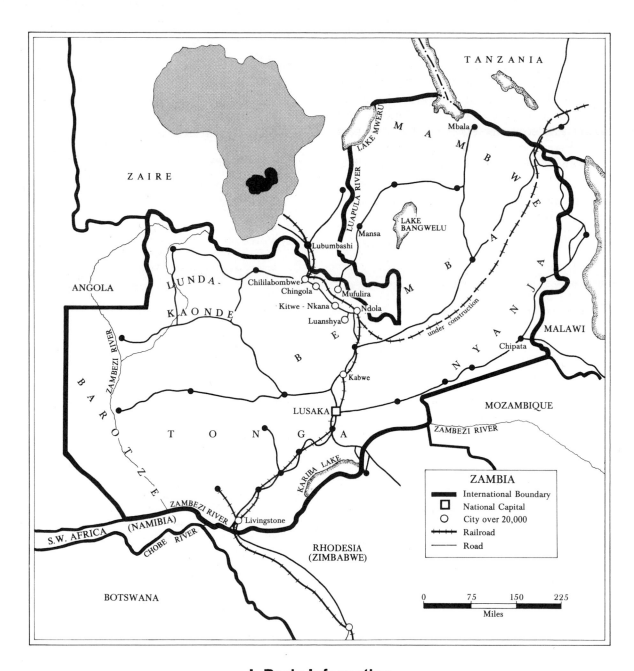

I. Basic Information

Date of Independence: October 24, 1964
Former Colonial Ruler: United Kingdom
Changes in Boundaries: Part of the Central African Federation, 1953–1963
Former Name: Northern Rhodesia

Population (1970): 4,300,000 (Census results)
Area Size (equivalent in U.S.): 288,000 sq. mi. (Texas)
Date of Last Census: 1969
Major Exports 1967 as Percent of Total Exports: copper —94 percent

II. Ethnic Patterns

The Kay classification (1967) is largely linguistic, while the Mitchell classification (1960–1964), which we have used, is modified to take account of cultural similarities. Our categories are at a middle level of abstraction, however, since they are based in part on locally recognized identity groupings. The European population of Zambia was 70,000 in 1965.

TABLE 32.1   Ethnic Units Over 5 Percent of Country Population

Ethnic Units	Estimated Ethnic Population 1967	Estimated Ethnic Percentage
a. Bemba Cluster	1,472,000	*37%*
1. Bemba (Awemba, Ayemba, Babeinba, Muemba, Wemba) i. Bisa, ii. Tabwa, iii. Kunda, iv. Senga	(599,000)	(15%)
2. Luapula i. Lunda (Luapula, Kazembe), ii. Chishinga, iii. Shila, iv. Bwile	(311,000)	(8%)
3. Lamba i. Lala, ii. Lamba, iii. Ambo, iv. Lima, v. Luano, vi. Swaka, vii. Limba, viii. Seba	(300,000)	(8%)
4. Aushi i. Ushi, ii. Ngumbo, iii. Mukulu, iv. Unga, v. Kabende	(260,000)	(7%)
b. Tonga Type	734,000	*19%*
1. Tonga (Batonga) i. Tonga, ii. Toka, iii. Gowa, iv. Fwe	(481,000)	(12%)
2. Lenje i. Lenje, ii. Sala, iii. Soli	(157,000)	(4%)
3. Ila i. Ila, ii. Leya, iii. Subiya, iv. Totela, v. Lumbu, vi. Lundwe	(94,000)	(2%)
c. Nyanja Type (Anyanja, Wanyanja) 1. Chewa i. Chewa, ii. Nsenga 2. Zambezi i. Chikunda 3. Ngoni	572,000	*15%*
d. Lunda-Kaonde Type	485,000	*12%*
1. Lunda-Luvale (Lunda-Alunda, Arunde, Balonde, Lounda, Valunda, Malhundo) i. Luvale, ii. Lunda (North-western), iii. Mbunda, iv. Luchazi, v. Mashashe, vi. Ndembu, vii. Chokwe	(355,000)	(9%)
2. Kaonde (Bakahonde, Baka-onde)	(127,000)	(3%)
e. Mambwe Cluster	327,000	*8%*
1. Mambwe Type i. Lungu, ii. Mambwe, iii. Winamwange, iv. Wiwa, v. Tambo	(209,000)	(5%)
2. Tumbuka Type i. Fungwe, ii. Kamanga, iii. Yombe, iv. Nthali, v. Hewe	(118,000)	(3%)
3. Nkoya Type i. Lambya, ii. Wandya, iii. Nyiha		
f. Barotze (Lozi, Barotse, Barozi, Barutse, Marotse, Rotse, Rozi) Type	280,000	*7%*
1. Luyana i. Kwangwa, ii. Kwandi, iii. Koma, iv. Nyengo, v. Simaa, vi. Mwenyi, vii. Imilangu, viii. Mashi, ix. Mbukushu, x. Ndundulu, xi. Lyuwa	(173,000)	(4%)
2. Lozi	(106,000)	(3%)

SOURCES: Clyde Mitchell, "The African Peoples," in *Handbook to the Federation of Rhodesia and Nyasaland*, ed. W. V. Brelsford (London: Cassell, 1960), pp. 117–181. Clyde Mitchell, *African Tribes and Languages of the Federation of Rhodesia and Nyasaland* (Salisbury: Federal Government Printer, 1964), Map. George Kay, *A Social Geography of Zambia* (London: University of London Press, 1967), p. 45.

III. Language Patterns

All of the languages of Zambia are Bantu. Bemba is probably the largest of these. Although the Bemba ethnic/cultural cluster includes 37 percent of the population, those who speak Bemba as a first language are probably only 15 percent of the total population. (Knappert suggests 20 percent; Rustow 33 percent.) Denny (1963) stresses that although Bemba is the major language, it is not a *lingua franca*. (Hence we retain the low estimated figure of 15 percent.) The second largest language is probably

Tonga, although Colson says they are the largest linguistic group. Those who speak Tonga as a first language probably constitute 12 percent of the population. English serves as a *lingua franca* and the official language.

TABLE 32.2   Language Patterns

1. Primacy
1st language	Bemba	(15%)
2nd language	Tonga	(12%)

2. Greenberg classification (all ethnic units in country over 5%)
Bemba	IA5
Tonga	IA5
Nyanja	IA5
Lunda	IA5
Mambwe	IA5
Barotze	IA5

3. *Lingua franca*   English
4. Official language   English

SOURCES: Elizabeth Colson, "The Assimilation of Aliens among Zambian Tonga," in *From Tribe to Nation in Africa*, eds. Ronald Cohen and John Middleton (Scranton, Pa.: Chandler Publishing Co., 1970). Neville Denny, "Languages and Education in Africa," in *Language in Africa*, ed. John Spencer (London: Cambridge University Press, 1963).

IV. Urban Patterns

Capital/largest city: Lusaka
Dominant ethnicity/language of capital
   Major vernacular: Bemba[1]
   Major ethnic group: Bemba[2]
   Major ethnic group as percent of capital's population:
   16% (1959)

TABLE 32.3   Growth of Capital/Largest City

Date	Lusaka
1920	2,000
1940	20,000
1950	80,000
1960	100,000
1966	170,000 UA

SOURCES: D. G. Bettison, *Numerical Data on African Dwellers in Lusaka* (Lusaka: Rhodes-Livingstone Institute, 1959), and the 1956 census of the Central African Federation. The most recent figure is from the *Europa Yearbook 1967*.

[1] Jan Knappert, "Language Problems of the New Nations of Africa," *African Quarterly*, 5 (1965): 95–105.

[2] D. G. Bettison, *Numerical Data on African Dwellers in Lusaka, Northern Rhodesia* (Lusaka: Rhodes-Livingstone Institute, 1959).

TABLE 32.4   Cities of 20,000 and Over

City	Size	Date
Lusaka	170,000 UA	1966
Kitwe-Nkana	144,000 UA	1966
Ndola	115,000 UA	1966
Mufulira	85,000	1965
Luanshya	81,000	1965
Chingola	65,000	1965
Kabwe	51,000	1965
Livingstone	37,000	1965
Chililabombwe	34,000	1965

SOURCE: *Europa Yearbook 1967*.

The 1963 census stated that the total population in "urban areas" was 667,540 or 19.6 percent of the population. According to the *Statesman's Yearbook 1968–69* the following cities were renamed in 1967:

New name	Former name
Mbala	Abercorn
Chililabombwe	Bancroft
Kabwe	Broken Hill
Mansa	Fort Rosebery
Chipata	Fort Jameson

V. Political Patterns

A. Political Parties and Elections*

Pre-independence Zambia was marked by a struggle over the problem of federation with Southern

* SOURCE: U.S. Department of the Army, *Area Handbook for Zambia* (Washington, D.C.: Government Printing Office, 1969).

Rhodesia and Nyasaland. The *African National Congress* (ANC) under the direction of Harry Nkumbula and the *United National Independence Party* (UNIP) led by Kenneth Kaunda were opposed to the federation while the *National Progress Party*

Figure 32.1 **Political Parties and Elections**

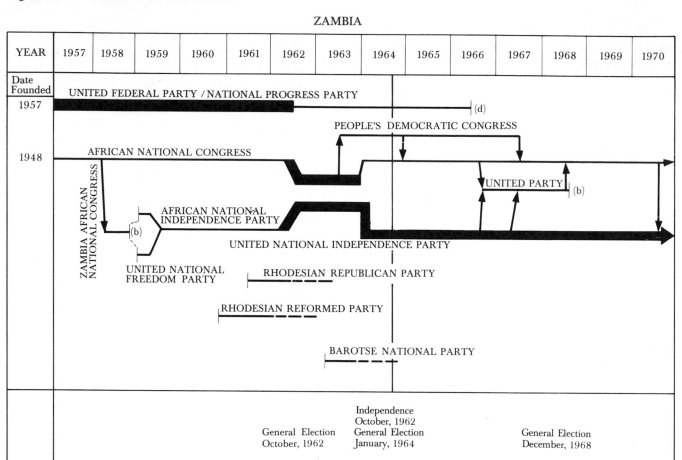

ZAMBIA

(NPP) (formerly known as the *United Federal Party*) favored union. Sir Roy Welensky's NPP lost the 1962 elections and a coalition government was formed between the rival ANC and UNIP with Kaunda at its head. This coalition proved to be unstable, and UNIP won the 1964 election and formed the new government itself. In the December 1968 elections UNIP won 81 seats and the ANC 24 in the Zambia Parliament. The ANC's main strength is in Barotseland.

TABLE 32.5 **Head of Government (Post Independence)**

Name	Dates in Office	Age (1971)	Ethnicity	Education	Former Occupation
1. Kenneth Kaunda (President)	1964–	43	Bemba	Secondary, Zambia Teacher's Certificate	Farmer, Teacher

B. Political Leadership

Kenneth Kaunda has led the government since independence. There was marked cabinet turnover in the 1964–65 period, but ethnic balance has remained unchanged.

TABLE 32.6 Cabinet Membership: Distribution by Ethnic Unit*

Ethnicity*	Independence Cabinet	1967 Cabinet
1. Bemba (37%)	33%	33%
2. Tonga (19)	17	22
3. Nyanja (15)	11	11
4. Lunda-Kaonde (12)	5.6	5.6
5. Mambwe (8)	0	0
6. Barotze (7)	22	22
7. Others (2)	11	5.6
N =	18	18

* Ethnic units arranged in rank order of size within country with the unit's percent of national population in parentheses.

VI. National Integration and Stability

The only coded instance of communal instability in Zambia has been the Lumpa rebellion. Tensions between the Lozi (Barotze), Ngoni and Tongas and the Bemba have been successfully managed so far by the government, although the advocacy of Barotze secession has a long history in Zambia.

TABLE 32.8 Communal Instability

Event and Date	Characteristics
1. Rebellion October 1964– November 1967	a. *Description*: The Lumpa Church of Alice Lenshina was founded in the 1950s as an African Christian faith-healing movement. Its main strength is among the Bemba in northern Zambia. It came into conflict with civil authorities in the pre-independence period. In the early 1960s it came into conflict with UNIP militants, and in 1963 Mrs. Lenshina forbade political activity on the part of her followers. Its religious exclusivism and its potential as a counter-force to UNIP apparently led to continued tensions which resulted in violent confrontations between the church and UNIP in 1963 and the government in July and August 1964. The Church was banned on August 3, 1964. On October 10, 1964 (the eve of Zambian independence) more than 60 members of the church were killed in Luangwa valley, raising the total killed on both sides to some 700 persons. On October 24, 1967, Mrs. Lenshina escaped from jail and more violence broke out. She was recaptured several days later. Many members of the church crossed into Congo (Kinshasa) in exile. b. *Participants*: The Lumpa Church. c. *Apparent Causes*: Tension between a militant religious group and UNIP militants who demanded cooperation with the government.

SOURCES: Gerald L. Caplan, "Barotseland: The Secessionist Challenge to Zambia," *Journal of Modern African Studies*, 6 (1968): 343–360. James W. Fernandez, "The Lumpa Uprising, Why?" *Africa Report*, 9 (November 1964): 30–32. Andrew D. Roberts, "The Lumpa Church of Alice Lenshina," in *Protest and Power in Black Africa*, eds. Robert I. Rotberg and Ali A. Mazrui (New York: Oxford, 1970), pp. 513–568.

VII. Selected References

GENERAL

Davies, D. H., et al. *Zambia in Maps*. London: Hodder & Stoughton, 1970.

Gann, Lewis H. *A History of Northern Rhodesia: Early Days to 1953*. London: Chatto & Windus, 1964.

Hall, Richard. *Zambia*. New York: Praeger, 1966.

Kay, George. *A Social Geography of Zambia.* London: University of London Press, 1967.

Rotberg, Robert I. *The Rise of Nationalism in Central Africa: The Making of Malawi and Zambia, 1873–1964.* Cambridge, Mass.: Harvard University Press, 1966.

Scarritt, James R. *Zambia.* Ithaca, N.Y.: Cornell University Press, forthcoming.

U.S. Department of the Army. *Area Handbook for Zambia.* Pamphlet No. 550–75. Washington, D.C.: Government Printing Office, 1969.

POLITICAL

Kaunda, Kenneth. *Zambia Shall Be Free: An Autobiography.* New York: Praeger, 1963.

Mulford, David C. *Zambia: The Politics of Independence 1957–1964.* London: Oxford University Press, 1967.

Rotberg, Robert I. "Tribalism and Politics in Zambia." *Africa Report,* 12 (December 1967): 29–35.

ECONOMIC

Baldwin, Robert E. *Economic Development and Export Growth: A Study of Northern Rhodesia.* Los Angeles and Berkeley: University of California Press, 1966.

de St. Jorre, John. "Zambia's Economy: Progress and Perils." *Africa Report,* 12 (December 1967): 36–39.

International Monetary Fund. "Zambia." In *Surveys of Africa Economies,* Vol. 4. Washington, D.C.: I.M.F., 1971.

Kay, G. "Agricultural Progress in Zambia," in *Environment and Land Use in Africa,* eds. M. F. Thomas and G. W. Whittington, pp. 495–524. London: Methuen, 1969.

SOCIAL

Brelsford, W. V. *The Tribes of Northern Rhodesia.* Lusaka: Northern Rhodesia Government Printer, 1956.

Mwanakatwe, J. M. *The Growth of Education in Zambia Since Independence.* London: Oxford University Press, 1969.

Powdermaker, Hortense. *Copper Town: Changing Africa. The Human Situation on the Rhodesian Copperbelt.* New York: Harper, 1962.

Taylor, John V., and Dorothea A. Lehmann, *Christians of the Copperbelt.* London: S.C.M., 1961.

Part III

Cross-National Research on Africa: Issues and Context

1. Theoretical Context and the Organization of the Data

The project out of which this book has grown was designed to investigate problems of African national integration and political instability. This chapter outlines our theoretical perspective and relates that perspective to the selection of data and organization in the Handbook.

Integration and instability are often employed as antonyms in the discourse of social scientists, and confusion results from this practice. The ambiguous identification of integration and stability is suggested by passages such as the following:

> By integration we mean the attainment, within a territory, of a "sense of community" and of institutions and practices strong enough and widespread enough to assure, for a "long" time, dependable expectations of "peaceful change" among its population.[1]

We prefer to make the conceptual distinction between integration and instability more definite, and to leave to theoretical and empirical research the problem of explaining the relationship between these two processes of national development.

Types of Political Integration

Integration is a process by which members of a social system (citizens for our purposes) develop linkages and cohesion so that the boundaries of the system persist over time and the boundaries of subsystems become less consequential in affecting behavior. In this process, members of the social system develop an escalating sequence of contact, cooperation, consensus, and community. Integration theory becomes relevant to the analysis of nations only if we can describe individual nations as being more or less integrated in operational terms. We have isolated four conceptual dimensions of integration on which nations may vary: (a) *Horizontal integration*: the linkages and communication between individuals and groups in positions of similar power or subordination. (b) *Vertical integration*: the linkages and communication between individuals and groups in positions of differential power or subordination. (c) *Value integration*: the congruency between the values held by individuals in the system under consideration. (d) *Centralization*: the structural facilities for the extension of central authority and coercion which effect or enforce compliance to the goals of the decision-makers in political systems.

Operational definitions of these dimensions of national integration are suggested throughout this Handbook. *Horizontal integration* is best measured in terms of the frequency of different kinds of transactions within the national system—particularly the movement and exchange of goods, persons, and messages.[2] In the absence of adequate aggregate data on domestic message flows, trade flows, or travel flows, it may be useful to operationalize the horizontal integration of nations in terms of their communication potential, or their facilities for different kinds of communication.

Reference to *vertical integration* in the literature on political development can be found in the frequent consideration of the mass-elite gap.[3] Unless the elite is able rapidly to communicate its decisions to the mass public, and is able to respond to the demands and feedback from that constituency, the cohesion of the political system is impaired. As Shils suggests,[4] political integration is a function of the inculcation of the core values of the elite population in the minds of those at the periphery of central decision-making institutions. Since, as he further suggests, the iden-

[1] Karl W. Deutsch, et al., "Political Community in the North Atlantic Area," in *International Political Communities. An Anthology* (New York: Doubleday Anchor Books, 1966), p. 2.

[2] See Karl W. Deutsch, "Transaction Flows as Indicators of Political Cohesion," *The Integration of Political Communities*, eds. Philip Jacob and James V. Toscano (New York: J. B. Lippincott Co., 1964), pp. 75–97.

[3] See Leonard Binder, "National Integration and Political Development," *American Political Science Review*, 57 (1964): 622–631; Myron Weiner, "Political Integration and Political Development," *The Annals*, 358 (1965): 52–64; and Claude Ake, *A Theory of Political Integration* (Homewood, Ill.: Dorsey Press, 1967).

[4] See Edward Shils, "Center and Periphery," in *The Logic of Personal Knowledge: Essays Presented to Michael Polanyi* (London: Routledge and Kegan Paul, 1961).

tities of the elite tend to become valued in themselves, we may develop operational measures of vertical integration in terms of the ethnic representativeness of elite groups, and of the degree to which the educational "status" of elites are achievable by the mass population.

Value integration or congruency is central to theories of political integration. Jacob stresses the theoretical primacy of values in the process of integration.

> From the standpoint of integration, one might say that the social norms represent, at the same time, the principal guarantor of the society and cohesiveness of the community in which they are held and the principal barrier to action intended to promote unity and cooperation across community lines. The more widely diffused and the more firmly implanted the social norms of a community, the more stable, predictable and cohesive it is likely to be; but at the same time, the more resistant it will be to political and social change except on terms which will allow it to preserve and extend its particular mix of social norms.[5]

Our operational approach to the distribution of social values in African nations is closely tied to the conceptualization of cultural pluralism.[6] Kuper and Smith distinguish between pluralism and plural societies,[7] reserving the latter term to denote societies in which the "ruling class" has a distinctive ethnic identity. We, however, are concerned with the more general case of pluralism in which two or more ethnic groups within a single territory maintain distinctive cultural systems, but interact for limited economic and political purposes.[8] The indicators of

cultural pluralism or value integration in this book relate to differences of language, religion, and ethnicity in the populations of black African nations. The operational treatment of ethnicity and cultural pluralism is particularly complex, and Chapter 4 of Part III is devoted to a lengthy discussion of this subject.

Finally, *centralization* as a dimension of national integration is related to the development of central political institutions which develop increasing capabilities for significantly affecting the distribution of resources and rewards throughout the national territory, and which increasingly establish a monopoly of control over the means of coercion.[9] Centralization can be operationalized in terms of the characteristics of political institutions[10] like parties, legislatures, legal systems, and bureaucracies, and in terms of the growth of coercive potential as measured by the size and financing of military and security forces.

The Organization of the Data

In our work on the theory of integration and its application to the analysis of political development in contemporary Africa, we have tried to select aggregate data which would be useful in measuring the major dimensions of nations which are hypothetically related to political integration and instability. The sixteen chapters of Part I of this book present the major results of this effort.

---

[5] Philip E. Jacob, "The Influence of Values in Political Integration," in *The Integration of Political Communities*, eds. Jacob and Teune, p. 243.

[6] Cultural pluralism as we use the term here should be sharply distinguished from the notion of political pluralism as the differentiation and non-cumulative distribution of power. Our sense of this term is close to that of Van den Berghe: "A society is pluralistic to the extent that it is structurally segmented and culturally diverse." Pierre Van den Berghe, "Towards a Sociology for Africa," *Social Forces*, 43 (October 1964): 11–18.

[7] See Leo Kuper and M. G. Smith, eds., *Pluralism in Africa* (Berkeley: University of California Press, 1969).

[8] Economic interaction was the condition stated in the classic definition of pluralism by Furnivall. "He sees such a society as arising as a result of the extension of commerce and trade, so that a market situation of a new type emerges in which those who participate do not share common values, customs and social institutions, but live for other than economic activities apart from one another in separate groups." John Rex, "The Plural Society in Sociological Theory," *British Journal of Sociology*, 19 (1959): 116. In post-colonial

situations, however, national political organization is an important addition to economic organization as a context for inter-ethnic interaction.

[9] This dimension of political integration has been most clearly underlined by Etzioni:

"A political community is a community that possesses three kinds of integration: (a) it has an effective control over the use of the means of violence . . . (b) it has a center of decision-making that is able to affect significantly the allocation of resources and rewards throughout the community; and (c) it is the dominant focus of political identification for the large majority of the politically-aware citizens."

Amitai Etzioni, *Political Unification: A Comparative Study of Leaders and Forces* (New York: Holt, Rinehart and Winston, 1965) p. 4.

[10] The importance of institutionalization in a more general sense than centralization is stressed by Samuel Huntington in his "Political Development and Political Decay," *World Politics* (1966): 378–414, and *Political Order in Changing Societies* (New Haven: Yale University Press, 1968).

A starting point in any analysis of political development is a consideration of the scale of the national unit. Chapter 1, on ecology and demography, presents data on the territorial size of nations, and the potential scale of national growth and importance in terms of population and geographical characteristics of each of the 32 nations. In Chapter 2, on language and religion, we discuss measures that are relevant to the operationalization of both cultural pluralism and communications potential as dimensions of national integration. Chapters 3, 4, 5, and 6 provide data on the economic resources and output of black African nations.

The data on education in Chapter 5 are particularly relevant to the analysis of changes in the mass-elite gap,[11] and the data on communications and transport in Chapter 6 are clearly relevant to the measurement of communications potential, and horizontal integration. Data in Chapter 7 (political regime characteristics), Chapter 8 (political parties and elections), and Chapter 9 (the extent of government influence) are related to the analysis of the centralization of the political authority, and the data in Chapter 10 (military and security systems) are useful for the analysis of coercive potential as a dimension of national integration.

Data on political instability are presented in Chapter 11, and may be used to investigate the relationship between different processes of integration and different forms of political instability. Chapters 12, 13, and 14 give data on different patterns of international relations, which may relate to the centralization of authority, the intensification of mass-elite discontinuities, the external support of domestic coercive potential, and to different patterns of domestic political instability. Chapters 15 and 16 contain information relating to urbanization and ethnicity. These data are placed at the end of Part I because they are collected by distinctive aggregation procedures where cities and tribes were the units of aggregation. The data in Chapter 15 are relevant to the analysis of urban-rural discontinuities which may be considered a particular case of pluralism or the mass-elite gap, but more obviously, these data indicate growth in the differentiation, communication, and interdependence of national populations.

[11] As a result of differential socialization experiences.

The ethnic data in Chapter 16 are directly related to the measurement of value congruence within national populations, although the collection and interpretation of these data is an extremely complicated matter, which is given extensive treatment in Chapter 4 of Part III.

Data Omissions

It is necessary to comment on some major categories of data which are relevant to our interests, but are nevertheless not reported, or not sufficiently well reported, in this book. Three categories of missing data are outstanding: (1) adequate time-series data; (2) data for units other than nations, urban centers, and ethnic groups; and (3) data on the colonial and pre-colonial experience.

(1) Any discussion of national political development, and any analysis of integration, is the more satisfactory as it relies on the explication of time-series relationships. Throughout this book, we have tried to emphasize temporal characteristics of the data, and to give rates of change and historical coverage for the variables as often as possible. Nevertheless, it will be clear that the bulk of the data in this book are relevant only to the post-independence period, and that on many conceptually critical dimensions we have little or no change data at all.[12]

(2) Political integration and instability are functions of the interaction, cohesion and conflict among numerous groups in national populations. Data aggregated as the sum of the characteristics of individuals, or a sample of all individuals, in the population are clearly inadequate in dealing with complex relationships between social actors whose characteristics are not reflected by the per capita aggregate for the population. This problem is discussed in the next chapter with reference to the treatment of ecological fallacies in explanations based on aggregate data, and here it is sufficient to observe that we

[12] Work is proceeding in certain areas but the compilation of pre-independence data is painstaking. We hope that other scholars working in this area might add their data to the Black Africa data bank and so make it available to other scholars through future editions of this Handbook and the data bank operation described in Appendices 1 and 2.

have tried to develop aggregate data on sub-national units such as urban centers and ethnic groups. In addition, we tried to get information on national interest groups, particularly labor unions, and political parties, which are institutions theoretically related to the centralization of authority, mass-elite linkage and value congruence in the national political system. We were not, however, able to collect systematic or sufficiently comprehensive data on these units for all nations.[13] An attempt at content analyzing selected writings of African political leaders in order to develop alternate measures of value congruence or ideological style was also a failure due to a lack of resources for handling the exorbitant costs of content analysis, and the lack of any reasonably comparable set of available documentation for each nation from which to sample observations. Finally, a very considerable effort has been invested in collecting background information on political elites. We have concentrated on the membership of the independence, pre-coup, post-coup, and 1967 cabinets in each nation. Our data on cabinet ethnicity is now all but complete, but there remain large gaps in the information on education, career-experience, former occupation, and the background of the parents of these elites.

Data descriptive of nations may and should be aggregated from the characteristics of sub-national units such as those we have just described—ethnic units, urban centers, political parties, trade unions, elite groups, etc. Characteristically, however, quantitative descriptions of nations are based on the aggregate characteristics of individuals, and are given in the form of a per capita average. As applied to theoretical analysis, such data are oftentimes misleading since they give no indication of the range of deviation from the measures of central tendency, or, put otherwise, of the level of inequality in the distribution of particular values in individual nations. In this respect, also, our data are not adequate, since the data necessary for constructing measures of inequality or giving indices of variance are not available to us. Ideally, we would want sufficiently

detailed information on personal income distribution, and data on land ownership which would facilitate the construction of indices of inequality in the distribution of income and real estate.[14] Apart from measures of deviation from a model of equal distribution of values to individuals, it would be particularly useful for theories of national integration to have data on the variation between regions in the distribution of values, but a satisfactory definition of "region" for comparative analysis is as difficult as is the disaggregation of available data by region.[15]

(3) The discussion so far of the omission of important categories of data from this book has been implicitly concerned with data relevant to "contemporary" black African political development. The discussion, and the book itself, is heavily oriented towards the post-independence period—i.e., the period in which our primary units of analysis, nation-states, were recognizable and relatively autonomous entities. Nevertheless, adequate time-sensitive analysis requires data for periods well in advance of the independence of these new nations, and different patterns of integration and instability are likely to reflect different patterns of colonial and pre-colonial development in the territories we now identify as nations. Since we do not have quantitative data on these periods, it will be important to indicate the possible sources of variation in contemporary political development which may in the future be well operationalized, and, therefore, analytically significant.

The Colonial Legacy: A Problem in Comparing African Nations

The most obvious, but perhaps least well explored, basis of variation in contemporary African political development is the origin of colonial rule.

... Only if we appreciate the very different approach to African society on the part of the British and French, can we

[13] Comprehensive data on African political parties for some of the nations covered in this book are being collected for the International Comparative Political Parties Project at Northwestern University under the direction of Kenneth Janda.

[14] See Hayward R. Alker, Jr., and Bruce M. Russett, "Indices for Comparing Inequality," in *Comparing Nations*, Merritt and Rokkan, pp. 349–372.

[15] See Juan J. Linz and Armando de Miguel, "Within-Nation Differences and Comparisons: The Eight Spains," and Erik Allardt, "Implications of Within-Nation Variations and Regional Imbalances for Cross-National Research," in *Comparing Nations*, Merritt and Rokkan, pp. 267–219 and 337–348.

understand the very different courses their political development has taken both during the struggle for independence and since.[16]

But the comparative analysis of colonialism is exceedingly complex and, although the broad differences between colonial policies of assimilation, indirect rule, and paternalism generally describe the differences between French, British, and German colonial practice, there is considerable variation in the degree of intervention in the pre-colonial African social and political structures that existed within the different territories governed by the same colonial power.[17] Therefore, instead of trying to force African political development into explanations of a colonial mold, it is advisable to consider the major dimensions of integration we use to describe contemporary African nations, and to suggest how variations in colonial practice inhibit or facilitate the integration of new nations.

The impact of colonial policy on the development of communication facilities in Africa was, of course, important yet, from another perspective, the economic basis of colonialism greatly inhibited the potential growth in this area. Railways and roads were developed for contact with economically profitable colonial hinterlands, but the exploitative basis of colonial economics was such that most of the railroads in West Africa necessary for the transportation of goods valued in Europe were built by the end of the first World War,[18] and relatively little expansion of transportation facilities took place in the inter-war years. What road-building there was after the 1920s was planned as an extension of the railroad and thus followed the quickest route to Europe to the neglect of the most economically productive linkages for the indigenous population of the territory. In terms of the development of communications facilities in Africa, it is therefore likely that the integration of contemporary states is more a function of the geographic dispersion of the products valued in Europe than of differences in European colonial practice.[19] Nevertheless, comparative data on the historical

growth of railroads, and the roads and telegraphs that were linked to them, would be important to the analysis of contemporary political development.

The impact of colonial policy on the pluralism of the territories partitioned in the "scramble for Africa" was perhaps as much a function of pre-colonial development as of differences in European practices. Where the territories ruled by colonial powers were already culturally heterogeneous, the effects of colonialism were often to intensify that heterogeneity. All colonial powers introduced European languages as forces for integration. The introduction of these European languages can be seen as inhibiting the integration of many African nations by adding an additional dimension to pre-existing linguistic pluralism. This is true also of the colonialists' religion. Christian missionary activity was generally less intrusive in French territories because of a well-entrenched legal tradition of the separation of church and state, but in all colonies the importation of the sectarianism of Christianity added to the cultural heterogeneity of the territories that were to become independent states.

A more variable impact of colonial policy on the integration of ethnically plural territories derives from the generally more "direct," "interventionist," or "centralized" character of colonial administration in the territories controlled by France, compared to the colonial administration practiced by Britain. British and French colonial administrations have been characterized as "indirect" and "direct," respectively,[20] although recent analysis is tending to blur the distinctions.[21] Indirect rule worked through traditional ethnic authorities in the fields of taxation, law, succession to leadership, and community boundaries. Traditional ethnic communities were allowed to continue under their leadership. A British "resident" (or, at a lower level, "district officer") was in an advisory position *vis-à-vis* the local authorities.[22] This policy had the effect of reinforcing existing language and ethnic groups. The French system of

[16] See Michael Crowder, *West Africa under Colonial Rule* (Evanston, Ill.: Northwestern University Press, 1968) p. 235.

[17] *Ibid.*, p. 112.

[19] *Ibid.*, p. 315.

[19] *Ibid.*, p. 274.

[20] See Michael Crowder, "Indirect Rule, French and British Style," *Africa*, 34 (1964): 197–205.

[21] See the articles in Michael Crowder and Obaro Ikine, eds., *West African Chiefs: their Changing Status Under Colonial Rule and Independence* (Ife, Nigeria: University of Ife Press, 1970).

[22] See, for example, Robert Heussler, *The British in Northern Nigeria* (London: Oxford University Press, 1968).

direct rule, by contrast, established administrative units which cut across traditional ethnic boundaries. While traditional leaders were often retained on stipend, they were regarded as functionaries, and did not have real power and, more often than was the case in British territories, African authorities were selected and appointed by the French rather than by traditional procedures. Administratve districts were organized into "circles" which were directly responsible to the territorial governors. The effects of these differences in policy may have been to decrease the degree of ethnic pluralism in African states inherited from French colonial rule, and to intensify that pluralism in territories ruled by the British. But in order to evaluate this hypothesis we need comparable data on the degree of intervention and restructuring characteristic of colonial administrations in all of the new African states.

The effects of colonial policy on elite formation, and on the "vertical" integration between elites and mass populations are far too complicated to detail here. In general, it might be argued that "more direct" forms of colonial administration widened the gap between elites and masses, and, therefore, that elite-mass tensions are likely to be more pronounced in former French territories than in other areas. But the differences between colonial policy seem less relevant than the similarity in colonial interference with traditional patterns of elite recruitment. Western education everywhere became a basis for access to new elite position, and the independent position of traditional economic elites was obliterated by the impact of the colonial economy.[23] The impact of education, in particular, was complicated by the tendency for education in French territories to be more narrowly distributed, but less restricted to families of traditional notables than in English colonial territories.[24] The changes in elite formation that resulted from colonial practice affected the centralization of authority in post-independence

Africa as much as they affected mass-elite relationships. In this regard, it is probable that French policy stimulated the growth of centralized political institutions more than was true of British colonial policy. The direct experience of African politicians in legislative institutions, both in France and in the colonial territories, and their recruitment to centralized colonial hierarchies, contrasts with the much more recent legislative experience in British colonies, where indirect rule generally encouraged decentralized patterns of administration.[25]

Finally, we should consider the impact of colonialism on the inheritance by African nations of facilities for coercion as an instrument of integration. The growth of military forces in colonial territories was affected by European aggression outside of Africa and by African resistance to colonial administration within the continent. In the first World War, the French used more African troops in Europe than did their British allies,[26] but both recruited extensively. In the second World War, after the end of the Vichy administration in French West Africa, over 100,000 African soldiers fought on the Allied front between 1943 and 1945 along with a very considerable number of troops from British colonies. African soldiers from French territories also saw action in the French wars in Southeast Asia and Algeria. Aside from this extensive military service, the armies developed in French territories were commanded by African officers sooner, and in greater numbers, than was the case in British territories.[27] This experience, coupled with the relatively undramatic movement to independence in French Colonial Africa as compared to the more vociferous and violent transition in British territories, may be interpreted as leading to more effective professional agencies of coercion in the

---

[23] The impact of colonialism on the role of indigenous economic elites was particularly strenuous, and is worth detailed investigation in the analysis of post-colonial economic development. See Crowder, *West African Chiefs*, p. 286.

[24] See Remi Clignet and Philip Foster, "French and British Colonial Education in Africa," *Comparative Education Review*, 8 (October 1964): 191–198, and their *The Fortunate Few* (Evanston, Ill.: Northwestern University Press, 1966).

[25] For details on the legislative experience of African politicians in France and in French territories see Ruth Schachter Morgenthau, *Political Parties in French-Speaking West Africa* (London: Oxford University Press, 1964). The effects of these differences in the institutionalization of territorial authority had repercussions on the style of anti-colonial struggle. See Crowder, *West African Chiefs*, p. 200.

[26] The French recruited some 200,000 men in West Africa, compared to the 30,000 recruited by the British in that area. Throughout Africa, however, the British recruited over 370,000 men, slightly under half of whom gained experience outside of their home territories. See Roger Murray, "Militarism in Africa," *New Left Review*, 38 (July–August 1966): 36–59.

[27] J. M. Lee, *African Armies and Civil Order* (London: Chatto & Windus, 1967), p. 39.

former French territories than in British-controlled areas. In all areas, however, army and police forces had to make the very difficult transition from agencies of colonial reaction against African nationalists to agencies of support for those men and organizations after independence.[28] Here again, the French colonial heritage may have been more conducive to the later abilities of African governments to enforce their will, since French colonial troops were not necessarily stationed in the territories from which they were recruited and French metropolitan troops and commanders remained stationed in Africa in large numbers after independence to support their "colleagues" in African armies in the maintenance of regimes loyal to the French "Community."[29]

Theory and Research

A special purpose of this Handbook is to facilitate the empirical analysis of political development in African nations by providing data to test theories explaining the integration and stability of political systems. In this chapter, we have sketched the theoretical context in which the data have been collected, and have indicated the limitations of the data in providing a composite picture of, or explanation of, political development in Africa. We discuss in the following

[28] See A. A. Mazrui and D. Rothchild, "The Soldier and the State in East Africa," *Western Political Quarterly*, 20 (1967).

[29] In 1964, the number of French garrisons in Africa was reduced involving a reduction in troops from 35,000 to 16,000. See *Africa Report* (November 1964).

chapters a range of methodological issues relating to the comparative analysis of African nations using the kinds of data we have included in the Handbook. It is important here to conclude by emphasizing that the adequacy of data and methodology in cross-national analysis can be evaluated *only* in terms of *theories* about the logical and hypothetical interrelationship of concepts which the data describe.

Although the elaboration of theory is not a concern of this Handbook,[30] we have had concepts and theories in mind in preparing the book, and the reader is advised to consider the central importance of theory to any satisfactory use of the data. In the words of Erik Allardt:

Theory is more important in cross-national research than in any other field. When doing national studies or studies of narrow subjects, the researcher may have hunches about the validity of his indicators or operational definitions. He is able to assess the face validity of his indicators. In comparative research, in which many and greatly varying environments are compared, it is not humanly possible to have hunches about the face validity of all indicators. Unless the researcher in cross-national research has a theory or some system of hypotheses which guide him, he will almost assuredly encounter a situation in which he regards as similar phenomena things which are actually different and which measure different things.[31]

[30] See, however, Donald George Morrison and Hugh Michael Stevenson, *Conflict and Change in African Political Development* (New York: The Free Press, forthcoming), for an attempt to develop a coherent theory that is tested with data on African nations.

[31] Erik Allardt, "Implications of Within-Nation Variations and Regional Imbalances for Cross-National Research," in *Comparing Nations*, eds. Richard L. Merritt and Stein Rokkan (New Haven: Yale University Press, 1966), p. 348.

2. Comparative Analysis of African Nations: On the Uses and Limitations of Cross-National Data

A detailed account of comparative methodology or cross-national research in the social sciences is not possible here, although such a work is needed.[1] It is important, however, to indicate the purposes of cross-national research and the possibilities and limitations of such research in Africa. The discussion here is designed primarily to speak to professional social scientists and "Africanists," some of whom may be either dubious of the value of comparative research using aggregate data on macro-social entities such as nations, or skeptical of the validity of quantitative, comparative analysis.

This chapter discusses the following questions: (1) Are nations comparable? (2) Why focus on black African nations, and what are the limitations of such a focus? (3) What kinds of approaches can be adopted to investigate questions about social life by comparing nations? (4) How accurately can one describe nations, and how much confidence can one have in the accuracy of generalizations based on the comparison of nations, and (5) how does one interpret such generalizations?

Nations as Units of Analysis in Comparative Research

Social science aims to establish generalizations about human behavior. All generalizations involve the comparison of two or more similar entities, and comparison is as basic to art as it is to science. A metaphor and a proposition both demand the comparison of entities which are not identical, but whose common properties may give us a richer knowledge of the individual entities. The need for comparison in the social sciences is well-illustrated by David McClelland:

> It is perhaps because I have spent time analyzing particular cases that I feel the need for generalizations and a comparative frame of reference. It is so easy to be mistaken if you analyze only a particular case. The clinical psychologist may decide, for example, that George is neurotic because his mother mistreated him. The detailed case record makes the point very clear. Yet might not the clinician's view of the case be quite different if he knew that mothers from George's social background generally mistreated their sons and that most of those sons did not become neurotic?[2]

Our concern with cross-national analysis is based on similar argument. It may well be argued that a *coup d'état* in Ghana, for example, was the result of a highly personalistic regime,[3] or the result of the inhibiting consequences of neo-colonialist manipulation of the Ghanaian economy,[4] but if we discover that other African countries that have equally personalistic regimes and suffer equally from foreign economic domination—for example, the Ivory Coast—do not have coups d'état, we may be less happy with such explanations, and search for factors other than personalism and neo-colonialism as explanations of all, or most, cases of coup d'état.

But this argument begs too many questions, the most important of which is: are nations comparable in the same sense as McClelland's individuals? What do Gambia and Zaire (Congo K.), for example, have in common? While this is a question for empirical analysis, it is also a question which must

---

[1] The best general review of comparative methodology is Robert M. Marsh, *Comparative Sociology* (New York: Harcourt, Brace and World, 1967), but a comprehensive analysis of cross-national research in political science would be a valuable complement to Marsh's broader focus on societies and the sociological and social anthropological literature. Adam Przeworski and Henry Teune, *The Logic of Comparative Social Inquiry* (New York: Wiley-Interscience, 1970) does much to meet this need on the level of theory and measurement. Some valuable discussions of methodology in cross-national research are contained in Richard L. Merritt and Stein Rokkan, eds., *Comparing Nations* (New Haven: Yale University Press, 1966), and in Stein Rokkan, ed., *Comparative Research across Cultures and Nations* (Paris: Mouton, 1968).

[2] David C. McClelland, *The Achieving Society* (New York: Van Nostrand, 1961), p. viii.

[3] See Henry C. Bretton, *The Rise and Fall of Kwame Nkrumah* (New York: Praeger, 1966).

[4] See Bob Fitch and Mary Oppenheimer, "Ghana: The End of an Illusion," *Monthly Review*, 18 (July–August, 1966).

be answered prior to the inclusion of these two countries in a sample of units for cross-national analysis. According to Przeworski and Teune:

> To study something "comparatively" often means that at some stage countries become units of analysis. However, the very choice of countries as units of analysis threatens the validity of the findings. Accumulated experience leads to the expectation that most of the third, or intervening, variables that alter the character of examined relationships are to be found at the level of the nation-state. Concepts are expected to have different meanings in different countries. Relationships are expected to differ more between countries than within a single country . . . The critical problem in cross-national research is that of identifying "equivalent" phenomena and analyzing the relationships between them in an "equivalent" fashion.[5]

The initial problem is to determine how much alike phenomena must be in order to be used as a basis for comparative generalization. This is as much a problem of unit equivalence as it is a problem of the equivalence of indicators (which Przeworski and Teune discuss). The common dictum that you cannot compare apples and oranges is frequently the point of arguments made against cross-national research, and it needs to be considered.

The Problem of Unit Equivalence

That apples and oranges are different entities is accepted by most people, but it is also accepted that both apples and oranges are fruits, and that certain generalizations for fruits will describe some aspects of both varieties. In set theoretic terms, the sets (a, b, c, d) and (x, b, y, d) have the subset (b, d) in common, and if we can make generalizations about the behavior of (b, d) we can say something about both sets, even though the interaction of the unique elements in each set may be such as to drastically limit the power of generalizations about (b, d). This then is the essential problem of unit equivalence in cross-national research: what number of characteristics do two or more nations have in common, and what are the limits of comparison and generalization imposed on cross-national research by the range of this commonality?

[5] Adam Przeworski and Henry Teune, "Equivalence in Cross-National Research," *Public Opinion Quarterly*, 30 (1966–67): 552.

There is no clear-cut answer to this problem, and perhaps it should be recognized as an unanswerable problem. The limits of unit equivalence are set by the goals of the researcher, and different levels of analysis are suitable modes of comparison for different problems and differences in data availability. There seems to be no *a priori* way to compare the range of non-equivalence in a set of individuals or in a set of national units. The conceptual equivalence of the units of analysis is a first-order assumption of any scientific investigation, and the fruitfulness of that assumption is determined by the degree to which generalizations based on a set of units provide satisfying results. Individuals have no more intrinsic "comparative" utility than nations. According to Kaplan:

> A scientist *may* use whatever concepts he *can* use, whatever ones he finds useful in fact. The restriction to which he is subject is only that what he says be capable of being checked by experience, or alternatively, capable of providing some guidance to action . . . The choice of locus (the selection of units of analysis) is subject to the demand of empirical anchorage, but not necessarily to that of physicalistic reduction. The behavior in behavioral science does not serve to limit the science's choice of conceptual base but only to emphasize its ultimate empiricism.[6]

If we take this open-ended and pragmatic approach to what Kaplan calls "the autonomy of inquiry" and "the autonomy of the conceptual base," it is nevertheless important to explain the selection of a particular set of units of analysis. For this Handbook, it is necessary to justify the concentration of national units in general, and African national units in particular.

The Equivalence of Nations

Nations as social entities are the subject of a very considerable conceptual and theoretical analysis.[7] For our purposes nations are geographically-bounded entities in which legal sovereignty is recognized to

[6] Abraham Kaplan, *The Conduct of Inquiry* (San Francisco: Chandler Publishing Co., 1964), p. 79.

[7] See the excellent discussion in Karl W. Deutsch, *Nationalism and Social Communication*, 2nd ed. (Cambridge: Massachusetts Institute of Technology Press, 1966).

be the prerogative of indigenous authorities. These parameters in the definition of nations change, of course, over time, but at any one time it is possible to establish the boundaries of a nation in these terms: what are the geographical frontiers of the national entity; who lives within those frontiers, and what proportion of them have the rights and obligations accruing to citizens; what institutions and officers are recognized as having the right to make rules for the behavior of citizens, and the right to enforce these rules in the event that citizens do not comply with them? These questions make clear the exclusively political character of nations—the laws which define them and the human relationships which sustain them are products of political action, and the importance of nations as subjects of academic study relates directly to the assumed importance of the impact of political decisions made by national authorities on the lives of people.

Our own evaluation of the importance of nations relates to the general historical development of nation-states as political entities, and, more particularly, to the development of nations in twentieth-century Africa. The growth of nationalism since the French Revolution has been a paradoxical conflict between an increasing institutionalization of the demands for individual liberty, fraternity, and equality, and an increasing alienation of individual and primary group autonomy to the more encompassing authority and coercive power of national governments. As men have expanded their conceptions of the scope of individual freedom so they have expanded the institutional means for the limitation of freedom, and nations born in revolution have all too easily given birth to totalitarianism.

The prospect of a resolution of this inherent conflict in the growth of nationalism has been the greatest stimulation to social scientists, who have heralded either the withering away of the state or the emergence of supra-national government. But as the dialectic continues, national citizenship becomes an increasingly unavoidable experience and the range of activities in which the life of the citizen is affected by national governments increases. The maintenance of territory, citizenship, and government as established in contemporary nations becomes increasingly a matter of life and death as the continued history of

struggles for national liberation or secession attests, and attempts at supra-national organization are founded on the fundamental assumption of the legitimacy of the principles of territorial integrity and internal sovereignty of nations.

The Development of African Nations

The recency of the African experience with independent nation-states has not made for any less concern with the centrality of nationalism in the political culture of Africa as compared to other places. Of the 32 countries considered in this Handbook, only Ethiopia and Liberia were independent prior to 1955. Sudan became independent in 1956, and in 1957 Ghana became the first all-black African state to emerge from the colonial era. By 1960, most of the French-speaking states and Nigeria had opted for complete independence. In the early 1960s, the British East and Central African states followed the West African example of independence.

In the 1950s and early 1960s, there was considerable controversy among African statesmen as to the appropriate boundaries for the independent African nations.[8] The boundaries inherited from the colonial era were regarded as artificial and, in fact, as a continuing symbol of colonialism. Proposals were made for larger groupings of states, ranging from regional units of neighboring states, to continent-wide Pan-Africanism. In July 1960, however, a series of events began to occur which polarized the African states: the Zairese army revolted against their Belgian officers, a coup occurred, Katanga attempted secession, and the Zairese civil war began, involving not only the world powers but other African states as well. During the period of the Katanga secession (1960–1963), African states were divided into two ideological groupings, centered at Monrovia and Casablanca, respectively.[9] Yet by

[8] See John N. Paden, "African Concepts of Nationhood," in *The African Experience*, eds. John N. Paden and Edward W. Soja, Vol. I (Evanson, Ill.: Northwestern University Press, 1970). Colin Legum, *Pan-Africanism: A Short Political Guide*, Revised edition (New York: Praeger, 1965) and Vincent Bakpetu Thompson, *Africa and Unity: The Evolution of Pan-Africanism* (London: Longmans, 1969).

[9] See William Zartman, *International Relations in the New African States* (Englewood Cliffs, N.J.: Prentice-Hall, 1966).

1963, it was clear to most African statesmen that such ideological division (which to some extent included disagreement about the means of Pan-African unification) was detrimental to their own goals as well as to Pan-Africanism. The Organization of African Unity (OAU), which was established in Addis Ababa in May, 1963, was a compromise between the Monrovia and Casablanca groups. It was agreed that the territorial boundaries of the African states should be regarded as inviolate, and boundary disputes were to be handled by a special commission of the OAU.[10] In return, the more radical states were assured that the continuing colonial situation in white-dominated southern Africa would receive priority attention by the OAU. In 1965, the African states refused to hold the OAU meeting in Ghana until the government had expelled the various "revolutionary" African governments-in-exile. By the time the OAU meeting was held in Accra (late 1965), it was clear that the principle of territorial integrity and non-subversion of fellow states was well-established.

Since 1963, as political, social, and economic sectors within the national systems of the new independent states became established so too did a sense of national self-interest. Often neighboring countries were in direct competition for sales of primary products on the world market, or were in competition for scarce capital investment resources. While some efforts at regional cooperation developed (notably the Entente between Ivory Coast, Upper Volta, Niger, and Dahomey), there was a strong counter-trend in the direction of weakening earlier ties between states (as in the East African Common Services Organization). With the growth and development of the OAU, there has been a clear reaffirmation of the goals of Pan-Africanism, but the goal of a united continent was premised primarily on the voluntary participation of existing national units. Thus far the position of the OAU participant states on every major issue of attempted secession, irredentism, or border dispute in Africa has been overwhelmingly to affirm the existing state boundaries despite the fact that several states officially recognized Biafra during her recent secession attempt.

[10] *Ibid.*

Africa and Cross-National Comparisons

Having argued that nations are comparable, why do we focus upon only a particular sub-set of nations in this Handbook? Zaire (Congo K.) and Gambia may be less comparable than either nation and Denmark. One pressing reason for the focus upon Africa is the present lack of aggregate data on Africa which makes it difficult to generalize about the universe of nations, since about one-third of all nations in the world are in Africa. Thus, in addition to our own concerns with national integration in Africa, this Handbook attempts to make some contribution to missing data problems in cross-national research.

A focus upon a particular region of the world makes sense in a more general way, however. Regions of the world, such as Africa, share certain uniformities in historical development which render their constituent countries especially comparable.[11] These uniformities may also present problems relatively unique to the region, such as tribal ethnicity in Africa, that require the attention of specialists. Thus a regional focus permits a more sophisticated use of regional and national data sources and findings. The regional focus also permits consideration of special factors which differentiate the nations in the region, such as the colonial legacy which we discussed briefly in the preceding chapter. The relevance of these factors in the comparison of nations is an empirical question which bears careful analysis, an analysis which is more likely to be successful in an enterprise of limited geographical scope such as this Handbook than in a data collection which makes no such distinctions.[12]

Five Approaches to Cross-National Analysis

If it is accepted that nations are social entities of

[11] For a consideration of the problems of regional variation in the universe of nation-states, see the chapter on "Regionalism versus Universalism in Comparing Nations," in *World Handbook of Political and Social Indicators*, Bruce M. Russett, et al. (New Haven: Yale University Press, 1964), pp. 322–340. For an argument for the collection of comprehensive data on another region, see Phillipe C. Schmitter, "New Strategies for the Comparative Analysis of Latin American Politics," *Latin American Research Review*, 4 (1969), 83–110.

[12] A data bank similar to this one for Africa has been compiled for Latin America by Phillipe Schmitter of the University of Chicago. It is hoped that an eventual consortium of regional data banks would contribute much to cross-national analysis. See Schmitter, *op. cit.*

Figure 2.1

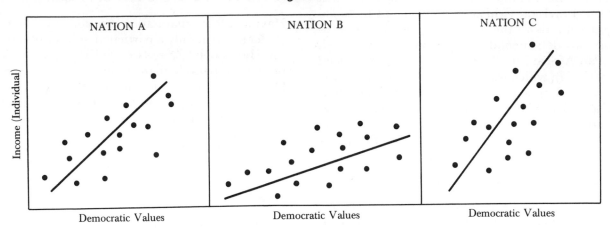

vital significance, and that they are conceptually equivalent as units of scientific and comparative analysis, there remains the question of what different procedures exist to compare nations, and what limitations are placed on our knowledge of national development by the selection of a particular research strategy.[13]

Consider the following question which has attracted some attention in the social sciences: *Do nations tend to become more democratic as they become economically more developed?* More simply stated, is there a relationship between democracy and wealth? In order to discuss possible answers to this question, we are going to ignore the problem of valid operationalization (measurement) of the concepts of wealth and democracy. If we assume that it is meaningful to quantify the concepts in many different ways, what quantitative evidence might provide an answer to our question? At least five possibilities suggest themselves.[14]

Method 1

We might argue that it is reasonable to suppose that democratic institutions will develop in nations in

which individuals hold democratic values and support the existence of such institutions. The answer to the question of whether or not there is a relationship between democracy and wealth in nations may be approached, therefore, in the following way: If in a number of nations people who are wealthier tend to support democratic practices more than people who are poorer, we might have some confidence in stating that nations tend to become more democratic as they become economically more developed.[15] In technical terms, we might present data as in Figure 2.1, in the form of regression lines for each nation.

In each nation the regression line is based on the

between the analyses. In all of the following discussion, we make the basic assumption that there are linear relationships between wealth and democracy, and that the best linear fit (regression line) for observations on these variables can be calculated. It should be clear in considering all the possibilities we outline, however, that given other equally plausible assumptions—e.g., that the relationship between these variables is non-linear—the interpretation of the same evidence could be radically different. Not only may there be curvilinear relationships between wealth and democracy, but the relationships between these variables may shift markedly over time, either in terms of great change in the form of the relationship, or in terms of step-jumps in the historical norm (or intercept) on which the relationship, whose form does not itself change much, is based. This should emphasize the crucial role of theory in the determination of the statistical model to which data is fitted.

[13] See Marsh, *Comparative Sociology*, for a review of the approaches to comparative analysis.

[14] This set of possibilities is intended to be neither exhaustive nor strictly comparable, but rather to suggest how a general problem related to the development of nations might be operationalized at different levels of analysis and to indicate certain communalities

[15] This argument has been clearly stated in the very influential work on the general question of the relationship between economic development and democracy by Seymour M. Lipset, *Political Man* (Garden City, N.Y.: Doubleday, Anchor Books, 1960). See especially the chapter on "Working Class Authoritarianism" as a special test of the general proposition.

Figure 2.2

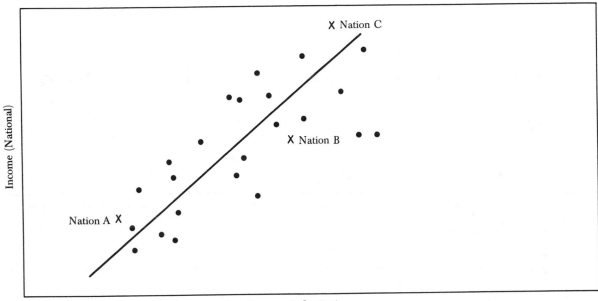

Democratic Institutions

plot of measures of income and democratic values for a sample of individuals in that nation. If we then discover that the form of the relationships (the slope of the regression line) in these countries are not significantly different,[16] or that they are all at least positive, we may argue that we have support for our hypothesis. If not, we may argue that national characteristics, or national political culture, is a significant intervening factor in the relationship between wealth and democracy,[17] and that we cannot generalize that nations tend to become more democratic as they become more economically developed.[18]

Method 2

In contrast to method 1, we might reason that although individual attitudes are critical to the support of democratic institutions, the presence or absence of such institutions in different nations can be observed, and that an answer to our question can be given if we observe that those nations which have more democratic institutions also tend to have greater degrees of economic development.[19] The evidence for such an answer would be presented in a form such as that suggested by Figure 2.2.

In this figure, the regression line states a relationship between aggregate income and democracy based on a plot of the levels of income and democracy in each of a sample of nations at a given point in time. The statistical association summarizing this relationship might be used as evidence for a positive answer to the question of whether or not there is a relationship between wealth and democracy. The nature of this answer, as compared to that provided by method 1 is, however, very different.[20]

[16] Tests of this kind can be made using Bartlett's X^2 test.

[17] The kind of argument we have in mind here is best exemplified in Gabriel Almond and Sidney Verba, *The Civic Culture* (Boston: Little, Brown, 1962).

[18] We might also argue that the assumption behind this method is based on a composition fallacy since the existence of democratic values among certain parts of the national population may be only marginally related to the construction and maintenance of democratic institutions.

[19] This is the form of the argument made most often in the literature, from Lipset's *Political Man* to a recent exploration of this question in Marvin E. Olsen, "Multivariate Analysis of National Political Development," *American Sociological Review*, 33 (1968): 699–712.

[20] Cross-national comparisons such as these do have certain critical comparability assumptions built into them which should be accepted before the hypothesis is evaluated. Most important is the neo-evolutionary view of the development of social and political systems whereby the temporal development of political and economic systems is reflected in the distribution of properties across states at a given point in time.

Figure 2.3

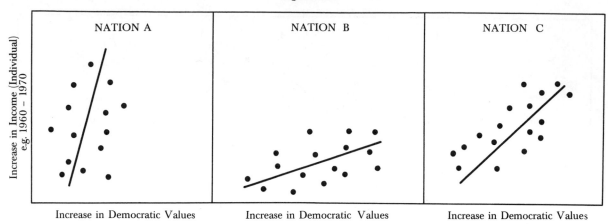

Figure 2.4

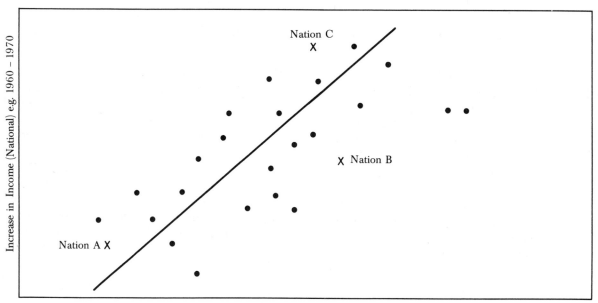

Increase in Democratic Institutions

Method 3

In both methods 1 and 2, we have failed to take temporal relationships into consideration and we have failed to take strict notice of the meaning of *become* in our question—do nations become more democratic as they become more wealthy? A slight but significant modification of method 1 would be to suggest that, if there is evidence in a number of nations that people tend increasingly to support democratic practices as they become wealthier, we should be relatively confident of a positive reply to our question. The evidence for such an answer would be in the form suggested in Figure 2.3.

Here the plot is based on observations of individuals at two different points in time, and each point on the graph indicates the amount of the increase in income, and in the degree of democratic

Figure 2.5

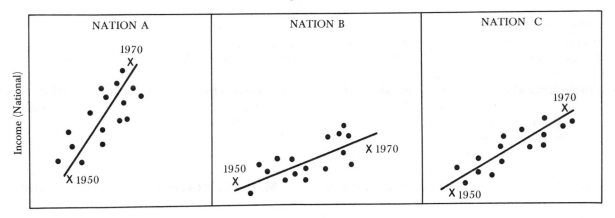

orientation of single individuals from time 1 to time 2. The interpretation of these data, and the decisions about the confidence in making a generalization from such data are the same as in Figure 2.1.[21]

Method 4

An adaptation of method 2 is similar to the procedure outlined in method 3. We may argue that if nations are observed to increase the democratic nature of their institutions as they become more wealthy in the same period of time, then we have reason to give a positive answer to our question.[22]

Method 5

The argument in method 4, as illustrated in Figure 2.4, is based on a very broad time period, and we may require more sensitive, detailed evidence of the pro-

cess by which nations change on the two variables, wealth and democracy. We might therefore consider evidence for each country in the form suggested by Figure 2.5.[23]

In this example, the statistical generalization is based on a plot in which each point represents a country's score on two variables in a particular year. The interpretation of such relationships is complicated by problems of the influence of trend and autocorrelation over time, but the general logic of the argument is, hopefully, clear.

Multi-Method Approach

Each of the five methods is a reasonable basis for making a generalization about nations. If the basic hypothesis was supported by all five methods, we would have reason to be confident in making the generalization that nations tend to become more democratic as they become more economically developed. If only one of the methods was used, positive results would provide some corroboration for the generalization. Positive results for methods 3, 4, and 5 would be more satisfying than positive results from methods 1 and 2, because the former would take into account the contaminating, but

[21] In this model, ignoring any time lag effects, the diagram examines changes in income and its relation to changes in democratic values. Assumptions as to the independence of the starting point for individual scores on each variable are important since end points of the distributions of the variables may be where many individuals are coded. Hence, changes in one direction may be more likely than in another direction. This is commonly known as the "regression effect."

[22] We ignore for the purposes of this outline the critical question of time-lags in theoretical relationships. In addition to the analysis of two change measures, one could suggest relationships between state descriptions of an entity (democratic institutions) and rates of change in a characteristic of the entity at time 2 (income from time 1 to time 2).

[23] As illustrated, the chronological time for which the data in nations A, B, and C is gathered is the same, but these periods may not represent comparable periods of institutional development for different nations.

omnipresent, influence of time. Positive results from methods 3 and 5 provide the strongest corroboration because they compare both the strength and form of the relationship. Nations may become more democratic as they become wealthier, but some nations may do so more rapidly than others, and it is the form of the statistical relationship, or the slope of the regression lines in Figures 2.3 and 2.5, which gives this additional dimension to our evidence.

One argument that does not seem tenable is that results from methods 1 and 3 are more satisfying than results from methods 2, 4, and 5. We cannot say on an *a priori* basis that inference from observations of individuals is necessarily preferable to inference from observations of nations as aggregate social entities. What is certain is that both levels of information are desirable, and that using only one level begs questions that cannot be resolved without reference to the other level. Unless we have results from both methods 1 and 2, we are in danger of committing ecological or composition fallacies in assuming that the results of the test indicated for method 1 will be similar to the tests for method 2. Individuals may tend to support democratic practices in proportion to their personal wealth, but in nations with large numbers of wealthy and democratically-oriented people, there may be a relative absence of democratic institutions. Likewise, nations which are wealthy and democratic may have citizens who are more likely to be democratic the less wealthy they are. Our approach, therefore, is to call for a *multi-method* approach to questions of national development, to recommend the use of various methods for which data are available, and to recommend the systematic collection of data which are presently not available but which are relevant to different methods of solving problems about social and political reality.

Social science does not *prove* anything: it seeks only to provide cumulative evidence for generalizations, and to subject generalizations to empirical tests which may refute them.[24] This Handbook aims, therefore, to provide the best data we can find to test such generalizations. The utility of the Handbook will be demonstrated by its application in cross-national research, and by its stimulation of the collection of new data and the posing of new questions about nations in Africa and throughout the world. Since the data collected in this book are appropriate primarily for national-level analysis, and particularly for cross-sectional comparisons of nations (methods 2 and 4), we should discuss briefly the major problems in assessing the meaning of generalizations based on such comparisons.[25]

Methodological Issues in Cross-National Generalization

In the most general ordinary-language sense, science attempts to provide accurate empirical descriptions of phenomena, and to make generalizations on the basis of such descriptions to future conditions of the phenomena.[26] The questions we ask in this section, therefore, relate to the possibility of accuracy in comparing nations with the data we have collected, and the intelligibility of interpreting statistical relationships between our measures of national characteristics as predictive either to future conditions of nations in Africa or to nations outside Africa.

Cross-national research seeks to evaluate hypothesized relationships by comparing characteristics of nations. Such relationships are normally based on the assumed, or empirically demonstrated, statistical associations between measures on a series of variables for a set of nations. Cross-national research typically follows the analytic paradigm suggested in Figure 2.4. We will confine the discussion of methodological problems to this basic model, shown again in Figure 2.6 representing a hypothesized relationship between economic development and political instability.

---

[24] See the discussion in Robert F. Winch and Donald T. Campbell, "Proof? No. Evidence? Yes. The Significance of Tests of Significance," *The American Sociologist*, 4 (1969): 140–143.

[25] This discussion is necessarily condensed, for details on different points the reader should consult Merritt and Rokkan, eds., *Comparing Nations*; Rokkan, ed., *Comparative Research Across Cultures and Nations*; Charles Louis Taylor, ed., *Aggregate Data Analysis: Political and Social Indicators in Cross-National Research* (The Hague: Mouton, 1968); and for a critical point of view see Oran Young, "Professor Russett: Industrious Tailor to a Naked Emperor," *World Politics*, 21 (April 1969): 486–511.

[26] Of course, in some cases theoretical predictions precede any observation of the phenomenon itself as in the prediction of the existence of Pluto before that planet was sighted.

Figure 2.6

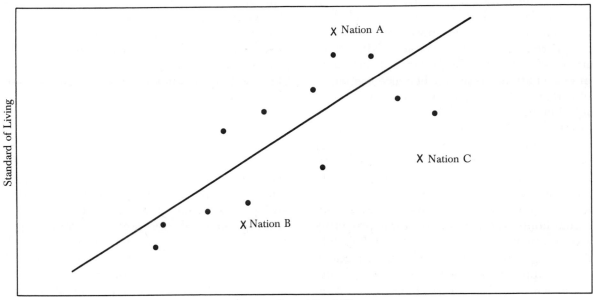

In this model, the nature of the relationship between change in national income and political instability in African nations is indicated by the regression line giving the best linear fit to the observations from which levels of instability can be predicted from a knowledge of levels of national standard of living. As illustrated here, the empirical relationships between these two variables is such that increasing levels of instability are associated with increasing standards of living for a set of nations A, B, . . . N.[27]

A generalization of this kind is subject to several limitations: (1) the validity and reliability of the aggregate data on which the empirical relationship is based, (2) the threat of "ecological" fallacies in inference across different units of analysis, (3) the limits of generalization from the set of nations used in the analysis to the universe of nations or to another time period, and (4) the difficulty of making causal inferences.

Validity and Reliability

If nations are to be accepted as legitimate units for social science research, related concepts and theories of interest to social science must be capable of measurement with valid and reliable data. In Figure 2.6, for example, we illustrate a theoretical relationship between national standard of living and political instability, and the problem is whether or not we can develop measures for national standards of living and political instability which will be valid and reliable. In this context, validity is the approximation of an indicator to the conceptual reality it is said to indicate: is it measuring what we want it to measure? Reliability is a measure of congruence between measures of the same indicator taken by different observers of the same conceptual reality: is the measure stable and repeatable? Since the problem of assessing reliability is discussed in the next chapter, we shall confine the discussion here to the problem of validity in cross-national measurement.

[27] The theoretical interest in these variables in the literature on cross-national research is considerable, although the empirical nature of the relationships between changes in the standard of living and political instability is by no means unambiguous. For a discussion of this and related hypotheses, see Donald G. Morrison and Hugh Michael Stevenson, *Conflict and Change in African Political Development* (New York: The Free Press, forthcoming).

The operational definition of a theoretical concept is a method of measurement for the concept. It is equivalent to the concept only in the vocabulary of operationalism.[28] Finding appropriate ways to measure theoretical concepts is one of the basic problems of social science. The problem of correspondence in cross-national research between aggregate data indicators and macro-theory concepts can be especially difficult.

Nations themselves are not directly observable, and the conceptual dimensions on which they vary are seldom easily equated with measures of some immediately observable characteristics. Macro theory is concerned with the properties of aggregates—groups of people of varying size and complexity. Commonly, the measures of these properties are aggregations from observations on individuals. The validity of such indices, based on aggregated data in the composition of a set of nations, is impaired by at least four possible sources of non-comparability in their measurement of concepts. These are: (1) differences in the way government agencies and researchers operationally define the same concepts; (2) differences in the coverage of the same concepts for different countries (the thoroughness, synchronization, and personnel involved in measurement); (3) error in the observations of different phenomena, even when the observations are made with similar thoroughness and operational definition; and (4) differences in the meaning and importance of similar phenomena in different countries.

The first of these difficulties concerns the lack of standardization in operational procedures used by agencies that collect aggregate data on nations. For example, in computing per capita national income, government agencies in different nations vary in the procedures they use to impute monetary values to goods and services that are not sold in the markets of countries with semi-subsistence economies.[29] The second difficulty relates to the availability and thoroughness of quantitative data that may be relevant to theoretically important concepts. Measures of health facilities and mortality, for example, may be considered fundamental to the measurement of standards of living, but data of this kind are not available for many African countries. When such data do exist, they are often very inadequate estimates. Thirdly, there is the related problem of error in available measurements, due to factors ranging from the political demand for growth on particular variables—especially those relating to standard of living—to the incapacity to collect data from anything but very unrepresentative samples of the national population.[30] Finally, there is the problem of the same indicators being very different in terms of their conceptual importance in different national contexts. The standard of living in a nation which has an almost entirely subsistence economy may be very inadequately measured by per capita income, but the same measure may be very descriptive of the standard of living in a more developed economy.[31]

These are serious difficulties, and some regard them as so serious that they recommend not using most available aggregate data on nations, and imply that most cross-national research is futile if such data have to be used.[32] But validity problems plague all social measurement, and it seems useful to ask what procedures regarded as important in other

---

[28] The classic statement of philosophical operationalism is in Percy W. Bridgman, *The Logic of Modern Physics* (New York: Macmillan, 1927). For a recent discussion of this issue, see Herbert M. Blalock, Jr., "The Measurement Problem: A Gap Between the Languages of Theory and Research," *Methodology in Social Research*, eds. H. Blalock, Jr., and A. Blalock (New York: McGraw-Hill, 1968), pp. 5–27.

[29] In general, national income accounts are calculated on the basis of categories recommended by the United Nations. For particular problems and references, see the discussion of income data in Part I, Chapter 4.

[30] See the discussion of these problems in Donal V. McGrenchan, "Comparative Social Research in the United Nations," *Comparing Nations*, eds. Merritt and Rokkan, pp. 525–544.

[31] A more specific example of this problem relates to the use of measures of vehicles per capita as an operationalization of horizontal integration, or communications potential in African nations. The difficulty is illustrated by Weinstein:

"Even though there is supposed to be one passenger vehicle for every 127 inhabitants (in Gabon), compared with one vehicle for every 180 in the four states of the former federation (AEF), only 6% of all vehicles are used for interior road transportation (in Gabon), compared with 25% in Chad."

Brian Weinstein, *Gabon: Nation Building on the Ogoowe* (Cambridge: Massachusetts Institute of Technology Press, 1966), p. 76.

[32] A particularly blunt critique was given by Arnold S. Feldman in a review of cross-national research in Latin America. See "The New Comparative Politics in Latin America: A Comment," commentary delivered to Latin American Studies Association, New York City, November 8, 1968. See also the commentary on D. P. Bwy, "Political Instability in Latin America: The Cross-Cultural Test of a Causal Model," *Latin American Research Review*, 3 (1968): 17–66.

styles of social research can be adopted to increase validity in cross-national research.

If it is accepted that no single indicator is a completely valid measure of a concept—i.e., that any indicator is only a partial representation of a conceptual phenomenon—there are nevertheless procedures which can be adopted to lend increased confidence to the validity of operationalized variables. Taken in isolation, a concept may be said to have a given meaning, and a number of alternative, equally valid, operationalizations. In cross-national analysis, the validity of a single indicator as a measure of some concept may vary for each nation being studied, and the validity of generalizations made about Africa with respect to that measure would be impossible to assess. One way out of this dilemma is to assess the equivalence of several indicators of the same concept, or to devise a composite index for measures of varying validity, which will minimize the invalidity of the single measures for particular countries. Thus:

> The problem of whether a concept can be measured cross-nationally by a set of identical indicators is empirical. Although complete equivalence is probably never possible, attempts can be made to measure equivalence if they are based on a set of indicators.[33]

This argument can be illustrated with reference to the concept of standard of living. Standard of living might be measured by GNP per capita, GDP per capita, agricultural productivity, price indices, the distribution of educational and medical facilities, the number of telephones, radios, automobiles and other consumer goods, or energy consumption. The validity of these measures of the single concept "standard of living" may be determined by the functional equivalence, or unidimensionality of this set of indicators for a sample of nations. Factor analytic tests for unidimensionality provide a means of testing the equivalence of the indicators in terms of their covariation. Those indicators which do not fall on a single factor have unique variance unexplained by the phenomenon being measured by that factor, which is to say that they appear to measure a dimension that is empirically unassociated with the concept in question. On the basis of such

tests for unidimensionality, one may select either a single representative variable from the loading pattern for the factor, or use a composite index such as factor scores based on all the information about factor structure.[34]

A related approach to the assessment of the validity of aggregate data as measures of social science concepts is derived from multi-method, multi-trait procedures of concept validation.[35] Concepts may be measured by different indicators, and conceptually similar indicators may be measured by different methods. The validity of different indicators can be assessed by the inter-correlation between the values for a particular indicator (trait) as obtained by different methods of observation: the greater the correlation, the greater the validity of the respective measures, or of their methods of operationalization. The assessment of the validity of aggregate data in these terms may be based on the intercorrelation between values of the same conceptual variable based on different sources of information, and on different methods of aggregation. The interrelationship between reliability and validity in these terms is underlined by Campbell and Fiske:

> Reliability is the agreement between two efforts to measure the same trait through maximally similar methods. Validity is represented in the agreement between two attempts to measure the same trait through maximally different methods.[36]

In the view of the above considerations, the data in Part I of this Handbook attempt to provide multiple operationalizations of similar concepts, and to provide data gathered by different observers and different aggregation procedures for conceptually similar variables.

To summarize: all measures of social phenomena are partially accurate in that they invariably involve a margin of error. This does not mean, however, that generalizations based on errorful data are necessarily erroneous; in fact, one can often

---

[33] Przeworski and Teune, "Equivalence in Cross-National Research," p. 556.

[34] For a detailed discussion, and for examples of this mode of index construction, see Morrison and Stevenson, *Conflict and Change in African Political Development*.

[35] See Donald T. Campbell and Donald W. Fiske, "Convergent and Discriminant Validation by the Multi trait—Multi method Matrix," *Psychological Bulletin*, 56 (1959): 82–105.

[36] *Ibid.*, p. 83.

take advantage of error in order to improve the data quality.[37] Unless one assumes that errors are more likely to be random in survey research data than in aggregate data, the methods of index construction and scaling developed from psychometric research[38] are amenable to cross-national research. Such indices may be used to partially neutralize the effects of error and increase construct validity, even when the actual error distribution is not known. Generalizations based on aggregate data descriptions of nations are, therefore, not necessarily less valid or reliable than generalizations based on any other unit of analysis. Instead of holding to a belief in what someone has called the doctrine of the immaculate perception, we should utilize all available data on our environment in order to find cumulative support for social theory, rather than search in vain for error-free and conceptually "pure" measures of social phenomena.

Ecological Fallacies

The ecological fallacy is commonly regarded as being the most clear-cut threat to research based on aggregate data. Ecological fallacies result from imputing the characteristics of a macro-system to its lower level components, and the logical problem is normally illustrated by the improper conclusion that relationships between two ecological variables (i.e. aggregate measures of a group, region, nation, etc.) are also characteristic of the same variables in their disaggregated form (i.e., measures of the component units of the macro-entity, commonly individuals). The most telling demonstration of the ecological fallacy was pointed out by William Robinson,[39] who showed in a dramatic example from the 1930 United States census, that the statistical relationship between color and literacy was .95 when aggregate descriptions of race and literacy for nine census regions were used, but that the same relationship was only .20

when the units of analysis were individuals and the variables used were measures of individual literacy and racial background. Any suggestion from the generalization based on aggregate data that individuals who were black were nearly certain to be relatively illiterate is fallacious. It is, however, proper to generalize that census regions with higher percentages of black residents are likely to have a higher percentage of illiteracy. This last observation is not usually stressed by critics of aggregate data analysis, but it should be emphasized as indicating that the ecological fallacy is not logically necessary to the use of aggregate data.[40]

If the ecological fallacy is not a *sina qua non* of aggregate data analysis, it is nevertheless a problem in most research of this kind because many relationships between aggregate entities, properly generalized only to aggregate entities at the same level, are in fact generalized to the component entities. Unless the generalization is treated as an hypothesis to be tested, with data on the component entities, or as the basis for a social reform which may be treated as an experiment to be evaluated with aggregate data, the ecological fallacy is likely to result.

Take, for example, the relationship between national standard of living and political instability. Theoretical explanations of political instability frequently deal with concepts such as systemic frustration or relative deprivation, which are operationalized in terms of levels or changes in the national standard of living.[41] Based on the assumption that individuals who are frustrated or relatively deprived will act out aggressive behavior, theories of national political instability frequently hypothesize that the lower the level of positive change in national standards of living, the greater the likelihood of political instability. To conclude from this kind of evidence alone that *individuals* whose standard of living is relatively low are most likely to engage in organized subversions of the political system is wrong, although it is often an attractive form of reasoning to those who hope that small-scale adjust-

[37] For a review of this argument, and its particular application to anthropological data, see Raoul Narrol, *Data Quality Control* (New York: The Free Press, 1962).

[38] For a thorough review of this field, see June C. Nunnally, *Psychometric Theory* (New York: McGraw-Hill, 1967).

[39] William S. Robinson, "Ecological Correlations and the Behavior of Individuals," *American Sociological Review*, 15 (1950): 351–357. Przeworski and Teune have an excellent discussion of this in *The Logic of Comparative Social Inquriy*, pp. 57–73.

[40] For an excellent summary of logical and data problems in cross-national research, see Erwin K. Schench, "Cross-National Comparisons Using Aggregate Data: Some Substantive and Methodological Problems," in *Comparing Nations*, eds. Merritt and Rokkan, pp. 131–167.

[41] See Part I, Chapter 11, for references.

Figure 2.7

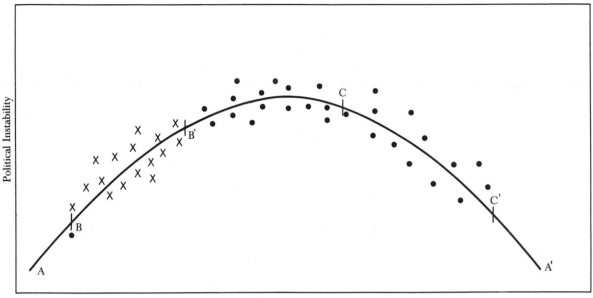

Standard of Living

ments in income distribution can maintain faltering political systems. Without data on the individual level, what can be concluded is only that there is a relationship between standard of living and political instability *in nations*.

With proper caution, ecological fallacies can be avoided in cross-national research. The theoretical advantage of macro-theoretical generalizations based on aggregate data has been most clearly established in economics and it is inadvisable to conclude that similar advantage will not be realized in other areas of social inquiry.

The Limits of Cross-National Generalization

If it is accepted that aggregate data descriptive of nations is not inherently less reliable or valid than survey data for operationalizing concepts in social theory, there are further restrictions on the kinds of generalizations that can be made in cross-national research using aggregate data. Looking again at Figure 2.6, we observe a relationship between national standard of living and political instability, the form of which is such that we would generalize that the greater the standard of living in African

nations, the greater the likelihood that they will experience some form of political instability. It is the purpose of this section to ask just what we can interpret such a generalization to mean.

The first question to be raised is *what relationship does the observation based on Figure 2.6, describing the experience of African nations, have to the experience of other, non-African nations?* The difficulties involved in answering such a question can be illustrated with reference to Figure 2.7.

In this figure we illustrate observations on the two variables under consideration for a hypothetical universe of nations. The observations marked "●" are for non-African nations; those marked "×" are for African nations. All these points represent observations which contain both a "true" score and measurement error,[42] so that the line AA' is the locus of all "true" scores on these variables for the universe of nations. The line BB' is the locus of the "true" scores for the sub-group of African nations in this illustration, and corresponds to the line drawn in Figure 2.6. Looking at these lines, we would generalize that there is a curvilinear relationship (AA') be-

[42] This "true" score is the observed score minus error due to measurement in that observation.

tween the standard of living and political instability in the universe of nations, such that at extreme levels of national standard of living there is a likelihood of relatively low political instability, but between these extremes the likelihood increases. The former generalization from Figure 2.6—that the likelihood of political instability for African nations increases with standard of living—is still true (BB'), but it is apparent that this relationship is not true for the universe of nations since the African nations do not represent a random sample of the world's nations.

The illustration in Figure 2.7 is intentional, although hypothetical. In the first place, curvilinear relationships are frequently hypothesized to exist for the universe of nations, and the illustrated relationship is theoretically intelligible[43] Second, it is important to make this likelihood apparent to users of this Handbook, and to users of any other set of cross-national data, since inasmuch as data for African nations are available, they are often reported in the tail of the distributions for "all" the nations of the world.[44] Furthermore, available handbooks have omitted data for many of the nations of Black Africa. There is a problem that generalizations for the universe of nations might take the form of the line CC' in Figure 2.7, which is as unrepresentative of the true relationship between standard of living and stability, as is the generalization based only on observations from Africa.[45]

This illustration suggests a number of qualifications that have to be made when cross-national generalizations are proposed from data on a set of nations that is less than the universe of nations, and which therefore does not represent fully the historical, ecological, and developmental differences in the

universe. The initial qualification is this: that if the set of nations used is taken from a theoretically homogeneous "region," any generalization of the relationship for that region to other nations may be seriously misleading. Second, if the selection of nations is not based on some regional definition of historical, ecological, or developmental homogeneity, statistical generalizations are likely to be misleading if applied to nations not included in the analysis. The way out of this latter problem is to take a random sample of the nations in the universe. This procedure is not adopted in the present state of the art of cross-national analysis, primarily because of the lack of adequate data on all nations likely to be randomly selected. In the absence of probability sampling, it is not appropriate to make generalizations from cross-national research to individual nations not included in the analysis,[46] and for the user of this Handbook, it is important to realize that any statistical relationship discovered in our data applies only to these 32 African nations, and that it should be regarded as having no known relationship to the general development of the nations of the world. Of course, it is the goal of social science to develop generalizations that apply to the universe of entities under consideration; in cross-national analysis we hope to make statements that apply to all nations. But, until available data permit either the analysis of the universe, or of strict probability samples of the nations of the universe, cross-national generalizations should be made with considerable caution.

---

[43] See, for example, Ivo K. Feierabend, Rosalind L. Feierabend, and Betty A. Nesvold, "Social Change and Political Violence: Cross-National Patterns," in *The History of Violence in America*, eds. Hugh Davis Graham and Ted Robert Gurr (New York: Bantam Books, 1969), pp. 632–687.

[44] See the data reported in Russett, et al., *World Handbook*, and Arthur S. Banks and Robert Textor, *A Cross-Polity Survey* (Cambridge: Massachusetts Institute of Technology Press, 1963).

[45] Of the major cross-national research published recently, Gurr includes 23 "non-Islamic" African countries in his analysis, the Feierabends include four of our countries, and Rummel includes only one. See Graham and Gurr, eds., *A History of Violence in America*, and Rudolph J. Rummel, "Indicators of Cross-National and International Patterns," *American Political Science Review*, 73 (September 1967): 145–172.

[46] This is particularly important when one considers the presentation of correlations, and factor analytic manipulations of these correlations, for sets of nations for which there are extensive missing data. Unless the missing data are distributed randomly, factor analytic models which require correlations to be comparable in terms of their being based on samples of the same universe are inappropriate, and generalizations from the individual correlations apply to different sets of nations, and cannot be considered to hold for countries not included in the calculations. Consider the set of nations for analysis in the following diagram, and the variables A, B, and C. As illustrated the sets of nations used in the calculation of r_{AB}, r_{BC}, and r_{AC} are all mutually exclusive.

Only the set of nations with observations for variable C has any possibility of being a random sample of the universe of nations, and therefore, statistical generalizations based on the mutually exclusive, non-random samples illustrated are not in any way comparable. While this is an extreme example, most correlations based on missing data are likely to have problems like those illustrated here, even if the sets of nations used in each correlation are not mutually exclusive.

Figure 2.8

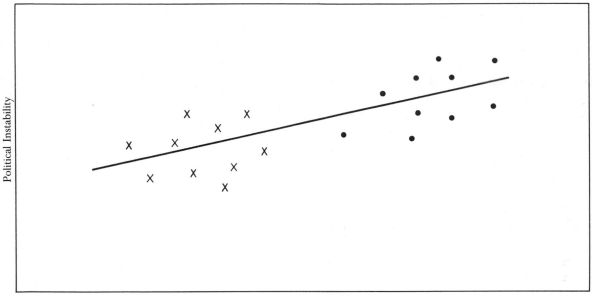

Standard of Living

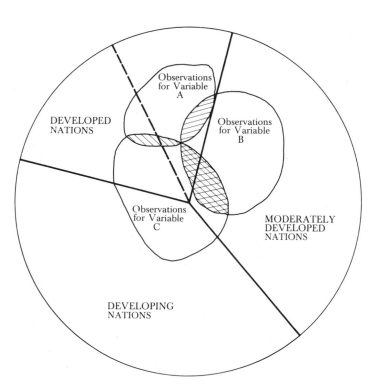

The second question to be asked about the generalization illustrated in Figure 2.6 is *what relationship does the observation that political instability increases with national standard of living have to the experience the same nations may have in future time?* If the generalization for Africa to the effect that increasing political instability varies with increased standards of living is true *ex post facto*, can we predict that the relationship will be true in the future?

An extrapolation of a generalization based on a particular cross-sectional observation of African nations is based on the assumption that although the values of the two variables will change, the relationship between them will not. This assumption, and/or empirical observation, is illustrated in Figure 2.8, where the observations marked "●" are data for a decade after independence, and those marked "×" are data of the kind we most commonly provide—i.e. data for the immediate post-independence period. As illustrated here, the form of the relationship between standard of living and political instability remains the same in the two decades after independence for African nations: throughout this period increasing political instability is associated with increasing levels in the national standard of living. But this illustration is entirely hypothetical. While many relations will not drastically change in the future, we can confidently expect some to be altered, since the decade after independence can be viewed as a "shaking out" phase of national development in which various institutions, which have not so far regularized national political behavior, develop this capability. It is important therefore to qualify all relationships found in data from this Handbook as holding for the time period on which the data is based, and holding in years ahead with less and less confidence. This of course is no more than common sense, and it applies to all predictions of human behavior, but it is a qualification that is particularly important for African nations at the present time.

The social scientist, and the student of national development, is not entirely at the mercy of time. There are many situations for which we can formulate theoretical expectations about the change in the relationship between two variables over time, and test that expectation over time.[47] These changes may be hypothesized in some cases as the result of the definition of a particular variable. For example, one aspect of an operational definition of standard of living can be the distribution of education opportunity, and we can expect that when education (at the primary level at least) reaches a saturation point for the relevant age group in the national population, the effects of changes in this variable are not likely to be as great, if they are noticeable at all, as were the effects of changes from a lower base level in time past. Considerations of the base value have, in fact, to be considered in any extrapolation of a relationship based on change variables. In the case of variables that do not have such clearly defined optimal distributions as education, the threshold levels at which relationships between two variables are likely to change in the future, as African political development progresses, can be hypothesized from empirical work on the universe of nations.[48]

[47] For a discussion of the very complex issues involved in the treatment of time in behavioral sciences, see C. W. Harris, ed., *Problems in Measuring Change* (Madison: University of Wisconsin Press, 1967).

[48] See the arguments for the differences in relationships between social, political and economic variables in sub-groups of the less-developed countries in Irma Adelman and Cynthia Taft Morris, *Society, Politics and Economic Development* (Baltimore: Johns Hopkins Press, 1967).

The Difficulty of Making Causal Inferences

We cannot go into the statistical techniques for analyzing questions like those we have discussed in this chapter. But it is clear that the inspection of correlation matrices, such as that given in an Appendix of this book, cannot serve as anything more than an heuristic guide to the explanation of dependent variables in the study of nations,[49] and as a basis for employing multivariate techniques which break down the relationships between pairs in a set of interrelated variables into the direct and indirect effects of each variable, taking intervening and exogenous effects into account. Whether one uses stepwise regression analysis,[50] predictions from simultaneous equations,[51] or path analysis,[52] the ultimate decisions about the causal relationships between variables measured in *ex post facto* research must be based on the theoretical reasons for the primacy of one variable over another in a hypothesized causal sequence. As in all matters of scientific analysis, statistical or methodological procedures of causal inference can only invalidate or lend convergent validation to theoretical statements of causal relationships.

Generalization from cross-national analysis based on the statistical relationship between aggregate measures of the characteristics of nations is, therefore, a difficult business. Theoretical coherence and durability in the form of tests based on data from

[49] A recent elaboration of this point is Edward R. Tufte "Improving Data Analysis in Political Science," *World Politics*, 21 (1969): 640–654.

[50] A discussion of this and other techniques is contained in Hayward R. Alker, Jr., "Statistics and Politics: The Need for Causal Data Analysis," in *Politics and the Social Sciences*, ed. Seymour Martin Lipset (New York: Oxford University Press, 1969), pp. 244–313.

[51] Basic reviews of simultaneous equation methods are A. S. Goldberger, *Econometric Theory* (New York: John Wiley, 1965) and J. Johnston, *Econometric Methods* (New York: McGraw-Hill, 1963). These techniques have been introduced to non-econometricians by Herbert Simon and Herbert Blalock. See Herbert Blalock, Jr., *Causal Inference in Non-Experimental Research* (Chapel Hill: North Carolina University Press, 1964).

[52] See Sewall Wright, "Path Coefficients and Path Regressions: Alternative or Complimentary Concepts," *Biometrics*, 16 (1960): 189–202; Otis Dudley Duncan, Jr., "Path Analysis: Sociological Examples," *American Journal of Sociology*, 72 (1966): 1–16; Kenneth Land, "Principles of Path Analysis," in *Sociological Methodology 1969*, ed. Edgar Borgatta (San Francisco: Jossey-Bass, 1969); and Richard P. Boyle, "Path Analysis and Ordinal Data," *American Journal of Sociology*, 75 (1970): 461–480.

different samples, different time periods, and different units of aggregation, and using multiple methods and multiple indicators, is the basis of scientific generalization. Quantitative data do not provide certainty, and statistical relationships do not imply deterministic relationships between variables. No single piece of aggregate data is completely accurate as a measure of a theoretical concept, and nations are not bound by the sins of aggregate data-gatherers or by the most confidently stated extrapolations from their past experience.

3. Data Reliability

Each of the chapters in Part I contains a brief evaluation of the reliability of the data in that chapter. Here we will discuss reliability in more general terms by examining the nature of the concept, the various types of threats to reliability, and some methods for reliability evaluation and control. Our focus is on the kinds of data presented in this book: comparative data at the national unit level.

The Nature of Reliability

In a work on research in psychology and education, Fred N. Kerlinger suggests three ways to approach the concept of reliability.[1] One view, focused on accuracy, is summed up by the question: Are the measures obtained accurate measures of the property measured? For example, we may question the accuracy of reported national income, given the potential error resulting from imputing the "product" of subsistence agriculture. In a second approach, reliability is determined from the stability of results from repeated measuring of a property using the same method or instruments. Here the concern is with the magnitude of agreement among independent measurements of reality. In a third approach, more relevant to psychological testing, an attempt is made to determine a possible error of measurement present in a set of data which have been obtained through the use of a single instrument.

We are principally concerned with the first type of reliability here because much of our data (in Part I) are *aggregate* (aggregated at the national unit level) originating, at least in raw form, in published documents and reports. However, the second aspect of reliability is clearly involved in the presentation of what may be termed *typological* data in this book. This type of data are generally measures of the number, frequency, or duration of similar events, persons, or objects which have been classified by some conceptual framework of mutually exclusive categories.[2] The latter type can be said to be "secondary data" in that quantitative measures come about through a judgmental process (i.e., coding) using descriptive information of diverse origins. It is apparent that in this work two types of data can be distinguished: those which must be judged in terms of (a) *source reliability*, largely but not exclusively related to aggregate data sources, and (b) *coder reliability*, which is a major consideration in the formulation of variables such as elite instability and those which relate to other characteristics of the political system.

Relationship of Reliability and Validity

Prior to a discussion of the practical evaluation of reliability, a related problem, that of *validity*, must be mentioned. Validity involves the question, "is the measure devised a satisfactory measure of the property intended for measurement?" At first glance this appears to be a re-statement of the question posed regarding accuracy as the prime concern of reliability, but there is an important distinction between the questions.

In a methodological article by Campbell and Fiske, who offer a schema for testing both validity and reliability, the following statement is made:

> Both reliability and validity concepts require that agreement between measures be demonstrated. A common denominator which most validity concepts share in contra-distinction to reliability is that this agreement represents the convergence of independent approaches.[3]

Therefore, while reliability concerns the stability and accuracy of a method of data collection and the corresponding accuracy of the quantitative results, irrespective of whether they are satisfactory measures of the theoretical concept or not, validity (or more

---

[1] Fred N. Kerlinger, *Foundations of Behavioral Research* (New York: Holt, Rinehart and Winston, 1966), pp. 432–443.

[2] Part II contains other types of data which pertain to national sub-systems and elite group members as units of analysis. Remarks on reliability are, of course, applicable to this latter group.

[3] Donald T. Campbell and Donald W. Fiske, "Convergent and Discriminant Validation by the Multitrait-Multimethod Matrix," *Psychological Bulletin*, 56 (1959): 81–105.

precisely, construct validity) concerns the power or success of methodologies in measuring specified concepts through the convergent results of differing methods.[4]

The previous chapter considers general problems of validity in cross-national research methodology. In this Handbook the problem of validity is most clearly apparent in the construction of indices or summary variables to measure complex theoretical concepts such as instability for which no available single indicator is adequate. These indices often consist of a composite of two or more aggregate or typological variables which are sometimes weighed according to the analyst's criteria. The several "political instability" measures offered in this book are of this type.[5] Political instability by any definition is a multi-faceted phenomenon involving events and behaviors of considerable variety. We found it necessary to specify three basic types of instability: elite, regime, and communal. The validity of our measure of elite instability in terms of coups d'état, may be partially ascertained through comparisons with other independent measures of the same phenomenon—measures of administrative discontinuity, elite turnover, or possibly electoral patterns. In our own use of factor analytic techniques, the fact that these similar indicators, chosen as measures of elite instability, loaded highly together on a factor which is orthogonal to that on which measures of mass or communal instability appeared, was reassuring in terms of the construct validity of these indices.[6]

[4] Campbell and Fiske (op. cit.) admit to this point, stating that correlations between similar tests (methodologies) are somewhere between measures of reliability and validity.

[5] An example of the difficulties involved in assessing the validity of complex indices of typological concepts is given in Part I, Chapter 11, where measures of "conspiracy" and "internal war" are compared with our measures of elite instability and communal instability. From the standpoint of face validity, these pairs of concepts should be closely related, and the measures based on them should be closely related. The fact that the relevant intercorrelations are low, or in the wrong direction, does not reflect on the reliability of the measures involved, which may be error free given different coding conventions, but does reflect seriously on the validity of measures of political instability in Africa.

[6] Examples of empirical studies which rely on constructed indices from several indicators include Irma Adelman and C. T. Morris, *Society, Politics and Economic Development* (Baltimore, Md.: Johns Hopkins Press, 1967); Arthur S. Banks and Robert B. Textor, *A Cross-Polity Survey* (Cambridge: Massachusetts Institute of Technology Press, 1963); and Raymond F. Bauer, *Social Indicators* (Cambridge: Massachusetts Institute of Technology Press, 1966).

In this Handbook we generally avoid labeling variables in terms of abstract concepts. "Total Christian Mission Stations per Million Population, ca. 1925" is used as a title for Table 2.15 instead of "Missionary Impact, 1920's." The use of the latter title would involve a number of assumptions about the ability of data on mission stations to measure missionary impact. For missionary impact, the number of converts per 1000 population would seem to be a more valid measure since it would be possible to have many mission stations but few converts and hence little "impact." One could further argue, however, that converts are only one aspect of the impact of the missionaries and that the number of children in missionary schools per million population is equally or more valid a measure (or operationalization) of the concept.

Source Reliability

Considering first the quality of quantitative and descriptive sources from which the bulk of our data are gathered and often directly transcribed, the apparent threats to reliability are many while the strategies open to the researcher for assessing the accuracy of his data are few. Often the fact that aggregate data are measured in seemingly unambiguous units—currencies, numbers of people, radios, etc.—tends in the mind of the user to give to the data an unwarranted degree of authority. A host of threats may in fact be present; unfortunately inaccuracies in "official" sources are neither all random nor, when systematic, totally unintentional. In addition, while international bodies such as those related to the United Nations may represent a higher degree of objectivity in the reporting of economic, educational, or demographic information, these organizations are to a large extent dependent upon the various national governments and trusteeship authorities for the supply of original data.

One of the frustrating aspects of gathering data on Africa is the fact that so many of the non-governmental data sources for comparative data such as *Africa 69/70, AID Economic Data Handbook, Europa Yearbook, Statesman's Yearbook*, Colin Legum's *Africa: A Handbook to the Continent*, present data without reference to the original source or to the date of the data. In the case of *Africa 69/70*, for instance, some of the urban data are quite up to date while the data for other cities are for 1960 or earlier.

When we have had to rely upon these sources for data, as in the case of acres of agricultural land per capita (Table 1.2), and where the sources differ, the procedure we have followed is to use the source which seems the most reliable on the basis of its recency, thoroughness, or its auspices. Where there seems to be a consensus on the part of the sources we sometimes took that consensus into account in assessing which figure to use. The difficulty with the latter procedure is that we have no way of knowing whether that consensus is the result of independent estimates or whether the sources have all used the same secondary source or whether the sources are all drawing upon each other in some incestuous way.

A few of the major threats to data reliability which relate to the original sources we have consulted are listed below:

(a) *Definitional non-equivalence and ambiguity*. From our experience in multiple source comparisons, especially for educational, economic, and military variable categories, wide divergencies in the definitional understanding of these measures is often the cause of otherwise irreconcilable differences in published figures. For education these largely stem from structural variations. The difficulty of comparing enrollment levels for both primary and secondary education due to definitional differences is cited in Part I, Chapter 5. In another sphere, while gross national product per capita appears to be a straightforward index of economic development, it is important to know in its computation whether a portion of the total represents an imputed value for activities in the traditional sector—bartering, subsistence farming, etc.—and how this estimate has been made.

(b) *Sampling error and collection techniques*. The problem of the use and representativeness of sampling techniques is magnified in developing nations. A common malady in data collection is a systematic bias (over-representation) for the modern sector of the national system, characterized by urbanism, greater control under the central political authority, and the exchange economy, as opposed to the rural,

traditional sector. Frequently the latter is merely estimated. Prior to independence, for example in many territories, uncertain estimates of enrollment in "bush schools" or uncontrolled facilities were added to actual counts of students in official and government inspected schools. In the same era, hindrances to cross-national comparability arose from contrasting methods of census taking in French and British areas. In the former, authorities employed various sampling techniques rather than attempting to survey the entire population.

(c) *Cyclical phenomena and seasonal variations*. Throughout this volume one finds variables explicitly identified by year. Except in instances where yearly values represent cumulative totals for the entire twelve-month period, the reliability of year by year comparisons is somewhat attenuated by within-year or seasonal fluctuations unless, in the case of regular variation, the date of measurement is approximately the same from year to year. (While time series comparability for one unit would then be strengthened, cross-national comparability is still open to question.) Most vulnerable to seasonal variation in terms of reliability are indices of change from one time period to another several years later since minor changes, which may reflect only the time of year at which the measure was taken, become magnified. Population figures are frequently affected by seasonal migration of traditional peoples who respect no artificial borders and also by participants in the modern sector who follow seasonal labor markets. One case in point exists in the Horn of Africa where large nomadic groups observe a regular schedule of migration from Somalia to Ethiopia to find fresh pastureland.

No less problematic than seasonal variations are cyclical phenomena influencing yearly measurements which may represent the high or low point in the cycle regardless of the long-term trend. Economic indices such as balance of trade measures and gross national product tend to reflect such cyclical patterns. One control for this phenomenon is offered in the use of cumulative figures covering several years or at least the total period of one cycle (e.g., cumulative balance of trade, 1963–1968, Table 13.15).

(d) *Differences in systematic development*. Should cross-national comparisons be made for particular years regardless of the degree of autonomy enjoyed by the political and economic systems involved? Only with trepidation are independent states such as Ethiopia and Liberia included in pre-1960 comparisons with colonial territories.[7] It may be argued (and here the threat may be more correctly interpreted as one aimed toward validity) that independent, colonial, and semi-autonomous units are noncomparable systems and that rankings which include the same are of questionable value. Should the theoretical implications of this kind of noncomparability impair the utility of these data in the present form for his purposes, the user has a partial solution in using year of independence as a comparative benchmark instead of "real" years. In Part I, Chapter 5, school enrollment data are given for two years before and after independence in an effort to avoid this problem (Table 5.7).

(e) *Intentional falsification.* Though difficult to document, there is every reason to suspect that on occasion both colonial administrators, and in recent years, public officials have been moved by political expediency to make adjustments in quantitative reports. Census figures, while crucial for social planning, are also used to determine political representation and thus are vulnerable to distorting influences. The Nigerian case, where the 1962 census was completely abrogated and the subsequent 1963 re-census widely criticized as a considerable over-count, is a dramatic case in point.[8]

Reliability Assessment

What follow are several guide-lines or strategies for reliability control which have been employed where applicable in the preparation of this volume. As suggested earlier, the careful discrimination among original data sources where more than one is available is of paramount importance. Selectivity may be based both on the reputed standards of the report-

ing organization and on the basis of agreement among acceptable sources. However, this would not preclude the necessity of further statistical testing to ascertain reliability.

In Part I we have followed the procedure of data evaluation utilizing factor analytic techniques and the inspection of cross-variable correlations. One may expect to find as an initial assurance of reliability, similar measures loading in factor analysis on the same dimension as well as high positive correlations among pairs of related variables. However, while negative or low product moment correlations among like measures may be strong evidence of low reliability, the presence of high positive correlations may be seen only as a test of the absence of *random* error. The presence of systematic error in both measures may, of course, produce correlations as high as those between indicators having identical values. For example, two measures of the same variable may correlate highly despite their different values when both of them are *consistently* exaggerated. The use of correlation as a test of reliability applies both to the question of source reliability and to coder reliability.

A more complex application of the correlational technique to establish reliability is one in which plausible bivariate relationships among dissimilar variables are tested. Such a comparison, made between indicators of aggregate educational attainment and literacy rates, was discussed in Part I. In this particular test, relationships across time demonstrated a predictable pattern of change in addition to close association. A related procedure, for cross-sectional as opposed to time-series data, is the use of scatter diagrams or the plotting of residuals from a best-fit linear regression. An example of residual plotting is the plot of newspapers per 1,000 and radios per 1,000 which correlate at .87, in the *World Handbook of Political and Social Indicators*, by Bruce M. Russett.[9] Outlying cases which show unusual deviation from the predicted location (the regression line) are not necessarily the product of unreliable data, but require additional verification through other sources.

The presence of time-series data in absolute values for individual units or nations facilitates additional

---

[7] While 1960 marks the year of independence for 17 of our 32 units, four were legally independent prior to 1958, while five did not achieve independence until after 1963.

[8] R. K. Udo, "Population and Politics in Nigeria," in *The Population of Tropical Africa*, eds. J. C. Caldwell and C. Okonjo (London: Longmans, 1968), pp. 97–105. See also the discussion in Appendix 5.

[9] Bruce M. Russett, et al., *World Handbook of Political and Social Indicators* (New Haven: Yale University Press, 1964), p. 118.

reliability evaluation. These measures, which include population totals, school enrollment, and economic indices, tend to change with geometric or incremental regularity annually, but they are also affected by historical events and trends in other spheres of activity. The marked relationship between world financial conditions and educational enrollment, for example, is discussed in Part I, Chapter 5. These data must therefore be assessed not only as they relate to other measures in cross-sectional analysis but, when possible, in the context of the total historical time continuum.

An important inter-coder variable which can affect the reliability of some data is conservatism in coding which introduces a degree of systematic difference, in addition to random disagreement between coders. With increased conservatism on the part of a coder, a greater number of "borderline cases" are excluded from the sample; as the difference between coders in terms of conservatism grows, the reliability coefficient diminishes. That the upward limits of reliability are in fact dependent upon the magnitude of difference in coder conservatism would imply that especially low coefficients may be explained in terms of this inter-coder variable.

At a relatively early stage in our data collection work an attempt was made to establish acceptable coder reliability for several quantitative measures relating to political conflict which had been collected for a separate study some months previously. We had hoped to use the same methods to supply data for years and political units not included in the original study. Our attempt to replicate the values for five indicators on five national units met with minimal success; the resulting coefficient was .58.[10] On this basis the attempt to supply the new data was discontinued and our efforts applied elsewhere. Upon later investigation and consultation with the author of the original study, several problems were isolated

as explanations for the lack of agreement. Although conservatism on the part of the second coder was a strong factor, the major problem was lack of definitional precision for each category. Another, perhaps unanticipated, cause, was the non-coincident favoring of one descriptive source over others among the four or five listed as original sources for coding.

Other results of a reliability check made for political parties' data are cited in Part I, Chapter 8. In this instance the measure of reliability was a product moment correlation. (Earlier remarks as to the limitations of the Pearson Product Moment Correlation as a coefficient of reliability—that it is not sensitive to positive systematic error—also apply here.) In this study for a random sampling of six countries out of 32, all variables were re-coded by a person other than the original coder. A correlational analysis was performed doubling the number of variables: the number of original variables being N, variable number 1 coded by a second coder becomes $N+1$ in the cross-correlation matrix. Correlations between variables 1 and $N+1 \ldots N$ and $N+N$ were then used as an initial indicator of inter-coder reliability.

Conclusion

Every attempt has been made in the process of preparing this data collection to ensure its accuracy. The enumeration of the various threats to reliability in this chapter should warn the researcher that data of this kind may pose severe reliability problems, however. Special attention should be paid to the information we provide regarding the reliability of specific sets of data in the various chapter introductions in Part I and in the introduction to Part II. Where analysis requires highly accurate data the researcher is advised to re-collect the data as a double check. It is hoped that future editions of this work can incorporate corrections, and readers are invited to send their suggestions to the authors.[11]

[10] See Ole Holsti, "The Quantitative Analysis of Content," in *Content Analysis*, ed. Robert C. North, et al. (Evanston, Ill.: Northwestern University Press, 1963), pp. 49–50, for a description of the procedures we followed.

[11] Corrections should be sent to Robert C. Mitchell, Department of Sociology, Swarthmore College, Swarthmore, Pa. 19081.

4. Ethnic Unit Classification and Analysis

In Part I, Chapter 16 and in each of the country profiles in Part II we have given information based on the ethnic composition of the populations of African nation-states. This information is not given to perpetuate esoteric interests in "traditional" or "primitive" societies, nor are we interested *per se* in exotic statistics on the number of different languages and tribes in the African continent and the national boundaries of their constituents. Rather the collection and presentation of these data are intended to inform the analysis of sociological theories of pluralism, integration, and other approaches to the continuing, but not unique, problems of national unity in Africa.

The utility of this information is critically dependent on the theoretical meaning and explanatory power of our concepts relating to ethnicity,[1] as well as the reliability, comparability, and reproducibility of the measures used to describe these concepts. The reader should note that our basic concept, the *ethnic unit*, is not the same thing as a tribe (or ethnic identity group), though ethnic units are made up of one or more tribes. This chapter, therefore, discusses: (1) the theoretical context of the ethnic data in this book, (2) the conceptualization of ethnicity and the theoretical equivalence of ethnic units used for the collection of this data, and (3) the operational procedures used by the authors for the classification and description of ethnic units listed here.

Ethnicity and National Integration

The theoretical relevance of our method of classifying the national ethnic units in Part II should be assessed in terms of the theory of integration, in which framework the authors set their data priorities for this Handbook. (See Part III, Chapter 1.) In the most abstract terms, integration has been defined as "a relationship among units in which they are mutually interdependent and jointly produce system properties which they would separately lack."[2] More loosely defined, integration is the degree of cohesion and consensus binding members of a social entity together, and as integration increases, there is a decrease in the salience of sub-unit boundaries or the lines of demarcation between members of the social entity. The theory of integration is the search for those behavioral relationships which increase or decrease the cohesion and consensus within social groupings, and the analysis of national integration is the search for those relationships which have an impact on the cohesion and consensus characteristic of the populations of nation-states.

By cohesion and consensus we refer principally to the degree to which members of a nation regard themselves as sharing a common identity and the degree to which they share common values. Whatever the relationship between values and identities in the process of integration, a major threat to consensus and cohesion in contemporary nation-states is thought to be the existence, within national boundaries, of ethnic groups (or "tribes") based on real or assumed blood ties, language, region, religion, or custom.[3] National integration in these terms means the shift in the locus of identity and loyalty from the ethnic group to the national population as a whole and to the formulation of some minimal set of shared values.

Despite the apparent importance of the role of ethnicity in African national integration, the empirical problems of analyzing ethnic heterogeneity are formidable. The problem, which we shall spend the bulk of this chapter discussing, is the empirical identification and comparability of ethnic groups. In order to decide whether there is more ethnic hetero-

---

[1] The word *ethnicity* is used here only to indicate the general focus of this chapter. It is in itself a concept that is more confusing than enlightening since it involves connotations of both ethnic identity and common culture, two subjects we feel it necessary to distinguish between in what follows.

[2] Karl W. Deutsch, *The Analysis of International Relations*, (Englewood Cliffs, N.J.: Prentice-Hall, 1968), p. 159.

[3] A very clear statement of this argument is found in Clifford Geertz, "The Integrative Revolution: Primordial Sentiments and Civic Politics in the New States," in *Old Societies and New States: The Quest for Modernity in Asia and Africa*, ed. Clifford Geertz (New York: The Free Press, 1963).

geneity in one nation than another, it is necessary to answer such apparently simple questions as: What is an ethnic group, and what are the boundaries between one ethnic group and another? The attempt to provide answers to these questions is generally phrased in terms of populations sharing common values and common identity. These two aspects of national integration require some elaboration at this point.

The question of the communality of values held by populations and the operational problem of measuring this value congruence is an important approach in the study of national integration.[4] In the simplest terms, values are the preferences individuals or groups have for particular social arrangements (e.g. polygyny vs. monogamy) or actions (e.g. negotiation vs. physical aggression in resolving marital conflicts). The fundamental hypothesis of structural-functional theories of the social system is that societies are distinguished from fluctuating aggregates of interacting individuals by the boundaries of value consensus to which members of the social system subscribe. Conflict theorists also presuppose some "rules of the game" which are accepted by the contending parties in an integrated society. The range of common values necessary for integration is not specified, but it seems that the range of minimal consensus for political integration is quite narrow. Two value dimensions are important in this context: (a) common values which define the purpose of community, and (b) common values that legitimate the exercise of power within the community—in particular, values that legitimate decision-making and conflict resolution procedures.

A second approach to the analysis of integration is one which focuses upon common identity. Identities are the recognition by individuals or groups that they are alike in some significant respect, and that this likeness distinguishes them from others. Individuals may hold multiple identities,[5] the primacy of which varies with the situation of the individual, and completely new identities may be assumed in new situations.[6]

In terms of identities, national integration is a process by which individuals recognize themselves to be members of the same nation. The movement "from tribe to nation"[7] is not, however, necessarily incompatible with the retention of sub-national ethnic identities. The identity shift is not an all or nothing phenomenon; the ethnic identities utilized by single individuals are not limited in number, nor should they be considered static. Thus, continued ethnic identity, under certain conditions, is not necessarily incompatible with national political integration; as Mercier argues:

> In the new states, ethnic identity does not always have a centrifugal effect. It can just as well be an integrative factor to the extent that the rules of a common game are explicitly or implicitly accepted. Ethnic diversity can, in many different ways, contribute to unification or be utilized toward that end.[8]

In considering the relationship between value congruence and common identity as aspects of national integration, it is important first to recapitulate the point made in the last paragraph that ethnic identities are not necessarily incompatible with a shared national identity. It may be supposed, however, that the growth of a shared national identity is contingent on the growth of a measure of value congruence between differently identified ethnic groups who, in Mazrui's words, assume increasingly "a capacity for constant discovery of areas of compatibility."[9] However, while national

---

[4] See the extended arguments in Karl W. Deutsch, "Integration and the Social System: Implications of Functional Analysis," and Philip E. Jacob, "The Influence of Values in Political Integration," in *The Integration of Political Communities*, eds. Jacob and James V. Toscano (New York: J. B. Lippincott Co., 1964), pp. 179–246.

[5] For a very clear theoretical argument for this statement, based on an analysis of international relations, see Harold Guetzkow, *Multiple Loyalties: Theoretical Approach to a Problem in International*

Organization (Princeton, N.J.: Center for Research on World Political Institutions, Princeton University, 1955).

[6] The evidence for situational ethnicity is primarily based on studies of urban ethnicity, of which two brilliant but contrasting examples are Arnold L. Epstein, *Politics in an Urban African Community* (Manchester, England: University Press, 1958), and Abner Cohen, *Custom and Politics in Urban Africa: A Study of Hausa Emmigrants in Yoruba Towns* (Berkeley: University of California Press, 1969).

[7] See Ronald Cohen and John Middleton, eds., *From Tribe to Nation: Studies in Incorporation Process* (Scranton, Pa.: Chandler Publishing Co., 1970) and P. H. Gulliver, ed., *Tradition and Transition in East Africa: Studies of the Tribal Element in the Modern Era* (Berkeley: University of California Press, 1969).

[8] Paul Mercier, "On the Meaning of 'Tribalism' in Black Africa," in *Africa: Social Problems of Change and Conflict*, ed. P. L. van der Berghe (San Francisco: Chandler Publishing Co., 1965), p. 486

[9] See the argument in Ali Mazrui, "Pluralism and National Integration," in *Pluralism in Africa*, eds. Leo Kuper and M. G. Smith,

identity may be facilitated by the relative cultural homogeneity of the ethnic groups in any nation, it cannot be said that such identity is a necessary consequence of value congruence. As Deutsch points out,

> The population of different territories might easily profess verbal attachment to the same set of values without having a sense of political community that leads to political integration. The kind of sense of community that is relevant for integration . . . turns out to be rather a matter of mutual sympathy and loyalty; of "we-feeling," trust, and mutual consideration; of partial identification in terms of self-images and interests; of mutually successful predictions of behavior and of cooperative action in accordance with it . . . [10]

At this stage in the empirical study of national integration it is not possible to determine the relative importance of, or relationship between, common values and shared identities in national populations. The approach taken here is to devise a method of assessing degrees of value congruence in ethnically heterogeneous African states rather than to assess the growth of a national identity. We adopt this strategy for theoretical and practical reasons.

Theoretically, as we have implied above, value congruence may be argued to precede national identity in that some minimal agreement on political values is necessary to produce the cooperation and mutual confidence that develop a sense of identity. The underlying hypothesis guiding this approach is, therefore, that the greater the value congruence amongst the ethnic groups within a nation, the greater the potential for their developing a shared national identity.

In practical terms, the available information on African populations, while highly unsatisfactory for determining contemporary identity groups (as we shall discuss below), does permit the classification of the groups identified by anthropologists into ethnic "units" that are homogeneous in terms of shared traditional cultural characteristics. For example, in contemporary Nigerian politics it may be argued that the critical identity groups in Western Nigerian

politics are the Yoruba sub-tribes (Ekiti, Ijebu, Oyo, etc.) rather than the broader Yoruba, non-Yoruba identities. But it is still relevant, in value congruence terms, to speak of a homogeneous Yoruba culture and the relative congruence between this and other traditional cultures in Nigeria may be thought of as an important factor influencing the development of Nigerian national integration.

In the rest of this chapter, then, we will discuss our approach to classifying ethnic units in black African nations on the basis of their internal cultural homogeneity. The development of this classification is the basis for our operationalizations of national ethnic pluralism given in Part I, Chapter 16. The composition of these ethnic units, their population and their geographic location is given for each nation in Part II.

The Comparability of Ethnic Units

The most extensive data on the cultural values of African peoples are contained in the work of anthropologists who have studied populations, variously described as "societies," "peoples," "ethnic groups" or "tribes." To the non-specialist there is hardly more difficulty in accepting the existence of "tribes" than in accepting the existence of nations and both words serve to bolster deep-seated prejudices. In the language of social scientists, however, the concept of "tribe," despite its apparent simplicity to the non-specialist, is a complex matter which has eluded satisfactory definition by anthropologists.[11] The conceptual confusion which bedevils the description of ethnic groups is particularly threatening to cross-national research which seeks to utilize ethnographic information. Aggregated data for cross-nation re-

---

(Berkeley: University of California Press, 1969). The quotation is from p. 334.

[10] Karl W. Deutsch, et al., "Political Community in the North Atlantic Area," in *International Political Communities—An Anthology* (New York: Doubleday Anchor Book, 1966), p. 17.

[11] The following is the conclusion of a contemporary student of anthropology: "If I had to select one word in the vocabulary of anthropology as the single most egregious case of meaninglessness, I would have to pass over 'tribe' in favor of 'race.' I am sure, however, that 'tribe' figures prominently on the list of putative technical terms ranked in order of degree of ambiguity." Morton H. Fried, *The Evolution of Political Society* (New York: Random House, 1967), p. 154. For further discussion, see other essays in *Essays on the Problem of Tribe*, ed. June Helm (Seattle: University of Washington Press, 1968), and Raoul Naroll, "The Culture-Bearing Unit in Cross-Cultural Surveys," in *Handbook of Method in Cultural Anthropology*, eds. Raoul Naroll and Ronald Cohen (New York: Natural History Press, 1970).

search must be based on the summary characteristics of groups of equivalent units, and aggregate ethnic data descriptive of nation-states is of little use if the unit of aggregation—the ethnic unit —is one thing in nation A and another in nation B. The aim of this section is, therefore, to investigate what James Fernandez has recently called "one of the most tangled areas in our taxonomies," in which "one man's tribe is another man's super-tribe and a third man's sub-tribe."[12]

The variety of analytic definitions of ethnic groups in the ethnographic literature is considerable, and the lack of correspondence in definitions is, of course, a major threat to the comparability of the units about which we "know" something. Summarizing the literature, Naroll finds at least ten different criteria proposed for the definition of ethnic units: (1) distribution of particular traits being studied; (2) territorial contiguity; (3) political organization; (4) language; (5) ecological adjustment; (6) local community structure; (7) widest relevant social unit; (8) native name; (9) common folklore or history and (10) ethnographer's units.[13]

Whichever of these criteria anthropologists use to define the boundaries of the populations they study, our assumption is that they base their field research on micro-societies that will in most cases correspond to functional identity groups. That is to say, the members of the population labelled X by the ethnographer will, with a high degree of probability, use the identity X in some situations, even if it is not their primary identity. It is impossible, however, to know whether ethnic groups studied by different anthropologists comprise populations for whom the identities given them by anthropologists have similar significance. It is not possible, therefore, to treat the groups named in ethnographies as equivalent identity groups, and to assess national integration in terms of the number of named-groups in a national population.[14] In addition, it is not clear that the named-groups in ethnographic literature correspond to culturally discrete populations. Apart from the situational and subjective relativity of ethnic identity, the effects of the diffusion of cultural traits from one named-group to another, further "fuzzes the discreteness of tribal units. Different tribes may in the process of historical diffusion turn out to be simple reiterations of the same entity and not truly discrete."[15]

In order to compare named-groups studied by anthropologists, social scientists interested in cross-cultural research have attempted, therefore, to establish criteria by which groups may be considered equivalent. Naroll, for example, specifies linguistic, political and interactional criteria to define comparable "culture-bearing units":

> People who are domestic speakers of a common distinct language and who belong either to the same state or the same contact group.[16]

This attempt relates directly to our problem: What conceptual approaches can be taken in order to abstract from the ethnographic literature a set of comparable units for *cross-national* research?

The requirements we selected for the classification of ethnic units for the countries in Black Africa are as follows: (1) each unit should be made up of people whose basic cultural characteristics are similar; (2) each unit should be of significant population size: i.e., units which comprise either more than 5 percent of the national population or more than one million people (within the country); (3) the set of ethnic units in each nation should be sufficiently inclusive to account for at least 80 percent of the total population; and (4) the set of ethnic units in each nation should reflect all major cultural variations represented in the national population. The demographic

---

[12] James W. Fernandez, "Contemporary African Religion: Confluents of Inquiry," in *Expanding Horizons in African Studies*, eds. Gwendolen M. Carter and Ann Paden (Evanston, Ill.: Northwestern University Press, 1969), p. 38.

[13] Naroll, "Culture-Bearing Unit," p. 726. For an earlier version of this, see Raoul R. Naroll, "On Ethnic Unit Classification," *Current Anthropology*, 5 (1964): 283–312. In this work Naroll elaborates six criteria: (1) distribution of particular traits being studied; (2) territorial contiguity; (3) political organization; (4) language; (5) ecological adjustment; (6) local community structure.

[14] For arguments in favor of using "named-groups" as identity groups see Michael Moerman, "Ethnic Identification in a Complex Civilization: Who are the Lue?" *American Anthropologist*, 67 (1965): 1215–1230.

[15] This is Galton's problem in the literature on cross-cultural analysis. See Raoul Naroll, "Two Solutions to Galton's Problem," *Philosophy of Science*, 28 (January 1961): 15–39, and Naroll and Roy G. D'Andrade, "Two Further Solutions to Galton's Problem, *American Anthropologist*, 65 (1963): 1053–1067.

[16] Naroll, "Culture-Bearing Unit," p. 731.

Figure 4.1 Hypothetical Cultural Value Data on Ethnic Identity Groups for Two Countries

Ethnic Identity Groups	NATION A			Ethnic Identity Groups	NATION B		
	Authority	Hierarchy	Distribution		Authority	Hierarchy	Distribution
EIG₁	1	2	1	EIG₁	1	1	1
EIG₂	1	2	1	EIG₂	1	1	1
EIG₃	2	1	5	EIG₃	2	3	3
EIG₄	3	4	6	EIG₄	2	3	3
EIG₅	3	4	6	EIG₅	3	2	2
Variance	.80	1.44	5.36	Variance	.56	.80	.80
	Total Variance 7.60				Total Variance 2.16		

EIG = Ethnic identity group
Authority, hierarchy, and distribution are ordinalized variables

requirements (2 and 3) require no further discussion until we come to the problem of finding demographic data on ethnic groups. The major question at this stage is how to aggregate ethnic identity groups to obtain ethnic units meeting these criteria.

Three Approaches to Aggregating Ethnic Identity Groups[17]

Let us consider three alternative approaches: (1) a single classification rule in which all identified ethnic identity groups which are identical on a set of cultural variables may be aggregated into a single unit; (2) an analysis of variance model in which identified ethnic identity groups are aggregated into single units whenever the cultural variance within the aggregate is less than a given percentage of the total variance for all identified ethnic groups being considered; (3) a cross-national research model, which is adopted here, in which the principles of aggregation in either (1) or (2) are modified by a consideration of the range of variation across the identified ethnic identity groups located *within a given national boundary.*

In this third approach ethnic distinctiveness is assessed not simply in terms of the cultural differences between ethnic identity groups, but in terms of the *range* of those differences relative to the range of difference within the national boundaries in which

[17] The term "ethnic identity group" will hereafter refer to a "named-group" from ethnographic case studies.

the identity groups are located. This is a somewhat complicated procedure. Let us illustrate this procedure by taking two hypothetical nations and their constituent ethnic identity groups as shown in Figure 4.1.

In these two national contexts, it is clear in qualitative terms that there is more cultural diversity (variance) in nation A than in nation B. There are, however, fundamental similarities in the cultural distribution of the two national populations. For each nation there are two sets of two culturally identical ethnic identity groups, and a single ethnic group that is different from all the others on each dimension. The identical *groups* could be grouped into a common *unit* at a higher level of abstraction by the single classification rule as one way of classifying national ethnic units.[18]

A modified approach, using the analysis of variance model, is to inspect the actual "distance" of the outlying identity groups from the other ethnic units. In nation A, it will be observed, the outlying identity group (EIG₃) differs markedly and not uniformly from the two pairs of identical groups. In nation B, the outlying group (EIG₅) is "closer" to one ethnic unit (EIG₃, EIG₄) than the other, and this is uniformly true.[19] Since we have already

[18] Giving the three units for country A: [EIG₁, EIG₂], [EIG₃], and [EIG₄, EIG₅] and for country B: [EIG₁, EIG₂], [EIG₃, EIG₄], and [EIG₅].

[19] That is, in nation A, when [EIG₄, EIG₅] is greater than [EIG₁, EIG₂] then [EIG₃] is not necessarily greater than [EIG₁, EIG₂], but in nation B, when [EIG₃, EIG₄] is greater than [EIG₁, EIG₂] then [EIG₅] is always greater than [EIG₁, EIG₂].

Figure 4.2 Ethnic Units: Model for the Definition of Levels of Inclusion for a Hypothetical Country.

Type of Ethnic Unit	Levels of Inclusion and Their Definitional Components		
	1. Common identity 2. Similar manifest culture 3. Similar value premises	1. Similar manifest culture 2. Similar value premises	1. Similar value premises
Ethnic Identity Group (EIG)	EIG_1 ———————————⟶		
Ethnic Type (ET)	EIG_2 EIG_3 EIG_4 ——————⟩ ET_1 ———————⟶		
Ethnic Cluster (EC)	EIG_5 EIG_6 EIG_7 ——⟩ ET_2 EIG_8 EIG_9 ——⟩ ET_3 EIG_{10}	⟩ EC_1 ——————⟶	
Analytical Continuum of Inclusion	Exclusive membership Multiple definitional components Concrete definitional criteria		Inclusive membership Few definitional components Abstract criteria ⟶

observed that the total variance in nation B is less than that in nation A, it may be more reflective of the national cultural diversity to include EIG_5 in the ethnic cluster it most closely approximates, giving two ethnic units in nation B.[20] In order to decide how to include identity groups into aggregate ethnic units in more complex cases than that illustrated here, one might decide on a decision-rule such as the following: Whenever the inclusion of an identity group in an ethnic unit means that the ratio of the variance in the ethnic unit to the total national variance is more than 15 percent, the identity group should not be included.

In countries with many more identity groups and greater cultural diversity than the hypothetical cases discussed here, the internal complexity of ethnic units may be much greater. For all countries, the classification of ethnic units may be viewed along two continua: scope of unit membership (ranging from exclusive to inclusive membership), and criteria of unit membership, both quantitative (from many to few definitional components) and qualitative (from concrete to abstract components). The three levels of inclusion on these continua that are relevant

[20] These two units being [EIG_1, EIG_2] and [EIG_3, EIG_4, EIG_5].

to the understanding of the ethnic units classified in this book are illustrated in Figure 4.2.

Group, Type, Cluster: Three Levels of Inclusion

The clustering of identity groups discussed above with reference to Figure 4.1 did not proceed beyond the first two levels of inclusion illustrated in Figure 4.2. This latter figure presents a hypothetical example of a national population from which ten named identity groups (EIG_1–EIG_{10}) have been selected for classification. Ideally, one's minimal units should be even more exclusive than those which operational limitations have obliged us to employ. Instead of starting with groups commonly identified as ethnic identity groups (tribes), the best starting point would be at the level of primary identity groups (i.e., sub-tribes, village clusters, etc.). Be this as it may, the identity groups which we do use out of necessity (such as Kikuyu and Kamba in Kenya) are assumed to be definable by three definitional components: shared identity (and language), similar institutions, and similar value premises.

We define our second level (Ethnic Type) by dropping the identity and language criteria, which leaves us with combinations of identity groups which are manifestly similar with respect to institutional organization as well as to the sharing of basic value premises. Our final level of inclusion (ethnic cluster) aggregates those types which, although somewhat variant in specific aspects of institutional organization, still are relatively culturally similar. The various groups which make up a cluster share similar metaphysical and social assumptions or value orientations.[21]

In the example shown in Figure 4.2, we present a classification which yields three basic ethnic units (EIG_1, ET_1 and EC_1). It happens that each unit has been established at a *different level of inclusion*. EIG_1 shares neither manifest cultural traits nor more abstract cultural premises with any other such population in the nation. It, therefore, stands alone as a distinct unit. EIG_2, EIG_3 and EIG_4 all have similar institutions which are likewise premised on similar assumptions and values, although this similarity has never been recognized and symbolized by a notion of common identity. There are, however, no other groups within the country which share similar value premises with these three groups. They have thus been grouped as a single type, ET_1. Finally EC_1 has been established from two types which share similar value premises, although their institutions differ from each other in certain significant respects.

Each ethnic unit in this country, then, although established at different levels of inclusion, represents

a population sharing a set of similar value premises which is significantly different from that of any other unit within the country. The major ambiguity arising from this discussion of Figure 4.2 is what is meant by "significant" similarity or difference. How similar must the institutions of two identity groups be to consider that they constitute a type? How similar must the value premises of two types be to consider them as one cluster? Given the quality and quantity of data we had to deal with in classifying the populations of 32 countries, it was impossible to set up rigid criteria to guide our judgments. Our decisions were more or less subjective, depending on the ethnic situation presented by each country, and the quality of its description in the ethnographic literature. An example which illustrates Figure 4.2 and the discussion of levels of inclusion is our classification of ethnic units in Dahomey.

Example of Dahomey

In this Handbook we have defined three major ethnic units in Dahomey and each of these units represents a different level of inclusion. The Yoruba correspond to our identity group level. Such groups as the various branches of the Egba Yoruba (the Holli, Dassa, Ketu, Manigri, Itsha, Chabe, and Anago) all speak closely related dialects of Yoruba. Their cultures are all highly similar at the institutional level, being characterized by a social organization including such features as large villages comprised of large extended patrilineal kin groups. These villages are organized into paramount chiefdoms in which authority is hierarchical and passed hereditarily to a patrilineal heir rather than a son. These societies recognize an hereditary aristocracy which rules over a class of freemen. As is common with most groups at this level of abstraction, the members of the group have a common sense of Egba Yoruba identity.

The peoples we have classified within the Fon type also manifest a high degree of cultural similarity, but they do not share a common identity. Historically the kingdoms of the Gun, the Adja and Wachi, the Aizo, and the Popo have been in relationships of varying degrees of autonomy with the Kingdom of Dahomey (Fon), but they have never considered

[21] A cluster being defined as a set of similar and aggregated ethnic types. It should be noticed that our use of the word "cluster" may be closer to the conventional meaning of culture *area* than culture *cluster* in the anthropological literature. ". . . . While the dividing point between the two is probably not always precise, two characteristics of the cluster tend to distinguish it from the area. The first of these is size; while it is conceivable that a culture cluster encompasses as large a geographic distribution as an area, this would seldom be the case, for the cluster pertains most directly to smaller groups of peoples whose culture shows a degree of unity rather than simple similarity as in a culture area. This is emphasized in the second difference between the two: The culture cluster involves a real commonality among the people concerned, with recognition of this commonality by the various groups. Thus the concept of the culture area is imposed upon the data by the ethnologist, while the concept of the culture cluster is both imposed by the ethnologist and recognized to varying degrees by the people concerned." Alan P. Merriam, "The Concept of Culture Clusters Applied to the Belgian Congo," *Southwestern Journal of Anthropology*, 15 (Winter 1959): 374. We have used the word cluster rather than area because we do not wish to attach any suggestion of geographic coherence to our ethnic units.

themselves one people. The Gun have always been relatively isolated from the Dahomeans due to their marsh environment. In many respects these groups are quite similar to our description of the Yoruba groups. They are different in that the family unit is restricted to independent polygynous families. What is more, political succession among the Fon type is guided by principles of patrilineality and primogeniture.

Our third group, which represents a cluster, is comprised of the Bargu, the Kilinga, and the Somba. These peoples all speak languages of the Bargu division of the Mossi-Grunshi branch of the Niger-Congo linguistic stock. They do not, however, share a common identity. They manifest a fair degree of similarity in numerous aspects of local communiy structure, e.g., neighborhoods of dispersed homesteads, each of which is comprised of a patrilineage. There are, however, marked differences in form at the higher levels of political organization. While the Bargu are organized as a centralized state and the Kilinga into paramount chiefdoms, the Somba have no political organization above the local community level. Be this as it may, we have grouped these people into a cluster because government at the Somba local level and government at the Bargu state level appear to be premised on similar assumptions. Among the Somba, local authority is centered in a *chef-de-terre* with ritual powers who administers the distribution and use of communally owned land. He is the eldest member of the founding lineage. Within the family, land and other property is held by the family head. Property transfer and political succession follow principles of patrilineality, with transferences moving from elder brother to younger brother. Such patterns are indicators of a notion of hierarchy in status relationships. These patterns and principles are also those of the other groups within the cluster. Although the level of political development varies within the Bargu cluster, the three major groups within it premise their political relationships on the same basic assumption.

What this means, therefore, is that for our purposes ethnic units are equivalent in terms of their cultural similarity in their national context, but that they differ greatly in terms of their salience and intelligibility to the individual citizen. Identity groups, types, and clusters may be classified as ethnic units in a given nation, and they are equivalent or comparable because the values shared within their constituent populations are sufficiently distinctive to distinguish them from other groups in the national population.

Therefore, an ethnic unit, as we define it for any African nation, is a culturally distinctive and numerically significant segment of the national population, in which individuals have similar values, the national distribution of which is such that (a) the rest of the population, or any other subset of it, has a different set of values in common, and (b) the degree of cultural diversity within the ethnic unit is substantially less than that within the total national population, and not substantially more than that in any other ethnic unit classified for the same nation.

Thus defined, ethnic units may be:

1. ethnic identity groups, in which individuals have values, institutions and identity in common;
2. ethnic types, in which individuals have values and institutions in common; or
3. ethnic clusters, in which individuals have values in common.

The preceding discussion is greatly simplified, and exceedingly abstract, in order to present the logic of equivalence between ethnic units as we conceptualize them for cross-national research purposes. The empirical problems involved in our application of this conceptual framework to the data on African ethnicity are discussed in the next section, which also includes a list of the units (identity groups, types, and clusters) we coded for the 32 black African nations.

Selection of Ethnic Units in African Nations

In attempting to implement the conceptual and methodological framework for the ethnic unit classification outlined in the previous section, we used the following general procedures:

a. Search out and compare all existing classifications of ethnic units by country to determine all major cultural distinctions within each national population.

b. Evaluate and revise existing classifications in terms of the cultural homogeneity and demographic significance of the ethnic units in their national context.

c. Provide quantitative data on the cultural characteristics of each unit finally selected. (These data are the basis for the measures of cultural variance for each nation given in Part I, Chapter 16.)

Location of Information

Available ethnic classifications of African populations tend to be based on either (i) maximal identity groups,[22] (ii) linguistic criteria,[23] (iii) geographic proximity or historical relatedness,[24] (iv) similarity with respect to multiple criteria.[25] The last of these is closest to our own interest, but even those classifications which purport to be based on a consideration of multiple criteria tend to be biased in favor of a single variable such as language, historical relatedness, political organization, ecological adaptation, or geographic proximity. Our task, at any rate, was to search the literature for ethnic classifications of all kinds, and to establish on what criteria they were based, and how significantly they diverged from our interest in ethnic units that are culturally and demographically distinctive in the national context.

The bibliographic references in Part II of this book indicate the sources which we found particularly helpful in locating ethnic classifications for each of the 32 countries discussed. Three sources of information can be grouped. First, we have recourse to the extensive case-study literature on individual African nations, and monographs such as Weinstein's

recent book on Gabon,[26] or one of the Area Handbooks[27] that provide ethnic classification on national populations. This literature is not directly written by or for anthropologists, but the focus on nations as entities agrees with our own, as does the concern for politically relevant categories.

Second, we have access to official reports and censuses containing statistical information in varying detail on the ethnic composition of national populations. Because we needed to couple our own ethnic unit classifications with reliable demographic data, we tended to be biased towards the use of official census categories if it was at all possible to find a correspondence between these and the categories used in culturally defined classifications. Where the census categories correspond to identity groups described in ethnographic sources, there is of course no problem. But some census classifications reflect the ascriptive categories employed by European administrators rather than indigenous categories or categories formulated by professional anthropologists.[28] In other cases, census categories are aggregate clusters of identity groups, which are not individually specified, and are aggregated according to criteria which are not fully explained in the census documentation.[29] Another difficulty posed by census classifications occurs when the populations of only the major identity groups in the country are reported,[30] which may inhibit the production of classifications that cover more than 80 percent of the population.

Finally, there are ethnic classifications which are the work of professional anthropologists. Based on

---

[22] The Kenya Census (1962) is an example of a list based on this criterion.

[23] The classification of ethnic groups for Liberia given in Colin Legum, ed., *Africa* (New York: Praeger, 1966), pp. 231–232, is of this kind.

[24] The classification for the ethnic groups of Tanganyika in J. P. Moffett, ed., *Handbook of Tanganyika*, 2nd ed. (Dar es Salaam: Government Printer, 1958), pp. 283–297, is largely based on geographical criteria.

[25] See the *Population Census of Ghana*, Special Report E-1, "Tribes in Ghana," (Accra: Census Office, 1964), pp. 1–5, for an example.

[26] Brian Weinstein, *Nation-Building on the Ogooué* (Cambridge: Massachusetts Institute of Technology Press, 1966), pp. 30–33.

[27] For example, U.S. Department of the Army, *Area Handbook for the Republic of the Sudan* (Washington, D.C.: Government Printing Office, 1960), pp. 51–74. At present these handbooks are available for a number of African countries including Burundi, Zaire (Congo K.), Ethiopia, Guinea, Ivory Coast, Kenya, Liberia, Nigeria, Rwanda, Senegal, Sudan, Tanzania, Uganda, and Zambia. Despite their curious auspices, these handbooks, which are written by scholars at American University, are generally comprehensive and relatively authoritative. They are also publicly available.

[28] See, for example, the censuses for Nyasaland and Northern Rhodesia which tended to classify populations into three categories— "European," "Asian," and "African."

[29] *Enquête démographique de la République du Congo* (Brazzaville, 1960), is an example.

[30] See *Étude Démographique par Sondage en Guinée*, 1954–1955 (Administration Générale des services de la France d'Outre-Mer, Services des Statistiques).

individual case studies of identity groups, these classifications range from detailed maps of the geographical location of identity groups,[31] to typological classifications in which identity groups are clustered according to some well defined principles. Although the former are useful for interpreting the national location of many classifications, the latter work is of most use to us. Of particular importance is the work of George Peter Murdock, whose comprehensive book, *Africa: Its Peoples and Their Culture History*,[32] is something of a *tour de force*. Based on a thorough review of the existing African ethnographic literature of a decade ago, Murdock developed a full classification system of African ethnic groups, relying especially on the criteria of historical and linguistic relatedness as a basis for combining identity groups into composite ethnic units. Although this work is idiosyncratic in some of its classifications, and is badly in need of updating in the light of recent anthropological field work and more recent linguistic classifications,[33] it is an invaluable aid for any work in ethnic unit clustering for Africa.

Summary Procedures for Ethnic Unit Classification

The search of the literature on ethnic unit classification produced a list for our countries of some 600 ethnic groups which are included in categories of varying inclusiveness and analytic definition. Because of the great variation in the detail of the classifications we found for different countries, this figure is in itself not particularly helpful. The list of identified groups does not mean that we have a comparable set of identity groups, defined at the same level of inclusion, for each country. If it had been possible to obtain such a list—say of N groups all defined as primary identity groups, and if there were compar-

ably detailed ethnographic case studies on each identified unit, it would have been possible to code each unit on a number of variables, and then follow our methodological outline for ethnic unit classification very precisely. Faced with the great variation in ethnic unit definition and case study information, however, we were bound to follow a far less precise procedure.

Dealing with each nation separately, we sought to evaluate the cultural content and demographic significance of each unit specified in available ethnic classifications. The ethnographic descriptions of each named group in a nation's population were searched, and, wherever possible, we made initial judgments about the coding for each group on our variables. These variables, operationalized as ordinal scales, are based to a large extent on the coding categories used by Murdock in his *Ethnographic Atlas*.[34] A significant proportion of this coding was, in fact, already available in Murdock's works,[35] and our own task was simplified in many cases to checking Murdock's judgments. In other cases, where Murdock has not published codings, or where more recent ethnographic material is available, we made our own judgments.

On the basis of this qualitative investigation of the cultural characteristics of each identified ethnic group within the national population, we proceeded to cluster groups that we judged to be culturally similar. The classification of ethnic types—the aggregation of culturally similar ethnic groups— was not, however, based on any precise quantitative rule. Wherever possible, our decisions about aggregation or typing were made on the basis of a comparison of each identified group on a set of multiple cultural characteristics. We had in some cases, however, to rely on judgments as to the overriding importance of linguistic, historical and geographical relationships, or the documentation on a widely perceived sense of communal identity said to be characteristic of a set of identified groups, whose cultural

[31] For example, Clyde Mitchell, *African Tribes and Languages of the Federation of Rhodesia and Nyasaland* (Map), (Salisbury: Federal Government Printer, 1964).

[32] George P. Murdock, *Africa: Its People and Their Culture History* (New York: McGraw-Hill, 1959).

[33] See Joseph Greenberg, *The Languages of Africa* (Bloomington: Indiana University Press, 1966), and Voegelin and Voegelin, "Languages of the World," in *Anthropological Linguistics*, March 1964 to April 1966. Apart from problems of linguistic classification, Murdock's classifications are eclectic in terms of the inclusiveness and criteria of selection, and his ethnographic sources range widely in historical time, and do not always reflect contemporary data.

[34] George P. Murdock, *Ethnographic Atlas* (Pittsburgh, Pa.: University of Pittsburgh Press, 1967).

[35] In addition to the *Ethnographic Atlas*, Murdock has published additional, corrected or expanded codings in the journal *Ethnology*, in which the material in the *Atlas* first appeared. We should record further our indebtedness to Professor Murdock's *African Cultural Summaries* (New Haven, Conn.: 1958), unpublished manuscript.

Figure 4.3 African Ethnic Units: Levels of Inclusion for Thirty-Two Countries

Country	Percent Country Population Classified	Relationship to Census Categories	Identity Group	Type	Cluster	Residual or "Shatter-Belt" Cluster
1. Botswana	90	1	Tswana			
2. Burundi	98	1		Rundi		
3. Cameroon	81	3	Fulani (Bororo)	Beti-Pahouin (Fang) Bassa-Bakoko (Douala) Baya-Mbum (Baya)	Highland Bantu	Kirdi (Masa)
4. Central African Republic (CAR)	90	1	Banda Baya Mandjia (Mandja) Mbum Mbaka (Bwaka)	Riverine		
5. Chad	91	4	Arab		Sudanic (Sara) Nilotic (Maba)* Saharan (Teda)	
6. Congo (Bra)	90	1	Kongo Téké M'Bété* Sanga	M'Bochi*		
7. Zaire (Congo K.)	84	4		Central Bantu (Kongo) Luba (Songye) Mongo Ngbandi-Ngbaka-Mbandja	Azandé–Mangbetu (Azandé) Kivu (Shi)	
8. Dahomey	93	2	Yoruba (Egba)	Fon	Bargu	
9. Ethiopia	96	4	Galla Amhara Somali Afar	Kafa-Sidamo	Nilotic	
10. Gabon	83	3	Fang	Eshira* M'Bété* Kota Omyènè (Mpongwe)		
11. Gambia	81	1	Mandingo (Malinké) Fulani (Bororo) Wolof Diola Serahuli (Soninké)			

Figure 4.3 African Ethnic Units: Levels of Inclusion for Thirty-Two Countries (*cont.*)

Country	Percent Country Population Classified	Relationship to Census Categories	Identity Group	Type	Cluster	Residual or "Shatter-Belt" Cluster
12. Ghana	82	1	Ewé Ga-Adangbe (Ga)		Akan (Ashanti) Mole-Dagbani (Gurensi)	
13. Guinea	97	2	Fulani (Foula Djallon)	Mandé-Fu (Kpellé)	Mandé (Malinké) West Atlantic (Kissi)	
14. Ivory Coast	95	1		Kru (Bété) Senufo Lagoon (Attie) Lobi	Akan (Baule) Mandé (Malinké) Peripheral Mandé (Gouro)	
15. Kenya	85	1	Luo		Western Bantu (Luhya) Coastal Bantu (Digo) Kalenjin (Nandi) Central Bantu (Kikuyu)	Other Eastern Nilotic (Masai)
16. Lesotho	95	1	Sotho			
17. Liberia	94	4	Vai	Mandé-Fu (Kpellé) Kru-Bassa (Kru)	Gola-Kissi (Gola)	
18. Malawi	94	3	Lomwe* Yao Ngoni	Tumbuka	Chewa	
19. Mali	98	4	Fulani (Boro) Tuareg (Asben) Songhai	Mandé (Bambara) Senufo Sarakolé (Soninké)		
20. Mauritania	95	2	Moors (Zenaga)	Tukulor-Fulani (Tukulor)		
21. Niger	93	1	Hausa Djerma-Songhai (Sunghai) Fulani (Bororo) Tuareg (Asben) Kanuri			
22. Nigeria	86	3	Yoruba Ibo	Hausa-Fulani (Hausa) Ibibio and Semi-Bantu (Ibibio) Kanuri and Kanuri- dominated peoples (Kanuri)		Tiv and Plateau (Tiv)
23. Rwanda	100	1		Rwanda		

Figure 4.3 African Ethnic Units: Levels of Inclusion for Thirty-Two Countries *(cont.)*

Country	Percent Country Population Classified	Relationship to Census Categories	Identity Group	Type	Cluster	Residual or "Shatter-Belt" Cluster
24. Senegal	94	2	Serer	Wolof Fulani-Tukulor (Bororo) Diola Mandé (Malinké)		
25. Sierra Leone	89	2		Temne Mendé Nuclear Mandé (Koranko)		
26. Somalia	95	4	Somali			
27. Sudan	95	3	Beja Arab (Kababish)	Darfur (Fur) Nuba (Mesakin)	Southern Nile (Dinka) Southwestern (Azandé)	
28. Tanzania	90	3		Nyamwesi (Sukuma) Interlacustrine Bantu (Haya) Northeast Coastal Bantu (Hadimu)	Central Bantu (Makonde) Rift (Gogo) Rufiji (Hehe) Nyakyusa (Nyakusa) Rukwa Cluster (Fipa) Kenya Highland Bantu (Chagga)	
29. Togo	91	4	Gurma	Ewé Kabré Moba Kotocoli*		Central Togo (Buem)
30. Uganda	94	3		Nilote (Lango) Lugbara	Eastern Lacustrine (Ganda) Western Lacustrine (Nyankole) Karamajong (Teso) Gisu	
31. Upper Volta	100	1	Mossi Fulani (Bororo) Gurma Busansi (Bisa)	Western Mandé (Bobo) Senufo Grunshi (Nankanse) Lobi		
32. Zambia	98	3		Tonga (Plateau Tonga) Nyanja (Chewa) Lunda-Kaonde (Luvale) Barotze (Lozi)	Mambwe Bemba	

KEY:

*= ethnic units not contained in Murdock, *Ethnographic Atlas*; coded by Handbook staff

( )— Murdock name of ethnic identity group on which we based our cultural variable coding

Relationship to official or census categories:
1 = based on census categories
2 = modified from census categories
3 = dissimilar from census categories
4 = census or ethnic codings in census not available

characteristics were not otherwise clearly defined. These judgments concerning the degree of cultural similarity between groups, and the significance of single variables in predicting to multivariate cultural congruity are partly summarized in Part II, but the results of the classification may be detailed here and exemplified by a discussion of the classification for a single nation.

For most countries, our threefold schema of identity groups, types, and clusters adequately describes the ethnic units which we classified from our comparisons of the cultural characteristics of ethnic groups identified in available ethnic unit classifications. In five countries, however, we utilized an additional conceptual category—the residual, or "shatter-belt" cluster—to describe a set of geographically contiguous ethnic groups, whose cultural experience varies in homogeneity, but who have received a common, out-group ascription or identity. The ethnic units we have classified for African nations are summarized in Figure 4.3, which shows the levels of inclusion, and the criteria for inclusion, characteristic of each unit. The classification may be further elaborated by an account of the selection of ethnic units for Cameroon.

Cameroon Example

Our starting point in developing the Cameroon classification was Victor T. LeVine's book, *The Cameroons: From Mandate to Independence*.[36] LeVine defines eleven ethnic groups in Cameroon. Several of LeVine's categories are based on Murdock:[37] Southern Nigerians, Northwestern and Coastal Bantu, Cameroon Highlanders, Plateau Nigerians, Eastern Nigritic, Fulani, and Pygmies.

Reviewing the ethnographic material on each of the identified groups within the clusters identified by Murdock and LeVine, we selected six culturally distinctive units, five of which correspond to Murdock's units, although we have labeled them differently to identify the ethnic group that we judge to be most typical of the cultural unit. Of the six units we have selected, the Fulani are a clear-cut identity

group. The Beti-Pahouin (Equatorial Bantu), the Bassa-Bakoko (Northwestern and Coastal Bantu), and the Baya-Mbum (Eastern Nigritic) are types, in our formulation. Each of these three units is made up of different identity groups which share a common culture. All of these three types are quite similar to each other with respect to principles of social and political organization. With few exceptions, the political level goes no higher than the local level. The local grouping is invariably a localized kin group residing in a compact village or hamlet. Principles of descent, inheritance, and succession are patrilineal. Our reasons for not carrying the classification of these types to the cluster level are primarily linguistic. The Baya-Mbum type speaks languages of the Eastern or Adamawa-Eastern subfamily of the Niger-Congo family, while the Beti-Pahouin and Bassa-Bakoko groups speak languages of the Bantu subfamily of the same stock. The Beti-Pahouin and Bassa-Bakoko types have not been clustered together because the latter type still maintain elements of their former matrilineality in their principles of social organization.

We have classified the peoples Murdock identifies as the Cameroon Highlanders as the Highland Bantu cluster. The distinct identity groups included in this cluster share similar basic value patterns and assumptions, while varying fairly widely in their more specific cultural forms as well as language forms. Specifically, there is rather wide variation in the level of political development. In all cases, villages are governed by an hereditary headman who is advised by a council of lineage heads. Some of the Highlander groups have no political organization above this level (Fia, Nen, Widekum), while the others are organized into states with paramount chiefs. These states tend to be small although the Mum, Nsaw, and some Bamiléké states attain substantial size. Regardless of size, all such states are characterized by divine kings, territorial courts, specialized officials, dual class stratification and prestigious queen-mothers.[38] With respect to community organization, the Highlanders all segment themselves into localized kin groups of varying degrees of inclusion. Principles of descent, inheritance, and succession are in all cases patrilineal.

[36] Victor T. LeVine, *The Cameroons: From Mandate to Independence* (Berkeley: University of California Press, 1964) See Chapter 1.
[37] Murdock, *Africa—Its Peoples and Their Culture History*.
[38] *Ibid.*, p. 241.

Finally, we have classified an ethnic "shatter-belt" cluster—the Kirdi—in which numerically small and culturally and linguistically distinct peoples have for social and administrative reasons come into increasingly direct association and received a common out-group ascription. Because of these out-group pressures and because of the generally low level of socio-political organization of the constituent units, these peoples are coming to share a more or less common culture.

It should be clear that the procedures for ethnic unit selection just described fall far short of the mathematical precision which our methodological discussion given above might indicate. In order to follow that conceptual and methodological framework in empirical work, we require complete data on the variable characteristics of each identified ethnic group within any given nation. As we have indicated, this is not possible, but the heuristic utility of the model may be illustrated by a highly quantitative experiment in ethnic cluster analysis that we applied to Zaire (Congo K.), a country for which relatively detailed information on ethnic identity groups is available.

Q-Factor Analysis of Zaire (Congo K.) Ethnic Groups

The human mind is probably incapable of assessing simultaneously all of the multiple dimensions and degrees of variation found among populations, and accurately judging thresholds of inclusion or exclusion for units defined in terms of cultural similarity. Through the use of computing machinery, the statistical techniques of Q-factor analysis can be employed to establish clusterings of units at different levels of similarity on the basis of patterns of variation across a range of variables. Such techniques have been used experimentally by others in culture trait analysis, and as an approach to a number of different ethnological problems.[39] We have applied this technique to the classification of the populations of Zaire (Congo K.).

Jan Vansina, in his *Introduction à l'Ethnographie du*

Congo (1965),[40] has looked at 250 Zairese ethnic groups, providing one of the most valuable attempts at a comprehensive ethnic classification of an African state. In considering this diversity of possible identity groups, Vansina is struck by the cultural unity of the Zairese population:

> This all too brief glance at the different cultures of the Congo has certainly given to the reader, as to the author, a growing sense of déjà vu. Institutions, beliefs, and even other traits, have become familiar to us by dint of their reappearing so often. The reason for this is that the cultural unity of the Congo around 1900 was far greater than most specialized ethnological studies would allow one to suppose. Such works, by their very nature, emphasize differences more than resemblances. Certainly, there existed 250 cultures, but all of them and in particular those of the Kivu and the Northwest, belonged to one single type. The Congo knows a single fundamental way of life, and rather than making these cultures mutually unintelligible, the diversities enriched the cultural heritage.[41]

The cultural unity of Zaire suggests the utility of clustering the 250 ethnic groups into a more parsimonious set of ethnic units, and Vansina has described a classification of 15 major ethnic types, or regions. The distribution of cultural regions classified by Vansina is shown in Figure 4.4 along with a much less detailed map of cultural clusters given earlier by Merriam.

Such classifications cannot help but suffer from the limitations inherent in any grouping derived from the individual researcher's attempt to perceive and interrelate multiple patterns of variation. Vansina himself recognizes the problems:

> . . . We have tried to group those peoples whose cultures seemed, objectively, to resemble each other the most. We have, thus, defined groups of peoples and culture regions which incorporate numerous groups. In more than one instance it was necessary to make comprises. . . . The absence of data and the fact that the author was only familiar with a portion of the Congolese cultures, constituted a major obstacle. Consequently, it was necessary to resolve certain cases through intuition or employing the most practical arrangement rather than following vigorously established criteria.[42]

Whatever the shortcomings of Vansina's knowledge,

[39] See R. M. Needham, "Computer Methods for Classification and Grouping," in *The Use of Computers in Anthropology*, ed. Dele Hymes (The Hague: Mouton, 1965), pp. 345-346, and H. E. Denver and K. F. Schuessler, "Factor Analysis of Ethnographic Data," *American Anthropologist*, 59 (1967), 655-663.

[40] Jan Vansina, *Introduction à l'Ethnographie du Congo* (Brussels: CRISP, Editions Universitaires du Congo, 1965)
[41] *Ibid.*, p. 223. (Our translation)
[42] *Ibid.*, p. 9. (Our translation)

Figure 4.4 Geographic Description of Ethnic Regions or Clusters in Zaire (Congo K.), as suggested by Merriam and Vansina.

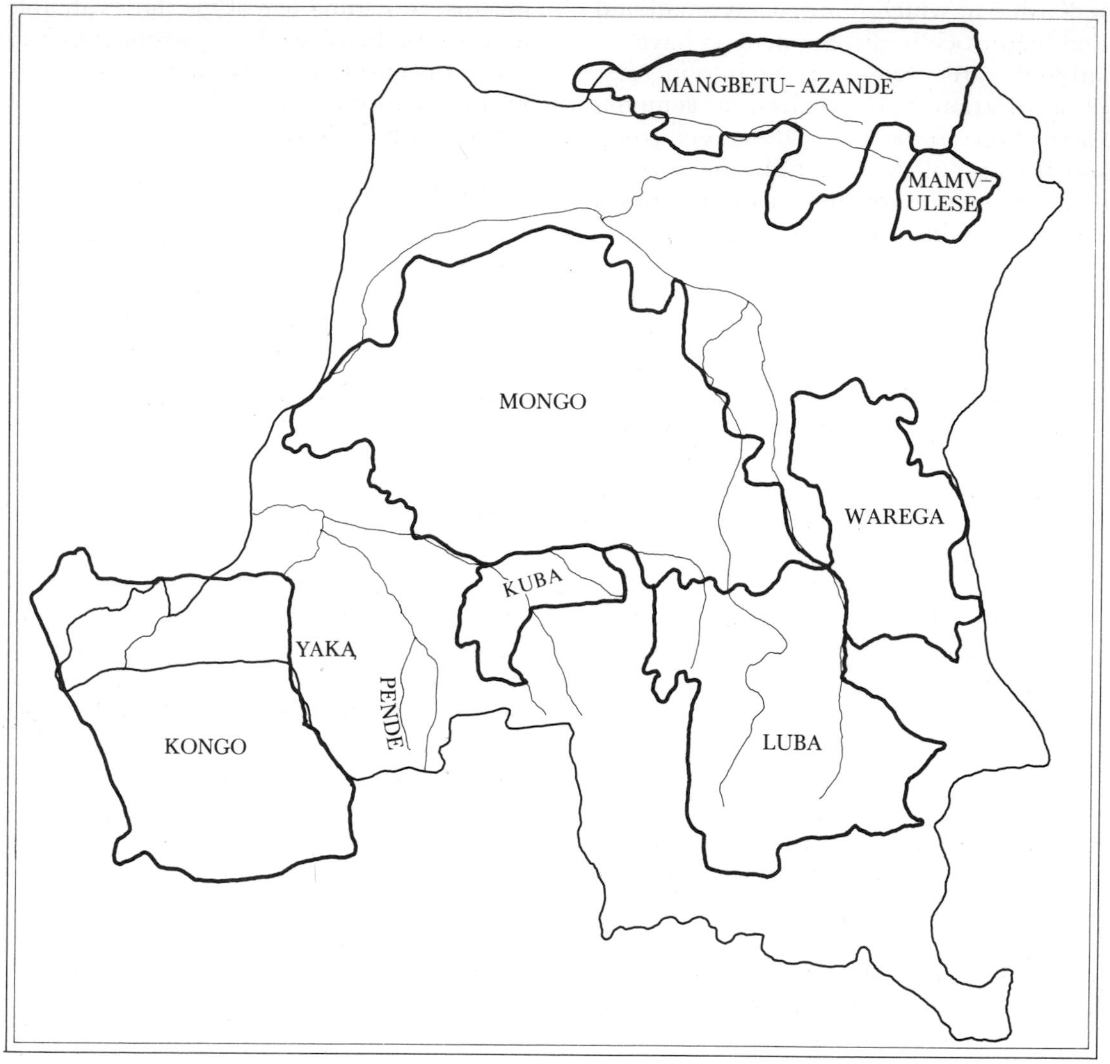

Alan P. Merriam, "The Concept of Culture Clusters Applied to the Belgian Congo," *Southwestern Journal of Anthropology*, 15 (Winter 1959), p. 347. Jan Vansina, *Introduction à l'Ethnographie du Congo* (Brussels: CRISP, Editions Universitaires du Congo, 1965).

intuition, and compromise, his outline of the cultural types in Zaire seems as good as the data will permit. What he has done may be considered a very well-informed, but not mathematically precise classification of 250 identity groups into 15 types, to use the vocabulary of this chapter.

Where Vansina groups peoples on the basis of historical, geographic, or linguistic grounds, we have

tried to adapt his work so as to present a less aggregated classification of 23 units which are more culturally coherent than the 15 already illustrated. Our adaptation is shown in Figure 4.5. Working on our adapted classification of 23 types, we selected the most prominent identity group in each type for which there was complete information on the 17 variables defined in Part I, Chapter 16. These

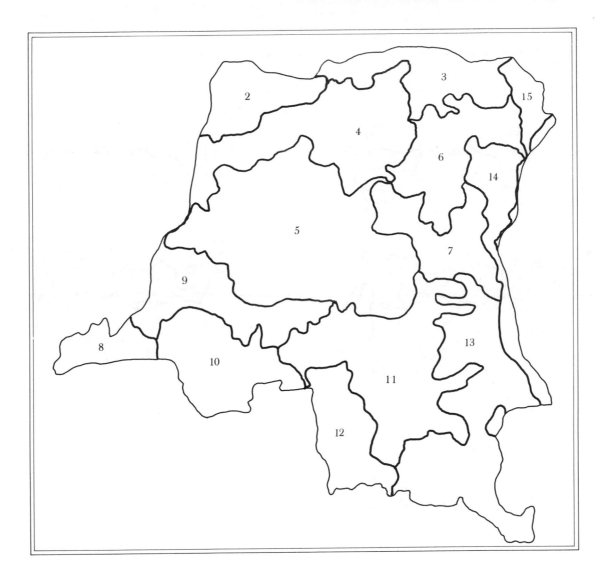

2 Région de l'Ubangi
3 Région de l'Uele
4 Région de l'Itimbiri-Ngiri
5 Région de la Cuvette Centrale
6 Région Balese-Komo
7 Région du Maniema
8 Région Kongo

9 Région du Bas Kasai
10 Région de l'entre Kwango-Kasai
11 Région du Kasai-Katanga
12 Région Lunda
13 Région Tanganyika-Haut Katanga
14 Région du Kivu
15 Région du Nord-Est

codings were then assumed to be the modal characteristics of the types, and using the data on 17 variables for 23 ethnic types we employed a Q-factor analysis routine to identify the most inclusive cultural clustering of these types. The aim of this experiment was to derive a set of ethnic units, more inclusive than Vansina's, and, in terms of cultural homogeneity, somewhere between the 23 distinctive types

and the unitary culture zone Vansina referred to earlier.

The clusters and factor loadings obtained from a four-factor solution are illustrated in Figure 4.5. The factor loadings indicate for each of the 23 ethnic types the degree to which it is similar to other types in the cluster. The higher the loading—from 0 to 1.0 —the greater the correspondence. The Q-factor

Figure 4.5 Ethnic Culture Clusters with Factor Analytic Loadings: The Example of Zaire (Congo K.).

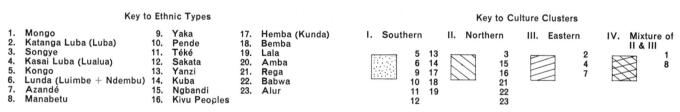

Ethnic Type Units (adapted from Vansina*)

Ethnic Culture Clusters with Factor Analytic Loading

Key to Ethnic Types		
1. Mongo	9. Yaka	17. Hemba (Kunda)
2. Katanga Luba (Luba)	10. Pende	18. Bemba
3. Songye	11. Téké	19. Lala
4. Kasai Luba (Lualua)	12. Sakata	20. Amba
5. Kongo	13. Yanzi	21. Rega
6. Lunda (Luimbe + Ndembu)	14. Kuba	22. Babwa
7. Azandé	15. Ngbandi	23. Alur
8. Manabetu	16. Kivu Peoples	

Key to Culture Clusters

I. Southern		II. Northern		III. Eastern		IV. Mixture of II & III	
5	13	3		2		1	
6	14	15		4		8	
9	17	16		7			
10	18	21					
11	19	22					
12		23					

* Jan Vansina, *Introduction à l'Ethnographie du Congo* (Brussels: CRISP, Editions Universitaires du Congo, 1965).

analysis technique was used to generate a variety of different solutions by varying the number of factors included in the solution, and by varying the number of variables used in the computation of the factor matrix. Results of the kind illustrated here might well lend precision to the final selection of ethnic units for cross-national research, although we will have to wait for more comprehensive numerical data on identified ethnic groups, and for means of comparing typological solutions based on statistical relationships found in different national samples of ethnic groups. In the meantime, the example discussed here may clarify our approach to cluster analysis, and, hopefully, stimulate further research.

Conclusion

We have described so far the process by which we selected ethnic units for African nations. We believe that the units we have listed in Figure 4.3, and in Part II, are comparable in that they each represent demographically and culturally distinctive populations within the national boundaries in which they are located. If we are correct in this belief, this data on ethnic unit classification provides a basis for the measurement of national integration in terms of the degree of ethnic pluralism, value congruence, or cultural variation characteristic of each of the 32 countries we have been concerned with in this Handbook.

In order to develop aggregate data for concepts like these,[43] we had to ascribe to each ethnic unit selected a coding representative of the modal characteristic of the culture cluster for any of our cultural variables. Where an ethnic unit is isomorphic with an identity group, we assign, of course, the coding of the identity group to the national ethnic unit. In cases where the ethnic unit is a type, cluster, or shatter-belt aggregate, we have assigned the coded characteristics of the largest identity group within the aggregate to the unit itself, or, in cases where we have evidence that the largest group in the aggregate is not the "most typical," we assign the variable scores of an identified group that is more typical of the ethnic unit. Furthermore, for some aggregates we were forced to use the only group for which complete data were available in order to generate unit codings.[44] In these ways, we have ascribed to each of our national ethnic units quantitative measures of their cultural characteristics, and utilizing this information we are able to develop aggregate indices of national variance of the kind discussed in Part I, Chapter 16.

Without the means for more precise quantitative evaluation of our ethnic unit classification, the comparability of the units we have selected in each nation is suspect, and the validity of our aggregate data on ethnic pluralism or cultural variance may be questioned. The most obvious difficulty relates to the selection of single units as "typical" of an aggregate ethnic unit. The judgments we have made fall short of a precise selection of the most typical group, and, at any rate, it would be preferable to give the aggregate entity a unique score reflective of some measure of central tendency for all the constituent groups on all the variables used for

classification. Another rather obvious difficulty is that the data we have used, whether for description of ethnic units or in the process of clustering units, are based on non-comparable temporal observations. Furthermore, whatever the reliability of the observations of the ethnographer we have consulted, there is the additional problem of the reliability of our own second-hand coding and judgment, which has not been systematically tested. Even more important as a threat to the validity of our data, is the fact that we have no precise indication that our units are equivalent in terms of their cultural distinctiveness in each nation. Our intention is that the population in each ethnic unit share a range of values in common, and that the values they share are different from those shared by other groups in the population. But we have no precise method of evaluating the correspondence of our selections in each nation to this intention. Finally, the ethnic units we have selected are appropriate for comparing variance between African countries but not necessarily for making statements about cultural variance in Black Africa as a whole, since our unit selection is based on within–country criteria.

Whatever the limitations of the data, or the conceptual and methodological approaches to it that we have discussed in this chapter, we believe that it is important to consider the complexity of African ethnicity in any research in that continent, and that it is imperative that cross-national research develop ethnic data for Africa that is comparable and theoretically relevant.[45] If the attempt discussed in this book is considerably less than ideal, we hope, at least, that it will stimulate future research along similar lines.

---

[43] The reader should consult Part I, Chapter 16 for this data, and additional commentary.

[44] The groups selected for representative codings for each ethnic unit are given in brackets in the summary classification in Figure 4.3, when the unit does not have the same label as the group coded.

[45] For a recent attack on the use of "tribalism" as the major explanatory variable for Black African countries by some "expatriate and African middle-class ideologists," see Archie Mafeja, "The Ideology of 'Tribalism'," *The Journal of Modern African Studies*, 9 (1971): 253–261. The emphasis here on ethnicity is meant to avoid some of the excesses of the analysis of "tribalism."

Appendix 1. African National Integration Project Data Bank

The African National Integration Project has arranged for the systematic collection and distribution of a larger set of data than is included in this book. Data descriptive of nations, ethnic groups, and elite individuals have been stored in the project's data bank in the following machine-readable files:

(1) *Black Africa File*: This file contains a data deck for 32 nations containing all the information given in the tables in Part I of this *Handbook*, plus an approximately equal number (155) of additional variables. A machine-readable codebook included in the file gives the definitions, sources, and data deck location of each variable.

(2) *African Nations File*: This file is the project's working data file, and contains, in addition to all the data in file (1), a large set of variables (over 1,000) for which data are either duplicates of the same variable from other sources, measures for different time periods, or relatively incomplete for the full set of 32 nations. New variables are being continuously added to this file, and a machine-readable codebook documents the variable definitions, data sources, and data deck locations.

(3) *African Ethnicity File*: This file contains data on the ethnic units given in Part II of this *Handbook*. The data are based on variables defined by George Peter Murdock and David Barrett, and these variables and sources are fully documented in the machine-readable codebook included in the file.

(4) *African Elite File*: This file contains data on the age, birthplace, ethnicity, and educational and occupational backgrounds of members of cabinets in 32 African nations at the date of independence (1967), and for the years in which *coups d'état* have occurred in any of these countries. The data deck gives the data on each individual cabinet member by nation and year, and a machine-readable codebook gives the definition and data deck location of variables.

Information regarding any of these files can be obtained from H. M. Stevenson, Institute for Behavioural Research, York University, Downsview, Canada. The *Black Africa File* is available at cost for immediate distribution to interested users of this *Handbook*, and is contained on a small 600-ft. magnetic tape. The other files will not be as easily available, since they are being continuously updated and changed, but, in response to requests for specific information on particular variables only, we will search the files and distribute the required information if it is available.

The following appendix gives some samples of the structure of the machine-readable codebook and data deck for the *Black Africa File*. Printouts of any of the other files would look substantially like these samples.

Appendix 2. Machine-Readable Codebook and Data: Samples

The following three pages from the machine-readable codebook for the *Black Africa File* give the format for the machine-readable codebook cards and the data cards. The third page contains the beginning of the codebook cards with the full reference for variable 01, Area in 1000 Square Kilometers, 1969. The reference to the *Handbook* gives an earlier version of its title.

```
STUDY SERIES 300--- AFRICAN DATA BANK FOR THE AFRICAN          1  300
   NATIONAL INTEGRATION PROJECT, NORTHWESTERN AND YORK UNIV.   1  300
   DIRECTORS ROBERT C. MITCHELL,(SWARTHMORE), DONALD G.        1  300
   MORRISON (YORK AND IBADAN), JOHN PADEN (NORTHWESTERN),      1  300
   HUGH MICHAEL STEVENSON (NORTHWESTERN AND YORK)              1  300


   ----------------------AFRICAN NATIONAL INTEGRATION PROJECT- 1 300
              NORTHWESTERN UNIVERSITY AND YORK UNIVERSITY      1 300

   * * * * * * * * * * * * * * * * * * * * * * * * * * * *      1  300


            REPORT NUMBER 2                                    1  300


MACHINE READABLE CODEBOOK FOR PART ONE OF THE BOOK            1  300
   DONALD G. MORRISON, ROBERT C. MITCHELL, JOHN N. PADEN,     1  300
   H. MICHAEL STEVENSON WITH LYNN FISCHER, JOESEPH KAUFERT,   1  300
   KENNETH E. LARRIMORE                                       1  300
   BLACK AFRICA A HANDBOOK FOR COMPARATIVE ANLAYSIS (FREE     1  300
   PRESS, NEW YORK, 1972)                                     1  300


            VERSION MAY 25, 1971                               1  300


   DISTRIBUTED BY THE DATA BANK SECTION OF THE INSTITUTE FOR  1 300
   BEHAVIOURAL RESEARCH, YORK UNIVERSITY, DOWNSVIEW, ONTARIO  1 300
   PROF. TOM ATKINSON, DIRECTOR OF THE DATA BANK              1 300
   * * * * * * * * * * * * * * * * * * * * * * * * * * * *      1  300




THIS STUDY CONTAINS APPROXIMATELY 327 VARIABLES COLLECTED     2  300
   FOR THE AFRICAN NATIONAL INTEGRATION PROJECT AT NORTH-     2  300
   WESTERN UNIVERSITY, PROGRAM OF AFRICAN STUDIES, AND COVERS 2  300
   32 INDEPENDENT COUNTRIES OF SUB-SAHARAN AFRICA.            2  300


THE VARIABLES HAVE BEEN GROUPED INTO 16 CATGORIES AS          3  300
   DETAILED BELOW IN TABLE 2.  FULL DEFINITIONS, PUNCHING LO- 3  300
   CATIONS, MISSING DATA, CODING PROCEDURES ARE INDICATED.    3  300

                                                              5  300
                                                              5  300
TABLE 1. COUNTRY CODE NUMBERS  * * * * * * * * * * * * * * *   5  300
                                                              5  300
   01 BOTSWANA      02 BURUNDI     03 CAMEROON    04 CAR       5  300
   05 CHAD          06 CONGO-BRA   07 CONGO-KIN   08 DAHOMEY   5  300
   09 ETHIOPIA      10 GABON       11 GAMBIA      12 GHANA     5  300
   13 GUINEA        14 IVORY COAST 15 KENYA       16 LESOTHO   5  300
   17 LIBERIA       18 MALAWI      19 MALI        20 MAURITANIA 5 300
   21 NIGER         22 NIGERIA     23 RWANDA      24 SENEGAL   5  300
   25 SIERRA LEONE  26 SOMALIA     27 SUDAN       28 TANZANIA  5  300
   29 TOGO          30 UGANDA      31 UPPER VOLTA 32 ZAMBIA    5  300
```

```
TABLE 2.  CATEGORY CODE NUMBERS * * * * * * * * * * * * *      5  300
   THE CATEGORY CODE NUMBERS APPEAR IN THE RIGHTMOST THREE    5  300
   COLUMNS ON CODE BOOK ENTRIES THAT PERTAIN TO THAT CATEGORY 5  300
   DATA CARDS FOR THAT CATEGORY HAVE THE LAST TWO DIGITS OF   5  300
   THE CATEGORY NUMBER IN COLS 78-79 OF EACH DATA CARD        5  300
                                                              5  300
301-- DEMOGRAPHY AND ECOLOGY                                  5  300
302-- CULTURAL PLURALISM, LANGUAGE AND RELIGION              5  300
303-- LABOR, ENERGY, AND INVESTMENT                          5  300
304-- SOCIAL AND ECONOMIC WELFARE                            5  300
305-- EDUCATION                                               5  300
306-- MASS COMMUNICATIONS AND TRANSPORTATION SYSTEMS         5  300
307-- POLITICAL REGIME CHARACTERISTICS                      5  300
308-- POLITICAL PARTIES AND ELECTIONS                        5  300
309-- EXTENT OF GOVERNMENT INFLUENCE                         5  300
310-- MILITARY AND SECURITY SYSTEMS                          5  300
311-- POLITICAL INSTABILITY                                  5  300
312-- INTERNATIONAL ECONOMIC AID                            5  300
313-- INTERNATIONAL TRADE                                    5  300
314-- INTERNATIONAL RELATIONS                               5  300
315-- URBAN PATTERNS                                         5  300
316-- ETHNIC PLURALISM                                       5  300


DATA CARD FORMAT                                             5  300
                                                              5  300
   ALL THE DATA CARDS HAVE A COMMON FORMAT FOR THE IDENTIFYIN 5  300
   G INFORMATION.  THIS IS AS FOLLOWS,                        5  300
                                                              5  300
      COL 1-6  COUNTRY NAME (FIRST SIX LETTERS)               5  300
          7-11 CATEGORY NAME (SHORT ACRONYM, SEE TABLE 2.)    5  300
          11-75 CONTAINS DATA OR BLANKS AS SPECIFIED          5  300
          76-77 COUNTRY NUMBER (SEE TABLE 1.)                 5  300
          78-79 CATEGORY NUMBER (SEE TABLE 2.)                5  300
             80 CARD NUMBER WITHIN CATEGORY                   5  300

   HENCE ALL REFERENCES TO COUNTRY, CATEGORY, AND CARD        5  300
   NUMBERS BELOW ARE TO NUMBERS ACTUALLY ON THE DATA CARDS.   5  300
                                                              5  300
STRUCTURE OF MACHINE READABLE CODEBOOK CARDS                 5  300
                                                              5  300
                                                              5  300
CATEGORY TITLE CARDS  (CARD TYPE 1, COL 75)                  5  300
   COL 1-3 CATEGORY NUMBER                                    5  300
       7-60 TITLE OF CATEGORY                                 5  300
       61-74 BLANK                                            5  300
       75    NUMBER 1                                         5  300
       78-80 STUDY NUMBER (SEE TABLE 2)                       5  300
                                                              5  300
                                                              5  300
VARIABLE NAME CARDS (CARD TYPE 7, COL 75)                    5  300
   COL 1-2 VARIABLE NUMBER IN THAT CATEGORY (ABITRARILY ASSIGNED) 5 300
       4-9 ABBREVIATED VARIABLE NAME (FOR COMPUTER ANALYSIS) 5  300
       11-60 SHORT DEFINITION (CONTINUE ON EXTRA CARDS AS NEED 5 300
```

```
THESE CARDS CONTAIN THE NUMBER WITHIN THE DATA CATEGORY          5   300
ASSIGNED TO THAT VARIABLE, A SIX COLUMN ACRONYM FOR THE          5   300
PURPOSE OF UNIFORM SHORT NAMES WHICH ARE REQUIRED IN MANY        5   300
COMPUTER PROGRAMS, AND A TITLE OF THE VARIABLE.  IF THE          5   300
TITLE IS NOT SUFFICIENT TO OPERATIONALLY DEFINE THE             5   300
VARIABLE, AN OPERATIONAL DEFINITION IS GIVEN ON A TYPE 8        5   300
CARD.                                                            5   300

VARIABLE DESCRIPTION CARDS -- (CARD TYPE 8, COL 75)              5   300
  1-DATA CARD COLUMN LOCATIONS AND TABLE NUMBER IN BOOK.         5   300
    THE FIRST CARD OF THE TYPE 8 CARDS GIVES THE CARD COLS.      5   300
    FOR THE DATA AND THE CARD NUMBER WITHIN THE DATA DECK        5   300
    FOR THAT CATEGORY OF DATA (E.G. CARD 2 IN THE LANGUAGE       5   300
    AND RELIGION DATA).  THE FORMAT IS AS FOLLOWS,  CARD COL     5   300
    UMN NUMBERS/ CARD NUMBER WITHIN CATEGORY.  (SEE DESCRIP      5   300
    TION OF DATA CARD FORMAT ABOVE)  THE CATEGORY NUMBER         5   300
    APPEARS IN COL 79-80 OF THE CODEBOOK CARD.                   5   300
    THIS INFORMATION IS FOLLOWED BY THE TABLE NUMBER IN THE      5   300
    BOOK OR THE LETTERS NIT (NOT IN TABLES IN THE BOOK)          5   300

  2-OPERATIONAL DEFINITION IF THE TITLE OF THE VARIABLE (SEE     5   300
    CARD TYPE 7) DOES NOT MAKE CLEAR THE DEFINITION OF THE       5   300
    VARIABLE, A CARD OR CARDS OF TYPE 8 ARE ADDED BEGINNING      5   300
    WITH THE LETTERS DEF--,  THESE CARDS GIVE A FULL OPERA-      5   300
    TIONAL DEFINITION OF THE VARIABLE                            5   300
  3- MISSING DATA  WHEN THERE IS NO MISSING DATA, THIS CARD      5   300
    MERELY STATES THIS DIRECTLY.  IF THERE IS MISSING DATA       5   300
    THEN THE COUNTRY NUMBERS (SEE TABLE 1) OF THE COUNTRIES      5   300
    WITHOUT DATA ARE GIVEN ON A CARD BEGINNING WITH THE          5   300
    WORDS MISSING DATA.                                          5   300
                                                                 5   300
                                                                 5   300
                                                                 5   300
                                                                 5   300
DATA SOURCE CARDS (CARD TYPE 9, IN COL 75)                       5   300
  THE SOURCES OF THE DATA ARE GIVEN ON CARD TYPE NUMBER 9.       5   300
    IF THE SOURCE IS GIVEN IN A TABLE IN PART 1 OF THE BOOK      5   300
    MORRISON, MITCHELL, PADEN, STEVENSON BLACK AFRICA A HAND     5   300
    BOOK FOR COMPARATIVE ANALYSIS, THEN THE BOOK IS GIVEN AS     5   300
    THE SOURCE.  IF THE DATA IS NOT DOCUMENTED IN THE BOOK,      5   300
    THEN THE DATA SOURCES ARE GIVEN ON CARD TYPE 9.  IF THE      5   300
    DATA COMES FROM SEVERAL SOURCES, COUNTRY NUMBERS ARE         5   300
    ATTACHED TO EACH SOURCE WHEN DATA CORRSPONDING TO THAT       5   300
    COUNTRY NUMBER CAME FROM THE SOURCE GIVEN.  (SEE TABLE 1     5   300
    FOR CORRESPONDENCE BETWEEN COUNTRY NUMBERS AND COUNTRY       5   300
    NAMES).                                                      5   300
                                                                 5   300
301    DEMOGRAPHY AND ECOLOGY                                    1   301
                                                                 1   301
                                                                 1   301
01 ARSSKM  AREA IN 1000 SQUARE KILOMETERS, 1969                 17   301
   COL 12-17/1           TABLE 1.1                               18   301
   DEF-- TOTAL AREA ENCLOSED WITHIN THE NATIONAL BOUNDARIES      18   301
   INCLUDING THAT COVERED BY WATER                               18   301
   NO MISSING DATA                                               18   301
   MORRISON,MITCHELL,PADEN,STEVENSON  BLACK AFRICA-- A HAND-    19   301
   BOOK FOR COMPARATIVE ANALYSIS (FREE PRESS, NEW YORK,1972)     19   301
02 WOP026  PERCENT WHITE POPULATION IN 1920 S TIMES 100         27   301
   COL 18-20/1           TABLE 1.7                               28   301
```

The following is a reproduction of the listing of all the data cards in the Black Africa File for Botswana.

```
BOTSWADEMOG    600 69 80   5     167    629 64   1   12.6                              01011
BOTSWALANGU 99990   2 34   1   4   2   2                                               01021
BOTSWARELIG 71   0 26   3 29       33214245 24 14 17                                   01022
BOTSWAECOND -0       -0 -0 -0 -0    2500       -0   2      -0 -0 91   1 -0 -0 -0 25     01031
BOTSWAECSOW  2 -0      -0   2 44 51      34 95116197 --8         57100     .8           01041
BOTSWAEDUCA  8000 10000 19000   19000   35225   46536   71557 27 30 51 44 70 8801051
BOTSWAEDUCA124     11      63   -14      3     77116122   5    641   1236 93 18217 01052
BOTSWAEDUCA  29123   75000   83000243351     444 59 32      36      54     500 45      01053
BOTSWAEDUCA   132     921  1854     3    17      32     240      88     967    110      01054
BOTSWAEDUCA639227135497257  88158  -0 40151162      0      17    17      5   7         01055
BOTSWAEDUCA 59 42 47     11 28 26     136 23 30 30   1713                              01056
BOTSWACOMMU  4    0   0 22 14 25  7   4 23   6 20 177   7 75   0   0 50 92346 57 4001061
BOTSWAPOLRE 31   5  .004  .010 43   3   2      -0 -0   3   5   3   2   5   6            01071
BOTSWAPOLPA  8 23 87   2     2   0   0   6   0   0   1   2   0   2 18 12 69             01081
BOTSWANATBU 40   2 -0 27 21      74   8   0   0 25 30   7 56        34 59               01091
BOTSWAMILIT  0   2   7   0   0   0   0      0   0   5      0   0   0   0   0   0 0118 -7 01101
BOTSWAPSTAB  1   1   0   1   3      0      0   1   0   0   0   0   0   0   0   0   0 01111
BOTSWAPSTAB  3   0      0      0   0   0   0   0   0      00                            01112
BOTSWAINAID 16  0.00    .33  0.00   0.00    .07 11.07 16.80    100   0 2270271201121
BOTSWATRCOM  0   1 10   5 96   1   0      0      0   0         18 22   5   5   1   5   3 301131
BOTSWAINREL  3   1 -0   1 -0 -0   0      0                                             01141
BOTSWAURBAN   -0 64      34 29   4 21 45367                                            01151
BOTSWAETHNI4.000.005.000.001.000.004.000.001.000.003.000.008.000.00                   01161
BOTSWAETHNI3.000.002.000.003.000.006.000.003.000.003.000.003.000.00                   01162
```

Appendix 3. Computer Program for Rank-Ordered Listing of the Data

```
C       INFORMATION TO USER----------                                    A    1
C                                                                        A    2
C       1.  GENERAL PROGRAM DESCRIPTION                                  A    3
C           PROGRAM RANKOR DESIGNED TO RETRIEVE SPECIFIC VARIABLES FROM  A    4
C           THE BLACK AFRICA HANDBOOK DATA COLLECTION.  PROGRAM PRODUCES A    5
C           RANK ORDERED TABLES ESSENTIALLY IDENTICAL TO THOSES FOUND IN A    6
C           PART I.                                                      A    7
C                                                                        A    8
C           SEVERAL SPECIFICATION CARDS FOLLOW THIS PROGRAM DECK BUT     A    9
C           PRECEDE THE DATA DECK.  THESE ARE---                         A   10
C           A.  PROBLEM CARD WITH NUMBER OF VARIABLES AND OTHER PARAMETERS A 11
C               (COLS 1-3), TOTAL NUMBER OF VARIABLES IN THIS RUN        A   12
C               (COLS 4-6), NUMBER OF VARIABLE FORMAT CARDS              A   13
C               (COLS 7-9), NUMBER OF SUBJECTS                           A   14
C           B.  FORMAT CARDS, F-TYPE , UP TO FIVE CARDS.        COLS 1-80 A   15
C               ARE AVAILABLE.                                           A   16
C           C.  COUNTRY NAME CARDS, 6 CARDS (STANDARD AS SHOWN HERE)     A   17
C           D.  CURRENT POPULATION CARDS, 2 CARDS (STANDARD AS SHOWN HERE) A 18
C               POPULATION SHOWN IN PERCENT OF TOTAL POPULATION IN SAME  A   19
C               ORDER AS COUNTRY NAMES.                                  A   20
C                                                                        A   21
C           VARIABLE NAME CARDS (ONE PER CARD) FOLLOW DATA DECK.         A   22
C                                                                        A   23
C       2.  SUMMARY OF INPUT ORDER-                                      A   24
C           (1) PROGRAM DECK                                             A   25
C           (2) PROBLEM CARD                                            A   26
C           (3) FORMAT CARDS, MAXIMUM OF 5                               A   27
C           (4) SIX COUNTRY NAME CARDS                                   A   28
C           (5) TWO POPULATION CARDS                                     A   29
C           (6) DATA DECK                                                A   30
C           (7) VARIABLE NAME CARDS   MAXIMUM OF 200                     A   31
C                                                                        A   32
C       3.  OPTION FOR 2ND AND 3RD COLUMNS IN EACH TABLE                 A   33
C           FOR TABULAR COMPARISONS BETWEEN VARIABLES, USER HAS OPTION OF A  34
C           ADDING A SECOND AND THIRD VARIABLE WHICH WILL CORRESPOND TO THE A 35
C           FIRST VARIABLE RANK ORDER.  FOR ADDITIONAL COLUMNS ENTER (RIGHT A 36
C           JUSTIFIED) VARIABLE NUMBER (IN ORDER OF DATA INPUT) IN COLUMNS A  37
C           71-75 (FOR A SECOND VARIABLE) AND COLUMNS 76-78 (FOR A THIRD  A   38
C           VARIABLE) ON EACH VARIABLE NAME CARD WHICH IDENTIFIES THE FIRST A 39
C           OR RANKED VARIABLE IN EACH TABLE.  IN ADDITION, IF ADDITIONAL A   40
C           VARIABLES ARE TO BE PRINTED WITH UP TO TWO PLACES TO THE RIGHT A  41
C           OF THE DECIMAL POINT, THEN COL 79 SHOULD HAVE A 2.  IF THE    A   42
C           RANKED VARIABLE IS TO HAVE ONE OR TWO PLACES TO THE RIGHT     A   43
C           OF THE DECIMAL POINT, THEN COL 80 SHOULD HAVE A 1 OR 2 RESPEC A   44
C           TIVELY.                                                      A   45
C                                                                        A   46
C       4.  OPTION FOR CHANGING OUTPUT FORMAT                            A   47
C           VALUES ARE PRINTED IN AN F8.0 FIELD UNLESS ALTERED BY USER.  A   48
C           TO CHANGE FIRST VARIABLE OUTPUT, PUNCH 1 FOR F8.1 AND 2 FOR  A   49
C           F8.2 IN COL 80 OF THE VARIABLE NAME CARD CORRESPONDING TO    A   50
C           VARIABLE FOR WHICH OUTPUT VARIATION REQUIRED.  TO CHANGE OUTPUT A 51
C           IN SECOND AND THIRD COLUMNS, ADJUST 4TH F-TYPE FIELD SPECIFI- A   52
C           CATION IN FORMAT STATEMENTS 25, 26, 27, 28, 29, 39 IN SUB OUTPU A 53
C                                                                        A   54
0001        DIMENSION FORMT(50), A(200,60), COUNM(60,3), TITLE(9), ISTOR(60), A 55
      1POPPC(60), B(200,60), LIST(60), COUND(60,3)
0002        DIMENSION P(10,60), IP(10,60), NSW(60)                       A   58
0003        EXTERNAL SIGN                                                A   57
```

```
0004              COMMON P                                              A   59
0005              EQUIVALENCE (P,IP)                                    A   60
0006              INTEGER OBSER                                         A   61
0007              REAL*8 FORMT,TITLE                                    A   62
0008              WRITE(6,99999)                                        1    4
0009            1 CONTINUE                                              A   63
0010            2 CONTINUE                                              A   64
0011              READ(5,30,END=18)NVAR,NVF,NCOUN                       A   65
0012              IF (NCOUN.EQ.0) NCOUN=32                              A   66
0013              POS=10.0                                              A   67
0014              IF (NVF.EQ.0) NVF=4                                   A   68
0015              NVF=NVF*10                                            A   69
0016              READ 19, (FORMT(I),I=1,NVF)                           A   70
0017              READ 20, ((COUNM(I,J),J=1,3),I=1,NCOUN)              A   71
0018              READ (5,21) (POPPC(I),I=1,NCOUN)                      A   72
0019              READ (5,FORMT) ((A(I,J),I=1,NVAR),J=1,NCOUN)          A   73
0020              DO 3 I=1,NVAR                                         A   74
0021              DO 3 J=1,NCOUN                                        A   75
0022              ISTOR(J)=0                                            A   76
0023            3 B(I,J)=A(I,J)                                         A   77
0024              DO 17 J=1,NVAR                                        A   78
0025              OBSER=NCOUN                                           A   79
0026              BIG=-1000.0                                           A   80
0027              BIG1=0.0                                              A   81
0028              SUMX=0.                                               A   82
0029              SUM2X=0.                                              A   83
0030              IZ=1                                                  A   84
0031              DO 7 I=1,NCOUN                                        A   85
0032              SUMX=SUMX+B(J,I)                                      A   86
0033              SUM2X=SUM2X+(B(J,I)**2)                               A   87
0034            4 CONTINUE                                              A   88
0035              DO 6 K=1,NCOUN                                        A   89
0036              IF (A(J,K).LE.BIG) GO TO 6                            A   90
0037              IF (ABS(A(J,K)).NE.0) GO TO 5                         A   91
0038              DATA=A(J,K)                                           A   92
0039              CHECK=SIGN(POS,DATA)                                  A   93
0040              IF (CHECK.GT.0.) GO TO 5                              A   94
0041              OBSER=OBSER-1                                         A   95
0042              LIST(IZ)=K                                            A   96
0043              IZ=IZ+1                                               A   97
0044              A(J,K)=-10000.                                        A   98
0045              GO TO 4                                               A   99
0046            5 ISTOR(I)=K                                            A  100
0047              BIG1=BIG                                              A  101
0048              BIG=A(J,K)                                            A  102
0049            6 CONTINUE                                              A  103
0050              IF (I.GT.OBSER) GO TO 7                               A  104
0051              IJ=ISTOR(I)                                           A  105
0052              A(J,IJ)=-10000.                                       A  106
0053            7 BIG=-1000.0                                           A  107
0054              IF (OBSER.LT.2) GO TO 16                              A  108
0055              SUMX=SUMX/OBSER                                       A  109
0056              SD=SQRT(SUM2X/OBSER-(SUMX*SUMX))                      A  110
0057              ITOP=ISTOR(1)                                         A  111
0058              IBOT=ISTOR(OBSER)                                     A  112
0059              RANGE=B(J,ITOP)-B(J,IBOT)                             A  113
0060              READ (5,22) (TITLE(I),I=1,9),N1,N2,N4,N3              A  114
0061              PRINT 23, (TITLE(I),I=1,9)                            A  115
```

```
0062            PRINT 24, RANGE,SUMX,SD                        A 116
0063            IF (N1.GT.0) GO TO 8                           A 117
0064            PRINT 25                                       A 118
0065            GO TO 9                                        A 119
0066          8 PRINT 26                                       A 120
0067          9 IRANGE=1                                       A 121
0068            NRNGE=0                                        A 122
0069            NPS=1                                          A 123
0070            POPCUM=0.0                                     A 124
0071            AINCR=RANGE*0.1                                A 125
0072            BOT=B(J,ITOP)-AINCR                            A 126
0073            DO 14 I=1,OBSER                                A 127
0074            IJ=ISTOR(I)                                    A 128
0075            IF (B(J,IJ).GT.BOT) GO TO 12                   A 129
0076         10 IRANGE=IRANGE+1                                A 130
0077            NPS=1                                          A 131
0078            IF (IRANGE.LE.10) GO TO 11                     A 132
0079            NPS=0                                          A 133
0080         11 BOT=BOT-AINCR                                  A 134
0081            IF (B(J,IJ).LT.BOT) GO TO 10                   A 135
0082         12 CONTINUE                                       A 136
0083            POPCUM=POPCUM+POPPC(IJ)                        A 137
0084            NSW(I)=NPS                                     A 138
0085            NPS=0                                          A 139
0086            P(1,I)=POPCUM                                  A 140
0087            P(2,I)=POPPC(IJ)                               A 141
0088            P(3,I)=I                                       A 142
0089            P(4,I)=COUNM(IJ,1)                             A 143
0090            P(5,I)=COUNM(IJ,2)                             A 144
0091            P(6,I)=COUNM(IJ,3)                             A 145
0092            P(7,I)=B(J,IJ)                                 A 146
0093            IP(8,I)=IRANGE                                 A 147
0094            IF (N1.LE.0) GO TO 13                          A 148
0095            P(9,I)=B(N1,IJ)                                A 149
0096            IF (N2.LE.0) GO TO 13                          A 150
0097            P(10,I)=B(N2,IJ)                               A 151
0098         13 CONTINUE                                       A 152
0099         14 CONTINUE                                       A 153
0100            CALL RANCK (OBSER)                             A 154
0101            CALL OUTPUT (OBSER,N2,N1,NSW,N3,N4)            A 155
0102            IF (OBSER.EQ.NCOUN) GO TO 17                   A 156
0103            PRINT 27                                       A 157
0104            KOUNT=NCOUN-OBSER                              A 158
0105            DO 15 I=1,KOUNT                                A 159
0106            IZ=LIST(I)                                     A 160
0107            COUND(I,1)=COUNM(IZ,1)                         A 161
0108            COUND(I,2)=COUNM(IZ,2)                         A 162
0109            COUND(I,3)=COUNM(IZ,3)                         A 163
0110         15 CONTINUE                                       A 164
0111            PRINT 28, ((COUND(IZ,K),K=1,3),IZ=1,KOUNT)     A 165
0112            GO TO 17                                       A 166
0113         16 CONTINUE                                       A 167
0114            READ (5,22) (TITLE(I),I=1,9),N1,N2,N3          A 168
0115            PRINT 23, (TITLE(I),I=1,9)                     A 169
0116            PRINT 29                                       A 170
0117         17 CONTINUE                                       A 171
0118            GO TO 2                                        A 172
          C                                                    A 173
```

```
0119            18 STOP                                                        A 174
        C                                                                      A 175
        C                                                                      A 176
0120            19 FORMAT (10A8)                                               A 177
0121            20 FORMAT (18A4)                                               A 178
0122            21 FORMAT (20F4.2)                                             A 179
0123            22 FORMAT (8A8,A6,I5,I3,2I1)                                   A 180
0124            23 FORMAT (1H1,8A8,A6)                                         A 181
0125            24 FORMAT (1H0/8H RANGE =,F12.2/8H MEAN = ,F12.2/22H STANDARD DEVIATI  A 182
                  10N = ,F12.2)                                                A 183
0126            25 FORMAT (1H0,/12H  POPULATION/51H     PERCENT          COUNTRY      A 184
                  1       RANGE  /49H            RANK    NAME            VALUE    DE   A 185
                  2CILE/13H CUM. COUNTRY/)                                     A 186
0127            26 FORMAT (1H0,/12H  POPULATION/51H     PERCENT          COUNTRY      A 187
                  1       RANGE  /49H            RANK    NAME            VALUE    DE   A 188
                  2CILE,7H  TOTAL/13H CUM. COUNTRY/)                           A 189
0128            27 FORMAT (//47H DATA NOT AVAILABLE FOR THE FOLLOWING COUNTRIES/)     A 190
0129            28 FORMAT (1H ,3A4,1X,3A4,1X,3A4,1X,3A4)                       A 191
0130            29 FORMAT (64H THERE IS NO DATA FOR THIS VARIABLE OR ONLY ONE OBSERVA  A 192
                  1TION     )                                                  A 193
0131            30 FORMAT(3I3)                                                 A 194
0132        99999 FORMAT(////,T40,27('* '),/' ',T40,'*',T92,'*',/' ',T40,'*',T48,   2      4
                  .'INSTITUTE   FOR  BEHAVIOURAL   RESEARCH',T92,'*'/' ',T40,'*',T52,  3      4
                  .'METHODS   &   ANALYSIS   SECTION',T92,'*'/' ',T40,'*',T92,'*'/ ' ', 4      4
                  .T40,'* PROGRAM:',T59,                                        5      4
                  .' R A N K O R'                                             6PROG  3
                  .,T92,'*'/' ',T40,'*',T92,'*'/' ',T40,'* WRITTEN FOR USE ON IBM/360  7      3
                  ./50  (YORK UNIVERSITY) *'/' ',T40,'* BY: ',               8     41
                  .'DONALD G. MORRISON'                                       9WRIT  2
                  ., T75,'DATE: ',                                           10      5
                  .'MAY 1971'                                                11DATE  3
                  .,T92,'*'/' ',T40,'*',T92,'*'/' ',T40,27('* '),////)       12      3
0133            END                                                           A 195-
```

Appendix 4. Correlation Matrix

The following matrix presents Pearson Product Moment Correlations for each of the variables in Part I by every other one. It is intended to provide a quick way to check bi-variate relationships between variables. The correlation coefficient varies between −1.00 and +1.00; the higher the coefficient the more the two variables co-vary. For example, the correlation coefficient between Public Investment Per Capita 1960 (PICF60, Table 3.8) and GNP Per Capita, 1963 (PCDG63, Table 4.3) is .76, indicating a strong relationship.

Each variable in the matrix is identified by a short (six-character) name and number. Most of these short names bear a discernible relationship to the name of the variable, but readers will have to use the table references to identify the variables initially.

MEANS AND STANDARD DEVIATIONS

VARIABLE (SHORT NAME)	TABLE REF. PART I	NUMBER OF OBSERVATIONS	MEAN	STANDARD DEVIATION
1 ARSSKM	1.1	32	597.4688	631.3840
2 WPOP26	1.7	29	0.1438	0.1640
3 WPOP60	1.8	31	0.4526	0.5724
4 NAGPOT	1.3	32	8.5938	4.0549
5 PEPHEC	1.2	32	14.6875	32.2755
6 POPE69	1.4	32	7076.3438	10744.7695
7 POPDE9	1.5	32	20.9375	24.0818
8 NATINR	1.6	32	2.6187	0.6582
9 PERVER	2.1	32	57.2813	22.5821
10 PERSEC	2.2	32	9.9437	24.0239
11 NULAPM	2.3	32	72.4063	80.3608
12 LANCLA	2.4	32	3.0313	2.3347
13 LINFRA	2.5	32	3.7813	1.0697
14 PRILAN	2.6	32	2.8438	0.9873
15 LANPOL	2.7	32	3.8438	1.9856
16 TRADPC	2.12	32	37.4688	20.5222
17 MUSLPC	2.8	32	30.5625	33.0151
18 PROTPC	2.10	32	12.3438	11.9801
19 ROMCPC	2.11	32	18.1563	17.6473
20 XNPERC	2.9	32	31.5938	25.4949
21 MSRC25	2.14	32	78.1563	94.9153
22 MSPR25	2.13	32	97.2813	118.4865
23 MSXN25	2.15	32	174.6250	173.8956
24 PECHAD	2.16	32	25.0000	22.5088
25 RCPCGN	2.18	31	16.3548	35.4387
26 AICMPO	2.17	32	12.8750	19.1020
27 TOEC38	3.5	30	192.5333	84.3613
28 PIPG60	3.9	28	73.6429	44.6544
29 PICF60	3.8	28	20.6786	25.3012

30	WGEN63	3.2	32	16254.6875	23611.3438
31	PCWE63	3.3	31	7.3871	4.5875
32	POSIND	3.6	30	9.5000	7.4127
33	AGLAB8	3.1	32	84.0938	9.0852
34	USIN65	3.10	32	1.7188	0.8884
35	PCEN66	3.4	30	87.5000	98.1198
36	DIFECG	3.11	30	2.7667	1.1043
37	GDCRG3	3.7	27	12.9925	7.0955
38	GDPD61	4.1	32	44.7813	62.9776
39	INAP60	4.7	30	128.6333	21.6882
40	COPR65	4.6	25	126.0800	20.0727
41	PCDG63	4.3	32	105.9063	64.7637
42	GNPA65	4.2	32	615.9688	918.7183
43	INPDOC	4.8	32	306.8125	205.9293
44	AUPHCH	4.9	32	11.9375	21.9324
45	GNPP68	4.4	32	120.6250	66.4752
46	PGNP18	4.5	32	1.1531	2.3378
47	PPCR30	5.1	32	15.0000	27.6429
48	PPCR53	5.2	32	36.6250	32.2348
49	PPCR60	5.3	32	58.4375	42.4773
50	PPCR65	5.5	32	81.2500	53.9594
51	PPCR16	5.6	32	51.7813	42.7225
52	PPCR17	5.7	32	43.0313	45.4614
53	PFEC60	5.8	32	30.7188	9.9230
54	SFEC60	5.12	32	20.6875	9.5392
55	SPCR50	5.9	32	6.0938	5.3843
56	SPCR66	5.10	32	54.5000	46.7602
57	SPCR12	5.11	32	105.8438	251.2281
58	EXPR65	5.18	32	525.7500	155.0652
59	PGDP65	5.19	32	28.7813	10.8323
60	PTGX65	5.20	32	162.8438	51.7071
61	HREA61	5.15	32	21.2813	18.0004
62	PPCRI4	5.4	32	94.1250	79.3236
63	PUTE66	5.22	32	47.0938	23.3920
64	PUTEIN	5.23	32	4.1875	31.2456
65	PTGXIN	5.21	30	-22.9000	77.6625
66	SSCP52	5.13	32	79.0313	63.7062
67	SSCPIN	5.14	32	183.7188	248.6576
68	LITR65	5.16	32	16.4375	13.3270
69	LITRIN	5.17	32	133.0313	167.6978
70	IMPRO7	6.8	32	54.7813	53.4408
71	CINSET	6.7	32	22.4063	25.3388
72	NMRT65	6.12	32	386.0000	386.4072
73	RADP66	6.1	32	35.1563	36.3718
74	RAPE06	6.2	32	274.3438	311.3223
75	NEPC65	6.3	32	41.0938	64.9085
76	NEPECA	6.4	32	19.4375	44.8229
77	TEPC68	6.5	32	32.0000	27.8753

78	TECH38	6.6	32	47.7500	55.3068
79	CVPE16	6.9	32	249.0625	195.5388
80	PECHCV	6.10	32	46.1875	53.7116
81	CARP16	6.11	32	37.9063	33.8082
82	LEGNOS	7.1	32	95.4063	72.8803
83	CABRPI	7.2	32	0.2296	0.2716
84	WAGPUB	7.3	29	31.2069	14.0874
85	LOCGOV	7.4	30	1.8333	0.7915
86	LAWTWO	7.5	31	1.8710	0.7184
87	LAWNOS	7.6	25	281.6399	558.5984
88	JUDREV	7.7	32	2.6563	0.7007
89	YOUNGI	7.8	32	3.5938	1.4997
90	YOUNGP	7.9	32	4.8125	2.1618
91	NOYRFO	8.1	32	25.2500	18.2085
92	NOVOIE	8.7	32	23.1250	12.5255
93	PEVORU	8.8	32	63.2500	25.5886
94	CHNOLP	8.3	30	-1.4000	3.3177
95	NOLEPA	8.2	32	5.8438	4.0569
96	NOPABN	8.6	31	2.8387	3.6249
97	TOSPME	8.4	32	2.6563	2.3086
98	LEGFRA	8.5	32	34.5313	25.6842
99	CGBC51	9.1	25	64.0000	45.0943
100	CGBC61	9.3	32	15.9688	13.0544
101	CGGC79	9.2	24	8.6250	4.0947
102	TAXD66	9.9	28	23.2500	11.2698
103	GREV66	9.7	32	19.0313	7.3066
104	GOSP61	9.4	32	16.4688	5.9459
105	TAXD36	9.10	24	1.1667	23.0513
106	GREV36	9.8	32	20.1563	23.0443
107	CREV36	9.11	32	35.8438	18.9637
108	GOEX68	9.5	32	29.4375	27.3106
109	GOSP38	9.6	30	22.7333	46.4498
110	DEFG65	10.7	32	98.8125	57.0724
111	TOTAID	10.11	32	6.6875	4.4391
112	NUMAID	10.10	32	2.6563	2.2663
113	TMAN67	10.1	32	70.8750	117.7232
114	AFARMF	10.9	32	2.5938	1.6434
115	DEFG67	10.6	32	22.6563	14.3967
116	CHDEFB	10.8	32	75.6250	92.1491
117	ARFPPO	10.3	32	100.5000	91.4006
118	CHARF7	10.2	32	72.3438	130.4295
119	INTSEC	10.4	32	89.8125	47.9108
120	CHINSE	10.5	32	6.2813	46.1073
121	TURMOL	11.4	32	11.0625	10.5278
122	ELITIN	11.2	32	7.1875	7.4550
123	KILLOG	11.5	32	3.2813	2.8082
124	COMWGT	11.3	32	6.7500	10.3954
125	AVERES	11.1	31	0.1932	0.1600

126	TOAAT8	12.1	32	66.3750	96.9754
127	PCAID8	12.2	32	1.1341	1.9701
128	AIDPC4	12.5	32	3.1187	6.5766
129	AIDPC8	12.6	32	2.0835	3.5510
130	CAPAD1	12.7	18	4.8405	4.6443
131	PCDAID	12.3	32	65.8438	267.5159
132	COMAID	12.9	32	23.1250	42.9837
133	CAPAD7	12.8	32	6.0656	7.6444
134	APCTO8	12.4	32	9.0190	8.0577
135	USTD62	13.13	32	10.0625	14.2850
136	USTD68	13.14	32	9.2813	9.1695
137	TMET62	13.10	30	40.4000	17.8916
138	TMET68	13.11	30	33.3667	15.4529
139	PCPREX	13.2	32	53.4688	21.0958
140	IMPCOM	13.12	32	1.8125	0.5923
141	TRPGN8	13.1	30	50.8333	28.8613
142	CUBATR	13.15	30	9.8667	46.2659
143	IMEQ62	13.4	32	28.1563	14.2401
144	EXAF68	13.6	32	13.3375	18.9497
145	IMAF68	13.5	31	9.5806	8.1108
146	7OPCEX	13.3	32	2.5938	1.4337
147	PCEXME	13.9	30	50.2333	26.2110
148	IMME25	13.7	24	45.2917	22.1310
149	EXME25	13.8	24	41.8333	25.9844
150	REGORG	14.3	32	6.5938	2.2981
151	MEMOR	14.5	21	125.2381	53.1507
152	MEMAME	14.4	32	7.4375	4.2875
153	DIPSEN	14.1	27	43.0370	47.4467
154	DIPREC	14.2	25	95.3600	60.0624
155	AOBJAG	14.7	32	28.9375	38.2377
156	MUCOSU	14.6	21	59.0000	56.8946
157	RECOC7	14.8	32	10.7188	9.5554
158	CH5067	15.8	30	186.9667	119.8073
159	MCITPM	15.4	32	15.4375	14.1192
160	LRCITP	15.5	32	231.5000	255.6175
161	PRLT4L	15.6	32	67.5938	21.8010
162	PRCT4L	15.7	32	65.5313	25.0818
163	URPC65	15.2	32	10.1875	7.5282
164	URPC55	15.1	32	44.4063	42.5038
165	UR5565	15.3	32	178.7500	102.4557
166	MOMARV	16.6	32	0.5509	0.7920
167	SETPAV	16.2	32	1.0750	0.8634
168	LEHIEV	16.4	32	0.4359	0.2186
169	HIEFAV	16.3	32	0.5203	0.3276
170	INHERV	16.5	32	1.3928	0.8792
171	AUTHOV	16.7	32	0.6844	0.4181
172	DECNV	16.1	32	1.0128	0.7340

C O R R E L A T I O N S

VARIABLE	1 ARSSKM	2 WPOP26	3 WPOP60	4 NAGPOT	5 PEPHEC	6 POPE69	7 POPDE9	8 NATINR	9 PERVER	10 PERSEC	11 NULAPM	12 LANCLA	13 LINFRA	14 PRILAN	15 LANPOL	TRADPC
1 ARSSKM	1.00															
2 WPOP26	0.03	1.00														
3 WPOP60	-0.01	0.66	1.00													
4 NAGPOT	0.08	0.03	0.38	1.00												
5 PEPHEC	0.16	0.53	0.08	-0.20	1.00											
6 POPE69	0.42	-0.16	-0.13	0.37	-0.17	1.00										
7 POPDE9	-0.38	-0.24	-0.29	-0.13	-0.30	0.25	1.00									
8 NATINR	-0.07	0.28	-0.06	-0.26	-0.06	0.05	0.02	1.00								
9 PERVER	-0.09	0.23	-0.27	-0.56	0.41	-0.15	0.17	0.26	1.00							
10 PERSEC	-0.11	0.61	0.00	-0.34	0.60	-0.17	-0.04	0.21	0.61	1.00						
11 NULAPM	-0.04	-0.02	0.26	0.38	-0.12	-0.22	-0.35	-0.31	-0.47	-0.20	1.00					
12 LANCLA	0.47	-0.36	-0.36	-0.09	-0.08	0.41	0.11	0.09	-0.03	-0.24	-0.23	1.00				
13 LINFRA	0.13	-0.12	-0.30	-0.35	-0.00	0.18	0.26	-0.03	-0.48	-0.10	-0.55	0.14	1.00			
14 PRILAN	0.50	0.16	-0.21	-0.06	-0.03	0.46	0.23	-0.05	0.16	-0.25	-0.37	0.58	0.52	1.00		
15 LANPOL	0.35	0.23	-0.22	-0.28	0.26	0.25	0.15	0.32	0.54	0.36	-0.28	-0.01	0.38	0.41	1.00	
16 TRADPC	-0.25	0.20	0.06	0.03	0.12	-0.26	-0.07	0.02	-0.30	0.01	0.27	-0.27	-0.29	-0.35	-0.23	1.00
17 MUSLPC	0.30	-0.30	-0.17	-0.21	-0.08	0.08	-0.21	0.04	-0.22	-0.15	-0.27	0.37	-0.14	-0.23	-0.02	-0.64
18 PROTPC	-0.21	0.33	0.10	0.23	0.04	0.07	0.10	-0.03	-0.48	0.38	0.11	-0.15	-0.15	-0.16	0.13	-0.06
19 ROMCPC	-0.18	0.16	0.19	0.22	-0.30	-0.00	0.41	-0.07	-0.03	0.04	0.17	-0.18	0.10	-0.03	0.15	0.00
20 XNPERC	-0.18	0.23	0.18	0.25	-0.20	0.10	0.33	-0.09	-0.04	0.19	0.14	-0.26	0.04	-0.00	0.22	0.00
21 MSRC25	-0.18	0.18	0.41	0.36	-0.16	-0.20	-0.15	-0.41	-0.30	0.08	0.46	-0.41	0.04	-0.24	-0.09	-0.07
22 MSPR25	-0.10	0.55	0.36	0.27	0.14	-0.13	-0.11	0.05	-0.02	0.45	0.25	-0.39	-0.36	-0.30	-0.05	0.25
23 MSXN25	-0.16	0.47	0.47	0.37	0.01	-0.20	-0.16	-0.19	-0.04	0.35	0.42	-0.49	-0.23	-0.33	-0.01	0.13
24 PECHAD	-0.16	0.25	0.25	0.20	-0.17	-0.02	0.26	-0.18	0.02	0.24	0.16	-0.31	0.16	-0.01	0.22	-0.30
25 RCPCGN	0.07	-0.10	-0.18	-0.28	-0.06	-0.10	-0.16	0.38	0.40	0.13	-0.19	0.02	0.08	-0.19	-0.09	-0.37
26 AICMPO	0.06	0.41	0.31	0.43	-0.05	0.05	-0.09	0.08	-0.16	0.08	0.15	-0.25	-0.24	-0.12	0.38	0.09
27 TOEC38	-0.11	-0.25	-0.25	-0.05	-0.08	-0.12	0.01	0.05	-0.03	-0.02	0.08	-0.15	-0.29	-0.18	-0.05	0.09
28 PIPG60	-0.16	0.02	-0.06	0.18	0.37	-0.30	-0.19	-0.28	-0.28	-0.19	0.17	-0.18	0.12	-0.08	0.31	-0.34
29 PICF60	-0.24	0.20	0.36	0.47	-0.01	-0.25	-0.21	-0.50	-0.11	-0.09	0.59	-0.29	-0.14	-0.27	-0.01	-0.07
30 WGEN63	0.54	0.18	0.15	0.49	-0.16	0.51	0.02	-0.17	-0.28	-0.19	-0.11	0.08	0.04	0.37	0.28	-0.05
31 PCWE63	0.08	0.22	0.54	0.56	-0.28	-0.13	-0.15	-0.24	-0.37	-0.27	0.15	-0.31	-0.24	-0.10	0.08	0.02
32 POSIND	0.20	0.44	0.41	0.63	-0.15	0.58	-0.04	0.11	-0.36	-0.29	-0.10	0.21	-0.29	0.18	-0.05	-0.06
33 AGLAB8	-0.03	-0.01	-0.33	-0.52	-0.24	-0.14	0.05	0.21	0.46	0.24	-0.09	0.21	-0.03	0.30	0.31	-0.05
34 USIN65	0.19	0.06	0.19	0.70	-0.23	0.42	-0.05	-0.11	-0.51	-0.28	0.42	-0.10	-0.27	0.02	-0.01	-0.11
35 PCEN66	-0.10	-0.17	-0.12	0.66	-0.04	-0.14	-0.28	-0.10	-0.45	-0.23	0.62	-0.33	-0.55	-0.33	-0.33	0.24
36 DIFECG	-0.08	-0.27	-0.33	-0.80	0.19	-0.29	0.11	0.16	0.50	0.34	-0.26	0.06	0.18	-0.05	0.11	0.06
37 GDCRG3	0.08	-0.04	-0.10	0.47	0.57	-0.12	-0.28	-0.38	-0.04	-0.14	0.46	-0.15	-0.26	-0.01	-0.03	-0.11
38 GDPD61	0.39	-0.09	-0.03	0.49	-0.19	0.94	0.21	0.09	-0.25	-0.20	-0.13	0.41	-0.03	0.35	0.31	-0.24
39 INAP60	-0.12	-0.13	-0.10	0.06	-0.05	-0.04	-0.06	0.48	0.10	0.42	-0.07	-0.02	-0.34	-0.24	-0.01	-0.15
40 CDPR65	-0.25	-0.17	-0.12	-0.37	0.00	-0.17	0.23	-0.01	0.21	0.37	-0.22	-0.16	0.04	-0.27	-0.33	-0.04
41 PCDG63	-0.17	0.05	0.49	0.63	-0.18	-0.21	-0.21	-0.40	-0.38	-0.27	0.68	-0.25	-0.47	-0.31	-0.05	0.06
42 GNPA65	0.31	-0.12	-0.04	0.49	-0.18	0.91	0.24	0.09	-0.26	-0.19	-0.13	0.39	-0.10	0.29	-0.07	-0.20
43 INPDDC	0.18	-0.38	-0.43	-0.55	-0.01	0.09	0.16	-0.00	-0.21	-0.08	-0.32	0.37	0.38	0.29	-0.13	0.01
44 AUPHCH	0.40	0.09	0.24	0.42	-0.16	0.18	-0.09	-0.01	-0.41	-0.24	0.01	-0.17	-0.04	0.07	-0.05	0.09
45 GNPP68	-0.18	0.15	0.59	0.63	-0.02	-0.25	-0.33	-0.40	-0.41	-0.18	0.64	-0.27	-0.56	-0.35	-0.33	0.11

C O R R E L A T I O N S

	1	2	3	4	5	6	7	8	9	10	11	12	13	14	15	15
VARIABLE	ARSSKM	WPOP26	WPOP60	NAGPOT	PEPHEC	POPE69	POPDE9	NATINR	PERVER	PERSEC	NULAPM	LANCLA	LINFRA	PRILAN	LANPOL	TRADPC
46 PGNP18	-0.05	-0.02	0.07	0.24	0.30	-0.14	-0.16	-0.11	0.04	-0.02	-0.05	-0.14	-0.09	0.02	0.11	-0.01
47 PPCR30	-0.20	0.39	0.07	-0.12	0.03	-0.10	0.12	0.26	0.21	0.65	-0.11	-0.24	-0.00	-0.14	0.17	-0.04
48 PPCR53	-0.21	0.39	0.29	0.25	-0.09	-0.09	0.06	0.05	-0.04	0.43	0.12	-0.37	-0.18	-0.32	0.01	-0.05
49 PPCR60	-0.22	0.41	0.40	0.37	-0.11	-0.08	0.02	-0.05	-0.10	0.37	0.21	-0.34	-0.17	-0.29	-0.02	0.07
50 PPCR65	-0.22	0.40	0.48	0.42	-0.01	-0.18	-0.10	-0.15	-0.20	0.30	0.37	-0.39	-0.37	-0.40	-0.15	0.18
51 PPCR16	0.20	-0.18	-0.05	-0.22	0.20	-0.22	-0.35	-0.21	-0.12	-0.13	0.16	0.19	-0.21	0.05	-0.32	0.04
52 PPCR17	0.32	-0.30	0.01	-0.23	0.19	-0.21	-0.33	-0.31	-0.00	-0.26	0.05	0.35	-0.08	0.26	-0.13	-0.19
53 PFEC60	-0.22	0.68	0.30	0.06	0.30	0.01	0.03	0.15	0.25	0.75	-0.11	-0.27	-0.05	-0.32	0.08	0.07
54 SFEC60	-0.37	0.52	0.16	-0.14	0.20	-0.11	0.12	0.11	0.36	0.58	-0.14	-0.22	0.02	-0.18	0.10	0.19
55 SPCR50	-0.31	0.04	0.15	0.19	-0.23	-0.08	0.04	-0.26	-0.04	0.03	0.10	-0.25	-0.08	-0.11	-0.08	-0.17
56 SPCR66	-0.28	-0.04	0.26	0.42	-0.23	-0.10	-0.02	-0.21	-0.39	-0.17	0.30	-0.23	-0.38	-0.30	-0.35	0.00
57 SPCR12	0.05	-0.07	0.11	0.10	0.37	-0.14	-0.23	-0.23	0.16	-0.00	-0.08	-0.08	0.07	0.12	0.09	-0.23
58 EXPR65	-0.20	0.31	0.15	-0.28	0.06	-0.16	0.22	0.48	0.28	0.17	-0.23	-0.03	0.01	0.07	0.25	0.13
59 PGDP65	-0.08	0.34	0.14	0.20	0.04	-0.17	0.24	-0.06	0.04	0.12	-0.02	-0.38	0.01	-0.04	-0.01	0.20
60 PTGX65	-0.05	-0.02	-0.32	0.08	-0.08	-0.03	0.29	0.01	0.14	0.24	-0.17	-0.05	0.19	0.07	0.09	0.18
61 HREA61	-0.19	-0.13	0.19	0.45	-0.25	-0.08	-0.14	-0.25	-0.19	-0.13	0.43	-0.11	-0.37	-0.32	-0.30	-0.01
62 PPCR14	0.14	-0.24	-0.11	0.02	0.06	0.01	-0.17	-0.16	-0.00	-0.18	-0.00	0.24	0.07	0.26	-0.22	-0.04
63 PUTE66	-0.10	-0.02	-0.03	-0.25	-0.10	-0.17	-0.03	0.12	-0.03	-0.01	-0.12	-0.09	0.07	-0.11	0.06	0.37
64 PUTEIN	0.08	0.05	-0.11	-0.38	0.21	0.10	0.08	0.18	0.32	0.27	-0.17	0.07	0.11	-0.11	0.30	0.21
65 PTGXIN	0.12	0.13	-0.09	-0.20	0.12	-0.43	-0.12	0.04	0.09	0.26	-0.00	-0.11	0.08	-0.08	0.04	0.01
66 SSCP52	-0.01	-0.22	-0.08	-0.05	-0.15	0.02	-0.05	0.01	-0.04	-0.14	-0.03	-0.06	0.01	-0.10	0.03	-0.39
67 SSCPIN	-0.02	0.09	0.10	0.15	-0.08	0.04	-0.00	0.21	-0.27	-0.06	0.14	-0.19	-0.29	-0.30	-0.11	0.03
68 LITR65	0.04	0.55	0.31	0.30	0.07	0.25	0.08	0.24	-0.07	0.50	-0.01	-0.19	-0.17	-0.06	0.20	0.05
69 LITRIN	-0.05	-0.15	0.26	0.25	-0.14	-0.04	-0.29	-0.12	-0.15	-0.12	0.35	-0.19	-0.17	-0.33	-0.23	-0.11
70 IMPR07	-0.36	-0.12	-0.19	0.06	-0.29	0.20	0.87	-0.09	-0.02	-0.10	-0.29	-0.02	0.15	0.14	0.04	0.09
71 CINSET	0.04	0.14	0.22	0.24	-0.16	0.21	-0.02	0.30	-0.05	-0.12	-0.21	-0.05	-0.20	0.02	0.06	-0.24
72 NMRT65	-0.28	-0.11	-0.05	0.23	-0.24	0.15	0.19	0.02	-0.30	-0.27	-0.15	-0.13	-0.08	-0.15	-0.19	0.32
73 RADP66	-0.38	-0.12	0.18	0.22	-0.20	-0.24	-0.06	-0.41	-0.20	-0.16	0.38	-0.23	-0.25	-0.22	-0.35	-0.20
74 RAPE06	0.02	-0.14	-0.09	-0.16	-0.10	-0.17	-0.20	0.10	0.00	0.04	-0.14	0.08	-0.06	-0.27	-0.11	-0.15
75 NEPC65	-0.11	-0.06	0.01	0.32	-0.20	-0.20	0.15	0.08	-0.29	-0.19	-0.00	-0.00	-0.42	-0.10	-0.15	0.01
76 NEPECA	0.02	-0.16	-0.05	0.09	-0.05	-0.07	-0.18	-0.08	-0.15	-0.06	0.36	-0.15	-0.26	-0.33	-0.10	0.18
77 TEPC68	-0.14	0.54	0.85	0.46	-0.05	-0.07	-0.27	-0.15	-0.28	-0.02	0.39	-0.37	-0.40	-0.30	-0.23	0.10
78 TECH38	0.22	0.03	-0.20	-0.25	0.36	-0.07	-0.16	-0.00	-0.35	0.32	-0.09	0.26	0.14	0.29	0.30	-0.18
79 CVPE16	-0.24	0.14	0.50	0.45	0.06	-0.33	-0.33	-0.34	-0.31	-0.09	0.45	-0.35	-0.54	-0.44	-0.49	-0.10
80 PECHCV	-0.18	-0.27	-0.26	0.08	0.07	-0.00	0.09	-0.13	-0.02	-0.07	0.00	0.07	-0.37	-0.16	-0.18	0.14
81 CARP16	-0.25	0.35	0.72	0.58	-0.09	-0.23	-0.26	-0.28	-0.43	-0.19	0.53	-0.38	-0.47	-0.33	-0.42	0.17
82 LEGNOS	0.52	-0.21	-0.16	0.15	-0.20	0.73	0.04	0.21	-0.04	-0.17	-0.18	0.52	0.15	0.47	0.19	-0.39
83 CABRPI	-0.17	-0.30	-0.14	0.10	-0.13	-0.20	0.03	-0.48	-0.30	-0.26	0.51	-0.10	-0.51	-0.17	-0.29	0.09
84 WAGPUB	-0.38	0.00	-0.19	-0.28	0.21	0.19	-0.24	0.16	0.22	0.22	-0.27	0.17	0.09	-0.12	0.24	-0.21
85 LOCGOV	-0.03	0.28	0.12	-0.10	0.11	0.13	0.25	0.27	0.03	0.07	-0.20	0.18	0.02	-0.01	-0.08	-0.10
86 LAWTWO	0.12	-0.04	-0.21	-0.17	0.18	-0.05	0.00	0.12	0.26	0.13	-0.09	0.10	-0.05	-0.13	0.19	-0.03
87 LAWNOS	-0.29	-0.28	-0.19	0.05	0.03	0.64	0.05	0.39	0.06	-0.12	-0.17	0.34	0.08	0.40	0.22	-0.50
88 JUDREV	-0.01	0.14	-0.12	-0.11	-0.09	0.17	0.24	0.30	0.18	-0.16	-0.16	-0.21	0.33	-0.01	0.38	0.02
89 YOUNGI	-0.29	0.34	0.41	0.24	0.22	-0.24	-0.24	-0.18	-0.04	0.21	0.12	-0.21	-0.10	-0.11	-0.20	-0.01
90 YOUNGP	-0.28	0.37	0.29	-0.21	0.07	-0.30	0.19	0.11	0.09	0.15	0.04	-0.19	0.11	-0.03	0.07	0.22

C O R R E L A T I O N S

VARIABLE	1 ARSSKM	2 WPOP26	3 WPOP60	4 NAGPOT	5 PEPHEC	6 POPE69	7 POPDE9	8 NATINR	9 PERVER	10 PERSEC	11 NULAPM	12 LANCLA	13 LINFRA	14 PRILAN	15 LANPOL	15 TRADPC
91 NOYRFO	-0.12	-0.16	0.02	0.38	-0.18	0.07	-0.13	-0.15	-0.17	-0.21	0.49	0.01	-0.28	-0.08	-0.24	-0.01
92 VOVOIE	-0.33	0.30	0.34	0.12	0.06	-0.31	-0.02	-0.03	-0.14	0.30	0.11	-0.17	-0.09	-0.17	-0.07	-0.30
93 PEVORU	-0.36	0.08	0.07	-0.13	0.30	-0.50	-0.08	0.05	0.16	0.05	0.11	-0.23	-0.25	-0.19	-0.20	-0.10
94 CHNOLP	-0.19	0.06	-0.02	-0.35	0.12	-0.36	-0.12	0.18	-0.30	0.18	0.15	0.14	-0.06	-0.08	0.03	-0.02
95 NOLEPA	0.29	0.18	0.09	0.30	-0.03	0.40	0.12	0.11	-0.07	0.10	-0.10	0.09	-0.10	-0.02	0.21	-0.22
96 VOPABN	0.47	-0.15	-0.11	0.26	-0.14	0.64	0.21	0.05	-0.20	-0.21	-0.12	0.34	0.15	0.27	0.23	-0.14
97 TOSPME	-0.12	0.20	0.24	0.07	-0.05	0.18	0.06	0.05	-0.11	0.02	-0.21	0.01	-0.08	-0.15	-0.08	-0.07
98 LEGFRA	-0.15	0.02	-0.12	0.14	-0.23	0.27	0.10	0.06	-0.11	0.04	-0.07	0.16	0.11	0.04	0.11	-0.10
99 CGBC51	-0.21	-0.05	0.13	0.39	-0.14	-0.13	-0.12	0.09	-0.27	-0.11	0.24	-0.14	-0.63	-0.37	-0.35	-0.17
100 CGBC61	-0.18	-0.06	0.33	0.38	-0.15	-0.16	-0.11	-0.05	-0.35	-0.28	0.16	-0.15	-0.60	-0.28	-0.43	-0.03
101 CGGC79	-0.13	0.23	0.45	0.16	-0.23	-0.17	0.05	-0.29	-0.32	-0.33	-0.16	-0.28	-0.30	-0.31	-0.33	0.44
102 TAXO66	0.16	0.29	0.29	0.17	0.09	0.22	0.14	-0.05	-0.15	-0.02	-0.05	-0.09	-0.21	0.21	0.07	-0.02
103 GREV66	0.12	0.37	0.60	0.42	0.06	-0.27	-0.45	-0.10	-0.41	-0.09	0.47	-0.43	-0.30	-0.31	-0.28	-0.08
104 GOSP61	-0.22	-0.24	0.07	0.28	-0.22	-0.22	-0.12	-0.08	-0.20	-0.36	-0.01	-0.21	-0.13	-0.18	-0.45	-0.11
105 TAXD36	0.00	-0.14	-0.16	0.17	-0.07	0.24	0.23	-0.10	-0.05	-0.02	-0.11	-0.17	0.09	-0.04	-0.01	-0.15
106 GREV36	0.16	0.06	0.02	-0.07	0.04	0.02	-0.26	0.14	0.03	0.04	0.21	-0.17	-0.05	-0.03	0.32	-0.01
107 CREV36	0.25	0.16	0.37	0.37	0.04	0.20	-0.36	0.03	-0.50	-0.15	0.40	-0.22	-0.47	-0.11	-0.04	-0.03
108 GOEX68	-0.14	0.48	0.77	0.58	0.14	-0.25	-0.34	-0.20	-0.40	-0.02	0.62	-0.38	-0.59	-0.42	-0.41	0.24
109 GOSP38	0.14	0.59	0.59	0.38	0.03	-0.12	-0.29	0.10	-0.45	-0.01	0.32	-0.22	-0.44	-0.22	-0.19	0.16
110 DEFG65	0.50	-0.43	-0.15	-0.04	-0.11	0.18	-0.25	-0.03	-0.15	-0.39	-0.11	0.50	0.16	0.19	0.04	-0.19
111 TOTAID	0.53	-0.22	-0.09	0.37	-0.28	0.57	-0.01	0.24	-0.14	-0.35	-0.17	0.19	0.08	0.36	0.28	-0.25
112 NUMAID	0.40	-0.18	-0.06	0.37	-0.26	0.72	0.07	0.25	-0.15	-0.28	-0.18	0.20	0.02	0.32	0.25	-0.29
113 TMAN67	0.52	-0.13	-0.06	0.41	-0.16	0.92	0.14	0.00	-0.21	-0.16	-0.18	0.28	0.17	0.38	0.29	-0.20
114 AFARMF	0.28	-0.39	-0.16	0.17	-0.29	0.30	0.06	-0.07	-0.11	-0.36	0.06	0.22	0.11	0.08	-0.05	-0.20
115 DEFG67	0.51	-0.17	0.19	0.23	-0.14	0.11	-0.38	-0.06	-0.23	-0.35	-0.07	0.15	0.20	0.13	-0.00	-0.23
116 CHDEFB	-0.03	-0.06	0.03	-0.07	-0.23	0.19	0.08	0.28	-0.24	-0.23	-0.04	-0.10	0.18	0.25	0.17	0.11
117 ARFPPO	-0.09	-0.16	0.16	0.40	-0.18	0.03	-0.24	-0.10	-0.15	-0.20	0.27	-0.19	-0.15	-0.27	-0.07	-0.14
118 CHARF7	-0.08	-0.20	-0.12	0.06	-0.12	0.43	0.23	-0.09	-0.03	-0.14	-0.12	0.24	-0.16	0.11	-0.11	-0.02
119 INTSEC	-0.11	0.31	0.50	0.26	0.06	-0.21	-0.32	-0.23	-0.17	-0.03	-0.28	-0.51	-0.21	-0.46	-0.12	-0.21
120 CHINSE	-0.11	-0.16	0.06	0.03	0.05	-0.13	-0.16	-0.31	-0.20	-0.07	-0.30	-0.02	-0.29	-0.03	-0.10	-0.10
121 TURMOL	0.37	-0.03	-0.13	0.42	-0.15	0.72	0.14	0.04	-0.25	-0.22	-0.12	0.33	-0.03	0.25	-0.02	-0.09
122 ELITIN	0.21	-0.25	-0.13	0.03	-0.28	0.20	0.25	-0.01	-0.17	-0.23	-0.01	0.10	0.15	-0.03	0.05	0.13
123 KILLOG	0.24	-0.12	-0.03	0.21	-0.21	0.58	0.38	-0.03	-0.04	-0.18	-0.15	0.31	0.29	0.48	0.25	-0.08
124 COMWGT	0.70	-0.11	-0.13	0.14	-0.13	0.69	0.06	0.03	-0.12	-0.18	-0.18	0.47	0.30	0.61	0.45	-0.21
125 AVERES	0.45	-0.17	-0.02	0.19	-0.11	0.09	0.03	-0.17	-0.07	-0.26	-0.04	-0.07	0.27	0.11	0.17	-0.19
126 TOAAT8	0.45	-0.09	-0.03	0.52	-0.15	0.60	0.01	-0.03	-0.31	-0.17	0.01	0.03	-0.04	0.20	-0.17	-0.09
127 PCAID8	-0.18	-0.15	-0.04	0.38	-0.14	-0.09	-0.07	0.14	-0.28	-0.05	-0.20	-0.25	-0.45	-0.33	-0.23	0.20
128 AIDPC4	0.28	-0.15	-0.08	0.52	-0.14	0.87	0.18	-0.03	-0.19	-0.14	-0.04	-0.30	0.06	0.28	0.05	-0.18
129 AIDPC8	0.20	-0.11	-0.02	0.54	-0.19	0.46	0.07	0.03	-0.37	-0.16	-0.04	-0.07	-0.19	0.02	-0.05	-0.00
130 CAPAD1	-0.28	0.06	-0.11	0.05	0.35	-0.19	-0.24	-0.23	0.20	0.31	0.39	-0.22	-0.19	-0.38	-0.14	0.22
131 PCDAID	-0.19	0.02	0.09	0.19	-0.01	-0.10	0.03	0.04	-0.17	0.01	0.09	-0.20	-0.29	-0.18	-0.15	0.23
132 COMAID	0.01	-0.13	-0.07	0.18	-0.15	0.17	-0.02	0.14	0.02	-0.08	-0.20	-0.18	0.05	-0.02	-0.10	-0.24
133 CAPAD7	-0.23	0.42	0.32	0.14	0.45	-0.30	-0.26	-0.26	-0.06	0.43	0.53	-0.35	-0.34	-0.38	-0.13	0.24
134 APCTO8	-0.27	0.37	0.46	0.24	0.33	-0.37	-0.33	-0.31	-0.00	0.37	0.40	-0.32	-0.38	-0.54	-0.25	0.11
135 USTD62	-0.08	-0.26	-0.19	0.05	-0.18	0.10	0.63	-0.13	-0.06	-0.17	0.03	0.02	0.15	0.30	-0.25	-0.01

	1	2	3	4	5	6	7	8	9	10	11	12	13	14	15	15
VARIABLE	ARSSKM	WPOP26	WPOP60	NAGPOT	PEPHEC	POPE69	POPDE9	NATINR	PERVER	PERSEC	NULAPM	LANCLA	LINFRA	PRILAN	LANPOL	TRADPC
135 USTD68	-0.07	-0.32	-0.18	0.21	-0.22	0.16	0.41	-0.24	-0.19	-0.25	0.23	-0.11	-0.09	0.14	0.13	-0.00
137 TMET62	-0.11	-0.38	0.19	0.10	-0.19	-0.13	-0.26	-0.34	-0.23	-0.47	0.33	-0.12	-0.25	-0.13	-0.43	-0.09
138 TMET68	-0.05	-0.32	0.26	0.00	-0.29	-0.11	-0.19	-0.29	-0.34	-0.50	0.20	-0.19	-0.23	-0.11	-0.49	-0.20
139 PCPREX	0.05	0.44	0.27	-0.17	-0.50	-0.28	0.02	-0.01	-0.18	-0.30	-0.00	-0.15	-0.03	0.07	0.07	0.12
140 IMPCOM	0.28	-0.29	-0.10	-0.16	-0.15	0.15	-0.24	0.19	-0.15	-0.35	-0.12	0.49	-0.07	0.22	-0.11	-0.02
141 TRPGN8	-0.26	0.32	0.46	0.45	0.07	-0.33	-0.27	-0.23	-0.27	-0.06	0.52	-0.53	-0.45	-0.45	-0.27	0.16
142 CUBATR	0.14	0.38	0.25	0.45	0.18	0.02	-0.17	-0.02	-0.17	0.01	0.41	-0.05	-0.25	0.02	0.08	-0.02
143 IMEQ62	0.14	-0.24	0.08	0.34	0.18	-0.06	-0.31	-0.37	-0.11	-0.31	0.29	-0.01	-0.05	0.06	-0.04	-0.13
144 EXAF68	-0.09	-0.15	-0.18	-0.33	-0.13	-0.09	-0.06	0.23	0.16	-0.11	-0.26	0.26	0.35	0.18	-0.11	0.27
145 IMAF68	-0.24	-0.11	-0.09	-0.39	-0.18	-0.17	0.10	0.30	0.08	-0.12	-0.25	0.02	0.27	0.03	-0.15	0.25
146 70PCEX	0.21	-0.18	-0.20	0.18	-0.29	0.37	-0.06	0.12	-0.10	-0.21	-0.13	0.25	0.07	0.16	0.11	-0.06
147 PCEXME	0.10	-0.34	0.03	0.13	-0.24	0.02	-0.08	-0.19	-0.47	-0.57	0.26	0.24	-0.25	0.10	-0.45	-0.08
148 IMME25	0.25	-0.31	0.02	0.47	-0.31	0.43	0.20	-0.08	-0.29	-0.60	0.01	0.40	-0.17	0.52	-0.02	-0.48
149 EXME25	0.02	-0.13	0.05	0.32	-0.33	0.27	0.32	0.10	-0.18	-0.47	-0.23	0.25	0.12	0.46	-0.05	-0.25
150 REGORG	0.07	-0.37	0.15	0.06	-0.34	-0.08	-0.37	-0.17	-0.40	-0.44	-0.29	0.19	-0.16	-0.17	-0.51	-0.08
151 MEMOR	0.27	0.06	0.01	0.32	-0.12	0.69	0.02	0.28	-0.06	-0.08	-0.34	0.49	-0.06	0.35	0.07	-0.41
152 MEMAME	-0.03	-0.42	0.06	0.12	-0.21	0.01	-0.21	-0.13	-0.29	-0.43	-0.18	0.19	-0.13	-0.05	-0.42	-0.11
153 DIPSEN	-0.12	-0.14	-0.08	0.34	-0.20	0.52	0.14	-0.04	-0.23	-0.09	-0.11	0.17	-0.28	-0.08	-0.15	-0.20
154 DIPREC	0.22	-0.15	-0.02	0.40	-0.31	0.61	0.45	0.23	-0.13	-0.02	-0.30	0.14	0.00	0.17	-0.05	-0.22
155 ADBJAG	0.30	-0.13	-0.11	0.02	-0.15	0.28	0.08	0.24	0.08	-0.08	-0.28	-0.09	0.18	-0.09	0.41	-0.32
156 MUCOSU	0.30	0.34	0.15	0.50	0.12	0.71	0.05	0.37	-0.17	-0.14	-0.25	0.36	-0.09	0.37	0.09	-0.13
157 RECOC7	0.28	-0.14	-0.00	0.27	-0.12	0.33	-0.10	0.12	-0.10	-0.29	-0.21	0.16	0.13	0.28	0.12	-0.12
158 CH5067	0.01	-0.19	-0.28	0.03	-0.04	-0.06	-0.13	0.12	0.08	0.08	0.06	0.22	0.06	0.14	-0.15	-0.19
159 MCITPM	-0.07	0.49	0.40	0.09	0.52	-0.09	-0.31	-0.20	0.05	0.40	0.41	-0.30	-0.27	-0.41	-0.07	-0.05
160 LRCITP	0.42	-0.02	0.14	0.52	-0.22	0.81	0.11	0.02	-0.34	-0.24	-0.18	-0.13	-0.05	0.31	0.14	-0.22
161 PRLT4L	-0.49	-0.33	-0.27	-0.15	-0.23	-0.30	0.41	-0.20	0.21	-0.03	-0.10	-0.22	0.19	0.06	0.11	-0.17
162 PRCT4L	-0.40	-0.37	-0.25	-0.13	-0.34	-0.23	0.39	-0.18	0.16	-0.13	-0.07	-0.19	0.21	0.12	0.11	-0.23
163 JRPC65	-0.06	0.42	0.71	0.35	0.13	-0.04	-0.32	-0.15	-0.30	-0.03	-0.43	-0.37	-0.42	-0.46	-0.27	-0.07
164 JRPC55	-0.04	0.32	0.75	0.41	-0.10	0.14	-0.17	-0.12	-0.37	-0.17	0.20	-0.19	-0.30	-0.22	-0.29	-0.06
165 JR5565	-0.18	-0.08	-0.29	-0.24	0.33	-0.32	-0.11	0.03	0.29	-0.18	0.10	-0.10	-0.08	-0.08	-0.02	-0.08
166 MOMARV	-0.07	-0.11	-0.05	0.18	-0.20	0.27	0.07	-0.11	-0.34	-0.24	0.18	-0.18	-0.22	-0.07	0.09	0.28
167 SETPAV	0.59	-0.21	-0.02	-0.11	-0.00	0.26	-0.29	-0.01	-0.22	-0.38	-0.13	0.57	-0.00	0.52	-0.03	-0.25
168 LEHIEV	0.18	-0.58	-0.06	0.39	-0.27	0.26	-0.23	-0.40	-0.67	-0.64	0.30	0.15	-0.20	0.05	-0.50	0.17
169 HIEFAV	0.33	-0.40	-0.08	0.14	-0.22	0.31	-0.15	-0.18	-0.53	-0.50	-0.03	0.25	-0.18	0.24	-0.18	0.15
170 INHERV	0.34	-0.33	0.06	0.45	-0.16	0.28	-0.24	-0.37	-0.34	-0.49	0.08	0.23	-0.08	0.18	-0.25	-0.19
171 AUTHOV	0.17	-0.34	0.06	0.14	-0.36	0.12	-0.19	-0.13	-0.66	-0.53	0.06	0.25	-0.20	0.03	-0.57	0.21
172 DECNV	0.39	-0.17	0.24	0.40	-0.22	0.22	-0.25	-0.26	-0.41	-0.42	0.17	0.08	-0.05	0.09	-0.21	-0.00

C O R R E L A T I O N S

VARIABLE	17 MUSLPC	18 PROTPC	19 ROMCPC	20 XNPERC	21 MSRC25	22 MSPR25	23 MSXN25	24 PECHAD	25 RCPCGN	26 AICMPD	27 TOEC38	28 PIPG60	29 PICF60	30 WGEN63	31 PCWE53	32 POSIND
17 MUSLPC	1.00															
18 PROTPC	-0.65	1.00														
19 ROMCPC	-0.69	0.52	1.00													
20 XNPERC	-0.77	0.79	0.89	1.00												
21 MSRC25	-0.34	0.27	0.59	0.50	1.00											
22 MSPR25	-0.48	0.59	0.26	0.43	0.33	1.00										
23 MSXN25	-0.51	0.54	0.50	0.56	0.76	0.86	1.00									
24 PECHAD	-0.72	0.63	0.91	0.94	0.65	0.43	0.64	1.00								
25 RCPCGN	0.51	-0.29	-0.28	-0.35	-0.13	-0.14	-0.17	-0.31	1.00							
26 AICMPD	-0.48	0.62	0.40	0.54	0.29	0.57	0.55	0.48	-0.24	1.00						
27 TOEC38	-0.04	0.12	-0.09	-0.00	-0.07	-0.05	-0.07	-0.10	-0.11	0.04	1.00					
28 PIPG60	0.22	-0.04	-0.01	-0.02	-0.40	0.02	0.25	-0.09	0.07	-0.14	-0.04	1.00				
29 PICF60	-0.18	-0.13	0.40	0.30	0.82	0.24	0.65	0.44	-0.13	-0.13	-0.06	0.70	1.00			
30 WGEN63	-0.22	0.30	0.30	0.33	0.03	0.21	0.16	0.23	-0.14	0.54	-0.03	-0.33	-0.19	1.00		
31 PCWE63	-0.44	0.44	0.61	0.59	0.66	0.50	0.72	0.62	-0.29	0.66	0.04	0.13	0.51	0.47	1.00	
32 POSIND	-0.15	0.39	0.12	0.25	0.01	0.21	0.14	0.09	-0.27	0.54	-0.12	-0.29	-0.06	0.58	0.23	1.00
33 AGLAB8	0.13	-0.18	-0.09	-0.13	-0.20	-0.14	-0.20	-0.08	0.24	-0.27	-0.40	0.12	-0.12	-0.38	-0.47	-0.42
34 USIN65	-0.20	0.16	0.05	0.18	0.16	0.25	0.26	0.07	-0.24	0.41	0.21	0.02	0.32	0.46	0.42	0.45
35 PCEN66	-0.29	0.26	0.18	0.21	0.47	0.75	0.77	0.24	-0.22	0.48	-0.03	0.25	0.58	0.13	0.55	0.34
36 DIFECG	0.16	-0.34	-0.14	-0.28	-0.30	-0.29	-0.37	-0.26	0.34	-0.47	0.02	-0.28	-0.44	-0.38	-0.43	-0.56
37 GDCRG3	0.04	0.17	-0.01	0.06	0.30	0.31	0.39	0.07	-0.26	0.20	0.21	0.62	0.55	-0.01	0.49	0.01
38 GDPD61	0.07	0.12	-0.02	0.10	-0.18	-0.09	-0.16	-0.06	-0.15	0.15	0.04	-0.31	-0.18	0.58	0.01	0.73
39 INAP60	0.19	-0.02	-0.11	-0.12	-0.17	-0.18	-0.22	-0.19	0.34	0.19	0.16	-0.03	-0.01	-0.09	-0.08	0.18
40 CDPR65	0.08	-0.20	-0.03	-0.07	-0.17	-0.41	-0.37	-0.08	0.11	-0.25	0.41	-0.09	-0.12	-0.29	-0.20	-0.12
41 PCDG63	-0.17	0.11	0.25	0.18	0.60	0.22	0.47	0.23	-0.18	0.32	0.25	0.29	0.76	0.07	0.74	0.21
42 GNPA65	0.08	0.10	-0.00	0.07	-0.19	-0.10	-0.18	-0.09	-0.15	0.12	0.11	-0.29	-0.16	0.50	-0.03	0.71
43 INPDOC	0.18	-0.38	-0.19	-0.24	-0.44	-0.42	-0.52	-0.21	0.05	-0.41	-0.04	-0.24	-0.38	-0.28	-0.54	-0.39
44 AUPHCH	-0.23	0.05	0.27	0.22	0.15	0.15	0.18	0.23	-0.12	0.49	0.13	-0.29	-0.07	0.77	0.45	0.27
45 GNPP68	-0.18	0.12	0.18	0.15	0.58	0.26	0.49	0.20	-0.26	0.36	0.10	0.37	0.72	-0.02	0.58	0.27

VARIABLE	17 MUSLPC	18 PROTPC	19 RDMCPC	20 XNPERC	21 MSRC25	22 MSPR25	23 MSXN25	24 PECHAD	25 RCPCGN	26 AICWPD	27 TOEC38	28 PIPG60	29 PICF60	30 WGEN63	31 PCWE53	32 POSIND
46 PGNP18	0.08	-0.09	-0.12	-0.10	0.01	0.07	0.06	-0.05	-0.24	0.07	-0.14	0.59	0.19	-0.13	0.01	-0.03
47 PPCR30	-0.36	0.62	0.33	0.50	0.25	0.67	0.59	0.51	-0.13	0.44	-0.00	0.12	0.07	0.01	0.15	0.15
48 PPCR53	-0.63	0.80	0.63	0.77	0.51	0.71	0.76	0.74	-0.26	0.66	0.21	0.01	0.32	0.26	0.67	0.35
49 PPCR60	-0.67	0.80	0.71	0.82	0.62	0.65	0.77	0.80	-0.33	0.71	-0.06	0.04	0.40	0.25	0.74	0.44
50 PPCR65	-0.66	0.71	0.63	0.72	0.60	0.59	0.72	0.70	-0.36	0.66	0.17	-0.03	0.41	0.19	0.73	0.40
51 PPCR16	0.32	-0.38	-0.44	-0.44	-0.24	-0.26	-0.31	-0.41	0.04	-0.22	0.37	-0.25	-0.10	-0.28	-0.18	-0.17
52 PPCR17	0.47	-0.51	-0.32	-0.44	-0.17	-0.38	-0.35	-0.36	0.01	-0.30	0.04	0.01	-0.05	-0.29	-0.13	-0.21
53 PFEC60	-0.33	0.55	0.22	0.38	0.35	0.60	0.60	0.39	-0.04	0.39	-0.07	0.05	0.32	-0.03	0.09	0.48
54 SFEC60	-0.38	0.51	0.18	0.32	0.24	0.41	0.40	0.28	-0.15	0.28	-0.02	-0.20	0.02	-0.06	0.05	0.34
55 SPCR50	-0.09	0.34	0.19	0.25	0.43	0.28	0.45	0.24	-0.12	0.27	0.13	-0.04	0.22	0.11	0.42	0.23
56 SPCR66	-0.16	0.26	0.17	0.21	0.31	0.10	0.23	0.17	-0.22	0.22	0.51	0.06	0.31	0.07	0.47	0.30
57 SPCR12	-0.25	-0.12	-0.13	-0.13	0.01	-0.03	-0.01	-0.07	-0.15	-0.07	-0.15	0.55	0.12	-0.20	-0.02	-0.06
58 EXPR65	-0.24	0.08	0.28	0.20	-0.11	0.25	0.11	-0.20	-0.04	-0.04	-0.24	-0.15	-0.30	-0.03	-0.14	-0.12
59 PGDP65	-0.47	0.38	0.45	0.42	-0.20	0.22	0.25	0.38	-0.32	0.44	0.15	0.02	0.13	0.35	0.45	0.14
60 PTGX65	-0.29	0.16	0.31	0.23	0.07	0.18	0.16	0.26	-0.32	0.21	0.14	-0.05	-0.09	0.12	0.08	-0.03
61 HREA61	-0.02	0.12	-0.00	0.03	0.25	0.15	0.24	0.03	-0.13	0.22	0.19	0.04	0.29	-0.02	0.44	0.20
62 PPCRI4	-0.32	-0.40	-0.28	-0.38	-0.20	-0.43	-0.41	-0.33	-0.05	-0.08	-0.17	0.02	-0.05	-0.19	-0.23	-0.00
63 PUTE66	-0.27	-0.09	0.15	0.05	0.08	-0.05	0.01	0.10	-0.22	-0.11	-0.11	-0.34	-0.16	-0.19	-0.13	-0.24
64 PUTEIN	-0.13	-0.06	0.01	0.01	-0.26	0.00	-0.14	0.07	-0.03	-0.10	0.07	-0.39	-0.42	-0.09	-0.18	-0.21
65 PTGXIN	0.14	-0.21	-0.13	-0.18	-0.09	0.10	0.02	-0.05	-0.09	0.06	0.16	0.15	-0.02	-0.13	-0.03	-0.43
66 SSCP52	0.56	-0.34	-0.41	-0.41	-0.10	-0.26	-0.23	-0.37	0.34	-0.27	0.20	0.23	-0.03	-0.11	-0.11	-0.13
67 SSCPIN	-0.09	0.27	-0.07	0.10	-0.10	0.23	0.11	-0.01	0.04	-0.01	0.35	0.26	0.13	0.04	0.05	-0.04
68 LITR65	-0.48	0.66	0.45	0.59	0.26	0.66	0.59	0.53	-0.26	0.71	-0.05	-0.22	0.01	0.47	0.44	0.70
69 LITRIN	0.09	-0.12	0.08	-0.02	0.30	-0.22	0.00	0.05	-0.21	0.07	-0.15	0.10	0.23	-0.17	0.30	0.06
70 IMPRO7	-0.37	0.22	0.49	0.41	0.02	0.04	0.04	0.36	-0.20	0.09	0.04	-0.18	-0.06	0.23	0.10	0.06
71 CINSET	-0.16	0.10	-0.10	-0.01	-0.17	-0.14	-0.19	-0.16	-0.10	0.29	0.32	-0.18	-0.12	0.38	0.15	0.60
72 NMRT65	-0.20	0.17	-0.10	-0.02	-0.08	0.01	-0.03	-0.14	-0.05	0.08	0.19	-0.19	-0.15	-0.13	-0.04	0.29
73 RADP66	-0.08	-0.20	-0.01	0.06	0.32	0.20	0.31	-0.06	-0.10	0.08	0.22	0.22	0.35	-0.13	-0.39	-0.03
74 RAPE06	0.14	-0.01	-0.10	-0.08	-0.06	0.05	-0.00	-0.08	-0.03	-0.04	-0.18	-0.17	-0.19	-0.07	-0.09	-0.07
75 NEPC65	-0.06	0.22	-0.02	0.08	-0.10	-0.06	-0.02	-0.10	-0.09	0.18	0.69	-0.20	-0.01	0.30	0.18	0.47
76 NEPECA	0.02	-0.00	-0.19	-0.15	-0.09	0.31	0.15	-0.15	-0.16	0.03	0.11	-0.18	-0.07	0.02	0.12	-0.18
77 TEPC68	-0.21	-0.20	-0.18	0.20	-0.50	0.36	0.51	0.24	-0.22	0.36	-0.05	0.30	0.56	0.04	0.51	-0.41
78 TECH38	0.27	-0.15	-0.23	-0.20	-0.06	-0.01	-0.04	-0.10	-0.24	-0.09	0.45	0.49	0.08	-0.29	-0.22	-0.24
79 CVPE16	0.06	-0.02	-0.13	-0.15	-0.28	-0.20	-0.28	-0.08	-0.08	-0.26	0.04	0.18	0.39	-0.10	0.44	-0.11
80 PECHCV	0.15	-0.14	-0.30	-0.31	-0.30	-0.01	-0.17	-0.34	-0.12	-0.05	-0.19	-0.20	-0.23	-0.11	-0.20	-0.08
81 CARP16	-0.20	0.15	0.12	0.12	0.51	0.31	0.48	0.15	-0.20	0.37	-0.07	0.28	0.64	0.06	0.55	0.36
82 LEGNOS	0.30	-0.10	-0.17	-0.07	-0.24	-0.20	-0.27	-0.15	0.31	-0.02	-0.06	-0.27	-0.23	0.31	-0.15	0.37
83 CABRPI	-0.11	-0.15	-0.06	0.08	-0.07	-0.01	-0.09	-0.10	-0.24	-0.04	0.45	-0.09	0.21	-0.11	-0.25	-0.16
84 WAGPUB	0.45	-0.22	-0.47	-0.42	-0.14	-0.16	-0.19	-0.42	-0.47	-0.26	0.04	-0.13	-0.29	-0.01	-0.41	-0.03
85 LOCGOV	0.22	-0.21	-0.34	-0.37	-0.22	-0.05	-0.16	-0.37	-0.20	-0.21	-0.19	-0.02	-0.13	-0.08	-0.24	0.07
86 LAWTWO	0.19	-0.01	-0.20	-0.20	-0.25	0.17	-0.02	-0.23	0.21	-0.00	0.17	0.05	-0.19	0.01	-0.09	-0.19
87 LAWNOS	0.40	-0.09	-0.30	-0.08	-0.29	-0.18	-0.30	-0.16	0.39	-0.10	0.01	-0.19	-0.18	0.01	-0.32	-0.22
88 JUDREV	-0.23	0.13	0.28	0.28	0.19	0.04	0.12	0.28	-0.21	-0.03	0.05	0.11	0.03	0.15	0.03	-0.07
89 YOUNGI	-0.14	0.32	0.05	0.19	0.20	0.30	0.31	0.23	-0.30	0.27	-0.13	0.49	0.41	-0.22	0.19	-0.10
90 YOUNGP	-0.40	0.22	0.43	0.33	0.23	0.06	0.17	0.36	-0.39	0.17	-0.17	0.15	0.15	-0.08	0.18	-0.08

C O R R E L A T I O N S

VARIABLE	17 MUSLPC	18 PROTPC	19 ROMCPC	20 XNPERC	21 MSRC25	22 MSPR25	23 MSXN25	24 PECHAD	25 RCPCGN	26 AICMPD	27 TOEC38	28 PIPG50	29 PICF50	30 WGEN63	31 PCWE53	32 POSIND
91 NOVRFO	-0.02	0.28	-0.09	0.01	0.14	0.31	0.29	-0.08	-0.01	0.18	0.03	0.07	0.24	0.10	0.30	0.18
92 VOVDIE	-0.11	0.02	0.24	0.14	0.33	0.28	0.37	0.28	-0.21	0.38	-0.15	0.31	0.37	-0.21	0.24	-0.00
93 PEVDRU	0.10	0.00	-0.14	-0.18	-0.13	0.03	-0.05	-0.20	0.10	-0.09	-0.10	0.19	0.07	-0.34	-0.05	-0.29
94 CHMOLP	0.23	-0.18	-0.28	-0.27	-0.08	-0.07	-0.09	-0.21	0.02	-0.35	-0.12	-0.35	0.12	-0.67	-0.25	-0.30
95 NOLEPA	-0.08	0.25	0.32	0.28	0.12	0.14	0.16	0.20	0.03	0.27	0.08	-0.16	-0.05	0.60	0.27	0.41
96 NOFABN	0.01	-0.01	0.18	0.08	-0.09	-0.14	-0.15	0.02	-0.02	0.04	-0.21	-0.30	-0.29	0.59	0.08	0.34
97 TOSPME	0.15	-0.06	-0.07	-0.13	-0.01	0.08	0.05	-0.16	-0.17	-0.00	-0.36	-0.22	-0.11	0.16	-0.12	0.35
98 LECFRA	-0.19	0.28	-0.37	0.33	0.23	0.10	0.20	0.29	0.07	0.24	-0.03	-0.13	-0.11	0.45	-0.17	0.27
99 CGEC51	0.08	0.34	-0.06	0.05	-0.06	0.14	0.09	-0.16	0.02	0.17	0.59	0.18	0.59	0.07	0.32	0.33
100 CGEC61	0.09	0.04	-0.10	-0.09	-0.05	0.02	-0.02	-0.18	-0.16	0.21	0.50	-0.06	0.07	0.09	0.35	0.36
101 CGCC79	-0.27	-0.05	0.05	-0.02	0.26	0.08	0.16	0.02	-0.37	0.44	0.21	-0.45	0.20	0.14	0.35	0.09
102 TAXD66	-0.32	0.49	0.18	0.42	-0.07	0.49	0.28	0.26	-0.17	0.41	0.17	-0.31	-0.07	0.46	0.29	0.38
103 GREV66	-0.05	0.05	0.05	0.01	0.35	0.34	0.42	0.08	0.02	0.28	-0.17	0.25	0.33	0.20	0.55	0.10
104 GOSP61	0.36	-0.19	-0.34	-0.37	-0.02	-0.19	-0.14	-0.38	0.03	-0.04	0.27	0.34	0.13	-0.05	0.13	0.06
105 TAXD36	-0.12	0.22	0.24	0.27	0.06	-0.03	0.01	0.16	0.06	0.19	0.36	-0.36	-0.07	0.39	0.11	0.16
106 GREV36	-0.21	0.16	0.25	0.28	0.08	-0.03	0.02	0.25	0.10	0.04	0.06	-0.05	-0.02	0.12	0.19	-0.13
107 CPEV36	-0.11	0.19	0.08	0.18	0.09	0.18	0.18	0.10	-0.02	0.21	0.05	0.01	0.13	0.30	0.27	0.27
108 GOEX68	-0.25	0.16	0.13	0.13	0.46	0.44	0.55	0.18	-0.20	0.32	0.06	0.32	0.67	-0.01	0.50	0.29
109 GOSP38	-0.31	0.26	0.27	0.29	-0.20	0.58	0.50	-0.31	-0.03	-0.31	-0.20	0.07	-0.23	-0.21	-0.41	0.22
110 DEFG65	0.38	-0.50	-0.23	-0.34	-0.27	-0.50	-0.49	-0.30	0.18	0.19	-0.18	-0.08	-0.24	0.06	-0.21	-0.01
111 TOTAID	0.16	-0.09	-0.02	-0.00	-0.14	-0.20	-0.21	-0.09	0.18	0.04	0.12	-0.31	-0.26	0.65	0.10	0.51
112 NUMAID	0.06	-0.07	-0.01	0.09	0.09	-0.17	-0.20	-0.05	0.08	0.11	0.20	-0.33	-0.26	0.61	-0.03	0.64
113 TMAN67	0.12	-0.00	-0.02	0.09	-0.15	-0.10	-0.15	0.01	-0.05	0.32	0.06	-0.28	-0.22	0.60	-0.01	0.50
114 AFARMF	0.37	-0.39	-0.27	-0.30	-0.20	-0.34	-0.34	-0.31	-0.20	-0.17	0.18	-0.02	0.01	0.09	-0.02	0.07
115 DEFG67	0.28	-0.33	-0.05	-0.17	-0.02	-0.25	-0.18	-0.09	-0.18	-0.06	-0.23	0.01	-0.13	0.33	0.18	0.14
116 CHOEFB	-0.21	0.09	0.24	0.19	0.07	-0.09	-0.02	0.17	-0.12	-0.10	-0.01	-0.22	-0.16	0.22	0.01	0.17
117 ARFPPD	-0.14	-0.07	-0.08	-0.07	0.15	0.11	0.15	-0.03	-0.30	-0.15	0.20	-0.11	0.20	0.18	0.37	0.06
118 CHARF7	-0.00	-0.03	0.08	0.02	-0.04	-0.26	-0.20	-0.04	-0.10	-0.18	0.07	-0.23	-0.18	0.03	-0.24	0.23
119 IN-SEC	-0.00	0.19	0.06	0.17	0.42	0.20	0.36	0.18	-0.17	-0.13	0.03	0.46	0.49	-0.04	0.38	0.01
120 CHINSE	-0.05	0.06	0.20	0.16	0.13	-0.03	0.03	0.23	-0.12	-0.03	-0.11	0.33	0.08	-0.13	-0.13	-0.09
121 TUFMOL	0.05	-0.02	-0.03	-0.01	-0.17	-0.06	-0.14	-0.10	-0.14	0.10	-0.10	-0.25	-0.17	0.47	0.02	0.61
122 EL-TIN	-0.14	-0.14	0.19	0.04	-0.01	-0.21	-0.15	0.06	-0.02	-0.05	0.06	-0.31	-0.22	0.26	-0.12	0.01
123 KILLOG	-0.22	0.11	0.39	0.35	0.01	0.04	-0.02	0.33	-0.31	0.16	-0.21	-0.18	-0.11	0.41	0.17	0.29
124 COMWGT	0.08	-0.06	-0.00	0.07	-0.20	-0.17	-0.23	0.04	-0.22	0.09	-0.01	-0.18	-0.24	0.53	0.05	0.32
125 AVERES	0.02	-0.12	-0.26	0.12	0.15	-0.13	-0.00	0.19	0.09	0.14	-0.02	-0.11	0.08	0.50	0.32	-0.18
126 TOAAT8	-0.04	0.14	-0.01	0.13	-0.10	0.18	0.07	0.05	-0.06	0.38	0.26	-0.31	-0.16	0.72	0.25	0.40
127 PCAID8	-0.08	0.12	-0.12	-0.05	0.00	0.18	0.13	-0.07	-0.05	0.46	0.38	-0.05	-0.11	0.51	0.25	0.04
128 AIBPC4	0.06	0.12	0.02	0.07	-0.09	0.03	-0.03	-0.04	-0.04	0.18	-0.19	-0.29	-0.17	0.51	-0.00	0.54
129 AIBPC8	-0.09	0.15	0.07	0.13	-0.06	-0.01	-0.04	-0.04	-0.11	0.52	-0.35	-0.29	-0.10	0.62	0.24	0.44
130 CAPADI	-0.01	0.28	-0.34	-0.18	-0.04	0.39	0.30	-0.21	-0.25	0.22	-0.12	-0.11	0.01	-0.17	-0.03	-0.07
131 PCBAID	-0.12	-0.03	-0.01	-0.03	0.01	-0.02	-0.01	-0.00	-0.16	0.34	0.07	0.06	0.10	-0.05	-0.09	0.01
132 COMAID	-0.14	-0.01	-0.12	0.01	-0.12	-0.17	-0.19	-0.06	-0.20	-0.01	0.38	0.08	-0.05	-0.10	-0.01	0.24
133 CAPAD7	-0.27	0.39	-0.00	0.15	0.27	0.59	0.55	0.18	-0.14	0.29	0.03	0.19	0.43	-0.21	0.28	-0.11
134 APETO8	-0.30	0.42	0.22	0.31	0.41	0.43	0.51	0.35	-0.07	0.29	-0.07	-0.15	0.42	-0.22	0.39	-0.08
135 US-D62	-0.22	0.02	0.34	0.30	-0.13	0.04	-0.04	0.29	-0.12	0.08	0.02	-0.12	-0.03	0.16	-0.17	-0.18

VARIABLE	17 MUSLPC	18 PROTPC	19 ROMCPC	20 XNPERC	21 MSRC25	22 MSPR25	23 MSXN25	24 PECHAD	25 RCPCGN	26 AICMPO	27 TOEC38	28 PIPG50	29 PICF50	30 WGEN63	31 PCWE63	32 POSIND
136 USTD68	-0.21	0.07	0.19	0.29	-0.12	0.00	-0.06	0.23	-0.13	0.06	0.19	-0.06	0.07	0.08	0.19	-0.07
137 TMET62	0.23	-0.34	-0.13	-0.24	0.15	-0.40	-0.18	-0.21	0.08	-0.23	-0.07	-0.03	0.18	-0.19	0.10	-0.12
138 TMET68	0.34	-0.37	-0.20	-0.30	0.05	-0.40	-0.23	-0.28	0.18	-0.23	-0.07	-0.25	0.04	-0.10	0.08	-0.09
139 PCPREX	0.06	-0.18	-0.13	-0.17	-0.16	0.24	0.08	-0.07	-0.03	-0.04	0.01	0.14	0.05	-0.14	-0.03	-0.21
140 IMPCOM	0.40	-0.43	-0.45	-0.50	-0.32	-0.27	-0.36	-0.50	0.06	-0.28	0.02	0.00	-0.20	-0.04	-0.21	-0.26
141 TRPGN8	-0.26	0.33	0.17	0.21	0.49	0.70	0.75	0.27	-0.02	0.41	-0.04	0.33	0.46	0.04	0.57	-0.00
142 CUBATR	-0.07	0.17	0.12	0.13	0.38	0.49	0.57	0.15	-0.01	0.29	0.00	0.37	0.56	0.24	0.34	-0.13
143 IMEQ62	0.26	-0.24	-0.23	-0.24	0.11	-0.09	-0.01	-0.18	-0.18	-0.14	-0.03	0.62	0.35	-0.12	0.15	-0.08
144 EXAF68	-0.07	-0.13	-0.08	-0.13	-0.16	-0.25	-0.25	-0.12	-0.03	-0.18	-0.09	-0.18	-0.21	-0.11	-0.24	-0.07
145 IMAF68	-0.18	0.01	0.11	0.03	-0.13	-0.19	-0.20	0.03	0.06	-0.23	-0.12	-0.16	-0.22	-0.10	-0.22	-0.20
146 70PCEX	-0.09	0.22	0.07	0.17	0.01	-0.12	-0.07	0.03	-0.06	0.16	-0.03	-0.21	-0.15	0.35	0.03	0.41
147 PCEXME	0.20	-0.41	-0.22	-0.33	-0.09	-0.34	-0.27	-0.35	-0.11	-0.30	-0.01	-0.17	-0.04	-0.09	-0.09	-0.09
148 IMME25	0.31	-0.03	-0.05	0.02	0.01	-0.23	-0.14	-0.12	0.17	-0.10	0.11	0.19	0.18	0.59	0.32	0.52
149 EXME25	0.26	-0.13	-0.09	-0.12	0.00	-0.20	-0.12	-0.17	0.12	-0.07	-0.16	0.13	0.04	0.50	0.11	0.41
150 REGORG	0.11	-0.32	-0.08	-0.22	0.11	-0.50	-0.29	-0.18	0.02	-0.10	0.01	-0.33	0.05	-0.13	0.12	0.07
151 MEMOR	0.25	0.26	-0.11	0.01	-0.22	-0.12	-0.22	-0.20	-0.05	0.26	0.17	-0.44	-0.28	0.54	-0.10	0.83
152 MEMAME	0.03	-0.28	-0.02	-0.15	0.04	-0.48	-0.31	-0.13	0.01	-0.12	-0.21	-0.30	-0.04	-0.12	-0.03	0.11
153 DIPSEN	0.22	0.04	-0.24	-0.12	-0.24	-0.10	-0.21	-0.26	-0.11	-0.02	0.55	-0.16	-0.07	0.19	-0.09	0.47
154 DIPREC	0.17	0.04	-0.13	-0.03	-0.26	-0.01	-0.17	-0.15	-0.15	0.16	0.32	-0.26	-0.20	0.47	-0.02	0.59
155 ADBJAG	0.09	-0.02	0.08	0.15	-0.14	-0.17	-0.19	0.11	0.41	0.11	0.32	-0.15	-0.23	0.39	0.07	0.08
156 MUCOSU	0.02	0.31	-0.05	0.07	-0.24	0.26	0.02	-0.14	-0.02	0.51	-0.17	-0.37	-0.26	0.66	-0.01	0.82
157 RECOC7	0.14	-0.13	-0.11	-0.10	-0.11	-0.14	-0.16	-0.15	-0.00	-0.11	-0.07	-0.03	-0.22	0.28	-0.00	0.44
158 CH5067	0.10	-0.03	0.12	0.05	0.05	-0.18	-0.09	0.03	-0.22	0.03	0.16	0.15	0.20	-0.10	-0.12	-0.06
159 MCITPM	-0.08	0.17	0.04	0.07	0.31	0.12	0.25	0.08	0.06	0.03	-0.04	0.14	0.44	-0.18	0.15	-0.09
160 LRCITP	0.02	0.10	0.06	0.16	-0.10	-0.08	-0.11	0.04	-0.13	0.32	0.04	-0.43	-0.23	0.74	0.15	0.69
161 PRLT4L	-0.00	0.05	0.18	0.15	0.15	0.07	0.13	0.20	-0.20	-0.02	0.23	0.31	0.12	-0.24	0.03	-0.47
162 PRCT4L	0.06	0.00	0.17	0.12	0.17	0.04	0.12	0.17	-0.18	-0.01	0.27	0.32	-0.04	-0.17	0.09	-0.44
163 URPC65	-0.10	0.10	0.09	0.08	0.32	0.11	0.24	0.07	-0.03	0.17	-0.00	-0.11	0.28	0.05	0.45	0.35
164 URPC55	0.00	0.02	0.09	0.04	0.24	0.08	0.17	0.04	-0.14	0.17	-0.14	-0.20	0.08	0.23	0.47	0.50
165 JR5565	-0.03	0.10	-0.10	-0.02	-0.03	-0.03	-0.03	-0.01	0.34	-0.26	-0.22	0.30	0.21	-0.38	-0.25	-0.56
166 MOMARV	-0.25	0.25	-0.15	0.10	-0.15	0.21	0.06	-0.06	-0.20	0.20	0.06	-0.21	-0.13	0.16	0.07	0.13
167 SETPAV	0.50	-0.37	-0.50	-0.45	-0.44	-0.33	-0.46	-0.50	-0.06	-0.19	-0.14	-0.16	-0.36	0.10	-0.25	0.17
168 LEHIEV	0.05	-0.09	-0.25	-0.21	-0.04	-0.13	-0.11	-0.28	-0.32	-0.10	0.12	-0.23	-0.03	0.14	0.04	0.23
169 HIEFAV	0.03	-0.06	-0.26	-0.16	-0.28	-0.05	-0.18	-0.25	-0.16	-0.02	0.04	-0.60	-0.49	0.37	0.02	0.32
170 INHERV	0.31	-0.15	-0.27	-0.23	0.03	-0.05	-0.02	-0.27	-0.21	-0.09	0.07	0.10	0.12	0.22	0.13	0.30
171 AUTHOV	0.12	-0.19	-0.29	-0.33	-0.22	-0.17	-0.24	-0.37	-0.15	-0.13	-0.16	-0.64	-0.45	0.17	-0.01	0.24
172 DECNV	0.00	-0.05	0.07	0.02	0.33	0.02	0.18	0.06	-0.18	0.15	0.03	-0.11	0.17	0.40	0.39	0.26

C O R R E L A T I O N S

	33	34	35	36	37	38	39	40	41	42	43	44	45	46	47	48
VARIABLE	AGLAB8	USIN65	PCEN66	DIFECG	GDCRG3	GDPD61	INAP60	COPR65	PCDG63	GNPA65	INPDOC	AUPHCH	GNPP68	PGNP18	PPCR30	PPCR53
33 AGLAB8	1.00															
34 USIN65	-0.42	1.00														
35 PCEN66	-0.33	0.52	1.00													
36 DIFECG	0.35	-0.61	-0.54	1.00												
37 GDCRG3	-0.17	0.34	0.46	-0.41	1.00											
38 GDPD61	-0.35	0.51	0.00	-0.39	-0.05	1.00										
39 INAP60	0.11	-0.08	0.10	-0.17	-0.06	0.06	1.00									
40 COPR65	-0.23	-0.20	-0.29	0.38	-0.22	-0.08	0.11	1.00								
41 PCDG63	-0.48	0.47	0.75	-0.52	0.57	-0.01	0.09	-0.06	1.00							
42 GNPA65	-0.36	0.49	0.02	-0.39	-0.03	0.99	0.13	-0.02	0.02	1.00						
43 INPDOC	0.46	-0.36	-0.59	0.60	-0.29	-0.08	-0.14	0.26	-0.54	-0.08	1.00					
44 AUPHCH	-0.52	0.40	0.17	-0.19	0.03	0.27	-0.20	-0.07	0.21	0.21	-0.16	1.00				
45 GNPP68	-0.40	0.37	0.78	-0.55	0.61	-0.07	0.17	-0.16	0.90	-0.03	-0.63	0.11	1.00			

C O R R E L A T I O N S

VARIABLE	33 AGLAB8	34 USIN65	35 PCEN66	36 DIFECG	37 GDCRG3	38 GDPD61	39 INAP60	40 CDPR65	41 PCDG53	42 GVPA65	43 INPDOC	44 AUPICH	45 GNPD68	46 PGNP18	47 PPCR30	48 PPCR53	49 PPCR60
46 FGNP18	0.10	0.00	0.17	-0.20	0.63	-0.17	0.11	-0.20	0.04	-0.14	-0.14	-0.04	0.34	1.00			
47 FPCR30	0.09	-0.12	0.33	-0.31	0.04	-0.11	0.01	-0.30	-0.17	-0.11	-0.20	-0.07	-0.08	0.04	1.00		
48 FPCR53	-0.38	0.14	0.49	-0.35	0.18	0.01	-0.11	-0.08	-0.23	-0.00	-0.43	0.28	0.24	-0.05	0.77	1.00	
49 FPCR60	-0.32	0.14	0.54	-0.44	0.16	0.01	-0.02	-0.16	0.32	-0.02	-0.49	0.21	0.38	-0.00	0.55	0.93	1.00
50 FPCR65	-0.47	0.22	0.58	-0.37	0.25	-0.03	-0.01	0.04	0.51	-0.02	-0.53	0.26	0.55	-0.05	0.45	0.86	
51 FPCR16	0.00	-0.01	-0.09	0.26	0.09	-0.18	-0.09	0.23	0.12	-0.14	0.34	-0.00	0.06	-0.18	-0.39	-0.36	
52 FPCR17	0.13	-0.25	-0.15	0.33	0.25	-0.20	-0.06	0.16	0.07	-0.07	0.42	-0.07	0.11	-0.16	-0.42	-0.46	
53 FEC60	-0.11	-0.03	-0.42	-0.37	-0.11	0.06	0.13	-0.23	-0.02	-0.07	-0.37	-0.09	0.08	-0.09	0.70	0.66	
54 FEC60	-0.05	-0.17	0.10	-0.01	-0.30	-0.07	-0.09	-0.09	-0.04	-0.06	-0.36	-0.24	0.02	-0.24	0.49	0.49	
55 FPCR50	-0.36	0.08	0.22	-0.22	0.01	0.00	-0.18	-0.11	-0.35	0.00	-0.65	0.02	0.37	-0.13	0.24	0.39	
56 FPCR66	-0.71	0.31	0.43	-0.43	0.19	0.13	0.07	0.30	0.62	0.18	-0.64	0.18	0.60	-0.11	0.00	0.37	
57 FPCR12	-0.03	-0.11	0.08	-0.05	0.67	-0.17	-0.12	0.03	0.03	-0.16	-0.09	-0.09	0.25	0.30	-0.04	-0.06	
58 EXPR65	0.28	-0.29	0.00	0.42	-0.11	-0.23	-0.05	-0.10	-0.33	-0.24	0.17	-0.08	-0.25	0.19	0.31	0.20	
59 GDP65	-0.31	0.11	0.12	-0.09	0.03	-0.07	-0.09	0.16	-0.15	-0.08	-0.24	0.37	0.09	-0.05	0.12	0.42	
60 TGX65	-0.15	0.05	-0.17	-0.04	0.02	-0.01	-0.24	0.19	-0.11	0.00	0.02	0.13	-0.18	-0.00	0.27	0.34	
61 AREA61	-0.51	0.25	-0.45	-0.41	0.29	0.08	0.08	-0.05	0.69	0.09	-0.53	-0.00	0.59	-0.09	-0.12	0.18	
62 PCR14	0.33	-0.05	-0.14	-0.06	0.03	-0.04	0.30	-0.07	-0.04	-0.01	0.32	-0.18	0.03	0.13	-0.34	-0.51	
63 UTE66	0.06	-0.10	-0.07	0.34	-0.25	-0.21	-0.07	0.15	-0.14	-0.21	0.20	-0.01	-0.13	-0.20	0.02	-0.06	
64 UTEIN	0.26	-0.39	-0.23	0.35	-0.22	0.01	0.04	0.21	-0.32	-0.03	0.44	-0.13	-0.28	-0.08	0.05	-0.09	
65 TGXIN	-0.02	-0.04	-0.04	0.00	0.06	-0.40	-0.11	0.25	-0.06	-0.41	0.10	-0.12	-0.11	0.00	0.12	-0.05	
66 SSCP52	-0.21	0.07	-0.03	-0.13	-0.13	0.07	0.15	0.30	0.06	0.08	-0.32	-0.09	0.05	-0.08	-0.20	-0.28	
67 SSCPIN	-0.28	0.26	0.31	-0.23	0.13	0.07	0.23	-0.00	0.05	0.12	-0.17	0.03	0.04	-0.02	0.22	0.24	
68 LITR65	-0.26	0.28	0.46	-0.50	0.06	0.34	0.05	-0.11	0.05	0.34	-0.43	0.32	0.14	-0.02	0.73	0.78	
69 LITRIN	-0.12	0.01	0.19	-0.11	0.08	-0.02	0.43	0.15	0.34	0.02	-0.15	-0.12	0.43	0.09	-0.25	-0.09	
70 IMPRO7	-0.16	0.03	-0.16	-0.01	-0.21	-0.20	-0.13	0.13	-0.04	0.23	-0.06	0.15	-0.14	-0.12	0.12	-0.20	
71 CINSET	-0.38	0.28	0.09	-0.36	-0.05	0.39	0.55	0.29	0.23	0.40	-0.33	0.19	0.15	-0.12	-0.13	0.01	
72 NMRT65	-0.51	0.25	0.02	-0.23	-0.09	0.22	-0.07	-0.13	0.07	0.23	-0.39	0.13	0.05	-0.05	-0.02	0.11	
73 RADP66	-0.34	0.14	0.37	-0.21	0.25	-0.14	-0.21	-0.08	0.54	-0.13	-0.50	-0.06	0.48	-0.11	0.01	0.19	
74 RAPE06	-0.00	-0.22	-0.21	-0.22	-0.31	-0.17	0.11	0.05	-0.12	-0.18	-0.04	-0.01	-0.11	-0.17	0.01	-0.03	
75 NEPC65	-0.65	0.44	0.19	-0.31	0.11	-0.45	0.15	0.35	0.36	0.50	-0.40	0.26	0.24	-0.19	-0.03	0.22	
76 NEPECA	-0.15	0.18	0.30	0.04	0.23	-0.06	-0.09	0.04	0.22	-0.06	-0.02	0.07	0.09	-0.15	-0.10	-0.03	
77 TEPC68	-0.40	0.26	0.81	-0.43	0.29	-0.05	-0.20	-0.07	0.63	-0.02	-0.61	0.08	0.78	0.18	0.08	0.33	
78 TECH38	0.35	-0.25	-0.14	-0.03	0.41	-0.13	-0.07	-0.20	-0.23	-0.11	0.18	0.31	-0.02	0.52	0.25	-0.03	
79 CVPE16	-0.31	-0.08	-0.60	-0.36	0.30	-0.19	0.28	-0.18	0.66	-0.14	-0.53	-0.02	0.76	0.19	-0.18	-0.03	
80 PECHCV	-0.13	-0.23	-0.07	0.10	-0.05	-0.01	0.22	-0.24	-0.02	-0.04	-0.07	-0.13	0.07	0.15	-0.22	-0.28	
81 CARP16	-0.34	0.37	0.82	-0.57	0.27	-0.08	0.22	-0.22	0.77	-0.05	-0.67	0.08	0.85	0.12	-0.07	0.18	
82 LEGNOS	0.03	0.36	-0.15	-0.15	-0.15	0.67	0.16	-0.22	-0.16	0.65	0.19	0.08	-0.24	-0.24	-0.15	-0.22	
83 CABRPI	-0.16	0.19	-0.13	0.02	-0.22	-0.09	-0.18	0.25	-0.43	-0.05	-0.07	-0.02	-0.28	-0.25	-0.21	-0.00	
84 WAGPUB	-0.17	-0.13	-0.32	0.19	-0.25	0.19	0.03	0.12	-0.28	0.17	-0.12	-0.02	-0.24	-0.18	-0.04	-0.14	
85 LDCGOV	-0.01	-0.06	0.04	0.06	-0.42	0.15	0.16	-0.16	-0.21	0.17	-0.13	-0.22	-0.11	-0.14	-0.09	-0.24	
86 LAWTWO	-0.14	-0.05	-0.01	0.30	0.20	-0.01	-0.04	0.17	-0.12	-0.02	0.07	-0.00	-0.13	-0.07	-0.02	-0.00	
87 LAWNOS	0.13	0.33	-0.19	-0.05	-0.05	0.53	0.08	-0.14	-0.22	0.53	0.26	-0.10	-0.23	-0.13	-0.18	-0.29	
88 JUDREV	0.00	0.15	-0.16	0.11	-0.24	0.10	-0.06	0.09	-0.27	0.09	-0.06	0.09	-0.25	-0.05	0.19	0.20	
89 YOUNGI	0.06	0.01	0.46	-0.47	-0.38	-0.28	-0.16	-0.17	0.27	-0.26	-0.23	-0.23	0.42	0.39	0.28	0.25	
90 YOUNGP	0.15	-0.30	0.10	0.13	-0.10	-0.28	-0.03	-0.04	-0.05	-0.28	-0.08	-0.04	0.10	0.11	0.31	0.28	

C O R R E L A T I O N S

VARIABLE	33 AGLAB8	34 USIN65	35 PCEN66	36 DIFECG	37 GDCRG3	38 GDPD61	39 INAP60	40 CDPR65	41 PCDG63	42 GNP465	43 INPDOC	44 AUP4CH	45 GNPP68	46 PGNP18	47 PPCR30	48 PPCR53
91 NOYRFO	-0.11	0.34	0.49	-0.30	0.40	0.13	-0.06	-0.38	0.48	0.12	-0.39	-0.10	0.37	-0.09	-0.03	0.07
92 VOVOIE	0.10	-0.10	0.41	-0.11	0.22	-0.26	0.13	0.00	0.27	-0.23	-0.14	-0.02	0.41	0.36	0.29	0.28
93 PEVORU	0.29	-0.29	0.14	0.16	0.41	-0.48	0.38	-0.02	0.13	-0.41	0.03	-0.33	0.18	0.28	-0.07	-0.18
94 CHNOLP	-0.46	-0.35	0.11	0.07	-0.07	-0.39	-0.30	-0.10	-0.09	-0.35	-0.05	-0.78	-0.05	-0.18	-0.11	-0.22
95 NOLEPA	-0.52	0.19	-0.01	-0.14	-0.08	-0.56	-0.11	-0.15	-0.08	0.51	-0.33	0.51	-0.01	-0.21	0.08	-0.39
96 NOPABN	-0.37	0.19	-0.19	-0.03	-0.14	0.66	-0.30	-0.09	-0.14	0.60	-0.07	0.46	-0.20	-0.15	-0.15	0.02
97 TOSPME	-0.09	-0.05	0.03	-0.06	-0.30	0.23	0.05	0.04	-0.07	0.22	-0.18	0.05	-0.03	-0.15	0.03	-0.03
98 LEGFRA	-0.24	0.13	0.46	-0.11	-0.34	0.34	-0.19	0.07	-0.04	0.29	-0.52	0.35	-0.12	-0.36	0.19	0.36
99 CGBC51	-0.63	0.31	0.46	-0.39	-0.49	0.15	0.28	0.34	0.68	0.20	-0.52	0.08	0.53	-0.16	0.04	0.47
100 CGBC61	-0.69	0.21	0.38	-0.28	0.33	0.12	0.27	0.28	0.58	0.17	-0.43	0.24	0.57	0.11	-0.18	0.14
101 CGGC79	-0.45	0.10	0.32	0.02	0.14	-0.04	-0.02	0.03	0.53	-0.02	-0.04	0.48	0.51	0.07	-0.25	0.23
102 TAXD66	-0.19	0.30	0.23	-0.10	0.28	-0.26	-0.15	-0.12	0.08	0.25	-0.03	0.35	0.25	-0.13	0.39	0.41
103 GREV66	-0.31	0.30	0.63	-0.28	0.24	-0.19	-0.04	-0.14	0.41	-0.21	-0.48	0.33	0.48	-0.13	-0.02	0.19
104 GDSP61	-0.41	0.11	0.19	-0.28	0.27	-0.10	0.28	0.12	0.33	-0.05	-0.35	0.01	0.33	0.23	-0.23	-0.16
105 TAXD36	-0.39	0.29	-0.22	0.06	0.17	0.30	-0.22	0.28	0.09	0.29	0.10	0.48	-0.14	-0.42	-0.09	0.21
106 GREV36	0.20	-0.00	-0.12	0.18	-0.13	-0.04	0.01	0.12	-0.09	-0.08	0.14	0.07	-0.11	-0.07	-0.07	0.04
107 CRFV36	-0.08	0.35	0.38	-0.28	0.15	-0.25	0.18	-0.07	-0.16	0.25	-0.22	0.31	0.25	0.10	0.04	0.14
108 GOEX68	-0.38	0.39	0.94	-0.53	0.46	-0.08	0.20	-0.10	0.77	-0.04	-0.59	0.11	0.85	0.18	0.02	0.29
109 GDSP38	-0.08	0.19	0.61	-0.32	0.03	-0.06	0.20	-0.12	0.23	-0.07	-0.26	0.22	0.31	0.09	0.45	0.44
110 DEFG65	-0.02	-0.06	-0.30	0.11	-0.02	0.15	-0.06	0.19	-0.11	0.10	0.38	0.17	-0.14	0.09	-0.48	-0.44
111 TOTAID	-0.28	0.40	-0.10	-0.33	-0.04	0.69	0.20	-0.02	-0.01	0.66	-0.08	0.39	-0.14	-0.15	-0.25	-0.15
112 NUMAID	-0.31	0.42	-0.09	-0.35	-0.06	0.77	0.24	-0.07	-0.01	0.76	-0.16	0.30	-0.19	-0.14	-0.15	-0.05
113 TMAN67	-0.32	0.53	-0.10	-0.34	-0.07	0.88	-0.09	-0.08	-0.10	0.84	-0.04	0.42	-0.03	-0.19	-0.14	-0.04
114 AFARMF	-0.28	0.43	-0.02	-0.17	-0.17	0.33	-0.02	0.34	0.23	0.32	0.18	0.10	-0.03	-0.19	-0.45	-0.37
115 DEFG67	-0.30	0.12	-0.00	-0.13	0.05	0.12	-0.09	0.15	-0.08	0.06	0.01	0.43	0.02	0.08	-0.35	-0.17
116 CHDEFB	-0.03	0.09	0.01	-0.19	-0.17	0.16	-0.01	-0.23	-0.07	0.15	-0.25	0.07	-0.04	-0.08	0.07	0.06
117 ARFPPO	-0.47	0.40	0.38	-0.30	0.34	0.11	0.09	0.13	0.53	0.09	-0.32	0.27	0.37	-0.01	-0.25	0.02
118 CHARF7	-0.17	0.10	-0.14	0.08	-0.14	0.43	-0.01	0.16	-0.10	0.45	-0.04	-0.04	-0.10	-0.10	-0.13	-0.04
119 INTSEC	-0.33	0.22	0.41	-0.20	0.09	-0.15	0.08	0.11	0.33	-0.16	-0.45	0.10	0.40	0.06	-0.02	0.25
120 CHINSE	-0.20	-0.32	-0.02	0.14	0.35	-0.18	-0.10	-0.15	-0.01	-0.17	-0.12	-0.05	0.09	0.40	-0.04	-0.12
121 TURMOL	-0.44	0.36	0.09	-0.27	-0.09	0.80	-0.11	-0.04	0.04	0.77	-0.09	0.36	-0.02	-0.13	-0.13	0.02
122 ELITIN	-0.49	0.12	-0.17	0.14	-0.29	0.25	-0.31	0.31	0.02	0.21	-0.06	0.41	-0.12	-0.29	-0.22	0.05
123 KILLOG	-0.07	0.19	-0.03	-0.04	-0.12	0.51	-0.33	0.02	-0.11	0.47	0.20	0.25	-0.15	-0.07	-0.03	0.09
124 COMWGT	-0.11	0.35	-0.17	-0.24	-0.15	0.64	-0.16	-0.08	-0.19	0.57	0.19	0.30	-0.24	-0.13	-0.13	-0.13
125 AVERES	-0.26	0.09	-0.09	0.00	0.16	0.07	-0.14	0.00	0.11	0.00	0.10	0.67	-0.05	-0.05	-0.25	0.02
126 TOAAT8	-0.48	0.67	0.13	-0.42	0.17	0.64	-0.16	-0.12	0.18	0.60	-0.15	0.65	-0.00	-0.15	-0.10	0.13
127 PCAID8	-0.23	0.30	0.33	-0.38	0.31	0.01	-0.45	-0.14	0.47	0.21	-0.29	0.19	-0.44	-0.12	-0.01	-0.09
128 AIDPC4	-0.19	0.45	0.04	-0.29	0.03	0.84	-0.07	-0.28	-0.01	0.82	-0.06	0.23	-0.09	-0.12	-0.11	-0.03
129 AIDPC8	-0.44	0.47	0.08	-0.44	0.11	0.56	-0.33	-0.05	0.24	0.58	-0.18	0.62	0.17	-0.01	-0.07	0.14
130 CAPAD1	0.14	0.03	0.25	0.03	0.44	-0.22	-0.11	-0.28	0.28	-0.22	-0.33	-0.23	0.25	-0.13	-0.25	0.00
131 PCDAID	0.10	-0.00	0.17	-0.24	0.10	-0.07	0.61	-0.20	0.16	-0.00	-0.09	0.02	0.35	0.38	-0.10	-0.04
132 COMAID	-0.34	0.36	-0.05	-0.28	0.02	0.23	0.23	0.55	0.05	0.25	-0.16	0.06	-0.04	-0.01	-0.13	-0.01
133 CAPAD7	-0.00	0.09	0.66	-0.17	0.54	-0.27	-0.16	-0.32	0.42	-0.25	-0.32	-0.15	0.45	0.05	0.24	0.32
134 APCTO8	-0.23	-0.09	0.53	-0.17	0.33	-0.28	0.03	-0.01	0.46	-0.27	-0.40	-0.11	0.54	-0.03	0.14	0.45
135 USTD62	0.11	0.22	0.00	-0.04	0.11	0.05	-0.18	0.05	0.11	0.03	0.14	-0.13	-0.09	-0.06	-0.13	-0.07

VARIABLE	33 AGLAB8	34 USIN65	35 PCEN66	36 DIFECG	37 GDCRG3	38 GDPD61	39 INAP60	40 COPR65	41 PCDG63	42 GNPA65	43 INPDOC	44 AUPHCH	45 GNPP68	46 PGNP18	47 PPCR30	48 PPCR53
136 USTD68	-0.05	0.44	0.08	-0.28	0.23	0.13	-0.10	0.14	0.24	0.14	0.01	0.10	0.08	-0.03	-0.15	-0.06
137 TMET62	-0.10	-0.14	0.03	0.17	0.04	-0.09	0.03	-0.03	0.35	-0.08	0.01	0.05	0.32	-0.02	-0.47	-0.30
138 TMET68	-0.17	-0.12	-0.02	0.19	-0.19	-0.07	0.06	-0.01	0.31	-0.07	0.08	0.11	0.22	-0.26	-0.47	-0.34
139 PCPREX	0.03	-0.02	0.25	0.04	0.28	-0.25	-0.21	0.22	0.07	-0.24	-0.03	0.04	0.05	0.12	-0.08	-0.05
140 IMPCOM	-0.10	0.14	0.03	-0.21	0.03	0.19	0.17	-0.04	0.01	0.20	-0.04	-0.15	0.04	0.15	-0.32	-0.39
141 TRPGN8	-0.24	0.18	0.72	-0.23	0.40	-0.26	-0.04	-0.33	0.55	-0.25	-0.63	0.19	0.65	0.29	0.35	0.51
142 CUBATR	0.08	0.47	0.57	-0.51	0.62	0.08	0.16	-0.56	0.48	0.06	-0.37	0.11	0.44	0.22	0.35	0.18
143 IMEQ62	-0.12	0.19	0.32	-0.25	0.79	-0.07	-0.17	-0.17	0.35	-0.07	-0.18	-0.01	0.45	0.67	-0.30	-0.23
144 EXAF68	0.36	-0.30	-0.28	0.32	-0.25	-0.17	-0.04	0.00	-0.28	-0.18	-0.55	-0.17	-0.30	-0.06	-0.09	-0.23
145 IMAF68	0.33	-0.52	-0.25	0.29	-0.35	-0.25	-0.16	0.05	-0.32	-0.24	-0.42	-0.16	-0.33	-0.14	-0.08	-0.10
146 70PCEX	0.02	0.14	-0.19	-0.09	-0.18	0.35	0.15	-0.29	-0.16	0.31	0.03	0.07	-0.14	-0.06	-0.05	0.03
147 PCEXME	-0.10	0.14	-0.01	0.14	-0.09	0.04	-0.22	-0.38	0.15	0.04	0.12	0.14	0.10	-0.04	-0.42	-0.33
148 IMME25	-0.20	0.39	0.12	-0.43	0.31	0.50	0.19	-0.35	0.33	0.49	-0.30	0.12	0.28	0.09	-0.33	-0.23
149 EXME25	-0.08	0.26	-0.07	-0.47	-0.02	0.28	0.20	-0.54	0.17	0.25	-0.43	0.03	0.17	0.12	-0.19	-0.26
150 REGORG	-0.22	-0.06	-0.04	0.08	-0.23	-0.01	0.15	0.15	0.32	0.00	-0.15	0.09	0.27	-0.29	-0.49	-0.25
151 MEMOR	-0.33	0.21	-0.10	-0.32	-0.20	0.84	0.21	0.07	-0.05	0.83	-0.20	0.23	-0.07	-0.35	0.04	0.12
152 MEMAME	-0.01	-0.17	-0.11	0.14	-0.09	0.03	0.18	-0.03	0.18	0.05	0.18	0.07	0.21	-0.01	-0.45	-0.27
153 DIPSEN	-0.60	0.46	0.06	-0.32	0.07	0.69	0.13	0.35	0.15	0.74	-0.08	0.15	0.02	-0.21	-0.15	0.12
154 DIPREC	-0.51	0.45	0.04	-0.40	-0.09	0.74	0.12	0.19	0.02	0.74	-0.09	0.30	-0.16	-0.24	-0.04	0.11
155 ADBJAG	-0.28	0.26	-0.21	-0.02	-0.12	0.28	0.17	0.42	-0.07	0.25	0.01	0.43	-0.21	-0.14	-0.15	0.02
156 MUCOSU	-0.09	0.44	0.17	-0.27	-0.15	0.77	0.14	-0.28	-0.14	0.74	-0.12	0.34	-0.10	-0.04	0.18	0.14
157 RECOC7	-0.25	0.23	-0.02	-0.21	0.05	0.33	-0.11	0.07	-0.07	0.31	-0.19	0.13	-0.04	0.18	-0.17	-0.10
158 CH5OO7	-0.17	0.01	-0.07	-0.12	0.19	-0.02	0.25	0.04	0.08	-0.02	-0.02	-0.04	-0.01	-0.20	-0.05	0.01
159 MCITPM	-0.07	0.01	-0.33	-0.00	0.12	-0.03	0.04	0.14	0.25	-0.01	-0.29	-0.16	0.33	-0.13	-0.05	0.12
160 LRCITP	-0.47	0.56	-0.00	-0.42	-0.09	0.85	0.00	-0.06	0.05	-0.81	-0.11	0.59	-0.05	-0.19	-0.15	0.05
161 PRLT4L	0.07	-0.11	-0.14	0.13	0.28	-0.35	-0.23	-0.01	0.05	-0.34	-0.03	-0.12	0.01	0.26	0.21	0.13
162 PRCT4L	0.03	-0.02	-0.11	0.12	0.31	-0.28	-0.21	0.00	0.08	-0.26	-0.00	-0.08	0.02	0.23	0.19	0.09
163 URPC65	-0.50	0.20	0.51	-0.19	-0.00	0.10	0.13	0.18	0.50	0.12	-0.47	0.14	0.54	-0.19	-0.19	0.17
164 URPC55	-0.62	0.18	0.46	-0.20	-0.15	0.29	0.03	0.11	0.40	-0.28	-0.42	0.26	0.45	-0.17	-0.19	0.16
165 UP5565	0.44	-0.18	-0.13	0.16	0.27	-0.43	0.17	-0.15	-0.04	-0.39	0.20	-0.35	-0.11	0.04	-0.00	-0.13
166 MOMARV	-0.11	0.52	0.11	-0.11	0.07	0.21	-0.10	-0.34	-0.00	0.19	-0.05	0.03	0.03	0.05	-0.04	-0.01
167 SETPAV	0.16	0.02	-0.18	0.09	-0.06	0.23	-0.10	-0.26	-0.26	0.18	0.36	0.07	-0.19	0.04	-0.29	-0.46
168 LEHIEV	-0.33	0.35	-0.17	-0.18	0.26	0.27	-0.31	-0.28	0.19	0.28	0.03	0.23	0.19	0.02	-0.31	-0.17
169 HIEFAV	-0.27	0.17	-0.07	-0.08	-0.07	0.32	-0.27	-0.20	-0.05	0.30	-0.05	0.32	-0.02	-0.11	-0.21	-0.17
170 INHERV	-0.42	0.35	0.20	-0.26	0.41	0.33	-0.25	-0.27	0.22	0.31	-0.05	0.19	0.19	0.11	-0.34	-0.14
171 AUTHOV	-0.31	0.02	-0.03	-0.04	-0.34	0.16	-0.18	-0.23	-0.00	0.15	0.02	0.19	-0.00	-0.30	-0.25	-0.21
172 DECNV	-0.37	0.19	0.28	-0.21	0.20	0.25	-0.01	-0.41	0.29	0.23	-0.11	0.43	0.32	0.02	-0.17	0.05

VARIABLE	49 PPCR60	50 PPCR65	51 PPCR16	52 PPCR17	53 PFEC50	54 SFEC60	55 SPCR50	56 SPCR66	57 SPCR12	58 EXPR65	59 PGDP65	60 PTGX65	61 HREA61	62 PPCR14	63 PUTE56	64 PUTEIN
49 PPCR60	1.00															
50 PPCR65	0.92	1.00														
51 PPCR16	-0.43	-0.14	1.00													
52 PPCR17	-0.41	-0.25	0.68	1.00												
53 PFEC50	0.62	0.53	0.53	-0.54	1.00											
54 SFEC60	0.48	0.45	-0.16	-0.44	0.77	1.00										
55 SPCR50	0.40	0.41	-0.12	-0.27	0.33	0.56	1.00									
56 SPCR66	0.36	0.55	0.08	-0.14	0.13	0.19	0.64	1.00								
57 SPCR12	-0.01	-0.00	0.01	0.43	-0.17	-0.23	-0.06	0.00	1.00							
58 EXPR65	0.16	-0.05	-0.23	-0.04	-0.10	-0.10	-0.28	-0.39	0.16	1.00						
59 PGDP65	0.42	0.49	-0.11	-0.28	0.23	0.34	0.20	0.25	-0.03	-0.09	1.00					
60 PTGX65	0.32	0.29	-0.13	-0.16	0.16	0.17	0.00	0.01	0.04	0.09	0.56	1.00				
61 HREA61	0.24	0.38	0.01	-0.06	-0.01	-0.17	0.47	0.62	-0.03	-0.36	-0.03	0.00	1.00			
62 PPCR14	-0.32	-0.29	0.28	0.54	-0.45	-0.43	-0.36	-0.24	-0.19	-0.25	-0.11	0.10	-0.12	1.00		
63 PUTE66	-0.10	-0.13	0.07	0.15	-0.08	-0.00	-0.17	-0.08	-0.12	0.43	-0.12	0.21	-0.10	0.12	1.00	
64 PUTEIN	-0.11	-0.10	0.03	0.10	-0.03	-0.04	-0.26	-0.22	-0.04	0.18	-0.15	-0.01	-0.14	-0.01	0.02	1.00
65 PTGXIN	-0.02	-0.03	0.22	0.20	-0.06	-0.21	-0.22	-0.03	-0.11	-0.04	0.20	0.53	-0.01	0.23	0.23	0.02
66 SSCP52	-0.34	-0.30	-0.02	-0.08	-0.17	-0.17	0.37	0.44	0.01	-0.47	-0.27	-0.31	0.30	-0.07	-0.24	-0.11
67 SSCPIN	0.09	0.66	-0.24	-0.35	0.12	-0.19	-0.16	0.24	-0.09	-0.03	-0.11	-0.22	-0.02	-0.33	-0.05	-0.12
68 LITR65	0.75	0.66	-0.36	-0.47	0.69	0.44	0.28	0.25	-0.07	-0.15	-0.33	0.31	-0.02	-0.29	-0.05	0.06
69 LITRIN	0.13	0.22	0.02	0.13	-0.11	-0.19	-0.00	0.21	0.18	-0.23	-0.01	-0.08	0.27	-0.38	0.00	0.00
70 IMPR07	0.18	0.08	-0.42	-0.42	-0.10	0.16	0.22	0.14	-0.24	0.09	0.39	0.33	-0.10	-0.23	-0.15	0.02
71 CINSET	-0.01	0.07	-0.01	-0.14	-0.00	0.08	0.19	0.38	-0.18	-0.25	0.11	-0.22	0.29	-0.03	-0.31	-0.20
72 NMRT65	0.06	0.04	-0.25	-0.35	-0.07	0.26	0.31	0.34	-0.13	-0.06	0.08	0.04	0.24	-0.26	0.12	-0.38
73 RADP66	0.18	0.28	0.13	-0.05	0.04	0.20	0.75	0.67	0.04	-0.33	0.02	0.22	0.62	-0.27	-0.25	-0.23
74 RAPE06	0.02	-0.00	0.07	0.09	0.03	0.00	0.08	-0.06	-0.11	-0.05	-0.23	-0.16	-0.03	-0.10	-0.17	-0.13
75 NEPC65	0.07	0.25	0.16	-0.16	0.08	0.14	0.39	0.72	0.19	-0.29	0.16	-0.00	0.35	-0.32	-0.18	-0.19
76 NEPECA	-0.09	-0.00	0.07	0.02	-0.20	-0.28	-0.05	0.10	-0.06	-0.06	-0.29	-0.14	0.37	-0.10	0.14	0.22
77 TEPC68	0.46	0.56	-0.08	-0.07	0.34	0.26	0.37	0.54	0.19	-0.08	-0.25	-0.25	0.33	-0.09	-0.12	-0.21
78 TECH38	-0.11	-0.19	0.09	0.28	0.11	0.03	-0.09	-0.23	0.48	0.04	-0.14	0.14	-0.17	0.10	-0.10	0.30
79 CVPE16	-0.16	-0.33	0.12	0.08	0.05	0.05	0.38	0.48	0.11	-0.37	-0.12	-0.20	0.64	0.15	-0.24	-0.12
80 PECHCV	-0.24	-0.20	0.02	0.06	-0.13	0.01	0.13	-0.05	-0.05	-0.19	-0.09	-0.09	0.30	0.13	-0.21	0.19
81 CARP16	0.35	0.46	-0.07	-0.13	0.18	0.17	0.46	0.55	0.01	-0.30	0.20	-0.28	0.49	0.02	-0.22	-0.32
82 LEGNOS	-0.22	-0.28	0.14	0.05	-0.07	-0.18	-0.17	-0.15	-0.17	-0.18	-0.30	-0.18	-0.10	0.13	-0.17	0.04
83 CABRPI	-0.04	0.19	0.40	0.25	-0.32	-0.13	0.26	0.39	-0.18	-0.38	0.11	-0.00	-0.35	0.05	-0.05	-0.09
84 WAGPUB	-0.25	-0.27	0.02	0.05	0.17	0.16	0.14	-0.01	-0.03	-0.25	-0.33	-0.20	-0.01	-0.19	0.02	-0.07
85 LOCGOV	-0.20	-0.25	-0.14	-0.19	0.28	0.21	0.04	0.01	-0.14	-0.02	-0.06	-0.11	-0.16	-0.01	-0.05	0.12
86 LAWTWO	-0.10	-0.09	-0.06	0.14	-0.05	-0.12	-0.09	-0.02	0.23	0.15	-0.13	0.04	0.07	-0.18	0.20	0.30
87 LAWNOS	-0.32	-0.32	-0.31	0.15	0.03	-0.18	-0.20	-0.15	0.04	-0.10	-0.42	-0.35	-0.17	-0.05	-0.19	0.16
88 JUDREV	0.15	0.04	-0.30	-0.51	0.33	0.22	0.09	-0.01	-0.10	0.10	-0.27	0.19	-0.44	-0.37	-0.00	0.03
89 YOUNGI	0.38	0.33	-0.18	-0.02	0.16	0.03	0.01	0.14	0.36	0.06	-0.05	-0.07	0.19	0.25	-0.08	-0.04
90 YOUNGP	0.37	0.26	-0.35	-0.05	0.18	0.26	0.06	-0.00	0.14	0.36	0.30	0.08	-0.22	0.01	0.34	0.17

C O R R E L A T I O N S

VARIABLE	49 PPCR60	50 PPCR65	51 PPCR16	52 PPCR17	53 PFEC60	54 SFEC60	55 SPCR50	56 SPCR66	57 SPCR12	58 EXPR65	59 PGDP65	60 PTGX55	61 HREA61	62 PPCR14	63 PUTE56	64 PUTEIN
91 NOYRFO	0.08	0.10	-0.06	-0.13	-0.08	0.08	0.38	0.29	-0.07	-0.21	-0.14	-0.25	0.62	-0.12	-0.17	-0.20
92 NOVOIE	0.39	0.36	-0.15	-0.06	0.21	0.10	0.12	0.10	0.28	-0.28	0.00	0.15	0.20	0.13	0.12	0.19
93 PEVBRU	-0.15	-0.06	0.18	0.20	-0.12	-0.11	-0.12	-0.12	0.21	0.26	0.00	-0.14	-0.04	-0.01	-0.01	0.00
94 CHNOLP	-0.15	-0.19	0.04	0.14	0.05	-0.14	-0.10	-0.12	0.16	-0.18	-0.33	-0.14	-0.12	0.15	0.22	0.11
95 NOLEPA	0.33	0.32	-0.34	-0.25	0.23	0.08	0.18	0.25	-0.11	-0.08	0.22	0.17	0.12	-0.39	-0.15	-0.02
96 NOPABN	0.02	-0.05	-0.35	-0.12	-0.10	-0.17	-0.06	-0.03	-0.02	-0.03	0.03	0.14	-0.00	-0.17	-0.02	0.01
97 TOSPME	0.00	-0.08	-0.28	-0.12	0.20	0.10	0.18	-0.05	-0.17	0.01	-0.29	-0.26	-0.05	-0.06	-0.05	-0.08
98 LEGFRA	0.36	0.25	-0.40	-0.31	0.18	0.13	0.32	-0.23	-0.30	-0.19	0.10	0.15	-0.01	-0.23	-0.03	-0.09
99 CGBC51	0.28	0.55	0.21	-0.09	0.08	0.08	0.43	0.81	-0.07	-0.36	0.19	0.05	0.59	-0.21	-0.29	-0.36
100 CGBC61	0.09	0.34	0.29	0.17	-0.10	-0.01	0.32	0.72	0.16	-0.20	0.19	-0.07	0.60	-0.09	-0.21	-0.20
101 CGGC79	0.19	0.35	0.18	0.12	0.04	0.15	0.13	0.20	-0.36	-0.11	0.32	0.00	0.33	-0.07	0.04	0.04
102 TAXD66	0.22	0.25	0.20	-0.05	0.26	0.18	0.17	0.09	-0.14	-0.06	0.27	-0.22	-0.15	-0.37	-0.33	0.03
103 GREV66	0.26	0.37	0.01	-0.09	0.07	-0.13	0.15	0.30	0.18	-0.12	0.32	-0.04	0.42	-0.03	-0.14	-0.20
104 GOSP61	-0.17	-0.08	0.08	-0.02	-0.20	-0.23	0.29	0.46	0.20	-0.35	0.20	0.04	0.38	0.16	-0.30	-0.47
105 TAXD36	0.06	0.18	0.23	-0.11	0.05	-0.04	0.09	0.14	-0.30	-0.11	0.24	0.18	-0.08	-0.29	-0.25	-0.09
106 GREV36	0.09	0.12	-0.09	-0.08	-0.19	-0.21	-0.23	-0.18	-0.10	0.11	-0.01	-0.12	-0.20	-0.04	0.03	0.25
107 CREV36	0.15	0.20	-0.02	-0.03	-0.05	-0.34	-0.08	0.09	-0.02	-0.06	-0.05	-0.22	-0.17	-0.37	-0.14	-0.08
108 GOEX68	0.39	0.37	-0.05	-0.04	0.26	-0.13	0.19	0.53	0.18	-0.14	0.20	-0.04	0.42	-0.03	-0.10	-0.20
109 GOSP38	0.48	0.44	-0.19	-0.10	0.22	-0.23	-0.17	0.09	-0.03	-0.12	0.12	-0.11	-0.06	0.05	-0.01	-0.09
110 DEFG65	-0.42	-0.40	0.16	0.45	-0.57	-0.61	-0.47	-0.24	-0.30	-0.02	-0.50	-0.24	-0.00	0.17	0.09	0.01
111 TOTAID	-0.19	-0.17	-0.08	-0.14	-0.19	-0.24	-0.05	0.06	-0.17	-0.26	-0.00	-0.02	0.05	-0.03	-0.21	-0.06
112 NUMAID	-0.08	-0.07	-0.11	-0.22	-0.07	-0.06	0.09	0.20	-0.19	-0.29	-0.04	-0.05	0.07	-0.10	-0.25	-0.33
113 TMAN67	-0.08	-0.12	-0.13	-0.18	-0.04	-0.23	-0.09	0.00	-0.12	-0.25	-0.14	-0.01	0.01	-0.06	-0.20	0.08
114 AFARMF	-0.43	-0.33	0.23	0.11	-0.41	-0.42	-0.25	0.08	-0.08	-0.35	-0.16	-0.04	0.32	-0.10	-0.19	-0.17
115 DEFG67	-0.13	-0.09	0.01	0.22	-0.42	-0.55	-0.27	0.00	0.26	-0.02	-0.16	-0.05	0.06	0.13	-0.05	-0.15
116 CHDEFB	-0.11	0.03	-0.29	-0.21	-0.06	-0.03	0.12	0.18	-0.09	-0.32	-0.28	-0.09	-0.10	-0.09	0.46	-0.06
117 ARFPPO	-0.00	0.11	-0.03	-0.06	-0.24	-0.32	0.09	0.39	0.06	-0.26	-0.17	-0.18	0.52	-0.13	-0.18	-0.13
118 CHARF7	-0.01	-0.02	-0.20	-0.01	-0.08	-0.01	0.02	0.14	0.03	-0.25	-0.32	-0.01	0.04	-0.24	-0.55	-0.03
119 INTSEC	0.28	0.36	-0.10	0.17	0.20	0.01	0.30	0.41	0.13	-0.13	0.13	-0.35	0.14	-0.02	-0.19	-0.32
120 CHINSE	0.19	0.15	-0.15	0.16	-0.02	-0.01	0.03	0.08	0.54	0.16	0.26	0.20	0.04	-0.13	-0.02	0.13
121 TURMOL	0.01	-0.02	-0.20	-0.07	-0.04	-0.06	-0.05	0.13	-0.02	-0.07	0.01	-0.01	0.21	-0.05	-0.17	-0.01
122 ELITIN	0.01	0.05	-0.14	-0.11	-0.20	-0.05	-0.02	0.22	-0.13	-0.07	0.22	0.25	0.23	-0.25	0.21	-0.06
123 KILLOG	0.17	0.05	-0.35	-0.02	-0.16	-0.15	-0.05	-0.07	0.04	0.09	0.05	0.18	-0.07	0.05	0.07	0.36
124 COMWGT	-0.12	-0.20	-0.12	0.02	-0.22	-0.28	-0.18	-0.09	-0.09	-0.22	-0.11	0.05	-0.09	0.10	-0.05	0.24
125 AVERES	-0.02	-0.05	-0.20	0.07	-0.34	-0.53	-0.24	-0.13	0.07	-0.11	0.24	0.08	-0.03	-0.04	-0.01	-0.07
126 TOAAT8	0.02	0.07	0.01	-0.22	-0.08	-0.23	0.04	-0.20	-0.17	-0.31	0.08	0.07	0.24	-0.19	-0.25	-0.02
127 PCAID8	0.09	0.17	0.04	-0.13	-0.06	-0.13	0.12	0.33	-0.14	-0.36	0.07	0.02	0.52	0.18	-0.15	-0.01
128 AIDPC4	0.02	-0.05	-0.24	-0.23	0.02	-0.11	-0.00	-0.05	-0.11	-0.13	-0.12	0.05	0.10	0.07	-0.18	0.01
129 AIDPC8	0.11	0.16	-0.04	-0.20	-0.02	-0.21	0.02	0.27	-0.19	-0.36	0.23	0.12	0.17	0.12	-0.22	-0.02
130 CAPAD1	0.05	0.11	0.06	-0.20	0.12	0.29	0.24	-0.02	-0.00	-0.10	-0.19	-0.19	0.55	-0.01	-0.23	-0.01
131 PCDAID	0.08	0.06	-0.10	-0.04	0.04	-0.08	-0.09	0.01	0.01	-0.13	0.12	0.02	0.04	0.39	-0.05	0.15
132 COMAID	-0.08	0.03	0.11	-0.17	-0.07	-0.07	0.08	0.40	0.07	-0.28	0.14	0.11	0.13	-0.03	-0.22	-0.22
133 CAPAD7	0.33	0.43	0.10	-0.07	0.37	0.33	0.18	0.17	0.10	-0.01	0.04	-0.14	0.41	-0.19	-0.18	0.13
134 APCTO8	0.56	0.71	0.06	0.00	0.40	0.36	0.26	0.37	-0.16	-0.02	0.14	-0.04	0.50	-0.17	-0.02	0.06
135 USTD62	-0.09	-0.09	-0.07	-0.11	-0.31	-0.22	-0.11	-0.04	-0.11	-0.11	0.18	-0.15	-0.11	-0.07	-0.13	-0.15

C O R R E L A T I O N S

VARIABLE	49 PPCR60	50 PPCR65	51 PPCR16	52 PPCR17	53 PFEC60	54 SFEC60	55 SPCR50	56 SPCR56	57 SPCR12	58 EXPR65	59 PGDP65	60 PTGX65	61 HREA61	62 PPCRI4	63 PUTE56	64 PUTEIN
136 USTD68	-0.09	-0.01	0.10	-0.09	-0.33	-0.27	-0.06	0.18	-0.06	-0.17	0.10	0.02	0.22	-0.04	-0.24	-0.00
137 TMET62	-0.21	-0.09	0.27	0.50	-0.45	-0.26	0.10	0.11	-0.14	-0.22	-0.18	-0.40	0.35	0.28	0.07	-0.05
138 TMET68	-0.28	-0.17	0.36	0.49	-0.43	-0.31	0.08	0.08	-0.10	-0.21	-0.30	-0.50	0.26	0.24	0.04	-0.15
139 PCPREX	-0.11	-0.02	0.23	0.29	-0.02	-0.09	-0.26	-0.04	0.34	0.18	-0.10	0.10	-0.10	0.11	-0.05	0.22
140 IMPCOM	-0.36	-0.31	0.15	0.21	-0.34	-0.23	-0.14	-0.07	0.11	-0.06	-0.33	0.03	-0.23	-0.26	-0.00	-0.23
141 TRPGN8	0.52	0.52	-0.20	-0.20	0.30	0.16	0.50	0.44	0.21	-0.05	0.18	-0.23	0.42	-0.30	-0.15	-0.15
142 CUBATR	0.18	0.10	-0.21	-0.13	0.23	-0.22	-0.04	-0.04	-0.04	0.01	-0.20	-0.24	0.06	-0.05	-0.11	-0.32
143 IMEQ62	-0.19	-0.12	0.06	0.29	-0.38	-0.39	-0.03	-0.13	-0.70	-0.08	-0.16	-0.18	0.31	0.07	-0.19	-0.24
144 EXAF68	-0.21	-0.29	0.09	0.05	-0.10	0.07	-0.23	-0.38	-0.19	0.23	-0.18	-0.08	-0.30	0.07	0.13	0.31
145 IMAF68	-0.10	-0.23	-0.19	-0.08	-0.05	-0.00	-0.22	-0.27	-0.23	0.26	-0.13	-0.20	-0.37	0.02	0.19	0.39
146 70PCEX	0.07	-0.01	-0.13	-0.25	0.06	0.16	0.13	-0.12	-0.31	-0.10	0.03	-0.05	-0.07	-0.13	-0.04	-0.22
147 PCEXME	-0.32	-0.23	0.37	0.40	-0.46	-0.34	-0.15	-0.08	-0.04	0.04	-0.16	-0.11	0.04	0.22	0.19	-0.42
148 IMME25	-0.18	-0.18	-0.05	0.07	-0.31	-0.27	0.31	0.27	0.04	-0.25	-0.19	-0.38	0.14	-0.03	-0.51	-0.39
149 EXME25	-0.20	-0.32	-0.31	-0.21	-0.15	-0.00	0.41	0.13	-0.09	-0.28	-0.23	-0.33	0.18	-0.08	-0.35	-0.53
150 REGORG	-0.11	0.05	0.41	0.46	-0.37	-0.22	-0.06	0.18	-0.14	-0.29	-0.20	-0.22	0.31	0.36	0.27	-0.04
151 MEMOR	0.04	-0.02	-0.09	-0.19	0.40	0.30	0.29	0.25	-0.34	-0.26	-0.15	-0.24	0.09	-0.14	-0.32	-0.16
152 MEMAME	-0.11	-0.11	0.26	0.48	-0.38	-0.22	-0.17	-0.03	-0.07	-0.04	-0.19	-0.17	0.16	-0.42	-0.30	-0.00
153 DIPSEN	-0.09	0.07	0.20	-0.16	0.27	0.01	0.06	0.45	-0.04	-0.41	0.04	0.13	0.30	-0.18	-0.25	-0.05
154 DIPREC	-0.05	0.00	-0.04	-0.37	0.32	0.06	0.02	0.26	-0.28	-0.28	0.20	0.28	0.22	-0.16	-0.28	-0.30
155 AOBJAG	-0.10	-0.06	-0.02	-0.14	-0.18	-0.28	-0.08	0.17	-0.07	-0.12	0.02	-0.11	-0.04	-0.23	-0.15	-0.05
156 MUCOSU	0.14	-0.02	-0.35	-0.43	0.39	0.11	0.01	-0.12	-0.23	0.06	-0.04	-0.20	-0.15	-0.01	-0.30	0.06
157 RECOC7	-0.12	-0.09	-0.03	-0.10	-0.15	-0.02	0.12	-0.15	-0.21	-0.00	0.06	0.09	-0.07	-0.09	-0.18	-0.34
158 CH5067	0.00	0.04	0.30	0.17	0.05	-0.10	-0.12	0.07	-0.06	-0.11	0.16	0.29	-0.13	-0.33	0.08	-0.31
159 MCITPM	0.21	0.39	0.14	-0.05	0.40	0.31	0.12	0.20	0.02	-0.18	0.14	-0.19	0.10	-0.07	-0.08	-0.05
160 LRCITP	0.04	0.04	-0.09	-0.19	-0.02	-0.14	0.03	0.13	-0.19	-0.24	0.06	-0.03	0.08	-0.04	-0.20	-0.10
161 PRLT4L	-0.07	-0.02	-0.15	-0.02	-0.15	-0.03	0.30	0.07	0.21	0.28	-0.01	0.25	0.11	-0.11	0.14	-0.12
162 PRCT4L	0.03	-0.06	-0.13	0.02	-0.21	-0.11	0.29	0.08	0.20	0.24	-0.04	0.21	0.08	-0.06	0.13	-0.14
163 JRPC65	0.29	0.51	0.11	-0.03	0.21	0.18	0.23	0.49	-0.01	-0.17	0.19	-0.23	0.38	-0.09	-0.04	-0.10
164 URPC55	0.27	0.42	0.00	0.00	0.14	0.13	0.30	0.48	-0.02	-0.10	0.18	-0.17	0.38	-0.09	-0.02	-0.08
165 UR5565	-0.19	-0.17	0.19	0.02	-0.02	-0.09	-0.31	-0.24	-0.02	-0.07	-0.13	-0.15	-0.21	0.07	-0.00	0.04
166 MOMARV	-0.01	-0.06	-0.10	-0.21	-0.09	-0.02	0.04	-0.07	-0.12	-0.02	-0.13	-0.21	0.02	-0.13	0.07	-0.14
167 SETPAV	-0.48	-0.48	0.46	0.57	-0.40	-0.33	-0.23	-0.28	-0.06	-0.11	-0.34	-0.38	-0.23	0.29	-0.08	-0.07
168 LEHIEV	-0.17	-0.09	0.27	0.25	-0.39	-0.33	0.06	0.19	0.06	-0.30	-0.13	-0.14	0.16	0.18	0.13	-0.34
169 HIEFAV	-0.21	-0.17	0.27	0.25	-0.29	-0.16	0.17	0.12	-0.06	-0.29	-0.18	-0.23	0.03	-0.00	-0.07	0.02
170 INHERV	-0.15	-0.06	0.27	0.31	-0.20	-0.23	0.13	0.17	0.22	-0.28	-0.07	-0.01	0.24	-0.04	0.00	-0.31
171 AUTHOV	-0.18	-0.12	0.27	0.20	-0.27	-0.13	0.10	0.12	-0.22	-0.24	-0.09	-0.07	0.12	0.22	0.05	-0.22
172 DECNV	0.10	0.13	0.09	0.17	-0.03	-0.16	0.18	0.18	-0.00	-0.23	-0.04	-0.12	0.10	-0.01	0.15	-0.10

C O R R E L A T I O N S

VARIABLE	65 PTGXIN	66 SSCP52	67 SSCPIN	68 LITR65	69 LITRIN	70 IMPRO7	71 CINSET	72 NMRT65	73 RADP66	74 RAPE06	75 NEPC65	76 NEPECA	77 TEPC68	78 TECH38	79 CVPE16	80 PECHCV
65 PTGXIN	1.00															
66 SSCP52	0.16	1.00														
67 SSCPIN	0.04	0.25	1.00													
68 LITR65	-0.02	-0.20	0.13	1.00												
69 LITRIN	-0.14	0.10	-0.12	-0.06	1.00											
70 IMPRO7	-0.19	-0.08	-0.02	0.22	-0.21	1.00										
71 CINSET	-0.22	0.30	0.12	0.13	0.07	-0.02	1.00									
72 NMRT65	-0.29	0.11	0.24	0.02	-0.23	0.34	0.27	1.00								
73 RADP66	-0.04	0.47	0.07	-0.03	0.03	0.03	0.07	0.12	1.00							
74 RAPE06	0.00	0.14	-0.06	-0.10	0.09	-0.08	0.02	0.03	-0.01	1.00						
75 NEPC65	-0.16	0.30	0.30	0.26	-0.20	0.24	0.65	0.47	0.34	-0.01	1.00					
76 NEPECA	0.28	0.18	0.21	-0.08	0.04	-0.18	-0.08	-0.03	0.27	0.02	0.08	1.00				
77 TEPC68	-0.17	0.07	0.22	0.32	0.39	-0.11	0.23	0.07	0.35	-0.16	0.18	-0.09	1.00			
78 TECH38	0.27	0.01	-0.11	0.03	-0.15	-0.26	-0.34	-0.40	-0.09	-0.28	-0.28	0.22	-0.08	1.00		
79 CVPE16	0.02	0.24	-0.03	-0.04	0.46	-0.15	0.15	-0.01	0.58	-0.01	0.09	0.22	0.61	-0.10	1.00	
80 PECHCV	-0.17	0.12	-0.21	-0.24	0.04	0.14	-0.06	0.08	0.18	0.21	-0.02	0.20	-0.18	-0.00	0.49	1.00
81 CARP16	-0.17	0.16	0.11	0.15	0.38	-0.05	0.27	0.14	0.51	-0.08	0.20	0.02	0.88	-0.22	0.79	0.07
82 LEGNOS	-0.25	0.09	0.04	0.04	0.07	-0.06	0.21	-0.02	-0.24	0.17	0.13	-0.07	-0.18	-0.04	-0.32	-0.09
83 CABRPI	0.07	0.10	0.01	-0.18	-0.05	0.08	0.02	-0.06	0.51	0.08	0.39	0.32	-0.02	-0.23	-0.31	0.28
84 WAGPUB	-0.03	0.53	0.04	-0.06	-0.11	-0.24	0.13	0.29	-0.15	0.44	0.15	0.00	-0.17	0.06	-0.22	0.04
85 LOCGOV	-0.03	0.32	0.18	0.03	0.04	0.26	-0.10	0.22	-0.04	0.08	-0.01	-0.14	0.22	0.07	0.08	0.12
86 LAWTWO	0.32	0.19	0.24	-0.04	-0.20	-0.06	-0.11	0.02	0.04	0.07	0.09	0.60	-0.16	0.13	-0.10	0.10
87 LAWNOS	-0.24	0.15	0.07	0.02	0.01	-0.13	0.08	-0.14	-0.11	0.14	0.10	-0.07	-0.20	0.19	-0.23	-0.04
88 JUDREV	-0.12	0.07	0.18	0.30	0.06	0.31	-0.11	0.07	-0.23	0.01	0.02	-0.32	0.03	0.04	-0.44	-0.40
89 YOUNGI	0.22	-0.07	0.17	0.15	0.09	-0.22	-0.00	-0.14	-0.23	-0.15	-0.19	-0.00	0.43	0.19	0.40	-0.11
90 YOUNGP	0.06	-0.24	-0.02	0.24	-0.04	0.21	-0.26	0.00	-0.05	-0.31	-0.26	-0.35	0.30	0.21	-0.03	-0.20

VARIABLE	65 PTGXIN	66 SSCP52	67 SSCPIN	68 LITR65	69 LITRIN	70 IMPRO7	71 CINSET	72 NMRT65	73 RADP66	74 RADE06	75 NEPC65	76 NEPECA	77 TEPC68	78 TECH38	79 CVPE16	80 PECHCV
91 NOYRFO	-0.56	0.12	0.12	-0.02	0.01	-0.10	0.11	0.23	0.59	-0.14	0.22	0.56	0.17	-0.22	0.37	0.26
92 VOVOIE	0.29	-0.07	-0.27	-0.27	0.15	-0.04	-0.15	-0.38	-0.19	-0.19	-0.22	0.01	0.32	-0.34	0.38	0.06
93 PEVORU	-0.02	-0.22	-0.02	-0.23	0.18	-0.10	-0.00	-0.17	0.08	-0.18	-0.15	0.20	0.08	-0.03	0.35	0.22
94 CHNOLP	0.14	0.14	0.12	-0.29	-0.11	-0.41	-0.18	-0.19	0.02	-0.17	-0.32	-0.02	0.14	-0.49	0.08	0.03
95 VOLEPA	-0.03	0.12	0.07	0.47	-0.11	0.26	0.25	0.12	-0.01	-0.19	0.39	-0.03	0.00	-0.17	-0.10	-0.06
96 VOPABN	-0.21	0.04	-0.04	0.21	-0.01	0.31	-0.02	0.26	-0.23	0.04	0.10	0.01	-0.20	-0.17	-0.28	0.00
97 TOSPME	-0.18	0.18	-0.12	0.15	-0.14	0.12	0.23	0.21	-0.02	0.35	0.12	0.13	-0.03	-0.32	-0.05	0.17
98 LEGFRA	0.00	0.20	0.04	0.38	-0.20	0.25	0.05	0.16	0.04	0.32	0.24	-0.07	-0.08	-0.21	-0.24	-0.12
99 CGBC51	0.09	0.35	0.51	0.20	0.03	-0.08	0.63	0.26	0.62	0.14	0.81	0.15	0.38	-0.32	0.37	0.02
100 CGBC61	-0.01	0.24	0.13	0.05	0.18	-0.01	0.58	0.28	0.49	-0.01	0.70	0.13	0.42	-0.19	0.57	0.17
101 CGGC79	-0.00	-0.24	-0.26	0.08	0.01	0.19	0.15	0.24	0.17	-0.24	0.17	0.04	0.40	-0.13	0.48	0.26
102 TAXD66	-0.30	-0.33	0.18	0.47	-0.39	0.20	0.29	0.02	0.18	-0.05	0.41	0.08	0.17	-0.24	-0.07	-0.08
103 GREV66	0.17	0.13	0.21	0.22	0.42	-0.24	-0.03	-0.14	0.27	0.32	-0.07	0.16	0.62	-0.20	0.52	-0.18
104 GOSP61	0.04	0.42	0.17	-0.23	0.30	-0.01	0.39	0.34	0.40	-0.14	0.31	0.00	0.29	-0.11	0.50	0.12
105 TAXD36	-0.09	-0.20	-0.14	0.18	-0.11	0.30	0.26	0.06	0.11	0.04	0.41	0.15	-0.30	-0.48	-0.22	-0.19
106 GREV36	-0.11	-0.13	0.03	0.02	0.24	-0.22	0.00	-0.43	-0.18	0.09	-0.20	-0.03	-0.09	-0.08	-0.14	-0.20
107 CREV36	-0.21	0.07	0.41	0.31	0.21	-0.26	0.17	-0.19	0.03	0.03	0.15	0.05	0.33	-0.16	0.17	-0.09
108 GOEX68	-0.01	0.02	0.29	0.27	0.36	-0.18	0.12	-0.02	0.36	-0.17	0.21	0.15	0.89	-0.12	0.70	-0.07
109 GOSP38	0.13	-0.13	0.43	0.45	0.16	-0.18	0.02	-0.22	-0.09	0.17	-0.06	0.11	0.51	-0.26	0.25	-0.15
110 DEFG65	0.05	0.10	-0.11	-0.45	0.03	-0.37	0.08	-0.12	-0.33	0.18	-0.12	0.15	-0.33	0.01	-0.25	-0.09
111 TOTAID	-0.31	0.15	0.07	0.08	0.09	0.02	0.56	0.19	-0.26	-0.01	0.39	0.01	-0.14	-0.28	-0.22	-0.07
112 NUMAID	-0.44	0.18	0.11	0.21	0.05	0.10	0.64	0.27	-0.18	-0.01	0.56	-0.07	-0.05	-0.24	-0.21	-0.04
113 TMAN67	-0.22	0.15	0.09	0.25	-0.03	0.14	0.28	0.10	-0.18	-0.12	0.27	0.04	-0.18	-0.11	-0.25	-0.09
114 AFARMF	0.08	0.29	0.08	-0.34	0.14	-0.08	0.34	0.06	-0.02	-0.10	0.26	0.36	-0.17	-0.23	-0.09	-0.17
115 DEFG67	0.16	0.17	-0.03	-0.14	0.30	-0.30	0.17	-0.10	-0.19	0.19	-0.09	0.15	0.00	-0.21	-0.05	-0.33
116 CHDEFB	-0.24	-0.06	0.11	0.16	-0.08	0.13	0.04	0.41	-0.07	-0.12	0.13	-0.03	0.01	-0.23	-0.28	-0.30
117 ARFPPO	0.06	0.41	0.20	-0.09	0.31	-0.15	0.33	0.09	0.33	0.11	0.27	0.61	0.17	-0.37	0.35	-0.01
118 CHARF7	-0.29	-0.07	-0.01	-0.05	0.03	-0.13	0.01	0.39	-0.10	-0.20	-0.03	0.05	-0.11	-0.17	-0.30	-0.12
119 INTSEC	0.04	0.41	0.44	0.07	0.30	-0.21	0.14	-0.07	0.42	-0.20	0.08	0.02	0.60	-0.26	0.40	-0.21
120 CHINSE	-0.03	-0.15	-0.00	-0.10	0.21	0.20	-0.21	-0.02	0.02	-0.11	-0.19	-0.05	0.19	-0.15	0.08	-0.01
121 TURMOL	-0.25	0.09	0.09	0.22	-0.08	0.15	0.25	0.31	-0.11	-0.07	0.32	-0.06	0.05	-0.13	-0.10	0.03
122 ELITIN	0.01	0.15	-0.00	-0.02	0.04	0.31	-0.03	0.39	-0.10	-0.02	0.18	0.05	-0.11	-0.20	-0.20	-0.10
123 KILLOG	-0.12	-0.13	-0.12	0.24	-0.12	0.38	-0.13	-0.10	-0.13	-0.20	-0.03	0.05	-0.09	0.00	-0.28	-0.06
124 COMWGT	0.02	0.14	0.07	0.14	-0.13	0.04	0.15	-0.06	-0.28	-0.20	0.07	-0.06	-0.17	0.18	-0.37	-0.24
125 AVERES	0.21	-0.00	0.10	-0.13	0.00	0.12	0.00	-0.07	-0.18	-0.04	-0.13	0.19	-0.16	-0.19	-0.07	-0.09
126 TOAAT8	-0.03	0.13	0.15	0.28	-0.14	0.12	0.35	0.18	0.07	-0.10	0.45	0.35	-0.12	-0.28	-0.02	-0.01
127 PCAID8	0.08	0.13	0.15	0.09	0.26	0.07	0.27	0.16	0.27	-0.12	0.27	0.38	0.12	-0.13	0.50	0.46
128 AIDPC4	-0.41	-0.05	-0.07	0.29	0.11	0.22	0.09	0.14	-0.07	-0.16	0.16	0.16	-0.14	-0.71	-0.07	0.16
129 AIDPC8	-0.10	0.02	0.10	0.34	0.17	0.26	0.47	0.21	-0.05	-0.15	0.44	0.05	-0.05	-0.25	0.22	0.19
130 CAPAD1	-0.19	0.00	-0.20	-0.06	0.10	-0.19	-0.13	0.08	0.42	-0.16	-0.12	0.65	-0.05	-0.24	0.57	0.59
131 PCDAID	-0.02	-0.09	0.02	0.09	0.39	0.14	0.08	-0.01	-0.13	-0.20	-0.10	-0.15	0.23	0.17	0.48	0.43
132 COMAID	0.06	0.39	0.22	0.02	0.16	-0.08	0.60	-0.13	0.03	-0.06	-0.51	-0.05	0.05	-0.22	-0.11	-0.31
133 CAPAD7	0.05	-0.14	-0.07	0.21	0.05	-0.20	-0.26	-0.15	0.46	-0.19	-0.10	0.43	0.37	0.08	0.51	0.15
134 APCTO8	0.09	-0.13	-0.03	0.19	0.32	-0.25	-0.11	-0.18	0.42	-0.16	-0.05	0.23	0.49	-0.08	0.59	0.13
135 USTD62	0.10	-0.06	-0.07	-0.08	-0.20	0.54	-0.03	-0.12	0.08	-0.25	0.04	0.27	-0.24	-0.18	-0.10	0.11

C O R R E L A T I O N S

VARIABLE	65 PTGXIN	66 SSCP52	67 SSCPIN	68 LITR65	69 LITRIN	70 IMPRO7	71 CINSET	72 NMRT65	73 RADP66	74 RADPEO6	75 NEPC65	76 NEPECA	77 TEPC68	78 TECH38	79 CVPE16	80 PECHCV
136 USTD68	0.02	0.08	0.09	-0.08	-0.04	0.33	0.13	-0.01	0.18	-0.13	0.25	0.25	-0.14	-0.23	-0.00	0.07
137 TMET62	-0.18	0.12	-0.22	-0.49	0.33	-0.24	0.02	-0.04	0.33	0.20	-0.06	0.01	0.12	-0.40	0.45	0.35
138 TMET68	-0.14	0.18	-0.16	-0.49	0.26	-0.14	0.13	0.08	0.35	0.34	-0.00	0.14	0.07	-0.19	0.41	0.24
139 PCPREX	0.51	0.00	0.01	0.10	-0.20	0.00	-0.19	-0.23	-0.01	-0.12	-0.06	0.18	0.14	0.19	0.07	-0.14
140 IMPCOM	0.01	0.22	-0.01	-0.28	0.05	-0.30	0.26	0.21	-0.16	0.05	-0.17	-0.05	-0.02	0.10	-0.03	0.01
141 TRPGN8	-0.13	0.16	0.23	0.28	0.18	-0.05	-0.13	0.03	0.61	0.01	0.05	0.30	0.62	-0.09	0.69	0.27
142 CUBATR	-0.07	-0.10	0.28	0.26	-0.13	-0.09	0.05	-0.01	0.03	-0.15	0.05	0.20	0.27	0.01	0.15	-0.12
143 IMEQ62	-0.08	0.16	0.05	-0.30	0.18	-0.32	-0.09	-0.03	-0.23	-0.35	-0.07	0.16	0.22	0.32	0.28	0.02
144 EXAF68	-0.19	-0.36	-0.25	-0.25	-0.15	-0.10	-0.05	-0.09	-0.28	-0.10	-0.22	-0.08	-0.25	-0.10	-0.33	-0.14
145 IMAF68	-0.21	-0.23	0.09	-0.17	-0.10	0.09	-0.07	0.04	-0.25	-0.02	-0.21	0.01	-0.18	-0.12	-0.25	-0.06
146 70PCEX	-0.49	-0.21	-0.04	0.02	-0.05	-0.07	0.32	0.18	-0.20	0.01	0.12	-0.24	-0.12	-0.10	-0.23	0.02
147 PCEXME	-0.10	-0.12	-0.08	-0.43	0.01	-0.07	-0.19	0.25	0.02	0.05	-0.05	-0.30	-0.07	-0.14	0.10	0.14
148 IMME25	-0.54	0.34	0.12	-0.12	0.05	0.33	0.44	0.23	0.34	0.15	0.45	-0.33	0.15	-0.17	0.05	0.06
149 EXME25	-0.47	0.43	-0.01	-0.15	-0.13	0.40	0.45	0.55	0.23	0.03	0.26	-0.46	0.13	-0.19	0.06	0.10
150 REGORG	-0.07	-0.00	-0.27	-0.39	0.51	-0.34	0.10	0.03	-0.04	0.22	-0.01	-0.01	0.10	-0.25	0.25	-0.02
151 MEMOR	-0.51	0.19	-0.05	0.54	-0.18	0.07	0.67	0.27	0.00	0.01	0.60	-0.16	-0.02	-0.09	-0.12	0.07
152 MEMAME	-0.26	-0.26	-0.40	-0.36	0.44	-0.21	-0.02	0.06	-0.13	0.16	-0.14	-0.09	-0.03	-0.21	0.18	0.23
153 DIPSEN	-0.02	0.35	0.49	0.31	-0.06	0.08	0.50	0.23	-0.14	-0.16	0.74	0.05	0.00	-0.06	0.00	-0.05
154 DIPREC	0.00	0.23	0.29	0.45	-0.14	0.27	0.58	0.19	-0.03	-0.32	0.57	0.02	-0.05	-0.15	-0.05	-0.08
155 ADBJAG	0.01	0.36	0.23	0.05	0.05	0.07	0.50	0.01	-0.14	0.22	0.37	0.12	-0.16	-0.31	-0.29	-0.27
155 MUCOSU	-0.48	-0.20	0.01	0.71	-0.18	0.12	0.38	0.12	-0.20	-0.09	0.26	-0.02	0.07	-0.19	-0.11	-0.10
157 RECOC7	-0.30	0.12	-0.07	0.02	0.04	-0.09	0.34	0.26	-0.12	-0.08	0.26	-0.21	0.06	-0.08	-0.18	-0.19
153 CH5067	0.28	-0.09	-0.04	0.04	0.07	0.02	-0.05	-0.11	-0.12	-0.06	0.10	-0.19	-0.14	0.03	-0.16	-0.16
159 MCITPM	-0.13	0.01	-0.04	0.19	0.42	-0.24	-0.09	-0.27	-0.19	-0.03	-0.07	-0.05	0.45	-0.02	0.38	-0.03
160 LRCITP	-0.28	0.04	0.01	0.32	-0.00	0.18	0.52	0.26	-0.11	-0.10	0.41	-0.04	-0.03	-0.35	-0.09	-0.09
161 PRLT4L	0.19	0.07	-0.11	-0.12	-0.24	0.37	-0.19	0.11	0.37	-0.20	-0.03	0.07	-0.23	0.14	-0.01	0.07
162 PRCT4L	0.15	0.11	-0.06	-0.10	-0.16	0.35	-0.13	0.10	0.36	-0.24	0.01	0.10	-0.18	0.12	-0.05	-0.04
163 URPC65	-0.16	0.13	0.04	0.20	0.58	-0.18	0.24	-0.00	0.30	-0.03	0.18	0.06	0.69	-0.36	0.58	-0.08
164 URPC55	-0.18	0.18	0.00	0.23	0.47	-0.05	0.29	-0.10	0.31	-0.03	0.21	0.00	0.67	-0.33	0.51	-0.07
165 UR5565	-0.01	-0.19	0.23	-0.32	-0.01	-0.14	-0.27	-0.14	-0.07	-0.05	-0.24	-0.08	-0.22	0.01	-0.08	-0.02
166 MOMARV	-0.31	-0.07	0.27	-0.01	-0.12	0.13	0.06	0.49	0.06	0.00	0.14	0.25	-0.01	-0.25	-0.04	0.11
167 SETPAV	-0.02	-0.06	-0.05	-0.30	-0.24	-0.44	0.08	-0.13	-0.12	-0.02	-0.05	-0.15	-0.14	0.29	-0.17	-0.30
168 LEHIEV	-0.30	-0.04	0.14	-0.21	0.03	-0.15	-0.07	0.40	0.19	-0.18	0.20	0.22	0.02	-0.20	0.12	-0.09
169 HIEFAV	-0.28	0.06	-0.02	-0.07	-0.22	-0.00	0.13	0.39	0.10	0.22	0.34	0.21	-0.11	-0.18	-0.01	-0.23
170 INHERV	0.00	0.08	0.09	-0.21	-0.09	-0.26	0.09	0.21	0.22	-0.10	0.24	0.19	0.08	0.01	0.13	0.03
171 AUTHOV	-0.13	0.03	-0.06	-0.16	0.08	-0.02	0.00	0.41	0.12	0.21	0.10	0.06	-0.01	-0.34	0.19	0.21
172 DECNV	-0.24	-0.09	0.08	0.03	0.18	-0.09	0.03	0.17	-0.05	-0.14	0.10	0.11	0.29	-0.08	0.21	0.00

C O R R E L A T I O N S

VARIABLE	81 CARP16	82 LEGNOS	83 CABRPI	84 WAGPUB	85 LOCGOV	86 LAWTWO	87 LAWNOS	88 JUDREV	89 YOUNGI	90 YOUNGP	91 NOYRFO	92 NOVOIE	93 PEVORU	94 CHNOLP	95 NOLEPA	96 NOPABN
81 CARP16	1.00															
82 LEGNOS	-0.21	1.00														
83 CABRPI	0.19	-0.23	1.00													
84 WAGPUB	-0.27	0.31	-0.23	1.00												
85 LOCGOV	0.16	0.24	-0.36	0.40	1.00											
86 LAWTWO	-0.26	-0.01	-0.01	0.36	0.20	1.00										
87 LAWNOS	-0.26	0.91	-0.13	0.26	0.21	-0.04	1.00									
88 JUDREV	-0.13	0.22	-0.39	0.15	0.37	-0.03	0.19	1.00								
89 YOUNGI	0.44	-0.32	-0.03	-0.44	-0.12	-0.09	-0.17	-0.38	1.00							
90 YOUNGP	0.15	-0.43	-0.21	-0.22	0.21	-0.00	-0.45	0.17	0.27	1.00						

C O R R E L A T I O N S

		81 CARP16	82 LEGNOS	83 CABRPI	84 WAGPUB	85 LOCGOV	86 LAWTWO	87 LAWNOS	88 JUDREV	89 YOUNGI	90 YOJNGP	91 NOYRFO	92 NOVOIE	93 PEVORU	94 CHNOLP	95 NOLEPA	96 NOPABN
91	NOYRFO	0.37	0.05	0.34	-0.12	-0.13	0.18	-0.02	-0.36	0.13	-0.22	1.00					
92	NOVOIE	0.30	-0.37	-0.12	-0.38	-0.06	0.02	-0.30	-0.20	0.56	0.41	-0.03	1.00				
93	PEVORU	0.14	-0.41	-0.14	-0.51	-0.11	0.02	-0.30	-0.32	0.30	0.05	0.19	0.15	1.00			
94	CHNOLP	-0.05	-0.15	-0.16	-0.01	0.21	0.10	-0.07	-0.14	0.28	0.20	0.09	0.19	0.29	1.00		
95	NOLEPA	-0.08	0.12	0.01	0.45	0.06	0.23	-0.05	0.16	-0.26	0.02	-0.10	-0.02	-0.51	-0.59	1.00	
96	NOPABN	-0.28	0.37	-0.20	0.49	0.17	0.21	0.12	0.18	-0.48	-0.01	-0.02	-0.27	-0.55	-0.50	0.74	1.00
97	TOSPME	-0.12	-0.03	-0.08	0.37	0.26	0.16	-0.08	-0.14	-0.04	0.02	-0.00	0.08	-0.15	-0.23	0.38	0.23
98	LEGFRA	-0.05	0.12	0.04	0.43	0.11	0.16	-0.12	0.26	-0.16	-0.16	-0.03	-0.02	-0.68	-0.43	0.73	0.53
99	CGBC51	0.40	-0.11	0.51	0.02	-0.26	0.05	-0.09	-0.24	0.11	-0.32	0.29	-0.13	0.13	-0.09	0.30	-0.14
100	CGBC61	0.44	-0.16	0.37	-0.09	-0.14	0.04	-0.13	-0.37	0.11	-0.15	0.24	0.11	0.21	-0.15	0.19	-0.07
101	CGGC79	0.39	-0.30	0.10	-0.13	-0.13	-0.03	-0.28	-0.27	-0.09	0.23	0.01	0.36	0.07	-0.31	0.08	0.07
102	TAXD66	0.10	0.21	0.24	-0.22	-0.20	0.01	0.34	0.03	-0.10	-0.12	0.15	-0.27	0.05	-0.43	0.11	-0.03
103	GREV66	0.60	-0.24	0.03	-0.23	0.08	-0.13	-0.34	0.09	0.22	0.03	0.13	0.13	0.17	-0.12	0.03	-0.05
104	GOSP61	0.40	-0.19	0.06	-0.10	0.06	-0.12	-0.30	-0.12	0.12	-0.22	0.25	-0.06	0.34	0.06	-0.22	-0.22
105	TAXD36	-0.27	0.13	0.21	-0.02	-0.37	0.04	0.18	0.19	-0.41	-0.39	-0.03	-0.23	-0.02	-0.74	0.40	0.23
106	GREV36	-0.11	-0.07	0.15	-0.22	-0.39	-0.25	-0.03	0.14	0.06	-0.01	-0.17	-0.04	-0.03	-0.21	0.15	-0.00
107	CREV36	0.30	0.09	0.23	-0.12	-0.18	-0.24	0.20	0.02	0.15	-0.01	0.04	-0.09	-0.00	-0.27	0.20	-0.06
108	GOEX68	0.86	-0.24	0.18	-0.28	-0.10	-0.11	-0.24	-0.13	0.47	0.14	0.29	0.33	0.21	0.11	-0.02	-0.25
109	GOSP38	0.45	-0.11	0.08	-0.28	-0.02	-0.12	-0.26	-0.09	0.43	0.10	-0.03	0.15	0.04	-0.02	0.10	-0.12
110	DEFG65	-0.35	-0.23	-0.15	0.31	-0.28	0.17	0.11	-0.32	-0.17	-0.34	-0.14	-0.14	-0.26	-0.02	0.10	0.34
111	TOTAID	-0.12	0.61	-0.11	0.26	-0.12	-0.12	0.41	0.17	-0.47	-0.52	0.07	-0.53	-0.33	-0.39	0.34	0.48
112	NUMAID	-0.06	0.60	-0.05	0.25	-0.06	-0.13	0.42	0.23	-0.43	-0.42	0.10	-0.51	-0.37	-0.36	0.39	0.44
113	TMAN67	-0.20	0.70	-0.16	0.27	-0.02	-0.01	0.62	0.16	-0.28	-0.42	0.22	-0.27	-0.57	-0.55	0.50	0.66
114	AFARMF	-0.10	0.42	-0.06	0.13	-0.13	-0.13	0.35	-0.10	-0.29	-0.61	-0.12	-0.31	-0.16	-0.08	0.00	0.21
115	DEFG67	-0.06	0.17	-0.27	0.15	-0.20	0.02	-0.06	-0.08	-0.02	-0.31	-0.11	-0.09	-0.21	-0.28	0.24	0.40
116	CHDEFB	-0.02	0.09	-0.24	0.03	0.09	-0.11	-0.04	0.18	-0.00	0.22	0.06	-0.12	-0.09	-0.00	0.04	0.22
117	ARFPPO	0.27	0.10	-0.14	0.08	-0.23	0.24	0.01	-0.20	-0.06	-0.52	0.46	0.02	-0.21	-0.20	0.17	0.15
118	CHARF7	-0.22	0.22	-0.19	0.27	0.16	0.25	0.16	0.07	0.32	0.15	0.08	-0.00	-0.21	-0.02	0.25	0.47
119	INTSEC	0.54	-0.16	0.11	0.08	0.09	0.00	-0.04	0.20	0.21	0.00	-0.00	0.07	-0.06	-0.04	0.15	-0.20
120	CHINSE	-0.00	-0.18	-0.24	-0.21	-0.01	0.26	-0.19	0.05	0.21	0.15	-0.12	0.19	0.14	0.07	-0.12	-0.00
121	TURMOL	-0.02	0.48	-0.13	0.31	0.18	0.05	0.34	-0.06	-0.18	-0.06	0.12	-0.15	-0.61	-0.37	0.59	0.75
122	ELITIN	-0.20	0.09	-0.06	0.38	0.08	0.15	-0.16	0.21	-0.54	-0.03	-0.06	-0.28	-0.55	-0.31	0.45	0.71
123	KILLOG	-0.15	0.29	-0.03	-0.17	0.03	0.23	0.19	0.07	0.01	0.19	0.00	0.19	-0.48	-0.36	0.40	0.54
124	COMWGT	-0.24	0.58	-0.16	0.19	0.06	0.07	0.40	0.11	-0.13	-0.13	-0.12	-0.20	-0.62	-0.24	0.35	0.54
125	AVERES	-0.15	-0.00	-0.06	0.06	-0.31	0.25	-0.31	-0.00	-0.20	-0.04	-0.11	-0.10	-0.17	-0.48	0.39	0.48
126	TOAAT8	-0.04	0.47	0.11	0.07	-0.20	0.09	0.38	0.00	-0.21	-0.53	0.27	-0.24	-0.35	-0.68	0.43	0.46
127	PCAID8	0.37	-0.05	0.26	-0.24	-0.13	0.01	-0.08	-0.30	0.19	-0.22	0.42	0.19	0.33	-0.14	-0.15	-0.19
128	AIDPC4	-0.09	0.58	-0.11	0.04	0.11	-0.01	0.45	0.00	-0.20	-0.33	0.33	-0.05	-0.26	-0.43	0.39	0.65
129	AIDPC8	0.13	0.31	0.04	-0.10	-0.12	-0.11	0.17	0.00	-0.13	-0.26	0.06	-0.05	-0.07	-0.62	0.34	0.33
130	CAPAD1	0.23	-0.19	0.26	0.04	-0.08	0.42	-0.06	-0.75	0.29	-0.28	0.69	0.15	0.43	0.06	-0.21	-0.17
131	PCDAID	0.34	-0.09	-0.10	-0.31	0.13	-0.21	-0.09	-0.05	0.23	0.22	-0.10	0.33	0.36	0.10	-0.28	-0.23
132	COMAID	0.01	0.26	0.03	0.10	-0.17	-0.12	0.28	-0.26	-0.44	-0.50	-0.10	-0.29	-0.15	-0.12	0.05	-0.13
133	CAPAD7	0.39	-0.30	0.24	-0.22	-0.05	0.14	-0.09	-0.28	0.44	0.10	0.52	0.34	0.35	0.17	-0.14	-0.29
134	APCTO8	0.46	-0.36	0.22	-0.14	-0.12	0.09	-0.22	-0.29	0.49	0.08	0.21	0.41	0.19	0.13	-0.08	-0.26
135	USTD62	-0.12	0.06	0.27	-0.52	-0.36	0.06	0.09	-0.05	-0.08	-0.12	0.17	0.03	0.09	-0.17	-0.07	-0.05

C O R R E L A T I O N S

VARIABLE	81 CARP16	82 LEGNOS	83 CABRPI	84 WAGPUB	85 LOCGOV	86 LAWTWO	87 LAWNOS	88 JUDREV	89 YJUNGI	90 YJJNGP	91 NOYRFD	92 NOVOIE	93 PEVORU	94 CHNOLP	95 NOLEPA	96 NOPABN
136 USTD68	0.02	0.17	0.45	-0.46	-0.41	-0.15	0.31	-0.05	-0.04	-0.33	0.21	-0.18	-0.00	-0.20	-0.13	-0.04
137 TMET62	0.26	-0.05	0.37	0.06	-0.14	-0.14	0.03	-0.45	-0.02	0.11	0.27	-0.01	0.05	-0.08	-0.05	0.02
138 TMET68	0.24	-0.06	0.35	0.10	-0.02	-0.15	0.11	-0.50	-0.08	-0.07	0.19	-0.10	0.11	-0.18	-0.04	-0.03
139 PCPREX	-0.01	-0.17	-0.05	-0.07	0.17	-0.23	0.00	-0.13	-0.27	-0.20	-0.14	-0.25	-0.18	0.02	-0.03	-0.11
140 IMPCOM	-0.01	0.27	-0.15	0.21	0.09	-0.06	0.08	-0.24	-0.02	-0.43	0.09	-0.15	-0.11	0.30	-0.15	-0.05
141 TRPGN8	0.69	-0.38	0.23	-0.22	-0.01	0.10	-0.32	-0.06	0.35	0.16	0.51	0.41	0.17	-0.02	0.02	-0.16
142 CUBATR	0.38	0.04	0.04	-0.13	-0.09	0.00	-0.04	-0.11	0.29	-0.07	0.39	0.12	0.22	0.03	0.01	-0.10
143 IMFQ62	-0.20	-0.14	-0.01	-0.12	-0.29	0.08	-0.09	-0.26	0.24	-0.16	0.34	0.12	0.20	0.20	-0.21	-0.00
144 EXAF68	-0.23	-0.03	-0.31	-0.21	-0.04	-0.06	-0.11	0.04	-0.04	0.10	-0.07	0.04	0.12	0.14	-0.38	-0.26
145 IMAF68	-0.18	-0.17	-0.26	-0.19	0.05	-0.01	-0.26	0.06	0.02	0.36	-0.10	-0.08	0.24	0.14	-0.32	-0.21
146 7OPCEX	-0.07	0.28	-0.15	0.06	-0.20	-0.21	0.08	0.15	-0.30	-0.26	0.09	-0.35	-0.18	-0.05	0.02	0.08
147 PCEXME	0.03	0.12	0.21	-0.02	0.03	-0.33	0.17	-0.31	-0.21	-0.07	0.04	-0.21	0.01	-0.09	-0.13	0.19
148 IMME25	0.26	0.49	0.22	-0.02	0.06	-0.15	0.49	0.01	-0.15	-0.39	0.59	-0.39	-0.05	-0.33	0.22	0.28
149 EXME25	0.31	0.29	-0.21	0.09	0.21	-0.32	0.11	0.02	-0.07	-0.23	0.56	-0.28	-0.04	-0.05	-0.05	0.15
150 REGORG	0.19	0.12	-0.13	0.10	-0.08	-0.19	-0.03	-0.31	-0.11	-0.02	-0.01	-0.03	-0.12	-0.01	0.07	0.07
151 MEMOR	-0.06	0.61	-0.11	0.43	0.12	0.03	0.41	-0.07	-0.18	-0.18	0.15	-0.15	-0.39	-0.38	0.61	0.46
152 MEMAME	-0.06	0.09	-0.02	-0.01	-0.17	-0.20	0.01	-0.35	-0.12	0.09	0.04	0.03	-0.05	-0.04	-0.11	0.14
153 DIPSEN	-0.06	0.37	0.16	0.21	0.09	0.06	0.37	0.00	-0.22	-0.50	0.04	-0.27	-0.29	-0.23	0.41	0.25
154 DIPREC	-0.09	0.37	-0.09	0.05	0.08	-0.04	0.26	0.04	-0.21	-0.48	0.02	-0.21	-0.26	-0.31	0.42	0.32
155 ADBJAG	-0.23	0.41	-0.08	0.30	-0.20	-0.13	0.41	0.33	-0.30	-0.41	-0.19	-0.30	-0.30	-0.46	0.33	0.28
156 MUCOSU	0.05	0.62	-0.30	0.08	0.27	0.11	0.43	0.04	-0.05	-0.05	0.23	0.05	-0.24	-0.43	0.45	0.46
157 RECOC7	-0.04	0.21	-0.22	0.13	-0.16	-0.27	0.07	0.13	-0.24	-0.40	0.05	-0.34	-0.23	-0.08	0.07	0.24
158 CH5067	-0.11	0.31	0.03	-0.01	0.04	-0.06	0.22	0.17	-0.11	-0.02	-0.06	-0.06	0.09	0.09	-0.12	-0.12
159 MCITPM	0.35	-0.15	0.13	0.10	0.20	-0.14	0.03	0.11	-0.10	-0.12	-0.01	0.09	0.12	0.03	0.18	-0.04
160 LRCITP	-0.01	0.57	-0.09	0.14	-0.08	-0.17	0.45	0.04	-0.24	-0.35	-0.03	0.27	-0.43	-0.69	0.52	0.59
161 PRLT4L	-0.13	-0.39	0.18	-0.34	-0.31	0.10	-0.29	-0.10	0.17	0.12	0.11	0.34	0.28	0.05	-0.22	-0.24
162 PRCT4L	-0.10	-0.28	0.16	-0.34	-0.29	0.11	-0.21	-0.03	0.11	0.09	0.14	0.28	0.27	0.04	-0.24	-0.21
163 JRPC65	0.60	-0.12	0.14	0.02	0.15	-0.12	-0.08	-0.07	0.11	0.06	0.07	0.09	0.05	-0.13	0.27	0.09
164 URPC55	0.55	0.00	0.00	0.02	0.26	-0.12	-0.04	-0.07	0.06	0.10	0.05	0.13	-0.14	-0.20	-0.37	0.28
165 UR5565	-0.16	-0.02	0.06	-0.18	-0.09	-0.06	0.12	0.04	0.17	-0.14	0.10	-0.23	-0.56	0.21	-0.50	-0.47
166 MOMARV	0.11	0.22	0.14	-0.03	0.04	0.11	0.32	0.08	-0.05	-0.14	0.32	-0.32	-0.04	-0.15	-0.15	0.06
167 SETPAV	-0.18	0.44	-0.04	0.21	0.02	0.00	0.46	-0.30	-0.13	-0.15	-0.04	-0.25	-0.19	-0.12	-0.15	0.08
168 LEHIEV	0.11	0.15	0.26	-0.02	-0.19	-0.06	0.10	-0.28	-0.15	-0.24	0.41	-0.37	-0.06	-0.19	-0.15	0.22
169 HIEFAV	-0.01	0.30	0.24	0.23	-0.04	0.07	0.25	-0.21	-0.31	-0.26	0.21	-0.47	-0.28	-0.35	0.05	0.28
170 INHERV	0.11	0.25	0.14	0.11	-0.07	0.25	0.23	-0.25	-0.09	-0.39	0.27	-0.23	-0.15	-0.05	0.04	0.15
171 AUTHOV	0.12	0.12	0.14	0.10	0.19	-0.23	-0.07	-0.30	-0.22	-0.16	0.14	-0.39	-0.11	-0.21	-0.05	0.26
172 DECNV	0.27	0.21	-0.07	0.05	0.01	0.07	0.00	-0.00	-0.22	-0.07	0.16	-0.17	-0.11	-0.18	-0.04	0.24

VARIABLE	97 TJSPME	98 LEGFRA	99 CGBC51	100 CGBC61	101 CGGC79	102 TAXD66	103 GREV66	104 GOSP61	105 TAXD36	106 GREV36	107 CREV36	108 GOEX68	109 GOSP38	110 DEFG55	111 TOTAID	112 NUMAID
97 TJSPME	1.00															
98 LEGFRA	0.42	1.00														
99 CGBC51	0.04	0.09	1.00													
100 CGBC61	0.01	-0.16	0.86	1.00												
101 CGGC79	0.02	-0.20	0.03	0.50	1.00											
102 TAXD66	-0.05	-0.08	0.21	0.25	0.20	1.00										
103 GREV66	-0.08	-0.06	0.21	0.23	0.05	0.05	1.00									
104 GOSP61	-0.15	-0.32	0.52	0.59	0.18	0.05	0.39	1.00								
105 TAXD36	0.15	0.15	0.35	0.24	0.25	0.53	-0.07	-0.04	1.00							
106 GREV36	-0.21	0.10	-0.06	-0.21	-0.26	-0.06	0.16	-0.30	0.13	1.00						
107 CREV36	-0.08	0.14	0.22	0.12	-0.14	0.31	0.49	-0.07	0.05	0.52	1.00					
108 GOEX68	-0.03	-0.15	0.57	0.46	0.41	0.15	0.68	0.26	-0.20	-0.06	0.41	1.00				
109 GOSP38	0.10	0.14	0.20	0.04	-0.32	0.18	0.60	-0.11	-0.33	0.30	0.67	0.61	1.00			
110 DEFG65	0.09	0.05	-0.12	-0.02	-0.08	-0.30	-0.20	-0.11	-0.01	0.09	-0.02	-0.29	-0.08	1.00		
111 TOTAID	0.04	0.16	0.22	0.12	-0.20	0.25	-0.05	0.13	0.34	0.12	0.24	-0.16	-0.00	0.31	1.00	
112 NUMAID	-0.09	0.25	0.33	0.20	-0.18	0.33	-0.13	0.10	0.33	0.09	0.28	-0.13	-0.04	0.18	0.94	1.00
113 TMAN67	-0.11	0.29	-0.04	-0.04	-0.04	0.24	-0.13	-0.16	0.37	0.09	0.25	-0.19	-0.08	0.28	0.72	0.70
114 AFARMF	-0.12	-0.17	0.26	0.21	0.05	-0.05	-0.05	0.28	0.28	-0.16	-0.18	-0.06	-0.26	0.50	0.50	0.39
115 DEFG67	0.01	0.11	0.04	0.11	-0.17	-0.25	0.36	0.18	0.12	0.25	0.16	0.01	0.25	0.71	0.42	0.23
116 CHDEFB	0.12	0.25	-0.09	-0.11	-0.32	-0.13	-0.06	-0.08	-0.09	0.02	0.11	-0.06	0.06	0.08	0.22	0.23
117 ARFPPO	-0.05	0.01	0.40	0.40	0.08	-0.08	0.30	0.34	-0.17	-0.17	0.09	0.31	0.11	0.31	0.33	0.22
118 CHARF7	0.21	0.29	-0.10	-0.04	-0.10	-0.26	-0.33	-0.16	0.08	-0.13	-0.09	-0.18	-0.27	0.21	0.15	0.21
119 INTSEC	0.07	0.15	0.38	0.18	-0.17	0.06	0.60	0.21	-0.03	-0.25	-0.47	0.52	0.46	-0.17	-0.12	-0.10
120 CHINSE	-0.28	-0.19	-0.34	-0.08	-0.10	-0.03	0.04	0.23	-0.11	-0.19	-0.34	0.03	-0.05	-0.06	-0.17	-0.19
121 TURMOL	0.22	0.40	-0.08	0.17	0.17	0.11	-0.11	-0.10	0.04	-0.14	0.15	0.01	0.03	0.26	0.49	0.53
122 ELITIN	-0.10	0.38	-0.04	0.08	0.30	-0.23	-0.02	-0.01	0.09	-0.10	-0.22	-0.17	-0.21	0.31	0.27	0.23
123 KILLOG	-0.11	0.46	-0.35	-0.24	-0.07	-0.12	-0.22	-0.43	0.03	0.13	0.04	-0.17	0.07	0.15	0.19	0.22
124 COMWGT	-0.10	0.34	-0.25	-0.21	-0.14	0.06	-0.19	-0.27	-0.05	0.19	0.14	-0.25	-0.00	0.39	0.53	0.51
125 AVERES	-0.05	0.23	-0.15	-0.04	0.30	0.04	0.14	-0.00	0.30	0.12	0.07	-0.12	-0.07	0.43	0.32	0.11
126 TOAATR	-0.03	0.20	0.24	0.23	0.18	0.44	0.08	0.04	0.55	0.05	0.24	-0.00	0.01	0.15	0.65	0.60
127 PCAID8	-0.18	-0.23	0.32	0.46	0.48	0.02	0.13	0.44	-0.05	-0.15	0.09	0.32	0.01	-0.22	0.05	0.06
128 AIDPC4	-0.19	-0.22	-0.09	-0.07	-0.04	0.14	-0.05	-0.08	0.31	-0.01	0.16	-0.09	-0.10	-0.04	0.53	0.52
129 AIDPC8	-0.01	0.11	0.27	0.38	0.45	0.26	0.07	0.26	0.48	-0.01	0.29	0.09	-0.00	-0.04	0.55	0.55
130 CAPAD1	0.10	-0.19	0.04	0.02	0.13	-0.04	0.08	0.05	0.02	-0.13	-0.23	0.14	-0.20	-0.24	-0.31	-0.32
131 PCDAID	-0.14	-0.33	-0.12	0.16	0.44	-0.12	0.07	0.27	-0.25	-0.10	0.12	0.25	0.08	-0.29	-0.10	-0.07
132 COMAID	-0.17	-0.02	0.55	0.32	-0.33	0.07	0.09	0.41	-0.31	-0.11	0.11	0.01	0.01	-0.09	0.53	0.57
133 CAPAD7	-0.17	-0.26	0.09	0.11	0.28	0.17	0.30	-0.09	-0.07	-0.01	0.07	0.55	0.17	-0.42	-0.50	-0.46
134 APCTD8	-0.01	-0.04	0.35	0.28	0.16	0.01	0.33	-0.08	-0.04	-0.09	0.06	0.58	0.36	-0.22	-0.44	-0.39
135 JSTD62	-0.26	-0.16	-0.09	-0.03	0.08	0.28	-0.17	-0.13	-0.28	-0.01	-0.20	-0.12	-0.11	-0.03	-0.09	0.03

C O R R E L A T I O N S

VARIABLE	97 TJSPME	98 LEGFRA	99 CGBC51	100 CGBC61	101 CGGC79	102 TAXD66	103 GREV66	104 GOSP61	105 TAXD36	106 GREV36	107 CREV36	108 GOEX58	109 GOSP38	110 DEFG65	111 TOTAID	112 NUMAID
136 JSTD68	-0.31	-0.21	0.20	0.15	0.01	0.35	-0.08	-0.01	0.27	0.07	0.08	0.03	-0.02	-0.00	0.24	0.23
137 TMET62	-0.19	-0.06	0.09	0.31	0.35	-0.16	0.02	0.13	-0.01	0.04	0.18	0.12	-0.07	0.18	-0.04	-0.09
138 TMET68	0.34	-0.07	0.11	0.34	0.38	-0.04	0.05	0.17	-0.13	-0.03	-0.13	-0.07	-0.03	-0.24	-0.02	-0.11
139 PCPREX	-0.04	-0.21	-0.03	0.07	0.10	-0.15	0.19	-0.13	-0.10	-0.15	-0.03	0.28	0.21	-0.13	-0.32	-0.38
140 IMPCOM	-0.12	-0.13	0.20	0.20	-0.32	-0.39	-0.04	-0.37	-0.50	-0.17	-0.15	-0.02	-0.01	-0.50	-0.35	0.31
141 TRPGN8	-0.02	0.04	0.24	-0.30	0.25	0.15	0.62	0.25	-0.20	0.01	0.35	0.68	0.41	-0.43	-0.30	-0.25
142 CUBATR	0.12	-0.00	0.10	-0.06	-0.08	0.18	0.21	-0.05	-0.06	-0.04	0.31	0.46	0.36	-0.09	0.10	0.02
143 IMEQ62	-0.35	-0.40	0.09	0.25	0.06	-0.19	0.28	0.40	-0.26	-0.06	0.08	0.29	-0.08	0.34	-0.02	-0.05
144 EXAF68	0.00	-0.15	-0.32	-0.27	0.02	-0.05	-0.34	-0.10	-0.06	0.06	-0.33	-0.34	-0.28	0.20	-0.09	-0.08
145 IMAF68	0.16	-0.05	-0.29	-0.26	-0.07	-0.01	-0.27	-0.10	-0.07	0.04	-0.10	-0.25	0.00	0.03	-0.10	-0.09
146 70PCEX	0.01	0.12	-0.01	-0.11	-0.09	0.17	-0.20	0.03	0.16	0.09	0.04	-0.28	-0.13	0.16	0.48	0.53
147 PCEXME	-0.12	-0.19	-0.05	0.17	0.30	-0.15	0.06	0.17	-0.09	-0.10	0.07	0.00	-0.07	0.22	-0.02	-0.13
148 IMME25	-0.08	0.12	0.35	0.31	-0.31	-0.38	-0.03	0.31	-0.10	0.01	0.26	0.07	0.01	0.14	0.63	0.63
149 EXME25	0.22	0.03	0.05	0.14	-0.11	0.06	-0.09	0.45	-0.19	-0.34	-0.11	-0.03	-0.17	0.08	0.49	0.45
150 REGORG	0.04	0.02	0.10	0.28	0.41	-0.36	-0.02	0.10	0.00	0.03	0.00	0.10	-0.07	0.43	0.04	0.00
151 MEMOR	0.46	0.48	0.31	0.30	0.07	0.37	-0.35	-0.08	0.40	-0.07	0.21	-0.14	-0.18	0.16	0.63	0.78
152 MEMAME	0.10	-0.08	-0.07	0.17	0.34	-0.28	-0.13	-0.01	0.02	-0.04	-0.00	-0.01	-0.13	0.39	0.05	0.02
153 DIPSEN	0.02	0.07	0.61	0.52	0.12	0.23	-0.13	0.28	0.43	-0.17	0.10	-0.10	-0.20	0.05	0.53	0.60
154 DIPREC	0.07	0.06	0.43	0.37	0.12	0.22	-0.07	0.29	0.46	-0.13	0.01	-0.03	-0.13	0.01	0.71	0.69
155 AOBJAG	-0.08	0.21	0.22	0.13	-0.14	0.22	-0.04	0.01	0.43	0.28	0.18	-0.21	-0.00	0.32	0.52	0.57
156 MUCOSU	0.45	0.37	-0.05	0.02	0.07	0.46	-0.03	-0.18	0.22	-0.02	0.37	-0.01	0.13	-0.05	0.47	0.56
157 RECOC7	-0.14	-0.04	0.19	0.17	-0.30	-0.05	-0.16	0.36	0.02	-0.02	0.06	-0.05	-0.03	-0.30	0.60	0.59
158 CH5067	-0.23	-0.05	0.19	-0.05	-0.12	-0.05	-0.05	0.03	0.16	-0.32	-0.12	-0.01	-0.07	-0.14	0.03	0.02
159 MCITPM	0.01	-0.03	0.10	0.04	0.04	-0.03	0.41	-0.13	0.07	0.31	0.32	0.49	0.21	-0.33	-0.24	-0.17
160 LRCITP	0.23	0.26	0.14	0.21	0.20	0.39	-0.02	0.00	0.53	0.04	0.30	-0.07	-0.01	0.19	0.75	0.74
161 PRLT4L	-0.15	-0.17	-0.01	0.07	0.14	-0.10	-0.22	0.21	0.12	-0.15	-0.38	-0.24	-0.42	-0.21	-0.35	-0.38
162 PRCT4L	-0.17	-0.19	-0.02	0.08	0.12	-0.05	-0.16	0.28	0.13	-0.15	-0.32	-0.22	-0.42	-0.19	-0.24	-0.28
163 URPC65	-0.12	-0.03	0.39	0.45	0.37	0.03	0.60	0.17	0.10	0.21	0.39	0.67	0.35	-0.18	-0.00	0.03
164 URPC55	0.25	0.08	0.33	0.50	0.43	0.10	0.54	0.22	0.05	0.03	0.29	0.55	0.31	-0.07	0.12	0.14
165 UR5565	-0.45	-0.40	-0.07	-0.28	-0.40	-0.03	-0.09	-0.02	0.01	0.18	-0.04	-0.03	-0.04	-0.18	-0.21	-0.28
166 MOMARV	0.06	-0.12	-0.10	-0.03	0.17	0.34	-0.09	-0.04	0.08	-0.02	0.14	-0.03	-0.07	-0.14	0.10	0.15
167 SETPAV	0.03	-0.11	-0.15	-0.00	-0.04	0.23	-0.12	-0.06	-0.19	-0.14	0.17	-0.22	-0.05	0.48	0.19	0.17
168 LEHIEV	-0.07	-0.07	0.09	0.22	0.21	0.15	-0.15	0.31	0.12	-0.24	0.24	0.09	0.23	0.23	0.23	0.21
169 HIEFAV	0.25	0.14	0.08	0.21	0.16	0.45	-0.11	0.01	0.17	-0.24	0.18	-0.14	-0.05	0.25	0.38	0.42
170 INHERV	0.07	-0.05	0.24	0.29	0.01	0.23	0.10	0.29	0.19	-0.38	-0.01	0.10	-0.06	0.29	0.33	0.27
171 AUTHOV	0.20	0.04	0.07	0.23	0.25	0.01	0.18	0.29	-0.05	-0.25	0.07	-0.02	0.05	0.16	0.15	0.13
172 DECNV	0.02	0.03	-0.10	0.15	0.31	0.25	0.22	0.17	-0.12	-0.27	0.15	0.23	0.09	0.14	0.35	0.29

C O R R E L A T I O N S

VARIABLE	113 TMAN67	114 AFARMF	115 DEFG67	116 CHDEFB	117 ARFPPO	118 CHARF7	119 INTSEC	120 CHINSE	121 TURMOL	122 ELITIN	123 KILLOG	124 COMWGT	125 AVERES	126 TOAAT8	127 PCAID8	128 AIDPC4
113 TMAN67	1.00															
114 AFARMF	0.45	1.00														
115 DEFG67	0.32	0.46	1.00													
116 CHDEFB	0.12	-0.16	0.18	1.00												
117 ARFPPO	0.28	0.63	0.56	-0.01	1.00											
118 CHARF7	0.33	0.06	0.06	0.63	0.04	1.00										
119 INTSEC	-0.06	-0.11	0.14	-0.14	0.31	-0.19	1.00									
120 CHINSE	-0.15	-0.05	0.15	-0.14	0.06	0.04	0.11	1.00								
121 TURMOL	0.71	0.31	0.26	0.05	0.18	0.38	-0.13	-0.07	1.00							
122 ELITIN	0.31	0.38	0.36	0.16	0.28	0.38	-0.12	0.11	0.52	1.00						
123 KILLOG	0.53	0.03	0.13	0.13	0.01	0.38	-0.17	0.25	0.56	0.28	1.00					
124 COMWGT	0.77	0.32	0.34	0.17	0.12	0.22	-0.15	-0.06	0.59	0.33	0.66	1.00				
125 AVERES	0.33	0.30	0.51	-0.08	0.37	-0.04	0.10	0.24	0.19	0.43	0.28	0.34	1.00			
126 TOAAT8	0.80	0.50	0.32	0.03	0.55	0.06	-0.02	-0.18	0.52	0.29	0.33	0.55	0.44	1.00		
127 PCAID8	0.02	0.18	-0.14	-0.15	0.45	-0.17	-0.05	-0.10	-0.06	-0.08	-0.22	-0.13	0.08	0.37	1.00	
128 AIDPC4	0.80	0.28	0.14	0.14	0.22	0.43	-0.21	-0.09	0.65	0.19	0.52	0.46	0.11	0.64	0.15	1.00
129 AIDPC8	0.58	0.24	0.13	0.01	0.31	-0.05	-0.08	-0.11	0.36	0.15	0.15	0.30	0.36	0.72	0.67	0.54
130 CAPAD1	-0.20	0.03	-0.19	-0.22	0.41	-0.03	-0.02	-0.19	-0.18	-0.21	-0.20	-0.38	-0.20	0.10	0.52	0.19
131 PCDAID	-0.13	-0.23	-0.29	-0.12	-0.12	-0.18	-0.08	0.06	-0.16	-0.25	-0.16	-0.13	-0.02	-0.10	0.69	-0.02
132 COMAID	0.31	0.49	0.32	0.02	0.40	-0.02	0.29	0.01	-0.07	-0.06	-0.14	0.15	-0.05	0.35	0.04	0.01
133 CAPAD7	-0.27	-0.19	-0.33	-0.23	0.22	-0.19	0.21	-0.02	-0.18	-0.25	-0.17	-0.34	-0.21	0.01	0.34	-0.02
134 APCT08	-0.32	-0.28	-0.08	-0.23	0.22	-0.14	0.46	0.24	-0.19	-0.17	-0.14	-0.41	-0.15	-0.16	0.13	-0.17
135 USTD62	0.18	0.35	-0.06	-0.05	0.24	-0.08	-0.26	0.09	-0.00	0.16	0.36	0.18	0.29	0.36	0.21	0.16

VARIABLE	113 TMAN67	114 AFARMF	115 DEFG67	116 CHDEFB	117 ARFPPO	118 CHARF7	119 INTSEC	120 CHNSE	121 TJRMOL	122 ELITIN	123 KILLOG	124 COMWGT	125 AVERES	126 TOAAT8	127 PCAID8	128 AIDPC4
136 USTD68	0.28	0.47	-0.03	-0.06	0.35	-0.16	-0.06	-0.09	0.04	0.11	0.15	0.18	0.14	0.47	0.31	0.13
137 TMET62	-0.15	-0.03	0.07	-0.12	0.08	0.06	0.15	-0.05	0.14	0.02	-0.06	-0.25	0.11	-0.19	0.08	-0.37
138 TMET68	-0.07	0.11	0.17	-0.05	0.18	0.02	0.15	-0.16	0.08	0.02	-0.15	-0.20	-0.14	-0.08	-0.11	-0.04
139 PCPREX	-0.15	0.03	0.03	-0.17	0.06	-0.20	-0.03	-0.01	0.02	-0.04	-0.03	-0.04	0.00	-0.01	-0.05	-0.21
140 IMPCOM	0.14	0.42	0.44	0.21	0.26	0.18	-0.24	-0.01	0.24	-0.15	-0.08	0.28	-0.19	0.07	-0.01	0.08
141 TRPGN8	-0.27	-0.36	-0.11	-0.08	0.35	-0.20	0.56	0.16	-0.10	-0.12	-0.07	-0.37	0.03	0.03	0.35	-0.07
142 CUBATR	0.05	0.03	-0.04	0.20	0.25	-0.07	0.10	-0.31	-0.07	-0.35	-0.10	0.01	0.15	0.20	0.23	0.13
143 IMEQ62	0.01	0.29	0.35	-0.05	0.42	-0.02	0.13	0.34	-0.02	-0.02	-0.07	-0.04	0.20	0.09	-0.14	0.04
144 EXAF68	-0.22	-0.04	-0.01	0.07	-0.28	-0.04	-0.42	0.10	-0.25	-0.23	0.03	-0.04	-0.17	-0.28	-0.19	-0.17
145 IMAF68	-0.33	-0.25	-0.10	0.29	-0.32	-0.00	-0.28	0.12	-0.27	-0.19	-0.01	-0.19	-0.03	-0.39	-0.14	-0.26
146 70PCEX	0.24	0.02	-0.03	0.11	-0.17	0.06	-0.09	-0.03	0.03	-0.06	-0.01	0.19	0.01	0.14	-0.06	0.22
147 PCEXME	0.00	0.09	0.11	0.07	-0.12	0.15	-0.15	-0.19	0.21	-0.22	-0.14	-0.05	0.04	-0.04	-0.01	0.09
148 IMME25	0.44	0.28	0.23	0.24	0.36	0.09	0.07	-0.02	0.30	-0.04	0.17	0.33	0.05	0.47	0.03	0.36
149 EXME25	0.24	0.20	0.15	0.45	0.26	0.12	-0.10	-0.08	0.18	0.01	-0.05	0.19	-0.07	0.25	0.10	0.22
150 REGORG	-0.06	0.22	0.33	0.02	0.14	0.15	-0.01	-0.06	0.13	0.26	-0.10	-0.02	-0.06	-0.13	-0.09	-0.37
151 MEMOR	0.62	0.09	0.02	0.16	0.02	0.35	-0.22	-0.24	0.76	0.04	0.38	0.43	-0.11	0.47	0.01	0.57
152 MEMAME	-0.08	0.03	0.20	0.10	-0.06	0.29	-0.23	0.03	0.15	0.15	-0.02	-0.17	-0.05	-0.20	0.05	0.07
153 DIPSEN	0.60	0.62	0.03	-0.17	0.28	0.17	-0.02	-0.16	0.54	0.21	0.04	0.31	-0.08	0.56	0.21	-0.41
154 DIPREC	0.70	0.63	0.17	0.07	0.27	0.11	-0.13	-0.14	0.55	0.19	0.19	0.43	0.49	0.68	0.19	0.54
155 AOBJAG	0.52	0.47	0.47	0.10	0.52	0.07	0.23	0.00	0.18	0.32	0.13	0.40		0.57	0.04	0.11
156 MUCOSU	0.60	-0.04	0.01	0.08	-0.04	0.25	-0.16	-0.20	0.73	-0.11	0.56	0.40	-0.03	0.50	0.05	0.73
157 RECOC7	0.33	0.33	0.48	0.25	-0.21	0.15	-0.05	0.12	0.30	-0.27	-0.00	0.25	-0.04	-0.27	-0.21	0.24
158 CH5067	-0.11	0.13	-0.15	0.05	-0.17	0.05	-0.17	-0.14	-0.14	-0.06	-0.22	-0.17	-0.05	-0.08	-0.07	-0.04
159 MCITPM	-0.09	-0.22	-0.15	-0.23	-0.01	-0.04	0.49	-0.13	-0.05	-0.10	-0.21	-0.24	-0.23	-0.16	-0.09	-0.03
160 LRCITP	0.89	0.38	0.32	0.15	0.27	0.27	-0.03	-0.20	0.69	0.28	0.39	0.59	0.32	0.81	0.13	0.74
161 PRLT4L	-0.26	-0.10	-0.24	0.11	0.05	0.09	-0.13	0.23	-0.40	-0.10	-0.00	-0.25	0.05	-0.10	0.19	-0.18
162 PRCT4L	-0.18	-0.00	-0.17	0.15	0.10	0.11	-0.13	0.22	-0.37	-0.08	-0.03	-0.15	0.08	-0.04	0.20	-0.12
163 URPC65	0.04	0.00	0.17	-0.06	0.30	0.04	0.56	-0.05	0.17	0.14	-0.15	-0.15	-0.08	0.05	0.08	0.09
164 JRPC55	0.20	0.03	-0.28	0.01	0.25	0.14	0.45	0.10	0.40	0.25	-0.11	0.04	-0.00	0.13	-0.02	0.23
165 UR5565	-0.34	-0.06	-0.20	0.01	0.01	-0.19	-0.01	0.01	-0.54	-0.38	-0.43	-0.35	-0.08	-0.20	-0.14	-0.24
166 MOMARV	0.24	0.09	-0.25	0.09	-0.08	0.12	0.06	-0.16	0.09	-0.02	0.07	0.13	-0.09	0.32	0.25	0.25
167 SETPAV	0.22	0.14	0.17	-0.07	-0.24	-0.05	-0.16	-0.15	0.26	-0.12	0.06	0.39	-0.01	0.07	-0.25	0.04
168 LEHIEV	0.22	0.22	0.14	0.17	-0.10	0.25	-0.07	0.02	0.28	0.17	0.15	0.09	0.04	0.28	0.18	0.33
169 HIEFAV	0.29	0.09	0.10	0.17	-0.00	0.04	-0.20	-0.11	0.32	0.15	0.08	0.27	0.19	0.37	0.05	0.21
170 INHERV	0.29	0.32	0.20	-0.06	0.15	0.11	0.09	0.20	0.24	-0.00	0.08	0.18	0.19	0.32	-0.04	-0.25
171 AUTHOV	0.07	0.07	0.21	0.18	-0.05	0.03	-0.18	-0.13	0.26	0.25	-0.08	0.03	-0.07	0.10	0.08	0.19
172 DECVV	0.22	0.05	0.16	0.17	0.08	0.12	0.07	0.25	0.13	0.12	0.08	0.16	0.37	0.25	0.15	0.21

C O R R E L A T I O N S

VARIABLE	129 AIDPC8	130 CAPAD1	131 PCDAID	132 COMAID	133 CAPAD7	134 APCT08	135 USTD62	136 JSTD68	137 TMET62	138 TMET68	139 PCPREX	140 IMP?M	141 TRPGN8	142 CUBATR	143 IMEQ62	144 EXAF68
129 AIDPC8	1.00															
130 CAPAD1	-0.08	1.00														
131 PCDAID	0.50	-0.14	1.00													
132 COMAID	0.24	-0.26	-0.19	1.00												
133 CAPAD7	-0.12	0.77	0.06	-0.34	1.00											
134 APCT08	-0.17	0.69	-0.01	-0.12	0.70	1.00										
135 JSTD62	0.16	0.12	-0.00	0.05	0.09	-0.14	1.00									

473

C O R R E L A T I O N S

VARIABLE	129 AIDPC8	130 CAPAD1	131 PCDAID	132 COMAID	133 CAPAD7	134 APCTD8	135 USTD62	136 USTD58	137 TMET62	138 TMET68	139 PCPREX	140 IMPCOM	141 TRPGN8	142 CUBATR	143 IMFO52	144 EXAF68
136 USTD68	0.25	0.07	0.01	0.36	0.09	-0.08	0.83	1.00								
137 TMET62	-0.01	-0.06	0.10	-0.22	-0.02	0.15	-0.26	-0.11	1.00							
138 TMET68	-0.05	-0.01	-0.04	-0.22	-0.10	0.06	-0.18	-0.07	0.85	1.00						
139 PCPREX	-0.18	-0.14	-0.09	-0.10	-0.38	0.13	0.26	0.18	-0.10	-0.07	1.00					
140 IMPCOM	-0.04	-0.15	-0.10	0.35	-0.36	-0.26	-0.16	-0.07	-0.10	-0.07	-0.13	1.00				
141 TRPGN8	0.03	0.52	0.19	-0.18	0.71	0.60	-0.03	-0.00	0.27	0.06	0.07	-0.27	1.00			
142 CUBATR	0.16	0.31	0.15	-0.18	0.36	0.01	0.09	0.08	-0.18	-0.09	0.10	0.01	0.30	1.00		
143 IMEQ62	-0.05	0.28	0.01	0.09	0.23	0.09	0.08	0.17	-0.15	-0.06	0.09	0.35	0.37	0.25	1.00	
144 EXAF68	-0.20	-0.09	-0.03	-0.15	-0.23	-0.26	-0.13	-0.31	-0.09	-0.07	-0.28	0.09	-0.35	-0.18	-0.17	1.00
145 IMAF68	-0.18	-0.22	0.10	-0.24	-0.23	-0.22	-0.11	-0.27	0.05	0.08	-0.19	-0.20	-0.19	-0.14	-0.34	0.79
146 7OPCEX	0.20	-0.22	0.00	0.16	-0.40	-0.23	-0.20	-0.15	-0.15	-0.15	-0.86	0.21	-0.20	0.01	-0.09	0.37
147 PCEXME	0.01	-0.45	0.02	-0.29	-0.20	-0.23	-0.11	-0.04	0.51	0.57	-0.08	0.29	-0.08	0.02	0.19	-0.11
148 IMME25	0.29	-0.41	-0.05	0.28	-0.44	-0.31	-0.53	-0.45	0.14	0.23	-0.30	0.41	0.05	0.43	0.25	-0.15
149 EXME25	0.19	-0.16	0.07	0.17	-0.47	-0.44	0.41	0.17	-0.02	0.13	-0.35	0.54	0.01	0.42	0.19	0.04
150 REGORG	0.07	-0.19	0.09	-0.07	-0.17	0.14	-0.34	-0.18	0.67	0.69	-0.28	0.20	-0.15	-0.30	-0.03	0.21
151 MEMOR	0.49	-0.05	-0.09	0.18	-0.25	-0.18	-0.25	-0.20	0.05	0.06	-0.30	0.15	-0.23	-0.02	-0.34	0.19
152 MEMAME	0.09	-0.08	-0.20	-0.23	-0.18	0.09	-0.24	-0.16	0.74	0.62	-0.29	0.11	-0.12	-0.24	-0.05	0.21
153 DIPSEN	0.50	-0.22	-0.09	0.54	-0.13	-0.10	-0.01	0.21	0.14	-0.10	-0.05	0.29	-0.25	0.14	-0.02	-0.25
154 DIPREC	0.59	-0.36	-0.06	0.51	-0.23	-0.25	0.26	0.23	-0.41	-0.25	-0.08	0.30	-0.33	-0.03	-0.12	-0.14
155 ADBJAG	0.40	-0.24	-0.20	0.69	-0.37	-0.23	0.28	0.40	-0.19	-0.07	-0.05	0.05	-0.18	-0.10	-0.05	-0.18
156 MUCOSU	0.48	0.14	0.03	-0.06	-0.08	-0.24	-0.08	-0.18	-0.16	-0.12	-0.13	0.01	-0.23	-0.25	-0.25	0.22
157 RECDC7	0.07	-0.31	-0.31	0.57	-0.39	-0.28	-0.07	-0.07	-0.21	-0.26	-0.26	0.65	-0.12	-0.14	-0.39	-0.01
158 CH5067	0.10	-0.25	0.07	0.15	-0.14	-0.11	0.06	0.10	-0.10	-0.11	0.11	0.02	-0.22	-0.14	-0.21	-0.12
159 MCITPM	-0.11	0.31	-0.01	-0.08	0.54	0.60	-0.31	-0.19	-0.13	0.06	0.16	0.35	0.37	-0.01	-0.01	-0.32
160 LRCITP	0.73	-0.19	-0.04	0.33	-0.28	-0.26	0.13	0.24	-0.00	0.12	-0.20	0.08	-0.22	0.06	-0.08	-0.21
161 PRLT4L	-0.08	0.16	0.06	-0.09	0.07	-0.09	0.41	0.24	-0.06	-0.03	0.03	-0.15	0.13	0.07	0.20	-0.05
162 PRCT4L	-0.03	0.07	0.07	-0.03	-0.01	-0.21	0.40	0.25	-0.06	-0.00	0.00	-0.11	0.11	0.13	0.22	-0.03
163 URPC65	0.12	0.18	0.04	0.10	0.37	0.57	-0.26	-0.09	0.31	0.39	0.10	-0.13	0.40	-0.06	0.04	-0.39
164 URPC55	0.17	-0.12	-0.01	0.07	0.14	0.40	-0.24	-0.16	0.33	0.39	0.05	-0.00	0.32	-0.17	0.03	-0.33
165 UR5565	-0.16	0.36	0.07	-0.01	0.31	0.09	0.10	0.14	-0.10	-0.09	0.10	-0.14	-0.01	0.27	0.05	-0.13
166 MOMARV	0.19	0.28	0.12	-0.01	0.10	-0.17	0.15	0.32	0.02	0.10	-0.21	-0.08	0.09	0.18	0.01	-0.05
167 SETPAV	-0.08	-0.36	-0.15	-0.09	-0.31	-0.38	-0.21	-0.13	0.25	0.32	-0.04	0.35	-0.31	-0.07	0.15	-0.17
168 LEHIEV	0.24	0.04	-0.03	-0.04	-0.05	-0.18	-0.16	0.04	0.35	0.33	-0.31	0.26	0.14	-0.06	0.37	-0.30
169 HIEFAV	0.24	-0.06	-0.10	-0.02	-0.23	-0.25	-0.08	0.11	0.28	0.35	-0.17	0.17	-0.03	-0.11	-0.02	-0.08
170 INHERV	0.11	-0.12	-0.22	0.14	-0.13	-0.02	-0.15	-0.05	0.22	0.21	-0.22	0.32	0.05	-0.12	0.37	-0.06
171 AUTHOV	0.15	-0.05	0.00	-0.15	-0.22	-0.17	-0.27	-0.15	0.35	0.53	-0.20	0.30	-0.07	-0.26	-0.11	0.06
172 DECNV	0.35	-0.30	0.18	-0.14	-0.12	-0.04	-0.22	-0.21	0.21	0.24	-0.36	0.04	0.22	0.23	0.17	-0.34

VARIABLE	145 IMAF68	146 7OPCEX	147 PCEXME	148 IMME25	149 EXME25	150 REGORG	151 MEMOR	152 MEMAME	153 DIPSEN	154 DIPREC	155 AOBJAG	156 MUCOSU	157 RECOC7	158 CH5067	159 MCITPM	160 LRCITP
145 IMAF68	1.00															
146 7OPCEX	0.17	1.00														
147 PCEXME	-0.22	-0.02	1.00													
148 IMME25	-0.18	0.33	0.26	1.00												
149 EXME25	0.01	0.39	0.23	0.75	1.00											
150 REGORG	0.13	0.09	0.46	0.01	-0.08	1.00										
151 MEMOR	-0.01	0.42	-0.24	0.72	0.35	0.09	1.00									
152 MEMAME	0.22	0.12	0.49	0.04	-0.04	0.83	0.12	1.00								
153 DIPSEN	-0.40	0.10	-0.01	0.27	0.00	-0.02	0.59	-0.23	1.00							
154 DIPREC	-0.29	0.22	-0.14	0.26	0.20	-0.23	0.63	-0.37	0.87	1.00						
155 AOBJAG	-0.13	0.11	-0.32	0.39	0.16	-0.07	0.29	-0.19	0.34	0.38	1.00					
156 MUCOSU	-0.04	0.36	-0.14	0.57	0.33	-0.22	0.76	-0.04	0.31	0.50	0.11	1.00				
157 RECOC7	-0.25	0.42	0.09	0.43	0.49	-0.07	0.29	-0.04	0.29	0.42	0.30	0.20	1.00			
158 CH5067	-0.10	-0.07	0.10	0.04	-0.09	0.08	-0.11	0.16	-0.05	-0.06	-0.02	-0.15	-0.11	1.00		
159 MCITPM	-0.32	-0.23	-0.08	-0.20	-0.43	0.09	-0.01	0.00	0.09	-0.11	-0.18	-0.04	-0.19	-0.05	1.00	
160 LRCITP	-0.28	-0.32	0.10	0.51	0.39	0.07	0.74	0.06	0.59	0.76	0.49	0.71	0.36	-0.11	-0.08	1.00
161 PRLT4L	-0.06	-0.19	0.04	-0.01	0.19	-0.32	-0.48	-0.22	-0.24	-0.21	-0.09	-0.48	-0.15	-0.05	-0.26	-0.26
162 PRCT4L	-0.04	-0.16	0.05	0.11	0.25	-0.29	-0.46	-0.23	-0.19	-0.14	-0.02	-0.43	-0.09	-0.02	-0.45	-0.18
163 URPC65	-0.32	-0.20	0.09	-0.01	-0.18	0.36	0.09	0.18	-0.23	-0.14	0.01	0.03	0.03	-0.22	0.78	0.20
164 JRPC55	-0.26	-0.13	0.15	0.13	0.01	0.36	0.26	0.20	0.29	0.31	0.01	0.23	0.16	-0.33	0.49	0.37
165 JR5565	0.24	-0.13	-0.01	-0.06	-0.11	-0.16	-0.50	-0.09	-0.33	-0.43	-0.02	-0.45	-0.26	-0.36	0.11	-0.43
166 MOMARV	-0.09	0.24	0.20	0.21	0.27	-0.10	-0.01	-0.08	0.03	-0.03	0.05	0.24	-0.05	-0.29	-0.17	0.27
167 SETPAV	-0.03	0.25	0.44	0.30	0.18	0.25	0.39	0.22	0.06	-0.01	-0.05	0.39	0.19	-0.01	-0.23	0.28
168 LEHIEV	-0.04	0.28	0.58	0.35	0.22	0.36	0.20	0.38	0.21	0.06	-0.17	0.24	0.29	-0.02	-0.19	0.28
169 HIEFAV	0.12	0.27	0.25	0.42	0.30	0.25	0.50	0.26	0.14	0.05	-0.08	0.35	0.20	-0.19	-0.35	0.37
170 INHERV	-0.23	0.33	0.28	0.38	0.21	0.18	0.24	0.15	0.36	0.33	-0.04	0.15	0.30	0.01	-0.22	0.30
171 AUTHOV	0.12	0.14	0.58	0.21	0.27	0.52	0.19	0.42	0.08	0.06	-0.25	0.13	0.10	-0.11	-0.17	0.24
172 DECNV	0.09	0.41	0.19	0.31	0.24	0.31	0.19	0.30	0.05	0.08	-0.01	0.18	0.12	0.00	-0.12	0.30

C O R R E L A T I O N S

VARIABLE	161 PRLT4L	162 PRCT4L	163 URPC65	164 URPC55	165 UR5565	166 MOMARV	167 SETPAV	168 LEHIEV	169 HIEFAV	170 INHERV	171 AUTHOV	172 DECNV
161 PRLT4L	1.00											
162 PRCT4L	0.97	1.00										
163 URPC65	-0.40	-0.39	1.00									
164 URPC55	-0.34	-0.29	0.88	1.00								
165 UR5565	0.12	0.08	-0.23	-0.55	1.00							
166 MOMARV	0.12	0.16	-0.06	-0.06	0.02	1.00						
167 SETPAV	-0.29	-0.22	-0.22	-0.03	-0.22	0.10	1.00					
168 LEHIEV	-0.08	0.00	0.03	0.12	-0.11	0.39	0.42	1.00				
169 HIEFAV	-0.22	-0.16	-0.12	0.07	-0.30	0.41	0.54	0.65	1.00			
170 INHERV	-0.06	-0.00	-0.02	0.18	-0.25	0.20	0.48	0.66	0.50	1.00		
171 AUTHOV	-0.25	-0.20	0.16	0.34	-0.28	0.19	0.40	0.57	0.69	0.36	1.00	
172 DECNV	-0.19	-0.08	0.12	0.28	-0.20	0.13	0.27	0.59	0.50	0.65	0.40	1.00

Appendix 5. Population Estimates

In order to calculate the *per capita* measures used in this Handbook it was necessary to obtain a complete set of yearly population estimates for the countries discussed for the years 1919–1969. Although the United Nations has published estimates going back in some cases year by year to 1940, population estimates for the total time period were unavailable to us and we were forced to calculate our own (Table A-1 on pp. 480–483). These estimates are the result of a crude attempt to develop a model of population growth based upon a few basic assumptions. As the quality of demographic data in Africa is still relatively low and the reliability of such variables as population growth rate, which we used to calculate our estimates, correspondingly questionable, our estimates should be used with extreme caution. We present them here so that the user of this Handbook can have access to the basis on which our *per capita* variables were calculated.[1]

Our estimates were calculated according to the following procedure:

1. We took the best available 1969 population figure for each country and multiplied it by an estimated growth rate for 1969.
2. We subtracted the result from the 1969 figure and got a 1968 population estimate.
3. We reduced the 1969 estimated growth rate by a constant factor, giving a 1968 growth rate.
4. We multiplied the new 1968 estimated population growth rate by the estimated 1968 population in order to get an estimate for 1967, etc.
5. In this process we used two different constants to reduce the growth rate, one for the first 21 years of the process (1969–1949) and the second for the remaining years to 1919.

The formula for our calculations is:

$$P_t = P_{1969}(1-d_t)^{1969-t}$$

where $d_t = d_{1969}(1-k)^{1969-t}$

[1] In Part I whenever data from a source were given in *per capita* form, we used the data as given. In other cases, where we have standardized the data by population, the estimates given in Table A1 were used.

d_{1969} is the estimated rate of natural increase
d_t is the population decrement for year t
P_t is the population estimate for year t
k is a for t between 1969 and 1949 and
k is b for t between 1948 and 1919
t is any year less than 1970

The values used in our calculations are:

	d_{1969} Rate of Natural Increase	k a	b
Botswana	2.6	.041	.014
Burundi	2.4	.093	.031
Cameroon	2.3	.053	.017
CAR	2.8	.092	.031
Chad	1.7	.052	.017
Congo (Brazzaville)	1.7	.052	.017
Zaire (Congo K.)*	2.5	.072	.024
Dahomey	3.1	.104	.035
Ethiopia	1.9	.062	.021
Gabon	.9	.020	.007
Gambia	2.1	.061	.021
Ghana	2.9	.080	.026
Guinea	2.8	.092	.031
ICoast	2.7	.076	.025
Kenya	3.4	.104	.035
Lesotho	3.3	.104	.035
Liberia	2.0	.052	.017
Malawi	2.6	.080	.026
Mauritania	2.1	.076	.025
Mali	2.3	.076	.025
Niger	3.5	.104	.035
Nigeria	2.6	.080	.026
Rwanda	3.5	.097	.032
Senegal	2.7	.092	.031
SLeone	1.5	.042	.014
Somalia	3.7	.097	.032
Sudan	3.2	.097	.032
Tanzania	3.2	.092	.031
Togo	3.0	.092	.031
Uganda*	2.8	.071	.024
UVolta	2.5	.052	.017
Zambia	3.5	.097	.032

* Based on 1967 data.

This procedure is based upon the following assumptions:

(1) *The appropriate base for decrementing African populations is the most recent population figure.* Only the

most recent African censuses can be regarded as "modern" in their methodologies and procedures. In the past decade the results of the "modern" censuses have indicated that the population totals given by earlier censuses often represented significant underestimates, although some, such as Sierra Leone and Liberia, were overestimates. This non-comparability between the most recent and the earlier censuses, and the superiority of the newer censuses, makes inadvisable the usual procedure of extrapolating between censuses to get population estimates for the intervening years.

The 1969 figures used in our calculations are, with few exceptions, from the *UN Demographic Yearbook 1969* (see Table 1.2). For Nigeria we have adopted a 1969 estimate of 56,700,000 while the figure reported in the *Yearbook* is 61,450,000. The larger figure is based upon the 1963 Nigerian census while ours is based upon the estimates of scholars who are critical of the 1963 Nigerian census. The Nigerian census experience, which included a 1962 census which was widely challenged and subsequently scrapped and a second 1963 census whose results paralleled the first one and were equally challenged despite the attempts on the part of the Government to institute more controls, is a sad chapter in African demography. Because it was widely believed that the political balance of power could be influenced by the census results, the huge growth in population reported by the 1962 and the 1963 censuses were greeted with suspicion by both the populace and the experts.[2] The UN is bound to accept those figures reported to it by its members while we are not. In this case we feel that according to the existing evidence the acceptance of the official Nigerian figures would seriously distort the *per capita* variables that we have calculated. Accordingly we have accepted the estimate of C. Okonjo that Nigeria had a population in mid-1962 of about 48 million.[3] Now that the military government has released some of the census data, it may be possible for demographers to arrive at a more accurate estimate of the quality of the 1963 census. For our urban data in this book we have been forced to use the figures reported in the 1963 census and in this instance alone we have used the official population figure to calculate the per capita urban variables.

(2) *It is possible and desirable to use estimated growth rates*[4] *to calculate the decrement for each year back over time.* If extrapolations between censuses are rejected as a method to obtain yearly population estimates, it is necessary to find some other way to decrement the population year by year. One way to do this is to use the available growth rate estimates for each country. The problem with this is that, at the present stage in the demographic study of African populations, their growth rates must be assumed to have relatively low reliability. The alternate procedure would be to use a common growth rate estimate for all countries. In choosing between the use of one estimated growth rate for all countries or a differential rate, we have chosen the latter procedure on the assumption that the available growth estimates represent at least in a crude way the differences between the growth rates of the various countries. Our procedure was to make an estimate of each country's population growth rate on the basis of the available estimates of growth rates for the late 1960s,[5] and then by a procedure of inspecting the population series 1960–1969 in the *UN Demographic Yearbook 1969*,[6] two standard decrements were estimated. For example, Botswana's 1969 population of 629,000 was decremented by a population growth rate of 2.6. The resulting 1968 estimate, 612,000 was decremented by a rate of 2.519 (2.6 − .041, the constant factor *a* for Botswana)

[2] Among the critical discussions of the 1962 and 1963 Nigerian censuses are: S. A. Aluko, "How Many Nigerians? An Analysis of Nigeria's Census Problems, 1901–1963," *Journal of Modern African Studies*, 3 (October 1965): 371–392. Chukuka Okonjo, "A Preliminary Medium Estimate of the 1962 Mid-year Population of Nigeria," in *The Population of Tropical Africa*, eds. J. C. Caldwell and C. Okonjo (London: Longmans, 1968), pp. 78–96; R. K. Udo, "Population and Politics in Nigeria: Problems of Census-Taking in the Nigerian Federation," in *ibid.*, pp. 97–105; and T. M. Yesufu, "The Politics and Economics of Nigeria's Population Census," in *ibid.*, pp. 106–116.

[3] Okonjo, in "A Preliminary Medium Estimate" discusses the various competing estimates and bases his "lower upper bound" on the number and distribution of the enumeration districts for the 1963 census.

[4] Meaning by this the rate of natural increase.

[5] R. K. Som, "Some Demographic Indicators for Africa," in *The Population of Tropical Africa*, pp. 187–198; and William Brass, et al., *The Demography of Tropical Africa* (Princeton, N.J.: Princeton University Press, 1968).

[6] *UN Demographic Yearbook 1969*, pp. 124–125.

to yield a 1967 estimate of 597,000, etc. For the 21st and following decrements, constant factor b is used; for Botswana it is .014.

(3) *Population growth rates have increased steadily over time, very slowly from 1919–1948 and much more rapidly since then.* In common with other developing countries the introduction of public health measures and the increasing availability of modern medicine has effected a reduction in death rates with a corresponding increase in the population growth rates of the countries in this Handbook.

It has been pointed out that the effect of these medical innovations has been most marked since the Second World War.[7] The procedure outlined

[7] J. C. Caldwell, "Introduction," in *The Population of Tropical Africa*, p. 14.

above for Botswana illustrates the way that our formula handles this simple model of population growth. The constant factors, a and b, reduce the growth rate for each year so that by the ninth decrement the estimated growth for Botswana is reduced from the original 2.6 to 2.2. Constant factor b, which is approximately *one-fourth* the size of constant factor a, reduces the growth rate much more slowly for the pre-1949 years so that the 1919 estimated growth rate is 1.4. This is a simplistic solution to a complicated situation, we realize, but it would appear to increase rather than decrease the reliability of our estimates.

TABLE A.1   Population Estimates for 32 African Nations, 1969–1919 (in thousands)

	BOTSWAN	BURUNDI	CAMEROO	CAR	CHAD	CONGO B	ZAIRE	DAHOMEY
1969	593	3340	5470	1459	3410	860	16353	2505
1968	578	3262	5347	1419	3353	845	15952	2430
1967	564	3188	5230	1382	3299	831	15573	2359
1966	550	3119	5117	1347	3247	817	15213	2293
1965	536	3054	5010	1313	3197	804	14872	2231
1964	524	2994	4908	1282	3150	792	14549	2172
1963	511	2937	4810	1253	3106	780	14244	2118
1962	500	2884	4716	1225	3063	769	13954	2066
1961	488	2834	4627	1200	3023	759	13681	2019
1960	478	2788	4542	1175	2985	749	13422	1974
1959	467	2745	4460	1153	2948	739	13178	1932
1958	457	2705	4383	1131	2914	730	12947	1893
1957	447	2669	4309	1111	2881	722	12730	1857
1956	438	2635	4238	1093	2851	713	12525	1823
1955	429	2604	4171	1076	2822	706	12332	1792
1954	421	2575	4107	1060	2795	699	12151	1763
1953	413	2550	4046	1045	2769	692	11982	1736
1952	405	2527	3988	1031	2745	685	11823	1711
1951	397	2506	3933	1019	2723	679	11675	1689
1950	390	2488	3881	1007	2702	674	11537	1668
1949	383	2473	3832	996	2683	669	11408	1650
1948	376	2459	3785	987	2666	664	11290	1633
1947	370	2448	3740	979	2650	660	11180	1618
1946	364	2438	3697	970	2634	655	11075	1604
1945	357	2429	3655	963	2619	651	10973	1591
1944	351	2420	3614	955	2605	647	10874	1578
1943	346	2412	3574	948	2591	643	10779	1566
1942	340	2405	3535	941	2577	640	10687	1554
1941	334	2399	3497	935	2564	636	10599	1543
1940	329	2394	3460	929	2552	633	10514	1533
1939	324	2389	3424	923	2540	629	10432	1523
1938	319	2385	3389	918	2528	626	10353	1514
1937	314	2382	3355	913	2517	623	10277	1506
1936	309	2379	3322	908	2507	620	10204	1498
1935	304	2377	3289	904	2496	617	10134	1490
1934	299	2376	3258	899	2487	614	10067	1484
1933	295	2376	3227	895	2478	612	10003	1477
1932	290	2376	3197	892	2469	609	9942	1472
1931	286	2378	3168	889	2461	607	9883	1466
1930	282	2379	3140	886	2453	604	9827	1462
1929	278	2382	3113	883	2445	602	9774	1457
1928	274	2386	3086	880	2439	600	9723	1454
1927	270	2390	3060	878	2432	598	9675	1451
1926	266	2395	3035	876	2426	596	9629	1448
1925	262	2400	3010	875	2420	595	9586	1446
1924	258	2407	2987	873	2415	593	9545	1444
1923	255	2414	2964	872	2410	591	9507	1443
1922	251	2422	2941	871	2406	590	9471	1443
1921	248	2430	2919	871	2402	589	9438	1443
1920	245	2440	2898	871	2398	587	9407	1443
1919	241	2450	2878	871	2395	586	9378	1444

	ETHIOPI	GABON	GAMBIA	GHANA	GUINEA	I COAST	KENYA	LESOTHO
1969	23457	473	343	8143	3702	4010	9948	385
1968	23020	469	336	7914	3601	3905	9621	857
1967	22604	465	329	7696	3506	3805	9314	830
1966	22210	461	323	7491	3417	3710	9026	805
1965	21836	457	317	7297	3333	3621	8755	782
1964	21481	453	311	7114	3254	3536	8502	760
1963	21144	450	306	6940	3179	3456	8264	739
1962	20826	446	300	6776	3109	3380	8041	720
1961	20525	443	295	6621	3044	3308	7831	702
1960	20241	439	291	6475	2982	3240	7635	685
1959	19973	436	286	6337	2924	3176	7452	669
1958	19721	433	282	6206	2871	3116	7280	655
1957	19483	430	278	6083	2820	3059	7119	641
1956	19261	428	274	5968	2773	3005	6969	628
1955	19052	425	271	5859	2729	2955	6829	616
1954	18858	422	267	5756	2689	2907	6699	605
1953	18677	420	264	5660	2651	2862	6578	594
1952	18509	417	261	5570	2616	2821	6466	585
1951	18353	415	259	5485	2584	2781	6362	576
1950	18211	413	256	5406	2555	2745	6266	568
1949	18080	411	254	5333	2528	2711	6178	560
1948	17961	409	251	5264	2504	2679	6098	554
1947	17855	407	249	5201	2483	2650	6025	548
1946	17752	405	247	5140	2462	2622	5954	542
1945	17654	403	246	5080	2443	2594	5887	536
1944	17560	401	244	5023	2424	2568	5822	531
1943	17470	399	242	4967	2406	2542	5760	526
1942	17385	397	240	4914	2389	2518	5701	521
1941	17303	396	239	4862	2373	2494	5644	516
1940	17225	394	237	4812	2357	2471	5590	512
1939	17152	392	235	4764	2343	2449	5538	507
1938	17082	391	234	4717	2329	2427	5488	503
1937	17016	389	233	4673	2316	2407	5441	500
1936	16953	388	231	4629	2304	2387	5396	496
1935	16895	386	230	4588	2293	2368	5354	492
1934	16840	384	229	4548	2282	2350	5313	489
1933	16789	383	227	4509	2272	2332	5275	486
1932	16742	382	226	4472	2263	2315	5239	483
1931	16698	380	225	4436	2255	2299	5205	481
1930	16658	379	224	4402	2247	2284	5173	478
1929	16621	377	223	4369	2240	2269	5143	476
1928	16588	376	222	4338	2234	2255	5114	474
1927	16559	375	221	4307	2228	2241	5088	472
1926	16533	374	221	4279	2224	2228	5064	470
1925	16511	372	220	4251	2219	2216	5041	468
1924	16492	371	219	4225	2216	2204	5021	467
1923	16476	370	218	4200	2213	2193	5002	466
1922	16464	369	218	4176	2211	2183	4985	464
1921	16456	368	217	4153	2210	2173	4970	464
1920	16450	367	217	4132	2209	2164	4956	463
1919	16449	366	216	4112	2209	2155	4945	462

	LIBERIA	MALAWI	MAURITA	MALI	NIGER	NIGERIA	RWANDA	SENEGAL
1969	1110	4130	1100	4745	3546	54000	3306	3670
1968	1088	4023	1077	4634	3426	52632	3194	3572
1967	1067	3923	1056	4529	3314	51338	3089	3479
1966	1048	3827	1036	4430	3208	50115	2990	3392
1965	1029	3737	1017	4337	3109	48960	2897	3310
1964	1011	3652	999	4248	3016	47868	2810	3233
1963	993	3572	982	4164	2929	46838	2728	3161
1962	977	3496	966	4085	2847	45866	2650	3093
1961	961	3424	951	4011	2770	44949	2578	3029
1960	946	3357	937	3940	2698	44085	2509	2969
1959	932	3293	924	3874	2630	43271	2445	2913
1958	918	3233	912	3812	2567	42506	2385	2861
1957	905	3177	900	3754	2508	41787	2328	2812
1956	893	3124	890	3699	2453	41113	2275	2767
1955	881	3075	880	3648	2401	40482	2225	2724
1954	870	3029	871	3600	2353	39891	2178	2685
1953	860	2985	863	3556	2309	39340	2135	2649
1952	850	2945	855	3515	2267	38828	2094	2615
1951	840	2907	848	3476	2228	38352	2056	2585
1950	832	2873	842	3441	2193	37913	2020	2557
1949	823	2841	837	3409	2160	37508	1988	2531
1948	815	2811	832	3380	2129	37136	1957	2509
1947	808	2784	828	3353	2102	36798	1929	2488
1946	801	2758	824	3327	2075	36472	1902	2469
1945	794	2733	820	3303	2050	36158	1875	2450
1944	787	2709	817	3279	2025	35856	1850	2433
1943	781	2686	813	3257	2002	35566	1826	2416
1942	774	2663	810	3235	1979	35287	1802	2400
1941	768	2642	807	3214	1957	35019	1780	2385
1940	762	2621	805	3195	1937	34763	1758	2371
1939	756	2601	802	3176	1917	34517	1737	2357
1938	751	2582	800	3158	1898	34282	1717	2345
1937	745	2564	798	3141	1880	34057	1697	2333
1936	740	2547	796	3124	1862	33843	1679	2322
1935	735	2530	795	3109	1846	33638	1661	2311
1934	730	2514	793	3095	1830	33444	1643	2302
1933	725	2499	792	3081	1815	33259	1627	2293
1932	720	2485	791	3068	1801	33083	1611	2285
1931	715	2471	790	3056	1787	32918	1596	2278
1930	711	2458	789	3045	1774	32761	1581	2271
1929	707	2446	789	3034	1762	32614	1568	2265
1928	703	2434	789	3025	1751	32475	1554	2260
1927	699	2423	789	3016	1740	32346	1542	2255
1926	695	2413	789	3008	1730	32225	1529	2252
1925	691	2403	789	3000	1721	32114	1518	2249
1924	688	2394	790	2994	1712	32011	1507	2246
1923	684	2386	791	2988	1704	31916	1497	2245
1922	681	2379	792	2983	1696	31830	1487	2244
1921	678	2372	793	2979	1690	31753	1477	2243
1920	675	2365	794	2975	1683	31684	1469	2244
1919	672	2359	796	2972	1678	31623	1460	2245

	SI LEON	SOMALI	SUDAN	TANZANI	TOGO	UGANDA	U VOLTA	ZAMBIA
1969	2439	2660	14355	12173	1724	7934	5054	3947
1968	2403	2564	13910	11796	1674	7718	4931	3814
1967	2368	2474	13491	11440	1626	7513	4813	3688
1966	2335	2389	13098	11105	1582	7318	4700	3570
1965	2304	2309	12727	10790	1540	7134	4593	3459
1964	2273	2234	12379	10492	1501	6959	4490	3355
1963	2244	2163	12052	10213	1463	6793	4391	3256
1962	2217	2097	11745	9949	1428	6635	4297	3164
1961	2190	2034	11456	9701	1395	6486	4207	3077
1960	2165	1975	11185	9468	1365	6344	4122	2996
1959	2141	1920	10930	9249	1336	6210	4039	2919
1958	2118	1868	10692	9042	1308	6083	3961	2847
1957	2097	1819	10469	8849	1283	5962	3886	2779
1956	2076	1774	10260	8667	1259	5849	3815	2716
1955	2056	1730	10065	8497	1237	5741	3746	2656
1954	2038	1690	9883	8337	1216	5639	3681	2601
1953	2020	1652	9713	8188	1196	5543	3619	2549
1952	2003	1617	9556	8049	1178	5452	3559	2500
1951	1988	1583	9410	7920	1162	5367	3503	2454
1950	1973	1552	9275	7799	1146	5286	3449	2412
1949	1959	1523	9151	7688	1132	5210	3398	2373
1948	1947	1496	9037	7585	1119	5140	3349	2336
1947	1935	1471	8933	7490	1107	5073	3302	2303
1946	1923	1447	8833	7398	1096	5009	3257	2270
1945	1912	1423	8737	7310	1085	4946	3213	2239
1944	1901	1400	8645	7225	1075	4886	3170	2209
1943	1890	1379	8556	7143	1065	4827	3128	2180
1942	1880	1358	8471	7065	1055	4771	3087	2152
1941	1870	1337	8390	6989	1046	4716	3047	2125
1940	1860	1318	8312	6916	1037	4663	3008	2099
1939	1851	1299	8237	6847	1028	4611	2971	2074
1938	1842	1280	8166	6780	1020	4561	2934	2049
1937	1833	1263	8097	6715	1013	4513	2898	2026
1936	1825	1246	8032	6653	1005	4466	2863	2004
1935	1816	1230	7970	6594	999	4421	2829	1983
1934	1809	1214	7911	6538	992	4378	2796	1962
1933	1801	1199	7855	6484	986	4335	2763	1942
1932	1794	1184	7802	6432	980	4295	2732	1924
1931	1787	1170	7751	6383	974	4255	2701	1905
1930	1780	1156	7703	6336	969	4217	2671	1888
1929	1773	1143	7658	6291	964	4181	2642	1871
1928	1767	1131	7616	6249	959	4145	2614	1856
1927	1761	1119	7577	6209	955	4111	2586	1840
1926	1755	1107	7540	6171	951	4078	2559	1826
1925	1750	1096	7505	6135	948	4047	2533	1812
1924	1745	1086	7473	6101	944	4016	2508	1799
1923	1740	1076	7444	6069	941	3987	2483	1787
1922	1735	1066	7417	6039	938	3959	2459	1775
1921	1731	1057	7392	6011	936	3932	2435	1764
1920	1727	1048	7370	5986	934	3906	2412	1753
1919	1723	1039	7351	5962	932	3882	2390	1743